NINTH EDITION

Financial Accounting

Robert Libby
Cornell University

Patricia A. Libby
Ithaca College

Frank Hodge
University of Washington

McGraw Hill Education

To: Herman and Doris Hargenrater
Oscar and Selma Libby
Laura Libby and Brian Plummer
Abby, Grace, and Claire Hodge

For more than 30 years, Dan Short has been an exceptional teacher, administrator, and textbook author. We have worked with Dan on *Financial Accounting* for more than 20 years. Over that period, he has been our mentor, trusted advisor, and coauthor. In fact, without Dan, we would never have completed our first edition. Dan is a truly gifted writer, has a great sense of humor, and we are proud to call him our friend. We wish Dan a well-earned and joyous retirement.

FINANCIAL ACCOUNTING, NINTH EDITION

Published by McGraw-Hill Education, 2 Penn Plaza, New York, NY 10121. Copyright © 2017 by McGraw-Hill Education. All rights reserved. Printed in the United States of America. Previous editions © 2014, 2011, and 2009. No part of this publication may be reproduced or distributed in any form or by any means, or stored in a database or retrieval system, without the prior written consent of McGraw-Hill Education, including, but not limited to, in any network or other electronic storage or transmission, or broadcast for distance learning.

Some ancillaries, including electronic and print components, may not be available to customers outside the United States.

This book is printed on acid-free paper.

5 6 7 8 9 LWI 21 20 19 18

ISBN 978-1-259-22213-9
MHID 1-259-22213-6

Senior Vice President, Products & Markets: *Kurt L. Strand*
Vice President, General Manager, Products & Markets: *Marty Lange*
Vice President, Content Design & Delivery: *Kimberly Meriwether David*
Managing Director: *Tim Vertovec*
Senior Brand Manager: *Natalie King*
Director, Product Development: *Rose Koos*
Director of Digital Content: *Patricia Plumb*
Lead Product Developer: *Ann Torbert*
Senior Product Developer: *Rebecca Mann*
Marketing Manager: *Kyle Burdette*
Market Development Manager: *Erin Chomat*
Senior Digital Product Analyst: *Xin Lin*
Director, Content Design & Delivery: *Linda Avenarius*

Program Manager: *Daryl Horrocks*
Content Project Managers: *Lori Koetters, Angela Norris*
Buyer: *Susan K. Culbertson*
Design: *Debra Kubiak*
Content Licensing Specialists: *Melissa Homer, Beth A. Thole*
Cover images: *Burrito: Dave Bradley Photography/Getty Images; Airplane: © Carlos E. Santa Maria/Shutterstock; Sandals: Teva/AP Images; Watch: © PG Pictures/Alamy; Boxes: Justin Sullivan/Getty Images; Soda: © Brent Hofacker/Shutterstock; Vegetables: © Adisa/Shutterstock; Coffee: © The McGraw-Hill Companies, Inc./Jill Braaten, photographer; Motorcycle: John B. Carnett/Getty Images; Background water image: © Tatiana Belova/Shutterstock*
Compositor: *SPi Global*
Printer: *LSC Communications/Willard*

All credits appearing on page or at the end of the book are considered to be an extension of the copyright page.

Library of Congress Cataloging-in-Publication Data

Names: Libby, Robert, author. | Libby, Patricia A., author. | Hodge, Frank, 1965- author.
Title: Financial accounting / Robert Libby, Patricia A. Libby, Frank Hodge.
Description: Ninth edition. | New York, NY : McGraw-Hill Education, 2017.
Identifiers: LCCN 2015036286 | ISBN 9781259222139 (alk. paper)
Subjects: LCSH: Accounting. | Corporations—Accounting. | Financial statements.
Classification: LCC HF5636 .L53 2017 | DDC 657—dc23 LC record available at http://lccn.loc.gov/2015036286

The Internet addresses listed in the text were accurate at the time of publication. The inclusion of a website does not indicate an endorsement by the authors or McGraw-Hill Education, and McGraw-Hill Education does not guarantee the accuracy of the information presented at these sites.

mheducation.com/highered

ABOUT THE AUTHORS

ROBERT LIBBY

Robert Libby is the David A. Thomas Professor of Accounting and Accounting Area Coordinator at Cornell University, where he teaches the introductory financial accounting course. He previously taught at the University of Illinois, Pennsylvania State University, the University of Texas at Austin, the University of Chicago, and the University of Michigan. He received his BS from Pennsylvania State University and his MAS and PhD from the University of Illinois; he also successfully completed the CPA exam (Illinois).

Bob was selected as the AAA Outstanding Educator in 2000 and received the AAA Outstanding Service Award in 2006 and the AAA Notable Contributions to the Literature Award in 1985 and 1996. He has received the Core Faculty Teaching Award multiple times at Cornell. Bob is a widely published author and researcher specializing in behavioral accounting. He has published numerous articles in *The Accounting Review; Journal of Accounting Research; Accounting, Organizations, and Society;* and other accounting journals. He has held a variety of offices, including vice president, in the American Accounting Association, and he is a member of the American Institute of CPAs and the editorial boards of *The Accounting Review* and *Accounting, Organizations, and Society.*

PATRICIA A. LIBBY

Patricia Libby is associate professor of accounting at Ithaca College, where she teaches the undergraduate financial accounting course. She previously taught graduate and undergraduate financial accounting at Eastern Michigan University and the University of Texas. Before entering academia, she was an auditor with Price Waterhouse (now PricewaterhouseCoopers) and a financial administrator at the University of Chicago. She is also faculty advisor to Beta Alpha Psi and Ithaca College Accounting Association. She received her BS from Pennsylvania State University, her MBA from DePaul University, and her PhD from the University of Michigan; she also successfully completed the CPA exam (Illinois).

Pat conducts research on using cases in the introductory course and other parts of the accounting curriculum. She has published articles in *The Accounting Review, Issues in Accounting Education,* and *The Michigan CPA.*

FRANK HODGE

Frank Hodge is the chair of the Accounting Department and the Harrington Family Endowed Professor at the University of Washington's Foster School of Business. Frank also serves in the President's Office as the University of Washington's Faculty Athletics Representative to the PAC-12 Conference and the National Collegiate Athletic Association.

Frank joined the faculty at the University of Washington in 2000. He earned his MBA and PhD degrees from Indiana University. Frank teaches financial accounting and financial statement analysis to undergraduate students, full-time MBA students, executive MBA students, and intercollegiate athletic administrators. Frank's research focuses on how individuals use accounting information to make investment decisions and how technology influences their information choices. Frank was one of six members of the Financial Accounting Standards Research Initiative team and has presented his research at the Securities and Exchange Commission. Frank is on the editorial boards of *The Accounting Review; Contemporary Accounting Research; and Accounting, Behavior and Organizations.* He also has published articles in *The Accounting Review; Contemporary Accounting Research; Accounting, Organizations, and Society; Accounting Horizons;* and several other journals. Frank lives in Seattle with his wife and two daughters.

New author Frank Hodge joins the award-winning author team of Bob Libby and Pat Libby to continue *Financial Accounting*'s best-selling tradition of helping the instructor and student become partners in learning. Libby/Libby/Hodge uses a remarkable learning approach that keeps students engaged and involved in the material from the first day of class.

Libby/Libby/Hodge's *Financial Accounting* maintains its leadership by focusing on three key attributes:

THE PIONEERING FOCUS COMPANY APPROACH

The Libby/Libby/Hodge authors' trademark focus company approach is the best method for helping students understand financial statements and the real-world implications of financial accounting for future managers. **This approach shows that accounting is relevant and motivates students by explaining accounting in a real-world context.** Throughout each chapter, the material is integrated around a familiar focus company, its decisions, and its financial statements. This provides the perfect setting for discussing the importance of accounting and how businesses use accounting information.

A BUILDING-BLOCK APPROACH TO TEACHING TRANSACTION ANALYSIS

Faculty agree the accounting cycle is the most critical concept to learn and master for students studying financial accounting. Libby/Libby/Hodge believes students struggle with the accounting cycle when transaction analysis is covered in one chapter. If students are exposed to the accounting equation, journal entries, and T-accounts for both balance sheet and income statement accounts in a single chapter, many are left behind and are unable to grasp material in the next chapter, which typically covers adjustments and financial statement preparation.

"The book does an excellent job of using real-world examples to highlight the importance of understanding financial accounting to students who may or may not be interested in pursuing accounting careers. I think this book will hold students' attention, without sacrificing the technical information that provides the foundation for further accounting coursework. ***Exceptionally well-written and nicely organized.****"*

—*Paul Hribar, University of Iowa*

The market-leading Libby/Libby/Hodge approach spreads transaction analysis coverage over two chapters so that students have the time to master the material. In Chapter 2 of *Financial Accounting*, students are exposed to the accounting equation and transaction analysis for investing and financing transactions that affect only balance sheet accounts. This

STUDENTS AND INSTRUCTORS

provides students with the opportunity to learn the basic structure and tools used in accounting in a simpler setting. In Chapter 3, students are exposed to more complex operating transactions that also affect income statement accounts. **By slowing down the introduction of transactions and giving students time to practice and gain mastery, this building-block approach leads to greater student success in their study of later topics in financial accounting such as adjusting entries.** After the students have developed an understanding of the complete accounting cycle and the resulting statements, Chapter 5 takes students through the corporate reporting and analysis process.

Accounting Cycle

Start Early	Compress Coverage	Extend Coverage (Libby/Libby/Hodge approach)
Overview of F/S and Users, B/S and I/S Transactions with Accounting Equation	Overview of F/S and Users	Overview of F/S and Users
	F/S, Ratios, and Conceptual Framework	**B/S** Transactions with Accounting Equation, Journal Entries, and T-accounts
B/S and I/S Transactions with Journal Entries and T-accounts	B/S and I/S Transactions with Accounting Equation, Journal Entries, and T-accounts	**B/S** and **I/S** Transactions with Accounting Equation, Journal Entries, and T-accounts
Adjustments, Closing Entries, F/S Preparation	Adjustments, Closing Entries, F/S Preparation	Adjustments, Closing Entries, F/S Preparation

This graphic shows a detailed comparison of the Libby/Libby/Hodge approach to the accounting cycle chapters compared to the approach taken by other financial accounting texts.

The authors' approach to introducing the accounting cycle has been tested in peer-reviewed, published research studies. One of these award-winning studies has shown that the accounting cycle approach used in this textbook yields learning gains that outpace approaches used in other textbooks by a significant margin.

POWERFUL TECHNOLOGY FOR TEACHING AND STUDY

Students have different learning styles and conflicting time commitments, so they want technology tools that will help them study more efficiently and effectively. The ninth edition includes the best technology available with Connect's latest features—SmartBook, Connect Insight, and new study, practice, and assessment materials.

> *"[Libby, Libby, Hodge] does a **great job explaining financial accounting concepts to college students on an introductory level.**"*
>
> —*Peggy O'Kelly, Northeastern University*

> *"The text has **some of the best discussions that I have seen in introductory texts of statement of cash flows and financial statement analysis topics.**"*
>
> —*Marilyn Misch, Pepperdine University*

v

Financial Accounting, 9e, offers a host of pedagogical tools that complement the different ways you like to teach and the ways your students like to learn. Some offer information and tips that help you present a complex subject; others highlight issues relevant to what your students read online or see on television. Either way, *Financial Accounting*'s pedagogical support will make a real difference in your course and in your students' learning.

FINANCIAL ANALYSIS — Interpreting Assets, Liabilities, and Stockholders' Equity on the Balance Sheet

Assessment of **Le-Nature's** assets was important to its creditors, **Wells Fargo Bank** and others, and its resources

A QUESTION OF ETHICS — Ethics and the Need for Internal Control

Some people are bothered by the recommendation that all well-run companies should have strong internal control does not

KEY RATIO ANALYSIS — Net Profit Margin

? **ANALYTICAL QUESTION**

FOCUS ON CASH FLOWS — Working Capital and Cash Flows

Many working capital accounts have a direct relationship to income-producing activities. Accounts

INTERNATIONAL PERSPECTIVE — The International Accounting Standards Board and Global Convergence of Accounting Standards

Financial accounting standards and disclosure requirements are adopted by national regulatory agencies. Since 2002, there has been substantial movement toward the adoption of **International Financial Reporting Standards (IFRS)** issued by the **International Accounting Standards Board (IASB).** Examples of jurisdictions requiring the use of IFRS currently include:

FINANCIAL ANALYSIS BOXES—These features tie important chapter concepts to real-world decision-making examples. They also highlight alternative viewpoints and add to the critical-thinking and decision-making focus of the text.

A QUESTION OF ETHICS BOXES—These boxes appear throughout the text, conveying the importance and the consequences of acting responsibly in business practice.

> *"Excellent book with **very good and clear writing, coverage, illustrations** and overall very student friendly."*
>
> —*Kashi Balachandran, New York University*

AND CONTENT

FOCUS ON CASH FLOWS BOXES—Each of the first eleven chapters includes a discussion and analysis of changes in the cash flows of the focus company and explores the decisions that caused those changes.

KEY RATIO ANALYSIS BOXES—Each box presents ratio analysis for the focus company in the chapter as well as for comparative companies. Cautions are also provided to help students understand the limitations of certain ratios.

INTERNATIONAL PERSPECTIVE BOXES—These boxes highlight the emergence of global accounting standards (IFRS) at a level appropriate for the introductory student.

Cash Flows from Operations, Net Income, and the Quality of Earnings

FOCUS ON CASH FLOWS

As presented in the previous chapters, the statement of cash flows explains the difference between the ending and beginning balances in the Cash account on the balance sheet during the accounting period. Put simply, the cash flow statement is a categorized list of all transactions of the period that affected the Cash account. The three categories are operating, investing, and financing activities. **Since no adjustments made in this chapter affected cash, the cash flow categories identified on the Cash T-account at the end of Chapter 3 remain the same.**

Many standard financial analysis texts warn analysts to look for unusual deferrals and accruals when they attempt to predict future periods' earnings. They often suggest that wide disparities between net income and cash flow from operations are a useful warning sign. For example, Subramanyan suggests the following:

Accounting accruals determining net income rely on estimates, deferrals, allocations, and valuations. These considerations sometimes allow more subjectivity than do the factors determining cash flows. For this reason we often relate cash flows from operations to net income in assessing its quality.

> "The textbook focuses on the key accounting concepts and is **written clearly so that it is easy for students to understand.**"
>
> —Rada Brooks, University of California Berkeley, Haas School of Business

> "The **real-life examples are an excellent way to draw in the student** and I thought that **the ethics components and IFRS components were an excellent addition.**"
>
> —Tammy Metzke, Milwaukee Area Technical College

PRACTICE IS KEY TO SUCCESS

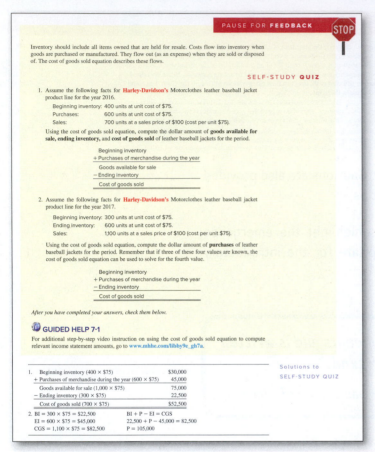

PAUSE FOR FEEDBACK AND SELF-STUDY QUIZ

Research shows that students learn best when they are actively engaged in the learning process. This active learning feature engages the student, provides interactivity, and promotes efficient learning. These quizzes ask students to pause at strategic points throughout each chapter to ensure they understand key points before moving ahead.

> "The **Pause for Feedback and Self-Study Quizzes give the student the opportunity to test their understanding of the material before moving forward** and also assist in breaking up the chapter into manageable sections."
>
> —Betty P. David, Francis Marion University

GUIDED HELP

Today's students have a wide variety of time commitments. And research shows that when they have difficulty understanding a key concept, they benefit most when help is available immediately. **Our unique Guided Help feature provides a narrated, animated, step-by-step walk-through of select topics covered in the Self-Study Quiz that students can view at any time through their mobile device or online. It also saves office hour time!**

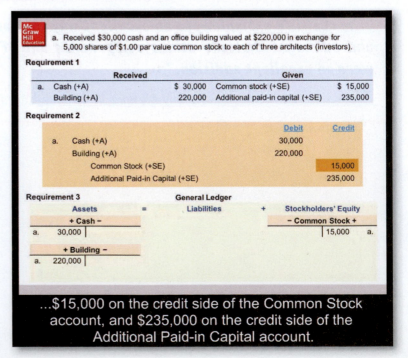

IN FINANCIAL ACCOUNTING

CHAPTER TAKE-AWAYS

End-of-chapter summaries complement the learning objectives outlined at the beginning of the chapter.

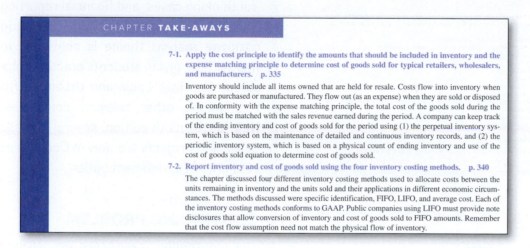

CHAPTER **TAKE-AWAYS**

7-1. Apply the cost principle to identify the amounts that should be included in inventory and the expense matching principle to determine cost of goods sold for typical retailers, wholesalers, and manufacturers. p. 335

Inventory should include all items owned that are held for resale. Costs flow into inventory when goods are purchased or manufactured. They flow out (as an expense) when they are sold or disposed of. In conformity with the expense matching principle, the total cost of the goods sold during the period must be matched with the sales revenue earned during the period. A company can keep track of the ending inventory and cost of goods sold for the period using (1) the perpetual inventory system, which is based on the maintenance of detailed and continuous inventory records, and (2) the periodic inventory system, which is based on a physical count of ending inventory and use of the cost of goods sold equation to determine cost of goods sold.

7-2. Report inventory and cost of goods sold using the four inventory costing methods. p. 340

The chapter discussed four different inventory costing methods used to allocate costs between the units remaining in inventory and the units sold and their applications in different economic circumstances. The methods discussed were specific identification, FIFO, LIFO, and average cost. Each of the inventory costing methods conforms to GAAP. Public companies using LIFO must provide note disclosures that allow conversion of inventory and cost of goods sold to FIFO amounts. Remember that the cost flow assumption need not match the physical flow of inventory.

COMPREHENSIVE PROBLEMS

Selected chapters include problems that cover topics from earlier chapters to refresh, reinforce, and build an integrative understanding of the course material.

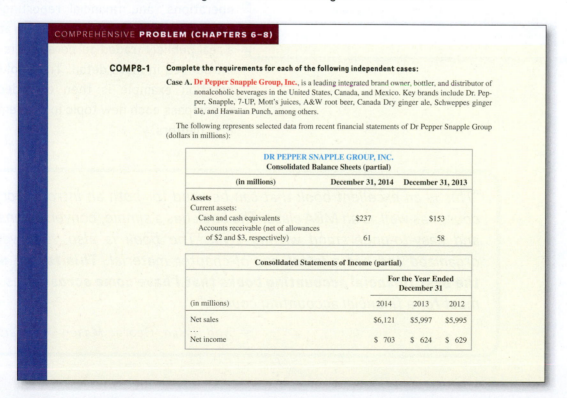

COMPREHENSIVE **PROBLEM (CHAPTERS 6–8)**

COMP8-1   **Complete the requirements for each of the following independent cases:**

Case A. **Dr Pepper Snapple Group, Inc.**, is a leading integrated brand owner, bottler, and distributor of nonalcoholic beverages in the United States, Canada, and Mexico. Key brands include Dr. Pepper, Snapple, 7-UP, Mott's juices, A&W root beer, Canada Dry ginger ale, Schweppes ginger ale, and Hawaiian Punch, among others.

The following represents selected data from recent financial statements of Dr Pepper Snapple Group (dollars in millions):

DR PEPPER SNAPPLE GROUP, INC. Consolidated Balance Sheets (partial)		
(in millions)	December 31, 2014	December 31, 2013
Assets		
Current assets:		
Cash and cash equivalents	$237	$153
Accounts receivable (net of allowances of $2 and $3, respectively)	61	58

Consolidated Statements of Income (partial)		
	For the Year Ended December 31		
(in millions)	2014	2013	2012
Net sales	$6,121	$5,997	$5,995
...			
Net income	$ 703	$ 624	$ 629

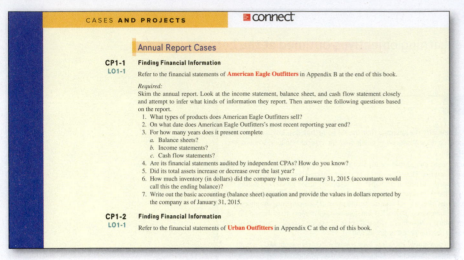

CASES AND PROJECTS

This section includes annual report cases, financial reporting and analysis cases, critical thinking cases, and financial reporting and analysis team projects. The real-world company analysis theme is continued in this section, giving students practice comparing American Eagle and Urban Outfitters among other relevant companies. **New** for the ninth edition: several of these Cases and Projects are now in Connect as auto-graded assignment option.

CONTINUING PROBLEM

The continuing case revolves around Penny's Pool Service & Supply, Inc., and its largest supplier, Pool Corporation, Inc. In the first five chapters, the continuing case follows the establishment, operations, and financial reporting for Penny's. In Chapter 5, Pool Corporation, a real publicly traded corporation, is also introduced in more detail. The Pool Corporation example is then extended to encompass each new topic in the remaining chapters.

*"This is an excellent book that can be used for both an introductory course as well as an MBA class. The book has a simple, conversational and easy-to-understand writing style. The book is also very well organized and has a lot of end-of-chapter material. **This is one of the best financial accounting books that I have come across.** It is a must for a financial accounting course."*

—Syed Hasan, George Mason University

WHAT'S NEW IN THE 9th EDITION?

In response to feedback and guidance from numerous financial accounting faculty, the authors have made many important changes to the ninth edition of *Financial Accounting*, including the following:

- Integrated **new focus companies** including **Amazon**, the world's largest Internet retailer; **Whole Foods Market**, a supermarket chain specializing in organic food; and **Graham Holdings Company**, a company that expands primarily through investing in other companies, including **Kaplan, Inc.**

- **Detailed edit of Chapters 9, 10, and 11** to use consistent terminology throughout each chapter and more closely link content to other chapters.

- **Expanded the number of Guided Help features** in the text to provide more of these narrated, animated, step-by-step examinations of select topics in the Self-Study Quizzes in each chapter.

- Reviewed, updated, and introduced new end-of-chapter material in each chapter to support new topics and learning objectives. In addition, other **new McGraw-Hill Connect®** **problem formats** include **General Ledger Problems** that auto-post from journal entries to T-accounts to trial balances, **Excel Simulations,** and **Interactive Presentations.**

- Added **new Annual Report Cases that can be auto-graded in Connect.** In addition, the **Cases and Projects** content from the book is also now available in Connect as either auto-graded or manually graded questions.

Chapter 1
Focus Company: Le-Nature's Inc.

- Chapter 1 is written around a recent accounting fraud that is exciting, yet simple. Students are introduced to the structure, content, and use of the four basic financial statements through the story of two brothers who founded **Le-Nature's Inc.,** a natural beverage company. Le-Nature's financial statements are used to support increases in borrowing for expansion. When actual sales do not live up to expectations, the brothers turn to financial statement fraud to cover up their failure, which emphasizes the importance of controls, responsible ethical conduct, and accurate financial reporting.

- **GUIDED HELP** feature provides all users of the text with free access to step-by-step video instruction on preparing a simple balance sheet, income statement, and statement of stockholders' equity for **LaCrosse Footwear**, a leading outdoor footwear company.

- More algorithmic exercises included in Connect®.

- *New* **CONTINUING PROBLEM** added to the end-of-chapter problems based on the activities of Penny's Pool Service & Supply and its supplier, **Pool Corporation**. These companies provide a consistent context for summarizing the key points emphasized in each chapter. In Chapter 1, students prepare a basic income statement, statement of stockholders' equity, and balance sheet based on Penny's estimates for the first year.

- *New* Annual Report Case that can be graded through Connect.

- New and updated real companies in end-of-chapter exercises, problems, and cases.

Chapter 2
Focus Company: Chipotle Mexican Grill

- Chapter 2 introduces the accounting cycle for **Chipotle Mexican Grill,** a trendy, yet relatively simple company. The chapter integrates financial information for investing and financing activities for the first quarter of 2015, resulting in the company's actual quarterly balance

sheet (with a few simplifications). This fast-casual restaurant does not utilize franchising, thus reducing the complexities found with most other competitors and allowing focused emphasis on transaction analysis, journal entries, T-accounts, and the structure of the balance sheet.

- Focus and contrast company data updated.

- Update of the conceptual framework to reflect the new definitions from the FASB.

- Simplified account titles that relate more closely to end-of-chapter material.

- T-accounts now follow each transaction to illustrate posting the effects, while marginal notes have been deleted for a cleaner visual approach.

- *New* additional **GUIDED HELP** feature provides free access to step-by-step video instruction applying transaction analysis to identify accounts and effects on the accounting equation. This is in addition to the existing Guided Help for recording, posting, and classifying accounts for financing and investing activities.

- *New* **CONTINUING PROBLEM** added to the end-of-chapter problems based on the activities of Penny's Pool Service & Supply and its supplier, **Pool Corporation**. These companies provide a consistent context for summarizing the key points emphasized in each chapter. In Chapter 2, students prepare journal entries, post to T-accounts, prepare a trial balance and classified balance sheet, identify investing and financing activities affecting cash flows, and compute and interpret the current ratio based on the balance sheet for Penny's Pool Service & Supply.
- *New and updated real companies*, as well as additional exercises on key concepts, in end-of-chapter exercises, problems, and cases.
- *New* Annual Report Case that can be graded through Connect.

Chapter 3
Focus Company: Chipotle Mexican Grill
- Chapter 3 builds on Chapter 2 by explaining and illustrating transaction analysis for operating activities for the first quarter of 2015 for **Chipotle Mexican Grill.** Students apply their knowledge of accounting concepts by preparing journal entries and posting to T-accounts using Chapter 2 transactions involving revenues and expenses.
- Focus and contrast company data updated.
- *New* concepts based on the FASB's Accounting Standards Updates for revenue recognition and expense recognition are incorporated in the chapter and end-of-chapter material.
- *New* additional **GUIDED HELP** feature provides free access to step-by-step video instruction applying transaction analysis to identify accounts and effects on the accounting equation. This is in addition to the existing Guided Help for identifying revenue and expense account titles and amounts for a given period.

XII

- *New* **CONTINUING PROBLEM** added to the end-of-chapter problems based on the activities of Penny's Pool Service & Supply and its supplier, **Pool Corporation**. These companies provide a consistent context for summarizing the key points emphasized in each chapter. In Chapter 3, students prepare journal entries, create a classified income statement, and calculate and analyze the net profit margin for Penny's Pool Service & Supply.
- *New and updated real companies*, as well as additional exercises on key concepts, in end-of-chapter exercises, problems, and cases.
- *New* Annual Report Case that can be graded through Connect.

Chapter 4
Focus Company: Chipotle Mexican Grill
- Chapter 4 builds on Chapters 2 and 3 by explaining and illustrating end-of-period adjustments, financial statements, and closing the records for the first quarter of 2015 for **Chipotle Mexican Grill.**
- Focus and contrast company data updated.
- The process for identifying and recording an adjustment at the end of the period has been modified to provide a logical progression—with the journal entry followed by the effects on the accounting equation, followed by posting the effects in the T-accounts—with less marginal clutter.
- *New* additional **GUIDED HELP** feature provides free access to step-by-step video instruction on recording a closing entry. This is in addition to the existing Guided Help for recording adjusting entries.
- *New* **CONTINUING PROBLEM** added to the end-of-chapter problems based on the activities of Penny's Pool Service & Supply and its supplier, **Pool Corporation**. These companies provide a consistent context for summarizing the key

points emphasized in each chapter. In Chapter 4, students prepare adjusting journal entries for Penny's Pool Service & Supply.
- *New and updated real companies*, as well as additional exercises on key concepts, in end-of-chapter exercises, problems, and cases.
- *New* Annual Report Case that can be graded through Connect.

Chapter 5
Focus Company: Apple Inc.
- Chapter 5 has been rewritten around the most recent financial statements and corporate governance and disclosure processes of **Apple Inc.,** students' favorite technology company.
- Focus and contrast company data updated.
- Focus of the chapter has been narrowed to three topics: details of the corporate governance and disclosure process; financial statement formats and important subtotals, totals, and additional disclosures; and the analysis of financial statements through gross profit, net profit, total asset turnover, and return on assets analysis.
- Fraud triangle provides the basis for the corporate governance discussion.
- *New* section on the effects of transactions on key ratios added to tie in the chapter to material in Chapters 2, 3, and 4.
- **GUIDED HELP** feature provides free access to step-by-step video instruction on preparing a detailed classified income statement and balance sheet from a trial balance for **Amazon.com**, the world's largest online retailer.
- More algorithmic exercises included in Connect.
- *Two new* **CONTINUING PROBLEMS** added to the end-of-chapter problems. The first asks students to evaluate the effects of key transactions on important statement subtotals and financial ratios

for Penny's Pool Service & Supply. The second introduces Penny's supplier, **Pool Corporation**, a public company, and asks students to prepare a detailed classified income statement and balance sheet and compute the gross profit percentage and return on assets ratios.

- *New* Annual Report Case that can be graded through Connect.
- *New and updated real companies* in end-of-chapter exercises, problems, and cases.

Chapter 6
Focus Company: Deckers Brands

- Focus and contrast company data updated.
- Content narrowed to three related topics: determinants of net sales, receivables valuation, and control of cash.
- Exhibits reorganized to better reflect the chapter flow.
- Coverage of bad debt recoveries increased.
- Coverage of electronic banking increased.
- *Two New* **GUIDED HELP** features provide free access to step-by-step video instruction on (1) preparing entries related to bad debts and determining their financial statement effects and (2) using aging to estimate bad debt expense.
- More algorithmic exercises included in Connect.
- *New* **CONTINUING PROBLEM** added to the end-of-chapter problems. Students are asked to make summary entries for bad debts and compute the amount to be reported as net sales for **Pool Corporation**, a public company.
- *New* Annual Report Case that can be graded through Connect.
- *New and updated real companies* in end-of-chapter exercises, problems, and cases.

Chapter 7
Focus Company: Harley-Davidson, Inc.

- Focus and contrast company data updated.
- Coverage of perpetual versus periodic inventory systems moved to section on cost of goods sold near the beginning of the chapter.
- *New* rules for applying lower-of-cost-or-market to inventories covered at an appropriate level for the introductory course.
- *Two New* **GUIDED HELP** features provide free access to step-by-step video instruction on (1) computation of goods available for sale and cost of goods sold and (2) computing cost of goods sold and ending inventory under FIFO and LIFO costing methods.
- Exhibits 7.4 and 7.5 revised to make it easier to see the effects of FIFO, LIFO, and average costing methods on the financial statements.
- **Supplement B** added to demonstrate the effects of determining FIFO and LIFO cost of goods sold under periodic versus perpetual inventory systems.
- More algorithmic exercises included in Connect.
- *New* **CONTINUING PROBLEM** added to the end-of-chapter problems. Students are asked to compute the effects of the LIFO/FIFO choice for inventory items with increasing and decreasing costs for **Pool Corporation**, a public company.
- *New* Annual Report Case that can be graded through Connect.
- *New and updated real companies* in end-of-chapter exercises, problems, and cases.

Chapter 8
Focus Company: Southwest Airlines

- Chapter 8 illustrates the acquisition, use, repair and improvement, and disposal of property, plant, and equipment, followed by an illustration of accounting and reporting for intangible assets and

natural resources, at several companies including **Cisco Systems**, **Walt Disney Company**, **Papa John's International**, and **International Paper**, among others.

- Focus and contrast company data updated.
- *New* additional **GUIDED HELP** feature provides free access to step-by-step video instruction on recording a disposal of an asset. This is in addition to the existing Guided Help for determining cost and creating depreciation schedules under straight-line, units-of-production, and declining-balance methods.
- *New* **CONTINUING PROBLEM** added to the end-of-chapter problems. Based on the activities of **Pool Corporation**, students are asked to determine cost; create depreciation schedules under straight-line, units-of-production, and declining-balance methods; and dispose of an asset.
- *New and updated real companies*, as well as additional exercises on key concepts, in end-of-chapter exercises, problems, and cases.
- *New* Annual Report Case that can be graded through Connect.

Chapter 9
Focus Company: Starbucks

- Focus company data updated. New contrast companies added.
- Complete revision of chapter content to more closely link content to other chapters and to use consistent terminology throughout the chapter.
- Updated present value discussion and graphics for both single amounts and annuities. Chapter now includes descriptions of how to calculate present values using tables, calculators, and Excel.
- *New* **GUIDED HELP** features teach students the steps required to compute present values using two popular calculator models (HP 10BII+ and HP 12C) and Excel.
- *New* **Supplement A** uses vivid graphics to display the steps required to compute

present values using two popular calculator models (HP 10BII+ and HP 12C) and Excel.

- *New* **CONTINUING PROBLEM** added to the end-of-chapter problems. Students are asked to record transactions that affect the liabilities section of the balance sheet for **Pool Corporation**, a public company.
- *New* Annual Report Case that can be graded through Connect.
- *New and updated real companies* in end-of-chapter exercises, problems, and cases.
- End-of-chapter material completely updated to seamlessly match the content of the chapter.

Chapter 10
Focus Company: **Amazon**
- *New* focus company and new contrast companies.
- Complete revision of chapter content to more closely link content to other chapters and to use consistent terminology throughout the chapter.
- *New* graphics that visually help students understand the timing of bond payments and the accounting for bonds.
- *New* **FINANCIAL ANALYSIS** feature describes bond ratings and bond rating agencies.
- Revised structure allows instructors to seamlessly assign accounting for bonds with or without the use of discount and premium accounts.
- *New* **GUIDED HELP** features walk students through (1) how to calculate the present value of a bond issued at a premium and (2) how to account for the bond over its life.
- *New* discussion of accounting for bond issuance costs.
- *New* **CONTINUING PROBLEM** added to the end-of-chapter problems. Students are asked to record bond transactions for **Pool Corporation**, a public company.

- *New* Annual Report Case that can be graded through Connect.
- *New and updated real companies* in end-of-chapter exercises, problems, and cases.
- End-of-chapter material completely updated to seamlessly match the content of the chapter.

Chapter 11
Focus Company: **Whole Foods Market**
- *New* focus company and new contrast companies.
- Complete revision of chapter content to more closely link content to other chapters and to use consistent terminology throughout the chapter.
- *New* discussion of stock splits effected in the form of a stock dividend.
- *New* **FINANCIAL ANALYSIS** feature on preferred stock.
- *New* **CONTINUING PROBLEM** added to the end-of-chapter problems. Students are asked to record transactions that affect the equity section of the balance sheet for **Pool Corporation**, a public company.
- *New* Annual Report Case that can be graded through Connect.
- *New and updated real companies* in end-of-chapter exercises, problems, and cases.
- End-of-chapter material completely updated to seamlessly match the content of the chapter.

Chapter 12
Focus Company: **National Beverage Corporation**
- Focus and contrast company data updated.
- *Two New* **GUIDED HELP** features provide free access to step-by-step video instruction on (1) preparing the operating section of the statement of cash flows using the indirect method and (2) preparing the investing and financing sections of the statement of cash flows.

- **Supplement C** and related problem material illustrate preparation of the complete statement of cash flows using the T-account approach.
- More algorithmic exercises included in Connect.
- *New* **CONTINUING PROBLEM** added to the end-of-chapter problems. Students are asked to prepare a complete statement of cash flows for **Pool Corporation**, a public company.
- *New* Annual Report Case that can be graded through Connect.
- *New and updated real companies* in end-of-chapter exercises, problems, and cases.

Chapter 13
Focus Company: **The Home Depot**
- Focus company data updated.
- Complete revision of chapter content to more closely link content to other chapters and to use consistent terminology throughout the chapter.
- *New* discussion of DuPont analysis.
- Ratio formulas in chapter updated to be consistent with formulas provided in previous chapters.
- *New* **CONTINUING PROBLEM** added to the end-of-chapter problems. Students are asked to download the latest financial statements for **Pool Corporation**, a public company, and compute various ratios discussed in the chapter.
- *New* Annual Report Case that can be graded through Connect.
- *New and updated real companies* in end-of-chapter exercises, problems, and cases.
- End-of-chapter material completely updated to seamlessly match the content of the chapter.

Appendix A
Focus Company: **Graham Holdings Company**
- *New focus company*, Graham Holdings Company, a company that expands

primarily through investing in other companies, including **Kaplan, Inc.** (top admissions test preparation organization). Accounting and reporting are discussed and illustrated for: (1) debt securities held to maturity, (2) passive investments using the fair value method, (3) investments involving significant influence using the equity method, and (4) investments in controlling interests.

- Focus and contrast company data updated.
- **GUIDED HELP** feature provides free access to step-by-step video instruction on accounting for and reporting available-for-sale securities as investments at fair value.
- *New* **CONTINUING PROBLEM** added to the end-of-chapter problems. Using the activities of **Pool Corporation**, students

are asked to record passive investments as trading securities and as available-for-sale securities over a three-year period.

- *New and updated real companies*, as well as additional exercises on key concepts, in end-of-chapter exercises, problems, and cases.
- *New* Annual Report Case that can be graded through Connect.

McGraw-Hill Connect®
Learn Without Limits

Connect is a teaching and learning platform that is proven to deliver better results for students and instructors.

Connect empowers students by continually adapting to deliver precisely what they need, when they need it, and how they need it, so your class time is more engaging and effective.

88% of instructors who use Connect require it; instructor satisfaction increases by 38% when Connect is required.

Course outcomes improve with Connect.

	With Connect	Without Connect
Exam Scores	80.4%	74.7%
Pass Rates	83.7%	72.9%
Attendance Rates	92.5%	74.5%
Retention Rates	87.5%	71.1%

■ With Connect ■ Without Connect

Using **Connect** improves passing rates by **10.8%** and retention by **16.4%**.

Analytics

Connect Insight®

Connect Insight is Connect's new one-of-a-kind visual analytics dashboard that provides at-a-glance information regarding student performance, which is immediately actionable. By presenting assignment, assessment, and topical performance results together with a time metric that is easily visible for aggregate or individual results, Connect Insight gives the user the ability to take a just-in-time approach to teaching and learning, which was never before available. Connect Insight presents data that helps instructors improve class performance in a way that is efficient and effective.

Connect helps students achieve better grades

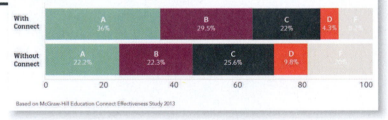

	A	B	C	D	F
With Connect	36%	29.5%	22%	4.3%	
Without Connect	22.2%	22.3%	25.6%	9.8%	20%

Based on McGraw-Hill Education Connect Effectiveness Study 2013

Adaptive

THE FIRST AND ONLY ADAPTIVE READING EXPERIENCE DESIGNED TO TRANSFORM THE WAY STUDENTS READ

More students earn **A's** and **B's** when they use McGraw-Hill Education **Adaptive** products.

SmartBook®

Proven to help students improve grades and study more efficiently, SmartBook contains the same content within the print book, but actively tailors that content to the needs of the individual. SmartBook's adaptive technology provides precise, personalized instruction on what the student should do next, guiding the student to master and remember key concepts, targeting gaps in knowledge and offering customized feedback, and driving the student toward comprehension and retention of the subject matter. Available on smartphones and tablets, SmartBook puts learning at the student's fingertips—anywhere, anytime.

Over **4 billion questions** have been answered, making McGraw-Hill Education products more intelligent, reliable, and precise.

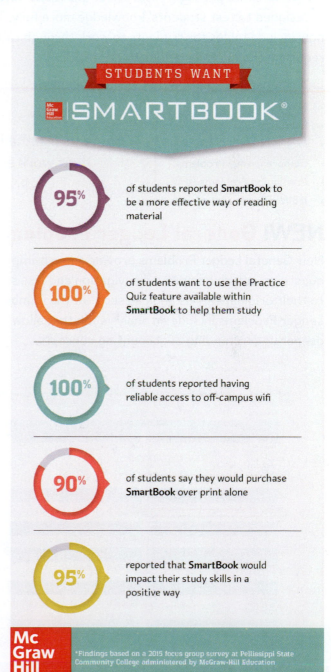

STUDENTS WANT

McGraw Hill Education **SMARTBOOK®**

95% of students reported **SmartBook** to be a more effective way of reading material

100% of students want to use the Practice Quiz feature available within **SmartBook** to help them study

100% of students reported having reliable access to off-campus wifi

90% of students say they would purchase **SmartBook** over print alone

95% reported that **SmartBook** would impact their study skills in a positive way

McGraw Hill Education

*Findings based on a 2015 focus group survey at Pellissippi State Community College administered by McGraw-Hill Education

Online Assignments

Connect helps students learn more efficiently by providing feedback and practice material when they need it, where they need it. Connect grades homework automatically and gives immediate feedback on any questions students may have missed. The extensive assignable, gradable end-of-chapter content includes a general journal application that looks and feels more like what you would find in a general ledger software package. Also, select questions have been redesigned to test students' knowledge more fully. They now include tables for students to work through rather than requiring that all calculations be done offline.

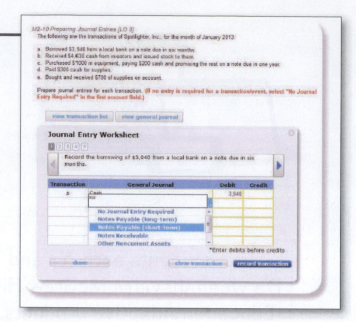

End-of-chapter questions in Connect include:

- Mini-Exercises
- Exercises
- Problems
- Comprehensive Problems
- Continuing Problems
- **NEW!** Cases and Projects

"Students like the flexibility that **Connect** offers . . . They can complete their work and catch up on lectures anytime and anywhere."

—Professor Lisa McKinney, M.T.A., CPA, University of Alabama

NEW! General Ledger Problems

New **General Ledger Problems** provide a much-improved student experience when working with accounting cycle questions, offering improved navigation and less scrolling. Students can audit their mistakes by easily linking back to their original entries and can see how the numbers flow through the various financial statements. Many General Ledger Problems include an analysis tab that allows students to demonstrate their critical thinking skills and a deeper understanding of accounting concepts.

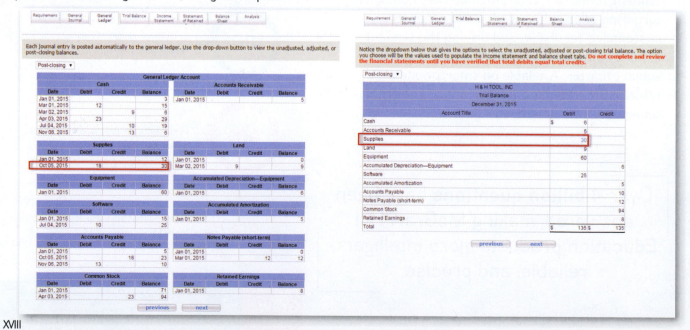

NEW! Interactive Presentations

The **Interactive Presentations** provide engaging narratives of all chapter learning objectives in an assignable and interactive online format. They follow the structure of the text and are organized to match the specific learning objectives within each chapter of *Financial Accounting*. The interactive presentations provide additional explanation and enhancement of material from the text chapter, allowing students to learn, study, and practice with instant feedback, at their own pace.

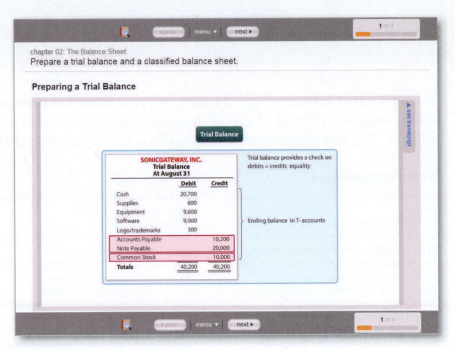

NEW! Excel Simulations

Simulated Excel Questions, assignable within Connect, allow students to practice their Excel skills—such as basic formulas and formatting—within the content of financial accounting. These questions feature animated, narrated Help and Show Me tutorials (when enabled), as well as automatic feedback and grading for both students and professors.

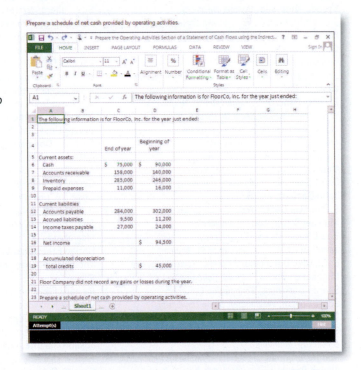

Guided Examples

The **Guided Examples** in Connect provide a narrated, animated, step-by-step walk-through of select exercises similar to those assigned. These short presentations can be turned on or off by instructors and provide reinforcement when students need it most.

> "As a student I need to interact with course material in order to retain it, and **Connect** offers a perfect platform for this kind of learning. Rather than just reading through textbooks, **Connect** has given me the tools to feel engaged in the learning process."
>
> —Jennah Epstein Kraus, Student, Bunker Hill Community College

ACKNOWLEDGMENTS

Many dedicated instructors have devoted their time and effort to help us make each edition better. We would like to acknowledge and thank all of our colleagues who have helped guide our development decisions for this and previous editions. This text would not be the success it is without the help of all of you.

Board of Reviewers

Dawn Addington, *Central New Mexico Community College*
Ajay Adhikari, *American University*
Gary Adna Ames, *Brigham Young University*
Peter Aghimien, *Indiana University—South Bend*
Nas Ahadiat, *California Polytechnic University*
John Ahern, *DePaul University*
Pervaiz Alam, *Kent State University*
Joyce Allen, *Xavier University*
Robert Allen, *University of Utah—Salt Lake City*
Vern Allen, *Central Florida Community College*
Bridget Anakwe, *Plattsburgh State University of New York*
Brenda Anderson, *Boston University*
Joseph Antenucci, *Youngstown State University*
Frank Aquilino, *Montclair State University*
Liz Arnold, *The Citadel*
Florence Atiase, *University of Texas—Austin*
Jane Baird, *Minnesota State University—Mankato*
Kashi R. Balachandran, *New York University*
Patricia Bancroft, *Bridgewater State University*
Yan Bao, *Frostburg State University*
Laurel Barfitt, *Delta State University*
Melody Barta, *Evergreen College*
Ira W. Bates, *Florida A&M University*
Deborah Beard, *Southeast Missouri State University*
Daisy Beck, *Louisiana State University*
John Bedient, *Albion College*
S. Douglas Beets, *Wake Forest University*
Michael Bitter, *Stetson University*
Eric Blazer, *Millersville University*
Janell Blazovich, *University of St. Thomas*
L. Charles Bokemeier, *Michigan State University*
Michael G. Booth, *Cabrillo College*
Sharon Borowicz, *Benedictine University*
Scott Boylan, *Washington & Lee University*
Mark Bradshaw, *Harvard Business School*
Christopher Brandon, *Indiana University—Purdue University Columbus*
Rodger Brannan, *University of Minnesota—Duluth*
Allison Brock, *Imperial Valley College*
Rada Brooks, *University of California at Berkeley*
Nina Brown, *Tarrant County College*
Amy Browning, *Ivy Technical Community College*
Helen Brubeck, *San Jose State University*
Terri Brunsdon, *The University of Akron*
Marci Butterfield, *University of Utah*
Catherine Byrne, *Boston College*
Kay Carnes, *Gonzaga University*
Nancy Cassidy, *Texas A&M University*

Michael Cathey, *The George Washington University*
Kam Chan, *Pace University*
Chiaho Chang, *Montclair State University*
Gretchen Charrier, *University of Texas—Austin*
Agnes Cheng, *University of Houston*
Antoinette Clegg, *Palm Beach Community College*
Anne Clem, *Iowa State University*
Jacklyn Collins, *University of Miami*
Judy Colwell, *Northern Oklahoma College*
Elizabeth Conner, *University of Colorado—Denver*
Teresa Conover, *University of North Texas*
Scott Creech, *Johnston Community College*
Marcia Croteau, *University of Maryland—Baltimore*
Sue Cullers, *Tarleton State University*
Dori Danko, *Grand Valley State University*
Betty David, *Francis Marion University*
Harold Davis, *Southeastern Louisiana University*
Paquita Davis-Friday, *Bernard M. Baruch College*
Marinus DeBruine, *Grand Valley State University*
Mark DeFond, *University of Southern California*
Elizabeth Demers, *University of Rochester*
Mingcherng Deng, *Columbia University*
Bettye Desselle, *Prairie View A&M University*
Carleton Donchess, *Bridgewater State University*
Debra Dragone, *University of Delaware*
Allan Drebin, *Northwestern University*
Carolyn Dreher, *Southern Methodist University*
Chan Du, *University of Massachusetts—Dartmouth*
Gene Elrod, *University of North Texas*
Sheri Erickson, *Minnesota State University—Moorehead*
Harlan Etheridge, *University of Louisiana—Lafayette*
Thomas Finnegan, *University of Illinois at Urbana—Champaign*
Richard Fleischman, *John Carroll University*
Virginia Fullwood, *Texas A&M University—Commerce*
Cheryl Furbee, *Cabrillo College*
Mohamed Gaber, *SUNY Plattsburgh*
Joseph Galante, *Millersville University of Pennsylvania*
Carolyn Galantine, *Pepperdine University*
Andy Garcia, *Bowling Green State University*
David Gelb, *Seton Hall University*
Lisa Gillespie, *Loyola University, Chicago*
Giorgio Gotti, *University of Massachusetts—Boston*
Anthony Greig, *Purdue University*
A. Kay Guess, *St. Edward's University*
Jeffrey Haber, *Iona College*
Leon Hanouille, *Syracuse University*
Russell Hardin, *Pittsburg State University*

Sheila Hardy, *Lafayette College*
Betty Harper, *Middle Tennessee State*
David Harr, *American University*
Bob Hartman, *University of Iowa*
Syed Hasan, *George Mason University*
Carla Hayn, *University of California—Los Angeles*
Haihong He, *California State University—Los Angeles*
Julie Head, *Indiana University*
Kenneth R. Henry, *Florida International University*
Siriyama Kanthi Herath, *Clark Atlanta University*
Ann Ownby Hicks, *North Park University*
Lori Holder-Webb, *University of Wisconsin*
Pamela Hopcroft, *Florida Community College*
Merle W. Hopkins, *University of Southern California*
Paul Hribar, *University of Iowa*
Courtland Huber, *University of Texas—Austin*
Dawn Hukai, *University of Wisconsin—River Falls*
Bob Hurt, *California State Polytechnic University—Pomona*
Carol Hutchinson, *AB Tech*
Constance M. Hylton, *George Mason University*
Marc Hyman, *University of California—Berkeley*
Laura Ilcisin, *University of Nebraska—Omaha*
Norma Jacobs, *Austin Community College*
Scott Jerris, *San Francisco State University*
Carol Johnson, *Oklahoma State University*
Eric Johnson, *Indiana University—Purdue University Columbus*
Shondra Johnson, *Bradley University*
Christopher Jones, *The George Washington University*
Matthew Josefy, *Texas A&M University*
John Karayan, *California State Polytechnic University—Pomona*
Robert Kasmir, *The George Washington University*
Beth Kern, *Indiana University—South Bend*
Irene Kim, *George Washington University*
Janet Kimbrell, *Oklahoma State University*
Janice Klimek, *University of Central Missouri*
Trevor Knox, *Muhlenberg College*
Dennis Lee Kovach, *Community College of Allegheny*
Tammy Kowalczyk, *Western Washington University*
Doug Kroll, *University of Notre Dame*
Charles Ladd, *University of St. Thomas*
Steven J. LaFave, *Augsburg College*
Christy Land, *Catawba Valley Community College*
Maria Leach, *Auburn University at Montgomery*
Terry Lease, *Sonoma State*
Marc Lebow, *Christopher Newport University*
Deborah Lee, *Northeastern State University*

Patsy Lee, *University of North Texas*
Christy Lefevers-Land, *Catawba Valley Community College*
Annette Leps, *Johns Hopkins University*
Seth Levine, *University of Miami*
Elliott Levy, *Bentley University*
Phil Lewis, *Eastern Michigan University*
June Li, *University of Wisconsin—River Falls*
Ling Lin, *University of Massachusetts—Dartmouth*
Daniel Litt, *University of California—Los Angeles*
Jack Little, *Cornell University*
Chao-Shin Liu, *University of Notre Dame*
Joshua Livnat, *New York University*
Lawrence Logan, *University of Massachusetts—Dartmouth*
Patricia Lopez, *Valencia Community College*
Barbara Lougee, *University of San Diego*
Joseph Lupino, *St. Mary's College of California*
Luann Lynch, *University of Virginia*
Mary MacAusland, *Cornell University*
Lori Mason-Olson, *University of Northern Iowa*
Josephine Mathias, *Mercer County Community College*
Larry McCabe, *Muhlenberg College*
Nick McGaughey, *San Jose State University*
Florence McGovern, *Bergen Community College*
Noel McKeon, *Florida Community College—Jacksonville*
Allison McLeod, *University of North Texas*
Michael G. McMillan, *Johns Hopkins University*
L. Kevin McNelis, *New Mexico State University*
Tammy Metzke, *Milwaukee Area Technical College*
Michael J. Meyer, *University of Notre Dame*
Paulette Miller, *Collin County Community College*
Tim Mills, *Eastern Illinois University*
Marilyn Misch, *Pepperdine University*
Birendra Mishra, *University of California at Riverside*
Earl Mitchell, *Santa Ana College*
Dennis P. Moore, *Worcester State College*
Haim Mozes, *Fordham University*
Brian Nagle, *Duquesne University*
Ramesh Narasimhan, *Montclair State University*
Presha Neidermeyer, *Union College*
Samir Nissan, *California Sate University—Chico*
Tom Nunamaker, *Washington State University*
Peggy O'Kelly, *Northeastern University*
John O'Shaughnessy, *San Francisco State University*
Janet L. O'Tousa, *University of Notre Dame*
Donald Pagach, *North Carolina State—Raleigh*
Susan Parker, *Santa Clara University*
Sharon Parrish, *Kentucky State University*
Kathy Petroni, *Michigan State University*
Catherine Plante, *University of New Hampshire*
Kay Poston, *Francis Marion University*

Grace Pownall, *Emory University*
Olga Quintanta, *University of Miami*
Rama Ramamurthy, *College of William & Mary*
Charles Ransom, *Oklahoma State University*
Keith Richardson, *Bellarmine University*
Brenda Richter, *Santa Barbara City College*
Laura Rickett, *Kent State University*
Brandi Roberts, *Southeastern Louisiana University*
Joanne Rockness, *University of North Carolina—Wilmington*
Lawrence Roman, *Cuyahoga Community College*
John Rossi III, *Moravian College*
John Rude, *Bloomsburg University*
Joan Ryan, *Clackamas Community College*
Karen Salmela, *University of Minnesota—Duluth*
Angela Sandberg, *Jacksonville State University*
Amy Santos, *Manatee Community College*
Maggie Schlerman, *Central College*
Andrew Schmidt, *Columbia University*
William Schmuhl, *University of Notre Dame*
Richard Schroeder, *University of North Carolina—Charlotte*
Joann Segovia, *Minnesota State University Moorhead*
Cindy Seipel, *New Mexico State University*
Ann Selk, *University of Wisconsin—Green Bay*
Kathleen Sevigny, *Bridgewater State College*
Howard Shapiro, *Eastern Washington University*
Warren Smock, *Ivy Technical Community College—Lafayette*
Billy Soo, *Boston College*
Sri Sridhanen, *Northwestern University*
David Stein, *Metropolitan State University*
Phillip Stocken, *Dartmouth College*
Dennis Stovall, *Grand Valley State University*
Joel Strong, *St. Cloud State University*
Gina Sturgill, *Concord College*
Susan Sullivan, *University of Massachusetts—Dartmouth*
Martin Taylor, *University of Texas—Arlington*
Mack Tennyson, *College of Charleston*
Peter Theuri, *Northern Kentucky University*
W. Stewart Thomas, *University of North Carolina—Pembroke*
Lynda Thompson, *Massasoit Community College*
Theresa Tiggeman, *University of the Incarnate Word*
Theodore Tully, *DeVry University*
Lana Tuss, *Chemeketa Community College*
Michael Ulinski, *Pace University*
Ingrid Ulstad, *University of Wisconsin—Eau Claire*
Marcia Veit, *University of Central Florida*
Charles Wain, *Babson College*
Rick Warne, *University of Cincinnati*
Charles Wasley, *University of Rochester*
Daniel Weddington, *Ohio University—Zanesville*

David Weiner, *University of San Francisco*
Patti Weiss, *John Carroll University*
Cheryl Westen, *Western Illinois University*
David Wiest, *Washington and Lee University*
Patrick Wilkie, *University of Virginia*
Jefferson Williams, *University of Michigan*
Wendy Wilson, *Southern Methodist University*
Peter Woodlock, *Youngstown State University*
Ron Woods, *North Seattle Community College*
Darryl Woolley, *University of Idaho*
Michael Yampuler, *University of Houston*
Kathryn Yarbrough, *University of North Carolina—Charlotte*
Zhang (May) Yue, *Northeastern University*
Xiao-Jun Zhang, *University of California at Berkeley*

We are grateful to the following individuals who helped develop, critique, and shape the extensive ancillary package: LuAnn Bean, Florida Institute of Technology; Jeannie Folk, College of DuPage; Julie Head, Indiana University; Shondra Johnson, Bradley University; Sara Kern, Gonzaga University; Nancy Lynch, West Virginia University; Mark McCarthy, East Carolina University; Barbara Muller, Arizona State University; Kristine Palmer, Longwood College; Ilene Leopold Persoff, Long Island University Post; Kevin Smith, Utah Valley University; Beth Woods, Accuracy Counts; and Teri Zuccaro, Clarke University.

We also have received invaluable input and support through the years from present and former colleagues and students. We also appreciate the additional comments, suggestions, and support of our students and our colleagues at Cornell University, Ithaca College, and University of Washington.

Last, we applaud the extraordinary efforts of a talented group of individuals at McGraw-Hill who made all of this come together. We would especially like to thank Tim Vertovec, our managing director; Natalie King, our senior brand manager; Rebecca Mann, our senior product developer; Kyle Burdette, our marketing manager; Daryl Horrocks, our program manager; Lori Koetters and Angela Norris, our project managers; Debra Kubiak, our designer; Susan Culbertson, our buyer; and Melissa Homer and Beth Thole, our content licensing specialists.

Robert Libby
Patricia A. Libby
Frank Hodge

CONTENTS IN BRIEF

Chapter 6

Reporting and Interpreting Sales Revenue, Receivables, and Cash 282

Chapter 7

Reporting and Interpreting Cost of Goods Sold and Inventory 332

Chapter 8

Reporting and Interpreting Property, Plant, and Equipment; Intangibles; and Natural Resources 388

Financial Accounting

Financial Statements and Business Decisions

Le-Nature's Inc. designed its business strategy to ride the growing wave of interest in noncarbonated beverages. And apparently its strategy was a huge success: Its financial statements reported growth in sales from $156 to $275 million in just three years. How did this small family-run business compete with the likes of Coke and Pepsi in this growing market? The business press suggested the first key to its success was manufacturing a broad range of products that fit into the fastest growing "healthy" segments: flavored waters, teas, and fruit drinks. Founder and CEO Gregory Podlucky said that an obsessive drive for quality and efficiency was just as critical. Matching customers' concerns for the environment and healthy living, Le-Nature's was praised as one of the first companies to switch to environmentally friendlier PET plastic bottles and to employ safe in-bottle pasteurization. Its 21st-century manufacturing operation in Latrobe, Pennsylvania, produced everything that goes into its products, from the injection-molded PET bottles to the final packaging. Complete control over the whole process assures quality and provides the flexibility to respond quickly to changes in customers' demands. When convenience stores moved to larger-sized drinks or school cafeterias switched from carbonated beverages to healthier drinks, Le-Nature's could change its production to meet the customers' needs. In August, the company opened a second new state-of-the-art manufacturing facility in Arizona to meet the apparent growing demand.

But here is the twist: Just three short months later, investigators discovered that Le-Nature's phenomenal sales growth was more fiction than fact. How could this seeming success story portrayed in the financial statements really be one of the most remarkable frauds in history?

Chapter 1 concentrates on the key financial statements that businesspeople rely upon when they evaluate a company's performance as well as the importance of accurate financial statements in making our economic system work. We discuss these issues in the context of Le-Nature's rise and fall.

Accounting knowledge will be valuable to you only if you can apply it in the real world. Learning is also easier when it takes place in real contexts. So at the beginning of each chapter we always provide some background about the business that will provide the context for the chapter discussion.

Learning Objectives

After studying this chapter, you should be able to:

1-1 Recognize the information conveyed in each of the four basic financial statements and the way that it is used by different decision makers (investors, creditors, and managers).

1-2 Identify the role of generally accepted accounting principles (GAAP) in determining financial statement content and how companies ensure the accuracy of their financial statements.

© James F. Quinn/LRT/Newscom

Le-Nature's Inc.

USING FINANCIAL STATEMENT INFORMATION TO MANAGE GROWTH

UNDERSTANDING THE BUSINESS

Le-Nature's Inc., our focus company for this chapter, was founded by Gregory Podlucky and his brother Jonathan, who initially were the sole owners or **stockholders** of the company. They were also the managers of the company. Using expertise gained working at their parents' brewery (**Stoney's Beer**), the brothers were early believers in the trend toward healthier, noncarbonated beverages. Like most entrepreneurs, their growth ambitions quickly outpaced their own financial resources. So they turned to banks, including **Wells Fargo Bank** and other lenders, to finance additional manufacturing facilities and equipment. Different units of Wells Fargo continued to arrange lending to Le-Nature's as the need arose, becoming its largest lender or **creditor.** Creditors make money on the loans by charging **interest.** The Podluckys also convinced others to buy stock in Le-Nature's. These individuals became part owners or stockholders along with the Podluckys. They hoped to receive a portion of what the company earned in the form of cash payments called **dividends** and to eventually sell their share of the company at a higher price than they paid. Creditors are more willing to lend and stock prices usually rise when creditors and investors expect the company to do well in the future. Both groups often judge future performance based on information in the company's financial statements.

The Accounting System

Managers (often called **internal decision makers**) need information about the company's business activities to manage the operating, investing, and financing activities of the firm. Stockholders and creditors (often called **external decision makers**) need information about these same business activities to assess whether

EXHIBIT 1.1

The Accounting System
and Decision Makers

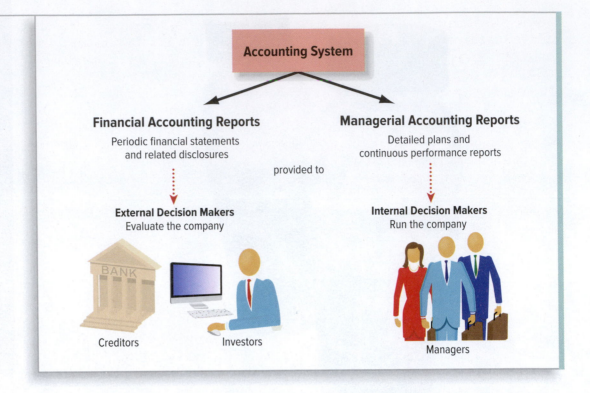

the company will be able to pay back its debts with interest and pay dividends. All businesses must have an **accounting** system that collects and processes financial information about an organization's business activities and reports that information to decision makers. **Le-Nature's** business activities included:

- **Financing Activities:** borrowing or paying back money to lenders and receiving additional funds from stockholders or paying them dividends.
- **Investing Activities:** buying or selling items such as plant and equipment used in the production of beverages.
- **Operating Activities:** the day-to-day process of purchasing raw tea and other ingredients from suppliers, manufacturing beverages, delivering them to customers, collecting cash from customers, and paying suppliers.

Exhibit 1.1 outlines the two parts of the accounting system. Internal managers typically require continuous, detailed information because they must plan and manage the day-to-day operations of the organization. Developing accounting information for internal decision makers, called **managerial** or **management accounting,** is the subject of a separate accounting course. The focus of this text is accounting for external decision makers, called **financial accounting,** and the four basic financial statements and related disclosures that are periodically produced by that system.

Why Study Financial Accounting?

No matter what your business career goals, you can't get away from financial accounting. You may want to work for an investment firm, a bank, or an accounting firm that would be involved in the financing of companies like **Le-Nature's**. We will focus much of our discussion on the perspectives of **investors, creditors,** and **preparers** of financial statements. However, you might not be aware that managers within the firm also make direct use of financial statements. For example, **marketing managers** and **credit managers** use customers' financial statements to decide whether to extend credit to their customers. **Supply chain managers** analyze suppliers'

ACCOUNTING
A system that collects and processes (analyzes, measures, and records) financial information about an organization and reports that information to decision makers.

financial statements to see whether the suppliers have the resources to meet demand and invest in future development. Both the employees' unions and company **human resource managers** use financial statements as a basis for contract negotiations over pay rates. Financial statement figures even serve as a basis for calculating employee bonuses. Regardless of the functional area of management in which you are employed, you will use financial statement data.

We begin with a brief but comprehensive overview of the information reported in the four basic financial statements and the people and organizations involved in their preparation and use. This overview provides a context in which you can learn the more detailed material presented in the chapters that follow. Then we will discuss the parties that are responsible for the accuracy of financial statements as well as the consequences of misstated financial statements. Le-Nature's stockholders and creditors used its financial statements to learn more about the company before making their investment and lending decisions. In doing so, they assumed that the statements accurately represented Le-Nature's financial condition.

Your Goals for Chapter 1

To understand the way in which creditors and stockholders used **Le-Nature's** financial statements, we must first understand what specific information is presented in the four basic financial statements for a company such as Le-Nature's. **PLEASE NOTE: Rather than trying to memorize the definitions of every term used in this chapter, try to focus your attention on learning the general content, structure, and use of the statements. Specifically:**

- **Content:** the categories of items (often called **elements**) reported on each of the four statements.
- **Structure:** the **equation** that shows how the elements within the statement are organized and related.
- **Use:** how the information is **used** by stockholders and creditors to make investment and lending decisions.

The Pause for Feedback–Self-Study Quizzes at key points in the chapter will help you assess whether you have reached these goals. Remember that since this chapter is an overview, each concept discussed here will be discussed again in Chapters 2 through 5.

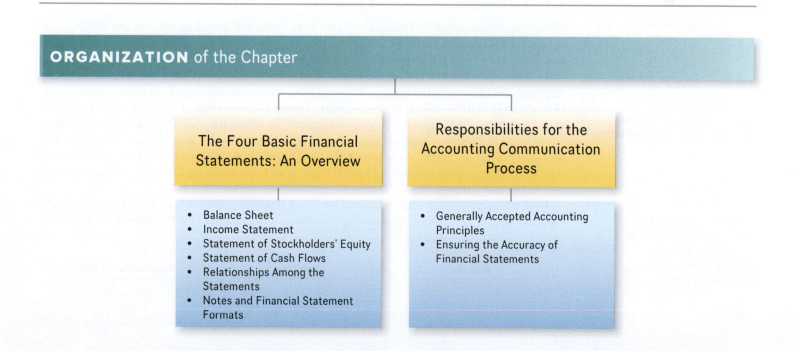

ORGANIZATION of the Chapter

The Four Basic Financial Statements: An Overview	Responsibilities for the Accounting Communication Process
• Balance Sheet • Income Statement • Statement of Stockholders' Equity • Statement of Cash Flows • Relationships Among the Statements • Notes and Financial Statement Formats	• Generally Accepted Accounting Principles • Ensuring the Accuracy of Financial Statements

THE FOUR BASIC FINANCIAL STATEMENTS: AN OVERVIEW

Four financial statements are normally prepared by profit-making organizations for use by investors, creditors, and other external decision makers.

1. On its **balance sheet, Le-Nature's** reports the economic resources it owns and the sources of financing for those resources.
2. On its **income statement,** Le-Nature's reports its ability to sell goods for more than their cost to produce and sell.
3. On its **statement of stockholders' equity,** Le-Nature's reports additional contributions or payments to investors and the amount of income the company reinvested for future growth.
4. On its **statement of cash flows,** Le-Nature's reports its ability to generate cash and how it was used.

The four basic statements can be prepared at any point in time (such as the end of the year, quarter, or month) and can apply to any time span (such as one year, one quarter, or one month). Like most companies, Le-Nature's prepared financial statements for external users (investors and creditors) at the end of each quarter (known as **quarterly reports**) and at the end of the year (known as **annual reports**).

The Balance Sheet

BALANCE SHEET (STATEMENT OF FINANCIAL POSITION)

Reports the amount of assets, liabilities, and stockholders' equity of an accounting entity at a point in time.

The purpose of the **balance sheet** is to report the financial position (amount of assets, liabilities, and stockholders' equity) of an accounting entity at a particular point in time. We can learn a great deal about what the balance sheet reports just by reading the statement from the top. The balance sheet **Le-Nature's Inc.** presented to creditors and stockholders is shown in Exhibit 1.2.

Structure

Notice that the **heading** specifically identifies four significant items related to the statement:

1. **Name of the entity,** Le-Nature's Inc.
2. **Title of the statement,** Balance Sheet.
3. **Specific date of the statement,** At December 31, 2012.
4. **Unit of measure,** (in millions of dollars).

ACCOUNTING ENTITY

The organization for which financial data are to be collected.

The organization for which financial data are to be collected, called an **accounting entity**, must be precisely defined. On the balance sheet, the business entity itself, not the business owners, is viewed as owning the resources it uses and being responsible for its debts. The heading of each statement indicates the time dimension of the report. The balance sheet is like a financial snapshot indicating the entity's financial position at a specific point in time—in this case, December 31, 2012—which is stated clearly on the balance sheet. Financial reports are normally denominated in the currency of the country in which they are located. U.S. companies report in U.S. dollars, Canadian companies in Canadian dollars, and Mexican companies in Mexican pesos. Le-Nature's statements report in millions of dollars. That is, they round the last six digits to the nearest **million** dollars. The listing of Cash $10.6 on Le-Nature's balance sheet actually means $10,600,000.

BASIC ACCOUNTING EQUATION (BALANCE SHEET EQUATION)

Assets = Liabilities + Stockholders' Equity.

Notice that Le-Nature's balance sheet has three major captions: assets, liabilities, and stockholders' equity. The **basic accounting equation**, often called the balance sheet equation, explains their relationship:

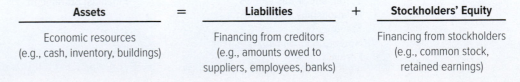

Assets	=	Liabilities	+	Stockholders' Equity
Economic resources (e.g., cash, inventory, buildings)		Financing from creditors (e.g., amounts owed to suppliers, employees, banks)		Financing from stockholders (e.g., common stock, retained earnings)

EXHIBIT 1.2

Balance Sheet

LE-NATURE'S INC.* Balance Sheet At December 31, 2012 (in millions of dollars)		EXPLANATION
		Name of the entity
		Title of the statement
		Specific date of the statement
		Unit of measure
Assets:		***Resources controlled by the company***
Cash	$ 10.6	*Amount of cash in the company's bank accounts*
Accounts receivable	6.6	*Amounts owed by customers from prior sales*
Inventories	51.2	*Ingredients and beverages ready for sale*
Property, plant, and equipment	459.0	*Factories, production equipment, and land*
Total assets	**$527.4**	***Total amount of company's resources***
Liabilities and stockholders' equity:		***Sources of financing for company's resources***
Liabilities		*Financing supplied by creditors*
Accounts payable	$ 26.0	*Amounts owed to suppliers for prior purchases*
Notes payable to banks	381.7	*Amounts owed to banks on written debt contracts*
Total liabilities	407.7	
Stockholders' equity		*Financing provided by stockholders*
Common stock	55.7	*Amounts invested in the business by stockholders*
Retained earnings	64.0	*Past earnings not distributed to stockholders*
Total stockholders' equity	119.7	
Total liabilities and stockholders' equity	**$527.4**	***Total sources of financing for company's resources***

The notes are an integral part of these financial statements.

The basic accounting equation shows what we mean when we refer to a company's **financial position:** the economic resources that the company owns and the sources of financing for those resources.

Elements

Assets are the economic resources owned by the entity. Le-Nature's lists four items under the category Assets. The exact items listed as assets on a company's balance sheet depend on the nature of its operations. But these are common names used by many companies. The four items listed by Le-Nature's are the economic resources needed to manufacture and sell beverages to retailers and vending companies. Each of these economic resources is expected to provide future benefits to the firm. To prepare to manufacture the beverages, Le-Nature's first needed cash to purchase land on which to build factories and install production machinery (property, plant, and equipment). Le-Nature's then began purchasing ingredients and producing beverages, which led to the balance assigned to inventories. When Le-Nature's sells its beverages to grocery stores and others, it sells them on credit and receives promises to pay called accounts receivable, which are collected in cash later.

Every asset on the balance sheet is initially measured at the total cost incurred to acquire it. Balance sheets do not generally show the amounts for which the assets could currently be sold.

Liabilities and stockholders' equity are the sources of financing for the company's economic resources. **Liabilities** indicate the amount of financing provided by creditors. They are the company's debts or obligations. Under the category Liabilities, Le-Nature's lists two items. The accounts payable arise from the purchase of goods

© Spaces Images/Blend Images

*Le-Nature's statements have been simplified for purposes of our discussion.

or services from suppliers on credit without a formal written contract (or a note). The notes payable to banks result from cash borrowings based on a formal written debt contract with banks.

Stockholders' equity indicates the amount of financing provided by owners of the business and reinvested earnings.[1] The investment of cash and other assets in the business by the stockholders is called common stock. The amount of earnings (profits) reinvested in the business (and thus not distributed to stockholders in the form of dividends) is called retained earnings.

In Exhibit 1.2, the Stockholders' Equity section reports two items. The founders and other stockholders' investment of $55.7 million is reported as common stock. Le-Nature's total earnings (or losses incurred) less all dividends paid to the stockholders since formation of the corporation equals $64 million and is reported as retained earnings. Total stockholders' equity is the sum of the common stock plus the retained earnings.

FINANCIAL ANALYSIS		Interpreting Assets, Liabilities, and Stockholders' Equity on the Balance Sheet

Assessment of **Le-Nature's** assets was important to its creditors, **Wells Fargo Bank** and others, and its stockholders because assets provide a basis for judging whether the company has sufficient resources available to operate. Assets are also important because they could be sold for cash in the event that Le-Nature's went out of business.

Le-Nature's debts are important because creditors and stockholders are concerned about whether the company has sufficient sources of cash to pay its debts. Le-Nature's debts were also relevant to Wells Fargo Bank's decision to lend money to the company because existing creditors share its claim against Le-Nature's assets. If a business does not pay its creditors, the creditors may force the sale of assets sufficient to meet their claims. The sale of assets often fails to cover all of a company's debts, and some creditors may take a loss.

Le-Nature's stockholders' equity is important to Wells Fargo Bank because creditors' claims legally come before those of owners. If Le-Nature's goes out of business and its assets are sold, the proceeds of that sale must be used to pay back creditors before the stockholders receive any money. Thus, creditors consider stockholders' equity a protective "cushion."

STOP   PAUSE FOR **FEEDBACK**

We just learned the **balance sheet** is a statement of financial position that reports dollar amounts for a company's assets, liabilities, and stockholders' equity at a specific point in time. These elements are related in the basic accounting equation: **Assets = Liabilities + Stockholders' Equity.** Before you move on, complete the following questions to test your understanding of these concepts.

SELF-STUDY **QUIZ**

1. **Le-Nature's** assets are listed in one section and **liabilities** and **stockholders' equity** in another. Notice that the two sections balance in conformity with the basic accounting

---

[1]A corporation is a business that is incorporated under the laws of a particular state. The owners are called **stockholders** or **shareholders.** Ownership is represented by shares of capital stock that usually can be bought and sold freely. The corporation operates as a separate legal entity, separate and apart from its owners. The stockholders enjoy limited liability; they are liable for the debts of the corporation only to the extent of their investments. Chapter Supplement A discusses forms of ownership in more detail.

equation. In the following chapters, you will learn that the basic accounting equation is the basic building block for the entire accounting process. Your task here is to verify that total assets ($527.4 million) is correct using the numbers for liabilities and stockholders' equity presented in Exhibit 1.2.

2. Learning which items belong in each of the balance sheet categories is an important first step in understanding their meaning. Without referring to Exhibit 1.2, mark each balance sheet item in the following list as an asset (A), a liability (L), or a stockholders' equity (SE) item.

_____ Accounts payable   _____ Property, plant, and equipment
_____ Accounts receivable   _____ Inventories
_____ Cash   _____ Notes payable
_____ Common stock   _____ Retained earnings

After you have completed your answers, check them below.

The Income Statement

Structure

The **income statement** (statement of income, statement of earnings, statement of operations, statement of comprehensive income[2]) reports the accountant's primary measure of performance of a business, revenues less expenses during the accounting period. While the term *profit* is used widely for this measure of performance, accountants prefer to use the technical terms **net income** or net earnings. **Le-Nature's** net income measures its success in selling beverages for more than the cost to generate those sales.

A quick reading of Le-Nature's income statement (Exhibit 1.3) indicates a great deal about its purpose and content. The heading identifies the name of the entity, the title of the report, and the unit of measure used in the statement. Unlike the balance sheet, however, which reports as of a certain date, the income statement reports for a specified period of time (for the year ended December 31, 2012). The time period covered by the financial statements (one year in this case) is called an **accounting period**. Notice that Le-Nature's income statement has three major captions: revenues, expenses, and net income. The income statement equation that describes their relationship is:

INCOME STATEMENT (STATEMENT OF INCOME, STATEMENT OF EARNINGS, STATEMENT OF OPERATIONS, STATEMENT OF COMPREHENSIVE INCOME)
Reports the revenues less the expenses of the accounting period.

ACCOUNTING PERIOD
The time period covered by the financial statements.

Revenues	−	Expenses	=	Net Income
(Cash and promises received from delivery of goods and services)		(Resources used to earn period's revenues)		(Revenues earned minus expenses incurred)

Elements

Companies earn **revenues** from the sale of goods or services to customers (in Le-Nature's case, from the sale of beverages). Revenues normally are amounts expected to be received for goods or services that have been delivered to a customer, **whether or not the customer has paid for the goods or services.** Retail stores such as **Walmart** and **McDonald's** often receive cash from consumers at the time of sale. However, when Le-Nature's delivers its beverages to retail stores, it receives a promise of future payment called an account receivable, which later is

Income Statement

Revenues
− Expenses
Net Income

---

1. Assets ($527.4) = Liabilities ($407.7) + Stockholders' Equity ($119.7) (in millions).
2. L, A, A, SE, A, A, L, SE (reading down the columns).

Solutions to
SELF-STUDY QUIZ

---

[2]Comprehensive income is sometimes presented in a separate statement. This advanced topic is discussed in Chapter 5.

EXHIBIT 1.3

Income Statement

LE-NATURE'S INC. **Income Statement** **For the Year Ended December 31, 2012** **(in millions of dollars)**		EXPLANATION
		Name of the entity
		Title of the statement
		Accounting period
		Unit of measure
Revenues		
Sales revenue	$275.1	Cash and promises received from sale of beverages
Expenses		
Cost of goods sold	140.8	Cost to produce beverages sold
Selling, general, and administrative		Other operating expenses (utilities, delivery
expenses	77.1	costs, etc.)
Interest expense	17.2	Cost of using borrowed funds
Income before income taxes	40.0	
Income tax expense	17.1	Income taxes on period's income before income taxes
Net income	$ 22.9	Revenues earned minus expenses incurred

The notes are an integral part of these financial statements.

collected in cash. In either case, the business recognizes total sales (cash and credit) as revenue for the period. Various terms are used in income statements to describe different sources of revenue (e.g., provision of services, sale of goods, rental of property). Le-Nature's lists only one, sales revenue, in its income statement.

Expenses represent the dollar amount of resources the entity used to earn revenues during the period. Expenses reported in one accounting period may actually be paid for in another accounting period. Some expenses require the payment of cash immediately while others require payment at a later date. Some may also require the use of another resource, such as an inventory item, which may have been paid for in a prior period. Le-Nature's lists four types of expenses on its income statement, which are described in Exhibit 1.3. These expenses include income tax expense, which, as a corporation, Le-Nature's must pay on the subtotal income before income taxes.

Net income or net earnings (often called "the bottom line") is the excess of total revenues over total expenses. If total expenses exceed total revenues, a net loss is reported.[3] We noted earlier that revenues are not necessarily the same as collections from customers and expenses are not necessarily the same as payments to suppliers. As a result, net income normally **does not equal** the net cash generated by operations. This latter amount is reported on the cash flow statement discussed later in this chapter.

FINANCIAL ANALYSIS   Analyzing the Income Statement: Beyond the Bottom Line

Investors and creditors such as **Wells Fargo Bank** closely monitor a firm's net income because it indicates the firm's ability to sell goods and services for more than they cost to produce and deliver. Investors buy stock when they believe that future earnings will improve and lead to dividends and the ability to sell their stock for more than they paid. Lenders also rely on future earnings to provide the resources to repay loans. The details of the statement also are important. For example, **Le-Nature's** had to sell more than $275 million worth of beverages to make just under $23 million. If a competitor were to lower prices just 10 percent, forcing Le-Nature's to do the same, its net income could easily turn into a net loss. These factors and others help investors and creditors estimate the company's future earnings.

---

[3]Net losses are normally noted by parentheses around the income figure.

As noted above, the **income statement** is a statement of operations that reports revenues, expenses, and net income for a stated period of time. To practice your understanding of these concepts, complete the following questions.

SELF-STUDY QUIZ

1. Learning which items belong in each of the income statement categories is an important first step in understanding their meaning. Without referring to Exhibit 1.3, mark each income statement item in the following list as a revenue (R) or an expense (E).

   _____ Cost of goods sold   _____ Sales revenue
   _____ Income tax   _____ Selling, general, and administrative

2. During the period 2012, **Le-Nature's** delivered beverages for which customers paid or promised to pay amounts totaling $275.1 million. During the same period, it collected $250.0 million in cash from its customers. Without referring to Exhibit 1.3, indicate which of these two amounts will be shown on Le-Nature's income statement as **sales revenue** for 2012. Why did you select your answer?

3. During the period 2012, Le-Nature's **produced** beverages with a total cost of production of $142.1 million. During the same period, it **delivered** to customers beverages that cost a total of $140.8 million to produce. Without referring to Exhibit 1.3, indicate which of the two numbers will be shown on Le-Nature's income statement as **cost of goods sold expense** for 2012. Why did you select your answer?

After you have completed your answers, check them below.

AP Photo/Keith Srakocic

Statement of Stockholders' Equity

Structure

Le-Nature's prepares a separate **statement of stockholders' equity**, shown in Exhibit 1.4. The heading identifies the name of the entity, the title of the report, and the unit of measure used in the statement. Like the income statement, the statement of stockholders' equity covers a specified period of time (the accounting period), which in this case is one year. The statement reports the changes in each of the company's stockholders' equity accounts during that period.

Le-Nature's had no changes in common stock during the period. Had it issued or repurchased common stock during the year, the transactions would be reported on separate lines. The retained earnings column reports the way that net income and the distribution of dividends affected the company's financial position during the accounting period. Net income earned during the year increases the balance of retained earnings, showing the relationship of

STATEMENT OF STOCKHOLDERS' EQUITY
Reports the way that net income and the distribution of dividends affected the financial position of the company during the accounting period.

Solutions to
SELF-STUDY QUIZ

1. E, E, R, E (reading down the columns).

2. Sales revenue in the amount of $275.1 million is recognized. Sales revenue is normally reported on the income statement when goods or services have been delivered to customers who have either paid or promised to pay for them in the future.

3. Cost of goods sold expense is $140.8. Expenses are the dollar amount of resources used up to earn revenues during the period. Only those beverages that have been delivered to customers have been used up.

LE-NATURE'S INC.
Statement of Stockholders' Equity
For the Year Ended December 31, 2012
(in millions of dollars)

	Common Stock	Retained Earnings	
Balance December 31, 2011	$55.7	$43.1	*Last period's ending balances*
Net income for 2012		22.9	*Net income reported on the income statement*
Dividends for 2012		(2.0)	*Dividends declared during the period*
Balance December 31, 2012	$55.7	$64.0	*Ending balances on the balance sheet*

The notes are an integral part of these financial statements.

EXPLANATION
Name of the entity
Title of the statement
Accounting period
Unit of measure

Statement of Stockholders' Equity
Beginning balance
+ Increases
− Decreases
Ending balance

the income statement to the balance sheet.[4] Declaring dividends to the stockholders decreases retained earnings.

The retained earnings equation that describes these relationships is:

Beginning Retained Earnings + Net Income − Dividends = Ending Retained Earnings

Elements

The statement starts with the beginning balances in the stockholders' equity accounts, lists the increases and decreases, and reports the resulting ending balances. The retained earnings portion of the statement in Exhibit 1.4 begins with Le-Nature's **beginning-of-the-year retained earnings.** The current year's **net income** reported on the income statement is added and the current year's **dividends** are subtracted from this amount. During 2012, Le-Nature earned $22.9 million, as shown on the income statement (Exhibit 1.3). This amount was added to the beginning-of-the-year retained earnings. Also, during 2012, Le-Nature's declared and paid a total of $2.0 million in dividends to its stockholders. This amount was subtracted in computing **end-of-the-year retained earnings** on the balance sheet. Note that retained earnings increased by the portion of income reinvested in the business ($22.9 million − $2.0 million = $20.9 million). The ending retained earnings amount of $64.0 million is the same as that reported in Exhibit 1.2 on Le-Nature's balance sheet. Thus, the retained earnings portion of the statement indicates the relationship of the income statement to the balance sheet.

FINANCIAL ANALYSIS   **Interpreting Retained Earnings**

Reinvestment of earnings, or retained earnings, is an important source of financing for **Le-Nature's**, representing more than 12 percent of its financing. Creditors such as **Wells Fargo Bank** closely monitor a firm's statement of stockholders' equity because the firm's policy on dividend payments to the stockholders affects its ability to repay its debts. Every dollar Le-Nature's pays to stockholders as a dividend is not available for use in paying back its debt to Wells Fargo. Investors examine retained earnings to determine whether the company is reinvesting a sufficient portion of earnings to support future growth.

---

[4]Net losses are subtracted.

The **statement of stockholders' equity** explains changes in stockholders' equity accounts, including the change in the retained earnings balance caused by net income and dividends during the reporting period. Check your understanding of these relationships by completing the following question.

SELF-STUDY QUIZ

1. Assume that a company's financial statements reported the following amounts: beginning retained earnings, $5,510; total assets, $20,450; dividends, $900; cost of goods sold expense, $19,475; and net income, $1,780. Without referring to Exhibit 1.4, compute ending retained earnings.

After you have completed your answer, check it below.

 GUIDED HELP 1-1

For additional step-by-step video instruction on preparing the balance sheet, income statement, and statement of stockholders' equity, go to **www.mhhe.com/libby9e_gh1**.

Statement of Cash Flows

Structure

Le-Nature's statement of cash flows is presented in Exhibit 1.5. The **statement of cash flows** (cash flow statement) divides Le-Nature's cash inflows and outflows (receipts and payments) into the three primary categories of cash flows in a typical business: cash flows from operating, investing, and financing activities. The heading identifies the name of the entity, the title of the report, and the unit of measure used in the statement. Like the income statement, the cash flow statement covers a specified period of time (the accounting period), which in this case is one year.

As discussed earlier in this chapter, reported revenues do not always equal cash collected from customers because some sales may be on credit. Also, expenses reported on the income statement may not be equal to the cash paid out during the period because expenses may be incurred in one period and paid for in another. Because the income statement does not provide information concerning cash flows, accountants prepare the statement of cash flows to report inflows and outflows of cash. The cash flow statement equation describes the causes of the change in cash reported on the balance sheet from the end of the last period to the end of the current period:

STATEMENT OF CASH FLOWS (CASH FLOW STATEMENT)
Reports inflows and outflows of cash during the accounting period in the categories of operating, investing, and financing.

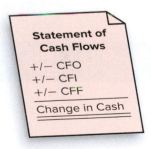

+/− Cash Flows from Operating Activities (CFO)

+/− Cash Flows from Investing Activities (CFI)

+/− Cash Flows from Financing Activities (CFF)

Change in Cash

+ Beginning Cash Balance

Ending Cash Balance

Note that each of the three cash flow sources can be positive or negative.

---

1. Beginning Retained Earnings ($5,510) + Net Income ($1,780) − Dividends ($900) = Ending Retained Earnings ($6,390).

Solutions to
SELF-STUDY QUIZ

EXHIBIT 1.5		

Statement of Cash Flows

LE-NATURE'S INC. **Statement of Cash Flows (Summary) For the Year Ended December 31, 2012 (in millions of dollars)**		**EXPLANATION**
		Name of the entity
		Title of the statement
		Accounting period
		Unit of measure
Cash flows from operating activities	$ 87.5	*Cash flows directly related to earning income*
Cash flows from investing activities	(125.5)	*Cash flows from purchase/sale of plant, equipment, & investments*
Cash flows from financing activities	47.0	*Cash flows from investors and creditors*
Net increase (decrease) in cash	9.0	***Change in cash during the period***
Cash balance December 31, 2011	1.6	*Last period's cash on the balance sheet*
Cash balance December 31, 2012	$ 10.6	***Ending cash on the balance sheet***

The notes are an integral part of these financial statements.

Elements

Cash flows from operating activities are cash flows that are directly related to earning income. For example, when customers pay Le-Nature's for the beverages it has delivered to them, it lists the amounts collected as cash collected from customers. When Le-Nature's pays salaries to its production employees or pays bills received from its tea suppliers, it includes the amounts in cash paid to suppliers and employees.

   Cash flows from investing activities include cash flows related to the acquisition or sale of the company's plant and equipment and investments. This year, Le-Nature's had only one cash outflow from investing activities, the purchase of additional manufacturing equipment to meet growing demand for its products.

   Cash flows from financing activities are cash flows directly related to the financing of the enterprise itself. They involve the receipt or payment of money to investors and creditors (except for suppliers). This year, Le-Nature's borrowed additional money from the bank to purchase most of the new manufacturing equipment. It also paid out dividends to the stockholders.[5]

FINANCIAL ANALYSIS		Interpreting the Cash Flow Statement

Bankers often consider the Operating Activities section to be most important because it indicates the company's ability to generate cash from sales to meet its current cash needs. Any amount left over can be used to pay back the bank debt or expand the company. Stockholders will invest in a company only if they believe that it will eventually generate more cash from operations than it uses so that cash will become available to pay dividends and expand.

STOP   PAUSE FOR **FEEDBACK**

The **statement of cash flows** reports inflows and outflows of cash for a stated period of time classified into three categories: operating, investing, and financing activities. Answer the following questions to test your understanding of the concepts involved.

---

[5]The complete statement of cash flows is discussed in Chapter 13.

1. During the period 2012, **Le-Nature's** delivered beverages to customers who paid or promised to pay a total of $275.1 million. During the same period, it collected $250.0 million in cash from customers. Which of the two amounts will be shown on Le-Nature's cash flow statement for 2012?

2. Your task here is to verify that Le-Nature's cash balance increased by $9.0 million during the year using the totals for cash flows from operating, investing, and financing activities presented in Exhibit 1.5. Recall the cash flow statement equation:

+/− Cash Flows from Operating Activities (CFO)
+/− Cash Flows from Investing Activities (CFI)
+/− Cash Flows from Financing Activities (CFF)
_____

Change in Cash

After you have completed your answers, check them below.

Relationships Among the Statements

Our discussion of the four basic financial statements has focused on what elements are reported in each statement, how the elements are related by the equation for each statement, and how the information is important to the decisions of investors, creditors, and others. We have also discovered how the statements, all of which are outputs from the same system, are related to one another. In particular, we learned:

❶ Net income from the income statement results in an increase in ending retained earnings on the statement of stockholders' equity.

❷ Ending retained earnings from the statement of stockholders' equity is one of the two components of stockholders' equity on the balance sheet.

❸ The change in cash on the cash flow statement added to the beginning-of-the-year balance in cash equals the end-of-year balance in cash on the balance sheet.

Thus, we can think of the income statement as explaining, through the statement of stockholders' equity, how the operations of the company improved or harmed the financial position of the company during the year. The cash flow statement explains how the operating, investing, and financing activities of the company affected the cash balance on the balance sheet during the year. These relationships are illustrated in Exhibit 1.6 for **Le-Nature's** financial statements.

Notes and Financial Statement Formats

At the bottom of each of **Le-Nature's** four basic financial statements is this statement: **"The notes are an integral part of these financial statements."** This is the accounting equivalent of the Surgeon General's warning on a package of cigarettes. It warns users that failure to

---

1. The firm recognizes $250.0 million on the cash flow statement because this number represents the actual cash collected from customers related to current and prior years' sales.

2.
+/− Cash Flows from Operating Activities (CFO)	$	87.5
+/− Cash Flows from Investing Activities (CFI)		(125.5)
+/− Cash Flows from Financing Activities (CFF)		47.0
Change in Cash	$	9.0

Solutions to
SELF-STUDY QUIZ

EXHIBIT 1.6

Relationships Among
Le-Nature's Statements

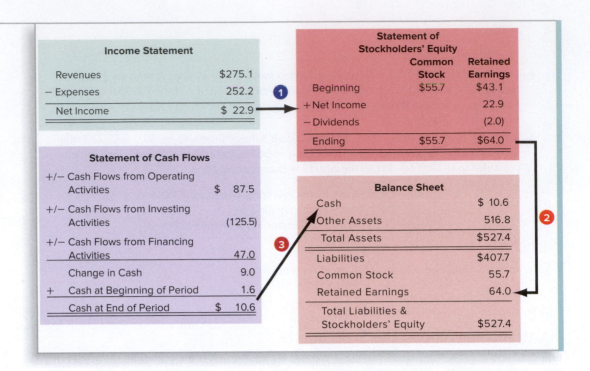

NOTES (FOOTNOTES)
Provide supplemental information about the financial condition of a company, without which the financial statements cannot be fully understood.

read the **notes** (or footnotes) to the financial statements will result in an incomplete picture of the company's financial health. Throughout this book, we will discuss many note disclosures because understanding their content is critical to understanding the company.

A few additional formatting conventions are worth noting here. Assets are listed on the balance sheet by ease of conversion to cash. Liabilities are listed by their maturity (due date). Most financial statements include the monetary unit sign (in the United States, the $) beside the first dollar amount in a group of items (e.g., the cash amount in the assets). Also, it is common to place a single underline below the last item in a group before a total or subtotal (e.g., land). For group totals (e.g., total assets), a dollar sign is placed beside each amount and a double underline is set below. The same conventions are followed in all four basic financial statements.

Summary of the Four Basic Financial Statements

We have learned a great deal about the content of the four basic financial statements. Exhibit 1.7 summarizes this information. Take a few minutes to review the information in the exhibit before you move on to the next section of the chapter.

LEARNING OBJECTIVE 1-2
Identify the role of generally accepted accounting principles (GAAP) in determining financial statement content and how companies ensure the accuracy of their financial statements.

RESPONSIBILITIES FOR THE ACCOUNTING COMMUNICATION PROCESS

For decision makers to use the information in **Le-Nature's** financial statements effectively, they have to know: (1) the information conveyed by the statements and the measurement rules applied in computing the numbers on the statements and (2) that the numbers on the statements are correct. The rules that determine the content and measurement rules of the statements are called **generally accepted accounting principles**, or GAAP.

Generally Accepted Accounting Principles

How Are Generally Accepted Accounting Principles Determined?

GENERALLY ACCEPTED ACCOUNTING PRINCIPLES (GAAP)
The measurement and disclosure rules used to develop the information in financial statements.

The accounting system in use today has a long history. Its foundations are normally traced back to the works of an Italian monk and mathematician, Fr. Luca Pacioli, published in 1494.

Financial Statement	Purpose	Structure	Examples of Content
Balance Sheet (Statement of Financial Position)	Reports the financial position (economic resources and sources of financing) of an accounting entity *at a point in time*.	**Balance Sheet** Assets = Liabilities + Stockholders' Equity	Cash, accounts receivable, plant and equipment, long-term debt, common stock
Income Statement (Statement of Income, Statement of Earnings, Statement of Operations)	Reports the accountant's primary measure of economic performance *during the accounting period*.	**Income Statement** Revenues − Expenses Net Income	Sales revenue, cost of goods sold, selling expense, interest expense
Statement of Stockholders' Equity	Reports changes in the company's common stock and retained earnings *during the accounting period*.	**Statement of Stockholders' Equity** Beginning Balance + Increases − Decreases Ending Balance	Beginning and ending stockholders' equity balances, stock issuances, net income, dividends
Statement of Cash Flows (Cash Flow Statement)	Reports inflows (receipts) and outflows (payments) of cash *during the accounting period* in the categories operating, investing, and financing.	**Statement of Cash Flows** +/− CFO +/− CFI +/− CFF Change in Cash	Cash collected from customers, cash paid to suppliers, cash paid to purchase equipment, cash borrowed from banks

EXHIBIT 1.7

Summary of the Four Basic
Financial Statements

However, prior to 1933, each company's management largely determined its financial reporting practices. Thus, little uniformity in practice existed among companies.

In the United States, Congress created the **Securities and Exchange Commission (SEC)** and gave it broad powers to determine the measurement rules for financial statements that companies issuing stock to the public (publicly traded companies) must provide to stockholders.[6] The SEC has worked with organizations of professional accountants and other interested parties to establish groups that are given the primary responsibilities to work out the detailed rules that become generally accepted accounting principles. Today, the **Financial Accounting Standards Board** (FASB) has this responsibility. The official pronouncements of the FASB are called the FASB **Accounting Standards Codification.**

Why Is GAAP Important to Managers and External Users?

Generally accepted accounting principles (GAAP) are of great interest to the companies that must prepare financial statements, their auditors, and the readers of the statements. Companies and their managers and owners are most directly affected by the information presented in

---

[6]Contrary to popular belief, these rules are different from those that companies follow when filing their income tax returns. We discuss these differences further in later chapters.

financial statements. Companies incur the cost of preparing the statements and bear the major economic consequences of their publication, which include, among others,

1. Effects on the selling price of a company's stock.

2. Effects on the amount of bonuses received by management and employees.

3. Loss of competitive information to other companies.

As a consequence of these and other concerns, changes in GAAP are actively debated, political lobbying often takes place, and final rules are a compromise among the wishes of interested parties. Most managers do not need to learn all the details included in these standards. Our approach is to focus on those details that have the greatest impact on the numbers presented in financial statements and are appropriate for an introductory course.

INTERNATIONAL PERSPECTIVE

The International Accounting Standards Board and Global Convergence of Accounting Standards

Financial accounting standards and disclosure requirements are adopted by national regulatory agencies. Since 2002, there has been substantial movement toward the adoption of **International Financial Reporting Standards (IFRS)** issued by the **International Accounting Standards Board (IASB).** Examples of jurisdictions requiring the use of IFRS currently include:

- **European Union (United Kingdom, Germany, France, the Netherlands, Belgium, Bulgaria, Poland, etc.)**
- **Australia and New Zealand**
- **Hong Kong (S.A.R. of China), Malaysia, and Republic of Korea**
- **Israel and Turkey**
- **Brazil and Chile**
- **Canada and Mexico**

In the United States, the Securities and Exchange Commission now allows foreign companies whose stock is traded in the United States to use IFRS, and it is considering the appropriateness of IFRS for U.S. domestic companies. To prepare you to deal with statements prepared under U.S. GAAP and IFRS, we will point out key differences between IFRS and U.S. GAAP starting in Chapter 5. The basic principles and practices we discuss in Chapters 1 through 4 apply equally to both sets of standards.

Source: IFRS Foundation 2015.

Ensuring the Accuracy of Financial Statements

What If the Numbers Are Wrong?

Shortly after the issuance of the statements presented in this chapter, **Le-Nature's** worked with the Wachovia Capital Markets group from **Wells Fargo Bank** to borrow an additional $285 million from various lenders. Why would lenders agree to risk such a large amount? Le-Nature's financial statements played a major role in the lenders' decisions to back the loan. The statements presented a picture of a growth company with amazing future prospects. Reported revenues grew from $40 to $275 million (or nearly 600 percent) in just six years! Reported income rose by 2,400 percent in the same period! Clearly, Le-Nature's looked like a good bet. But if the numbers are wrong, all bets are off.

The truth about Le-Nature's was revealed when several non-family-member stockholders suspected that all was not right and filed a lawsuit seeking an independent trustee to examine the company. Court records reveal an amazing story. According to the bankruptcy custodian, reported annual sales of $274 million were really about $32 million. Gregory Podlucky and his co-conspirators forged checks, invoices, and revenue and expense records to massively overstate revenues and profits. The $10.6 million its balance sheet claimed for cash turned out to be $1.8 million and the company had written checks totaling $2.9 million against that balance. The balance sheet also understated liabilities by $200 million. The company was never a real success—**it was all fake.**

Le Nature's—Reported versus Actual Sales

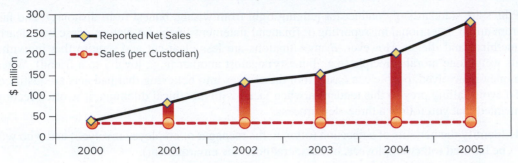

Podlucky was borrowing more and more money and using it to pay off his earlier creditors (this is called a **Ponzi scheme**). At the same time, he was stealing cash to support a lavish lifestyle. When the trustee arrived, Podlucky and his bodyguard were feverishly shredding documents. Federal agents found $20 million in gems, diamond-encrusted watches, and gold, silver, and platinum jewelry in safes in a secret room at the Latrobe plant. Podlucky had also spent more than $10 million of company money on his 25,000-square-foot mansion that was under construction. A sample of the resulting newspaper headlines follows:

Market Predicts Le-Nature's Is All Washed Up

Grand jury hears LeNature's ex-accountant's testimony

Debt holders sue Wachovia over Le Nature's Loan

Ex-LeNature's exec found guilty of fraud

Le-Nature's Fraud: 2 More Sentenced In $800M Fraud

Ex-Pa. soft-drink CEO gets 20 years in prison

Accountant Guilty of helping CEO Commit Fraud

© Sean Stipp, The Tribune-Review/AP Images

While this crime may read like a fantastic novel, the consequences for many were severe. This was the largest fraud ever heard in the Federal District Court of Western Pennsylvania. The final prison tally is listed below.

The Prison Tally	
Defendant	**Sentence**
Gregory Podlucky, CEO	20 years in federal prison
Robert Lynn, President	15 years in federal prison
Andrew Murin, Consultant	10 years in federal prison
Jonathan Podlucky, COO	5 years in federal prison
Karla Podlucky (CEO's wife)	4¼ years in federal prison
G. Jesse Podlucky (CEO's son)	9 years in federal prison
Donald Pollinger, Businessman	5 years in federal prison
Tammy Jo Andreycak, Bookkeeper	5 years in federal prison

Crime clearly did not pay for Podlucky and his co-conspirators.

Ethical Conduct

Ethics are standards of conduct for judging right from wrong, honest from dishonest, and fair from unfair. Intentional misreporting of financial statements in the Le-Nature's case was clearly unethical and illegal. However, many situations are less clear-cut and require that individuals weigh one moral principle (e.g., honesty) against another (e.g., loyalty to a friend). When money is involved, people can easily fool themselves into believing that bad acts are justified. To avoid falling prey to this tendency, when faced with an ethical dilemma, it is often recommended that you follow a three-step process:

1. Identify the benefits of a decision (often to the manager or employee involved) and who will be harmed (other employees, owners, creditors, the environment).
2. Identify alternative courses of action.
3. Choose the one you would like your family and friends to see reported on your local news. That is usually the ethical choice.

In the Le-Nature's case, Podlucky and his co-conspirators clearly did not follow this process. Little besides the jewelry and the Latrobe plant were left to satisfy Le-Nature's over $800 million in debts. The nonfamily stockholders lost all of their money. Over 240 plant workers lost their jobs. And the town of Latrobe, Pennsylvania, suffered a severe economic blow.

Responsibility and the Need for Controls

As a manager in a business, you are responsible for setting up systems to prevent and detect unethical behavior. Primary responsibility for the information in the financial statements lies with management, represented by the highest officer of the company and the highest financial officer. Companies should take three important steps to assure investors that the company's records are accurate: (1) they should maintain a system of controls over both the records and the assets of the company, (2) they should hire outside independent auditors to **audit** the fairness of the financial statements, and (3) they should form a committee of the board of directors to oversee the integrity of these other safeguards. These safeguards failed in Le-Nature's case. The company had no controls, the independent auditors were duped by management, and the board included only Podlucky's cronies. We will discuss the roles of management, auditors, and directors in more detail in Chapter 5.

AUDIT
An examination of the financial reports to ensure that they represent what they claim and conform with generally accepted accounting principles.

Three steps to ensure the accuracy of records:

System of Controls   External Auditors   Board of Directors

Those responsible for fraudulent financial statements are subject to criminal and civil penalties. As noted above, those criminally liable at Le-Nature's are serving a total of more than 70 years in prison and have been forced to forfeit all of their assets to be paid to creditors who suffered losses. The auditors who missed the fraud agreed to pay $50 million to the creditors and Wachovia Capital Markets, which marketed the loans, agreed to pay $80 million. The bottling equipment company that provided false documents to support Le-Nature's loans has paid a $15 million fine and $110 million in restitution. Other civil suits are still in process.

Although financial statement fraud is a fairly rare event, the misrepresentations in Le-Nature's statements aptly illustrate the importance of fairly presented financial statements to investors and creditors. Although most managers and owners act in an honest and responsible fashion, this incident, and the much larger frauds at **Enron** and **WorldCom**, are stark reminders of the economic consequences of lack of fair presentation in financial reports. All three companies were forced into bankruptcy when their fraudulent financial reporting practices were brought to light. Penalties against Enron and WorldCom's audit firm, **Arthur Andersen**, also led to its bankruptcy and dissolution. Thousands lost their jobs.

DEMONSTRATION CASE

At the end of most chapters, one or more demonstration cases are presented. These cases provide an overview of the primary issues discussed in the chapter. Each demonstration case is followed by a recommended solution. You should read the case carefully and then prepare your own solution before you study the recommended solution. This self-evaluation is highly recommended. The introductory case presented here reviews the elements reported on the income statement, statement of stockholders' equity, and balance sheet and how the elements within the statements are related.

Pier 1 Imports, Inc., sells a wide variety of furniture, decorative home furnishings, dining and kitchen goods, bath and bedding accessories, candles, gifts, and other specialty items for the home through over 1,000 retail stores in North America. Its merchandise largely consists of items that feature a significant degree of handcraftsmanship and are mostly imported directly from foreign suppliers. Following is a list of the financial statement items and amounts adapted from a recent Pier 1 income statement and balance sheet. The numbers are presented in millions of dollars for the current year ended February 28. Assume that the company did not pay dividends, issue stock, or retire stock during the year. Retained earnings at the beginning of the year was $193.

Accounts payable	$237	Long-term debt	94
Accounts receivable	15	Net income	100
Cash	301	Net sales	1,401
Common stock	120	Properties, net	92
Cost of sales	861	Retained earnings	293
Income before income taxes	103	Selling, general, and administrative expenses	432
Income tax expense	3	Total assets	744
Interest expense	5	Total liabilities	331
Inventories	336	Total liabilities and shareholders' equity	744
		Total shareholders' equity	413

Required:

1. Prepare a balance sheet, income statement, and a statement of stockholders' equity for the year following the formats in Exhibits 1.2, 1.3, and 1.4.

2. Specify what information these three statements provide.

3. Indicate the other statement that would be included in Pier 1's annual report.

4. Securities regulations require that Pier 1's statements be subject to an independent audit. Suggest why Pier 1 might voluntarily subject its statements to an independent audit if there were no such requirement.

SUGGESTED SOLUTION

1.

PIER 1 IMPORTS, INC.	
Balance Sheet	
At February 28, Current Year	
(in millions of dollars)	

Assets	
Cash	$301
Accounts receivable	15
Inventories	336
Properties, net	92
Total assets	**$744**
Liabilities and shareholders' equity	
Liabilities:	
Accounts payable	$237
Long-term debt	94
Total liabilities	331
Shareholders' equity:	
Common stock	120
Retained earnings	293
Total shareholders' equity	413
Total liabilities and	
shareholders' equity	**$744**

PIER 1 IMPORTS, INC.	
Income Statement	
For the Year Ended February 28, Current Year	
(in millions of dollars)	

Net sales	$1,401
Cost of sales	861
Selling, general, and	
administrative expense	432
Interest expense	5
Income before income taxes	103
Income tax expense	3
Net income	$ 100

PIER 1 IMPORTS, INC.		
Statement of Stockholders' Equity		
For the Year Ended February 28, Current Year		
(in millions of dollars)		

	Common Stock	Retained Earnings
Balance February 28, prior year	$120	$193
+ Net income	—	100
− Dividends	—	—
Balance February 28, current year	$120	$293

2. The balance sheet reports the amount of assets, liabilities, and stockholders' equity of an accounting entity at a point in time. The income statement reports the accountant's primary measure of performance of a business, revenues less expenses, during the accounting period. The statement of stockholders' equity reports on changes in the stockholders' equity accounts during the accounting period.

3. Pier 1 would also present a statement of cash flows.

4. Users will have greater confidence in the accuracy of financial statement information if they know that the people who audited the statements were required to meet professional standards of ethics and competence.

Chapter Supplement A

Types of Business Entities

This textbook emphasizes **accounting for profit-making business entities.** The three main types of business entities are sole proprietorship, partnership, and corporation. A **sole proprietorship** is an unincorporated business owned by one person; it usually is small in size and is common in the service, retailing, and farming industries. Often the owner is the manager. Legally, the business and the owner are not separate entities. Accounting views the business as a separate entity, however, that must be accounted for separately from its owner.

A **partnership** is an unincorporated business owned by two or more persons known as **partners.** The agreements between the owners are specified in a partnership contract. This contract deals with matters such as division of income each reporting period and distribution of resources of the business on termination of its operations. A partnership is not legally separate from its owners. Legally, each partner in a general partnership is responsible for the debts of the business (each general partner has **unlimited liability**). The partnership, however, is a separate business entity to be accounted for separately from its several owners.

A **corporation** is a business incorporated under the laws of a particular state. The owners are called **stockholders** or **shareholders.** Ownership is represented by shares of capital stock that usually can be bought and sold freely. When the organizers file an approved application for incorporation, the state issues a charter. This charter gives the corporation the right to operate as a separate legal entity, separate and apart from its owners. The stockholders enjoy **limited liability.** Stockholders are liable for the corporation's debts only to the extent of their investments. The corporate charter specifies the types and amounts of capital stock that can be issued. Most states require a minimum of two or three stockholders and a minimum amount of resources to be contributed at the time of organization. The stockholders elect a governing board of directors, which in turn employs managers and exercises general supervision of the corporation. Accounting also views the corporation as a separate business entity that must be accounted for separately from its owners. Limited liability companies (**LLCs**) and limited liability partnerships (**LLPs**) have many characteristics similar to corporations.

In terms of economic importance, the corporation is the dominant form of business organization in the United States. This dominance is caused by the many advantages of the corporate form: (1) limited liability for the stockholders, (2) continuity of life, (3) ease in transferring ownership (stock), and (4) opportunities to raise large amounts of money by selling shares to a large number of people. The primary disadvantage of a corporation is that its income may be subject to double taxation (income is taxed when it is earned and again when it is distributed to stockholders as dividends). In this textbook, we emphasize the corporate form of business. Nevertheless, the accounting concepts and procedures that we discuss also apply to other types of businesses.

Chapter Supplement B

Employment in the Accounting Profession Today

Since 1900, accounting has attained the stature of professions such as law, medicine, engineering, and architecture. As with all recognized professions, accounting is subject to professional competence requirements, is dedicated to service to the public, requires a high level of academic study, and rests on a common body of knowledge. An accountant may be licensed as a certified public accountant, or CPA. This designation is granted only on completion of requirements specified by the state that issues the license. Although CPA requirements vary among states, they include a college degree with a specified number of accounting courses, good character, professional experience, and successful completion of a professional examination. The CPA examination is prepared by the American Institute of Certified Public Accountants.

Accountants (including CPAs) commonly are engaged in professional practice or are employed by businesses, government entities, nonprofit organizations, and so on. Accountants employed in these activities may take and pass a professional examination to become a certified management accountant, or CMA (the CMA examination is administered by the Institute of Management Accountants), or a certified internal auditor, or CIA (the CIA examination is administered by the Institute of Internal Auditors).

Practice of Public Accounting

Although an individual may practice public accounting, usually two or more individuals organize an accounting firm in the form of a partnership (in many cases, a limited liability partnership, or LLP). Accounting firms vary in size from a one-person office, to regional firms, to the Big Four firms (**Deloitte & Touche**, **Ernst & Young**, **KPMG**, and **PricewaterhouseCoopers**), which have hundreds of offices located worldwide. Accounting firms usually render three types of services: audit or assurance services, management consulting services, and tax services.

Audit or Assurance Services

Audit or assurance services are independent professional services that improve the quality of information for decision makers. The most important assurance service performed by the CPA in public practice is financial statement auditing. The purpose of an audit is to lend credibility to the financial reports, that is, to ensure that they fairly represent what they claim. An audit involves an examination of the financial reports (prepared by the management of the entity) to ensure that they conform with GAAP. Other areas of assurance services include electronic commerce integrity and security and information systems reliability.

Management Consulting Services

Many independent CPA firms offer management consulting services. These services usually are accounting based and encompass such activities as the design and installation of accounting, data processing, and profit-planning and control (budget) systems; financial advice; forecasting; inventory controls; cost-effectiveness studies; and operational analysis. To maintain their independence, CPAs are prohibited from performing certain consulting services for the public companies that they audit.

Tax Services

CPAs in public practice usually provide income tax services to their clients. These services include both tax planning as a part of the decision-making process and the determination of the income tax liability (reported on the annual income tax return). Because of the increasing complexity of state and federal tax laws, a high level of competence is required, which CPAs specializing in taxation can provide. The CPA's involvement in tax planning often is quite significant. Most major business decisions have significant tax impacts; in fact, tax-planning considerations often govern certain business decisions.

Employment by Organizations

Many accountants, including CPAs, CMAs, and CIAs, are employed by profit-making and nonprofit organizations. An organization, depending on its size and complexity, may employ from a few to hundreds of accountants. In a business enterprise, the chief financial officer (usually a vice president or controller) is a member of the management team. This responsibility usually entails a wide range of management, financial, and accounting duties.

In a business entity, accountants typically are engaged in a wide variety of activities, such as general management, general accounting, cost accounting, profit planning and control (budgeting), internal auditing, and information systems management. A primary function of the accountants in organizations is to provide data that are useful for internal managerial decision making and for controlling operations. The functions of external reporting, tax planning, control of assets, and a host of related responsibilities normally are also performed by accountants in industry.

Employment in the Public and Not-for-Profit Sector

The vast and complex operations of governmental units, from the local to the international level, create a need for accountants. The same holds true for other not-for-profit organizations such as hospitals and universities. Accountants employed in the public and not-for-profit sector perform functions similar to those performed by their counterparts in private organizations. The Government Accountability Office (GAO) and the regulatory agencies, such as the SEC and Federal Communications Commission (FCC), also use the services of accountants in carrying out their regulatory duties.

CHAPTER TAKE-AWAYS

1-1. Recognize the information conveyed in each of the four basic financial statements and the way that it is used by different decision makers (investors, creditors, and managers). p. 6

The **balance sheet** is a statement of financial position that reports dollar amounts for the assets, liabilities, and stockholders' equity at a specific point in time.

The **income statement** is a statement of operations that reports revenues, expenses, and net income for a stated period of time.

The **statement of stockholders' equity** explains changes in stockholders' equity accounts (common stock and retained earnings) that occurred during a specific period of time.

The **statement of cash flows** reports inflows and outflows of cash for a stated period of time.

The statements are used by investors and creditors to evaluate different aspects of the firm's financial position and performance.

1-2. Identify the role of generally accepted accounting principles (GAAP) in determining financial statement content and how companies ensure the accuracy of their financial statements. p. 16

GAAP refers to the measurement rules used to develop the information in financial statements. Knowledge of GAAP is necessary for accurate interpretation of the numbers in financial statements.

Management has primary responsibility for the accuracy of a company's financial information. Auditors are responsible for expressing an opinion on the fairness of the financial statement presentations based on their examination of the reports and records of the company.

Users will have confidence in the accuracy of financial statement numbers only if the people associated with their preparation and audit have reputations for ethical behavior and competence. Management and auditors can also be held legally liable for fraudulent financial statements.

In this chapter, we studied the basic financial statements that communicate financial information to external users. Chapters 2, 3, and 4 provide a more detailed look at financial statements and examine how to translate data about business transactions into these statements. Learning how to translate back and forth between business transactions and financial statements is the key to using financial statements in planning and decision making. Chapter 2 begins our discussion of the way that the accounting function collects data about business transactions and processes the data to provide periodic financial statements, with emphasis on the balance sheet. To accomplish this purpose, Chapter 2 discusses key accounting concepts, the accounting model, transaction analysis, and analytical tools. We examine the typical business activities of an actual service-oriented company to demonstrate the concepts in Chapters 2, 3, and 4.

FINDING **FINANCIAL INFORMATION**

Balance Sheet

Assets = Liabilities + Stockholders' Equity

Income Statement

Revenues
− Expenses
Net Income

Statement of Stockholders' Equity

Beginning balance
+ Increases
− Decreases
Ending balance

Statement of Cash Flows

+/− Cash Flows from Operating Activities
+/− Cash Flows from Investing Activities
+/− Cash Flows from Financing Activities
Net Change in Cash

KEY **TERMS**

Accounting   p. 4
Accounting Entity   p. 6
Accounting Period   p. 9
Audit   p. 20
Balance Sheet (Statement of
   Financial Position)   p. 6

Basic Accounting Equation
   (Balance Sheet Equation)   p. 6
Generally Accepted Accounting
   Principles (GAAP)   p. 16
Income Statement (Statement of Income,
   Statement of Earnings, Statement

of Operations, or Statement of
   Comprehensive Income)   p. 9
Notes (Footnotes)   p. 16
Statement of Cash Flows (Cash Flow
   Statement)   p. 13
Statement of Stockholders' Equity   p. 11

QUESTIONS

1. Define **accounting.**
2. Briefly distinguish financial accounting from managerial accounting.
3. The accounting process generates financial reports for both internal and external users. Identify some of the groups of users.
4. Briefly distinguish investors from creditors.
5. What is an accounting entity? Why is a business treated as a separate entity for accounting purposes?
6. Complete the following:

Name of Statement	Alternative Title
a. Income statement	a. _____
b. Balance sheet	b. _____
c. Audit report	c. _____

7. What information should be included in the heading of each of the four primary financial statements?
8. What are the purposes of (a) the income statement, (b) the balance sheet, (c) the statement of cash flows, and (d) the statement of stockholders' equity?

9. Explain why the income statement and the statement of cash flows are dated "For the Year Ended December 31," whereas the balance sheet is dated "At December 31."
10. Briefly explain the importance of assets and liabilities to the decisions of investors and creditors.
11. Briefly define **net income** and **net loss.**
12. Explain the equation for the income statement. What are the three major items reported on the income statement?
13. Explain the equation for the balance sheet. Define the three major components reported on the balance sheet.
14. Explain the equation for the statement of cash flows. Explain the three major components reported on the statement of cash flows.
15. Explain the equation for retained earnings. Explain the four major items reported on the statement of stockholders' equity related to retained earnings.
16. The financial statements discussed in this chapter are aimed at **external** users. Briefly explain how a company's **internal** managers in different functional areas (e.g., marketing, purchasing, human resources) might use financial statement information from their own and other companies.
17. Briefly describe the way that accounting measurement rules (generally accepted accounting principles) are determined in the United States.
18. Briefly explain the responsibility of company management and the independent auditors in the accounting communication process.
19. (Supplement A) Briefly differentiate between a sole proprietorship, a partnership, and a corporation.
20. (Supplement B) List and briefly explain the three primary services that CPAs in public practice provide.

MULTIPLE-CHOICE **QUESTIONS**

1. Which of the following is **not** one of the four basic financial statements?
   a. Balance sheet
   b. Audit report
   c. Income statement
   d. Statement of cash flows
2. As stated in the audit report, or **Report of Independent Accountants,** the primary responsibility for a company's financial statements lies with
   a. The owners of the company.
   b. Independent financial analysts.
   c. The auditors.
   d. The company's management.
3. Which of the following is true?
   a. FASB creates SEC.
   b. GAAP creates FASB.
   c. SEC creates AICPA.
   d. FASB creates U.S. GAAP.
4. Which of the following regarding retained earnings is false?
   a. Retained earnings is increased by net income and decreased by a net loss.
   b. Retained earnings is a component of stockholders' equity on the balance sheet.
   c. Retained earnings is an asset on the balance sheet.
   d. Retained earnings represents earnings not distributed to stockholders in the form of dividends.
5. Which of the following is **not** one of the four items required to be shown in the heading of a financial statement?
   a. The financial statement preparer's name.
   b. The title of the financial statement.
   c. The unit of measure in the financial statement.
   d. The name of the business entity.
6. Which of the following statements regarding the statement of cash flows is true?
   a. The statement of cash flows separates cash inflows and outflows into three major categories: operating, investing, and financing.
   b. The ending cash balance shown on the statement of cash flows must agree with the amount shown on the balance sheet for the same fiscal period.
   c. The total increase or decrease in cash shown on the statement of cash flows must agree with the "bottom line" (net income or net loss) reported on the income statement.
   d. Both (a) and (b) are true.
   e. All of the above.

7. Which of the following is **not** a typical note included in an annual report?
   a. A note describing the auditor's opinion of the management's past and future financial planning for the business.
   b. A note providing more detail about a specific item shown in the financial statements.
   c. A note describing the accounting rules applied in the financial statements.
   d. A note describing financial disclosures about items not appearing in the financial statements.
8. Which of the following is true regarding the income statement?
   a. The income statement is sometimes called the **statement of operations.**
   b. The income statement reports revenues, expenses, and liabilities.
   c. The income statement reports only revenue for which cash was received at the point of sale.
   d. The income statement reports the financial position of a business at a particular point in time.
9. Which of the following is false regarding the balance sheet?
   a. The accounts shown on a balance sheet represent the basic accounting equation for a particular business entity.
   b. The retained earnings balance shown on the balance sheet must agree with the ending retained earnings balance shown on the statement of stockholders' equity.
   c. The balance sheet reports the changes in specific account balances over a period of time.
   d. The balance sheet reports the amount of assets, liabilities, and stockholders' equity of an accounting entity at a point in time.
10. Which of the following regarding GAAP is true?
   a. U.S. GAAP is the body of accounting knowledge followed by all countries in the world.
   b. Changes in GAAP can affect the interests of managers and stockholders.
   c. GAAP is the abbreviation for generally accepted auditing procedures.
   d. Changes to GAAP must be approved by the Senate Finance Committee.

MINI-EXERCISES

Matching Elements with Financial Statements

M1-1
LO1-1

Match each element with its financial statement by entering the appropriate letter in the space provided.

Element	Financial Statement
___ (1) Expenses	A. Balance sheet
___ (2) Cash flow from investing activities	B. Income statement
___ (3) Assets	C. Statement of stockholders' equity
___ (4) Dividends	D. Statement of cash flows
___ (5) Revenues	
___ (6) Cash flow from operating activities	
___ (7) Liabilities	
___ (8) Cash flow from financing activities	

Matching Financial Statement Items to Financial Statement Categories

M1-2
LO1-1

Mark each item in the following list as an asset (A), liability (L), or stockholders' equity (SE) item that would appear on the balance sheet or a revenue (R) or expense (E) item that would appear on the income statement.

___ (1) Retained earnings	___ (6) Inventories
___ (2) Accounts receivable	___ (7) Interest expense
___ (3) Sales revenue	___ (8) Accounts payable
___ (4) Property, plant, and equipment	___ (9) Land
___ (5) Cost of goods sold expense	

M1-3
LO1-2

Identifying Important Accounting Abbreviations

The following is a list of important abbreviations used in the chapter. These abbreviations also are used widely in business. For each abbreviation, give the full designation. The first one is an example.

Abbreviation	Full Designation
(1) CPA	Certified Public Accountant
(2) GAAP	_____
(3) SEC	_____
(4) FASB	_____

EXERCISES

E1-1
LO1-1, 1-2

Matching Definitions with Terms or Abbreviations

Match each definition with its related term or abbreviation by entering the appropriate letter in the space provided.

Term or Abbreviation	Definition
___ (1) SEC	A. A system that collects and processes financial information about an organization and reports that information to decision makers.
___ (2) Audit	
___ (3) Sole proprietorship	B. Measurement of information about an entity in terms of the dollar or other national monetary unit.
___ (4) Corporation	
___ (5) Accounting	C. An unincorporated business owned by two or more persons.
___ (6) Accounting entity	D. The organization for which financial data are to be collected (separate and distinct from its owners).
___ (7) Audit report	
___ (8) Publicly traded	E. An incorporated entity that issues shares of stock as evidence of ownership.
___ (9) Partnership	
___ (10) FASB	F. An examination of the financial reports to ensure that they represent what they claim and conform with generally accepted accounting principles.
___ (11) CPA	
___ (12) Unit of measure	
___ (13) GAAP	G. Certified public accountant.
	H. An unincorporated business owned by one person.
	I. A report that describes the auditor's opinion of the fairness of the financial statement presentations and the evidence gathered to support that opinion.
	J. Securities and Exchange Commission.
	K. Financial Accounting Standards Board.
	L. A company with stock that can be bought and sold by investors on established stock exchanges.
	M. Generally accepted accounting principles.

E1-2
LO1-1

Matching Financial Statement Items to Financial Statement Categories

According to its annual report, **P&G**'s billion-dollar brands include Pampers, Tide, Ariel, Always, Pantene, Bounty, Charmin, Downy, Olay, Crest, Vicks, Gillette, Duracell, and others. The following are items taken from its recent balance sheet and income statement. Note that different companies use slightly different titles for the same item. Mark each item in the following list as an asset (A), liability (L), or stockholders' equity (SE) item that would appear on the balance sheet or a revenue (R) or expense (E) item that would appear on the income statement.

___ (1) Accounts receivable

___ (2) Cash and cash equivalents

___ (3) Net sales

___ (4) Debt due within one year

___ (5) Taxes payable

___ (6) Retained earnings

___ (7) Cost of products sold

___ (8) Selling, general, and administrative expense

___ (9) Income taxes

___ (10) Accounts payable

___ (11) Trademarks and other intangible assets

___ (12) Property, plant, and equipment

___ (13) Long-term debt

___ (14) Inventories

___ (15) Interest expense

Matching Financial Statement Items to Financial Statement Categories

E1-3
LO1-1

Tootsie Roll Industries is engaged in the manufacture and sale of candy. Major products include Tootsie Roll, Tootsie Roll Pops, Tootsie Pop Drops, Tootsie Flavor Rolls, Charms, and Blow-Pop lollipops. The following items were listed on Tootsie Roll's recent income statement and balance sheet. Mark each item from the balance sheet as an asset (A), liability (L), or shareholders' equity (SE) item and mark each item from the income statement as a revenue (R) or expense (E) item.

___ (1) Bank loans

___ (2) Selling, marketing, and administrative expenses

___ (3) Accounts payable

___ (4) Dividends payable

___ (5) Retained earnings

___ (6) Cash and cash equivalents

___ (7) Accounts receivable

___ (8) Provision for income taxes*

___ (9) Product cost of goods sold

___ (10) Machinery and equipment

___ (11) Net product sales

___ (12) Inventories

___ (13) Trademarks

___ (14) Buildings

___ (15) Land

___ (16) Income taxes payable

___ (17) Rental and royalty costs

___ (18) Investments (in other companies)

Preparing a Balance Sheet

E1-4
LO1-1

Honda Motor Corporation of Japan is a leading international manufacturer of automobiles, motorcycles, all-terrain vehicles, and personal watercraft. As a Japanese company, it follows Japanese GAAP and reports its financial statements in billions of yen (the sign for yen is ¥). Its recent balance sheet contained the following items (in billions). Prepare a balance sheet as of March 31, current year, solving for the missing amount. (**Hint:** Exhibit 1.2 in the chapter provides a good model for completing this exercise.)

Cash and cash equivalents	¥ 1,279
Common stock	259
Accounts payable and other current liabilities	3,568
Inventories	900
Investments	640
Long-term debt	2,043
Net property, plant, and equipment	1,939
Other assets	6,025
Other liabilities	1,377
Retained earnings	4,324
Total assets	11,571
Total liabilities and stockholders' equity	?
Trade accounts, notes, and other receivables	788

Completing a Balance Sheet and Inferring Net Income

E1-5
LO1-1

Carlos Ramirez and Camila Garza organized New World Book Store as a corporation; each contributed $80,000 cash to start the business and received 4,000 shares of common stock. The store completed its first year of operations on December 31, current year. On that date, the following financial items for the year were determined: December 31, current year, cash on hand and in the bank, $75,600; December 31, current year, amounts due from customers from sales of books, $39,000; unused portion of store and office equipment, $73,000; December 31, current year, amounts owed to publishers for books purchased, $12,000; one-year note payable to a local bank for $3,000. No dividends were declared or paid to the stockholders during the year.

*In the United States, "provision for income taxes" is most often used as a synonym for "income tax expense."

Required:
1. Complete the following balance sheet as of the end of the current year.
2. What was the amount of net income for the year? (**Hint:** Use the retained earnings equation [Beginning Retained Earnings + Net Income − Dividends = Ending Retained Earnings] to solve for net income.)

Assets		**Liabilities**	
Cash	$	Accounts payable	$
Accounts receivable		Note payable	
Store and office equipment		Interest payable	300
		Total liabilities	$
		Stockholders' Equity	
		Common stock	
		Retained earnings	12,300
		Total stockholders' equity	
Total assets	$	Total liabilities and stockholders' equity	$

E1-6
LO1-1

Analyzing Revenues and Expenses and Preparing an Income Statement

Assume that you are the owner of Campus Connection, which specializes in items that interest students. At the end of January of the current year, you find (for January only) this information:

a. Sales, per the cash register tapes, of $150,000, plus one sale on credit (a special situation) of $2,500.
b. With the help of a friend (who majored in accounting), you determine that all of the goods sold during January cost $70,000 to purchase.
c. During the month, according to the checkbook, you paid $37,000 for salaries, rent, supplies, advertising, and other expenses; however, you have not yet paid the $900 monthly utilities for January on the store and fixtures.

Required:
On the basis of the data given (disregard income taxes), what was the amount of net income for January? Show computations. (**Hint:** A convenient form to use has the following major side captions: Revenue from Sales, Expenses, and the difference—Net Income.)

E1-7
LO1-1

Preparing an Income Statement and Inferring Missing Values

Walgreen Co. is one of the nation's leading drugstore chains. Its recent income statement contained the following items (in millions). Prepare an income statement for the year ended August 31, current year. (**Hint:** First order the items as they would appear on the income statement and then confirm the values of the subtotals and totals. Exhibit 1.3 in the chapter provides a good model for completing this exercise.)

Cost of sales	$51,692
Provision for income taxes*	1,580
Interest expense	71
Net earnings	2,714
Net sales	72,184
Pretax income	4,294
Selling, general, and administration expense	16,561
Other income	434
Total expenses	68,324
Total revenues/income	72,618

E1-8
LO1-1

Analyzing Revenues and Expenses and Completing an Income Statement

Neighborhood Realty, Incorporated, has been operating for three years and is owned by three investors. S. Bhojraj owns 60 percent of the total outstanding stock of 9,000 shares and is the managing executive in

*In the United States, "provision for income taxes" is a common synonym for "income tax expense."

charge. On December 31, current year, the following financial items for the entire year were determined: commissions earned and collected in cash, $150,900, plus $16,800 uncollected; rental service fees earned and collected, $20,000; salaries expense paid, $62,740; commissions expense paid, $35,330; payroll taxes paid, $2,500; rent paid, $2,475 (not including December rent yet to be paid); utilities expense paid, $1,600; promotion and advertising paid, $7,750; income taxes paid, $24,400; and miscellaneous expenses paid, $500. There were no other unpaid expenses at December 31. Also during the year, the company paid the owners "out-of-profit" cash dividends amounting to $12,000. Complete the following income statement:

Revenues	
Commissions earned	$ _____
Rental service fees	_____
Total revenues	$ _____
Expenses	
Salaries expense	_____
Commission expense	_____
Payroll tax expense	_____
Rent expense	_____
Utilities expense	_____
Promotion and advertising expense	_____
Miscellaneous expenses	_____
Total expenses (excluding income taxes)	$ _____
Pretax income	
Income tax expense	_____
Net income	$50,180

Inferring Values Using the Income Statement and Balance Sheet Equations

E1-9
LO1-1

Review the chapter explanations of the income statement and the balance sheet equations. Apply these equations in each independent case to compute the two missing amounts for each case. Assume that it is the end of the first full year of operations for the company. (**Hint:** Organize the listed items as they are presented in the balance sheet and income statement equations and then compute the missing amounts.)

Independent Cases	Total Revenues	Total Expenses	Net Income (Loss)	Total Assets	Total Liabilities	Stockholders' Equity
A	$93,500	$76,940	$	$140,200	$66,500	$
B		75,834	14,740	107,880		77,500
C	68,120	76,430		98,200	69,850	
D		55,804	21,770		20,300	78,680
E	84,840	75,320			25,520	80,000

Inferring Values Using the Income Statement and Balance Sheet Equations

E1-10
LO1-1

Review the chapter explanations of the income statement and the balance sheet equations. Apply these equations in each independent case to compute the two missing amounts for each case. Assume that it is the end of the first full year of operations for the company. (**Hint:** Organize the listed items as they are presented in the balance sheet and income statement equations and then compute the missing amounts.)

Independent Cases	Total Revenues	Total Expenses	Net Income (Loss)	Total Assets	Total Liabilities	Stockholders' Equity
A	$242,300	$196,700	$	$253,500	$ 75,000	$
B		176,500	29,920	590,000		350,600
C	73,500	91,890		260,400	190,760	
D	35,840		9,840		190,430	97,525
E	224,130	209,500			173,850	360,100

E1-11

LO1-1

Preparing an Income Statement and Balance Sheet

Painter Corporation was organized by five individuals on January 1 of the current year. At the end of January of the current year, the following monthly financial data are available:

Total revenues	$305,000
Total expenses (excluding income taxes)	189,000
Income tax expense (all unpaid as of January 31)	35,000
Cash balance, January 31	65,150
Receivables from customers (all considered collectible)	44,700
Merchandise inventory (by inventory count at cost)	94,500
Payables to suppliers for merchandise purchased from them	
(will be paid during February of the current year)	25,950
Common stock	62,400

No dividends were declared or paid during January.

Required:

Complete the following two statements:

PAINTER CORPORATION	
Income Statement	
For the Month of January, Current Year	
Total revenues	$ _____
Less: Total expenses (excluding income tax)	_____
Pretax income	_____
Less: Income tax expense	_____
Net income	$ _____

PAINTER CORPORATION	
Balance Sheet	
At January 31, Current Year	
Assets	
Cash	$ _____
Receivables from customers	_____
Merchandise inventory	_____
Total assets	$ _____
Liabilities	
Payables to suppliers	$ _____
Income taxes payable	_____
Total liabilities	_____
Stockholders' Equity	
Common stock	_____
Retained earnings	_____
Total stockholders' equity	_____
Total liabilities and stockholders' equity	$ _____

E1-12

LO1-1

Preparing an Income Statement and Balance Sheet

Clay Corporation was organized on January 1, current year. At the end of the current year, the following financial data are available:

Total revenues	$299,000
Total expenses (excluding income taxes)	184,000
Income tax expense (all unpaid as of January 31)	34,500
Cash	70,150
Receivables from customers (all considered collectible)	34,500
Merchandise inventory (by inventory count at cost)	96,600
Payables to suppliers for merchandise purchased from	
them (will be paid during the following year)	26,450
Common stock	59,800

No dividends were declared or paid during the first year.

Required:
Complete the following two statements:

CLAY CORPORATION	
Income Statement	
For the Current Year	
Total revenues	$ _____
Less: Total expenses (excluding income tax)	_____
Pretax income	_____
Less: Income tax expense	_____
Net income	$ _____

CLAY CORPORATION	
Balance Sheet	
At December 31, Current Year	
Assets	
Cash	$ _____
Receivables from customers	_____
Merchandise inventory	_____
Total assets	$ _____
Liabilities	
Payables to suppliers	$ _____
Income taxes payable	_____
Total liabilities	_____
Stockholders' Equity	
Common stock	_____
Retained earnings	_____
Total stockholders' equity	_____
Total liabilities and stockholders' equity	$ _____

Preparing a Statement of Stockholders' Equity

E1-13
LO1-1

Clint's Stonework Corporation was organized on January 1, 2015. For its first two years of operations, it reported the following:

Net income for 2015	$ 31,000
Net income for 2016	42,000
Dividends for 2015	14,200
Dividends for 2016	18,700
Total assets at the end of 2015	130,000
Total assets at the end of 2016	250,000
Common stock at the end of 2015	100,000
Common stock at the end of 2016	100,000

Required:
On the basis of the data given, prepare a statement of stockholders' equity for 2016. Show computations.

Focus on Cash Flows: Matching Cash Flow Statement Items to Categories

E1-14
LO1-1

The following items were taken from a recent cash flow statement. Note that different companies use slightly different titles for the same item. Without referring to Exhibit 1.5, mark each item in the list as a cash flow from operating activities (O), investing activities (I), or financing activities (F). Place parentheses around the letter if it is a cash outflow.

___ (1) Purchases of property, plant, and equipment

___ (2) Cash received from customers

___ (3) Cash paid for dividends to stockholders

___ (4) Cash paid to suppliers

___ (5) Income taxes paid

___ (6) Cash paid to employees

___ (7) Cash proceeds received from sale of investment in another company

___ (8) Repayment of borrowings

PROBLEMS

P1-1
LO1-1

Preparing an Income Statement, Statement of Stockholders' Equity, and Balance Sheet (AP1-1)

Assume that you are the president of Highlight Construction Company. At the end of the first year of operations (December 31), the following financial data for the company are available:

Cash	$ 25,600
Receivables from customers (all considered collectible)	10,800
Inventory of merchandise (based on physical count and priced at cost)	81,000
Equipment owned, at cost less used portion	42,000
Accounts payable owed to suppliers	46,140
Salary payable (on December 31, this was owed to an employee who will be paid on January 10)	2,520
Total sales revenue	128,400
Expenses, including the cost of the merchandise sold (excluding income taxes)	80,200
Income taxes expense at 30% × Pretax income; all paid during the current year	?
Common stock (December 31)	87,000
Dividends declared and paid during the current year	10,000
(Note: The beginning balances in Common Stock and Retained Earnings are zero because it is the first year of operations.)	

Required:

Using the financial statement exhibits in the chapter as models and showing computations:

1. Prepare a summarized income statement for the year.
2. Prepare a statement of stockholders' equity for the year.
3. Prepare a balance sheet at December 31.

P1-2
LO1-1

Analyzing a Student's Business and Preparing an Income Statement (AP1-2)

During the summer between his junior and senior years, James Cook needed to earn sufficient money for the coming academic year. Unable to obtain a job with a reasonable salary, he decided to try the lawn care business for three months. After a survey of the market potential, James bought a used pickup truck on June 1 for $1,800. On each door he painted "James Cook Lawn Service, Phone 471-4487." He also spent $900 for mowers, trimmers, and tools. To acquire these items, he borrowed $3,000 cash by signing a note payable promising to pay the $3,000 plus interest of $78 at the end of the three months (ending August 31).

By the end of the summer, James had done a lot of work and his bank account looked good. This prompted him to wonder how much profit the business had earned.

A review of the check stubs showed the following: Bank deposits of collections from customers totaled $15,000. The following checks had been written: gas, oil, and lubrication, $1,050; pickup repairs, $250; mower repair, $110; miscellaneous supplies used, $80; helpers, $5,400; payroll taxes, $190; payment for assistance in preparing payroll tax forms, $25; insurance, $125; telephone, $110; and $3,078 to pay off the note including interest (on August 31). A notebook kept in the pickup, plus some unpaid bills, reflected that customers still owed him $700 for lawn services rendered and that he owed $180 for gas and oil (credit card charges). He estimated that the cost for use of the truck and the other equipment (called **depreciation**) for three months amounted to $600.

Required:

1. Prepare a quarterly income statement for James Cook Lawn Service for the months June, July, and August. Use the following main captions: Revenues from Services, Expenses, and Net Income. Assume that the company will not be subject to income tax.
2. Do you see a need for one or more additional financial reports for this company for the quarter and thereafter? Explain.

Comparing Income with Cash Flow (Challenging) (AP1-3)

P1-3
LO1-1

Huang Trucking Company was organized on January 1. At the end of the first quarter (three months) of operations, the owner prepared a summary of its activities as shown in item (*a*) of the following table:

Summary of Transactions	Computation of	
	Income	Cash
a. Services performed for customers, $66,000, of which $11,000 remained uncollected at the end of the quarter.	+$66,000	+$55,000
b. Cash borrowed from the local bank, $56,000 (one-year note).		
c. Small service truck purchased at the end of the quarter to be used in the business for two years starting the next quarter: Cost, $12,500 cash.		
d. Wages earned by employees, $25,000, of which one-half remained unpaid at the end of the quarter.		
e. Service supplies purchased for use in the business, $3,800 cash, of which $900 were unused (still on hand) at the end of the quarter.		
f. Other operating expenses, $38,000, of which $6,500 remained unpaid at the end of the quarter.		
g. Based only on these transactions, compute the following for the quarter: Income (or loss) Cash inflow (or outflow)		

Required:

1. For items (*b*) through (*g*), enter what you consider to be the correct amounts. Enter a zero when appropriate. The first transaction is illustrated.
2. For each transaction, explain the basis for your response in requirement (1).

Evaluating Data to Support a Loan Application (Challenging)

P1-4
LO1-1

On January 1 of the current year, three individuals organized Northwest Company as a corporation. Each individual invested $10,000 cash in the business. On December 31 of the current year, they prepared a list of resources owned (assets) and debts owed (liabilities) to support a company loan request for $70,000 submitted to a local bank. None of the three investors had studied accounting. The two lists prepared were as follows:

Company Resources

Cash	$ 12,000
Service supplies inventory (on hand)	7,000
Service trucks (four, practically new)	57,000
Personal residences of organizers (three houses)	190,000
Service equipment used in the business (practically new)	30,000
Bills due from customers (for services already completed)	15,000
Total	$311,000

Company Obligations

Unpaid wages to employees	$ 19,000
Unpaid taxes	8,000
Owed to suppliers	10,000
Owed on service trucks and equipment (to a finance company)	45,000
Loan from organizer	10,000
Total	$ 92,000

Required:

Prepare a short memo in which you discuss the following:

1. Which of these items do not belong on the balance sheet? (Bear in mind that the company is considered to be separate from the owners.)
2. What additional questions would you raise about the measurement of items on the list? Explain the basis for each question.
3. If you were advising the local bank on its loan decision, which amounts on the list would create special concerns? Explain the basis for each concern and include any recommendations that you have.
4. In view of your responses to (1) and (2), what do you think the amount of stockholders' equity (i.e., assets minus liabilities) of the company would be? Show your computations.

ALTERNATE PROBLEMS

AP1-1
LO1-1

Preparing an Income Statement, Statement of Stockholders' Equity, and Balance Sheet (P1-1)

Assume that you are the president of Influence Corporation. At the end of the first year (December 31) of operations, the following financial data for the company are available:

Cash	$ 13,150
Receivables from customers (all considered collectible)	10,900
Inventory of merchandise (based on physical count and priced at cost)	27,000
Equipment owned, at cost less used portion	66,000
Accounts payable owed to suppliers	31,500
Salary payable (on December 31, this was owed to an employee who will be paid on January 10)	1,500
Total sales revenue	100,000
Expenses, including the cost of the merchandise sold (excluding income taxes)	68,500
Income taxes expense at 30% × Pretax income; all paid during December of the current year	?
Common stock at the end of the current year	62,000

No dividends were declared or paid during the current year. The beginning balances in Common stock and Retained earnings are zero because it is the first year of operations.

Required:

Using the financial statement exhibits in the chapter as models and showing computations:

1. Prepare a summarized income statement for the year.
2. Prepare a statement of stockholders' equity for the year.
3. Prepare a balance sheet at year-end.

AP1-2
LO1-1

Analyzing a Student's Business and Preparing an Income Statement (P1-2)

Upon graduation from high school, Sam List immediately accepted a job as an electrician's assistant for a large local electrical repair company. After three years of hard work, Sam received an electrician's license and decided to start his own business. He had saved $12,000, which he invested in the business. First, he transferred this amount from his savings account to a business bank account for List Electric Repair Company, Incorporated. His lawyer had advised him to start as a corporation. He then purchased a used panel truck for $9,000 cash and secondhand tools for $1,500; rented space in a small building; inserted an ad in the local paper; and opened the doors on October 1. Immediately, Sam was very busy; after one month, he employed an assistant.

Although Sam knew practically nothing about the financial side of the business, he realized that a number of reports were required and that costs and collections had to be controlled carefully. At the end of the year, prompted in part by concern about his income tax situation (previously he had to report only salary), Sam recognized the need for financial statements. His wife Janet developed some financial statements for the business. On December 31, with the help of a friend, she gathered the following data for the three months just ended. Bank account deposits of collections for electric repair services totaled $32,000. The following checks had been written: electrician's assistant, $7,500; payroll taxes, $175; supplies purchased and used on jobs, $9,500; oil, gas, and maintenance on truck, $1,200; insurance, $700; rent, $500; utilities and telephone, $825; and miscellaneous expenses (including advertising), $600. Also, uncollected bills to customers for electric repair services amounted to $3,500. The $250 rent for December had not been paid. Sam estimated the cost of using the truck and tools (depreciation) during the three months to be $1,200. Income taxes for the three-month period were $3,930.

Required:

1. Prepare a quarterly income statement for List Electric Repair for the three months October through December. Use the following main captions: Revenues from Services, Expenses, Pretax Income, and Net Income.
2. Do you think that Sam may need one or more additional financial reports for the quarter and thereafter? Explain.

Comparing Income with Cash Flow (Challenging) (P1-3)

AP1-3
LO1-1

Choice Chicken Company was organized on January 1. At the end of the first quarter (three months) of operations, the owner prepared a summary of its activities as shown in transaction (*a*) of the following table:

Summary of Transactions	Computation of	
	Income	Cash
a. Services performed for customers, $85,000, of which $15,000 remained uncollected at the end of the quarter.	+$85,000	+$70,000
b. Cash borrowed from the local bank, $25,000 (one-year note).		
c. Small service truck purchased at the end of the quarter to be used in the business for two years starting the next quarter: Cost, $8,000 cash.		
d. Wages earned by employees, $36,000, of which one-sixth remained unpaid at the end of the quarter.		
e. Service supplies purchased for use in the business, $4,000 cash, of which $1,000 were unused (still on hand) at the end of the quarter.		
f. Other operating expenses, $31,000, of which one-half remained unpaid at the end of the quarter.		
g. Based only on these transactions, compute the following for the quarter: Income (or loss) Cash inflow (or outflow)		

Required:

1. For items (*b*) through (*g*), enter what you consider to be the correct amounts. Enter a zero when appropriate. The first transaction is illustrated.
2. For each transaction, explain the basis for your response in requirement (1).

CONTINUING **PROBLEM**

CON1-1   Financial Statements for a New Business Plan

Penny Cassidy is considering forming her own pool service and supply company, Penny's Pool Service & Supply, Inc. (PPSS). She has decided to incorporate the business to limit her legal liability. She expects to invest $20,000 of her own savings and receive 1,000 shares of common stock. Her plan for the first year of operations forecasts the following amounts at December 31, the end of the current year: Cash in bank, $2,900; amounts due from customers for services rendered, $2,300; pool supplies inventory, $4,600; equipment, $28,000; amounts owed to **Pool Corporation, Inc.**, a pool supply wholesaler, $3,500; note payable to the bank, $5,000. Penny forecasts first-year sales of $60,000, wages of $24,000, cost of supplies used of $8,200, other administrative expenses of $4,500, and income tax expense of $4,000. She expects to pay herself a $10,000 dividend as the sole stockholder of the company.

Required:
If Penny's estimates are correct, what would the following first-year financial statements look like for Penny's Pool Service & Supply (use Exhibits 1.2, 1.3, and 1.4 as models)?
1. Income statement
2. Statement of stockholders' equity
3. Balance sheet

CASES **AND PROJECTS**

Annual Report Cases

CP1-1   Finding Financial Information
LO1-1
Refer to the financial statements of **American Eagle Outfitters** in Appendix B at the end of this book.

Required:
Skim the annual report. Look at the income statement, balance sheet, and cash flow statement closely and attempt to infer what kinds of information they report. Then answer the following questions based on the report.
1. What types of products does American Eagle Outfitters sell?
2. On what date does American Eagle Outfitters's most recent reporting year end?
3. For how many years does it present complete
   a. Balance sheets?
   b. Income statements?
   c. Cash flow statements?
4. Are its financial statements audited by independent CPAs? How do you know?
5. Did its total assets increase or decrease over the last year?
6. How much inventory (in dollars) did the company have as of January 31, 2015 (accountants would call this the ending balance)?
7. Write out the basic accounting (balance sheet) equation and provide the values in dollars reported by the company as of January 31, 2015.

CP1-2   Finding Financial Information
LO1-1
Refer to the financial statements of **Urban Outfitters** in Appendix C at the end of this book.

Required:

1. What is the amount of net income for the most recent year?
2. What amount of revenue was earned in the most recent year?
3. How much inventory (in dollars) does the company have as of January 31, 2015?
4. By what amount did cash and cash equivalents* change during the most recent year?
5. Who is the auditor for the company?

Comparing Companies within an Industry

Refer to the financial statements of **American Eagle Outfitters** in Appendix B and **Urban Outfitters** in Appendix C.

CP1-3
LO1-1

Required:

1. Total assets is a common measure of the size of a company. Which company had the higher total assets at the end of the most recent year? (**Note: Some companies will label a year that has a January year-end as having a fiscal year-end dated one year earlier. For example, a January 2015 year-end may be labeled as Fiscal 2014 since the year actually has more months that fall in the 2014 calendar year than in the 2015 calendar year.**)
2. Net sales is also a common measure of the size of a company. Which company had the higher net sales for the most recent year?
3. Growth during a period is calculated as:

$$\frac{\text{Ending amount} - \text{Beginning amount}}{\text{Beginning amount}} \times 100 = \text{Growth rate}$$

Which company had the higher growth in total assets during the most recent year? Which company had the higher growth in net sales during the most recent year?

Financial Reporting and Analysis Case

Using Financial Reports: Identifying and Correcting Deficiencies in an Income Statement and Balance Sheet

CP1-4
LO1-1

Performance Corporation was organized on January 1, 2015. At the end of 2015, the company had not yet employed an accountant; however, an employee who was "good with numbers" prepared the following statements at that date:

PERFORMANCE CORPORATION	
December 31, 2015	
Income from sales of merchandise	$180,000
Total amount paid for goods sold during 2015	(90,000)
Selling costs	(25,000)
Depreciation (on service vehicles used)	(12,000)
Income from services rendered	52,000
Salaries and wages paid	(62,000)

---

*Cash equivalents** are short-term investments readily convertible to cash whose value is unlikely to change.

PERFORMANCE CORPORATION	
December 31, 2015	
Resources	
Cash	$ 32,000
Merchandise inventory (held for resale)	42,000
Service vehicles	50,000
Retained earnings (profit earned in 2015)	32,250
Grand total	$156,250
Debts	
Payables to suppliers	$ 17,750
Note owed to bank	25,000
Due from customers	13,000
Total	$ 55,750
Supplies on hand (to be used in rendering services) $15,000	
Accumulated depreciation* (on service vehicles) 12,000	
Common stock, 6,500 shares 65,000	
Total	92,000
Grand total	$147,750

This represents the portion of the service vehicles that has been used up to date.

Required:

1. List all deficiencies that you can identify in these statements. Give a brief explanation of each one.
2. Prepare a proper income statement (correct net income is $32,250 and income tax expense is $10,750) and balance sheet (correct total assets are $140,000).

Critical Thinking Cases

CP1-5

LO1-2

Making Decisions as an Owner: Deciding about a Proposed Audit

You are one of three partners who own and operate Mary's Maid Service. The company has been operating for seven years. One of the other partners has always prepared the company's annual financial statements. Recently you proposed that the statements be audited each year because it would benefit the partners and preclude possible disagreements about the division of profits. The partner who prepares the statements proposed that his Uncle Ray, who has a lot of financial experience, can do the job and at little cost. Your other partner remained silent.

Required:

1. What position would you take on the proposal? Justify your response.
2. What would you strongly recommend? Give the basis for your recommendation.

CP1-6

LO1-2

Evaluating an Ethical Dilemma: Ethics and Auditor Responsibilities

A key factor that an auditor provides is independence. The **AICPA Code of Professional Conduct** states that "a member in public practice should be independent in fact and appearance when providing auditing and other attestation services."

Required:

Do you consider the following circumstances to suggest a lack of independence? Justify your position. (Use your imagination. Specific answers are not provided in the chapter.)

1. Jack Jones is a partner with a large audit firm and is assigned to the **Ford** audit. Jack owns 10 shares of Ford.

2. Melissa Chee has invested in a mutual fund company that owns 500,000 shares of **Sears** stock. She is the auditor of Sears.

3. Bob Franklin is a clerk/typist who works on the audit of **AT&T**. He has just inherited 50,000 shares of AT&T stock. (Bob enjoys his work and plans to continue despite his new wealth.)

4. Nancy Sodoma worked on weekends as the controller for a small business that a friend started. Nancy quit the job in midyear and now has no association with the company. She works full time for a large CPA firm and has been assigned to do the audit of her friend's business.

5. Mark Jacobs borrowed $100,000 for a home mortgage from First City National Bank. The mortgage was granted on normal credit terms. Mark is the partner in charge of the First City audit.

Financial Reporting and Analysis Team Project

Team Project: Examining an Annual Report

CP1-7

As a team, select an industry to analyze. *Yahoo! Finance* provides lists of industries at **biz.yahoo .com/p/industries.html**. Click on an industry for a list of companies in that industry. Alternatively, go to Google Finance at **www.google.com/finance**, search for a company you are interested in, and you will be presented with a list including that company and its competitors. Each team member should acquire the annual report or 10-K for one publicly traded company in the industry, with each member selecting a different company (the SEC EDGAR service at **www.sec.gov** and the company's investor relations website itself are good sources).

Required:

On an individual basis, each team member should write a short report answering the following questions about the selected company. Discuss any patterns across the companies that you as a team observe. Then, as a team, write a short report comparing and contrasting your companies.

1. What types of products or services does it sell?
2. On what day of the year does its fiscal year end?
3. For how many years does it present complete
   a. Balance sheets?
   b. Income statements?
   c. Cash flow statements?
4. Are its financial statements audited by independent CPAs? If so, indicate who performs the audit.
5. Did its total assets increase or decrease over last year? By what percentage? (Percentage change is calculated as [Current year − Last year] ÷ Last year. Show supporting computations.)
6. Did its net income increase or decrease over last year? By what percentage?

Investing and Financing Decisions and the Accounting System

Steve Ells is a classically trained chef who is often called one of the most innovative men in the world of food. He is the founder, chairman of the board, and co-chief executive officer of **Chipotle Mexican Grill**, a leader in the fastest-growing segment of the restaurant industry, now called "fast-casual." In 1993, this entrepreneur opened his first restaurant in a former Dolly Madison ice cream store in Denver, Colorado. His vision was a restaurant that serves food fast but uses higher-quality fresh ingredients and cooking techniques found in finer restaurants. As of December 31, 2014, the Chipotle chain had over 1,770 restaurants in the United States, Canada, England, France, and Germany. In addition, the company has expanded its business model to include nine **ShopHouse Southeast Asian Kitchen** and two **Pizzeria Locale** restaurants. It plans to open about 200 additional restaurants in 2015.

How did Chipotle grow so fast? It did so in two stages. First, in 1999, **McDonald's Corporation** became the majority stockholder by investing about $360 million in Chipotle. This provided funding for its tremendous early growth from 19 stores to nearly 490 restaurants

Learning Objectives

After studying this chapter, you should be able to:

2-1   Define the objective of financial reporting, the elements of the balance sheet, and the related key accounting assumptions and principles.

2-2   Identify what constitutes a business transaction and recognize common balance sheet account titles used in business.

2-3   Apply transaction analysis to simple business transactions in terms of the accounting model: Assets = Liabilities + Stockholders' Equity.

2-4   Determine the impact of business transactions on the balance sheet using two basic tools: Journal entries and T-accounts.

2-5   Prepare a trial balance and simple classified balance sheet, and analyze the company using the current ratio.

2-6   Identify investing and financing transactions and demonstrate how they impact cash flows.

AP Photo/Matt York

by the end of 2005. Then, in January 2006, Chipotle "went public." In its IPO, or initial public offering, it issued stock to the public for the first time. That stock is listed on the New York Stock Exchange as CMG. McDonald's also sold its ownership in Chipotle for nearly $1.4 billion—a handsome profit of over $1 billion. Comparing its balance sheet from 2005 to 2014 highlights the company's amazing 549 percent growth since becoming a public company:

(in millions of dollars)

	Assets	=	Liabilities	+	Stockholders' Equity
End of 2014	$2,546		$534		$2,012
End of 2005	392		83		309
Change	+$2,154		+$451		+$1,703

This growth was stimulated in part by Ells's evolving vision that "fresh is not enough anymore." He has committed Chipotle to serving naturally raised pork, chicken, and beef; using no-trans-fat cooking oil; serving cheese and sour cream products that are free of synthetic bovine growth hormones; using certified organic beans and locally grown organic produce when in season; and serving preservative-free corn and flour tortillas. In an even more dramatic show of commitment to sustainability, in 2009, Chipotle built the first-ever free-standing restaurant to receive the highest rating (LEED Platinum) from the U.S. Green

Building Council,[1] a start toward other sustainable renovations and projects. In 2011, the company created the Chipotle Cultivate Foundation to expand philanthropic work surrounding sustainable agriculture.

As it continues to evolve, Chipotle's recent annual report states its vision is now "to change the way people think about and eat fast food." The belief is that providing good food and service is good business.

UNDERSTANDING THE BUSINESS

The "fast-casual" segment of the $2.1 trillion restaurant industry generates approximately $40 billion in sales annually. What identifies a restaurant as fast-casual? Typically, customers still order at the register as in a fast-food restaurant, but the food is made to order, typically in view of the customers and without full table service, and it is served in modern and upscale surroundings, with checks typically ranging between $8 and $16. **Chipotle Mexican Grill** has been a leader in this segment.

Franchising is common in chain restaurants. The largest restaurant to use franchising is **Subway**, with over 39,000 restaurants—all franchised. Franchising involves selling the right to use or sell a product or service to another. This is an easy way for someone to start his or her own business because the franchisor (the seller, such as **Panera Bread**) often provides site location, design, marketing, and management training support in exchange for initial franchise fees and ongoing royalty fees usually based on weekly sales. At Panera Bread, for example, only 48 percent of the stores are company-owned.

Unlike most restaurant chains, however, Chipotle does not franchise the business. All restaurants are company-owned. Developing a new site, usually on rented property, costs on average about $900,000. In 2014, Chipotle spent nearly $253 million on new and renovated property and equipment. The creation of new restaurants to meet consumer demand for healthier food options explains most of the changes in Chipotle's assets and liabilities from year to year. To understand how the result of Chipotle Mexican Grill's growth strategy is communicated in the balance sheet, we must answer the following questions:

- What business activities cause changes in the balance sheet amounts from one period to the next?
- How do specific business activities affect each of the balance sheet amounts?
- How do companies keep track of the balance sheet amounts?

In this chapter, we focus on some typical asset acquisition activities (often called **investing activities**), along with related **financing activities,** such as borrowing funds from creditors or selling stock to investors to provide the cash necessary to acquire the assets. We examine those activities that affect only balance sheet amounts. Operating activities that affect both the income statement and the balance sheet are covered in Chapters 3 and 4. To begin, let's return to the basic concepts introduced in Chapter 1.

---

[1]See **www.greenbeanchicago.com** and **https://www.usgbc.org/ShowFile.aspx?DocumentID=6953** for more information.

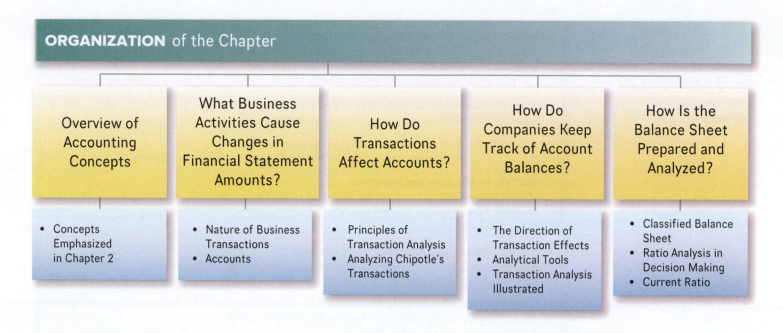

ORGANIZATION of the Chapter

Overview of Accounting Concepts	What Business Activities Cause Changes in Financial Statement Amounts?	How Do Transactions Affect Accounts?	How Do Companies Keep Track of Account Balances?	How Is the Balance Sheet Prepared and Analyzed?
• Concepts Emphasized in Chapter 2	• Nature of Business Transactions • Accounts	• Principles of Transaction Analysis • Analyzing Chipotle's Transactions	• The Direction of Transaction Effects • Analytical Tools • Transaction Analysis Illustrated	• Classified Balance Sheet • Ratio Analysis in Decision Making • Current Ratio

OVERVIEW OF ACCOUNTING CONCEPTS

Because learning and remembering **how** the accounting process works is much easier if you know **why** it works a certain way, we begin by discussing key accounting terms and concepts. They are part of a **conceptual framework** developed over many years and synthesized by the Financial Accounting Standards Board (FASB) to provide a structure for developing accounting standards. Exhibit 2.1 provides an overview of the key concepts in the framework that will be discussed in each of the next four chapters. A clear understanding of these accounting concepts will be helpful as you study, and they will also help you in future chapters as we examine more complex business activities.

Concepts Emphasized in Chapter 2

Objective of Financial Reporting

The **primary objective of financial reporting to external users** is to provide financial information about the reporting entity that is useful to existing and potential investors, lenders, and other creditors in making decisions about providing resources to the entity. The users of accounting information are all expected to have a reasonable understanding of accounting concepts and procedures—which may be one of the reasons you are studying accounting. Of course, as we discussed in Chapter 1, many other groups, such as suppliers and customers, also use external financial statements.

Most users are interested in information to help them **assess the amount, timing, and uncertainty of a business's future cash inflows and outflows.** For example, creditors and potential creditors need to assess an entity's ability to (1) pay interest on a loan over time and also (2) pay back the principal on the loan when it is due. Investors and potential investors want to assess the entity's ability to (1) pay dividends in the future and (2) be successful so that the stock price rises, enabling investors to sell their stock for more than they paid. Information about a company's economic resources, claims against its resources, and activities that change these items provides insight into cash flows and a company's financial strengths and weaknesses.

Qualitative Characteristics of Useful Information

For accounting information to be useful, it must be relevant and be a faithful representation. **Relevant information** is capable of influencing decisions by allowing users to assess past activities and/or predict future activities. To be reported, the information should also be

LEARNING OBJECTIVE 2-1
Define the objective of financial reporting, the elements of the balance sheet, and the related key accounting assumptions and principles.

PRIMARY OBJECTIVE OF FINANCIAL REPORTING TO EXTERNAL USERS
To provide useful economic information about a business to help external parties make sound financial decisions.

RELEVANT INFORMATION
Information that can influence a decision; it is timely and has predictive and/or feedback value.

EXHIBIT 2.1

Financial Accounting and
Reporting Conceptual
Framework

Objective of Financial Reporting to External Users: (in Ch. 2)
To provide financial information about the reporting entity that is useful to existing and potential investors, lenders, and other creditors in making decisions about providing resources to the entity
➤ **Pervasive Cost-Benefit Constraint:** Benefits of providing information should outweigh its costs

Fundamental Qualitative Characteristics of Useful Information: (in Ch. 2)
Relevance (including materiality) and Faithful Representation

   Attributes That Enhance Qualitative Characteristics:
   Comparability (including consistency), Verifiability, Timeliness, and Understandability

Elements to Be Measured and Reported:
Assets, Liabilities, Stockholders' Equity, Investments by Owners, and Distributions to Owners (in Ch. 2)
Revenues, Expenses, Gains, and Losses (in Ch. 3)
Comprehensive Income (in Ch. 5)

Recognition, Measurement, and Disclosure Concepts:
Assumptions: Separate Entity, Going Concern, and Monetary Unit (in Ch. 2)
               Time Period (in Ch. 3)

Principles: Mixed-Attribute Measurement (in Ch. 2)
          Revenue Recognition and Expense Recognition (in Ch. 3)
          Full Disclosure (in Ch. 5)

FAITHFUL REPRESENTATION
Requires that the information be complete, neutral, and free from error.

SEPARATE ENTITY ASSUMPTION
States that business transactions are separate from the transactions of the owners.

GOING CONCERN ASSUMPTION
States that businesses are assumed to continue to operate into the foreseeable future (also called the continuity assumption).

MONETARY UNIT ASSUMPTION
States that accounting information should be measured and reported in the national monetary unit without any adjustment for changes in purchasing power.

MIXED-ATTRIBUTE MEASUREMENT MODEL
Applied to measuring different assets and liabilities of the balance sheet.

COST (HISTORICAL COST)
The cash-equivalent value of an asset on the date of the transaction.

material in amount, depending on the nature of the item and company. **Faithful representation** requires that the information be complete, neutral, and free from error. Comparability, verifiability, timeliness, and understandability are qualitative characteristics that enhance the usefulness of information that is relevant and faithfully represented. For example, our discussions of ratio analysis will emphasize the importance of comparing ratios for the same company over time, as well as with those of competitors. Such comparisons are valid only if the information is prepared on a consistent and comparable basis. These characteristics of useful information guide the FASB in deciding what financial information should be reported.

Recognition and Measurement Concepts

Before we discuss accountants' definitions for the elements of the balance sheet, we should consider three assumptions and a measurement concept that underlie much of our application of these definitions. First we make the **separate entity assumption**, which states that each business's activities must be accounted for separately from the activities of its owners, all other persons, and other entities. This means, for example, that, when an owner purchases property for personal use, the property is not an asset of the business. Second, under the **going concern assumption** (also called the **continuity assumption**), unless there is evidence to the contrary, we assume that the business will continue operating into the foreseeable future, long enough to meet its contractual commitments and plans. This means, for example, that if there was a high likelihood of bankruptcy, then its assets should be valued and reported on the balance sheet as if the company were to be liquidated (that is, discontinued, with all of its assets sold and all debts paid). Under the **monetary unit assumption**, each business entity accounts for and reports its financial results primarily in terms of the national monetary unit (e.g., dollars in the United States, yen in Japan, and euros in Germany), without any adjustment for changes in purchasing power (e.g., inflation).

Finally, accountants measure the elements of the balance sheet using what is called a **mixed-attribute measurement model**. Most balance sheet elements are recorded at their **cost (historical cost)**, which is the cash-equivalent value on the date of the transaction. For example, assets are initially recorded at the cash paid plus the dollar value of all noncash considerations on the exchange date, such as the trade-in value of a used asset. We will discuss the conditions under which these values are adjusted to other amounts, such as their market value, starting in Chapter 6 of this text. With these assumptions in mind, we are now ready to discuss accountants' definitions of the elements of the balance sheet.

Elements of the Balance Sheet

The four financial statements—balance sheet, income statement, statement of stockholders' (shareholders' or owners') equity, and statement of cash flows—along with the notes to the statements provide the structure for the information communicated to users. As we learned in Chapter 1, assets, liabilities, and stockholders' equity are the elements of a corporation's balance sheet. The conceptual framework defines them as follows.

Assets are probable future economic benefits owned or controlled by an entity as a result of past transactions or events. In other words, they are the economic resources the entity acquired to use in operating the company in the future. As shown in **Chipotle's** balance sheet presented in Exhibit 2.2, most companies list assets **in order of liquidity,** or how soon an asset is expected by management to be turned into cash or used. Notice that several of Chipotle's assets are categorized as **current assets**. Current assets are those resources that Chipotle will use or turn into cash within one year (the next 12 months). Chipotle's current assets include Cash, Short-Term Investments (in the stocks and bonds of other companies), Accounts Receivable (due from customers and others), Supplies (to make and serve the food), Prepaid Expenses (for rent, insurance, and advertising paid in advance of use), and Other Current Assets (a summary of several smaller accounts). For manufacturers that produce and sell goods and merchandisers who sell already-completed goods, Inventory (for goods to be sold) would also be listed after Accounts Receivable. Inventory is always considered a current asset, regardless of how long it takes to produce and sell the inventory. These are typical titles used by most entities.

All other assets are considered long term (or noncurrent). That is, they are to be used or turned into cash after the coming year. For Chipotle, that includes property and equipment (Land, Buildings, and Equipment), Long-Term Investments (in the stocks and bonds of other companies), and Intangibles (nonphysical assets such as trademarks and patents). Intangibles are discussed in detail in Chapter 8.

Liabilities are defined as probable future sacrifices of economic benefits arising from present obligations of a business to transfer cash or other assets or to provide services as a result of past transactions or events. Entities that a company owes money to are called **creditors.**

Similar to how assets are reported in order of liquidity, liabilities are usually listed on the balance sheet **in order of maturity** (how soon an obligation is to be paid). Liabilities that Chipotle will need to pay or settle within the coming year (with cash, goods, other current assets, or services) are classified as **current liabilities**. Chipotle's current liabilities include Accounts Payable (to suppliers), Unearned Revenue (for unredeemed gift cards that have been purchased by customers), and Accrued Expenses Payable (more specifically, Wages Payable and Utilities Payable, although additional accrued liabilities may include Interest Payable and Taxes Payable, among others). Distinguishing current assets and current liabilities assists external users of the financial statements in assessing the amounts and the timing of future cash flows.

Long-term obligations are summarized as Other Liabilities that may include Notes Payable (written promises to pay the amount borrowed and interest as specified in the agreement) and other obligations, such as to employee pension plans and long-term capital leases. These and other liabilities will be discussed in more detail in subsequent chapters.

Stockholders' equity (also called **shareholders' equity** or **owners' equity**) is the residual interest in the assets of the entity after subtracting liabilities. It is a combination of the financing provided by the owners and by business operations.

- **Financing Provided by Owners** is referred to as **contributed capital.** Owners invest in the business by providing cash and sometimes other assets and receive in exchange shares of stock as evidence of ownership. The largest investors in Chipotle Mexican Grill are financial institutions (mutual funds, pension funds, etc.). The directors and executive officers also own stock, as do other corporate employees and the general public.

EXHIBIT 2.2

Chipotle Mexican Grill, Inc., Balance Sheet

CHIPOTLE MEXICAN GRILL, INC.
Consolidated Balance Sheet*
December 31, 2014
(in thousands of dollars, except per share data)

EXPLANATIONS

"Consolidated" means all subsidiaries are combined
Point in time for which the balance sheet was prepared

ASSETS
Current Assets:

Cash	$ 419,500	
Short-term investments	338,600	*Ownership of other companies' stocks and bonds*
Accounts receivable	34,800	*Amounts due from customers and others*
Supplies	15,300	*Food, beverage, and packaging supplies on hand*
Prepaid expenses	70,300	*Rent, advertising, and insurance paid in advance*
Total current assets	878,500	

Current assets

Property and equipment:

Land	11,100	
Buildings	1,267,100	
Equipment	442,500	*Includes furniture and fixtures*
Total cost	1,720,700	*Cost of property and equipment at date of acquisition*
Accumulated depreciation	(613,700)	*Amount of cost used in past operations*
Net property and equipment	1,107,000	
Long-term investments	496,100	*Ownership of other companies' stocks and bonds*
Intangible assets	64,700	*Rights, such as patents, trademarks, and licenses*
Total assets	$2,546,300	

Noncurrent assets

LIABILITIES AND STOCKHOLDERS' EQUITY
Current Liabilities:

Accounts payable	$ 69,600	*Amount due to suppliers*
Unearned revenue	16,800	*Unredeemed gift cards*
Accrued expenses payable:		
Wages payable	73,900	*Amount due to employees*
Utilities payable	85,400	*Amount due for electric, gas, and telephone usage*
Total current liabilities	245,700	
Other liabilities	288,200	*Summary of liabilities due beyond one year*
Total liabilities	533,900	

Current liabilities

Noncurrent liabilities

Stockholders' Equity:

Common stock ($0.01 par value)	400	*Total par value of stock issued by company to investors*
Additional paid-in capital	290,200	*Excess of amount received from investors over par*
Retained earnings	1,721,800	*Undistributed earnings reinvested in the company*
Total stockholders' equity	2,012,400	
Total liabilities and stockholders' equity	$2,546,300	

Stockholders' equity

*The information has been adapted from actual statements and simplified for this chapter.

RETAINED EARNINGS
Cumulative earnings of a company that are not distributed to the owners and are reinvested in the business.

- **Financing Provided by Operations** is referred to as **earned capital** or **retained earnings**.[2] When companies earn profits, they can be distributed to owners as dividends or reinvested in the business. The portion of profits reinvested in the business is called retained earnings. Companies with a growth strategy often pay little or no dividends to retain funds for expansion. A look at Chipotle's balance sheet (Exhibit 2.2) indicates that its growth has been financed by substantial reinvestment of earnings ($1,721.8 million).

---

[2]Retained earnings can increase only from profitable operations, but they decrease when a firm has a loss or pays dividends.

We just learned the elements of the balance sheet (assets, liabilities, and stockholders' equity) and how assets and liabilities are usually classified (current or noncurrent). Current assets (including inventory) are expected to be used or turned into cash within the next 12 months and current liabilities are expected to be paid or satisfied within the next 12 months with cash, services, or other current assets.

SELF-STUDY QUIZ

The following is a list of items from a recent balance sheet of **Panera Bread Company**. Indicate on the line provided whether each of the following is usually categorized on the balance sheet as a current asset (CA), noncurrent asset (NCA), current liability CL), noncurrent liability (NCL), or stockholders' equity (SE).

____ *a.* Retained Earnings   ____ *f.* Properties (buildings and equipment)
____ *b.* Prepaid Expenses   ____ *g.* Trade Accounts Receivable
____ *c.* Accounts Payable   ____ *h.* Long-Term Debt
____ *d.* Inventories   ____ *i.* Accrued Expenses
____ *e.* Additional Paid-in Capital

After you have completed your answers, check them below.

Unrecorded but Valuable Assets and Liabilities

FINANCIAL ANALYSIS

Many very valuable intangible **assets,** such as trademarks, patents, and copyrights that are developed inside a company (not purchased), are **not reported** on the balance sheet. For example, **General Electric**'s balance sheet reveals no listing for the GE trademark because it was developed internally over time through research, development, and advertising (it was not purchased). Likewise, the **Coca-Cola Company** does not report any asset for its patented Coke formula, although it does report more than $6.5 billion in various trademarks that it has purchased.

Nearly all companies have some form of off-balance-sheet financing—obligations **not reported** as **liabilities** on the balance sheet. For many companies, renting facilities or equipment can fall into this category, and it can be quite significant. For example, **Delta Air Lines** included in a note to the financial statements in a recent annual report that over $11.1 billion in future cash flows of aircraft rental leases were not reported on the balance sheet as debt, an amount equal to nearly 25 percent of its total liabilities that were reported on the balance sheet. This also illustrates the importance of reading the notes, not just the financial statements, when analyzing a company's financial information and predicting future cash flows.

Now that we have reviewed the basic elements of the balance sheet and related recognition and measurement concepts as part of the conceptual framework, let's see what economic activities cause changes in the amounts reported on the balance sheet.

WHAT BUSINESS ACTIVITIES CAUSE CHANGES IN FINANCIAL STATEMENT AMOUNTS?

Nature of Business Transactions

Accounting focuses on certain events that have an economic impact on the entity. Those events that are recorded as part of the accounting process are called **transactions**. The first step in translating the results of business events to financial statement numbers is determining which events to include. As the definitions of assets and liabilities indicate, only economic resources

LEARNING OBJECTIVE 2-2

Identify what constitutes a business transaction and recognize common balance sheet account titles used in business.

TRANSACTION

(1) An exchange between a business and one or more external parties to a business or (2) a measurable internal event such as the use of assets in operations.

a. SE; *b.* CA; *c.* CL; *d.* CA; *e.* SE; *f.* NCA; *g.* CA; *h.* NCL; *i.* CL

Solutions to
SELF-STUDY QUIZ

and debts **resulting from past transactions** are recorded on the balance sheet. Transactions include two types of events:

1. **External events:** These are **exchanges** of assets, goods, or services by one party for assets, services, or promises to pay (liabilities) from one or more other parties. Examples include the purchase of a machine from a supplier, sale of merchandise to customers, borrowing of cash from a bank, and investment of cash in the business by the owners.

2. **Internal events:** These include certain events that are not exchanges between the business and other parties but nevertheless have a direct and measurable effect on the entity. Examples include using up insurance paid in advance and using buildings and equipment over several years.

Throughout this textbook, the word *transaction* is used in the broad sense to include both types of events.

Some important events that have a future economic impact on a company, however, are **not** reflected in the financial statements. In most cases, signing a contract is not considered to be an accounting transaction because it involves **only the exchange of promises,** not of assets such as cash, goods, services, or property. For example, assume that **Chipotle** signs an employment contract with a new regional manager. From an accounting perspective, no transaction has occurred because no exchange of assets, goods, or services has been made. Each party to the contract has exchanged promises—the manager agrees to work; Chipotle agrees to pay the manager for the work. For each day the new manager works, however, the exchange of services for pay results in a transaction that Chipotle must record. Because of their importance, long-term employment contracts, leases, and other commitments may need to be disclosed in notes to the financial statements.

Accounts

ACCOUNT

A standardized format that organizations use to accumulate the dollar effect of transactions on each financial statement item.

To accumulate the dollar effect of transactions on each financial statement item, organizations use a standardized format called an **account**. The resulting balances are kept separate for financial statement purposes. To facilitate the recording of transactions, each company establishes a **chart of accounts,** a list of all account titles and their unique numbers. The accounts are usually organized by financial statement element, with asset accounts listed first, followed by liability, stockholders' equity, revenue, and expense accounts in that order. Exhibit 2.3 lists

EXHIBIT 2.3

Typical Account Titles

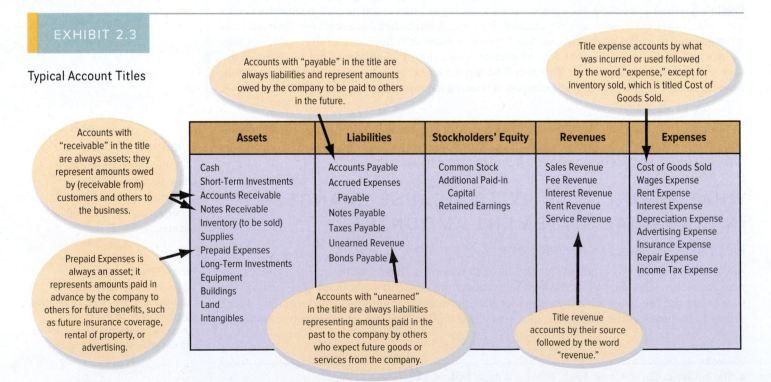

various account titles that are quite common and are used by most companies. The exhibit also provides special notes to help you in learning account titles. When you are completing assignments and are unsure of an account title, refer to this listing for help.

Every company creates its own chart of accounts to fit the nature of its business activities. For example, a small lawn care service may have an asset account titled Lawn Mowing Equipment, but a large corporation such as **Dell** is unlikely to report such an account. These differences in accounts will become more apparent as we examine the balance sheets of various companies. Because each company has its own chart of accounts, you should **not** try to memorize a typical chart of accounts but focus instead on understanding the nature of each typical account. Then when you see a company that uses a slightly different title, you will understand what it means. For example, some companies use the terms Trade Accounts Receivable (same as Accounts Receivable) or Merchandise Inventory (same as Inventory). In homework problems, you will either be given the account names or be expected to select appropriate names, similar to the ones in Exhibit 2.3. Once you select a name for an account, you must use that exact name in all transactions affecting that account.

The accounts you see in the financial statements of most large corporations are actually summations (or aggregations) of a number of specific accounts in their recordkeeping system. For example, **Chipotle** keeps separate accounts for food, beverage, and packaging supplies but combines them under Supplies on the balance sheet. Other Accrued Expenses Payable summarizes several accounts with smaller balances and may include Interest Payable and Utilities Payable.

HOW DO TRANSACTIONS AFFECT ACCOUNTS?

Managers' business decisions often result in transactions that affect the financial statements. For example, decisions to expand the number of stores, advertise a new product, change an employee benefit package, and invest excess cash would all affect the financial statements. Sometimes these decisions have unintended consequences as well. The decision to purchase additional inventory for cash in anticipation of a major sales initiative, for example, will increase inventory and decrease cash. But if there is no demand for the additional inventory, the lower cash balance will also reduce the company's ability to pay its other obligations.

Because business decisions often involve an element of risk, managers should understand exactly how transactions impact the financial statements. The process for determining the effects of transactions is called **transaction analysis.**

Principles of Transaction Analysis

Transaction analysis is the process of studying a transaction to determine its economic effect on the entity in terms of the accounting equation (also known as the **fundamental accounting model**). We outline the process in this section of the chapter and create a visual tool representing the process (the transaction analysis model). The basic accounting equation and two principles are the foundation for this model. Recall from Chapter 1 that the basic accounting equation for a business that is organized as a corporation is as follows:

> **Assets (A) = Liabilities (L) + Stockholders' Equity (SE)**

The two principles underlying the transaction analysis process follow:

- Every transaction affects at least two accounts; correctly identifying those accounts and the direction of the effect (whether an increase or a decrease) is critical.

- The accounting equation must remain in balance after each transaction.

Success in performing transaction analysis depends on a clear understanding of these principles. Study the following material well.

LEARNING OBJECTIVE 2-3
Apply transaction analysis to simple business transactions in terms of the accounting model: Assets = Liabilities + Stockholders' Equity.

TRANSACTION ANALYSIS
The process of studying a transaction to determine its economic effect on the business in terms of the accounting equation.

Dual Effects

The idea that every transaction has **at least two effects** on the basic accounting equation is known as the **dual effects** concept.[3] Most transactions with external parties involve an **exchange** by which the business **entity both receives something and gives up something in return.** For example, suppose **Chipotle** purchased tomatoes for cash. In this exchange, Chipotle would receive food supplies (an increase in an asset) and in return would give up cash (a decrease in an asset).

A	=	L	+	SE
+/−				

Transaction	Chipotle Received	Chipotle Gave
Purchased tomatoes for cash	**Supplies** (asset account increased)	**Cash** (asset account decreased)

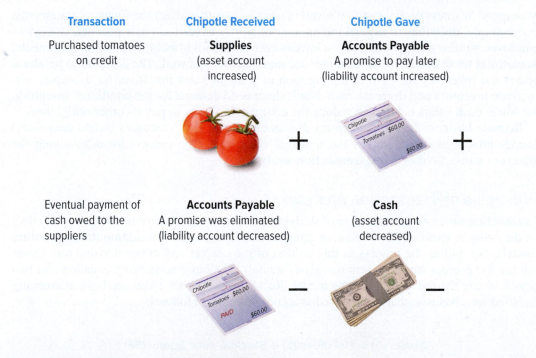

In analyzing this transaction, we determined that the accounts affected were Supplies and Cash. However, most supplies are purchased on credit (that is, money is owed to suppliers). In that case, Chipotle would engage in **two** separate transactions at different points in time:

A	=	L	+	SE
+		+		

Transaction	Chipotle Received	Chipotle Gave
Purchased tomatoes on credit	**Supplies** (asset account increased)	**Accounts Payable** A promise to pay later (liability account increased)

A	=	L	+	SE
−		−		

	Accounts Payable	Cash
Eventual payment of cash owed to the suppliers	**Accounts Payable** A promise was eliminated (liability account decreased)	**Cash** (asset account decreased)

Tomatoes: Jill Fromer/Photodisc/Getty Images; Invoice: Digital Stock/Corbis; Money: Jules Frazier/Photodisc/Getty Images

Balancing the Accounting Equation

Notice in the previous tomato purchase illustrations that the accounting equation for each transaction remained in balance. The accounting equation must remain in balance after each transaction. That is, total assets (resources) must equal total liabilities and stockholders' equity

---

[3]From this concept, accountants have developed what is known as the *double-entry system* of recordkeeping.

(claims to resources). If all correct accounts have been identified and the appropriate direction of the effect on each account has been determined, the equation should remain in balance.

Systematic transaction analysis for investing and financing activities includes the following steps:

Step 1: Ask → **What was received and what was given?**

- **Identify the account affected by title** (e.g., Cash and Notes Payable). Remember: *Make sure that at least two accounts change.*
- **Classify each account by type:** Asset (A), Liability (L), or Stockholders' Equity (SE) (e.g., Cash is an asset).
- **Determine the direction of the effect:** Did the account increase (+) or decrease (−)?

Step 2: Verify → **Is the accounting equation in balance? (A = L + SE)**

Analyzing Chipotle's Transactions

To illustrate the use of the transaction analysis process, let's consider transactions of **Chipotle** that are also common to most businesses. Remember that this chapter presents transactions that affect only the balance sheet accounts. Assume that Chipotle engages in the **following events during the first quarter of 2015,** the first three months following the balance sheet in Exhibit 2.2. Account titles are from that balance sheet, and remember that, for simplicity, **all amounts are in thousands, except per share data:**

(*a*) **Chipotle issued (sold) 10,000 additional shares of common stock with a par value of $0.01 per share at a market value of $0.37 per share, receiving $3,700 in cash from investors.** Each share of common stock usually has a nominal (low) **par value** printed on the face of the certificate. Par value is a legal amount per share established by the board of directors; it has no relationship to the market price of the stock. Its significance is that it establishes the minimum amount that a stockholder must contribute. Chipotle's common stock has a par value of $0.01 per share, and in this transaction, each share sold for $0.37 per share. When a corporation issues common (capital) stock, the amount received affects separate accounts:

- **Common Stock** for the number of shares issued times the par value per share (10,000 shares × $0.01 par value per share = $100)
- **Additional Paid-in Capital** (or **Paid-in Capital** or **Contributed Capital in Excess of Par**) for the excess received above par (10,000 shares × $0.36 excess over par value per share = $3,600)
- Cash or other considerations for the market value of the shares given (10,000 shares × $0.37 market value per share = $3,700)

PAR VALUE
(1) The nominal value per share of capital stock as specified in the corporate charter.
(2) Also, another name for bond principal, or the maturity amount of a bond.

COMMON STOCK
The basic voting stock issued by a corporation.

ADDITIONAL PAID-IN CAPITAL (PAID-IN CAPITAL, CONTRIBUTED CAPITAL IN EXCESS OF PAR)
The amount of contributed capital less the par value of the stock.

Step 1: What was received and what was given (account name, type of account, amount, and direction of effect)?

Received: Cash (+A) $3,700

Given: Additional stock shares:
Common Stock (+SE) $100 *(10,000 shares × $.01 per share)*
Additional Paid-in Capital (+SE) $3,600 *(10,000 shares × $0.36 per share)*

Assets				=	Liabilities			+	Stockholders' Equity		
Cash	Investments	Property and Equipment	Intangible Assets		Notes Payable	Dividends Payable	Other Liabilities		Common Stock	Additional Paid-in Capital	Retained Earnings
(a) +3,700				=					+100	+3,600	

Step 2: Is the accounting equation in balance? Assets $3,700 = Liabilities $0 + Stockholders' Equity $3,700

(b) **Chipotle borrowed $2,000 from its local bank, signing a note to be paid in three years.**

Step 1: **What was received and what was given** (account name, type of account, amount, and direction of effect)?

    Received: Cash (+A) $2,000   **Given:** Long-Term Notes
                                         Payable (+L) $2,000

		Assets		=		Liabilities		+		Stockholders' Equity	
Cash	Investments	Property and Equipment	Intangible Assets		Notes Payable	Dividends Payable	Other Liabilities		Common Stock	Additional Paid-in Capital	Retained Earnings
(a) +3,700				=					+100	+3,600	
(b) +2,000				=	+2,000						

Step 2: **Is the accounting equation in balance?** Assets $2,000 = Liabilities $2,000 + Stockholders' Equity $0

Companies that need cash to buy or build additional facilities often seek funds by selling stock to investors as in transaction *(a)* or by borrowing from creditors as in transaction *(b)*. Any transactions with stockholders (usually issuing additional stock and paying dividends) and transactions with banks (borrowing and repaying loans) are **financing** activities.

(c) **Chipotle purchased $10,000 in additional land, $8,200 in new buildings, $33,800 in new equipment, and $3,700 in additional intangible assets; paid $53,400 in cash and signed a short-term note payable for the remainder owed ($2,300).**

Step 1: **What was received and what was given** (account name, type of account, amount, and direction of effect)?

    Received: Land (+A) $10,000   **Given:** Cash (−A) $53,400
                Buildings (+A)   8,200   Short-Term Notes Payable (+L) 2,300
                Equipment (+A)   33,800
                Intangible Assets (+A)   3,700

		Assets		=		Liabilities		+		Stockholders' Equity	
Cash	Investments	Property and Equipment	Intangible Assets		Notes Payable	Dividends Payable	Other Liabilities		Common Stock	Additional Paid-in Capital	Retained Earnings
(a) +3,700				=					+100	+3,600	
(b) +2,000				=	+2,000						
(c) −53,400		+52,000	+3,700	=	+2,300						

Step 2: **Is the accounting equation in balance?** Assets $2,300 = Liabilities $2,300 + Stockholders' Equity $0

Purchasing and selling property and equipment and investments in the stock of other companies are **investing** activities. In the investing transaction *(c)*, notice that more than two accounts were affected.

(d) **Chipotle paid $2,300 on the short-term note payable in *(c)* above and $2,300 on other noncurrent liabilities (ignore interest).**

Step 1: **What was received and what was given** (account name, type of account, amount, and direction of effect)?

    Received: Reduction in amount due: **Given:** Cash (−A) $4,600
                Short-Term Notes Payable (−L) $2,300
                Other Liabilities (−L) 2,300

		Assets		=		Liabilities		+		Stockholders' Equity	
Cash	Investments	Property and Equipment	Intangible Assets		Notes Payable	Dividends Payable	Other Liabilities		Common Stock	Additional Paid-in Capital	Retained Earnings
(a) +3,700				=					+100	+3,600	
(b) +2,000				=	+2,000						
(c) −53,400		+52,000	+3,700	=	+2,300						
(d) −4,600				=	−2,300		−2,300				

Step 2: **Is the accounting equation in balance?** Assets −$4,600 = Liabilities −$4,600 + Stockholders' Equity $0

(e) **Chipotle purchased the stock of other companies as investments, paying $44,000 cash; of this, $9,000 was in short-term investments and $35,000 was in long-term investments.**

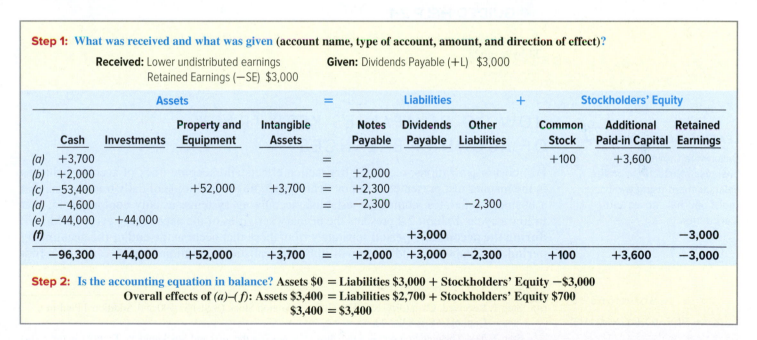

Step 1: **What was received and what was given** (account name, type of account, amount, and direction of effect)?

Received: Short-Term Investments (+A) $9,000   **Given:** Cash (−A) $44,000
Long-Term Investments (+A)   35,000

	Assets				=	Liabilities			+	Stockholders' Equity		
	Cash	Investments	Property and Equipment	Intangible Assets		Notes Payable	Dividends Payable	Other Liabilities		Common Stock	Additional Paid-in Capital	Retained Earnings
(a)	+3,700				=					+100	+3,600	
(b)	+2,000				=	+2,000						
(c)	−53,400		+52,100	+3,700	=	+2,300						
(d)	−4,600				=	−2,300		−2,300				
(e)	−44,000	+44,000										

Step 2: Is the accounting equation in balance? **Assets $0 = Liabilities $0 + Stockholders' Equity $0**

(f) Chipotle does not pay dividends, but instead reinvests profits into growing the business. However, for illustration purposes, **assume Chipotle's board of directors declared that the Company will pay $3,000 in cash as dividends to shareholders next quarter.**

Step 1: **What was received and what was given** (account name, type of account, amount, and direction of effect)?

Received: Lower undistributed earnings   **Given:** Dividends Payable (+L) $3,000
Retained Earnings (−SE) $3,000

	Assets				=	Liabilities			+	Stockholders' Equity		
	Cash	Investments	Property and Equipment	Intangible Assets		Notes Payable	Dividends Payable	Other Liabilities		Common Stock	Additional Paid-in Capital	Retained Earnings
(a)	+3,700				=					+100	+3,600	
(b)	+2,000				=	+2,000						
(c)	−53,400		+52,000	+3,700	=	+2,300						
(d)	−4,600				=	−2,300		−2,300				
(e)	−44,000	+44,000										
(f)							+3,000					−3,000
	−96,300	+44,000	+52,000	+3,700	=	+2,000	+3,000	−2,300		+100	+3,600	−3,000

Step 2: Is the accounting equation in balance? **Assets $0 = Liabilities $3,000 + Stockholders' Equity −$3,000**
Overall effects of (a)–(f): Assets $3,400 = Liabilities $2,700 + Stockholders' Equity $700
$3,400 = $3,400

PAUSE FOR FEEDBACK

STOP

Transaction analysis involves identifying accounts affected in a transaction (by title), recognizing that at least two accounts are affected, classifying the accounts (asset, liability, or stockholders' equity), and determining the direction of the effect on the account (increase or decrease). If all accounts and effects are correct, then the fundamental accounting equation (A = L + SE) will remain in balance. **Practice is the most effective way to develop your transaction analysis skills.**

SELF-STUDY QUIZ

Review the analysis in events (*a*) through (*f*) above, complete the analysis of the following transactions, and indicate the effects in the chart below. Answer from the standpoint of the business.

(*a*) **Paul Knepper contributes $50,000 cash to establish Florida Flippers, Inc., a new scuba business organized as a corporation; in exchange, he receives 25,000 shares of stock with a par value of $0.10 per share.**

Step 1: Identify and classify accounts and effects.

Received: _____   Given: _____

Step 2: Is the accounting equation in balance?   Yes or No? _____

(*b*) **Florida Flippers buys a small building near the ocean for $250,000, paying $25,000 cash and signing a 10-year note payable for the rest.**

Step 1: Identify and classify accounts and effects.

Received: _____   Given: _____

Step 2: Is the accounting equation in balance?   Yes or No? _____

After you have completed your answers, check them below. If your answers did not agree with ours, we recommend that you go back to each event to make sure that you have completed each of the steps of transaction analysis.

 **GUIDED HELP 2-1**

For additional step-by-step video instruction on analyzing transaction effects, go to **www.mhhe.com/libby9e_gh2a**.

LEARNING OBJECTIVE 2-4

Determine the impact of business transactions on the balance sheet using two basic tools: Journal entries and T-accounts.

HOW DO COMPANIES KEEP TRACK OF ACCOUNT BALANCES?

For most organizations, recording transaction effects and keeping track of account balances in the manner just presented is impractical. To handle the multitude of daily transactions that a business generates, companies establish accounting systems, usually computerized, that follow a cycle. Exhibit 2.4 presents the primary activities of the **accounting cycle** performed **during the accounting period** separately from those that occur at the **end of the accounting period.** In Chapters 2 and 3, we will illustrate realistic transactions during **Chipotle**'s first

---

Solutions to
SELF-STUDY QUIZ

(*a*) Step 1: Received: Cash (+A) $50,000; Given: Common Stock (+SE) $2,500 and Additional Paid-in Capital (+SE) $47,500.

Step 2: Yes. The equation remains in balance; Assets (on the left) and Stockholders' Equity (on the right) increase by the same amount, $50,000.

(*b*) Step 1: Received: Building (+A) $250,000; Given: Cash (−A) $25,000 and Notes Payable (+L) $225,000.

Step 2: Yes. Assets (on the left) increase by $225,000 and Liabilities (on the right) increase by $225,000.

	Assets		=	Liabilities	+	Stockholders' Equity	
	Cash	Building		Notes Payable		Common Stock	Additional Paid-in Capital
(*a*)	+50,000		=			+2,500	+47,500
(*b*)	−25,000	+250,000	=	+225,000			

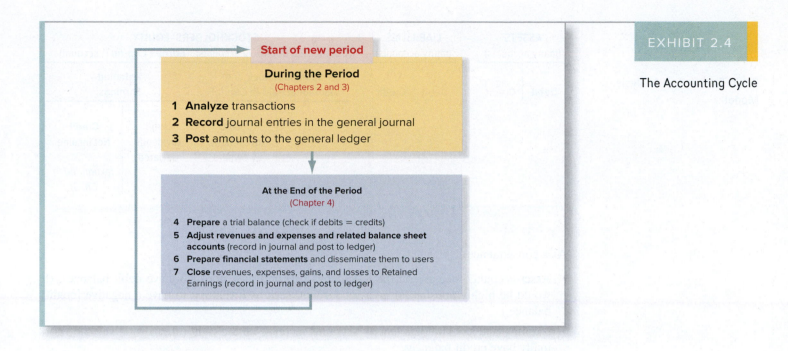

EXHIBIT 2.4

The Accounting Cycle

quarter of 2015. In Chapter 4, we will complete the accounting cycle by discussing and illustrating activities at the end of the period to adjust the records, prepare financial statements, and finally close the accounting records.

During the accounting period, transactions that result in exchanges between the company and other external parties are analyzed to determine the accounts and effects. The effects are recorded first in the **general journal,** a listing in chronological order of each transaction's effects. To determine account balances, the accounts are updated by posting the effects listed in the general journal to the respective accounts in the **general ledger,** a record of effects to and balances of each account.

These formal records are based on two very important tools used by accountants: journal entries and T-accounts. From the standpoint of accounting systems design, these analytical tools are a more efficient way to reflect the effects of transactions, determine account balances, and prepare financial statements. As future business managers, you should develop your understanding and use of these tools in financial analysis. For those studying accounting, this knowledge is the foundation for an understanding of the accounting system and future accounting coursework. After we explain how to perform transaction analysis using these tools, we illustrate their use in financial analysis.

ACCOUNTING CYCLE
The process used by entities to analyze and record transactions, adjust the records at the end of the period, prepare financial statements, and prepare the records for the next cycle.

The Direction of Transaction Effects

As we saw earlier in this chapter, transaction effects increase and decrease assets, liabilities, and stockholders' equity accounts. To reflect these effects efficiently, we need to structure the transaction analysis model in a manner that shows the **direction** of the effects. As shown in Exhibit 2.5, each account is set up as a "T" with the following structure:

- **Increases in asset accounts are on the left** because assets are on the left side of the accounting equation (A = L + SE).
- **Increases in liability and stockholders' equity accounts are on the right** because they are on the right side of the accounting equation (A = L + SE).

Also notice that:

- The term **debit** (dr for short) always refers to the **left** side of the T.
- The term **credit** (cr for short) always refers to the **right** side of the T.

DEBIT
The left side of an account.

CREDIT
The right side of an account.

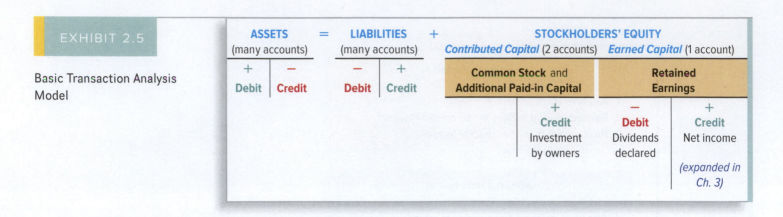

EXHIBIT 2.5

Basic Transaction Analysis Model

As a consequence:

- Asset accounts increase on the left (debit) side and they normally have debit balances. (It would be highly unusual for an asset account, such as Inventory, to have a negative [credit] balance.)
- Liability and stockholders' equity accounts increase on the right (credit) side and they normally have credit balances.

In summary:

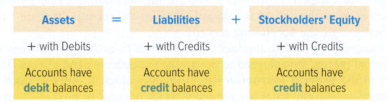

In Chapter 3, we will add revenue and expense account effects to Retained Earnings in our model. Until then, as you are learning to perform transaction analysis, **you should refer to the transaction analysis model in Exhibit 2.5 often until you can construct it on your own without assistance.**

Many students have trouble with accounting because they forget that the term **debit** is simply the **left** side of an account and the term **credit** is simply the **right** side of an account. Perhaps someone once told you that you were a credit to your school or your family. As a result, you may think that credits are good and debits are bad. Such is not the case. Just remember that **debit is on the left** and **credit is on the right.**

If you have identified the correct accounts and effects through transaction analysis, the accounting equation will remain in balance. **The total dollar value of all debits will equal the total dollar value of all credits** in a transaction. For an extra measure of assurance, add this equality check (Debits = Credits) to the transaction analysis process.

STOP   PAUSE FOR **FEEDBACK**

From Exhibit 2.5, we learned that each account can increase and decrease. In the transaction analysis model, the effect of a transaction on each element can be represented with a T with one side increasing and the other side decreasing. Asset accounts on the left side of the fundamental accounting equation increase their balances on the left side of the T. Liability and stockholders' equity accounts are on the right side of the fundamental accounting equation and increase their balance on the right side of the T. In accounting, the left side of the T is called the debit side and the right is called the credit side. Most accounts have a balance on the positive side.

Analytical Tools

The Journal Entry

In a bookkeeping system, transactions are recorded in chronological order in a **general journal** (or, simply, journal). After analyzing the business documents (such as purchase invoices, receipts, and cash register tapes) that describe a transaction, the bookkeeper enters the effects on the accounts in the journal using debits and credits. The **journal entry**, then, is an accounting method for expressing the effects of a transaction on accounts. It is written in a debits-equal-credits format. To illustrate, we refer back to event (*a*) in **Chipotle**'s transaction analyis in the previous section.

> **JOURNAL ENTRY**
> An accounting method for expressing the effects of a transaction on accounts in a debits-equal-credits format.

(*a*) **Chipotle issued (sold) 10,000 additional shares of common stock with a par value of $0.01 per share at a market value of $0.37 per share, receiving $3,700 in cash from investors.**

The journal entry for event (*a*) in the Chipotle illustration is as follows:

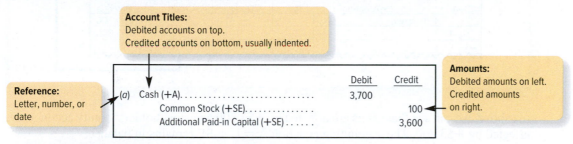

Notice the following:

- It is useful to include a date or some form of reference for each transaction. The debited accounts are written first (on top) with the amounts recorded in the left column. The credited accounts are written below the debits and are usually indented in manual records; the credited amounts are written in the right column. The order of the debited accounts or credited accounts does not matter, as long as the debits are on top and the credits are on the bottom and indented to the right.

- Total debits ($3,700) equal total credits ($100 + $3,600 = $3,700).

- Three accounts are affected by this transaction. Any journal entry that affects more than two accounts is called a **compound entry.** Many transactions in this and subsequent chapters require a compound journal entry.

- As you can see in the illustration of a formal bookkeeping system in Exhibit 2.6, an additional line is written below the journal entry as an explanation of the transaction. For simplicity, explanations will not be included in this text.

While you are learning to perform transaction analysis, use the symbols A, L, and SE next to each account title, as in the preceding journal entry. Specifically identifying accounts as assets (A), liabilities (L), or stockholders' equity (SE) clarifies the transaction analysis and makes journal entries easier to write. For example, if Cash is to be increased, we write Cash (+A). Throughout subsequent chapters, we include the direction of the effect along with the symbol to help you understand the effects of each transaction on the financial statements. In transaction

EXHIBIT 2.6

Posting Transaction Effects from the Journal to the Ledger

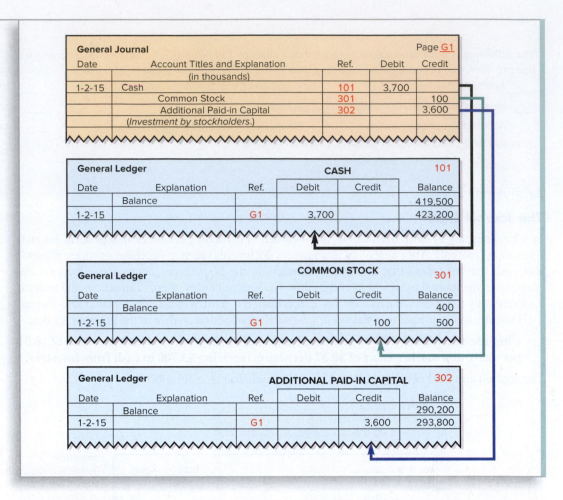

(*a*) above, we can see that assets are affected by +$3,700 and stockholders' equity accounts are affected by +$3,700. The accounting equation A = L + SE remains in balance.

A note of caution: Many students try to memorize journal entries without understanding or using the transaction analysis model. As more detailed transactions are presented in subsequent chapters, the task becomes increasingly more difficult. In the long run, **memorizing, understanding, and using the transaction analysis model** presented here will save you time and prevent confusion.

The T-Account

By themselves, journal entries do not provide the balances in accounts. After the journal entries have been recorded, the bookkeeper **posts** (transfers) the dollar amounts to each account affected by the transaction to determine the new account balances. (In most computerized accounting systems, this happens automatically.)

As a group, the accounts are called a **general ledger.** In the manual accounting system used by some small organizations, the ledger is often a three-ring binder with a separate page for each account. In a computerized system, accounts are stored on a disk. See Exhibit 2.6 for an illustration of a journal page and the related ledger pages. Note that the cash effects from the journal entry have been posted to the Cash ledger page.

One very useful tool for summarizing the transaction effects and determining the balances for individual accounts is a **T-account**, a simplified representation of a ledger account. Exhibit 2.7 shows the T-accounts for Chipotle's Cash and Common Stock accounts based on Event (*a*). Notice that, for Cash, which is classified as an asset, increases are shown on the left and decreases appear on the right side of the T-account. For Common Stock, however, increases are shown on the right and decreases on the left since Common Stock is a stockholders' equity account. Many small businesses still use handwritten or manually maintained accounts in this T-account format. Computerized systems retain the concept but not the format of the T-account.

T-ACCOUNT

A tool for summarizing transaction effects for each account, determining balances, and drawing inferences about a company's activities.

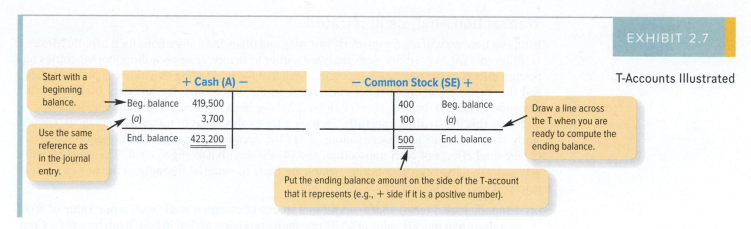

EXHIBIT 2.7

T-Accounts Illustrated

Start with a beginning balance.

Use the same reference as in the journal entry.

+ Cash (A) −	
Beg. balance 419,500	
(a) 3,700	
End. balance 423,200	

− Common Stock (SE) +	
	400 Beg. balance
	100 (a)
	500 End. balance

Draw a line across the T when you are ready to compute the ending balance.

Put the ending balance amount on the side of the T-account that it represents (e.g., + side if it is a positive number).

In Exhibit 2.7, notice that the ending balance is indicated on the positive side with a double underline. To find the account balances, we can express the T-accounts as equations:

	Cash	Common Stock
Beginning balance	$419,500	$ 400
+ "+" side	+ 3,700	+100
− "−" side	− 0	− 0
Ending balance	$423,200	$ 500

A word on terminology: The words **debit** and **credit** may be used as verbs, nouns, and adjectives. For example, we can say that Chipotle's Cash account was debited (verb) when stock was issued to investors, meaning that the amount was entered on the left side of the T-account. Or we can say that a credit (noun) was entered on the right side of an account. Common Stock may be described as a credit account (adjective). These terms will be used instead of **left** and **right** throughout the rest of this textbook. The next section illustrates the steps to follow in analyzing the effects of transactions, recording the effects in journal entries, and determining account balances using T-accounts.

Inferring Business Activities from T-Accounts

FINANCIAL ANALYSIS

T-accounts are useful primarily for instructional and analytical purposes. In many cases, we will use T-accounts to determine what transactions a company engaged in during a period. For example, the primary transactions affecting Accounts Payable for a period are purchases of assets on account from suppliers and cash payments to suppliers. If we know the beginning and ending balances of Accounts Payable and all the amounts that were purchased on credit during a period, we can determine the amount of cash paid. A T-account analysis would include the following:

− Accounts Payable (L) +		
	600	Beg. bal.
Cash payments to suppliers ?	1,500	Purchases on account
	300	End. bal.

Solution:

Beginning Balance	+	Purchases on Account	−	Cash Payments to Suppliers	=	Ending Balance
$600	+	$1,500	−	?	=	$ 300
		$2,100	−	?	=	$ 300
				?	=	$1,800

Transaction Analysis Illustrated

In this section, we will use the quarterly investing and financing transactions for **Chipotle Mexican Grill** (events [a] to [f]) that were analyzed earlier to demonstrate recording journal entries and posting effects to the relevant T-accounts. Note that the accounting equation remains in balance and that debits equal credits after each entry. In the T-accounts, the amounts from Chipotle's December 31, 2014, balance sheet (Exhibit 2.2) have been inserted as the beginning balances.

Study this illustration carefully, including the explanations of transaction analysis. Careful study is **essential** to an understanding of (1) the accounting model, (2) transaction analysis, (3) the dual effects of each transaction, and (4) the dual-balancing system. The most effective way to learn these critical concepts, which are basic to material throughout the rest of the text, is to practice, practice, practice.

(a) **Chipotle issued (sold) 10,000 additional shares of common stock with a par value of $0.01 per share at a market value of $0.37 per share, receiving $3,700 in cash from investors. Common stock is recorded at par (10,000 shares × $0.01 par value per share) and Additional Paid-in Capital is recorded for the excess over par value (10,000 shares × $0.36 per share).**

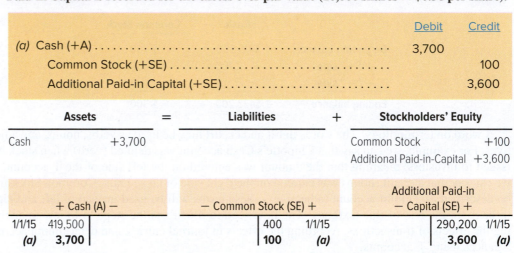

The effects reflected in the journal entry have been posted to the appropriate T-accounts. Notice that if an account was debited such as Cash, that effect was written in the debit column of the Cash T-account. Similarly, if an account was credited such as Common Stock, that effect was written in the credit column of the T-account. Also notice that the January 1, 2015, beginning balances are the same as the ending balances at December 31, 2014, (see Exhibit 2.2) and are indicated on the respective positive side of the account—assets have debit balances and liabilities and stockholders' equity accounts have credit balances.

(b) **Chipotle borrowed $2,000 from its local bank, signing a note to be paid in three years.** Since Notes Payable is a new account not listed on the December 31, 2014, balance sheet in Exhibit 2.2, its beginning balance is $0.

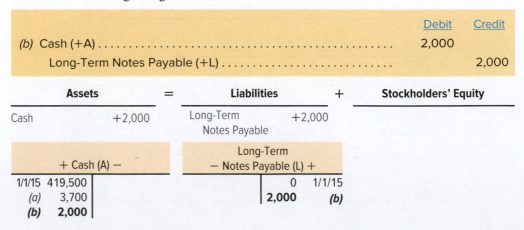

(c) **Chipotle purchased $10,000 in additional land, $8,200 in new buildings, $33,800 in new equipment, and $3,700 in additional intangible assets; paid $53,400 in cash and signed a short-term note payable for the remainder owed ($2,300).**

	Debit	Credit
(c) Land (+A)	10,000	
Buildings (+A)	8,200	
Equipment (+A)	33,800	
Intangible Assets (+A)	3,700	
Cash (−A)		53,400
Short-Term Notes Payable (+L)		2,300

Assets	=	Liabilities	+	Stockholders' Equity
Land +10,000		Short-Term		
Buildings +8,200		Notes Payable +2,300		
Equipment +33,800				
Intangible assets +3,700				
Cash −53,400				

+ Cash (A) −			+ Land (A) −			+ Buildings (A) −	
1/1/15 419,500			1/1/15 11,100			1/1/15 1,267,100	
(a) 3,700	**53,400**	(c)	(c) **10,000**			(c) **8,200**	
(b) 2,000							

+ Equipment (A) −			Intangible + Assets (A) −			Short-Term − Notes Payable (L) +	
1/1/15 442,500			1/1/15 64,700				0 1/1/15
(c) **33,800**			(c) **3,700**				**2,300** (c)

(d) **Chipotle paid $2,300 on the short-term note payable in (c) above and $2,300 on other noncurrent liabilities (ignore interest).**

	Debit	Credit
(d) Short-Term Notes Payable (−L)	2,300	
Other Liabilities (−L)	2,300	
Cash (−A)		4,600

Assets	=	Liabilities	+	Stockholders' Equity
Cash −4,600		Short-Term		
		Notes Payable −2,300		
		Other Liabilities −2,300		

+ Cash (A) −			Short-Term − Notes Payable (L) +			− Other Liabilities (L) +	
1/1/15 419,500				0 1/1/15			288,200 1/1/15
(a) 3,700	53,400	(c)	(d) **2,300**	2,300	(c)	(d) **2,300**	
(b) 2,000	**4,600**	(d)					

(e) **Chipotle purchased the stock of other companies as investments, paying $44,000 cash; of this, $9,000 was in short-term investments and $35,000 was in long-term investments.**

	Debit	Credit
(e) Short-Term Investments (+A)	9,000	
Long-Term Investments (+A)	35,000	
Cash (−A)		44,000

Assets	=	Liabilities	+	Stockholders' Equity
Short-Term Investments +9,000				
Long-Term Investments +35,000				
Cash −44,000				

+ Cash (A) −			Short-Term + Investments (A) −		Long-Term + Investment (A) −	
1/1/15 419,500			1/1/15 338,600		1/1/15 496,100	
(a) 3,700	53,400	(c)	(e) 9,000		(e) 35,000	
(b) 2,000	4,600	(d)				
	44,000	(e)				

(f) Chipotle does not pay dividends, but instead reinvests profits into growing the business. However, for illustration purposes, **assume Chipotle's board of directors declared that the Company will pay $3,000 in cash as dividends to shareholders next quarter.** Because Dividends Payable was not listed on the December 31, 2014, balance sheet (see Exhibit 2.2), it has a $0 balance on January 1, 2015.

	Debit	Credit
(f) Retained Earnings (−SE)	3,000	
Dividends Payable (+L)		3,000

Assets	=	Liabilities	+	Stockholders' Equity
		Dividends Payable +3,000		Retained Earnings −3,000

− Dividends Payable (L) +		− Retained Earnings (SE) +	
	0 1/1/15		1,721,800 1/1/15
3,000	(f)	(f) 3,000	

Now we determine the balances in the T-accounts that changed during the quarter. Each T-account is listed with the beginning balances and transaction effects with references. Then a line is drawn across the T-account after the last transaction effect with the balance indicated below the summation line on the positive side:

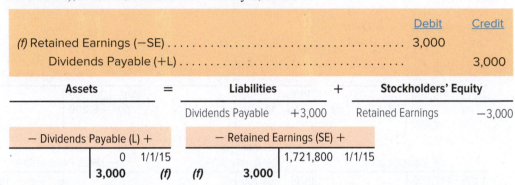

+ Cash (A) −			+ Short-Term Investments (A) −		+ Land (A) −	
1/1/15 419,500			1/1/15 338,600		1/1/15 11,100	
(a) 3,700	53,400	(c)	(e) 9,000		(c) 10,000	
(b) 2,000	4,600	(d)	347,600		21,100	
	44,000	(e)				
323,200						

+ Buildings (A) −		+ Equipment (A) −		+ Intangible Assets (A) −		+ Long-Term Investments (A) −	
1/1/15 1,267,100		1/1/15 442,500		1/1/15 64,700		1/1/15 496,100	
(c) 8,200		(c) 33,800		(c) 3,700		(e) 35,000	
1,275,300		476,300		68,400		531,100	

Short-Term − Notes Payable (L) +			Long-Term − Notes Payable (L) +			Dividends − Payable (L) +			− Other Liabilities (L) +	
	0	1/1/15		0	1/1/15		0	1/1/15		288,200 1/1/15
(d) 2,300	2,300	(c)		2,000	(b)		3,000	(f)	(d) 2,300	
	0			2,000			3,000			285,900

− Common Stock (SE) +		− Additional Paid-in Capital (SE) +		− Retained Earnings (SE) +	
	400 1/1/15		290,200 1/1/15		1,721,800 1/1/15
	100 (a)		3,600 (a)	(f) 3,000	
	500		293,800		1,718,800

PAUSE FOR **FEEDBACK**

STOP

Accountants analyze and then record transactions in the general journal in chronological order in journal entry form. Debited accounts are written on top with amounts in the left column and credited accounts are written on the bottom with amounts in the right column. Then the effects are posted in the general ledger (similar to a T-account). Each page of the ledger represents a different account that has a debit (left) side and a credit (right) side. To post transaction effects, the amount for each account in a journal entry is written in the appropriate debit or credit column on the ledger page to obtain account balances. Refer to Exhibit 2.5 for the transaction analysis model.

SELF-STUDY QUIZ

Record the following transactions and post the effects to the T-accounts. Because this is a new company, all T-accounts start with a beginning balance of $0.

(a) **Paul Knepper contributes $50,000 cash to establish Florida Flippers, Inc., a new scuba business organized as a corporation; he receives in exchange 25,000 shares of stock with a $0.10 per share par value.**

		Debit	Credit
(a) _____ ( )..................		_____	
_____ ( )..................			
_____ ( )..................			_____

(b) **Florida Flippers buys a small building near the ocean for $250,000, paying $25,000 in cash and signing a 10-year note payable for the rest.**

		Debit	Credit
(b) _____ ( )..................		_____	
_____ ( )..................			
_____ ( )..................			_____

Cash		Buildings		Notes Payable		Common Stock		Additional Paid-in Capital	
Beg. 0		Beg. 0			0 Beg.		0 Beg.		0 Beg.

After you have completed your answers, check them below.

GUIDED HELP 2-2

For additional step-by-step video instruction on analyzing, recording, and posting transaction effects and classifying accounts, go to **www.mhhe.com/libby9e_gh2b**.

(a) Cash (+A) 50,000
   Common Stock (+SE) .... 2,500 [25,000 shares × $0.10 par]
   Additional Paid-in Capital (+SE)........ 47,500

(b) Buildings (+A) 250,000
   Cash (−A) 25,000
   Notes Payable (+L) 225,000

+ Cash −				+ Buildings −			− Notes Payable +			− Common Stock +			− Additional Paid-in Capital +	
Beg. 0				Beg. 0				0 Beg.			0 Beg.			0 Beg.
(a) 50,000	25,000	*(b)*		*(b)* 250,000				225,000 *(b)*			2,500 *(a)*			47,500 *(a)*
25,000				250,000				225,000			2,500			47,500

LEARNING OBJECTIVE 2-5

Prepare a trial balance and simple classified balance sheet, and analyze the company using the current ratio.

TRIAL BALANCE

A list of all accounts with their balances to provide a check on the equality of the debits and credits.

HOW IS THE BALANCE SHEET PREPARED AND ANALYZED?

Although no operating activities occurred yet (they will be illustrated in Chapter 3), it is possible to create a balance sheet based solely on the investing and financing activities recorded above. Usually, businesses will create a **trial balance** spreadsheet first for internal purposes before preparing statements for external users. A trial balance lists the names of the T-accounts in one column, usually in financial statement order (assets, liabilities, stockholders' equity, revenues, and expenses), with their ending debit or credit balances in the next two columns. Debit balances are indicated in the left column and credit balances are indicated in the right column. Then the two columns are totaled to provide a check on the equality of the debits and credits. Errors in a computer-generated trial balance may exist if wrong accounts and/or amounts are used in the journal entries.[4]

Chipotle's trial balance follows. The account balances that did not change are taken from the December 31, 2014, balance sheet in Exhibit 2.2. The accounts that did change due to the investing and financing transactions illustrated in this chapter are shaded; their balances are taken from the T-accounts summarized at the end of the previous section.

CHIPOTLE MEXICAN GRILL—TRIAL BALANCE
(based on investing and financing transactions only during the first quarter ended March 31, 2015)

(in thousands)	Debit	Credit
Cash	323,200	
Short-term investments	347,600	
Accounts receivable	34,800	
Supplies	15,300	
Prepaid expenses	70,300	
Land	21,100	
Buildings	1,275,300	
Equipment	476,300	
Accumulated depreciation		613,700
Long-term investments	531,100	
Intangible assets	68,400	
Accounts payable		69,600
Unearned revenue		16,800
Dividends payable		3,000
Wages payable		73,900
Utilities payable		85,400
Short-term notes payable		0
Long-term notes payable		2,000
Other liabilities		285,900
Common stock		500
Additional paid-in capital		293,800
Retained earnings		1,718,800
Total	**3,163,400**	**3,163,400**

---

[4]In homework assignments, if you have an error in your trial balance (the two column totals are not equal), errors can be traced and should be corrected before adjusting the records. To find errors, reverse your steps. Check that:

- You copied the ending balances in all of the T-accounts (both amount and whether a debit or credit) correctly to the trial balance.
- You computed the ending balances in the T-accounts correctly.
- You posted the transaction effects correctly from the journal entries to the T-accounts (amount, account, and whether a debit or credit).
- You prepared the journal entries correctly (amount, account, and whether a debit or credit).

Classified Balance Sheet

The balance sheet in Exhibit 2.8 was prepared from the trial balance as shown above. As a formal statement for external users, it needs a good heading (name of the company, title of the statement, date, and if the dollars are in thousands or millions). Notice in Exhibit 2.8 several additional features:

- The assets and liabilities are **classified** into two categories: **current** and **noncurrent.** Current assets are those to be used or turned into cash within the upcoming year, whereas

EXHIBIT 2.8

Chipotle Mexican Grill's First Quarter 2015 Balance Sheet (based on investing and financing activities only)

CHIPOTLE MEXICAN GRILL, INC.
Consolidated Balance Sheets
(in thousands of dollars, except per share data)

	March 31, 2015	December 31, 2014
ASSETS		
Current Assets:		
Cash	$ 323,200	$ 419,500
Short-term investments	347,600	338,600
Accounts receivable	34,800	34,800
Supplies	15,300	15,300
Prepaid expenses	70,300	70,300
Total current assets	791,200	878,500
Property and equipment:		
Land	21,100	11,100
Buildings	1,275,300	1,267,100
Equipment	476,300	442,500
Total cost	1,772,700	1,720,700
Accumulated depreciation	(613,700)	(613,700)
Net property and equipment	1,159,000	1,107,000
Long-term investments	531,100	496,100
Intangible assets	68,400	64,700
Total assets	**$2,549,700**	**$2,546,300**
LIABILITIES AND STOCKHOLDERS' EQUITY		
Current Liabilities:		
Accounts payable	$ 69,600	$ 69,600
Unearned revenue	16,800	16,800
Dividends payable	3,000	—
Accrued expenses payable:		
Wages payable	73,900	73,900
Taxes payable	85,400	85,400
Total current liabilities	248,700	245,700
Notes payable	2,000	—
Other liabilities	285,900	288,200
Total liabilities	536,600	533,900
Stockholders' Equity:		
Common stock ($0.01 par value per share)	500	400
Additional paid-in capital	293,800	290,200
Retained earnings	1,718,800	1,721,800
Total stockholders' equity	2,013,100	2,012,400
Total liabilities and stockholders' equity	**$2,549,700**	**$2,546,300**

noncurrent assets are those that will last longer than one year. Current liabilities are those obligations to be paid or settled within the next 12 months with current assets.

- Dollar signs are indicated at the top and bottom of the asset section and top and bottom of the liabilities and shareholders' equity section. More than that tends to look messy.

- The statement includes **comparative data.** That is, it compares the account balances at December 31, 2014, with those at March 31, 2015. When multiple periods are presented, the most recent balance sheet amounts are usually listed on the left.

- Unlike **Chipotle**, most companies do not provide a total liabilities line on the balance sheet. To determine total liabilities on those statements, add total current liabilities and each of the noncurrent liabilities.

INTERNATIONAL PERSPECTIVE

Understanding Foreign Financial Statements

Although IFRS differs from GAAP, they use the same system of analyzing, recording, and summarizing the results of business activities that you have learned in this chapter. One place where IFRS differs from GAAP is in the formatting of financial statements.

Financial statements prepared using GAAP and IFRS include the same elements (assets, liabilities, revenues, expenses, etc.). However, a single, consistent format has not been mandated. Consequently, various formats have evolved over time, with those in the United States differing from those typically used internationally. The formatting differences include:

	GAAP	IFRS
Balance Sheet Order	**Assets:**	**Assets:**
	Current	Noncurrent
Similar accounts are	Noncurrent	Current
shown, but the order of	**Liabilities:**	**Stockholders' Equity**
liquidity (for assets) and	Current	**Liabilities:**
the order of maturity (for	Noncurrent	Noncurrent
liabilities) differ	**Stockholders' Equity**	Current

On the balance sheet, GAAP begins with current items whereas IFRS begins with noncurrent items. Consistent with this, **assets are listed in decreasing order of liquidity under GAAP, but internationally assets are usually listed in increasing order of liquidity.** IFRS similarly emphasizes longer-term financing sources by listing equity before liabilities and, within liabilities, by listing noncurrent liabilities before current liabilities (**decreasing time to maturity**). The key to avoiding confusion is to be sure to **pay attention to the subheadings** in the statement. Any account under the heading "liabilities" must be a liability.

Ratio Analysis in Decision Making

Why do the classifications of current and noncurrent on the balance sheet matter? Users of financial information compute a number of ratios in analyzing a company's past performance and financial condition as input in predicting its future potential. How ratios change over time and how they compare to the ratios of the company's competitors or industry averages provide valuable information about a company's strategies for its operating, investing, and financing activities. We introduce here the first of many ratios that will be presented throughout the rest of this textbook, with a final summary of ratio analysis in Chapter 13.

Current Ratio

? ANALYTICAL QUESTION

Does the company have the short-term resources to pay its short-term debt?

% RATIO AND COMPARISONS

$$\text{Current Ratio} = \frac{\text{Current Assets}}{\text{Current Liabilities}}$$

The 2014 ratio for **Chipotle** is (dollars in thousands):

$$\frac{\$878,500}{\$245,700} = 3.575$$

COMPARISONS OVER TIME Chipotle Mexican Grill, Inc.		
2014	**2013**	**2012**
3.575	3.344	2.925

COMPARISONS WITH COMPETITORS	
Panera Bread, Inc.	**Fiesta Restaurant Group, Inc.**
2014	**2014**
1.152	0.713
Vies for top fast-casual restaurant	Owns Pollo Tropical and Taco Cabana

💡 INTERPRETATIONS

In General   The current ratio is a very common ratio. Creditors and security analysts use the current ratio to measure the ability of the company to pay its short-term obligations with short-term assets. Generally, the higher the ratio, the more cushion a company has to pay its current obligations if future economic conditions take a downturn. While a ratio above 1.0 normally suggests good liquidity, today, many strong companies use sophisticated management techniques to minimize funds invested in current assets and, as a result, have current ratios below 1.0. Likewise, when compared to others in the industry, too high of a ratio may suggest inefficient use of resources.

Focus Company Analysis   Over time, the current ratio for Chipotle shows a high level of liquidity, well above 1.0, and the ratio has risen each year since 2012. Chipotle has high growth strategies requiring cash to fund expansion.

Compared with competitors, **Panera Bread**, vying with Chipotle as the top fast-casual restaurant, also maintains a current ratio above 1.0, and both companies report cash as the largest current asset. The ratio for Chipotle is much higher than for **Fiesta Restaurant Group**, which reports a current ratio below 1.0. Fiesta Restaurant Group owns and franchises two quick-service brands: **Pollo Tropical**, featuring a tropical and Caribbean-style menu, and **Taco Cabana**, offering Mexican fast food. Fiesta expects growth, but franchising (that is, selling rights to others to operate restaurants under the company brands) does not require the cash flow levels needed for company-owned facilities. It is also likely that all of these companies have sophisticated cash management systems that enable them to maintain lower cash balances.

Reuters reports that the fast-casual sector of the restaurant industry has an average current ratio of 1.73 while the broader restaurant industry's average is 1.23. Compared to the sector average, Chipotle has sufficient current assets to pay short-term obligations (adequate liquidity), while Panera Bread and Fiesta Restaurant Group have current ratios below the industry average, suggesting these companies may rely on sufficient cash flows generated during the year to meet current obligations.

A Few Cautions   The current ratio may be a misleading measure of liquidity if significant funds are tied up in assets that cannot be easily converted into cash. A company with a high current ratio might still have liquidity problems if the majority of its current assets consists of slow-moving inventory. Analysts also recognize that managers can manipulate the current ratio by engaging in certain transactions just before the close of the fiscal year. In most cases, for example, the current ratio can be improved by paying creditors immediately prior to the preparation of financial statements.

Selected Focus Companies' Current Ratios

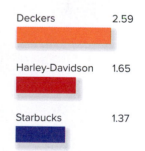

Deckers	2.59
Harley-Davidson	1.65
Starbucks	1.37

We just learned that the current ratio measures a company's ability to pay short-term obligations with short-term assets—a liquidity measure. It is computed by dividing current assets by current liabilities. A ratio above 1.0 is normally considered good, although some may need a higher ratio and others with good cash management systems can have a ratio below 1.0 (i.e., more current liabilities than current assets).

SELF-STUDY QUIZ

Yum! Brands, Inc., is the world's largest quick-service restaurant company that develops, franchises, and operates 41,000 units in more than 125 countries and territories through three restaurant concepts (KFC, Pizza Hut, and Taco Bell). The company reported the following balances on its recent balance sheets (in millions). Compute Yum! Brands's current ratio for fiscal years 2012, 2013, and 2014.

(dollars in millions)

	Current Assets	Current Liabilities	Current Ratio
Fiscal year 2014	$1,646	$2,411	_____
Fiscal year 2013	1,691	2,265	_____
Fiscal year 2012	1,925	2,279	_____

What do these results suggest about Yum! Brands's liquidity in the current year and over time?

After you have completed your answers, check them below.

FOCUS ON CASH FLOWS

Investing and Financing Activities

LEARNING OBJECTIVE 2-6
Identify investing and financing transactions and demonstrate how they impact cash flows.

As discussed in Chapter 1, companies report cash inflows and outflows over a period in their **statement of cash flows,** which is divided into three categories: operating, investing, and financing activities:

- Operating activities are covered in Chapter 3.
- Investing activities include buying and selling noncurrent assets and investments.
- Financing activities include borrowing and repaying debt, including short-term bank loans; issuing and repurchasing stock; and paying dividends.

Only transactions affecting cash are reported on the statement. An important step in constructing and analyzing the statement of cash flows is identifying the various transactions as operating (O), investing (I), or financing (F). Let's analyze the Cash T-account for **Chipotle**'s transactions in this chapter. Refer to transactions *(a)–(f)* illustrated earlier in this chapter, and remember, **you must see cash in the transaction for it to affect the statement of cash flows.**

			+ Cash (A) −				
		1/1/15	419,500				
From investors	+F	(a)	3,700	53,400	(c)	−I	For noncurrent assets
From bank	+F	(b)	2,000	4,600	(d)	−F	To pay notes payable and other liabilities
				44,000	(e)	−I	For investments in other companies
			323,200				

Solutions to
SELF-STUDY QUIZ

Current Ratio:					
Fiscal year 2014	$1,646	÷	$2,411	=	0.683
Fiscal year 2013	1,691	÷	2,265	=	0.747
Fiscal year 2012	1,925	÷	2,279	=	0.845

Yum! Brands's current ratio is below 1.0 and falling over the three years, suggesting the company has a low level of liquidity—insufficient current assets to settle short-term obligations. However, as a cash-oriented business and with a strong cash management system, Yum! Brands's current ratio below 1.0 is not a concern.

PAUSE FOR **FEEDBACK**   STOP

As we discussed, every transaction affecting cash can be classified either as an operating (discussed in Chapter 3), investing, or financing effect. Investing effects relate to purchasing/selling investments or property and equipment or lending funds to/receiving repayment from others. Financing effects relate to borrowing or repaying banks, issuing stock to investors, repurchasing stock from investors, or paying dividends to investors.

SELF-STUDY QUIZ

Indicate whether the following transactions from a recent annual statement of cash flows for **Apple, Inc.**, were investing (I) or financing (F) activities and the direction of their effects on cash (+ for increases; − for decreases):

Transactions	Type of Activity (I or F)	Effect on Cash Flows (+ or −)
1. Purchased investments	_____	_____
2. Issued common stock	_____	_____
3. Acquired property, plant, and equipment	_____	_____
4. Sold investments	_____	_____
5. Purchased intangible assets (e.g., patents)	_____	_____

After you have completed your answers, check them below.

DEMONSTRATION CASE

On April 1, 2016, three ambitious college students started Terrific Lawn Maintenance Corporation. A summary of transactions completed through April 7, 2016, for Terrific Lawn Maintenance Corporation follows:

a. Issued 500 shares of stock (1,500 shares in total) with a par value of $0.10 per share to each of the three investors in exchange for $9,000 cash.

b. Acquired rakes and other hand tools (equipment) with a list price of $690 for $600; paid the hardware store $200 cash and signed a three-month note for the balance.

c. Ordered three lawn mowers and two edgers from XYZ Lawn Supply, Inc., for $4,000.

d. Purchased four acres of land for the future site of a storage garage; paid cash, $5,000.

e. Received the mowers and edgers that had been ordered, signing a note to pay XYZ Lawn Supply in full in 18 months.

f. Sold for $1,250 one acre of land to the city for a park. Accepted a note from the city for payment by the end of the month.

g. One of the owners borrowed $3,000 from a local bank for personal use.

Required:

1. Set up T-accounts for Cash, Notes Receivable (from the city), Equipment (hand tools and mowing equipment), Land, Short-Term Notes Payable (to the hardware store), Long-Term Notes Payable (to the equipment supply company), Common Stock, and Additional Paid-in Capital. Beginning balances are $0; indicate these beginning balances in the T-accounts. Analyze each transaction using the process outlined in the chapter with the transaction analysis model, and prepare journal entries in chronological order. Enter the effects of the transactions in the appropriate T-accounts; identify each amount with its letter in the preceding list. Compute ending balances for each T-account.

---

1. **I** −   2. **F** +   3. **I** −   4. **I** +   5. **I** −

Solutions to
SELF-STUDY QUIZ

Assets	=	Liabilities	+	Stockholders' Equity	
(many accounts)		(many accounts)		Contributed Capital (2 accounts) Earned Capital (1 account)	

+	−	−	+	Common Stock and Additional Paid-in Capital	Retained Earnings	
Debit	Credit	Debit	Credit			

	+	−	+
	Credit	Debit	Credit
	Investment by owners	Dividends declared	Net income

2. Use the balances in the T-accounts developed in the previous requirement to prepare a classified balance sheet for Terrific Lawn Maintenance Corporation at April 7, 2016.

3. Identify transactions (a)–(g) as investing or financing activities affecting cash flows and the direction of each effect. Use +I for investing inflow, −I for investing outflow, +F for financing inflow, and −F for financing outflow.

Check your answers with the solution in the following section.

SUGGESTED SOLUTION

1. Transaction Analysis:

Received:	Given:
a. Cash (+A) $9,000	Common Stock (+SE) $150
	(1,500 shares × $0.10 par value per share)
	Additional Paid-in Capital (+SE) $8,850 ($9,000 − $150)
b. Equipment (+A) $600	Cash (−A) $200
	Short-Term Notes Payable (+L) $400
c. Not a transaction—a promise to pay for a promise to deliver from the supplier	
d. Land (+A) $5,000	Cash (−A) $5,000
e. Equipment (+A) $4,000	Long-Term Notes Payable (+L) $4,000
f. Notes Receivable (+A) $1,250 Land (−A) $1,250 (1/4 of the $5,000 cost of the land)	
g. Not a transaction of the business—separate-entity assumption	

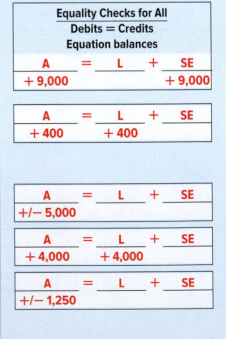

Journal Entries	Debit	Credit
(a) Cash (+A)...	9,000	
Common Stock (+SE)...........................		150
Additional Paid-in Capital (+SE).................		8,850
(b) Equipment (+A).....................................	600	
Cash (−A).......................................		200
Short-Term Notes Payable (+L)		400
(c) No transaction		
(d) Land (+A)...	5,000	
Cash (−A).......................................		5,000
(e) Equipment (+A).....................................	4,000	
Long-Term Notes Payable (+L)...................		4,000
(f) Notes Receivable (+A)	1,250	
Land (−A).......................................		1,250
(g) No transaction		

Equality Checks for All
Debits = Credits
Equation balances

A	=	L	+	SE
+ 9,000				+ 9,000

A	=	L	+	SE
+ 400		+ 400		

A	=	L	+	SE
+/− 5,000				

A	=	L	+	SE
+ 4,000		+ 4,000		

A	=	L	+	SE
+/− 1,250				

T-Accounts:

+ Cash (A) −			
4/1/16	0		
(a)	9,000	200	(b)
		5,000	(d)
	3,800		

+ Notes Receivable (A) −			
4/1/16	0		
(f)	1,250		
	1,250		

+ Equipment (A) −			
4/1/16	0		
(b)	600		
(e)	4,000		
	4,600		

+ Land (A) −			
4/1/16	0		
(d)	5,000	1,250	(f)
	3,750		

Short-Term − Notes Payable (L) +			
		0	4/1/16
		400	(b)
		400	

Long-Term − Notes Payable (L) +			
		0	4/1/16
		4,000	(e)
		4,000	

− Common Stock (SE) +			
		0	4/1/16
		150	(a)
		150	

Additional Paid-in − Capital (SE) +			
		0	4/1/16
		8,850	(a)
		8,850	

2. Classified Balance Sheet:

TERRIFIC LAWN MAINTENANCE CORPORATION
Balance Sheet
April 7, 2016

Assets	
Current Assets:	
Cash	$ 3,800
Notes receivable	1,250
Total current assets	5,050
Equipment	4,600
Land	3,750
Total assets	**$13,400**
Liabilities and Stockholders' Equity	
Current Liabilities:	
Short-term notes payable	$ 400
Total current liabilities	400
Long-term notes payable	4,000
Total liabilities	4,400
Stockholders' Equity:	
Common stock ($0.10 par)	150
Additional paid-in capital	8,850
Total stockholders' equity	9,000
Total liabilities and stockholders' equity	**$13,400**

3. Cash Flows:

+ Cash (A) −			
4/1/16	0		
(a)	9,000	200	(b)
		5,000	(d)
	3,800		

Only transactions *(a)*, *(b)*, and *(d)* affect cash flows (as shown in the Cash T-account).

(a) +F for $9,000

(b) −I for $200

(d) −I for $5,000

CHAPTER TAKE-AWAYS

2-1. Define the objective of financial reporting, the elements of the balance sheet, and the related key accounting assumptions and principles.   p. 45

Objective:

- The primary objective of financial reporting to external users is to provide financial information about the reporting entity that is useful to existing and potential investors, lenders, and other creditors in making decisions about providing resources to the entity.

Qualitative characteristics of useful financial information:

- Relevance (including materiality) allows users to assess past activities and/or predict future activities.
- Faithful representation requires information to be complete, neutral, and free from error.
  - To enhance its qualitative characteristics, information should also be comparable (to other companies and over time), verifiable, timely, and understandable.

Key recognition, measurement, and disclosure concepts:

Assumptions—

- Separate entity assumption—Transactions of the business are accounted for separately from transactions of the owner.
- Going concern assumption—A business is expected to continue to operate into the foreseeable future.
- Monetary unit assumption—Financial information is reported in the national monetary unit without adjustment for changes in purchasing power.

Principles—

- Mixed-attribute measurement model—Most balance sheet elements are recorded following the historical cost (or cost) principle—financial statement elements should be recorded at the cash-equivalent cost on the date of the transaction; however, these values may be adjusted to other amounts, such as market value, depending on certain conditions.

Elements of the balance sheet:

- Assets—Probable future economic benefits owned or controlled by the entity as a result of past transactions.
- Liabilities—Probable future sacrifices of economic benefits arising from present obligations of a business as a result of past transactions.

- Stockholders' equity—Residual interest of owners in the assets of the entity after settling liabilities; the financing provided by the owners (contributed capital) and by business operations (earned capital).

2-2. Identify what constitutes a business transaction and recognize common balance sheet account titles used in business.   p. 49

- An exchange of cash, goods, or services for cash, goods, services, or promises between a business and one or more external parties to a business (not the exchange of a promise for a promise),

or

- A measurable internal event, such as adjustments for the use of assets in operations.

An account is a standardized format that organizations use to accumulate the dollar effects of transactions related to each financial statement item. Typical balance sheet account titles include the following:

- *Assets:* Cash, Accounts Receivable, Inventory, Prepaid Expenses, Investments, Property (buildings and land) and Equipment, and Intangibles (rights without physical substance).
- *Liabilities:* Accounts Payable, Notes Payable, Accrued Expenses Payable, Unearned Revenues, and Taxes Payable.
- *Stockholders' Equity:* Common Stock, Additional Paid-in Capital, and Retained Earnings.

2-3. Apply transaction analysis to simple business transactions in terms of the accounting model: Assets = Liabilities + Stockholders' Equity.   p. 51

To determine the economic effect of a transaction on an entity in terms of the accounting equation, each transaction must be analyzed to determine the accounts (at least two) that are affected. In an exchange, the company receives something and gives up something. If the accounts, direction of the effects, and amounts are correctly analyzed, the accounting equation will stay in balance. The transaction analysis model is:

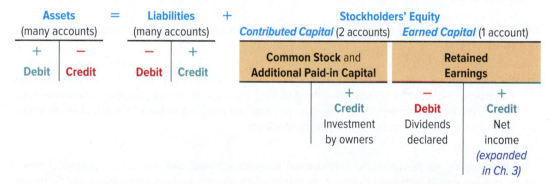

Systematic transaction analysis includes (1) determining the accounts that were received and were given in the exchange, including the type of each account (A, L, or SE), the amounts, and the direction of the effects, and (2) determining that the accounting equation remains in balance.

2-4. Determine the impact of business transactions on the balance sheet using two basic tools: Journal entries and T-accounts.   p. 56

- Journal entries express the effects of a transaction on accounts in a debits-equal-credits format. The accounts and amounts to be debited are listed first. Then the accounts and amounts to be credited are listed below the debits and indented, resulting in debit amounts on the left and credit amounts on the right. Each entry needs a reference (date, number, or letter).

	Debit	Credit
(a) Cash (+A)...	62,300	
Common Stock (+SE)		100
Additional Paid-in Capital (+SE)......................		62,200

- T-accounts summarize the transaction effects for each account. These tools can be used to determine balances and draw inferences about a company's activities.

+ (dr)	Assets	(cr) −		− (dr)	Liabilities and Stockholders' Equity	(cr) +
Beginning balance						Beginning balance
Increases		Decreases		Decreases		Increases
Ending balance						Ending balance

2-5. Prepare a trial balance and simple classified balance sheet, and analyze the company using the current ratio. p. 66

A trial balance lists all accounts and their balances, with debit balances in the left column and credit balances in the right column. The two columns are added to determine if debits equal credits.

Classified balance sheets are structured as follows:

- Assets are categorized as current assets (those to be used or turned into cash within the year, with inventory always considered a current asset) and noncurrent assets, such as long-term investments, property and equipment, and intangible assets.

- Liabilities are categorized as current liabilities (those that will be paid with current assets) and long-term liabilities.

- Stockholders' equity accounts are listed as Common Stock (number of shares × par value per share) and Additional Paid-in Capital (number of shares × excess of market value over par value per share) first, followed by Retained Earnings (earnings reinvested in the business).

The current ratio (Current Assets ÷ Current Liabilities) measures a company's liquidity, that is, the ability of the company to pay its short-term obligations with current assets.

2-6. Identify investing and financing transactions and demonstrate how they impact cash flows. p. 70

A statement of cash flows reports the sources and uses of cash for the period by the type of activity that generated the cash flow: operating, investing, and financing. Investing activities include purchasing and selling long-term assets and making loans and receiving principal repayments from others. Financing activities include borrowing from and repaying to banks the principal on loans, issuing and repurchasing stock, and paying dividends.

In this chapter, we discussed the fundamental accounting model and transaction analysis. Journal entries and T-accounts were used to record the results of transaction analysis for investing and financing decisions that affect balance sheet accounts. In Chapter 3, we continue our detailed look at the financial statements, in particular the income statement. The purpose of Chapter 3 is to build on your knowledge by discussing the measurement of revenues and expenses and illustrating the transaction analysis of operating decisions.

KEY **RATIO**

Current ratio measures the ability of the company to pay its short-term obligations with current assets. Although a ratio above 1.0 indicates sufficient current assets to meet obligations when they come due, many companies with sophisticated cash management systems have ratios below 1.0 (see the "Key Ratio Analysis" box in the How Is the Balance Sheet Prepared and Analyzed? section):

$$\text{Current Ratio} = \frac{\text{Current Assets}}{\text{Current Liabilities}}$$

FINDING **FINANCIAL INFORMATION**

Balance Sheet

Current Assets
  Cash
  Short-term investments
  Accounts receivable
  Notes receivable
  Inventory
  Prepaid expenses

Noncurrent Assets
  Long-term investments
  Property and equipment
  Intangibles

Current Liabilities
  Accounts payable
  Accrued expenses payable
  Short-term notes payable
  Unearned revenue

Noncurrent Liabilities
  Long-term debt (notes payable)

Stockholders' Equity
  Common stock
  Additional paid-in capital
  Retained earnings

Income Statement
To be presented in Chapter 3

Statement of Cash Flows

Operating Activities
  To be presented in Chapter 3

Investing Activities
  + Sales of noncurrent assets and investments for cash
  − Purchases of noncurrent assets and investments for cash
  − Loans to others
  + Receipt of loan principal payments from others

Financing Activities
  + Borrowing from banks
  − Repayment of loan principal to banks
  + Issuance of stock
  − Repurchasing stock
  − Dividends paid

Notes
To be discussed in future chapters

KEY **TERMS**

Account   p. 50
Accounting Cycle   p. 56
Additional Paid-in Capital (Paid-in Capital, Contributed Capital in Excess of Par)   p. 53
Assets   p. 47
Common Stock   p. 53
Cost (Historical Cost)   p. 46
Credit   p. 57
Current Assets   p. 47
Current Liabilities   p. 47

Debit   p. 57
Faithful Representation   p. 46
Going Concern Assumption   p. 46
Journal Entry   p. 59
Liabilities   p. 47
Mixed-Attribute Measurement Model   p. 46
Monetary Unit Assumption   p. 46
Par Value   p. 53
Primary Objective of Financial Reporting to External Users   p. 45

Relevant Information   p. 45
Retained Earnings   p. 48
Separate Entity Assumption   p. 46
Stockholders' Equity (Shareholders' or Owners' Equity)   p. 47
T-account   p. 60
Transaction   p. 49
Transaction Analysis   p. 51
Trial Balance   p. 66

QUESTIONS

1. What is the primary objective of financial reporting for external users?
2. Define the following:
   a. Asset
   b. Current asset
   c. Liability
   d. Current liability
   e. Additional paid-in capital
   f. Retained earnings

3. Explain what the following accounting terms mean:
   a. Separate entity assumption
   b. Monetary unit assumption
   c. Going concern assumption
   d. Historical cost
4. Why are accounting assumptions necessary?
5. For accounting purposes, what is an account? Explain why accounts are used in an accounting system.
6. What is the fundamental accounting model?
7. Define a business transaction in the broad sense, and give an example of two different kinds of transactions.
8. Explain what *debit* and *credit* mean.
9. Briefly explain what is meant by *transaction analysis*. What are the two steps in transaction analysis?
10. What two accounting equalities must be maintained in transaction analysis?
11. What is a journal entry?
12. What is a T-account? What is its purpose?
13. How is the current ratio computed and interpreted?
14. What transactions are classified as investing activities in a statement of cash flows? What transactions are classified as financing activities?

MULTIPLE-CHOICE QUESTIONS

1. If a publicly traded company is trying to maximize its perceived value to decision makers external to the corporation, the company is most likely to understate which of the following on its balance sheet?
   a. Assets
   b. Common Stock
   c. Retained Earnings
   d. Liabilities
2. Which of the following is not an asset?
   a. Investments
   b. Land
   c. Prepaid Expense
   d. Additional Paid-in Capital
3. Total liabilities on a balance sheet at the end of the year are $150,000, retained earnings at the end of the year are $80,000, net income for the year is $60,000, common stock is $40,000, and additional paid-in capital is $20,000. What amount of total assets would be reported on the balance sheet at the end of the year?
   a. $290,000
   b. $270,000
   c. $205,000
   d. $15,000
4. The dual effects concept can best be described as follows:
   a. When one records a transaction in the accounting system, at least two effects on the basic accounting equation will result.
   b. When an exchange takes place between two parties, both parties must record the transaction.
   c. When a transaction is recorded, both the balance sheet and the income statement must be impacted.
   d. When a transaction is recorded, one account will always increase and one account will always decrease.
5. The T-account is a tool commonly used for analyzing which of the following?
   a. Increases and decreases to a single account in the accounting system.
   b. Debits and credits to a single account in the accounting system.
   c. Changes in specific account balances over a time period.
   d. All of the above describe how T-accounts are used by accountants.
6. Which of the following describes how assets are listed on the balance sheet?
   a. In alphabetical order
   b. In order of magnitude, lowest value to highest value
   c. From most liquid to least liquid
   d. From least liquid to most liquid

7. The Cash T-account has a beginning balance of $21,000. During the year, $100,000 was debited and $110,000 was credited to the account. What is the ending balance of Cash?
   a. $11,000 debit balance
   b. $11,000 credit balance
   c. $31,000 credit balance
   d. $31,000 debit balance

8. Which of the following statements are true regarding the balance sheet?
   1. One cannot determine the true fair market value of a company by reviewing its balance sheet.
   2. Certain internally generated assets, such as a trademark, are not reported on a company's balance sheet.
   3. A balance sheet shows only the ending balances, in a summarized format, of all balance sheet accounts in the accounting system as of a particular date.
   a. None are true.
   b. Statements 1 and 2 only are true.
   c. Statements 2 and 3 only are true.
   d. All statements are true.

9. At the end of a recent year, **The Gap, Inc.**, reported total assets of $7,422 million, current assets of $4,309 million, total liabilities of $4,667, current liabilities of $2,128 million, and stockholders' equity of $2,755 million. What is its current ratio and what does this suggest about the company?
   a. The ratio of 1.59 suggests that The Gap has liquidity problems.
   b. The ratio of 2.02 suggests that The Gap has sufficient liquidity.
   c. The ratio of 1.59 suggests that The Gap has greater current assets than current liabilities.
   d. The ratio of 2.02 suggests that The Gap is not able to pay its short-term obligations with current assets.

10. Which of the following is *not* a financing activity on the statement of cash flows?
    a. When the company lends money.
    b. When the company borrows money.
    c. When the company pays dividends.
    d. When the company issues stock to shareholders.

MINI-EXERCISES

Matching Definitions with Terms

M2-1
LO2-1, 2-4

Match each definition with its related term by entering the appropriate letter in the space provided. There should be only one definition per term (that is, there are more definitions than terms).

Term	Definition
___ (1) Going concern assumption	A. = Liabilities + Stockholders' Equity.
___ (2) Historical cost	B. Reports assets, liabilities, and stockholders' equity.
___ (3) Credits	C. Accounts for a business separate from its owners.
___ (4) Assets	D. Increase assets; decrease liabilities and stockholders' equity.
___ (5) Account	E. An exchange between an entity and other parties.
	F. The concept that businesses will operate into the foreseeable future.
	G. Decrease assets; increase liabilities and stockholders' equity.
	H. The concept that assets should be recorded at the amount paid on the date of the transaction.
	I. A standardized format used to accumulate data about each item reported on financial statements.

M2-2

LO2-1, 2-2, 2-3, 2-4

Matching Definitions with Terms

Match each definition with its related term by entering the appropriate letter in the space provided. There should be only one definition per term (that is, there are more definitions than terms).

Term	Definition
___ (1) Journal entry	A. Accounting model.
___ (2) A = L + SE, and	B. Four periodic financial statements.
Debits = Credits	C. The two equalities in accounting that aid in providing
___ (3) Assets = Liabilities +	accuracy.
Stockholders' Equity	D. The results of transaction analysis in accounting format.
___ (4) Liabilities	E. The account that is debited when money is borrowed
___ (5) Income statement, balance sheet,	from a bank.
statement of stockholders' equity,	F. Probable future economic benefits owned by an entity.
and statement of cash flows	G. Cumulative earnings of a company that are not
	distributed to the owners.
	H. Every transaction has at least two effects.
	I. Probable debts or obligations to be paid with assets
	or services.

M2-3

LO2-2

Identifying Events as Accounting Transactions

For each of the following events, which ones result in an exchange transaction for Dittman Company (Y for yes and N for no)?

___ (1) Six investors in Dittman Company sold their stock to another investor.

___ (2) The founding owner, Megan Dittman, purchased additional stock in another company.

___ (3) The company borrowed $2,500,000 from a local bank.

___ (4) Dittman Company purchased a machine that it paid for by signing a note payable.

___ (5) The company lent $300,000 to a supplier.

___ (6) Dittman Company ordered supplies from **Staples** to be delivered next week.

M2-4

LO2-2

Classifying Accounts on a Balance Sheet

The following are the accounts of Rosa-Perez Company:

___ (1) Accounts Payable   ___ (9) Long-Term Investments

___ (2) Accounts Receivable   ___ (10) Notes Payable (due in three years)

___ (3) Buildings   ___ (11) Notes Receivable (due in six months)

___ (4) Cash   ___ (12) Prepaid Rent

___ (5) Common Stock   ___ (13) Retained Earnings

___ (6) Land   ___ (14) Supplies

___ (7) Merchandise Inventory   ___ (15) Utilities Payable

___ (8) Income Taxes Payable   ___ (16) Wages Payable

In the space provided, classify each as it would be reported on a balance sheet. Use:

CA for current asset   CL for current liability   SE for stockholders' equity

NCA for noncurrent asset   NCL for noncurrent liability

M2-5

LO2-3

Determining Financial Statement Effects of Several Transactions

For each of the following transactions of Dennen, Inc., for the month of January, indicate the accounts, the amounts, and the direction of the effects on the accounting equation. A sample is provided.

a. *(Sample)* Borrowed $30,000 from a local bank.

b. Lent $10,000 to an affiliate; accepted a note due in one year.

c. Sold to investors 100 additional shares of stock with a par value of $0.10 per share and a market price of $5 per share; received cash.

d. Purchased $15,000 of equipment, paying $5,000 cash and signing a note for the rest due in one year.

e. Declared and paid $2,000 in dividends to stockholders.

Assets		=	Liabilities		+	Stockholders' Equity
a. Sample: Cash	+30,000		Notes Payable	+30,000		

Identifying Increase and Decrease Effects on Balance Sheet Elements

M2-6
LO2-4

Complete the following table by entering either the word *increase* or *decrease* in each column.

	Debit	Credit
Assets	_____	_____
Liabilities	_____	_____
Stockholders' equity	_____	_____

Identifying Debit and Credit Effects on Balance Sheet Elements

M2-7
LO2-4

Complete the following table by entering either the word *debit* or *credit* in each column.

	Increase	Decrease
Assets	_____	_____
Liabilities	_____	_____
Stockholders' equity	_____	_____

Recording Simple Transactions

M2-8
LO2-4

For each transaction in M2-5 (including the sample), write the journal entry in the proper form.

Completing T-Accounts

M2-9
LO2-4

For each transaction in M2-5 (including the sample), post the effects to the appropriate T-accounts and determine ending account balances. Beginning balances are provided.

Cash			Notes Receivable			Equipment	
Beg. bal. 900			Beg. bal. 1,000			Beg. bal. 15,100	

Notes Payable			Common Stock			Additional Paid-in Capital	
	Beg. bal. 3,000			Beg. bal. 1,000			Beg. bal. 3,000

Retained Earnings	
	Beg. bal. 10,000

Preparing a Trial Balance

M2-10
LO2-5

Complete M2-9, and then prepare a trial balance for Dennen, Inc., as of January 31.

Preparing a Simple Classified Balance Sheet

M2-11
LO2-5

Starting with the beginning balances in M2-9 and given the transactions in M2-5 (including the sample), prepare a balance sheet for Dennen, Inc., as of January 31, classified into current and noncurrent assets and liabilities.

Computing and Interpreting the Current Ratio

M2-12
LO2-5

Calculate the current ratio for Sal's Taco Company at the end of 2013 and 2014, based on the following data:

	Current Assets	Current Liabilities
End of 2013	$280,000	$155,000
End of 2014	$270,000	$250,000

What does the result suggest about the company over time? What can you say about Sal's Taco Company's ratio when compared to **Chipotle**'s 2014 ratio?

M2-13
LO2-6

Identifying Transactions as Investing or Financing Activities on the Statement of Cash Flows

For the transactions in M2-5 (including the sample), identify each as an investing (I) activity or financing (F) activity on the statement of cash flows.

EXERCISES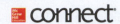

E2-1
LO2-1, 2-2, 2-3, 2-4

Matching Definitions with Terms

Match each definition with its related term by entering the appropriate letter in the space provided. There should be only one definition per term (that is, there are more definitions than terms).

Term	Definition
____ (1) Transaction	A. Economic resources to be used or turned into cash within one year.
____ (2) Going concern assumption	
____ (3) Balance sheet	B. Reports assets, liabilities, and stockholders' equity.
____ (4) Liabilities	C. Business transactions are accounted for separately from the transactions of the owners.
____ (5) Assets = Liabilities + Stockholders' Equity	
	D. Increase assets; decrease liabilities and stockholders' equity.
____ (6) Notes payable	E. An exchange between an entity and other parties.
____ (7) Common stock	F. The concept that businesses will operate into the foreseeable future.
____ (8) Historical cost	
____ (9) Account	G. Decrease assets; increase liabilities and stockholders' equity.
____ (10) Dual effects	H. The concept that assets should be recorded at the amount paid on the exchange date.
____ (11) Retained earnings	
____ (12) Current assets	I. A standardized format used to accumulate data about each item reported on financial statements.
____ (13) Separate entity assumption	
____ (14) Par value	J. Amounts owed from customers.
____ (15) Debits	K. The fundamental accounting model.
____ (16) Accounts receivable	L. Represents the shares issued at par value.
____ (17) Monetary unit assumption	M. The account that is credited when money is borrowed from a bank.
____ (18) Faithful representation	
____ (19) Relevance	N. The concept that states that accounting information should be measured and reported in the national monetary unit without adjustment for changes in purchasing power.
____ (20) Stockholders' equity	

O. Cumulative earnings of a company that are not distributed to the owners.

P. Probable debts or obligations to be settled with assets or services.

Q. Every transaction has at least two effects on the accounting equation.

R. Financing provided by owners and by business operations.

S. The concept to exercise care not to overstate assets and revenues or understate liabilities and expenses.

T. Useful information has predictive and feedback value.

U. Relatively small amounts not likely to influence users' decisions are to be recorded in the most cost-beneficial way.

V. Probable economic resources expected to be used or turned into cash beyond the next 12 months.

W. Useful information should be complete, neutral, and free from error.

X. A legal amount per share.

Identifying Account Titles

E2-2
LO2-2

The following are independent situations.

a. A new company is formed and sells 100 shares of $1 par value stock for $12 per share to investors.
b. A company purchases for $18,000 cash a new delivery truck that has a list, or sticker, price of $21,000.
c. A women's clothing retailer orders 30 new display stands for $300 each for future delivery.
d. A company orders and receives 10 personal computers for office use for which it signs a note promising to pay $25,000 within three months.
e. A construction company signs a contract to build a new $500,000 warehouse for a corporate customer. At the signing, the corporation writes a check for $50,000 to the construction company as the initial payment for the construction (receiving construction in progress). Answer from the standpoint of the corporation (not the construction company).
f. A publishing firm purchases for $40,000 cash the copyright (an intangible asset) to a manuscript for an introductory accounting text.
g. A manufacturing firm declares a $100,000 cash dividend to be distributed to stockholders next period.
h. A company purchases a piece of land for $50,000 cash. An appraiser for the buyer values the land at $52,500.
i. A manufacturing company acquires the patent (an intangible asset) on a new digital satellite system for television reception, paying $500,000 cash and signing a $400,000 note payable due in one year.
j. A local company is a sole proprietorship (one owner); its owner buys a car for $10,000 for personal use. Answer from the local company's point of view.
k. A company purchases 100 shares of **Apple Inc.** common stock as an investment for $5,000 cash.
l. A company borrows $1,000 from a local bank and signs a six-month note for the loan.
m. A company pays $1,500 principal on its note payable (ignore interest).

Required:
1. Indicate the appropriate account titles, if any, affected in each of the preceding events. Consider what is received and what is given.
2. At what amount would you record the truck in (b)? The land in (h)? What measurement principle are you applying?
3. For (c), what accounting concept did you apply? For (j), what accounting concept did you apply?

Classifying Accounts and Their Usual Balances

E2-3
LO2-2, 2-4

As described in a recent annual report, **Verizon Communications** provides wireless voice and data services across one of the most extensive wireless networks in the United States. Verizon now serves more than 100 million customers, making it the largest wireless service provider in the United States in terms of the total number of customers. The following are accounts from a recent balance sheet for Verizon:

(1) Accounts Receivable	(6) Long-Term Investments
(2) Retained Earnings	(7) Plant, Property, and Equipment
(3) Accrued Expenses Payable	(8) Accounts Payable
(4) Prepaid Expenses	(9) Short-Term Investments
(5) Common Stock	(10) Long-Term Debt

Required:
For each account, indicate (1) whether the account is usually classified as a current asset (CA), noncurrent asset (NCA), current liability (CL), noncurrent liability (NCL), or stockholders' equity (SE) item and (2) whether the account usually has a debit or credit balance.

Determining Financial Statement Effects of Several Transactions

E2-4
LO2-3

The following events occurred for Johnson Company:

a. Received investment of cash by organizers and distributed to them 1,000 shares of $1 par value common stock with a market price of $40 per share.
b. Purchased $15,000 of equipment, paying $3,000 in cash and owing the rest on accounts payable to the manufacturer.
c. Borrowed $10,000 cash from a bank.
d. Loaned $800 to an employee who signed a note.
e. Purchased $13,000 of land; paid $4,000 in cash and signed a mortgage note for the balance.

Required:

For each of the events *(a)* through *(e)*, perform transaction analysis and indicate the account, amount, and direction of the effect (+ for increase and − for decrease) on the accounting equation. Check that the accounting equation remains in balance after each transaction. Use the following headings:

Event	Assets	=	Liabilities	+	Stockholders' Equity

E2-5

LO2-3

Determining Financial Statement Effects of Several Transactions

Nike, Inc., with headquarters in Beaverton, Oregon, is one of the world's leading manufacturers of athletic shoes and sports apparel. The following activities occurred during a recent year. The amounts are rounded to millions.

a. Purchased additional buildings for $172 and equipment for $270; paid $432 in cash and signed a long-term note for the rest.
b. Issued 100 shares of $2 par value common stock for $345 cash.
c. Declared $145 in dividends to be paid in the following year.
d. Purchased additional short-term investments for $7,616 cash.
e. Several Nike investors sold their own stock to other investors on the stock exchange for $84.
f. Sold $4,313 in short-term investments for $4,313 in cash.

Required:

1. For each of the events *(a)* through *(f)*, perform transaction analysis and indicate the account, amount, and direction of the effect on the accounting equation. Check that the accounting equation remains in balance after each transaction. Use the following headings:

Event	Assets	=	Liabilities	+	Stockholders' Equity

2. Explain your response to event *(e)*.

E2-6

LO2-4

Recording Investing and Financing Activities

Refer to E2-4.

Required:

For each of the events *(a)* through *(e)* in E2-4, prepare journal entries, checking that debits equal credits.

E2-7

LO2-4

Recording Investing and Financing Activities

Refer to E2-5.

Required:

1. For each of the events *(a)* through *(f)* in E2-5, prepare journal entries, checking that debits equal credits.
2. Explain your response to event *(e)*.

E2-8

LO2-4

Recording Investing and Financing Activities

Kelsey Baker founded **GolfDeals.com** at the beginning of February. **GolfDeals.com** sells new and used golf equipment online. The following events occurred in February.

a. Borrowed $30,000 cash from a bank, signing a note due in three years.
b. Received investment of cash by organizers and distributed to them 500 shares of $0.10 par value common stock with a market price of $30 per share.
c. Purchased a warehouse for $115,000, paying $23,000 in cash and signing a note payable for the balance on a 10-year mortgage.
d. Purchased computer and office equipment for $20,000, paying $4,000 in cash and owing the rest on accounts payable to the manufacturers.
e. Loaned $1,000 to an employee who signed a note due in three months.
f. Paid $2,000 to the manufacturers in *(d)* above.
g. Purchased short-term investments for $10,000 cash.

Required:
For each of the events (*a*) through (*g*), prepare journal entries, checking that debits equal credits.

Analyzing the Effects of Transactions in T-Accounts

E2-9
LO2-4

Granger Service Company, Inc., was organized by Ted Granger and five other investors. The following activities occurred during the year:

a. Received $70,000 cash from the investors; each was issued 8,400 shares of common stock with a par value of $0.10 per share.
b. Purchased equipment for use in the business at a cost of $18,000; one-fourth was paid in cash and the company signed a note for the balance (due in six months).
c. Signed an agreement with a cleaning service to pay $120 per week for cleaning the corporate offices next year.
d. Received an additional contribution from investors who provided $3,000 in cash and land valued at $15,000 in exchange for 1,000 shares of stock in the company.
e. Lent $2,500 to one of the investors, who signed a note due in six months.
f. Ted Granger borrowed $7,000 for personal use from a local bank, signing a one-year note.

Required:
1. Create T-accounts for the following accounts: Cash, Notes Receivable, Equipment, Land, Notes Payable, Common Stock, and Additional Paid-in Capital. Beginning balances are $0. For each of the transactions (*a*) through (*f*), record the effects of the transaction in the appropriate T-accounts. Include good referencing and totals for each T-account.
2. Using the balances in the T-accounts, fill in the following amounts for the accounting equation:

   Assets $_____   =   Liabilities $_____   +   Stockholders' Equity $_____

3. Explain your response to events (*c*) and (*f*).

Analyzing the Effects of Transactions in T-Accounts

E2-10
LO2-4

Precision Builders Construction Company was incorporated by Chris Stoschek. The following activities occurred during the year:

a. Received from three investors $60,000 cash and land valued at $35,000; each investor was issued 1,000 shares of common stock with a par value of $0.10 per share.
b. Purchased construction equipment for use in the business at a cost of $36,000; one-fourth was paid in cash and the company signed a note for the balance (due in six months).
c. Lent $2,500 to one of the investors, who signed a note due in six months.
d. Chris Stoschek purchased a truck for personal use; paid $5,000 down and signed a one-year note for $22,000.
e. Paid $12,000 on the note for the construction equipment in (*b*) (ignore interest).

Required:
1. Create T-accounts for the following accounts: Cash, Notes Receivable, Equipment, Land, Notes Payable, Common Stock, and Additional Paid-in Capital. Beginning balances are $0. For each of the transactions (*a*) through (*e*), record the effects of the transaction in the appropriate T-accounts. Include good referencing and totals for each T-account.
2. Using the balances in the T-accounts, fill in the following amounts for the accounting equation:

   Assets $_____   =   Liabilities $_____   +   Stockholders' Equity $_____

3. Explain your response to event (*d*).
4. Compute the market value per share of the stock issued in (*a*).

E2-11

LO2-4, 2-5

Inferring Investing and Financing Transactions and Preparing a Balance Sheet

During its first week of operations ending January 7, FastTrack Sports Inc. completed six transactions with the dollar effects indicated in the following schedule:

Accounts	Dollar Effect of Each of the Six Transactions						Ending Balance
	1	2	3	4	5	6	
Cash	$15,000	$75,000	$(5,000)	$(4,000)	$(9,500)		
Notes receivable (short-term)				4,000			
Store fixtures					9,500		
Land			16,000			$4,000	
Notes payable (due in three months)		75,000	11,000			4,000	
Common stock (15,000 shares)	1,500						
Additional paid-in capital	13,500						

Required:

1. Write a brief explanation of transactions (1) through (6). Explain any assumptions that you made.
2. Compute the ending balance in each account and prepare a classified balance sheet for FastTrack Sports Inc. on January 7.

E2-12

LO2-4, 2-5

Inferring Investing and Financing Transactions and Preparing a Balance Sheet

During its first month of operations in March, Volz Cleaning, Inc., completed six transactions with the dollar effects indicated in the following schedule:

Accounts	Dollar Effect of Each of the Six Transactions						Ending Balance
	1	2	3	4	5	6	
Cash	$45,000	$(8,000)	$(2,000)	$(7,000)	$3,000	$(4,000)	
Investments (short-term)				7,000	(3,000)		
Notes receivable (due in six months)			2,000				
Computer equipment						$4,000	
Delivery truck		35,000					
Notes payable (due in 10 years)		27,000					
Common stock (3,000 shares)	6,000						
Additional paid-in capital	39,000						

Required:

1. Write a brief explanation of transactions (1) through (6). Explain any assumptions that you made.
2. Compute the ending balance in each account and prepare a classified balance sheet for Volz Cleaning, Inc., at the end of March.

E2-13

LO2-4

Recording Journal Entries

Nathanson Corporation was organized on May 1. The following events occurred during the first month.

a. Received $70,000 cash from the five investors who organized Nathanson Corporation. Each investor received 100 shares of $10 par value common stock.
b. Ordered store fixtures costing $15,000.
c. Borrowed $18,000 cash and signed a note due in two years.
d. Purchased $11,000 of equipment, paying $1,500 in cash and signing a six-month note for the balance.
e. Lent $2,000 to an employee who signed a note to repay the loan in three months.
f. Received and paid for the store fixtures ordered in (b).

Required:

Prepare journal entries for transactions (a) through (f). (Remember that debits go on top and credits go on the bottom, indented.) Be sure to use good referencing and categorize each account as an asset (A), liability (L), or stockholders' equity (SE) item. If a transaction does not require a journal entry, explain the reason.

Recording Journal Entries

E2-14
LO2-4

BMW Group, headquartered in Munich, Germany, manufactures several automotive brands including BMW Group, MINI, and Rolls-Royce. Financial information is reported in the euro (€) monetary unit using International Financial Reporting Standards (IFRS) as applicable to the European Union. The following activities were adapted from the annual report of the BMW Group; amounts are in millions of euros.

a. Declared €1,508 in dividends to be paid next month.
b. Ordered €2,598 of equipment.
c. Paid €852 in dividends declared in prior months.
d. Borrowed €5,899 in cash from banks.
e. Sold equipment at its cost of €53 for cash.
f. Received the equipment ordered in event (b), paying €2,250 in cash and signing a note for the balance.
g. Purchased investments for €2,616 cash.

Required:
Prepare journal entries for transactions (a) through (g). Be sure to use good referencing and categorize each account as an asset (A), liability (L), or stockholders' equity (SE) item. If a transaction does not require a journal entry, explain the reason.

Analyzing the Effects of Transactions Using T-Accounts and Interpreting the Current Ratio as a Manager of the Company

E2-15
LO2-4, 2-5

Higgins Company began operations last year. You are a member of the management team investigating expansion ideas that will require borrowing funds from banks. At the start of the current year, Higgins's T-account balances were as follows:

Assets:

Cash		Short-Term Investments		Property and Equipment	
5,000		2,500		3,000	

Liabilities:

Short-Term Notes Payable		Long-Term Notes Payable	
	2,200		800

Stockholders' Equity:

Common Stock		Additional Paid-in Capital		Retained Earnings	
	500		4,000		3,000

Required:
1. Using the data from these T-accounts, determine the amounts for the following on January 1 of the current year:

   Assets $_____ = Liabilities $_____ + Stockholders' Equity $_____

2. Enter the following transactions for the current year in the T-accounts:
   (a) Borrowed $4,000 from a local bank, signing a note due in three years.
   (b) Sold $1,500 of the investments for $1,500 cash.
   (c) Sold one-half of the property and equipment for $1,500 in cash.
   (d) Declared and paid $800 in cash dividends to stockholders.

3. Compute ending balances in the T-accounts to determine amounts for the following on December 31 of the current year:

   Assets $_____ = Liabilities $_____ + Stockholders' Equity $_____

4. Calculate the current ratio at December 31 of the current year. If the industry average for the current ratio is 1.50, what does your computation suggest to you about Higgins Company? Would you suggest that Higgins Company increase its short-term liabilities? Why or why not?

E2-16

LO2-5

Preparing a Balance Sheet

Refer to E2-15.

Required:
From the ending balances in the T-accounts in E2-15, prepare a classified balance sheet at December 31 of the current year in good form.

E2-17

LO2-4, 2-5

Analyzing the Effects of Transactions Using T-Accounts, Preparing a Balance Sheet, and Evaluating the Current Ratio over Time as a Bank Loan Officer

Strauderman Delivery Company, Inc., was organized in 2016 in Wisconsin. The following transactions occurred during the year:

a. Received cash from investors in exchange for 10,000 shares of stock (par value of $1.00 per share) with a market value of $4 per share.
b. Purchased land in Wisconsin for $16,000, signing a one-year note (ignore interest).
c. Bought two used delivery trucks for operating purposes at the start of the year at a cost of $10,000 each; paid $4,000 cash and signed a note due in three years for the rest (ignore interest).
d. Paid $1,000 cash to a truck repair shop for a new motor for one of the trucks. (**Hint:** Increase the account you used to record the purchase of the trucks since the productive life of the truck has been improved.)
e. Sold one-fourth of the land for $4,000 to Pablo Development Corporation, which signed a six-month note.
f. Stockholder Melissa Strauderman paid $27,600 cash for a vacant lot (land) in Canada for her personal use.

Required:
1. Set up appropriate T-accounts with beginning balances of zero for Cash, Short-Term Notes Receivable, Land, Equipment, Short-Term Notes Payable, Long-Term Notes Payable, Common Stock, and Additional Paid-in Capital. Using the T-accounts, record the effects of transactions (a) through (f) by Strauderman Delivery Company.
2. Prepare a trial balance at December 31, 2016.
3. Prepare a classified balance sheet for Strauderman Delivery Company at December 31, 2016.
4. At the end of the next two years, Strauderman Delivery Company reported the following amounts on its balance sheets:

	December 31, 2017	December 31, 2018
Current Assets	$52,000	$ 47,000
Long-Term Assets	38,000	73,000
Total Assets	**90,000**	**120,000**
Short-Term Notes Payable	23,000	40,000
Long-Term Notes Payable	17,000	20,000
Total Liabilities	**40,000**	**60,000**
Stockholders' Equity	**50,000**	**60,000**

Compute the company's current ratio for 2016, 2017, and 2018. What is the trend and what does this suggest about the company?
5. At the beginning of year 2019, Strauderman Delivery Company applied to your bank for a $50,000 short-term loan to expand the business. The vice president of the bank asked you to review the information and make a recommendation on lending the funds based solely on the results of the current ratio. What recommendation would you make to the bank's vice president about lending the money to Strauderman Delivery Company?

E2-18

LO2-4

Explaining the Effects of Transactions on Balance Sheet Accounts Using T-Accounts

Waltman Furniture Repair Service, a company with two stockholders, began operations on June 1. The following T-accounts indicate the activities for the month of June.

Cash (A)				Notes Receivable (A)			Tools and Equipment (A)		
6/1	0			6/1	0		6/1	0	
a.	20,000	b.	1,800	b.	1,800		a.	5,000	d.	900
d.	900	c.	10,000						

Building (A)		Notes Payable (L)		Common Stock (100,000 shares) (SE)	
6/1	0		6/1	0		6/1	0
c.	40,000		c.	30,000		a.	2,000

Additional Paid-in Capital (SE)	
	6/1	0
	a.	23,000

Required:

Explain events (*a*) through (*d*) that resulted in the entries in the T-accounts. That is, for each account, what transactions made it increase and/or decrease?

Inferring Typical Investing and Financing Activities in Accounts

E2-19
LO2-4

The following T-accounts indicate the effects of normal business transactions:

Equipment			Notes Receivable			Notes Payable		
1/1	500		1/1	150			100	1/1
	250	?		?	225	?	170	
12/31	100		12/31	170			160	12/31

Required:
1. Describe the typical investing and financing transactions that affect each T-account. That is, what economic events occur to make each of these accounts increase and decrease?
2. For each T-account, compute the missing amounts.

Identifying Investing and Financing Activities Affecting Cash Flows

E2-20
LO2-6

Foot Locker, Inc., is a large global retailer of athletic footwear and apparel selling directly to customers and through the Internet. It includes the Foot Locker family of stores, Champs Sports, Footaction, Runners Point, and Sidestep. The following are several of Foot Locker's investing and financing activities as reflected in a recent annual statement of cash flows.

a. Capital expenditures (for property, plant, and equipment).
b. Repurchases of common stock from investors.
c. Sale of short-term investments.
d. Issuance of common stock.
e. Purchases of short-term investments.
f. Dividends paid on common stock.

Required:
For activities (*a*) through (*f*), indicate whether the activity is investing (I) or financing (F) and the direction of the effect on cash flows (+ for increases cash; − for decreases cash).

Identifying the Investing and Financing Activities Affecting Cash Flows

E2-21
LO2-6

Starwood Hotels & Resorts Worldwide, Inc., is one of the world's largest hotel and leisure companies, with more than 1,200 properties in 100 countries. Starwood owns, operates, and franchises hotels, resorts, and residences with the following brands: St. Regis®, The Luxury Collection®, W®, Westin®, Le Méridien®, Sheraton®, Four Points® by Sheraton, Aloft®, and Element®. Information adapted from the company's recent annual statement of cash flows indicates the following investing and financing activities during that year (simplified, in millions of dollars):

a.	Additional borrowing from banks	$1,290
b.	Purchase of investments	1
c.	Sale of assets and investments (assume sold at cost)	806
d.	Issuance of stock	70
e.	Purchases of property, plant, and equipment	327
f.	Payment of debt principal	108
g.	Dividends paid	735
h.	Receipt of principal payment on a note receivable	5

Required:

For activities (*a*) through (*h*), indicate whether the activity is investing (I) or financing (F) and the direction of the effects on cash flows (+ for increases cash; − for decreases cash).

E2-22
LO2-2, 2-5, 2-6

Finding Financial Information as a Potential Investor

You are considering investing the cash you inherited from your grandfather in various stocks. You have received the annual reports of several major companies.

Required:

For each of the following items, indicate where you would locate the information in an annual report. The information may be in more than one location.

1. Total current assets.
2. Amount of debt principal repaid during the year.
3. Summary of significant accounting policies.
4. Cash received from sales of noncurrent assets.
5. Amount of dividends paid during the year.
6. Short-term obligations.
7. Date of the statement of financial position.

PROBLEMS

P2-1
LO2-1, 2-2, 2-4

Identifying Accounts on a Classified Balance Sheet and Their Normal Debit or Credit Balances (AP2-1)

Exxon Mobil Corporation explores, produces, refines, markets, and supplies crude oil, natural gas, and petroleum products in the United States and around the world. The following are accounts from a recent balance sheet of Exxon Mobil Corporation:

	Balance Sheet Classification	Debit or Credit Balance
(1) Notes and Loans Payable (short-term)	_____	_____
(2) Materials and Supplies	_____	_____
(3) Common Stock	_____	_____
(4) Patents (an intangible asset)	_____	_____
(5) Income Taxes Payable	_____	_____
(6) Long-Term Debt	_____	_____
(7) Marketable Securities (short-term investments)	_____	_____
(8) Property, Plant, and Equipment	_____	_____
(9) Retained Earnings	_____	_____
(10) Notes and Accounts Receivable (short-term)	_____	_____
(11) Investments (long-term)	_____	_____
(12) Cash and Cash Equivalents	_____	_____
(13) Accounts Payable	_____	_____
(14) Crude Oil Products and Merchandise	_____	_____
(15) Additional Paid-in Capital	_____	_____

Required:

For each account, indicate how it normally should be categorized on a classified balance sheet. Use CA for current asset, NCA for noncurrent asset, CL for current liability, NCL for noncurrent liability, and SE for stockholders' equity. Also indicate whether the account normally has a debit or credit balance.

P2-2
LO2-2, 2-3, 2-5

Determining Financial Statement Effects of Various Transactions (AP2–2)

East Hill Home Healthcare Services was organized by four friends who each invested $10,000 in the company and, in turn, was issued 8,000 shares of $1.00 par value stock. To date, they are the only stockholders. At the end of last year, the accounting records reflected total assets of $700,000 ($50,000 cash; $500,000 land; $50,000 equipment; and $100,000 buildings), total liabilities of $200,000 (short-term notes payable $100,000 and long-term notes payable $100,000), and stockholders' equity of $500,000

($20,000 common stock, $80,000 additional paid-in capital, and $400,000 retained earnings). During the current year, the following summarized events occurred:

a. Sold 9,000 additional shares of stock to the original organizers for a total of $90,000 cash.
b. Purchased a building for $60,000, equipment for $15,000, and four acres of land for $14,000; paid $9,000 in cash and signed a note for the balance (due in 15 years). (**Hint:** Five different accounts are affected.)
c. Sold one acre of land acquired in (b) for $3,500 cash to another company.
d. Purchased short-term investments for $18,000 cash.
e. One stockholder reported to the company that 300 shares of his East Hill stock had been sold and transferred to another stockholder for $3,000 cash.
f. Lent one of the shareholders $5,000 for moving costs and received a signed six-month note from the shareholder.

Required:

1. Was East Hill Home Healthcare Services organized as a sole proprietorship, a partnership, or a corporation? Explain the basis for your answer.
2. During the current year, the records of the company were inadequate. You were asked to prepare the summary of transactions shown above. To develop a quick assessment of their economic effects on East Hill Home Healthcare Services, you have decided to complete the tabulation that follows and to use plus (+) for increases and minus (−) for decreases for each account. The first event is used as an example.

		ASSETS					=	LIABILITIES		+	STOCKHOLDERS' EQUITY		
Cash	Short-Term Investments	Notes Receivable	Land	Buildings	Equipment			Short-Term Notes Payable	Long-Term Notes Payable		Common Stock	Additional Paid-in Capital	Retained Earnings
Beg. 50,000			500,000	100,000	50,000		=	100,000	100,000		20,000	80,000	400,000
(a) +90,000							=				+9,000	+81,000	

3. Did you include the transaction between the two stockholders—event (e)—in the tabulation? Why?
4. Based only on the completed tabulation, provide the following amounts (show computations):
   a. Total assets at the end of the year.
   b. Total liabilities at the end of the year.
   c. Total stockholders' equity at the end of the year.
   d. Cash balance at the end of the year.
   e. Total current assets at the end of the year.
5. Compute the current ratio for the current year. What does this suggest about the company?

Recording Transactions in T-Accounts, Preparing the Balance Sheet from a Trial Balance, and Evaluating the Current Ratio (AP2-3)

P2-3

LO2-2, 2-4, 2-5

Cougar Plastics Company has been operating for three years. At December 31 of last year, the accounting records reflected the following:

Cash	$22,000	Accounts payable	$15,000
Investments (short-term)	3,000	Accrued liabilities payable	4,000
Accounts receivable	3,000	Notes payable (short-term)	7,000
Inventory	20,000	Long-term notes payable	47,000
Notes receivable (long-term)	1,000	Common stock	10,000
Equipment	50,000	Additional paid-in capital	80,000
Factory building	90,000	Retained earnings	31,000
Intangibles	5,000		

During the current year, the company had the following summarized activities:

a. Purchased short-term investments for $10,000 cash.
b. Lent $5,000 to a supplier, who signed a two-year note.
c. Purchased equipment that cost $18,000; paid $5,000 cash and signed a one-year note for the balance.
d. Hired a new president at the end of the year. The contract was for $85,000 per year plus options to purchase company stock at a set price based on company performance.
e. Issued an additional 2,000 shares of $0.50 par value common stock for $11,000 cash.
f. Borrowed $9,000 cash from a local bank, payable in three months.
g. Purchased a patent (an intangible asset) for $3,000 cash.
h. Built an addition to the factory for $24,000; paid $8,000 in cash and signed a three-year note for the balance.
i. Returned defective equipment to the manufacturer, receiving a cash refund of $1,000.

Required:
1. Create T-accounts for each of the accounts on the balance sheet and enter the end-of-year balances as the beginning balances for the current year.
2. Record each of the events for the current year in T-accounts (including referencing) and determine the ending balances.
3. Explain your response to event (*d*).
4. Prepare a trial balance at December 31 of the current year.
5. Prepare a classified balance sheet at December 31 of the current year.
6. Compute the current ratio for the current year. What does this suggest about Cougar Plastics?

P2-4
LO2-6

Identifying Effects of Transactions on the Statement of Cash Flows (AP2-4)

Refer to P2-3.

Required:
Using events (*a*) through (*i*) in P2-3, indicate whether each is an investing (I) or financing (F) activity for the year and the direction of the effect on cash flows (+ for increase and − for decrease). If there is no effect on cash flows, write NE.

P2-5
LO2-2, 2-4, 2-5

Recording Transactions, Preparing Journal Entries, Posting to T-Accounts, Preparing the Balance Sheet, and Evaluating the Current Ratio

Apple Inc., headquartered in Cupertino, California, designs, manufactures, and markets mobile communication and media devices, personal computers, and portable digital music players and sells a variety of related software and services. The following is Apple's (simplified) balance sheet from a recent year (fiscal year ending on the last Saturday of September).

APPLE INC.	
Consolidated Balance Sheet	
September 27, 2014	
(dollars in millions)	
ASSETS	
Current assets:	
Cash	$ 13,844
Short-term investments	11,233
Accounts receivable	17,460
Inventories	2,111
Other current assets	23,883
Total current assets	68,531
Long-term investments	130,162
Property, plant, and equipment, net	20,624
Other noncurrent assets	12,522
Total assets	$231,839
LIABILITIES AND STOCKHOLDERS' EQUITY	
Current liabilities:	
Accounts payable	$ 30,196
Accrued expenses	18,453
Unearned revenue	8,491
Short-term notes payable	6,308
Total current liabilities	63,448
Long-term debt	28,987
Other noncurrent liabilities	27,857
Total liabilities	120,292
Shareholders' equity:	
Common stock ($0.00001 par value)	1
Additional paid-in capital	23,312
Retained earnings	88,234
Total shareholders' equity	111,547
Total liabilities and shareholders' equity	$231,839

Assume that the following transactions (in millions) occurred during the next fiscal year (ending on September 26, 2015):

a. Borrowed $18,266 from banks due in two years.
b. Purchased additional investments for $21,000 cash; one-fifth were long term and the rest were short term.
c. Purchased property, plant, and equipment; paid $9,571 in cash and signed a short-term note for $1,410.
d. Issued additional shares of common stock for $1,469 in cash; total par value was $1 and the rest was in excess of par value.
e. Sold short-term investments costing $18,810 for $18,810 cash.
f. Declared $11,126 in dividends to be paid at the beginning of the next fiscal year.

Required:
1. Prepare a journal entry for each transaction. Use the account titles in the Apple balance sheet.
2. Create T-accounts for each balance sheet account and include the September 27, 2014, balances; create a new account Dividends Payable with a $0 beginning balance. Post each journal entry to the appropriate T-accounts.
3. Prepare a balance sheet from the T-account ending balances for Apple at September 26, 2015, based on these transactions.
4. Compute Apple's current ratio for the year ending on September 26, 2015. What does this suggest about the company?

Identifying the Investing and Financing Activities Affecting the Statement of Cash Flows

P2-6
LO2-6

Refer to P2-5.

Required:
For each of the activities (*a*)–(*f*), indicate whether the activity is investing (I) or financing (F) and the direction and amount of the effect on cash flows (+ for increases; − for decreases). If the activity does not affect the statement of cash flows, indicate no effect (NE).

ALTERNATE PROBLEMS

Identifying Accounts on a Classified Balance Sheet and Their Normal Debit or Credit Balances (P2-1)

AP2-1
LO2-1, 2-2, 2-4

According to a recent Form 10-K report of **Mattel, Inc.**, the company "designs, manufactures, and markets a broad variety of toy products worldwide." Mattel's brands include Barbie, Hot Wheels, Fisher-Price toys, and American Girl brand dolls and accessories. The following are several of the accounts from a recent balance sheet:

	Balance Sheet Classification	Debit or Credit Balance
(1) Prepaid Expenses		
(2) Inventories		
(3) Accounts Receivable		
(4) Long-Term Debt		
(5) Cash and Equivalents		
(6) Goodwill (an intangible asset)		
(7) Accounts Payable		
(8) Income Taxes Payable		
(9) Property, Plant, and Equipment		
(10) Retained Earnings		
(11) Additional Paid-in Capital		
(12) Short-Term Borrowings		
(13) Accrued Liabilities		
(14) Common Stock		

Required:
Indicate how each account normally should be categorized on a classified balance sheet. Use CA for current asset, NCA for noncurrent asset, CL for current liability, NCL for noncurrent liability, and SE for stockholders' equity. Also indicate whether the account normally has a debit or credit balance.

AP2-2

LO2-2, 2-3, 2-5

Determining Financial Statement Effects of Various Transactions (P2-2)

Adamson Incorporated is a small manufacturing company that makes model trains to sell to toy stores. It has a small service department that repairs customers' trains for a fee. The company has been in business for five years. At the end of the company's prior fiscal year ending on December 31, the accounting records reflected total assets of $500,000 (cash, $120,000; equipment, $70,000; buildings, $310,000), total liabilities of $200,000 (short-term notes payable, $140,000; long-term notes payable, $60,000), and total stockholders' equity of $300,000 (common stock [par value $1.00 per share], $20,000; additional paid-in capital, $200,000; retained earnings, $80,000). During the current year, the following summarized events occurred:

a. Borrowed $110,000 cash from the bank and signed a 10-year note.
b. Purchased equipment for $30,000, paying $3,000 in cash and signing a note due in six months for the balance.
c. Issued an additional 10,000 shares of capital stock for $100,000 cash.
d. Purchased a delivery truck (equipment) for $10,000; paid $5,000 cash and signed a short-term note payable for the remainder.
e. Lent $2,000 cash to the company president, Clark Adamson, who signed a note with terms showing the principal plus interest due in one year.
f. Built an addition on the factory for $200,000 and paid cash to the contractor.
g. Purchased $85,000 in long-term investments.
h. Returned a $3,000 piece of equipment purchased in (b) because it proved to be defective; received a reduction of its short-term note payable.
i. A stockholder sold $5,000 of his capital stock in Adamson Incorporated to his neighbor.

Required:
1. Was Adamson Incorporated organized as a sole proprietorship, a partnership, or a corporation? Explain the basis for your answer.
2. During the current year, the records of the company were inadequate. You were asked to prepare the summary of transactions shown above. To develop a quick assessment of their economic effects on Adamson Incorporated, you have decided to complete the tabulation that follows and to use plus (+) for increases and minus (−) for decreases for each account. The first transaction is used as an example.

		ASSETS			=	LIABILITIES		+	STOCKHOLDERS' EQUITY		
Cash	Notes Receivable	Long-Term Investments	Equipment	Buildings		Short-Term Notes Payable	Long-Term Notes Payable		Common Stock	Additional Paid-in Capital	Retained Earnings
Beg. 120,000			70,000	310,000	=	140,000	60,000		20,000	200,000	80,000
(*a*) +110,000					=		+110,000				

3. Did you include event (*i*) in the tabulation? Why?
4. Based on beginning balances plus the completed tabulation, provide the following amounts (show computations):
   a. Total assets at the end of the year.
   b. Total liabilities at the end of the year.
   c. Total stockholders' equity at the end of the year.
   d. Cash balance at the end of the year.
   e. Total current assets at the end of the year.
5. Compute the current ratio for the current year. What does this suggest about the company?

AP2-3

LO2-2, 2-4, 2-5

Recording Transactions in T-Accounts, Preparing the Balance Sheet, and Evaluating the Current Ratio (P2-3)

Ethan Allen Interiors, Inc., is a leading manufacturer and retailer of home furnishings in the United States and abroad. The following is adapted from Ethan Allen's recent annual financial report (fiscal year ending on June 30). Amounts are in thousands.

Cash and cash equivalents	$ 78,519	Accounts payable	$ 26,958
Short-term investments	12,909	Accrued expenses payable	127,639
Accounts receivable	15,036	Long-term debt (includes the	
Inventories	141,692	current portion of $19)	165,032
Prepaid expenses and		Other long-term liabilities	27,009
other current assets	20,372	Common stock ($0.01 par value)	484
Property, plant, and equipment	294,853	Additional paid-in capital	359,728
Intangibles	45,128	Retained earnings	501,908
Other assets	19,816	Other stockholders' equity items	(580,433)

Assume that the following events occurred in the first quarter ended September 30 of the next fiscal year:

a. Issued 1,600 additional shares of stock for $1,020 in cash.
b. Purchased $3,400 in additional intangibles for cash.
c. Ordered $43,500 in wood and other raw materials for the manufacturing plants.
d. Sold equipment at its cost for $4,020 cash.
e. Purchased $2,980 in short-term investments for cash.
f. Purchased property, plant, and equipment; paid $1,830 in cash and signed additional long-term notes for $9,400.
g. Sold at cost other assets for $310 cash.
h. Declared $300 in dividends.

Required:
1. Create T-accounts for each of the accounts on the balance sheet, including a new account Dividends Payable; enter the balances at June 30 as the beginning balances for the quarter.
2. Record each of the transactions for the first quarter ended September 30 in the T-accounts (including referencing) and determine the ending balances.
3. Explain your response to event (c).
4. Prepare a trial balance at September 30.
5. Prepare a classified balance sheet at September 30.
6. Compute the current ratio for the quarter ended September 30. What does this suggest about Ethan Allen Interiors, Inc.?

Identifying Effects of Transactions on the Statement of Cash Flows (P2-4)

Refer to AP2-3.

Required:
Using the events (a) through (h) in AP2-3, indicate whether each transaction is an investing (I) or financing (F) activity for the quarter and the direction and amount of the effect on cash flows (+ for increase and − for decrease). If there is no effect on cash flows, write NE.

AP2-4
LO2-6

 **connect**   CONTINUING **PROBLEM**

Accounting for the Establishment of a New Business (the Accounting Cycle)

Penny Cassidy has decided to start her business, Penny's Pool Service & Supply, Inc. (PPSS). There is much to do when starting a new business. Here are some transactions that have occurred in the business in March.

a. Received $25,000 cash and a large delivery van with a value of $36,000 from Penny, who was given 4,000 shares of $0.05 par value common stock in exchange.
b. Purchased land with a small office and warehouse by paying $10,000 cash and signing a 10-year mortgage note payable to the local bank for $80,000. The land has a value of $18,000 and the building's value is $72,000. Use separate accounts for land and buildings.
c. Purchased a new computer from **Dell** for $2,500 cash and office furniture for $4,000, signing a short-term note payable in six months.

CON2-1
LO2-4, 2-5, 2-6

d. Hired a receptionist for the office at a salary of $1,500 per month, starting in April.
e. Paid $1,000 on the note payable to the bank at the end of March (ignore interest).
f. Purchased short-term investments in the stock of other companies for $5,000 cash.
g. Ordered $10,000 in inventory from **Pool Corporation, Inc.**, a pool supply wholesaler, to be received in April.

Required:
1. For each of the events (*a*) through (*g*), prepare journal entries if a transaction of the business exists, checking that debits equal credits. If a transaction does not exist, explain why there is no transaction for the business.
2. Create T-accounts, and post each of the transactions to determine balances at March 31. Because this is a new business, beginning balances are $0.
3. Prepare a trial balance on March 31 to check that debits equal credits after the transactions are posted to the T-accounts.
4. From the trial balance, prepare a classified balance sheet (with current assets and current liabilities sections) at March 31 (before the beginning of operations in April).
5. For each of the events (*a*) through (*g*), indicate if it is an investing activity (I) or financing activity (F), and the direction (+ for increases; − for decreases) and amount of the effect on cash flows using the following structure. Write NE if there is no effect on cash flows.

	Type of Activity (I, F, or NE)	Effect on Cash Flows (+ or − and amount)
(*a*)	_____	_____
(*b*) etc.	_____	_____

6. Calculate the current ratio at March 31. What does this ratio indicate about the ability of PPSS to pay its current liabilities?

CASES **AND PROJECTS**

Annual Report Cases

CP2-1

LO2-1, 2-2, 2-5, 2-6

Finding Financial Information

Refer to the financial statements of **American Eagle Outfitters** in Appendix B at the end of this book.

Required:
1. Is the company a corporation, a partnership, or a sole proprietorship? How do you know?
2. The company shows on the balance sheet that inventories are worth $278,972,000. Does this amount represent the expected selling price? Why or why not?
3. List the types of current obligations this company has. You need not provide the amounts.
4. Compute the company's current ratio and explain its meaning.
5. How much cash did the company spend on purchasing property and equipment each year (capital expenditures)? Where did you find the information?

CP2-2

LO2-1, 2-2, 2-5, 2-6

Finding Financial Information

Refer to the financial statements of **Urban Outfitters** in Appendix C at the end of this book.

Required:
1. Use the company's balance sheet to determine the amounts in the accounting equation (A = L + SE) as of January 31, 2015.
2. If the company were liquidated at the end of the current year (January 31, 2015), are the shareholders guaranteed to receive $1,327,969,000?

3. What are the company's noncurrent liabilities?
4. What is the company's current ratio?
5. Did the company have a cash inflow or outflow from investing activities? Of how much?

Comparing Companies within an Industry

CP2-3
LO2-2, 2-5, 2-6

Refer to the financial statements of American Eagle Outfitters in Appendix B, Urban Outfitters in Appendix C, and the Industry Ratio Report in Appendix D at the end of this book.

Required:

1. Compute the current ratio for both companies. Compared to the industry average (from the Industry Ratio Report), are these two companies more or less able to satisfy short-term obligations with current assets? How is the current ratio influenced by these companies' choice to rent space instead of buying it?
2. In the most recent year, how much cash, if any, was spent buying back (repurchasing) each company's own common stock?
3. How much, if any, did each company pay in dividends for the most recent year?
4. What account title or titles does each company use to report any land, buildings, and equipment it may have?

Financial Reporting and Analysis Cases

Broadening Financial Research Skills: Locating Financial Information on the SEC's Database

CP2-4
LO2-2, 2-5, 2-6

The Securities and Exchange Commission (SEC) regulates companies that issue stock on the stock market. It receives financial reports from public companies electronically under a system called EDGAR (Electronic Data Gathering and Retrieval Service). Using the Internet, anyone may search the database for the reports that have been filed.

Using your Web browser, access the EDGAR database at **www.sec.gov**. To search the database, click on "Company Filings" at the top of the page. Then type in "**chipotle**" for the company name in the search window, and press enter.

Required:

To look at SEC filings, type in "10-Q" in the space indicating "Filing Type" and press enter. Skim down the left side until you locate the Form 10-Q (quarterly report) filed October 21, 2014. Click on the "Documents" for that report, click on the 10-Q document (first item), and skim to the Table of Contents.

1. Click on "Financial Statements" and skim to the "Condensed Consolidated Balance Sheets."
   a. What was the amount of Chipotle's total assets for the most recent quarter reported?
   b. Did current liabilities increase or decrease since December 31, 2013?
   c. Compute the current ratio. How does it compare to the ratio indicated for Chipotle Mexican Grill in the chapter at December 31, 2014? What does this suggest about the company?
2. Skim to the Chipotle "Consolidated Statements of Cash Flow."
   a. What amount did Chipotle spend on "leasehold improvements, property and equipment" for the quarter ended September 30, 2014? (Leasehold improvements are major renovations, such as adding elevators, to rented property.)
   b. What was the total amount of cash flows used in financing activities?

Using Financial Reports: Evaluating the Reliability of a Balance Sheet

CP2-5
LO2-1, 2-5

Frances Sabatier asked a local bank for a $50,000 loan to expand her small company. The bank asked Frances to submit a financial statement of the business to supplement the loan application. Frances prepared the following balance sheet.

FS COMPUTING
Balance Sheet
June 30, 2016

Assets

Cash and investments	$ 9,000
Inventory	30,000
Equipment	46,000
Personal residence (monthly payments, $2,800)	300,000
Remaining assets	20,000
Total assets	**$405,000**

Liabilities

Short-term debt to suppliers	$ 62,000
Long-term debt on equipment	38,000
Total debt	100,000
Stockholders' equity	305,000
Total liabilities and stockholders' equity	**$405,000**

Required:

The balance sheet has several flaws. However, there is at least one major deficiency. Identify it and explain its significance.

CP2-6

LO2-2, 2-4, 2-5

Using Financial Reports: Analyzing the Balance Sheet

Recent balance sheets are provided for **Twitter, Inc.**, a global platform for real-time public self-expression and conversation.

TWITTER, INC.
Consolidated Balance Sheets
(In thousands, unless otherwise specified)

	December 31, 2014	December 31, 2013
ASSETS		
Current assets		
Cash and cash equivalents	$1,510,724	$ 841,010
Short-term investments	2,111,154	1,393,044
Accounts receivable	418,454	247,328
Prepaid expenses and other current assets	215,521	93,297
Total current assets	4,255,853	2,574,679
Property and equipment, net	557,019	332,662
Intangible assets	727,581	441,104
Other noncurrent assets	42,629	17,795
Total assets	$5,583,082	$3,366,240

TWITTER, INC.
Consolidated Balance Sheets
(In thousands, unless otherwise specified)
(Continued)

	December 31, 2014	December 31, 2013
LIABILITIES AND STOCKHOLDERS' EQUITY		
Current liabilities		
Accounts payable	$ 53,241	$ 27,994
Accrued and other current liabilities	228,233	110,310
Capital leases, short-term	112,320	87,126
Total current liabilities	393,794	225,430
Notes payable	1,376,020	
Capital leases, long-term	118,950	110,520
Other long-term liabilities	67,915	80,284
Total liabilities	1,956,679	416,234
Stockholders' equity		
Common stock ($0.000005 par value)	3	3
Additional paid-in capital	5,208,870	3,944,952
Accumulated deficit	(1,582,470)	(994,949)
Total stockholders' equity	3,626,403	2,950,006
Total liabilities and stockholders' equity	$5,583,082	$3,366,240

Required:

1. Is Twitter a corporation, sole proprietorship, or partnership? Explain the basis of your answer.
2. Use the company's balance sheet to determine the amounts in the accounting equation (A = L + SE) at the end of the most recent year.
3. Calculate the company's current ratio on December 31, 2014, and on December 31, 2013. Interpret the ratios that you calculated. What other information would make your interpretation more useful?
4. Prepare the journal entry the company will make in 2015 when it pays its 2014 accounts payable due at year-end.
5. Does the company appear to have been profitable over its years in business? On what account are you basing your answer? Assuming no dividends were paid, how much was net income (or net loss) in the most recent year? If it is impossible to determine without an income statement, state so.

Critical Thinking Cases

Making a Decision as a Financial Analyst: Preparing and Analyzing a Balance Sheet

Your best friend from home writes you a letter about an investment opportunity that has come her way. A company is raising money by issuing shares of stock and wants her to invest $20,000 (her recent inheritance from her great-aunt's estate). Your friend has never invested in a company before and, knowing that you are a financial analyst, asks that you look over the balance sheet and send her some advice. An **unaudited** balance sheet, in only moderately good form, is enclosed with the letter.

CP2-7
LO2-1, 2-5

DEWEY, CHEETUM, AND HOWE, INC.
Balance Sheet
For the Most Recent Year Ending December 31

Accounts receivable	$ 8,000
Cash	1,000
Inventory	8,000
Furniture and fixtures	52,000
Delivery truck	12,000
Buildings (estimated market value)	98,000
Total assets	**$179,000**
Accounts payable	$ 16,000
Payroll taxes payable	13,000
Notes payable (due in three years)	15,000
Mortgage payable	50,000
Total liabilities	**$ 94,000**
Contributed capital (issued 2,000 shares,	$ 80,000
$2 par value per share)	
Retained earnings	5,000
Total stockholders' equity	**$ 85,000**

There is only one disclosure note, and it states that the building was purchased for $65,000, has been depreciated by $5,000 on the books, and still carries a mortgage (shown in the liability section). The note also states that, in the opinion of the company president, the building is "easily worth $98,000."

Required:
1. Draft a new balance sheet for your friend, correcting any errors you note. (If any of the account balances need to be corrected, you may need to adjust the retained earnings balance correspondingly.) If there are no errors or omissions, so state.
2. Write a letter to your friend explaining the changes you made to the balance sheet, if any, and offer your comments on the company's apparent financial condition based only on this information. Suggest other information your friend might want to review before coming to a final decision on whether to invest.

CP2-8   Evaluating an Ethical Dilemma: Analyzing Management Incentives

In July 2004, the U.S. government filed civil and criminal charges against four former executives of Netherlands-based **Ahold**'s subsidiary **U.S. Foodservice, Inc.**, an operator of supermarkets such as Bi-Lo and Giant Food Stores. Two of the four executives have pleaded guilty, and the other two were indicted. The alleged widespread fraud included recording completely fictitious revenues for false promotions and persuading vendors to confirm to auditors the false promotional payments. U.S. Attorney David Kelley suggested the fraud was motivated by the greed of the executives to reap fat bonuses if the company met certain financial goals. The auditors did not uncover the fraud.

Required:
1. Describe the parties who were harmed or helped by this fraud.
2. Explain how greed may have contributed to the fraud.
3. Why do you think the independent auditors failed to catch the fraud?

Financial Reporting and Analysis Team Project

CP2-9
LO2-2, 2-5, 2-6

Team Project: Analysis of Balance Sheets and Ratios

Working together as a team, select an industry to analyze. Yahoo Finance provides lists of industries at **biz.yahoo.com/p/industries.html**. Click on an industry for a list of companies in that industry. Alternatively, go to Google Finance at **www.google.com/finance**, search for a company you are interested in, and you will be presented with a list including that company and its competitors. Each team member should acquire the annual report or 10-K for one publicly traded company in the industry, with each member selecting a different company (the SEC EDGAR service at **www.sec.gov** or the company's investor relations website itself are good sources).

Required:

On an individual basis, each team member should write a short report answering the following questions about the selected company. Discuss any patterns across the companies that you as a team observe. Then, as a team, write a short report comparing and contrasting your companies.

1. For the most recent year, what are the top three asset accounts by size? What percentage is each of total assets? (Calculated as Asset A ÷ Total Assets)

2. What are the major investing and financing activities (by dollar size) for the most recent year? (Look at the Statement of Cash Flows.)

3. Ratio Analysis:
   a. What does the current ratio measure in general?
   b. Compute the current ratio for each of the last three years. (You may find prior years' information in the section of the annual report or 10-K called "Selected Financial Information" or you may search for prior years' annual reports.)
   c. What do your results suggest about the company?
   d. If available, find the industry ratio for the most recent year, compare it to your results, and discuss why you believe your company differs or is similar to the industry ratio.

Operating Decisions and the Accounting System

Chipotle Mexican Grill's philosophy of "Food with Integrity" guides its operating decisions. "Food with Integrity" entails finding and serving high-quality sustainably and organically raised food. It also includes showing respect for animals, the environment, and people involved in the operations. The company keeps operations simple, offering a few menu items (burritos, burrito bowls, tacos, and salads). Within these items, customers can choose from four meats, two types of beans and rice, and a variety of additional items such as salsa, guacamole, cheese, and lettuce—creating hundreds of options. The focused menu allows Chipotle to concentrate on the source of the food items, a challenging activity given the smaller and often costlier market for organic meats, produce, and dairy products. Anticipating changes in these food costs and sources is critical to determining menu prices and controlling costs.

To control quality and increase efficiency, the company purchases key ingredients such as meat, beans, and tortillas from a small number of suppliers and other raw materials from approved sources. Twenty-two independently owned and operated regional distribution centers purchase from these suppliers and then deliver the items as needed to the Chipotle restaurants in each region.

The second highest cost for Chipotle, as with most restaurants, is hiring and developing employees. The food is prepared from scratch on stoves and grills, not with microwaves

Learning Objectives

After studying this chapter, you should be able to:

3-1 Describe a typical business operating cycle and explain the necessity for the time period assumption.

3-2 Explain how business activities affect the elements of the income statement.

3-3 Explain the accrual basis of accounting and apply the revenue and expense recognition principles to measure income.

3-4 Apply transaction analysis to examine and record the effects of operating activities on the financial statements.

3-5 Prepare a classified income statement.

3-6 Compute and interpret the net profit margin ratio.

chapter 3

Bloomberg/Getty Images

FOCUS COMPANY:

Chipotle Mexican Grill

IT'S MORE THAN MEAT, GUACAMOLE, AND TORTILLAS

www.chipotle.com

and other automated cooking techniques. Each employee is trained in all aspects of preparing the food—from grilling, to making fresh salsa, to cooking rice—and creating a positive interactive experience for customers. The company has numerous incentives to develop strong leadership, with about 90 percent of salaried management and about 98 percent of hourly management promoted from within the company.

Chipotle also competes using marketing strategies. Chipotle spends less on expensive national advertising campaigns than larger restaurant chains and much more on strategic promotional activities to make connections with neighborhoods and explain how Chipotle is different. Most activities are innovative, such as the award-winning two-minute animated video "Back to the Start" that aired during the 2012 Grammy Awards; the Cultivate Chicago festival featuring indie bands, artisanal food, wine producers, and high-profile chefs; and the Chipotle Truck, which travels to various locations, including new store openings, and sells almost a full menu of Chipotle items from the food trailer. As stated in its 2014 annual report:

> Collectively, these efforts and our excellent restaurant teams have helped us create considerable word-of-mouth publicity as our customers learn more about us and share with others. This approach allows us to build awareness and loyalty with relatively low advertising expenditures, even in a competitive category, and to differentiate Chipotle as a company that is committed to doing the right thing in every facet of our business.

UNDERSTANDING THE BUSINESS

The restaurant industry is extremely competitive. For example, in February 2012, **McDonald's Corporation** announced a requirement that suppliers need to phase out stalls that restrict the movement of pregnant pigs, a change made in direct response to **Chipotle**'s TV video on its ethical stance aired at the Grammy Awards. **Taco Bell** announced in July 2012 the creation of a Cantina Bell™ menu featuring "gourmet" food items such as the Cantina Burrito and Cantina Bowl. **Jack in the Box, Inc.**, is expanding its **Qdoba Mexican Grill** chain to compete in the fast-casual segment of the industry that is dominated by Mexican restaurants.

Restaurants have to manage economic downturns and shifts in consumer tastes for healthier food choices while facing the competition. Recent trends in mobile technology apps for ordering, customer payment, and loyalty program management; equipment improvements, such as 1,000-degree ovens for baking two-minute pizzas; and the tremendous expansion of fast-casual restaurant concepts provide challenges. Based on their projections of these forces, companies set goals for their performance. Published income statements provide the primary basis for comparing projections to the actual results of operations. To understand how business plans and the results of operations are reflected on the income statement, we need to answer the following questions:

1. How do business activities affect the income statement?
2. How are business activities measured?
3. How are business activities reported on the income statement?

In this chapter we focus on Chipotle's operating activities that involve the sale of food to the public. The results of these activities are reported on the income statement.

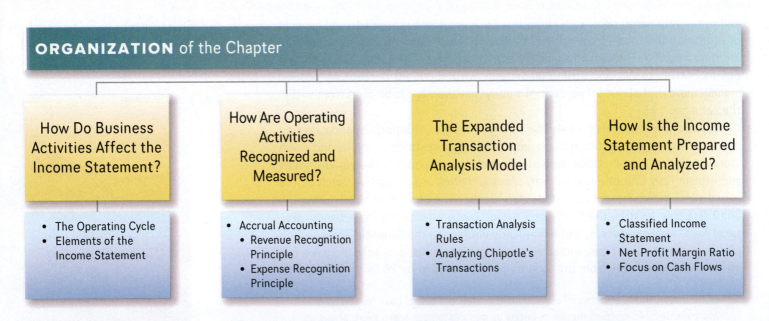

ORGANIZATION of the Chapter

How Do Business Activities Affect the Income Statement?	How Are Operating Activities Recognized and Measured?	The Expanded Transaction Analysis Model	How Is the Income Statement Prepared and Analyzed?

• The Operating Cycle
• Elements of the Income Statement
	• Accrual Accounting
	  • Revenue Recognition Principle
	  • Expense Recognition Principle
		• Transaction Analysis Rules
		• Analyzing Chipotle's Transactions
			• Classified Income Statement
			• Net Profit Margin Ratio
			• Focus on Cash Flows

HOW DO BUSINESS ACTIVITIES AFFECT THE INCOME STATEMENT?

The Operating Cycle

LEARNING OBJECTIVE 3-1
Describe a typical business operating cycle and explain the necessity for the time period assumption.

The long-term objective for any business is to **turn cash into more cash.** If a company is to stay in business, this excess cash must be generated from operations (that is, from the activities for which the business was established), not from borrowing money or selling long-lived assets.

Companies (1) acquire inventory and the services of employees and (2) sell inventory or services to customers. The **operating (cash-to-cash) cycle** begins when a company receives goods to sell, pays for them, and sells to customers (or, in the case of a service company, has employees work to provide services to customers); it ends when customers pay cash to the company. The length of time for completion of the operating cycle depends on the nature of the business.

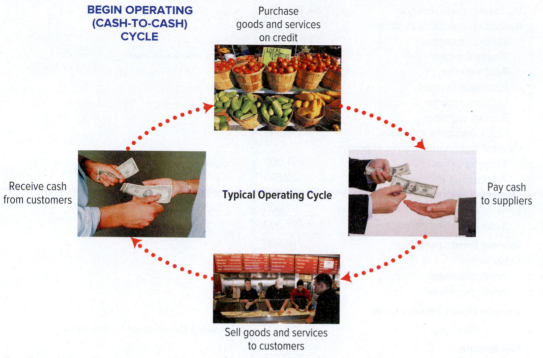

BEGIN OPERATING (CASH-TO-CASH) CYCLE

Purchase goods and services on credit

Receive cash from customers

Typical Operating Cycle

Pay cash to suppliers

Sell goods and services to customers

Top: Digital Vision/Getty Images; Left: Digital Stock/Corbis; Right: Tetra Images/Getty Images; Bottom: Jeff Kowalsky/Bloomberg/Getty Images

The operating cycle for **Chipotle** is relatively short. It spends cash to purchase fresh ingredients, prepares the food, and sells it to customers for cash. In some companies, inventory is paid for well before it is sold. **Toys R Us**, for example, builds its inventory for months preceding the year-end holiday season. It borrows funds from banks to pay for the inventory and repays the loans with interest when it receives cash from customers. In other companies, cash is received from customers well after a sale takes place. For example, furniture retailers often allow customers to make monthly payments over several years. Shortening the operating cycle by creating incentives that encourage customers to buy sooner and/or pay faster improves a company's cash flows.

Until a company ceases its activities, the operating cycle is repeated continuously. However, decision makers require information periodically about the company's financial condition and performance. As indicated in the conceptual framework in Exhibit 2.1, to measure income for a specific period of time, accountants follow the **time period assumption**, which assumes that the long life of a company can be reported in shorter time periods, such as months, quarters, and years.[1] Two types of issues arise in reporting periodic income to users:

1. Recognition issues: **When** should the effects of operating activities be recognized (recorded)?

2. Measurement issues: **What amounts** should be recognized?

Before we examine the rules accountants follow in resolving these issues, however, let's examine the elements of the income statement that are affected by operating activities.

---

[1]In addition to the audited annual statements, most businesses prepare quarterly financial statements (also known as **interim reports** covering a three-month period) for external users. The Securities and Exchange Commission requires public companies to do so.

EXHIBIT 3.1

Chipotle Mexican Grill's
Income Statement

CHIPOTLE MEXICAN GRILL, INC.
Consolidated Statement of Income*
For the Year ended December 31, 2014
(in thousands of dollars, except per share data)

Restaurant sales revenue	$4,108,300
Restaurant operating expenses:	
Supplies expense	1,421,000
Wages expense	904,400
Rent expense	230,900
Insurance expense	118,000
Utilities expense	60,700
Repairs expense	35,200
Other operating expenses	338,300
General and administrative expenses:	
Training expense	151,000
Advertising expense	20,500
Depreciation expense	110,500
Loss on disposal of assets	7,000
Total operating expenses	3,397,500
Income from operations	710,800
Other items:	
Interest revenue	4,200
Interest expense	(700)
Income before income taxes	714,300
Income tax expense	269,000
Net income	$ 445,300
Earnings per share	$14.35

Includes salaries expense (Wages expense)

Includes pre-opening costs (Training expense)

Also called Provision for Income Taxes (Income tax expense)

= *$445,300,000 Net Income ÷ 31,038,000 weighted average number of common stock shares outstanding (per 2014 annual report)*

Operating activities (central focus of business)

Peripheral activities (not central focus of business)

**The information has been adapted from actual statements and simplified for this chapter.*

Elements of the Income Statement

Exhibit 3.1 shows a recent income statement for **Chipotle**, simplified for the purposes of this chapter. It has multiple subtotals, such as **operating income** and **income before income taxes.** This format is known as **multiple step** and is very common.[2] In fact, you can tell if a company uses the multiple-step format if you see the Operating Income (also called Income from Operations) subtotal. As we discuss the elements of the income statement, also refer to the conceptual framework outlined in Exhibit 2.1.

Operating Revenues

REVENUES
Increases in assets or settlements of liabilities from the major or central ongoing operations of the business.

Revenues are defined as increases in assets or settlements of liabilities from the major or **central ongoing operations** of the business. Operating revenues result from the sale of goods or the rendering of services as the central focus of the business. When Chipotle sells tacos to consumers, it has **earned** revenue. When revenue is earned, assets, usually Cash or Accounts Receivable, often increase. Sometimes if a customer pays for goods or services in advance, a liability account, usually Unearned (or Deferred) Revenue, is created. At this point, no revenue

---

[2]Another common format, **single step,** reorganizes all accounts from the multiple-step format. All revenues and gains are listed together and all expenses and losses except taxes are listed together. The expense subtotal is then subtracted from the revenue subtotal to arrive at income before income taxes, the same subtotal as on the multiple-step statement.

has been earned. There is simply a receipt of cash in exchange for a promise to provide a good or service in the future. When the company provides the promised goods or services to the customer, then the revenue is recognized and the liability eliminated.

Many companies generate revenues from a variety of sources. For example, **General Motors** reports revenues from its automotive sales as well as from providing financing to customers. In the restaurant industry, many companies, such as **McDonald's Corporation**, have company-owned stores but also sell franchise rights. The franchisor (seller) reports revenues from both the sales of food in company-owned stores and the fees from franchisees. Chipotle does not sell franchises. Therefore, the company generates revenue from one source—sales of food orders to customers—that is reported in the **Restaurant Sales Revenue** account.

Operating Expenses

Some students confuse the terms **expenditures** and **expenses.** An expenditure is any outflow of cash for any purpose, whether to buy equipment, pay off a bank loan, or pay employees their wages. **Expenses** are outflows or the using up of assets or increases in liabilities from **ongoing operations** incurred to generate revenues during the period. Therefore, **not all cash expenditures are expenses, but expenses are necessary to generate revenues.**

Chipotle's employees make and serve food. The company uses electricity to operate equipment and light its facilities, and it uses food and paper supplies. Without incurring these expenses, Chipotle could not generate revenues. Expenses may be incurred before, after, or at the same time as cash is paid. When an expense is incurred, assets such as Supplies decrease (are used up) **or** liabilities such as Wages Payable or Utilities Payable increase. The following are Chipotle's primary operating expenses:

Restaurant Operating Expenses:

- **Supplies Expense.** In Chipotle's restaurant operations, any food ingredients or beverage and packaging supplies that are used to produce and sell meals are expensed as they are used. For Chipotle, this is its largest expense at $1,421,000,000 in 2014. In companies with a manufacturing or merchandising focus, the most significant expense is usually Cost of Goods Sold (or Cost of Sales), representing the cost of inventory used in generating sales.

- **Wages Expense.** When salaried and hourly employees work and generate sales for Chipotle, the company incurs an expense, although wages and salaries will be paid later. Wages Expense of $904,400,000 is Chipotle's second largest expense. In purely service-oriented companies in which no products are produced or sold, the cost of having employees generate revenues is usually the largest expense. For example, **Federal Express** reported over $16 billion in salaries expense for the year ended May 31, 2014.

- **Rent Expense, Insurance Expense, Utilities Expense, and Repairs Expense.** Renting facilities, insuring property and equipment at the stores, using utilities, and repairing and maintaining facilities and equipment are typical expenses related to operating stores. Usually, rent and insurance are paid before occupying the facilities, but utilities and repairs are paid after occupying the facilities.

- **Other Operating Expenses.** These expenses include a variety of accounts with smaller dollar balances.

General and Administrative Expenses: General and Administrative Expenses include costs of training employees and managers, advertising, and other expenses not directly related to operating stores. These often include expenses such as renting headquarters facilities and paying executive salaries.

Depreciation Expense: When a company uses buildings and equipment to generate revenues, a part of the cost of these assets is reported as an expense called Depreciation Expense. Chapter 8 discusses methods for estimating the amount of depreciation expense.

Losses (Gains) on Disposal of Assets: Companies sell property, plant, and equipment from time to time to maintain modern facilities. When assets other than investments are sold or disposed of for more than their undepreciated cost, **gains** result. If they are sold or disposed of for less than the undepreciated cost, **losses** result. In 2014, Chipotle reported a loss on disposal of assets of $7,000,000. Note that selling short- or long-term investments above or below cost also results in gains or losses, but these are not reported in the Operating Expenses section of the multiple-step income statement. Instead, they are reported in Other Items as discussed in the next section.

Operating revenues less operating expenses equals **Operating Income** (also called Income from Operations)—a measure of the profit from central ongoing operations.

Other Items

Not all activities affecting an income statement are central to ongoing operations. Any revenues, expenses, gains, or losses that result from these other activities are not included as part of operating income but are instead categorized as Other Items. Typically, these include the following:

- **Interest Revenue** (or **Investment Revenue, Investment Income,** or **Dividend Revenue**). Using excess cash to purchase stocks or bonds in other companies is an investing activity for Chipotle, not the central operation of making and selling fresh Mexican food. Therefore, any interest or dividends earned on investments in other companies is not included as operating revenue.

- **Interest Expense.** Likewise, since borrowing money is a financing activity, any cost of using that money (called interest) is not an operating expense. Except for financial institutions, incurring interest expense and earning interest revenue are **not** the central operations of most businesses, including Chipotle. We say these are peripheral (normal but not central) transactions.

- **Losses (Gains) on Sale of Investments.** When investments are sold for more (or less) than the original cost, a gain (or loss) results and is reported as an Other Item on the income statement. In 2014, Chipotle did not report any gains or losses from selling investments.

Income Tax Expense

Adding (subtracting) other items to (from) operating income gives a subtotal of **Income before Income Taxes** (or Pretax Income). Income Tax Expense (also called **Provision for Income Taxes**) is the last expense listed on the income statement before determining net income. All profit-making corporations are required to compute income taxes owed to federal, state, and foreign governments. Income tax expense is calculated as a percentage of pretax income determined by applying the tax rates of the federal, state, local, and foreign taxing authorities. Chipotle's effective tax rate in 2014 was 37.7 percent ($269,000,000 in income tax expense divided by $714,300,000 in income before income taxes). This indicates that, for every dollar of income before taxes that Chipotle made in 2014, the company paid nearly $0.38 to taxing authorities.

Earnings per Share

Corporations are required to disclose earnings per share on the income statement or in the notes to the financial statements. This ratio is widely used in evaluating the operating performance and profitability of a company. At this introductory level, we can compute earnings per share simply as net income divided by the weighted average number of shares of stock outstanding (Net Income ÷ Weighted Average Number of Shares of Stock Outstanding). Please note, however, that the calculation of the ratio is actually much more complex and beyond the scope of this course. For simplicity, we use the $445,300,000 net income in Exhibit 3.1 as the numerator and 31,038,000 weighted average number of shares computed by Chipotle as the denominator. For 2014, Chipotle reported $14.35 in earnings for each share of stock owned by investors.

Income Statement Differences

Under IFRS, the income statement is usually titled the Statement of Operations. There is also a difference in how expenses may be reported:

	GAAP	IFRS
Presentation of Expenses		
• Similar expenses are reported, but they may be grouped in different ways.	Public companies categorize expenses by business **function** (e.g., production, research, marketing, general operations).	Companies can categorize expenses by either **function or nature** (e.g., salaries, rent, supplies, electricity).

In addition, foreign companies often use account titles that differ from those used by U.S. companies. For example, **GlaxoSmithKline** (a UK pharmaceutical company), **Parmalat** (an Italian food producer of milk, dairy products, and fruit-based beverages), and **Unilever** (a UK- and Netherlands-based company supplying food, home, and personal care products such as Hellman's mayonnaise, Dove soap, and Popsicle treats) use the term *turnover* to refer to sales revenue, *finance income* for income from investments, and *finance cost* for interest expense. **BMW Group**, on the other hand, reports *revenues* and uses *financial result* for the difference between income from investments and interest expense. All four companies follow IFRS.

HOW ARE OPERATING ACTIVITIES RECOGNIZED AND MEASURED?

You probably determine your personal financial position by the cash balance in your bank account. Your financial performance is measured as the difference between your cash balance at the beginning of the period and the cash balance at the end of the period (that is, whether you end up with more or less cash). If you have a higher cash balance, cash receipts exceeded cash disbursements for the period. Many local retailers, medical offices, and other small businesses use **cash basis accounting**, in which revenues are recorded when cash is received and expenses are recorded when cash is paid, regardless of when the revenues are earned or the expenses incurred. This basis produces net operating cash flow information that is often quite adequate for organizations that do not need to report to external users. The following table illustrates the application of cash basis accounting for the first three years of a new business, Cade Company:

CASH BASIS
Income Measurement
Revenues (= cash receipts)
−Expenses (= cash payments)
Net Income (cash basis)

CASH BASIS ACCOUNTING
Records revenues when cash is received and expenses when cash is paid.

Cade Company Income Statements	Year 1	Year 2	Year 3	Total
Sales on credit	$ 60,000	$ 60,000	$ 60,000	$180,000
Cash receipts from customers	$ 20,000	$70,000	$90,000	$180,000
Cash disbursements for:				
Salaries to employees	(30,000)	(30,000)	(30,000)	(90,000)
Insurance for 3 years	(12,000)	(0)	(0)	(12,000)
Supplies	(3,000)	(7,000)	(5,000)	(15,000)
Net operating cash flows	**$(25,000)**	**$33,000**	**$55,000**	**$ 63,000**

In this illustration, $60,000 in sales was earned each year by Cade Company. However, because the sales were on account, customers spread out their payments over three years. Salaries to employees were paid in full each year. Insurance was prepaid at the beginning of the first year for equal coverage over the three years. Supplies were purchased on credit and used evenly over the three years. However, the company paid part of the first-year purchases in the second year.

Using cash basis accounting may lead to an incorrect interpretation of future company performance. Simply looking at the first year, investors and creditors might interpret the negative cash flows as a problem with the company's ability to generate cash flows in the future. However, the other two years show positive cash flows. Likewise, performance over time appears uneven, when in actuality it is not. Sales were earned evenly each year, although collections from customers were not. The years in which insurance and supplies were paid for are not the same as the years in which these resources were used.

Accrual Accounting

Financial statements created under cash basis accounting normally postpone or accelerate recognition of revenues and expenses long before or after goods and services are produced and delivered (when cash is received or paid). They also do not necessarily reflect all assets or liabilities of a company on a particular date. For these reasons, cash basis financial statements are not very useful to external decision makers. Therefore, generally accepted accounting principles require **accrual basis accounting** for financial reporting.

In accrual basis accounting, revenues and expenses are recognized when the transaction that causes them occurs, not necessarily when cash is received or paid. That is, **revenues are recognized when they are earned and expenses when they are incurred to generate revenues.**

Using the same information for Cade Company, we can apply the accrual basis of accounting.

ACCRUAL BASIS ACCOUNTING

Records revenues when earned and expenses when incurred, regardless of the timing of cash receipts or payments.

ACCRUAL BASIS
Income Measurement
Revenues (= when earned)
−Expenses (= when incurred)
Net Income (accrual basis)

Cade Company Income Statements	Year 1	Year 2	Year 3	Total
Sales revenue (earned)	$60,000	$60,000	$60,000	$180,000
Expenses (resources used or incurred):				
Salaries expense	(30,000)	(30,000)	(30,000)	(90,000)
Insurance expense	(4,000)	(4,000)	(4,000)	(12,000)
Supplies expense	(5,000)	(5,000)	(5,000)	(15,000)
Net income	**$21,000**	**$21,000**	**$21,000**	**$63,000**

Regardless of when cash is received, Cade Company reported revenues when earned. Likewise, the company used insurance coverage and supplies evenly over the three years, despite prepaying the entire amount of insurance at the beginning of the first year and paying part of the first year's purchases in the second year. The $21,000 net income in the first year is a better predictor of future cash flows and performance than net operating cash flows reported under cash basis accounting. The two basic accounting principles that determine when revenues and expenses are recorded under accrual basis accounting are the **revenue recognition principle** and the **expense recognition principle** (also called the **matching principle**).

Revenue Recognition Principle

REVENUE RECOGNITION PRINCIPLE

Revenues are recognized (1) when the company transfers promised goods or services to customers (2) in the amount it expects to receive.

The core **revenue recognition principle** specifies both the timing and amount of revenue to be recognized during an accounting period. It requires that a company recognize revenue:

1. **When the company transfers promised goods or services to customers**
2. **In the amount it expects to receive.**

When **Chipotle** delivers food to customers, it recognizes revenue **regardless of when cash is received.** Exhibit 3.2 illustrates that revenue is earned when the business delivers goods or services,

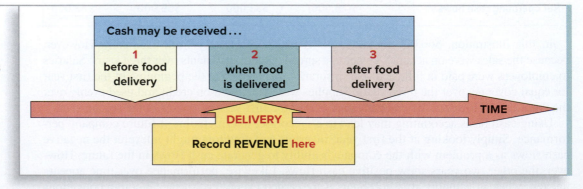

EXHIBIT 3.2

Recording Revenues versus Cash Receipts

although cash can be received from customers (1) in a period **before** delivery, (2) in the **same** period as delivery, or (3) in a period **after** delivery. Let's see how to handle each of these cases.

1 > **Cash is received *before* the goods or services are delivered.** Chipotle sells gift cards to customers for cash in exchange for the promise to provide future food orders. Since Chipotle has not at that point delivered food, it records **no revenue.** Instead, it creates a liability account (Unearned Revenue) representing the amount of food service owed to the customers. Later, when customers redeem their gift cards and Chipotle delivers the food, it earns and records the revenue while reducing the liability account since it has satisfied its promise to deliver.

On receipt of a $100 cash deposit:

Cash (+A)	100	
Unearned Revenue (+L)		100

On delivery of ordered food:

Unearned Revenue (−L)	100	
Restaurant Sales Revenue (+R, +SE).....		100

2 > **Cash is received *in the same period as* the goods or services are delivered.** As is a typical timing of cash receipts and revenue recognition in the restaurant industry, Chipotle receives cash from most customers within a few minutes of them receiving their food. Chipotle delivers the food to the customer as ordered in exchange for cash, **earning revenue** in the process.

On delivery of ordered food for $12 cash:

Cash (+A)	12	
Restaurant Sales Revenue (+R, +SE)		12

3 > **Cash is received *after* the goods or services are delivered.** When a business sells goods or services on account, the revenue is earned when the goods or services are delivered, not when cash is received at a later date. Let's assume that, to boost business, Chipotle agrees to deliver food ordered by select customers, such as departments at area colleges or local businesses. These customers pay for the food order when Chipotle bills them at the end of the month, rather than when they receive the food. When delivered, Chipotle records both Restaurant Sales Revenue and the asset Accounts Receivable, representing the customer's promise to pay in the future for past food deliveries. When the customer pays its monthly bill, Chipotle will increase its Cash account and decrease Accounts Receivable.

On delivery of ordered food for $50 on account:

Accounts Receivable (+A)	50	
Restaurant Sales Revenue (+R, +SE)		50

On receipt of cash after delivery:

Cash (+A)	50	
Accounts Receivable (−A)		50

Companies usually disclose their revenue recognition practices in the financial statement note titled Significant Accounting Policies. The following excerpt from Note 1 to recent financial statements describes how Chipotle recognizes its revenue:

1. DESCRIPTION OF BUSINESS AND SUMMARY OF SIGNIFICANT ACCOUNTING POLICIES

Revenue Recognition

Revenue from restaurant sales is recognized when food and beverage products are sold . . . The Company sells gift cards which do not have an expiration date . . . The Company recognizes revenues from gift cards when: (i) the gift card is redeemed by the customer; or (ii) the Company determines the likelihood of the gift card being redeemed by the customer is remote (gift card breakage) . . . The determination of the gift card breakage rate is based upon Company-specific historical redemption patterns.

CHIPOTLE MEXICAN GRILL

REAL WORLD EXCERPT:

Annual Report

Revenue Recognition for More Complex Customer Contracts		FINANCIAL ANALYSIS

The FASB and IASB issued a new revenue recognition accounting standard effective for 2018 financial statements. As indicated earlier, the standard requires a company to recognize revenue when it transfers goods and services to customers in the amount it expects to receive. The standard also specifies how to handle more complex contracts with customers. The standard specifies five steps to recognizing revenue:

1. Identify the contract between the company and customer.
2. Identify the performance obligations (promised goods and services).
3. Determine the transaction price.

4. Allocate the transaction price to the performance obligations.
5. Recognize revenue when each performance obligation is satisfied (or over time if a service is provided over time).

For example, when **Dell** sells computers and a one-year warranty together in a single sale, it will determine the separate obligations (selling a computer and selling a warranty service) and split the sales price among them. Dell will then recognize the revenue allocated to the computer when it is delivered, and it will recognize one-twelfth of the revenue from the warranty each month it is in force. Accounting for complex sales transactions is covered in more detail in intermediate accounting courses.

PAUSE FOR **FEEDBACK**

We just learned the **revenue recognition principle's** criteria: Recognize revenue (1) when the company transfers promised goods or services to customers (2) in the amount it expects to receive.

SELF-STUDY **QUIZ**

Complete this quiz now to make sure you can apply the revenue recognition principle. The following transactions are samples of typical monthly operating activities of **Papa John's International, Inc.** (dollars in thousands), a company that makes and delivers pizza and sells franchises. If revenue is to be recognized in **January,** indicate the title of the revenue account and the amount of revenue to be recognized. For account titles, name the revenue account based on the nature of the transaction. For example, sales to customers are Restaurant Sales Revenue and sales of franchises are Franchise Fee Revenue.

ACTIVITY	REVENUE ACCOUNT TITLE	AMOUNT OF REVENUE RECOGNIZED IN JANUARY
(a) In January, Papa John's company-owned restaurants sold food to customers for $32,000 cash.		
(b) In January, Papa John's sold new franchises for $625 cash, providing $400 in services to these new franchisees during January; the remainder of services will be provided over the next three months.		
(c) In January, Papa John's received $210 in cash from customers as deposits on large orders to be delivered in February.		
(d) In January, Papa John's delivered $1,630 to select customers on account; the customers will pay when billed at the end of January.		
(e) In January, customers paid $1,200 on account to Papa John's from December deliveries of pizza.		
(f) In January, Papa John's delivered $385 to customers who provided deposits in December.		

After you have completed your answers, check them below.

Solutions to
SELF-STUDY QUIZ

Revenue Account Title	Amount of Revenue Recognized in January
(a) Restaurant Sales Revenue	$32,000
(b) Franchise Fee Revenue	$ 400
(c) No revenue earned in January	—
(d) Restaurant Sales Revenue	$ 1,630
(e) No revenue earned in January	—
(f) Restaurant Sales Revenue	$ 385

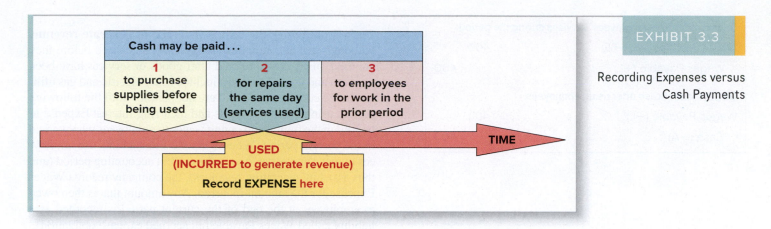

EXHIBIT 3.3

Recording Expenses versus
Cash Payments

Expense Recognition Principle

The **expense recognition principle** (also called the **matching principle**) requires that costs incurred to generate revenues be recognized in the same period—a matching of costs with benefits. For example, when Chipotle's restaurants provide food service to customers, revenue is earned. The costs of generating the revenue include expenses incurred such as these:

- Salaries and wages to employees who worked **during the period**
- Utilities for the electricity used **during the period**
- Food, beverage, and packaging supplies used **during the period**
- Facilities rental **during the period**
- Grills and other equipment used **during the period**

EXPENSE RECOGNITION PRINCIPLE (OR MATCHING PRINCIPLE)
Requires that expenses be recorded when incurred in earning revenue.

As with revenues and cash receipts, expenses are recorded as incurred, **regardless of when cash is paid.** Cash may be paid (1) **before,** (2) **during,** or (3) **after** an expense is incurred (see Exhibit 3.3). An entry will be made on the date the expense is incurred and another on the date the cash is paid, if they occur at different times. Let's see how to handle each of these cases related to the expense recognition principle.

1 **Cash is paid** *before* **the expense is incurred to generate revenue.** Companies purchase many assets that are used to generate revenues in future periods. Examples include buying insurance for future coverage, paying rent for future use of space, and acquiring supplies and equipment for future use. When revenues are generated in the future, the company records an expense for the portion of the cost of the assets used—costs are matched with the benefits. As an example, Chipotle buys paper supplies (napkins, bags, cups, etc.) in one month but uses them the following month. When acquired, the supplies are recorded as an asset called Supplies because they will benefit future periods. When they are used the following month, Supplies Expense is recorded for the month and the asset Supplies is reduced to the balance yet to be used. Similarly, rent, insurance, and advertising that are prepaid are often recorded in an asset account called Prepaid Expenses and expensed when used.

On payment of $200 cash for supplies:		
Supplies (+A)	200	
Cash (−A)		200
On subsequent use of half of the supplies:		
Supplies Expense (+E, −SE)	100	
Supplies (−A)		100

2 **Cash is paid** *in the same period* **as the expense is incurred to generate revenue.** Expenses are sometimes incurred and paid for in the period in which they arise. An example is paying for repairs on grills the day of the service. If Chipotle spends $275 cash to repair grills so that food can be prepared to sell, an expense is incurred and recorded (Repairs Expense).

On payment of $275 cash for repair service:		
Repairs Expense (+E, −SE)	275	
Cash (−A)		275

On use of $400 in employees' services during the period:		
Wages Expense (+E, −SE)	400	
Wages Payable (+L)		400
On payment of cash after using employees:		
Wages Payable (−L)...................	400	
Cash (−A)		400

 3 **Cash is paid *after* the cost is incurred to generate revenue.** Although rent and supplies are typically purchased before they are used, many costs are paid after goods or services have been received and used. Examples include using electric and gas utilities in the current period that are not paid for until the following period, using borrowed funds and incurring Interest Expense to be paid in the future, and owing wages to employees who worked in the current period. When Chipotle's restaurants use employees to make and serve food in the current accounting period (and thus assist in generating revenues), the company records Wages Expense for the amount incurred. Any amount that is then owed to employees at the end of the current period is recorded as a liability called Wages Payable (an accrued expense obligation).

PAUSE FOR **FEEDBACK**

The **expense recognition principle** (or matching principle) requires that costs incurred to generate revenues be recognized in the same period—that costs are matched with the revenues they generate. Regardless of when cash is paid, expense is recorded when incurred.

SELF-STUDY **QUIZ**

Complete this quiz now to make sure you can apply the expense recognition principle. The following transactions are samples of typical monthly operating activities of **Papa John's International, Inc.** (dollars in thousands). If an expense is to be recognized in **January,** indicate the title of the expense account and the amount of expense to be recognized.

ACTIVITY	EXPENSE ACCOUNT TITLE	AMOUNT OF EXPENSE RECOGNIZED IN JANUARY
(a) At the beginning of January, Papa John's restaurants paid $3,000 in rent for the months of January, February, and March.		
(b) In January, Papa John's paid suppliers $10,000 on account for supplies received in December.		
(c) In January, the food and paper products supplies used in making and selling pizza products to customers was $9,500. The supplies were purchased in December on account.		
(d) In late January, Papa John's received a $400 utility bill for electricity used in January. The bill will be paid in February.		

After you have completed your answers, check them below.

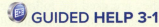 **GUIDED HELP 3-1**

For additional step-by-step video instruction on identifying revenue and expense accounts and amounts for a given period, go to **www.mhhe.com/libby9e_gh3a**.

Solutions to
SELF-STUDY QUIZ

Expense Account Title	Amount of Expense Recognized in January
(a) Rent Expense	$1,000 ($3,000 ÷ 3 months)
(b) No expense in January	Supplies will be expensed when used.
(c) Supplies Expense	$9,500
(d) Utilities Expense	$ 400

A QUESTION OF ETHICS

Management's Incentives to Violate Accounting Rules

Investors in the stock market base their decisions on their expectations of a company's future earnings. When companies announce quarterly and annual earnings information, investors evaluate how well the companies have met expectations and adjust their investing decisions accordingly. Companies that fail to meet expectations often experience a decline in stock price. Thus, managers are motivated to produce earnings results that meet or exceed investors' expectations to bolster stock prices. Greed may lead some managers to make unethical accounting and reporting decisions, often involving falsifying revenues and expenses. While this sometimes fools people for a short time, it rarely works in the long run and often leads to very bad consequences.

Fraud is a criminal offense for which managers may be sentenced to jail. Samples of fraud cases, a few involving faulty revenue and expense accounting, are shown below. Just imagine what it must have been like to be 65-year-old Bernie Ebbers or 21-year-old Barry Minkow, both sentenced to 25 years in prison for accounting fraud.

The CEO	The Fraud	Conviction/Plea	The Outcome
Elaine Martin, 67 **MarCon, Inc.**	Failed to record sales of used materials.	Convicted, February 2014	Sentenced to 7 years
Annette Bongiorno, 62, and **Joann Crupi,** 49 **Madoff Investment Securities**	Recorded trades of securities in the wrong accounting period as part of a Ponzi scheme.	Convicted, December 2014	Sentenced to 6 years each; forfeit a total of $188.9 billion
Bernard Madoff, 71 **Madoff Investment Securities**	Scammed $50 billion from investors in a Ponzi scheme (in which investors receive "returns" from money paid by subsequent investors).	Confessed, December 2008	Sentenced to 150 years
Bernie Ebbers, 65 **Worldcom**	Recorded $11 billion in operating expenses as if they were assets.	Convicted, July 2005	Sentenced to 25 years
Sanjay Kumar, 44 **Computer Associates**	Recorded sales in the wrong accounting period.	Pleaded guilty, April 2006	Sentenced to 12 years
Martin Grass, 49 **Rite Aid Corporation**	Recorded rebates from drug companies before they were earned.	Pleaded guilty, June 2003	Sentenced to 8 years
Barry Minkow, 21 **ZZZZ Best**	Made up customers and sales to show profits when, in reality, the company was a sham.	Convicted, December 1988	Sentenced to 25 years

Many others are affected by accounting fraud. Shareholders lose stock value, employees may lose their jobs (and pension funds, as in the case of **Enron**), and customers and suppliers may become wary of dealing with a company operating under the cloud of fraud. As a manager, you may face an ethical dilemma in the workplace. The ethical decision is the one you will be proud of 20 years later.

THE EXPANDED TRANSACTION ANALYSIS MODEL

We have discussed the variety of business activities affecting the income statement and how they are measured. Now we need to determine how these business activities are recorded in the accounting system and reflected in the financial statements. Chapter 2 covered investing and financing activities that affect assets, liabilities, and contributed capital. We now expand the transaction analysis model to include operating activities.

Transaction Analysis Rules

The complete transaction analysis model presented in Exhibit 3.4 includes **all five elements:** assets, liabilities, stockholders' equity, revenues, and expenses. Recall that the Retained Earnings account is the accumulation of all past revenues and expenses minus any income distributed to stockholders as dividends (that is, earnings not retained in the business).[3] When net income is positive, Retained Earnings increases; a net loss decreases Retained Earnings.

---

[3]Instead of reducing Retained Earnings directly when dividends are declared, companies may use the account Dividends Declared, which has a debit balance.

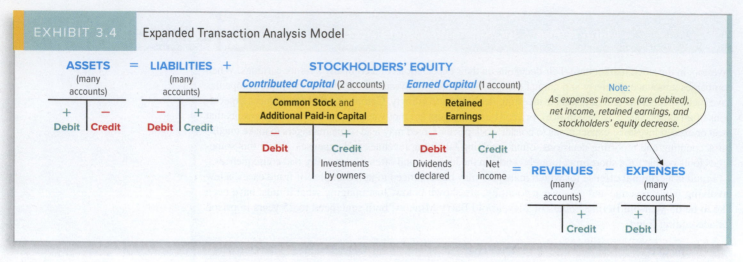

EXHIBIT 3.4   Expanded Transaction Analysis Model

Some students attempt to memorize journal entries in the introductory accounting course. However, they are often overwhelmed by the number and complexity of transactions as the course progresses. To avoid this pitfall, you should instead be able to construct the transaction analysis model in Exhibit 3.4 on your own without assistance and use it to analyze transactions. It will be very beneficial in completing assignments and analyzing more complex transactions in future chapters. Now let's study Exhibit 3.4 carefully to remember how the model is constructed and to understand the impact of operating activities on both the balance sheet and income statement:

- All accounts can increase or decrease, although revenues and expenses tend to increase throughout a period. For accounts on the left side of the accounting equation, the increase symbol + is written on the left side of the T-account. For accounts on the right side of the accounting equation, the increase symbol + is written on the right side of the T-account, **except for expenses, which increase on the left side of the T-account.**

- Debits (dr) are written on the left of each T-account and credits (cr) are written on the right.

- Every transaction affects at least two accounts.

- Revenues increase stockholders' equity through the account Retained Earnings and therefore have **credit** balances. Recording revenue results in either increasing an asset (such as Cash or Accounts Receivable) or decreasing a liability (such as Unearned Subscriptions Revenue).

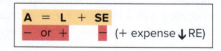

- Expenses decrease net income, thus decreasing Retained Earnings and stockholders' equity. Therefore, they have **debit** balances (opposite of the balance in Retained Earnings). That is, to increase an expense, you debit it, thereby decreasing net income and Retained Earnings. Recording an expense results in either decreasing an asset (such as Supplies when used) or increasing a liability (such as Wages Payable when money is owed to employees).

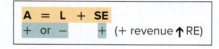

- When revenues exceed expenses, the company reports net income, increasing Retained Earnings and stockholders' equity. However, when expenses exceed revenues, a net loss results that decreases Retained Earnings and thus stockholders' equity.

In summary:

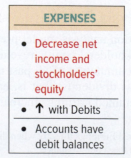

The steps to follow in analyzing transactions presented in Chapter 2 are now modified to determine the effects of earning revenues and incurring expenses. Now, as shown in Exhibit 3.5, when a transaction occurs, the questions to ask are:

Step 1: Ask → Was a revenue earned by delivering goods or services?
    If so, credit the revenue account and debit the appropriate accounts for what was received.

or Ask → Was an expense incurred to generate a revenue in the current period?
    If so, debit the expense account and credit the appropriate accounts for what was given.

or Ask → If no revenue was earned or expense incurred, what was received and given?

- **Identify the accounts affected by title** (e.g., Cash and Notes Payable).
    Remember: *Make sure that at least two accounts change.*
- **Classify them by type of account:** asset (A), liability (L), stockholders' equity (SE), revenue/gain (R), or expense/loss (E).
- **Determine the direction of the effect.** Did the account increase (+) or decrease (−)?

Step 2: Verify → Is the accounting equation in balance? (A = L + SE)

EXHIBIT 3.5

Transaction Analysis Steps

Analyzing Chipotle's Transactions

Now we continue operating activities for **Chipotle Mexican Grill**, building on the company's trial balance presented in Exhibit 3.6 (and at the end of Chapter 2). It included only investing and financing transactions occurring during the first quarter of 2015.

EXHIBIT 3.6

Chipotle Mexican Grill's Trial Balance

CHIPOTLE MEXICAN GRILL		
Trial Balance		
(based on investing and financing transactions during the first quarter ended March 31, 2015)		
(in thousands)	**Debit**	**Credit**
Cash	323,200	
Short-term investments	347,600	
Accounts receivable	34,800	
Supplies	15,300	
Prepaid expenses	70,300	
Land	21,100	
Buildings	1,275,300	
Equipment	476,300	
Accumulated depreciation		613,700
Long-term investments	531,100	
Intangible assets	68,400	
Accounts payable		69,600
Unearned revenue		16,800
Dividends payable		3,000
Wages payable		73,900
Utilities payable		85,400
Short-term notes payable		0
Long-term notes payable		2,000
Other liabilities		285,900
Common stock		500
Additional paid-in capital		293,800
Retained earnings		1,718,800
Total	**3,163,400**	**3,163,400**

Using the transaction analysis steps in Exhibit 3.5, we now analyze, record, and post to the T-accounts the effects of this chapter's operating activities that also occurred during the first quarter. The T-accounts begin with the **trial balance amounts** in Exhibit 3.6. All amounts are in thousands of dollars, except per share information. You should notice, in each journal entry, that

- When a revenue or expense is recorded, we insert (+R, +SE) for revenues and (+E, −SE) for expenses to emphasize the effect of the transaction on the accounting equation and to help you see that the equation remains in balance.
- Debits equal credits—another check you should make when preparing journal entries.

In Chapter 4, we complete the accounting cycle with the activities at the end of the quarter (on March 31).

(1) **Chipotle purchased food, beverage, and packaging supplies costing $369,800, paying $289,800 in cash and owing the rest on account.**

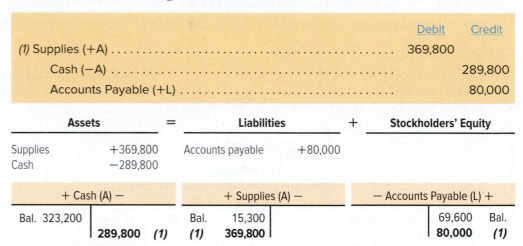

(2) **At the beginning of January, Chipotle paid $79,700 cash in advance for prepaid expenses for rent, insurance, and advertising.**

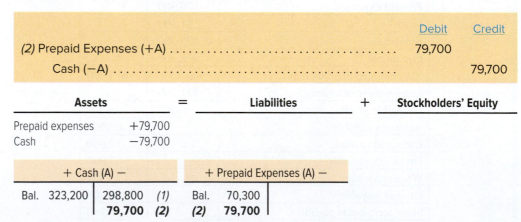

(3) **During the first quarter, Chipotle sold food to customers for $1,071,700; $25,700 was sold to universities on account (to be paid by the universities next quarter) and the rest was received in cash in the stores. NOTE:** To measure revenues and expenses in a period, these accounts begin with a $0 balance; notice they are not listed on the trial balance in Exhibit 3.6 because they have no balance yet.

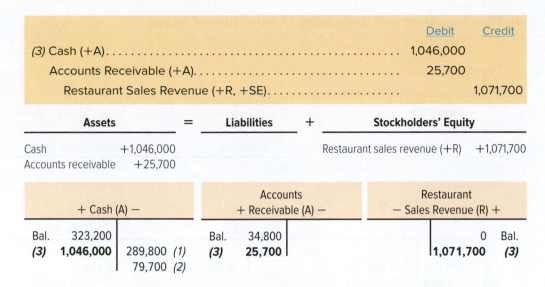

	Debit	Credit
(3) Cash (+A)...	1,046,000	
Accounts Receivable (+A)................................	25,700	
Restaurant Sales Revenue (+R, +SE).......................		1,071,700

Assets	=	Liabilities	+	Stockholders' Equity
Cash +1,046,000				Restaurant sales revenue (+R) +1,071,700
Accounts receivable +25,700				

+ Cash (A) −		Accounts + Receivable (A) −		Restaurant − Sales Revenue (R) +	
Bal. 323,200		Bal. 34,800		0 Bal.	
(3) **1,046,000**	289,800 *(1)*	*(3)* **25,700**		1,071,700 *(3)*	
	79,700 *(2)*				

(4) **Chipotle paid $40,800 for management training expenses.**

	Debit	Credit
(4) Training Expense (+E, −SE).............................	40,800	
Cash (−A)...		40,800

Assets	=	Liabilities	+	Stockholders' Equity
Cash −40,800				Training expense (+E) −40,800

+ Cash (A) −		+ Training Expense (E) −	
Bal. 323,200		Bal. 0	
(3) 1,046,000	289,800 *(1)*	*(4)* **40,800**	
	79,700 *(2)*		
	40,800 *(4)*		

(5) **Chipotle paid employees $177,000 for work this quarter and $73,900 for work last quarter** (recorded last quarter as Wages Expense and Wages Payable).

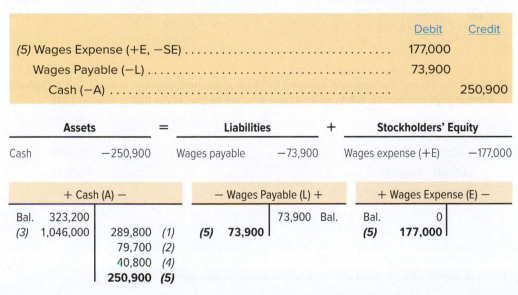

	Debit	Credit
(5) Wages Expense (+E, −SE).................................	177,000	
Wages Payable (−L).....................................	73,900	
Cash (−A)...		250,900

Assets	=	Liabilities	+	Stockholders' Equity
Cash −250,900		Wages payable −73,900		Wages expense (+E) −177,000

+ Cash (A) −		− Wages Payable (L) +		+ Wages Expense (E) −	
Bal. 323,200			73,900 Bal.	Bal. 0	
(3) 1,046,000	289,800 *(1)*	*(5)* **73,900**		*(5)* **177,000**	
	79,700 *(2)*				
	40,800 *(4)*				
	250,900 *(5)*				

(6) **Chipotle sold for cash land costing $9,000 at a loss of $4,200.**[4]

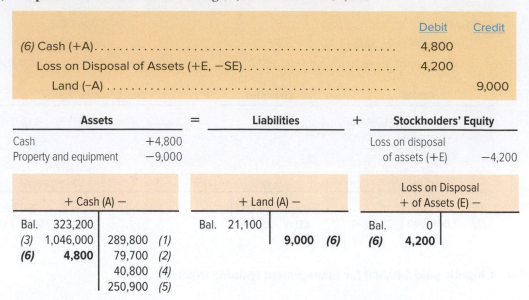

	Debit	Credit
(6) Cash (+A)...	4,800	
Loss on Disposal of Assets (+E, −SE)......................	4,200	
Land (−A)...		9,000

Assets		=	Liabilities	+	Stockholders' Equity	
Cash	+4,800				Loss on disposal	
Property and equipment	−9,000				of assets (+E)	−4,200

+ Cash (A) −			+ Land (A) −		Loss on Disposal + of Assets (E) −	
Bal. 323,200			Bal. 21,100		Bal. 0	
(3) 1,046,000	289,800 *(1)*			9,000 *(6)*	*(6)* 4,200	
(6) **4,800**	79,700 *(2)*					
	40,800 *(4)*					
	250,900 *(5)*					

(7) **Chipotle received $39,000 cash from customers paying on their accounts.**

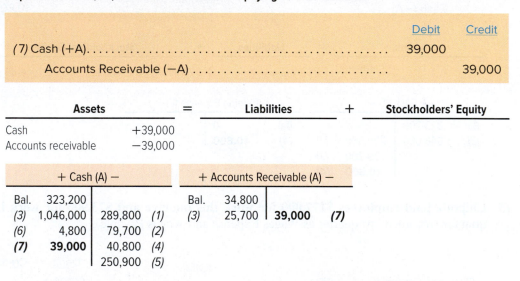

	Debit	Credit
(7) Cash (+A)..	39,000	
Accounts Receivable (−A)..................................		39,000

Assets		=	Liabilities	+	Stockholders' Equity
Cash	+39,000				
Accounts receivable	−39,000				

+ Cash (A) −			+ Accounts Receivable (A) −		
Bal. 323,200			Bal. 34,800		
(3) 1,046,000	289,800 *(1)*		*(3)* 25,700	39,000 *(7)*	
(6) 4,800	79,700 *(2)*				
(7) **39,000**	40,800 *(4)*				
	250,900 *(5)*				

(8) **During the quarter, Chipotle paid suppliers $73,500 on accounts payable. It also paid $35,900 on utilities payable and $28,400 in income taxes incurred for part of the first quarter of 2015.**

	Debit	Credit
(8) Accounts Payable (−L).....................................	73,500	
Utilities Payable (−L).....................................	35,900	
Income Tax Expense (+E, −L)...............................	28,400	
Cash (−A)...		137,800

---

[4]This is an example of a peripheral activity; it will be covered in more depth in Chapter 8.

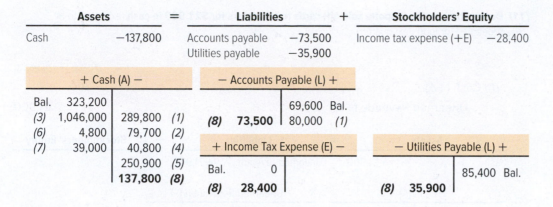

Assets	=	Liabilities	+	Stockholders' Equity
Cash −137,800		Accounts payable −73,500 Utilities payable −35,900		Income tax expense (+E) −28,400

	+ Cash (A) −		
Bal.	323,200		
(3)	1,046,000	289,800	(1)
(6)	4,800	79,700	(2)
(7)	39,000	40,800	(4)
		250,900	(5)
		137,800	**(8)**

− Accounts Payable (L) +		
	69,600	Bal.
(8) 73,500	80,000	(1)

+ Income Tax Expense (E) −	
Bal. 0	
(8) 28,400	

− Utilities Payable (L) +		
	85,400	Bal.
(8) 35,900		

(9) Chipotle paid $75,400 for utilities used during the quarter and paid $18,700 for repairs and maintenance of its facilities and equipment during the quarter.

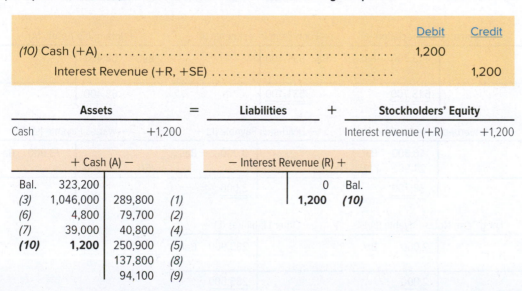

		Debit	Credit
(9) Utilities Expense (+E, −SE).		75,400	
Repairs Expense (+E, −SE).		18,700	
Cash (−A)			94,100

Assets	=	Liabilities	+	Stockholders' Equity
Cash −94,100				Utilities expense (+E) −75,400 Repairs expense (+E) −18,700

	+ Cash (A) −		
Bal.	323,200		
(3)	1,046,000	289,800	(1)
(6)	4,800	79,700	(2)
(7)	39,000	40,800	(4)
		250,900	(5)
		137,800	(8)
		94,100	**(9)**

+ Utilities Expense (E) −	
Bal. 0	
(9) 75,400	

+ Repairs Expense (E) −	
Bal. 0	
(9) 18,700	

(10) Chipotle received $1,200 cash as interest revenue earned during the quarter.

		Debit	Credit
(10) Cash (+A).		1,200	
Interest Revenue (+R, +SE)			1,200

Assets	=	Liabilities	+	Stockholders' Equity
Cash +1,200				Interest revenue (+R) +1,200

	+ Cash (A) −		
Bal.	323,200		
(3)	1,046,000	289,800	(1)
(6)	4,800	79,700	(2)
(7)	39,000	40,800	(4)
(10)	**1,200**	250,900	(5)
		137,800	(8)
		94,100	(9)

− Interest Revenue (R) +		
	0	Bal.
	1,200	**(10)**

(11) During the quarter, Chipotle sold gift cards to customers for $21,900 in cash (expected to be redeemed for food next quarter).

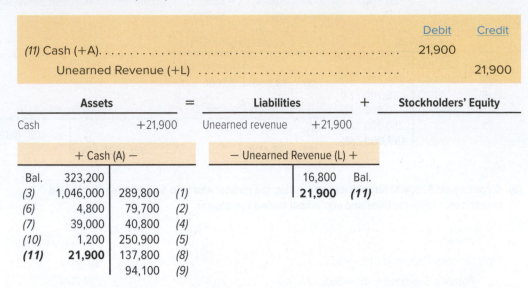

	Debit	Credit
(11) Cash (+A)...	21,900	
Unearned Revenue (+L)		21,900

Assets	=	Liabilities	+	Stockholders' Equity
Cash +21,900		Unearned revenue +21,900		

+ Cash (A) −				− Unearned Revenue (L) +	
Bal.	323,200			16,800	Bal.
(3)	1,046,000	289,800	(1)	**21,900**	**(11)**
(6)	4,800	79,700	(2)		
(7)	39,000	40,800	(4)		
(10)	1,200	250,900	(5)		
(11)	**21,900**	137,800	(8)		
		94,100	(9)		

Now we determine the balances in the T-accounts that changed.

Balance Sheet Accounts:

+ Cash (A) −			
Bal.	323,200		
(3)	1,046,000	289,800	(1)
(6)	4,800	79,700	(2)
(7)	39,000	40,800	(4)
(10)	1,200	250,900	(5)
(11)	21,900	137,800	(8)
		94,100	(9)
	543,000		

+ Short-Term Investments (A) −	
Bal. 347,600	
347,600	

+ Accounts Receivable (A) −			
Bal.	34,800		
(3)	25,700	39,000	(7)
	21,500		

+ Supplies (A) −		
Bal.	15,300	
(1)	369,800	
	385,100	

Prepaid + Expenses (A) −		
Bal.	70,300	
(2)	79,700	
	150,000	

+ Land (A) −			
Bal.	21,100		
		9,000	(6)
	12,100		

+ Buildings (A) −	
Bal. 1,275,300	
1,275,300	

+ Equipment (A) −	
Bal. 476,300	
476,300	

− Accumulated Depreciation +	
	613,700 Bal.
	613,700

+ Long-Term Investments (A) −	
Bal. 531,100	
531,100	

+ Intangible Assets (A) −	
Bal. 68,400	
68,400	

− Accounts Payable (L) +			
		69,600	Bal.
(8)	73,500	80,000	(1)
		76,100	

− Unearned Revenue (L) +	
	16,800 Bal.
	21,900 (11)
	38,700

− Dividends Payable (L) +	
	3,000 Bal.
	3,000

− Wages Payable (L) +		
		73,900 Bal.
(5)	73,900	
		0

− Utilities Payable (L) +		
		85,400 Bal.
(8)	35,900	
		49,500

− Long-Term Notes Payable (L) +	
	2,000 Bal.
	2,000

− Other Liabilities (L) +	
	285,900 Bal.
	285,900

− Common Stock (SE) +		− Additional Paid-in Capital (SE) +		− Retained Earnings (SE) +	
	500 Bal.		293,800 Bal.		1,718,800 Bal.
	500		293,800		1,718,800

Income Statement Accounts:

− Restaurant Sales Revenue (R) +		− Interest Revenue (R) +	
	0 Bal.		0 Bal.
	1,071,700 (3)		1,200 (10)
	1,071,700		1,200

+ Wages Expense (E) −		+ Utilities Expense (E) −		+ Repairs Expense (E) −		+ Training Expense (E) −	
Bal. 0		Bal. 0		Bal. 0		Bal. 0	
(5) 177,000		(9) 75,400		(9) 18,700		(4) 40,800	
177,000		75,400		18,700		40,800	

+ Loss on Disposal of Assets (E) −		+ Income Tax Expense (E) −	
Bal. 0		Bal. 0	
(6) 4,200		(8) 28,400	
4,200		28,400	

PAUSE FOR **FEEDBACK**   STOP

We just illustrated the steps in analyzing and recording transactions, including those involving earning revenue and incurring expenses.

Transaction Analysis Steps:

Step 1: **Ask →** **Was a revenue earned by delivering goods or services?**
  If so, credit the revenue account and debit the appropriate accounts for what was received.

or **Ask →** **Was an expense incurred to generate a revenue in the current period?**
  If so, debit the expense account and credit the appropriate accounts for what was given.

or **Ask →** **If no revenue was earned or expense incurred, what was received and given?**
  • **Identify the accounts affected by title** (e.g., Cash and Notes Payable).
    Remember: *Make sure that at least two accounts change.*
  • **Classify them by type of account:** asset (A), liability (L), stockholders' equity (SE), revenue/gain (R), or expense/loss (E).
  • **Determine the direction of the effect.** Did the account increase (+) or decrease (−)?
Step 2: Verify → **Is the accounting equation in balance?** (A = L + SE)

SELF-STUDY **QUIZ**

Now it's your turn. Analyze and record the journal entries for each of the selected **June** transactions for Florida Flippers, Inc., a scuba diving and instruction business. Then post the effects to the T-accounts. Account titles and beginning balances are provided in the T-accounts that follow. Be sure to check that debits equal credits in each journal entry and that the accounting equation remains in balance.

  a. In June, new customers paid Florida Flippers $8,200 in cash for diving trips; $5,200 was for trips made in June, and the rest is for trips that will be provided in July.
  b. In June, customers paid $3,900 in cash for instruction they received in May.
  c. At the beginning of June, Florida Flippers paid a total of $6,000 cash for insurance to cover the months of June, July, and August.

d. In June, Florida Flippers paid $4,000 in wages to employees who worked in June.

	ACCOUNT TITLES	DEBIT	CREDIT
a.			
b.			
c.			
d.			

+ Cash (A) −			+ Accounts Receivable (A) −			+ Prepaid Insurance (A) −	
Beg. 25,000			Beg. 4,500			Beg. 0	
End.			End.			End.	

− Unearned Revenue (L) +		− Diving Trip Revenue (R) +		+ Wages Expense (E) −	
	0 Beg.		0 Beg.	Beg. 0	
	End.		End.	End.	

After you have completed your answers, check them below.

Solutions to SELF-STUDY QUIZ

	Account Titles	Debit	Credit
a.	Cash (+A)	8,200	
	Diving Trip Revenue (+R, +SE)		5,200
	Unearned Revenue (+L)		3,000
b.	Cash (+A)	3,900	
	Accounts Receivable (−A)		3,900
c.	Prepaid Insurance (+A)	6,000	
	Cash (−A)		6,000
d.	Wages Expense (+E, −SE)	4,000	
	Cash (−A)		4,000

+ Cash (A) −				+ Accounts Receivable (A) −			+ Prepaid Insurance (A) −	
Beg.	25,000			Beg. 4,500			Beg. 0	
(*a*)	8,200	6,000	(*c*)		3,900 (*b*)		(*c*) 6,000	
(*b*)	3,900	4,000	(*d*)					
End.	27,100			End. 600			End. 6,000	

− Unearned Revenue (L) +		− Diving Trip Revenue (R) +		+ Wages Expense (E) −	
	0 Beg.		0 Beg.	Beg. 0	
	3,000 (*a*)		5,200 (*a*)	(*d*) 4,000	
	3,000 End.		5,200 End.	End. 4,000	

GUIDED HELP 3-2

For additional step-by-step video instruction on analyzing, recording, and posting transaction effects, go to **www.mhhe.com/libby9e_gh3b**.

HOW IS THE INCOME STATEMENT PREPARED AND ANALYZED?

As we discussed in Chapter 2, companies can prepare financial statements at any point in time. Before we consider creating any statements for **Chipotle**, however, we must first determine that the debits equal credits after all of the transactions illustrated above by generating a trial balance. Accounts are listed in financial statement order: assets, liabilities, stockholders' equity, revenues/gains, and expenses/losses.

LEARNING OBJECTIVE 3-5
Prepare a classified income statement.

CHIPOTLE MEXICAN GRILL Unadjusted Trial Balance For the first quarter ended March 31, 2015		
(in thousands)	Debit	Credit
Cash	543,000	
Short-term investments	347,600	
Accounts receivable	21,500	
Supplies	385,100	
Prepaid expenses	150,000	
Land	12,100	
Buildings	1,275,300	
Equipment	476,300	
Accumulated depreciation		613,700
Long-term investments	531,100	
Intangible assets	68,400	
Accounts payable		76,100
Unearned revenue		38,700
Dividends payable		3,000
Wages payable		0
Utilities payable		49,500
Long-term notes payable		2,000
Other liabilities		285,900
Common stock		500
Additional paid-in capital		293,800
Retained earnings		1,718,800
Restaurant sales revenue		1,071,700
Interest revenue		1,200
Wages expense	177,000	
Utilities expense	75,400	
Repairs expense	18,700	
Training expense	40,800	
Loss on disposal of assets	4,200	
Income tax expense	28,400	
Total	**4,154,900**	**4,154,900**

Although debits do equal credits, why is the trial balance labeled "unadjusted"? Does it make sense that supplies were purchased during the quarter, but no Supplies Expense was recorded to show the amount of supplies used? How likely is it that gift cards were sold, but none were redeemed by customers during the quarter? And didn't Chipotle use property and equipment during the quarter to generate revenues? The answer to all of these questions is that **no end-of-period adjustments have been made yet** to reflect all revenues earned and expenses incurred during the quarter. Therefore, the trial balance is **unadjusted** until adjustments are made, as we discuss in Chapter 4.

CLASSIFIED INCOME STATEMENT

The following classified income statement (that is, it is categorized into operating activities and peripheral activities) is presented to highlight the structure **but note that, because it is based on unadjusted balances, it would not be presented to external users.**

CHIPOTLE MEXICAN GRILL, INC.
Consolidated Statement of Income
UNADJUSTED
For the Quarter ended March 31, 2015
(in thousands of dollars)

Restaurant sales revenue	$1,071,700
Restaurant operating expenses:	
Wages expense	177,000
Utilities expense	75,400
Repairs expense	18,700
General and administrative expenses:	
Training expense	40,800
Loss on disposal of assets	4,200
Total operating expenses	316,100
Income from operations	755,600
Other items:	
Interest revenue	1,200
Income before income taxes	756,800
Income tax expense	28,400
Net income	$ 728,400

When comparing this statement with **Chipotle**'s 2014 income statement in Exhibit 3.1, we notice that the income from operations for the first quarter ($755,600) exceeds all income from operations for 2014 ($710,800). Since a more representative amount for one quarter would be about 25 percent, obviously, numerous adjustments are necessary to revenues and expenses, such as the use of food, packaging, and beverage supplies to generate revenue during the quarter and renting facilities for the quarter. We would not want to use the information for analysis until it has been adjusted. Instead, we use the 2014 income statement in Exhibit 3.1 to determine how effective Chipotle's management is at generating profit.

KEY RATIO ANALYSIS	Net Profit Margin

 ANALYTICAL QUESTION

How effective is management in generating profit on every dollar of sales?

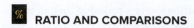 **RATIO AND COMPARISONS**

$$\text{Net Profit Margin} = \frac{\text{Net Income}}{\text{Net Sales (or Operating Revenues)*}}$$

*Net sales is sales revenue less any returns from customers and other reductions. For companies in the service industry, total operating revenues is equivalent to net sales.

The 2014 ratio for **Chipotle** using reported amounts (from Exhibit 3.1) is (dollars in thousands):

$$\frac{\$445,300}{\$4,108,300} = 0.1084 \text{ or } 10.84\%$$

COMPARISONS OVER TIME Chipotle Mexican Grill, Inc.			COMPARISONS WITH COMPETITORS	
			Panera Bread, Inc.	Fiesta Restaurant Group, Inc.
2014	**2013**	**2012**	**2014**	**2014**
0.1084	0.1019	0.1018	0.0709	0.0592

Selected Focus Companies' Net Profit Margin Ratios for 2014

Apple	21.6%
Harley-Davidson	13.6%
Southwest Airlines	6.1%

INTERPRETATIONS

In General   Net profit margin measures how much of every sales dollar generated during the period is profit. A rising net profit margin signals more efficient management of sales and expenses. Differences among industries result from the nature of the products or services provided and the intensity of competition. Differences among competitors in the same industry reflect how each company responds to changes in competition (and demand for the product or service) and changes in managing sales volume, sales price, and costs. Financial analysts expect well-run businesses to maintain or improve their net profit margin over time.

Focus Company Analysis   Chipotle's net profit margin increased over the three-year period of 2012 to 2014. As indicated by management in the annual report, revenue increases were due primarily to an increase in customer visits and a menu price increase, as well as opening new restaurants each year. Food costs continued to increase as well, primarily costs related to beef, avocados, and dairy. Acquiring "Food with Integrity" (naturally raised, free of preservatives and growth hormones) is challenging and costlier than using traditional food products and sources. On the other hand, labor and occupancy costs (including utilities, repairs, and rent) grew at a lower rate than sales due to higher average sales per restaurant. Chipotle's management did a better job of generating revenues and controlling labor and occupancy costs in 2014.

Panera Bread and **Fiesta Restaurant Group** each had a lower net profit margin than Chipotle. Chipotle's is nearly 53 percent higher than Panera Bread's. This suggests that Chipotle has greater effectiveness in generating sales, mostly by a high growth in establishing nearly 200 new restaurants and higher menu prices, while controlling costs. Panera Bread, on the other hand, experienced labor and occupancy costs in 2014 that grew at a higher rate than operating revenues, despite opening new restaurants and selling additional franchises. Fiesta Restaurant Group is much smaller in size, which suggests lower economies of scale. In 2014, the Group experienced, as a percentage of operating revenues, lower food and labor costs that were offset by higher repairs and insurance costs. Differences in business strategies and size explain some of the wide variation in the ratio analysis.

A Few Cautions   The decisions that management makes to maintain the company's net profit margin in the current period may have negative long-run implications. Analysts should perform additional analysis of the ratio to identify trends in each component of revenues and expenses. This involves dividing each line on the income statement by net sales. Statements presented with these percentages are called **common-sized income statements.** Changes in the percentages of the individual components of net income provide information on shifts in management's strategies.

Operating Activities	FOCUS ON CASH FLOWS

In this chapter, we focus on cash flows from operating activities: **cash from** operating sources, primarily customers, and **cash to** suppliers and others involved in operations. The accounts most often associated with operating activities are current assets, such as Accounts Receivable, Inventories, and Prepaid Expenses, and current liabilities, such as Accounts Payable, Wages Payable, and Unearned Revenue.

As discussed in Chapter 2, companies report cash inflows and outflows over a period of time in their **statement of cash flows.** This statement is divided into three categories:

- **O** — Operating activities include those primarily with customers and suppliers, and interest payments and earnings on investments.
- **I** — Investing activities include buying and selling noncurrent assets and investments.
- **F** — Financing activities include borrowing and repaying debt, including short-term bank loans; issuing and repurchasing stock; and paying dividends.

Only transactions affecting cash are reported on the statement. An important step in constructing and analyzing the statement of cash flows is identifying the various transactions as operating, investing, or financing. Let's analyze the Cash T-account for **Chipotle**'s transactions in this chapter, adding to transactions *(a)*—*(f)* from Chapter 2. Refer to transactions *(1)*—*(11)* illustrated earlier in the chapter, and remember, **if you see Cash in a transaction, it will be reflected on the statement of cash flows.**

			+ Cash (A) −				
		1/1/15	419,500				
From investors	**+F**	*(a)*	3,700	53,400	*(c)*	**−I**	**For purchases of noncurrent assets**
From bank	**+F**	*(b)*	2,000	4,600	*(d)*	**−F**	**For debt payment to banks**
				44,000	*(e)*	**−I**	**For investment in other companies**
From customers	**+O**	*(3)*	1,046,000	289,800	*(1)*	**−O**	**For supplies**
From asset disposal	**+I**	*(6)*	4,800	79,700	*(2)*	**−O**	**For prepaid assets**
From customers	**+O**	*(7)*	39,000	40,800	*(4)*	**−O**	**For training**
From investments	**+O**	*(10)*	1,200	250,900	*(5)*	**−O**	**To employees**
From customers	**+O**	*(11)*	21,900	137,800	*(8)*	**−O**	**To suppliers and for taxes**
				94,100	*(9)*	**−O**	**For utilities and maintenance**
			543,000				

PAUSE FOR **FEEDBACK**

As we discussed, every transaction affecting cash can be classified either as an operating, investing, or financing effect.

Operating effects relate to receipts of cash from customers, payments to suppliers (employees, utilities, and other suppliers of goods and services for operating the business), and any interest paid or investment income received.

Investing effects relate to purchasing/selling investments or property and equipment or lending funds to/receiving repayment from others.

Financing effects relate to borrowing or repaying banks, issuing stock to investors, repurchasing stock from investors, or paying dividends to investors.

SELF-STUDY **QUIZ**

Mattel, Inc., designs, manufactures, and markets a broad variety of toys (e.g., Barbie, Hot Wheels, Fisher-Price brands, and American Girl dolls) worldwide. Indicate whether these transactions from a recent statement of cash flows were operating (O), investing (I), or financing (F) activities and the direction of their effects on cash (+ for increases in cash; − for decreases in cash):

TRANSACTIONS	TYPE OF ACTIVITY (O, I, OR F)	EFFECT ON CASH FLOWS (+ OR −)
1. Purchases of property, plant, and equipment		
2. Receipts from customers		
3. Payments of dividends		
4. Payments to employees		
5. Receipts of investment income		

After you have completed your answers, check them below.

DEMONSTRATION   CASE

This case is a continuation of the Terrific Lawn Maintenance Corporation case introduced in Chapter 2. In that chapter, the company was established and supplies, property, and equipment were purchased. Terrific Lawn is now ready for business. The balance sheet at April 7, 2016, based on the first week of investing and financing activities (from Chapter 2) is as follows:

TERRIFIC LAWN MAINTENANCE CORPORATION
Balance Sheet
April 7, 2016

Assets	
Current Assets:	
Cash	$ 3,800
Notes receivable	1,250
Total current assets	5,050
Equipment	4,600
Land	3,750
Total assets	**$13,400**
Liabilities and Stockholders' Equity	
Current Liabilities:	
Short-term notes payable	$ 400
Total current liabilities	400
Long-term notes payable	4,000
Total liabilities	4,400
Stockholders' Equity:	
Common stock ($0.10 par)	150
Additional paid-in capital	8,850
Total stockholders' equity	9,000
Total liabilities and stockholders' equity	**$13,400**

1. I −   2. O +   3. F −   4. O −   5. O +

The additional following activities occurred during the rest of April 2016:

a. Purchased and used during April gasoline for mowers and edgers, paying $90 in cash at a local gas station.

b. In early April, received from the city $1,600 cash in advance for lawn maintenance service for April through July ($400 each month). (Record the entire amount as Unearned Revenue.)

c. In early April, purchased $300 of insurance covering six months, April through September. (Record the entire payment as Prepaid Expenses.)

d. Mowed lawns for residential customers who are billed every two weeks. A total of $5,200 of service was billed in April.

e. Residential customers paid $3,500 on their accounts.

f. Paid wages every two weeks. Total cash paid in April was $3,900.

g. Received a bill for $320 from the local gas station for additional gasoline purchased on account and used in April. The bill will be paid in May.

h. Paid $700 principal and $40 interest on notes owed to XYZ Lawn Supply.

i. Paid $100 on accounts payable.

j. Collected $1,250 principal and $12 interest on the note owed by the city to Terrific Lawn Maintenance Corporation.

Required:

1. a. On a separate sheet of paper, set up T-accounts for Cash, Accounts Receivable, Notes Receivable, Prepaid Expenses, Equipment, Land, Accounts Payable, Short-Term Notes Payable, Long-Term Notes Payable, Unearned Revenue (same as deferred revenue), Common Stock, Additional Paid-in Capital, Retained Earnings, Mowing Revenue, Interest Revenue, Wages Expense, Fuel Expense, and Interest Expense. Beginning balances for the balance sheet accounts should be taken from the preceding balance sheet. Beginning balances for operating accounts are $0. Indicate these balances on the T-accounts.

   b. Analyze each transaction, referring to the expanded transaction analysis model presented in this chapter.

   c. On a separate sheet of paper, prepare journal entries in chronological order and indicate their effects on the accounting model (Assets = Liabilities + Stockholders' Equity). Include the equality checks: (1) Debits = Credits and (2) the accounting equation is in balance.

   d. Enter the effects of each transaction in the appropriate T-accounts. Identify each amount with its letter in the preceding list of activities.

   e. Compute balances in each of the T-accounts.

2. On the Cash T-account, identify each transaction as O for operating activity, I for investing activity, or F for financing activity.

3. Use the amounts in the T-accounts to prepare an unadjusted classified income statement for Terrific Lawn Maintenance Corporation for the month ended April 30, 2016. (Adjustments to accounts will be presented in Chapter 4.)

Now check your answers with the following suggested solution.

SUGGESTED SOLUTION

1. *b*. and *c*. Transaction analysis and journal entries:

Journal Entries	Debits	Credits
(a) Fuel Expense (+E, −SE)	90	
Cash (−A)		90
(b) Cash (+A).	1,600	
Unearned Revenue (+L)		1,600
(c) Prepaid Expenses (+A)	300	
Cash (−A)		300
(d) Accounts Receivable (+A).	5,200	
Mowing Revenue (+R, +SE).		5,200
(e) Cash (+A).	3,500	
Accounts Receivable (−A)		3,500
(f) Wages Expense (+E, −SE).	3,900	
Cash (−A)		3,900
(g) Fuel Expense (+E, −SE)	320	
Accounts Payable (+L)		320
(h) Interest Expense (+E, −SE).	40	
Long-Term Notes Payable (−L).	700	
Cash (−A)		740
(i) Accounts Payable (−L)	100	
Cash (−A)		100
(j) Cash (+A)	1,262	
Notes Receivable (−A)		1,250
Interest Revenue (+R, +SE).		12

Assets	=	Liabilities	+	Stockholders' Equity	
−90				+E	−90
+1,600		+1,600			
+300					
−300					
+5,200				+R	+5,200
+3,500					
−3,500					
−3,900				+E	−3,900
		+320		+E	−320
−740		−700		+E	−40
−100		−100			
+1,262				+R	+12
−1,250					

Equality Checks

For each journal entry: Debits = Credits   For each transaction analysis: Equation balances

1. *a*., *d*., and *e*. T-Accounts:

Assets

+ Cash (A) −			
Beg.	3,800		
(b)	1,600	90	(a)
(e)	3,500	300	(c)
(j)	1,262	3,900	(f)
		740	(h)
		100	(i)
	5,032		

+ Accounts Receivable (A) −			
Beg.	0		
(d)	5,200	3,500	(e)
	1,700		

+ Notes Receivable (A) −			
Beg.	1,250		
		1,250	(j)
		0	

+ Prepaid Expenses (A) −		+ Equipment (A) −		+ Land (A) −	
Beg.	0	Beg.	4,600	Beg.	3,750
(c)	300				
	300		4,600		3,750

Liabilities

− Accounts Payable (L) +			− Short-Term Notes Payable (L) +			− Unearned Revenue (L) +		
		0 Beg.			400 Beg.			0 Beg.
(i)	100	320 (g)					1,600	(b)
		220			400			1,600

− Long-Term Notes Payable (L) +		
		4,000 Beg.
(h)	700	
		3,300

Stockholders' Equity

− Common Stock (SE) +		− Additional Paid-in Capital (SE) +		− Retained Earnings (SE) +	
	150 Beg.		8,850 Beg.		0 Beg.
	150		8,850		0

Revenues

− Mowing Revenue (R) +		− Interest Revenue (R) +	
	0 Beg.		0 Beg.
	5,200 (d)		12 (j)
	5,200		12

Expenses

+ Wages Expense (E) −		+ Fuel Expense (E) −		+ Interest Expense (E) −	
Beg.	0	Beg.	0	Beg.	0
(f)	3,900	(a)	90	(h)	40
	3,900	(g)	320		40
			410		

2. Cash flow activities identified (O = operating, I = investing, and F = financing):

		+ Cash (A) −				
		Beg.	3,800			
From customers	**+O**	(b)	1,600	90	(a)	**−O** For fuel
From customers	**+O**	(e)	3,500	300	(c)	**−O** For insurance
$12 for interest **+O**; $1,250 for principal	**+I**	(j)	1,262	3,900	(f)	**−O** To employees
				740	(h)	**−O** $40 for interest; **−F** $700 for principal
				100	(i)	**−O** To suppliers
			5,032			

3. Income Statement:

TERRIFIC LAWN MAINTENANCE CORPORATION
Unadjusted Income Statement
For the Month Ended April 30, 2014

Mowing revenue	$5,200
Operating expenses:	
Wages expense	3,900
Fuel expense	410
Total operating expenses	4,310
Income from operations	890
Other items:	
Interest revenue	12
Interest expense	(40)
Income before taxes	862
Income tax expense	0
Net income	$ 862

To be computed and recorded after adjustments are made to revenue and expense accounts (Chapter 4)

CHAPTER **TAKE-AWAYS**

3-1. Describe a typical business operating cycle and explain the necessity for the time period assumption.   p. 104

- The operating cycle, or cash-to-cash cycle, is the time needed to purchase goods or services from suppliers, sell the goods or services to customers, and collect cash from customers.

- Time period assumption—to measure and report financial information periodically, we assume the long life of a company can be cut into shorter periods.

3-2. Explain how business activities affect the elements of the income statement.   p. 106

- Elements of the income statement:
  a. Revenues—increases in assets or settlements of liabilities from major or central ongoing operations.
  b. Expenses—decreases in assets or increases in liabilities from major or central ongoing operations.
  c. Gains—increases in assets or settlements of liabilities from peripheral activities.
  d. Losses—decreases in assets or increases in liabilities from peripheral activities.

3-3. Explain the accrual basis of accounting and apply the revenue and expense recognition principles to measure income.   p. 110

In accrual basis accounting, revenues are recognized when earned and expenses are recognized when incurred.

- Revenue recognition principle—recognize revenues (1) when the company transfers promised goods or services to customers (2) in the amount it expects to receive.

- Expense recognition principle (matching)—recognize expenses when they are incurred in generating revenue (a matching of costs with benefits).

3-4. Apply transaction analysis to examine and record the effects of operating activities on the financial statements.   p. 115

The expanded transaction analysis model includes revenues and expenses:

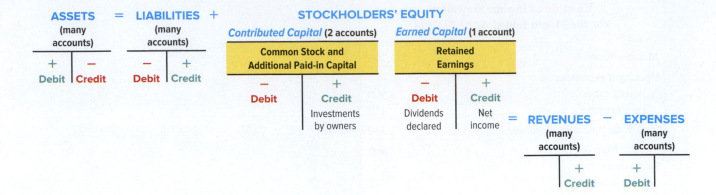

3-5. Prepare a classified income statement.   p. 125

Until the accounts have been updated to include all revenues earned and expenses incurred in the period (due to a difference in the time when cash is received or paid), the financial statements are unadjusted:

- Classified income statement—net income is needed to determine ending Retained Earnings; classifications include Operating Revenues, Operating Expenses (to determine Operating Income), Other Items (to determine Pretax Income), Income Tax Expense, Net Income (or Net Loss), and Earnings per Share.

3-6. Compute and interpret the net profit margin ratio.   p. 127

The net profit margin ratio (Net Income [or Net Loss] ÷ Net Sales [or Operating Revenues]) measures the profit generated per dollar of sales (operating revenues). The higher the ratio, the more effective the company is at generating revenues and/or controlling costs.

In this chapter, we discussed the operating cycle and accounting concepts relevant to income determination: the time period assumption, definitions of the income statement elements (revenues, expenses, gains, and losses), the revenue recognition principle, and the expense recognition principle. The accounting principles are defined in accordance with the accrual basis of accounting, which requires revenues to be recorded when earned and expenses to be recorded when incurred in the process of generating revenues. We expanded the transaction analysis model introduced in Chapter 2 by adding revenues and expenses and prepared an unadjusted classified income statement. In Chapter 4, we discuss the activities that occur at the end of the accounting period: the adjustment process, the preparation of adjusted financial statements, and the closing process.

KEY RATIO

Net profit margin ratio measures the profit generated per dollar of sales (operating revenues). A high ratio suggests that a company is generating revenues and/or controlling expenses effectively. The ratio is computed as follows (see the "Key Ratio Analysis" box in the Classified Income Statement section):

$$\text{Net Profit Margin Ratio} = \frac{\text{Net Income}}{\text{Net Sales (or Operating Revenues)}}$$

FINDING **FINANCIAL INFORMATION**

Balance Sheet

Current Assets
  Cash
  Short-term investments
  Accounts and notes receivable
  Inventory (goods to be sold)
  Supplies
  Prepaid expenses

Noncurrent Assets
  Long-term investments
  Land
  Buildings
  Equipment
  (Accumulated depreciation)
  Intangible assets

Current Liabilities
  Accounts payable
  Short-term notes payable
  Accrued expenses payable
  (e.g., wages, taxes)
  Unearned revenue

Noncurrent Liabilities
  Long-term notes payable
  Long-term debt

Stockholders' Equity
  Common stock
  Additional paid-in capital
  Retained earnings

Income Statement

Revenues (operating)
  Sales (from various operating activities)

Expenses (operating)
  Cost of goods sold (used inventory)
  Rent, wages, depreciation, insurance, etc.
  Losses (gains) on disposal of assets

Operating Income
Other Items
  Interest expense
  Interest revenue
  Losses (gains) on sale of investments

Pretax Income
  Income tax expense

Net Income
Earnings per Share

Statement of Cash Flows

Operating Activities
  + Cash from customers
  + Cash from interest and dividends
  – Cash to suppliers
  – Cash to employees
  – Interest paid
  – Income taxes paid

Notes

Under Summary of Significant Accounting Policies
  Description of the company's revenue recognition policy.

KEY **TERMS**

Accrual Basis Accounting   p. 110
Cash Basis Accounting   p. 109
Expense Recognition Principle
  (or Matching Principle)   p. 113
Expenses   p. 107

Gains   p. 108
Losses   p. 108
Operating (Cash-to-Cash) Cycle   p. 105
Operating Income (Income from
  Operations)   p. 108

Revenue Recognition Principle   p. 110
Revenues   p. 106
Time Period Assumption   p. 105

QUESTIONS

1. Describe a typical business operating cycle.
2. Explain what the time period assumption means.
3. Write the income statement equation and define each element.
4. Explain the difference between
   a. Revenues and gains.
   b. Expenses and losses.
5. Define **accrual accounting** and contrast it with cash basis accounting.
6. What criteria must normally be met for revenue to be recognized under accrual basis accounting?
7. Explain the expense recognition principle.
8. Explain why stockholders' equity is increased by revenues and decreased by expenses.

9. Explain why revenues are recorded as credits and expenses are recorded as debits.

10. Complete the following matrix by entering either **debit** or **credit** in each cell:

Item	Increase	Decrease
Revenues		
Losses		
Gains		
Expenses		

11. Complete the following matrix by entering either **increase** or **decrease** in each cell:

Item	Debit	Credit
Revenues		
Losses		
Gains		
Expenses		

12. Identify whether the following transactions affect cash flow from operating, investing, or financing activities, and indicate the effect of each on cash (+ for increase and − for decrease). If there is no cash flow effect, write "None."

Transaction	Operating, Investing, or Financing Effect on Cash	Direction of the Effect on Cash
Cash paid to suppliers		
Sale of goods on account		
Cash received from customers		
Purchase of investments		
Cash paid for interest		
Issuance of stock for cash		

13. State the equation for the net profit margin ratio and explain how it is interpreted.

MULTIPLE-CHOICE QUESTIONS

1. Which of the following is **not** a specific account in a company's chart of accounts?
   a. Gain on Sale of Assets
   b. Interest Revenue
   c. Net Income
   d. Unearned Revenue

2. Which of the following is **not** one of the criteria that normally must be met for revenue to be recognized according to the revenue recognition principle for accrual basis accounting?
   a. Cash has been collected.
   b. Services have been performed.
   c. Goods have been transferred.
   d. The amount the company expects to receive is determinable.

3. The expense recognition principle controls
   a. Where on the income statement expenses should be presented.
   b. When costs are recognized as expenses on the income statement.
   c. The ordering of current assets and current liabilities on the balance sheet.
   d. How costs are allocated between Cost of Sales (sometimes called Cost of Goods Sold) and general and administrative expenses.

4. When expenses exceed revenues in a given period,
    a. Retained earnings are not impacted.
    b. Retained earnings are decreased.
    c. Retained earnings are increased.
    d. One cannot determine the impact on retained earnings without additional information.

5. On January 1, 2017, Anson Company started the year with a $300,000 credit balance in Retained Earnings, a $50,000 balance in Common Stock, and a $300,000 balance in Additional Paid-in Capital. During 2017, the company earned net income of $45,000, declared a dividend of $15,000, and issued 900 additional shares of stock (par value of $1 per share) for $10,000. What is total stockholders' equity on December 31, 2017?
    a. $692,500.
    b. $695,000.
    c. $690,000.
    d. None of the above.

6. During 2016, CliffCo Inc. incurred operating expenses of $250,000, of which $150,000 was paid in cash; the balance will be paid in January 2017. Transaction analysis of operating expenses for 2016 should reflect only the following:
    a. Decrease stockholders' equity, $150,000; decrease assets, $150,000.
    b. Decrease assets, $250,000; decrease stockholders' equity, $250,000.
    c. Decrease stockholders' equity, $250,000; decrease assets, $150,000; increase liabilities, $100,000.
    d. Decrease assets, $250,000; increase liabilities, $100,000; decrease stockholders' equity, $150,000.
    e. None of the above is correct.

7. Which of the following is the entry to be recorded by a law firm when it receives a $2,000 retainer from a new client at the initial client meeting?
    a. Debit to Cash, $2,000; credit to Legal Fees Revenue, $2,000.
    b. Debit to Accounts Receivable, $2,000; credit to Legal Fees Revenue, $2,000.
    c. Debit to Unearned Revenue, $2,000; credit to Legal Fees Revenue, $2,000.
    d. Debit to Cash, $2,000; credit to Unearned Revenue, $2,000.
    e. Debit to Unearned Revenue, $2,000; credit to Cash, $2,000.

8. You have observed that the net profit margin ratio for a retail chain has increased steadily over the last three years. The **most** likely explanation is which of the following?
    a. Salaries for upper management as a percentage of total expenses have decreased over the last three years.
    b. A successful advertising campaign increased sales companywide, but with no increases in operating expenses.
    c. New stores were added throughout the last three years, and sales increased as a result of the additional new locations.
    d. The company began construction of a new, larger main office location three years ago that was put into use at the end of the second year.

9. Cash payments for salaries are reported in what section of the statement of cash flows?
    a. Operating.
    b. Investing.
    c. Financing.
    d. None of the above.

10. This period a company collects $100 cash on an account receivable from a customer for a sale last period. How would the receipt of cash impact the following two financial statements this period?

	Income Statement	Statement of Cash Flows
a.	Revenue + $100	Inflow from investing
b.	No impact	Inflow from operations
c.	Revenue − $100	Inflow from operations
d.	No impact	Inflow from financing

MINI-**EXERCISES**

M3-1
LO3-1, 3-2, 3-3

Matching Definitions with Terms

Match each definition with its related term by entering the appropriate letter in the space provided. There should be only one definition per term (that is, there are more definitions than terms).

Term	Definition
___ (1) Losses	A. Record revenues when earned and measurable (when the company transfers promised goods or services to customers, it should record the amount it expects to receive).
___ (2) Expense recognition principle	
___ (3) Revenues	
___ (4) Time period assumption	B. The time it takes to purchase goods or services from suppliers, sell goods or services to customers, and collect cash from customers.
___ (5) Operating cycle	
	C. Record expenses when incurred in earning revenue.
	D. Decreases in assets or increases in liabilities from central ongoing operations.
	E. Report the long life of a company in shorter time periods.
	F. Increases in assets or decreases in liabilities from central ongoing operations.
	G. Decreases in assets or increases in liabilities from peripheral transactions.

M3-2
LO3-3

Reporting Cash Basis versus Accrual Basis Income

Skidmore Music Company had the following transactions in March:

a. Sold instruments to customers for $18,000; received $8,000 in cash and the rest on account. The cost of the instruments was $9,000.

b. Purchased $4,000 of new instruments inventory; paid $1,000 in cash and owed the rest on account.

c. Paid $900 in wages to employees who worked during the month.

d. Received $5,000 from customers as deposits on orders of new instruments to be sold to the customers in April.

e. Received a $300 bill for March utilities that will be paid in April.

Complete the following statements:

Cash Basis Income Statement		Accrual Basis Income Statement	
Revenues		Revenues	
Cash sales		Sales to customers	
Customer deposits			
Expenses		Expenses	
Inventory purchases		Cost of sales	
Wages paid		Wages expense	
		Utilities expense	
Net income	_____	Net income	_____

M3-3
LO3-2, 3-3

Identifying Revenues

The following transactions are July activities of Craig's Bowling, Inc., which operates several bowling centers (for games and equipment sales). If revenue is to be recognized in **July,** indicate the revenue account title and amount. If revenue is not to be recognized in July, explain why.

Activity	Revenue Account Title and Amount
a. Craig's collected $15,000 from customers for games played in July.	
b. Craig's sold bowling merchandise inventory from its pro shop for $8,000; received $3,000 in cash and customers owed the rest on account. (See M3-4[*e*] for the cost of goods sold [expense] related to these sales.)	
c. Craig's received $4,000 from customers who purchased merchandise in June on account.	
d. The men's and ladies' bowling leagues gave Craig's a deposit of $2,500 for the upcoming fall season.	

Identifying Expenses

M3-4
LO3-2, 3-3

The following transactions are July activities of Craig's Bowling, Inc., which operates several bowling centers (for games and equipment sales). If expense is to be recognized in **July,** indicate the expense account title and amount. If expense is not to be recognized in July, explain why.

Activity	Expense Account Title and Amount
e. Craig's provided to customers bowling merchandise inventory costing Craig's $6,800. (See M3-3[*b*] for the sale related to this use of merchandise).	
f. Craig's paid $800 on the electricity bill for June (recorded as an expense in June).	
g. Craig's paid $3,500 to employees for work in July.	
h. Craig's purchased $1,500 in insurance for coverage from July 1 to October 1. (Part is an expense for July and part is a prepaid expense to be used in future months.)	
i. Craig's paid $700 to plumbers for repairing a broken pipe in the restrooms.	
j. Craig's received the July electricity bill for $900 to be paid in August.	

Recording Revenues

M3-5
LO3-4

For each of the transactions in M3-3, write the journal entry in good form.

Recording Expenses

M3-6
LO3-4

For each of the transactions in M3-4, write the journal entry in good form.

Determining the Financial Statement Effects of Operating Activities Involving Revenues

M3-7
LO3-4

The following transactions are July activities of Craig's Bowling, Inc., which operates several bowling centers (for games and equipment sales). For each of the following transactions, complete the tabulation, indicating the amount and effect (+ for increase and − for decrease) of each transaction. (Remember that $A = L + SE$; $R − E = NI$; and NI affects SE through Retained Earnings.) Write NE if there is no effect. The first transaction is provided as an example.

	BALANCE SHEET			INCOME STATEMENT		
Transaction	Assets	Liabilities	Stockholders' Equity	Revenues	Expenses	Net Income
a. Craig's collected $15,000 from customers for games played in July.	+15,000	NE	+15,000	+15,000	NE	+15,000
b. Craig's sold bowling merchandise inventory from its pro shop for $8,000; received $3,000 in cash and customers owed the rest on accvount. (See M3-4[e] for the cost of goods sold [expense] related to these sales.)						
c. Craig's received $4,000 from customers who purchased merchandise in June on account.						
d. The men's and ladies' bowling leagues gave Craig's a deposit of $2,500 for the upcoming fall season.						

M3-8

LO3-4

Determining the Financial Statement Effects of Operating Activities Involving Expenses

The following transactions are July activities of Craig's Bowling, Inc., which operates several bowling centers (for games and equipment sales). For each of the following transactions, complete the tabulation, indicating the amount and effect (+ for increase and − for decrease) of each transaction. (Remember that $A = L + SE; R − E = NI$; and NI affects SE through Retained Earnings.) Write NE if there is no effect. The first transaction is provided as an example.

	BALANCE SHEET			INCOME STATEMENT		
Transaction	Assets	Liabilities	Stockholders' Equity	Revenues	Expenses	Net Income
e. Craig's provided to customers bowling merchandise inventory costing Craig's $6,800. (See M3-3[b] for the sale related to this use of merchandise.)	−6,800	NE	−6,800	NE	+6,800	−6,800
f. Craig's paid $800 on the electricity bill for June (recorded as an expense in June).						
g. Craig's paid $3,500 to employees for work in July.						
h. Craig's purchased $1,500 in insurance for coverage from July 1 to October 1. (Part is an expense for July and part is a prepaid expense to be used in future months.)						
i. Craig's paid $700 to plumbers for repairing a broken pipe in the restrooms.						
j. Craig's received the July electricity bill for $900 to be paid in August.						

M3-9

LO3-5

Preparing a Simple Income Statement

Given the transactions in M3-7 and M3-8 (including the examples), prepare an income statement for Craig's Bowling, Inc., for the month of July.

M3-10

LO3-5

Identifying the Operating Activities in a Statement of Cash Flows

Given the transactions in M3-7 and M3-8 (including the examples), indicate how the transactions will affect the statement of cash flows for Craig's Bowling, Inc., for the month of July. Create a table similar to the one below for transactions (*a*) through (*j*). Use O for operating, I for investing, and F for financing activities and indicate the direction of their effects on cash (+ for increases in cash; − for decreases in cash). Also include the amount of cash to be reported on the statement. If there is no effect on the statement of cash flows, write NE.

Transaction	Type of Activity (O, I, or F)	Effect on Cash Flows (+ or − and amount)
a.		
b.		
etc.		

Computing and Explaining the Net Profit Margin Ratio

The following data are from annual reports of Jen's Jewelry Company:

	2018	2017	2016
Total assets	$ 60,000	$ 53,000	$ 41,000
Total liabilities	14,000	11,000	6,000
Total stockholders' equity	46,000	42,000	35,000
Sales revenue	163,000	151,000	132,000
Net income	51,000	40,000	25,000

Compute Jen's net profit margin ratio for each year. What do these results suggest to you about Jen's Jewelry Company?

M3-11

LO3-6

EXERCISES

Matching Definitions with Terms

Match each definition with its related term by entering the appropriate letter in the space provided. There should be only one definition per term (that is, there are more definitions than terms).

E3-1

LO3-1, 3-2, 3-3

Term	Definition
___ (1) Expenses	A. Report the long life of a company in shorter periods.
___ (2) Gains	B. Record expenses when incurred in earning revenue.
___ (3) Revenue recognition principle	C. The time it takes to purchase goods or services from suppliers, sell goods or services to customers, and collect cash from customers.
___ (4) Cash basis accounting	
___ (5) Unearned revenue	
___ (6) Operating cycle	D. Record revenues when earned and expenses when incurred.
___ (7) Accrual basis accounting	E. Increases in assets or decreases in liabilities from peripheral transactions.
___ (8) Prepaid expenses	
___ (9) Revenues − Expenses = Net Income	F. An asset account used to record cash paid before expenses have been incurred.
___ (10) Ending Retained Earnings = Beginning Retained Earnings + Net Income − Dividends Declared	G. Record revenues when earned and measurable (when the company transfers promised goods or services to customers, and in the amount the company expects to receive).
	H. Decreases in assets or increases in liabilities from peripheral transactions.
	I. Record revenues when received and expenses when paid.
	J. The income statement equation.
	K. Decreases in assets or increases in liabilities from central ongoing operations.
	L. The retained earnings equation.
	M. A liability account used to record cash received before revenues have been earned.

E3-2

LO3-3

Reporting Cash Basis versus Accrual Basis Income

Payson Sports, Inc., sells sports equipment to customers. Its fiscal year ends on December 31. The following transactions occurred in the current year:

a. Purchased $250,000 of new sports equipment inventory; paid $90,000 in cash and owed the rest on account.
b. Paid employees $180,300 in wages for work during the year; an additional $3,700 for the current year's wages will be paid in January of the next year.
c. Sold sports equipment to customers for $750,000; received $500,000 in cash and owed the rest on account. The cost of the equipment was $485,000.
d. Paid $17,200 cash for utilities for the year.
e. Received $70,000 from customers as deposits on orders of new winter sports equipment to be sold to the customers in January of the next year.
f. Received a $1,930 utilities bill for December of the current year that will be paid in January of the next year.

Required:

1. Complete the following statements:

Cash Basis Income Statement		**Accrual Basis Income Statement**	
Revenues		Revenues	
Cash sales		Sales to customers	
Customer deposits			
Expenses		Expenses	
Inventory purchases		Cost of sales	
Wages paid		Wages expense	
Utilities paid	_____	Utilities expense	_____
Net income	═══════	Net income	═══════

2. Which basis of accounting (cash or accrual) provides more useful information to investors, creditors, and other users? Why?

E3-3

LO3-2, 3-3

Identifying Revenues

Revenues are normally recognized when the company transfers promised goods or services in the amount the company expects to receive. The amount recorded is the cash-equivalent sales price. The following transactions occurred in **September:**

a. A popular ski magazine company receives a total of $12,345 today from subscribers. The subscriptions begin in the next fiscal year. Answer from the magazine company's standpoint.
b. On September 1 of the current year, a bank lends $1,500 to a company; the note principal and $150 ($1,500 × 10 percent) annual interest are due in one year. Answer from the bank's standpoint.
c. **Fucillo Automotive Group** (offering a wide variety of car and truck brands) sells a Ford F-150 truck with a list, or "sticker," price of $48,050 for $46,500 cash.
d. **Macy's** department store orders 1,000 men's shirts for $15 each for future delivery from **PVH Corp.**, manufacturer of IZOD, ARROW, Van Heusen, Calvin Klein, and Tommy Hilfiger apparel. The terms require payment in full within 30 days of delivery. Answer from PVH Corp.'s standpoint.
e. PVH Corp. completes production of the shirts described in (d) and delivers the order. Answer from PVH's standpoint.
f. PVH Corp. receives payment from Macy's for the events described in (d) and (e). Answer from PVH's standpoint.
g. A customer purchases a ticket from **American Airlines** for $780 cash to travel the following January. Answer from American Airlines's standpoint.
h. **Ford Motor Company** issues $15 million in new common stock.
i. **Michigan State University** receives $19,500,000 cash for 80,000 five-game season football tickets.
j. Michigan State plays the first football game referred to in (i).
k. **Precision Builders** signs a contract with a customer for the construction of a new $1,500,000 warehouse. At the signing, Precision receives a check for $200,000 as a deposit on the future construction. Answer from Precision's standpoint.
l. A customer orders and receives 10 personal computers from **Dell**; the customer promises to pay $9,600 within three months. Answer from Dell's standpoint.
m. **Sears**, a retail store, sells a $300 lamp to a customer who charges the sale on his Sear's credit card. Answer from Sears's standpoint.

Required:

For each of the transactions, if revenue is to be recognized in September, indicate the revenue account title and amount. If revenue is not to be recognized in September, explain why.

Identifying Expenses

E3-4
LO3-2, 3-3

Revenues are normally recognized when a company transfers promised goods or services to customers in the amount the company expects to receive. Expense recognition is guided by an attempt to match the costs associated with the generation of those revenues to the same time period. The following transactions occurred in **January:**

a. **McGraw-Hill Education** uses $3,800 worth of electricity and natural gas in its headquarters building for which it has not yet been billed.

b. At the beginning of January, **Turner Construction Company** pays $963 for magazine advertising to run in monthly publications each of the first three months of the year.

c. **Dell** pays its computer service technicians $403,000 in salaries for the two weeks ended January 7. Answer from Dell's standpoint.

d. The **University of Florida** orders 60,000 season football tickets from its printer and pays $8,340 in advance for the custom printing. The first game will be played in September. Answer from the university's standpoint.

e. The campus bookstore receives 500 accounting texts at a cost of $160 each. The terms indicate that payment is due within 30 days of delivery.

f. During the last week of January, the campus bookstore sold 500 accounting texts received in (*e*) at a sales price of $230 each.

g. **Fucillo Automotive Group** pays its salespersons $13,800 in commissions related to December automobile sales. Answer from Fucillo's standpoint.

h. On January 31, Fucillo Automotive Group determines that it will pay its salespersons $15,560 in commissions related to January sales. The payment will be made in early February. Answer from Fucillo's standpoint.

i. A new grill is purchased and installed at a **Wendy's** restaurant at the end of the day on January 31; a $12,750 cash payment is made on that day.

j. **Destiny USA** (formerly Carousel Mall in Syracuse, NY) had janitorial supplies costing $3,500 in storage. An additional $2,600 worth of supplies was purchased during January. At the end of January, $1,400 worth of janitorial supplies remained in storage.

k. An **Iowa State University** employee works eight hours, at $15 per hour, on January 31; however, payday is not until February 3. Answer from the university's point of view.

l. Wang Company paid $4,800 for a fire insurance policy on January 1. The policy covers 12 months beginning on January 1. Answer from Wang's point of view.

m. Derek Incorporated has its delivery van repaired in January for $600 and charges the amount on account.

n. Hass Company, a farm equipment company, receives its phone bill at the end of January for $154 for January calls. The bill has not been paid to date.

o. Martin Company receives and pays in January a $2,034 invoice (bill) from a consulting firm for services received in January. Answer from Martin's standpoint.

p. Parillo's Taxi Company pays a $595 invoice from a consulting firm for services received and recorded in December.

q. **PVH Corp.**, manufacturer of IZOD, ARROW, Van Heusen, Calvin Klein, and Tommy Hilfiger apparel, completes production of 450 men's shirts ordered by **Macy's** department stores at a cost of $10 each and delivers the order. Answer from PVH Corp.'s standpoint.

Required:

For each of the transactions, if an expense is to be recognized in January, indicate the expense account title and the amount. If an expense is not to be recognized in January, indicate why.

Determining Financial Statement Effects of Various Transactions

E3-5
LO3-4

Amazon.com, Inc., headquartered in Seattle, WA, started its electronic commerce business in 1995 and expanded rapidly. The following transactions occurred during a recent year (dollars in millions):

a. Issued stock for $6 cash (example).

b. Purchased equipment costing $6,320, paying $4,893 in cash and charging the rest on account.

c. Paid $513 in principal and $91 in interest expense on long-term debt.

   d. Earned $88,988 in sales revenue; collected $87,949 in cash with the customers
      owing the rest on account.
   e. Incurred $10,766 in shipping expenses, all on credit.
   f. Paid $28,241 cash on accounts owed to suppliers.
   g. Incurred $4,332 in marketing expenses; paid cash.
   h. Collected $620 in cash from customers paying on account.
   i. Borrowed $6,359 in cash as long-term debt.
   j. Used inventory costing $62,752 when sold to customers.
   k. Paid $177 in income tax recorded as an expense in the prior year.

Required:

For each of the transactions, complete the tabulation, indicating the effect (+ for increase and − for
decrease) of each transaction. (Remember that A = L + SE; R − E = NI; and NI affects SE through
Retained Earnings.) Write NE if there is no effect. The first transaction is provided as an example.

	BALANCE SHEET			INCOME STATEMENT		
Transaction	Assets	Liabilities	Stockholders' Equity	Revenues	Expenses	Net Income
(*a*) (example)	+6	NE	+6	NE	NE	NE

E3-6 **Determining Financial Statement Effects of Various Transactions**

LO3-4

Wolverine World Wide, Inc., manufactures military, work, sport, and casual footwear and leather accessories under a variety of brand names, such as Hush Puppies, Wolverine, Merrell, Stride Rite, and Bates,
to a global market. The following transactions occurred during a recent year. Dollars are in thousands.

   a. Issued common stock to investors for $14,083 cash (example).
   b. Purchased $878,418 of additional inventory on account.
   c. Borrowed $11,000.
   d. Sold $1,409,068 of products to customers on account; cost of the products sold was $852,316.
   e. Paid cash dividends of $22,737.
   f. Purchased for cash $19,397 in additional property, plant, and equipment.
   g. Incurred $386,540 in selling expenses, paying three-fourths in cash and owing the rest on account.
   h. Earned $370 interest on investments, receiving 90 percent in cash.
   i. Incurred $1,395 in interest expense to be paid at the beginning of next year.

Required:

For each of the transactions, complete the tabulation, indicating the effect (+ for increase and − for
decrease) of each transaction. (Remember that A = L + SE; R − E = NI; and NI affects SE through
Retained Earnings.) Write NE if there is no effect. The first transaction is provided as an example.

	BALANCE SHEET			INCOME STATEMENT		
Transaction	Assets	Liabilities	Stockholders' Equity	Revenues	Expenses	Net Income
(*a*) (example)	+14,083	NE	+14,083	NE	NE	NE

E3-7 **Recording Journal Entries**

LO3-4

Sysco, formed in 1969, is North America's largest marketer and distributor of food service products,
serving approximately 425,000 restaurants, hotels, schools, hospitals, and other institutions. The following summarized transactions are typical of those that occurred in a recent year (dollars are in millions).

   a. Purchased plant and equipment for $636 in cash.
   b. Borrowed $181 from a bank, signing a short-term note.
   c. Provided $39,323 in service to customers during the year, with $28,558 on account and the rest
      received in cash.

d. Paid $32,074 cash on accounts payable.

e. Purchased $32,305 inventory on account.

f. Paid payroll, $3,500 during the year.

g. Received $39,043 on account paid by customers.

h. Purchased and used fuel of $750 in delivery vehicles during the year (paid for in cash).

i. Declared $597 in dividends at the end of the year to be paid the following year.

j. Incurred $68 in utility usage during the year; paid $55 in cash and owed the rest on account.

Required:

For each of the transactions, prepare journal entries. Determine whether the accounting equation remains in balance and debits equal credits after each entry.

Recording Journal Entries

E3-8

LO3-4

Vail Resorts, Inc., owns and operates five premier year-round ski resort properties (Vail Mountain, Beaver Creek Resort, Breckenridge Mountain, and Keystone Resort, all located in the Colorado Rocky Mountains, and Heavenly Valley Mountain Resort, located in the Lake Tahoe area of California/Nevada). The company also owns a collection of luxury hotels, resorts, and lodging properties. The company sells lift tickets, ski lessons, and ski equipment. The following hypothetical **December** transactions are typical of those that occur at the resorts.

a. Borrowed $2,300,000 from the bank on December 1, signing a note payable due in six months.

b. Purchased a new snowplow for $98,000 cash on December 31.

c. Purchased ski equipment inventory for $35,000 on account to sell in the ski shops.

d. Incurred $62,000 in routine maintenance expenses for the chairlifts; paid cash.

e. Sold $390,000 of January through March season passes and received cash.

f. Sold a pair of skis from a ski shop to a customer for $800 on account. (The cost of the skis was $500). (**Hint:** Record two entries.)

g. Sold daily lift passes in December for a total of $320,000 in cash.

h. Received a $3,500 deposit on a townhouse to be rented for five days in January.

i. Paid half the charges incurred on account in (c).

j. Received $400 on account from the customer in (f).

k. Paid $245,000 in wages to employees for the month of December.

Required:

1. Prepare journal entries for each transaction. (Remember to check that debits equal credits and that the accounting equation is in balance after each transaction.)

2. Assume that Vail Resorts had a $1,000 balance in Accounts Receivable at the beginning of December. Determine the ending balance in the Accounts Receivable account at the end of December based on transactions (a) through (k). Show your work in T-account format.

Recording Journal Entries

E3-9

LO3-4

Blaine Air Transport Service, Inc., has been in operation for three years. The following transactions occurred in February:

February 1	Paid $275 for rent of hangar space in February.
February 2	Purchased fuel costing $490 on account for the next flight to Dallas.
February 4	Received customer payment of $820 to ship several items to Philadelphia next month.
February 7	Flew cargo from Denver to Dallas; the customer paid $910 for the air transport.
February 10	Paid $175 for an advertisement in the local paper to run on February 19.
February 14	Paid pilot $2,300 in wages for flying in January (recorded as expense in January).
February 18	Flew cargo for two customers from Dallas to Albuquerque for $3,800; one customer paid $1,600 cash and the other asked to be billed.
February 25	Purchased on account $2,550 in spare parts for the planes.
February 27	Declared a $200 cash dividend to be paid in March.

Required:

Prepare journal entries for each transaction. Be sure to categorize each account as an asset (A), liability (L), stockholders' equity (SE), revenue (R), or expense (E).

E3-10

LO3-3, 3-4

Analyzing the Effects of Transactions in T-Accounts and Computing Cash Basis versus Accrual Basis Net Income

Stacey's Piano Rebuilding Company has been operating for one year. At the start of the second year, its income statement accounts had zero balances and its balance sheet account balances were as follows:

Cash	$ 6,400	Accounts payable	$ 9,600
Accounts receivable	32,000	Unearned revenue	3,840
Supplies	1,500	Long-term note payable	48,500
Equipment	9,500	Common stock	1,600
Land	7,400	Additional paid-in capital	7,000
Building	25,300	Retained earnings	11,560

Required:

1. Create T-accounts for the balance sheet accounts and for these additional accounts: Rebuilding Fees Revenue, Rent Revenue, Wages Expense, and Utilities Expense. Enter the beginning balances.
2. Enter the following transactions for January of the second year into the T-accounts, using the letter of each transaction as the reference:
   a. Rebuilt and delivered five pianos in January to customers who paid $19,000 in cash.
   b. Received a $600 deposit from a customer who wanted her piano rebuilt.
   c. Rented a part of the building to a bicycle repair shop; received $850 for rent in January.
   d. Received $7,200 from customers as payment on their accounts.
   e. Received an electric and gas utility bill for $400 to be paid in February.
   f. Ordered $960 in supplies.
   g. Paid $2,300 on account in January.
   h. Received from the home of Stacey Eddy, the major shareholder, a $920 tool (equipment) to use in the business in exchange for 100 shares of $1 par value stock.
   i. Paid $16,500 in wages to employees who worked in January.
   j. Declared and paid a $2,200 dividend (reduce Retained Earnings and Cash).
   k. Received and paid cash for the supplies in (*f*).
3. Using the data from the T-accounts, amounts for the following at the end of January of the second year were

   Revenues $ _____ − Expenses $ _____ = Net Income $ _____

   Assets $ _____ = Liabilities $ _____ + Stockholders' Equity $ _____

4. What is net income if Stacey's used the cash basis of accounting? Why does this differ from accrual basis net income (in requirement 3)?

E3-11

LO3-5

Preparing an Income Statement

Refer to E3-10.

Required:

Use the ending balances in the T-accounts in E3-10 to prepare in good form an income statement for January of the second year (ignore income taxes).

E3-12

LO3-5

Identifying Activities Affecting the Statement of Cash Flows

Refer to E3-10.

Required:

Use the transactions in E3-10 to identify the operating (O), investing (I), and financing (F) activities and the direction (+ for increase, − for decrease) and amount of the effect. If there is no effect, use NE.

Analyzing the Effects of Transactions in T-Accounts and Computing Cash Basis versus Accrual Basis Net Income

E3-13
LO3-3, 3-4

At January 1 (beginning of its fiscal year), Conover, Inc., a financial services consulting firm, reported the following account balances (in thousands of dollars, except number of shares and par value per share):

Cash	$1,900	Accounts payable	$ 210
Short-term investments	410	Unearned revenue	1,320
Accounts receivable	3,570	Salaries payable	870
Supplies	150	Short-term note payable	780
Prepaid expenses	4,720	Common stock ($1 par value)	50
Office equipment	1,530	Additional paid-in capital	6,560
Accumulated depreciation—office equipment*	(480)	Retained earnings	2,010

This account has a credit balance representing the portion of the cost of the equipment used in the past.

Required:
1. Create T-accounts for the balance sheet accounts and for these additional accounts: Consulting Fees Revenue, Interest Revenue, Salaries Expense, and Utilities Expense. Enter the beginning balances of the balance sheet accounts; Conover's income statement accounts had zero balances.
2. Enter the following transactions for the current year into the T-accounts, using the letter of each transaction as the reference:
   a. Received $9,500 cash for consulting services rendered.
   b. Issued 10,000 additional shares of common stock at a market price of $120 per share.
   c. Purchased $640 of equipment, paying 25 percent in cash and owing the rest on a short-term note.
   d. Received $890 from clients for consulting services to be performed in the next year.
   e. Bought $470 of supplies on account.
   f. Incurred and paid $1,800 in utilities for the current year.
   g. Consulted for clients in the current year for fees totaling $1,620, due from clients in the next year.
   h. Received $2,980 from clients paying on their accounts.
   i. Incurred $6,210 in salaries in the current year, paying $5,300 and owing the rest (to be paid next year).
   j. Purchased $1,230 in short-term investments and paid $800 for insurance coverage beginning in the next fiscal year.
   k. Received $10 in interest revenue earned in the current year on short-term investments.
3. Using the data from the T-accounts, amounts for the following at the end of the current year were

   Revenues $ _____ − Expenses $ _____ = Net Income $ _____

   Assets $ _____ = Liabilities $ _____ + Stockholders' Equity $ _____

4. What would net income be if Conover, Inc., used the cash basis of accounting? Why does this differ from accrual basis net income (in requirement 3)?

Preparing an Income Statement

E3-14
LO3-5

Refer to E3-13.

Required:
Use the ending balances in the T-accounts in E3-13 to prepare in good form an income statement for the current year ended December 31. (Ignore income taxes.)

Analyzing the Effects of Transactions in T-Accounts

E3-15
LO3-4

Lisa Frees and Amelia Ellinger have been operating a catering business for several years. In March, the partners plan to expand by opening a retail sales shop. They have decided to form the business as a corporation called Traveling Gourmet, Inc. The following transactions occurred in March:

a. Received $80,000 cash from each of the two shareholders to form the corporation, in addition to $2,000 in accounts receivable, $5,300 in equipment, a van (equipment) appraised at a fair value of $13,000, and $1,200 in supplies. Gave the two owners each 500 shares of common stock with a par value of $1 per share.
b. Purchased a vacant store for sale in a good location for $360,000, making a $72,000 cash down payment and signing a 10-year mortgage from a local bank for the rest.
c. Borrowed $50,000 from the local bank on a 10 percent, one-year note.
d. Purchased and used food and paper supplies costing $10,830 in March; paid cash.

e. Catered four parties in March for $4,200; $1,600 was billed, and the rest was received in cash.

f. Made and sold food at the retail store for $11,900 cash.

g. Received a $420 telephone bill for March to be paid in April.

h. Paid $363 in gas for the van in March.

i. Paid $6,280 in wages to employees who worked in March.

j. Paid a $300 dividend from the corporation to each owner.

k. Purchased $50,000 of equipment (refrigerated display cases, cabinets, tables, and chairs) and renovated and decorated the new store for $20,000 (added to the cost of the building); paid cash.

Required:

1. Set up appropriate T-accounts for Cash, Accounts Receivable, Supplies, Equipment, Building, Accounts Payable, Note Payable, Mortgage Payable, Common Stock, Additional Paid-in Capital, Retained Earnings, Food Sales Revenue, Catering Sales Revenue, Supplies Expense, Utilities Expense, Wages Expense, and Fuel Expense.

2. Record in the T-accounts the effects of each transaction for Traveling Gourmet, Inc., in March. Identify the amounts with the letters starting with (*a*). Compute ending balances.

E3-16

LO3-5

Preparing an Income Statement, Identifying Cash Flow Effects, and Analyzing Results

Refer to E3-15.

Required:

Use the balances in the completed T-accounts in E3-15 to respond to the following:

1. Prepare an income statement in good form for the month of March.

2. Identify operating (O), investing (I), and financing (F) activities affecting cash flows. Include the direction and amount of the effect. If there is no effect on cash flows, use NE.

3. What do you think about the success of this company based on the results of the first month of operations? (**Hint:** Compare net income to cash flows from operations.)

E3-17

LO3-2, 3-3, 3-4, 3-5

Inferring Operating Transactions and Preparing an Income Statement and Balance Sheet

Kate's Kite Company (a corporation) sells and repairs kites from manufacturers around the world. Its stores are located in rented space in malls and shopping centers. During its first month of operations ended April 30, Kate's Kite Company completed eight transactions with the dollar effects indicated in the following schedule:

Accounts	DOLLAR EFFECT OF EACH OF THE EIGHT TRANSACTIONS								Ending Balance
	(a)	(b)	(c)	(d)	(e)	(f)	(g)	(h)	
Cash	$82,000	$(15,400)	$(6,200)	$9,820		$(1,300)	$(2,480)	$3,960	
Accounts Receivable				4,180					
Inventory			24,800	(7,000)					
Prepaid Expenses							1,860		
Store Fixtures		15,400							
Accounts Payable			18,600		$1,480				
Unearned Revenue								2,510	
Common Stock ($1 par value)	10,000								
Additional Paid-in Capital	72,000								
Sales Revenue				14,000				1,450	
Cost of Sales				7,000					
Wages Expense						1,300			
Rent Expense							620		
Utilities Expense					1,480				

Required:
1. Write a brief explanation of transactions (*a*) through (*h*). Include any assumptions that you made.
2. Compute the ending balance in each account and prepare an income statement and a classified balance sheet for Kate's Kite Company on April 30.

Analyzing the Effects of Transactions Using T-Accounts and Interpreting the Net Profit Margin Ratio as a Financial Analyst

E3-18

LO3-4, 3-6

Massa Company, which has been operating for three years, provides marketing consulting services worldwide for dot-com companies. You are a financial analyst assigned to report on the Massa management team's effectiveness at managing its assets efficiently. At the start of 2016 (its fourth year), Massa's T-account balances were as follows. Dollars are in thousands.

Assets

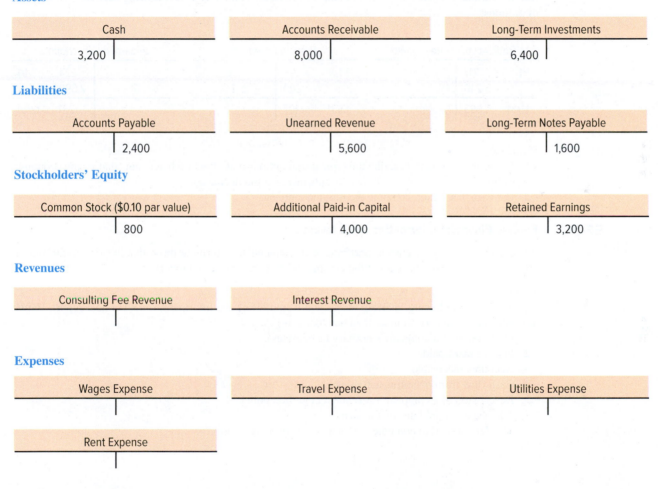

Cash		Accounts Receivable		Long-Term Investments	
3,200		8,000		6,400	

Liabilities

Accounts Payable		Unearned Revenue		Long-Term Notes Payable	
	2,400		5,600		1,600

Stockholders' Equity

Common Stock ($0.10 par value)		Additional Paid-in Capital		Retained Earnings	
	800		4,000		3,200

Revenues

Consulting Fee Revenue		Interest Revenue	

Expenses

Wages Expense		Travel Expense		Utilities Expense	

Rent Expense	

Required:
1. Using the data from these T-accounts, amounts for the following on January 1, 2016, were:

Assets $ _____ = Liabilities $ _____ + Stockholders' Equity $ _____

2. Enter in the T-accounts the following transactions for 2016:
   a. Provided $58,000 in services to clients who paid $48,000 in cash and owed the rest on account.
   b. Received $5,600 cash from clients on account.
   c. Received $400 in cash as interest revenue on investments.
   d. Paid $36,000 in wages, $12,000 in travel, $7,600 in rent, and $1,600 on accounts payable.
   e. Received $1,600 in cash from clients in advance of services Massa will provide next year.
   f. Received a utility bill for $800 for 2016 services.
   g. Declared and paid $480 in dividends to stockholders.

3. Compute ending balances in the T-accounts to determine amounts for the following on December 31, 2016:

Revenues $ _____ − Expenses $ _____ = Net Income $ _____

Assets $ _____ = Liabilities $ _____ + Stockholders' Equity $ _____

4. Calculate the net profit margin ratio for 2016. If the company had a net profit margin ratio of 2.9 percent in 2015 and 2.5 percent in 2014, what does your computation suggest to you about Massa Company? What would you say in your report?

E3-19
LO3-4

Inferring Transactions and Computing Effects Using T-Accounts

A recent annual report of **Gannett Co., Inc.**, an international diversified media and marketing solutions company that currently includes numerous television stations, newspapers (such as *USA Today*), and Internet businesses (such as Cars.com and Career-Builder) included the following accounts. Dollars are in millions:

Trade Accounts Receivable			Prepaid Expenses			Unearned Subscriptions		
1/1	717		1/1	95			224	1/1
	5,240	?		203	?	?	2,690	
12/31	693		12/31	107			231	12/31

Required:
1. For each T-account, describe the typical transactions that affect each account (that is, the economic events that occur to make these accounts increase and decrease).
2. For each T-account, compute the missing amounts.

E3-20
LO3-5, 3-6

Finding Financial Information as an Investor

You are evaluating your current portfolio of investments to determine those that are not performing to your expectations. You have all of the companies' most recent annual reports.

Required:
For each of the following, indicate where you would locate the information in an annual report. (**Hint:** The information may be in more than one location.)
1. Description of a company's primary business(es).
2. Income taxes paid.
3. Accounts receivable.
4. Cash flow from operating activities.
5. Description of a company's revenue recognition policy.
6. The inventory sold during the year.
7. The data needed to compute the total net profit margin ratio.

PROBLEMS

P3-1
LO3-4

Recording Nonquantitative Journal Entries (AP3-1)

The following list includes a series of accounts for Sanjeev Corporation, which has been operating for three years. These accounts are listed and numbered for identification. Following the accounts is a series of transactions. For each transaction, indicate the account(s) that should be debited and credited by entering the appropriate account number(s) to the right of each transaction. If no journal entry is needed, write **none** after the transaction. The first transaction is used as an example.

Account No.	Account Title	Account No.	Account Title
1	Cash	10	Income Taxes Payable
2	Accounts Receivable	11	Common Stock
3	Supplies	12	Additional Paid-in Capital
4	Prepaid Expenses	13	Retained Earnings
5	Equipment	14	Service Revenue
6	Patents	15	Operating Expenses (wages, supplies)
7	Accounts Payable	16	Income Tax Expense
8	Note Payable	17	Interest Expense
9	Wages Payable		

Transactions	Debit	Credit
a. Example: Purchased equipment for use in the business; paid one-third cash and signed a note payable for the balance.	5	1, 8
b. Paid cash for salaries and wages earned by employees this period.		
c. Paid cash on accounts payable for expenses incurred last period.		
d. Purchased supplies to be used later; paid cash.		
e. Performed services this period on credit.		
f. Collected cash on accounts receivable for services performed last period.		
g. Issued stock to new investors.		
h. Paid operating expenses incurred this period.		
i. Incurred operating expenses this period to be paid next period.		
j. Purchased a patent (an intangible asset); paid cash.		
k. Collected cash for services performed this period.		
l. Used some of the supplies on hand for operations.		
m. Paid three-fourths of the income tax expense incurred for the year; the balance will be paid next year.		
n. Made a payment on the equipment note in (a); the payment was part principal and part interest expense.		
o. On the last day of the current period, paid cash for an insurance policy covering the next two years.		

Recording Journal Entries (AP3-2)

P3-2
LO3-4

Ryan Terlecki organized a new Internet company, CapUniverse, Inc. The company specializes in base-ball-type caps with logos printed on them. Ryan, who is never without a cap, believes that his target market is college and high school students. You have been hired to record the transactions occurring in the first two weeks of operations.

a. Issued 2,000 shares of $0.01 par value common stock to investors for cash at $20 per share.
b. Borrowed $60,000 from the bank to provide additional funding to begin operations; the note is due in two years.
c. Paid $1,500 for the current month's rent of a warehouse and another $1,500 for next month's rent.
d. Paid $2,400 for a one-year fire insurance policy on the warehouse (recorded as a prepaid expense).
e. Purchased furniture and fixtures for the warehouse for $15,000, paying $3,000 cash and the rest on account. The amount is due within 30 days.
f. Purchased for $2,800 cash **The University of Pennsylvania**, **Notre Dame**, **The University of Texas at Austin**, and **Michigan State University** baseball caps as inventory to sell online.
g. Placed advertisements on **Google** for a total of $350 cash.
h. Sold caps totaling $1,700, half of which was charged on account. The cost of the caps sold was $900. (**Hint:** Make two entries.)
i. Made full payment for the furniture and fixtures purchased on account in (e).
j. Received $210 from a customer on account.

Required:

For each of the transactions, prepare journal entries. Be sure to categorize each account as an asset (A), liability (L), stockholders' equity (SE), revenue (R), or expense (E). Note that transaction (h) will require two entries, one for revenue and one for the related expense.

P3-3
LO3-4

Determining Financial Statement Effects of Various Transactions and Identifying Cash Flow Effects (AP3-3)

According to its annual report, **The Wendy's Company** is "one quick-service restaurant that is 'A Cut Above,'" serving hamburgers and other fresh food items including salads, chicken sandwiches, and baked potatoes in more than 6,500 restaurants worldwide. The company operates its own restaurants and sells franchises to others. The following activities were inferred from a recent annual report.

a. Purchased food and paper products; paid part in cash and the rest on account.
b. Purchased additional investments.
c. Incurred restaurant operating costs in company-owned facilities; paid part in cash and the rest on account.
d. Served food to customers for cash.
e. Used food and paper products.
f. Paid cash dividends.
g. Sold franchises, receiving part in cash and the rest in notes due from franchisees.
h. Paid interest on debt incurred and due during the period.

Required:
1. For each of the transactions, complete the tabulation, indicating the effect (+ for increase and − for decrease) of each transaction. (Remember that A = L + SE; R − E = NI; and NI affects SE through Retained Earnings.) Write NE if there is no effect. The first transaction is provided as an example.

	BALANCE SHEET			INCOME STATEMENT		
Transaction	**Assets**	**Liabilities**	**Stockholders' Equity**	**Revenues**	**Expenses**	**Net Income**
(*a*) (example)	+/−	+	NE	NE	NE	NE

2. Where, if at all, would each transaction be reported on the statement of cash flows? Use O for operating activities, I for investing activities, F for financing activities, and NE if the transaction would not be included on the statement.

P3-4
LO3-4, 3-5, 3-6

Analyzing the Effects of Transactions Using T-Accounts, Preparing an Income Statement, and Evaluating the Net Profit Margin Ratio as a Manager (AP3-4)

Kaylee James, a connoisseur of fine chocolate, opened Kaylee's Sweets in Collegetown on February 1. The shop specializes in a selection of gourmet chocolate candies and a line of gourmet ice cream. You have been hired as manager. Your duties include maintaining the store's financial records. The following transactions occurred in February, the first month of operations.

a. Received four shareholders' contributions totaling $30,200 cash to form the corporation; issued 400 shares of $0.10 par value common stock.
b. Paid three months' rent for the store at $1,750 per month (recorded as prepaid expenses).
c. Purchased and received candy for $6,000 on account, due in 60 days.
d. Purchased supplies for $1,560 cash.
e. Negotiated and signed a two-year $11,000 loan at the bank, receiving cash at the time.
f. Used the money from (*e*) to purchase a computer for $2,750 (for recordkeeping and inventory tracking); used the balance for furniture and fixtures for the store.
g. Placed a grand opening advertisement in the local paper for $400 cash; the ad ran in the current month.
h. Made sales on Valentine's Day totaling $3,500; $2,675 was in cash and the rest on accounts receivable. The cost of the candy sold was $1,600.
i. Made a $550 payment on accounts payable.
j. Incurred and paid employee wages of $1,300.
k. Collected accounts receivable of $600 from customers.
l. Made a repair to one of the display cases for $400 cash.
m. Made cash sales of $1,200 during the rest of the month. The cost of the candy sold was $600.

Required:

1. Set up appropriate T-accounts for Cash, Accounts Receivable, Supplies, Inventory, Prepaid Expenses, Equipment, Furniture and Fixtures, Accounts Payable, Notes Payable, Common Stock, Additional Paid-in Capital, Sales Revenue, Cost of Goods Sold (expense), Advertising Expense, Wage Expense, and Repair Expense. All accounts begin with zero balances.
2. Record in the T-accounts the effects of each transaction for Kaylee's Sweets in February, referencing each transaction in the accounts with the transaction letter. Show the ending balances in the T-accounts. Note that transactions (*h*) and (*m*) require two types of entries, one for revenue recognition and one for the expense.
3. Prepare an income statement at the end of the first month of operations ended February 28.
4. Write a short memo to Kaylee offering your opinion on the results of operations during the first month of business.
5. After three years in business, you are being evaluated for a promotion. One measure is how effectively you managed the sales and expenses of the business. The following data are available:

	2018*	2017	2016
Total assets	$88,000	$58,500	$52,500
Total liabilities	49,500	22,000	18,500
Total stockholders' equity	38,500	36,500	34,000
Net sales revenue	93,500	82,500	55,000
Net income	22,000	11,000	4,400

At the end of 2018, Kaylee decided to open a second store, requiring loans and inventory purchases prior to the store's opening in early 2019.

Compute the net profit margin ratio for each year and evaluate the results. Do you think you should be promoted? Why?

Identifying Cash Flow Effects (AP3-5)

Refer to P3-4.

Required:
For the transactions listed in P3-4, indicate the type of effect on cash flows (O for operating, I for investing, and F for financing) and the direction (+ for increase and − for decrease) and amount of the effect. If there is no effect, write NE.

P3-5
LO3-5

Analyzing the Effects of Transactions Using T-Accounts, Preparing an Income Statement, and Evaluating the Net Profit Margin Ratio (AP3-6)

Following are account balances (in millions of dollars) from a recent **FedEx** annual report, followed by several typical transactions. Assume that the following are account balances on May 31 (end of the prior fiscal year):

P3-6
LO3-4, 3-5, 3-6

Account	Balance		Account	Balance
Property and equipment (net)	$15,543		Receivables	$4,581
Retained earnings	12,716		Other current assets	610
Accounts payable	1,702		Cash	2,328
Prepaid expenses	329		Spare parts, supplies, and fuel	437
Accrued expenses payable	1,894		Other noncurrent liabilities	5,616
Long-term notes payable	1,667		Other current liabilities	1.286
Other noncurrent assets	3,557		Additional paid-in capital	2,472
Common stock ($0.10 par value)	32			

These accounts are not necessarily in good order and have normal debit or credit balances. Assume the following transactions (in millions) occurred the next fiscal year beginning June 1 (the current year):

a. Provided delivery service to customers, receiving $21,704 in accounts receivable and $17,600 in cash.
b. Purchased new equipment costing $3,434; signed a long-term note.

c. Paid $13,864 cash to rent equipment and aircraft, with $10,136 for rental this year and the rest for rental next year.

d. Spent $3,864 cash to maintain and repair facilities and equipment during the year.

e. Collected $24,285 from customers on account.

f. Repaid $350 on a long-term note (ignore interest).

g. Issued 20 shares of additional stock for $16.

h. Paid employees $15,276 during the year.

i. Purchased for cash and used $8,564 in fuel for the aircraft and equipment during the year.

j. Paid $784 on accounts payable.

k. Ordered $88 in spare parts and supplies.

Required:

1. Prepare T-accounts for May 31 of the current year from the preceding list; enter the respective beginning balances. You will need additional T-accounts for income statement accounts; enter zero for beginning balances.

2. For each transaction, record the current year's transaction effects in the T-accounts. Label each using the letter of the transaction. Compute ending balances.

3. Prepare an income statement for the current year ended May 31.

4. Compute the company's net profit margin ratio for the current year ended May 31. What do the results suggest to you about FedEx?

P3-7

LO3-4

Recording Journal Entries and Identifying Cash Flow Effects

Cedar Fair, L.P. (Limited Partnership) is one of the largest regional amusement park operators in the world, owning eleven amusement parks, three outdoor water parks, one indoor water park, and five hotels. The parks include **Cedar Point** in Ohio; **Valleyfair** near Minneapolis/St. Paul; **Dorney Park** and **Wildwater Kingdom** near Allentown, Pennsylvania; **Worlds of Fun** in Kansas City; **Great America** in Santa Clara, California; and **Canada's Wonderland** near Toronto, Canada, among others. The following are summarized transactions similar to those that occurred in a recent year. Dollars are in thousands.

a. Guests at the parks paid $596,042 cash in admissions.

b. The primary operating expenses for the year were employee wages of $433,416, with $401,630 paid in cash and the rest to be paid to employees in the following year.

c. Cedar Fair paid $47,100 principal on long-term notes payable.

d. The parks sells merchandise in park stores. The cash received during the year for sales was $365,693. The cost of the inventory sold during the year was $92,057.

e. Cedar Fair purchased and built additional rides and other equipment during the year, paying $90,190 in cash.

f. Guests may stay in the parks at accommodations owned by the company. During the year, accommodations revenue was $82,994; $81,855 was paid by the guests in cash and the rest was owed on account.

g. Interest incurred and paid on long-term debt was $153,326.

h. The company purchased $147,531 in inventory for the park stores during the year, paying $119,431 in cash and owing the rest on account.

i. Advertising costs for the parks were $140,426 for the year; $134,044 was paid in cash, and the rest was owed on account.

j. Cedar Fair paid $11,600 on accounts payable during the year.

Required:

1. For each of these transactions, record journal entries. Use the letter of each transaction as its reference. Note that transaction (d) will require two entries, one for revenue recognition and one for the related expense.

2. Use the following chart to identify whether each transaction results in a cash flow effect from operating (O), investing (I), or financing (F) activities, and indicate the direction and amount of the effect on cash (+ for increase and − for decrease). If there is no cash flow effect, write **none.** The first transaction is provided as an example.

Transaction	Operating, Investing, or Financing Effect	Direction and Amount of the Effect (in thousands)
(a)	O	+596,042

Recording Nonquantitative Journal Entries (P3-1)

AP3-1

LO3-4

The following is a series of accounts for Kruger & Laurenzo, Incorporated, which has been operating for two years. The accounts are listed and numbered for identification. Following the accounts is a series of transactions. For each transaction, indicate the account(s) that should be debited and credited by entering the appropriate account number(s) to the right of each transaction. If no journal entry is needed, write **none** after the transaction. The first transaction is given as an example.

Account No.	Account Title	Account No.	Account Title
1	Cash	9	Wages Payable
2	Accounts Receivable	10	Income Taxes Payable
3	Supplies	11	Common Stock
4	Prepaid Expenses	12	Additional Paid-in Capital
5	Buildings	13	Retained Earnings
6	Land	14	Service Revenue
7	Accounts Payable	15	Other Expenses (wages, supplies, interest)
8	Mortgage Payable	16	Income Tax Expense

	Transactions	Debit	Credit
a.	*Example:* Issued stock to new investors.	1	11, 12
b.	Incurred and recorded operating expenses on credit to be paid next period.	_____	_____
c.	Purchased on credit but did not use supplies this period.	_____	_____
d.	Performed services for customers this period on credit.	_____	_____
e.	Prepaid a fire insurance policy this period to cover the next 12 months.	_____	_____
f.	Purchased a building this period by making a 20 percent cash down payment and signing a mortgage loan for the balance.	_____	_____
g.	Collected cash this year for services rendered and recorded in the prior year.	_____	_____
h.	Collected cash for services rendered this period.	_____	_____
i.	Paid cash this period for wages earned and recorded last period.	_____	_____
j.	Paid cash for operating expenses charged on accounts payable in the prior period.	_____	_____
k.	Paid cash for operating expenses incurred in the current period.	_____	_____
l.	Made a payment on the mortgage loan, which was part principal repayment and part interest.	_____	_____
m.	This period a shareholder sold some shares of her stock to another person for an amount above the original issuance price.	_____	_____
n.	Used supplies on hand to clean the offices.	_____	_____
o.	Recorded income taxes for this period to be paid at the beginning of the next period.	_____	_____
p.	Declared and paid a cash dividend this period.	_____	_____

Recording Journal Entries (P3-2)

AP3-2

LO3-4

Jimmy Langenberger is the president of TemPro, Inc., a company that provides temporary employees for not-for-profit companies. TemPro has been operating for five years; its revenues are increasing with each passing year. You have been hired to help Jimmy analyze the following transactions for the first two weeks of April:

a. Billed the local **United Way** office $23,500 for temporary services provided.

b. Paid $3,005 for supplies purchased and recorded on account last period.

c. Purchased supplies for the office for $2,600 on account.

d. Purchased a new computer for the office costing $3,800 cash.

e. Placed an advertisement in the local paper for $1,400 cash.

f. Paid employee wages of $11,900. Of this amount, $3,800 had been earned by employees and recorded in the Wages Payable account in the prior period.

g. Issued 3,000 additional shares of common stock for cash at $45 per share in anticipation of building a new office. The common stock had a par value of $0.50 per share.

h. Received $12,500 on account from the local United Way office for the services provided in (a).

i. Billed Family & Children's Service $14,500 for services rendered.

j. Purchased land as the site of a future office for $10,000. Paid $3,000 cash as a down payment and signed a note payable for the balance.

k. Received the April telephone bill for $1,950 to be paid next month.

Required:

For each of the transactions, prepare journal entries. Be sure to categorize each account as an asset (A), liability (L), stockholders' equity (SE), revenue (R), or expense (E).

AP3-3
LO3-4

Determining Financial Statement Effects of Various Transactions and Identifying Cash Flow Effects (P3-3)

Barnes & Noble is the nation's largest bookseller and a leading retailer of digital media and electronic products, including the Nook for eReading. The following activities were inferred from a recent annual report.

a. *Example:* Incurred expenses; paid part in cash and part on credit.

b. Paid interest on long-term debt.

c. Sold merchandise to customers on account. (**Hint:** Indicate the effects of the sale; then reduce inventory for the amount sold—two transactions.)

d. Sold equipment for cash for more than its cost.

e. Collected cash on account.

f. Used supplies.

g. Repaid long-term debt principal.

h. Received interest on investments.

i. Purchased equipment; paid part in cash and part on credit.

j. Paid cash on account.

k. Issued additional stock.

l. Paid rent to mall owners.

Required:

1. For each of the transactions, complete the tabulation, indicating the effect (+ for increase and − for decrease) of each transaction. (Remember that A = L + SE; R − E = NI; and NI affects SE through Retained Earnings.) Write NE if there is no effect. The first transaction is provided as an example.

	BALANCE SHEET			**INCOME STATEMENT**		
Transaction	**Assets**	**Liabilities**	**Stockholders' Equity**	**Revenues**	**Expenses**	**Net Income**
(a) (example)	−	+	−	NE	+	−

2. For each transaction, indicate where, if at all, it would be reported on the statement of cash flows. Use O for operating activities, I for investing activities, F for financing activities, and NE if the transaction would not be included on the statement.

AP3-4
LO3-4, 3-5, 3-6

Analyzing the Effects of Transactions Using T-Accounts, Preparing an Income Statement, and Evaluating the Net Profit Margin Ratio as a Manager (P3-4)

Alpine Stables, Inc., is established in Denver, Colorado, on April 1, 2017, to provide stables, care for animals, and grounds for riding and showing horses. You have been hired as the new assistant controller. The following transactions for April 2017 are provided for your review.

a. Received contributions from five investors of $60,000 in cash ($12,000 each), a barn valued at $100,000, land valued at $90,000, and supplies valued at $12,000. Each investor received 3,000 shares of stock with a par value of $0.01 per share.

b. Built a small barn for $62,000. The company paid half the amount in cash on April 1, 2017, and signed a three-year note payable for the balance.

c. Provided $35,260 in animal care services for customers, all on credit.

d. Rented stables to customers who cared for their own animals; received cash of $13,200.

e. Received from a customer $2,400 to board her horse in May, June, and July (record as unearned revenue).

f. Purchased hay and feed supplies on account for $3,810 to be used in the summer.

g. Paid $1,240 in cash for water utilities incurred in the month.

h. Paid $2,700 on accounts payable for previous purchases.

i. Received $10,000 from customers on accounts receivable.

j. Paid $6,000 in wages to employees who worked during the month.

k. At the end of the month, purchased a two-year insurance policy for $3,600.

l. Received an electric utility bill for $1,800 for usage in April; the bill will be paid next month.

m. Paid $100 cash dividend to each of the five investors at the end of the month.

Required:

1. Set up appropriate T-accounts. All accounts begin with zero balances.
2. Record in the T-accounts the effects of each transaction for Alpine Stables in April, referencing each transaction in the accounts with the transaction letter. Show the ending balances in the T-accounts.
3. Prepare an income statement for April.
4. Write a short memo to the five owners offering your opinion on the results of operations during the first month of business.
5. After three years in business, you are being evaluated for a promotion to chief financial officer. One measure is how effectively you have managed the revenues and expenses of the business. The following annual data are available:

	2019*	2018	2017
Total assets	$480,000	$320,000	$300,000
Total liabilities	125,000	28,000	30,000
Total stockholders' equity	355,000	292,000	270,000
Operating revenue	450,000	400,000	360,000
Net income	50,000	30,000	(10,000)

At the end of 2019, Alpine Stables decided to build an indoor riding arena for giving lessons year-round. The company borrowed construction funds from a local bank in 2019, and the arena was opened in early 2020.

Compute the net profit margin ratio for each year and evaluate the results. Do you think you should be promoted? Why?

Identifiying Cash Flow Effects (P3-5)

Refer to AP3-4.

Required:
For the transactions listed in AP3-4, indicate the type of activity (O for operating, I for investing, and F for financing) and the direction (+ for increase, − for decrease) and amount of the effect. If the transaction had no effect on cash flows, write NE.

Analyzing the Effects of Transactions Using T-Accounts, Preparing an Income Statement, and Evaluating the Net Profit Margin Ratio (P3-6)

The following are the summary account balances from a recent balance sheet of **Exxon Mobil Corporation**. The accounts have normal debit or credit balances, but they are not necessarily listed in good order. The amounts are shown in millions of dollars for the end of the prior year. Assume the year-end is December 31.

AP3-5

LO3-5

AP3-6

LO3-4, 3-5, 3-6

Cash	$ 12,664	Short-term investments	$ 404
Long-term notes payable	7,711	Retained earnings	151,232
Accounts receivable	38,642	Accounts payable	57,067
Inventories	11,665	Income tax payable	12,727
Other long-term debt	83,481	Prepaid expenses	3,359
Property and equipment, net	214,664	Long-term investments	34,333
Common stock	9,512	Other assets and intangibles	9,092
Other current assets	6,229	Short-term notes payable	9,322

The following is a list of hypothetical transactions for January of the current year (in millions of dollars):

a. Purchased on account $1,610 of new equipment.
b. Received $3,100 on accounts receivable.
c. Received and paid $3 for utility bills.
d. Earned $39,780 in sales on account with customers; cost of sales was $5,984.
e. Paid employees $1,238 for wages earned during the month.
f. Paid three-fourths of the income taxes payable.
g. Purchased $23 in supplies on account (include in Inventories).
h. Prepaid $82 to rent a warehouse next month.
i. Paid $10 of other long-term debt principal and $1 in interest expense on the debt.
j. Purchased a patent (an intangible asset) for $6 cash.

Required:

1. Prepare T-accounts for December 31 of the current year from the preceding list; enter the beginning balances. You will need additional T-accounts for income statement accounts; enter zero for beginning balances.
2. For each transaction, record the effects in the T-accounts. Label each using the letter of the transaction. Compute ending balances. (**Note:** Record two transactions in (*d*), one for revenue recognition and one for the expense.)
3. Prepare an income statement for January of the current year.
4. Compute the company's net profit margin ratio for the month ended January 31 of the current year. What does it suggest to you about Exxon Mobil Corporation?

CONTINUING **PROBLEM**

CON3-1

LO3-4, 3-5, 3-6

Accounting for Operating Activities in a New Business (the Accounting Cycle)

Penny's Pool Service & Supply, Inc. (PPSS) had the following transactions related to operating the business in its first year's busiest quarter ended September 30:

a. Placed and paid for $2,600 in advertisements with several area newspapers (including the online versions), all of which ran in the newspapers during the quarter.
b. Cleaned pools for customers for $19,200, receiving $16,000 in cash with the rest owed by customers who will pay when billed in October.
c. Paid **Pool Corporation, Inc.**, a pool supply wholesaler, $10,600 for inventory received by PPSS in May.
d. As an incentive to maintain customer loyalty, PPSS offered customers a discount for prepaying next year's pool cleaning service. PPSS received $10,000 from customers who took advantage of the discount.
e. Paid the office receptionist $4,500, with $1,500 owed from work in the prior quarter and the rest from work in the current quarter. Last quarter's amount was recorded as an expense and a liability Wages Payable.
f. Had the company van repaired, paying $310 to the mechanic.

g. Paid $220 for phone, water, and electric utilities used during the quarter.
h. Received $75 cash in interest earned during the current quarter on short-term investments.
i. Received a property tax bill for $600 for use of the land and building in the quarter; the bill will be paid next quarter.
j. Paid $2,400 for the next quarter's insurance coverage.

Required:
1. For each of the events, prepare journal entries, checking that debits equal credits.
2. Based only on these quarterly transactions, prepare a classified income statement (with income from operations determined separately from other items) for the quarter ended September 30.
3. Calculate the net profit margin ratio at September 30. What does this ratio indicate about the ability of PPSS to control operations?

CASES **AND PROJECTS**

Annual Report Cases

Finding Financial Information

Refer to the financial statements of **American Eagle Outfitters** in Appendix B at the end of the book.

CP3-1
LO3-2, 3-4, 3-6

Required:
1. State the amount of the largest expense on the income statement for the year ended January 31, 2015, and describe the transaction represented by the expense.
2. Assuming that all net sales are on credit, how much cash did American Eagle Outfitters collect from customers?* (**Hint:** Use a T-account of accounts receivable to infer collection.)
3. A shareholder has complained that "more dividends should be paid because the company had net earnings of $80,322,000. Since this amount is all cash, more of it should go to the owners." Explain why the shareholder's assumption that earnings equal net cash inflow is valid. If you believe that the assumption is **not** valid, state so and support your position concisely.
4. Describe and contrast the purpose of an income statement versus a balance sheet.
5. Compute the company's net profit margin for each year presented. Explain its meaning.

Finding Financial Information

Refer to the financial statements of **Urban Outfitters** in Appendix C at the end of the book.

CP3-2
LO3-2, 3-4, 3-6

Required:
1. What is the company's revenue recognition policy? (**Hint:** Look in the notes to the financial statements.)
2. Assuming that $50 million of cost of sales was due to noninventory purchase expenses (distribution and occupancy costs), how much inventory did the company buy during the year? (**Hint:** Use a T-account of inventory to infer how much was purchased.)
3. Calculate selling, general, and administrative expenses as a percent of sales for each year presented. By what percent did these expenses increase or decrease from fiscal years ended 2014 and 2015 and between 2013 and 2014? (**Hint:** Percentage Change = [Current Year Amount − Prior Year Amount] ÷ Prior Year Amount.)
4. Compute the company's net profit margin for each year presented and explain its meaning.

---

*Note that most retailers settle sales in cash at the register and would not have accounts receivable related to sales unless they had layaway or private credit. For American Eagle, the accounts receivable on the balance sheet primarily relates to amounts owed from landlords for their construction allowances for building new American Eagle stores in malls.

CP3-3

LO3-2, 3-4, 3-6

Comparing Companies within an Industry

Refer to the financial statements of **American Eagle Outfitters** in Appendix B, **Urban Outfitters** in Appendix C, and the Industry Ratio Report in Appendix D at the end of this book.

Required:
1. By what title does each company call its income statement? Explain what "Consolidated" means.
2. Which company had higher net income for the fiscal year?
3. Compute the net profit margin ratio for both companies for the year. Which company is managing revenues and expenses more effectively?
4. Compare the net profit margin ratio for both companies for the most recent year presented to the industry average. On average, are these two companies managing sales and expenses better or worse than their competitors?
5. How much cash was provided by operating activities for each year by each company? What was the percentage change in operating cash flows (1) from fiscal year ended 2013 to 2014 and (2) from fiscal year ended 2014 to 2015? (**Hint:** Percentage Change = [Current Year Amount − Prior Year Amount] ÷ Prior Year Amount.)

Financial Reporting and Analysis Cases

CP3-4

LO3-6

Analyzing a Company over Time

Refer to the annual report for **American Eagle Outfitters** in Appendix B.

Required:
1. The annual report or 10-K report for American Eagle Outfitters provides selected financial data for the last five years. Compute the net profit margin ratio for each of the years presented. Use income from continuing operations in place of net income. (**Hint:** See Item 6 from the 10-K, which is disclosed within the annual report for the data.) **Note:** Some companies will label a year that has a January year-end as having a fiscal year-end dated one year earlier. For example, a January 2015 year-end may be labeled as Fiscal 2014 since the year actually has more months that fall in the 2014 calendar year than in the 2015 calendar year.
2. In Chapter 2, we discussed the current ratio. This ratio is computed in Item 6. Observe the trends over time for both the net profit margin and the current ratio. What do they suggest about American Eagle Outfitters?

CP3-5

LO3-3

Interpreting the Financial Press

The October 4, 2004, edition of *BusinessWeek* presented an article titled "Fuzzy Numbers" on issues related to accrual accounting and its weaknesses that have led some corporate executives to manipulate estimates in their favor, sometimes fraudulently. You can access the article at **www.bloomberg.com/bw/stories/2004-10-03/fuzzy-numbers**.

Required:
Read the article and then answer the following questions:
1. What is accrual accounting?
2. What does the article's title "Fuzzy Numbers" mean?
3. What does the article suggest about the reforms adopted by Congress and the SEC?

Critical Thinking Cases

CP3-6

LO3-3, 3-4, 3-5

Making a Decision as a Bank Loan Officer: Analyzing and Restating Financial Statements That Have Major Deficiencies (Challenging)

Julio Estela started and operated a small boat repair service company during the current year. He is interested in obtaining a $100,000 loan from your bank to build a dry dock to store boats for customers in the winter months. At the end of the year, he prepared the following statements based on information stored in a large filing cabinet:

ESTELA COMPANY		
Profit for the Current Year		
Service fees collected during the current year		$ 55,000
Cash dividends received		10,000
Total		65,000
Expense for operations paid during the current year	$22,000	
Cash stolen	500	
New tools purchased during the current year (cash paid)	1,000	
Supplies purchased for use on service jobs (cash paid)	3,200	
Total		26,700
Profit		$ 38,300
Assets Owned at the End of the Current Year		
Cash in checking account		$ 29,300
Building (at current market value)		32,000
Tools and equipment		18,000
Land (at current market value)		30,000
Stock in ABC Industrial		130,000
Total		$239,300

The following is a summary of completed transactions:

a. Received the following contributions (at fair value) to the business from the owner when it was started in exchange for 1,000 shares of $1 par value common stock in the new company:

Building	$21,000	Land	$20,000
Tools and equipment	17,000	Cash	1,000

b. Earned service fees during the current year of $87,000; of the cash collected, $20,000 was for deposits from customers on work to be done by Julio in the next year.

c. Received the cash dividends on shares of ABC Industrial stock purchased by Julio Estela six years earlier (the stock was not owned by the company).

d. Incurred expenses during the current year of $61,000.

e. Determined amount of supplies on hand (unused) at the end of the current year as $700.

Required:

1. Did Julio prepare the income statement on a cash basis or an accrual basis? Explain how you can tell. Which basis should be used? Explain why.
2. Reconstruct the correct entries under accrual accounting principles and post the effects to T-accounts.
3. Prepare an accrual-based income statement. Explain (using footnotes) the reason for each change that you make to the income statement.
4. What additional information would assist you in formulating your decision regarding the loan to Julio?
5. Based on the revised statements and additional information needed, write a letter to Julio explaining your decision at this time regarding the loan.

Evaluating an Ethical Dilemma

CP3-7

LO3-3

Mike Lynch is the manager of an upstate New York regional office for an insurance company. As the regional manager, his compensation package comprises a base salary, commissions, and a bonus when the region sells new policies in excess of its quota. Mike has been under enormous pressure lately, stemming largely from two factors. First, he is experiencing a mounting personal debt due to a family member's illness. Second, compounding his worries, the region's sales of new policies have dipped below the normal quota for the first time in years.

You have been working for Mike for two years, and like everyone else in the office, you consider yourself lucky to work for such a supportive boss. You also feel great sympathy for his personal problems over the last few months. In your position as accountant for the regional office, you are only too aware of the drop in new policy sales and the impact this will have on the manager's bonus. While you are working late at year-end, Mike stops by your office.

Mike asks you to change the manner in which you have accounted for a new property insurance policy for a large local business. A substantial check for the premium came in the mail on December 31, the last day of the reporting year. The premium covers a period beginning on January 5. You deposited the check and correctly debited Cash and credited an **unearned revenue** account. Mike says, "Hey, we have the money this year, so why not count the revenue this year? I never did understand why you accountants are so picky about these things anyway. I'd like you to change the way you have recorded the transaction. I want you to credit a *revenue* account. And anyway, I've done favors for you in the past, and I am asking for such a small thing in return." With that, he leaves for the day.

Required:
1. How should you handle this situation?
2. What are the ethical implications of Mike's request?
3. Who are the parties who would be helped or harmed if you complied with the request?
4. If you fail to comply with his request, how will you explain your position to him in the morning?

Financial Reporting and Analysis Team Project

CP3-8
LO3-2, 3-3, 3-6

Team Project: Analysis of Income Statements and Ratios

As a team, select an industry to analyze. Yahoo Finance provides lists of industries at **biz.yahoo.com/p/industries.html**. Click on an industry for a list of companies in that industry. Alternatively, go to Google Finance at **www.google.com/finance**, search for a company you are interested in, and you will be presented with a list including that company and its competitors. Each team member should acquire the annual report or 10-K for one publicly traded company in the industry, with each member selecting a different company (the SEC EDGAR service at **www.sec.gov** and the company's investor relations website itself are good sources).

Required:
On an individual basis, each team member should write a short report answering the following questions about the selected company. Discuss any patterns across the companies that you as a team observe. Then, as a team, write a short report comparing and contrasting your companies.
1. For the most recent year, what is (are) the major revenue account(s)? What percentage is each to total operating revenues? (Calculated as Revenue A ÷ Total revenues.)
2. For the most recent year, what is (are) the major expense account(s)? What percentage is each to total operating expenses? (Calculated as Expense A ÷ Total expenses.)
3. Ratio Analysis:
   a. What does the net profit margin ratio measure in general?
   b. Compute the ratio for the last three years.
   c. What do your results suggest about the company?
   d. If available, find the industry ratio for the most recent year, compare it to your results, and discuss why you believe your company differs or is similar to the industry ratio.
4. Describe the company's revenue recognition policy, if reported (usually in the Significant Accounting Policies note to the financial statements).
5. The ratio of Cash from Operating Activities divided by Net Income measures how liberal (that is, speeding up revenue recognition or delaying expense recognition) or conservative (that is, taking care not to record revenues too early or expenses too late) management is in choosing among various revenue and expense recognition policies. A ratio above 1.0 suggests more conservative policies; a ratio below 1.0 suggests more liberal policies. Compute the ratio for each of the last three years. What do your results suggest about the company's choice of accounting policies?

Adjustments, Financial Statements, and the Quality of Earnings

The end of the accounting period is a very busy time for **Chipotle Mexican Grill**. Although the last day of the fiscal year for Chipotle falls on the last day of December each year, the financial statements are not distributed to users until management and the external auditors (independent CPAs) make many critical evaluations.

- Management must ensure that the correct amounts are reported on the balance sheet and income statement. This often requires estimations, assumptions, and judgments about the timing of revenue and expense recognition and values for assets and liabilities.

- The auditors have to (1) assess the strength of the controls established by management to safeguard the company's assets and ensure the accuracy of the financial records and (2) evaluate the appropriateness of estimates and accounting principles used by management in determining revenues and expenses.

Managers of most companies understand the need to present financial information fairly so as not to mislead users. However, since end-of-period adjustments are the most complex portion of the annual recordkeeping process, they are prone to error. External auditors examine the company's records on a test, or sample, basis. To maximize the chance of detecting any errors significant enough to affect users' decisions, CPAs allocate more of their testing to transactions most likely to be in error.

Several accounting research studies have documented the most error-prone transactions for medium-size manufacturing companies. End-of-period adjustment errors, such as failure to provide adequate product warranty liability, failure to include items that should be

Learning Objectives

After studying this chapter, you should be able to:

4-1 Explain the purpose of adjustments and analyze the adjustments necessary at the end of the period to update balance sheet and income statement accounts.

4-2 Present an income statement with earnings per share, a statement of stockholders' equity, and a balance sheet.

4-3 Compute and interpret the total asset turnover ratio.

4-4 Explain the closing process.

© SchulteProductions/iStockphoto

expensed, and end-of-period transactions recorded in the wrong period (called cut-off errors), are in the top category and thus receive a great deal of attention from auditors.

For 2014, Chipotle's year-end estimation and auditing process took until February 4, 2015, the date on which the auditor Ernst & Young LLP completed the audit work and signed its audit opinion. At that point, the financial statements were made available to the public.

UNDERSTANDING THE BUSINESS

Managers are responsible for preparing financial statements that will be useful to investors, creditors, and others. Financial information is most useful for analyzing the past and predicting the future when it is considered by users to be of **high quality.** High-quality information is information that is relevant (that is, material and able to influence users' decisions) and a faithful representation of what is being reported (that is, complete, free from error, and unbiased in portraying economic reality).

Users expect revenues and expenses to be reported in the proper period based on the revenue recognition and expense recognition principles discussed in Chapter 3. Revenues are to be recorded when earned, and expenses are to be recorded when incurred, regardless of when cash receipts or payments occur. Many operating activities take place over a period of time or over several periods, such as using insurance that has been prepaid or owing wages to employees for past work. Because recording these and similar activities daily is often very costly, most companies wait until the end of the period (usually monthly, quarterly, or annually) to make **adjustments** to record related revenues and expenses in the correct period. These entries update the records and are the focus of this chapter.

In this chapter, we emphasize the use of the same analytical tools illustrated in Chapters 2 and 3 (T-accounts and journal entries) to understand how common adjustments are analyzed and recorded at the end of the accounting period. These tools provide the foundation for understanding adjustments that require additional estimation and judgments by management, which we discuss in future chapters. Then, in this chapter, we prepare financial statements using adjusted accounts, and finally, we illustrate how to prepare the accounting records for the next period by performing a process called **closing the books.**

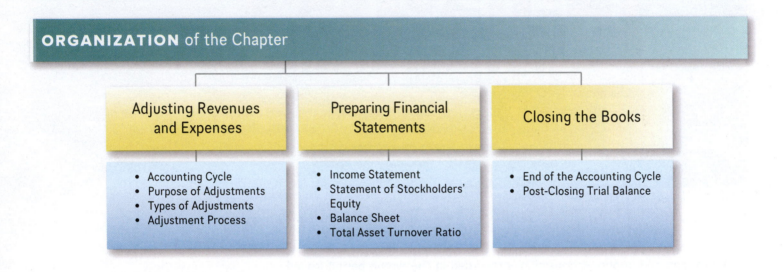

ORGANIZATION of the Chapter

Adjusting Revenues and Expenses
- Accounting Cycle
- Purpose of Adjustments
- Types of Adjustments
- Adjustment Process

Preparing Financial Statements
- Income Statement
- Statement of Stockholders' Equity
- Balance Sheet
- Total Asset Turnover Ratio

Closing the Books
- End of the Accounting Cycle
- Post-Closing Trial Balance

ADJUSTING REVENUES AND EXPENSES

Accounting Cycle

Exhibit 4.1 presents the basic steps in the **accounting cycle.** As initially discussed in Chapter 2, the accounting cycle is the process followed by entities to analyze and record transactions, adjust the records at the end of the period, prepare financial statements, and prepare the records for the next cycle. **During** the accounting period, transactions that result in exchanges between the company and other external parties are analyzed and recorded in the general journal in chronological order (journal entries), and the related accounts are updated in the general ledger (T-accounts), similar to our Chipotle illustrations in Chapters 2 and 3. In this chapter, we examine the **end-of-period** steps that focus primarily on adjustments to record revenues and expenses in the proper period and to update the balance sheet accounts for reporting purposes.

Purpose of Adjustments

Accounting systems are designed to record most recurring daily transactions, particularly those involving cash. As cash is received or paid, it is recorded in the accounting system. In general, this focus on cash works well, especially when cash receipts and payments occur in the same period as the activities that produce revenues and expenses. However, cash is not always received in the period in which the company earns revenue; likewise, cash is not always paid in the period in which the company incurs an expense.

How does the accounting system record revenues and expenses when one transaction is needed to record a cash receipt or payment and another transaction is needed to record revenue when it is earned or an expense when it is incurred? The solution to the problem created by such differences in timing is to record adjusting entries at the end of every accounting period, so that

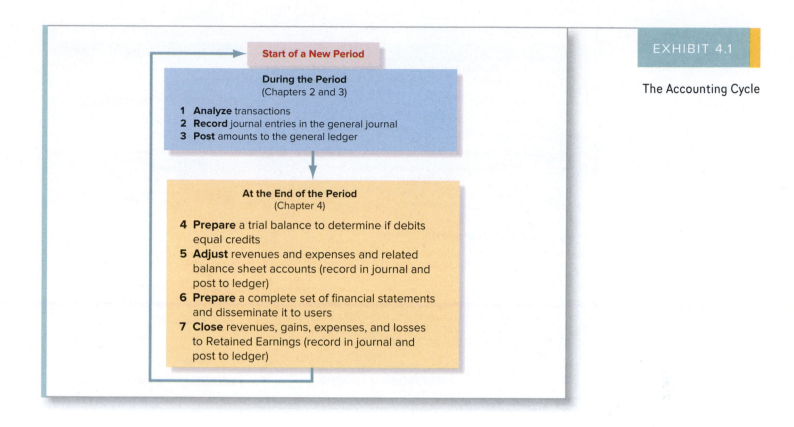

EXHIBIT 4.1

The Accounting Cycle

- Revenues are recorded when they are earned (the **revenue recognition principle**),
- Expenses are recorded when they are incurred to generate revenue (the **expense recognition principle**),
- **Assets** are reported at amounts that represent the probable future benefits remaining at the end of the period, and
- **Liabilities** are reported at amounts that represent the probable future sacrifices of assets or services owed at the end of the period.

Companies wait until the **end of the accounting period** to adjust their accounts in this way because adjusting the records daily would be very costly and time-consuming. Adjusting entries are required every time a company wants to prepare financial statements for external users.

Types of Adjustments

Exhibit 4.2 describes the four types of adjustments (two in which cash was already received or paid and two in which cash will be received or paid). Because of the timing of the cash receipts or payments, each of these types of adjustments involves two entries:

- One for the cash receipt or payment either before or after the end of the period.
- One for the adjustment to record the revenue or expense in the proper period (the adjusting entry).

In practice, almost every account, **except Cash,** could require an adjustment. Rather than trying to memorize an endless list of specific examples, you should focus instead on learning the general types of adjustments that are needed and the process that is used to determine how to adjust the accounts. We will illustrate the process involved in analyzing and adjusting the accounts by reviewing all the adjustments needed for **Chipotle Mexican Grill** before preparing the financial statements for the first quarter of 2015 based on adjusted balances.

EXHIBIT 4.2

Four Types of
Adjustments

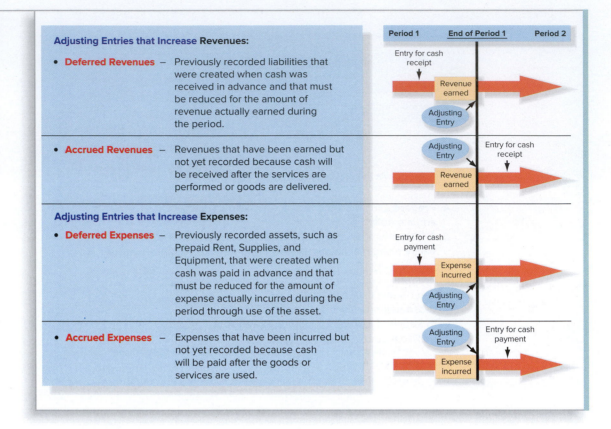

Adjusting Entries that Increase Revenues:

- **Deferred Revenues** — Previously recorded liabilities that were created when cash was received in advance and that must be reduced for the amount of revenue actually earned during the period.

- **Accrued Revenues** — Revenues that have been earned but not yet recorded because cash will be received after the services are performed or goods are delivered.

Adjusting Entries that Increase Expenses:

- **Deferred Expenses** — Previously recorded assets, such as Prepaid Rent, Supplies, and Equipment, that were created when cash was paid in advance and that must be reduced for the amount of expense actually incurred during the period through use of the asset.

- **Accrued Expenses** — Expenses that have been incurred but not yet recorded because cash will be paid after the goods or services are used.

Adjustment Process

In analyzing adjustments at the end of the period, there are three steps:

EXHIBIT 4.3

Adjustment Process

Step 1: Ask: **Was revenue earned or an expense incurred that is not yet recorded?**

If the answer is YES, credit the revenue account or debit the expense account in the adjusting entry.

Step 2: Ask: **Was the related cash received or paid in the past or will it be received or paid in the future?**

If cash **was received** in the past, a deferred revenue (liability) account was recorded in the past → Now, reduce the liability account (usually Unearned Revenue) that was recorded when cash was received because some or all of the liability has been earned since then.

If cash **will be received** in the future → Increase the receivable account (such as Interest Receivable or Rent Receivable) to record what is owed by others to the company (creating an accrued revenue).

If cash **was paid** in the past, a deferred expense account (asset) was created in the past → Now reduce the asset account (such as Supplies or Prepaid Expenses) that was recorded in the past because some of or the entire asset has been used since then.

If cash **will be paid** in the future → Increase the payable account (such as Interest Payable or Wages Payable) to record what is owed by the company to others (creating an accrued expense).

NOTE: Cash is never included in the adjusting entry because it was recorded already in the past or will be recorded in the future.

Step 3: **Compute the amount of revenue earned or expense incurred.** Sometimes the amount is given or known, sometimes it must be computed, and sometimes it must be estimated.

In summary, the pattern that results when the adjusting entry is recorded is as follows:

When revenue is earned:	When expense is incurred:
If cash was received and previously recorded, the adjusting entry is	If cash was paid and previously recorded, the adjusting entry is
DEFERRED REVENUE	DEFERRED EXPENSE
Unearned Revenue (−L) xx	Expense (+E, −SE)........................... xx
Revenue (+R, +SE) xx	Prepaid Expense (−A)....................... xx
OR	OR
If cash will be received, the adjusting entry is	If cash will be paid, the adjusting entry is
ACCRUED REVENUE	ACCRUED EXPENSE
Receivable (+A) xx	Expense (+E, −SE) xx
Revenue (+R, +SE) xx	Payable (+L) xx

Now let's illustrate the adjustment process for **Chipotle** at the end of the first quarter of 2015. We start by reviewing the unadjusted trial balance from Chapter 3:

EXHIBIT 4.4

Unadjusted Trial Balance

CHIPOTLE MEXICAN GRILL
Unadjusted Trial Balance
For the first quarter ended March 31, 2015

(in thousands)	Debit	Credit
Cash	543,000	
Short-term investments	347,600	
Accounts receivable	21,500	
Supplies	385,100	
Prepaid expenses	150,000	
Land	12,100	
Buildings (*at cost*)	1,275,300	
Equipment (*at cost*)	476,300	
Accumulated depreciation (*used cost*)		613,700
Long-term investments	531,100	
Intangible assets	68,400	
Accounts payable		76,100
Unearned revenue		38,700
Dividends payable		3,000
Wages payable		0
Utilities payable		49,500
Long-term notes payable		2,000
Other liabilities		285,900
Common stock		500
Additional paid-in capital		293,800
Retained earnings		1,718,800
Restaurant sales revenue		1,071,700
Interest revenue		1,200
Wages expense	177,000	
Utilities expense	75,400	
Repairs expense	18,700	
Training expense	40,800	
Loss on disposal of assets	4,200	
Income tax expense	28,400	
Total	**4,154,900**	**4,154,900**

From a review of the unadjusted trial balance, we identify several accounts that may need an adjustment:

- One deferred revenue account:
  Unearned Revenue representing the amount received from customers on gift cards. A portion may have been earned during the quarter.

- One accrued revenue:
  Additional interest on investments may have been earned but not yet received by the end of the quarter.

- Four deferred expense accounts:
  Supplies of food, beverage, and packaging were used during the period.
  Prepaid Expenses relating to rent, insurance, and advertising paid in the past were partially used during the period.
  Buildings were used during the period to generate revenue.
  Equipment was also used during the period to generate revenue. Because buildings and equipment were used during the quarter, we must make an adjustment to reflect that in the Accumulated Depreciation account representing the cost of the buildings and equipment that has been allocated (used) in the past.

- Four accrued expenses:
  Wages, utilities, interest on notes payable, and income taxes may need to be adjusted for amounts incurred during the quarter but not yet paid.

We follow the three-step adjustment process outlined in Exhibit 4.3 to illustrate how to apply the process. For each of the following adjustments, we shorten the term **adjusting journal entry** to AJE for ease of labeling. Also, note that the beginning balance in each T-account is taken from the unadjusted trial balance in Exhibit 4.4. Finally, as you learned in Chapters 2 and 3, it is important to continue to check that debits equal credits in each entry and that the accounting equation remains in balance. In the following adjustments, all entries and the accounting equation are in balance.

Deferred Revenues

DEFERRED (UNEARNED) REVENUES
Previously recorded liabilities (from collecting cash from customers in the past) that need to be adjusted at the end of the period to reflect the amount of revenue earned by providing goods or services over time to customers.

When a customer pays for goods or services before the company delivers them, the company records the amount of cash received in a **deferred (unearned) revenue** account. This unearned revenue is a liability representing the company's promise to perform or deliver the goods or services in the future. Recognition of (recording) the revenue is postponed (deferred) until the company meets its obligation.

AJE 1   Unearned Revenue Chipotle received cash last period from customers purchasing gift cards and recorded an increase in Cash and an increase in Unearned Revenues, a liability, to recognize the business's obligation to provide future services to customers. During the first quarter of 2015, customers redeemed a portion of the gift cards for $17,300 in food service.

| Step 1: | **Was revenue earned that is not yet recorded? Yes.** When customers redeemed their gift cards during the quarter, Chipotle provided food service. Therefore, Chipotle earned $17,300 in Restaurant Sales Revenue that is not yet recorded by the end of the quarter. **Record an increase in the revenue account.** |

| Step 2: | **Was the related cash received in the past or will it be received in the future? In the past.** The Unearned Revenue account was created when cash was received in the past. At the end of the quarter, there is a $38,700 balance in the account. However, it is too large because a portion of it has been earned. Therefore, **reduce the unearned revenue account** for the amount earned. |

| Step 3: | **Compute the amount of revenue earned.** The amount of the revenue that was earned is given as $17,300. **Record $17,300** in the adjusting journal entry. |

	Debit	Credit
(AJE 1) Unearned Revenue (−L)	17,300	
Restaurant Sales Revenue (+R, +SE).........		17,300

Assets	=	Liabilities	+	Stockholders' Equity	
		Unearned revenue −17,300		Restaurant sales revenue (+R) +17,300	

− Unearned Revenue (L) +				− Restaurant Sales Revenue (R) +		
	38,700	Bal.			1,071,700	Bal.
(AJE 1) 17,300					17,300	(AJE 1)
	21,400				1,089,000	

NOTE: The beginning balance for each T-account is from the 3/31/15 unadjusted trial balance in Exhibit 4.4.

Additional examples of deferred revenues include magazine subscription sales by publishing companies; season tickets sold in advance to sporting events, plays, and concerts by these types of organizations; air flight tickets sold in advance by airlines; and rent received in advance by landlords. Each of these requires an adjusting entry at the end of the accounting period to report the amount of revenue earned during the period.

Accrued Revenues

Sometimes companies perform services or provide goods (that is, earn revenue) before customers pay. Because the cash that is owed for these goods and services has not yet been received and the customers have not yet been billed, the revenue that was earned may not have been recorded. Revenues that have been earned but have not yet been recorded at the end of the accounting period are called **accrued revenues**.

AJE 2   **Interest on Investments** Investments owned by Chipotle earned $200 in additional interest revenue for the quarter, but the cash will be received in the next quarter.

Step 1:   **Was revenue earned that is not yet recorded? Yes.** Investments earned an additional amount of interest during the quarter, but no interest revenue has yet been recorded. Therefore, revenue is understated in the current quarter. **Record an increase in the revenue account.**

Step 2:   **Was the related cash received in the past or will it be received in the future? In the future.** Chipotle will receive the cash from the interest revenue in the next quarter. Because cash will be received, a new account (a receivable) needs to be increased. **Increase Interest Receivable.**

Step 3:   **Compute the amount of revenue earned.** The amount of the revenue that was earned is given. **Record $200** in the adjusting journal entry.

ACCRUED REVENUES
Previously unrecorded revenues that need to be adjusted at the end of the accounting period to reflect the amount earned and its related receivable account.

	Debit	Credit
(AJE 2) Interest Receivable (+A)	200	
Interest Revenue (+R, +SE)		200

Assets	=	Liabilities	+	Stockholders' Equity	
Interest receivable +200				Interest Revenue (+R) +200	

+ Interest Receivable (A) −				− Interest Revenue (R) +		
Bal.	0				1,200	Bal.
(AJE 2)	200				200	(AJE 2)
	200				1,400	

Deferred Expenses

Assets represent resources with probable future benefits to the company. Many assets are used over time to generate revenues, including supplies, buildings, equipment, and prepaid expenses

DEFERRED EXPENSES
Previously acquired assets that need to be adjusted at the end of the accounting period to reflect the amount of expense incurred in using the asset to generate revenue.

for insurance, advertising, and rent. These assets are **deferred expenses** (that is, recording the expenses for using these assets is deferred to the future). At the end of every period, an adjustment must be made to record the amount of the asset that was used during the period.

AJE 3 **Supplies** Supplies include food, beverage, and paper products for Chipotle. At the end of the quarter, Chipotle counted $16,100 in supplies on hand, but the Supplies account indicated a balance of $385,100 (from the unadjusted trial balance in Exhibit 4.4).

Step 1: **Was expense incurred that is not yet recorded? Yes.** Supplies were used during the quarter to generate revenue, but no entry has been made to record the amount used. Expenses are understated. **Record an increase in the Supplies Expense account.**

Step 2: **Was the related cash paid in the past or will it be paid in the future? In the past.** Chipotle purchased supplies during the quarter and recorded the acquisition in the Supplies account. Some of these supplies have been used during the quarter, but no entry has been made yet to reduce the account. Assets are overstated. **Record a decrease in the Supplies account.**

Step 3: **Compute the amount of expense incurred.** The easiest way to determine the dollar amount of supplies used is to add the dollar amount of supplies available at the beginning of the period plus any purchases made during the period, and then subtract the dollar amount of supplies remaining on hand at the end of the period.

Computation of Supplies Expense	
Beginning balance—Supplies	$ 15,300
+ Purchases during quarter	369,800
Unadjusted balance at end of quarter	385,100
− Amount on hand at end of quarter	(16,100)
Supplies used during quarter	$369,000

The balance of Supplies on the unadjusted trial balance is $385,100, which includes the beginning balance for the quarter ($15,300) and the purchases during the quarter ($369,800). With $16,100 remaining on hand, the amount of supplies used during the period is $369,000. **Record $369,000 in the adjusting entry.**

	Debit	Credit
(AJE 3) Supplies Expense (+E, −SE)	369,000	
Supplies (−A)		369,000

Assets	=	Liabilities	+	Stockholders' Equity	
Supplies −369,000				Supplies expense (+E) −369,000	

+ Supplies (A) −			+ Supplies Expense (E) −	
Bal. 385,100			Bal. 0	
	369,000 (AJE 3)		(AJE 3) 369,000	
16,100			369,000	

AJE 4 **Prepaid Expenses** Among a few other times, the Prepaid Expenses account includes:

- $88,000 paid at the beginning of the quarter for rental of facilities at $22,000 per month,
- $48,000 for insurance coverage for six months beginning January 1, 2015, and
- $3,400 for advertising during the quarter.

Step 1: **Was expense incurred that is not yet recorded? Yes.** A portion of the rent and insurance and all of the advertising have been used during the quarter to generate revenue, but no entry has been made to record the amount used. Expenses are understated. **Record these expenses separately as Rent Expense, Insurance Expense, and Advertising Expense.**

Step 2:   **Was the related cash paid in the past or will it be paid in the future? In the past.** Chipotle prepaid rent, insurance, and advertising at the beginning of the quarter. These provided probable future benefits and were recorded as an asset Prepaid Expenses. Because a portion of these prepaid expenses have been used during the quarter, but no entry has been made yet to reflect that, the Prepaid Expenses account is overstated. **Record a decrease in Prepaid Expenses.**

Step 3:   **Compute the amount of expense incurred.** The computations for each are as follows:

- Rent: $22,000 per month × 3 months in the quarter = $66,000 used
- Insurance: ($48,000 prepaid × 3 months in the quarter) ÷ 6 months coverage = $24,000 used
- Advertising: All during the quarter = $3,400 used

Record a total of $93,400.

	Debit	Credit
(AJE 4) Rent Expense (+E, −SE)	66,000	
Insurance Expense (+E, −SE).	24,000	
Advertising Expense (+E, −SE)	3,400	
Prepaid Expenses (−A)		93,400

Assets		=	Liabilities	+	Stockholders' Equity	
Prepaid expenses	−93,400				Rent expense (+E)	−66,000
					Insurance expense (+E)	−24,000
					Advertising expense (+E)	−3,400

+ Prepaid Expenses (A) −					+ Rent Expense (E) −		
Bal.	150,000			Bal.	0		
		93,400	*(AJE 4)*	*(AJE 4)*	66,000		
	56,600				66,000		

+ Insurance Expense (E) −				+ Advertising Expense (E) −		
Bal.	0			Bal.	0	
(AJE 4)	24,000			*(AJE 4)*	3,400	
	24,000				3,400	

AJE 5   **Buildings and Equipment** In Exhibit 4.4, we noted that Buildings and Equipment accounts are listed at **cost.** Buildings and equipment accounts increase by the cost of the assets when they are **acquired** and decrease by the cost of the assets when they are **sold.** However, these assets are also **used** over time to generate revenue. Thus, a part of their cost should be expensed in the same period (following the expense recognition principle). Accountants say that buildings and equipment, but not land, **depreciate** over time as they are used (land does not depreciate or get used up in an accounting sense). In accounting, **depreciation is an allocation of the cost of buildings and equipment over their estimated useful lives to the organization.**

To keep track of the asset's historical cost, the amount that has been used is not subtracted directly from the asset account. Instead, it is accumulated in a new kind of account called a **contra-account.** Contra-accounts are accounts that are **directly linked to another account, but with an opposite balance.** For Buildings and Equipment, the contra-account for the total cost used to date is called **Accumulated Depreciation** (noted in Exhibit 4.4). Accumulated Depreciation increases with the amount of depreciation expense for the period and decreases when an asset is sold for the portion used in prior periods. This is the first of several contra-accounts you will learn throughout the text. We will designate contra-accounts with an X in front of the type of account to which it is related. For example, this first contra-account will be shown as Accumulated Depreciation (XA).

CONTRA-ACCOUNT
An account that is an offset to, or reduction of, the primary account.

NET BOOK VALUE (CARRYING OR BOOK VALUE)
The acquisition cost of an asset less accumulated depreciation, depletion, or amortization.

Since assets have debit balances, Accumulated Depreciation has a credit balance. On the balance sheet, the amount that is reported for total property and equipment is its **net book value** (also called the **book value** or **carrying value**), which equals the ending balance in the Land, Buildings, and Equipment accounts (total cost of property and equipment) minus the ending balance in the Accumulated Depreciation account (used cost of buildings and equipment).

+ Property and Equipment (A) −		− Accumulated Depreciation (XA) +		Amount reported on the balance sheet
Beginning bal. Buy (cost)	Sell (cost)	Accumulated portion of asset cost used when sold	Beginning bal. Portion of asset cost used during period	
Ending bal.		−	Ending bal.	= Net book value

For Chipotle, based on unadjusted balances (from Exhibit 4.4 with dollars in thousands), land, buildings, and equipment have a total cost of $1,763,700 and Accumulated Depreciation has a credit balance of $613,700. On the balance sheet, property and equipment would be reported net of those two amounts as follows:

Property and equipment (net of accumulated depreciation of $613,700)	$1,150,000

Depreciation is discussed in much greater detail in Chapter 8. Until then, we will give you the amount of depreciation estimated by the company. Chipotle estimates depreciation to be $122,400 per year.

Step 1: **Was expense incurred that is not yet recorded? Yes.** The company used buildings and equipment during the first quarter of 2015. However, no expense has yet been recorded, so expenses are understated. **Record an increase in the expense account, Depreciation Expense.**

Step 2: **Was the related cash paid in the past or will it be paid in the future? In the past.** Chipotle purchased buildings and equipment in the past to be used over several years. The acquisitions were recorded in the asset accounts, which maintain the historical cost of the assets. The amount to be used in the future (net book value) must now be reduced for the depreciation for the first quarter of 2015. **Reduce the net book value by increasing the contra-account Accumulated Depreciation.**

Step 3: **Compute the amount of expense incurred.** The property and equipment have been used to generate revenue for the quarter. Thus, we need to calculate one quarter of Depreciation Expense:

Depreciation expense for the quarter = $122,400 for the year (given) × 1/4 of the year
= $30,600

	Debit	Credit
(AJE 5) Depreciation Expense (+E, −SE).	30,600	
Accumulated Depreciation (+XA, −A).		30,600

Assets	= Liabilities +	Stockholders' Equity
Accumulated depreciation (+XA) −30,600		Depreciation expense (+E) −30,600

+ Depreciation Expense (E) −		− Accumulated Depreciation (XA) +	
Bal.	0	613,700	Bal.
(AJE 5)	**30,600**	**30,600**	*(AJE 5)*
	30,600	644,300	

Accrued Expenses

Numerous expenses are incurred in the current period without being paid for until the next period. Common examples include Wages Expense for the wages owed to employees, Interest Expense incurred on debt, and Utilities Expense for the water, gas, and electricity used during the period. These **accrued expenses** accumulate (accrue) over time but are not recognized until the end of the period in an adjusting entry.

AJE 6 **Wages** Chipotle's employees earned $67,200 in wages for working two days at the end of the quarter. They will be paid in the next quarter.

Step 1: **Was expense incurred that is not yet recorded? Yes.** The company used employee labor near the end of the first quarter of 2015. However, no expense has yet been recorded, so expenses are understated. **Record an increase in Wages Expense.**

Step 2: **Was the related cash paid in the past or will it be paid in the future? In the future.** Chipotle will pay the employees in the next quarter, but no liability has yet been recorded. Liabilities are understated. **Record an increase in Wages Payable.**

Step 3: **Compute the amount of expense incurred.** The amount of wages owed to employees is given. **Record $67,200 in the adjusting entry.**

	Debit	Credit
(AJE 6) Wages Expense (+E, −SE)	67,200	
Wages Payable (+L)		67,200

Assets	=	Liabilities	+	Stockholders' Equity	
		Wages payable +67,200		Wages expense (+E)	−67,200

+ Wages Expense (E) −			− Wages Payable (L) +	
Bal.	177,000		0	Bal.
(AJE 6)	67,200		67,200	(AJE 6)
	244,200		67,200	

AJE 7 **Interest on Debt** Chipotle borrowed $2,000 in long-term notes payable and had other interest-bearing obligations of $14,000 (of the $285,900 in Other Liabilities) at the beginning of the quarter. There are two components when borrowing (or lending) money: **principal** (the amount borrowed or loaned) and **interest** (the cost of borrowing or lending). The interest rate on Chipotle's borrowings is 5.0 percent. Long-Term Notes Payable and a portion of Other Liabilities (the principal) were recorded properly when the money was borrowed. Their balances do not need to be adjusted. However, interest expense is incurred by Chipotle over time as the money is used, and it will be paid in the future.

Step 1: **Was expense incurred that is not yet recorded? Yes.** Chipotle used borrowed funds during the quarter, but the expense has not yet been recognized. Expenses are understated. **Record an increase in the Interest Expense account.**

Step 2: **Was the related cash paid in the past or will it be paid in the future? In the future.** Chipotle will pay interest on the debt in the future. Because cash is owed, a payable account needs to be increased. **Record an increase in Interest Payable.**

Step 3: **Compute the amount of expense incurred. NOTE: Unless told otherwise, the interest rate on loans to others and debt is always given as an annual percentage.** The following table gives the formula for computing interest for any part of a year:

Principal	×	Annual Interest Rate	×	Fraction of Year (since last computation)	=	Interest for the Period
$16,000	×	0.05	×	3 months ÷ 12 months	=	$200

Chipotle had $16,000 in interest-bearing debt for the first quarter (3 out of 12 months). **Record $200 in the adjusting entry.**

ACCRUED EXPENSES
Previously unrecorded expenses that need to be adjusted at the end of the accounting period to reflect the amount incurred and its related payable account.

	Debit	Credit
(AJE 7) Interest Expense (+E, −SE)	200	
Interest Payable (+L)		200

Assets	=	Liabilities		+	Stockholders' Equity	
		Interest payable	+200		Interest expense (+E)	−200

+ Interest Expense (E) −			− Interest Payable (L) +	
Bal.	0		0	Bal.
(AJE 7)	200		200	(AJE 7)
	200		200	

AJE 8   Utilities Most organizations receive utility bills after using utility services such as electricity, natural gas, and telephone. Chipotle received a utility bill for $14,900 for usage during the quarter. The bill will be paid next quarter.

Step 1: **Was expense incurred that is not yet recorded? Yes.** Chipotle used the utilities during the first quarter but has not yet recorded the expense. Expenses are understated. **Record an increase in Utilities Expense.**

Step 2: **Was the related cash paid in the past or will it be paid in the future? In the future.** Chipotle will pay next quarter the utility bill owed for usage in the first quarter. The liability is understated. **Increase the Utilities Payable account.**

Step 3: **Compute the amount of expense incurred.** The amount of the utilities incurred in the first quarter is given. **Record $14,900 in the adjusting entry.**

	Debit	Credit
(AJE 8) Utilities Expense (+E, −SE).................	14,900	
Utilities Payable (+L)....................		14,900

Assets	=	Liabilities		+	Stockholders' Equity	
		Utilities payable	+14,900		Utilities expense (+E)	−14,900

+ Utilities Expense (E) −			− Utilities Payable (L) +	
Bal.	75,400		49,500	Bal.
(AJE 8)	14,900		14,900	(AJE 8)
	90,300		64,400	

AJE 9   Income Taxes The final adjusting entry is to record the accrual of income taxes that will be paid in the next quarter. This requires computing adjusted pretax income and applying the appropriate tax rate.

Step 1: **Was expense incurred that is not yet recorded? Yes.** Chipotle incurred taxes on its quarterly income. Until an adjusting entry is recorded at the end of the period based on all adjusted revenues, gains, expenses, and losses, total expenses on the income statement are understated. **Record an increase in Income Tax Expense.**

Step 2: **Was the related cash paid in the past or will it be paid in the future? In the future.** Income taxes from the first quarter are due by the end of the second quarter. So the liabilities on the balance sheet must be increased. **Record an increase in Income Taxes Payable.**

Step 3: **Compute the amount of expense incurred.** Income taxes are computed on the pretax income after all other adjustments. First determine adjusted pretax income:

	Revenues and Gains	−	Expenses and Losses	
On unadjusted trial balance	$1,072,900		$316,100	← Excludes $28,400 of income tax expense already recorded during the quarter
AJE 1	17,300			
AJE 2	200			
AJE 3			369,000	
AJE 4			93,400	← Rent $66,000 + Insurance $24,000 + Advertising $3,400
AJE 5			30,600	
AJE 6			67,200	
AJE 7			200	
AJE 8			14,900	
	$1,090,400	−	$891,400	= **$199,000** Pretax Income

Chipotle estimated a tax rate of 38.4 percent for the quarter, with the taxes not yet paid due next quarter. Computation of the quarterly income tax expense:

Pretax income $199,000 × Income tax rate 0.384 = Income tax expense for the quarter $76,400 (rounded)

Less: Income taxes paid for the quarter   28,400

Income tax expense to be recorded $48,000

Record $48,000 in the adjusting entry.

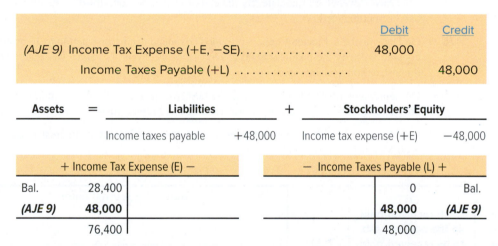

		Debit	Credit
(AJE 9) Income Tax Expense (+E, −SE)...............		48,000	
Income Taxes Payable (+L)			48,000

Assets	=	Liabilities	+	Stockholders' Equity
		Income taxes payable +48,000		Income tax expense (+E) −48,000

+ Income Tax Expense (E) −		− Income Taxes Payable (L) +	
Bal.	28,400	0	Bal.
(AJE 9)	48,000	48,000	(AJE 9)
	76,400	48,000	

In all of the above adjustments, you may have noticed that **the Cash account was never adjusted.** The cash has already been received or paid by the end of the period, or it will be received or paid in the next period. Adjustments are required to record revenues and expenses in the proper period because the cash part of the transaction is at a different point in time. In addition, **each adjusting entry always included one income statement account and one balance sheet account.** Now it's your turn to practice the adjustment process.

PAUSE FOR **FEEDBACK**

STOP

Adjustments are necessary at the end of the accounting cycle to record all revenues and expenses in the proper period and to reflect the proper valuation for assets and liabilities.

- **Deferred revenues** (liabilities) have balances at the end of the period because cash was received before it was earned. If all or part of the liability has been satisfied by the end of the period, revenue needs to be recorded and the liability reduced.

(continued)

- **Accrued revenue** adjustments are necessary when the company has earned revenue but the cash will be received in the next period. Since nothing has yet been recorded, revenue needs to be recognized and an asset (a receivable) increased.

- **Deferred expenses** (assets) have balances at the end of the period because cash was paid in the past by the company for the assets. If all or part of the asset has been used to generate revenues in the period, an expense needs to be recorded and the asset reduced.

- **Accrued expense** adjustments are necessary when the company has incurred an expense but the cash will be paid in the next period. Since nothing has yet been recorded, an expense needs to be recognized and a liability (a payable) increased.

SELF-STUDY QUIZ

For practice, complete the following adjustments using the three-step process outlined in the chapter: (1) Determine if revenue was earned or an expense incurred; (2) determine if cash was received or paid in the past or will be received or paid in the future; and (3) compute the amount.

Florida Flippers, a scuba diving and instruction business, completed its first year of operations on December 31.

AJE 1: Florida Flippers received $6,000 from customers on November 15 for diving trips to the Bahamas in December and January of the next year. The $6,000 was recorded in Unearned Revenue on that date. By the end of December, one-third of the diving trips had been completed.

AJE 2: On December 31, Florida Flippers provided advanced diving instruction to 10 customers who will pay the business $800 in January of next year. No entry was made when the instruction was provided.

AJE 3: On September 1, Florida Flippers paid $24,000 for insurance for the 12 months beginning on September 1. The amount was recorded as Prepaid Insurance on September 1.

AJE 4: On March 1, Florida Flippers borrowed $300,000 at 12 percent. Interest is payable each March 1 for three years.

	(1) Revenue earned or expense incurred?	(2) Cash received/paid in the past or cash to be received/paid in the future?	(3) Amount	Adjusting Journal Entry		
				Accounts	Debit	Credit
AJE 1						
AJE 2						
AJE 3						
AJE 4						

After you have completed your answers, check them at the bottom of the next page.

 **GUIDED HELP 4-1**

For additional step-by-step video instruction on recording adjusting entries, go to **www.mhhe.com/ libby9e_gh4a**.

Adjustments and Incentives

Owners and managers of companies are most directly affected by the information presented in financial statements. If the financial performance and condition of the company appear strong, the company's stock price rises. Shareholders usually receive dividends and increase their investment value. Managers often receive bonuses based on the strength of a company's financial performance, and many in top management are compensated with options to buy their company's stock at prices below market value. The higher the market value, the more compensation they earn. When actual performance lags behind expectations, managers and owners may be tempted to manipulate accruals and deferrals to make up part of the difference. For example, managers may record cash received in advance of being earned as revenue in the current period or may fail to accrue certain expenses at year-end.

Evidence from studies of large samples of companies indicates that some managers do engage in such behavior. This research is borne out by enforcement actions of the Securities and Exchange Commission against companies and sometimes against their auditors. In January 2003, an SEC study reported that, in a five-year period, there were 227 enforcement investigations. Of these, "126 involved improper revenue recognition and 101 involved improper expense recognition. . . . Of the 227 enforcement matters during the Study period, 157 resulted in charges against at least one senior manager. . . . Furthermore, the Study found that 57 enforcement matters resulted in charges for auditing violations. . . ." (p. 47).[*]

In many of these cases, the firms involved, their managers, and their auditors are penalized for such actions. Furthermore, owners suffer because news of an SEC investigation negatively affects the company's stock price.

_____

[*] These statistics are reported in the Securities and Exchange Commission's study "Report Pursuant to Section 704 of the Sarbanes-Oxley Act of 2002," January 27, 2003.

PREPARING FINANCIAL STATEMENTS

As you learned in Chapter 1, the financial statements are interrelated—that is, the numbers from one statement flow into the next statement. The following illustration highlights the interconnections among the statements using the fundamental accounting equation.

Also notice special labels for the accounts. Balance sheet accounts are considered **permanent,** indicating that they retain their balances from the end of one period to the beginning of the next. Revenue, expense, gain, and loss accounts are **temporary** accounts because their balances accumulate for a period but start with a zero balance at the beginning of the next period. These labels will be discussed in the section on closing the books, which follows our presentation of **Chipotle**'s financial statements.

> **LEARNING OBJECTIVE 4-2**
> Present an income statement with earnings per share, a statement of stockholders' equity, and a balance sheet.

Solutions to

SELF-STUDY QUIZ

	(1) Revenue earned or expense incurred?	(2) Cash received/paid in the past or cash to be received/paid in the future?	(3) Amount	Adjusting Journal Entry		
				Accounts	Debit	Credit
AJE 1	Diving Trip Revenue earned	Received in past: *Unearned Revenue*	$6,000 × 1/3 = $2,000 earned	Unearned Revenue (−L) Diving Trip Revenue (+R, +SE)	2,000	2,000
AJE 2	Instruction Revenue earned	To be received: *Accrued Revenue*	$800 earned (given)	Accounts Receivable (+A) Instruction Revenue (+R, +SE)	800	800
AJE 3	Insurance Expense incurred	Paid in past: *Prepaid Expense*	$24,000 × 4 months/ 12 months = $8,000 used	Insurance Expense (+E, −SE) Prepaid Insurance (−A)	8,000	8,000
AJE 4	Interest Expense incurred	To be paid: *Accrued Expense*	$300,000 × 0.12 × 10/12 = $30,000 incurred and owed	Interest Expense (+E, −SE) Interest Payable (+L)	30,000	30,000

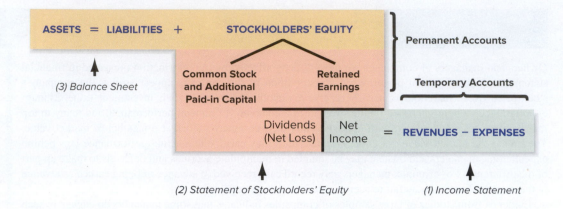

Starting on the bottom right, notice that

- Revenues minus expenses yields net income (assuming it is positive) on the **Income Statement.**
- Net income (or net loss) and dividends to stockholders affect Retained Earnings and any additional issuances of stock during the period affect the balance in Common Stock and Additional Paid-in Capital, all of which appear on the **Statement of Stockholders' Equity.**
- Stockholders' Equity is a component of the **Balance Sheet.**

Thus, if a number on the income statement changes or is in error, it will impact the other statements.

Another way of presenting the relationships among the statements follows.

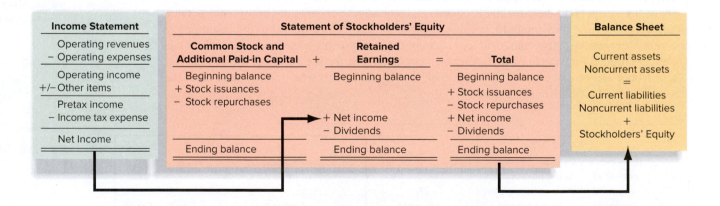

Before we prepare a complete set of financial statements, let's update Chipotle's trial balance to reflect the adjustments, providing us with the adjusted balances needed for the statements. The spreadsheet in Exhibit 4.5 has three sets of debit-credit columns: One for the unadjusted balances as shown in Exhibit 4.4, then the effects of the adjustments AJE 1 through AJE 9, and, finally, the adjusted balances that are determined by adding or subtracting the adjustment across each row. Again, we note that the total debits equal the total credits in each of the sets. Also notice that nearly every revenue and expense account was adjusted, and several new accounts were created during the adjustment process at the end of the period (e.g., Interest Receivable and Depreciation Expense). It is from these adjusted balances that we will prepare an income statement, a statement of stockholders' equity (which includes a column for Retained Earnings), and a balance sheet.

Chipotle Mexican Grill's Trial Balance Spreadsheet   **EXHIBIT 4.5**

CHIPOTLE MEXICAN GRILL
Trial Balance Spreadsheet
For the first quarter ended March 31, 2015
(in thousands of dollars)

NOTE: Cash did not change because cash is never adjusted.

	Unadjusted		Adjustments			Adjusted	
	Debit	Credit		Debit	Credit	Debit	Credit
Cash	543,000					543,000	
Short-term investments	347,600					347,600	
Accounts receivable	21,500					21,500	
Interest receivable			AJE 2	200		200	
Supplies	385,100		AJE 3		369,000	16,100	
Prepaid expenses	150,000		AJE 4		93,400	56,600	
Land	12,100					12,100	
Buildings	1,275,300					1,275,300	
Equipment	476,300					476,300	
Accumulated depreciation		613,700	AJE 5		30,600		644,300
Long-term investments	531,100					531,100	
Intangible assets	68,400					68,400	
Accounts payable		76,100					76,100
Unearned revenue		38,700	AJE 1	17,300			21,400
Dividends payable		3,000					3,000
Wages payable			AJE 6		67,200		67,200
Utilities payable		49,500	AJE 8		14,900		64,400
Interest payable			AJE 7		200		200
Income taxes payable			AJE 9		48,000		48,000
Long-term notes payable		2,000					2,000
Other liabilities		285,900					285,900
Common stock		500					500
Additional paid-in capital		293,800					293,800
Retained earnings		1,718,800					1,718,800
Restaurant sales revenue		1,071,700	AJE 1		17,300		1,089,000
Interest revenue		1,200	AJE 2		200		1,400
Supplies expense			AJE 3	369,000		369,000	
Wages expense	177,000		AJE 6	67,200		244,200	
Rent expense			AJE 4	66,000		66,000	
Insurance expense			AJE 4	24,000		24,000	
Utilities expense	75,400		AJE 8	14,900		90,300	
Repairs expense	18,700					18,700	
Training expense	40,800					40,800	
Advertising expense			AJE 4	3,400		3,400	
Depreciation expense			AJE 5	30,600		30,600	
Loss on disposal of assets	4,200					4,200	
Interest expense			AJE 7	200		200	
Income tax expense	28,400		AJE 9	48,000		76,400	
Total	**4,154,900**	**4,154,900**		**640,800**	**640,800**	**4,316,000**	**4,316,000**

Income Statement

The income statement is prepared first because net income is a component of Retained Earnings. The first quarter 2015 income statement for **Chipotle** based on the adjusted trial balance follows.

CHIPOTLE MEXICAN GRILL, INC. **Consolidated Statement of Income** **For the quarter ended March 31, 2015** **(in thousands of dollars, except per share data)**	
Restaurant sales revenue	$1,089,000
Restaurant operating expenses:	
Supplies expense	369,000
Wages expense	244,200
Rent expense	66,000
Insurance expense	24,000
Utilities expense	90,300
Repairs expense	18,700
General and administrative expenses:	
Training expense	40,800
Advertising expense	3,400
Depreciation expense	30,600
Loss on disposal of assets	4,200
Total operating expenses	891,200
Income from operations	197,800
Other items:	
Interest revenue	1,400
Interest expense	(200)
Income before income taxes	199,000
Income tax expense	76,400
Net income	$ 122,600
Earnings per share (for the quarter)	$ 2.45

You will note that the earnings per share (EPS) ratio is reported on the income statement. It is widely used in evaluating the operating performance and profitability of a company, and it is the only ratio required to be disclosed on the statement or in the notes to the statements. The actual computation of the ratio is quite complex and appropriate for more advanced accounting courses. In this text, we simplify the earnings per share computation as:

$$\text{Earnings per Share}^* = \frac{\text{Net income}}{\text{Average number of shares of common stock outstanding}^\dagger \text{ during the period}}$$

The denominator in the EPS ratio is the average number of shares outstanding (the number at the beginning of the period plus the number at the end of the period, divided by 2). For Chipotle Mexican Grill, the number of shares at the end of 2014 was 40,000,000 and we recorded an additional issuance of 10,000,000 shares at the beginning of the quarter. Therefore, the average number of shares outstanding was 50,000,000 the entire quarter.

$$\text{EPS} = \frac{\$122,600,000 \text{ net income for the quarter}}{50,000,000 \text{ average number of shares outstanding}} = \$2.45 \text{ for the quarter}$$

If this quarterly EPS is repeated in the next three quarters, an annual EPS of $9.80 is expected. This would not be as high as the 2014 EPS of $14.35, suggesting issues of controlling revenues

---

*If there are preferred dividends (discussed in Chapter 11), the amount is subtracted from net income in the numerator. In addition, the denominator is the weighted average of shares outstanding, a complex computation.

†Outstanding shares are those that are currently held by the shareholders.

and expenses. For example, Chipotle experienced lower sales due to a low supply of pork for carnitas, a popular burrito ingredient. It also paid higher prices due to the higher cost of organic avocados supplied from one source in California. The lower EPS may also result from issuing additional shares of common stock at a greater rate than the increase in net income.

Statement of Stockholders' Equity

The final total from the income statement, net income, is carried forward to the Retained Earnings column of the statement of stockholders' equity. To this, the additional elements of the statement are added. Dividends declared and an additional stock issuance (from prior chapters) are also included in the statement:

CHIPOTLE MEXICAN GRILL, INC.
Consolidated Statement of Stockholders' Equity
For the quarter ended March 31, 2015
(in thousands of dollars)

	Common Stock	Additional Paid-in Capital	Retained Earnings	Total Stockholders' Equity	
Balance at December 31, 2014	$400	$290,200	$1,721,800	$2,012,400	
Additional stock issuance	100	3,600		3,700	← From transaction (a) in Ch. 2
Net income			122,600	122,600	← From the income statement
Dividends declared			(3,000)	(3,000)	← From transaction (f) in Ch. 2
Balance at March 31, 2015	$500	$293,800	$1,841,400	$2,135,700	← On the balance sheet

Balance Sheet

The ending balances for Common Stock, Additional Paid-in Capital, and Retained Earnings from the statement of stockholders' equity are included on the balance sheet that follows. You will notice that the contra-asset account, Accumulated Depreciation (used cost), has been subtracted from the total of the land, buildings, and equipment accounts (at cost) to reflect **net book value** (or carrying value) at month-end for balance sheet purposes. Also recall that assets are listed in order of liquidity, and liabilities are listed in order of due dates. Current assets are those used or turned into cash within one year (as well as inventory). Current liabilities are obligations to be paid with current assets within one year. We present the balances at the end of 2014 and the balances at the end of the first quarter of 2015.

Cash Flows from Operations, Net Income, and the Quality of Earnings	FOCUS ON CASH FLOWS

As presented in the previous chapters, the statement of cash flows explains the difference between the ending and beginning balances in the Cash account on the balance sheet during the accounting period. Put simply, the cash flow statement is a categorized list of all transactions of the period that affected the Cash account. The three categories are operating, investing, and financing activities. **Since no adjustments made in this chapter affected cash, the cash flow categories identified on the Cash T-account at the end of Chapter 3 remain the same.**

Many standard financial analysis texts warn analysts to look for unusual deferrals and accruals when they attempt to predict future periods' earnings. They often suggest that wide disparities between net income and cash flow from operations are a useful warning sign. For example, Subramanyan suggests the following:

> Accounting accruals determining net income rely on estimates, deferrals, allocations, and valuations. These considerations sometimes allow more subjectivity than do the factors determining cash flows. For this reason we often relate cash flows from operations to net income in assessing its quality.

Some users consider earnings of higher quality when the ratio of cash flows from operations divided by net income is greater. This derives from a concern with revenue recognition or expense accrual criteria yielding high net income but low cash flows (emphasis added).[*]

The cash flows from operations to net income ratio is illustrated and discussed in more depth in Chapter 12.

[*]K. Subramanyan, *Financial Statement Analysis* (New York: McGraw-Hill/Irwin, 2009), p. 412.

CHIPOTLE MEXICAN GRILL, INC. Consolidated Balance Sheets (in thousands of dollars, except per share data)	March 31, 2015	December 31, 2014
ASSETS		
Current Assets:		
Cash	$ 543,000	$ 419,500
Short-term investments	347,600	338,600
Accounts receivable	21,500	34,800
Interest receivable	200	—
Supplies	16,100	15,300
Prepaid expenses	56,600	70,300
Total current assets	985,000	878,500
Property and equipment:		
Land	12,100	11,100
Buildings	1,275,300	1,267,100
Equipment	476,300	442,500
Total cost	1,763,700	1,720,700
Accumulated depreciation	(644,300)	(613,700)
Net property and equipment	1,119,400	1,107,000
Long-term investments	531,100	496,100
Intangible assets	68,400	64,700
Total assets	**$2,703,900**	$2,546,300
LIABILITIES AND STOCKHOLDERS' EQUITY		
Current Liabilities:		
Accounts payable	$ 76,100	$ 69,600
Unearned revenue	21,400	16,800
Dividends payable	3,000	—
Accrued expenses payable:		
Wages payable	67,200	73,900
Utilities payable	64,400	85,400
Interest payable	200	—
Income taxes payable	48,000	—
Total current liabilities	280,300	245,700
Long-term notes payable	2,000	—
Other liabilities	285,900	288,200
Total liabilities	568,200	533,900
Stockholders' Equity:		
Common stock ($0.10 par per share)	500	400
Additional paid-in capital	293,800	290,200
Retained earnings	1,841,400	1,721,800
Total stockholders' equity	2,135,700	2,012,400
Total liabilities and stockholders' equity	**$2,703,900**	$2,546,300

| Total Asset Turnover Ratio | | KEY RATIO ANALYSIS |

 ANALYTICAL QUESTION

How efficient is management in using assets (its resources) to generate sales?

 RATIO AND COMPARISONS

$$\text{Total Asset Turnover Ratio} = \frac{\text{Net Sales (or Operating Revenues)}}{\text{Average Total Assets}^*}$$

*To compute "average": (Beginning balance + Ending balance)/÷2

The 2014 ratio for **Chipotle** is (dollars in thousands):

$$\frac{\$4,108,269}{\$2,277,782.50^*} = 1.804$$

*($2,009,280 + $2,546,285) ÷ 2 (from 2014 10-K)

COMPARISONS OVER TIME			COMPARISONS WITH COMPETITORS	
Chipotle Mexican Grill, Inc.			**Panera Bread, Inc.**	**Fiesta Restaurant Group, Inc.**
2014	**2013**	**2012**	**2014**	**2014**
1.804	1.748	1.766	1.635	1.806

 INTERPRETATIONS

In General   The total asset turnover ratio measures how efficient management is at using assets to generate sales. Over time or compared to competitors, the higher the asset turnover is, the more efficient assets are being utilized to generate revenues. A company's products or services and business strategy contribute significantly to its asset turnover ratio. However, when competitors are similar, management's ability to control the firm's assets is vital in determining its success. Stronger financial performance improves the asset turnover ratio.

Creditors and security analysts use this ratio to assess a company's effectiveness at controlling both current and noncurrent assets. In a well-run business, creditors expect the ratio on a quarterly basis to fluctuate due to seasonal upswings and downturns. For example, as inventory is built up prior to a heavy sales season, companies need to borrow funds. The asset turnover ratio declines with this increase in assets. Eventually, the season's high sales provide the cash needed to repay the loans. The asset turnover ratio then rises with the increased sales.

Focus Company Analysis   Chipotle's total asset turnover ratio has increased slightly since 2012, suggesting an increase in management efficiency in using assets to generate operating revenues. Compared to its competitors, Chipotle's total asset turnover ratio is higher than that for **Panera Bread**, but equivalent to the ratio for the **Fiesta Restaurant Group**. This is due in part to differences in business strategies. Chipotle and Panera are the two largest fast-casual restaurant chains. Chipotle's recent growth strategy is to open a higher percentage of new stores annually than Panera. Adding new restaurants by Panera increases total assets (the denominator of the ratio), but the increase in its sales (the numerator) may lag behind until the stores are more well-established. In fact, Chipotle's total asset turnover ratio has remained about the same over five years of continued growth, whereas Panera Bread's ratio has fallen slightly and the ratio for Fiesta Restaurant Group, which is much smaller, has increased.

A Few Cautions   While the total asset turnover ratio may decrease due to seasonal fluctuations, a declining ratio may also be caused by changes in corporate policies leading to a rising level of assets. Examples include relaxing credit policies for new customers or reducing collection efforts in accounts receivable. A detailed analysis of the changes in the key components of assets is needed to determine the causes of a change in the asset turnover ratio and thus management's decisions.

CLOSING THE BOOKS
End of the Accounting Cycle

The ending balance in each of the asset, liability, and stockholders' equity accounts becomes the beginning account balance for the next period. These accounts, called **permanent (real) accounts**, are not reduced to a zero balance at the end of the accounting period. For example, the ending Cash balance of the prior accounting period is the beginning Cash balance of the next accounting period. The only time a permanent account has a zero balance is when the item it represents is no longer owned or owed.

On the other hand, revenue, expense, gain, and loss accounts are used to accumulate data for the **current accounting period only;** they are called **temporary (nominal) accounts**. The final step in the accounting cycle, closing the books, is done to prepare income statement accounts for the next accounting cycle. Therefore, at the end of each period, the balances in the temporary accounts are transferred, or **closed,** to the Retained Earnings account by recording a closing entry.

The **closing entries** have two purposes:

1. To transfer the balances in the temporary accounts (income statement accounts) to Retained Earnings.[1]

2. To establish a zero balance in each of the temporary accounts to start the accumulation in the next accounting period.

In this way, the income statement accounts are again ready for their temporary accumulation function for the next period. The closing entry is dated the last day of the accounting period, entered in the usual debits-equal-credits format (in the journal), and immediately posted to the ledger (or T-accounts). **Temporary accounts with debit balances are credited and temporary accounts with credit balances are debited.** The net amount, equal to net income, affects Retained Earnings.

To illustrate the process, we create an example using just a few accounts. The journal entry amounts are taken from the adjusted balances in the T-accounts:

TEMPORARY (NOMINAL) ACCOUNTS
Income statement (and sometimes dividends declared) accounts that are closed to Retained Earnings at the end of the accounting period.

CLOSING ENTRIES
Made at the end of the accounting period to transfer balances in temporary accounts to Retained Earnings and to establish a zero balance in each of the temporary accounts.

Revenues and gains have credit balances. Close them with debits.

	Debit	Credit
Sales Revenue (–R)...................	100	
Gain on Sale of Assets (–R)...........	30	
Wages Expense (–E)................		40
Loss on Sale of Assets (–E).........		10
Retained Earnings (+SE)...........		80

Expenses and losses have debit balances. Close them with credits.

= Net income

CE is short for *closing entry.*

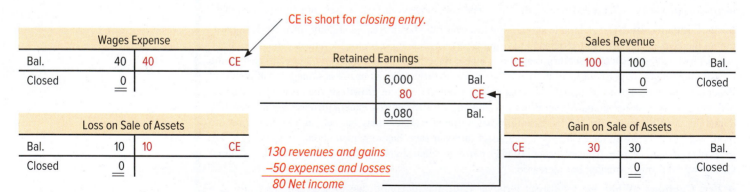

Wages Expense			
Bal.	40	40	CE
Closed	0		

Retained Earnings	
	6,000 Bal.
	80 CE
	6,080 Bal.

Sales Revenue			
CE	100	100	Bal.
		0	Closed

Loss on Sale of Assets			
Bal.	10	10	CE
Closed	0		

130 revenues and gains
−50 expenses and losses
80 Net income

Gain on Sale of Assets			
CE	30	30	Bal.
		0	Closed

We will now prepare the closing entry (CE) for **Chipotle** at March 31, 2015, although companies close their records only at the end of the fiscal year.[2] These amounts are taken from the adjusted trial balance in Exhibit 4.5.

---

[1]Companies may close income statement accounts to a special temporary summary account, called **Income Summary,** which is then closed to Retained Earnings.

[2]Most companies use computerized accounting software to record journal entries, produce trial balances and financial statements, and close the books.

(CE)	Debit	Credit
Restaurant Sales Revenue (−R)	1,089,000	
Interest Revenue (−R)	1,400	
Supplies Expense (−E)		369,000
Wages Expense (−E)		244,200
Rent Expense (−E)		66,000
Insurance Expense (−E)		24,000
Utilities Expense (−E)		90,300
Repairs Expense (−E)		18,700
Training Expense (−E)		40,800
Advertising Expense (−E)		3,400
Depreciation Expense (−E)		30,600
Loss on Disposal of Assets (−E)		4,200
Interest Expense (−E)		200
Income Tax Expense (−E)		76,400
Retained Earnings (+SE)		122,600

PAUSE FOR FEEDBACK — STOP

The process of closing the books (after adjustments) includes making all temporary account balances (from the income statement) zero and transferring the difference to Retained Earnings. The following is an adjusted trial balance from a recent year for **Toys R Us**. Dollars are in millions. Record the journal entry at the end of the accounting cycle to close the books.

SELF-STUDY QUIZ

	DEBIT	CREDIT
Cash	783	
Accounts receivable	251	
Merchandise inventories	1,781	
Buildings	7,226	
Accumulated depreciation		3,039
Other assets	1,409	
Accounts payable		1,412
Accrued expenses payable		847
Long-term debt		5,447
Other liabilities		979
Common stock		19
Retained earnings (accumulated deficit)	399	
Sales revenue		13,724
Interest revenue		16
Gain on sale of business		5
Other income		130
Cost of sales	8,976	
Selling, general, and administrative expenses	3,968	
Depreciation expense	399	
Interest expense	419	
Income tax expense	7	
Totals	25,618	25,618

Closing entry:

(continued)

After you have completed your answers, check them with the solutions below.

 GUIDED HELP 4-2

For additional step-by-step video instruction on recording a closing entry at the end of a given period, go to **www.mhhe.com/libby9e_gh4b**.

Post-Closing Trial Balance

POST-CLOSING TRIAL BALANCE
Prepared as an additional step in the accounting cycle to check that debits equal credits and all temporary accounts have been closed.

After the closing process is complete, all income statement accounts have a zero balance. These accounts are then ready for recording revenues and expenses in the new accounting period. The ending balance in Retained Earnings now is up-to-date (matches the amount on the balance sheet) and is carried forward as the beginning balance for the next period.

As an additional step of the accounting information processing cycle, a **post-closing trial balance** should be prepared as a check that debits still equal credits and that all temporary accounts have been closed. It would have the structure of the trial balance with only balance sheet accounts with balances. The accounting cycle for the period is now complete.

DEMONSTRATION CASE

We take our final look at the accounting activities of Terrific Lawn Maintenance Corporation by illustrating the activities at the end of the accounting cycle: the adjustment process, financial statement preparation, and the closing process. No adjustments had been made to the accounts to reflect all revenues earned and expenses incurred in April. The trial balance for Terrific Lawn on April 30, 2016, based on the unadjusted balances in Chapter 3, is as follows:

TERRIFIC LAWN MAINTENANCE CORPORATION
Unadjusted Trial Balance at April 30, 2016

	Debit	Credit
Cash	5,032	
Accounts receivable	1,700	
Prepaid expenses	300	

**Solutions to
SELF-STUDY QUIZ**

	Debit	Credit
Sales revenue (−R)	13,724	
Interest revenue (−R)	16	
Gain on sale of business (−R)	5	
Other income (−R)	130	
Cost of sales (−E)		8,976
Selling, general, and administrative expenses (−E)		3,968
Depreciation expense (−E)		399
Interest expense (−E)		419
Income tax expense (−E)		7
Retained earnings (+SE)		106

	Debit	Credit
Equipment *(cost)*	4,600	
Accumulated depreciation *(used cost)*		0
Land	3,750	
Accounts payable		220
Wages payable		0
Utilities payable		0
Short-term notes payable		400
Interest payable		0
Income tax payable		0
Unearned revenue		1,600
Long-term notes payable		3,300
Common stock		150
Additional paid-in capital		8,850
Retained earnings		0
Mowing revenue		5,200
Interest revenue		12
Wages expense	3,900	
Fuel expense	410	
Insurance expense	0	
Utilities expense	0	
Depreciation expense	0	
Interest expense	40	
Income tax expense	0	
Total	**19,732**	**19,732**

Additional information follows:

a. The $1,600 in Unearned Revenue represents four months of service from April through July.

b. Prepaid Expenses includes insurance costing $300 for coverage for six months (April through September).

c. Mowers, edgers, rakes, and hand tools (equipment) have been used in April to generate revenues. The company estimates $300 in depreciation each year.

d. Wages have been paid through April 28. Employees worked the last two days of April and will be paid in May. Wages accrue at $200 per day.

e. An extra telephone line was installed in April at an estimated cost of $52, including hookup and usage charges. No entry has yet been recorded. The bill will be received and paid in May.

f. Interest accrues on the outstanding short-term and long-term notes payable at an annual rate of 12 percent. The $3,700 total in principal has been outstanding all month.

g. The estimated income tax rate for Terrific Lawn is 35 percent. Round to the nearest dollar.

Required:

1. Prepare the adjusting journal entries for April, using the account titles shown in the trial balance. In your analysis, be sure to use the three-step process outlined in this chapter: (1) Determine if a revenue was earned or an expense incurred that needs to be recorded for the period, (2) determine whether cash was or will be received or paid, and (3) compute the amount.

2. Prepare an adjusted trial balance.

3. Prepare an income statement, statement of stockholders' equity, and balance sheet from the amounts in the adjusted trial balance. Include earnings per share on the income statement. The company issued 1,500 shares.

4. Prepare the closing entry for April 30, 2016.

5. Compute the following ratios for the month (round to three decimal places):

    a. Current ratio

    b. Net profit margin

    c. Total asset turnover

Now you can check your answers with the following solutions.

SUGGESTED SOLUTION

1. Adjusting entries

AJE	Debit	Credit
a. Unearned Revenue (−L)	400	
Mowing Revenue (+R, +SE)		400
$1,600 × 1/4 = $400 earned in April		
b. Insurance Expense (+E, −SE)	50	
Prepaid Expenses (−A)		50
$300 × 1/6 = $50 insurance used in April		
c. Depreciation Expense (+E, −SE)	25	
Accumulated Depreciation (+XA, −A)		25
$300 × 1/12 = $25 depreciation in April		
d. Wages Expense (+E, −SE)	400	
Wages Payable (+L)		400
$200 per day × 2 days = $400 incurred in April		
e. Utilities Expense (+E, −SE)	52	
Utilities Payable (+L)		52
$52 is estimated as incurred in April		
f. Interest Expense (+E, −SE)	37	
Interest Payable (+L)		37
$3,700 principal × 0.12 annual rate × 1/12 = $37 interest incurred in April		
g. Income Tax Expense (+E, −SE)	244	
Income Tax Payable (+L)		244

	Revenues	Expenses	
Unadjusted balances	$5,212	$4,350	
AJE (a)	400		
AJE (b)		50	
AJE (c)		25	
AJE (d)		400	
AJE (e)		52	
AJE (f)		37	
Adjusted balances	$5,612 —	$4,914 =	$698 Pretax Income
			× 0.35 tax rate
			$244 (rounded)

2. Adjusted trial balance

TERRIFIC LAWN MAINTENANCE CORPORATION
Adjusted Trial Balance at April 30, 2016

	Debit	Credit
Cash	5,032	
Accounts receivable	1,700	
Prepaid expenses	250	
Equipment (*cost*)	4,600	
Accumulated depreciation (*used cost*)		25
Land	3,750	
Accounts payable		220
Wages payable		400
Utilities payable		52
Short-term notes payable		400
Interest payable		37
Income tax payable		244
Unearned revenue		1,200
Long-term notes payable		3,300
Common stock		150
Additional paid-in capital		8,850
Retained earnings		0
Mowing revenue		5,600
Interest revenue		12
Wages expense	4,300	
Fuel expense	410	
Insurance expense	50	
Utilities expense	52	
Depreciation expense	25	
Interest expense	77	
Income tax expense	244	
Total	**20,490**	**20,490**

3. Financial statements:

TERRIFIC LAWN MAINTENANCE CORPORATION
Income Statement
For the Month Ended April 30, 2016

Operating revenues:	
Mowing revenue	$5,600
Operating expenses:	
Wages expense	4,300
Fuel expense	410
Insurance expense	50
Utilities expense	52
Depreciation expense	25
	4,837
Operating income	763
Other items:	
Interest revenue	12
Interest expense	(77)
Pretax income	698
Income tax expense	244
Net Income	$ 454
Earnings per share (for the month)	
($454 ÷ 1,500 shares)	$ 0.30

TERRIFIC LAWN MAINTENANCE CORPORATION
Statement of Stockholders' Equity
For the Month Ended April 30, 2016

	Common Stock	Additional Paid-in Capital	Retained Earnings	Total
Beginning April 1, 2016	$ 0	$ 0	$ 0	$ 0
Stock issuance	150	8,850		9,000
Net income			454	454
Dividends declared			0	0
Balance, April 30, 2016	$150	$8,850	$454	$9,454

TERRIFIC LAWN MAINTENANCE CORPORATION
Balance Sheet
April 30, 2016

Assets		**Liabilities**	
Current Assets:		Current Liabilities:	
Cash	$ 5,032	Accounts payable	$ 220
Accounts receivable	1,700	Wages payable	400
Prepaid expenses	250	Utilities payable	52
Total current assets	6,982	Short-term notes payable	400
		Interest payable	37
		Income tax payable	244
		Unearned revenue	1,200
		Total current liabilities	2,553
Equipment (net of $25		Long-term notes payable	3,300
accumulated depreciation)	4,575	**Stockholders' Equity**	
Land	3,750	Common stock	150
		Additional paid-in capital	8,850
		Retained earnings	454
		Total stockholders' equity	9,454
		Total liabilities and	
Total assets	$15,307	**stockholders' equity**	$15,307

4. Closing entry:

Mowing Revenue (−R)	5,600	
Interest Revenue (−R)	12	
Wages Expense (−E)		4,300
Fuel Expense (−E)		410
Insurance Expense (−E)		50
Utilities Expense (−E)		52
Depreciation Expense (−E)		25
Interest Expense (−E)		77
Income Tax Expense (−E)		244
Retained Earnings (+SE)		454

5. Ratios:

$a.$ Current Assets $= \dfrac{\text{Current Assets}}{\text{Current Liabilities}} = \dfrac{\$6{,}982}{\$2{,}553} = 2.735$

$b.$ Net Profit Margin for April $= \dfrac{\text{Net Income}}{\text{Net Sales (or Operating Revenues)}} = \dfrac{\$454}{\$5{,}600} = 0.081 \text{ or } 8.1\%$

$c.$ Total Asset Turnover for April $= \dfrac{\text{Net Sales (or Operating Revenues)}}{\text{Average Total Assets}} = \dfrac{\$5{,}600}{\$7{,}653.50*} = 0.732$

*(Beginning \$0 + Ending \$15,307) ÷ 2 = \$7,653.50

CHAPTER TAKE-AWAYS

4-1. Explain the purpose of adjustments and analyze the adjustments necessary at the end of the period to update balance sheet and income statement accounts. p. 166

- Adjusting entries are necessary at the end of the accounting period to measure income properly, correct errors, and provide for adequate valuation of balance sheet accounts. There are four types:
  a. Deferred revenues—previously recorded liabilities created when cash was received before being earned that must be adjusted for the amount of revenue earned during the period.
  b. Accrued revenues—revenues that were earned during the period but have not yet been recorded (cash will be received in the future).
  c. Deferred expenses—previously recorded assets (Prepaid Rent, Supplies, and Equipment) that must be adjusted for the amount of expense incurred during the period.
  d. Accrued expenses—expenses that were incurred during the period but have not yet been recorded (cash will be paid in the future).

The analysis involves:

Step 1: Determining if revenue was earned or an expense was incurred. Record an increase in the revenue or expense account.

Step 2: Determining whether cash was received or paid in the past or will be received or paid in the future. If in the past, the existing asset or liability is overstated and needs to be reduced. If in the future, the related receivable or payable account needs to be increased.

Step 3: Computing the amount of revenue earned or expense incurred in the period.

- Recording adjusting entries has no effect on the Cash account.

4-2. Present an income statement with earnings per share, a statement of stockholders' equity, and a balance sheet.   p. 179

Adjusted account balances are used in preparing the following financial statements:

- Income Statement: Revenues − Expenses = Net Income (including earnings per share, computed as net income divided by the average number of shares of common stock outstanding during the period). It may be classified into a section on operating revenues and expenses followed by a section on other items (primarily interest revenue, interest expense, and gains and losses on investments).

- Statement of Stockholders' Equity: (Beginning Contributed Capital + Stock Issuances − Stock Repurchases) + (Beginning Retained Earnings + Net Income − Dividends Declared) = Ending Total Stockholders' Equity.

- Balance Sheet: Assets = Liabilities + Stockholders' Equity. It is often classified into current assets followed by noncurrent assets and current liabilities followed by noncurrent liabilities.

4-3. Compute and interpret the total asset turnover ratio.   p. 185

The total asset turnover ratio (Net Sales (or Operating Revenues) ÷ Average Total Assets) measures sales generated per dollar of assets. A rising total asset turnover signals more efficient management of assets.

4-4. Explain the closing process.   p. 185

Temporary accounts (revenues, expenses, gains, and losses) are closed to a zero balance at the end of the accounting period to allow for the accumulation of income items in the following period and to update Retained Earnings for the period's net income. To close these accounts, debit each revenue and gain account, credit each expense and loss account, and record the difference (equal to net income) to Retained Earnings.

Closing Entry:		
Each revenue	xx	
Each gain	xx	
Each expense		xx
Each loss.................................		xx
Retained earnings		xx
(assumes net income is positive)		

This chapter discussed the important steps in the accounting cycle that take place at year-end. These include the adjustment process, the preparation of the basic financial statements, and the closing process that prepares the records for the next accounting period. This end to the internal portions of the accounting cycle, however, is just the beginning of the process of communicating accounting information to external users.

In the next chapter, we take a closer look at more sophisticated financial statements and related disclosures. We also examine the process by which financial information is disseminated to professional analysts, investors, the Securities and Exchange Commission, and the public, and the role each plays in analyzing and interpreting the information. These discussions will help you consolidate much of what you have learned about the financial reporting process from previous chapters. It will also preview many of the important issues we address in later chapters. These later chapters include many other adjustments that involve difficult and complex estimates about the future, such as estimates of customers' ability to make payments to the company for purchases on account, the useful lives of new machines, and future amounts that a company may owe on warranties of products sold in the past. Each of these estimates and many others can have significant effects on the stream of net earnings that companies report over time.

KEY **RATIO**

Total asset turnover measures the sales generated per dollar of assets. A high or rising ratio suggests that the company is managing its assets more efficiently. It is computed as follows (see the "Key Ratio Analysis" box in the Preparing Financial Statements section):

$$\text{Total Asset Turnover} = \frac{\text{Net Sales (or Operating Revenues)}}{\text{Average Total Assets}}$$

FINDING **FINANCIAL INFORMATION**

Balance Sheet

Current Assets

Accrued revenues include:
  Interest receivable
  Rent receivable
Deferred expenses include:
  Supplies
  Prepaid insurance, rent,
  and advertising

Noncurrent Assets

Deferred expenses include:
  Buildings

Equipment
Intangible assets

Current Liabilities

Accrued expenses include:
  Interest payable
  Wages payable
  Utilities payable
  Income tax payable
Deferred revenues include:
  Unearned revenue

Income Statement

Revenues
Increased by adjusting entries

Expenses
Increased by adjusting entries

Pretax Income
Income tax expense

Net Income

Notes

In Various Notes (if not on the balance sheet)
Details of accrued expenses payable
Interest paid and income taxes paid

Statement of Cash Flows

Adjusting Entries Do Not Affect Cash

KEY **TERMS**

Accrued Expenses   p. 175
Accrued Revenues   p. 171
Adjusting Entries   p. 166
Closing Entries   p. 186
Contra-Account   p. 173

Deferred Expenses   p. 172
Deferred (Unearned) Revenues   p. 170
Net Book Value (Book Value, Carrying
  Value)   p. 174
Permanent (Real) Accounts   p. 185

Post-Closing Trial Balance   p. 188
Temporary (Nominal) Accounts   p. 186

QUESTIONS

1. What is the purpose of recording adjusting entries?
2. List the four types of adjusting entries, and give an example of each type.
3. What is a contra-asset? Give an example of one.
4. Explain how the financial statements relate to each other.
5. What is the equation for each of the following statements: (*a*) income statement, (*b*) balance sheet, and (*c*) statement of stockholders' equity?
6. Explain the effect of adjusting entries on cash.
7. How is earnings per share computed and interpreted?
8. How is the total asset turnover ratio computed and interpreted?
9. What are the purposes for closing the books?
10. Differentiate among (*a*) permanent, (*b*) temporary, (*c*) real, and (*d*) nominal accounts.
11. Explain why the income statement accounts are closed but the balance sheet accounts are not.
12. What is a post-closing trial balance? Is it a useful part of the accounting information processing cycle? Explain.

MULTIPLE-CHOICE QUESTIONS

1. Which of the following accounts would **not** appear in a closing entry?
   a. Salary Expense
   b. Interest Income
   c. Accumulated Depreciation
   d. Retained Earnings

2. Which account is least likely to appear in an adjusting journal entry?
   a. Cash
   b. Interest Receivable
   c. Property Tax Expense
   d. Salaries Payable

3. On October 1, 2017, the $12,000 premium on a one-year insurance policy for the building was paid and recorded as Prepaid Insurance. On December 31, 2017 (end of the accounting period), what adjusting entry is needed?

   a. Insurance Expense (+E)   2,000
      Prepaid Insurance (−A)   2,000

   b. Insurance Expense (+E)   3,000
      Prepaid Insurance (−A)   3,000

   c. Prepaid Insurance (+A)   3,000
      Insurance Expense (−E)   3,000

   d. Prepaid Insurance (+A)   9,000
      Insurance Expense (−E)   9,000

4. On June 1, 2016, Oakcrest Company signed a three-year $110,000 note payable with 9 percent interest. Interest is due on June 1 of each year beginning in 2017. What amount of interest expense should be reported on the income statement for the year ended December 31, 2016?
   a. $5,250
   b. $9,900
   c. $4,950
   d. $5,775

5. Failure to make an adjusting entry to recognize accrued salaries payable would cause which of the following?
   a. An understatement of expenses, liabilities, and stockholders' equity.
   b. An understatement of expenses and liabilities and an overstatement of stockholders' equity.
   c. An overstatement of assets and stockholders' equity.
   d. An overstatement of assets and liabilities.

6. An adjusted trial balance
   a. Shows the ending account balances in a "debit" and "credit" format before posting the adjusting journal entries.
   b. Is prepared after closing entries have been posted.
   c. Shows the ending account balances resulting from the adjusting journal entries in a "debit" and "credit" format.
   d. Is a tool used by financial analysts to review the performance of publicly traded companies.

7. JJ Company owns a building. Which of the following statements regarding depreciation as used by accountants is false?
   a. As depreciation is recorded, stockholders' equity is reduced.
   b. Depreciation is an estimated expense to be recorded over the building's estimated useful life.
   c. As depreciation is recorded, the net book value of the asset is reduced.
   d. As the value of the building decreases over time, it "depreciates."

8. At the beginning of the current year, Donna Company had $1,000 of supplies on hand. During the current year, the company purchased supplies amounting to $6,400 (paid for in cash and debited to Supplies). At the end of the current year, a count of supplies reflected $2,000. The adjusting entry Donna Company would record at the end of the current year to adjust the Supplies account would include a
   a. Debit to Supplies for $2,000.
   b. Credit to Supplies Expense for $5,400.
   c. Credit to Supplies for $5,400.
   d. Debit to Supplies Expense for $4,400.

9. According to GAAP, what ratio must be reported on the financial statements or in the notes to the statements?
   a. Earnings per share ratio.
   b. Return on equity ratio.
   c. Net profit margin ratio.
   d. Current ratio.

10. If a company is successful in acquiring several large buildings at the end of the year, what is the effect on the total asset turnover ratio?
  a. The ratio will increase.
  b. The ratio will not change.
  c. The ratio will decrease.
  d. Either (a) or (c).

connect   MINI-**EXERCISES**

Preparing a Trial Balance

M4-1
LO4-1

Hagadorn Company has the following adjusted accounts and balances at year-end (June 30):

Accounts Payable	$ 250		Interest Expense	$ 70
Accounts Receivable	420		Interest Income	60
Accrued Expenses Payable	160		Inventories	710
Accumulated Depreciation	250		Land	300
Additional Paid-in Capital	300		Long-Term Debt	1,460
Buildings and Equipment	1,400		Prepaid Expenses	30
Cash	175		Salaries Expense	640
Common Stock	100		Sales Revenue	2,400
Cost of Sales	780		Rent Expense	460
Depreciation Expense	150		Retained Earnings	150
Income Taxes Expense	135		Unearned Fees	90
Income Taxes Payable	50			

Prepare an adjusted trial balance in good form for the Hagadorn Company at June 30.

Matching Definitions with Terms

M4-2
LO4-1

Match each definition with its related term by entering the appropriate letter in the space provided.

Definition	Term
____ (1) A revenue not yet earned; collected in advance.	A. Accrued expense
____ (2) Rent not yet collected; already earned.	B. Deferred expense
____ (3) Property taxes incurred; not yet paid.	C. Accrued revenue
____ (4) Rent revenue collected; not yet earned.	D. Deferred revenue
____ (5) An expense incurred; not yet paid or recorded.	
____ (6) Office supplies on hand to be used next accounting period.	
____ (7) An expense not yet incurred; paid in advance.	
____ (8) A revenue earned; not yet collected.	

Matching Definitions with Terms

M4-3
LO4-1

Match each definition with its related term by entering the appropriate letter in the space provided.

Definition	Term
____ (1) At year-end, service revenue of $1,000 was collected in cash but was not yet earned.	A. Accrued expense
	B. Deferred expense
____ (2) Interest of $550 on a note receivable was earned at year-end, although collection of the interest is not due until the following year.	C. Accrued revenue
	D. Deferred revenue
____ (3) At year-end, wages payable of $5,600 had not been recorded or paid.	
____ (4) Office supplies were purchased during the year for $700, and $100 of them remained on hand (unused) at year-end.	

M4-4

LO4-1

Recording Adjusting Entries (Deferred Accounts)

In each of the following transactions (*a*) through (*c*) for Romney's Marketing Company, use the three-step process illustrated in the chapter to record the adjusting entry at the end of the current year. The process includes (1) determining if revenue was earned or an expense was incurred, (2) determining whether cash was received or paid in the past or will be received or paid in the future, and (3) computing the amount of the adjustment.

a. Collected $1,200 rent for the period December 1 of the current year to April 1 of next year, which was credited to Unearned Rent Revenue on December 1.
b. Purchased a machine for $32,000 cash on January 1. The company estimates annual depreciation at $3,200.
c. Paid $5,000 for a two-year insurance premium on July 1 of the current year; debited Prepaid Insurance for that amount.

M4-5

LO4-1

Determining Financial Statement Effects of Adjusting Entries (Deferred Accounts)

For each of the transactions in M4-4, indicate the amounts and the direction of effects of the adjusting entry on the elements of the balance sheet and income statement. Using the following format, indicate + for increase, − for decrease, and NE for no effect.

	BALANCE SHEET			INCOME STATEMENT		
Transaction	Assets	Liabilities	Stockholders' Equity	Revenues	Expenses	Net Income
a.						
b.						
c.						

M4-6

LO4-1

Recording Adjusting Entries (Accrued Accounts)

In each of the following transactions (*a*) through (*c*) for Romney's Marketing Company, use the three-step process illustrated in the chapter to record the adjusting entry at the end of the current year. The process includes (1) determining if revenue was earned or an expense was incurred, (2) determining whether cash was received or paid in the past or will be received or paid in the future, and (3) computing the amount of the adjustment.

a. Estimated electricity usage at $450 for December; to be paid in January of next year.
b. On September 1 of the current year, loaned $6,000 to an officer who will repay the loan principal and interest in one year at an annual interest rate of 14 percent.
c. Owed wages to 10 employees who worked four days at $200 each per day at the end of the current year. The company will pay employees at the end of the first week of next year.

M4-7

LO4-1

Determining Financial Statement Effects of Adjusting Entries (Accrued Accounts)

For each of the transactions in M4-6, indicate the amounts and the direction of effects of the adjusting entry on the elements of the balance sheet and income statement. Using the following format, indicate + for increase, − for decrease, and NE for no effect.

	BALANCE SHEET			INCOME STATEMENT		
Transaction	Assets	Liabilities	Stockholders' Equity	Revenues	Expenses	Net Income
a.						
b.						
c.						

Reporting an Income Statement with Earnings per Share

M4-8
LO4-2

Romney's Marketing Company has the following adjusted trial balance at the end of the current year. No dividends were declared. However, 500 shares ($0.10 par value per share) issued at the end of the year for $3,000 are included below:

	Debit	Credit
Cash	1,500	
Accounts receivable	2,200	
Interest receivable	100	
Prepaid insurance	1,600	
Long-term notes receivable	2,800	
Equipment	15,290	
Accumulated depreciation		3,000
Accounts payable		2,400
Accrued expenses payable		3,920
Income taxes payable		2,700
Unearned rent revenue		500
Common stock (800 shares)		80
Additional paid-in capital		3,620
Retained earnings		2,000
Sales revenue		38,500
Interest revenue		100
Rent revenue		800
Wages expense	19,500	
Depreciation expense	1,800	
Utilities expense	380	
Insurance expense	750	
Rent expense	9,000	
Income tax expense	2,700	
Total	57,620	57,620

Prepare a multistep income statement in good form for the current year. Include earnings per share (rounded to two decimal places).

Reporting a Statement of Stockholders' Equity

M4-9
LO4-2

Refer to M4-8. Prepare a statement of stockholders' equity in good form for the current year.

Reporting a Balance Sheet and Explaining the Effects of Adjustments on the Statement of Cash Flows

M4-10
LO4-2

1. Refer to M4-8. Prepare a classified balance sheet in good form for the end of the current year.
2. Explain how the adjustments in M4-4 and M4-6 affected the operating, investing, and financing activities on the statement of cash flows.

Analyzing Total Asset Turnover

M4-11
LO4-3

Compute total assets for Romney's Marketing Company based on the adjusted trial balance in M4-8. Then compute the company's total asset turnover (rounded to two decimal places) for the current year, assuming total assets at the end of the prior year were $16,050.

Recording Closing Entries

M4-12
LO4-4

Refer to the adjusted trial balance for Romney's Marketing Company in M4-8. Prepare the closing entry at the end of the current year.

EXERCISES

E4-1
LO4-1

Preparing a Trial Balance

Paige Consultants, Inc., provides marketing research for clients in the retail industry. The company had the following unadjusted balances at the end of the current year:

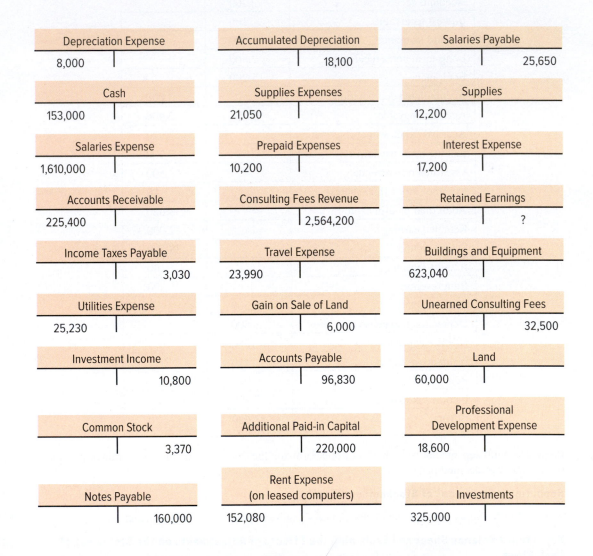

Depreciation Expense	Accumulated Depreciation	Salaries Payable
8,000	18,100	25,650

Cash	Supplies Expenses	Supplies
153,000	21,050	12,200

Salaries Expense	Prepaid Expenses	Interest Expense
1,610,000	10,200	17,200

Accounts Receivable	Consulting Fees Revenue	Retained Earnings
225,400	2,564,200	?

Income Taxes Payable	Travel Expense	Buildings and Equipment
3,030	23,990	623,040

Utilities Expense	Gain on Sale of Land	Unearned Consulting Fees
25,230	6,000	32,500

Investment Income	Accounts Payable	Land
10,800	96,830	60,000

Common Stock	Additional Paid-in Capital	Professional Development Expense
3,370	220,000	18,600

Notes Payable	Rent Expense (on leased computers)	Investments
160,000	152,080	325,000

Required:

Prepare in good form an unadjusted trial balance for Paige Consultants, Inc., at the end of the current year.

E4-2
LO4-1, 4-4

Identifying Adjusting Entries from Unadjusted Trial Balance

In a recent annual report, **Hewlett-Packard Company** states, "We are a leading global provider of products, technologies, software, solutions and services to individual consumers, small- and medium-sized businesses ('SMBs') and large enterprises, including customers in the government, health and education sectors." Its offerings span personal computing and other access drivers, imaging and printing-related products and services, enterprise information technology infrastructure, and multivendor customer services. Following is a trial balance listing accounts that Hewlett-Packard uses. Assume that the balances are unadjusted at the end of a recent fiscal year ended October 31.

HEWLETT-PACKARD COMPANY
Unadjusted Trial Balance
(dollars in millions)
For the year ended October 31

	Debit	Credit
Cash	8,000	
Accounts receivable	21,400	
Inventory	7,500	
Other current assets	14,100	
Property, plant, and equipment	25,500	
Accumulated depreciation		13,200
Other assets	66,200	
Short-term note payable		8,100
Accounts payable		14,800
Accrued liabilities		19,100
Deferred revenue		7,400
Income tax payable		1,000
Long-term debt		22,600
Other liabilities		17,500
Common stock		200
Additional paid-in capital		7,000
Retained earnings		24,700
Product revenue		84,800
Service revenue		42,000
Interest revenue		400
Cost of products	65,200	
Cost of services	32,100	
Interest expense	1,000	
Research and development expense	3,300	
Selling, general, and administrative expense	13,500	
Other expenses	3,100	
Income tax expense	1,900	
Total	262,800	262,800

Required:
1. Based on the information in the unadjusted trial balance, list types of adjustments on the balance sheet that may need to be adjusted at October 31 and the related income statement account for each (no computations are necessary). You may need to make assumptions.
2. Which accounts should be closed at the end of the year? Why?

Recording Adjusting Entries

E4-3

LO4-1

Diane Company completed its first year of operations on December 31. All of the year's entries have been recorded except for the following:

a. At year-end, employees earned wages of $4,000, which will be paid on the next payroll date in January of next year.

b. At year-end, the company had earned interest revenue of $1,500. The cash will be collected March 1 of the next year.

Required:

1. What is the annual reporting period for this company?
2. Identify whether each transaction results in adjusting a deferred or an accrued account. Using the process illustrated in the chapter, prepare the required adjusting entry for transactions (*a*) and (*b*). Include appropriate dates and write a brief explanation of each entry.
3. Why are these adjustments made?

E4-4
LO4-1

Recording Adjusting Entries

Elana's Traveling Veterinary Services, Inc., completed its first year of operations on December 31. All of the year's entries have been recorded except for the following:

a. On March 1 of the current year, the company borrowed $60,000 at a 10 percent interest rate to be repaid in five years.
b. On the last day of the current year, the company received a $360 utility bill for utilities used in December. The bill will be paid in January of next year.

Required:

1. What is the annual reporting period for this company?
2. Identify whether each transaction results in adjusting a deferred or an accrued account. Using the process illustrated in the chapter, prepare the required adjusting entry for transactions (*a*) and (*b*). Include appropriate dates and write a brief explanation of each entry.
3. Why are these adjustments made?

E4-5
LO4-1, 4-2

Recording Adjusting Entries and Reporting Balances in Financial Statements

Aubrae Company is making adjusting entries for the year ended December 31 of the current year. In developing information for the adjusting entries, the accountant learned the following:

a. A two-year insurance premium of $4,800 was paid on October 1 of the current year for coverage beginning on that date. The bookkeeper debited the full amount to Prepaid Insurance on October 1.
b. At December 31 of the current year, the following data relating to Shipping Supplies were obtained from the records and supporting documents.

Shipping supplies on hand, January 1 of the current year	$13,000
Purchases of shipping supplies during the current year	75,000
Shipping supplies on hand, counted on December 31 of the current year	20,000

Required:

1. Using the process illustrated in the chapter, record the adjusting entry for insurance at December 31 of the current year.
2. Using the process illustrated in the chapter, record the adjusting entry for supplies at December 31 of the current year, assuming that the shipping supplies purchased during the current year were debited in full to the account Shipping Supplies.
3. What amount should be reported on the current year's income statement for Insurance Expense? For Shipping Supplies Expense?
4. What amount should be reported on the current year's balance sheet for Prepaid Insurance? For Shipping Supplies?

E4-6
LO4-1, 4-2

Recording Adjusting Entries and Reporting Balances in Financial Statements

Gauge Construction Company is making adjusting entries for the year ended March 31 of the current year. In developing information for the adjusting entries, the accountant learned the following:

a. The company paid $1,800 on January 1 of the current year to have advertisements placed in the local monthly neighborhood paper. The ads were to be run from January through June. The bookkeeper debited the full amount to Prepaid Advertising on January 1.
b. At March 31 of the current year, the following data relating to Construction Equipment were obtained from the records and supporting documents.

Construction equipment (at cost)	$340,000
Accumulated depreciation (through March 31 of the prior year)	132,000
Estimated annual depreciation for using the equipment	34,000

Required:

1. Using the process illustrated in the chapter, record the adjusting entry for advertisements at March 31 of the current year.
2. Using the process illustrated in the chapter, record the adjusting entry for the use of construction equipment during the current year.
3. What amount should be reported on the current year's income statement for Advertising Expense? For Depreciation Expense?
4. What amount should be reported on the current year's balance sheet for Prepaid Advertising? For Construction Equipment (at net book value)?

Determining Financial Statement Effects of Adjusting Entries

Refer to E4-3 and E4-5.

E4-7
LO4-1

Required:

For each of the transactions in E4-3 and E4-5, indicate the amount and the direction of effects of the adjusting entry on the elements of the balance sheet and income statement. Using the following format, indicate + for increase, − for decrease, and NE for no effect.

	BALANCE SHEET			INCOME STATEMENT		
Transaction	Assets	Liabilities	Stockholders' Equity	Revenues	Expenses	Net Income
E4-3 (a)						
E4-3 (b)						
E4-5 (a)						
E4-5 (b)						

Recording Seven Typical Adjusting Entries

Dittman's Variety Store is completing the accounting process for the current year just ended, December 31. The transactions during the year have been journalized and posted. The following data with respect to adjusting entries are available:

E4-8
LO4-1

a. Wages earned by employees during December, unpaid and unrecorded at December 31, amounted to $2,700. The last payroll was December 28; the next payroll will be January 6.
b. Office supplies on hand at January 1 of the current year totaled $450. Office supplies purchased and debited to Office Supplies during the year amounted to $500. The year-end count showed $275 of supplies on hand.
c. One-fourth of the basement space is rented to Heald's Specialty Shop for $560 per month, payable monthly. At the end of the current year, the rent for November and December had not been collected or recorded. Collection is expected in January of the next year.
d. The store used delivery equipment all year that cost $60,500; $12,100 was the estimated annual depreciation.
e. On July 1 of the current year, a two-year insurance premium amounting to $2,400 was paid in cash and debited in full to Prepaid Insurance. Coverage began on July 1 of the current year.
f. The remaining basement of the store is rented for $1,600 per month to another merchant, M. Carlos, Inc. Carlos sells compatible, but not competitive, merchandise. On November 1 of the current year, the store collected six months' rent in the amount of $9,600 in advance from Carlos; it was credited in full to Unearned Rent Revenue when collected.
g. Dittman's Variety Store operates a repair shop to meet its own needs. The shop also does repairs for M. Carlos. At the end of the current year, Carlos had not paid $800 for completed repairs. This amount has not yet been recorded as Repair Shop Revenue. Collection is expected during January of next year.

Required:

1. Identify each of these transactions as a deferred revenue, deferred expense, accrued revenue, or accrued expense.
2. Prepare the adjusting entries that should be recorded for Dittman's Variety Store at December 31 of the current year.

E4-9

LO4-1

Recording Seven Typical Adjusting Entries

John's Boat Yard, Inc., repairs, stores, and cleans boats for customers. It is completing the accounting process for the year just ended on November 30. The transactions for the past year have been journalized and posted. The following data with respect to adjusting entries at year-end are available:

a. John's winterized (cleaned and covered) three boats for customers at the end of November but did not record the service for $3,300.

b. On October 1, John's paid $2,200 to the local newspaper for an advertisement to run every Thursday for 12 weeks. All ads have been run except for three Thursdays in December to complete the 12-week contract.

c. John's borrowed $300,000 at an 11 percent annual interest rate on April 1 of the current year to expand its boat storage facility. The loan requires John's to pay the interest quarterly until the note is repaid in three years. John's paid quarterly interest on July 1 and October 1.

d. The Johnson family paid John's $4,500 on November 1 to store its sailboat for the winter until May 1 of the next fiscal year. John's credited the full amount to Unearned Storage Revenue on November 1.

e. John's used boat-lifting equipment that cost $180,000; $18,000 was the estimated depreciation for the current year.

f. Boat repair supplies on hand at the beginning of the current year totaled $18,900. Repair supplies purchased and debited to Supplies during the year amounted to $45,200. The year-end count showed $15,600 of the supplies on hand.

g. Wages of $5,600 earned by employees during November were unpaid and unrecorded at November 30. The next payroll date will be December 5 of the next fiscal year.

Required:

1. Identify each of these transactions as a deferred revenue, deferred expense, accrued revenue, or accrued expense.
2. Prepare the adjusting entries that should be recorded for John's at November 30, end of the current year.

E4-10

LO4-1

Determining Financial Statement Effects of Seven Typical Adjusting Entries

Refer to E4-8.

Required:
For each of the transactions in E4-8, indicate the amount and the direction of effects of the adjusting entry on the elements of the balance sheet and income statement. Using the following format, indicate + for increase, − for decrease, and NE for no effect.

	BALANCE SHEET			INCOME STATEMENT		
Transaction	**Assets**	**Liabilities**	**Stockholders' Equity**	**Revenues**	**Expenses**	**Net Income**
a.						
b.						
c.						
(etc.)						

E4-11

LO4-1

Determining Financial Statement Effects of Seven Typical Adjusting Entries

Refer to E4-9.

Required:
For each of the transactions in E4-9, indicate the amount and the direction of effects of the adjusting entry on the elements of the balance sheet and income statement. Using the following format, indicate + for increase, − for decrease, and NE for no effect.

	BALANCE SHEET			INCOME STATEMENT		
Transaction	**Assets**	**Liabilities**	**Stockholders' Equity**	**Revenues**	**Expenses**	**Net Income**
a.						
b.						
c.						
(etc.)						

Recording Transactions Including Adjusting and Closing Entries (Nonquantitative)

E4-12
LO4-1, 4-4

The following accounts are used by Britt's Knits, Inc.

Codes	Accounts	Codes	Accounts
A	Cash	J	Common Stock and Additional Paid-in Capital
B	Office Supplies	K	Retained Earnings
C	Accounts Receivable	L	Service Revenue
D	Office Equipment	M	Interest Revenue
E	Accumulated Depreciation	N	Wage Expense
F	Note Payable	O	Depreciation Expense
G	Wages Payable	P	Interest Expense
H	Interest Payable	Q	Supplies Expense
I	Unearned Service Revenue	R	None of the above

Required:

For each of the following nine independent situations, prepare the journal entry by entering the appropriate code(s) and amount(s). The first transaction is used as an example.

		DEBIT		CREDIT	
Independent Situations	**Code**	**Amount**	**Code**	**Amount**	
a. Accrued wages, unrecorded and unpaid at year-end, $400 (example).	N	400	G	400	
b. Service revenue earned but not yet collected at year-end, $600.					
c. Dividends declared and paid during the year, $900.					
d. Office supplies on hand during the year, $400; supplies on hand at year-end, $160.					
e. Service revenue collected in advance and not yet earned, $800.					
f. Depreciation expense for the year, $1,000.					
g. At year-end, interest on note payable not yet recorded or paid, $220.					
h. Balance at year-end in Service Revenue account, $56,000. Prepare the closing entry at year-end.					
i. Balance at year-end in Interest Expense account, $460. Prepare the closing entry at year-end.					

E4-13
LO4-1, 4-2

Determining Financial Statement Effects of Three Adjusting Entries

Daniel Company started operations on January 1 of the current year. It is now December 31, the end of the current annual accounting period. The part-time bookkeeper needs your help to analyze the following three transactions:

a. During the year, the company purchased office supplies that cost $3,000. At the end of the year, office supplies of $800 remained on hand.

b. On January 1 of the current year, the company purchased a special machine for cash at a cost of $25,000. The machine's cost is estimated to depreciate at $2,500 per year.

c. On July 1, the company paid cash of $1,000 for a two-year premium on an insurance policy on the machine; coverage began on July 1 of the current year.

Required:
Complete the following schedule with the amounts that should be reported for the current year:

Selected Balance Sheet Accounts at December 31	Amount to Be Reported
Assets	
Equipment	$ _____
Accumulated depreciation	_____
Net book value of equipment	_____
Office supplies	_____
Prepaid insurance	_____

Selected Income Statement Accounts for the Year Ended December 31	
Expenses	
Depreciation expense	$ _____
Office supplies expense	_____
Insurance expense	_____

E4-14
LO4-1

Determining Financial Statement Effects of Adjustments for Interest on Two Notes

Note 1: On April 1, 2017, Warren Corporation received a $30,000, 10 percent note from a customer in settlement of a $30,000 open account receivable. According to the terms, the principal of the note and interest are payable at the end of 12 months. The annual accounting period for Warren ends on December 31, 2017.

Note 2: On August 1, 2017, to meet a cash shortage, Warren Corporation obtained a $30,000, 12 percent loan from a local bank. The principal of the note and interest expense are payable at the end of six months.

Required:
For the relevant transaction dates of each note, indicate the amounts and the direction of effects on the elements of the balance sheet and income statement. Using the following format, indicate + for increase, − for decrease, and NE for no effect. (**Reminder**: Assets = Liabilities + Stockholders' Equity; Revenues − Expenses = Net Income; and Net Income accounts are closed to Retained Earnings, a part of Stockholders' Equity.)

	BALANCE SHEET			INCOME STATEMENT		
Date	Assets	Liabilities	Stockholders' Equity	Revenues	Expenses	Net Income
Note 1						
April 1, 2017						
December 31, 2017						
March 31, 2018						
Note 2						
August 1, 2017						
December 31, 2017						
January 31, 2018						

Inferring Transactions

E4-15
LO4-1

Deere & Company is the world's leading producer of agricultural equipment; a leading supplier of a broad range of industrial equipment for construction, forestry, and public works; a producer and marketer of a broad line of lawn and grounds care equipment; and a provider of credit, managed health care plans, and insurance products for businesses and the general public. The following information is from a recent annual report (in millions of dollars):

Income Taxes Payable			Dividends Payable			Interest Payable		
	Beg. bal.	154		Beg. bal.	127		Beg. bal.	190
(a) ?	(b)	1,424	(c) ?	(d)	634	(e) 759	(f)	?
	End. bal.	166		End. bal.	168		End. bal.	191

Required:

1. Identify the nature of each of the transactions (*a*) through (*f*). Specifically, what activities cause the accounts to increase and decrease?
2. For transactions (*a*), (*c*), and (*f*), compute the amount.

Analyzing the Effects of Errors on Financial Statement Items

E4-16
LO4-1

Cohen & Boyd, Inc., publishers of movie and song trivia books, made the following errors in adjusting the accounts at year-end (December 31):

a. Did not accrue $1,400 owed to the company by another company renting part of the building as a storage facility.
b. Did not record $15,000 depreciation on the equipment costing $115,000.
c. Failed to adjust the Unearned Fee Revenue account to reflect that $1,500 was earned by the end of the year.
d. Recorded a full year of accrued interest expense on a $17,000, 9 percent note payable that has been outstanding only since November 1.
e. Failed to adjust Prepaid Insurance to reflect that $650 of insurance coverage has been used.

Required:

1. For each error, prepare (*a*) the adjusting journal entry that was made, if any, and (*b*) the adjusting journal entry that should have been made at year-end.
2. Using the following headings, indicate the effect of each error and the amount of the effect (that is, the difference between the entry that was or was not made and the entry that should have been made). Use O if the effect overstates the item, U if the effect understates the item, and NE if there is no effect. (**Reminder:** Assets = Liabilities + Stockholders' Equity; Revenues − Expenses = Net Income; and Net Income accounts are closed to Retained Earnings, a part of Stockholders' Equity.)

	BALANCE SHEET			INCOME STATEMENT		
Transaction	Assets	Liabilities	Stockholders' Equity	Revenues	Expenses	Net Income
a.						
b.						
c.						
(etc.)						

Analyzing the Effects of Adjusting Entries on the Income Statement and Balance Sheet

E4-17
LO4-1, 4-2

On December 31, Fawzi Company prepared an income statement and balance sheet and failed to take into account four adjusting entries. The income statement, prepared on this incorrect basis, reflected pretax income of $65,000. The balance sheet (before the effect of income taxes) reflected total assets, $185,000; total liabilities, $90,000; and stockholders' equity, $95,000. The data for the four adjusting entries follow:

a. Wages amounting to $37,000 for the last three days of December were not paid and not recorded (the next payroll will be at the beginning of next year).
b. Depreciation of $19,000 for the year on equipment that cost $190,000 was not recorded.

c. Rent revenue of $10,500 was collected on December 1 of the current year for office space for the period December 1 to February 28 of the next year. The $10,500 was credited in full to Unearned Rent Revenue when collected.

d. Income taxes were not recorded. The income tax rate for the company is 30 percent.

Required:

Complete the following tabulation to correct the financial statements for the effects of the four errors (indicate deductions with parentheses):

Items	Net Income	Total Assets	Total Liabilities	Stockholders' Equity
Balances reported	$65,000	$185,000	$90,000	$95,000
Additional adjustments:				
a. Wages				
b. Depreciation				
c. Rent revenue				
Adjusted balances				
d. Income taxes				
Correct balances				

E4-18

LO4-1, 4-2

Recording the Effects of Adjusting Entries and Reporting a Corrected Income Statement and Balance Sheet

On December 31, the bookkeeper for Grillo Company prepared the following income statement and balance sheet summarized here but neglected to consider three adjusting entries.

	As Prepared	Effects of Adjusting Entries	Corrected Amounts
Income Statement			
Revenues	$ 97,000		
Expenses	(73,000)		
Income tax expense			
Net income	$ 24,000		
Balance Sheet			
Assets			
Cash	$ 20,000		
Accounts receivable	22,000		
Rent receivable			
Equipment	50,000		
Accumulated depreciation	(10,000)		
	$ 82,000		
Liabilities			
Accounts payable	$ 10,000		
Income taxes payable			
Stockholders' Equity			
Common stock	10,000		
Additional paid-in capital	30,000		
Retained earnings	32,000		
	$ 82,000		

Data on the three adjusting entries follow:

a. Rent revenue of $2,500 earned in December of the current year was neither collected nor recorded.
b. Depreciation of $4,500 on the equipment for the current year was not recorded.
c. Income tax expense of $5,100 for the current year was neither paid nor recorded.

Required:

1. Prepare the three adjusting entries that were omitted. Use the account titles shown in the income statement and balance sheet data.
2. Complete the two columns to the right in the preceding tabulation to show the effects of the adjusting entries and the corrected amounts on the income statement and balance sheet.

Reporting a Correct Income Statement with Earnings per Share to Include the Effects of Adjusting Entries and Evaluating Total Asset Turnover as an Auditor

E4-19
LO4-1, 4-2, 4-3

Jay, Inc., a party rental business, completed its first year of operations on December 31. Because this is the end of the annual accounting period, the company bookkeeper prepared the following tentative income statement:

Income Statement	
Rental revenue	$109,000
Expenses:	
Salaries and wages expense	26,500
Maintenance expense	12,000
Rent expense	8,800
Utilities expense	4,300
Gas and oil expense	3,000
Miscellaneous expenses (items not listed elsewhere)	1,000
Total expenses	55,600
Income	$ 53,400

You are an independent CPA hired by the company to audit the company's accounting systems and review the financial statements. In your audit, you developed additional data as follows:

a. Wages for the last three days of December amounting to $730 were not recorded or paid.
b. Jay estimated telephone usage at $440 for December, but nothing has been recorded or paid.
c. Depreciation on rental autos, amounting to $24,000 for the current year, was not recorded.
d. Interest on a $15,000, one-year, 8 percent note payable dated October 1 of the current year was not recorded. The 8 percent interest is payable on the maturity date of the note.
e. Maintenance expense excludes $1,100, representing the cost of maintenance supplies used during the current year.
f. The Unearned Rental Revenue account includes $4,100 of revenue to be earned in January of next year.
g. The income tax expense is $5,800. Payment of income tax will be made next year.

Required:

1. For items (a) through (g), what adjusting entry should Jay record at December 31? If none is required, explain why.
2. Prepare a corrected income statement for the current year in good form, including earnings per share (rounded to two decimal places), assuming that 7,000 shares of stock are outstanding all year. Show computations.
3. Assume the beginning of the year balance for Jay's total assets was $58,020 and its ending balance for total assets was $65,180. Compute the total asset turnover ratio (rounded to two decimal places) based on the corrected information. What does this ratio suggest? If the average total asset turnover ratio for the industry is 2.31, what might you infer about Jay, Inc.?

E4-20

LO4-1

Recording Four Adjusting Entries and Completing the Trial Balance Worksheet

Green Valley Company prepared the following trial balance at the end of its first year of operations ending December 31. To simplify the case, the amounts given are in thousands of dollars.

Account Titles	UNADJUSTED Debit	UNADJUSTED Credit	ADJUSTMENTS Debit	ADJUSTMENTS Credit	ADJUSTED Debit	ADJUSTED Credit
Cash	20					
Accounts receivable	13					
Prepaid insurance	8					
Machinery	85					
Accumulated depreciation						
Accounts payable		11				
Wages payable						
Income taxes payable						
Common stock (4,000 shares)		4				
Additional paid-in capital		67				
Retained earnings	6					
Revenues (not detailed)		82				
Expenses (not detailed)	32					
Totals	164	164				

Other data not yet recorded at December 31 include:

a. Insurance expired during the current year, $7.
b. Wages payable, $4.
c. Depreciation expense for the current year, $9.
d. Income tax expense, $11.

Required:
1. Prepare the adjusting entries for the current year.
2. Complete the trial balance Adjustments and Adjusted columns.

E4-21

LO4-2

Reporting an Income Statement, Statement of Stockholders' Equity, and Balance Sheet

Refer to E4-20.

Required:
Using the adjusted balances for Green Valley Company in E4-20, prepare an income statement, statement of stockholders' equity, and balance sheet for the current year.

E4-22

LO4-4

Recording Closing Entries

Refer to E4-20.

Required:
1. What are the purposes of "closing the books" at the end of the accounting period?
2. Using the adjusted balances for Green Valley Company in E4-20, prepare the closing entry for the current year.

 **PROBLEMS**

Preparing a Trial Balance (AP4-1)

Papa John's International Inc. operates and franchises pizza delivery and carryout restaurants world-wide. The following is an alphabetical list of accounts and amounts reported in a recent year's set of financial statements. The accounts have normal debit or credit balances and the dollars are rounded to the nearest thousand.

P4-1
LO4-1

Accounts payable	$ 38,832	Intangible assets	$ 82,007
Accounts receivable	56,047	Interest expense	4,077
Accrued expenses payable	58,293	Interest revenue	702
Accumulated depreciation	337,524	Inventories	27,394
Additional paid-in capital	47,912	Land	32,880
Advertising expense	63,463	Long-term debt	230,451
Buildings and leasehold improvements	203,621	Long-term notes receivable	12,801
Cash	20,122	Other assets	42,530
Common stock	433	Other long-term liabilities	64,063
Cost of sales	732,391	Prepaid expenses and other current assets	36,812
Depreciation expense	39,965	Rent and utilities expense	215,696
Equipment	320,480	Retained earnings	?
General and administrative expenses	148,789	Restaurant and franchise sales revenue	1,598,149
Income tax expense	40,940	Salaries and benefits expense	280,215
Income tax receivable	9,527	Short-term notes receivable	6,106
Income taxes payable	9,637	Unearned revenue	4,257

Required:
1. Prepare an adjusted trial balance.
2. How did you determine the amount for retained earnings?

Recording Adjusting Entries (AP4-2)

All of the current year's entries for Zimmerman Company have been made, except the following adjusting entries. The company's annual accounting year ends on December 31.

P4-2
LO4-1

a. On September 1 of the current year, Zimmerman collected six months' rent of $8,400 on storage space. At that date, Zimmerman debited Cash and credited Unearned Rent Revenue for $8,400.

b. On October 1 of the current year, the company borrowed $18,000 from a local bank and signed a one-year, 12 percent note for that amount. The principal and interest are payable on the maturity date.

c. Depreciation of $2,500 must be recognized on a service truck purchased in July of the current year at a cost of $15,000.

d. Cash of $3,000 was collected on November of the current year for services to be rendered evenly over the next year beginning on November 1 of the current year. Unearned Service Revenue was credited when the cash was received.

e. On November 1 of the current year, Zimmerman paid a one-year premium for property insurance, $9,000, for coverage starting on that date. Cash was credited and Prepaid Insurance was debited for this amount.

f. The company earned service revenue of $4,000 on a special job that was completed December 29 of the current year. Collection will be made during January of the next year. No entry has been recorded.

g. At December 31 of the current year, wages earned by employees totaled $14,000. The employees will be paid on the next payroll date in January of the next year.

h. On December 31 of the current year, the company estimated it owed $500 for this year's property taxes on land. The tax will be paid when the bill is received in January of next year.

Required:

1. Indicate whether each transaction relates to a deferred revenue, deferred expense, accrued revenue, or accrued expense.
2. Give the adjusting entry required for each transaction at December 31 of the current year.

P4-3   **Recording Adjusting Entries (AP4-3)**

LO4-1

Martin Towing Company is at the end of its accounting year ending December 31. The following data that must be considered were developed from the company's records and related documents:

a. On January 1 of the current year, the company purchased a new hauling van at a cash cost of $28,000. Depreciation estimated at $3,500 for the year has not been recorded for the current year.

b. During the current year, office supplies amounting to $1,000 were purchased for cash and debited in full to Supplies. At the end of last year, the count of supplies remaining on hand was $500. The inventory of supplies counted on hand at the end of the current year was $150.

c. On December 31 of the current year, Lanie's Garage completed repairs on one of the company's trucks at a cost of $2,600; the amount is not yet recorded by Martin and by agreement will be paid during January of next year.

d. On December 31 of the current year, property taxes on land owned during the current year were estimated at $1,800. The taxes have not been recorded and will be paid in the next year when billed.

e. On December 31 of the current year, the company completed towing service for an out-of-state company for $4,000 payable by the customer within 30 days. No cash has been collected, and no journal entry has been made for this transaction.

f. On July 1 of the current year, a three-year insurance premium on equipment in the amount of $900 was paid and debited in full to Prepaid Insurance on that date. Coverage began on July 1 of the current year.

g. On October 1 of the current year, the company borrowed $13,000 from the local bank on a one-year, 12 percent note payable. The principal plus interest is payable at the end of 12 months.

h. The income before any of the adjustments or income taxes was $30,000. The company's federal income tax rate is 30 percent. (**Hint:** Compute adjusted pre-tax income based on (*a*) through (*g*) to determine income tax expense.)

Required:

1. Indicate whether each transaction relates to a deferred revenue, deferred expense, accrued revenue, or accrued expense.
2. Prepare the adjusting entry required for each transaction at December 31 of the current year.

P4-4   **Determining Financial Statement Effects of Adjusting Entries (AP4-4)**

LO4-1

Refer to the information regarding Zimmerman Company in P4-2.

Required:

1. Indicate whether each transaction relates to a deferred revenue, deferred expense, accrued revenue, or accrued expense.
2. Using the following headings, indicate the effect of each adjusting entry and the amount of the effect. Use + for increase, − for decrease, and NE for no effect. (**Reminder:** Assets = Liabilities + Stockholders' Equity; Revenues − Expenses = Net Income; and Net Income accounts are closed to Retained Earnings, a part of Stockholders' Equity.)

	BALANCE SHEET			INCOME STATEMENT		
Transaction	Assets	Liabilities	Stockholders' Equity	Revenues	Expenses	Net Income
a.						
b.						
c.						
(etc.)						

Determining Financial Statement Effects of Adjusting Entries (AP4-5)

P4-5
LO4-1

Refer to the information regarding Martin Towing Company in P4-3.

Required:

1. Indicate whether each transaction relates to a deferred revenue, deferred expense, accrued revenue, or accrued expense.
2. Using the following headings, indicate the effect of each adjusting entry and the amount of each. Use + for increase, − for decrease, and NE for no effect. (**Reminder:** Assets = Liabilities + Stockholders' Equity; Revenues − Expenses = Net Income; and Net Income accounts are closed to Retained Earnings, a part of Stockholders' Equity.)

	BALANCE SHEET			INCOME STATEMENT		
Transaction	Assets	Liabilities	Stockholders' Equity	Revenues	Expenses	Net Income
a.						
b.						
c.						
(etc.)						

Inferring Year-End Adjustments, Computing Earnings per Share and Total Asset Turnover, and Recording Closing Entries (AP4-6)

P4-6
LO4-1, 4-3, 4-4

Ramirez Company is completing the information processing cycle at its fiscal year-end on December 31. Following are the correct balances at December 31 for the accounts both before and after the adjusting entries.

	Trial Balance, December 31 of the Current Year					
	Before Adjusting Entries		Adjustments		After Adjusting Entries	
Items	Debit	Credit	Debit	Credit	Debit	Credit
a. Cash	13,500				13,500	
b. Accounts receivable					1,820	
c. Prepaid insurance	850				720	
d. Equipment	168,280				168,280	
e. Accumulated depreciation, equipment		42,100				48,100
f. Income taxes payable						1,380
g. Common stock and additional paid-in capital		112,000				112,000
h. Retained earnings, January 1		19,600				19,600
i. Service revenue		64,400				66,220
j. Salary expense	55,470				55,470	
k. Depreciation expense					6,000	
l. Insurance expense					130	
m. Income tax expense					1,380	
	238,100	238,100			247,300	247,300

Required:

1. Compare the amounts in the columns before and after the adjusting entries to reconstruct the adjusting entries made in the current year. Provide an explanation of each.
2. Compute the amount of net income assuming that it is based on the amounts (*a*) before adjusting entries and (*b*) after adjusting entries. Which net income amount is correct? Explain why.
3. Compute earnings per share (rounded to two decimal places), assuming that 3,000 shares of stock are outstanding all year.
4. Compute the total asset turnover ratio (rounded to two decimal places), assuming total assets at the beginning of the year were $110,000. If the industry average is 0.49, what does this suggest to you about Ramirez Company?
5. Record the closing entry at December 31 of the current year.

P4-7
LO4-1, 4-2, 4-4

Recording Adjusting and Closing Entries and Preparing a Balance Sheet and Income Statement Including Earnings per Share (AP4-7)

Tunstall, Inc., a small service company, keeps its records without the help of an accountant. After much effort, an outside accountant prepared the following unadjusted trial balance as of the end of the annual accounting period on December 31:

Account Titles	Debit	Credit
Cash	42,000	
Accounts receivable	11,600	
Supplies	900	
Prepaid insurance	800	
Service trucks	19,000	
Accumulated depreciation		9,200
Other assets	8,300	
Accounts payable		3,000
Wages payable		
Income taxes payable		
Note payable (3 years; 10% interest due each December 31)		17,000
Common stock (5,000 shares outstanding)		400
Additional paid-in capital		19,000
Retained earnings		6,000
Service revenue		61,360
Remaining expenses (not detailed; excludes income tax)	33,360	
Income tax expense		
Totals	115,960	115,960

Data not yet recorded at December 31 included:

a. The supplies count on December 31 reflected $300 in remaining supplies on hand to be used in the next year.
b. Insurance expired during the current year, $800.
c. Depreciation expense for the current year, $3,700.
d. Wages earned by employees not yet paid on December 3, $640.
e. Income tax expense, $5,540.

Required:

1. Record the adjusting entries.
2. Prepare an income statement and a classified balance sheet that include the effects of the preceding five transactions.
3. Record the closing entry.

Preparing a Trial Balance (P4-1)

Starbucks Corporation purchases and roasts high-quality whole bean coffees and sells them along with fresh-brewed coffees, Italian-style espresso beverages, a variety of pastries and confections, coffee-related accessories and equipment, and a line of premium teas. In addition to sales through its company-operated retail stores, Starbucks also sells coffee and tea products through other channels of distribution. The following is a simplified list of accounts and amounts reported in recent financial statements. The accounts have normal debit or credit balances, and the dollars are rounded to the nearest million. The fiscal year ends on September 30.

AP4-1

LO4-1

Accounts Payable	$ 540	Inventories	$ 966
Accounts Receivable	387	Long-Term Investments	479
Accrued Liabilities	1,536	Long-Term Liabilities	897
Accumulated Depreciation	3,808	Net Revenues	11,903
Additional Paid-in Capital	39	Other Current Assets	230
Cash	1,148	Other Long-Lived Assets	730
Common Stock	2	Other Operating Expenses	402
Cost of Sales	4,949	Prepaid Expenses	162
Depreciation Expense	523	Property, Plant, and Equipment	6,163
General and Administrative Expense	636	Retained Earnings	?
Income Tax Expense	563	Short-Term Investments	903
Interest Expense	33	Store Operating Expenses	3,665
Interest Income	116		

Required:
1. Prepare an adjusted trial balance at September 30.
2. How did you determine the amount for retained earnings?

Recording Adjusting Entries (P4-2)

Hannah Company's annual accounting year ends on June 30. All of the entries for the current year have been made, except the following adjusting entries:

AP4-2

LO4-1

a. On March 30 of the current year, Hannah paid a six-month premium for property insurance, $3,200, for coverage starting on that date. Cash was credited and Prepaid Insurance was debited for this amount.

b. On June 1 of the current year, Hannah collected two months' maintenance revenue of $450. At that date, Hannah debited Cash and credited Unearned Maintenance Revenue for $450.

c. At June 30 of the current year, wages of $900 were earned by employees but not yet paid. The employees will be paid on the next payroll date in July, the beginning of the next fiscal year.

d. Depreciation of $3,000 must be recognized on a service truck that cost $15,000 when purchased on July 1 of the current year.

e. Cash of $4,200 was collected on May 1 of the current year for services to be rendered evenly over the next year beginning on May 1 of the current year. Unearned Service Revenue was credited when the cash was received.

f. On February 1 of the current year, the company borrowed $18,000 from a local bank and signed a one-year, 9 percent note for that amount, with the principal and interest payable on the maturity date.

g. On June 30 of the current year, the company estimated that it owed $500 in property taxes on land it owned in the second half of the current fiscal year. The taxes will be paid when billed in August of the next fiscal year.

h. The company earned service revenue of $2,000 on a special job that was completed June 29 of the current year. Collection will be made during July and no entry has been recorded.

Required:

1. Indicate whether each transaction relates to a deferred revenue, deferred expense, accrued revenue, or accrued expense.
2. Prepare the adjusting entry required for each transaction at June 30.

AP4-3
LO4-1

Recording Adjusting Entries (P4-3)

Bill's Catering Company is at its accounting year-end on December 31. The following data that must be considered were developed from the company's records and related documents:

a. During the current year, office supplies amounting to $1,200 were purchased for cash and debited in full to Supplies. At the beginning of the year, the count of supplies on hand was $450; at the end of the year, the count of supplies on hand was $400.

b. On December 31 of the current year, the company catered an evening gala for a local celebrity. The $7,500 bill is due from the customer by the end of January of next year. No cash has been collected, and no journal entry has been made for this transaction.

c. On October 1 of the current year, a one-year insurance premium on equipment in the amount of $1,200 was paid and debited in full to Prepaid Insurance on that date. Coverage began on November 1 of the current year.

d. On December 31 of the current year, repairs on one of the company's delivery vans were completed at a cost estimate of $600; the amount has not yet been paid or recorded by Bill's. The repair shop will bill Bill's Catering at the beginning of January of next year.

e. In November of the current year, Bill's Catering signed a lease for a new retail location, providing a down payment of $2,100 for the first three months' rent that was debited in full to Prepaid Rent. The lease began on December 1 of the current year.

f. On July 1 of the current year, the company purchased new refrigerated display counters at a cash cost of $18,000. Depreciation of $2,600 has not been recorded for the current year.

g. On November 1 of the current year, the company loaned $4,000 to one of its employees on a one-year, 12 percent note. The principal plus interest is payable by the employee at the end of 12 months.

h. The income before any of the adjustments or income taxes was $22,400. The company's federal income tax rate is 30 percent. (**Hint:** Compute adjusted pre-tax income based on (*a*) through (*g*) to determine income tax expense.)

Required:

1. Indicate whether each transaction relates to a deferred revenue, deferred expense, accrued revenue, or accrued expense.
2. Prepare the adjusting entry required for each transaction at December 31 of the current year.

AP4-4
LO4-1

Determining Financial Statement Effects of Adjusting Entries (P4-4)

Refer to the information regarding Hannah Company in AP4-2.

Required:

1. Indicate whether each transaction relates to a deferred revenue, deferred expense, accrued revenue, or accrued expense.
2. Using the following headings, indicate the effect of each adjusting entry and the amount of the effect. Use + for increase, − for decrease, and NE for no effect. (**Reminder:** Assets = Liabilities + Stockholders' Equity; Revenues − Expenses = Net Income; and Net Income accounts are closed to Retained Earnings, a part of Stockholders' Equity.)

	BALANCE SHEET			INCOME STATEMENT		
Transaction	Assets	Liabilities	Stockholders' Equity	Revenues	Expenses	Net Income
a.						
b.						
(etc.)						

AP4-5
LO4-1

Determining Financial Statement Effects of Adjusting Entries (P4-5)

Refer to the information regarding Bill's Catering Company in AP4-3.

Required:

1. Indicate whether each transaction relates to a deferred revenue, deferred expense, accrued revenue, or accrued expense.
2. Using the following headings, indicate the effect of each adjusting entry and the amount of each. Use + for increase, − for decrease, and NE for no effect. (**Reminder:** Assets = Liabilities + Stockholders' Equity; Revenues − Expenses = Net Income; and Net Income accounts are closed to Retained Earnings, a part of Stockholders' Equity.)

	BALANCE SHEET			INCOME STATEMENT		
Transaction	Assets	Liabilities	Stockholders' Equity	Revenues	Expenses	Net Income
a.						
b.						
(etc.)						

Inferring Year-End Adjustments, Computing Earnings per Share and Total Asset Turnover, and Recording Closing Entries (P4-6)

AP4-6
LO4-1, 4-3, 4-4

Taos Company is completing the information processing cycle at the end of its fiscal year on December 31. Following are the correct balances at December 31 of the current year for the accounts both before and after the adjusting entries for the current year.

Trial Balance, December 31 of the Current Year						
	Before Adjusting Entries		Adjustments		After Adjusting Entries	
Items	Debit	Credit	Debit	Credit	Debit	Credit
a. Cash	18,000				18,000	
b. Accounts receivable					1,500	
c. Prepaid rent	1,200				800	
d. Property, plant, and equipment	208,000				208,000	
e. Accumulated depreciation		52,500				70,000
f. Income taxes payable						6,500
g. Unearned revenue		16,000				8,000
h. Common stock and additional paid-in capital		110,000				110,000
i. Retained earnings, January 1		21,700				21,700
j. Service revenue		83,000				92,500
k. Salary expense	56,000				56,000	
l. Depreciation expense					17,500	
m. Rent expense					400	
n. Income tax expense					6,500	
	283,200	283,200			308,700	308,700

Required:

1. Compare the amounts in the columns before and after the adjusting entries to reconstruct the adjusting entries made in the current year. Provide an explanation of each.
2. Compute the amount of net income, assuming that it is based on the amount (a) before adjusting entries and (b) after adjusting entries. Which net income amount is correct? Explain why.
3. Compute earnings per share (rounded to two decimal places), assuming that 5,000 shares of stock are outstanding.
4. Assuming total assets were $136,000 at the beginning of the year, compute the total asset turnover ratio (rounded to two decimal places). What does this suggest to you about Taos Company?
5. Record the closing entry at December 31 of the current year.

AP4-7
LO4-1, 4-2, 4-4

Recording Adjusting and Closing Entries and Preparing a Balance Sheet and Income Statement Including Earnings per Share (P4-7)

South Bend Repair Service Co. keeps its records without the help of an accountant. After much effort, an outside accountant prepared the following unadjusted trial balance as of the end of the annual accounting period on December 31:

Account Titles	Debit	Credit
Cash	19,600	
Accounts receivable	7,000	
Supplies	1,300	
Prepaid insurance	900	
Equipment	27,000	
Accumulated depreciation		12,000
Other assets	5,100	
Accounts payable		2,500
Wages payable		
Income taxes payable		
Note payable (two years; 12% interest due each December 31)		5,000
Common stock (3,000 shares outstanding all year)		300
Additional paid-in capital		15,700
Retained earnings		10,300
Service revenue		48,000
Remaining expenses (not detailed; excludes income tax)	32,900	
Income tax expense		
Totals	93,800	93,800

Data not yet recorded at December 31 of the current year include:

a. Depreciation expense for the current year, $3,000.
b. Insurance expired during the current year, $450.
c. Wages earned by employees but not yet paid on December 31 of the current year, $2,100.
d. The supplies count at the end of the current year reflected $800 in remaining supplies on hand to be used in the next year.
e. Income tax expense was $3,150.

Required:
1. Record the adjusting entries.
2. Prepare an income statement and a classified balance sheet for the current year to include the effects of the preceding five transactions.
3. Record the closing entry.

CONTINUING **PROBLEM**

CON4-1

Adjusting Accounts at Year-End (the Accounting Cycle)

Penny's Pool Service & Supply, Inc. (PPSS) is completing the accounting process for the year just ended, December 31 of the current year. The transactions during the year have been journalized and posted. The following data with respect to adjusting entries are available:

a. PPSS owed $7,500 in wages to the office receptionist and three assistants for working the last 10 days in December. The employees will be paid in January of next year.
b. On October 1 of the current year, PPSS received $24,000 from customers who prepaid pool cleaning service for one year beginning on November 1 of the current year.
c. The company received a $520 utility bill for December utility usage. It will be paid in January of the next year.

d. PPSS borrowed $30,000 from a local bank on May 1 of the current year, signing a one-year, 10 percent note. The note and interest are due on May 1 of next year.

e. On December 31 of the current year, PPSS cleaned and winterized a customer's pool for $800, but the service was not yet recorded on December 31.

f. On August 1 of the current year, PPSS purchased a two-year insurance policy for $4,200, with coverage beginning on that date. The amount was recorded as Prepaid Insurance when paid.

g. On December 31 of the current year, PPSS had $3,100 of pool cleaning supplies on hand. During the current year, PPSS purchased supplies costing $23,000 from **Pool Corporation, Inc.**, and had $2,400 of supplies on hand on December 31 of the prior year.

h. PPSS estimated that depreciation on its buildings and equipment was $8,300 for the year.

i. At December 31 of the current year, $110 of interest on investments was earned that will be received in the next year.

Required:

Prepare adjusting entries for Penny's Pool Service & Supply, Inc., on December 31 of the current year.

COMPREHENSIVE PROBLEMS (CHAPTERS 1–4)

Recording Transactions (Including Adjusting and Closing Entries), Preparing Financial Statements, and Performing Ratio Analysis

COMP4-1
LO4-1, 4-2, 4-3, 4-4

Brothers Mike and Tim Hargen began operations of their tool and die shop (H & H Tool, Inc.) on January 1, 2016. The annual reporting period ends December 31. The trial balance on January 1, 2017, follows:

Account Titles	Debit	Credit
Cash	6,000	
Accounts receivable	5,000	
Supplies	13,000	
Land		
Equipment	78,000	
Accumulated depreciation (on equipment)		8,000
Other assets (not detailed to simplify)	7,000	
Accounts payable		
Wages payable		
Interest payable		
Income taxes payable		
Long-term notes payable		
Common stock (8,000 shares, $0.50 par value)		4,000
Additional paid-in capital		80,000
Retained earnings		17,000
Service revenue		
Depreciation expense		
Supplies expense		
Wages expense		
Interest expense		
Income tax expense		
Remaining expenses (not detailed to simplify)		
Totals	109,000	109,000

Transactions during 2017 follow:

a. Borrowed $15,000 cash on a five-year, 8 percent note payable, dated March 1, 2017.
b. Purchased land for a future building site; paid cash, $13,000.
c. Earned $215,000 in revenues for 2017, including $52,000 on credit and the rest in cash.
d. Sold 4,000 additional shares of capital stock for cash at $1 market value per share on January 1, 2017.
e. Incurred $114,000 in Remaining Expenses for 2017, including $20,000 on credit and the rest paid in cash.
f. Collected accounts receivable, $34,000.
g. Purchased other assets, $15,000 cash.
h. Purchased supplies on account for future use, $27,000.
i. Paid accounts payable, $26,000.
j. Signed a three-year $33,000 service contract to start February 1, 2018.
k. Declared and paid cash dividends, $25,000.

Data for adjusting entries:

l. Supplies counted on December 31, 2017, $18,000.
m. Depreciation for the year on the equipment, $10,000.
n. Interest accrued on notes payable (to be computed).
o. Wages earned by employees since the December 24 payroll but not yet paid, $16,000.
p. Income tax expense, $11,000, payable in 2018.

Required:

1. Set up T-accounts for the accounts on the trial balance and enter beginning balances.
2. Prepare journal entries for transactions (a) through (k) and post them to the T-accounts.
3. Journalize and post the adjusting entries (l) through (p).
4. Prepare an income statement (including earnings per share rounded to two decimal places), statement of stockholders' equity, and balance sheet.
5. Identify the type of transaction for (a) through (k) for the statement of cash flows (O for operating, I for investing, F for financing), and the direction and amount of the effect.
6. Journalize and post the closing entry.
7. Compute the following ratios (rounded to two decimal places) for 2017 and explain what the results suggest about the company:
   a. Current ratio
   b. Total asset turnover
   c. Net profit margin

COMP4-2

LO4-1, 4-2, 4-3, 4-4

Recording Transactions (Including Adjusting and Closing Entries), Preparing Financial Statements, and Performing Ratio Analysis

Josh and Kelly McKay began operations of their furniture repair shop (Furniture Refinishers, Inc.) on January 1, 2016. The annual reporting period ends December 31. The trial balance on January 1, 2017, was as follows:

Account Titles	Debit	Credit
Cash	5,000	
Accounts receivable	4,000	
Supplies	2,000	
Small tools	6,000	
Equipment		
Accumulated depreciation (on equipment)		
Other assets (not detailed to simplify)	9,000	
Accounts payable		7,000
Notes payable		
Wages payable		
Interest payable		
Income taxes payable		
Unearned revenue		

(Continued)

Account Titles	Debit	Credit
Common stock (60,000 shares, $0.10 par value)		6,000
Additional paid-in capital		9,000
Retained earnings		4,000
Service revenue		
Depreciation expense		
Wages expense		
Interest expense		
Income tax expense		
Remaining expenses (not detailed to simplify)		
Totals	26,000	26,000

Transactions during 2017 follow:

a. Borrowed $20,000 cash on July 1, 2017, signing a one-year, 10 percent note payable.
b. Purchased equipment for $18,000 cash on July 1, 2017.
c. Sold 10,000 additional shares of capital stock for cash at $0.50 market value per share at the beginning of the year.
d. Earned $70,000 in revenues for 2017, including $14,000 on credit and the rest in cash.
e. Incurred remaining expenses of $35,000 for 2017, including $7,000 on credit and the rest paid with cash.
f. Purchased additional small tools, $3,000 cash.
g. Collected accounts receivable, $8,000.
h. Paid accounts payable, $11,000.
i. Purchased $10,000 of supplies on account.
j. Received a $3,000 deposit on work to start January 15, 2018.
k. Declared and paid a cash dividend, $10,000.

Data for adjusting entries:

l. Supplies of $4,000 and small tools of $8,000 were counted on December 31, 2017 (debit Remaining Expenses).
m. Depreciation for 2017, $2,000.
n. Interest accrued on notes payable (to be computed).
o. Wages earned since the December 24 payroll but not yet paid, $3,000.
p. Income tax expense was $4,000, payable in 2018.

Required:

1. Set up T-accounts for the accounts on the trial balance and enter beginning balances.
2. Prepare journal entries for transactions (a) through (k) and post them to the T-accounts.
3. Journalize and post the adjusting entries (l) through (p).
4. Prepare an income statement (including earnings per share rounded to two decimal places), statement of stockholders' equity, and balance sheet.
5. Identify the type of transaction for (a) through (k) for the statement of cash flows (O for operating, I for investing, F for financing), and the direction and amount of the effect.
6. Journalize and post the closing entry.
7. Compute the following ratios (rounded to two decimal places) for 2017 and explain what the results suggest about the company:
   a. Current ratio
   b. Total asset turnover
   c. Net profit margin

CASES AND PROJECTS

Annual Report Cases

CP4-1
LO4-2, 4-3, 4-4

Finding Financial Information

Refer to the financial statements of **American Eagle Outfitters** in Appendix B at the end of this book.

Required:
(**Hint:** The notes to the financial statements may be helpful for many of these questions.)

1. How much cash did the company pay for income taxes in its 2014 fiscal year (for the year ended January 31, 2015)?
2. What was the company's best quarter in terms of sales in its 2014 fiscal year? Where did you find this information?
3. Give the closing entry for the Other Income (net) account.
4. What does Accounts Receivable consist of? Provide the names of the accounts and their balances as of January 31, 2015. Where did you find this information?
5. Compute the company's total asset turnover ratio (rounded to three decimal places) for the three years reported. What does the trend suggest to you about American Eagle Outfitters?

CP4-2
LO4-2, 4-3, 4-4

Finding Financial Information

Refer to the financial statements of **Urban Outfitters** in Appendix C at the end of this book.

Required:

1. How much is in the Prepaid Expenses and Other Current Assets account at the end of the most recent year (for the year ended January 31, 2015)? Where did you find this information?
2. What did the company report for Deferred Rent and Other Liabilities at January 31, 2015? Where did you find this information?
3. What is the difference between prepaid rent and deferred rent?
4. Describe in general terms what accrued liabilities are.
5. What would generate the interest income that is reported on the income statement?
6. What company accounts would not have balances on a post-closing trial balance?
7. Prepare the closing entry, if any, for Prepaid Expenses.
8. What is the company's earnings per share (basic only) for the three years reported?
9. Compute the company's total asset turnover ratio (rounded to three decimal places) for the three years reported. What does the trend suggest to you about Urban Outfitters?

CP4-3
LO4-2, 4-3

Comparing Companies within an Industry and Over Time

Refer to the financial statements of **American Eagle Outfitters** in Appendix B, **Urban Outfitters** in Appendix C, and the Industry Ratio Report in Appendix D at the end of this book.

Required:

1. What was Advertising Expense for each company for the most recent year? Where did you find this information?
2. Compute the percentage of Advertising Expense to Net Sales ratio (rounded to two decimal places) for most recent year for both companies. Which company incurred the higher percentage? Show computations. Are you able to perform the same comparison for the previous two years? If so, show the computations. If not, explain why not.
3. Compare the Advertising Expense to Net Sales ratio for the most recent year computed in requirement (2) to the industry average found in the Industry Ratio Report (Appendix D). Were these two companies spending more or less than their average competitor on advertising (on a relative basis)? What does this ratio tell you about the general effectiveness of each company's advertising strategy?
4. Both companies include a note to the financial statements explaining the accounting policy for advertising. How do the policies differ, if at all?
5. Compute each company's total asset turnover ratio (rounded to three decimal places) for the three years reported. What do your results suggest to you about each company over time and in comparison to each other?

6. Compare each company's total asset turnover ratio for the most recent year to the industry average total asset turnover ratio in the Industry Ratio Report (Appendix D). Were these two companies performing better or worse than the average company in the industry?

Financial Reporting and Analysis Cases

Computing Amounts on Financial Statements and Finding Financial Information

CP4-4

LO4-1, 4-2

The following information was provided by the records of Liberty Circle Apartments (a corporation) at the end of the current annual fiscal period, December 31:

Rent

a. Rent revenue collected in cash during the current year for occupancy in the current year, $500,000.
b. Rent revenue earned for occupancy in December of the current year; not collected until the following year, $10,000.
c. In December of the current year, rent revenue collected in advance for January of the following year, $14,000.

Salaries

d. Cash payment in January of the current year to employees for work in December of the prior year (accrued in the prior year), $6,000.
e. Salaries incurred and paid during the current year, $70,000.
f. Salaries earned by employees during December of the current year that will be paid in January of the next year, $3,000.
g. Cash advances to employees in December of the current year for salaries that will be earned in January of the next year, $2,000.

Supplies

h. Maintenance supplies on January 1 of the current year (balance on hand), $7,000.
i. Maintenance supplies purchased for cash during the current year, $8,000.
j. Maintenance supplies counted on December 31 of the current year $2,000.

Required:
For each of the following accounts, compute the balance to be reported in the current year, the statement the account will be reported on, and the effect (direction and amount) on cash flows (+ for increases cash and − for decreases cash). (**Hint:** Create T-accounts to determine balances.)

Account	Current Year Balance	Financial Statement	Effect on Cash Flows
1. Rent revenue			
2. Salary expense			
3. Maintenance supplies expense			
4. Rent receivable			
5. Receivables from employees			
6. Maintenance supplies			
7. Unearned rent revenue			
8. Salaries payable			

Using Financial Reports: Inferring Adjusting Entries and Information Used in Computations and Recording Closing Entries

CP4-5

LO4-1, 4-4

The pre-closing balances in the T-accounts of Naim Company at the end of the third year of operations follow. The the current year's adjusting entries are identified by letters.

Cash	
Bal. 25,000	

Note Payable (6%)	
	Bal. 10,000

Common Stock (10,000 shares)	
	Bal. 10,000

Maintenance Supplies	
Bal. 800	(a) 500

Interest Payable	
	(b) 600

Retained Earnings	
	Bal. 12,000

Service Equipment	
Bal. 90,000	

Income Taxes Payable	
	(f) 13,020

Service Revenue	
	Bal. 214,000
	(c) 10,000

Accumulated Depreciation, Service Equipment	
	Bal. 21,000
	(d) 9,000

Wages Payable	
	(e) 400

Expenses	
Bal. 160,000	
(a) 500	
(b) 600	
(d) 9,000	
(e) 400	
(f) 13,020	

Remaining Assets	
Bal. 44,800	

Unearned Revenue	
(c) 10,000	Bal. 13,600

Additional Paid-in Capital	
	Bal. 40,000

Required:

1. Develop three trial balances for Naim Company using the following format:

	UNADJUSTED TRIAL BALANCE		ADJUSTED TRIAL BALANCE		POST-CLOSING TRIAL BALANCE	
Account	Debit	Credit	Debit	Credit	Debit	Credit

2. Write an explanation for each adjusting entry.
3. Record the closing journal entry at the end of the current year.
4. What was the average income tax rate for the current year?
5. What was the average issue (sale) price per share of the common stock?

CP4-6

LO4-1, 4-2

Using Financial Reports: Analyzing the Effects of Adjustments

Carey Land Company, a closely held corporation, invests in commercial rental properties. Carey's annual accounting period ends on December 31. At the end of each year, numerous adjusting entries must be made because many transactions completed during current and prior years have economic effects on the financial statements of the current and future years. Assume that the current year is 2018.

Required:

This case concerns four transactions that have been selected for your analysis. Answer the questions for each.

Transaction (a): On January 1, 2016, the company purchased office equipment costing $14,000 for use in the business. The company estimates that the equipment's cost should be allocated at $1,000 annually.
1. Over how many accounting periods will this transaction directly affect Carey's financial statements? Explain.
2. How much depreciation expense was reported on the 2016 and 2017 income statements?
3. How should the office equipment be reported on the 2018 balance sheet?
4. Would Carey make an adjusting entry at the end of each year during the life of the equipment? Explain your answer.

Transaction (b): On September 1, 2018, Carey collected $30,000 rent on office space. This amount represented the monthly rent in advance for the six-month period September 1, 2018, through February 28, 2019. Unearned Rent Revenue was increased (credited) and Cash was increased (debited) for $30,000.

1. Over how many accounting periods will this transaction affect Carey's financial statements? Explain.
2. How much rent revenue on this office space should Carey report on the 2018 income statement? Explain.
3. Did this transaction create a liability for Carey as of the end of 2018? Explain. If yes, how much?
4. Should Carey make an adjusting entry on December 31, 2019? Explain why. If your answer is yes, prepare the adjusting entry.

Transaction (c): On December 31, 2018, Carey owed employees unpaid and unrecorded wages of $7,500 because the employees worked the last three days in December 2018. The next payroll date is January 5, 2019.

1. Over how many accounting periods will this transaction affect Carey's financial statements? Explain.
2. How will this $7,500 affect Carey's 2018 income statement and balance sheet?
3. Should Carey make an adjusting entry on December 31, 2018? Explain why. If your answer is yes, prepare the adjusting entry.

Transaction (d): On January 1, 2018, Carey agreed to supervise the planning and subdivision of a large tract of land for a customer, J. Signanini. This service job that Carey will perform involves four separate phases. By December 31, 2018, three phases had been completed to Signanini's satisfaction. The remaining phase will be performed during 2019. The total price for the four phases (agreed on in advance by both parties) was $60,000. Each phase involves about the same amount of services. On December 31, 2018, Carey had collected no cash for the services already performed.

1. Should Carey record any service revenue on this job for 2018? Explain why. If yes, how much?
2. If your answer to part (1) is yes, should Carey make an adjusting entry on December 31, 2018? If yes, prepare the entry. Explain.
3. What entry will Carey make when it completes the last phase, assuming that the full contract price is collected on the completion date, February 15, 2019?

Using Financial Reports: Analyzing Financial Information in a Sale of a Business (Challenging)

CP4-7
LO4-1, 4-2

Crystal Mullinex owns and operates Crystal's Day Spa and Salon, Inc. She has decided to sell the business and retire. She has had discussions with a representative from a regional chain of day spas. The discussions are at the complex stage of agreeing on a price. Among the important factors have been the financial statements of the business. Crystal's secretary, Kenya, under Crystal's direction, maintained the records. Each year they developed a statement of profits on a cash basis; no balance sheet was prepared. Upon request, Crystal provided the other company with the following statement for 2018 prepared by Kenya:

CRYSTAL'S DAY SPA AND SALON, INC. Statement of Profits 2018		
Spa fees collected		$1,215,000
Expenses paid:		
Rent for office space	$130,000	
Utilities expense	43,600	
Telephone expense	12,200	
Salaries expense	562,000	
Supplies expense	31,900	
Miscellaneous expenses	12,400	
Total expenses		792,100
Profit for the year		$ 422,900

Upon agreement of the parties, you have been asked to examine the financial figures for 2018. The other company's representative said, "I question the figures because, among other things, they appear to be on a 100 percent cash basis." Your investigations revealed the following additional data at December 31, 2018:

a. Of the $1,215,000 in spa fees collected in 2018, $142,000 was for services performed prior to 2018.
b. At the end of 2018, spa fees of $29,000 for services performed during the year were uncollected.
c. Office equipment owned and used by Crystal cost $205,000. Depreciation was estimated at $20,500 annually.
d. A count of supplies at December 31, 2018, reflected $5,200 worth of items purchased during the year that were still on hand. Also, the records for 2017 indicated that the supplies on hand at the end of that year were $3,125.
e. At the end of 2018, the secretary whose salary is $18,000 per year had not been paid for December because of a long trip that extended to January 15, 2019.
f. The December 2018 telephone bill for $1,400 has not been recorded or paid. In addition, the $12,200 amount on the statement of profits includes payment of the December 2017 bill of $1,800 in January 2018.
g. The $130,000 office rent paid was for 13 months (it included the rent for January 2019).

Required:
1. On the basis of this information, prepare a corrected income statement for 2018 (ignore income taxes). Show your computations for any amounts changed from those in the statement prepared by Crystal's secretary. (**Suggestion:** Format solution with four column headings: Items; Cash Basis per Crystal's Statement, $; Explanation of Changes; and Corrected Basis, $.)
2. Write a memo to support your schedule prepared in requirement (1). The purpose should be to explain the reasons for your changes and to suggest other important items that should be considered in the pricing decision.

Critical Thinking Cases

CP4-8

LO4-1, 4-2, 4-3

Using Financial Reports: Evaluating Financial Information as a Bank Loan Officer

Stoscheck Moving Corporation has been in operation since January 1, 2017. It is now December 31, 2017, the end of the annual accounting period. The company has not done well financially during the first year, although revenue has been fairly good. The three stockholders manage the company, but they have not given much attention to recordkeeping. In view of a serious cash shortage, they have applied to your bank for a $30,000 loan. You requested a complete set of financial statements. The following 2017 annual financial statements were prepared by a clerk and then were given to the bank.

STOSCHECK MOVING CORP.	
Balance Sheet	
At December 31, 2017	
Assets	
Cash	$ 2,000
Receivables	3,000
Supplies	4,000
Equipment	40,000
Prepaid insurance	6,000
Remaining assets	27,000
Total assets	$82,000
Liabilities	
Accounts payable	$ 9,000
Stockholders' Equity	
Common stock (10,000 shares outstanding)	35,000
Retained earnings	38,000
Total liabilities and stockholders' equity	$82,000

STOSCHECK MOVING CORP.	
Income Statement	
For the Period Ended December 31, 2017	
Transportation revenue	$85,000
Expenses:	
Salaries expense	17,000
Supplies expense	12,000
Other expenses	18,000
Total expenses	47,000
Net income	$38,000

After briefly reviewing the statements and "looking into the situation," you requested that the statements be redone (with some expert help) to "incorporate depreciation, accruals, inventory counts, income taxes, and so on." As a result of a review of the records and supporting documents, the following additional information was developed:

a. The Supplies of $4,000 shown on the balance sheet has not been adjusted for supplies used during 2017. A count of the supplies on hand on December 31, 2017, showed $1,800 worth of supplies remaining.

b. The insurance premium paid in 2017 was for years 2017 and 2018. The total insurance premium was debited in full to Prepaid Insurance when paid in 2017 and no adjustment has been made.

c. The equipment cost $40,000 when purchased January 1, 2017. It had an estimated annual depreciation of $8,000. No depreciation has been recorded for 2017.

d. Unpaid (and unrecorded) salaries at December 31, 2017, amounted to $3,200.

e. At December 31, 2017, transportation revenue collected in advance amounted to $7,000. This amount was credited in full to Transportation Revenue when the cash was collected earlier during 2017.

f. The income tax rate is 35 percent.

Required:

1. Record the six adjusting entries required on December 31, 2017, based on the preceding additional information.

2. Recast the preceding statements after taking into account the adjusting entries. You do not need to use classifications on the statements. Suggested form for the solution:

| | | CHANGES | | |
Items	Amounts Reported	Debit	Credit	Corrected Amounts
(List here each item from the two statements)				

3. Omission of the adjusting entries caused:
   a. Net income to be overstated or understated (select one) by $ _____.
   b. Total assets on the balance sheet to be overstated or understated (select one) by $_____.
   c. Total liabilities on the balance sheet to be overstated or understated (select one) by $ _____.

4. For both the unadjusted and adjusted balances, calculate these ratios for the company: (*a*) earnings per share (rounded to two decimal places) and (*b*) total asset turnover (rounded to three decimal places). There were 10,000 shares outstanding all year. Explain the causes of the differences and the impact of the changes on financial analysis.

5. Write a letter to the company explaining the results of the adjustments, your analysis, and your decision regarding the loan.

Evaluating the Effect of Adjusting Unearned Subscriptions on Cash Flows and Performance as a Manager

CP4-9
LO4-1

You are the regional sales manager for Miga News Company. Miga is making adjusting entries for the year ended March 31, 2018. On September 1, 2017, customers in your region paid $36,000 cash for three-year magazine subscriptions beginning on that date. The magazines are published and mailed to customers monthly. These were the only subscription sales in your region during the year.

Required:

1. What amount should be reported as cash from operations on the statement of cash flows for the year ended March 31, 2018?

2. What amount should be reported on the income statement for subscriptions revenue for the year ended March 31, 2018?

3. What amount should be reported on the March 31, 2018, balance sheet for unearned subscriptions revenue?

4. Prepare the adjusting entry at March 31, 2018, assuming that the subscriptions received on September 1, 2017, were recorded for the full amount in Unearned Subscriptions Revenue.

5. The company expects your region's annual revenue target to be $9,000.
   a. Evaluate your region's performance, assuming that the revenue target is based on cash sales.
   b. Evaluate your region's performance, assuming that the revenue target is based on accrual accounting.

Financial Reporting and Analysis Team Project

CP4-10

LO4-1, 4-2, 4-3

Team Project: Analysis of Accruals, Earnings per Share, and Net Profit Margin

As a team, select an industry to analyze. Yahoo Finance provides lists of industries at **biz.yahoo.com/p/ industries.html**. Click on an industry for a list of companies in that industry. Alternatively, go to Google Finance at **www.google.com/finance**, search for a company you are interested in, and you will be presented with a list including that company and its competitors. Each team member should acquire the annual report or 10-K for one publicly traded company in the industry, with each member selecting a different company (the SEC EDGAR service at **www.sec.gov** and the company's investor relations website itself are good sources).

Required:

On an individual basis, each team member should write a short report answering the following questions about the selected company. Discuss any patterns across the companies that you as a team observe. Then, as a team, write a short report comparing and contrasting your companies.

1. From the income statement, what is the company's basic earnings per share for each of the last three years?
2. Ratio analysis:
   a. What does the total asset turnover ratio measure in general?
   b. Compute the total asset turnover ratio (rounded to three decimal places) for the last three years.
   c. What do your results suggest about the company? (You may refer to the Management Discussion and Analysis section of the 10-K or annual report to read what the company says about the reasons for any change over time.)
   d. If available, find the industry ratio for the most recent year, compare it to your results, and discuss why you believe your company differs or is similar to the industry ratio.
3. List the accounts and amounts of accrued expenses payable on the most recent balance sheet. (You may find the detail in the notes to the statements.) What is the ratio of the total accrued expenses payable to total liabilities?

Communicating and Interpreting Accounting Information

t is the rare person today who has not been affected by **Apple** products and services. From the first commercially viable personal computer, the Apple II introduced in 1977, to the raft of mobile communication and media devices, personal computers, software, and iStore content that we all use today, Apple has fundamentally changed the way we work, play, and interact. Apple Inc. the company is a far cry from the startup incorporated by Steve Jobs, Steve Wozniak, and a group of venture capitalists in 1977. Its 1977 sales of $1 million rose to $1 billion by 1982 and exceeded *$180 billion* in 2014. To accomplish this feat, Apple didn't just invent new products; it created whole new product categories such as the personal music player, the smartphone, and the tablet. And its laserlike focus on superior ease-of-use; seamless integration of hardware, software, and content; innovative design; and frequent updating make it very difficult for others to compete.

Apple's financial statements reflect its phenomenal sales and profit growth and convey this information to the stock market. Apple's stock price increased more than sevenfold over the last six years in response to news of its success.

Financial statement information will only affect a company's stock price if the market believes in the integrity of the financial communication process. As a publicly traded company, Apple Inc. is required to provide detailed information in regular filings with the Securities and Exchange Commission. As the certifying officers of the company, current President and CEO Timothy Cook and Senior Vice President and Chief Financial Officer Luca Maestri are responsible for the accuracy of the filings. The board of directors and auditors monitor

Learning Objectives

After studying this chapter, you should be able to:

5-1 Recognize the people involved in the accounting communication process (regulators, managers, directors, auditors, information intermediaries, and users), their roles in the process, and the guidance they receive from legal and professional standards.

5-2 Identify the steps in the accounting communication process, including the issuance of press releases, annual reports, quarterly reports, and SEC filings, as well as the role of electronic information services in this process.

5-3 Recognize and apply the different financial statement and disclosure formats used by companies in practice and analyze the gross profit percentage.

5-4 Analyze a company's performance based on return on assets and its components and the effects of transactions on financial ratios.

chapter 5

MacFormat Magazine/Getty Image

FOCUS COMPANY:

Apple Inc.

COMMUNICATING FINANCIAL
INFORMATION AND CORPORATE
STRATEGY

www.apple.com

the integrity of the system that produces the disclosures. Integrity in communication with investors and other users of financial statements is key to maintaining relationships with suppliers of capital.

UNDERSTANDING THE BUSINESS

Apple Inc.'s best-known products and services are the iPhone®, iPad®, Mac®, iPod®, and the iTunes Store®. The company sells its products and services worldwide through its own Apple Store retail and online stores, as well as through third-party cellphone companies such as **AT&T** and **Verizon** and retailers such as **Best Buy**. Components for its products are produced by outsourcing partners in the United States, Asia, and Europe. Final assembly of the company's products is currently performed in the company's manufacturing facility in Ireland and by outsourcing partners, primarily located in Asia. Apple invests considerable sums in research and development, marketing, and advertising and is known for introducing new and innovative products long before the end of existing products' life cycles.

Apple also invests in **corporate governance**: procedures designed to ensure that the company is managed in the interests of the shareholders. Much of its corporate governance system is aimed at ensuring integrity in the financial reporting process. Good corporate governance eases the company's access to capital, lowering both the costs of borrowing (interest rates) and the perceived riskiness of Apple's stock.

Apple knows that when investors lose faith in the truthfulness of a firm's accounting numbers, they also normally punish the company's stock. Disclosure of an accounting fraud causes, on average, a 20 percent drop in the price of a company's stock. The extreme accounting scandals at **Le-Nature's Inc.** (discussed in Chapter 1), **Enron**, and

CORPORATE GOVERNANCE
The procedures designed to ensure that the company is managed in the interests of the shareholders.

SARBANES-OXLEY ACT
A law that strengthens U.S. financial reporting and corporate governance regulations.

WorldCom caused their stock to become worthless. In an attempt to restore investor confidence, Congress passed the Public Accounting Reform and Investor Protection Act (the **Sarbanes-Oxley Act**), which strengthens financial reporting and corporate governance for public companies.

A QUESTION OF ETHICS		The Fraud Triangle

THE FRAUD TRIANGLE

Three conditions are necessary for financial statement fraud to occur. There must be (1) an incentive to commit fraud, (2) the opportunity to commit fraud, and (3) the ability to rationalize the misdeed. These conditions make up what antifraud experts call the fraud triangle. A good system of corporate governance is designed to address these conditions. Clear lines of responsibility and sure and severe punishment counteract incentives to commit fraud. Strong internal controls and oversight by directors and auditors reduce opportunity to commit fraud. A strong code of ethics, ethical actions by those at the top of the organization, fair dealings with employees, and rewards for whistle-blowing make it more difficult for individuals to rationalize fraud. Financial statement users also have a role to play in preventing fraud. While even the savviest user can still be surprised by fraudulent reports in some cases, accounting knowledge and healthy skepticism are the best protection from such surprises.

Chapters 2 through 4 focused on the mechanics of preparing the income statement, balance sheet, statement of stockholders' equity, and cash flow statement. Based on your better understanding of financial statements, we will next take a closer look at the people involved and the regulations that govern the process that conveys accounting information to statement users in the Internet age. We will also take a more detailed look at statement formats and additional disclosures provided in financial reports to help you learn how to find relevant information. Finally, we will examine a general framework for assessing a company's business strategy and performance based on these reports.

ORGANIZATION of the Chapter

Players in the Accounting Communication Process	The Disclosure Process	A Closer Look at Financial Statement Formats and Notes	ROA Analysis: A Framework for Evaluating Company Performance
• Regulators (SEC, FASB, PCAOB, Stock Exchanges) • Managers (CEO, CFO, and Accounting Staff) • Boards of Directors (Audit Committee) • Auditors • Information Intermediaries: Information Services and Financial Analysts • Users: Institutional and Private Investors, Creditors, and Others	• Press Releases • Annual Reports and Form 10-K • Quarterly Reports and Form 10-Q • Other SEC Reports	• Classified Balance Sheet • Classified Income Statement • Gross Profit Percentage • Statement of Stockholders' Equity • Statement of Cash Flows • Notes to Financial Statements • Voluntary Disclosures	• Return on Assets (ROA) • ROA Profit Driver Analysis and Business Strategy • How Transactions Affect Ratios

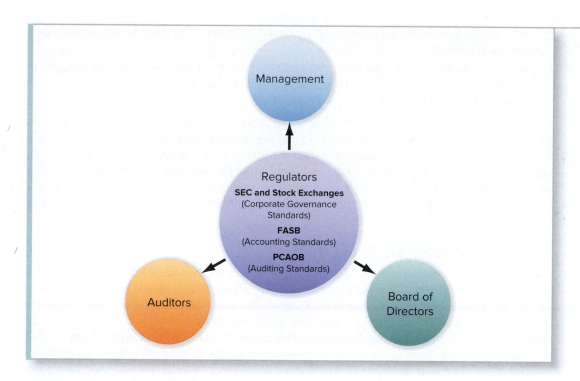

EXHIBIT 5.1

Ensuring the Integrity of
Financial Information

PLAYERS IN THE ACCOUNTING COMMUNICATION PROCESS

Exhibit 5.1 summarizes the major actors involved in ensuring the integrity of the financial reporting process.

Regulators (SEC, FASB, PCAOB, Stock Exchanges)

The mission of the U.S. **Securities and Exchange Commission (SEC)** is to protect investors and maintain the integrity of the securities markets. As part of this mission, the SEC oversees the work of the **Financial Accounting Standards Board (FASB)**, which sets generally accepted accounting principles (GAAP), and the **Public Company Accounting Oversight Board (PCAOB)**, which sets auditing standards for independent auditors (CPAs) of public companies.

The SEC staff also reviews the reports filed with it for compliance with its standards, investigates irregularities, and punishes violators. During 2009 through 2014, the SEC brought 651 enforcement actions related to financial fraud and issuer financial reporting.[1] As a consequence, a number of high-profile company officers have recently been fined and sentenced to jail. Consequences to the company can include enormous financial penalties as well as bankruptcy, as in the cases of **Le-Nature's**, **Enron**, and **WorldCom**. You can read about recent SEC enforcement actions at:

www.sec.gov/divisions/enforce/friactions.shtml

Managers (CEO, CFO, and Accounting Staff)

The primary responsibility for the information in **Apple**'s financial statements and related disclosures lies with management, specifically the highest officer in the company, often called the **chief executive officer** (CEO), and the highest officer associated with the financial and accounting side of the business, often called the **chief financial officer** (CFO). At Apple and all public companies, these two officers must personally certify that:

- Each report filed with the Securities and Exchange Commission does not contain any untrue material statement or omit a material fact and fairly presents in all material respects the financial condition, results of operations, and cash flows of the company.

---

[1]Source: **www.sec.gov/news/newsroom/images/enfstats.pdf**.

LEARNING OBJECTIVE 5-1

Recognize the people involved in the accounting communication process (regulators, managers, directors, auditors, information intermediaries, and users), their roles in the process, and the guidance they receive from legal and professional standards.

SECURITIES AND EXCHANGE COMMISSION (SEC)
The U.S. government agency that determines the financial statements that public companies must provide to stockholders and the measurement rules that they must use in producing those statements.

FINANCIAL ACCOUNTING STANDARDS BOARD (FASB)
The private sector body given the primary responsibility to work out the detailed rules that become generally accepted accounting principles.

PUBLIC COMPANY ACCOUNTING OVERSIGHT BOARD (PCAOB)
The private sector body given the primary responsibility to work out detailed auditing standards.

- There are no significant deficiencies and material weaknesses in the internal controls over financial reporting.
- They have disclosed to the auditors and audit committee of the board any weaknesses in internal controls or any fraud involving management or other employees who have a significant role in financial reporting.

Executives who knowingly certify false financial reports are subject to a fine of $5 million and a 20-year prison term. The members of the **accounting staff,** who actually prepare the details of the reports, also bear professional responsibility for the accuracy of this information, although their legal responsibility is smaller. Their future professional success depends heavily on their reputation for honesty and competence. Accounting managers responsible for financial statements with material errors are routinely fired and often have difficulty finding other employment.

Board of Directors (Audit Committee)

BOARD OF DIRECTORS
Elected by the shareholders to represent their interests; its audit committee is responsible for maintaining the integrity of the company's financial reports.

As **Apple**'s statement on corporate governance indicates, the **board of directors** (elected by the stockholders) oversees the chief executive officer and other senior management in the competent and ethical operation of Apple on a day-to-day basis and assures that the long-term interests of shareholders are being served. The **audit committee** of the board, which must be composed of nonmanagement (independent) directors with financial knowledge, is responsible for ensuring that processes are in place for maintaining the integrity of the company's accounting, financial statement preparation, and financial reporting. It is responsible for hiring the company's independent auditors. Members of the audit committee meet separately with the auditors to discuss management's compliance with their financial reporting responsibilities.

Auditors

UNQUALIFIED (CLEAN) AUDIT OPINION
Auditor's statement that the financial statements are fair presentations in all material respects in conformity with GAAP.

The SEC requires publicly traded companies to have their statements and their control systems over the financial reporting process audited by an independent registered public accounting firm (independent auditor) following auditing standards established by the PCAOB. Many privately owned companies also have their statements audited. By signing an **unqualified (clean) audit opinion**, a CPA firm assumes part of the financial responsibility for the fairness of the financial statements and related presentations. This opinion, which adds credibility to the statements, is also often required by agreements with lenders and private investors. Subjecting the company's statements to independent verification reduces the risk that the company's financial condition is misrepresented in the statements. As a result, rational investors and lenders should lower the rate of return (interest) they charge for providing capital. Examples of an unqualified audit opinion are presented under Report of Independent Registered Public Accounting Firm in Appendix B and Appendix C of this text.

Ernst & Young is currently **Apple**'s auditor. Ernst & Young, **Deloitte**, **KPMG**, and **PricewaterhouseCoopers** make up what are referred to as the "Big 4" CPA firms. Each of these firms employs thousands of CPAs in offices scattered throughout the world. They audit the great majority of publicly traded companies as well as many that are privately held. Some public companies and most private companies are audited by smaller CPA firms. A list of the auditors for selected focus companies follows.

Focus Company	Industry	Auditor
Starbucks	Coffee	Deloitte & Touche
Deckers Brands	Footwear	KPMG
Whole Foods Market	Food Retail	Ernst & Young

Information Intermediaries: Information Services and Financial Analysts

Students often view the communication process between companies and financial statement users as a simple process of mailing the report to individual shareholders who read the report and then make investment decisions based on what they have learned. This simple picture is far from today's reality. Now most investors rely on company websites, information services, and financial analysts to gather and analyze information.

Companies actually file their SEC forms electronically through the EDGAR (Electronic Data Gathering, Analysis, and Retrieval) Service, which is sponsored by the SEC. Each fact in the report is now tagged to identify its source and meaning using a language called **XBRL.** Users can retrieve information from EDGAR within 24 hours of its submission, long before it is available through the mail. EDGAR is a free service available on the Web under "Filings & Forms" at:

www.sec.gov

Most companies also provide direct access to their financial statements and other information over the Web. You can contact **Apple** at:

investor.apple.com

Information services allow investors to gather their own information about the company and monitor the recommendations of a variety of analysts. Financial analysts and other sophisticated users obtain much of the information they use from the wide variety of commercial online information services. Fee-based services such as **Compustat** and **Thomson Reuters** provide broad access to financial statements and news information. A growing number of other resources offering a mixture of free and fee-based information exist on the Web. These include:

www.google.com/finance   **finance.yahoo.com**   **www.marketwatch.com**
www.bloomberg.com

Exhibit 5.2 suggests the wide range of information about Apple available on the Google Finance website. It includes stock price and financial statement information, news accounts, and important future events related to Apple. Note that the financial information at the bottom of the exhibit matches the income statement information and ratio calculations for Apple and its two largest competitors presented later in this chapter. To see what has happened to Apple since this chapter was written, go to **www.google.com/finance?q=NASDAQ:AAPL**. Look at the "Related Companies" section to see how Apple has fared compared to its competitors. Click on "Financials" on the top left menu to review the most recent financial statements.

Financial analysts receive accounting reports and other information about the company from electronic information services. They also gather information through conversations with company executives and visits to company facilities and competitors. The results of their analyses are combined into analysts' reports. Analysts' reports normally include forecasts of future quarterly and annual earnings per share and share price; a buy, hold, or sell recommendation for the company's shares; and explanations for these judgments. In making their **earnings forecasts**, the analysts rely heavily on their knowledge of the way the accounting system translates business events into the numbers on a company's financial statements, which is the subject matter of this text. Individual analysts often specialize in particular industries (such as sporting goods or energy companies). Analysts are regularly evaluated based on the accuracy of their forecasts, as well as the profitability of their stock

EARNINGS FORECASTS
Predictions of earnings for future accounting periods, prepared by financial analysts.

EXHIBIT 5.2	Google Finance Information on Apple

APPLE REAL WORLD EXCERPT: Google Finance

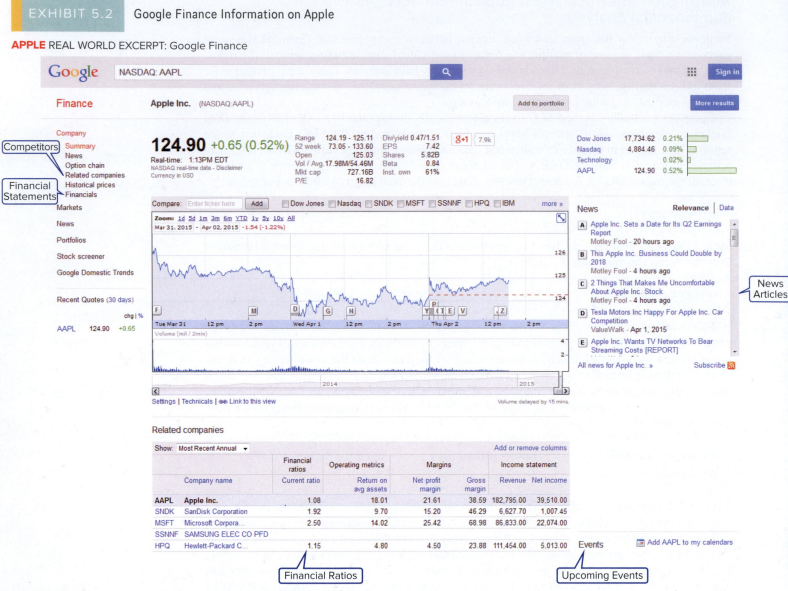

Google and the Google logo are registered trademarks of Google Inc., used with permission.

picks. A sample of these forecasts and stock recommendations for Apple at the time this chapter was written follow:

Firm	Stock Recommendation	Earnings per Share Forecast for 2015	Earnings per Share Forecast for 2016
Credit Suisse–NA	Buy	8.82	9.89
Oppenheimer & Co.	Strong Buy	8.73	9.76
Wells Fargo	Hold	8.58	8.86
BGC Partners	Hold	8.49	9.08
Consensus of 46 analysts	Buy	8.61	9.26

Analysts often work in the research departments of brokerage and investment banking houses such as Credit Suisse, mutual fund companies such as **Fidelity Investments**, and investment advisory services such as **Value Line** that sell their advice to others. Through their reports and recommendations, analysts are transferring their knowledge of accounting, the company, and the industry to customers who lack this expertise.

Information Services and Your Job Search

Information services have become the primary tool for professional analysts who use them to analyze competing firms. Information services are also an important source of information for job seekers. Potential employers expect job applicants to demonstrate knowledge of their companies during an interview, and electronic information services are an excellent source of company information. The best place to begin learning about potential employers is to visit their websites. Be sure to read the material in the employment section and the investor relations section of the site. To learn more about electronic information services, contact the business or reference librarian at your college or university or explore the websites discussed in this section.

Users: Institutional and Private Investors, Creditors, and Others

Institutional investors include pension funds (associated with companies, unions, or government agencies); mutual funds; and endowment, charitable foundation, and trust funds (such as the endowment of your college or university). These institutional stockholders usually employ their own analysts, who also rely on the information intermediaries just discussed. Institutional shareholders control the majority of publicly traded shares of U.S. companies. For example, at the time this chapter is being written, institutional investors own 61 percent of **Apple** stock. Apple's three largest institutional investors follow:

Institution	Approximate Ownership
Vanguard Group Inc.	5.70%
State Street Corp.	4.22%
FMR LLC	3.07%

Most small investors own stock in companies such as Apple indirectly through mutual and pension funds.

Private investors include large individual investors such as the venture capitalists who originally invested directly in Apple, as well as small retail investors who buy shares of publicly traded companies through brokers such as **Fidelity**. Retail investors normally lack the expertise to understand financial statements and the resources to gather data efficiently. They often rely on the advice of information intermediaries or turn their money over to the management of mutual and pension funds (institutional investors).

Lenders, or **creditors**, include suppliers, banks, commercial credit companies, and other financial institutions that lend money to companies. Lending officers and financial analysts in these organizations use the same public sources of information. They also use additional financial information (e.g., monthly statements) that companies often agree to provide as part of the lending contract. Lenders are the primary external user group for financial statements of private companies. Institutional and private investors also become creditors when they buy a company's publicly traded bonds.

Financial statements also play an important role in the relationships between suppliers and customers. Customers evaluate the financial health of suppliers to determine whether they will be reliable, up-to-date sources of supply. Suppliers evaluate their customers to estimate their future needs and ability to pay debts. Competitors also attempt to learn useful information about a company from its statements. The potential loss of competitive advantage is one of the costs of public financial disclosures. Accounting regulators consider these costs as well as the direct costs of preparation when they consider requiring new disclosures. **Cost-effectiveness** requires the benefits of accounting for and reporting information to outweigh the costs. Small amounts do not have to be reported separately or accounted for precisely according to GAAP if they would not influence users' decisions. Accountants usually designate such items and amounts as **immaterial.** Determining **material amounts** is often very subjective.

INSTITUTIONAL INVESTORS
Managers of pension, mutual, endowment, and other funds that invest on the behalf of others.

PRIVATE INVESTORS
Individuals who purchase shares in companies.

LENDERS (CREDITORS)
Suppliers and financial institutions that lend money to companies.

COST-EFFECTIVENESS
Requires that the benefits of accounting for and reporting information should outweigh the costs.

MATERIAL AMOUNTS
Amounts that are large enough to influence a user's decision.

In this section, we learned the roles of different parties in the accounting communication process and the guidance they receive from legal and professional standards. Management of the reporting company decides the appropriate format and level of detail to present in its financial reports. Independent audits increase the credibility of the information. Directors monitor managers' compliance with reporting standards and hire the auditor. The SEC staff reviews public financial reports for compliance with legal and professional standards and punishes violators. Financial statement announcements from public companies usually are first transmitted to users through electronic information services. Analysts play a major role in making financial statement and other information available to average investors through their stock recommendations and earnings forecasts. Before you move on, complete the following exercise to test your understanding of these concepts.

SELF-STUDY **QUIZ**

Match the key terms in the left column with their definitions in the right column.

1. Material amount	*a.* Management primarily responsible for accounting information.
2. CEO and CFO	*b.* An independent party who verifies financial statements.
3. Financial analyst	*c.* Amount large enough to influence users' decisions.
4. Auditor	*d.* Reporting only information that provides benefits in excess of costs.
5. Cost-effectiveness	*e.* An individual who analyzes financial information and provides advice.

After you have completed your answers, check them below.

LEARNING OBJECTIVE 5-2

Identify the steps in the accounting communication process, including the issuance of press releases, annual reports, quarterly reports, and SEC filings, as well as the role of electronic information services in this process.

PRESS RELEASE

A written public news announcement normally distributed to major news services.

THE DISCLOSURE PROCESS

As noted in our discussion of information services and information intermediaries, the accounting communication process includes more steps and participants than one would envision in a world in which annual and quarterly reports are simply mailed to shareholders. SEC regulation FD, for "Fair Disclosure," requires that companies provide all investors equal access to all important company news. Managers and other insiders are also prohibited from trading their company's shares based on nonpublic (insider) information so that no party benefits from early access.

Press Releases

To provide timely information to external users and to limit the possibility of selective leakage of information, **Apple** and other public companies announce quarterly and annual earnings through a **press release** as soon as the verified figures (audited for annual and reviewed for quarterly earnings) are available. Apple normally issues its earnings press releases within four weeks of the end of the accounting period. The announcements are sent electronically to the major print and electronic news services, including Dow Jones, Thomson Reuters, and Bloomberg, which make them immediately available to subscribers. Exhibit 5.3 shows an excerpt from a typical earnings press release for Apple that includes key financial figures. This excerpt is followed by management's discussion of the results and condensed income statements and balance sheets, which will be included in the formal report to shareholders, distributed after the press release.

Many companies, including Apple, follow these press releases with a **conference call** during which senior managers answer analysts' questions about the quarterly results. These calls are open to the investing public. Listening to these recordings is a good way to learn about a company's business strategy and its expectations for the future, as well as key factors that analysts consider when they evaluate a company.

1. *c;* 2. *a;* 3. *e;* 4. *b;* 5. *d.*

Earnings Press Release
Excerpt for Apple Inc.

APPLE REPORTS RECORD FIRST-QUARTER RESULTS

Highest-Ever Revenue and Earnings Drive 48% Increase in EPS

Growth Led by Record Revenue from iPhone, Mac, and App Store

CUPERTINO, California—January 27, 2015—Apple® today announced financial results for its fiscal 2015 first quarter ended December 27, 2014. The Company posted record quarterly revenue of $74.6 billion and record quarterly net profit of $18 billion, or $3.06 per diluted share. These results compare to revenue of $57.6 billion and net profit of $13.1 billion, or $2.07 per diluted share, in the year-ago quarter. Gross margin was 39.9 percent compared to 37.9 percent in the year-ago quarter. International sales accounted for 65 percent of the quarter's revenue.

The results were fueled by all-time record revenue from iPhone® and Mac® sales as well as record performance of the App Store℠. iPhone unit sales of 74.5 million also set a new record.

"We'd like to thank our customers for an incredible quarter, which saw demand for Apple products soar to an all-time high," said Tim Cook, Apple's CEO. "Our revenue grew 30 percent over last year to $74.6 billion, and the execution by our teams to achieve these results was simply phenomenal."

Apple press release, January 27, 2015.

APPLE

REAL WORLD EXCERPT:

Press Release

How Does the Stock Market React to Earnings Announcements?

FINANCIAL ANALYSIS

For actively traded stocks such as **Apple**, most of the stock market reaction (stock price increases and decreases from investor trading) to the news in the press release usually occurs quickly. Recall that a number of analysts follow Apple and regularly predict the company's earnings. When the actual earnings are published, the market reacts not to the amount of earnings, but to the difference between expected earnings and actual earnings. This amount is called **unexpected earnings.** In January, analysts expected Apple to report quarterly profit of $2.60 per share. In its press release presented in Exhibit 5.3, Apple's actual earnings per share for the quarter ended up being $3.06 per share. Unexpected earnings (Actual − Expected) were thus $0.46 per share ($3.06 − $2.60) and, as a result, the share price opened at $8 the next day, a 7 percent increase.

Companies such as Apple also issue press releases concerning other important events such as new product announcements. Press releases related to annual earnings and quarterly earnings often precede the issuance of the quarterly or annual report by 15 to 45 days. This time is necessary to prepare the additional detail and to distribute those reports.

Annual Reports and Form 10-K

For privately held companies, **annual reports** are relatively simple documents photocopied on white bond paper. They normally include only the following:

1. Four basic financial statements: income statement, balance sheet, stockholders' equity or retained earnings statement, and cash flow statement.

2. Related notes (footnotes).

3. Report of Independent Accountants (Auditor's Opinion) if the statements are audited.

The annual reports of public companies filed on **Form 10-K** are significantly more elaborate mainly because of additional SEC reporting requirements. SEC reports are normally referred

FORM 10-K
The annual report that publicly traded companies must file with the SEC.

to by number (for example, the "10-K"). The principal components of the financial disclosures in the 10-K include:

Item 1. **Business:** Description of business operations and company strategy.

Item 6. **Selected Financial Data:** Summarized financial data for a 5-year period.

Item 7. **Management's Discussion and Analysis of Financial Condition and Results of Operations:** Management's views on the causes of its successes and failures during the reporting period and the risks it faces in the future.

Item 8. **Financial Statements and Supplemental Data:** The four basic financial statements and related notes, the report of management, and the auditor's report (Report of Independent Registered Public Accounting Firm).

Except for the Management's Discussion and Analysis, most of these elements have been covered in earlier chapters. This element includes an explanation of key figures on the financial statements and the risks the company faces in the future. The Form 10-K also provides a more detailed description of the business, including its products, product development, sales and marketing, manufacturing, and competitors. It also lists properties owned or leased, any legal proceedings it is involved in, and significant contracts it has signed.

Quarterly Reports and Form 10-Q

FORM 10-Q
The quarterly report that publicly traded companies must file with the SEC.

Quarterly reports for private companies include condensed financial statements providing fewer details than annual statements and only key notes to the statements. They are not audited and so are marked **unaudited.** Often the cash flow statement, statement of stockholders' equity, and some notes to the financial statements are omitted. Private companies normally prepare quarterly reports for their lenders. Public companies file their quarterly reports on **Form 10-Q** with the SEC. The Form 10-Q contains most of the information items provided in the financial section (PART II) of the 10-K and some additional items.

Other SEC Reports

FORM 8-K
The report used by publicly traded companies to disclose any material event not previously reported that is important to investors.

Public companies must file other reports with the SEC. These include the current event reports **Form 8-K**, which is used to disclose any material event not previously reported that is important to investors (e.g., auditor changes, mergers). Other filing requirements for public companies are described on the SEC website.

A CLOSER LOOK AT FINANCIAL STATEMENT FORMATS AND NOTES

LEARNING OBJECTIVE 5-3
Recognize and apply the different financial statement and disclosure formats used by companies in practice and analyze the gross profit percentage.

The financial statements shown in previous chapters provide a good introduction to their content and structure. In this section, we will discuss three additional characteristics of financial statements and the related disclosures that are designed to make them more useful to investors, creditors, and analysts:

- **Comparative financial statements.** To allow users to compare performance from period to period, companies report financial statement values for the current period and one or more prior periods. **Apple** and most U.S. companies present two years' balance sheets and three years' income statements, cash flow statements, and statements of stockholders' equity.

- **Additional subtotals and classifications in financial statements.** You should not be confused when you notice slightly different statement formats used by different companies. In this section, we will focus on similarities and differences in the classifications and line items presented on Apple's and **Chipotle**'s balance sheet, income statement, and cash flow statement.

- **Additional disclosures.** Most companies present voluminous notes that are necessary to understand a company's performance and financial condition. In addition, certain complex transactions require additional statement disclosures. We take a closer look at some of Apple's note disclosures to prepare you for more detailed discussions in the remaining chapters in this text.

Classified Balance Sheet

Exhibit 5.4 shows the September 27, 2014, balance sheet for **Apple**. This balance sheet looks very similar in structure to the balance sheet for **Chipotle** presented in Chapter 4, but it is presented for two years to ease comparisons over time. The statement classifications (current vs. noncurrent assets and current vs. noncurrent liabilities) play a major role in our discussion of ratio analysis (e.g., the current ratio in Chapter 2).

EXHIBIT 5.4

Balance Sheet of Apple Inc.

APPLE INC.
Consolidated Balance Sheets
(in millions except number of shares, which are in thousands)*

	September 27, 2014	September 28, 2013
ASSETS		
Current assets:		
Cash and cash equivalents	$ 13,844	$ 14,259
Short-term marketable securities	11,233	26,287
Accounts receivable, less allowances of $86 and		
$99, respectively	17,460	13,102
Inventories	2,111	1,764
Deferred tax assets	4,318	3,453
Vendor non-trade receivables	9,759	7,539
Other current assets	9,806	6,882
Total current assets	68,531	73,286
Long-term marketable securities	130,162	106,215
Property, plant, and equipment, net	20,624	16,597
Goodwill	4,616	1,577
Acquired intangible assets, net	4,142	4,179
Other assets	3,764	5,146
Total assets	$231,839	$207,000
LIABILITIES AND SHAREHOLDERS' EQUITY		
Current liabilities:		
Accounts payable	$ 30,196	$ 22,367
Accrued expenses	18,453	13,856
Deferred revenue	8,491	7,435
Commercial paper	6,308	0
Total current liabilities	63,448	43,658
Deferred revenue—non-current	3,031	2,625
Long-term debt	28,987	16,960
Other non-current liabilities	24,826	20,208
Total liabilities	120,292	83,451
Commitments and contingencies		
Shareholders' equity:		
Common stock and additional paid-in capital,		
$0.00001 par value; 12,600,000 shares authorized;		
5,866,161 and 6,294,494 shares issued and		
outstanding, respectively	24,395	19,293
Retained earnings	87,152	104,256
Total shareholders' equity	111,547	123,549
Total liabilities and shareholders' equity	$231,839	$207,000

Apple's statements have been simplified for purposes of our discussion.

APPLE
REAL WORLD EXCERPT:
Annual Report

Assets that will be used or turned into cash within one year

Assets that will be used or turned into cash beyond one year

Obligations that will be paid or settled within one year

Obligations that will be paid or settled after one year

} *Capital contributed by shareholders*
} *Earnings reinvested in the company*

Apple's balance sheet contains an item, not included in Chipotle's, that is worthy of additional discussion. **Intangible assets** (discussed in Chapter 8) have no physical existence and a long life. Examples are patents, trademarks, copyrights, franchises, and goodwill from purchasing other companies. Most intangibles (except goodwill, trademarks, and other intangibles with indefinite lives) are amortized as they are used in a manner similar to the depreciation of tangible assets (Amortization Expense is debited and the contra-asset Accumulated Amortization is credited). Just as tangible fixed assets are reported net of accumulated depreciation, **intangible assets are reported net of accumulated amortization** on the balance sheet. **Goodwill** is a more general intangible asset representing the excess of the price paid for another company over the value of its identifiable assets. It is discussed in more detail in Chapter 8.

Also recall our discussion of deferred revenues from Chapter 4. These are liabilities created when customers pay for goods or services before the company delivers them. In Apple's balance sheet, **deferred revenues show up in two places: current liabilities and noncurrent liabilities.** They both relate primarily to product warranties that Apple includes with its products. The deferred revenues related to repairs Apple expects to provide during the next year are classified as current. Those that relate to repairs to be provided in later years are classified as noncurrent.

When you first look at a new set of financial statements, try not to be confused by differences in terminology. When interpreting line items you have never seen before, be sure to consider their description **and their classification.**

Classified Income Statement

Apple's 2014 consolidated income statement is reprinted in Exhibit 5.5. It presents the income statement followed by earnings per share for three years, as required by the SEC. Apple's income statement includes one subtotal not included in **Chipotle**'s. Like many manufacturing and merchandising (retail and wholesale) companies that sell goods, Apple reports the subtotal **Gross Profit** (gross margin), which is the difference between net sales and cost of goods sold. **It is important to note that regardless of whether a company reports a gross profit subtotal, the income statement presents the same information.** Another subtotal—**Operating Income** (also called Income from Operations)—is computed by subtracting operating expenses from gross profit.

Nonoperating (other) Items are revenues, expenses, gains, and losses that do not relate to the company's primary operations. Examples include interest income, interest expense, and gains and losses on the sale of investments. These nonoperating items are added to or subtracted from income from operations to obtain **Income before Income Taxes**, also called Pretax Earnings. At this point, Provision for Income Taxes (Income Tax Expense) is subtracted to obtain Net Income. Some companies show fewer subtotals on their income statements. No difference exists in the revenue, expense, gain, and loss items reported using the different formats. Only the categories and subtotals differ.

When a major component of a business is sold or abandoned, income or loss from that component earned before the disposal, as well as any gain or loss on disposal, is included as **Discontinued Operations.** The item is presented separately because it is not useful in predicting the future income of the company given its nonrecurring nature. If discontinued operations are reported, an additional subtotal is presented before this item for Income from Continuing Operations.

Finally, **earnings per share** is reported. Simple computations of earnings per share (EPS) are as follows:

$$\text{Earnings per Share} = \frac{\text{Net Income*}}{\begin{array}{c}\text{Average Number of Shares of Common Stock}\\\text{Outstanding during the Period}\end{array}}$$

GROSS PROFIT (GROSS MARGIN)
Net sales less cost of goods sold.

OPERATING INCOME (INCOME FROM OPERATIONS)
Net sales less cost of goods sold and other operating expenses.

INCOME BEFORE INCOME TAXES (PRETAX EARNINGS)
Revenues minus all expenses except income tax expense.

---

*If there are preferred dividends (discussed in Chapter 11), the amount is subtracted from net income in the numerator.

EXHIBIT 5.5

Income Statement of Apple Inc.

APPLE

REAL WORLD EXCERPT:

Annual Report

APPLE INC.
Consolidated Statements of Operations*
(in millions except number of shares which are in thousands and per share amounts)

Three years ended September 27, 2014	2014	2013	2012	
Net sales	$182,795	$170,910	$156,508	
Cost of sales	112,258	106,606	87,846	
Gross profit	70,537	64,304	68,662	
Operating expenses:				Operating activities (central focus of the business)
Research and development	6,041	4,475	3,381	
Selling, general, and administrative	11,993	10,830	10,040	
Total operating expenses	18,034	15,305	13,421	
Operating income	52,503	48,999	55,241	Peripheral activities (not the main focus of the business)
Other income/(expense), net	980	1,156	522	
Income before provision for income taxes	53,483	50,155	55,763	
Provision for income taxes	13,973	13,118	14,030	Income tax expense
Net income	$ 39,510	$ 37,037	$ 41,733	
Earnings per share:				
Basic	$ 6.49	$ 5.72	$ 6.38	= Net Income/Average Number of Shares Outstanding
Shares used in computing earnings per share:				
Basic	6,085,572	6,477,320	6,543,726	

Apple's statements have been simplified for purposes of our discussion.

Statement of Comprehensive Income

FINANCIAL ANALYSIS

Both the FASB and the IASB require an additional statement entitled the Statement of Comprehensive Income, which can be presented separately or in combination with the income statement. When presented separately, the statement starts with Net Income, the bottom line of the income statement. Following this total would be the components of other comprehensive income. The Net Income and Other Comprehensive Income items are then combined to create a total called Comprehensive Income (the bottom line for this statement). The following summarizes the information **Apple** presented in a recent quarterly report. Other Comprehensive Income items include fair value changes on certain marketable securities, which are discussed in Appendix A, as well as other items discussed in more advanced accounting classes.

APPLE INC.
Consolidated Statement of Comprehensive Income
Three months ended December 28, 2014 (in millions)

Net income	$18,024
Other comprehensive (loss)/income	
Change in foreign currency translation	(66)
Change in unrecognized gains/losses on derivative instruments	1,417
Change in unrealized gains/losses on marketable securities	(470)
Comprehensive income	$18,905

PAUSE FOR **FEEDBACK**

As **Apple**'s statements suggest, most statements are classified and include subtotals that are relevant to analysis. On the balance sheet, the most important distinctions are between current and noncurrent assets and liabilities. On the income statement, the subtotals gross profit and income from operations are most important. So the next step in preparing to analyze financial statements is to see if you understand the effects of transactions you have already studied on these subtotals. The following questions will test your ability to do so.

SELF-STUDY **QUIZ**

1. Complete the following tabulation, indicating the **direction** (+ for increase, − for decrease, and NE for no effect) **and amount** of the effect of each transaction. Consider each item independently. (**Hint:** Prepare journal entries for each transaction. Then consider the balance sheet or income statement classification of each account affected to come up with your answers.)

   a. Recorded and paid rent expense of $200.

   b. Recorded the sale of services on account for $400.

Transaction	Current Assets	Gross Profit	Income from Operations
a.			
b.			

After you have completed your answers, check them below.

 GUIDED HELP 5-1

For additional step-by-step video instruction on preparing the balance sheet and income statement from a trial balance, go to **www.mhhe.com/libby9e_gh5**.

KEY RATIO ANALYSIS	Gross Profit Percentage

The key subtotals on the income statement we just discussed also play a major role in financial ratio analysis. As we noted above, net sales less cost of goods sold equals the subtotal **gross profit** or **gross margin.** Analysts often examine gross profit as a percentage of sales (the gross profit or gross margin percentage).

 ANALYTICAL QUESTION

How effective is management in selling goods and services for more than the costs to purchase or produce them?

 RATIO AND COMPARISONS

The gross profit percentage ratio is computed as follows:

$$\text{Gross Profit Percentage} = \frac{\text{Gross Profit*}}{\text{Net Sales}}$$

*Gross Profit = Net Sales − Cost of Sales

Solutions to SELF-STUDY QUIZ

1. *a.* Rent expense (+E, −SE)   200
        Cash (−A)   200
        −200, NE, −200

   b. Accounts receivable (+A)   400
        Sales revenue (+R, +SE)   400
        +400, +400, +400

The ratio for 2014 for **Apple** is:

$$\frac{\$70{,}537}{\$182{,}795} = 0.386\ (38.6\%)$$

COMPARISONS OVER TIME			COMPARISON WITH COMPETITOR
Apple			HP
2012	2013	2014	2014
43.9%	37.6%	38.6%	23.4%

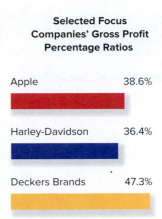

Selected Focus Companies' Gross Profit Percentage Ratios

Apple	38.6%
Harley-Davidson	36.4%
Deckers Brands	47.3%

INTERPRETATIONS

In General   The gross profit percentage measures a company's ability to charge premium prices and produce goods and services at low cost. All other things equal, a higher gross profit results in higher net income.

   Business strategy, as well as competition, affects the gross profit percentage. Companies pursuing a product-differentiation strategy use research and development and product promotion activities to convince customers of the superiority or distinctiveness of the company's products. This allows them to charge premium prices, producing a higher gross profit percentage. Companies following a low-cost strategy rely on more efficient management of production to reduce costs and increase the gross profit percentage. Managers, analysts, and creditors use this ratio to assess the effectiveness of the company's product development, marketing, and production strategy.

Focus Company Analysis   Apple's gross profit percentage has remained fairly steady over the past three years and remains well above that of its competitor, **HP**. At the beginning of the chapter, we discussed key elements of Apple's business strategy that focused on introducing new integrated technologies, product lines, and styles, as well as managing production and inventory costs. Each of these elements can have a large effect on gross profit. Its Form 10-K indicates that its various product lines have different gross profit percentages and that a large increase in iPhone sales increased the overall gross profit percentage. Introducing new products with higher initial cost structures can decrease gross profit percentage.

A Few Cautions   To assess the company's ability to sustain its gross profits, you must understand the sources of any change in the gross profit percentage. For example, an increase in margin resulting from increased sales of high-margin new products can be eroded by actions of competitors or increases in component costs for popular products. Also, higher prices must often be sustained with higher R&D and advertising costs, which reduce net income and can offset any increase in gross profit. This has not been the case for Apple in recent years as we will see later in the chapter. Apple's astonishing gross profit results in an industry-leading net profit margin and return on assets.

Statement of Stockholders' Equity

The statement of stockholders' (shareholders') equity reports the changes in each of the company's stockholders' equity accounts during the accounting period. Exhibit 5.6 presents **Apple**'s 2014 consolidated statement of stockholders' equity. The statement has a column for each stockholders' equity account and one for the effect on total stockholders' equity. (Apple combines the common stock account and additional paid-in capital accounts.) The first row of the statement starts with the beginning balances in each account, which correspond to the prior year's ending balances on the balance sheet. Each row that follows lists each event that occurred during the period that affected any stockholders' equity accounts. Apple reported net income of $39,510 for the year, which increases retained earnings. Apple declared dividends of $11,215, which is subtracted from retained earnings. Apple issued 60,344 shares of common stock during the year and received $5,102 million for the issuance. **Note that the number of shares and the dollar amount are both listed. It is important not to confuse them.** Apple also repurchased and retired shares. This topic is discussed in Chapter 11. The final row lists the ending balances in the accounts, which correspond to the ending balances on the balance sheet. Public companies must present information for the prior three years in their statements

EXHIBIT 5.6

Statement of Stockholders' Equity

APPLE INC.
Consolidated Statements of Shareholders' Equity (partial)*
(in millions, except number of shares, which are reflected in thousands)

	Common Stock and Additional Paid-In Capital		Retained Earnings	Total Shareholders' Equity
	Shares	Amount		
Balances as of September 28, 2013	6,294,494	$19,293	$104,256	$123,549
Net income	–	–	39,510	39,510
Other comprehensive income/(loss)	–	–	–	–
Dividends and dividend equivalents declared	–	–	(11,215)	(11,215)
Stock issued	60,344	5,102		5,102
Stock repurchased	(488,677)	–	(45,399)	(45,399)
Balances as of September 27, 2014	**5,866,161**	**$24,395**	**$ 87,152**	**$111,547**

Apple's statements have been simplified for purposes of our discussion.

of stockholders' equity. So Apple's 2012 and 2013 statements would be presented above the information shown in Exhibit 5.6.

Statement of Cash Flows

We introduced the three cash flow statement classifications in prior chapters:

Cash Flows from Operating Activities. This section reports cash flows associated with earning income.

Cash Flows from Investing Activities. Cash flows in this section are associated with the purchase and sale of (1) productive assets (other than inventory) and (2) investments in other companies.

Cash Flows from Financing Activities. These cash flows are related to financing the business through borrowing and repaying loans from financial institutions, stock (equity) issuances and repurchases, and dividend payments.

Exhibit 5.7 presents **Apple**'s 2014 consolidated statement of cash flows. The first section (Cash Flows from Operating Activities) can be reported using either the **direct** or **indirect** method. For Apple, this first section is reported using the indirect method, which presents a reconciliation of net income on an accrual basis to cash flows from operations.

The Operating Activities section prepared using the indirect method helps the analyst understand the **causes of differences** between a company's net income and its cash flows. Net income and cash flows from operating activities can be quite different. Remember that the income statement is prepared under the accrual concept. Revenues are recorded when earned without regard to when the related cash flows occur. Likewise, expenses are matched with revenues and recorded in the same period without regard to when the related cash flows occur.

In the indirect method, the Operating Activities section starts with net income computed under the accrual concept and then eliminates noncash items, leaving cash flow from operating activities:

> **Net income**
> **+/−Adjustments for noncash items**
> **Cash provided by operating activities**

The items listed between these two amounts explain the reasons they differ. For example, since no cash is paid during the current period for Apple's depreciation expense reported on the income

APPLE INC.
Consolidated Statements of Cash Flows*
(in millions)

Three years ended September 27, 2014	2014	2013	2012
Cash and cash equivalents, beginning of the year	$ 14,259	$ 10,746	$ 9,815
Operating activities:			
Net income	39,510	37,037	41,733
Adjustments to reconcile net income to cash generated by operating activities:			
Depreciation	7,946	6,757	3,277
Other noncash items	5,210	3,394	6,145
Changes in operating assets and liabilities:	7,047	6,478	(299)
Cash generated by operating activities	59,713	53,666	50,856
Investing activities:			
Purchases of marketable securities	(217,128)	(148,489)	(151,232)
Proceeds from sales/maturities of marketable securities	208,111	124,447	112,805
Payments for acquisition of property, plant, and equipment	(13,336)	(8,661)	(8,645)
Payments for acquisition of intangible assets	(242)	(911)	(1,107)
Other investing activities	16	(160)	(48)
Cash used in investing activities	(22,579)	(33,774)	(48,227)
Financing activities:			
Proceeds from issuance of common stock	730	530	665
Dividends paid	(11,126)	(10,564)	(2,488)
Repurchase of common stock	(45,399)	(22,860)	0
Other financing activities	18,246	16,515	125
Cash used in financing activities	(37,549)	(16,379)	(1,698)
Increase/(decrease) in cash and cash equivalents	(415)	3,513	931
Cash and cash equivalents, end of the year	$ 13,844	$ 14,259	$ 10,746
Supplemental cash flow disclosure			
Cash paid for income taxes, net	$ 10,026	$ 9,128	$ 7,682
Cash paid for interest	$ 339	$ 0	$ 0

* Apple's statements have been simplified for purposes of our discussion.

EXHIBIT 5.7

Cash Flow Statement of Apple

APPLE

REAL WORLD EXCERPT:

Annual Report

Cash flows associated with earning income computed by eliminating noncash items from net income

Cash flows associated with purchase and sale of productive assets and investments

Cash flows associated with borrowing and repaying loans, issuing and repurchasing stock, and dividends

} *Total change in cash*
} *End of year cash on balance sheet*

statement, this amount is added back to net income to eliminate its effect. Similarly, increases and decreases in certain assets and liabilities (called operating assets and liabilities) also account for some of the difference between net income and cash flow from operations. For example, sales on account increase net income as well as the current asset accounts receivable, but sales on account do not increase cash. As we cover different portions of the income statement and balance sheet in more detail in Chapters 6 through 11, we will also discuss the relevant sections of the cash flow statement. Then we discuss the complete cash flow statement in detail in Chapter 12.

Notes to Financial Statements

While the numbers reported on the various financial statements provide important information, users require additional details to facilitate their analysis. All financial reports include additional information in notes that follow the statements. **Apple**'s 2014 notes include three types of information:

1. Descriptions of the key accounting rules applied to the company's statements.

2. Additional detail supporting reported numbers.

3. Relevant financial information not disclosed on the statements.

Accounting Rules Applied in the Company's Statements

One of the first notes is typically a summary of significant accounting policies. As you will see in your study of subsequent chapters, generally accepted accounting principles (GAAP) permit companies to select from alternative methods for measuring the effects of transactions. The summary of significant accounting policies tells the user which accounting methods the company has adopted. Apple's accounting policy for property, plant, and equipment is as follows:

NOTE 1 – SUMMARY OF SIGNIFICANT ACCOUNTING POLICIES

Property, Plant, and Equipment

Property, plant, and equipment are stated at cost. Depreciation is computed by use of the straight-line method over the estimated useful lives of the assets, which for buildings is the lesser of 30 years or the remaining life of the underlying building; between two to five years for machinery and equipment, including product tooling and manufacturing process equipment; and the shorter of lease terms or ten years for leasehold improvements.

We will discuss alternative depreciation methods in Chapter 8. Without an understanding of the various accounting methods used, it is impossible to analyze a company's financial results effectively.

Additional Detail Supporting Reported Numbers

The second category of notes provides supplemental information concerning the data shown on the financial statements. Among other information, these notes may show revenues broken out by geographic region or business segment, describe unusual transactions, and/or offer expanded detail on a specific classification. For example, in Note 3, Apple indicates the makeup of property, plant, and equipment presented on the balance sheet.

NOTE 3 – CONSOLIDATED FINANCIAL STATEMENT DETAILS

Property, Plant, and Equipment

	2014	2013
Land and buildings	$ 4,863	$ 3,309
Machinery, equipment, and internal-use software	29,639	21,242
Leasehold improvements	4,513	3,968
Gross property, plant, and equipment	39,015	28,519
Accumulated depreciation and amortization	(18,391)	(11,922)
Net property, plant, and equipment	$20,624	$16,597

Relevant Financial Information Not Disclosed on the Statements

The final category includes information that impacts the company financially but is not shown on the statements. Examples include information on legal matters and contractual agreements that do not result in an asset or liability on the balance sheet. In Note 10, Apple disclosed the details of its commitments under supply agreements, which total over $27 billion and are not shown as a liability on the balance sheet.

NOTE 10 – CONSOLIDATED FINANCIAL STATEMENT DETAILS

Other Commitments

As of September 27, 2014, the Company had outstanding off-balance sheet third-party manufacturing commitments and component purchase commitments of $24.5 billion.

In addition to the off-balance sheet commitments mentioned above, the Company had outstanding obligations of $3.4 billion as of September 27, 2014, which consisted mainly of commitments to acquire capital assets, including product tooling and manufacturing process equipment, and commitments related to advertising, R&D, Internet and telecommunications services and other obligations.

APPLE

REAL WORLD EXCERPT:

Annual Report

Voluntary Disclosures

GAAP and SEC regulations set only the minimum level of required financial disclosures. Many companies provide important disclosures beyond those required. For example, in its annual report, 10-K, and recent earnings press release, **Apple** discloses sales by major product category, which helps investors track the success of new products.

	2014	2013	2012
Net sales by Product:			
iPhone	$101,991	$ 91,279	$ 78,692
iPad	30,283	31,980	30,945
Mac	24,079	21,483	23,221
iPod	2,286	4,411	5,615
iTunes, software, and services	18,063	16,051	12,890
Accessories	6,093	5,706	5,145
Total net sales	$182,795	$170,910	$156,508

APPLE

REAL WORLD EXCERPT:

Annual Report

Differences in Accounting Methods Acceptable under IFRS and U.S. GAAP

INTERNATIONAL PERSPECTIVE

Financial accounting standards and disclosure requirements are adopted by national regulatory agencies. Many countries, including the members of the European Union, have adopted International Financial Reporting Standards (IFRS) issued by the International Accounting Standards Board (IASB). IFRS are similar to U.S. GAAP, but there are several important differences. A partial list of the differences at the time this chapter is being written is presented below, along with the chapter in which these issues will be addressed:

(continued)

Difference	U.S. GAAP	IFRS	Chapter
Last-in first-out (LIFO) method for inventory	Permitted	Prohibited	7
Reversal of inventory write-downs	Prohibited	Required	7
Basis for property, plant, and equipment	Historical cost	Fair value or historical cost	8
Development costs	Expensed	Capitalized	8
Debt to be refinanced	Current	Noncurrent	9
Recognition of contingent liabilities	Probable	More likely than not	9
Stockholders' equity accounts	Common stock	Share capital	11
	Paid-in capital	Share premium	
Interest received on cash flow statement	Operating	Operating or investing	12
Interest paid on cash flow statement	Operating	Operating or financing	12

The FASB and IASB are working together to eliminate some of these differences.

RETURN ON ASSETS ANALYSIS: A FRAMEWORK FOR EVALUATING COMPANY PERFORMANCE

Evaluating company performance is the primary goal of financial statement analysis. Company managers, as well as competitors, use financial statements to better understand and evaluate a company's business strategy. Analysts, investors, and creditors use these same statements to judge company performance when they estimate the value of the company's stock and its creditworthiness. Our discussion of the financial data contained in accounting reports has now reached the point where we can develop an overall framework for using those data to evaluate company performance. The most general framework for evaluating company performance is called return on assets (ROA) analysis.

KEY RATIO ANALYSIS	Return on Assets (ROA)

 ANALYTICAL QUESTION

During the period, how well has management used the company's total investment in assets financed by both debt holders and stockholders?

 RATIO AND COMPARISONS

$$\text{Return on Assets} = \frac{\text{Net Income*}}{\text{Average Total Assets}^\dagger}$$

The 2014 ratio for **Apple**:

$$\frac{\$39,510}{(\$207,000 + \$231,839) \div 2} = 0.180 \ (18.0\%)$$

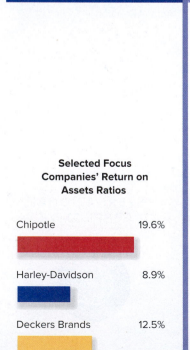

Selected Focus Companies' Return on Assets Ratios

Chipotle — 19.6%

Harley-Davidson — 8.9%

Deckers Brands — 12.5%

COMPARISONS OVER TIME			COMPARISON WITH COMPETITOR
Apple			HP
2012	2013	2014	2014
28.5%	19.3%	18.0%	4.8%

💡 **INTERPRETATIONS**

In General   ROA measures how much the firm earned for each dollar of investment in assets. It is the broadest measure of profitability and management effectiveness, independent of financing strategy. Firms with higher ROA are doing a better job of selecting and managing investments, all other things equal. Since it is independent of the source of financing (debt vs. equity), it can be used to evaluate performance at any level within the organization. It is often computed on a division-by-division or product line basis and used to evaluate division or product line managers' relative performance.

Focus Company Analysis   The decrease in return on assets between 2012 and 2014 was mainly due to an increase in average assets accompanied by consistent net income. Specifically, marketable securities have increased dramatically over the last three years. As a result, Apple has increased dividends and continued a stock buyback program to return the excess assets to shareholders.

A Few Cautions   Like all ratios, the key to interpreting change is to dig deeper to understand the reason for each change. Our next topic, ROA Profit Driver Analysis and Business Strategy, is aimed at doing just that.

---

*In more complex return on assets analyses, interest expense (net of tax) and noncontrolling interest are added back to net income in the numerator of the ratio, since the measure assesses return on capital independent of its source.

† Average Total Assets = (Beginning Total Assets + Ending Total Assets) ÷ 2.

ROA Profit Driver Analysis and Business Strategy

Effective analysis of **Apple**'s performance also requires understanding **why** its ROA differs both from prior levels and from those of its competitors. ROA profit driver analysis (also called **ROA decomposition** or **DuPont analysis**) breaks down ROA into the two factors shown in Exhibit 5.8. These factors are often called **profit drivers** or **profit levers** because they describe the two ways that management can improve ROA. They are measured by the key ratios you learned in Chapters 3 and 4.

1. **Net profit margin = Net Income ÷ Net Sales.** It measures how much of every sales dollar is profit. It can be increased by

   a. Increasing sales volume.
   b. Increasing sales price.
   c. Decreasing cost of goods sold and operating expenses.

2. **Total asset turnover = Net Sales ÷ Average Total Assets.** It measures how many sales dollars the company generates with each dollar of assets (efficiency of use of assets). It can be increased by

   a. Centralizing distribution to reduce inventory kept on hand.
   b. Consolidating production facilities in fewer factories to reduce the amount of assets necessary to generate each dollar of sales.

EXHIBIT 5.8

ROA Profit Driver Analysis

These two ratios report on the effectiveness of the company's operating and investing activities, respectively.

Successful manufacturers often follow one of two business strategies. The first is a **high-value** or **product-differentiation** strategy. Companies following this strategy rely on research and development and product promotion to convince customers of the superiority or distinctiveness of their products. This allows the company to charge higher prices and earn a higher net profit margin. The second is a **low-cost strategy,** which relies on efficient management of accounts receivable, inventory, and productive assets to produce high asset turnover.

The ROA profit driver analysis presented in Exhibit 5.9 indicates the sources of Apple's ROA and compares them to the same figures for **HP**. **Apple** follows a classic **high-value strategy,** developing a reputation for the most innovative products in its markets. The success of this strategy is evident in its market-leading **net profit margin** of 0.216 or **21.6%.** This means that 21.6 cents of every sales dollar is net profit. This compares with HP's 4.5% net profit margin.

HP primarily follows a **low-cost strategy** by offering excellent products and service at competitive prices. The efficiency of HP's operations is evident in its higher **total asset turnover** of **1.067** compared to Apple's 0.883. Apple has produced a much higher ROA than HP because its phenomenal net profit margin more than offsets its lower total asset turnover, and its stock price has responded accordingly.

If Apple follows the same strategy it has in the past, the secret to maintaining its ROA must be continued product development to support premium selling prices. In 2014, Apple made major strides in new product development and the success of its new product introductions bodes well for a high ROA in the longer term. As the preceding discussion indicates, a company can take many different actions to try to affect its profit drivers. To understand the impact of these actions, financial analysts disaggregate each of the profit drivers into more detailed ratios. For example, the total asset turnover ratio is further disaggregated into turnover ratios for specific assets such as accounts receivable, inventory, and fixed assets. We will develop our understanding of these more specific ratios in the next seven chapters of the book. Then, in Chapter 13, we will combine the ratios in a comprehensive review.

How Transactions Affect Ratios

Apple and other companies know that investors and creditors follow their key financial ratios closely. Changes in ROA and its components can have a major effect on a company's stock price and interest rates that lenders charge. As a consequence, company managers closely follow the effects of their actual and planned transactions on these same key financial ratios. We have already learned how to determine the effects of transactions on key subtotals on the income statement and balance sheet (gross profit, current assets, etc.). So we are only one step away from being able to compute the effects of transactions on ratios. The following three-step process will help you do so:

1. **Journalize the transaction to determine its effects on various accounts,** just as we did in Chapters 2 through 4.

2. **Determine which accounts belong to the financial statement subtotals or totals in the numerator (top) and denominator (bottom) of the ratio and the direction of their effects.**

3. **Evaluate the combined effects from step 2 on the ratio.**

EXHIBIT 5.9	ROA Profit Drivers	Formulas	Apple	HP
	Net Profit Margin	Net Income/Net Sales	0.216	0.045
Apple vs. HP ROA Profit Driver Analysis	× Total Asset Turnover	× Net Sales/Average Total Assets	0.833	1.067
	= Return on Assets	= Net Income/Average Total Assets	0.180	0.048

Let's try a few examples to get a feel for the process. What would be the effect of the following transactions on the following ratios (ignoring taxes)? The examples we will consider illustrate that the effect depends on what part of the ratio, numerator (top) and/or denominator (bottom), is affected. We need to consider three cases.

What if only the numerator or denominator is affected?

Example 1: Apple incurred an additional $1,000 in research and development expense paid for in cash (all numbers in millions). What would be the effect on the **net profit margin** ratio? The entry would be:

Research and development expense (+E, −SE)..................... 1,000	
Cash (−A)	1,000

Note that the transaction would decrease the numerator Net Income and have no effect on the denominator Net Sales. The ratio was 0.216 (using numbers from Exhibit 5.5). It would decrease to 0.211 as follows.

	Net Income	÷	Net Sales	=	Net Profit Margin
As reported:	$39,510	÷	$182,795	=	0.216
Transaction effect:	−1,000		–		
After transaction:	$38,510	÷	$182,795	=	0.211

This example illustrates a general point about the effect of transactions on ratios. If a transaction **only** affects the numerator **or** denominator of the ratio, it will have the following effects on the ratio:

Ratio Changes Given Changes in Numerator *or* Denominator	
Numerator	**Ratio**
Increases	Increases
Decreases	Decreases
Denominator	
Increases	Decreases
Decreases	Increases

What if both the numerator and denominator are affected but by different amounts?

Example 2: Consider the same transaction as in Example 1. What would be the effect on the **return on assets** ratio? Note that the transaction would decrease the numerator Net Income by $1,000. It would also **decrease the ending** total assets by $1,000 but have **no effect on beginning** total assets. So the denominator, **average** total assets, would only decrease by $500:

$$\text{Avg. Total Assets} = (\$207,000 + \$231,839 - \$1,000) \div 2 = \$218,920$$

The ratio was 0.180 in Exhibit 5.9. It would decrease as follows:

	Net Income	÷	Avg. Total Assets	=	Return on Assets
As reported:	$39,510	÷	$219,420	=	0.180
Transaction effect:	−1,000		−500		
After transaction:	$38,510	÷	$218,920	=	0.176

This example illustrates a second general point about the effect of transactions on ratios. If a transaction affects the numerator by more than it affects the denominator, or if it affects the denominator by more than it affects the numerator, you must compute the effect with the numbers given.

What if the numerator and denominator are affected by the same amount?

Example 3: Apple paid $4,000 of accounts payable in cash (all numbers in millions). What would be the effect on the **current ratio?** The entry would be:

Accounts payable (−L)	4,000
Cash (−A)	4,000

Note that the transaction would decrease the numerator, Current Assets, and the denominator, Current Liabilities, by the same amount. The ratio was 1.08 (using numbers from Exhibit 5.4). It would increase as follows.

	Current Assets	÷	Current Liabilities	=	Current Ratio
As reported:	$68,531	÷	$63,448	=	1.08
Transaction effect:	−4,000		−4,000		
After transaction:	$64,531	÷	$59,448	=	1.09

This example illustrates a third general point about the effect of transactions on ratios. **If a transaction affects the numerator and denominator of the ratio by the same amount, the effect will depend on whether the original ratio value was greater or less than 1.00:**

Ratio Changes Given *Same* Change in Numerator *and* Denominator

Numerator and Denominator	Ratio < 1	Ratio > 1
Increase both	Increases	Decreases
Decrease both	Decreases	Increases

PAUSE FOR **FEEDBACK**

ROA measures how well management used the company's invested capital during the period. Its two determinants, net profit margin and asset turnover, indicate why ROA differs from prior levels or the ROAs of competitors. They also suggest strategies to improve ROA in future periods. The effect of an individual transaction on a financial ratio depends on its effects on both the numerator and denominator of the ratio.

SELF-STUDY **QUIZ**

0.0　0.50　1.00　1.50

2014　　2013
▮ Apple　▮ Apple

1. We used profit driver analysis in Exhibit 5.9 to explain why a company has an ROA different from its competitors at a single point in time. This type of analysis is called **cross-sectional analysis.** Profit driver analysis can also be used to explain how changes in net profit margin (Net Income/Net Sales) and total asset turnover (Net Sales/Average Total Assets) changed **Apple's** ROA over time. This type of analysis is often called **time-series analysis.** Following is the recent year's ROA analysis for Apple Inc. Using profit driver analysis, explain how Apple has increased its ROA.

ROA Profit Drivers	2014	2013
Net Income/Net Sales	0.216	0.217
× Net Sales/Average Total Assets	0.833	0.892
= Net Income/Average Total Assets	0.180	0.193

2. What would be the **direction** of the effect of the following transactions on the following ratios (+ for increase, − for decrease, and NE for no effect)? Consider each item independently.

   a. Recorded and paid rent expense of $200.

   b. Recorded the sale of services on account for $400.

Transaction	Gross Profit Margin	Return on Assets	Current Ratio
a.			
b.			

After you have completed your answers, check them below.

DEMONSTRATION   CASE

Complete the following requirements before proceeding to the suggested solution. **Microsoft Corporation** is the developer of a broad line of computer software, including the Windows operating systems and Word (word processing) and Excel (spreadsheet) programs. Following is a list of the financial statement items and amounts adapted from a recent Microsoft income statement and balance sheet. These items have normal debit and credit balances and are reported in millions of dollars. For that year, 8,299 million (weighted average) shares of stock were outstanding. The company closed its books on June 30, 2014.

Accounts payable	$ 7,432	Other current liabilities	$ 9,464
Accounts receivable (net)	19,544	Other income, net	61
Accrued compensation	4,797	Other investments	14,597
Cash and short-term investments	85,709	Other noncurrent assets	30,530
Common stock and paid-in capital	68,366	Property, plant, and equipment (net)	13,011
Cost of goods sold	26,934	Provision for income taxes	5,746
General and administrative	4,948	Research and development	11,381
Income taxes payable	782	Retained earnings	21,418
Long-term liabillities	36,975	Sales and marketing	15,811
Net revenue	86,833	Unearned revenue	23,150
Other current assets	8,993		

Required:

1. Prepare in good form a classified (multiple-step) income statement (showing gross profit, operating income, income before income taxes, net income, and earnings per share) and a classified balance sheet for the year.

2. Compute the company's ROA. Briefly explain its meaning using ROA profit driver analysis. (Microsoft's total assets at the beginning of the year were $142,431 million.)

3. If Microsoft had an additional $1,500 in general and administrative expenses (paid for in cash), what would be the effect on its ROA (increase, decrease, or no effect)?

---

1. Apple's 1.3% decline (19.3% − 18.0%) in ROA resulted from a decline in its total asset turnover. The management discussion and analysis in its 10-K indicates that most of this decrease resulted from increases in total assets, mainly marketable securities.

2. *a.* Rent expense (+E, −SE)   200   *b.* Accounts receivable (+A)   400
       Cash (−A)   200   Sales revenue (+R, +SE)   400
           NE, −, −   +, +, +

Solutions to
SELF-STUDY QUIZ

SUGGESTED SOLUTION

1.

MICROSOFT CORPORATION Income Statement For the Year Ended June 30, 2014 (In millions, except per share amounts)	
Net revenue	$86,833
Cost of goods sold	26,934
Gross profit	59,899
Operating expenses:	
Research and development	11,381
Sales and marketing	15,811
General and administrative	4,948
Total operating expenses	32,140
Operating income	27,759
Nonoperating income and expenses:	
Other income, net	61
Income before income taxes	27,820
Provision for income taxes	5,746
Net income	$22,074
Earnings per share	$ 2.66

MICROSOFT CORPORATION Balance Sheet June 30, 2014 (In millions)	
ASSETS	
Current assets	
Cash and short-term investments	$ 85,709
Accounts receivable (net)	19,544
Other current assets	8,993
Total current assets	114,246
Noncurrent assets:	
Property, plant, and equipment (net)	13,011
Other investments	14,597
Other noncurrent assets	30,530
Total assets	$172,384
LIABILITIES AND STOCKHOLDERS' EQUITY	
Current liabilities	
Accounts payable	$ 7,432
Accrued compensation	4,797
Income taxes payable	782
Unearned revenue	23,150
Other current liabilities	9,464
Total current liabilities	45,625
Long-term liabilities	36,975
Stockholders' equity:	
Common stock and paid-in capital	68,366
Retained earnings	21,418
Total stockholders' equity	89,784
Total liabilities and stockholders' equity	$172,384

2.

Fiscal Year Ending June 30, 2014	
Net Income/Net Sales	0.25
× Net Sales/Average Total Assets	0.55
= Net Income/Average Total Assets	0.14

For the year ended June 30, Microsoft earned an ROA of 14 percent. Microsoft maintains high profit margins, earning $0.25 of net income for every $1 of net sales, but the company has a lower asset efficiency with only $0.55 in sales generated for each $1 of assets. The analysis also indicates Microsoft's dominance of the computer software business, which allows the company to charge premium prices for its products.

3.

General and administrative expenses (+E, −SE)	1,500	
Cash (−A)		1,500

The numerator Net Income would decrease by $1,500 and the denominator Average Total Assets would decrease by $750. As a consequence, ROA would decrease.

CHAPTER **TAKE-AWAYS**

5-1. Recognize the people involved in the accounting communication process (regulators, managers, directors, auditors, information intermediaries, and users), their roles in the process, and the guidance they receive from legal and professional standards. p. 233

Management of the reporting company must decide on the appropriate format (categories) and level of detail to present in its financial reports. Independent audits increase the credibility of the information. Directors monitor managers' compliance with reporting standards and hire the auditor. Financial statement announcements from public companies usually are first transmitted to users through electronic information services. The SEC staff reviews public financial reports for compliance with legal and professional standards, investigates irregularities, and punishes violators. Analysts play a major role in making financial statement and other information available to average investors through their stock recommendations and earnings forecasts.

5-2. Identify the steps in the accounting communication process, including the issuance of press releases, annual reports, quarterly reports, and SEC filings, as well as the role of electronic information services in this process. p. 238

Earnings are first made public in press releases. Companies follow these announcements with annual and quarterly reports containing statements, notes, and additional information. Public companies must file additional reports with the SEC, including the 10-K, 10-Q, and 8-K, which contain more details about the company. Electronic information services are the key source of dissemination of this information to sophisticated users.

5-3. Recognize and apply the different financial statement and disclosure formats used by companies in practice and analyze the gross profit percentage. p. 240

Most statements are classified and include subtotals that are relevant to analysis. On the balance sheet, the most important distinctions are between current and noncurrent assets and liabilities. On the income and cash flow statements, the distinction between operating and nonoperating items is most important. The notes to the statements provide descriptions of the accounting rules applied, add more information about items disclosed on the statements, and present information about economic events not included in the statements.

5-4. Analyze a company's performance based on return on assets and its components and the effects of transactions on financial ratios. p. 250

ROA measures how well management used the company's invested capital during the period. Its two determinants, net profit margin and asset turnover, indicate why ROA differs from prior levels or the ROAs of competitors. They also suggest strategies to improve ROA in future periods. The effect of an individual transaction on a financial ratio depends on its effects on both the numerator and denominator of the ratio.

In Chapter 6, we will begin our in-depth discussion of individual items presented in financial statements. We will start with two of the most liquid assets, cash and accounts receivable, and transactions that involve revenues and certain selling expenses. Accuracy in revenue recognition and the related recognition of cost of goods sold (discussed in Chapter 7) are the most important determinants of the accuracy—and, thus, the usefulness—of financial statements. We will also introduce concepts related to the management and control of cash and receivables, a critical business function. A detailed understanding of these topics is crucial to future managers, accountants, and financial analysts.

KEY **RATIOS**

Gross profit percentage measures the excess of sales prices over the costs to purchase or produce the goods or services sold as a percentage. It is computed as follows (see the "Key Ratio Analysis" box in the A Closer Look at Financial Statement Formats and Notes section):

$$\text{Gross Profit Percentage} = \frac{\text{Gross Profit}}{\text{Net Sales}}$$

Return on assets (ROA) measures how much the firm earned for each dollar of investment. It is computed as follows (see the "Key Ratio Analysis" box in the Return on Assets section):

$$\text{Return on Assets} = \frac{\text{Net Income}}{\text{Average Total Assets}}$$

FINDING FINANCIAL INFORMATION

Balance Sheet

Assets (by order of liquidity)
   Current assets (short-term)
   Noncurrent assets
     Total assets

Liabilities (by order of time to maturity)
   Current liabilities (short-term)
   Long-term liabilities
     Total liabilities

Stockholders' equity (by source)
   Common stock and Additional paid-in capital (by owners)
   Retained earnings (accumulated earnings minus accumulated dividends declared)
     Total stockholders' equity
     Total liabilities and stockholders' equity

Income Statement

   Net sales
− Cost of goods sold

   Gross margin
− Operating expenses

   Income from operations
+/− Nonoperating revenues/expenses and gains/losses

   Income before income taxes
− Income tax expense

   Net income

   Earnings per share

Statement of Stockholders' Equity

	Common Stock	Add'l Paid-in Capital	Retained Earnings	Total Stockholders' Equity
Beginning balance	xx	xx	xx	xx
Net income			xx	xx
Dividends declared			(xx)	(xx)
Stock issued	xx	xx		xx
Stock retired	(xx)	(xx)		(xx)
Ending balance	xx	xx	xx	xx

Statement of Cash Flows

Operating activities:
   Net income
   +/− Adjustments for noncash items
   Cash provided by operating activities

Investing activities:

Financing activities:

Notes

Key Classifications
   Descriptions of accounting rules applied in the statements
   Additional detail supporting reported numbers
   Relevant financial information not disclosed on the statements

KEY TERMS

Board of Directors   p. 234
Corporate Governance   p. 231
Cost-Effectiveness   p. 237
Earnings Forecasts   p. 235
Financial Accounting Standards Board (FASB)   p. 233

Form 8-K   p. 240
Form 10-K   p. 239
Form 10-Q   p. 240
Gross Profit (Gross Margin)   p. 242
Income before Income Taxes (Pretax Earnings)   p. 242

Institutional Investors   p. 237
Lenders (Creditors)   p. 237
Material Amounts   p. 237
Operating Income (Income from Operations)   p. 242
Press Release   p. 238

QUESTIONS

1. Describe the roles and responsibilities of management and independent auditors in the financial reporting process.
2. Define the following three users of financial accounting disclosures and the relationships among them: (a) financial analysts, (b) private investors, and (c) institutional investors.
3. Briefly describe the role of information services in the communication of financial information.
4. Explain what a material amount is.
5. What basis of accounting (cash or accrual) does GAAP require on the (a) income statement, (b) balance sheet, and (c) statement of cash flows?
6. Briefly explain the normal sequence and form of financial reports produced by private companies in a typical year.
7. Briefly explain the normal sequence and form of financial reports produced by public companies in a typical year.
8. What are the four major subtotals or totals on the income statement?
9. List the six major classifications reported on a balance sheet.
10. For property, plant, and equipment, as reported on the balance sheet, explain (a) cost, (b) accumulated depreciation, and (c) net book value.
11. Briefly explain the major classifications of stockholders' equity for a corporation.
12. What are the three major classifications on a statement of cash flows?
13. What are the three major categories of notes or footnotes presented in annual reports? Cite an example of each.
14. Briefly define return on assets and what it measures.

MULTIPLE-CHOICE QUESTIONS

1. If average total assets increase, but net income, net sales, and average stockholders' equity remain the same, what is the impact on the return on assets ratio?
   a. Increases.
   b. Decreases.
   c. Remains the same.
   d. Cannot be determined without additional information.
2. If a company plans to differentiate its products by offering low prices and discounts for items packaged in bulk (like a discount retailer that requires memberships for its customers), which component in the ROA profit driver analysis is the company attempting to boost?
   a. Net profit margin.   c. Financial leverage.
   b. Asset turnover.   d. All of the above.
3. If a company reported the following items on its income statement (cost of goods sold $6,000, income tax expense $2,000, interest expense $500, operating expenses $3,500, sales revenue $14,000), what amount would be reported for the subtotal "income from operations"?
   a. $8,000   c. $4,500
   b. $2,000   d. $4,000
4. Which of the following is one of the possible nonrecurring items that must be shown in a separate line item **below** the Income from Continuing Operations subtotal in the income statement?
   a. Gains and losses from the sale of fixed assets.   c. Extraordinary items.
   b. Discontinued operations.   d. Both a and b.
5. Which of the following reports is filed annually with the SEC?
   a. Form 10-Q   c. Form 8-K
   b. Form 10-K   d. Press release

6. Which of the following would normally **not** be found in the notes to the financial statements?
   a. Accounting rules applied in the company's financial statements.
   b. Additional detail supporting numbers reported in the company's financial statements.
   c. Relevant financial information not presented in the company's financial statements.
   d. All of the above would be found in the notes to the financial statements.

7. Which of the following is **not** a normal function of a financial analyst?
   a. Issue earnings forecasts.
   b. Examine the records underlying the financial statements to certify their conformance with GAAP.
   c. Make buy, hold, and sell recommendations on companies' stock.
   d. Advise institutional investors on their securities holdings.

8. The classified balance sheet format allows one to ascertain quickly which of the following?
   a. The most valuable asset of the company.
   b. The specific due date for all liabilities of the company.
   c. What liabilities must be paid within the upcoming year.
   d. None of the above.

9. When a company issues stock with a par value, what columns are typically presented in the statement of stockholders' equity?
   a. Common Stock; Additional Paid-In Capital; and Property, Plant, and Equipment, Net.
   b. Cash; and Property, Plant, and Equipment, Net.
   c. Common Stock; Additional Paid-In Capital; and Retained Earnings.
   d. Common Stock; Additional Paid-In Capital; and Cash.

10. Net income was $850,000. Beginning and ending assets were $8,500,000 and $9,600,000, respectively. What was the return on assets (ROA)?
    a. 9.39%   c. 9.94%
    b. 10.59%   d. 10.41%

MINI-**EXERCISES**

M5-1   **Matching Players in the Accounting Communication Process with Their Definitions**

LO5-1   Match each player with the related definition by entering the appropriate letter in the space provided.

Players	Definitions
___ (1) Independent auditor	A. Adviser who analyzes financial and other economic information to form forecasts and stock recommendations.
___ (2) CEO and CFO	B. Institutional and private investors and creditors (among others).
___ (3) Users	C. Chief executive officer and chief financial officer who have primary responsibility for the information presented in financial statements.
___ (4) Financial analyst	D. Independent CPA who examines financial statements and attests to their fairness.

M5-2   **Identifying the Disclosure Sequence**

LO5-2   Indicate the order in which the following disclosures or reports are normally issued by public companies.

No.	Title
_____	Form 10-K
_____	Earnings press release
_____	Annual report

Finding Financial Information: Matching Financial Statements with the Elements of Financial Statements

M5-3
LO5-3

Match each financial statement with the items presented on it by entering the appropriate letter in the space provided.

Elements of Financial Statements	Financial Statements
___ (1) Expenses	A. Income statement
___ (2) Cash from operating activities	B. Balance sheet
___ (3) Losses	C. Cash flow statement
___ (4) Assets	D. None of the above
___ (5) Revenues	
___ (6) Cash from financing activities	
___ (7) Gains	
___ (8) Owners' equity	
___ (9) Liabilities	
___ (10) Assets personally owned by a stockholder	

Determining the Effects of Transactions on Balance Sheet and Income Statement Categories

M5-4
LO5-3

Complete the following tabulation, indicating the sign of the effect (+ for increase, − for decrease, and NE for no effect) of each transaction. Consider each item independently.

a. Recorded sales on account of $300 and related cost of goods sold of $200.
b. Recorded advertising expense of $10 incurred but not paid for.

Transaction	Current Assets	Gross Profit	Current Liabilities
(a)			
(b)			

Determining Financial Statement Effects of Sales and Cost of Goods Sold and Issuance of Stock

M5-5
LO5-3

Using the following categories, indicate the effects of the following transactions. Use + for increase and − for decrease and indicate the accounts affected and the amounts.

a. Sales on account were $1,800 and related cost of goods sold was $1,200.
b. Issued 5,000 shares of $1 par value stock for $60,000 cash.

Event	Assets	=	Liabilities	+	Stockholders' Equity
(a)					
(b)					

Recording Sales and Cost of Goods Sold and Issuance of Stock

M5-6
LO5-3

Prepare journal entries for each transaction listed in M5-5.

Computing and Interpreting Return on Assets

M5-7
LO5-4

Saunders, Inc., recently reported the following December 31 amounts in its financial statements (dollars in thousands):

	Current Year	Prior Year
Gross profit	$ 200	$120
Net income	100	40
Total assets	1,000	800
Total shareholders' equity	800	600

Compute return on assets for the current year. What does this ratio measure?

EXERCISES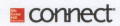

E5-1
LO5-1

Matching Players in the Accounting Communication Process with Their Definitions

Match each player with the related definition by entering the appropriate letter in the space provided.

Players	Definitions
___ (1) Financial analyst	A. Financial institution or supplier that lends money to the company.
___ (2) Creditor	
___ (3) Independent auditor	B. Chief executive officer and chief financial officer who have primary responsibility for the information presented in financial statements.
___ (4) Private investor	
___ (5) SEC	C. Manager of pension, mutual, and endowment funds that invest on the behalf of others.
___ (6) Information service	
___ (7) Institutional investor	D. Securities and Exchange Commission, which regulates financial disclosure requirements.
___ (8) CEO and CFO	
	E. A company that gathers, combines, and transmits (paper and electronic) financial and related information from various sources.
	F. Adviser who analyzes financial and other economic information to form forecasts and stock recommendations.
	G. Individual who purchases shares in companies.
	H. Independent CPA who examines financial statements and attests to their fairness.

E5-2
LO5-2

Matching Definitions with Information Releases Made by Public Companies

Following are the titles of various information releases. Match each definition with the related release by entering the appropriate letter in the space provided.

Information Release	Definitions
___ (1) Form 10-Q	A. Report of special events (e.g., auditor changes, mergers) filed by public companies with the SEC.
___ (2) Quarterly report	
___ (3) Press release	B. Brief unaudited report for quarter normally containing summary income statement and balance sheet.
___ (4) Annual report	
___ (5) Form 10-K	C. Quarterly report filed by public companies with the SEC that contains additional unaudited financial information.
___ (6) Form 8-K	
	D. Written public news announcement that is normally distributed to major news services.
	E. Annual report filed by public companies with the SEC that contains additional detailed financial information.
	F. Report containing the four basic financial statements for the year, related notes, and often statements by management and auditors.

E5-3
LO5-2

Finding Financial Information: Matching Information Items to Financial Reports

Following are information items included in various financial reports. Match each information item with the report(s) where it would most likely be found by entering the appropriate letter(s) in the space provided.

Information Item	Report
___ (1) Summarized financial data for 5-year period.	A. Form 10-Q
___ (2) Notes to financial statements.	B. Annual report
___ (3) The four basic financial statements for the year.	C. Form 8-K
___ (4) Summarized income statement information for the quarter.	D. Press release
___ (5) Detailed discussion of the company's competition.	E. Quarterly report
___ (6) Initial announcement of hiring of new vice president for sales.	F. Form 10-K
___ (7) Initial announcement of quarterly earnings.	G. None of the
___ (8) Description of those responsible for the financial statements.	above
___ (9) Complete quarterly income statement, balance sheet, and cash flow statement.	
___ (10) Announcement of a change in auditors.	

Ordering the Classifications on a Typical Balance Sheet

E5-4
LO5-3

Following is a list of classifications on the balance sheet. Number them in the order in which they normally appear on a balance sheet.

No.	Title
___	Long-term liabilities
___	Current liabilities
___	Long-term investments
___	Intangible assets
___	Common stock and additional paid-in capital
___	Current assets
___	Retained earnings
___	Property, plant, and equipment
___	Other noncurrent assets

Preparing a Classified Balance Sheet

E5-5
LO5-3

Campbell Soup Company is the world's leading maker and marketer of soup and sells other well-known brands of food in 120 countries. Presented here are the items listed on its recent balance sheet (dollars in millions) presented in alphabetical order:

Accounts payable	$ 585	Other assets	$ 136
Accounts receivable	560	Other current assets	152
Accrued expenses	619	Other current debt	785
Cash and cash equivalents	484	Other noncurrent liabilities	3,777
Common stock, $0.0375 par value	351	Property, plant, and equipment, net	2,103
Intangible assets	2,660	Retained earnings	745
Inventories	767		

Required:
Prepare a classified consolidated balance sheet for Campbell Soup for the current year (ended July 31) using the categories presented in the chapter.

Preparing and Interpreting a Classified Balance Sheet with Discussion of Terminology (Challenging)

E5-6
LO5-3

Snyder's-Lance manufactures, markets, and distributes a variety of snack food products including pretzels, sandwich crackers, kettle chips, cookies, potato chips, tortilla chips, other salty snacks, sugar wafers, nuts, and restaurant-style crackers. These items are sold under trade names including Snyder's of Hanover, Lance, Cape Cod, Krunchers!, Jays, Tom's, Archway, and others. Presented here are the items listed on its recent balance sheet (dollars in millions) in alphabetical order:

Accounts payable	$ 52,930	Other assets (noncurrent)	$ 21,804
Accounts receivable, net	143,238	Other current assets	96,983
Accrued compensation	29,248	Other intangible assets, net	376,062
Additional paid-in capital	730,338	Other long-term liabilities	219,114
Cash and cash equivalents	20,841	Other payables and accrued	
Common stock, 67,820,798 shares		liabilities	68,712
outstanding	56,515	Prepaid expenses and other	20,705
Goodwill	367,853	Property, plant, and equipment, net	313,043
Inventories	106,261	Retained earnings	51,738
Long-term debt	253,939	Short-term debt	4,256

Required:

1. Prepare a classified consolidated balance sheet for Snyder's-Lance for the current year (ended December 31) using the categories presented in the chapter.
2. Three of the items end in the term **net.** Explain what this term means in each case.

E5-7

LO5-3

Preparing a Classified (Multiple-Step) Income Statement

Macy's, Inc., operates the two best-known high-end department store chains in North America: Macy's and Bloomingdale's. The following data (in millions) were taken from its recent annual report for the year ended February 1:

Cost of sales	$16,725
Federal, state, and local income tax expense	804
Interest expense	390
Interest income	2
Net sales	27,931
Other operating expenses	88
Selling, general, and administrative expenses	8,440

Required:

Prepare a complete classified (multiple-step) consolidated statement of income for the company (showing gross margin, operating income, and income before income taxes).

E5-8

LO5-3

Preparing a Classified (Multiple-Step) Income Statement and Computing the Gross Profit Percentage

The following data were taken from the records of Township Corporation at December 31 of the current year:

Sales revenue	$85,000
Gross profit	30,000
Selling (distribution) expense	7,000
Administrative expense	?
Pretax income	13,000
Income tax rate	35%
Shares of stock outstanding	2,500

Required:

Prepare a complete classified (multiple-step) income statement for the company (showing both gross profit and income from operations). Show all computations. (**Hint:** Set up the side captions or rows starting with sales revenue and ending with earnings per share; rely on the amounts and percentages given to infer missing values.) What is the gross profit percentage?

Preparing a Classified (Multiple-Step) Income Statement (Challenging)

Most people know **Hewlett Packard Company (HP)** as a leading supplier of personal computers, printers and scanners, and storage and networking products for large and small customers alike. However, HP also is a major provider of technology consulting, outsourcing, and services to business, educational, and government organizations. Finally, HP also provides financing for products and services to its larger customers. As a consequence, its income statement shows three sources of operating revenues (goods/services/financing) and three related costs of goods/services/financing provided to customers. Presented below are the items adapted from its recent income statement for the year ended October 31 (in millions, except per share amounts). Net earnings per share was $3.78 and the weighted-average shares used in the computation was 2,319.

Acquisition-related charges	$ 293	Product sales	$84,799
Amortization of purchased intangible assets	1,484	Provision for taxes	2,213
Cost of financing	302	Research and development	2,959
Cost of products	65,064	Restructuring charges	1,144
Cost of services	30,590	Selling, general, and administrative	12,718
Financing income	418	Service sales	40,816
Interest expense	505		

Required:
1. Recognizing that HP has three sources of operating revenues, prepare a classified (multiple-step) income statement for HP following the format and using the subtotals presented in Exhibit 5.5. (**Hint:** The term "charge" is a synonym for "expense.")
2. Which source of operating revenues produces the highest gross profit?

E5-9
LO5-3

Inferring Income Statement Values

Supply the missing dollar amounts for the current year income statement of NexTech Company for each of the following independent cases. (**Hint:** Organize each case in the format of the classified or multiple-step income statement discussed in the chapter. Rely on the amounts given to infer the missing values.)

E5-10
LO5-3

	Case A	Case B	Case C	Case D	Case E
Sales revenue	$800	$600	$500	$?	$?
Selling expense	?	50	80	350	240
Cost of goods sold	?	150	?	500	320
Income tax expense	?	30	20	50	20
Gross margin	375	?	?	?	440
Pretax income	200	300	?	200	?
Administrative expense	125	?	70	120	80
Net income	150	?	50	?	100

Inferring Income Statement Values

Supply the missing dollar amounts for the current year income statement of BGT Company for each of the following independent cases. (**Hint:** Organize each case in the format of the classified or multiple-step income statement discussed in the chapter. Rely on the amounts given to infer the missing values.)

E5-11
LO5-3

	Case A	Case B	Case C	Case D	Case E
Sales revenue	$770	$?	$?	$600	$1,050
Pretax income	?	?	150	130	370
Income tax expense	65	210	60	45	?
Cost of goods sold	?	320	125	250	?
Gross margin	?	880	?	?	630
Selling expense	90	275	45	70	?
Net income	115	275	?	?	240
Administrative expense	200	120	80	?	175

E5-12

LO5-3

Stock Issuances and the Statement of Stockholders' Equity

In a recent year, **Coach, Inc.**, a designer and marketer of handbags and other accessories, issued 12,100 shares of its $0.01 par value stock for $344,000 (these numbers are rounded). These additional shares were issued under an employee stock option plan. Prepare the line on the statement of stockholders' equity that would reflect this transaction. The statement has the following columns:

Common Stock		Additional Paid-in Capital	Retained Earnings	Total Stockholders' Equity
Shares	Amount			

E5-13

LO5-3

Inferring Stock Issuances and Cash Dividends from Changes in Stockholders' Equity

The Kroger Co. is one of the largest retailers in the United States and also manufactures and processes some of the food for sale in its supermarkets. Kroger reported the following January 31 balances in its statement of stockholders' equity (dollars in millions):

	Current Year	Prior Year
Common stock	$ 959	$ 958
Paid-in capital	3,427	3,394
Retained earnings	8,571	8,225

During the current year, Kroger reported net income of $602.

Required:
1. How much did Kroger declare in dividends for the year?
2. Assume that the only other transaction that affected stockholders' equity during the current year was a single stock issuance. Recreate the journal entry reflecting the stock issuance.

E5-14

LO5-3

Determining the Effects of Transactions on Balance Sheet and Income Statement Categories

Hasbro is one of the world's leading toy manufacturers and the maker of such popular board games as Monopoly, Scrabble, and Clue, among others. Listed here are selected aggregate transactions from a recent year (dollars in millions). Complete the following tabulation, indicating the sign (+ for increase, − for decrease, and NE for no effect) and amount of the effect of each transaction. Consider each item independently.

a. Recorded sales on account of $4,285.6 and related cost of goods sold of $1,836.3.
b. Issued debt due in six months with a principal amount of $500.0.
c. Incurred research and development expense of $197.6, which was paid in cash.

Transaction	Current Assets	Gross Profit	Current Liabilities
a.			
b.			
c.			

E5-15

LO5-3

Determining the Effects of Transactions on Balance Sheet, Income Statement, and Statement of Cash Flows Categories

Listed here are selected aggregate transactions for ModernStyle Furniture Company from the first quarter of a recent year (dollars in millions). Complete the following tabulation, indicating the sign (+ for increase, − for decrease, and NE for no effect) and amount of the effect of each additional transaction. Consider each item independently.

a. Recorded collections of cash from customers owed on open account of $40.8.
b. Repaid $5.6 in principal on line of credit with a bank with principal payable within one year.

Transaction	Current Assets	Gross Profit	Current Liabilities	Cash Flow from Operating Activities
a.				
b.				

Preparing a Simple Statement of Cash Flows Using the Indirect Method

E5-16

LO5-3

Avalos Corporation is preparing its annual financial statements at December 31 of the current year. Listed here are the items on its statement of cash flows presented in alphabetical order. Parentheses indicate that a listed amount should be subtracted on the cash flow statement. The beginning balance in cash was $25,000 and the ending balance was $50,000.

Cash borrowed on three-year note	$30,000
Decrease in accounts payable	(3,000)
Decrease in inventory	1,000
Increase in accounts receivable	(9,000)
Land purchased	(36,000)
Net income	25,000
New delivery truck purchased for cash	(7,000)
Stock issued for cash	24,000

Required:
Prepare the current year statement of cash flows for Avalos Corporation. The section reporting cash flows from operating activities should be prepared using the indirect method discussed in the chapter.

Analyzing and Interpreting Return on Assets

E5-17

LO5-4

Tiffany & Co. is one of the world's premier jewelers and a designer of other fine gifts and housewares. Presented here are selected income statement and balance sheet amounts (dollars in thousands).

	Current Year	Prior Year
Net sales	$3,642,937	$3,085,290
Net income	439,190	368,403
Average shareholders' equity	2,263,190	2,030,357
Average total assets	3,947,331	3,612,015

Required:
1. Compute ROA for the current and prior years and explain the meaning of the change.
2. Explain the major cause(s) of the change in ROA using ROA profit driver analysis.

Analyzing and Evaluating Return on Assets from a Security Analyst's Perspective

E5-18

LO5-4

Papa John's is one of the fastest-growing pizza delivery and carry-out restaurant chains in the country. Presented here are selected income statement and balance sheet amounts (dollars in thousands).

	Current Year	Prior Year
Net sales	$1,217,882	$1,126,397
Net income	59,387	55,425
Average shareholders' equity	212,711	246,119
Average total assets	403,162	394,143

Required:
1. Compute ROA for the current and prior years and explain the meaning of the change.
2. Would security analysts more likely increase or decrease their estimates of share value on the basis of this change? Explain.

Determining the Effects of Transactions on Ratios

E5-19

LO5-4

What would be the **direction** of the effect of the following transactions on the following ratios (+ for increase, − for decrease, and NE for no effect)? Consider each item independently.

a. Repaid principal of $2,000 on a long-term note payable with the bank.
b. Recorded rent expense of $100 paid for in cash.

Transaction	Net Profit Margin	Return on Assets	Current Ratio
a.			
b.			

PROBLEMS

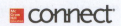

P5-1
LO5-1,5-2

Matching Transactions with Concepts

Following are the concepts of accounting covered in Chapters 2 through 5. Match each transaction or definition with its related concept by entering the appropriate letter in the space provided. Use one letter for each blank.

Concepts	Transactions/Definitions

Concepts

____ (1) Users of financial statements

____ (2) Objective of financial statements

Qualitative Characteristics

____ (3) Relevance

____ (4) Reliability

Assumptions

____ (5) Separate entity

____ (6) Continuity

____ (7) Unit of measure

____ (8) Time period

Elements of Financial Statements

____ (9) Revenues

____ (10) Expenses

____ (11) Gains

____ (12) Losses

____ (13) Assets

____ (14) Liabilities

____ (15) Stockholders' equity

Principles

____ (16) Cost

____ (17) Revenue

____ (18) Matching

____ (19) Full disclosure

Constraints of Accounting

____ (20) Materiality threshold

____ (21) Cost-effectiveness

____ (22) Conservatism constraint

____ (23) Special industry practices

Transactions/Definitions

A. Recorded a $2,000 sale of merchandise on credit.

B. Counted (inventoried) the unsold items at the end of the period and valued them in dollars.

C. Acquired a vehicle for use in operating the business.

D. Reported the amount of depreciation expense because it likely will affect statement users' decision making.

E. The investors, creditors, and others interested in the business.

F. Used special accounting approaches because of the uniqueness of the industry.

G. Sold and issued bonds payable of $3 million.

H. Used services from outsiders; paid cash for some and put the remainder on credit.

I. Engaged an outside independent CPA to audit the financial statements.

J. Sold an asset at a loss that was a peripheral or incidental transaction.

K. Established an accounting policy that sales revenue shall be recognized only when ownership to the goods sold passes to the customer.

L. To design and prepare the financial statements to assist the users in making decisions.

M. Established a policy not to include in the financial statements the personal financial affairs of the owners of the business.

N. Sold merchandise and services for cash and on credit during the year; then determined the cost of those goods sold and the cost of rendering those services.

O. The user value of a special financial report exceeds the cost of preparing it.

P. Valued an asset, such as inventory, at less than its purchase cost because the replacement cost is less.

Q. Dated the income statement "For the Year Ended December 31, 2017."

R. Paid a contractor for an addition to the building with $15,000 cash and $20,000 market value of the stock of the company ($35,000 was deemed to be the cash-equivalent price).

S. Acquired an asset (a pencil sharpener that will have a useful life of five years) and recorded it as an expense when purchased for $1.99.

T. Disclosed in the financial statements all relevant financial information about the business; necessitated the use of notes to the financial statements.

U. Sold an asset at a gain that was a peripheral or incidental transaction.

V. Assets of $600,000 − Liabilities of $400,000 = ?

W. Accounting and reporting assume a "going concern."

Matching Definitions with Balance Sheet–Related Terms

P5-2
LO5-2

Following are terms related to the balance sheet that were discussed in Chapters 2 through 5. Match each definition with its related term by entering the appropriate letter in the space provided.

Terms	Definitions
____ (1) Capital in excess of par	A. Nearness of assets to cash (in time).
____ (2) Assets	B. Liabilities expected to be paid out of current assets normally within the next year.
____ (3) Retained earnings	C. All liabilities not classified as current liabilities.
____ (4) Book value	D. Total assets minus total liabilities.
____ (5) Other assets	E. Probable future economic benefits owned by the entity from past transactions.
____ (6) Shares outstanding	F. Debts or obligations from past transactions to be paid with assets or services.
____ (7) Shareholders' equity	G. Assets expected to be collected in cash within one year or the operating cycle, if longer.
____ (8) Liquidity	H. Assets that do not have physical substance.
____ (9) Normal operating cycle	I. Balance of the Common Stock account divided by the par value per share.
____ (10) Current assets	J. A miscellaneous category of assets.
____ (11) Current liabilities	K. Sum of the annual depreciation expense on an asset from its acquisition to the current date.
____ (12) Long-term liabilities	L. Asset offset account (subtracted from asset).
____ (13) Fixed assets	M. Accumulated earnings minus accumulated dividends.
____ (14) Liabilities	N. Property, plant, and equipment.
____ (15) Contra-asset account	O. Same as carrying value; cost less accumulated depreciation to date.
____ (16) Accumulated depreciation	P. Amount of contributed capital less the par value of the stock.
____ (17) Intangible assets	Q. The average cash-to-cash time involved in the operations of the business.
	R. None of the above.

Preparing a Balance Sheet and Analyzing Some of Its Parts (AP5-1)

P5-3
LO5-3

Exquisite Jewelers is developing its annual financial statements for the current year. The following amounts were correct at December 31, current year: cash, $58,000; accounts receivable, $71,000; merchandise inventory, $154,000; prepaid insurance, $1,500; investment in stock of Z Corporation (long-term), $36,000; store equipment, $67,000; used store equipment held for disposal, $9,000; accumulated depreciation, store equipment, $19,000; accounts payable, $52,500; long-term note payable, $42,000; income taxes payable, $9,000; retained earnings, $164,000; and common stock, 100,000 shares outstanding, par value $1.00 per share (originally sold and issued at $1.10 per share).

Required:
1. Based on these data, prepare a December 31, current year, balance sheet. Use the following major captions (list the individual items under these captions):
   a. Assets: Current Assets, Long-Term Investments, Fixed Assets, and Other Assets.
   b. Liabilities: Current Liabilities and Long-Term Liabilities.
   c. Stockholders' Equity: Contributed Capital and Retained Earnings.
2. What is the net book value of the store equipment? Explain what this value means.

P5-4
LO5-3

Preparing a Statement of Stockholders' Equity (AP5-2)

At the end of the prior annual reporting period, Barnard Corporation's balance sheet showed the following:

BARNARD CORPORATION Balance Sheet At December 31, Prior Year	
Stockholders' Equity	
Contributed capital	
Common stock (par $15; 5,500 shares)	$ 82,500
Paid-in capital	13,000
Total contributed capital	95,500
Retained earnings	44,000
Total stockholders' equity	$139,500

During the current year, the following selected transactions (summarized) were completed:

a. Sold and issued 1,000 shares of common stock at $35 cash per share (at year-end).
b. Determined net income, $37,000.
c. Declared and paid a cash dividend of $2 per share on the beginning shares outstanding.

Required:
Prepare a statement of stockholders' equity for the year ended December 31, current year. Be sure to show both the dollar amount and number of shares of common stock.

P5-5
LO5-3

Preparing a Classified (Multiple-Step) Income Statement and Interpreting the Gross Profit Percentage

Aeropostale, Inc., is a mall-based specialty retailer of casual apparel and accessories. The company concept is to provide the customer with a focused selection of high-quality, active-oriented fashions at compelling values. The items reported on its income statement for a recent year (ended March 31) are presented here (dollars in thousands) in alphabetical order:

Cost of goods sold	$1,733,916
Interest expense	417
Net revenue	2,342,260
Other selling, general, and administrative expenses	494,829
Provision for income taxes	43,583
Weighted average shares outstanding	81,208

Required:
Prepare a classified (multiple-step) consolidated income statement (showing gross profit, operating income, and income before income taxes). Include a presentation of basic earnings per share. What is the gross profit percentage? Explain its meaning.

P5-6
LO5-3

Preparing Both an Income Statement and a Balance Sheet from a Trial Balance (AP5-3)

Jordan Sales Company (organized as a corporation on April 1, 2014) has completed the accounting cycle for the second year, ended March 31, 2016. Jordan also has completed a correct trial balance as follows:

Account Titles	Debit	Credit
JORDAN SALES COMPANY		
Trial Balance		
At March 31, 2016		
Cash	$ 58,000	
Accounts receivable	49,000	
Office supplies inventory	1,000	
Automobiles (company cars)	34,000	
Accumulated depreciation, automobiles		$ 14,000
Office equipment	3,000	
Accumulated depreciation, office equipment		1,000
Accounts payable		22,000
Income taxes payable		0
Salaries and commissions payable		2,000
Note payable, long-term		33,000
Capital stock (par $1; 33,000 shares)		33,000
Paid-in capital		5,000
Retained earnings (on April 1, 2015)		7,500
Dividends declared and paid during the current year	10,500	
Sales revenue		99,000
Cost of goods sold	33,000	
Operating expenses (detail omitted to conserve time)	19,000	
Depreciation expense (on autos and including $500 on office equipment)	8,000	
Interest expense	1,000	
Income tax expense (not yet computed)		
Totals	$216,500	$216,500

Required:

Complete the financial statements as follows:

a. Classified (multiple-step) income statement for the reporting year ended March 31, 2016. Include income tax expense, assuming a 25 percent tax rate. Use the following subtotals: Gross Profit, Total Operating Expenses, Income from Operations, Income before Income Taxes, and Net Income, and show EPS.

b. Classified balance sheet at the end of the reporting year, March 31, 2016. Include (1) income taxes for the current year in Income Taxes Payable and (2) dividends in Retained Earnings. Use the following captions (list each item under these captions):

Assets	**Stockholders' Equity**
Current assets	Contributed capital
Noncurrent assets	Retained earnings
Liabilities	
Current liabilities	
Long-term liabilities	

Determining and Interpreting the Effects of Transactions on Income Statement Categories and Return on Assets (AP5-4)

P5-7

LO5-3, 5-4

Creative Technology, a computer hardware company based in Singapore, developed the modern standard for computer sound cards in the early 1990s. Recently, Creative has released a line of portable audio products to directly compete with **Apple**'s popular iPod. Presented here is a recent income statement (dollars in millions).

Net sales	$ 231
Costs and expenses	
Cost of sales	182
Research and development	66
Selling, general, and administrative	62
Operating income (loss)	(79)
Interest and other income (expenses), net	27
Income (loss) before provision (benefit) for income taxes	(52)
Provision (benefit) for income taxes	(5)
Net income (loss)	$ (47)

The company's beginning and ending assets were $403 and $342, respectively.

Required:

Listed here are hypothetical **additional** transactions. Assuming that they **also** occurred during the fiscal year, complete the following tabulation, indicating the sign of the effect of each **additional** transaction (+ for increase, − for decrease, and NE for no effect). Consider each item independently and ignore taxes. (**Hint:** Construct the journal entry for each transaction before evaluating its effect.)

a. Recorded sales on account of $400 and related cost of goods sold of $300.
b. Incurred additional research and development expense of $100, which was paid in cash.
c. Issued additional shares of common stock for $260 cash.
d. Declared and paid dividends of $90.

Transaction	Gross Profit	Operating Income	Return on Assets
a.			
b.			
c.			
d.			

P5-8

LO5-4

Determining the Effects of Transactions on Ratios

Mateo Inc. is a retailer of men's and women's clothing aimed at college-age customers. Listed below are additional transactions that Mateo was considering at the end of the accounting period.

Required:

Listed below are additional transactions that occurred during the fiscal year. Complete the following tabulation, indicating the sign of the effect of each additional transaction (+ for increase, − for decrease, and NE for no effect). Consider each item independently and ignore taxes. (**Hint:** Construct the journal entry for each transaction before evaluating its effect.)

a. Borrowed $3,000 on a line of credit with the bank.
b. Incurred salary expense of $1,000 paid for in cash.
c. Provided $2,000 of services on account.
d. Purchased $700 of inventory on account.
e. Sold $500 of goods on account. The related cost of goods sold was $300. Gross profit margin was 45 percent before this sale.

Transaction	Total Asset Turnover	Return on Assets	Gross Profit Percentage
a.			
b.			
c.			
d.			
e.			

Preparing a Multiple-Step Income Statement with Discontinued Operations

P5-9
LO5-3

Newell Rubbermaid Inc. manufactures and markets a broad array of office products, tools and hardware, and home products under a variety of brand names, including Sharpie, Paper Mate, Rolodex, Rubbermaid, Levolor, and others. The items reported on its income statement for the year ended December 31, 2011, are presented here (dollars in thousands) in alphabetical order:

Cost of Products Sold	$3,659.4
Income Tax Expense	17.9
Interest and Other Nonoperating Expense	104.7
Loss on Sale of Discontinued Operations, Net of Income Taxes	(9.4)
Net Sales	5,864.6
Other Expense	432.7
Selling, General, and Administrative Expenses	1,515.3

Required:

Using appropriate headings and subtotals, prepare a multiple-step consolidated income statement (showing gross profit, operating income, and any other subheadings you deem appropriate).

ALTERNATE PROBLEMS

Preparing a Balance Sheet and Analyzing Some of Its Parts (P5-3)

AP5-1
LO5-3

TangoCo is developing its annual financial statements for the current year. The following amounts were correct at December 31, current year: cash, $48,800; investment in stock of PIL Corporation (long-term), $36,400; store equipment, $67,200; accounts receivable, $71,820; inventory, $154,000; prepaid rent, $1,120; used store equipment held for disposal, $9,800; accumulated depreciation, store equipment, $13,440; income taxes payable, $9,800; long-term note payable, $32,000; accounts payable, $58,800; retained earnings, $165,100; and common stock, 100,000 shares outstanding, par value $1 per share (originally sold and issued at $1.10 per share).

Required:

1. Based on these data, prepare a December 31, current year balance sheet. Use the following major captions (list the individual items under these captions):
   a. Assets: Current Assets and Noncurrent Assets.
   b. Liabilities: Current Liabilities and Long-Term Liabilities.
   c. Stockholders' Equity: Contributed Capital and Retained Earnings.
2. What is the net book value of the store equipment? Explain what this value means.

Preparing a Statement of Stockholders' Equity (P5-4)

AP5-2
LO5-3

At the end of the prior annual reporting period, Mesa Industries's balance sheet showed the following:

MESA INDUSTRIES Balance Sheet At December 31, Prior Year	
Stockholders' Equity	
Common stock (par $15; 7,000 shares)	$105,000
Additional paid-in capital	9,000
Retained earnings	48,000
Total stockholders' equity	$162,000

During the current year, the following selected transactions (summarized) were completed:

a. Sold and issued 1,500 shares of common stock at $26 cash per share (at year-end).
b. Determined net income, $46,000.
c. Declared and paid a cash dividend of $1 per share on the beginning shares outstanding.

Required:
Prepare a statement of stockholders' equity for the year ended December 31, current year. Be sure to show both the dollar amount and number of shares of common stock.

AP5-3
LO5-3

Preparing Both an Income Statement and a Balance Sheet from a Trial Balance (P5-6)

Dynamite Sales (organized as a corporation on September 1, 2013) has completed the accounting cycle for the second year, ended August 31, 2015. Dynamite also has completed a correct trial balance as follows:

DYNAMITE SALES Trial Balance At August 31, 2015		
Account Titles	**Debit**	**Credit**
Cash	$ 47,700	
Accounts receivable	38,320	
Office supplies	270	
Company vehicles (delivery vans)	27,000	
Accumulated depreciation, company vehicles		$ 9,000
Equipment	2,700	
Accumulated depreciation, equipment		900
Accounts payable		16,225
Income taxes payable		0
Salaries payable		1,350
Long-term debt		25,000
Capital stock (par $1; 29,000 shares)		29,000
Paid-in capital		4,500
Retained earnings (on September 1, 2014)		6,615
Dividends declared and paid during the current year	7,200	
Sales revenue		81,000
Cost of goods sold	27,000	
Operating expenses (detail omitted to conserve time)	16,200	
Depreciation expense (on vehicles and equipment)	4,950	
Interest expense	2,250	
Income tax expense (not yet computed)		
Totals	$173,590	$173,590

Required:
Complete the financial statements, as follows:

a. Classified (multiple-step) income statement for the reporting year ended August 31, 2015. Include income tax expense, assuming a 30 percent tax rate. Use the following subtotals: Gross Profit, Total Operating Expenses, Income from Operations, Income before Income Taxes, and Net Income, and show EPS.

b. Classified balance sheet at the end of the reporting year, August 31, 2015. Include (1) income taxes for the current year in Income Taxes Payable and (2) dividends in Retained Earnings. Use the following captions (list each item under these captions).

Assets

Current assets
Noncurrent assets

Liabilities

Current liabilities
Long-term liabilities

Stockholders' Equity

Contributed capital
Retained earnings

Determining and Interpreting the Effects of Transactions on Income Statement Categories and Return on Assets (P5-7)

AP5-4
LO5-3, 5-4

Avon Products, Inc., is a leading manufacturer and marketer of beauty products and related merchandise. The company sells its products in 110 countries through a combination of direct selling and use of individual sales representatives. Presented here is a recent income statement (dollars in millions).

Net sales	$11,292
Costs and expenses	
Cost of sales	4,149
Selling, general, and administrative	6,288
Operating income (loss)	855
Interest and other income (expenses), net	(125)
Income (loss) before provision (benefit) for income taxes	730
Provision (benefit) for income taxes	216
Net income (loss)	$ 514

Avon's beginning and ending total assets were $7,874 and $7,735, respectively.

Required:

1. Listed below are hypothetical **additional** transactions. Assuming that they **also** occurred during the fiscal year, complete the following tabulation, indicating the sign of the effect of each **additional** transaction (+ for increase, − for decrease, and NE for no effect). Consider each item independently and ignore taxes.

   a. Recorded and received additional interest income of $7.
   b. Purchased $80 of additional inventory on open account.
   c. Recorded and paid additional advertising expense of $16.
   d. Issued additional shares of common stock for $40 cash.

Transaction	Operating Income (Loss)	Net Income	Return on Assets
a.			
b.			
c.			
d.			

2. Assume that next period, Avon does not pay any dividends, does not issue or retire stock, and earns 20 percent more than during the current period. If total assets increase by 5 percent, will Avon's ROA next period be higher, lower, or the same as in the current period? Why?

CON5-1   Evaluating the Impact of Transactions on Statement Categories and Ratios

After completing her first year of operations, Penny Cassidy used a number of ratios to evaluate the performance of Penny's Pool Service & Supply, Inc. She was particularly interested in the effects of the following transactions from the last quarter:

a. Paid herself a dividend of $10,000 as the sole stockholder.
b. Recorded advance payments from customers of $2,000.
c. Paid the current month's rent in cash, $500.
d. Purchased a new truck for $14,000 and signed a note payable for the whole amount. The truck was not placed in service until January 2015.
e. Recorded depreciation expense on office equipment of $600.
f. Accrued interest expense on the note payable to the bank was $400.

Required:
(**Hint:** Construct the journal entry for each transaction before evaluating its effect.)
  1. Complete the following table, indicating the effects of each transaction on each financial statement category listed. Indicate the amount and use + for increase, − for decrease, and NE for no effect.

Transaction	Gross Profit	Operating Income (Loss)	Current Assets
a.			
etc.			

  2. Complete the following table, indicating the sign of the effects of each transaction on the financial ratio listed. Use + for increase, − for decrease, and NE for no effect.

Transaction	Net Profit Margin	Total Asset Turnover	Return on Assets
a.			
etc.			

CON5-2   Preparing an Income Statement and Balance Sheet and Computing Gross Profit Percentage and Return on Assets for a Public Company

Pool Corporation, Inc., is the world's largest wholesale distributor of swimming pool supplies and equipment. It is a publicly traded corporation that trades on the NASDAQ exchange under the symbol POOL.

It sells these products to swimming pool repair and service businesses like Penny's Pool Service & Supply, Inc., swimming pool builders, and retail swimming pool stores. The majority of these customers are small, family-owned businesses like Penny's. Its trial balance and additional information adapted from a recent year ended December 31 are presented below. All numbers are in thousands.

Cash and cash equivalents	$ 17,487	
Receivables, net	110,555	
Product inventories, net	386,924	
Prepaid expenses and other current assets	23,035	
Property and equipment, net	41,394	
Intangible assets	188,841	
Other noncurrent assets, net	30,386	
Accounts payable		$ 177,437
Accrued expenses and other current liabilities		53,398
Current portion of long-term debt		22
Long-term debt		247,300
Other long-term liabilities		40,719
Common stock		47
Additional paid-in capital		173,180
Retained earnings		34,526
Net sales		1,793,318
Cost of sales	1,261,728	
Selling and administrative expenses	406,523	
Interest expense	7,755	
Provision for income taxes	45,319	
	$2,519,947	$2,519,947

Required:
1. Prepare a classified income statement (with earnings per share) and balance sheet for the current year. Number of shares outstanding used in computation of earnings per share was 48,158.
2. Compute gross profit percentage and return on assets. Total assets at the beginning of the year was $728,545.

 **connect**

CASES AND PROJECTS

Annual Report Cases

Finding Financial Information

Refer to the financial statements of **American Eagle Outfitters** given in Appendix B at the end of this book. At the bottom of each statement, the company warns readers to "Refer to Notes to Consolidated Financial Statements." The following questions illustrate the types of information that you can find in the financial statements and accompanying notes. (**Hint:** Use the notes.)

CP5-1
LO5-2, 5-3, 5-4

Required:
1. What items were included as noncurrent assets on the balance sheet?
2. How much land did the company own at the end of the most recent reporting year?
3. What percentage of current liabilities were "Unredeemed store value cards and gift certificates" during the current year (round to one decimal place)?
4. At what point were website sales recognized as revenue?
5. The company reported cash flows from operating activities of $338,426,000. However, its net income was only $80,322 for the year. What was the largest single cause of the difference?

6. What was the highest stock price for the company during fiscal 2014? (**Note:** Some companies will label a year that has a January year-end as having a fiscal year-end dated one year earlier. For example, a January 2015 year-end may be labeled as Fiscal 2014 since the year actually has more months that fall in the 2014 calendar year than in the 2015 calendar year.)

7. Calculate the company's ROA for fiscal 2014 and 2013. Did it increase or decrease or stay the same?

CP5-2
LO5-2, 5-3

Finding Financial Information

Refer to the financial statements of **Urban Outfitters** given in Appendix C at the end of this book. At the bottom of each statement, the company warns readers that "The accompanying notes are an integral part of these financial statements." The following questions illustrate the types of information that you can find in the financial statements and accompanying notes. (**Hint:** Use the notes.)

Required:

1. What subtotals does Urban Outfitters report on its income statement?
2. The company spent $229,804,000 on capital expenditures (property, plant, and equipment) and $405,659,000 purchasing investments during the most recent year. Were operating activities or financing activities the major source of cash for these expenditures?
3. What was the company's largest asset (net) at the end of the most recent year?
4. How does the company account for costs associated with developing its websites?
5. Over what useful lives are buildings depreciated?
6. What portion of gross "Property and Equipment" is composed of "Buildings"?
7. Compute the company's gross profit percentage for the most recent two years. Has it risen or fallen? Explain the meaning of the change.

CP5-3
LO5-4

Comparing Companies within an Industry

Refer to the financial statements of **American Eagle Outfitters** (Appendix B) and **Urban Outfitters** (Appendix C) and the Industry Ratio Report (Appendix D) at the end of this book.

Required:

1. Compute return on assets for the most recent year. Which company provided the highest return on invested capital during the current year?
2. Use ROA profit driver analysis to determine the cause(s) of any differences. How might the ownership versus the rental of property, plant, and equipment affect the total asset turnover ratio?
3. Compare the ROA profit driver analysis for American Eagle Outfitters and Urban Outfitters to the ROA profit driver analysis for their industry. Where does American Eagle Outfitters outperform or underperform the industry? Where does Urban Outfitters outperform or underperform the industry?

Financial Reporting and Analysis Case

CP5-4
LO5-3

Using Financial Reports: Financial Statement Inferences

The following amounts were selected from the annual financial statements for Genesis Corporation at December 31, 2015 (end of the third year of operations):

From the 2015 income statement:	
Sales revenue	$275,000
Cost of goods sold	(170,000)
All other expenses (including income tax)	(95,000)
Net income	$ 10,000

From the December 31, 2015, balance sheet:	
Current assets	$ 90,000
All other assets	212,000
Total assets	$302,000

Current liabilities	$ 40,000
Long-term liabilities	66,000
Capital stock (par $10)	100,000
Paid-in capital	16,000
Retained earnings	80,000
Total liabilities and stockholders' equity	$302,000

Required:

Analyze the data on the 2015 financial statements of Genesis by answering the questions that follow. Show computations.

1. What was the gross margin on sales?
2. What was the amount of EPS?
3. If the income tax rate was 25 percent, what was the amount of pretax income?
4. What was the average sales price per share of the capital stock?
5. Assuming that no dividends were declared or paid during 2015, what was the beginning balance (January 1, 2015) of retained earnings?

Critical Thinking Cases

Making Decisions as a Manager: Evaluating the Effects of Business Strategy on Return on Assets

CP5-5

LO5-4

Sony is a world leader in the manufacture of consumer and commercial electronics as well as in the entertainment and insurance industries. Its ROA has decreased over the last three years.

Required:

Indicate the most likely effect of each of the changes in business strategy on Sony's ROA for the next period and future periods (+ for increase, − for decrease, and NE for no effect), assuming all other things are unchanged. Explain your answer for each. Treat each item independently.

a. Sony decreases its investment in research and development aimed at products to be brought to market in more than one year.
b. Sony begins a new advertising campaign for a movie to be released during the next year.

Strategy Change	Current Period ROA	Future Periods' ROA
a.		
b.		

Making a Decision as an Auditor: Effects of Errors on Income, Assets, and Liabilities

CP5-6

LO5-1, 5-3

Megan Company (not a corporation) was careless about its financial records during its first year of operations, 2013. It is December 31, 2013, the end of the annual accounting period. An outside CPA has examined the records and discovered numerous errors, all of which are described here. Assume that each error is independent of the others.

Required:

Analyze each error and indicate its effect on 2013 and 2014 net income, assets, and liabilities if not corrected. Do not assume any other errors. Use these codes to indicate the effect of each dollar amount: O = overstated, U = understated, and NE = no effect. Write an explanation of your analysis of each transaction to support your response. The first transaction is used as an example.

	Effect on					
	Net Income		Assets		Liabilities	
Independent Errors	2013	2014	2013	2014	2013	2014
1. Depreciation expense for 2013, not recorded in 2013, $950.	O $950	NE	O $950	O $950	NE	NE
2. Wages earned by employees during 2013 not recorded or paid in 2013 but recorded and paid in 2014, $500.						
3. Revenue earned during 2013 but not collected or recorded until 2014, $600.						
4. Amount paid in 2013 and recorded as expense in 2013 but not an expense until 2014, $200.						
5. Revenue collected in 2013 and recorded as revenue in 2013 but not earned until 2014, $900.						
6. Sale of services and cash collected in 2013. Recorded as a debit to Cash and as a credit to Accounts Receivable, $300.						
7. On December 31, 2013, bought land on credit for $8,000; not recorded until payment was made on February 1, 2014.						

Following is a sample explanation of the first error:

Failure to record depreciation in 2013 caused depreciation expense to be too low; therefore, income was overstated by $950. Accumulated depreciation also is too low by $950, which causes assets to be overstated by $950 until the error is corrected.

CP5-7
LO5-1, 5-3

Evaluating an Ethical Dilemma: Management Incentives and Fraudulent Financial Statements

Netherlands-based **Royal Ahold** ranks among the world's three largest food retailers. In the United States it operates the **Stop & Shop** and **Giant** supermarket chains. Dutch and U.S regulators and prosecutors have brought criminal and civil charges against the company and its executives for overstating earnings by more than $1 billion. The nature of the fraud is described in the following excerpt:

Two Former Execs of Ahold Subsidiary Plead Not Guilty to Fraud

NEW YORK (AP)—Two former executives pleaded not guilty Wednesday to devising a scheme to inflate the earnings of U.S. Foodservice Inc., a subsidiary of Dutch supermarket giant Royal Ahold NV. Former chief financial officer Michael Resnick and former chief marketing officer Mark Kaiser entered their pleas in a Manhattan federal court, a day after prosecutors announced fraud and conspiracy charges against them.

The government contends they worked together to boost the company's earnings by $800 million from 2000 to 2003 by reporting fake rebates from suppliers—and sweetened their own bonuses in the process. Two other defendants have already pleaded guilty in the alleged scheme: Timothy Lee, a former executive vice president, and William Carter, a former vice president. Both are set for sentencing in January. Netherlands-based Ahold's U.S. properties include the Stop & Shop and Giant supermarket chains. U.S. Foodservice is one of the largest distributors of food products in the country, providing to restaurants and cafeterias.

Ahold said last year it had overstated its earnings by more than $1 billion, mostly because of the fraud at U.S. Foodservice. Its stock lost 60 percent of its value, and about $6 billion in market value evaporated.

From Associated Press, July 28, 2004. Copyrighted 2004. Associated Press. 260587:0318PF.

Required:

Using more recent news reports (*The Wall Street Journal Index, Factiva,* and *Bloomberg Business News* are good sources), answer the following questions.

1. Whom did the courts and regulatory authorities hold responsible for the misstated financial statements?
2. Did the company cooperate with investigations into the fraud? How did this affect the penalties imposed against the company?
3. How might executive compensation plans that tied bonuses to accounting earnings have motivated unethical conduct in this case?

Financial Reporting and Analysis Team Project

Analyzing the Accounting Communication Process

As a team, select an industry to analyze. Yahoo Finance provides lists of industries at **biz.yahoo.com/p/ industries.html**. Click on an industry for a list of companies in that industry. Alternatively, go to Google Finance at **www.google.com/finance** and search for a company you are interested in. You will be presented with a list including that company and its competitors. Each team member should acquire the annual report or 10-K for one publicly traded company in the industry, with each member selecting a different company (the SEC EDGAR service at **www.sec.gov** and the company's investor relations website itself are good sources).

CP5-8
LO5-1, 5-2, 5-3, 5-4

Required:

On an individual basis, each team member should write a short report answering the following questions about the selected company. Discuss any patterns across the companies that you as a team observe. Then, as a team, write a short report comparing and contrasting your companies.

1. What formats are used to present the
   a. Balance Sheets?
   b. Income Statements?
   c. Operating Activities section of the Statement of Cash Flows?
2. Find one footnote for each of the following and describe its contents in brief:
   a. An accounting rule applied in the company's statements.
   b. Additional detail about a reported financial statement number.
   c. Relevant financial information but with no number reported in the financial statements.
3. Using electronic sources, find one article reporting the company's annual earnings announcement. When is it dated and how does that date compare to the balance sheet date?
4. Using electronic sources, find two analysts' reports for your company.
   a. Give the date, name of the analyst, and his or her recommendation from each report.
   b. Discuss why the recommendations are similar or different. Look at the analysts' reasoning for their respective recommendations.
5. Using the SEC EDGAR website (**www.sec.gov**), what is the most recent document filed by your company with the SEC (e.g., 8-K, S-1) and what did it say in brief?
6. Ratio analysis:
   a. What does the return on total assets ratio measure in general?
   b. Compute the ROA ratio for the last three years.
   c. What do your results suggest about the company?
   d. If available, find the industry ratio for the most recent year, compare it to your results, and discuss why you believe your company differs from or is similar to the industry ratio.
7. Use the ROA profit driver analysis to determine the cause(s) of any differences in the ROA ratio over the last three years. (Remember that you computed the three profit driver ratios in the last three chapters.)

Reporting and Interpreting Sales Revenue, Receivables, and Cash

Founded by then University of California, Santa Barbara, student Doug Otto, **Deckers Brands** is best known for its Teva® sports sandals and the UGG® brand sheepskin boots. Deckers has become a major player in the casual, outdoor, and athletic footwear market by building on the needs of hikers, trail runners, kayakers, surfers, and whitewater rafters for comfort, function, and performance. Its growth strategy requires building brand recognition by developing and introducing additional innovative footwear that satisfies the company's high standards. Building the brands allows Deckers to maintain a loyal consumer following and penetrate new markets. It also has allowed Deckers to continue to grow during the worst recession in more than 25 years.

There is a second key component to Deckers's successful growth strategy. Success in the ultracompetitive footwear market requires careful matching of production schedules to customers' needs and careful management of customer receivables. Deckers's successful focus on brand development, product innovation, and working capital management has allowed the company to report the highest gross profit in its history.

UNDERSTANDING THE BUSINESS

Planning **Deckers**'s growth strategy requires careful coordination of sales activities, as well as cash collections from customers. Much of this coordination revolves around allowing consumers to use credit cards, providing business customers discounts for early payment, and allowing sales returns and allowances under certain circumstances—strategies that motivate customers to buy its products and make payment for their purchases. These

Learning Objectives

After studying this chapter, you should be able to:

6-1 Analyze the impact of credit card sales, sales discounts, and sales returns on the amounts reported as net sales.

6-2 Estimate, report, and evaluate the effects of uncollectible accounts receivable (bad debts) on financial statements.

6-3 Analyze and interpret the receivables turnover ratio and the effects of accounts receivable on cash flows.

6-4 Report, control, and safeguard cash.

Teva®/AP Images

activities affect **net sales** revenue, the top line on the income statement. Coordinating sales and cash collections from customers also involves managing bad debts, which affect selling, general, and administrative expenses on the income statement and **cash** and **accounts receivable** on the balance sheet. Net sales, accounts receivable, and cash are the focus of this chapter. We will also introduce the receivables turnover ratio as a measure of the efficiency of credit-granting and collection activities. Finally, since the cash collected from customers is also a tempting target for fraud and embezzlement, we will discuss how accounting systems commonly include controls to prevent and detect such misdeeds.

*Deckers Brands has not verified the data nor the information contained in this text. Therefore, investors should not rely on this information in making any assessments of the company for investment or other such purposes.

ORGANIZATION of the Chapter

Accounting for Net Sales Revenue	Measuring and Reporting Receivables	Reporting and Safeguarding Cash
• Motivating Sales and Collections • Credit Card Sales to Consumers • Sales Discounts to Businesses • Sales Returns and Allowances • Reporting Net Sales	• Classifying Receivables • Accounting for Bad Debts • Reporting Accounts Receivable and Bad Debts • Estimating Bad Debts • Control over Accounts Receivable • Receivables Turnover Ratio	• Cash and Cash Equivalents Defined • Cash Management • Internal Control of Cash • Reconciliation of the Cash Accounts and the Bank Statements

ACCOUNTING FOR NET SALES REVENUE

As indicated in Chapter 3, the **revenue recognition principle** requires that revenues be recorded when the company transfers goods and services to customers, in the amount it expects to receive. For sellers of goods, sales revenue is recorded when title and risks of ownership transfer to the buyer.[1] The point at which title (ownership) changes hands is determined by the shipping terms in the sales contract. When goods are shipped **FOB (free on board) shipping point,** title changes hands at shipment, and the buyer normally pays for shipping. When they are shipped **FOB destination,** title changes hands on delivery, and the seller normally pays for shipping. Revenues from goods shipped FOB shipping point are normally recognized at shipment. Revenues from goods shipped FOB destination are normally recognized at delivery.

Service companies most often record sales revenue when they have provided services to the buyer. Companies disclose the revenue recognition rule they follow in the footnote to the financial statements entitled Summary of Significant Accounting Policies. In that note, **Deckers** reports the following:

DECKERS BRANDS

REAL WORLD EXCERPT:

Annual Report

> NOTES TO CONSOLIDATED FINANCIAL STATEMENTS
>
> **1. Summary of Significant Accounting Policies**
>
> *Revenue Recognition*
>
> The Company recognizes wholesale, eCommerce, and international distributor revenue when products are shipped and retail revenue at the point of sale. All sales are recognized when the customer takes title and assumes risk of loss, collection of the related receivable is reasonably assured, persuasive evidence of an arrangement exists, and the sales price is fixed or determinable.

The appropriate **amount** of revenue to record is **the amount it expects to receive.**

---

[1]Starting in 2018, the new revenue recognition standard will be in effect. It will not change revenue recognition in a significant manner for simple sales of goods, which dominate Deckers's revenues.

Motivating Sales and Collections

Some sales practices differ depending on whether sales are made to businesses or consumers. **Deckers** sells footwear and apparel to other **businesses** (retailers), including Athlete's Foot and Eastern Mountain Sports, which then sell the goods to consumers. It also operates its own Internet and retail stores that sell footwear directly to **consumers.**

Deckers uses a variety of methods to motivate both groups of customers to buy its products and make payment for their purchases. The principal methods include (1) allowing consumers to use credit cards to pay for purchases, (2) providing business customers direct credit and discounts for early payment, and (3) allowing returns from all customers under certain circumstances. These methods, in turn, affect the way we compute **net sales revenue.**

LEARNING OBJECTIVE 6-1
Analyze the impact of credit card sales, sales discounts, and sales returns on the amounts reported as net sales.

Credit Card Sales to Consumers

Deckers accepts cash or credit card payment for its retail store and Internet sales. Deckers's managers decided to accept credit cards (mainly Visa, Mastercard, and American Express) for a variety of reasons:

1. Increasing customer traffic.

2. Avoiding the costs of providing credit directly to consumers, including recordkeeping and bad debts (discussed later).

3. Lowering losses due to bad checks.

4. Avoiding losses from fraudulent credit card sales. (As long as Deckers follows the credit card company's verification procedure, the credit card company [e.g., Visa] absorbs any losses.)

5. Receiving money faster. (Since credit card receipts can be directly deposited in its bank account, Deckers receives its money faster than it would if it provided credit directly to consumers.)

The credit card company charges a fee for the service it provides. When Deckers deposits its credit card receipts in the bank, it might receive credit for only 97 percent of the sales price. The credit card company is charging a 3 percent fee (the **credit card discount**) for its services. If daily credit card sales were $3,000, Deckers would report the following:

CREDIT CARD DISCOUNT
Fee charged by the credit card company for its services.

Sales revenue	$3,000
Less: Credit card discounts (0.03 × 3,000)	90
Net sales (reported on the income statement)	$2,910

Some companies report credit card discounts as part of selling, general, and administrative expenses.

Sales Discounts to Businesses

Most of **Deckers**'s sales to businesses are credit sales on open account; that is, there is no formal written promissory note or credit card. When Deckers sells footwear to retailers on credit, credit terms are printed on the sales document and invoice (bill) sent to the customer.

Early Payment Incentive

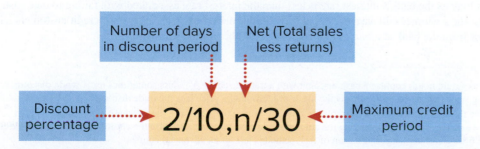

Often credit terms are abbreviated. For example, if the full price is due within 30 days of the invoice date, the credit terms would be noted as **n/30.** Here, the **n** means the sales amount **net** of, or less, any sales returns.

In some cases, a **sales discount** (often called a cash discount) is granted to the purchaser to encourage early payment.[2] For example, Deckers may offer terms of 2/10, n/30, which means that the customer may deduct 2 percent from the invoice price if cash payment is made within 10 days from the date of sale. If cash payment is not made within the 10-day discount period, the full sales price (less any returns) is due within a maximum of 30 days.

Deckers offers this sales discount to encourage customers to pay more quickly. This provides two benefits to Deckers:

1. Prompt receipt of cash from customers reduces the necessity to borrow money to meet operating needs.

2. Since customers tend to pay bills providing discounts first, a sales discount also decreases the chances that the customer will run out of funds before Deckers's bill is paid.

Companies commonly record sales discounts taken by subtracting the discount from sales if payment is made **within** the discount period (the usual case).[3] For example, if credit sales of $1,000 are recorded with terms 2/10, n/30 and payment of $980 ($1,000 × 0.98 = $980) is made within the discount period, net sales of the following amount would be reported:

Sales revenue	$1,000
Less: Sales discounts (0.02 × $1,000)	20
Net sales (reported on the income statement)	$ 980

If payment is made after the discount period, the full $1,000 would be reported as net sales. Accounting for sales discounts is discussed in more detail in the Supplement at the end of this chapter.

SALES (OR CASH) DISCOUNT
Cash discount offered to encourage prompt payment of an account receivable.

FINANCIAL ANALYSIS	To Take or Not to Take the Discount, That Is the Question

Customers usually pay within the discount period because the savings are substantial. With terms 2/10, n/30, customers save 2 percent by paying 20 days early (on the 10th day instead of the 30th). This translates into a 37 percent annual interest rate. To calculate the annual interest rate, first compute the interest rate for the discount period. When the 2 percent discount is taken, the customer pays only 98 percent of the gross sales price. For example, on a $100 sale with terms 2/10, n/30, $2 would be saved and $98 would be paid 20 days early.

The interest rate for the 20-day discount period and the annual interest rate are computed as follows:

$$\frac{\text{Amount Saved}}{\text{Amount Paid}} = \text{Interest Rate for 20 Days} \qquad \text{Interest Rate for 20 Days} \times \frac{365 \text{ days}}{20 \text{ days}} = \text{Annual Interest Rate}$$

$$\frac{\$2}{\$98} = 2.04\% \text{ for 20 Days} \qquad\qquad 2.04\% \times \frac{365 \text{ days}}{20 \text{ days}} = 37.23\% \text{ Annual Interest Rate}$$

As long as the bank's interest rate is less than the interest rate associated with failing to take cash discounts, the customer will save by taking the cash discount. For example, even if credit customers had to borrow from the bank at a rate as high as 15 percent, they would save a great deal.

---

[2] It is important not to confuse a cash discount with a trade discount. Vendors sometimes use a **trade discount** for quoting sales prices; the sales price is the list or printed catalog price **less** the trade discount.

[3] We use the gross method in all examples in this text. Some companies use the alternative net method, which records sales revenue after deducting the amount of the cash discount. Because the choice of method has little effect on the financial statements, discussion of this method is left for an advanced course.

Sales Returns and Allowances

Retailers and consumers have a right to return unsatisfactory or damaged merchandise and receive a refund or an adjustment to their bill. Such returns are often accumulated in a separate account called **Sales Returns and Allowances** and must be deducted from gross sales revenue in determining net sales. This account informs **Deckers**'s managers of the volume of returns and allowances and thus provides an important measure of the quality of customer service. Assume that **Fontana's Shoes** of Ithaca, New York, buys 40 pairs of sandals (at $50 each) from Deckers for $2,000 on account. Before paying for the sandals, Fontana's discovers that 10 pairs of sandals are not the color ordered and returns them to Deckers.[4] Deckers computes net sales as follows:

SALES RETURNS AND ALLOWANCES
A reduction of sales revenues for return of or allowances for unsatisfactory goods.

Sales revenue	$2,000
Less: Sales returns and allowances (10 × $50)	500
Net sales (reported on the income statement)	$1,500

Cost of goods sold related to the 10 pairs of sandals would also be reduced.

Reporting Net Sales

On the company's books, credit card discounts, sales discounts, and sales returns and allowances are accounted for separately to allow managers to monitor the costs of credit card use, sales discounts, and returns. Using the numbers in the preceding examples, the amount of net sales reported on the income statement is computed in the following manner:

Sales revenue	$6,000
Less: Credit card discounts (a contra-revenue)	90
Sales discounts (a contra-revenue)	20
Sales returns and allowances (a contra-revenue)	500
Net sales (included on the first line of the income statement)	$5,390

Net sales to all customers is the top line reported on **Deckers**'s income statement, presented in Exhibit 6.1. Deckers indicates in its revenue recognition footnote that the appropriate subtractions are made.

NET SALES
The top line reported on the income statement. Net Sales = Sales Revenue − (Credit card discounts + Sales discounts + Sales returns and allowances).

DECKERS OUTDOOR CORPORATION AND SUBSIDIARIES
Consolidated Statements of Comprehensive Income
Three Years Ended December 31, 2013, 2012, 2011
(amounts in thousands)

	2013	2012	2011
Net sales	$1,556,618	$1,414,398	$1,377,283
Cost of sales	820,135	782,244	698,288
Gross profit	736,483	632,154	678,995
Selling, general, and administrative expenses	528,586	445,206	394,157
Income from operations	207,897	186,948	284,838
Other income (expense)	(2,340)	(2,830)	424
Income before income taxes	205,557	184,118	285,262
Income taxes	59,868	55,104	83,404
Net income	$ 145,689	$ 129,014	$ 201,858

---

[4]Alternatively, Deckers might offer Fontana's a $200 allowance to keep the wrong-color sandals. If Fontana's accepts the offer, Deckers reports $200 as sales returns and allowances.

DECKERS BRANDS

REAL WORLD EXCERPT:

Annual Report

NOTES TO CONSOLIDATED FINANCIAL STATEMENTS

1. Summary of Significant Accounting Policies

Revenue Recognition

. . . allowances for estimated returns, discounts . . . are provided for when related revenue is recorded.

In 2013, Deckers disclosed that it provided its customers with $47,285,000 in sales discounts based on meeting certain order, shipment, and payment timelines.

PAUSE FOR **FEEDBACK**

In the last section, we learned to analyze the impact of **credit card sales, sales discounts,** and **sales returns,** all of which reduce the amounts reported as net sales. Both credit card discounts and sales or cash discounts promote faster receipt of cash. Sales returns and allowances include refunds and adjustments to customers' bills for defective or incorrect merchandise.

Before you move on, complete the following questions to test your understanding of these concepts.

SELF-STUDY **QUIZ**

1. Assume that **Deckers** sold $30,000 worth of footwear to various retailers with terms 1/10, n/30 and half of that amount was paid within the discount period. Gross catalog and Internet sales were $5,000 for the same period; 80 percent of these sales were paid for with credit cards with a 3 percent discount and the rest were paid for with cash. Compute net sales for the period.

    _____

    _____

2. During the first quarter of 2013, Deckers's net sales totaled $263,760, and cost of sales was $140,201. What was Deckers's gross profit for the first quarter of 2013?

    _____

    _____

After you have completed your answers, check them below.

Solutions to SELF-STUDY QUIZ

1. Gross Sales		$35,000
Less: Sales Discounts (0.01 × 1/2 × $30,000)		150
Credit Card Discounts (0.03 × 0.80 × $5,000)		120
Net Sales		$34,730

2. Net Sales	$263,760	
Cost of Sales	140,201	
Gross Profit	$123,559	

MEASURING AND REPORTING RECEIVABLES

Classifying Receivables

Receivables may be classified in three common ways. First, they may be classified as either an account receivable or a note receivable. An **account receivable** is created by a credit sale on an open account. For example, an account receivable is created when **Deckers** sells shoes on open account to **Fontana's Shoes** in Ithaca, New York. A **note receivable** is a promise in writing (a formal document) to pay (1) a specified amount of money, called the **principal,** at a definite future date known as the maturity date and (2) a specified amount of **interest** at one or more future dates. The interest is the amount charged for use of the principal.

Second, receivables may be classified as trade or nontrade receivables. A **trade receivable** is created in the normal course of business when a sale of merchandise or services on credit occurs. A **nontrade receivable** arises from transactions other than the normal sale of merchandise or services. For example, if Deckers loaned money to a new vice president to help finance a home at the new job location, the loan would be classified as a nontrade receivable. Third, in a classified balance sheet, receivables also are classified as either **current** or **noncurrent** (short term or long term), depending on when the cash is expected to be collected. Like many companies, Deckers reports only one type of receivable account, Trade Accounts Receivable, from customers and classifies the asset as a current asset because the accounts receivable are all due to be paid within one year.

ACCOUNTS RECEIVABLE (TRADE RECEIVABLES, RECEIVABLES)
Open accounts owed to the business by trade customers.

NOTES RECEIVABLE
Written promises that require another party to pay the business under specified conditions (amount, time, interest).

Foreign Currency Receivables

INTERNATIONAL PERSPECTIVE

Export (international) sales are a growing part of the U.S. economy. For example, international sales amounted to 33.0 percent of **Deckers**'s revenues in 2013. Most export sales to businesses are on credit. When a buyer agrees to pay in its local currency, Deckers cannot add the resulting accounts receivable, which are denominated in foreign currency, directly to its U.S. dollar accounts receivable. Deckers's accountants must first convert them to U.S. dollars using the end-of-period exchange rate between the two currencies. For example, if a French department store owed Deckers €20,000 (euros, the common currency of the European Monetary Union) on December 31, 2014, and each euro was worth US$1.20 on that date, it would add US$24,000 to its accounts receivable on the balance sheet.

Selected Foreign Currency Exchange Rates (in US$)

Mexican Peso	$0.07
Singapore Dollar	$0.75
Euro	$1.20

Accounting for Bad Debts

For billing and collection purposes, **Deckers** keeps a separate accounts receivable account for each retailer that resells its footwear and apparel (called a **subsidiary account**). The accounts receivable amount on the balance sheet represents the total of these individual customer accounts.

When Deckers extends credit to its commercial customers, it knows that some of these customers will not pay their debts. The expense recognition principle requires recording of bad debt expense in the **same** accounting period in which the related sales are made. This presents an important accounting problem. Deckers may not learn which particular customers will not pay until the **next** accounting period. So, at the end of the period of sale, it normally does not know which customers' accounts receivable are bad debts.

LEARNING OBJECTIVE 6-2
Estimate, report, and evaluate the effects of uncollectible accounts receivable (bad debts) on financial statements.

ALLOWANCE METHOD
Bases bad debt expense on an estimate of uncollectible accounts.

Deckers resolves this problem by using the **allowance method** to measure bad debt expense. The allowance method is based on **estimates** of the expected amount of bad debts. Two primary steps in employing the allowance method are:

1. Making the end-of-period adjusting entry to record estimated bad debt expense.

2. Writing off specific accounts determined to be uncollectible during the period.

Recording Bad Debt Expense Estimates

BAD DEBT EXPENSE (DOUBTFUL ACCOUNTS EXPENSE, UNCOLLECTIBLE ACCOUNTS EXPENSE, PROVISION FOR UNCOLLECTIBLE ACCOUNTS)
Expense associated with estimated uncollectible accounts receivable.

Bad debt expense (doubtful accounts expense, uncollectible accounts expense, provision for uncollectible accounts) is the expense associated with estimated uncollectible accounts receivable. An **adjusting journal entry at the end of the accounting period** records the bad debt estimate. For the year ended December 31, 2013, Deckers estimated bad debt expense to be $115,101 (all numbers in thousands of dollars) and made the following adjusting entry:

Bad debt expense (+E, −SE)................................	115,101	
Allowance for doubtful accounts (+XA, −A).................		115,101

Assets	=	Liabilities	+	Stockholders' Equity	
Allowance for doubtful accounts −115,101				Bad debt expense (+E) −115,101	

The Bad Debt Expense is included in the category "Selling" expenses on the income statement. It decreases net income and stockholders' equity. Accounts Receivable could not be credited in the journal entry because there is no way to know which customers' accounts receivable are involved. So the credit is made, instead, to a contra-asset account called **Allowance for Doubtful Accounts** (Allowance for Bad Debts or Allowance for Uncollectible Accounts). As a contra-asset, the balance in Allowance for Doubtful Accounts is always subtracted from the balance of the asset Accounts Receivable. Thus, the entry decreases the net book value of Accounts Receivable and total assets.

ALLOWANCE FOR DOUBTFUL ACCOUNTS (ALLOWANCE FOR BAD DEBTS, ALLOWANCE FOR UNCOLLECTIBLE ACCOUNTS)
Contra-asset account containing the estimated uncollectible accounts receivable.

Writing Off Specific Uncollectible Accounts

Throughout the year, when it is determined that a customer will not pay its debts (e.g., due to bankruptcy), the write-off of that individual bad debt is recorded through a journal entry. Now that the specific uncollectible customer account receivable has been identified, it can be removed with a credit. At the same time, we no longer need the related estimate in the contra-asset Allowance for Doubtful Accounts, which is removed by a debit. The journal entry summarizing Deckers's total write-offs of $115,119 during 2013 follows:

Allowance for doubtful accounts (−XA, +A)....................	115,119	
Accounts receivable (−A)................................		115,119

Assets	=	Liabilities	+	Stockholders' Equity
Allowance for doubtful accounts +115,119				
Accounts receivable −115,119				

Notice that this journal entry did **not affect any income statement accounts.** It did not record a bad debt expense because the estimated expense was recorded with an adjusting entry in the period of sale. Also, the entry did **not change the net book value of accounts receivable** since the decrease in the asset account (Accounts Receivable) was offset by the decrease in the contra-asset account (Allowance for Doubtful Accounts). Thus, it also did not affect total assets.

| Bad Debt Recoveries | FINANCIAL ANALYSIS |

When a company receives a payment on an account that has already been written off, the journal entry to write off the account is reversed to put the receivable back on the books, and the collection of cash is recorded. For example, if the previously written-off amount was $677, it would make the following entries:

Accounts receivable (+A)..	677	
Allowance for doubtful accounts (+XA, −A).....................		677
Cash (+A)	677	
Accounts receivable (−A).....................................		677

Note that these entries, like the original write-off, do not affect total assets or net income. Only the estimate of bad debts affects these amounts.

Summary of the Accounting Process

It is important to remember that accounting for bad debts is a two-step process:

Step	Timing	Accounts Affected	Financial Statement Effects	
1. Record estimated bad debts adjustment	End of period in which sales are made	Bad Debt Expense (E) ↑	Net Income ↓	
		Allowance for Doubtful Accounts (XA) ↑	Assets (Accounts Receivable, Net) ↓	
2. Identify and write off actual bad debts	Throughout period as bad debts become known	Accounts Receivable (A) ↓	Net Income	No effect
		Allowance for Doubtful Accounts (XA) ↓	Assets (Accounts Receivable, Net)	

Deckers's complete 2013 accounting process for bad debts can now be summarized in terms of the changes in Accounts Receivable (Gross) and the Allowance for Doubtful Accounts:[5]

Accounts Receivable Dec. 31, 2013

Accounts Receivable (Gross) (A)	$209,081
Allowance for Doubtful Accounts (XA)	25,068
Accounts Receivable (Net) (A)	$184,013

Accounts Receivable (Gross) (A)			
Beginning balance	215,842	Collections on account	1,448,260
Sales on account	1,556,618	Write-offs	115,119
Ending balance	209,081		

Allowance for Doubtful Accounts (XA)			
		Beginning balance	25,086
		Bad debt expense	
Write-offs	115,119	adjustment	115,101
		Ending balance	25,068

[5]This assumes that all sales are on account.

Accounts Receivable (Gross) includes the total accounts receivable, both collectible and uncollectible. The balance in the Allowance for Doubtful Accounts is the portion of the accounts receivable balance the company estimates to be uncollectible. Accounts Receivable (Net) reported on the balance sheet is the portion of the accounts the company expects to collect (or its estimated net realizable value).

Reporting Accounts Receivable and Bad Debts

Analysts who want information on **Deckers**'s receivables will find Accounts Receivable, net of allowance for doubtful accounts (the **net book value**), of $184,013 and $190,756 for 2013 and 2012, respectively, reported on the balance sheet (Exhibit 6.2). Deckers reports the balance in the Allowance for Doubtful Accounts ($25,068 in 2013 and $25,086 in 2012) within the account title. Other companies report the balance in the Allowance for Doubtful Accounts in a note. Accounts Receivable (Gross), the total accounts receivable, can be computed by adding the two amounts together.

The amounts of bad debt expense and accounts receivable written off for the period, if material, are reported on a schedule that publicly traded companies must include in their Annual Report Form 10-K filed with the SEC. Exhibit 6.3 presents this schedule from Deckers's 2013 filing.

EXHIBIT 6.2

Accounts Receivable on the Partial Balance Sheet

DECKERS BRANDS

REAL WORLD EXCERPT:
Annual Report

DECKERS OUTDOOR CORPORATION AND SUBSIDIARIES
Consolidated Balance Sheets
December 31, 2013 and 2012
(amounts in thousands)

	2013	2012
ASSETS		
Current assets:		
Cash and cash equivalents	$237,125	$110,247
Trade accounts receivable, net of allowances of $25,068 and $25,086 as of December 31, 2013, and December 31, 2012, respectively	184,013	190,756
Inventories	260,791	300,173
Prepaid expenses	14,980	14,092
Other current assets	112,514	59,028
Deferred tax assets	19,881	17,290
Total current assets	$829,304	$691,586

EXHIBIT 6.3

Accounts Receivable Valuation Schedule (Form 10-K)

DECKERS BRANDS

REAL WORLD EXCERPT:
Annual Report

DECKERS OUTDOOR CORPORATION AND SUBSIDIARIES
Valuation and Qualifying Accounts
Three Years Ended December 31, 2013, 2012, 2011
(amounts in thousands)

	Balance at Beginning of Year	Additions	Deductions	Balance at End of Year
December 31, 2013	$25,086	$115,101	$115,119	$25,068
December 31, 2012	21,692	96,931	93,537	25,086
December 31, 2011	13,772	75,995	68,075	21,692

PAUSE FOR FEEDBACK   STOP

When receivables are material, companies must employ the allowance method to account for uncollectibles. These are the steps in the process:

a. The end-of-period adjusting entry to record the estimate of bad debt expense and *increase* the allowance for doubtful accounts.

b. Writing off specific accounts determined to be uncollectible during the period to eliminate the specific uncollectible account receivable and *decrease* the allowance for doubtful accounts.

The adjusting entry reduces net income as well as net accounts receivable. The write-off affects neither. Before you move on, complete the following questions to test your understanding of these concepts.

SELF-STUDY QUIZ

In a recent year, **Crocs, Inc.,** a major **Deckers** competitor, had a beginning credit balance in the Allowance for Doubtful Accounts of $3,973 (all numbers in thousands of dollars). It wrote off accounts receivable totaling $1,535 during the year and made a bad debt expense adjustment for the year of $2,204.

1. What adjusting journal entry did Crocs make for bad debts at the end of the year?
2. Make the journal entry summarizing Crocs's total write-off of bad debts during the year.
3. Compute the balance in the Allowance for Doubtful Accounts at the end of the year.

After you have completed your answers, check them below.

 GUIDED HELP 6-1

For additional step-by-step video instruction on preparing journal entries related to bad debts, go to **www.mhhe.com/libby9e_gh6a**.

Estimating Bad Debts

The bad debt expense amount recorded in the end-of-period adjusting entry often is estimated based on either (1) a percentage of total credit sales for the period or (2) an aging of accounts receivable. Both methods are acceptable under GAAP and are widely used. The percentage of credit sales method is simpler to apply, but the aging method is generally more accurate. Many companies use the simpler method on a weekly or monthly basis and use the more accurate method on a monthly or quarterly basis to check the accuracy of the earlier estimates. In our example, both methods produce exactly the same estimate, which rarely occurs in practice.

Percentage of Credit Sales Method

The **percentage of credit sales method** bases bad debt expense on the historical percentage of credit sales that result in bad debts. The average percentage of credit sales that result in bad debts can be computed by dividing total bad debt losses by total **credit** sales. A company that has been operating for some years has sufficient experience to project probable future bad debt

PERCENTAGE OF CREDIT SALES METHOD
Bases bad debt expense on the historical percentage of credit sales that result in bad debts.

Solutions to

SELF-STUDY QUIZ

1. Bad debt expense (+E, −SE)   2,204
      Allowance for doubtful accounts (+XA, −A)   2,204
2. Allowance for doubtful accounts (−XA, +A)   1,535
      Accounts receivable (−A)   1,535
3. Beginning Balance + Bad Debt Expense Estimate − Write-Offs = Ending Balance,
   $3,973 + 2,204 − 1,535 = $4,642

losses. For example, if we assume that, during the year 2014, **Deckers** expected bad debt losses of 1.0 percent of credit sales, and its credit sales were $1,500,000, it would estimate the current year's bad debts as:

Credit sales	$1,500,000
× **Bad debt loss rate** (1.0%)	× 0.01
Bad debt expense	$ 15,000

This amount would be directly recorded as Bad Debt Expense (and an increase in Allowance for Doubtful Accounts) in the current year. Our beginning balance in the Allowance for Doubtful Accounts for 2014 would be the ending balance for 2013. Assuming write-offs during 2014 of $17,068, the ending balance is computed as follows:

Beginning balance	$25,068
+ Bad debt expense	15,000
− Write-offs	17,068
Ending balance	$23,000

Percent of credit sales estimate

Allowance for Doubtful Accounts (XA)			
		2014 Beginning balance	25,068
2014 Write-offs	17,068	2014 Bad debt expense adjustment	15,000
		2014 Ending balance	? = 23,000

Aging of Accounts Receivable

The **aging of accounts receivable method** relies on the fact that, as accounts receivable become older and more overdue, it is less likely that they will be collected. For example, a receivable that was due in 30 days but has not been paid after 120 days is less likely to be collected, on average, than a similar receivable that remains unpaid after 45 days.

If Deckers split its assumed 2014 ending balance in accounts receivable (gross) of $230,000 into three age categories, it would first examine the individual customer accounts receivable and sort them into the three age categories. Based on prior experience, management would then **estimate** the probable bad debt loss rates for each category: for example, not yet due, 2 percent; 1 to 90 days past due, 10 percent; over 90 days, 30 percent.

As illustrated in the aging schedule below, this would result in an estimate of total uncollectible amounts of $23,000, the **estimated ending balance** that **should be** in the Allowance for Doubtful Accounts. From this, the adjustment to record Bad Debt Expense (and an increase in Allowance for Doubtful Accounts) for 2014 would be computed as follows:

Aging Schedule 2014

Aged Accounts Receivable		Estimated Percentage Uncollectible		Estimated Amount Uncollectible
Not yet due	$115,000	× 2%	=	$ 2,300
Up to 90 days past due	69,000	× 10%	=	6,900
Over 90 days past due	46,000	× 30%	=	13,800
Estimated ending balance in Allowance for Doubtful Accounts				$23,000
Less: Balance in Allowance for Doubtful Accounts before adjustment (25,068 − 17,068)				8,000
Bad Debt Expense for the year				$15,000

Allowance for Doubtful Accounts (XA)			
		2014 Beginning balance	25,068
2014 Write-offs	17,068	2014 Bad debt expense adjustment	?
		2014 Ending balance	23,000

= 15,000

Total estimated uncollectible accounts

Comparison of the Two Methods

It is important to recognize that the approach to recording bad debt expense using the percentage of credit sales method is different from that for the aging method:

- **Percentage of credit sales.** Directly compute the amount to be recorded as **Bad Debt Expense** on the **income statement** for the period in the adjusting journal entry.
- **Aging of Accounts Receivable.** Compute the **estimated ending balance** we would like to have in the **Allowance for Doubtful Accounts** on the **balance sheet** after we make the necessary adjusting entry. The **difference** between the current balance in the account and the estimated balance is recorded as the adjusting entry for Bad Debt Expense for the period.

In either case, the balance sheet presentation for 2014 would show Accounts Receivable, less Allowance for Doubtful Accounts, of $207,000 ($230,000 − $23,000).

Actual Write-Offs Compared with Estimates

Deckers's Form 10-K provides particularly clear information on its approach to estimating uncollectible accounts and the potential effect of any errors in those estimates:

CRITICAL ACCOUNTING POLICIES

Allowance for Doubtful Accounts

We provide a reserve against trade accounts receivable for estimated losses that may result from customers' inability to pay. We determine the amount of the reserve by analyzing known uncollectible accounts, aged trade accounts receivables, economic conditions and forecasts, historical experience and the customers' credit-worthiness. . . . Our use of different estimates and assumptions could produce different financial results. For example, a 1.0 percent change in the rate used to estimate the reserve for the accounts we consider to have credit risk and not specifically identified as uncollectible would change the allowance for doubtful accounts at December 31, 2013, by approximately $1,000.

DECKERS BRANDS

REAL WORLD EXCERPT:
Form 10-K

If uncollectible accounts actually written off differ from the estimated amount previously recorded, a higher or lower amount is recorded in the next period to make up for the previous period's error in estimate. **When estimates are found to be incorrect, financial statement values for prior annual accounting periods are not corrected.**

Control over Accounts Receivable

Many managers forget that extending credit will increase sales volume, but unless the related receivables are collected, they do not add to the bottom line. Companies that emphasize sales without monitoring the collection of credit sales soon find much of their current assets tied up in accounts receivable. The following practices can help minimize bad debts:

1. Require approval of customers' credit history by a person independent of the sales and collections functions.
2. Age accounts receivable periodically and contact customers with overdue payments.
3. Reward both sales and collections personnel for speedy collections so that they work as a team.

To assess the effectiveness of overall credit-granting and collection activities, managers and analysts often compute the receivables turnover ratio.

KEY RATIO ANALYSIS		Receivables Turnover Ratio

LEARNING OBJECTIVE 6-3

Analyze and interpret the receivables turnover ratio and the effects of accounts receivable on cash flows.

 ANALYTICAL QUESTION

How effective are credit-granting and collection activities?

% RATIO AND COMPARISONS

The receivables turnover ratio is computed as follows (see Exhibits 6.1 and 6.2):

$$\text{Receivables Turnover} = \frac{\text{Net Sales}^*}{\text{Average Net Trade Accounts Receivable}^\dagger}$$

The 2013 receivables turnover ratio for **Deckers:**

$$\frac{\$1,556,618}{(190,756 + 184,013)/2} = 8.3$$

COMPARISONS OVER TIME			COMPARISONS WITH COMPETITORS	
Deckers			Skechers U.S.A.	Crocs
2011	**2012**	**2013**	**2013**	**2013**
8.9	7.4	8.3	8.4	12.1

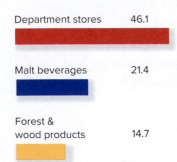

Selected Industry Comparisons: Receivables Turnover Ratio

Department stores   46.1

Malt beverages   21.4

Forest & wood products   14.7

INTERPRETATIONS

In General   The receivables turnover ratio reflects how many times average trade receivables are recorded and collected during the period. The higher the ratio, the faster the collection of receivables. A higher ratio benefits the company because it can invest the money collected to earn interest income or reduce borrowings to reduce interest expense. Overly generous payment schedules and ineffective collection methods keep the receivables turnover ratio low. Analysts and creditors watch this ratio because a sudden decline may mean that a company is extending payment deadlines in an attempt to prop up lagging sales or is even recording sales that will later be returned by customers. Many managers and analysts compute the related number **average collection period** or **average days sales in receivables,** which is equal to 365 ÷ Receivables Turnover Ratio. It indicates the average time it takes a customer to pay its accounts. For Deckers, the amount would be computed as follows for 2013:

$$\text{Average Collection Period} = \frac{365}{\text{Receivables Turnover}} = \frac{365}{8.3} = 44.0 \text{ days}$$

Focus Company Analysis   Deckers's receivables turnover increased from a 2011 high of 8.9 to 8.3 in 2013. This indicates that the company is taking more time to convert its receivables into cash. Compared to the receivables turnover ratios of its competitors, Deckers's ratio is below those of **Skechers** and **Crocs**.

A Few Cautions   Since differences across industries and between firms in the manner in which customer purchases are financed can cause dramatic differences in the ratio, a particular firm's ratio should be compared only with its prior years' figures or with other firms in the same industry following the same financing practices.

Since the amount of net credit sales is normally not reported separately, most analysts use net sales in this equation.

†*Average Net Trade Accounts Receivable = (Beginning Net Trade Accounts Receivable + Ending Net Trade Accounts Receivable) ÷ 2.*

Accounts Receivable

FOCUS ON
CASH FLOWS

The change in accounts receivable can be a major determinant of a company's cash flow from operations. While the income statement reflects the revenues of the period, the cash flow from operating activities reflects cash collections from customers. Since sales on account increase the balance in accounts receivable and cash collections from customers decrease the balance in accounts receivable, the change in accounts receivable from the beginning to the end of the period is the difference between sales and collections.

EFFECT ON STATEMENT OF CASH FLOWS

In General   When there is a net **decrease in accounts receivable** for the period, cash collected from customers is more than revenue; thus, the decrease must be **added** in computing cash flows from operations. When a net **increase in accounts receivable** occurs, cash collected from customers is less than revenue; thus, the increase must be **subtracted** in computing cash flows from operations.*

	Effect on Cash Flows
Operating activities (indirect method)	
Net income	$ xxx
Adjusted for	
Add accounts receivable decrease	+
or	
Subtract accounts receivable increase	−

Focus Company Analysis   The excerpt below shows the Operating Activities section of **Deckers**'s statement of cash flows. Collections outpaced sales growth during 2013 to result in a decrease in Deckers's balance in receivables. This decrease is added in reconciling net income to cash flow from operating activities because revenues are lower than cash collected from customers for 2013. When receivables increase, the amount of the increase in receivables is subtracted in reconciling net income to cash flow from operating activities because cash collected from customers is lower than revenues.

	2013
Cash flows from operating activities	
Net income	$145,689
Adjustments to reconcile net income to net cash provided by operating activities:	
....	. . .
Changes in operating assets and liabilities:	
Trade accounts receivable, net of provision for doubtful accounts	6,743
Inventories	39,382
	. . .
	. . .
Net cash provided by operating activities	$262,125

*For companies with receivables in foreign currency or business acquisitions/dispositions, the change reported on the cash flow statement will not equal the change in the accounts receivable reported on the balance sheet.

PAUSE FOR **FEEDBACK**

When using the **percentage of sales method,** you directly compute the bad debt expense for the period by multiplying the amount of credit sales by the bad debt loss rate. With the **aging method,** you compute the estimated ending balance in the allowance and solve for the bad debt expense. This process involves multiplying the amount in each age category by the estimated percentage uncollectible to produce the estimated ending balance in the allowance for doubtful accounts. The difference between the estimated ending balance and the balance in the allowance before the adjustment becomes the bad debt expense for the year. Before you move on, try an example of the more difficult aging method computations based on **Crocs**'s numbers reported in an earlier year.

SELF-STUDY **QUIZ**

1. In an earlier year, **Deckers**'s competitor Crocs reported a beginning balance in the Allowance for Doubtful Accounts of $5,262. It also wrote off bad debts amounting to $2,551 during the year. At the end of the year, it computed total estimated uncollectible accounts using the aging method to be $3,973 (all numbers in thousands of dollars). What amount did Crocs record as bad debt expense for the period? (**Solution approach:** Use the Allowance for Doubtful Accounts T-account or the following equation to solve for the missing value.)

Allowance for Doubtful Accounts (XA)	

Estimated ending balance in Allowance for Doubtful Accounts   _____
Less: Current balance in Allowance for Doubtful Accounts   _____
Bad Debt Expense for the year   ══════

The accounts receivable turnover ratio measures the effectiveness of credit-granting and collection activities. Faster turnover means faster receipt of cash from your customers. To test whether you understand this concept, answer the following question:

2. Indicate whether **granting later payment deadlines** (e.g., 60 days instead of 30 days) will most likely **increase** or **decrease** the accounts receivable turnover ratio. Explain.

After you have completed your answers, check them below.

 GUIDED HELP 6-2

For additional step-by-step video instruction on estimating and reporting bad debts using the aging method, go to **www.mhhe.com/libby9e_gh6b**.

Solutions to
SELF-STUDY QUIZ

1.

Allowance for Doubtful Accounts (XA)			
		Beginning balance	5,262
Write-offs	2,551	Bad debt expense (solve)	1,262
		Ending balance	3,973

Estimated ending balance in Allowance for Doubtful Accounts   3,973
Less: Current balance in Allowance for Doubtful Accounts ($5,262 − $2,551)   2,711
Bad Debt Expense for the year $1,262

2. Granting later payment deadlines will most likely **decrease** the accounts receivable turnover ratio because later collections from customers will increase the average accounts receivable balance (the denominator of the ratio), decreasing the ratio.

REPORTING AND SAFEGUARDING CASH

Cash and Cash Equivalents Defined

Cash is defined as money or any instrument that banks will accept for deposit and immediate credit to a company's account, such as a check, money order, or bank draft. **Cash equivalents** are investments with original maturities of three months or less that are readily convertible to cash and whose value is unlikely to change (that is, they are not sensitive to interest rate changes). Typical instruments included as cash equivalents are bank certificates of deposit and Treasury bills that the U.S. government issues to finance its activities.

Like most companies, **Deckers** combines all of its bank accounts and cash equivalents into one amount, Cash and Cash Equivalents, on the balance sheet. It also reports that the book values of cash equivalents on the balance sheet equal their fair market values—which we should expect given the nature of the instruments (investments whose value is unlikely to change).

Cash Management

Many businesses receive a large amount of cash, checks, and credit card receipts from their customers each day. Anyone can spend cash, so management must develop procedures to safeguard the cash it uses in the business. Effective cash management involves more than protecting cash from theft, fraud, or loss through carelessness. Other cash management responsibilities include:

1. Accurate accounting so that reports of cash flows and balances may be prepared.
2. Controls to ensure that enough cash is available to meet (*a*) current operating needs, (*b*) maturing liabilities, and (*c*) unexpected emergencies.
3. Prevention of the accumulation of excess amounts of idle cash. Idle cash earns no revenue. Therefore, it is often invested in securities to earn a return until it is needed for operations.

Internal Control of Cash

The term **internal controls** refers to the process by which a company safeguards its assets and provides reasonable assurance regarding the reliability of the company's financial reporting, the effectiveness and efficiency of its operations, and its compliance with applicable laws and regulations. Internal control procedures should extend to all assets: cash, receivables, investments, plant and equipment, and so on. Controls that ensure the accuracy of the financial records are designed to prevent inadvertent errors and outright fraud. Because internal control increases the reliability of the financial statements, it is reviewed by the outside independent auditor.

Because cash is the asset most vulnerable to theft and fraud, a significant number of internal control procedures should focus on cash. You have already observed internal control procedures for cash, although you may not have known it at the time. At most movie theaters, one employee sells tickets and another employee collects them. Having one employee do both jobs would be less expensive, but that single employee could easily steal cash and admit a patron without issuing a ticket. If different employees perform the tasks, a successful theft requires the participation of both.

Effective internal control of cash should include the following:

1. Separation of duties.
   - *a.* Complete separation of the jobs of receiving cash and disbursing cash.
   - *b.* Complete separation of the procedures of accounting for cash receipts and cash disbursements.
   - *c.* Complete separation of the physical handling of cash and all phases of the accounting function.

Juice Images/Alamy

2. Prescribed policies and procedures.

  a. Require that all cash receipts be deposited in a bank daily. Keep any cash on hand under strict control.

  b. Require separate approval of the purchases and the actual cash payments. Prenumbered checks should be used. Special care must be taken with payments by **electronic funds transfers** since they involve no controlled documents (checks).

  c. Assign the responsibilities for cash payment approval and check-signing or electronic funds transfer transmittal to different individuals.

  d. Require monthly reconciliation of bank accounts with the cash accounts on the company's books (discussed in detail in the next section).

A QUESTION OF ETHICS	Ethics and the Need for Internal Control

Some people are bothered by the recommendation that all well-run companies should have strong internal control procedures. These people believe that control procedures suggest that management does not trust the company's employees. Although the vast majority of employees are trustworthy, employee theft does cost businesses billions of dollars each year. Interviews with convicted felons indicate that in many cases they stole from their employers because they thought that it was easy and that no one cared (there were no internal control procedures).

Many companies have a formal code of ethics that requires high standards of behavior in dealing with customers, suppliers, fellow employees, and the company's assets. Although each employee is ultimately responsible for his or her own ethical behavior, internal control procedures can be thought of as important value statements from management.

Reconciliation of the Cash Accounts and the Bank Statements

Content of a Bank Statement

BANK STATEMENT
A monthly report from a bank that shows deposits recorded, checks cleared, other debits and credits, and a running bank balance.

Proper use of the bank accounts can be an important internal cash control procedure. Each month, the bank provides the company (the depositor) with a **bank statement** that lists (1) each paper or electronic deposit recorded by the bank during the period, (2) each paper or electronic check cleared by the bank during the period, and (3) the balance in the company's account. The bank statement also shows the bank charges or deductions (such as service charges) made directly to the company's account by the bank. A typical bank statement for ROW.COM, Inc., is shown in Exhibit 6.4.

Exhibit 6.4 lists four items that need explanation. Notice the $500 and $100 items listed in the Checks and Debits column and coded **EFT**.[6] This is the code for **electronic funds transfers.** ROW.COM pays its electricity and insurance bills using electronic checking. When it orders the electronic payments, it records these items on the company's books in the same manner as a paper check. So no additional entry is needed.

Notice that listed in the Checks and Debits column there is a deduction for $18 coded **NSF.** This entry refers to a check for $18 received from a customer and deposited by ROW.COM with its bank. The bank processed the check through banking channels to the customer's bank, but the account did not have sufficient funds to cover the check. The customer's bank therefore returned it to ROW.COM's bank, which then charged it back to ROW.COM's account. This type of check often is called an **NSF check** (not sufficient funds). The NSF check is now a receivable; consequently, ROW.COM must make an entry to debit Receivables and credit Cash for the $18.

---

[6]These codes vary among banks.

EXHIBIT 6.4

Example of a Bank Statement

Notice the $6 listed on June 30 in the Checks and Debits column and coded **SC.** This is the code for bank service charges. The bank statement included a memo by the bank explaining this service charge (which was not documented by a check). ROW.COM must make an entry to reflect this $6 decrease in the bank balance as a debit to a relevant expense account, such as Bank Service Expense, and a credit to Cash.

Notice the $20 listed on June 18 in the Deposits and Credits column and coded **INT** for interest earned. The bank pays interest on checking account balances, and it increased ROW.COM's account for interest earned during the period. ROW.COM must record the interest by making an entry to debit Cash and credit Interest Income for the $20.

Need for Reconciliation

A **bank reconciliation** is the process of comparing (reconciling) the ending cash balance in the company's records and the ending cash balance reported by the bank on the monthly bank statement. A bank reconciliation should be completed at the end of each month. Usually, the ending cash balance as shown on the bank statement does not agree with the ending cash balance shown by the related Cash ledger account on the books of the company. For example, the Cash ledger account of ROW.COM showed the following at the end of June (ROW.COM has only one checking account):

BANK RECONCILIATION
Process of verifying the accuracy of both the bank statement and the cash accounts of a business.

Cash (A)			
June 1 balance	7,753.40		
June deposits	5,830.00	June payments	4,543.40
Ending balance	9,040.00		

The $8,322.20 ending cash balance shown on the bank statement (Exhibit 6.4) differs from the $9,040.00 ending balance of cash shown on the books of ROW.COM. Most of this difference exists because of timing differences in the recording of transactions:

1. Some transactions affecting cash were recorded in the books of ROW.COM but were not shown on the bank statement.

2. Some transactions were shown on the bank statement but had not been recorded in the books of ROW.COM.

Some of the difference may also be caused by errors in recording transactions.

The most common causes of differences between the ending bank balance and the ending book balance of cash are as follows:

1. **Outstanding checks.** These are checks written by the company and recorded in the company's ledger as credits to the Cash account that have not cleared the bank (they are not shown on the bank statement as a deduction from the bank balance). The outstanding checks are identified by comparing the list of canceled checks on the bank statement with the record of checks (such as check stubs or a journal) maintained by the company.

2. **Deposits in transit.** These are deposits sent to the bank by the company and recorded in the company's ledger as debits to the Cash account. The bank has not recorded these deposits (they are not shown on the bank statement as an increase in the bank balance). Deposits in transit usually happen when deposits are made one or two days before the close of the period covered by the bank statement. Deposits in transit are determined by comparing the deposits listed on the bank statement with the company deposit records.

3. **Bank service charges.** These are expenses for bank services listed on the bank statement but not recorded on the company's books.

4. **NSF checks.** These are "bad checks" or "bounced checks" that have been deposited but must be deducted from the company's cash account and rerecorded as accounts receivable.

5. **Interest.** This is the interest paid by the bank to the company on its bank balance.

6. **Errors.** Both the bank and the company may make errors, especially when the volume of cash transactions is large.

Bank Reconciliation Illustrated

The company should make a bank reconciliation immediately after receiving each bank statement. The general format for the bank reconciliation follows:

Ending cash balance per books	$xxx	Ending cash balance per bank statement	$xxx
+ Interest paid by bank	xx	+ Deposits in transit	xx
− NSF checks/Service charges	xx	− Outstanding checks	xx
± Company errors	xx	± Bank errors	xx
Ending correct cash balance	$xxx	Ending correct cash balance	$xxx

Exhibit 6.5 shows the bank reconciliation prepared by ROW.COM for the month of June to reconcile the ending bank balance ($8,322.20) with the ending book balance ($9,040.00). On the completed reconciliation, the correct cash balance is $9,045.00. This correct balance is the amount that should be shown in the Cash account after the reconciliation. Since ROW.COM has only one checking account and no cash on hand, it is also the correct amount of cash that should be reported on the balance sheet.[7]

ROW.COM followed these steps in preparing the bank reconciliation:

1. **Identify the outstanding checks.** A comparison of the checks and electronic payments listed on the bank statement with the company's record of all checks drawn and electronic

[7]In this example, there were no outstanding checks or deposits in transit at the end of May.

EXHIBIT 6.5

Bank Reconciliation Illustrated

ROW.COM, INC.
Bank Reconciliation
For the Month Ending June 30, 2016

Company's Books		Bank Statement	
Ending cash balance		Ending cash balance	
per books	$9,040.00	per bank statement	$8,322.20
Additions		Additions	
Interest paid by the bank	20.00	Deposit in transit	1,800.00
Error in recording payment	9.00		
	9,069.00		10,122.20
Deductions		Deductions	
NSF check of R. Smith	18.00	Outstanding checks	1,077.20
Bank service charges	6.00		
Ending correct cash balance	$9,045.00	Ending correct cash balance	$9,045.00

payments made showed the following checks were still outstanding (had not cleared the bank) at the end of June:

Check No.	Amount
121	$ 145.00
123	815.00
131	117.20
Total	$1,077.20

This total was entered on the reconciliation as a deduction from the bank account. These checks will be deducted by the bank when they clear the bank.

2. **Identify the deposits in transit.** A comparison of the deposit slips on hand with those listed on the bank statement revealed that a deposit of $1,800 made on June 30 was not listed on the bank statement. This amount was entered on the reconciliation as an addition to the bank account. It will be added by the bank when it records the deposit.

3. **Record bank charges and credits:**
   a. Interest received from the bank, $20—entered on the bank reconciliation as an addition to the book balance; it already has been included in the bank balance.
   b. NSF check of R. Smith, $18—entered on the bank reconciliation as a deduction from the book balance; it has been deducted from the bank statement balance.
   c. Bank service charges, $6—entered on the bank reconciliation as a deduction from the book balance; it has been deducted from the bank balance.

4. **Determine the impact of errors.** At this point, ROW.COM found that the reconciliation did not balance by $9. Upon checking the journal entries made during the month, the electronic payment on 6-09 for $100 to pay an account payable was found. The payment was recorded in the company's accounts as $109. Therefore, $9 (i.e., $109 − $100) must be added to the book cash balance on the reconciliation; the bank cleared the electronic payment for the correct amount, $100.

Note that in Exhibit 6.5 the two sections of the bank reconciliation now agree at a correct cash balance of $9,045.00.

A bank reconciliation as shown in Exhibit 6.5 accomplishes two major objectives:

1. It checks the accuracy of the bank balance and the company cash records, which involves developing the correct cash balance. The correct cash balance (plus cash on hand, if any) is the amount of cash that is reported on the balance sheet.

2. It identifies any previously unrecorded transactions or changes that are necessary to cause the company's Cash account(s) to show the correct cash balance. Any transactions or changes on the **company's books side** of the bank reconciliation need journal entries. Therefore, the following journal entries based on the company's books side of the bank reconciliation (Exhibit 6.5) must be entered into the company's records:

Accounts of ROW.COM

(a) Cash (+A)	20	
Interest income (+R, +SE)		20
To record interest by bank.		
(b) Accounts receivable (+A)	18	
Cash (−A)		18
To record NSF check.		
(c) Bank service expense (+E, −SE)	6	
Cash (−A)		6
To record service fees charged by bank.		
(d) Cash (+A)	9	
Accounts payable (+L)		9
To correct error made in recording a check payable to a creditor.		

Assets		=	Liabilities	+	Stockholders' Equity	
Cash (+20, −18, −6, +9)	+5		Accounts payable	+9	Interest income (+R)	+20
Accounts receivable	+18				Bank service expense (+E)	−6

Notice again that all of the additions and deductions on the company's books side of the reconciliation need journal entries to update the Cash account. The additions and deductions on the bank statement side do not need journal entries because they will work out automatically when they clear the bank.

PAUSE FOR FEEDBACK

Cash is the most liquid of all assets, flowing continually into and out of a business. As a result, a number of critical control procedures, including the **reconciliation** of bank accounts, should be applied. Also, management of cash may be critically important to decision makers who must have cash available to meet current needs yet must avoid excess amounts of idle cash that produce no revenue. To see if you understand the basics of a bank reconciliation, answer the following questions:

SELF-STUDY QUIZ

Indicate which of the following items discovered while preparing a company's bank reconciliation will result in adjustment of the cash balance on the balance sheet.

1. Outstanding checks.
2. Deposits in transit.
3. Bank service charges.
4. NSF checks that were deposited.

After you have completed your answers, check them at the bottom of the next page.

EPILOGUE

As we noted at the beginning of the chapter, **Deckers** recognized that to turn growth into profits, it had to (1) continually refresh its product lines by introducing new technologies, new styles, and new product categories; (2) become a leaner and more nimble manufacturer, taking advantage of lower-cost, more flexible production locations; and (3) focus attention on inventory management and collections of accounts receivable since an uncollected account is of no value to the company. Each of these efforts is aimed at increasing net sales and/or decreasing cost of goods sold, thereby increasing gross profit. The first quarter of 2014 was a mixed bag for Deckers. Sales increased, but net income declined compared to the first quarter of 2013, and resulted in a net loss. You can evaluate the further success of the company's strategy by going to the Web at **www.deckers.com** to check Deckers's latest annual and quarterly reports.

DEMONSTRATION   CASE A

(Complete the requirements before proceeding to the suggested solutions.) Wholesale Warehouse Stores sold $950,000 in merchandise during 2016. Of this amount, $400,000 was on credit with terms 2/10, n/30 (75 percent of these amounts were paid within the discount period), $500,000 was paid with credit cards (there was a 3 percent credit card discount), and the rest was paid in cash. On December 31, 2016, the Accounts Receivable balance was $80,000. The beginning balance in the Allowance for Doubtful Accounts was $9,000 and $6,000 of bad debts was written off during the year.

Required:

1. Compute net sales for 2016, assuming that sales and credit card discounts are treated as contra-revenues.

2. Assume that Wholesale uses the percentage of sales method for estimating bad debt expense and that it estimates that 2 percent of credit sales will produce bad debts. Record bad debt expense for 2016.

3. Assume instead that Wholesale uses the aging of accounts receivable method and that it estimates that $10,000 worth of current accounts is uncollectible. Record bad debt expense for 2016.

SUGGESTED SOLUTION

1. Both sales discounts and credit card discounts should be subtracted from sales revenues in the computation of net sales.

Sales revenue	$950,000
Less: Sales discounts (0.02 × 0.75 × $400,000)	6,000
Credit card discounts (0.03 × $500,000)	15,000
Net sales	$929,000

2. The percentage estimate of bad debts should be applied to credit sales. Cash sales never produce bad debts.

Bad debt expense (+E, −SE) (0.02 × $400,000)	8,000	
Allowance for doubtful accounts (+XA, −A)		8,000

Assets	=	Liabilities	+	Stockholders' Equity
Allowance for				Bad debt
doubtful accounts −8,000				expense (+E) −8,000

3. Bank service charges are deducted from the company's account; thus, cash must be reduced and an expense must be recorded.

4. NSF checks that were deposited were recorded on the books as increases in the cash account; thus, cash must be decreased and the related accounts receivable increased if payment is still expected.

3. The entry made when using the aging of accounts receivable method is the estimated balance minus the current balance.

Estimated ending balance in Allowance for Doubtful Accounts	$10,000
Less: Current balance in Allowance for Doubtful Accounts ($9,000 − $6,000)	3,000
Bad Debt Expense for the year	$ 7,000

Bad debt expense (+E, −SE)..	7,000	
Allowance for doubtful accounts (+XA, −A)......................		7,000

Assets	=	Liabilities	+	Stockholders' Equity	
Allowance for				Bad debt	
doubtful accounts	−7,000			expense (+E)	−7,000

DEMONSTRATION CASE B

(Complete the requirements before proceeding to the suggested solution that follows.) Heather Ann Long, a freshman at a large state university, has just received her first checking account statement. This was her first chance to attempt a bank reconciliation. She had the following information to work with:

Bank balance, September 1	$1,150
Deposits during September	650
Checks cleared during September	900
Bank service charge	25
Bank balance, October 1	875

Heather was surprised that the deposit of $50 she made on September 29 had not been posted to her account and was pleased that her rent check of $200 had not cleared her account. Her checkbook balance was $750.

Required:

1. Complete Heather's bank reconciliation.

2. Why is it important for individuals such as Heather and businesses to do a bank reconciliation each month?

SUGGESTED SOLUTION

1. Heather's bank reconciliation:

Heather's Books		**Bank Statement**	
October 1 cash balance	$750	October 1 cash balance	$875
Additions		Additions	
None		Deposit in transit	50
Deductions		Deductions	
Bank service charge	(25)	Outstanding check	(200)
Correct cash balance	$725	Correct cash balance	$725

2. Bank statements, whether personal or business, should be reconciled each month. This process helps ensure that a correct balance is reflected in the customer's books. Failure to reconcile a bank statement increases the chance that an error will not be discovered and may result in bad checks being written. Businesses must reconcile their bank statements for an additional reason: The correct balance that is calculated during reconciliation is recorded on the balance sheet.

Chapter Supplement

Recording Discounts and Returns

In this chapter, both **credit card discounts** and **cash discounts** have been recorded as contra-revenues. For example, if the credit card company is charging a 3 percent fee for its service and **Deckers**'s Internet credit card sales are $3,000 for January 2, Deckers will record the following:

Cash (+A)	2,910	
Credit card discount (+XR, −R, −SE)..............................	90	
Sales revenue (+R, +SE)		3,000

Assets	=	Liabilities	+	Stockholders' Equity	
Cash +2,910				Sales revenue (+R)	+3,000
				Credit card discount (+XR)	−90

Similarly, if credit sales of $1,000 are recorded with terms 2/10, n/30 ($1,000 × 0.98 = $980), and payment is made within the discount period, Deckers will record the following:

Accounts receivable (+A)...	1,000	
Sales revenue (+R, +SE)		1,000

Assets	=	Liabilities	+	Stockholders' Equity	
Accounts receivable +1,000				Sales revenue (+R)	+1,000

Cash (+A)	980	
Sales discount (+XR, −R, −SE).....................................	20	
Accounts receivable (−A)......................................		1,000

Assets	=	Liabilities	+	Stockholders' Equity	
Cash +980				Sales discount (+XR)	−20
Accounts receivable −1,000					

Sales returns and allowances should always be treated as a contra-revenue. Assume that **Fontana's Shoes** of Ithaca, New York, buys 40 pairs of sandals from Deckers for $2,000 on account. On the date of sale, Deckers makes the following journal entry:

Accounts receivable (+A)...	2,000	
Sales revenue (+R, +SE)		2,000

Assets	=	Liabilities	+	Stockholders' Equity	
Accounts receivable +2,000				Sales revenue (+R)	+2,000

Before paying for the sandals, however, Fontana's discovers that 10 pairs of sandals are not the color ordered and returns them to Deckers. On that date Deckers records:

Sales returns and allowances (+XR, −R, −SE)......................	500	
Accounts receivable (−A)......................................		500

Assets	=	Liabilities	+	Stockholders' Equity	
Accounts receivable −500				Sales returns and allowances (+XR)	−500

In addition, the related cost of goods sold entry for the 10 pairs of sandals would be reversed.

CHAPTER **TAKE-AWAYS**

6-1. Analyze the impact of credit card sales, sales discounts, and sales returns on the amounts reported as net sales.   p. 285

Both **credit card discounts** and **sales** or **cash discounts** can be recorded either as contra-revenues or as expenses. When recorded as contra-revenues, they reduce net sales. **Sales returns and allowances,** which should always be treated as a contra-revenue, also reduce net sales.

6-2. Estimate, report, and evaluate the effects of uncollectible accounts receivable (bad debts) on financial statements.   p. 289

When receivables are material, companies must employ the allowance method to account for uncollectibles. These are the steps in the process:

a. The end-of-period adjusting entry to record bad debt expense estimates.

b. Writing off specific accounts determined to be uncollectible during the period.

The adjusting entry reduces net income as well as net accounts receivable. The write-off affects neither.

6-3. Analyze and interpret the receivables turnover ratio and the effects of accounts receivable on cash flows.   p. 296

a. **Receivables turnover ratio**—This ratio measures the effectiveness of credit-granting and collection activities. It reflects how many times average trade receivables were recorded and collected during the period. Analysts and creditors watch this ratio because a sudden decline in it may mean that a company is extending payment deadlines in an attempt to prop up lagging sales or is recording sales that later will be returned by customers.

b. **Effects on cash flows**—When a net decrease in accounts receivable for the period occurs, cash collected from customers is always more than revenue, and cash flows from operations increase. When a net increase in accounts receivable occurs, cash collected from customers is always less than revenue. Thus, cash flows from operations decline.

6-4. Report, control, and safeguard cash.   p. 299

Cash is the most liquid of all assets, flowing continually into and out of a business. As a result, a number of critical control procedures, including the reconciliation of bank accounts, should be applied. Also, management of cash may be critically important to decision makers, who must have cash available to meet current needs yet must avoid excess amounts of idle cash that produce no revenue.

Closely related to recording revenue is recording the cost of what was sold. Chapter 7 will focus on transactions related to inventory and cost of goods sold. This topic is important because cost of goods sold has a major impact on a company's gross profit and net income, which are watched closely by investors, analysts, and other users of financial statements. Increasing emphasis on quality, productivity, and costs have further focused production managers' attention on cost of goods sold and inventory. Since inventory cost figures play a major role in product introduction and pricing decisions, they also are important to marketing and general managers. Finally, since inventory accounting has a major effect on many companies' tax liabilities, this is an important place to introduce the effect of taxation on management decision making and financial reporting.

KEY **RATIO**

Receivables turnover ratio measures the effectiveness of credit-granting and collection activities. It is computed as follows (see the "Key Ratio Analysis" box in the Measuring and Reporting Receivables section):

$$\text{Receivables Turnover} = \frac{\text{Net Sales}}{\text{Average Net Trade Accounts Receivable}}$$

FINDING **FINANCIAL INFORMATION**

Balance Sheet

Under Current Assets
  Accounts receivable (net of allowance for doubtful accounts)

Income Statement

Revenues
  Net sales (sales revenue less discounts and sales returns and allowances)

Expenses
  Selling expenses (including bad debt expense)

Statement of Cash Flows

Under Operating Activities (indirect method)
  Net income
  + decreases in accounts receivable (net)
  − increases in accounts receivable (net)

Notes

Under Summary of Significant Accounting Policies
  Revenue recognition policy

Under a Separate Note on Form 10-K
  Bad debt expense and write-offs of bad debts

KEY **TERMS**

Accounts Receivable (Trade Receivables or Receivables)   p. 289
Aging of Accounts Receivable Method   p. 294
Allowance for Doubtful Accounts (Allowance for Bad Debts or Allowance for Uncollectible Accounts)   p. 290
Allowance Method   p. 290

Bad Debt Expense (Doubtful Accounts Expense, Uncollectible Accounts Expense, or Provision for Uncollectible Accounts)   p. 290
Bank Reconciliation   p. 301
Bank Statement   p. 300
Cash   p. 299
Cash Equivalents   p. 299

Credit Card Discount   p. 285
Internal Controls   p. 299
Net Sales   p. 287
Notes Receivable   p. 289
Percentage of Credit Sales Method   p. 293
Sales (or Cash) Discount   p. 286
Sales Returns and Allowances   p. 287

QUESTIONS

1. Explain the difference between sales revenue and net sales.
2. What is gross profit or gross margin on sales? In your explanation, assume that net sales revenue was $100,000 and cost of goods sold was $60,000.
3. What is a credit card discount? How does it affect amounts reported on the income statement?
4. What is a sales discount? Use 1/10, n/30 in your explanation.
5. What is the distinction between sales allowances and sales discounts?
6. Differentiate accounts receivable from notes receivable.
7. Which basic accounting principle is the allowance method of accounting for bad debts designed to satisfy?
8. Using the allowance method, is bad debt expense recognized in (a) the period in which sales related to the uncollectible account are made or (b) the period in which the seller learns that the customer is unable to pay?
9. What is the effect of the write-off of bad debts (using the allowance method) on (a) net income and (b) accounts receivable, net?
10. Does an increase in the receivables turnover ratio generally indicate faster or slower collection of receivables? Explain.
11. Define cash and cash equivalents in the context of accounting. Indicate the types of items that should be included and excluded.
12. Summarize the primary characteristics of an effective internal control system for cash.

13. Why should cash-handling and cash-recording activities be separated? How is this separation accomplished?
14. What are the purposes of a bank reconciliation? What balances are reconciled?
15. Briefly explain how the total amount of cash reported on the balance sheet is computed.
16. (Chapter Supplement) Under the gross method of recording sales discounts discussed in this chapter, is the amount of sales discount taken recorded (*a*) at the time the sale is recorded or (*b*) at the time the collection of the account is recorded?

MULTIPLE-CHOICE QUESTIONS

1. Sales discounts with terms 2/10, n/30 mean:
   a. 10 percent discount for payment within 30 days.
   b. 2 percent discount for payment within 10 days, or the full amount (less returns) due within 30 days.
   c. Two-tenths of a percent discount for payment within 30 days.
   d. None of the above.
2. Gross sales total $300,000, one-half of which were credit sales. Sales returns and allowances of $15,000 apply to the credit sales, sales discounts of 2 percent were taken on all of the net credit sales, and credit card sales of $100,000 were subject to a credit card discount of 3 percent. What is the dollar amount of net sales?
   a. $227,000   c. $279,300
   b. $229,800   d. $240,000
3. A company has been successful in reducing the amount of sales returns and allowances. At the same time, a credit card company reduced the credit card discount from 3 percent to 2 percent. What effect will these changes have on the company's net sales, all other things equal?
   a. Net sales will not change.   c. Net sales will decrease.
   b. Net sales will increase.   d. Either (b) or (c).
4. When a company using the allowance method writes off a specific customer's $100,000 account receivable from the accounting system, which of the following statements are true?
   1. Total stockholders' equity remains the same.
   2. Total assets remain the same.
   3. Total expenses remain the same.
   a. 2   c. 1 and 2
   b. 1 and 3   d. 1, 2, and 3
5. You have determined that Company X estimates bad debt expense with an aging of accounts receivable schedule. Company X's estimate of uncollectible receivables resulting from the aging analysis equals $250. The beginning balance in the allowance for doubtful accounts was $220. Write-offs of bad debts during the period were $180. What amount would be recorded as bad debt expense for the current period?
   a. $180   c. $210
   b. $250   d. $220
6. Upon review of the most recent bank statement, you discover that you recently received an "insufficient funds check" from a customer. Which of the following describes the actions to be taken when preparing your bank reconciliation?

	Balance per Books	**Balance per Bank Statement**
a.	No change	Decrease
b.	Decrease	Increase
c.	Decrease	No change
d.	Increase	Decrease

7. Which of the following is **not** a step toward effective internal control over cash?
   a. Require signatures from a manager and one financial officer on all checks.
   b. Require that cash be deposited daily at the bank.
   c. Require that the person responsible for removing the cash from the register have no access to the accounting records.
   d. All of the above are steps toward effective internal control.

8. When using the allowance method, as bad debt expense is recorded,
    a. Total assets remain the same and stockholders' equity remains the same.
    b. Total assets decrease and stockholders' equity decreases.
    c. Total assets increase and stockholders' equity decreases.
    d. Total liabilities increase and stockholders' equity decreases.
9. Which of the following best describes the proper presentation of accounts receivable in the financial statements?
    a. Gross accounts receivable plus the allowance for doubtful accounts in the asset section of the balance sheet.
    b. Gross accounts receivable in the asset section of the balance sheet and the allowance for doubtful accounts in the expense section of the income statement.
    c. Gross accounts receivable less bad debt expense in the asset section of the balance sheet.
    d. Gross accounts receivable less the allowance for doubtful accounts in the asset section of the balance sheet.
10. Which of the following is **not** a component of net sales?
    a. Sales returns and allowances   c. Cost of goods sold
    b. Sales discounts   d. Credit card discounts

MINI-EXERCISES

Reporting Net Sales with Sales Discounts

Merchandise invoiced at $9,500 is sold on terms 1/10, n/30. If the buyer pays within the discount period, what amount will be reported on the income statement as net sales?

M6-1
LO6-1

Reporting Net Sales with Sales Discounts, Credit Card Discounts, and Sales Returns

Total gross sales for the period include the following:

Credit card sales (discount 3%)	$ 9,400
Sales on account (2/15, n/60)	$12,000

Sales returns related to sales on account were $650. All returns were made before payment. One-half of the remaining sales on account were paid within the discount period. The company treats all discounts and returns as contra-revenues. What amount will be reported on the income statement as net sales?

M6-2
LO6-1

Recording Bad Debts

Prepare journal entries for each transaction listed.

a. During the period, bad debts are written off in the amount of $14,500.
b. At the end of the period, bad debt expense is estimated to be $16,000.

M6-3
LO6-2

Determining Financial Statement Effects of Bad Debts

Using the following categories, indicate the effects of the following transactions. Use + for increase and − for decrease and indicate the accounts affected and the amounts.

a. At the end of the period, bad debt expense is estimated to be $15,000.
b. During the period, bad debts are written off in the amount of $9,500.

M6-4
LO6-2

Assets	=	Liabilities	+	Stockholders' Equity

M6-5
LO6-3

Determining the Effects of Credit Policy Changes on Receivables Turnover Ratio

Indicate the most likely effect of the following changes in credit policy on the receivables turnover ratio (+ for increase, − for decrease, and NE for no effect).

a. Granted credit with shorter payment deadlines.
b. Increased effectiveness of collection methods.
c. Granted credit to less creditworthy customers.

M6-6
LO6-4

Matching Reconciling Items to the Bank Reconciliation

Indicate whether the following items would be added (+) or subtracted (−) from the company's books or the bank statement during the construction of a bank reconciliation.

Reconciling Item	Company's Books	Bank Statement
a. Outstanding checks		
b. Bank service charge		
c. Deposit in transit		

M6-7

(Chapter Supplement) Recording Sales Discounts

A sale is made for $6,000; terms are 3/10, n/30. At what amount should the sale be recorded under the gross method of recording sales discounts? Give the required entry. Also give the collection entry, assuming that it is during the discount period.

EXERCISES

E6-1
LO6-1

Reporting Net Sales with Credit Sales and Sales Discounts

During the months of January and February, Hancock Corporation sold goods to three customers. The sequence of events was as follows:

Jan.	6	Sold goods for $1,500 to S. Green and billed that amount subject to terms 2/10, n/30.
	6	Sold goods to M. Munoz for $850 and billed that amount subject to terms 2/10, n/30.
	14	Collected cash due from S. Green.
Feb.	2	Collected cash due from M. Munoz.
	28	Sold goods for $500 to R. Reynolds and billed that amount subject to terms 2/10, n/45.

Required:
Assuming that Sales Discounts is treated as a contra-revenue, compute net sales for the two months ended February 28.

E6-2
LO6-1

Reporting Net Sales with Credit Sales, Sales Discounts, and Credit Card Sales

The following transactions were selected from the records of OceanView Company:

July	12	Sold merchandise to Customer R, who charged the $3,000 purchase on his Visa credit card. Visa charges OceanView a 2 percent credit card fee.
	15	Sold merchandise to Customer S at an invoice price of $9,000; terms 3/10, n/30.
	20	Sold merchandise to Customer T at an invoice price of $4,000; terms 3/10, n/30.
	23	Collected payment from Customer S from July 15 sale.
Aug.	25	Collected payment from Customer T from July 20 sale.

Required:

Assuming that Sales Discounts and Credit Card Discounts are treated as contra-revenues, compute net sales for the two months ended August 31.

Reporting Net Sales with Credit Sales, Sales Discounts, Sales Returns, and Credit Card Sales

E6-3
LO6-1

The following transactions were selected from among those completed by Cadence Retailers in November and December:

Nov.	20	Sold 20 items of merchandise to Customer B at an invoice price of $5,500 (total); terms 3/10, n/30.
	25	Sold two items of merchandise to Customer C, who charged the $400 sales price on her Visa credit card. Visa charges Cadence Retailers a 2 percent credit card fee.
	28	Sold 10 identical items of merchandise to Customer D at an invoice price of $9,000 (total); terms 3/10, n/30.
	29	Customer D returned one of the items purchased on the 28th; the item was defective, and credit was given to the customer.
Dec.	6	Customer D paid the account balance in full.
	20	Customer B paid in full for the invoice of November 20, 2013.

Required:

Assume that Sales Returns and Allowances, Sales Discounts, and Credit Card Discounts are treated as contra-revenues; compute net sales for the two months ended December 31.

Determining the Effects of Credit Sales, Sales Discounts, Credit Card Sales, and Sales Returns and Allowances on Income Statement Categories

E6-4
LO6-2

Brazen Shoe Company records Sales Returns and Allowances, Sales Discounts, and Credit Card Discounts as contra-revenues. Complete the following tabulation, indicating the effect (+ for increase, − for decrease, and NE for no effect) and amount of the effects of each transaction, including related cost of goods sold.

July	12	Sold merchandise to customer at factory store who charged the $300 purchase on her American Express card. American Express charges a 1 percent credit card fee. Cost of goods sold was $175.
July	15	Sold merchandise to Customer T at an invoice price of $5,000; terms 3/10, n/30. Cost of goods sold was $2,500.
July	20	Collected cash due from Customer T.
July	21	Before paying for the order, a customer returned shoes with an invoice price of $1,000, and cost of goods sold was $600.

Transaction	Net Sales	Cost of Goods Sold	Gross Profit
July 12			
July 15			
July 20			
July 21			

Evaluating the Annual Interest Rate Implicit in a Sales Discount with Discussion of Management Choice of Financing Strategy

E6-5
LO6-1

Clark's Landscaping bills customers subject to terms 3/10, n/50.

Required:

1. Compute the annual interest rate implicit in the sales discount. (Round to two decimal places.)
2. If his bank charges 15 percent interest, should the customer borrow from the bank so that he can take advantage of the discount? Explain your recommendation.

E6-6
LO6-1

Reporting Bad Debt Expense and Accounts Receivable

At the end of the prior year, Durney's Outdoor Outfitters reported the following information.

Accounts Receivable, Dec. 31 prior year

Accounts Receivable (Gross) (A)	$48,067
Allowance for Doubtful Accounts (XA)	8,384
Accounts Receivable (Net) (A)	$39,683

During the current year, sales on account were $304,423, collections on account were $289,850, write-offs of bad debts were $6,969, and the bad debt expense adjustment was $4,685.

Required:
Show how the amounts related to Accounts Receivable and Bad Debt Expense would be reported on the income statement and balance sheet for the current year. (**Hint:** Complete the Accounts Receivable and Allowance for Doubtful Accounts T-accounts to determine the balance sheet values.) Disregard income tax considerations.

E6-7
LO6-2

Recording Bad Debt Expense Estimates and Write-Offs Using the Percentage of Credit Sales Method

During the current year, Adams Assembly, Inc., recorded credit sales of $1,300,000. Based on prior experience, it estimates a 1 percent bad debt rate on credit sales.

Required:
Prepare journal entries for each transaction:

a. On September 29 of the current year, an account receivable for $4,000 from March of the current year was determined to be uncollectible and was written off.
b. The appropriate bad debt expense adjustment was recorded for the current year.

E6-8
LO6-2

Recording Bad Debt Expense Estimates and Write-Offs Using the Percentage of Credit Sales Method

During the current year, Sun Electronics, Incorporated, recorded credit sales of $5,000,000. Based on prior experience, it estimates a 2 percent bad debt rate on credit sales.

Required:
Prepare journal entries for each transaction:

a. On November 13 of the current year, an account receivable for $98,000 from a prior year was determined to be uncollectible and was written off.
b. At year-end, the appropriate bad debt expense adjustment was recorded for the current year.

E6-9
LO6-2

Determining Financial Statement Effects of Bad Debts Using the Percentage of Credit Sales Method

Using the following categories, indicate the effects of the transactions listed in E6-8. Use + for increase and − for decrease and indicate the accounts affected and the amounts.

Assets	=	Liabilities	+	Stockholders' Equity

Recording and Determining the Effects of Bad Debt Transactions on Income Statement Categories Using the Percentage of Credit Sales Method

E6-10
LO6-2

During the current year, Giatras Electronics recorded credit sales of $680,000. Based on prior experience, it estimates a 3.5 percent bad debt rate on credit sales.

Required:

1. Prepare journal entries for each of the following transactions.
   a. On October 28 of the current year, an account receivable for $2,800 from a prior year was determined to be uncollectible and was written off.
   b. At year-end, the appropriate bad debt expense adjustment was recorded for the current year.
2. Complete the following tabulation, indicating the amount and effect (+ for increase, − for decrease, and NE for no effect) of each transaction.

Transaction	Net Sales	Gross Profit	Income from Operations
a.			
b.			

Computing Bad Debt Expense Using Aging Analysis

E6-11
LO6-2

Lin's Dairy uses the aging approach to estimate bad debt expense. The ending balance of each account receivable is aged on the basis of three time periods as follows: (1) not yet due, $22,000; (2) up to 120 days past due, $6,500; and (3) more than 120 days past due, $2,800. Experience has shown that for each age group, the average loss rate on the amount of the receivables at year-end due to uncollectibility is (1) 3 percent, (2) 14 percent, and (3) 34 percent, respectively. At the end of the current year, the Allowance for Doubtful Accounts balance is $1,200 (credit) before the end-of-period adjusting entry is made.

Required:
What amount should be recorded as Bad Debt Expense for the current year?

Recording and Reporting a Bad Debt Estimate Using Aging Analysis

E6-12
LO6-2

Casilda Company uses the aging approach to estimate bad debt expense. The ending balance of each account receivable is aged on the basis of three time periods as follows: (1) not yet due, $50,000; (2) up to 180 days past due, $14,000; and (3) more than 180 days past due, $4,000. Experience has shown that for each age group, the average loss rate on the amount of the receivables at year-end due to uncollectibility is (1) 3 percent, (2) 12 percent, and (3) 30 percent, respectively. At December 31, the end of the current year, the Allowance for Doubtful Accounts balance is $200 (credit) before the end-of-period adjusting entry is made.

Required:

1. Prepare the appropriate bad debt expense adjusting entry for the current year.
2. Show how the various accounts related to accounts receivable should be shown on the December 31, current year, balance sheet.

Recording and Reporting a Bad Debt Estimate Using Aging Analysis

E6-13
LO6-2

Chou Company uses the aging approach to estimate bad debt expense. The ending balance of each account receivable is aged on the basis of three time periods as follows: (1) not yet due, $295,000; (2) up to 120 days past due, $55,000; and (3) more than 120 days past due, $18,000. Experience has shown that for each age group, the average loss rate on the amount of the receivables at year-end due to uncollectibility is (1) 2.5 percent, (2) 11 percent, and (3) 30 percent, respectively. At December 31, the end of the current year, the Allowance for Doubtful Accounts balance is $100 (credit) before the end-of-period adjusting entry is made.

Required:

1. Prepare the appropriate bad debt expense adjusting entry for the current year.
2. Show how the various accounts related to accounts receivable should be shown on the December 31, current year, balance sheet.

E6-14

LO6-2

Interpreting Bad Debt Disclosures

Siemens is one of the world's largest electrical engineering and electronics companies. Headquartered in Germany, the company has been in business for over 160 years and operates in 190 countries. In a recent annual report, it disclosed the following information concerning its allowance for doubtful accounts (euros in millions denoted as €):

Balance at Beginning of Period	Charged to Costs and Expenses	Amounts Written Off	Balance at End of Period
€993	€213	€(201)	€1,005

Required:

1. Record summary journal entries related to the allowance for doubtful accounts for the current year.
2. If Siemens had written off an additional €10 million of accounts receivable during the period, how would receivables, net, and net income have been affected? Explain why.

E6-15

LO6-2

Interpreting Bad Debt Disclosures

Skechers designs and markets lifestyle and performance footwear for men, women, and children. Its products are sold through department stores and specialty and Internet retailers. In a recent annual report, it disclosed the following information concerning its allowance for doubtful accounts (in thousands):

Balance at Beginning of Period	Charged to Costs and Expenses	Amounts Written Off	Balance at End of Period
$5,980	$6,284	$(6,823)	$5,441

Required:

1. Record summary journal entries related to the allowance for doubtful accounts for the current year.
2. If Skechers had written off $15 million less of accounts receivable during the period, how would receivables, net, and net income have been affected? Explain why.

E6-16

LO6-2

Inferring Bad Debt Write-Offs and Cash Collections from Customers

On its recent financial statements, Hassell Fine Foods reported the following information about net sales revenue and accounts receivable (amounts in thousands):

	Current Year	Prior Year
Accounts receivable, net of allowances of $153 and $117	$13,589	$11,338
Net revenues	60,420	51,122

According to its Form 10-K, Hassell recorded bad debt expense of $88 and there were no bad debt recoveries during the current year. (**Hint:** Refer to the summary of the effects of accounting for bad debts on the Accounts Receivable (Gross) and the Allowance for Doubtful Accounts T-accounts. Use the T-accounts to solve for the missing values.)

Required:

1. What amount of bad debts was written off during the current year?
2. Based on your answer to requirement (1), solve for cash collected from customers for the current year, assuming that all of Hassell's sales during the period were on open account.

Inferring Bad Debt Write-Offs and Cash Collections from Customers

E6-17
LO6-3

Microsoft develops, produces, and markets a wide range of computer software, including the Windows operating system. On its recent financial statements, Microsoft reported the following information about net sales revenue and accounts receivable (amounts in millions).

	Current Year	Prior Year
Accounts receivable, net of allowances of $333 and $375	$14,987	$13,014
Net revenues	69,943	62,484

According to its Form 10-K, Microsoft recorded bad debt expense of $14 and there were no bad debt recoveries during the current year. (**Hint:** Refer to the summary of the effects of accounting for bad debts on the Accounts Receivable (Gross) and the Allowance for Doubtful Accounts T-accounts. Use the T-accounts to solve for the missing values.)

Required:
1. What amount of bad debts was written off during the current year?
2. Based on your answer to requirement (1), solve for cash collected from customers for the current year, assuming that all of Microsoft's sales during the period were on open account.

Inferring Bad Debt Expense and Determining the Impact of Uncollectible Accounts on Income and Working Capital

E6-18
LO6-2

A recent annual report for **Target** contained the following information (dollars in thousands) at the end of its fiscal year:

	Year 2	Year 1
Accounts receivable	$6,357,000	$6,843,000
Less: Allowance for doubtful accounts	430,000	690,000
	$5,927,000	$6,153,000

A footnote to the financial statements disclosed that uncollectible accounts amounting to $414,000 and $854,000 were written off as bad debts during Year 2 and Year 1, respectively. Assume that the tax rate for Target was 30 percent.

Required:
1. Determine the bad debt expense for Year 2 based on the preceding facts. (**Hint:** Use the Allowance for Doubtful Accounts T-account to solve for the missing value.)
2. **Working capital** is defined as current assets minus current liabilities. How was Target's working capital affected by the write-off of $414,000 in uncollectible accounts during Year 2? What impact did the recording of bad debt expense have on working capital in Year 2?
3. How was net income affected by the $414,000 write-off during Year 2? What impact did recording bad debt expense have on net income for Year 2?

Recording, Reporting, and Evaluating a Bad Debt Estimate Using the Percentage of Credit Sales Method

E6-19
LO6-2

During the current year, Robby's Camera Shop had sales revenue of $170,000, of which $75,000 was on credit. At the start of the current year, Accounts Receivable showed a $16,000 debit balance, and the Allowance for Doubtful Accounts showed a $900 credit balance. Collections of accounts receivable during the current year amounted to $60,000.

Data during the current year follow:

a. On December 31 an Account Receivable (J. Doe) of $1,700 from a prior year was determined to be uncollectible; therefore, it was written off immediately as a bad debt.
b. On December 31, on the basis of experience, a decision was made to continue the accounting policy of basing estimated bad debt losses on 1.5 percent of credit sales for the year.

Required:
1. Give the required journal entries for the two items on December 31, the end of the accounting period.
2. Show how the amounts related to Accounts Receivable and Bad Debt Expense would be reported on the income statement and balance sheet for the current year. Disregard income tax considerations.
3. On the basis of the data available, does the 1.5 percent rate appear to be reasonable? Explain.

E6-20

LO6-2

Recording, Reporting, and Evaluating a Bad Debt Estimate Using the Percentage of Credit Sales Method

During the current year, Bob's Ceramics Shop had sales revenue of $60,000, of which $25,000 was on credit. At the start of the current year, Accounts Receivable showed a $3,500 debit balance, and the Allowance for Doubtful Accounts showed a $300 credit balance. Collections of accounts receivable during the current year amounted to $18,000.

Data during the current year follow:

a. On December 31, an Account Receivable (Toby's Gift Shop) of $550 from a prior year was determined to be uncollectible; therefore, it was written off immediately as a bad debt.
b. On December 31, on the basis of experience, a decision was made to continue the accounting policy of basing estimated bad debt losses on 2 percent of credit sales for the year.

Required:
1. Give the required journal entries for the two items on December 31, the end of the accounting period.
2. Show how the amounts related to Accounts Receivable and Bad Debt Expense would be reported on the income statement and balance sheet for the current year. Disregard income tax considerations.
3. On the basis of the data available, does the 2 percent rate appear to be reasonable? Explain.

E6-21

LO6-2

Recording, Reporting, and Evaluating a Bad Debt Estimate Using Aging Analysis

Brown Cow Dairy uses the aging approach to estimate bad debt expense. The ending balance of each account receivable is aged on the basis of three time periods as follows: (1) not yet due, $14,000; (2) up to 120 days past due, $4,500; and (3) more than 120 days past due, $2,500. Experience has shown that for each age group, the average loss rate on the amount of the receivables at year-end due to uncollectibility is (1) 2 percent, (2) 12 percent, and (3) 30 percent, respectively. At December 31 (end of the current year), the Allowance for Doubtful Accounts balance is $800 (credit) before the end-of-period adjusting entry is made.

Data during the current year follow:

a. During December, an Account Receivable (Patty's Bake Shop) of $750 from a prior sale was determined to be uncollectible; therefore, it was written off immediately as a bad debt.
b. On December 31, the appropriate adjusting entry for the year was recorded.

Required:
1. Give the required journal entries for the two items listed above.
2. Show how the amounts related to Accounts Receivable and Bad Debt Expense would be reported on the income statement and balance sheet for the current year. Disregard income tax considerations.
3. On the basis of the data available, does the estimate resulting from the aging analysis appear to be reasonable? Explain.

E6-22

LO6-3

Computing and Interpreting the Receivables Turnover Ratio

A recent annual report for **FedEx** contained the following data:

	(dollars in thousands)	
	Current Year	**Previous Year**
Accounts receivable	$ 4,763,000	$4,329,000
Less: Allowance for doubtful accounts	182,000	166,000
Net accounts receivable	$ 4,581,000	$4,163,000
Net sales (assume all on credit)	$39,304,000	

Required:
1. Determine the receivables turnover ratio and average days sales in receivables for the current year.
2. Explain the meaning of each number.

Computing and Interpreting the Receivables Turnover Ratio

A recent annual report for **Dell, Inc.**, contained the following data:

	(dollars in thousands)	
	Current Year	**Previous Year**
Accounts receivable	$ 6,539,000	$6,589,000
Less: Allowance for doubtful accounts	63,000	96,000
Net accounts receivable	$ 6,476,000	$6,493,000
Net sales (assume all on credit)	$62,071,000	

E6-23
LO6-3

Required:
1. Determine the receivables turnover ratio and average days sales in receivables for the current year.
2. Explain the meaning of each number.

Interpreting the Effects of Sales Declines and Changes in Receivables on Cash Flow from Operations

E6-24
LO6-3

Stride Rite Corporation manufactures and markets shoes under the brand names Stride Rite, Keds, and Sperry Top-Sider. Three recent years produced a combination of declining sales revenue and net income culminating in a net loss of $8,430,000. Each year, however, Stride Rite was able to report positive cash flows from operations. Contributing to that positive cash flow was the change in accounts receivable. The current and prior year balance sheets reported the following:

	(dollars in thousands)	
	Current Year	**Previous Year**
Accounts and notes receivable, less allowances	$48,066	$63,403

Required:
1. On the current year's cash flow statement (indirect method), how would the change in accounts receivable affect cash flow from operations? Explain why it would have this effect.
2. Explain how declining sales revenue often leads to (*a*) declining accounts receivable and (*b*) cash collections from customers being higher than sales revenue.

Preparing Bank Reconciliation, Entries, and Reporting Cash

E6-25
LO6-4

Bentley Company's June 30 bank statement and June ledger accounts for cash are summarized below:

BANK STATEMENT			
	Checks	**Deposits**	**Balance**
Balance, June 1			$ 6,500
Deposits during June		$16,200	22,700
Checks cleared during June	$16,600		6,100
Bank service charges	40		6,060
Balance, June 30			6,060

Cash (A)				
June 1	Balance	6,500	June	Checks written	19,000
June	Deposits	18,100			

Required:

1. Reconcile the bank account. A comparison of the checks written with the checks that have cleared the bank shows outstanding checks of $2,400. A deposit of $1,900 is in transit at the end of June.
2. Give any journal entries that should be made as a result of the bank reconciliation.
3. What is the balance in the Cash account after the reconciliation entries?
4. What is the total amount of cash that should be reported on the balance sheet at June 30?

E6-26

LO6-4

Preparing Bank Reconciliation, Entries, and Reporting Cash

The September 30 bank statement for Bennett Company and the September ledger accounts for cash are summarized here:

BANK STATEMENT			
	Checks	**Deposits**	**Balance**
Balance, September 1			$ 6,500
Deposits recorded during September		$26,900	33,400
Checks cleared during September	$27,400		6,000
NSF checks—Betty Brown	170		5,830
Bank service charges	60		5,770
Balance, September 30			5,770

Cash (A)				
Sept. 1	Balance	6,500	Sept. Checks written	28,900
Sept.	Deposits	28,100		

No outstanding checks and no deposits in transit were carried over from August; however, there are deposits in transit and checks outstanding at the end of September.

Required:

1. Reconcile the bank account.
2. Give any journal entries that should be made as the result of the bank reconciliation.
3. What should the balance in the Cash account be after the reconciliation entries?
4. What total amount of cash should the company report on the September 30 balance sheet?

E6-27

(Chapter Supplement) Recording Credit Sales, Sales Discounts, Sales Returns, and Credit Card Sales

The following transactions were selected from among those completed by Hailey Retailers in the current year:

Nov.	20	Sold two items of merchandise to Customer B, who charged the $450 sales price on her Visa credit card. Visa charges Hailey a 2 percent credit card fee.
	25	Sold 14 items of merchandise to Customer C at an invoice price of $2,800 (total); terms 2/10, n/30.
	28	Sold 12 identical items of merchandise to Customer D at an invoice price of $7,200 (total); terms 2/10, n/30.
	30	Customer D returned one of the items purchased on the 28th; the item was defective, and credit was given to the customer.
Dec.	6	Customer D paid the account balance in full.
	30	Customer C paid in full for the invoice of November 25.

Required:

Give the appropriate journal entry for each of these transactions, assuming the company records sales revenue under the gross method. Do not record cost of goods sold. Compute Net Sales.

 **PROBLEMS**

Reporting Net Sales and Expenses with Discounts, Returns, and Bad Debts (AP6-1)

P6-1
LO6-1, 6-2

The following data were selected from the records of Sykes Company for the year ended December 31, current year.

Balances January 1, current year	
Accounts receivable (various customers)	$120,000
Allowance for doubtful accounts	8,000

In the following order, except for cash sales, the company sold merchandise and made collections on credit terms 2/10, n/30 (assume a unit sales price of $500 in all transactions and use the gross method to record sales revenue).

Transactions during 2014

a. Sold merchandise for cash, $235,000.
b. Sold merchandise to R. Smith; invoice price, $11,500.
c. Sold merchandise to K. Miller; invoice price, $26,500.
d. Two days after purchase date, R. Smith returned one of the units purchased in (b) and received account credit.
e. Sold merchandise to B. Sears; invoice price, $24,000.
f. R. Smith paid his account in full within the discount period.
g. Collected $98,000 cash from customer sales on credit in prior year, all within the discount periods.
h. K. Miller paid the invoice in (c) within the discount period.
i. Sold merchandise to R. Roy; invoice price, $19,000.
j. Three days after paying the account in full, K. Miller returned seven defective units and received a cash refund.
k. After the discount period, collected $6,000 cash on an account receivable on sales in a prior year.
l. Wrote off a prior year account of $3,000 after deciding that the amount would never be collected.
m. The estimated bad debt rate used by the company was 1.5 percent of credit sales net of returns.

Required:

1. Using the following categories, indicate the effect of each listed transaction, including the write-off of the uncollectible account and the adjusting entry for estimated bad debts (ignore cost of goods sold). Indicate the sign and amount of the effect or use "NE" for "no effect." The first transaction is used as an example.

	Sales Revenue	Sales Discounts (taken)	Sales Returns and Allowances	Bad Debt Expense
(a)	+235,000	NE	NE	NE

2. Show how the accounts related to the preceding sale and collection activities should be reported on the 2014 income statement. (Treat sales discounts as a contra-revenue.)

Recording Bad Debts and Interpreting Disclosure of Allowance for Doubtful Accounts (AP6-2)

P6-2
LO6-2

Peet's Coffee & Tea, Inc., is a specialty coffee roaster and marketer of branded fresh-roasted whole bean coffee. It recently disclosed the following information concerning the Allowance for Doubtful Accounts on its Form 10-K Annual Report submitted to the Securities and Exchange Commission.

A summary of the Allowance for Doubtful Accounts is as follows (dollars in thousands):

Allowance for Doubtful Accounts	Balance at Beginning of Period	Additions (Charges) to Expense	Write-Offs	Balance at End of Period
Year 1	$128	$?	$ 0	$132
Year 2	132	187	?	283
Year 3	283	42	201	124

Required:

1. Record summary journal entries related to bad debts for Year 3.
2. Supply the missing dollar amounts noted by (?) for Year 1 and Year 2.

P6-3

LO6-2

Determining Bad Debt Expense Based on Aging Analysis (AP6-3)

Blue Skies Equipment Company uses the aging approach to estimate bad debt expense at the end of each accounting year. Credit sales occur frequently on terms n/60. The balance of each account receivable is aged on the basis of three time periods as follows: (1) not yet due, (2) up to one year past due, and (3) more than one year past due. Experience has shown that for each age group, the average loss rate on the amount of the receivable at year-end due to uncollectibility is (a) 3 percent, (b) 9 percent, and (c) 28 percent, respectively.

At December 31, 2014 (end of the current accounting year), the Accounts Receivable balance was $48,700, and the Allowance for Doubtful Accounts balance was $920 (credit). In determining which accounts have been paid, the company applies collections to the oldest sales first. To simplify, only five customer accounts are used; the details of each on December 31, 2014, follow:

B. Brown—Account Receivable				
Date	Explanation	Debit	Credit	Balance
3/11/2013	Sale	13,000		13,000
6/30/2013	Collection		3,000	10,000
1/31/2014	Collection		3,800	6,200
D. Donalds—Account Receivable				
2/28/2014	Sale	21,000		21,000
4/15/2014	Collection		8,000	13,000
11/30/2014	Collection		6,000	7,000
N. Napier—Account Receivable				
11/30/2014	Sale	8,000		8,000
12/15/2014	Collection		1,000	7,000
S. Strothers—Account Receivable				
3/2/2012	Sale	4,000		4,000
4/15/2012	Collection		4,000	–0–
9/1/2013	Sale	9,000		9,000
10/15/2013	Collection		4,500	4,500
2/1/2014	Sale	21,000		25,500
3/1/2014	Collection		5,000	20,500
12/31/2014	Sale	4,000		24,500
T. Thomas—Account Receivable				
12/30/2014	Sale	4,000		4,000

Required:

1. Compute the total accounts receivable in each age category.
2. Compute the estimated uncollectible amount for each age category and in total.

3. Give the adjusting entry for bad debt expense at December 31, 2014.
4. Show how the amounts related to accounts receivable should be presented on the 2014 income statement and balance sheet.

Preparing an Income Statement and Computing the Receivables Turnover Ratio with Discounts, Returns, and Bad Debts (AP6-4)

P6-4

LO6-1, 6-2, 6-3

Tungsten Company, Inc., sells heavy construction equipment. There are 10,000 shares of capital stock outstanding. The annual fiscal period ends on December 31. The following condensed trial balance was taken from the general ledger on December 31, current year:

Account Titles	Debit	Credit
Cash	$ 33,600	
Accounts receivable (net)	14,400	
Inventory, ending	52,000	
Operational assets	40,000	
Accumulated depreciation		$ 16,800
Liabilities		24,000
Capital stock		72,000
Retained earnings, January 1, current year:		9,280
Sales revenue		147,100
Sales returns and allowances	5,600	
Cost of goods sold	78,400	
Selling expense	14,100	
Administrative expense	15,400	
Bad debt expense	1,600	
Sales discounts	6,400	
Income tax expense	7,680	
Totals	$269,180	$269,180

Required:

1. Beginning with the amount for net sales, prepare an income statement (showing both gross profit and income from operations). Treat sales discounts and sales returns and allowances as a contra-revenue.
2. The beginning balance in Accounts Receivable (net) was $16,000. Compute the receivables turnover ratio and explain its meaning.

Preparing a Bank Reconciliation and Related Journal Entries

P6-5

LO6-4

The bookkeeper at Jefferson Company has not reconciled the bank statement with the Cash account, saying, "I don't have time." You have been asked to prepare a reconciliation and review the procedures with the bookkeeper.

The April 30, current year, bank statement and the April ledger accounts for cash showed the following (summarized):

BANK STATEMENT			
	Checks	Deposits	Balance
Balance, April 1, current year			$31,000
Deposits during April		$37,100	68,100
Interest collected		1,180	69,280
Checks cleared during April	$43,000		26,280
NSF check—A. B. Wright	160		26,120
Bank service charges	50		26,070
Balance, April 30, current year			26,070

Cash (A)				
Apr. 1 Balance	23,500	Apr. Checks written	41,100
Apr. Deposits	41,500		

A comparison of checks written before and during April with the checks cleared through the bank showed outstanding checks at the end of April of $5,600 (including $3,700 written before and $1,900 written during April). No deposits in transit were carried over from March, but a deposit was in transit at the end of April.

Required:

1. Prepare a detailed bank reconciliation for April.
2. Give any required journal entries as a result of the reconciliation. Why are they necessary?
3. What was the balance in the Cash account in the ledger on May 1, current year?
4. What total amount of cash should be reported on the balance sheet at the end of April?

P6-6

LO6-4

Computing Outstanding Checks and Deposits in Transit and Preparing a Bank Reconciliation and Journal Entries (AP6-5)

The August current year bank statement for Allison Company and the August current year ledger account for cash follow:

	BANK STATEMENT		
Date	**Checks and EFTs**	**Deposits**	**Balance**
Aug. 1			$17,510
2	$ 320		17,190
3		$11,700	28,890
4	430		28,460
5	270		28,190
9	880		27,310
10	250 EFT		27,060
15		4,000	31,060
21	350		30,710
24	20,400		10,310
25		6,500	16,810
30	850 EFT		15,960
30		2,350*	18,310
31	120†		18,190

*$2,350 interest collected.
†Bank service charge.

Cash (A)				
Aug. 1 Balance	16,490	Checks written and electronic funds transfers		
Deposits		Aug. 2	EFT 250	
Aug. 2	11,700	4	880	
12	4,000	15	280	
24	6,500	17	510	
31	5,200	18	EFT 850	
		20	350	
		23	20,400	

Outstanding checks at the end of July were for $270, $430, and $320. No deposits were in transit at the end of July.

Required:

1. Compute the deposits in transit at the end of August by comparing the deposits on the bank statement to the deposits listed on the cash ledger account.
2. Compute the outstanding checks at the end of August by comparing the checks listed on the bank statement with those on the cash ledger account and the list of outstanding checks at the end of July.
3. Prepare a bank reconciliation for August.

4. Give any journal entries that the company should make as a result of the bank reconciliation. Why are they necessary?

5. What total amount of cash should be reported on the August 31, current year, balance sheet?

(Chapter Supplement) Recording Sales, Returns, and Bad Debts **P6-7**

Use the data presented in P6-1, which were selected from the records of Sykes Company for the year ended December 31, current year.

Required:

1. Give the journal entries for these transactions, including the write-off of the uncollectible account and the adjusting entry for estimated bad debts. Do not record cost of goods sold. Show computations for each entry.

2. Show how the accounts related to the preceding sale and collection activities should be reported on the current year income statement. (Treat sales discounts as a contra-revenue.)

ALTERNATE **PROBLEMS**

Reporting Net Sales and Expenses with Discounts, Returns, and Bad Debts (P6-1)

AP6-1
LO6-1, 6-2

The following data were selected from the records of Sharkim Company for the year ended December 31, current year.

Balances January 1, current year:	
Accounts receivable (various customers)	$116,000
Allowance for doubtful accounts	5,200

In the following order, except for cash sales, the company sold merchandise and made collections on credit terms 2/10, n/30 (assume a unit sales price of $500 in all transactions and use the gross method to record sales revenue).

Transactions during 2014

a. Sold merchandise for cash, $227,000.
b. Sold merchandise to Karen Corp.; invoice price, $12,000.
c. Sold merchandise to White Company; invoice price, $23,500.
d. Karen paid the invoice in (b) within the discount period.
e. Sold merchandise to Cavendish Inc.; invoice price, $26,000.
f. Two days after paying the account in full, Karen returned one defective unit and received a cash refund.
g. Collected $88,200 cash from customer sales on credit in prior year, all within the discount periods.
h. Three days after purchase date, White returned seven of the units purchased in (c) and received account credit.
i. White paid its account in full within the discount period.
j. Sold merchandise to Delta Corporation; invoice price, $18,500.
k. Cavendish (e) paid its account in full after the discount period.
l. Wrote off a prior year account of $2,400 after deciding that the amount would never be collected.
m. The estimated bad debt rate used by the company was 4 percent of credit sales net of returns.

Required:

1. Using the following categories, indicate the effect of each listed transaction, including the write-off of the uncollectible account and the adjusting entry for estimated bad debts (ignore cost of goods sold). Indicate the sign and amount of the effect or use "NE" to indicate "no effect." The first transaction is used as an example.

	Sales Revenue	Sales Discounts (taken)	Sales Returns and Allowances	Bad Debt Expense
(a)	+227,000	NE	NE	NE

2. Show how the accounts related to the preceding sale and collection activities should be reported on the 2014 income statement. (Treat sales discounts as a contra-revenue.)

AP6-2

LO6-2

Recording Bad Debts and Interpreting Disclosure of Allowance for Doubtful Accounts (P6-2)

Under various registered brand names, **Saucony, Inc**., and its subsidiaries develop, manufacture, and market bicycles and component parts, athletic apparel, and athletic shoes. It recently disclosed the following information concerning the allowance for doubtful accounts on its Form 10-K Annual Report submitted to the Securities and Exchange Commission.

Schedule II				
Valuation and Qualifying Accounts (dollars in thousands)				
Allowances for Doubtful Accounts	**Balance at Beginning of Year**	**Additions Charged to Costs and Expenses**	**Deductions from Reserve**	**Balance at End of Year**
Year 3	$1,108	$6,014	$5,941	(?)
Year 2	2,406	(?)	5,751	$1,108
Year 1	2,457	4,752	(?)	2,406

Required:
1. Record summary journal entries related to bad debts for Year 3.
2. Supply the missing dollar amounts noted by (?) for Year 1, Year 2, and Year 3.

AP6-3

LO6-2

Determining Bad Debt Expense Based on Aging Analysis (P6-3)

Briggs & Stratton Engines Inc. uses the aging approach to estimate bad debt expense at the end of each accounting year. Credit sales occur frequently on terms n/45. The balance of each account receivable is aged on the basis of four time periods as follows: (1) not yet due, (2) up to 6 months past due, (3) 6 to 12 months past due, and (4) more than one year past due. Experience has shown that for each age group, the average loss rate on the amount of the receivable at year-end due to uncollectibility is (*a*) 1 percent, (*b*) 5 percent, (*c*) 20 percent, and (*d*) 50 percent, respectively.

At December 31, 2014 (end of the current accounting year), the Accounts Receivable balance was $39,500, and the Allowance for Doubtful Accounts balance was $1,550 (credit). In determining which accounts have been paid, the company applies collections to the oldest sales first. To simplify, only five customer accounts are used; the details of each on December 31, 2014, follow:

Date	Explanation	Debit	Credit	Balance
R. Devens—Account Receivable				
3/13/2014	Sale	19,000		19,000
5/12/2014	Collection		10,000	9,000
9/30/2014	Collection		7,000	2,000
C. Howard—Account Receivable				
11/01/2013	Sale	31,000		31,000
06/01/2014	Collection		20,000	11,000
12/01/2014	Collection		5,000	6,000
D. McClain—Account Receivable				
10/31/2014	Sale	12,000		12,000
12/10/2014	Collection		8,000	4,000

(continued)

T. Skibinski—Account Receivable				
05/02/2014	Sale	15,000		15,000
06/01/2014	Sale	10,000		25,000
06/15/2014	Collection		15,000	10,000
07/15/2014	Collection		10,000	0
10/01/2014	Sale	26,000		26,000
11/15/2014	Collection		16,000	10,000
12/15/2014	Sale	4,500		14,500
H. Wu—Account Receivable				
12/30/2014	Sale	13,000		13,000

Required:

1. Compute the total accounts receivable in each age category.
2. Compute the estimated uncollectible amount for each age category and in total.
3. Give the adjusting entry for bad debt expense at December 31, 2014.
4. Show how the amounts related to accounts receivable should be presented on the 2014 income statement and balance sheet.

Preparing an Income Statement and Computing the Receivables Turnover Ratio with Discounts, Returns, and Bad Debts (P6-4)

AP6-4
LO6-1, 6-2, 6-3

Perry Corporation is a local grocery store organized seven years ago as a corporation. At that time, a total of 10,000 shares of common stock were issued to the three organizers. The store is in an excellent location, and sales have increased each year. At the end of the current year, the bookkeeper prepared the following statement (assume that all amounts are correct; note the incorrect terminology and format):

PERRY CORPORATION Profit and Loss December 31, current year		
	Debit	**Credit**
Sales		$184,000
Cost of goods sold	$ 98,000	
Sales returns and allowances	9,000	
Selling expense	17,000	
Administrative and general expense	18,000	
Bad debt expense	2,000	
Sales discounts	8,000	
Income tax expense	10,900	
Net profit	21,100	
Totals	$184,000	$184,000

Required:

1. Beginning with the amount of net sales, prepare an income statement (showing both gross profit and income from operations). Treat sales discounts as a contra-revenue.
2. The beginning and ending balances in accounts receivable were $16,000 and $18,000, respectively. Compute the receivables turnover ratio and explain its meaning.

Computing Outstanding Checks and Deposits in Transit and Preparing a Bank Reconciliation and Journal Entries (P6-6)

AP6-5
LO6-4

The December 31, current year, bank statement for Rivas Company and the December current year ledger accounts for cash follow.

BANK STATEMENT			
Date	Checks and EFTs	Deposits	Balance
Dec. 1			$48,000
2	$400; 300	$17,000	64,300
4	7,000; 90		57,210
6	120; 180; 1,600 EFT		55,310
11	500; 1,200; 70	28,000	81,540
13	480; 700; 1,900		78,460
17	12,000; 8,000 EFT		58,460
23	60; 23,500	36,000	70,900
26	900; 2,650		67,350
28	2,200; 5,200		59,950
30	17,000; 1,890; 300*	19,000	59,760
31	1,650; 1,350; 150†	5,250‡	61,860

*NSF check, J. Left, a customer.
†Bank service charge.
‡Interest collected.

Cash (A)						
Dec. 1	Balance	64,100	Checks written during December:			
Deposits			60	5,000	2,650	
Dec. 11		28,000	17,000	5,200	1,650	
23		36,000	700	1,890	2,200	
30		19,000	3,500	EFT 1,600	7,000	
31		13,000	1,350	120	300	
			180	90	480	
			12,000	23,500	EFT 8,000	
			70	500	1,900	
			900	1,200		

The November current year bank reconciliation showed the following: correct cash balance at November 30, $64,100; deposits in transit on November 30, $17,000; and outstanding checks on November 30, $400 + $500 = $900.

Required:
1. Compute the deposits in transit December 31, current year, by comparing the deposits on the bank statement to the deposits listed on the cash ledger account and the list of deposits in transit at the end of November.
2. Compute the outstanding checks at December 31, current year, by comparing the checks listed on the bank statement with those on the cash ledger account and the list of outstanding checks at the end of November.
3. Prepare a bank reconciliation at December 31, current year.
4. Give any journal entries that should be made as a result of the bank reconciliation made by the company. Why are they necessary?
5. What total amount of cash should be reported on the December 31, current year, balance sheet?

CONTINUING **PROBLEM**    connect

CON6-1   **Computing Net Sales and Recording Bad Debt Estimates and Write-offs**

Pool Corporation, Inc., is the world's largest wholesale distributor of swimming pool supplies and equipment.

Required:
1. Pool Corp. reported the following information related to bad debt estimates and write-offs for the current year. Prepare journal entries for the bad debt expense adjustment and total write-offs of bad debts for the current year.

Allowance for doubtful accounts:

Balance at beginning of year	$ 7,102
Bad debt expense	2,958
Write-offs	(4,160)
Balance at end of year	$ 5,900

2. Pool Corp. reduces net sales by the amount of sales returns and allowances, cash discounts, and credit card fees. Bad debt expense is recorded as part of selling and administrative expense. Assume that gross sales revenue for the month was $137,256, bad debt expense was $146, sales discounts were $1,134, sales returns were $856, and credit card fees were $1,849. What amount would Pool Corp. report for net sales for the month?

 connect   CASES **AND PROJECTS**

Annual Report Cases

Finding Financial Information

Refer to the financial statements of **American Eagle Outfitters** given in Appendix B at the end of this book.

Required:
1. What does the company include in its category of cash and cash equivalents? How close do you think the disclosed amount is to actual fair market value? (**Hint:** The notes may be helpful in answering this question.)
2. What expenses does American Eagle Outfitters subtract from net sales in the computation of gross profit? How does this differ from **Deckers**'s practice and how might it affect the manner in which you interpret the gross profit?
3. Compute American Eagle Outfitters's receivables turnover ratio for the current year. What characteristics of its business might cause it to be so high?

CP6-1
LO6-1, 6-2, 6-4

Finding Financial Information

Refer to the financial statements of **Urban Outfitters** given in Appendix C at the end of this book.

Required:
1. How much cash and cash equivalents does the company report at the end of the current year?
2. What was the change in accounts receivable and how did it affect net cash provided by operating activities for the current year?
3. Which types of customers account for most of the company's accounts receivable? Did bad debts expense increase or decrease between 2013 and 2014? How did you know?
4. Where does the company disclose its revenue recognition policy? When does the company record revenues for the "sale" of gift cards?

CP6-2
LO6-2, 6-4

Comparing Companies within an Industry

Refer to the financial statements of **American Eagle Outfitters** (Appendix B) and **Urban Outfitters** (Appendix C) and the Industry Ratio Report (Appendix D) at the end of this book.

Required:
1. Compute the receivables turnover ratio for both companies for the most recent year.
2. What do you think explains the difference in the ratios? Consider to whom the amounts are owed.
3. Compare the receivables turnover ratio for each company for the most recent reporting year to the industry average. Are these two companies doing better or worse than the industry average?

CP6-3
LO6-2, 6-4

Critical Thinking Cases

CP6-4

Evaluating an Ethical Dilemma: Management Incentives, Revenue Recognition, and Sales with the Right of Return

Symbol Technologies, Inc., was a fast-growing maker of bar-code scanners. According to the federal charges, Tomo Razmilovic, the CEO at Symbol, was obsessed with meeting the stock market's expectation for continued growth. His executive team responded by improperly recording revenue and allowances for returns, as well as a variety of other tricks, to overstate revenues by $230 million and pretax earnings by $530 million. What makes this fraud nearly unique is that virtually the whole senior management team is charged with participating in the six-year fraud. Five have pleaded guilty, another eight are under indictment, and the former CEO has fled the country to avoid prosecution. The exact nature of the fraud is described in the following excerpt dealing with the guilty plea by the former vice president for finance:

Ex-Official at Symbol Pleads Guilty

A former finance executive at Symbol Technologies Inc. pleaded guilty to participating in a vast accounting fraud that inflated revenue at the maker of bar-code scanners by roughly 10%, or $100 million a year, from 1999 through 2001.

. . .

The criminal information and civil complaint filed yesterday accused Mr. Asti and other high-level executives of stuffing the firm's distribution channel with phony orders at the end of each quarter to meet revenue and earnings targets. Under generally accepted accounting practices, revenue can be booked only when the products are shipped to a customer. Symbol's customers include delivery services and grocery stores.

Investigators alleged that Mr. Asti and others engaged in "candy" deals, where Symbol bribed resellers with a 1% fee to "buy" products from a distributor at the end of a quarter, which Symbol would later buy back. Symbol then allegedly would convince the distributor to order more products from the company to satisfy the newly created inventory void.

The SEC said the inflated revenue figures helped boost Symbol's stock price, as well as enriching Mr. Asti. He allegedly sold thousands of shares of Symbol stock, which he received from exercising stock options, when the stock was trading at inflated levels.

Source: Kara Scannell, *The Wall Street Journal,* March 26, 2003. Copyright © 2003 by Dow Jones & Co. Used with permission.

Required:

1. What facts, if any, presented in the article suggest that Symbol violated the revenue recognition principle?
2. Assuming that Symbol did recognize revenue when goods were shipped, how could it have properly accounted for the fact that customers had a right to cancel the contracts (make an analogy with accounting for bad debts)?
3. What do you think may have motivated management to falsify the statements? Why was management concerned with reporting continued growth in net income?
4. Explain who was hurt by management's unethical conduct.
5. Assume that you are the auditor for other firms. After reading about the fraud, what types of transactions would you pay special attention to in the audit of your clients in this industry? What ratio might provide warnings about possible channel stuffing?

CP6-5

LO6-4

Evaluating Internal Control

Cripple Creek Company has one trusted employee who, as the owner said, "handles all of the bookkeeping and paperwork for the company." This employee is responsible for counting, verifying, and recording cash receipts and payments; making the weekly bank deposit; preparing checks for major expenditures (signed by the owner); making small expenditures from the cash register for daily expenses; and collecting accounts receivable. The owners asked the local bank for a $20,000 loan. The bank asked that an audit be performed covering the year just ended. The independent auditor (a local CPA), in a private conference with the owner, presented some evidence of the following activities of the trusted employee during the past year.

a. Cash sales sometimes were not entered in the cash register, and the trusted employee pocketed approximately $50 per month.

b. Cash taken from the cash register (and pocketed by the trusted employee) was replaced with expense memos with fictitious signatures (approximately $12 per day).

c. A $300 collection on an account receivable of a valued out-of-town customer was pocketed by the trusted employee and was covered by making a $300 entry as a debit to Sales Returns and a credit to Accounts Receivable.

d. An $800 collection on an account receivable from a local customer was pocketed by the trusted employee and was covered by making an $800 entry as a debit to Allowance for Doubtful Accounts and a credit to Accounts Receivable.

Required:
1. What was the approximate amount stolen during the past year?
2. What would be your recommendations to the owner?

Financial Reporting and Analysis Team Project

Team Project: Analyzing Revenues and Receivables

CP6-6
LO6-2, 6-3

As a team, select an industry to analyze. Yahoo Finance provides lists of industries at **biz.yahoo.com/p/ industries.html**. Click on an industry for a list of companies in that industry. Alternatively, go to Google Finance at **www.google.com/finance** and search for a company you are interested in. You will be presented with a list including that company and its competitors. Each team member should acquire the annual report or 10-K for one publicly traded company in the industry, with each member selecting a different company (the SEC EDGAR service at **www.sec.gov** and the company's investor relations website itself are good sources).

Required:
On an individual basis, each team member should write a short report answering the following questions about the selected company. Discuss any patterns across the companies that you as a team observe. Then, as a team, write a short report comparing and contrasting your companies.
1. If your company lists receivables in its balance sheet, what percentage of total assets does receivables represent for each of the last three years? If your company does not list receivables, discuss why this is so.
2. Ratio analysis
   a. What does the receivables turnover ratio measure in general?
   b. If your company lists receivables, compute the ratio for the last three years.
   c. What do your results suggest about the company?
   d. If available, find the industry ratio for the most recent year, compare it to your results, and discuss why you believe your company differs or is similar to the industry ratio.
3. If your company lists receivables, use the 10-K to determine what additional disclosure is available concerning the allowance for doubtful accounts. (Usually the information is in a separate schedule, Item 15.)
   a. What is bad debt expense as a percentage of sales for the last three years?
4. What is the effect of the change in receivables on cash flows from operating activities for the most recent year (that is, did the change increase or decrease operating cash flows)? Explain your answer.

Reporting and Interpreting Cost of Goods Sold and Inventory

The **Harley-Davidson** eagle trademark was once known best as a popular request in tattoo parlors. Now, Harley-Davidson dominates the heavyweight motorcycle market in North America with a 53.3 percent market share. Harley is also a market leader in Canada, Japan, and Australia and is a growing presence in Europe.

But the heavyweight king took a major hit from the worldwide economic downturn that started in 2008. Harley responded with an aggressive plan to enhance profitability through continuous improvement in manufacturing, product development, and business operations. These plans are aimed at shortening product development lead times and implementing flexible manufacturing at its Wisconsin, Missouri, and Pennsylvania facilities, which reduce costs and allow the company to better respond to the needs of the dealer network.

Controlling inventory quality, quantities, and cost are key to maintaining gross profit margin. Introducing new products to stay ahead of major competitors **Honda** and **BMW** and providing a premium dealer experience to all of Harley's customers will also increase gross margin. Finally, selecting appropriate accounting methods for inventory can have a dramatic effect on the amount Harley-Davidson pays in income taxes. Harley produced strong financial

Learning Objectives

After studying this chapter, you should be able to:

7-1 Apply the cost principle to identify the amounts that should be included in inventory and the expense matching principle to determine cost of goods sold for typical retailers, wholesalers, and manufacturers.

7-2 Report inventory and cost of goods sold using the four inventory costing methods.

7-3 Decide when the use of different inventory costing methods is beneficial to a company.

7-4 Report inventory at the lower of cost or market (LCM).

7-5 Evaluate inventory management using the inventory turnover ratio.

7-6 Compare companies that use different inventory costing methods.

7-7 Understand methods for controlling inventory, analyze the effects of inventory errors on financial statements, and analyze the effects of inventory on cash flows.

Gary Gardiner/Bloomberg via Getty Images

Harley-Davidson, Inc.

BUILDING A LEGEND INTO A
WORLD-CLASS MANUFACTURER

www.harley-davidson.com

results in 2014, but continuous improvement in all of these areas will be necessary for the Harley-Davidson eagle to continue its rise.

UNDERSTANDING THE BUSINESS

The cost and quality of inventory are concerns faced by all modern manufacturers and merchandisers and so we turn our attention to **cost of goods sold** (cost of sales, cost of products sold) on the income statement and **inventory** on the balance sheet. Exhibit 7.1 presents the relevant excerpts from **Harley-Davidson**'s financial statements that include these accounts. Note that Cost of Goods Sold is subtracted from Net Sales to produce Gross Profit on its income statement. On the balance sheet, Inventory is a current asset; it is reported below Cash, Marketable Securities, and Accounts and Finance Receivables because it is less liquid than those assets.

The primary goals of inventory management are to have sufficient quantities of high-quality inventory available to serve customers' needs while minimizing the costs of carrying inventory (production, storage, obsolescence, and financing). Low quality leads to customer dissatisfaction, returns, and a decline in future sales. Also, purchasing or producing too few units of a hot-selling item causes stock-outs, which mean lost sales revenue and decreases in customer satisfaction. Conversely, purchasing too many units of a slow-selling item increases storage costs as well as interest costs on short-term borrowings used to finance the purchases. It may even lead to losses if the merchandise cannot be sold at normal prices.

The accounting system plays three roles in the inventory management process. First, the system must provide accurate information for preparation of periodic financial statements and tax returns. Second, it must provide up-to-date information on inventory quantities and costs to facilitate ordering and manufacturing

EXHIBIT 7.1

Income Statement and
Balance Sheet Excerpts

HARLEY-DAVIDSON, INC.

REAL WORLD EXCERPT:

Annual Report

HARLEY-DAVIDSON, INC.
Consolidated Statements of Income
(In thousands)*

Years Ended December 31,	2014	2013	2012
Net Sales	$5,567,681	$5,258,290	$4,942,582
Cost of Goods Sold	3,542,601	3,395,918	3,222,394
Gross Profit	$2,025,080	$1,862,372	$1,720,188

HARLEY-DAVIDSON, INC.
Consolidated Balance Sheets
(In thousands)*

	2014	2013
Assets		
Current Assets		
Cash and cash equivalents	$ 906,680	$1,066,612
Marketable securities	57,325	99,009
Accounts receivable, net	247,621	261,065
Finance receivables, net	1,916,635	1,773,686
Inventories	448,871	424,507
Deferred income taxes	89,916	103,625
Other current assets	281,047	260,299
Total current assets	$3,948,095	$3,988,803

Harley-Davidson's statements have been simplified for purposes of our discussion.

decisions. Third, because inventories are subject to theft and other forms of misuse, the system must also provide the information needed to help protect these important assets.

Harley's mix of product lines makes it a particularly good example for this chapter. Although best known as a **manufacturer** of motorcycles, Harley also purchases and resells completed products such as its popular line of Motorclothes apparel. In the second case, it acts as a **wholesaler.** Both the motorcycle and Motorclothes product lines are sold to the company's network of independent dealers. From an accounting standpoint, these independent dealers are Harley-Davidson's customers. The independent dealers are the **retailers** who sell the products to the public.

We begin this chapter with a discussion of the makeup of inventory, the important choices management must make in the financial and tax reporting process, and how these choices affect the financial statements and taxes paid. Then we discuss how managers and analysts evaluate the efficiency of inventory management. Finally, we briefly discuss how accounting systems are organized to keep track of inventory quantities and costs for decision making and control. This topic will be the principal subject matter of your managerial accounting course.

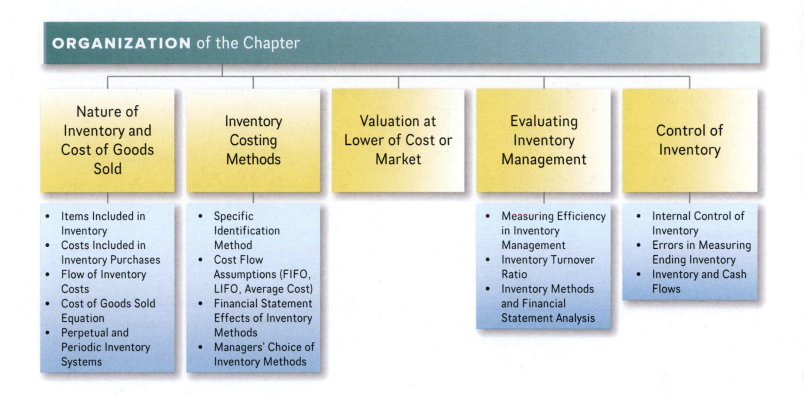

NATURE OF INVENTORY AND COST OF GOODS SOLD

Items Included in Inventory

Inventory is tangible property that is (1) held for sale in the normal course of business or (2) used to produce goods or services for sale. Inventory is reported on the balance sheet as a current asset because it normally is used or converted into cash within one year or the next operating cycle. The types of inventory normally held depend on the characteristics of the business.

Merchandisers (wholesale or retail businesses) hold the following:

Merchandise inventory   Goods (or merchandise) held for resale in the normal course of business. The goods usually are acquired in a finished condition and are ready for sale without further processing.

For **Harley-Davidson**, merchandise inventory includes the Motorclothes line and the parts and accessories it purchases for sale to its independent dealers.

Manufacturing businesses hold three types of inventory:

Raw materials inventory   Items acquired for processing into finished goods. These items are included in raw materials inventory until they are used, at which point they become part of work in process inventory.

Work in process inventory   Goods in the process of being manufactured but not yet complete. When completed, work in process inventory becomes finished goods inventory.

Finished goods inventory   Manufactured goods that are complete and ready for sale.

Inventories related to Harley-Davidson's motorcycle manufacturing operations are recorded in these accounts.

LEARNING OBJECTIVE 7-1

Apply the cost principle to identify the amounts that should be included in inventory and the expense matching principle to determine cost of goods sold for typical retailers, wholesalers, and manufacturers.

INVENTORY

Tangible property held for sale in the normal course of business or used in producing goods or services for sale.

MERCHANDISE INVENTORY

Goods held for resale in the ordinary course of business.

RAW MATERIALS INVENTORY

Items acquired for the purpose of processing into finished goods.

WORK IN PROCESS INVENTORY
Goods in the process of being manufactured.

FINISHED GOODS INVENTORY
Manufactured goods that are complete and ready for sale.

HARLEY-DAVIDSON, INC.

REAL WORLD EXCERPT:

Annual Report

Harley-Davidson's recent inventory note reports the following:

HARLEY-DAVIDSON, INC.
Notes to Consolidated Financial Statements

2. ADDITIONAL BALANCE SHEET AND CASH FLOWS INFORMATION
(dollars in thousands)

	December 31,	
	2014	**2013**
Inventories:		
Components at the lower of FIFO cost or market:		
Raw materials and work in process	$151,254	$140,302
Motorcycle finished goods	230,309	205,416
Parts and accessories and general merchandise	117,210	127,515

Note that Harley-Davidson combines the raw materials and work in process into one number. Other companies separate the two components. The parts and accessories and general merchandise category includes purchased parts and Motorclothes and other accessories that make up merchandise inventory.[1]

Costs Included in Inventory Purchases

Goods in inventory are initially recorded at cost. Inventory cost includes the sum of the costs incurred in bringing an article to usable or salable condition and location. When **Harley-Davidson** purchases raw materials and merchandise inventory, the amount recorded should include the invoice price to be paid plus other expenditures related to the purchase, such as freight charges to deliver the items to its warehouses (**freight-in**) and inspection and preparation costs. Any **purchase returns and allowances** or **purchase discounts** taken are subtracted. In general, the company should cease accumulating purchase costs when the raw materials are **ready for use** or when the merchandise inventory is **ready for shipment.** Any additional costs related to selling the inventory to the dealers, such as marketing department salaries and dealer training sessions, are incurred after the inventory is ready for use. So they should be included in selling, general, and administrative expenses in the period in which they are incurred.

FINANCIAL ANALYSIS	Applying the Materiality Constraint in Practice

Incidental costs such as inspection and preparation costs often are not material in amount (see the discussion of materiality in Chapter 5) and do not have to be assigned to the inventory cost. Thus, for practical reasons, many companies use the invoice price, less returns and discounts, to assign a unit cost to raw materials or merchandise and record other indirect expenditures as a separate cost that is reported as an expense.

Flow of Inventory Costs

The flow of inventory costs for merchandisers (wholesalers and retailers) is relatively simple, as Exhibit 7.2A shows. When merchandise is purchased, the merchandise inventory account is increased. When the goods are sold, cost of goods sold is increased and merchandise inventory is decreased.

---

[1]These do not add up to the balance reported in Exhibit 7.1 because they do not include the LIFO adjustment discussed later.

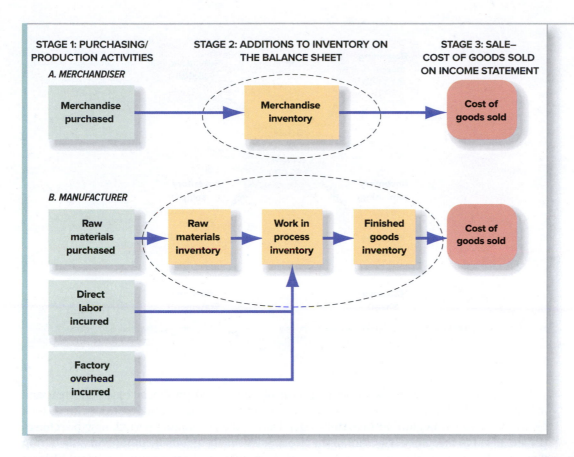

EXHIBIT 7.2

Flow of Inventory Costs

The flow of inventory costs in a manufacturing environment is more complex, as diagrammed in Exhibit 7.2B. First, **raw materials** (also called **direct materials**) must be purchased. For **Harley-Davidson**, these raw materials include steel and aluminum castings, forgings, sheet, and bars, as well as certain motorcycle component parts produced by its small network of suppliers, including carburetors, batteries, and tires. When they are used, the cost of these materials is removed from the raw materials inventory and added to the work in process inventory.

Two other components of manufacturing cost, direct labor and factory overhead, are also added to the work in process inventory when they are used. **Direct labor** cost represents the earnings of employees who work directly on the products being manufactured. **Factory overhead** costs include all other manufacturing costs. For example, the factory supervisor's salary and the cost of heat, light, and power to operate the factory are included in factory overhead. When the motorcycles are completed and ready for sale, the related amounts in work in process inventory are transferred to finished goods inventory. When the finished goods are sold, cost of goods sold increases, and finished goods inventory decreases.

As Exhibit 7.2 indicates, there are three stages to inventory cost flows for both merchandisers and manufacturers. The first involves purchasing and/or production activities. In the second stage, these activities result in additions to inventory accounts on the balance sheet. In the third stage, the inventory items are sold and the amounts become cost of goods sold expense on the income statement. Since the flow of inventory costs from merchandise inventory and finished goods to cost of goods sold are very similar, we will focus the rest of our discussion on merchandise inventory.

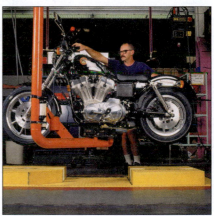

H. Mark Weidman Photography/Alamy

DIRECT LABOR
The earnings of employees who work directly on the products being manufactured.

FACTORY OVERHEAD
Manufacturing costs that are not raw material or direct labor costs.

Cost of Goods Sold Equation

Cost of goods sold (CGS) expense is directly related to sales revenue. Sales revenue during an accounting period is the number of units sold multiplied by the sales price. Cost of goods sold is the same number of units multiplied by their unit costs.

Cost of Goods Sold for Merchandise Inventory

Beginning inventory
+ Purchases of merchandise during the year
_____
Goods available for sale
− Ending inventory
_____
Cost of goods sold
_____

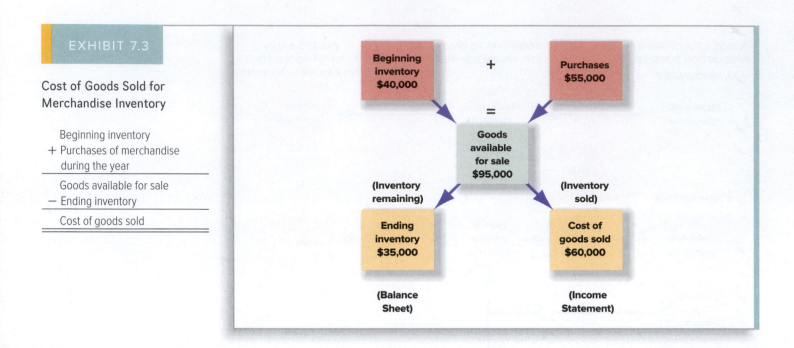

GOODS AVAILABLE FOR SALE
The sum of beginning inventory and purchases (or transfers to finished goods) for the period.

COST OF GOODS SOLD EQUATION
BI + P − EI = CGS.

Let's examine the relationship between cost of goods sold on the income statement and inventory on the balance sheet. **Harley-Davidson** starts each accounting period with a stock of inventory called **beginning inventory** (BI). During the accounting period, new **purchases** (P) are added to inventory. The sum of the two amounts is the **goods available for sale** during that period. What remains unsold at the end of the period becomes **ending inventory** (EI) on the balance sheet. The portion of goods available for sale that is sold becomes **cost of goods sold** on the income statement. The ending inventory for one accounting period then becomes the beginning inventory for the next period. The relationships between these various inventory amounts are brought together in the **cost of goods sold equation**:

$$BI + P - EI = CGS$$

To illustrate, assume that Harley-Davidson began the period with $40,000 worth of Motor-clothes in beginning inventory, purchased additional merchandise during the period for $55,000, and had $35,000 left in inventory at the end of the period. These amounts are combined as follows to compute cost of goods sold of $60,000:

Beginning inventory	$40,000
+ Purchases of merchandise during the year	55,000
Goods available for sale	95,000
− Ending inventory	35,000
Cost of goods sold	$60,000

These same relationships are illustrated in Exhibit 7.3 and can be represented in the merchandise inventory T-account as follows:

Merchandise Inventory (A)			
Beginning inventory	40,000		
Add: Purchases of inventory	55,000	Deduct: Cost of goods sold	60,000
Ending inventory	35,000		

If three of these four values are known, either the cost of goods sold equation or the inventory T-account can be used to solve for the fourth value.

PAUSE FOR FEEDBACK

Inventory should include all items owned that are held for resale. Costs flow into inventory when goods are purchased or manufactured. They flow out (as an expense) when they are sold or disposed of. The cost of goods sold equation describes these flows.

SELF-STUDY QUIZ

1. Assume the following facts for **Harley-Davidson**'s Motorclothes leather baseball jacket product line for the year 2016.

   Beginning inventory: 400 units at unit cost of $75.
   Purchases: 600 units at unit cost of $75.
   Sales: 700 units at a sales price of $100 (cost per unit $75).

   Using the cost of goods sold equation, compute the dollar amount of **goods available for sale, ending inventory,** and **cost of goods sold** of leather baseball jackets for the period.

   | Beginning inventory |
   | + Purchases of merchandise during the year |
   | Goods available for sale |
   | − Ending inventory |
   | Cost of goods sold |

2. Assume the following facts for **Harley-Davidson**'s Motorclothes leather baseball jacket product line for the year 2017.

   Beginning inventory: 300 units at unit cost of $75.
   Ending inventory: 600 units at unit cost of $75.
   Sales: 1,100 units at a sales price of $100 (cost per unit $75).

   Using the cost of goods sold equation, compute the dollar amount of **purchases** of leather baseball jackets for the period. Remember that if three of these four values are known, the cost of goods sold equation can be used to solve for the fourth value.

   | Beginning inventory |
   | + Purchases of merchandise during the year |
   | − Ending inventory |
   | Cost of goods sold |

After you have completed your answers, check them below.

GUIDED HELP 7-1

For additional step-by-step video instruction on using the cost of goods sold equation to compute relevant income statement amounts, go to http://www.mhhe.com/libby9e_7a.

Solutions to
SELF-STUDY QUIZ

1.		
Beginning inventory (400 × $75)	$30,000	
+ Purchases of merchandise during the year (600 × $75)	45,000	
Goods available for sale (1,000 × $75)	75,000	
− Ending inventory (300 × $75)	22,500	
Cost of goods sold (700 × $75)	$52,500	

2. BI = 300 × $75 = $22,500   BI + P − EI = CGS
   EI = 600 × $75 = $45,000   22,500 + P − 45,000 = 82,500
   CGS = 1,100 × $75 = $82,500   P = 105,000

Perpetual and Periodic Inventory Systems

The amount of purchases for the period is always accumulated in the accounting system. The amount of cost of goods sold and ending inventory can be determined by using one of two different inventory systems: perpetual or periodic.

Perpetual Inventory System

PERPETUAL INVENTORY SYSTEM

An inventory system in which a detailed inventory record is maintained, recording each purchase and sale during the accounting period.

To this point in the text, all journal entries for purchase and sale transactions have been recorded using a perpetual inventory system. In a **perpetual inventory system**, purchase transactions are recorded directly in an inventory account. When each sale is recorded, a companion cost of goods sold entry is made, decreasing inventory and recording cost of goods sold. You have already experienced the starting point for that process when your purchases are scanned at the checkout counter at **Walmart** or **Target**. Not only does that process determine how much you must pay the cashier, it also removes the sold items from the store inventory records. As a result, information on cost of goods sold and ending inventory is available on a continuous (perpetual) basis.

In a perpetual inventory system, a detailed record is maintained for each type of merchandise stocked, showing (1) units and cost of the beginning inventory, (2) units and cost of each purchase, (3) units and cost of the goods for each sale, and (4) units and cost of the goods on hand at any point in time. This up-to-date record is maintained on a transaction-by-transaction basis. Most modern companies could not survive without this information. As noted at the beginning of the chapter, cost and quality pressures brought on by increasing competition, combined with dramatic declines in the cost of computers, have made sophisticated perpetual inventory systems a requirement at all but the smallest companies. As a consequence, we will continue to focus on perpetual inventory systems throughout the book.

Periodic Inventory System

PERIODIC INVENTORY SYSTEM

An inventory system in which ending inventory and cost of goods sold are determined at the end of the accounting period based on a physical inventory count.

Under the **periodic inventory system**, no up-to-date record of inventory is maintained during the year. An actual physical count of the goods remaining on hand is required at the **end of each period.** The number of units of each type of merchandise on hand is multiplied by unit cost to compute the dollar amount of the ending inventory. Cost of goods sold is calculated using the cost of goods sold equation.

Because the amount of inventory is not known until the end of the period when the inventory count is taken, the amount of cost of goods sold cannot be reliably determined until the inventory count is complete. The primary disadvantage of a periodic inventory system is the lack of inventory information. Managers are not informed about low or excess stock situations.

INVENTORY COSTING METHODS

LEARNING OBJECTIVE 7-2

Report inventory and cost of goods sold using the four inventory costing methods.

In the Motorclothes example presented in the Self-Study Quiz, the cost of all units of the leather baseball jackets was the same—$75. If inventory costs normally did not change, this would be the end of our discussion. As we are all aware, however, the prices of most goods do change. In recent years, the costs of many manufactured items such as automobiles and motorcycles have risen gradually. In some industries such as computers, costs of production have dropped dramatically along with retail prices.

When inventory costs have changed, which inventory items are treated as sold or remaining in inventory can turn profits into losses and cause companies to pay or save millions in taxes. A simple example will illustrate these dramatic effects. Do not let the simplicity of our example mislead you. It applies broadly to actual company practices.

Assume that a **Harley-Davidson** dealer made the following purchases:

Jan. 1   Had beginning inventory of two units of a Model A leather jacket at $70 each.

Jan. 12   Purchased four units of the Model A leather jacket at $80 each.

Jan. 14   Purchased one unit of the Model A leather jacket at $100.

Jan. 15   Sold four units of the Model A leather jacket for $120 each.

Note that the **cost of the leather jacket rose** rapidly during January. On January 15, four units are sold for $120 each and revenues of $480 are recorded. What amount is recorded as cost of goods sold? The answer depends on which specific goods we assume are sold. Four generally accepted inventory costing methods are available for determining cost of goods sold:

1. Specific identification.

2. First-in, first-out (FIFO).

3. Last-in, first-out (LIFO).

4. Average cost.

The four inventory costing methods are alternative ways to assign the total dollar amount of goods available for sale between (1) ending inventory and (2) cost of goods sold. The first method identifies individual items that remain in inventory or are sold. The remaining three methods assume that the inventory costs follow a certain flow.

Specific Identification Method

When the **specific identification method** is used, the cost of each item sold is individually identified and recorded as cost of goods sold. This method requires keeping track of the purchase cost of each item. In the leather jacket example, any four of the items could have been sold. If we assume that one of the $70 items, two of the $80 items, and the one $100 item have been sold, the cost of those items ($70 + $80 + $80 + $100) would become cost of goods sold ($330). The cost of the remaining items would be ending inventory.

The specific identification method is impractical when large quantities of similar items are stocked. On the other hand, when dealing with expensive unique items such as houses or fine jewelry, this method is appropriate. As a consequence, most inventory items are accounted for using one of three cost flow assumptions.

SPECIFIC IDENTIFICATION METHOD
An inventory costing method that identifies the cost of the specific item that was sold.

Cost Flow Assumptions

The **choice of an inventory costing method is NOT based on the physical flow of goods** on and off the shelves. That is why they are called **cost flow assumptions.** A useful tool for representing inventory cost flow assumptions is a bin, or container. Try visualizing these inventory costing methods as flows of inventory in and out of the bin.

First-In, First-Out Method

The **first-in, first-out method**, frequently called **FIFO**, assumes that the earliest goods purchased (the first ones in) are the first goods sold, and the last goods purchased are left in ending inventory. Under FIFO, cost of goods sold and ending inventory are computed as if the flows in and out of the FIFO inventory bin in Exhibit 7.4A had taken place. First, each purchase is treated as if it were deposited in the bin from the top in sequence (two units of beginning inventory at $70 followed by purchases of four units at $80 and one unit at $100), producing goods available for sale of $560. Each good sold is then removed from the *bottom* in sequence (two units at $70 and two at $80); **first in is first out.** These goods totaling $300 become cost of goods sold (CGS). The remaining units (two units at $80 and one unit at $100 = $260) become ending inventory. FIFO allocates the **oldest** unit costs **to cost of goods sold** and the **newest** unit costs **to ending inventory.**

FIRST-IN, FIRST-OUT (FIFO) METHOD
An inventory costing method that assumes that the first goods purchased (the first in) are the first goods sold.

Cost of Goods Sold Calculation (FIFO)		
Beginning inventory	(2 units at $70 each)	$140
+ Purchases	(4 units at $80 each)	320
	(1 unit at $100)	100
Goods available for sale		560
− Ending inventory	(2 units at $80 each and 1 unit at $100)	260
Cost of goods sold	(2 units at $70 each and 2 units at $80 each)	$300

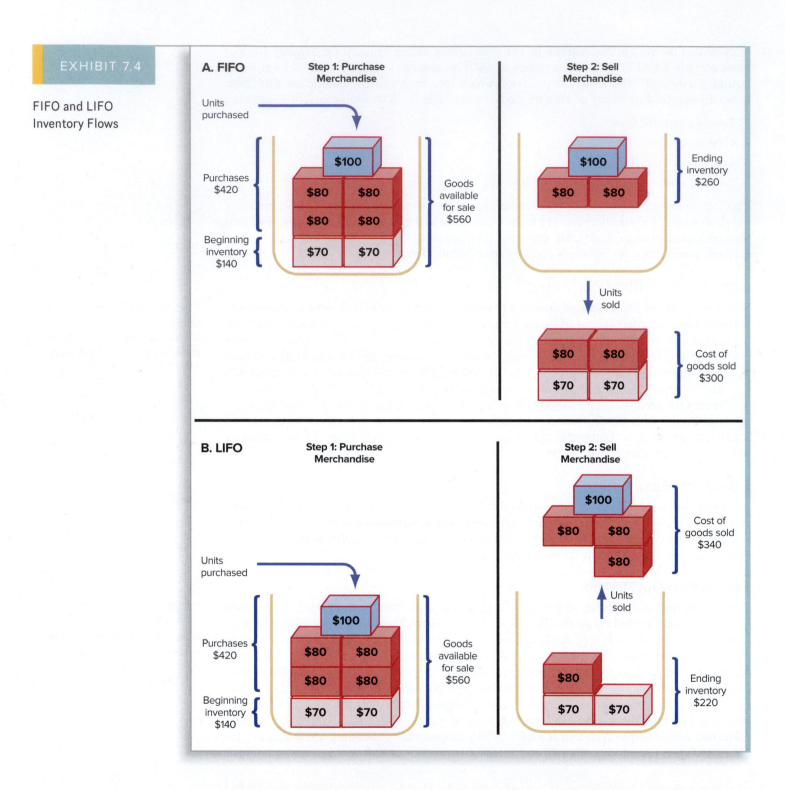

Last-In, First-Out Method

The **last-in, first-out method**, often called **LIFO**, assumes that the most recently purchased goods (the last ones in) are sold first and the oldest units are left in ending inventory. It is illustrated by the LIFO inventory bin in Exhibit 7.4B. As in FIFO, each purchase is treated as if it were deposited in the bin from the top (two units of beginning inventory at $70 followed by purchases of four units at $80 and one unit at $100), resulting in the goods available for sale of $560. Unlike FIFO, however, each good sold is treated as if it were removed from the *top* in sequence (one unit at $100 followed by three units at $80). These goods totaling $340 become cost of goods sold (CGS). The remaining units (one at $80 and two at $70 = $220) become ending inventory. LIFO allocates the **newest** unit costs **to cost of goods sold** and the **oldest** unit costs to ending inventory.

Cost of Goods Sold Calculation (LIFO)		
Beginning inventory	(2 units at $70 each)	$140
+ Purchases	(4 units at $80 each)	320
	(1 unit at $100)	100
Goods available for sale		560
− Ending inventory	(2 units at $70 each and 1 unit at $80)	220
Cost of goods sold	(3 units at $80 each and 1 unit at $100)	$340

The LIFO cost flow assumption is the exact opposite of the FIFO cost flow assumption:

	FIFO	LIFO
Cost of goods sold on income statement	Oldest unit costs	Newest unit costs
Inventory on balance sheet	Newest unit costs	Oldest unit costs

Average Cost Method

The **average cost method** (weighted average cost method) uses the weighted average unit cost of the goods available for sale for both cost of goods sold and ending inventory. The weighted average unit cost of the goods available for sale is computed as follows.

AVERAGE COST METHOD
Uses the weighted average unit cost of the goods available for sale for both cost of goods sold and ending inventory.

Number of Units	×	Unit Cost	=	Total Cost
2	×	$ 70	=	$140
4	×	$ 80	=	320
1	×	$100	=	100
7				$560

$$\text{Average cost} = \frac{\text{Cost of Goods Available for Sale}}{\text{Number of Units Available for Sale}}$$

$$\text{Average cost} = \frac{\$560}{7 \text{ Units}} = \$80 \text{ per Unit}$$

Cost of goods sold and ending inventory are assigned the same weighted average cost per unit of $80.

Cost of Goods Sold Calculation (Average Cost)		
Beginning inventory	(2 units at $70 each)	$140
+ Purchases	(4 units at $80 each)	320
	(1 unit at $100)	100
Goods available for sale	(7 units at $80 average cost each)	560
− Ending inventory	(3 units at $80 average cost each)	240
Cost of goods sold	(4 units at $80 average cost each)	$320

Perpetual Inventory Systems and Cost Flow Assumptions in Practice

You should have noted that, in our example, all inventory units were purchased before a sale was made and cost of goods sold recorded. In reality, most companies make numerous purchases and sales of the same inventory item throughout the accounting period. How can we apply our simple example to these circumstances given that companies normally employ perpetual inventory systems?

First, it is important to know that FIFO inventory and cost of goods sold are the same whether computed on a perpetual or periodic basis. Second, accounting systems that keep track of the costs of individual items normally do so on a FIFO or average cost basis, regardless of the cost flow assumption used for financial reporting. As a consequence, companies that wish to report under LIFO convert the outputs of their perpetual inventory system to LIFO with an adjusting entry at the end of each period. By waiting until the end of the period to calculate this LIFO adjustment, LIFO ending inventory and cost of goods sold are calculated *as if* all purchases during the period were recorded before cost of goods sold was calculated and recorded. In other words, our simple example of how to calculate cost of goods sold applies even though a company actually tracks the number of units bought and sold on a perpetual basis.[2]

INTERNATIONAL PERSPECTIVE

LIFO and International Comparisons

While U.S. GAAP allows companies to choose between FIFO, LIFO, and average cost inventory accounting methods, International Financial Reporting Standards (IFRS) currently prohibit the use of LIFO. U.S. GAAP also allows different inventory accounting methods to be used for different types of inventory items and even for the same item in different locations. IFRS requires that the same method be used for all inventory items that have a similar nature and use. These differences can create comparability problems when one attempts to compare companies across international borders. For example, **Ford** uses LIFO to value most U.S. inventories and average cost or FIFO for non–U.S. inventories, while **Honda** (of Japan) uses FIFO for all inventories. Each individual country's tax laws determine the acceptability of different inventory methods for tax purposes.

Financial Statement Effects of Inventory Methods

Each of the four alternative inventory costing methods is in conformity with GAAP and the tax law. To understand why managers choose different methods in different circumstances, we must first understand their effects on the income statement and balance sheet. Exhibit 7.5 summarizes the financial statement effects of the FIFO, LIFO, and average cost inventory methods in our example. Remember that the methods differ only in the dollar amount of goods available for sale allocated to cost of goods sold versus ending inventory. For that reason, the method that gives the highest ending inventory amount also gives the lowest cost of goods sold and the highest gross profit, income tax expense, and income amounts, and vice versa. The weighted average cost method generally gives income and inventory amounts that are between the FIFO and LIFO extremes.

In our example, recall that unit costs were increasing. **When unit costs are rising, LIFO produces lower income and a lower inventory valuation than FIFO.** Even in inflationary times, some companies' costs decline. **When unit costs are declining, LIFO produces higher income and higher inventory valuation than FIFO.** These effects, which hold as long as inventory quantities are constant or rising,[3] are summarized in the following table:

---

[2]We show an example comparing calculation of cost of goods sold under perpetual versus periodic FIFO and LIFO in Chapter Supplement B.

[3]The impact of a decline in inventory **quantity** on LIFO amounts is discussed in Supplement A to this chapter.

	FIFO	LIFO	Average Cost
Effect on the Income Statement			
Sales	$480	$480	$480
Cost of goods sold	300	340	320
Gross profit	180	140	160
Other expenses	80	80	80
Income before income taxes	100	60	80
Income tax expense (25%)	25	15	20
Net income	$ 75	$ 45	$ 60
Effect on the Balance Sheet			
Inventory	$260	$220	$240

EXHIBIT 7.5

Financial Statement Effects of Inventory Costing Methods

Increasing Costs: Normal Financial Statement Effects

	FIFO	LIFO
Cost of goods sold on income statement	Lower	Higher
Net income	Higher	Lower
Income taxes	Higher	Lower
Inventory on balance sheet	Higher	Lower

Decreasing Costs: Normal Financial Statement Effects

	FIFO	LIFO
Cost of goods sold on income statement	Higher	Lower
Net income	Lower	Higher
Income taxes	Lower	Higher
Inventory on balance sheet	Lower	Higher

Managers' Choice of Inventory Methods

What motivates companies to choose different inventory costing methods? Most managers choose accounting methods based on two factors:

1. Net income effects (managers prefer to report higher earnings for their companies).

2. Income tax effects (managers prefer to pay the least amount of taxes allowed by law as late as possible—the **least–latest rule of thumb**).

Any conflict between the two motives is normally resolved by choosing one accounting method for external financial statements and a different method for preparing the company's tax return. The choice of inventory costing methods is a special case, however, because of what is called the **LIFO conformity rule:** If LIFO is used on the U.S. income tax return, it must also be used to calculate inventory and cost of goods sold for the financial statements.

Increasing Cost Inventories

- **For inventory with increasing costs, LIFO is used on the tax return because it normally results in lower income taxes.**

LEARNING OBJECTIVE 7-3
Decide when the use of different inventory costing methods is beneficial to a company.

This is illustrated in Exhibit 7.5, where income before income taxes was lowered from $100 under FIFO to $60 under LIFO. On the income tax expense line, this lowers income taxes from $25 under FIFO to $15 under LIFO, generating cash tax savings of $10 under LIFO.[4] The LIFO conformity rule leads companies to adopt LIFO for **both** tax and financial reporting purposes for increasing cost inventories located in the United States. **Harley-Davidson** is a fairly typical company facing increasing costs. It has saved approximately $17 million in taxes from the date it adopted the LIFO method through 2014.

For inventory located in countries that do not allow LIFO for tax purposes or that do not have a LIFO conformity rule, companies with increasing costs most often use FIFO or average cost to report higher income on the income statement.

Decreasing Cost Inventories

- **For inventory with decreasing costs, FIFO is most often used for both the tax return and financial statements.**

Using this method (along with lower of cost or market valuation, discussed later) produces the lowest tax payments for companies with decreasing cost inventories. Many high-technology companies are facing declining costs. In such circumstances, the FIFO method, in which the oldest, most expensive goods become cost of goods sold, produces the highest cost of goods sold, the lowest pretax earnings, and thus the lowest income tax liability. For example, **Apple** and **HP** account for inventories using the FIFO method.

Since most companies in the same industry face similar cost structures, clusters of companies in the same industries often choose the same accounting method.

Consistency in Use of Inventory Methods

It is important to remember that regardless of the physical flow of goods, a company can use any of the inventory costing methods. Also, a company is not required to use the same inventory costing method for all inventory items, and no particular justification is needed for the selection of one or more of the acceptable methods. Harley-Davidson, and most large companies, use different inventory methods for different inventory items. However, accounting rules require companies to apply their accounting methods on a consistent basis over time. A company is not permitted to use LIFO one period, FIFO the next, and then go back to LIFO. A change in method is allowed only if the change will improve the measurement of financial results and financial position.

A QUESTION OF ETHICS **LIFO and Conflicts between Managers' and Owners' Interests**

We have seen that the selection of an inventory method can have significant effects on the financial statements. Company managers may have an incentive to select a method that is not consistent with the owners' objectives. For example, during a period of rising prices, using LIFO may be in the best interests of the owners because LIFO often reduces a company's tax liability. However, if managers' compensation is tied to reported profits, they may prefer FIFO, which typically results in higher profits.

While a well-designed compensation plan should reward managers for acting in the best interests of the owners, that is not always the case. Clearly, a manager who selects an accounting method that is not optimal for the company solely to increase his or her compensation is engaging in questionable ethical behavior.

---

[4]In theory, LIFO cannot provide permanent tax savings because (1) when inventory levels drop or (2) costs drop, the income effect reverses and the income taxes deferred must be paid. The economic advantage of deferring income taxes in such situations is due to the fact that interest can be earned on the money that otherwise would be paid as taxes for the current year.

PAUSE FOR **FEEDBACK**

Four different inventory costing methods may be used to allocate costs between the units remaining in inventory and the units sold, depending on economic circumstances. The methods include specific identification, FIFO, LIFO, and average cost. Each of the inventory costing methods conforms to GAAP. Remember that the cost flow assumption need not match the physical flow of inventory. The following questions test your understanding of the FIFO and LIFO methods.

SELF-STUDY QUIZ

1. Compute cost of goods sold and pretax income for **2015** under the FIFO and LIFO accounting methods. Assume that a company's beginning inventory and purchases for 2015 included:

Beginning inventory	10 units @ $ 6 each
Purchases January	5 units @ $10 each
Purchases May	5 units @ $12 each

   During 2015, 15 units were sold for $20 each, and other operating expenses totaled $100.

2. Compute cost of goods sold and pretax income for **2016** under the FIFO and LIFO accounting methods. (**Hint:** The 2015 ending inventory amount from Part 1 becomes the 2016 beginning inventory amount.) Assume that the company's purchases for 2016 included:

Purchases March	6 units @ $13 each
Purchases November	5 units @ $14 each

   During 2016, 10 units were sold for $24 each, and other operating expenses totaled $70.

3. Which method would you recommend that the company adopt? Why?

After you have completed your answers, check them below.

 **GUIDED HELP 7-2**

For additional step-by-step video instruction on computing ending inventory and cost of goods sold using different cost flow assumptions, go to **http://www.mhhe.com/libby9e_7b**.

Solutions to
SELF-STUDY QUIZ

1.

2015	FIFO	LIFO		FIFO	LIFO
Beginning inventory	$ 60	$ 60	Sales revenue (15 × $20)	$300	$300
Purchases (5 × $10) + (5 × $12)	110	110	Cost of goods sold	110	140
Goods available for sale	170	170	Gross profit	190	160
Ending inventory*	60	30	Other expenses	100	100
Cost of goods sold	$110	$140	Pretax income	$ 90	$ 60

*FIFO ending inventory = (5 × $12) = $60
   Cost of goods sold = (10 × $6) + (5 × $10) = $110
LIFO ending inventory = (5 × $6) = $30
   Cost of goods sold = (5 × $12) + (5 × $10) + (5 × $6) = $140

2.

2016	FIFO	LIFO		FIFO	LIFO
Beginning inventory	$ 60	$ 30	Sales revenue (10 × $24)	$240	$240
Purchases (6 × $13) + (5 × $14)	148	148	Cost of goods sold	125	135
Goods available for sale	208	178	Gross profit	115	105
Ending inventory†	83	43	Other expenses	70	70
Cost of goods sold	$125	$135	Pretax income	$ 45	$ 35

†FIFO ending inventory = (5 × $14) + (1 × $13) = $83
   Cost of goods sold = (5 × $12) + (5 × $13) = $125
LIFO ending inventory = (5 × $6) + (1 × $13) = $43
   Cost of goods sold = (5 × $14) + (5 × $13) = $135

3. LIFO would be recommended because it produces lower pretax income and lower taxes when inventory costs are rising.

VALUATION AT LOWER OF COST OR MARKET (NET REALIZABLE VALUE)

LEARNING OBJECTIVE 7-4
Report inventory at the lower of cost or market (LCM).

NET REALIZABLE VALUE
The expected sales price less selling costs (e.g., repair and disposal costs).

LOWER OF COST OR MARKET (LCM)
Valuation method departing from the cost principle; it serves to recognize a loss when net realizable value drops below cost.

Inventories should be measured initially at their purchase cost in conformity with the cost principle. When the **net realizable value** (sales price less costs to sell) of goods remaining in ending inventory falls below cost, these goods must be assigned a unit cost equal to their current estimated net realizable value. This rule is known as measuring inventories at the **lower of cost or market** (LCM or lower of cost or net realizable value).

This departure from the cost principle is based on the **conservatism** constraint, which requires special care to avoid overstating assets and income. It is particularly important for two types of companies: (1) high-technology companies such as **HP** that manufacture goods for which costs of production and selling price are declining and (2) companies such as **American Eagle Outfitters** that sell seasonal goods such as clothing, the value of which drops dramatically at the end of each selling season (fall or spring).

Under LCM, companies recognize a "holding" loss in the period in which the net realizable value of an item drops, rather than in the period the item is sold. The holding loss is the difference between the purchase cost and the lower net realizable value. It is added to the cost of goods sold for the period. To illustrate, assume that HP had the following in the current period ending inventory:

Item	Quantity	Cost per Item	Net Realizable Value (Market) per Item	Lower of Cost or Market per Item	Total Lower of Cost or Market
Intel chips	1,000	$250	$200	$200	1,000 × $200 = $200,000
Disk drives	400	100	110	100	400 × $100 = 40,000

The 1,000 Intel chips should be recorded in the ending inventory at the current net realizable value ($200) because it is **lower** than the cost ($250). HP makes the following journal entry to record the write-down:

Cost of goods sold (+E, −SE) (1,000 × $50)	50,000	
Inventory (−A)		50,000

Assets	=	Liabilities	+	Stockholders' Equity	
Inventory −50,000				Cost of Goods Sold (+E) −50,000	

Since the market price of the disk drives ($110) is higher than the original cost ($100), no write-down is necessary. The drives remain on the books at their cost of $100 per unit ($40,000 in total). Recognition of holding gains on inventory is not permitted by GAAP.

The write-down of the Intel chips to market produces the following effects on the income statement and balance sheet:

Effects of LCM Write-Down	Current Period	Next Period (if sold)
Cost of goods sold	Increase $50,000	Decrease $50,000
Pretax income	Decrease $50,000	Increase $50,000
Ending inventory on balance sheet	Decrease $50,000	Unaffected

Note that the effects in the period of sale are the opposite of those in the period of the write-down. Lower of cost or market changes only the timing of cost of goods sold. It transfers cost of goods sold from the period of sale to the period of write-down.

Note that in the two examples that follow, both **Harley-Davidson**, which is a mixed LIFO company, and HP, which is a FIFO company, report the use of lower of cost or market for financial statement purposes.[5]

---

[5]For tax purposes, lower of cost or market may be applied with all inventory costing methods except LIFO.

HARLEY-DAVIDSON, INC.
Notes to Consolidated Financial Statements
1. SUMMARY OF SIGNIFICANT ACCOUNTING POLICIES

Inventories—Inventories are valued at the lower of cost or market. Substantially all inventories located in the United States are valued using the last-in, first-out (LIFO) method. Other inventories totaling $232.8 million at December 31, 2014, and $210.7 million at December 31, 2013, are valued at the lower of cost or market using the first-in, first-out (FIFO) method.

HARLEY-DAVIDSON, INC.

REAL WORLD EXCERPT:

Annual Report

HEWLETT-PACKARD COMPANY AND SUBSIDIARIES
Notes to Consolidated Financial Statements
NOTE 1: Summary of Significant Accounting Policies

Inventory

HP values inventory at the lower of cost or market. . . . Adjustments to reduce the cost of inventory to its net realizable value are made, if required, for estimated excess, obsolete or impaired balances. Inventories are stated at the lower of cost or market with cost being determined on a first-in, first-out basis.

HEWLETT-PACKARD

REAL WORLD EXCERPT:

Annual Report

EVALUATING INVENTORY MANAGEMENT

Measuring Efficiency in Inventory Management

As noted at the beginning of the chapter, the primary goals of inventory management are to have sufficient quantities of high-quality inventory available to serve customers' needs while minimizing the costs of carrying inventory (production, storage, obsolescence, and financing). The inventory turnover ratio is an important measure of the company's success in balancing these conflicting goals.

> **LEARNING OBJECTIVE 7-5**
> Evaluate inventory management using the inventory turnover ratio.

Inventory Turnover   **KEY RATIO ANALYSIS**

 **ANALYTICAL QUESTION**

How efficient are inventory management activities?

% RATIO AND COMPARISONS

$$\text{Inventory Turnover} = \frac{\text{Cost of Goods Sold}}{\text{Average Inventory}}$$

The 2014 ratio for **Harley-Davidson** (see Exhibit 7.1 for the inputs to the equation):

$$\frac{\$3,542,601}{(\$448,871 + 424,507)/2} = 8.1$$

COMPARISONS OVER TIME			COMPARISONS WITH COMPETITORS	
Harley-Davidson			Polaris	Honda Motor
2012	2013	2014	2014	2014
7.9	8.3	8.1	6.4	7.0

(continued)

Selected Focus Companies' Inventory Turnover

National Beverage	10.19
Home Depot	4.72
Deckers	2.92

💡 INTERPRETATIONS

In General The inventory turnover ratio reflects how many times average inventory was produced and sold during the period. A higher ratio indicates that inventory moves more quickly through the production process to the ultimate customer, reducing storage and obsolescence costs. Because less money is tied up in inventory, the excess can be invested to earn interest income or reduce borrowing, which reduces interest expense. More efficient purchasing and production techniques, such as just-in-time inventory, as well as high product demand cause this ratio to be high. Analysts and creditors also watch the inventory turnover ratio because a sudden decline may mean that a company is facing an unexpected drop in demand for its products or is becoming sloppy in its production management. Many managers and analysts compute the related number average days to sell inventory, which, for Harley-Davidson, is equal to:

$$\text{Average Days to Sell Inventory} = \frac{365}{\text{Inventory Turnover}} = \frac{365}{8.1} = 45.1 \text{ days}$$

It indicates the average time it takes the company to produce and deliver inventory to customers.

Focus Company Analysis Harley-Davidson's inventory turnover was generally stable from 2012 to 2014, fluctuating around a ratio of 8.1 during those three years. Harley's ratio is higher than that of related company **Polaris** and also higher than that of giant Japanese auto and motorcycle manufacturer **Honda**.

A Few Cautions Differences across industries in purchasing, production, and sales processes cause dramatic differences in this ratio. For example, restaurants such as **Papa John's**, which must turn over their perishable inventory very quickly, tend to have much higher inventory turnover. A particular firm's ratio should be compared only with its figures from prior years or with figures for other firms in the same industry.

STOP PAUSE FOR **FEEDBACK**

The inventory turnover ratio measures the efficiency of inventory management. It reflects how many times average inventory was produced and sold during the period. Analysts and creditors watch this ratio because a sudden decline may mean that a company is facing an unexpected drop in demand for its products or is becoming sloppy in its production management. When a net **decrease in inventory** for the period occurs, sales are more than purchases; thus, the decrease must be **added** in computing cash flows from operations. When a net **increase in inventory** for the period occurs, the opposite is true. Before you move on, complete the following questions to test your understanding of these concepts.

SELF-STUDY **QUIZ**

Refer to the Key Ratio Analysis for **Harley-Davidson**'s inventory turnover. Based on the computations for 2014, answer the following question. If Harley-Davidson had been able to manage its inventory more efficiently and decrease purchases and ending inventory by $10,000 for 2014, would its inventory turnover ratio have increased or decreased? Explain.

After you have completed your answer, check it below.

LEARNING OBJECTIVE 7-6

Compare companies that use different inventory costing methods.

Inventory Methods and Financial Statement Analysis

What would analysts do if they wanted to compare two companies that prepared their statements using different inventory accounting methods? Before meaningful comparisons could be made, one company's statements would have to be converted to a comparable basis. Making such a conversion is eased by the requirement that U.S. public companies using LIFO also

Solutions to
SELF-STUDY QUIZ

Inventory turnover would have increased because the denominator of the ratio (average inventory) would have decreased by $5,000.

$$\frac{\$3,542,601}{(\$448,871 + \$414,507)/2} = 8.2$$

EXHIBIT 7.6

Financial Statement Effects of
Inventory Costing Methods

HARLEY-DAVIDSON, INC.
Notes to Consolidated Financial Statements
2. ADDITIONAL BALANCE SHEET AND CASH FLOWS INFORMATION
(in thousands)

	December 31,	
	2014	**2013**
Inventories:		
. . .		
Inventory at FIFO	$498,773	$473,233
Excess of FIFO over LIFO cost	49,902	48,726
Inventory at LIFO	$448,871	$424,507

←—LIFO Reserve

←—*Inventory reported
on the balance sheet*

HARLEY-DAVIDSON, INC.

REAL WORLD EXCERPT:

Annual Report

report beginning and ending inventory on a FIFO basis in the notes if the FIFO values are materially different. We can use this information along with the cost of goods sold equation to convert the balance sheet and income statement to the FIFO basis.

Converting the Income Statement to FIFO

Recall that the choice of a cost flow assumption affects how goods available for sale are allocated to ending inventory and cost of goods sold. It does not affect the recording of purchases. Ending inventory will be different under the alternative methods, and, because last year's ending inventory is this year's beginning inventory, beginning inventory will also be different:

Beginning inventory	**Different**
+ Purchases of merchandise during the year	**Same**
− Ending inventory	**Different**
Cost of goods sold	**Different**

This equation suggests that if we know the differences between a company's inventory valued at LIFO and FIFO for both beginning and ending inventory, we can compute the difference in cost of goods sold. Exhibit 7.6 shows **Harley-Davidson**'s 2014 disclosure of the differences between LIFO and FIFO values for beginning and ending inventory. These amounts, referred to as the **LIFO reserve** or "Excess of FIFO over LIFO," are disclosed by LIFO users in their inventory footnotes.

Using Harley-Davidson's LIFO reserve values reported in the footnote presented in Exhibit 7.6, we see that cost of goods sold would have been $1,176 **lower** had it used FIFO.

LIFO RESERVE
A contra-asset for the excess of
FIFO over LIFO inventory.

Beginning LIFO Reserve (Excess of FIFO over LIFO)	$48,726
− Less: Ending LIFO Reserve (Excess of FIFO over LIFO)	−49,902
Difference in Cost of Goods Sold under FIFO	($1,176)

Since FIFO cost of goods sold expense is **lower,** income before income taxes would have been $1,176 **higher.** Income taxes would be that amount times its tax rate of 35 percent **higher** had it used FIFO.

Difference in pretax income under FIFO	$1,176
Tax rate	× .35
Difference in taxes under FIFO	$ 412

Combining the two effects, net income would be increased by the change in cost of goods sold of $1,176 and decreased by the change in income tax expense of $412, resulting in an overall increase in net income of $764.

Decrease in Cost of Goods Sold Expense (*Income increases*)	$ 1,176
Increase in Income Tax Expense (*Income decreases*)	(412)
Increase in Net Income	$ 764

These Harley-Davidson computations are for 2014. It is important to note that even companies that usually face increasing costs occasionally face decreasing costs. For example, during 2000, Harley-Davidson's costs of new inventory declined due to manufacturing efficiencies. As a result, even though LIFO usually **saves** the company taxes, Harley paid **extra** taxes in 2000.

Converting Inventory on the Balance Sheet to FIFO

You can adjust the inventory amounts on the balance sheet to FIFO by substituting the FIFO values in the note ($498,773 and $473,233 for 2014 and 2013, respectively) for the LIFO values (see Exhibit 7.6). Alternatively, you can add the LIFO reserve to the LIFO value on the balance sheet to arrive at the same numbers.

FINANCIAL ANALYSIS	**LIFO and Inventory Turnover Ratio**

For many LIFO companies, the inventory turnover ratio can be deceptive. Remember that, for these companies, the beginning and ending inventory numbers that make up the denominator of the ratio will be artificially small because they reflect old lower costs. Consider **Deere & Co.**, manufacturer of John Deere farm, lawn, and construction equipment. Its inventory note lists the following values:

DEERE & COMPANY
REAL WORLD EXCERPT:
Annual Report

DEERE & COMPANY		
Notes to Consolidated Financial Statements		
(dollars in millions)		
	2014	**2013**
Inventories:		
Total FIFO value	$5,738	$6,464
Adjustment to LIFO basis	1,528	1,529
Inventories	$4,210	$4,935

John Deere's cost of goods sold for 2014 was $24,775.8 million. If the ratio were computed using the reported LIFO inventory values for the ratio, it would be

$$\text{Inventory Turnover Ratio} = \frac{\$24{,}775.8}{(\$4{,}210 + \$4{,}935)/2} = 5.4$$

Converting cost of goods sold (the numerator) to a FIFO basis and using the more current FIFO inventory values in the denominator, it would be

$$\text{Inventory Turnover Ratio} = \frac{\$24{,}775.8 + 1}{(\$5{,}738 + \$6{,}464)/2} = 4.1$$

Note that the major difference between the two ratios is in the denominator. FIFO inventory values are roughly 36 percent higher than the LIFO values. The LIFO beginning and ending inventory numbers are artificially small because they reflect older lower costs.

The selection of an inventory costing method is important because it will affect reported income, income tax expense (and hence cash flow), and the inventory valuation reported on the balance sheet. In a period of rising prices, FIFO normally results in a higher income and higher taxes than LIFO; in a period of falling prices, the opposite occurs. The choice of methods is normally made to minimize taxes. Answer the following question to practice converting cost of goods sold and pretax income from the LIFO to the FIFO method for a company facing increasing prices.

SELF-STUDY QUIZ

In a recent year, **Caterpillar Inc.,** a major manufacturer of farm and construction equipment, reported pretax earnings of "$6,725 million. Its inventory note indicated "if the FIFO (first-in, first-out) method had been in use, inventories would have been $2,422 and $2,575 higher than reported at the end of the current and prior year, respectively." (The amounts noted are for the LIFO reserve.) Convert pretax earnings for the current year from a LIFO to a FIFO basis.

Beginning LIFO Reserve (Excess of FIFO over LIFO)	_____
Less: Ending LIFO Reserve (Excess of FIFO over LIFO)	_____
Difference in cost of goods sold under FIFO	========
Pretax income (LIFO)	_____
Difference in pretax income under FIFO	_____
Pretax income (FIFO)	========

After you have completed your answers, check them below.

CONTROL OF INVENTORY

Internal Control of Inventory

After cash, inventory is the asset second most vulnerable to theft. Efficient management of inventory to avoid the cost of stock-outs and overstock situations is also crucial to the profitability of most companies. As a consequence, a number of control features focus on safeguarding inventories and providing up-to-date information for management decisions. Key among these are:

LEARNING OBJECTIVE 7-7
Understand methods for controlling inventory, analyze the effects of inventory errors on financial statements, and analyze the effects of inventory on cash flows.

1. Separation of responsibilities for inventory accounting and physical handling of inventory.
2. Storage of inventory in a manner that protects it from theft and damage.
3. Limiting access to inventory to authorized employees.
4. Maintaining perpetual inventory records (described earlier in this chapter).
5. Comparing perpetual records to periodic physical counts of inventory.

Errors in Measuring Ending Inventory

As the cost of goods sold equation indicates, a direct relationship exists between ending inventory and cost of goods sold because items not in the ending inventory are assumed to have been sold. Thus, the measurement of ending inventory quantities and costs affects both the balance sheet (assets) and the income statement (cost of goods sold, gross profit, and net income). The measurement of ending inventory affects not only the net income for that period but also the net income for the next accounting period. This two-period effect occurs because the ending inventory for one period is the beginning inventory for the next accounting period.

Greeting card maker **Gibson Greetings** overstated its net income by 20 percent because one division overstated ending inventory for the year. You can compute the effects of the error on both the current year's and the next year's income before taxes using the cost of goods sold

Alistair Berg/Digital Vision/Getty Images

Solutions to
SELF-STUDY QUIZ

Beginning LIFO Reserve	$2,575	Pretax income (LIFO)	$6,725
Less: Ending LIFO Reserve	2,422	Difference in pretax income	(153)
Difference in cost of goods sold	$ 153	Pretax income (FIFO)	$6,572

equation. Assume that ending inventory was overstated by $10,000 due to a clerical error that was not discovered. This would have the following effects in the current year and next year:

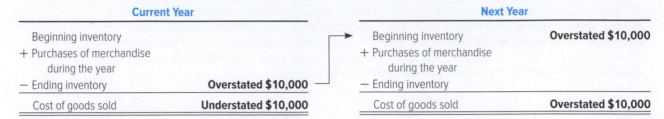

Current Year		Next Year	
Beginning inventory		Beginning inventory	**Overstated $10,000**
+ Purchases of merchandise during the year		+ Purchases of merchandise during the year	
− Ending inventory	**Overstated $10,000**	− Ending inventory	
Cost of goods sold	**Understated $10,000**	Cost of goods sold	**Overstated $10,000**

Because cost of goods sold was understated, **income before taxes would be overstated** by $10,000 in the **current year.** And, since the current year's ending inventory becomes next year's beginning inventory, it would have the following effects the next year. Because cost of goods sold was overstated, **income before taxes would be understated** by $10,000 in the **next year.**

Each of these errors would flow into retained earnings so that at the end of the current year, retained earnings would be overstated by $10,000 (less the related income tax expense). This error would be offset in the next year, and retained earnings and inventory at the end of next year would be correct.

In this example, we assumed that the overstatement of ending inventory was inadvertent, the result of a clerical error. However, inventory fraud is a common form of financial statement fraud.

PAUSE FOR FEEDBACK

An error in the measurement of ending inventory affects cost of goods sold on the current period's income statement and ending inventory on the balance sheet. Because this year's ending inventory becomes next year's beginning inventory, it also affects cost of goods sold in the following period by the same amount but in the opposite direction. These relationships can be seen through the cost of goods sold equation (BI + P − EI = CGS).

SELF-STUDY QUIZ

Assume that it is now the end of 2016 and Benson Inc. is undergoing its first audit by an independent CPA. The annual income statement prepared by the company is presented here. Assume further that the independent CPA discovers that the ending inventory for 2016 was understated by $15,000. Correct and reconstruct the income statement in the space provided.

	For the Year Ended December 31	
	2016 Uncorrected	**2016 Corrected**
Sales revenue	$750,000	
Cost of goods sold		
Beginning inventory	$ 45,000	
Add purchases	460,000	_____
Goods available for sale	505,000	
Less ending inventory	40,000	_____
Cost of goods sold	465,000	_____
Gross margin on sales	285,000	
Operating expenses	275,000	
Pretax income	10,000	_____
Income tax expense (20%)	2,000	
Net income	$ 8,000	_____

After you have completed your answers, check them at the bottom of the next page.

Inventory and Cash Flows

When companies expand production to meet increases in demand, this increases the amount of inventory reported on the balance sheet. However, when companies overestimate demand for a product, they usually produce too many units of the slow-selling item. This increases storage costs as well as the interest costs on short-term borrowings that finance the inventory. It may even lead to losses if the excess inventory cannot be sold at normal prices. The cash flow statement often provides the first sign of such problems.

Inventory	FOCUS ON CASH FLOWS

As with a change in accounts receivable, a change in inventories can have a major effect on a company's cash flow from operations. Cost of goods sold on the income statement may be more or less than the amount of cash paid to suppliers during the period. Since most inventory is purchased on open credit (borrowing from suppliers is normally called *accounts payable*), reconciling cost of goods sold with cash paid to suppliers requires consideration of the changes in both the Inventory and Accounts Payable accounts.

The simplest way to think about the effects of changes in inventory is that buying (increasing) inventory eventually decreases cash, while selling (decreasing) inventory eventually increases cash. Similarly, borrowing from suppliers, which increases accounts payable, increases cash. Paying suppliers, which decreases accounts payable, decreases cash.

EFFECT ON STATEMENT OF CASH FLOWS

In General   When a net **decrease in inventory** for the period occurs, sales are greater than purchases; thus, the decrease must be **added** in computing cash flows from operations.

When a net **increase in inventory** for the period occurs, sales are less than purchases; thus, the increase must be **subtracted** in computing cash flows from operations.

When a net **decrease in accounts payable** for the period occurs, payments to suppliers are greater than new purchases; thus, the decrease must be **subtracted** in computing cash flows from operations.

When a net **increase in accounts payable** for the period occurs, payments to suppliers are less than new purchases; thus, the increase must be **added** in computing cash flows from operations.

	Effect on Cash Flows
Operating activities (indirect method)	
Net income	$xxx
Adjusted for	
Add inventory **decrease**	+
or	
Subtract inventory **increase**	−
Add accounts payable **increase**	+
or	
Subtract accounts payable **decrease**	−

(continued)

Solutions to

SELF-STUDY QUIZ

Sales revenue		$750,000
Cost of goods sold		
Beginning inventory	$ 45,000	
Add purchases	460,000	
Goods available for sale	505,000	
Less ending inventory	55,000	
Cost of goods sold		450,000
Gross margin on sales		300,000
Operating expenses		275,000
Pretax income		25,000
Income tax expense (20%)		5,000
Net income		$ 20,000

Note: An ending inventory error in one year affects pretax income by the amount of the error. In the next year, the ending inventory error affects pretax income again by the same amount, but in the opposite direction.

Focus Company Analysis   When the inventory balance increases during the period, as was the case at **Harley-Davidson** in 2014, the company has purchased or produced more inventory than it has sold. Thus, the increase is subtracted in the computation of cash flow from operations. Conversely, when the inventory balance decreases during the period, the company has sold more inventory than it purchased or produced. Thus, the decrease is added in the computation of cash flow from operations. When the accounts payable balance increases during the period, the company has borrowed more from suppliers than it has paid them (or postponed payments). Thus, the increase is added in the computation of cash flow from operations.*

HARLEY-DAVIDSON, INC.
Consolidated Statement of Cash Flows
Year Ended December 31, 2014
(dollars in thousands)

	2014
Cash flows from operating activities:	
Net Income	$ 844,611
Adjustments to reconcile net income to net cash provided by operating activities:	
Depreciation	179,300
. . . .	
Changes in current assets and current liabilities:	
. . . .	
Inventories	(50,866)
Accounts payable and accrued liabilities	19,128
. . . .	
Total Adjustments	$ 302,066
Net cash (used by) provided by continuing operating activities	$1,146,677

*For companies with foreign currency or business acquisitions/dispositions, the amount of the change reported on the cash flow statement will not equal the change in the accounts reported on the balance sheet.

DEMONSTRATION   CASE

(Complete the requirements before proceeding to the suggested solution that follows.) This case reviews the application of the FIFO and LIFO inventory costing methods and the inventory turnover ratio.

Balent Appliances distributes a number of household appliances. One product, microwave ovens, has been selected for case purposes. Assume that the following summarized transactions were completed during the year ended December 31, 2016, in the order given (assume that all transactions are cash):

	Units	Unit Cost
a. Beginning inventory	11	$200
b. New inventory purchases	9	220
c. Sales (selling price, $420)	8	?

Required:

1. Compute the following amounts, assuming the application of the FIFO and LIFO inventory costing methods:

	Ending Inventory		Cost of Goods Sold	
	Units	Dollars	Units	Dollars
FIFO				
LIFO				

2. Assuming that inventory cost was expected to follow current trends, which method would you suggest that Balent select to account for these inventory items? Explain your answer.

3. Assuming that other operating expenses were $500 and the income tax rate is 25 percent, prepare the income statement for the period using your selected method.

4. Compute the inventory turnover ratio for the current period using your selected method. What does it indicate?

SUGGESTED SOLUTION

1.

	Ending Inventory		Cost of Goods Sold	
	Units	Dollars	Units	Dollars
FIFO	12	$2,580	8	$1,600
LIFO	12	$2,420	8	$1,760

Computations

Beginning inventory (11 units × $200)	$2,200
+ Purchases (9 units × $220)	1,980
Goods available for sale	$ 4,180

FIFO inventory (costed at end of period)

Goods available for sale (from above)	$ 4,180
− Ending inventory [(9 units × $220) + (3 units × $200)]	2,580
Cost of goods sold (8 units × $200)	$1,600

LIFO inventory (costed at end of period)

Goods available for sale (from above)	$ 4,180
− Ending inventory [(11 units × $200) + (1 unit × $220)]	2,420
Cost of goods sold (8 units × $220)	$ 1,760

2. LIFO should be selected. Because costs are rising, LIFO produces higher cost of goods sold, lower pretax income, and lower income tax payments. It is used on the tax return and income statement because of the LIFO conformity rule.

3.

BALENT APPLIANCES
Statement of Income
Year Ended December 31, 2016

Sales	$3,360
Cost of goods sold	1,760
Gross profit	1,600
Other expenses	500
Income before income taxes	1,100
Income tax expense (25%)	275
Net income	$ 825

Computations

Sales = 8 × $420 = $3,360

4. Inventory turnover ratio = Cost of Goods Sold ÷ Average Inventory

  = $1,760 ÷ [($2,200 + $2,420) ÷ 2 = $2,310]

  = 0.76

The inventory turnover ratio reflects how many times average inventory was produced or purchased and sold during the period. Thus, Balent Appliances purchased and sold its average inventory less than one time during the year.

Chapter Supplement A

LIFO Liquidations

When a LIFO company sells more inventory than it purchases or manufactures, items from beginning inventory become part of cost of goods sold. This is called a **LIFO liquidation**. When inventory costs are rising, these lower-cost items in beginning inventory produce a higher gross profit, higher taxable income, and higher taxes when they are sold. We illustrate this process by continuing our **Harley-Davidson** Model A leather baseball jacket example into its second year.

Financial Statement Effects of LIFO Liquidations

Recall that, in its first year of operation, the store purchased units for $70, $80, and $100 in sequence (see Exhibit 7.4). Then, the $100 unit and three of the $80 units were sold under LIFO, leaving one $80 unit and two $70 units in ending inventory. We will continue this illustration into a second year. The ending inventory from Year 1 becomes the beginning inventory for Year 2.

First, we assume that in Year 2, the **Harley-Davidson** store purchases a total of **three** inventory units at the current $120 price, the sales price has been raised to $140, and **three** units are sold. Using LIFO, the units are allocated to ending inventory and cost of goods sold as follows.

Cost of Goods Sold Calculation (LIFO with three units purchased and three units sold)		
Beginning inventory	(2 units at $70 each and 1 unit at $80)	$220
+ Purchases	(3 units at $120 each)	360
Goods available for sale		580
− Ending inventory	(2 units at $70 each and 1 unit at $80)	220
Cost of goods sold	(3 units at $120 each)	$360

Given that revenue is $140 per unit, the gross profit on the three newly purchased units is 3 units × $20 = $60.

Now assume instead that the store purchases only *two* additional units at $120 each. Using LIFO, these two new $120 units and the old $80 unit would become cost of goods sold.

Cost of Goods Sold Calculation (LIFO with two units purchased and three units sold)		
Beginning inventory	(2 units at $70 each and 1 unit at $80)	$220
+ Purchases	(2 units at $120 each)	240
Goods available for sale		460
− Ending inventory	(2 units at $70 each)	140
Cost of goods sold	(2 units at $120 each and 1 unit at $80)	$320

Given that revenue is $140 per unit, the gross profit on the newly purchased units is 2 units × $20 = $40. Since the cost of the old unit is only $80, the gross profit on this one unit is $60 ($140 − $80) instead of $20, raising total gross profit to $100. The complete income statement effects are reflected below.

	No Liquidation (purchase 3 units)	Liquidation (purchase 2 units)
Effect on the Income Statement		
Sales	$420	$420
Cost of goods sold	360	320
Gross profit	60	100
Other expenses	48	48
Income before income taxes	12	52
Income tax expense (25%)	3	13
Net income	$ 9	$ 39

This $40 change is the **pretax effect of the LIFO liquidation.** Given the assumed tax rate of 25 percent, taxes paid are $10 (0.25 × $40) higher than if no liquidation had taken place.

In practice, LIFO liquidations and extra tax payments can be avoided even if purchases of additional inventory take place **after** the sale of the item it replaces. Tax law allows LIFO to be applied **as if** all purchases during an accounting period took place before any sales and cost of goods sold were recorded. Thus, temporary LIFO liquidations can be eliminated by purchasing additional inventory before year-end. Most companies apply LIFO in this manner.

Chapter Supplement B

FIFO and LIFO Cost of Goods Sold under Periodic versus Perpetual Inventory Systems

The purpose of this supplement is to compare the calculation of FIFO and LIFO cost of goods sold under a periodic versus a perpetual inventory system. As we noted in the chapter, calculations of FIFO cost of goods sold will always be the same under both systems. However, calculations of LIFO cost of goods sold will usually differ in a manner that causes the company to pay higher income taxes when inventory costs are rising if it uses the perpetual computation. Consider the following company purchase and sale data for the month of January. Note that beginning inventory is 2,000 units, purchases are 14,000 units, and sales are 9,000 units.

	Units	Unit Cost
January 1 Beginning inventory	2,000	$20.60
January 5 Sold	1,000	
January 13 Purchased	6,000	22.00
January 17 Sold	3,000	
January 25 Purchased	8,000	25.10
January 27 Sold	5,000	

FIFO (First-in, First-out)

FIFO assumes that the oldest goods are the first ones sold. Using a **periodic inventory** calculation, the 9,000 **oldest goods available during the month** would include the 2,000 in beginning inventory, the 6,000 purchased on January 13, and 1,000 of the units purchased January 25. Cost of goods sold would be calculated as follows:

Cost of Goods Sold		
Units	Unit Cost	Total Cost
2,000	$20.60	$ 41,200
6,000	22.00	132,000
1,000	25.10	25,100
Total		$198,300

Using a **perpetual inventory** calculation, we would compute the cost of goods sold for each sale separately using the **oldest goods available at the time of each sale.**

Cost of Goods Sold			
Date of Sale	Units	Unit Cost	Total Cost
Jan. 5	1,000	$20.60	$ 20,600
Jan. 17	1,000	20.60	20,600
	2,000	22.00	44,000
Jan. 27	4,000	22.00	88,000
	1,000	25.10	25,100
Total			$198,300

Note that cost of goods sold is $198,300 using both computations. This is true because the oldest goods available during the month are the same as the oldest goods available at the time of each sale. This will always be true.

LIFO (Last-in, First-out)

LIFO assumes that the newest goods are the first ones sold. Using a **periodic inventory** calculation, the 9,000 **newest goods available during the month** would include the 8,000 units purchased January 25 and 1,000 of the units purchased on January 13. Cost of goods sold would be calculated as follows:

	Cost of Goods Sold	
Units	**Unit Cost**	**Total Cost**
8,000	$25.10	$200,800
1,000	22.00	22,000
Total		$222,800

Using a **perpetual inventory** calculation, we would compute the cost of goods sold for each sale separately using the **newest goods available at the time of each sale.**

	Cost of Goods Sold		
Date of Sale	**Units**	**Unit Cost**	**Total Cost**
Jan. 5	1,000	$20.60	$ 20,600
Jan. 17	3,000	22.00	66,000
Jan. 27	5,000	25.10	125,500
Total			$212,100

Note that cost of goods sold is higher using the periodic computation. This is true because the newest goods available during the month are **not** the same as the newest goods available at the time of each sale. **When costs are rising, the periodic calculation will always produce the same or a higher value for cost of goods sold than the perpetual calculation.** In this case, the periodic calculation gives you a $10,700 higher value for cost of goods sold ($222,800 − $212,100). This higher value will result in a $10,700 lower amount for income before taxes. If the tax rate is 35 percent, the company would end up paying $3,745 less in taxes for the current year (0.35 × $10,700).

Why You Won't See LIFO Perpetual Calculations in Practice

This added tax savings from the periodic calculation illustrated above is one of the two reasons you will rarely if ever see LIFO perpetual calculations in practice in medium- to large-sized companies. The other reason relates to the complexity and cost of the calculations. Even if a company's perpetual inventory information system is sophisticated enough to instantaneously record the arrival of new inventory, it is unlikely that it will have sufficient information concerning invoice pricing, returns, allowances, and discounts to instantaneously compute a unit cost for those goods. Also, consider the number of calculations of goods available for sale that would have to be made by a company that has numerous sales and purchases of many different inventory items. This makes it very costly or impossible for most companies to apply LIFO using a perpetual calculation. Instead, companies keep perpetual inventory records on a FIFO basis and then make an end-of-period adjusting entry using the periodic calculation to convert both inventory on the balance sheet and cost of goods sold on the income statement to a LIFO basis.

Chapter Supplement C

Additional Issues in Measuring Purchases

Purchase Returns and Allowances

PURCHASE RETURNS AND ALLOWANCES
A reduction in the cost of purchases associated with unsatisfactory goods.

Purchased goods may be returned to the vendor if they do not meet specifications, arrive in damaged condition, or are otherwise unsatisfactory. **Purchase returns and allowances** require a reduction in the cost of inventory purchases and the recording of a cash refund or a reduction in the liability to the vendor. For example, assume that **Harley-Davidson** returned to a supplier damaged harness boots that cost $1,000. The return would be recorded as follows:

| Accounts payable (−L) (or Cash +A) .... | 1,000 | |
| Inventory (−A) .... | | 1,000 |

Assets	=	**Liabilities**	+	**Stockholders' Equity**
Inventory	−1,000	Accounts Payable	−1,000	

Purchase Discounts

Cash discounts must be accounted for by both the seller and the buyer (accounting by the seller was discussed in Chapter 6). When merchandise is bought on credit, terms such as 2/10, n/30 are sometimes specified. That is, if payment is made within 10 days from the date of purchase, a 2 percent cash discount known as the **purchase discount** is granted. If payment is not made within the discount period, the full invoice cost is due 30 days after the purchase.

PURCHASE DISCOUNT
Cash discount received for prompt payment of an account.

Assume that on January 17, **Harley-Davidson** bought goods that had a $1,000 invoice price with terms 2/10, n/30. The purchase would be recorded as follows (using what is called the **gross method**):

Date of Purchase

| Jan. 17 | Inventory (+A) .... | 1,000 | |
| | Accounts payable (+L) .... | | 1,000 |

Assets	=	**Liabilities**	+	**Stockholders' Equity**
Inventory	+1,000	Accounts Payable	+1,000	

Date of Payment, within the Discount Period

Jan. 26	Accounts payable (−L)	1,000	
	Inventory (−A)		20
	Cash (−A)		980

Assets	=	**Liabilities**	+	**Stockholders' Equity**
Inventory	−20	Accounts Payable	−1,000	
Cash	−980			

If for any reason Harley-Davidson did not pay within the 10-day discount period, the following entry would be needed:

Date of Payment, after the Discount Period

| Feb. 1 | Accounts payable (−L)........................ | 1,000 | |
| | Cash (−A) .... | | 1,000 |

Assets	=	**Liabilities**	+	**Stockholders' Equity**
Cash	−1,000	Accounts Payable	−1,000	

7-1. Apply the cost principle to identify the amounts that should be included in inventory and the expense matching principle to determine cost of goods sold for typical retailers, wholesalers, and manufacturers.   p. 335

Inventory should include all items owned that are held for resale. Costs flow into inventory when goods are purchased or manufactured. They flow out (as an expense) when they are sold or disposed of. In conformity with the expense matching principle, the total cost of the goods sold during the period must be matched with the sales revenue earned during the period. A company can keep track of the ending inventory and cost of goods sold for the period using (1) the perpetual inventory system, which is based on the maintenance of detailed and continuous inventory records, and (2) the periodic inventory system, which is based on a physical count of ending inventory and use of the cost of goods sold equation to determine cost of goods sold.

7-2. Report inventory and cost of goods sold using the four inventory costing methods.   p. 340

The chapter discussed four different inventory costing methods used to allocate costs between the units remaining in inventory and the units sold and their applications in different economic circumstances. The methods discussed were specific identification, FIFO, LIFO, and average cost. Each of the inventory costing methods conforms to GAAP. Public companies using LIFO must provide note disclosures that allow conversion of inventory and cost of goods sold to FIFO amounts. Remember that the cost flow assumption need not match the physical flow of inventory.

7-3. Decide when the use of different inventory costing methods is beneficial to a company.   p. 345

The selection of an inventory costing method is important because it will affect reported income, income tax expense (and hence cash flow), and the inventory valuation reported on the balance sheet. In a period of rising prices, FIFO normally results in higher income and higher taxes than LIFO; in a period of falling prices, the opposite occurs. The choice of methods is normally made to minimize taxes.

7-4. Report inventory at the lower of cost or market (LCM).   p. 348

Ending inventory should be measured based on the lower of actual cost or net realizable value (LCM basis). This practice can have a major effect on the statements of companies facing declining costs. Damaged, obsolete, and out-of-season inventory should also be written down to their current estimated net realizable value if below cost. The LCM adjustment increases cost of goods sold, decreases income, and decreases reported inventory in the year of the write-down.

7-5. Evaluate inventory management using the inventory turnover ratio.   p. 349

The inventory turnover ratio measures the efficiency of inventory management. It reflects how many times average inventory was produced and sold during the period. Analysts and creditors watch this ratio because a sudden decline may mean that a company is facing an unexpected drop in demand for its products or is becoming sloppy in its production management.

7-6. Compare companies that use different inventory costing methods.   p. 350

These comparisons can be made by converting the LIFO company's statements to FIFO. Public companies using LIFO must disclose the differences between LIFO and FIFO values for beginning and ending inventory. These amounts are often called the LIFO reserve. The beginning LIFO reserve minus the ending LIFO reserve equals the difference in cost of goods sold under FIFO. Pretax income is affected by the same amount in the opposite direction. This amount times the tax rate is the tax effect.

7-7. Understand methods for controlling inventory, analyze the effects of inventory errors on financial statements, and analyze the effects of inventory on cash flows.   p. 353

Various control procedures can limit inventory theft or mismanagement. An error in the measurement of ending inventory affects cost of goods sold on the current period's income statement and ending inventory on the balance sheet. Because this year's ending inventory becomes next year's beginning inventory, it also affects cost of goods sold in the following period by the same amount but in the opposite direction. These relationships can be seen through the cost of goods sold equation (BI + P − EI = CGS). When a net **decrease in inventory** for the period occurs, sales are more than purchases; thus, the decrease must be **added** in computing cash flows from operations. When a net **increase in inventory** for the period occurs, sales are less than purchases; thus, the increase must be **subtracted** in computing cash flows from operations.

In this and previous chapters, we discussed the current assets of a business. These assets are critical to operations, but many of them do not directly produce value. In Chapter 8, we will discuss the noncurrent assets property, plant, and equipment; intangibles that are the elements of productive capacity; and natural resources. Many of the noncurrent assets produce value, such as a factory that manufactures cars. These assets present some interesting accounting problems because they benefit a number of accounting periods.

KEY **RATIO**

Inventory turnover ratio measures the efficiency of inventory management. It reflects how many times average inventory was produced and sold during the period (see the "Key Ratio Analysis" box in the Evaluating Inventory Management section):

$$\text{Inventory Turnover} = \frac{\text{Cost of Goods Sold}}{\text{Average Inventory}}$$

FINDING **FINANCIAL INFORMATION**

Balance Sheet

Under Current Assets
   Inventories

Income Statement

Expenses
   Cost of goods sold

Statement of Cash Flows

Under Operating Activities (indirect method):

Net income
   − increases in inventory
   + decreases in inventory
   + increases in accounts payable
   − decreases in accounts payable

Notes

Under Summary of Significant Accounting
   Policies:
     Description of management's choice of
     inventory accounting policy (FIFO, LIFO,
     LCM, etc.)

In Separate Note
   If not listed on balance sheet, components
     of inventory (merchandise, raw materials,
     work in progress, finished goods)
   If using LIFO, LIFO reserve (excess of FIFO
     over LIFO)

KEY **TERMS**

Average Cost Method   p. 343
Cost of Goods Sold Equation   p. 338
Direct Labor   p. 337
Factory Overhead   p. 337
Finished Goods Inventory   p. 335
First-In, First-Out (FIFO) Method   p. 341
Goods Available for Sale   p. 338

Inventory   p. 335
Last-In, First-Out (LIFO) Method   p. 342
LIFO Liquidation   p. 358
LIFO Reserve   p. 351
Lower of Cost or Market (LCM)   p. 348
Merchandise Inventory   p. 335
Net Realizable Value   p. 348

Periodic Inventory System   p. 340
Perpetual Inventory System   p. 340
Purchase Discount   p. 361
Purchase Returns and Allowances   p. 360
Raw Materials Inventory   p. 335
Specific Identification Method   p. 341
Work in Process Inventory   p. 335

QUESTIONS

1. Why is inventory an important item to both internal (management) and external users of financial statements?
2. What are the general guidelines for deciding which items should be included in inventory?
3. Explain the application of the cost principle to an item in the ending inventory.
4. Define goods available for sale. How does it differ from cost of goods sold?
5. Define beginning inventory and ending inventory.
6. The chapter discussed four inventory costing methods. List the four methods and briefly explain each.
7. Explain how income can be manipulated when the specific identification inventory costing method is used.
8. Contrast the effects of LIFO versus FIFO on reported assets (i.e., the ending inventory) when (a) prices are rising and (b) prices are falling.
9. Contrast the income statement effect of LIFO versus FIFO (i.e., on pretax income) when (a) prices are rising and (b) prices are falling.
10. Contrast the effects of LIFO versus FIFO on cash outflow and inflow.
11. Explain briefly the application of the LCM concept to the ending inventory and its effect on the income statement and balance sheet when market is lower than cost.
12. When a perpetual inventory system is used, unit costs of the items sold are known at the date of each sale. In contrast, when a periodic inventory system is used, unit costs are known only at the end of the accounting period. Why are these statements correct?

MULTIPLE-CHOICE QUESTIONS

1. Consider the following information: ending inventory, $24,000; sales, $250,000; beginning inventory, $30,000; selling and administrative expenses, $70,000; and purchases, $90,000. What is cost of goods sold?
   a. $86,000
   b. $94,000
   c. $96,000
   d. $84,000
2. The inventory costing method selected by a company will affect
   a. The balance sheet.
   b. The income statement.
   c. The statement of retained earnings.
   d. All of the above.
3. Which of the following is **not** a component of the cost of inventory?
   a. Administrative overhead
   b. Direct labor
   c. Raw materials
   d. Factory overhead
4. Consider the following information: beginning inventory, 10 units @ $20 per unit; first purchase, 35 units @ $22 per unit; second purchase, 40 units @ $24 per unit; 50 units were sold. What is cost of goods sold using the **FIFO** method of inventory costing?
   a. $1,090
   b. $1,060
   c. $1,180
   d. $1,200
5. Consider the following information: beginning inventory, 10 units @ $20 per unit; first purchase, 35 units @ $22 per unit; second purchase, 40 units @ $24 per unit; 50 units were sold. What is cost of goods sold using the **LIFO** method of inventory costing?
   a. $1,090
   b. $1,060
   c. $1,180
   d. $1,200
6. An increasing inventory turnover ratio
   a. Indicates a longer time span between the ordering and receiving of inventory.
   b. Indicates a shorter time span between the ordering and receiving of inventory.
   c. Indicates a shorter time span between the purchase and sale of inventory.
   d. Indicates a longer time span between the purchase and sale of inventory.

7. If the ending balance in accounts payable decreases from one period to the next, which of the following is true?
   a. Cash payments to suppliers exceeded current period purchases.
   b. Cash payments to suppliers were less than current period purchases.
   c. Cash receipts from customers exceeded cash payments to suppliers.
   d. Cash receipts from customers exceeded current period purchases.
8. Which of the following regarding the lower of cost or market rule for inventory are true?
   (1) The lower of cost or market rule is an example of the historical cost principle.
   (2) When the net realizable value of inventory drops below the cost shown in the financial records, net income is reduced.
   (3) When the net realizable value of inventory drops below the cost shown in the financial records, total assets are reduced.

   a. (1)   c. (2) and (3)
   b. (2)   d. All three
9. Which inventory method provides a better matching of current costs with sales revenue on the income statement and outdated values for inventory on the balance sheet?
   a. FIFO   c. LIFO
   b. Average cost   d. Specific identification
10. Which of the following is false regarding a perpetual inventory system?
    a. Physical counts are not needed since records are maintained on a transaction-by-transaction basis.
    b. The balance in the inventory account is updated with each inventory purchase and sale transaction.
    c. Cost of goods sold is increased as sales are recorded.
    d. The account Purchases is not used as inventory is acquired.

MINI-**EXERCISES**

Matching Inventory Items to Type of Business

Match the type of inventory with the type of business in the following matrix:

M7-1
LO7-1

	TYPE OF BUSINESS	
Type of Inventory	**Merchandising**	**Manufacturing**
Work in process		
Finished goods		
Merchandise		
Raw materials		

Recording the Cost of Purchases for a Merchandiser

Select Apparel purchased 90 new shirts and recorded a total cost of $2,258 determined as follows:

M7-2
LO7-1

Invoice cost	$1,800
Shipping charges	185
Import taxes and duties	165
Interest (6.0%) on $1,800 borrowed to finance the purchase	108
	$2,258

Required:
Make the needed corrections in this calculation. Give the journal entry (or entries) to record this purchase in the correct amount, assuming a perpetual inventory system. Show computations.

M7-3

LO7-1

Identifying the Cost of Inventories for a Manufacturer

Operating costs incurred by a manufacturing company become either (1) part of the cost of inventory to be expensed as cost of goods sold at the time the finished goods are sold or (2) expenses at the time they are incurred. Indicate whether each of the following costs belongs in category (1) or (2).

___ *a.* Wages of factory workers
___ *b.* Costs of raw materials purchased
___ *c.* Sales salaries
___ *d.* Heat, light, and power for the factory building
___ *e.* Heat, light, and power for the headquarters office building

M7-4

LO7-1

Inferring Purchases Using the Cost of Goods Sold Equation

JCPenney Company, Inc., is a major retailer with department stores in all 50 states. The dominant portion of the company's business consists of providing merchandise and services to consumers through department stores that include catalog departments. In a recent annual report, JCPenney reported cost of goods sold of $11,042 million, ending inventory for the current year of $2,916 million, and ending inventory for the previous year of $3,213 million.

Required:

Is it possible to develop a reasonable estimate of the merchandise purchases for the year? If so, prepare the estimate; if not, explain why.

M7-5

LO7-2

Matching Financial Statement Effects to Inventory Costing Methods

Indicate whether the FIFO or LIFO inventory costing method normally produces each of the following effects under the listed circumstances.

a. Declining costs
   Highest net income _____
   Highest inventory _____

b. Rising costs
   Highest net income _____
   Highest inventory _____

M7-6

LO7-3

Matching Inventory Costing Method Choices to Company Circumstances

Indicate whether the FIFO or LIFO inventory costing method would normally be selected when inventory costs are rising. Explain why.

M7-7

LO7-4

Reporting Inventory under Lower of Cost or Market

Wood Company had the following inventory items on hand at the end of the year:

	Quantity	Cost per Item	Net Realizable Value per Item
Item A	70	$110	$100
Item B	30	60	85

Computing the lower of cost or market on an item-by-item basis, determine what amount would be reported on the balance sheet for inventory.

M7-8

LO7-5

Determining the Effects of Inventory Management Changes on Inventory Turnover Ratio

Indicate the most likely effect of the following changes in inventory management on the inventory turnover ratio (use + for increase, − for decrease, and NE for no effect).

___ *a.* Have parts inventory delivered daily by suppliers instead of weekly.
___ *b.* Extend payments for inventory purchases from 15 days to 30 days.
___ *c.* Shorten production process from 10 days to 8 days.

Determining the Financial Statement Effects of Inventory Errors

Assume the prior year ending inventory was understated by $50,000. Explain how this error would affect the prior year and current year pretax income amounts. What would be the effects if the prior year ending inventory were overstated by $50,000 instead of understated?

M7-9
LO7-7

connect

EXERCISES

Analyzing Items to Be Included in Inventory

E7-1
LO7-1

Based on its physical count of inventory in its warehouse at year-end, December 31 of the current year, Madison Company planned to report inventory of $34,500. During the audit, the independent CPA developed the following additional information:

a. Goods from a supplier costing $700 are in transit with UPS on December 31 of the current year. The terms are FOB shipping point (explained in the "Required" section). Because these goods had not yet arrived, they were excluded from the physical inventory count.
b. Madison delivered samples costing $1,800 to a customer on December 27 of the current year, with the understanding that they would be returned to Madison on January 15 of the next year. Because these goods were not on hand, they were excluded from the inventory count.
c. On December 31 of the current year, goods in transit to customers, with terms FOB shipping point, amounted to $6,500 (expected delivery date January 10 of the next year). Because the goods had been shipped, they were excluded from the physical inventory count.
d. On December 31 of the current year, goods in transit to customers, with terms FOB destination, amounted to $1,500 (expected delivery date January 10 of the next year). Because the goods had been shipped, they were excluded from the physical inventory count.

Required:
Madison's accounting policy requires including in inventory all goods for which it has title. Note that the point where title (ownership) changes hands is determined by the shipping terms in the sales contract. When goods are shipped "FOB shipping point," title changes hands at shipment and the buyer normally pays for shipping. When they are shipped "FOB destination," title changes hands on delivery, and the seller normally pays for shipping. Begin with the $34,500 inventory amount and compute the correct amount for the ending inventory. Explain the basis for your treatment of each of the preceding items. (**Hint:** Set up three columns: Item, Amount, and Explanation.)

Inferring Missing Amounts Based on Income Statement Relationships

E7-2
LO7-1

Supply the missing dollar amounts for the income statement for each of the following independent cases. (**Hint:** In Case B, work from the bottom up.)

	Case A	Case B	Case C
Net sales revenue	$7,500	$?	$5,000
Beginning inventory	$11,200	$ 7,000	$ 4,000
Purchases	4,500	?	9,500
Goods available for sale	?	15,050	13,500
Ending inventory	9,000	11,050	?
Cost of goods sold	?	?	4,200
Gross profit	?	800	?
Expenses	300	?	700
Pretax income (loss)	$ 500	($200)	$ 100

Inferring Missing Amounts Based on Income Statement Relationships

E7-3
LO7-1

Supply the missing dollar amounts for the income statement for each of the following independent cases:

Cases	Sales Revenue	Beginning Inventory	Purchases	Total Available	Ending Inventory	Cost of Goods Sold	Gross Profit	Expenses	Pretax Income (Loss)
A	$ 650	$100	$700	$?	$500	$?	$?	$200	$?
B	1,100	200	900	?	?	?	?	150	150
C	?	150	?	?	300	200	400	100	?
D	800	?	550	?	300	?	?	200	200
E	1,000	?	900	1,100	?	?	500	?	(50)

E7-4

LO7-1

Inferring Merchandise Purchases

Abercrombie and Fitch is a leading retailer of casual apparel for men, women, and children. Assume that you are employed as a stock analyst and your boss has just completed a review of the new Abercrombie annual report. She provided you with her notes, but they are missing some information that you need. Her notes show that the ending inventory for Abercrombie in the current and previous years was $569,818,000 and $385,857,000, respectively. Net sales for the current year were $4,158,058,000. Cost of goods sold was $1,639,188,000. Net income was $127,658,000. For your analysis, you determine that you need to know the amount of purchases for the year.

Required:

Can you develop the information from her notes? Explain and show calculations. (**Hint:** Use the cost of goods sold equation or the inventory T-account to solve for the needed value.)

E7-5

LO7-2

Calculating Ending Inventory and Cost of Goods Sold under FIFO, LIFO, and Average Cost

Penn Company uses a periodic inventory system. At the end of the annual accounting period, December 31 of the current year, the accounting records provided the following information for product 1:

	Units	Unit Cost
Inventory, December 31, prior year	2,000	$5
For the current year:		
Purchase, March 21	5,000	6
Purchase, August 1	3,000	8
Inventory, December 31, current year	4,000	

Required:

Compute ending inventory and cost of goods sold for the current year under FIFO, LIFO, and average cost inventory costing methods. (**Hint:** Set up adjacent columns for each case.)

E7-6

LO7-2

Calculating Ending Inventory and Cost of Goods Sold under FIFO, LIFO, and Average Cost

Hamilton Company uses a periodic inventory system. At the end of the annual accounting period, December 31 of the current year, the accounting records provided the following information for product 1:

	Units	Unit Cost
Inventory, December 31, prior year	2,000	$5
For the current year:		
Purchase, March 21	6,000	4
Purchase, August 1	4,000	2
Inventory, December 31, current year	3,000	

Required:

Compute ending inventory and cost of goods sold under FIFO, LIFO, and average cost inventory costing methods. (**Hint:** Set up adjacent columns for each case.)

Analyzing and Interpreting the Financial Statement Effects of LIFO and FIFO

E7-7
LO7-2, 7-3

Broadhead Company uses a periodic inventory system. At the end of the annual accounting period, December 31 of the current year, the accounting records provided the following information for product 2:

	Units	Unit Cost
Inventory, December 31, prior year	3,000	$ 9
For the current year:		
Purchase, April 11	9,000	10
Purchase, June 1	7,000	15
Sales ($50 each)	10,000	
Operating expenses (excluding income tax expense) $195,000		

Required:
1. Prepare a separate income statement through pretax income that details cost of goods sold for (*a*) Case A: FIFO and (*b*) Case B: LIFO. For each case, show the computation of the ending inventory and cost of goods sold. (**Hint:** Set up adjacent columns for each case.)
2. Compare the pretax income and the ending inventory amounts between the two cases. Explain the similarities and differences.
3. Which inventory costing method may be preferred for income tax purposes? Explain.

Analyzing and Interpreting the Financial Statement Effects of LIFO and FIFO

E7-8
LO7-2, 7-3

Beck Inc. uses a periodic inventory system. At the end of the annual accounting period, December 31 of the current year, the accounting records provided the following information for product 2:

	Units	Unit Cost
Inventory, December 31, prior year	7,000	$ 11
For the current year:		
Purchase, March 5	19,000	9
Purchase, September 19	10,000	5
Sale ($28 each)	8,000	
Sale ($30 each)	16,000	
Operating expenses (excluding income tax expense) $400,000		

Required:
1. Prepare a separate income statement through pretax income that details cost of goods sold for (*a*) Case A: FIFO and (*b*) Case B: LIFO. For each case, show the computation of the ending inventory and cost of goods sold. (**Hint:** Set up adjacent columns for each case.)
2. Compare the pretax income and the ending inventory amounts between the two cases. Explain the similarities and differences.
3. Which inventory costing method may be preferred for income tax purposes? Explain.

Evaluating the Choice among Three Alternative Inventory Methods Based on Cash Flow Effects

E7-9
LO7-2, 7-3

Following is partial information for the income statement of Audio Solutions Company under three different inventory costing methods, assuming the use of a periodic inventory system:

	FIFO	LIFO	Average Cost
Cost of goods sold			
Beginning inventory (400 units @ $28)	$11,200	$11,200	$11,200
Purchases (475 units @ $35)	16,625	16,625	16,625
Goods available for sale			
Ending inventory (525 units)			
Cost of goods sold	$	$	$
Sales, 350 units; unit sales price, $50			
Expenses, $1,700			

Required:

1. Compute cost of goods sold under the FIFO, LIFO, and average cost inventory costing methods.
2. Prepare an income statement through pretax income for each method.
3. Rank the three methods in order of income taxes paid (favorable cash flow) and explain the basis for your ranking.

E7-10

LO7-2, 7-3

Evaluating the Choice among Three Alternative Inventory Methods Based on Cash Flow Effects

Following is partial information for the income statement of Arturo Technologies Company under three different inventory costing methods, assuming the use of a periodic inventory system:

	FIFO	LIFO	Average Cost
Cost of goods sold			
Beginning inventory (400 units @ $30)	$12,000	$12,000	$12,000
Purchases (400 units @ $20)	8,000	8,000	8,000
Goods available for sale			
Ending inventory (500 units)			
Cost of goods sold	$	$	$
Sales, 300 units; unit sales price, $50			
Expenses, $2,500			

Required:

1. Compute cost of goods sold under the FIFO, LIFO, and average cost inventory costing methods.
2. Prepare an income statement through pretax income for each method.
3. Rank the three methods in order of preference based on income taxes paid (favorable cash flow) and explain the basis for your ranking.

E7-11

LO7-2, 7-3

Evaluating the Choice among Three Alternative Inventory Methods Based on Income and Cash Flow Effects

Daniel Company uses a periodic inventory system. Data for the current year: beginning merchandise inventory (ending inventory December 31, prior year), 2,000 units at $38; purchases, 8,000 units at $40; expenses (excluding income taxes), $194,500; ending inventory per physical count at December 31, current year, 1,800 units; sales, 8,200 units; sales price per unit, $75; and average income tax rate, 30 percent.

Required:

1. Compute cost of goods sold and prepare income statements under the FIFO, LIFO, and average cost inventory costing methods. Use a format similar to the following:

		INVENTORY COSTING METHOD		
Cost of Goods Sold	Units	FIFO	LIFO	Average Cost
Beginning inventory		$	$	$
Purchases				
Goods available for sale				
Ending inventory				
Cost of goods sold		$	$	$

Income Statement	FIFO	LIFO	Average Cost
Sales revenue	$	$	$
Cost of goods sold			
Gross profit			
Expenses			
Pretax income			
Income tax expense			
Net income	$	$	$

2. Between FIFO and LIFO, which method is preferable in terms of (*a*) net income and (*b*) income taxes paid (cash flow)? Explain.
3. What would your answer to requirement (2) be, assuming that prices were falling? Explain.

Reporting Inventory at Lower of Cost or Market

E7-12
LO7-4

Jones Company is preparing the annual financial statements dated December 31 of the current year. Ending inventory information about the five major items stocked for regular sale follows:

	ENDING INVENTORY, CURRENT YEAR		
Item	Quantity on Hand	Unit Cost When Acquired (FIFO)	Net Realizable Value (Market) at Year-End
A	50	$15	$12
B	80	30	40
C	10	48	52
D	70	25	30
E	350	10	5

Required:
Compute the valuation that should be used for the current year ending inventory using the LCM rule applied on an item-by-item basis. (**Hint:** Set up columns for Item, Quantity, Total Cost, Total Market, and LCM Valuation.)

Reporting Inventory at Lower of Cost or Market

E7-13
LO7-4

Parson Company was formed on January 1 of the current year and is preparing the annual financial statements dated December 31, current year. Ending inventory information about the four major items stocked for regular sale follows:

	ENDING INVENTORY, CURRENT YEAR		
Item	Quantity on Hand	Unit Cost When Acquired (FIFO)	Net Realizable Value (Market) at Year-End
A	30	$20	$15
B	55	40	44
C	35	52	55
D	15	27	32

Required:
1. Compute the valuation that should be used for the current year ending inventory using the LCM rule applied on an item-by-item basis. (**Hint:** Set up columns for Item, Quantity, Total Cost, Total Market, and LCM Valuation.)
2. What will be the effect of the write-down of inventory to lower of cost or market on cost of goods sold for the year ended December 31, current year?

Analyzing and Interpreting the Inventory Turnover Ratio

E7-14
LO7-5

Dell Inc. is the leading manufacturer of personal computers. In a recent year, it reported the following in dollars in millions:

Net sales revenue	$62,071
Cost of sales	48,260
Beginning inventory	1,301
Ending inventory	1,404

Required:
1. Determine the inventory turnover ratio and average days to sell inventory for the current year.
2. Explain the meaning of each number.

E7-15
LO7-5, 7-6

Analyzing and Interpreting the Effects of the LIFO/FIFO Choice on Inventory Turnover Ratio

The records at the end of January of the current year for Young Company showed the following for a particular kind of merchandise:

Beginning Inventory at FIFO: 19 Units @ $16 = $304

Beginning Inventory at LIFO: 19 Units @ $12 = $228

January Transactions	Units	Unit Cost	Total Cost
Purchase, January 9	25	$13	$325
Purchase, January 20	50	19	950
Sale, January 21 (at $38 per unit)	40		
Sale, January 27 (at $39 per unit)	25		

Required:
Compute the inventory turnover ratio for the month of January under the FIFO and LIFO inventory costing methods (show computations and round to the nearest dollar). Which costing method is the more accurate indicator of the efficiency of inventory management? Explain.

E7-16
LO7-6

Analyzing Notes to Adjust Inventory from LIFO to FIFO

The following note was contained in a recent **Ford Motor Company** annual report:

NOTE 8. INVENTORIES—AUTOMOTIVE SECTOR		
Inventories at December 31 were as follows (dollars in millions)		
	Current Year	Previous Year
Raw material, work in process, & supplies	$2,847	$2,812
Finished products	3,982	3,970
Total inventories at FIFO	6,829	6,782
Less LIFO adjustment	(928)	(865)
Total	$5,901	$5,917
About one-third of inventories were determined under the last-in, first-out method.		

Required:
1. What amount of ending inventory would have been reported in the current year if Ford had used only FIFO?
2. The cost of goods sold reported by Ford for the current year was $113,345 million. Determine the cost of goods sold that would have been reported if Ford had used only FIFO for both years.
3. Explain why Ford management chose to use LIFO for certain of its inventories.

E7-17
LO7-6

Analyzing Notes to Adjust Inventory from LIFO to FIFO

Snyder's-Lance is a leading snack-food company. The following note was contained in its recent annual report:

NOTE 4. INVENTORIES		
Inventories at year-end consisted of the following: (in thousands)		
	Current Year	Prior Year
Finished goods	$23,227	$21,910
Raw materials	11,556	7,701
Supplies, etc.	15,293	14,297
Total inventories at FIFO cost	50,076	43,908
Less: adjustment to reduce FIFO cost to LIFO cost	(6,964)	(5,249)
Total inventories	$43,112	$38,659

Required:
1. What amount of ending inventory would have been reported in the current year if Snyder's-Lance had used only FIFO?
2. The cost of goods sold reported by Snyder's-Lance for the current year was $531,528 thousand. Determine the cost of goods sold that would have been reported if Snyder's-Lance had used only FIFO for both years.
3. Explain why Snyder's-Lance management chose to use LIFO for certain of its inventories.

Analyzing the Effect of an Inventory Error Disclosed in an Actual Note to a Financial Statement

E7-18
LO7-7

Several years ago, the financial statements of **Gibson Greeting Cards**, now part of **American Greetings**, contained the following note:

> On July 1, the Company announced that it had determined that the inventory . . . had been overstated. . . . The overstatement of inventory . . . was $8,806,000. *(Gibson Greeting Cards Annual Report)*

Gibson reported an incorrect net income amount of $25,852,000 for the year in which the error occurred and the income tax rate was 39.3 percent.

Required:
1. Compute the amount of net income that Gibson reported after correcting the inventory error. Show computations.
2. Assume that the inventory error was not discovered. Identify the financial statement accounts that would have been incorrect (*a*) for the year the error occurred and (*b*) for the subsequent year. State whether each account was understated or overstated.

Analyzing and Interpreting the Impact of an Inventory Error

E7-19
LO7-7

Grants Corporation prepared the following two income statements (simplified for illustrative purposes):

	First Quarter		Second Quarter	
Sales revenue		$11,000		$18,000
Cost of goods sold				
Beginning inventory	$4,000		$ 3,800	
Purchases	3,000		13,000	
Goods available for sale	7,000		16,800	
Ending inventory	3,800		9,000	
Cost of goods sold		3,200		7,800
Gross profit		7,800		10,200
Expenses		5,000		6,000
Pretax income		$ 2,800		$ 4,200

During the third quarter, it was discovered that the ending inventory for the first quarter should have been $4,400.

Required:
1. What effect did this error have on the combined pretax income of the two quarters? Explain.
2. Did this error affect the EPS amounts for each quarter? (See Chapter 5 for discussion of EPS.) Explain.
3. Prepare corrected income statements for each quarter.
4. Set up a schedule with the following headings to reflect the comparative effects of the correct and incorrect amounts on the income statement:

	First Quarter			**Second Quarter**		
Income Statement Item	Incorrect	Correct	Error	Incorrect	Correct	Error

E7-20   **Interpreting the Effect of Changes in Inventories and Accounts Payable on Cash Flow from**
LO7-7   **Operations**

In its recent annual report, **PepsiCo** included the following information in its balance sheets (dollars in millions):

CONSOLIDATED BALANCE SHEETS		
	Current Year	**Previous Year**
. . .		
Inventories	$ 3,827	$ 3,372
. . .		
Accounts payable	11,757	10,923

Required:
Explain the effects of the changes in inventory and accounts payable on cash flow from operating activities for the current year.

E7-21   **(Chapter Supplement A) Analyzing the Effects of a Reduction in the Amount of LIFO Inventory**

In its annual report, **ConocoPhillips** reported that the company decreased its inventory levels during 2011. ConocoPhillips's 2011 financial statements contain the following note:

> In 2011, a liquidation of LIFO inventory values increased net income attributable to ConocoPhillips $160 million, of which $155 million was attributable to the R&M segment.

Required:
1. Explain why the reduction in inventory quantity increased net income for ConocoPhillips.
2. If ConocoPhillips had used FIFO, would the reductions in inventory quantity during the two years have increased net income? Explain.

E7-22   **(Chapter Supplement B) FIFO and LIFO Cost of Goods Sold under Periodic versus Perpetual**
Inventory Systems

Assume that a retailer's beginning inventory and purchases of a popular item during January included: (1) 300 units at $7 in beginning inventory on January 1, (2) 450 units at $8 purchased on January 8, and (3) 750 units at $9 purchased on January 29. The company sold 350 units on January 12 and 550 units on January 30.

Required:
1. Calculate the cost of goods sold for the month of January under (*a*) FIFO (periodic calculation), (b) FIFO (perpetual calculation), (c) LIFO (periodic calculation), and (d) LIFO (perpetual calculation).
2. Which cost flow assumption would you recommend to management and why? Which calculation approach, periodic or perpetual, would you recommend and why?

(Chapter Supplement C) Recording Sales and Purchases with Cash Discounts

E7-23

Scott's Cycles sells merchandise on credit terms of 2/15, n/30. A sale invoiced at $1,500 (cost of sales $975) was made to Shannon Allen on February 1. The company uses the gross method of recording sales discounts.

Required:
1. Give the journal entry to record the credit sale. Assume use of the perpetual inventory system.
2. Give the journal entry, assuming that the account was collected in full on February 9.
3. Give the journal entry, assuming, instead, that the account was collected in full on March 2.

On March 4, the company purchased bicycles and accessories from a supplier on credit, invoiced at $9,000; the terms were 3/10, n/30. The company uses the gross method to record purchases.

Required:
4. Give the journal entry to record the purchase on credit. Assume use of the perpetual inventory system.
5. Give the journal entry, assuming that the account was paid in full on March 12.
6. Give the journal entry, assuming, instead, that the account was paid in full on March 28.

PROBLEMS

Analyzing Items to Be Included in Inventory

P7-1
LO7-1

Travis Company has just completed a physical inventory count at year-end, December 31 of the current year. Only the items on the shelves, in storage, and in the receiving area were counted and costed on a FIFO basis. The inventory amounted to $80,000. During the audit, the independent CPA developed the following additional information:

a. Goods costing $900 were being used by a customer on a trial basis and were excluded from the inventory count at December 31 of the current year.

b. Goods in transit on December 31 of the current year, from a supplier, with terms FOB destination (explained in the "Required" section), cost $900. Because these goods had not yet arrived, they were excluded from the physical inventory count.

c. On December 31 of the current year, goods in transit to customers, with terms FOB shipping point, amounted to $1,700 (expected delivery date January 10 of next year). Because the goods had been shipped, they were excluded from the physical inventory count.

d. On December 28 of the current year, a customer purchased goods for cash amounting to $2,650 and left them "for pickup on January 3 of next year." Travis Company had paid $1,750 for the goods and, because they were on hand, included the latter amount in the physical inventory count.

e. On the date of the inventory count, the company received notice from a supplier that goods ordered earlier at a cost of $3,550 had been delivered to the transportation company on December 27 of the current year; the terms were FOB shipping point. Because the shipment had not arrived by December 31 of the current year, it was excluded from the physical inventory count.

f. On December 31 of the current year, the company shipped $700 worth of goods to a customer, FOB destination. The goods are expected to arrive at their destination no earlier than January 8 of next year. Because the goods were not on hand, they were not included in the physical inventory count.

g. One of the items sold by the company has such a low volume that management planned to drop it last year. To induce Travis Company to continue carrying the item, the manufacturer-supplier provided the item on a "consignment basis." This means that the manufacturer-supplier retains ownership of the item, and Travis Company (the consignee) has no responsibility to pay for the items until they are sold to a customer. Each month, Travis Company sends a report to the manufacturer on the number sold and remits cash for the cost. At the end of December of the current year, Travis Company had six of these items on hand; therefore, they were included in the physical inventory count at $950 each.

Required:

Assume that Travis's accounting policy requires including in inventory all goods for which it has title. Note that the point where title (ownership) changes hands is determined by the shipping terms in the sales contract. When goods are shipped "FOB shipping point," title changes hands at shipment and the buyer normally pays for shipping. When they are shipped "FOB destination," title changes hands on delivery, and the seller normally pays for shipping. Begin with the $80,000 inventory amount and compute the correct amount for the ending inventory. Explain the basis for your treatment of each of the preceding items. (**Hint:** Set up three columns: Item, Amount, and Explanation.)

P7-2
LO7-2

Analyzing the Effects of Four Alternative Inventory Methods (AP7-1)

Kirtland Corporation uses a periodic inventory system. At the end of the annual accounting period, December 31, the accounting records for the most popular item in inventory showed the following:

Transactions	Units	Unit Cost
Beginning inventory, January 1	400	$3.00
Transactions during the year:		
a. Purchase, January 30	300	3.40
b. Purchase, May 1	460	4.00
c. Sale ($5 each)	(160)	
d. Sale ($5 each)	(700)	

Required:

Compute the amount of (*a*) goods available for sale, (*b*) ending inventory, and (*c*) cost of goods sold at December 31, under each of the following inventory costing methods (show computations and round to the nearest dollar):

1. Average cost (round the average cost per unit to the nearest cent).
2. First-in, first-out.
3. Last-in, first-out.
4. Specific identification, assuming that the first sale was selected two-fifths from the beginning inventory and three-fifths from the purchase of January 30. Assume that the second sale was selected from the remainder of the beginning inventory, with the balance from the purchase of May 1.

P7-3
LO7-2, 7-3

Evaluating Four Alternative Inventory Methods Based on Income and Cash Flow (AP7-2)

At the end of January of the current year, the records of Donner Company showed the following for a particular item that sold at $16 per unit:

Transactions	Units	Amount
Inventory, January 1	500	$2,365
Purchase, January 12	600	3,600
Purchase, January 26	160	1,280
Sale	(370)	
Sale	(250)	

Required:

1. Assuming the use of a periodic inventory system, prepare a summarized income statement through gross profit for the month of January under each method of inventory: (*a*) average cost, (*b*) FIFO, (*c*) LIFO, and (*d*) specific identification. For specific identification, assume that the first sale was

selected from the beginning inventory and the second sale was selected from the January 12 purchase. Round the average cost per unit to the nearest cent. Show the inventory computations in
detail.

2. Of FIFO and LIFO, which method results in the higher pretax income? Which method results in the
higher EPS?
3. Of FIFO and LIFO, which method results in the lower income tax expense? Explain, assuming a 30
percent average tax rate.
4. Of FIFO and LIFO, which method produces the more favorable cash flow? Explain.

Analyzing and Interpreting Income Manipulation under the LIFO Inventory Method

P7-4

LO7-2, 7-3

Pacific Company sells electronic test equipment that it acquires from a foreign source. During the year,
the inventory records reflected the following:

	Units	Unit Cost	Total Cost
Beginning inventory	20	$12,000	$240,000
Purchases	42	10,000	420,000
Sales (47 units at $24,500 each)			

Inventory is valued at cost using the LIFO inventory method.

Required:
1. Complete the following income statement summary using the LIFO method and the periodic inventory system (show computations):

Sales revenue	$ _____
Cost of goods sold	_____
Gross profit	_____
Expenses	300,000
Pretax income	$ _____
Ending inventory	$ _____

2. The management, for various reasons, is considering buying 20 additional units before the December 31 year-end, at $9,000 each. Restate the income statement (and ending inventory), assuming that
this purchase is made on December 31.
3. How much did pretax income change because of the decision on December 31? Assuming that the
unit cost of test equipment is expected to continue to decline during the following year, is there any
evidence of income manipulation? Explain.

Evaluating the LIFO and FIFO Choice When Costs Are Rising and Falling (AP7-3)

P7-5

LO7-2, 7-3

Income is to be evaluated under four different situations as follows:

a. Prices are rising:
    (1) Situation A: FIFO is used.
    (2) Situation B: LIFO is used.
b. Prices are falling:
    (1) Situation C: FIFO is used.
    (2) Situation D: LIFO is used.

The basic data common to all four situations are: sales, 500 units for $15,000; beginning inventory, 300 units; purchases, 400 units; ending inventory, 200 units; and operating expenses, $4,000. The following tabulated income statements for each situation have been set up for analytical purposes:

| | PRICES RISING | | PRICES FALLING | |
	Situation A FIFO	Situation B LIFO	Situation C FIFO	Situation D LIFO
Sales revenue	$15,000	$15,000	$15,000	$15,000
Cost of goods sold:				
Beginning inventory	3,300	?	?	?
Purchases	4,800	?	?	?
Goods available for sale	8,100	?	?	?
Ending inventory	2,400	?	?	?
Cost of goods sold	5,700	?	?	?
Gross profit	9,300	?	?	?
Expenses	4,000	4,000	4,000	4,000
Pretax income	5,300	?	?	?
Income tax expense (30%)	1,590	?	?	?
Net income	$ 3,710			

Required:
1. Complete the preceding tabulation for each situation. In Situations A and B (prices rising), assume the following: beginning inventory, 300 units at $11 = $3,300; purchases, 400 units at $12 = $4,800. In Situations C and D (prices falling), assume the opposite; that is, beginning inventory, 300 units at $12 = $3,600; purchases, 400 units at $11 = $4,400. Use periodic inventory procedures.
2. Analyze the relative effects on pretax income and net income as demonstrated by requirement (1) when prices are rising and when prices are falling.
3. Analyze the relative effects on the cash position for each situation.
4. Would you recommend FIFO or LIFO? Explain.

P7-6

LO7-4

Evaluating the Income Statement and Cash Flow Effects of Lower of Cost or Market

Jaffa Company prepared its annual financial statements dated December 31 of the current year. The company applies the FIFO inventory costing method; however, the company neglected to apply LCM to the ending inventory. The preliminary current year income statement follows:

Sales revenue		$300,000
Cost of goods sold		
Beginning inventory	$ 33,000	
Purchases	184,000	
Goods available for sale	217,000	
Ending inventory (FIFO cost)	50,450	
Cost of goods sold		166,550
Gross profit		133,450
Operating expenses		62,000
Pretax income		71,450
Income tax expense (30%)		21,435
Net income		$ 50,015

Assume that you have been asked to restate the current year financial statements to incorporate LCM. You have developed the following data relating to the current year ending inventory:

Item	Quantity	Acquisition Cost Unit	Acquisition Cost Total	Net Realizable Value (Market)
A	3,050	$3	$ 9,150	$4
B	1,500	5.5	8,250	3.5
C	7,100	1.5	10,650	3.5
D	3,200	7	22,400	4
			$50,450	

Required:
1. Restate this income statement to reflect LCM valuation of the current year ending inventory. Apply LCM on an item-by-item basis and show computations.
2. Compare and explain the LCM effect on each amount that was changed on the income statement in requirement (1).
3. What is the conceptual basis for applying LCM to merchandise inventories?
4. Thought question: What effect did LCM have on the current year cash flow? What will be the long-term effect on cash flow?

Evaluating the Effects of Manufacturing Changes on Inventory Turnover Ratio and Cash Flows from Operating Activities

P7-7
LO7-5, 7-7

Mears and Company has been operating for five years as an electronics component manufacturer specializing in cellular phone components. During this period, it has experienced rapid growth in sales revenue and in inventory. Mr. Mears and his associates have hired you as Mears's first corporate controller. You have put into place new purchasing and manufacturing procedures that are expected to reduce inventories by approximately one-third by year-end. You have gathered the following data related to the changes:

(dollars in thousands)	Beginning of Year	End of Year (projected)
Inventory	$582,500	$384,610
		Current Year (projected)
Cost of goods sold		$7,283,566

Required:
1. Compute the inventory turnover ratio based on two different assumptions:
   a. Those presented in the preceding table (a decrease in the balance in inventory).
   b. No change from the beginning-of-the-year inventory balance.
2. Compute the effect of the projected change in the balance in inventory on cash flow from operating activities for the year (indicate the sign and amount of effect).
3. On the basis of the preceding analysis, write a brief memo explaining how an increase in inventory turnover can result in an increase in cash flow from operating activities. Also explain how this increase can benefit the company.

Evaluating the Choice between LIFO and FIFO Based on an Inventory Note

P7-8
LO7-6

An annual report for **International Paper Company** included the following note:

The last-in, first-out inventory method is used to value most of International Paper's U.S. inventories . . . If the first-in, first-out method had been used, it would have increased total inventory balances by approximately $350 million and $334 million at December 31, 2011, and 2010, respectively.

For the year 2011, International Paper Company reported net income (after taxes) of $1,341 million. At December 31, 2011, the balance of International Paper Company's retained earnings account was $3,330 million.

Required:

1. Determine the amount of net income that International Paper would have reported in 2011 if it had used the FIFO method (assume a 30 percent tax rate).
2. Determine the amount of retained earnings that International Paper would have reported at the end of 2011 if it always had used the FIFO method (assume a 30 percent tax rate).
3. Use of the LIFO method reduced the amount of taxes that International Paper had to pay in 2011 compared with the amount that would have been paid if International Paper had used FIFO. Calculate the amount of this reduction (assume a 30 percent tax rate).

P7-9

LO7-7

Analyzing and Interpreting the Effects of Inventory Errors (AP7-4)

The income statement for Pruitt Company summarized for a four-year period shows the following:

	2016	2017	2018	2019
Sales revenue	$2,025,000	$2,450,000	$2,700,000	$2,975,000
Cost of goods sold	1,505,000	1,627,000	1,782,000	2,113,000
Gross profit	520,000	823,000	918,000	862,000
Expenses	490,000	513,000	538,000	542,000
Pretax income	30,000	310,000	380,000	320,000
Income tax expense (30%)	9,000	93,000	114,000	96,000
Net income	$ 21,000	$ 217,000	$ 266,000	$ 224,000

An audit revealed that in determining these amounts, the ending inventory for 2017 was overstated by $18,000. The company uses a periodic inventory system.

Required:

1. Recast the income statements to reflect the correct amounts, taking into consideration the inventory error.
2. Compute the gross profit percentage for each year (*a*) before the correction and (*b*) after the correction.
3. What effect would the error have had on the income tax expense assuming a 30 percent average rate?

P7-10

(Chapter Supplement A) Analyzing LIFO and FIFO When Inventory Quantities Decline Based on an Actual Note

In a recent annual report, **General Electric** reported the following in its inventory note:

December 31 (dollars in millions)	Current Year	Prior Year
Raw materials and work in progress	$5,603	$5,515
Finished goods	2,863	2,546
Unbilled shipments	246	280
	8,712	8,341
Less revaluation to LIFO	(2,226)	(2,076)
LIFO value of inventories	$6,486	$6,265

It also reported a $23 million change in cost of goods sold due to "lower inventory levels."

Required:

1. Compute the increase or decrease in the pretax operating profit (loss) that would have been reported for the current year had GE employed FIFO accounting for all inventory for both years.
2. Compute the increase or decrease in pretax operating profit that would have been reported had GE employed LIFO but not reduced inventory quantities during the current year.

Analyzing the Effects of Four Alternative Inventory Methods (P7-2)

AP7-1

LO7-2

Dixon Company uses a periodic inventory system. At the end of the annual accounting period, December 31, the accounting records for the most popular item in inventory showed the following:

Transactions	Units	Unit Cost
Beginning inventory, January 1	390	$32.00
Transactions during the current period:		
a. Purchase, February 20	700	34.25
b. Purchase, June 30	460	37.00
c. Sale ($50 each)	(70)	
d. Sale ($50 each)	(750)	

Required:

Compute the cost of (*a*) goods available for sale, (*b*) ending inventory, and (*c*) goods sold at December 31 under each of the following inventory costing methods (show computations and round to the nearest dollar):

1. Average cost (round average cost per unit to the nearest cent).
2. First-in, first-out.
3. Last-in, first-out.
4. Specific identification, assuming that the first sale was selected two-fifths from the beginning inventory and three-fifths from the purchase of February 20. Assume that the second sale was selected from the remainder of the beginning inventory, with the balance from the purchase of June 30.

Evaluating Four Alternative Inventory Methods Based on Income and Cash Flow (P7-3)

AP7-2

LO7-2, 7-3

At the end of January of the current year, the records of NewRidge Company showed the following for a particular item that sold at $16 per unit:

Transactions	Units	Amount
Inventory, January 1	120	$ 960
Purchase, January 12	380	3,420
Purchase, January 26	200	2,200
Sale	(100)	
Sale	(140)	

Required:

1. Assuming the use of a periodic inventory system, prepare a summarized income statement through gross profit for January under each method of inventory: (*a*) weighted average cost, (*b*) FIFO, (*c*) LIFO, and (*d*) specific identification. For specific identification, assume that the first sale was selected from the beginning inventory and the second sale was selected from the January 12 purchase. Show the inventory computations (including for ending inventory) in detail.
2. Of FIFO and LIFO, which method results in the higher pretax income? Which method results in the higher EPS?
3. Of FIFO and LIFO, which method results in the lower income tax expense? Explain, assuming a 30 percent average tax rate.
4. Of FIFO and LIFO, which method produces the more favorable cash flow? Explain.

Evaluating the LIFO and FIFO Choice When Costs Are Rising and Falling (P7-5)

AP7-3

LO7-2, 7-3

Income is to be evaluated under four different situations as follows:
a. Prices are rising:
   (1) Situation A: FIFO is used.
   (2) Situation B: LIFO is used.
b. Prices are falling:
   (1) Situation C: FIFO is used.
   (2) Situation D: LIFO is used.

The basic data common to all four situations are: sales, 510 units for $13,260; beginning inventory, 340 units; purchases, 410 units; ending inventory, 240 units; and operating expenses, $5,000. The following tabulated income statements for each situation have been set up for analytical purposes:

	PRICES RISING		PRICES FALLING	
	Situation A FIFO	Situation B LIFO	Situation C FIFO	Situation D LIFO
Sales revenue	$13,260	$13,260	$13,260	$13,260
Cost of goods sold:				
Beginning inventory	3,060	?	?	?
Purchases	4,100	?	?	?
Goods available for sale	7,160	?	?	?
Ending inventory	2,400	?	?	?
Cost of goods sold	4,760	?	?	?
Gross profit	8,500	?	?	?
Expenses	5,000	5,000	5,000	5,000
Pretax income	3,500	?	?	?
Income tax expense (30%)	1,050	?	?	?
Net income	$ 2,450			

Required:
1. Complete the preceding tabulation for each situation. In Situations A and B (prices rising), assume the following: beginning inventory, 340 units at $9 = $3,060; purchases, 410 units at $10 = $4,100. In Situations C and D (prices falling), assume the opposite; that is, beginning inventory, 340 units at $10 = $3,400; purchases, 410 units at $9 = $3,690. Use periodic inventory procedures.
2. Analyze the relative effects on pretax income and net income as demonstrated by requirement (1) when prices are rising and when prices are falling.
3. Analyze the relative effects on the cash position for each situation.
4. Would you recommend FIFO or LIFO? Explain.

AP7-4

LO7-7

Analyzing and Interpreting the Effects of Inventory Errors (P7-9)

The income statements for four consecutive years for Colca Company reflected the following summarized amounts:

	2016	2017	2018	2019
Sales revenue	$60,000	$63,000	$65,000	$68,000
Cost of goods sold	39,000	43,000	44,000	46,000
Gross profit	21,000	20,000	21,000	22,000
Expenses	16,000	17,000	17,000	19,000
Pretax income	$ 5,000	$ 3,000	$ 4,000	$ 3,000

Subsequent to development of these amounts, it has been determined that the physical inventory taken on December 31, 2017, was understated by $2,000.

Required:
1. Recast the income statements to reflect the correct amounts, taking into consideration the inventory error.
2. Compute the gross profit percentage for each year (*a*) before the correction and (*b*) after the correction.
3. What effect would the error have had on the income tax expense, assuming a 30 percent average rate?

Evaluating the Choice of Inventory Method When Costs Are Rising and Falling   **CON7-1**

Pool Corporation, Inc., reported in its recent annual report that "In 2010, our industry experienced some price deflation. . . . In 2011, our industry experienced more normalized price inflation of approximately 2% overall despite price deflation for certain chemical products." This suggests that in some years Pool's overall inventory costs rise, and in some years they fall. Furthermore, in many years, the costs of some inventory items rise while others fall. Assume that Pool has only two product items in its inventory this year. Purchase and sale data are presented below.

Transaction	Inventory Item A		Inventory Item B	
	Units	Unit Cost	Units	Unit Cost
Beginning inventory	40	$6	40	$6
Purchases, February 7	80	8	80	5
Purchases, March 16	100	9	100	3
Sales, April 28	160		160	

Required:
1. Compute cost of goods sold for each of the two items separately using the FIFO and LIFO inventory costing methods.
2. Between FIFO and LIFO, which method is preferable in terms of (*a*) net income and (*b*) income taxes paid (cash flow)? Answer the question for each item separately. Explain.

Annual Report Cases

Finding Financial Information   **CP7-1**
                                           LO7-1, 7-2, 7-5
Refer to the financial statements of **American Eagle Outfitters** given in Appendix B at the end of this book.

Required:
1. How much inventory does the company hold at the end of the most recent year?
2. Estimate the amount of merchandise that the company purchased during the current year. (**Hint:** Use the cost of goods sold equation and ignore "certain buying, occupancy, and warehousing expenses.")
3. What method does the company use to determine the cost of its inventory?
4. Compute the inventory turnover ratio for the current year. What does an inventory turnover ratio tell you?

Finding Financial Information   **CP7-2**
                                           LO7-2, 7-4, 7-5, 7-7
Refer to the financial statements of **Urban Outfitters** given in Appendix C at the end of this book.

Required:
1. The company uses lower of cost or market to account for its inventory. At the end of the year, do you expect the company to write its inventory down to replacement cost or net realizable value? Explain your answer.
2. What method does the company use to determine the cost of its inventory?

3. If the company overstated ending inventory by $10 million for the year ended January 31, 2015, what would be the corrected value for Income before Income Taxes?
4. Compute the inventory turnover ratio for the current year. What does an inventory turnover ratio tell you?

CP7-3

LO7-5

Comparing Companies within an Industry

Refer to the financial statements of **American Eagle Outfitters** (Appendix B) and **Urban Outfitters** (Appendix C) and the Industry Ratio Report (Appendix D) at the end of this book.

Required:
1. Compute the inventory turnover ratio for both companies for the current year. What do you infer from the difference?
2. Compare the inventory turnover ratio for both companies to the industry average. Are these two companies doing better or worse than the industry average in turning over their inventory?

Financial Reporting and Analysis Cases

CP7-4

LO7-1

Using Financial Reports: Interpreting the Effect of Charging Costs to Inventory as Opposed to Current Operating Expenses

Dana Holding Corporation designs and manufactures component parts for the vehicular, industrial, and mobile off-highway original equipment markets. In a recent annual report, Dana's inventory note indicated the following:

> Dana changed its method of accounting for inventories effective January 1 . . . to include in inventory certain production-related costs previously charged to expense. This change in accounting principle resulted in a better matching of costs against related revenues. The effect of this change in accounting increased inventories by $23.0 and net income by $12.9.

Required:
1. Under Dana's previous accounting method, certain production costs were recognized as expenses on the income statement in the period they were incurred. When will they be recognized under the new accounting method?
2. Explain how including these costs in inventory increased both inventories and net income for the year.

CP7-5

LO7-5, 7-6

Using Financial Reports: Interpreting Effects of the LIFO/FIFO Choice on Inventory Turnover

In its annual report, **Caterpillar, Inc.**, a major manufacturer of farm and construction equipment, reported the following information concerning its inventories:

> Inventories are stated at the lower of cost or market. Cost is principally determined using the last-in, first-out (LIFO) method. The value of inventories on the LIFO basis represented about 65% of total inventories at December 31, 2011, and about 70% of total inventories at December 31, 2010 and 2009.
>
> If the FIFO (first-in, first-out) method had been in use, inventories would have been $2,422 million, $2,575 million, and $3,022 million higher than reported at December 31, 2011, 2010, and 2009, respectively.

On its balance sheet, Caterpillar reported:

	2011	2010	2009
Inventories	$14,544	$9,587	$6,360

	2011	2010	2009
Cost of goods sold	$43,578	$30,367	$23,886

Required:

As a recently hired financial analyst, you have been asked to analyze the efficiency with which Caterpillar has been managing its inventory and to write a short report. Specifically, you have been asked to compute inventory turnover for 2011 based on FIFO and LIFO and to compare the two ratios with two standards: (1) Caterpillar for the prior year 2010 and (2) its chief competitor, **John Deere**. For 2011, John Deere's inventory turnover was 4.2 based on FIFO and 5.9 based on LIFO. In your report, include:

1. The appropriate ratios computed based on FIFO and LIFO.
2. An explanation of the differences in the ratios across the FIFO and LIFO methods.
3. An explanation of whether the FIFO or LIFO ratios provide a more accurate representation of the companies' efficiency in use of inventory.

Critical Thinking Cases

Making a Decision as a Financial Analyst: Analysis of the Effect of a Change to LIFO

CP7-6
LO7-6

A press release for **Seneca Foods** (licensee of the **Libby's** brand of canned fruits and vegetables) included the following information:

> The current year's net earnings were $8,019,000 or $0.65 per diluted share, compared with $32,067,000 or $2.63 per diluted share, last year. These results reflect the Company's decision to implement the LIFO (last-in, first-out) inventory valuation method effective December 30, 2007 (fourth quarter). The effect of this change was to reduce annual pretax earnings by $28,165,000 and net earnings by $18,307,000 or $1.50 per share ($1.49 diluted) below that which would have been reported using the Company's previous inventory method. The Company believes that in this period of significant inflation, the use of the LIFO method better matches current costs with current revenues. This change also results in cash savings of $9,858,000 by reducing the Company's income taxes, based on statutory rates. If the Company had remained on the FIFO (first-in, first-out) inventory valuation method, the pretax results, less non-operating gains and losses, would have been an all-time record of $42,644,000, up from $40,009,000 in the prior year.

Required:

As a new financial analyst at a leading Wall Street investment banking firm, you are assigned to write a memo outlining the effects of the accounting change on Seneca's financial statements. Assume a 35 percent tax rate. In your report, be sure to include the following:

1. Why did management adopt LIFO?
2. By how much did the change affect pretax earnings and ending inventory? Verify that the amount of the tax savings listed in the press release is correct.
3. As an analyst, how would you react to the decrease in income caused by the adoption of LIFO? Consider all of the information in the press release.

Evaluating an Ethical Dilemma: Earnings, Inventory Purchases, and Management Bonuses

CP7-7

Micro Warehouse was a computer software and hardware online and catalog sales company.* A 1996 *Wall Street Journal* article disclosed the following:

MICRO WAREHOUSE IS REORGANIZING TOP MANAGEMENT

Micro Warehouse Inc. announced a "significant reorganization" of its management, including the resignation of three senior executives. The move comes just a few weeks after the Norwalk, Conn., computer catalogue sales company said it overstated earnings by $28 million since 1992 as a result of accounting irregularities. That previous disclosure prompted a flurry of shareholder lawsuits against the company. In addition, Micro Warehouse said it is cooperating with an "informal inquiry" by the Securities and Exchange Commission.

Source: Stephan E. Frank, *The Wall Street Journal*, November 21, 1996, p. B2. Copyright © 1996 by Dow Jones & Co. Used with permission.

Its Form 10-Q quarterly report filed with the Securities and Exchange Commission two days before indicated that inaccuracies involving understatement of purchases and accounts payable in current and prior

*Micro Warehouse declared bankruptcy in 2003.

periods amounted to $47.3 million. It also indicated that, as a result, $2.2 million of executive bonuses for 1995 would be rescinded. Micro Warehouse's total tax rate is approximately 40.4 percent. Both cost of goods sold and executive bonuses are fully deductible for tax purposes.

Required:

As a new staff member at Micro Warehouse's auditing firm, you are assigned to write a memo outlining the effects of the understatement of purchases and the rescinding of the bonuses. In your report, be sure to include the following:

1. The total effect on pretax and after-tax earnings of the understatement of purchases.
2. The total effect on pretax and after-tax earnings of the rescinding of the bonuses.
3. An estimate of the percentage of after-tax earnings management is receiving in bonuses.
4. A discussion of why Micro Warehouse's board of directors may have decided to tie managers' compensation to reported earnings and the possible relation between this type of bonus scheme and the accounting errors.

Financial Reporting and Analysis Team Project

CP7-8

LO7-2, 7-3, 7-5, 7-7

CP7-8 Team Project: Analyzing Inventories

As a team, select an industry to analyze. Yahoo Finance provides lists of industries at **biz.yahoo.com/p/industries.html**. Click on an industry for a list of companies in that industry. Alternatively, go to Google Finance at **www.google.com/finance** and search for a company you are interested in. You will be presented with a list including that company and its competitors. Each team member should acquire the annual report or 10-K for one publicly traded company in the industry, with each member selecting a different company (the SEC EDGAR service at **www.sec.gov** and the company's investor relations website itself are good sources).

Required:

On an individual basis, each team member should write a short report answering the following questions about the selected company. Discuss any patterns across the companies that you as a team observe. Then, as a team, write a short report comparing and contrasting your companies.

1. If your company lists inventories in its balance sheet, what percentage of total assets does inventories represent for each of the last three years? If your company does not list inventories, discuss why this is so.
2. If your company lists inventories, what inventory costing method is applied to U.S. inventories?
   a. What do you think motivated this choice?
   b. If the company uses LIFO, how much higher or lower would net income before taxes be if it had used FIFO or a similar method instead?
3. Ratio Analysis:
   a. What does the inventory turnover ratio measure in general?
   b. If your company reports inventories, compute the ratio for the last three years.
   c. What do your results suggest about the company?
   d. If available, find the industry ratio for the most recent year, compare it to your results, and discuss why you believe your company differs or is similar to the industry ratio.
4. What is the effect of the change in inventories on cash flows from operating activities for the most recent year (that is, did the change increase or decrease operating cash flows)? Explain your answer.

Reporting and Interpreting Property, Plant, and Equipment; Intangibles; and Natural Resources

As of December 31, 2014, **Southwest Airlines** operated 665 Boeing 737 aircraft, providing service to 93 domestic and international destinations, and was the largest U.S. air carrier in number of originating passengers boarded. Southwest is a capital-intensive company with more than $14 billion in property, plant, and equipment reported on its balance sheet. In fiscal year 2014, Southwest spent nearly $1.8 billion on aircraft and other flight equipment as well as ground equipment. Since the demand for air travel is seasonal, with peak demand occurring during the summer months, planning for optimal productive capacity in the airline industry is very difficult. Southwest's managers must determine how many aircraft are needed in which cities at what points in time to fill all seats demanded. Otherwise, the company loses revenue (not enough seats) or incurs higher costs (too many seats).

Demand is also highly sensitive to general economic conditions and other events beyond the control of the company. Even the best corporate planners could not have predicted the September 11, 2001, terrorist attacks against the United States that rocked the airline industry. The war in Iraq led to further declines in the demand for air travel. In response to

Learning Objectives

After studying this chapter, you should be able to:

8-1 Define, classify, and explain the nature of long-lived productive assets and interpret the fixed asset turnover ratio.

8-2 Apply the cost principle to measure the acquisition and maintenance of property, plant, and equipment.

8-3 Apply various cost allocation methods as assets are held and used over time.

8-4 Explain the effect of asset impairment on the financial statements.

8-5 Analyze the disposal of property, plant, and equipment.

8-6 Apply measurement and reporting concepts for intangible assets and natural resources.

8-7 Explain how the acquisition, use, and disposal of long-lived assets impact cash flows.

Larry MacDougal/AP Photos

the precipitous drop in demand, many airlines accelerated retirement of various aircraft, temporarily grounded aircraft, and considered delaying the purchase of new aircraft. Then, a worsening global economic environment provided more challenges for the airline industry. With fuel prices more than tripling between 2000 and 2014, many carriers were forced to reduce capacity.

UNDERSTANDING THE BUSINESS

One of the major challenges managers of most businesses face is forecasting the company's long-term productive capacity—that is, predicting the amount of plant and equipment it will need. If managers underestimate the need, the company will not be able to produce enough goods or services to meet demand and will miss an opportunity to earn revenue. On the other hand, if they overestimate the need, the company will incur excessive costs that will reduce its profitability.

The airline industry provides an outstanding example of the difficulty of planning for and analyzing productive capacity. If an airplane takes off from Kansas City, Missouri, en route to New York City with empty seats, the economic value associated with those seats is lost for that flight. There is obviously no way to sell the seat to a customer after the airplane has left the gate. Unlike a manufacturer, an airline cannot "inventory" seats for the future.

Likewise, if an unexpectedly large number of people want to board a flight, the airline must turn away some customers. You might be willing to buy a television set from **Best Buy** even if you had to wait one week for delivery, but you probably wouldn't book a flight home on Thanksgiving weekend on an airline that told you no seats were available. You would simply pick another airline or use a different mode of transportation.

Southwest has a number of large competitors with familiar names such as **American**, **United Continental**, **JetBlue**, and **Delta**. Southwest's 10-K report mentions that the company "currently competes with other airlines on virtually all of South-west's scheduled routes."

Much of the battle for passengers in the airline industry is fought in terms of property, plant, and equipment. Passengers want convenient schedules (which requires a large number of aircraft), and they want to fly on new, modern airplanes. Because airlines have such a large investment in equipment but no opportunity to inventory unused seats, they work very hard to fill their aircraft to capacity for each flight. Southwest's Annual Report for 2014 describes the keys to its ability to offer lower fares and generous frequent flyer benefits.

SOUTHWEST AIRLINES

REAL WORLD EXCERPT:

Annual Report

> A key component of the Company's business strategy has historically been its low-cost structure, which was designed to allow Southwest to profitably charge low fares. Adjusted for stage length, Southwest has lower unit costs, on average, than the vast majority of major domestic carriers. The Company's low-cost structure has historically been facilitated by Southwest's use of a single aircraft type, the Boeing 737, an operationally efficient point-to-point route structure, and highly productive Employees. Southwest's use of a single aircraft type has allowed for simplified scheduling, maintenance, flight operations, and training activities.

As you can see from this discussion, issues surrounding property, plant, and equipment have a pervasive impact on a company in terms of strategy, pricing decisions, and profitability. Managers devote considerable time to planning optimal levels of productive capacity, and financial analysts closely review a company's statements to determine the impact of management's decisions.

This chapter is organized according to the life cycle of long-lived assets—acquisition, use, and disposal. First, we will discuss the measuring and reporting issues related to land, buildings, and equipment. Then we will discuss the measurement and reporting issues for intangible assets and natural resources. Among the issues we will discuss are the maintenance, use, and disposal of property and equipment over time and the measurement and reporting of assets considered impaired in their ability to generate future cash flows.

ORGANIZATION of the Chapter

Acquisition and Maintenance of Plant and Equipment	Use, Impairment, and Disposal of Plant and Equipment	Intangible Assets and Natural Resources
• Classifying Long-Lived Assets • Measuring and Recording Acquisition Cost • Fixed Asset Turnover Ratio • Repairs, Maintenance, and Improvements	• Depreciation Concepts • Alternative Depreciation Methods • How Managers Choose • Measuring Asset Impairment • Disposal of Property, Plant, and Equipment	• Acquisition and Amortization of Intangible Assets • Acquisition and Depletion of Natural Resources

ACQUISITION AND MAINTENANCE OF PLANT AND EQUIPMENT

Exhibit 8.1 shows the asset section of the balance sheet from **Southwest**'s annual report for the fiscal year ended December 31, 2014. Over 70 percent of Southwest's total assets are flight and ground equipment. Southwest also reports other assets with probable long-term benefits. Let's begin by classifying these assets.

Classifying Long-Lived Assets

The resources that determine a company's productive capacity are often called **long-lived assets**. These assets, which are listed as noncurrent assets on the balance sheet, may be either tangible or intangible and have the following characteristics:

1. **Tangible assets** have physical substance; that is, they can be touched. The three kinds of long-lived tangible assets are:

   a. **Land** used in operations. As is the case with **Southwest**, land often is not shown as a separate item on the balance sheet.

   b. **Buildings, fixtures, and equipment** used in operations. For Southwest, this category includes aircraft, ground equipment to service the aircraft, and office space. (*Note:* Land, buildings, fixtures, and equipment are also called **property, plant, and equipment** or **fixed assets.**)

   c. **Natural resources** used in operations. Southwest does not report any natural resources on its balance sheet. However, companies in other industries report natural resources such as timber tracts and silver mines.

2. **Intangible assets** are long-lived assets without physical substance that confer specific rights on their owner. Examples are patents, copyrights, franchises, licenses, and trademarks. Southwest reports $970 million of goodwill on its balance sheet.

Measuring and Recording Acquisition Cost

Under the cost principle, all reasonable and necessary expenditures made in acquiring and preparing an asset for use (or sale, as in the case of inventory) **should be recorded as the cost of the asset.** We say that the expenditures are **capitalized** when they are recorded as part of the cost of an asset instead of as expenses in the current period. Any sales taxes, legal

LEARNING OBJECTIVE 8-1
Define, classify, and explain the nature of long-lived productive assets and interpret the fixed asset turnover ratio.

LONG-LIVED ASSETS
Tangible and intangible resources owned by a business and used in its operations over several years.

TANGIBLE ASSETS
Assets that have physical substance.

INTANGIBLE ASSETS
Assets that have special rights but not physical substance.

Plant and Equipment as a Percent of Total Assets for Selected Focus Companies

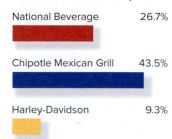

National Beverage	26.7%
Chipotle Mexican Grill	43.5%
Harley-Davidson	9.3%

EXHIBIT 8.1

Southwest Airlines's Asset Section of the Balance Sheet

SOUTHWEST AIRLINES
REAL WORLD EXCERPT:
Annual Report

SOUTHWEST AIRLINES CO.
Consolidated Balance Sheets (partial)
December 31, 2014 and 2013

Assets (*dollars in millions*)	2014	2013
Current assets: (*summarized*)	$ 4,404	$ 4,456
Property and equipment, at cost:		
Flight equipment	18,473	16,937
Ground property and equipment	2,853	2,666
Deposits on flight equipment purchase contracts	566	764
Assets constructed for others	621	453
	22,513	20,820
Less allowance for depreciation and amortization	8,221	7,431
Total property and equipment	14,292	13,389
Goodwill	970	970
Other assets	534	530
Total assets	$20,200	$19,345

fees, transportation costs, and installation costs are then added to the purchase price of the asset. However, special discounts are subtracted and any interest charges associated with the purchase are expensed as incurred.

KEY RATIO ANALYSIS

Selected Focus Companies' Fixed Asset Turnover Ratios

Chipotle Mexican Grill — 3.99

Deckers — 10.40

Apple — 9.82

Fixed Asset Turnover

? ANALYTICAL QUESTION

How effectively is management utilizing fixed assets to generate revenues?

% RATIO AND COMPARISONS

$$\text{Fixed Asset Turnover} = \frac{\text{Net Sales (or Operating Revenues)}}{\text{Average Net Fixed Assets*}}$$

The 2014 ratio for **Southwest** is (dollars in millions):

Operating Revenues $18,605 ÷ [($13,389 + $14,292) ÷ 2] = 1.34 times

COMPARISONS OVER TIME			COMPARISONS WITH COMPETITORS	
Southwest Airlines			Delta	United Continental Holdings
2012	2013	2014	2014	2014
0.92	0.90	1.34	1.84	2.07

 INTERPRETATIONS

In General   The fixed asset turnover ratio measures the sales dollars generated by each dollar of fixed assets used. A high rate normally suggests effective management. An increasing rate over time signals more efficient fixed asset use. Creditors and security analysts use this ratio to assess a company's effectiveness in generating sales from its fixed assets.

Focus Company Analysis   Southwest's fixed asset turnover ratio increased between 2012 and 2014. Although at first glance it appears that Southwest is less efficient than **Delta** and **United Continental Holdings**, this is not the case. Their higher fixed asset turnover is due to the greater age of their fleet (a higher percentage has been depreciated) and the fact that more planes are leased in such a way that they do not appear as fixed assets on the balance sheet.

A Few Cautions   A lower or declining fixed asset turnover rate may indicate that a company is expanding (by acquiring additional productive assets) in anticipation of higher future sales. An increasing ratio could also signal that a firm has cut back on capital expenditures due to a downturn in business. This is not the case at Southwest, which continues to expand its fleet. As a consequence, appropriate interpretation of the fixed asset turnover ratio requires an investigation of related activities.

*[Beginning + Ending Fixed Asset Balance (net of accumulated depreciation)] ÷ 2.

LEARNING OBJECTIVE 8-2

Apply the cost principle to measure the acquisition and maintenance of property, plant, and equipment.

In addition to purchasing buildings and equipment, a company may acquire undeveloped land, typically with the intent to build a new factory or office building. When a company purchases land, all of the incidental costs of the purchase, such as title fees, sales commissions, legal fees, title insurance, delinquent taxes, and surveying fees, should be included in its cost.

Sometimes a company purchases an old building or used machinery for the business operations. Renovation and repair costs incurred by the company prior to the asset's use should be included as a part of its cost. Also, when purchasing land, buildings, and equipment as a group (known as a *basket purchase*), the total cost is allocated to each asset in proportion to the asset's market value relative to the total market value of the assets as a whole.

For the sake of illustration, let's assume that **Southwest** purchased a new 737 aircraft from **Boeing** on January 1, 2017 (the beginning of Southwest's fiscal year), for a list price of $78 million. Let's also assume that Boeing offered Southwest a discount of $4 million for signing the purchase agreement. That means the price of the new plane to Southwest would actually be $74 million. In addition, Southwest paid $200,000 to have the plane delivered and $800,000 to prepare the new plane for use. The amount recorded for the purchase, called the **acquisition cost**, is the net cash amount paid for the asset or, when noncash assets are used as payment, the fair value of the asset given or asset received, whichever can be more clearly determined (called the **cash equivalent price**). Southwest would calculate the acquisition cost of the new aircraft as follows:

ACQUISITION COST
The net cash equivalent amount paid or to be paid for an asset.

Invoice price	$78,000,000
Less: Discount from Boeing	4,000,000
Net cash invoice price	74,000,000
Add: Transportation charges paid by Southwest	200,000
Preparation costs paid by Southwest	800,000
Cost of the aircraft (added to the asset account)	$75,000,000

For Cash

Assuming that Southwest paid cash for the aircraft and related transportation and costs, the transaction is recorded as follows:

Flight Equipment (+A)	75,000,000	
Cash (−A)		75,000,000

Assets		=	Liabilities	+	Stockholders' Equity
Flight Equipment	+75,000,000				
Cash	−75,000,000				

It might seem unusual for Southwest to pay cash to purchase new assets that cost $75 million, but this is often the case. When it acquires productive assets, a company may pay with cash that was generated from operations or cash recently borrowed. It also is possible for the seller to finance the purchase on credit.

For Debt

Now let's assume that Southwest signed a note payable for the new aircraft and paid cash for the transportation and preparation costs. In that case, Southwest would record the following journal entry:

Flight Equipment (+A)	75,000,000	
Cash (−A)		1,000,000
Notes Payable (+L)		74,000,000

Assets		=	Liabilities		+	Stockholders' Equity
Flight Equipment	+75,000,000		Notes Payable	+74,000,000		
Cash	−1,000,000					

Commercial airlines often utilize financing schemes that include leasing aircraft. Shorter-term leases, called **operating leases,** provide airlines with flexibility in managing fleet size and obsolescence, which can occur with changes in environmental and noise-level laws in various countries. Operating leases are not reported on the balance sheet as liabilities and the assets are not included in fixed assets. On the other hand, longer-term leases, called **financing leases** or **capital leases,** are in essence the acquisition of assets that are reported on the balance sheet along with the lease obligations, allowing for companies to take advantage of tax benefits. At December 31, 2014, Southwest Airlines disclosed the following regarding its leasing commitments:

NOTES TO CONSOLIDATED FINANCIAL STATEMENTS

7. Leases

The majority of the Company's terminal operations space, as well as 174 aircraft . . . were under operating leases at December 31, 2014 . . . Future minimum lease payments under capital leases and noncancelable operating leases and rentals to be received under subleases with initial or remaining terms in excess of one year at December 31, 2014, were:

(in millions)	Capital Leases	Operating Leases
2015	$ 33	$ 753
2016	42	715
2017	45	671
2018	44	573
2019	43	502
Thereafter	202	1,802
Total minimum lease payments	$409	$5,016

Additional discussion of leases is provided in Chapter 9.

For Equity (or Other Noncash Considerations)

Noncash consideration, such as the company's common stock or a right given by the company to the seller to purchase the company's goods or services at a special price, might also be part of the transaction. When noncash consideration is included in the purchase of an asset, the cash-equivalent cost (fair value of the asset given or received) is determined.

Assume that Southwest gave Boeing 1,000,000 shares of its $1.00 par value common stock with a market value of $50 per share and paid the balance in cash. The journal entry and transaction effects follow:

1,000,000 shares × $1 par →
1,000,000 shares × $49 excess →
($50 market value − $1 par)

Flight Equipment (+A)	75,000,000	
Common Stock (+SE)		1,000,000
Additional Paid-in Capital (+SE)		49,000,000
Cash (−A)		25,000,000

Assets		=	Liabilities	+	Stockholders' Equity	
Flight Equipment	+75,000,000				Common Stock	+1,000,000
Cash	−25,000,000				Additional Paid-In Capital	+49,000,000

By Construction

In some cases, a company may construct an asset for its own use instead of buying it from a manufacturer. When a company does so, the cost of the asset includes all the necessary costs associated with construction, such as labor, materials, and, in most situations, a portion of the interest incurred during the construction period, called **capitalized interest**. The amount of interest expense that is capitalized is recorded by debiting the asset and crediting cash when the interest is paid. The amount of interest to be capitalized is a complex computation discussed in detail in other accounting courses.

CAPITALIZED INTEREST
Interest expenditures included in the cost of a self-constructed asset.

Capitalizing labor, materials, and a portion of interest expense has the effect of increasing assets, decreasing expenses, and increasing net income. Let's assume Southwest constructed a new hangar, paying $600,000 in labor costs and $1,300,000 in supplies and materials. Southwest also paid $100,000 in interest expense during the year related to the construction project:

Building (+A)	2,000,000	
Cash (−A)		2,000,000

Capitalized Expenditures:

Wages paid	$ 600,000
Supplies paid	1,300,000
Interest paid	100,000

Assets		=	Liabilities	+	Stockholders' Equity
Building	+2,000,000				
Cash	−2,000,000				

American Airlines includes a note on capitalized interest in a recent annual report:

NOTES TO CONSOLIDATED FINANCIAL STATEMENTS

5. **Basis of Presentation and Summary of Significant Accounting Policies:**

(e) Operating Property and Equipment

Operating property and equipment are recorded at cost. Interest expense related to the acquisition of certain property and equipment, including aircraft purchase deposits, is capitalized as an additional cost of the asset. Interest capitalized for the years ended December 31, 2014, 2013, and 2012 was $61 million, $47 million, and $50 million, respectively.

AMERICAN AIRLINES GROUP
REAL WORLD EXCERPT:
2014 Annual Report

PAUSE FOR FEEDBACK   STOP

We just learned how to measure the cost of operational assets acquired under various methods. In general, all necessary and reasonable costs to ready the asset for its intended use are part of the cost of the asset. Assets can be acquired with cash, with debt, and/or with the company's stock (at market value).

SELF-STUDY QUIZ

It's your turn to apply these concepts by answering the following questions. In a recent year, **McDonald's Corporation** purchased property, plant, and equipment priced at $2.7 billion. Assume that the company also paid $216 million for sales tax; $20 million for transportation costs; $12 million for installation and preparation of the property, plant, and equipment before use; and $1 million in maintenance contracts to cover repairs to the property, plant, and equipment during use.

(continued)

1. Compute the acquisition cost for the property, plant, and equipment.

2. How did you account for the sales tax, transportation costs, and installation costs? Explain.

3. Under the following independent assumptions, indicate the effects of the acquisition on the accounting equation. Use + for increase and − for decrease and indicate the accounts and amounts:

	ASSETS	LIABILITIES	STOCKHOLDERS' EQUITY
a. Paid 30 percent in cash and the rest by signing a note payable.			
b. Issued 10 million shares of common stock ($0.01 per share par value) at a market price of $100 per share and paid the balance in cash.			

After you have completed your answers, check them below.

Repairs, Maintenance, and Improvements

Most assets require substantial expenditures during their lives to maintain or enhance their productive capacity. These expenditures include cash outlays for ordinary repairs and maintenance, major repairs, replacements, and additions. Expenditures that are made after an asset has been acquired are classified as follows:

ORDINARY REPAIRS AND MAINTENANCE
Expenditures that maintain the productive capacity of an asset during the current accounting period only and are recorded as expenses.

1. **Ordinary repairs and maintenance** are expenditures that maintain the productive capacity of the asset during the current accounting period only. These expenditures are recurring in nature, involve relatively small amounts at each occurrence, and do not directly increase the productive life, operating efficiency, or capacity of the asset. These cash outlays are recorded as **expenses** in the current period.

In the case of **Southwest Airlines**, examples of ordinary repairs would include changing the oil in the aircraft engines, replacing the lights in the control panels, and fixing torn fabric on passenger seats. Although the cost of individual ordinary repairs is relatively small, in the aggregate these expenditures can be substantial. In 2014, Southwest paid $978 million for aircraft maintenance and repairs. This amount was reported as an expense on its income statement. The following summary entry represents how these expenditures would have been recorded by Southwest:

Solutions to
SELF-STUDY QUIZ

1. **Property, Plant, and Equipment (PPE)**

Acquisition cost	$2,700,000,000
Sales tax	216,000,000
Transportation	20,000,000
Installation	12,000,000
Total	$2,948,000,000

Because the maintenance contracts are not necessary to ready the assets for use, they are not included in the acquisition cost.

2. Sales tax and transportation and installation costs are capitalized because they are reasonable and necessary for getting the asset ready for its intended use.

3.

	Assets		Liabilities		Stockholders' Equity	
a. PPE	+2,948,000,000	Note Payable	+2,063,600,000			
Cash	−884,400,000					
b. PPE	+2,948,000,000				Common Stock	+100,000
Cash	−1,948,000,000				Additional Paid-In Capital	+999,900,000

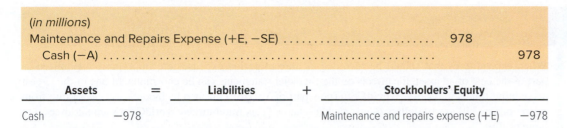

(in millions)		
Maintenance and Repairs Expense (+E, −SE)	978	
Cash (−A)		978

Assets	=	Liabilities	+	Stockholders' Equity	
Cash	−978			Maintenance and repairs expense (+E)	−978

2. **Improvements** are expenditures that increase the productive life, operating efficiency, or capacity of the asset. These **capital expenditures** are added to the appropriate asset accounts (that is, they are capitalized). They occur infrequently, involve large amounts of money, and increase an asset's economic usefulness in the future through either increased efficiency or longer life. Examples include additions, major overhauls, complete reconditioning, and major replacements and improvements, such as the complete replacement of an engine on an aircraft.

IMPROVEMENTS
Expenditures that increase the productive life, operating efficiency, or capacity of an asset and are recorded as increases in asset accounts, not as expenses.

Assume that Southwest spent $300 million in 2016 to modify the exterior of its aircraft to reduce fuel consumption, resulting in 9 percent greater fuel efficiency and lower operating costs. The summary entry below represents how these expenditures would have been recorded by Southwest:

(in millions)		
Flight Equipment (+A)	300	
Cash (−A)		300

Assets	=	Liabilities	+	Stockholders' Equity
Flight equipment	+300			
Cash	−300			

In many cases, no clear line distinguishes improvements (assets) from ordinary repairs and maintenance (expenses). In these situations, managers must exercise professional judgment and make a subjective decision. Capitalizing expenses will increase assets and net income in the current year, lowering future years' income by the amount of the annual depreciation. On the other hand, for tax purposes, expensing the amount in the current period will lower taxes immediately. Because the decision to capitalize or expense is subjective, auditors review the items reported as capital expenditures and ordinary repairs and maintenance closely.

To avoid spending too much time classifying additions and improvements (capital expenditures) and repair expenses (revenue expenditures), some companies develop simple policies to govern the accounting for these expenditures. For example, one large computer company expenses all individual items that cost less than $1,000. Such policies are acceptable because immaterial (relatively small dollar) amounts will not affect users' decisions when analyzing financial statements.

AP Photo/The Yuma Daily Sun, Craig Fry

FINANCIAL ANALYSIS		WorldCom: Hiding Billions in Expenses through Capitalization

When expenditures that should be recorded as current period expenses are improperly capitalized as part of the cost of an asset, the effects on the financial statements can be enormous. In one of the largest accounting frauds in history, **WorldCom** (now part of **Verizon**) inflated its income and cash flows from operations by billions of dollars in just such a scheme. This fraud turned WorldCom's actual losses into large profits.

Over five quarters in 2001 and 2002, the company initially announced that it had capitalized $3.8 billion that should have been recorded as operating expenses. By early 2004, auditors discovered $74.4 billion in necessary restatements (reductions to previously reported pretax income) for 2000 and 2001.

Accounting for expenses as capital expenditures increases current income because it spreads a single period's operating expenses over many future periods as depreciation expense. It increases cash flows from operations by moving cash outflows from the operating section to the investing section of the cash flow statement.

STOP   PAUSE FOR **FEEDBACK**

Practice these applications for operational assets as they are used over time: repairing or maintaining (expensed in current period) and adding to or improving (capitalized as part of the cost of the asset).

SELF-STUDY **QUIZ**

A building that originally cost $400,000 has been used over the past 10 years and needs continual maintenance and repairs. For each of the following expenditures, indicate whether it should be expensed in the current period or capitalized as part of **the cost of the asset.**

	Expense or Capitalize?
1. Major replacement of electrical wiring throughout the building.	_____
2. Repairs to the front door of the building.	_____
3. Annual cleaning of the filters on the building's air-conditioning system.	_____
4. Significant repairs due to damage from an unusual and infrequent flood.	_____

After you have completed your answers, check them below.

USE, IMPAIRMENT, AND DISPOSAL OF PLANT AND EQUIPMENT

Depreciation Concepts

LEARNING OBJECTIVE 8-3
Apply various cost allocation methods as assets are held and used over time.

Except for land, which is considered to have an unlimited life, a long-lived asset with a limited useful life, such as an airplane, represents the prepaid cost of a bundle of future services or benefits. The **expense principle** requires that a portion of an asset's cost be allocated as an expense in the same period that revenues are generated by its use. **Southwest Airlines** earns

Solutions to
SELF-STUDY QUIZ

1. Capitalize   2. Expense   3. Expense   4. Capitalize

revenue when it provides air travel service and incurs an expense when using its aircraft to generate the revenue.

The term used to identify the matching of the cost of using buildings and equipment with the revenues they generate is **depreciation**. Thus, depreciation is **the process of allocating the cost of buildings and equipment over their productive lives using a systematic and rational method.**

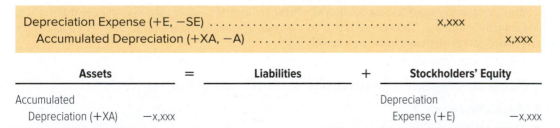

Using the asset→Depreciation Expense each year

DEPRECIATION
The process of allocating the cost of buildings and equipment (but not land) over their productive lives using a systematic and rational method.

Students often are confused by the concept of depreciation as accountants use it. In accounting, depreciation is a process of **cost allocation,** not a process of determining an asset's current market value or worth. When an asset is depreciated, the remaining balance sheet amount **probably does not represent its current market value.** On balance sheets subsequent to acquisition, the undepreciated cost is not measured on a market or fair value basis.

An adjusting journal entry is needed at the end of each period to reflect the use of buildings and equipment for the period:

| Depreciation Expense (+E, −SE) .... | x,xxx | |
| Accumulated Depreciation (+XA, −A) .... | | x,xxx |

Assets	=	Liabilities	+	Stockholders' Equity	
Accumulated				Depreciation	
Depreciation (+XA) −x,xxx				Expense (+E) −x,xxx	

The amount of depreciation recorded during each period is reported on the income statement as **Depreciation Expense.** The amount of depreciation expense accumulated since the acquisition date is reported on the balance sheet as a contra-account, **Accumulated Depreciation,** and deducted from the related asset's cost. The net amount on the balance sheet is called **net book value** or **carrying value.** The **net book value** (or **carrying** or **book value**) of a long-lived asset is its acquisition cost less the accumulated depreciation from the acquisition date to the balance sheet date.

NET BOOK VALUE (CARRYING OR BOOK VALUE)
The acquisition cost of an asset less accumulated depreciation, depletion, or amortization.

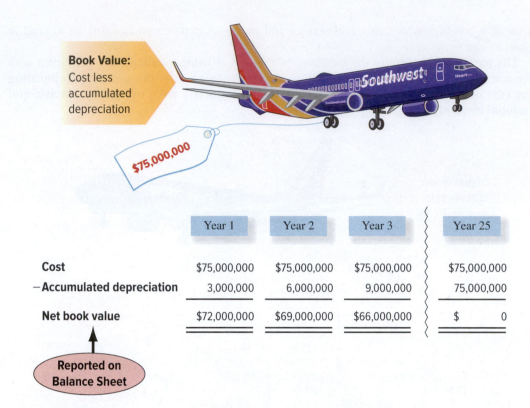

Book Value:
Cost less accumulated depreciation

$75,000,000

	Year 1	Year 2	Year 3	Year 25
Cost	$75,000,000	$75,000,000	$75,000,000	$75,000,000
−Accumulated depreciation	3,000,000	6,000,000	9,000,000	75,000,000
Net book value	$72,000,000	$69,000,000	$66,000,000	$ 0

Reported on Balance Sheet

From Exhibit 8.1 in the previous section, we see that Southwest's acquisition cost for property and equipment is $22,513 million at the end of 2014. The accumulated depreciation and amortization on the property and equipment is $8,221 million (amortization is the name for allocating costs of intangible assets and is discussed later in the chapter). Thus, the book value is reported at $14,292 million. Southwest also reported depreciation and amortization expense of $938 million on its income statement for 2014.

FINANCIAL ANALYSIS

 Book Value as an Approximation of Remaining Life

Book Value as a Percentage of Original Cost

Southwest   63%

United Continental   71%

JetBlue   78%

Some analysts compare the book value of assets to their original cost as an approximation of their remaining life. If the book value of an asset is 100 percent of its cost, it is a new asset; if the book value is 25 percent of its cost, the asset has about 25 percent of its estimated life remaining. In **Southwest**'s case, the book value of its property and equipment is 63 percent of its original cost, compared to 71 percent for **United Continental** and 78 percent for **JetBlue Airways**.

This comparison suggests that Southwest's flight equipment is older than the equipment at JetBlue and United Continental. This comparison is only a rough approximation and is influenced by some of the accounting issues discussed in the next section.

To calculate depreciation expense, three amounts are required for each asset:

1. Acquisition cost.

2. **Estimated** useful life to the company.

3. **Estimated** residual (or salvage) value at the end of the asset's useful life to the company.

Notice that the asset's useful life and residual value are estimates. Therefore, **depreciation expense is an estimate.**

Estimated useful life represents management's estimate of the asset's useful **economic life** to the company rather than its total economic life to all potential users. The asset's expected physical life is often longer than the company intends to use the asset. Economic life may be

ESTIMATED USEFUL LIFE
The expected service life of an asset to the present owner.

expressed in terms of years or units of capacity, such as the number of hours a machine is expected to operate or the number of units it can produce. Southwest's aircraft fleet is expected to fly for more than 25 years, but Southwest wants to offer its customers a high level of service by replacing its older aircraft with modern equipment. For accounting purposes, Southwest uses a 23- to 25-year estimated useful life. The subsequent owner of the aircraft (likely a regional airline) would use an estimated useful life based on its own policies.

| Differences in Estimated Lives | FINANCIAL ANALYSIS |
| within a Single Industry | |

Notes to recent actual financial statements of various airline companies reveal the following estimates for the useful lives of flight equipment:

Company	Estimated Life (in years)
Southwest	23 to 25
United Continental	25 to 30
Singapore Airlines	15

The differences in the estimated lives may be attributed to a number of factors such as the type of aircraft used by each company, equipment replacement plans, operational differences, and the degree of management's conservatism. In addition, given the same type of aircraft, companies that plan to use the equipment over fewer years may estimate higher residual values than companies that plan to use the equipment longer. For example, Singapore Airlines uses a residual value of 10 percent over a relatively short useful life for its passenger aircraft, compared to as low as 5 percent for **Delta Air Lines** over as much as a 30-year useful life.

Differences in estimated lives and residual values of assets can have a significant impact on a comparison of the profitability of the competing companies. Analysts must be certain to identify the causes of differences in depreciable lives.

Residual (or **salvage**) **value** represents management's estimate of the amount the company expects to recover upon disposal of the asset at the end of its estimated useful life. The residual value may be the estimated value of the asset as salvage or scrap or its expected value if sold to another user. In the case of Southwest's aircraft, residual value may be the amount it expects to receive when it sells the asset to a small regional airline that operates older equipment. The notes to Southwest's financial statements indicate that the company estimates residual value to be between 0 and 20 percent of the cost of the asset, depending on the asset.

RESIDUAL (OR SALVAGE) VALUE
The estimated amount to be recovered by the company, less disposal costs, at the end of an asset's estimated useful life.

Alternative Depreciation Methods

Because of significant differences among companies and the assets they own, accountants have not been able to agree on a single best method of depreciation. As a result, managers may choose from several acceptable depreciation methods that match depreciation expense with the revenues generated in a period. They may also choose different methods for specific assets or groups of assets. Once selected, the method should be applied consistently over time to enhance comparability of financial information. We will discuss the three most common depreciation methods:

1. Straight-line (the most common, used by more than 98 percent of companies for many or all of their assets).

2. Units-of-production.

3. Declining-balance.

To illustrate each method, let's assume that **Southwest Airlines** acquired a new service vehicle (ground equipment) on January 1, 2016. The relevant information is shown in Exhibit 8.2.

Data for Illustrating the
Computation of Depreciation
under Alternative Methods

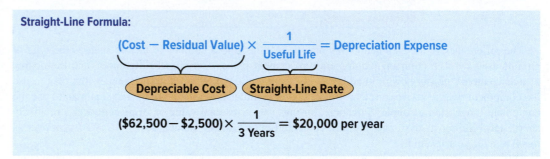

SOUTHWEST AIRLINES
Acquisition of a New Service Vehicle

Cost, purchased on January 1, 2016	$62,500	
Estimated residual value	$ 2,500	
Estimated useful life		3 years **OR** 100,000 miles
Actual miles driven in:	Year 2016	30,000 miles
	Year 2017	50,000 miles
	Year 2018	20,000 miles

Straight-Line Method

STRAIGHT-LINE DEPRECIATION
Method that allocates the depreciable cost of an asset in equal periodic amounts over its useful life.

More companies, including Southwest, use **straight-line depreciation** in their financial statements than all other methods combined. Under the straight-line method, an equal portion of an asset's depreciable cost is allocated to each accounting period over its estimated useful life. Using the information in Exhibit 8.2, the formula to estimate annual depreciation expense follows:

Straight-Line Formula:

$$(\text{Cost} - \text{Residual Value}) \times \frac{1}{\text{Useful Life}} = \text{Depreciation Expense}$$

Depreciable Cost   Straight-Line Rate

$$(\$62,500 - \$2,500) \times \frac{1}{3 \text{ Years}} = \$20,000 \text{ per year}$$

In this formula, "Cost minus Residual Value" is the amount to be depreciated, also called the **depreciable cost.** The formula "1 ÷ Useful Life" is the **straight-line rate.** Using the data provided in Exhibit 8.2, the depreciation expense for Southwest's new service vehicle would be $20,000 per year.

Companies often create a **depreciation schedule** that shows the computed amount of depreciation expense each year over the entire useful life of the asset. You can use computerized spreadsheet programs, such as Excel, to create the depreciation schedule. Using the data in Exhibit 8.2 and the straight-line method, Southwest's depreciation schedule follows:

Straight-Line Expense

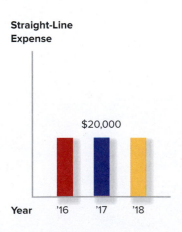

$20,000

| Year | '16 | '17 | '18 |

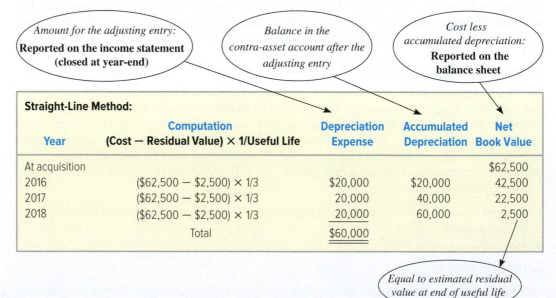

Amount for the adjusting entry:
Reported on the income statement
(closed at year-end)

Balance in the contra-asset account after the adjusting entry

Cost less accumulated depreciation:
Reported on the balance sheet

Straight-Line Method:

Year	Computation (Cost − Residual Value) × 1/Useful Life	Depreciation Expense	Accumulated Depreciation	Net Book Value
At acquisition				$62,500
2016	($62,500 − $2,500) × 1/3	$20,000	$20,000	42,500
2017	($62,500 − $2,500) × 1/3	20,000	40,000	22,500
2018	($62,500 − $2,500) × 1/3	20,000	60,000	2,500
	Total	$60,000		

Equal to estimated residual value at end of useful life

Notice that

- Depreciation expense is a constant amount each year.
- Accumulated depreciation increases by an equal amount each year.
- Net book value decreases by the same amount each year until it equals the estimated residual value.

This is the reason for the name **straight-line method.** Notice, too, that the adjusting entry can be prepared from this schedule, and the effects on the income statement and balance sheet are known. Southwest Airlines uses the straight-line method for all of its assets. The company reported depreciation and amortization expense in the amount of $938 million for 2014, equal to 5 percent of the airline's revenues for the year. Most companies in the airline industry use the straight-line method.

Units-of-Production Method

The **units-of-production depreciation** method relates depreciable cost to total estimated productive output. The formula to estimate annual depreciation expense under this method is as follows:

UNITS-OF-PRODUCTION DEPRECIATION
Method that allocates the depreciable cost of an asset over its useful life based on the relationship of its periodic output to its total estimated output.

Units-of-Production Formula:

$$\frac{\text{(Cost} - \text{Residual Value)}}{\text{Estimated Total Production}} \times \frac{\text{Actual}}{\text{Production}} = \text{Depreciation Expense}$$

$$\frac{(\$62,500 - \$2,500)}{100,000 \text{ miles}} = \$0.60 \text{ per mile depreciation rate}$$

$$\$0.60 \text{ per mile} \times 30,000 \text{ actual miles in 2016} = \underline{\$18,000} \text{ for 2016}$$

Dividing the depreciable cost by the estimated total production yields the **depreciation rate per unit of production,** which is then multiplied by the actual production for the period to determine depreciation expense. In our illustration, for every mile that the new vehicle is driven, Southwest would record depreciation expense of $0.60. Based on the information in Exhibit 8.2, the depreciation schedule for the service vehicle under the units-of-production method would appear as follows:

Units-of-Production Method:

Year	Computation [(Cost − Residual Value)/Total Estimated Production] × Actual Production	Depreciation Expense	Accumulated Depreciation	Net Book Value
At acquisition	RATE			$62,500
2016	$.60 per mile × 30,000 miles	$18,000	$18,000	44,500
2017	$.60 per mile × 50,000 miles	30,000	48,000	14,500
2018	$.60 per mile × 20,000 miles	12,000	60,000	2,500
		$60,000		

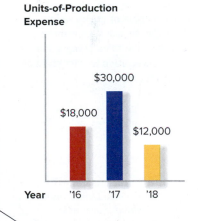

Units-of-Production Expense

Equal to estimated residual value at end of useful life

Notice that, from period to period, depreciation expense, accumulated depreciation, and book value vary directly with the units produced. In the units-of-production method, depreciation expense is a **variable expense** because it varies directly with production or use.

You might wonder what happens if the total estimated productive output differs from actual total output. Remember that the estimate is management's best guess of total output. If any difference occurs at the end of the asset's life, the final adjusting entry to depreciation expense should be for the amount needed to bring the asset's net book value equal to the asset's estimated residual value. For example, if, in 2018, Southwest's service vehicle ran 25,000 actual miles, the same amount of depreciation expense, $12,000, would be recorded.

Although Southwest does not use the units-of-production method, the **Exxon Mobil Corporation**, a major energy company that explores, produces, transports, and sells crude oil and natural gas worldwide, does, as a note to the company's annual report explains.

EXXONMOBIL

REAL WORLD EXCERPT:

2014 Annual Report

> **NOTES TO CONSOLIDATED FINANCIAL STATEMENTS**
>
> **1. Summary of Accounting Policies**
>
> **Property, Plant and Equipment.** Depreciation, depletion and amortization, based on cost less estimated salvage value of the asset, are primarily determined under either the unit-of-production method or the straight-line method, which is based on estimated asset service life taking obsolescence into consideration. . . . Acquisition costs of proved properties are amortized using a unit-of-production method, computed on the basis of total proved oil and gas reserves.

The units-of-production method is based on an estimate of an asset's total future productive capacity or output, which is difficult to determine. This is another example of the degree of subjectivity inherent in accounting.

Declining-Balance Method

DECLINING-BALANCE DEPRECIATION
Method that allocates the net book value (cost minus accumulated depreciation) of an asset over its useful life based on a multiple of the straight-line rate, thus assigning more depreciation to early years and less depreciation to later years of an asset's life.

If an asset is considered to be more efficient or productive when it is newer, managers might choose the **declining-balance depreciation** method to match a higher depreciation expense with higher revenues in the early years of an asset's life and a lower depreciation expense with lower revenues in the later years. We say, then, that this is an **accelerated depreciation** method. Although accelerated methods are seldom used for financial reporting purposes, the method that is used more frequently than others is the declining-balance method.

Declining-balance depreciation is based on applying a rate exceeding the straight-line rate to the asset's net book value over time. The rate is often double (two times) the straight-line rate and is termed the **double-declining-balance rate.** For example, if the straight-line rate is 10 percent ($1 \div 10$ years) for a 10-year estimated useful life, then the declining-balance rate is 20 percent ($2 \times$ the straight-line rate). Other typical acceleration rates are 1.5 times and 1.75 times. The double-declining-balance rate is adopted most frequently by companies employing an accelerated method, so we will use it in our illustration, with information from Exhibit 8.2.

Double-Declining-Balance Formula:

$$(\text{Cost} - \text{Accumulated Depreciation}) \times \frac{2}{\text{Useful Life}} = \text{Depreciation Expense}$$

Accumulated Depreciation increases over time

$$(\$62,500 - \$0 \text{ in } 2016) \times \frac{2}{3 \text{ years}} = \$41,667 \text{ in the first year}$$

There are two important differences between this method and the others described previously:

1. Notice that accumulated depreciation, not residual value, is included in the formula. Since accumulated depreciation increases each year, net book value (Cost minus Accumulated Depreciation) decreases. The double-declining rate is applied to a lower net book value each year, resulting in a decline in depreciation expense over time.

2. As with the other methods, the net book value should not be depreciated below the residual value:

- Occasionally, before the end of the estimated useful life, if the annual computation reduces net book value below residual value, only the amount of depreciation expense needed to make net book value equal to residual value is recorded, and no additional depreciation expense is computed in subsequent years.
- More likely, in the last year of the asset's estimated useful life, whatever amount is needed to bring net book value to residual value is recorded, regardless of the amount of the computation.

Computation of double-declining-balance depreciation expense is illustrated in the depreciation schedule:

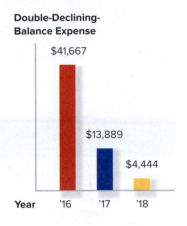

Double-Declining-Balance Expense

Year	Computation [(Cost − Accumulated Depreciation) × 2/Useful Life]	Depreciation Expense	Accumulated Depreciation	Net Book Value
At acquisition				$62,500
2016	($62,500 − $0) × 2/3	$41,667	$41,667	$20,833
2017	($62,500 − $41,667) × 2/3	13,889	55,556	6,944
2018	($62,500 − $55,556) × 2/3	~~4,629~~	~~60,185~~	~~2,315~~
		4,444	60,000	2,500
Total		$60,000		

Computed amount is too large

Equal to estimated residual value at end of useful life

The calculated depreciation expense for 2018 ($4,629) is not the same as the amount actually reported on the income statement ($4,444). An asset should never be depreciated below the point at which net book value equals its residual value. The asset owned by Southwest has an estimated residual value of $2,500. If depreciation expense were recorded in the amount of $4,629, the book value of the asset would be less than $2,500. The correct depreciation expense for year 2018 is therefore $4,444, the amount that will reduce the book value to exactly $2,500. To determine the amount to record in 2018, indicate the amount needed for net book value ($2,500), determine what the balance in accumulated depreciation should be to yield the $60,000 ($62,500 cost − $2,500 residual value), and compute the amount of depreciation expense necessary to increase the balance in accumulated depreciation to $60,000 ($60,000 balance needed in accumulated depreciation − $55,556 prior balance in accumulated depreciation).

Companies in industries that expect fairly rapid obsolescence of their equipment use the declining-balance method. **Toyota** is one of the companies that uses this method, as a note to its annual report shows.

NOTES TO CONSOLIDATED FINANCIAL STATEMENTS

2. Summary of significant accounting policies:

Property, plant and equipment —
. . . Depreciation of property, plant and equipment is mainly computed on the declining-balance method for the parent company and Japanese subsidiaries and on the straight-line method for foreign subsidiary companies at rates based on estimated useful lives of the respective assets according to general class, type of construction and use. The estimated useful lives range from 2 to 65 years for buildings and from 2 to 20 years for machinery and equipment.

TOYOTA MOTOR CORPORATION

REAL WORLD EXCERPT:

2014 Annual Report

As this note indicates, companies may use different depreciation methods for different classes of assets. Under the consistency principle, they are expected to apply the same methods to those assets over time.

In Summary

The three depreciation methods, computations, and the differences in depreciation expense over time for each method are summarized as follows:

Method	Computation	Depreciation Expense
Straight-line	(Cost − Residual Value) × 1/Useful Life	Equal amounts each year
Units-of-production	[(Cost − Residual Value)/Estimated Total Production] × Annual Production	Varying amounts based on production level
Double-declining-balance	(Cost − Accumulated Depreciation) × 2/Useful Life	Declining amounts over time

---

FINANCIAL ANALYSIS

Impact of Alternative Depreciation Methods

Summary Depreciation Expense

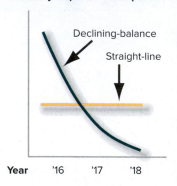

Year   '16   '17   '18

Assume that you are comparing two companies that are exactly the same, except that one uses accelerated depreciation and the other uses the straight-line method. Which company would you expect to report a higher net income? Actually, this question is a bit tricky. The answer is that you cannot say for certain which company's income would be higher.

The accelerated methods report higher depreciation and therefore lower net income during the early years of an asset's life. As the age of the asset increases, this effect reverses. Therefore, companies that use accelerated depreciation report lower depreciation expense and higher net income during the later years of an asset's life. The nearby graph illustrates the pattern of depreciation over the life of an asset for the straight-line and declining-balance methods discussed in this chapter. When the curve for the accelerated method falls below the line for the straight-line method, the accelerated method produces a higher net income than the straight-line method. However, total depreciation expense by the end of the asset's life is the same for each method.

Users of financial statements must understand the impact of alternative depreciation methods used over time. **Differences in depreciation methods rather than real economic differences can cause significant variation in reported net incomes.**

STOP   PAUSE FOR **FEEDBACK**

The three cost allocation methods discussed in this section are:

- Straight-line: (Cost − Residual Value) × 1/Useful Life
- Units-of-production: [(Cost − Residual Value)/Estimated Total Production] × Annual Production
- Double-declining-balance: (Cost − Accumulated Depreciation) × 2/Useful Life

Practice these methods using the following information.

SELF-STUDY **QUIZ**

Assume that **Southwest** has acquired new computer equipment at a cost of $240,000. The equipment has an estimated life of six years, an estimated operating life of 50,000 hours, and an estimated residual value of $30,000. Determine depreciation expense for the first full year under each of the following methods:

1. Straight-line method.
2. Units-of-production method (assume the equipment ran for 8,000 hours in the first year).
3. Double-declining-balance method.

After you have completed your answers, check them below.

 GUIDED HELP 8-1

For additional step-by-step video instruction on using the three cost allocation methods discussed in this section, go to **www.mhhe.com/libby9e_gh8a**.

Increased Profitability Due to an Accounting Adjustment? Reading the Notes	FINANCIAL ANALYSIS

Financial analysts are particularly interested in changes in accounting estimates because they can have a large impact on a company's before-tax operating income. In 2001, **Singapore Airlines** disclosed in its annual report that it had increased the estimated useful life of its aircraft from 10 to 15 years to reflect a change in its aircraft replacement policy. The change reduced depreciation expense for the year by $265 million and would reduce expenses by a similar amount each year over the remaining life of the aircraft. Analysts pay close attention to this number because it represents increased profitability due merely to an accounting adjustment.

Component Allocation	INTERNATIONAL PERSPECTIVE

Under IFRS, the cost of an individual asset's components is allocated among each significant component and then depreciated separately over that component's useful life. For example, **British Airways** (now merged into **International Airlines Group**) depreciates the body and engines over 18 to 25 years and the cabin interior modifications over 5 years.

How Managers Choose

Financial Reporting

For financial reporting purposes, corporate managers must determine which depreciation method provides the best matching of revenues and expenses for any given asset. If the asset is expected to provide benefits evenly over time, then the straight-line method is preferred. Managers also find this method to be easy to use and to explain. If no other method is more systematic or rational, then the straight-line method is selected. Also, during the early years of an asset's life, the straight-line method reports higher income than the accelerated methods do. For these reasons, the straight-line method is, by far and away, the most common.

On the other hand, certain assets produce more revenue in their early lives because they are more efficient than in later years. In this case, managers select an accelerated method to allocate cost.

Solutions to
SELF-STUDY QUIZ

1. ($240,000 − $30,000) × 1/6 = $35,000
2. [($240,000 − $30,000) ÷ 50,000] × 8,000 = $33,600
3. ($240,000 − $0) × 2/6 = $80,000

Tax Reporting

Southwest Airlines, like most public companies, maintains two sets of accounting records. Both sets of records reflect the same transactions, but the transactions are accounted for using two different sets of measurement rules. One set is prepared under GAAP for reporting to stockholders. The other set is prepared to determine the company's tax obligation under the Internal Revenue Code. The reason that the two sets of rules are different is simple: The objectives of GAAP and the Internal Revenue Code differ.

Financial Reporting (GAAP)	Tax Reporting (IRC)
The objective of financial reporting is to provide economic information about a business that is useful in projecting future cash flows of the business. Financial reporting rules follow generally accepted accounting principles.	The objective of the Internal Revenue Code is to raise sufficient revenues to pay for the expenditures of the federal government. Many of the Code's provisions are designed to encourage certain behaviors that are thought to benefit society (e.g., contributions to charities are made tax deductible to encourage people to support worthy programs).

In some cases, differences between the Internal Revenue Code and GAAP leave the manager no choice but to maintain separate records. In other cases, the differences are the result of management choice. When given a choice among acceptable tax accounting methods, managers apply what is called the **least and the latest rule.** All taxpayers want to pay the lowest amount of tax that is legally permitted and at the latest possible date. If you had the choice of paying $100,000 to the federal government at the end of this year or at the end of next year, you would choose the end of next year. By doing so, you could invest the money for an extra year and earn a significant return on the investment.

A QUESTION OF ETHICS

Two Sets of Books

When they first learn that companies maintain two sets of books, some people question the ethics or legality of the practice. In reality, **it is both legal and ethical to maintain separate records for tax and financial reporting purposes. However, these records must reflect the same transactions.** Understating revenues or overstating expenses on a tax return can result in financial penalties and/or imprisonment. Accountants who aid tax evaders also can be fined or imprisoned and lose their professional licenses.

Similarly, by maintaining two sets of books, corporations can defer (delay) paying millions and sometimes billions of dollars in taxes. The following companies reported significant gross deferred tax obligations in 2014. Much of these deferrals were due to differences in asset cost allocation methods:

Company	Deferred Tax Liabilities	Percentage Due to Applying Different Cost Allocation Methods
Southwest Airlines	$4,328 million	99%
PepsiCo	$7,348 million	30
Hertz	$3,685 million	74
Marriott International	$18 million	56

Most corporations use the IRS-approved Modified Accelerated Cost Recovery System (MACRS) to calculate depreciation expense for their tax returns. MACRS is similar to the declining-balance method and is applied over relatively short asset lives to yield high depreciation expense in the early years. The high depreciation expense reported under MACRS reduces a corporation's taxable income and therefore the amount it must pay in taxes. MACRS provides an incentive for corporations to invest in modern property, plant, and equipment in order to be competitive in world markets. However, **it is not acceptable for financial reporting purposes.**

Measuring Asset Impairment

As we discussed in Chapter 2, assets are defined as economic resources with probable future benefits acquired in an exchange transaction. On the date of the exchange, an asset is measured at historical cost. However, later in its useful life, when an asset is not expected to generate sufficient cash flows (probable future benefits) at least equal to its book value, we say the asset's book value is impaired. Corporations must review long-lived tangible and intangible assets for possible impairment. Two steps are necessary:

> **LEARNING OBJECTIVE 8-4**
> Explain the effect of asset impairment on the financial statements.

Step 1: Test for Impairment **Impairment** occurs when events or changed circumstances cause the estimated future cash flows (future benefits) of these assets to fall below their book value.

> If net book value > Estimated future cash flows, then the asset is impaired

Step 2: Computation of Impairment Loss For any asset considered to be impaired, companies recognize a loss for the difference between the asset's book value and its **fair value** (a market concept).

> Impairment Loss = Net Book Value − Fair Value

That is, the asset is **written down** to fair value.

To illustrate measuring impairment losses, let's assume that **Southwest** did a review for asset impairment and identified an aircraft with the following information:

Step 1: Test	Net book value	$10,000,000	
	Estimated future cash flows	8,000,000	**Step 2: If impaired, loss**
	Fair value	7,500,000	

Step 1: Since the net book value of $10 million exceeds the estimated future cash flows of $8 million, then the asset is impaired because it is not expected to generate future benefits equal to its net book value. When impaired, proceed to Step 2.

Step 2: If impaired, the amount of the impairment loss is the difference between net book value and the asset's fair value. For Southwest, determining fair value includes using published sources and third-party bids to obtain the value of the asset. If the asset's fair value was $7,500,000, then the loss is calculated as $2,500,000 ($10,000,000 net book value less $7,500,000 fair value). The following journal entry would be recorded:

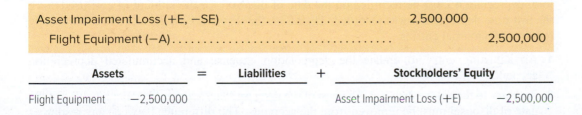

Asset Impairment Loss (+E, −SE)	2,500,000	
Flight Equipment (−A)		2,500,000

Assets	=	Liabilities	+	Stockholders' Equity	
Flight Equipment	−2,500,000			Asset Impairment Loss (+E)	−2,500,000

Although Southwest did not report asset impairment losses in its recent annual report, it did report in notes to the financial statements that it follows the practice of reviewing assets for impairment:

SOUTHWEST AIRLINES

REAL WORLD EXCERPT:

2014 Annual Report

> The Company evaluates its long-lived assets used in operations for impairment when events and circumstances indicate that the undiscounted cash flows to be generated by that asset are less than the carrying amounts of the asset and may not be recoverable. Factors that would indicate potential impairment include, but are not limited to, significant decreases in the market value of the long-lived asset(s), a significant change in the long-lived asset's physical condition, and operating or cash flow losses associated with the use of the long-lived asset. If an asset is deemed to be impaired, an impairment loss is recorded for the excess of the asset book value in relation to its estimated fair value.

Sears Holdings Corporation, which owns and operates approximately 2,400 **Kmart** and **Sears** stores in the United States and Canada, reported impairment losses on its fixed assets in its annual report for the 2013 fiscal year ended February 1, 2014:

SEARS HOLDINGS CORPORATION

REAL WORLD EXCERPT:

Fiscal Year 2013 Annual Report

> ### NOTE 13—STORE CLOSING CHARGES, SEVERANCE COSTS AND IMPAIRMENTS
>
> *Long-Lived Assets*
>
> In accordance with accounting standards governing the impairment or disposal of long-lived assets, we performed an impairment test of certain of our long-lived assets (principally the value of buildings and other fixed assets associated with our stores) due to events and changes in circumstances during 2013, 2012 and 2011 that indicated an impairment might have occurred. . . . As a result of this impairment testing, the Company recorded impairment charges of $220 million, $35 million and $16 million during 2013, 2012 and 2011, respectively.

The impairment loss in addition to a decline in revenues and an increase in expenses in fiscal year 2011 resulted in Sears Holdings Corporation reporting a net loss of over $3 billion, the first loss since Kmart and Sears merged in March 2005. The company also reported net losses of more than $0.9 and $1.3 billion in fiscal years 2012 and 2013 respectively.

Disposal of Property, Plant, and Equipment

LEARNING OBJECTIVE 8-5

Analyze the disposal of property, plant, and equipment.

In some cases, a business may **voluntarily** decide not to hold a long-lived asset for its entire life. The company may drop a product from its line and no longer need the equipment that was used to produce it, or managers may want to replace a machine with a more efficient one. These disposals include sales, trade-ins, and retirements. When **Southwest** disposes of an old aircraft, the company may sell it to a cargo airline or regional airline. A business may also dispose of an asset **involuntarily,** as the result of a casualty such as a storm, fire, or accident.

Disposals of long-lived assets seldom occur on the last day of the accounting period. Therefore, depreciation must be recorded on the date of disposal for the amount of cost used since the last time depreciation was recorded. Therefore, the disposal of a depreciable asset usually requires two journal entries:

1. An adjusting entry to update the depreciation expense and accumulated depreciation accounts.

2. An entry to record the disposal. The cost of the asset **and** any accumulated depreciation at the date of disposal must be removed from the accounts. The difference between any resources

received on disposal of an asset and its book value at the date of disposal is treated as a gain or loss on the disposal of the asset. This gain (or loss) is reported on the income statement. It is not an operating revenue (or expense), however, because it arises from peripheral or incidental activities rather than from central operations. Gains and losses from disposals are usually shown as a separate item on the income statement.

Juan Silva/The Image Bank/Getty Images

Assume that at the end of year 17, Southwest sold an aircraft that was no longer needed because of the elimination of service to a small city. The aircraft was sold for $11 million cash. The original cost of the flight equipment of $30 million was depreciated using the straight-line method over 25 years with no residual value ($1.2 million depreciation expense per year). The last accounting for depreciation was at the end of Year 16; thus, depreciation expense must be recorded for Year 17. The computations are:

Cash received		$11,000,000
Original cost of flight equipment	$30,000,000	
Less: Accumulated depreciation ($1,200,000 × 17 years)	20,400,000	
Book value at date of sale		9,600,000
Gain on sale of flight equipment		$ 1,400,000

The entries and effects of the transaction on the date of the sale are as follows:

1. Update depreciation expense for Year 17:

Depreciation Expense (+E, −SE)	1,200,000	
Accumulated Depreciation (+XA, −A)		1,200,000

2. Record the sale:

Cash (+A)	11,000,000	
Accumulated Depreciation (−XA, +A)	20,400,000	
Flight Equipment (−A)		30,000,000
Gain on Sale of Assets (+Gain, +SE)		1,400,000

Assets		=	Liabilities	+	Stockholders' Equity	
(1) Accumulated					Depreciation	
Depreciation (+XA)	−1,200,000				Expense (+E)	−1,200,000
(2) Cash	+11,000,000				Gain on Sale of Asset (+R)	+1,400,000
Flight Equipment	−30,000,000					
Accumulated						
Depreciation (−XA)	+20,400,000					

PAUSE FOR **FEEDBACK**

STOP

We learned that, when disposing of an operational asset, you must first record depreciation expense for usage of the asset since the last time it was recorded. Then eliminate the asset at cost and its related accumulated depreciation. The difference between the cash received, if any, and the net book value of the asset is either a gain or loss on disposal.

(continued)

SELF-STUDY QUIZ

Now let's assume the same facts as illustrated in the example above except that the asset was sold for $2,000,000 cash. Prepare the two entries on the date of the sale:

1. Update depreciation expense for Year 17:

2. Record the sale:

	Assets	=	Liabilities	+	Stockholders' Equity

(1)

(2)

After you have completed your answers, check them below.

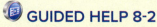 **GUIDED HELP 8-2**

For additional step-by-step video instruction on recording a disposal of an asset, go to **www.mhhe .com/libby9e_gh8b**.

INTANGIBLE ASSETS AND NATURAL RESOURCES

Acquisition and Amortization of Intangible Assets

Intangible assets are increasingly important resources for organizations. An intangible asset, like any other asset, has value because of certain rights and privileges often conferred by law on its owner. Unlike tangible assets such as land and buildings, however, an intangible asset has no material or physical substance. Instead, the majority of intangible assets usually are evidenced by a legal document. The most common types of intangible assets are the following:

- Goodwill (recognized in a business combination)
- Trademarks
- Copyrights

Solutions to
SELF-STUDY QUIZ

(1)	Depreciation Expense (+E, −SE)	1,200,000	
	Accumulated Depreciation (+XA, −A)		1,200,000
(2)	Cash (+A)	2,000,000	
	Accumulated Depreciation (−XA, +A)	20,400,000	
	Loss on Sale of Flight Equipment (+Loss, −SE)	7,600,000	
	Flight Equipment (−A)		30,000,000

	Assets		=	Liabilities	+	Stockholders' Equity	
(1)	Accumulated Depreciation	−1,200,000				Depreciation Expense	−1,200,000
(2)	Flight Equipment	−30,000,000				Loss on Sale of Asset	−7,600,000
	Accumulated Depreciation	+20,400,000					
	Cash	+2,000,000					

- Technology
- Patents
- Franchises
- Licenses and operating rights
- Others, including customer lists/relationships, noncompete covenants, and contracts and agreements

Accounting for intangible assets has become increasingly important due to the tremendous expansion in computer information systems and Web technologies and the frenzy in companies purchasing other companies at high prices, with the expectation that these intangible resources will provide significant future benefits to the company. Intangible assets are recorded **at historical cost only if they have been purchased.** If these assets are developed internally by the company, they are expensed when incurred. Upon acquisition of intangible assets, managers determine whether the separate intangibles have definite or indefinite lives:

- **Definite Life.** The cost of an intangible asset with a definite life is allocated on a **straight-line basis** each period over its useful life in a process called **amortization** that is similar to depreciation. Most companies do not estimate a residual value for their intangible assets. Amortization expense is included on the income statement each period and the intangible assets are reported at cost less accumulated amortization on the balance sheet.

AMORTIZATION
Systematic and rational allocation of the acquisition cost of an intangible asset over its useful life.

Let's assume a company purchases a patent for $800,000 and intends to use it for 20 years. The adjusting entry to record $40,000 in patent amortization expense ($800,000 ÷ 20 years) is as follows:

Patent Amortization Expense (+E, −SE)	40,000	
Patents (−A) (or Accumulated Amortization +XA, −A)[1]		40,000

Assets		=	Liabilities	+	Stockholders' Equity	
Patents (or Accumulated Amortization +XA)	−40,000				Patent Amortization Expense (+E)	−40,000

- **Indefinite Life.** Intangible assets with indefinite lives are **not amortized.** Instead, these assets must be reviewed at least annually for possible impairment of value by first using qualitative factors to determine whether it is more likely than not (that is, it is greater than a 50 percent likelihood) that the fair value of the indefinite-life intangible is less than its carrying amount. Qualitative factors can include, for example, negative effects due to increases in costs, decreases in cash flows beyond expectations, an economic downturn, or deterioration in the industry. If it is more likely, then the two-step process described in the previous section under "Measuring Asset Impairment" is followed to determine the amount of the impairment loss.

Goodwill

By far the most frequently reported intangible asset is **goodwill (cost in excess of net assets acquired)**. The term **goodwill,** as used by most business people, means the favorable reputation that a company has with its customers. Goodwill arises from factors such as customer confidence, reputation for good service or quality goods, location, outstanding management team, and financial standing. From its first day of operations, a successful business continually builds goodwill. In this context, the goodwill is said to be **internally generated** and is not reported as an asset (i.e., it was not purchased).

GOODWILL (COST IN EXCESS OF NET ASSETS ACQUIRED)
For accounting purposes, the excess of the purchase price of a business over the fair value of the acquired business's assets and liabilities.

---

[1]Consistent with the procedure for recording depreciation, an accumulated amortization account may be used. In practice, however, most companies credit the asset account directly for periodic amortization. This procedure is also typically used for natural resources, which are discussed in the next section.

The only way to report goodwill as an asset is to purchase another business. Often the purchase price of the business exceeds the fair value of all of its net assets (assets minus liabilities). Why would a company pay more for a business as a whole than it would pay if it bought the assets individually? The answer is to obtain its goodwill. You could easily buy modern bottling equipment to produce and sell a new cola drink, but you would not make as much money as you would if you acquired the goodwill associated with Coke or Pepsi brand names.

For accounting purposes, goodwill is defined as the difference between the purchase price of a company as a whole and the fair value of its net assets. For example, in 2006, **Cedar Fair**, the Ohio-based owner and operator of numerous amusement and water parks and hotels throughout North America, bought five theme parks from **Paramount Parks**. The total purchase price that Cedar Fair agreed to pay ($1.2 billion) exceeded the fair value of Paramount's net assets ($890 million). As shown below, Cedar Fair paid this extra $310 million to acquire the goodwill associated with the theme parks' businesses.

Cedar Fair's Purchase of Paramount Parks	In Millions
Purchase price	$1,200
— Fair value of assets purchased and liabilities assumed:	
Current assets	70
Property and equipment	1,000
Intangible assets	80
Debt and other liabilities	(260)
Net assets, at fair value	**890**
Goodwill	**$ 310**

In many acquisitions, the amount recorded as Goodwill can be very large. For example, **Cisco Systems**, which designs, manufactures, and sells Internet-based networking and other products and services, has completed several acquisitions since 2009. Of the nearly $17.1 billion total cost of these acquisitions, $11.4 billion was recorded as Goodwill. That is over 47 percent of the $24.2 billion in Goodwill reported on Cisco's July 26, 2014, balance sheet and the second largest asset reported.

Goodwill is considered to have an indefinite life and, as described in the previous section, must be tested for possible impairment for indefinite-life intangibles. Cisco reported the following policy:

CISCO SYSTEMS, INC.

REAL WORLD EXCERPT:

2014 Annual Report

2. Summary of Significant Accounting Policies

Goodwill and Purchased Intangible Assets

Goodwill is tested for impairment on an annual basis in the fourth fiscal quarter and, when specific circumstances dictate, between annual tests. When impaired, the carrying value of goodwill is written down to fair value.

Trademarks

TRADEMARK

An exclusive legal right to use a special name, image, or slogan.

A **trademark** is a special name, image, or slogan identified with a product or a company; it is protected by law. Trademarks are among the most valuable assets a company can own. For example, most of us cannot imagine the **Walt Disney Company** without Mickey Mouse. Similarly, you probably enjoy your favorite soft drink more because of the image that has been built up around its name than because of its taste. Many people can identify the shape of a corporate logo as quickly as they can recognize the shape of a stop sign. Although trademarks are valuable assets, they are rarely seen on balance sheets. The reason is simple; intangible assets are not recorded unless they are purchased. Companies often spend millions of dollars developing trademarks, but most of those expenditures are recorded as expenses rather than being capitalized as an intangible asset.

Copyrights

A **copyright** gives the owner the exclusive right to publish, use, and sell a literary, musical, or artistic piece for a period not exceeding 70 years after the author's death.[2] The book you are reading has a copyright to protect the publisher and authors. It is against the law, for example, for an instructor to copy several chapters from this book and hand them out in class. A copyright that is purchased is recorded at cost.

Technology

The number of companies reporting a **technology** intangible asset continues to rise. Computer software and Web development costs are becoming increasingly significant. At December 31, 2014, **IBM Corporation** reported $696 million in capitalized software and $1,298 million in completed technology (over 64 percent of its intangible assets excluding goodwill) on its balance sheet and disclosed the following in the notes to the financial statements:

D. Hurst/Alamy

COPYRIGHT
Exclusive right to publish, use, and sell a literary, musical, or artistic work.

TECHNOLOGY
Includes costs for computer software and Web development.

INTERNATIONAL BUSINESS MACHINES CORPORATION

REAL WORLD EXCERPT:

2014 Annual Report

Note A.

SIGNIFICANT ACCOUNTING POLICIES

Software Costs

Costs that are related to the conceptual formulation and design of licensed software programs are expensed as incurred to research, development and engineering expense; costs that are incurred to produce the finished product after technological feasibility has been established are capitalized as an intangible asset. Capitalized amounts are amortized on a straight-line basis over periods ranging up to three years and are recorded in software cost within cost of sales. . . .

   The company capitalizes certain costs that are incurred to purchase or to create and implement internal-use software programs, including software coding, installation, testing and certain data conversions. These capitalized costs are amortized on a straight-line basis over periods ranging up to two years and are recorded in selling, general and administrative expense.

| Research and Development Costs: Not an Intangible Asset Under U.S. GAAP | FINANCIAL ANALYSIS |

Note in the IBM excerpt above that costs to formulate and design licensed software programs are **expensed** as incurred to research, development, and engineering expense. In addition, if an intangible asset is developed internally, the cost of development normally is recorded as **research and development expense.** For example, **Abbott Laboratories** (a manufacturer of pharmaceutical and nutritional products) recently reported it spends about $1.5 billion annually on research to discover new products. These amounts were reported as expenses, not assets, because research and development expenditures typically do not possess sufficient probability of resulting in measurable future cash flows. If Abbott Labs had spent an equivalent amount to purchase patents for new products from other drug companies, it would have recorded the expenditures as assets.

---

[2]In general, the limit is 70 years beyond the death of an author. For anonymous authors, the limit is 95 years from the first publication date. For more detail, go to **copyright.gov**.

Patents

PATENT
Granted by the federal government for an invention; gives the owner the exclusive right to use, manufacture, and sell the subject of the patent.

A **patent** is an exclusive right granted by the federal government for a period of 20 years, typically granted to a person who invents a new product or discovers a new process.[3] The patent enables the owner to use, manufacture, and sell both the subject of the patent and the patent itself. It prevents a competitor from simply copying a new invention or discovery until the inventor has had time to earn an economic return on the new product. Without the protection of a patent, inventors likely would be unwilling to search for new products. Patents are recorded at their purchase price or, if **developed internally,** at only their registration and legal costs because GAAP requires the immediate expensing of research and development costs.

Franchises

FRANCHISE
A contractual right to sell certain products or services, use certain trademarks, or perform activities in a geographical region.

Franchises may be granted by the government or a business for a specified period and purpose. A city may grant one company a franchise to distribute gas to homes for heating purposes, or a company may sell franchises, such as the right to operate a **KFC** restaurant (owned by **Yum! Brands**). Franchise agreements are contracts that can have a variety of provisions. They usually require an investment by the franchisee; therefore, they should be accounted for as intangible assets. The life of the franchise agreement depends on the contract. It may be a single year or an indefinite period. For example, **Papa John's International**, a franchisor, has over 4,600 stores around the world, and about 84 percent are franchises. The franchise agreement covers a 10-year term that is renewable for another 10 years. In the United States, to obtain a new Papa John's franchise, a franchisee pays an initial franchise fee of $25,000 to Papa John's. This amount is then recorded by the franchisee as an intangible asset.

Licenses and Operating Rights

LICENSES AND OPERATING RIGHTS
Obtained through agreements with governmental units or agencies; permit owners to use public property in performing their services.

Southwest Airlines's intangible assets are included on the balance sheet presented in Exhibit 8.1 as *other assets.* They primarily represent leasehold rights to airport-owned gates. Others include operating rights, which are authorized landing slots regulated by the government that are in limited supply at many airports. They are intangible assets that can be bought and sold by the airlines. Other types of **licenses and operating rights** that grant permission to companies include using airwaves for radio and television broadcasts and land for cable and telephone lines.

INTERNATIONAL PERSPECTIVE   Differences in Accounting for Tangible and Intangible Assets

IFRS differs from GAAP somewhat in accounting for tangible and intangible assets. Two of the most significant differences are summarized below. IFRS allows companies the option of reporting these assets at fair value (e.g., appraisals), provided they use the fair value method consistently each year. The primary argument in favor of revaluation is that the historical cost of an asset purchased 15 to 20 years ago is not meaningful because of the impact of inflation. In contrast, GAAP requires tangible and intangible assets to be recorded at cost and not revalued for later increases in asset values. A primary argument against the revaluation is the lack of objectivity involved in estimating an asset's current cost.

IFRS also requires companies to capitalize the costs of developing intangible assets, such as prototypes for making new products or tools. GAAP, on the other hand, generally expenses such development costs because of the uncertainty of their value.

---

[3]For more details, go to **http://www.uspto.gov/web/offices/pac/doc/general/index.html#patent**.

	GAAP	IFRS
Cost versus Fair Value	• Must record at **cost** • Adjust for depreciation/amortization and impairment • Do not record increases in value	• Choose between either **cost or fair value** • Adjust for depreciation/amortization and impairment • **If using fair value, record increases in value**
Research and Development	• **Expense all costs** of researching and developing intangible assets	• Expense research costs, but **capitalize measurable costs of developing intangible assets**

Until the United States adopts IFRS, you should carefully read the financial statement notes of any non–U.S. company you analyze. **Euro Disney** and the **LEGO Group** reported in 2014 that they chose to use historical costs, but they could have chosen instead to use fair value.

Acquisition and Depletion of Natural Resources

You are probably most familiar with large companies that are involved in manufacturing (**Ford Motor Corporation**, **Stanley Black & Decker**), distribution (**Sears Holdings**, **Home Depot**), or services (**FedEx®**, **Marriott International**). A number of large companies, some of which are less well known, develop raw materials and products from **natural resources**, including mineral deposits such as gold or iron ore, oil wells, and timber tracts. These resources are often called **wasting assets** because they are depleted (i.e., physically used up). Companies that develop natural resources are critical to the economy because they produce essential items such as lumber for construction, fuel for heating and transportation, and food for consumption. Because of the significant effect they can have on the environment, these companies attract considerable public attention. Concerned citizens often read the financial statements of companies involved in the exploration for oil, coal, and various ores to determine the amount of money they spend to protect the environment.

When natural resources are acquired or developed, they are recorded in conformity with the **cost principle.** As a natural resource is used up, its acquisition cost must be apportioned among the periods in which revenues are earned in conformity with the **expense principle.** The term **depletion** describes the process of allocating a natural resource's cost over the period of its exploitation.[4] The units-of-production method is often applied to compute depletion.

When a natural resource such as an oil well is depleted, the company obtains inventory (oil). Because depleting the natural resource is necessary to obtain the inventory, the depletion computed during a period is not expensed immediately, but is **capitalized** as part of the cost of the inventory. Only when the inventory is sold does the company record an expense (Cost of Goods Sold). Consider the following illustration:

A timber tract costing $530,000 is depleted over its estimated cutting period based on a "cutting" rate of approximately 20 percent per year as in the following entry. Note that the amount of the natural resource that is depleted is capitalized as inventory, not expensed. When the inventory is sold, the cost of goods sold will be included as an expense on the income statement.

NATURAL RESOURCES
Assets occurring in nature, such as mineral deposits, timber tracts, oil, and gas.

DEPLETION
Systematic and rational allocation of the cost of a natural resource over the period of its exploitation.

Inventory (+A).	106,000	
Timber Tract (−A) (or Accumulated Depletion +XA, −A)		106,000

Assets		=	Liabilities	+	Stockholders' Equity
Inventory	+106,000				
Timber Tract (or Accumulated Amortization +XA)	−106,000				

[4]Consistent with the procedure for recording depreciation, an accumulated depletion account may be used. In practice, however, most companies credit the asset account directly for periodic depletion.

International Paper's 2014 balance sheet lists Forestlands of $507 million as an important natural resource. The following is an excerpt of the related footnote describing the accounting policies for the company's natural resource:

INTERNATIONAL PAPER

REAL WORLD EXCERPT:

2014 Annual Report

> NOTES TO CONSOLIDATED FINANCIAL STATEMENTS
>
> NOTE 1 SUMMARY OF BUSINESS AND SIGNIFICANT ACCOUNTING POLICIES
>
> *FORESTLANDS*
>
> At December 31, 2014, International Paper and its subsidiaries owned or managed approximately 334,000 acres of forestlands in Brazil, and through licenses and forest management agreements, had harvesting rights on government-owned forestlands in Russia. Costs attributable to timber are expensed as trees are cut. The rate charged is determined annually based on the relationship of incurred costs to estimated current merchantable volume.

FOCUS ON CASH FLOWS

Productive Assets and Depreciation

LEARNING OBJECTIVE 8-7

Explain how the acquisition, use, and disposal of long-lived assets impact cash flows.

EFFECT ON STATEMENT OF CASH FLOWS

The indirect method for preparing the operating activities section of the statement of cash flows involves reconciling net income on the accrual basis (reported on the income statement) to cash flows from operations. This means that, among other adjustments, (1) revenues and expenses that do not involve cash and (2) gains and losses that relate to investing or financing activities (not operations) should be eliminated.

When depreciation is recorded, no cash payment is made (i.e., there is no credit to Cash). Because depreciation expense (a noncash expense) is subtracted in calculating net income on the income statement, it must be added back to net income to eliminate its effect. Likewise, because any gain (or loss) on the sale of long-lived assets (an investing activity) is added (or subtracted) to determine net income, it must be subtracted from (or added to) net income to eliminate its effect.

In General   The acquisition, sale, and depreciation of long-term assets are reflected on a company's cash flow statement as indicated in the following table:

	Effect on Cash Flows
Operating activities (indirect method)	
Net income	$xxx
Adjusted for: Depreciation and amortization expense	+
Gains on sale of long-lived assets	−
Losses on sale of long-lived assets	+
Losses due to asset impairment write-downs	+
Investing activities	
Purchase of long-lived assets	−
Sale of long-lived assets	+

Focus Company Analysis   The following is a condensed version of **Southwest**'s statement of cash flows for 2014. Buying and selling long-lived assets are investing activities. In 2014, Southwest used $1,748 million in cash to purchase flight equipment and ground property and equipment.

Southwest did not sell any flight or ground equipment during the year. Selling long-lived assets is not an operating activity. Therefore, any gains (losses) on sales of long-term assets that were included in net income must be deducted from (added to) net income in the operating activities section to eliminate the effect of the sale. Unless they are large, these gain and loss adjustments normally are not specifically highlighted on the statement of cash flows. Southwest did not list any gains or losses as adjustments in 2014.

In capital-intensive industries such as airlines, depreciation is a significant noncash expense. In Southwest's case, depreciation and amortization expense is usually the single largest adjustment to net income in determining cash flows from operations. For example, in 2014, the adjustment for depreciation and amortization expense was 32 percent of operating cash flows.

SOUTHWEST AIRLINES CO.	
Consolidated Statement of Cash Flows (partial)	
For the Year Ended December 31, 2014	
(*In millions*)	
	2014
Cash Flows from Operating Activities:	
Net income	$ 1,136
Adjustments to reconcile net income to cash provided by operating activities:	
Depreciation and amortization	938
Other (*summarized*)	828
Net cash provided by (used in) operating activities	2,902
Cash Flows from Investing Activities:	
Capital expenditures (*purchases of property and equipment*)	(1,748)
Other (*summarized*)	21
Net cash used in investing activities	(1,727)

A Misinterpretation

Some analysts misinterpret the meaning of a noncash expense, saying that "cash is provided by depreciation." Although depreciation is added in the operating section of the statement of cash flows, **depreciation is not a source of cash.** Cash from operations can be provided only by selling goods and services. A company with a large amount of depreciation expense does not generate more cash compared with a company that reports a small amount of depreciation expense, assuming that they are exactly the same in every other respect. While depreciation expense reduces the amount of reported net income for a company, it does not reduce the amount of cash generated by the company because it is a noncash expense. Remember that the effects of recording depreciation are a reduction in stockholders' equity and a reduction in fixed assets, not in cash. That is why, on the statement of cash flows, depreciation expense is added back to net income on an accrual basis to compute cash flows from operations (on a cash basis).

Although depreciation is a noncash expense, the **depreciation for tax purposes can affect a company's cash flows.** Depreciation is a deductible expense for income tax purposes. The higher the amount of depreciation recorded by a company for tax purposes, the lower the company's taxable income and the taxes it must pay. Because taxes must be paid in cash, a reduction in a company's results reduces the company's cash outflows (that is, lower net income leads to lower tax payments).

DEMONSTRATION CASE A

(Resolve the requirements before proceeding to the suggested solution that follows.) Diversified Industries started as a residential construction company. In recent years, it has expanded into heavy construction, ready-mix concrete, construction supplies, and earth-moving services. Assume the company completed the following transactions during 2016. Amounts have been simplified.

2016

Jan. 1   The management decided to buy a 10-year-old building for $175,000 and the land on which it was situated for $130,000. It paid $100,000 in cash and signed a mortgage note payable for the rest.

Jan. 12   Paid $38,000 in renovation costs on the building prior to use.

July 10   Paid $1,200 for ordinary repairs on the building.

Dec. 31   Year-end adjustments:

a.   The building will be depreciated on a straight-line basis over an estimated useful life of 30 years. The estimated residual value is $33,000.

b.   Diversified purchased another company several years ago at $100,000 over the fair value of the net assets acquired. The goodwill has an indefinite life.

c.   At the beginning of the year, the company owned equipment with a cost of $650,000 and accumulated depreciation of $150,000. The equipment is being depreciated using the double-declining-balance method, with a useful life of 20 years and no residual value.

d.   At year-end, the company tested its long-lived assets for possible impairment of their value. It identified a piece of old excavation equipment with a cost of $156,000 and remaining book value of $120,000. Due to its smaller size and lack of safety features, the old equipment has limited use. The future cash flows are expected to be $40,000 and the fair value is determined to be $35,000. Goodwill was found not to be impaired.

December 31, 2016, is the end of the annual accounting period.

Required:

1. Indicate the accounts affected and the amount and direction (+ for increase and − for decrease) of the effect of each of the preceding events (Jan. 1, Jan. 12, July 10, and adjustments *a* through *d*) on the financial statement categories at the end of the year. Use the following headings:

Date	Assets	=	Liabilities	+	Stockholders' Equity

2. Record the December 31 adjusting journal entries (*a*) and (*c*) only.

3. Show the December 31, 2016, balance sheet classification and amount reported for each of the following items:

Fixed assets—land, building, and equipment
Intangible asset—goodwill

4. Assuming that the company had operating revenues of $1,000,000 for the year and a net book value of $500,000 for fixed assets at the beginning of the year, compute the fixed asset turnover ratio. Explain its meaning.

SUGGESTED SOLUTION

1. Effects of events (with computations):

Date	Assets		=	Liabilities		+	Stockholders' Equity	
Jan. 1	Cash	−100,000		Note Payable	+205,000			
	Land	+130,000						
	Building	+175,000						
Jan. 12 (1)	Cash	−38,000						
	Building	+38,000						
July 10 (2)	Cash	−1,200					Repairs Expense	−1,200
Dec. 31 *a* (3)	Accumulated						Depreciation	
	Depreciation (+XA)	−6,000					Expense	−6,000
Dec. 31 *b* (4)	No entry							
Dec. 31 *c* (5)	Accumulated						Depreciation	
	Depreciation (+XA)	−50,000					Expense	−50,000
Dec. 31 *d* (6)	Equipment	−85,000					Loss Due to Asset	
							Impairment	−85,000

(1) Capitalize the $38,000 expenditure because it is necessary to prepare the asset for use.

(2) This is an ordinary repair and should be expensed.

(3)

Cost of Building		Straight-Line Depreciation
Initial purchase price	$175,000	($213,000 cost − $33,000 residual value) ×
Repairs prior to use	38,000	1/30 years = **$6,000** annual depreciation
Acquisition cost	$213,000	

(4) Goodwill has an indefinite life and is therefore not amortized. We will test for impairment later.

(5) **Double-declining-balance depreciation**

($650,000 cost − $150,000 accumulated depreciation) × 2/20 years = **$50,000** depreciation for 2016.

(6) **Asset impairment**

Impairment Test: The book value of old equipment, $120,000, exceeds expected future cash flows, $40,000. The asset is impaired.

Impairment Loss	
Book value	$120,000
Less: Fair value	−35,000
Loss due to impairment	$ 85,000

2. Adjusting entries at December 31, 2016:

a.

| Depreciation Expense (+E, −SE) | 6,000 | |
| Accumulated Depreciation (+XA, −A) | | 6,000 |

b.

| Depreciation Expense (+E, −SE) | 50,000 | |
| Accumulated Depreciation (+XA, −A) | | 50,000 |

3. Partial balance sheet, December 31, 2016:

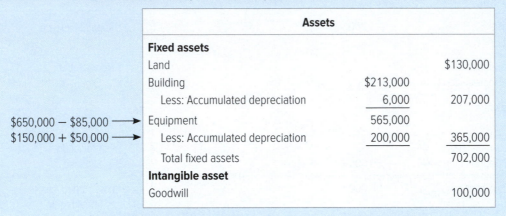

Assets		
Fixed assets		
Land		$130,000
Building	$213,000	
Less: Accumulated depreciation	6,000	207,000
Equipment	565,000	
Less: Accumulated depreciation	200,000	365,000
Total fixed assets		702,000
Intangible asset		
Goodwill		100,000

$650,000 − $85,000 ⟶ Equipment
$150,000 + $50,000 ⟶ Less: Accumulated depreciation

4. Fixed asset turnover ratio:

$$\frac{\text{Operating Revenues (Net Sales)}}{\text{(Beginning Net Fixed Asset Balance + Ending Net Fixed Asset Balance)} \div 2} = \frac{\$1,000,000}{(\$500,000 + 702,000) \div 2} = 1.66$$

This construction company is capital intensive. The fixed asset turnover ratio measures the company's efficiency at using its investment in property, plant, and equipment to generate sales.

DEMONSTRATION **CASE B**

In 2017, Diversified Industries, a residential construction company, acquired a gravel pit (designated Gravel Pit No. 1) to support its construction operations. The company completed the following transactions during 2017 related to the gravel pit. Amounts have been simplified and the company's fiscal year ends on December 31.

June 19   Bought Gravel Pit No.1 for $50,000 cash. It was estimated that 100,000 cubic yards of gravel could be removed.

Aug. 1   Paid $10,000 for costs of preparing the new gravel pit for exploitation.

Nov. 10   12,000 cubic yards of gravel were removed from Gravel Pit No. 1 to be used or sold in 2018.

Required:

Record the June 19, August 1, and November 10 transactions.

SUGGESTED SOLUTION

Date	Accounts		
June 19	Gravel Pit No. 1 (+A)	50,000	
	Cash (−A)		50,000
Aug. 1	Gravel Pit No. 1 (+A)	10,000	
	Cash (−A)		10,000
Nov. 10*	Inventory—Gravel (+A)	7,200	
	Gravel Pit No. 1 (−A)		7,200

*Cost of Gravel Pit

Initial purchase price	$50,000
Preparation costs	10,000
Total cost	$60,000

Units-of-Production Depletion

Depletion Rate: $60,000 cost ÷ 100,000 estimated production = $0.60 per unit

Depletion Expense: $0.60 per unit × 12,000 actual production = $7,200

Capitalize the depletion to gravel inventory.

Chapter Supplement

Changes in Depreciation Estimates

Depreciation is based on two estimates: useful life and residual value. These estimates are made at the time a depreciable asset is acquired. As experience with the asset accumulates, one or both of these initial estimates may need to be revised. In addition, any improvements that extend the asset's useful life may be added to the original acquisition cost at some time during the asset's use. When it is clear that either estimate should be revised to a material degree or that the asset's cost has changed, the undepreciated asset balance (less any residual value at that date) should be apportioned over the remaining estimated life from the current year into the future. This is called a prospective **change in estimate.**

To compute the new depreciation expense due to a change in estimate for any of the depreciation methods described here, substitute the net book value for the original acquisition cost, the new residual value for the original amount, and the estimated remaining life in place of the original estimated life. As an illustration, the formula using the straight-line method follows.

Original Straight-Line Formula Modified for a Change in Estimate:

$$(\text{Cost} - \text{Residual Value}) \times \frac{1}{\text{Useful Life}} = \text{Original Depreciation Expense}$$

$$(\text{Net Book Value} - \text{New Residual Value}) \times \frac{1}{\text{Remaining Life}} = \text{Revised Depreciation Expense}$$

Assume **Southwest** purchased an aircraft for $60,000,000 with an estimated useful life of 20 years and estimated residual value of $3,000,000. Shortly after the start of Year 5, Southwest changed the

Straight-Line Depreciation Expense with a Change in Estimate

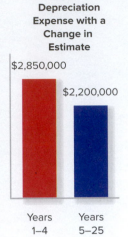

Years 1–4   Years 5–25

initial estimated life to 25 years and lowered the estimated residual value to $2,400,000. At the end of Year 5, the computation of the new amount for depreciation expense is as follows:

Original depreciation expense

$$(\$60,000,000 - \$3,000,000) \times 1/20 = \$\ 2,850,000 \text{ per year}$$
$$\times\ 4 \text{ years}$$

Accumulated depreciation at the end of year 4: $11,400,000

Net book value at the end of year 4		**Remaining Life**	
Acquisition cost	$60,000,000	New estimated life	25 years
Less: Accumulated depreciation	11,400,000	In the past	4 years
Net book value	$48,600,000	Remaining	21 years

Depreciation in years 5 through 25 based on changes in estimates

$$\text{(Net Book Value} - \text{New Residual Value)} \times \text{1/Remaining Years} = \text{New Depreciation Expense}$$

$$(\$48,600,000 - \$2,400,000) \times 1/21 \text{ years} = \$2,200,000 \text{ per year}$$

Companies may also change depreciation methods (for example, from declining balance to straight line). Such a change requires significantly more disclosure because it violates the consistency principle, which requires that accounting information reported in the financial statements should be comparable across accounting periods. Under GAAP, changes in accounting estimates and depreciation methods should be made only when a new estimate or accounting method "better measures" the periodic income of the business.

STOP

PAUSE FOR **FEEDBACK**

When management changes an estimate used in a depreciation computation, the net book value at the time of the change minus any expected residual value is allocated over the remaining life of the asset.

SELF-STUDY **QUIZ**

Assume that **Southwest Airlines** owned a service truck that originally cost $100,000. When purchased at the beginning of 2013, the truck had an estimated useful life of 10 years with no residual value. At the beginning of 2018, after operating the truck for five years, Southwest determined that the remaining life was only two more years. Southwest uses the straight-line method.

1. What is the truck's net book value at the beginning of 2018?
2. Based on this change in estimate, what amount of depreciation should be recorded each year over the remaining life of the asset?

After you have completed your answers, check them below.

Solutions to
SELF-STUDY QUIZ

1. (Cost $100,000 − Residual Value $0) × 1/10 = $10,000 Original Annual Depreciation
   $10,000 Annual Depreciation Expense × 5 Years = $50,000 Accumulated Depreciation
   Net Book Value After 5 Years = Cost $100,000 − Accumulated Depreciation $50,000 = $50,000
2. (Net Book Value $50,000 − Residual Value $0) × 1/2 (remaining life) = $25,000 Depreciation Expense per Year

8-1. Define, classify, and explain the nature of long-lived productive assets and interpret the fixed asset turnover ratio.   p. 391

a. Productive assets are those that a business retains for long periods of time for use in the course of normal operations rather than for sale. They may be divided into tangible assets (land, buildings, equipment, natural resources) and intangible assets (including goodwill, patents, and franchises).

b. The cost allocation method utilized affects the amount of net property, plant, and equipment that is used in the computation of the fixed asset turnover ratio. Accelerated methods reduce book value and increase the turnover ratio.

8-2. Apply the cost principle to measure the acquisition and maintenance of property, plant, and equipment.   p. 392

The acquisition cost of property, plant, and equipment is the cash-equivalent purchase price plus all reasonable and necessary expenditures made to acquire and prepare the asset for its intended use. These assets may be acquired using cash, debt, or stock or through self-construction. Expenditures made after the asset is in use are either additions and improvements or ordinary repairs (expenses):

a. **Ordinary repairs and maintenance** provide benefits during the current accounting period only. Amounts are debited to appropriate current expense accounts when the expenses are incurred.

b. **Improvements** provide benefits for one or more accounting periods beyond the current period. Amounts are debited to the appropriate asset accounts (they are capitalized) and depreciated, depleted, or amortized over their useful lives.

8-3. Apply various cost allocation methods as assets are held and used over time.   p. 398

Cost allocation methods: In conformity with the expense principle, cost less any estimated residual value is allocated to periodic expense over the periods benefited. Because of depreciation, the net book value of an asset declines over time and net income is reduced by the amount of the expense. Common depreciation methods include straight-line (a constant amount over time), units-of-production (a variable amount over time), and double-declining-balance (a decreasing amount over time).

a. Depreciation—buildings and equipment.

b. Amortization—intangibles.

c. Depletion—natural resources.

8-4. Explain the effect of asset impairment on the financial statements.   p. 409

When events or changes in circumstances reduce the estimated future cash flows of long-lived assets below their book value, the book values should be written down (by recording a loss) to the fair value of the assets.

8-5. Analyze the disposal of property, plant, and equipment.   p. 410

When assets are disposed of through sale or abandonment,

a. Record additional depreciation since the last adjustment was made.

b. Remove the cost of the old asset and its related accumulated depreciation, depletion, or amortization.

c. Recognize the cash proceeds.

d. Recognize any gain or loss when the asset's net book value is not equal to the cash received.

8-6. Apply measurement and reporting concepts for intangible assets and natural resources.   p. 412

The cost principle should be applied in recording the acquisition of intangible assets and natural resources. Intangibles with definite useful lives are amortized using the straight-line method. Intangibles with indefinite useful lives, including goodwill, are not amortized, but are reviewed at least annually for impairment. Report intangibles at net book value on the balance sheet. Natural resources should be depleted (usually by the units-of-production method) usually with the amount of the depletion expense capitalized to an inventory account.

8-7. Explain how the acquisition, use, and disposal of long-lived assets impact cash flows.   p. 418

Depreciation expense is a noncash expense that has no effect on cash. It is added back to net income on the statement of cash flows to determine cash from operations. Acquiring and disposing of long-lived assets are investing activities.

In previous chapters, we discussed business and accounting issues related to the assets that a company holds. In Chapters 9, 10, and 11, we shift our focus to the other side of the balance sheet to see how managers finance business operations and the acquisition of productive assets. We discuss various types of liabilities in Chapters 9 and 10 and examine stockholders' equity in Chapter 11.

KEY RATIO

The **fixed asset turnover ratio** measures how efficiently a company utilizes its investment in property, plant, and equipment over time. Its ratio can then be compared to competitors' ratios. The fixed asset turnover ratio is computed as follows (see the "Key Ratio Analysis" box in the Acquisition and Maintenance of Plant and Equipment section):

$$\text{Fixed Asset Turnover} = \frac{\text{Net Sales (or Operating Revenues)}}{\text{Average Net Fixed Assets}}$$

FINDING FINANCIAL INFORMATION

Balance Sheet

Under Noncurrent Assets
Property, plant, and equipment (net of
   accumulated depreciation)
Natural resources (net of accumulated depletion)
Intangibles (net of accumulated amortization,
   if any)

Income Statement

Under Operating Expenses
Depreciation, depletion, and amortization
   expense **or** included in
Selling, general, and administrative expenses and
Cost of goods sold (with the amount for
   depreciation expense disclosed in a note)

Statement of Cash Flows

Under Operating Activities (indirect method)
Net income
+ Depreciation and amortization expense
− Gains on sales of assets
+ Losses on sales of assets

Under Investing Activities
+ Sales of assets for cash
− Purchases of assets for cash

Notes

Under Summary of Significant Accounting Policies
Description of management's choice for depreciation
   and amortization methods, including useful lives,
   and the amount of annual depreciation expense, if
   not listed on the income statement.

Under a Separate Footnote
If not specified on the balance sheet, a listing of the
   major classifications of long-lived assets at cost and
   the balance in accumulated depreciation, depletion,
   and amortization.

KEY TERMS

Acquisition Cost   p. 393
Amortization   p. 413
Capitalized Interest   p. 395
Copyright   p. 415

Declining-Balance Depreciation   p. 404
Depletion   p. 417
Depreciation   p. 399
Estimated Useful Life   p. 400

Franchise   p. 416
Goodwill (Cost in Excess of Net Assets
   Acquired)   p. 413
Improvements   p. 397

QUESTIONS

1. Define **long-lived assets.** Why are they considered to be a "bundle of future services"?
2. How is the fixed asset turnover ratio computed? Explain its meaning.
3. What are the classifications of long-lived assets? Explain each.
4. Under the cost measurement concept, what amounts should be included in the acquisition cost of a long-lived asset?
5. Describe the relationship between the expense recognition principle and accounting for long-lived assets.
6. Distinguish between ordinary repairs and improvements. How is each accounted for?
7. Distinguish among depreciation, depletion, and amortization.
8. In computing depreciation, three values must be known or estimated; identify and explain the nature of each.
9. The estimated useful life and residual value of a long-lived asset relate to the current owner or user rather than all potential users. Explain this statement.
10. What type of depreciation expense pattern is used under each of the following methods and when is its use appropriate?
    a. The straight-line method.
    b. The units-of-production method.
    c. The double-declining-balance method.
11. Over what period should an addition to an existing long-lived asset be depreciated? Explain.
12. What is **asset impairment**? How is it accounted for?
13. When equipment is sold for more than net book value, how is the transaction recorded? For less than net book value? What is **net book value**?
14. Define **intangible asset.** What period should be used to amortize an intangible asset with a definite life?
15. Define **goodwill.** When is it appropriate to record goodwill as an intangible asset?
16. Why is depreciation expense added to net income (indirect method) on the statement of cash flows?

MULTIPLE-CHOICE QUESTIONS

1. Miga Company and Porter Company both bought a new delivery truck on January 1, 2014. Both companies paid exactly the same cost, $30,000, for their respective vehicles. As of December 31, 2017, the net book value of Miga's truck was less than Porter Company's net book value for the same vehicle. Which of the following is an acceptable explanation for the difference in net book value?
   a. Miga Company estimated a lower residual value, but both estimated the same useful life and both elected straight-line depreciation.
   b. Both companies elected straight-line depreciation, but Miga Company used a longer estimated life.
   c. Because GAAP specifies rigid guidelines regarding the calculation of depreciation, this situation is not possible.
   d. Miga Company is using the straight-line method of depreciation, and Porter Company is using the double-declining-balance method of depreciation.
2. Leslie, Inc., followed the practice of depreciating its building on a straight-line basis. A building was purchased in 2016 and had an estimated useful life of 25 years and a residual value of $20,000.

The company's depreciation expense for 2016 was $15,000 on the building. What was the original cost of the building?

a. $395,000

b. $500,000

c. $520,000

d. Cannot be determined from the information given.

3. Maks, Inc., uses straight-line depreciation for all of its depreciable assets. Maks sold a used piece of machinery on December 31, 2017, that it purchased on January 1, 2016, for $10,000. The asset had a five-year life, zero residual value, and $2,000 accumulated depreciation as of December 31, 2016. If the sales price of the used machine was $7,500, the resulting gain or loss upon the sale was which of the following amounts?

a. Loss of $500   d. Gain of $1,500

b. Gain of $500   e. No gain or loss upon the sale.

c. Loss of $1,500

4. Under what method(s) of depreciation is an asset's **net book value** the depreciable base (the amount to be depreciated)?

a. Straight-line method   c. Units-of-production method

b. Declining-balance method   d. All of the above

5. What assets should be amortized using the straight-line method?

a. Intangible assets with definite lives   c. Natural resources

b. Intangible assets with indefinite lives   d. All of the above

6. A company wishes to report the highest earnings possible for financial reporting purposes. Therefore, when calculating depreciation,

a. It will follow the MACRS depreciation tables prescribed by the IRS.

b. It will select the shortest lives possible for its assets.

c. It will select the lowest residual values for its assets.

d. It will estimate higher residual values for its assets.

7. How many of the following statements regarding goodwill are true?

- Goodwill is not reported unless purchased in an exchange.
- Goodwill must be reviewed annually for possible impairment.
- Impairment of goodwill results in a decrease in net income.

a. Three

b. Two

c. One

d. None

8. Company X is going to retire equipment that is fully depreciated with no residual value. The equipment will simply be disposed of, not sold. Which of the following statements is *false*?

a. Total assets will not change as a result of this transaction.

b. Net income will not be impacted as a result of this transaction.

c. This transaction will not impact cash flow.

d. All of the above statements are true.

9. When recording depreciation, which of the following statements is *true*?

a. Total assets increase and stockholders' equity increases.

b. Total assets decrease and total liabilities increase.

c. Total assets decrease and stockholders' equity increases.

d. None of the above are true.

10. (Chapter Supplement) Irish Industries purchased a machine for $65,000 and is depreciating it with the straight-line method over a life of 10 years, using a residual value of $3,000. At the beginning of the sixth year, a major overhaul was made costing $5,000, and the total estimated useful life was extended to 13 years with a residual value of $3,000. Depreciation expense for Year 6 is:

a. $1,885   d. $3,625

b. $2,000   e. $4,500

c. $3,250

Classifying Long-Lived Assets and Related Cost Allocation Concepts

For each of the following long-lived assets, indicate its nature and the related cost allocation concept. Use the following symbols:

M8-1
LO8-1, 8-3, 8-6

Nature		Cost Allocation Concept	
L	Land	DR	Depreciation
B	Building	DP	Depletion
E	Equipment	A	Amortization
NR	Natural resource	NO	No cost allocation
I	Intangible	O	Other
O	Other		

Asset	Nature	Cost Allocation	Asset	Nature	Cost Allocation
(1) Tractors	____	____	(6) Operating license	____	____
(2) Land in use	____	____	(7) Production plant	____	____
(3) Timber tract	____	____	(8) Trademark	____	____
(4) Warehouse	____	____	(9) Silver mine	____	____
(5) New engine for old machine	____	____	(10) Land held for sale	____	____

Computing and Evaluating the Fixed Asset Turnover Ratio

The following information was reported by Young's Air Cargo Service for 2014:

M8-2
LO8-1

Net fixed assets (beginning of year)	$1,500,000
Net fixed assets (end of year)	2,300,000
Net operating revenues for the year	3,600,000
Net income for the year	1,600,000

Compute the company's fixed asset turnover ratio (rounded to two decimal places) for the year. What can you say about Young's ratio when compared to **Southwest**'s 2014 ratio?

Identifying Capital Expenditures and Expenses

For each of the following items, enter the correct letter to the left to show the type of expenditure. Use the following:

M8-3
LO8-2

Type of Expenditure		Transactions
C	Capital expenditure	____ (1) Purchased a patent, $4,300 cash.
E	Expense	____ (2) Paid $10,000 for monthly salaries.
N	Neither	____ (3) Paid cash dividends, $20,000.
		____ (4) Purchased a machine, $7,000; gave a long-term note.
		____ (5) Paid three-year insurance premium, $900.
		____ (6) Paid for routine maintenance, $200, on credit.
		____ (7) Paid $400 for ordinary repairs.
		____ (8) Paid $6,000 for improvements that lengthened the asset's productive life.
		____ (9) Paid $20,000 cash for addition to old building.

M8-4
LO8-3

Computing Book Value (Straight-Line Depreciation)

Calculate the book value of a three-year-old machine that has a cost of $31,000, an estimated residual value of $1,000, and an estimated useful life of five years. The company uses straight-line depreciation.

M8-5
LO8-3

Computing Book Value (Double-Declining-Balance Depreciation)

Calculate the book value of a three-year-old machine that has a cost of $55,000, an estimated residual value of $5,000, and an estimated useful life of five years. The company uses double-declining-balance depreciation. Round to the nearest dollar.

M8-6
LO8-3

Computing Book Value (Units-of-Production Depreciation)

Calculate the book value of a three-year-old machine that has a cost of $26,000, an estimated residual value of $1,000, and an estimated useful life of 50,000 machine hours. The company uses units-of-production depreciation and ran the machine 3,200 hours in Year 1; 7,050 hours in Year 2; and 7,500 hours in Year 3.

M8-7
LO8-4

Identifying Asset Impairment

For each of the following scenarios, indicate whether an asset has been impaired (Y for yes and N for no) and, if so, the amount of loss that should be recorded.

	Book Value	Estimated Future Cash Flows	Fair Value	Is Asset Impaired?	Amount of Loss
a. Machine	$ 15,500	$ 10,000	$ 9,500		
b. Copyright	$ 31,000	$ 41,000	$ 37,900		
c. Factory building	$ 58,000	$ 29,000	$ 27,000		
d. Building	$227,000	$227,000	$200,000		

M8-8
LO8-5

Recording the Disposal of a Long-Lived Asset (Straight-Line Depreciation)

As part of a major renovation at the beginning of the year, Bonham's Bakery sold shelving units (store fixtures) that were 10 years old for $1,800 cash. The original cost of the shelves was $6,500 and they had been depreciated on a straight-line basis over an estimated useful life of 12 years with an estimated residual value of $800. Record the sale of the shelving units.

M8-9
LO8-6

Computing Goodwill and Patents

Elizabeth Pie Company has been in business for 50 years and has developed a large group of loyal restaurant customers. Giant Bakery Inc. has made an offer to buy Elizabeth Pie Company for $5,000,000. The book value of Elizabeth Pie's recorded assets and liabilities on the date of the offer is $4,300,000 with a fair value of $4,500,000. Elizabeth Pie also (1) holds a patent for a pie crust fluting machine that the company invented (the patent with a fair value of $300,000 was never recorded by Elizabeth Pie because it was developed internally) and (2) estimates goodwill from loyal customers to be $310,000 (also never recorded by the company). Should Elizabeth Pie Company management accept Giant Bakery's offer of $5,000,000? If so, compute the amount of goodwill that Giant Bakery should record on the date of the purchase.

M8-10
LO8-7

Preparing the Statement of Cash Flows

Garrett Company had the following activities for a recent year ended December 31: Sold land that cost $20,000 for $20,000 cash; purchased $181,000 of equipment, paying $156,000 in cash and signing a note payable for the rest; and recorded $5,500 in depreciation expense for the year. Net income for the year was $18,000. Prepare the operating and investing sections of a statement of cash flows for the year based on the data provided.

Preparing a Classified Balance Sheet

E8-1
LO8-1

The following is a list of account titles and amounts (dollars in millions) from a recent annual report of **Hasbro, Inc.**, a leading manufacturer of games, toys, and interactive entertainment software for children and families:

Buildings and improvements	$234	Machinery, equipment, and software	$ 504
Prepaid expenses and other current assets	392	Accumulated depreciation	509
Allowance for doubtful accounts	16	Inventories	340
Other noncurrent assets	658	Other intangibles	1,123
Accumulated amortization (other intangibles)	798	Land and improvements	7
Cash and cash equivalents	893	Accounts receivable	1,111
Goodwill	593		

Required:
Prepare the asset section of the balance sheet for Hasbro, Inc., classifying the assets into Current Assets; Property, Plant, and Equipment (net); and Other Assets.

Computing and Interpreting the Fixed Asset Turnover Ratio from a Financial Analyst's Perspective

E8-2
LO8-1

The following data were included in a recent **Apple Inc.** annual report ($ in millions):

In millions	2011	2012	2013	2014
Net sales	$108,249	$156,508	$170,910	$182,795
Net property, plant, and equipment	7,777	15,452	16,597	20,624

Required:
1. Compute Apple's fixed asset turnover ratio for 2012, 2013, and 2014. Round your answers to two decimal points.
2. How might a financial analyst interpret the results?

Computing and Recording Cost and Depreciation of Assets (Straight-Line Depreciation)

E8-3
LO8-2, 8-3

Shahia Company bought a building for $82,000 cash and the land on which it was located for $107,000 cash. The company paid transfer costs of $9,000 ($3,000 for the building and $6,000 for the land). Renovation costs on the building were $21,000.

Required:
1. Give the journal entry to record the purchase of the property, including all relevant expenditures. Assume that all transactions were for cash and that all purchases occurred at the start of the year.
2. Compute straight-line depreciation at the end of one year, assuming an estimated 10-year useful life and a $15,000 estimated residual value.
3. What would be the net book value of the property (land and building) at the end of Year 2?

Determining Financial Statement Effects of an Asset Acquisition and Depreciation (Straight-Line Depreciation)

E8-4
LO8-2, 8-3

During Year 1, Ashkar Company ordered a machine on January 1 at an invoice price of $21,000. On the date of delivery, January 2, the company paid $6,000 on the machine, with the balance on credit at 10 percent interest due in six months. On January 3, it paid $1,000 for freight on the machine. On January 5, Ashkar paid installation costs relating to the machine amounting to $2,500. On July 1, the company paid the balance due on the machine plus the interest. On December 31 (the end of the accounting period), Ashkar recorded depreciation on the machine using the straight-line method with an estimated useful life of 10 years and an estimated residual value of $4,000.

Required (round all amounts to the nearest dollar):
1. Indicate the effects (accounts, amounts, and + or −) of each transaction (on January 1, 2, 3, and 5 and July 1) on the accounting equation. Use the following schedule:

Date	Assets	=	Liabilities	+	Stockholders' Equity

2. Compute the acquisition cost of the machine.
3. Compute the depreciation expense to be reported for Year 1.
4. What impact does the interest paid on the 10 percent note have on the cost of the machine? Under what circumstances can interest expense be included in acquisition cost?
5. What would be the net book value of the machine at the end of Year 2?

E8-5
LO8-2, 8-3

Determining Financial Statement Effects of an Asset Acquisition and Depreciation (Straight-Line Depreciation)

Steve's Outdoor Company purchased a new delivery van on January 1 for $45,000 plus $3,800 in sales tax. The company paid $12,800 cash on the van (including the sales tax), with the $36,000 balance on credit at 8 percent interest due in nine months (on September 30). On January 2, the company paid cash of $700 to have the company name and logo painted on the van. On September 30, the company paid the balance due on the van plus the interest. On December 31 (the end of the accounting period), Steve's Outdoor recorded depreciation on the van using the straight-line method with an estimated useful life of 5 years and an estimated residual value of $4,500.

Required (round all amounts to the nearest dollar):
1. Indicate the effects (accounts, amounts, and + or −) of each transaction (on January 1, 2, and September 30) on the accounting equation. Use the following schedule:

Date	Assets	=	Liabilities	+	Stockholders' Equity

2. Compute the acquisition cost of the van.
3. Compute the depreciation expense to be reported for Year 1.
4. What impact does the interest paid on the 8 percent note have on the cost of the van? Under what circumstances can interest expense be included in acquisition cost?
5. What would be the net book value of the van at the end of Year 2?

E8-6
LO8-2, 8-3

Recording Depreciation and Repairs (Straight-Line Depreciation)

Manrow Growers, Inc., owns equipment for sowing and harvesting its organic fruit, vegetables, and tree nuts that are sold to local restaurants and grocery stores. At the beginning of 2016, an asset account for the company showed the following balances:

Equipment	$350,000
Accumulated depreciation through 2015	132,000

During 2016, the following expenditures were incurred for the equipment:

Routine maintenance and repairs on the equipment	$ 5,000
Major overhaul of the equipment that improved efficiency on January 1, 2016	42,000

The equipment is being depreciated on a straight-line basis over an estimated life of 10 years with a $20,000 estimated residual value. The annual accounting period ends on December 31.

Required:
1. Give the adjusting entry that was made at the end of 2015 for depreciation on the equipment.
2. Starting at the beginning of 2016, what is the remaining estimated life?
3. Give the journal entries to record the two expenditures during 2016.

Recording Depreciation and Repairs (Straight-Line Depreciation)

Hulme Company operates a small manufacturing facility as a supplement to its regular service activities. At the beginning of 2017, an asset account for the company showed the following balances:

Manufacturing equipment	$120,000
Accumulated depreciation through 2016	57,600

During 2017, the following expenditures were incurred for the equipment:

Routine maintenance and repairs on the equipment	$ 1,000
Major overhaul of the equipment that improved efficiency on January 2, 2017	13,000

The equipment is being depreciated on a straight-line basis over an estimated life of 15 years with a $12,000 estimated residual value. The annual accounting period ends on December 31.

Required:
1. Give the adjusting entry that was made at the end of 2016 for depreciation on the manufacturing equipment.
2. Starting at the beginning of 2017, what is the remaining estimated life?
3. Give the journal entries to record the two expenditures during 2017.

Determining Financial Statement Effects of Depreciation and Repairs (Straight-Line Depreciation)

Refer to the information in E8-7.

Required:
Indicate the effects (accounts, amounts, and + or −) of the items below on the accounting equation. Use the following schedule:

Date	Assets	=	Liabilities	+	Stockholders' Equity

1. The adjustment for depreciation at the end of 2016.
2. The two expenditures during 2017.

Computing Depreciation under Alternative Methods

Assume **Purity Ice Cream Company, Inc.**, in Ithaca, NY, bought a new ice cream maker at the beginning of the year at a cost of $9,000. The estimated useful life was four years, and the residual value was $1,000. Assume that the estimated productive life of the machine was 16,000 hours. Actual annual usage was 5,500 hours in Year 1; 3,800 hours in Year 2; 3,200 hours in Year 3; and 3,500 hours in Year 4.

Required:
1. Complete a separate depreciation schedule for each of the alternative methods. Round your answers to the nearest dollar.
   a. Straight-line.
   b. Units-of-production (use four decimal places for the per unit output factor).
   c. Double-declining-balance.

Method: _____				
Year	Computation	Depreciation Expense	Accumulated Depreciation	Net Book Value
At acquisition				
1				
2				
etc.				

2. Assuming that the machine was used directly in the production of one of the products that the company manufactures and sells, what factors might management consider in selecting a preferable depreciation method in conformity with the expense principle?

E8-10

LO8-3

Computing Depreciation under Alternative Methods

Strong Metals Inc. purchased a new stamping machine at the beginning of the year at a cost of $950,000. The estimated residual value was $50,000. Assume that the estimated useful life was five years and the estimated productive life of the machine was 300,000 units. Actual annual production was as follows:

Year	Units
1	70,000
2	67,000
3	50,000
4	73,000
5	40,000

Required:

1. Complete a separate depreciation schedule for each of the alternative methods. Round your answers to the nearest dollar.
   a. Straight-line.
   b. Units-of-production.
   c. Double-declining-balance.

Method:_____				
Year	Computation	Depreciation Expense	Accumulated Depreciation	Net Book Value
At acquisition				
1				
2				
etc.				

2. Assuming that the machine was used directly in the production of one of the products that the company manufactures and sells, what factors might management consider in selecting a preferable depreciation method in conformity with the expense principle?

E8-11

LO8-3

Computing Depreciation under Alternative Methods

At the beginning of the year, Palermo Brothers, Inc., purchased a new plastic water bottle making machine at a cost of $45,000. The estimated residual value was $5,000. Assume that the estimated useful life was four years and the estimated productive life of the machine was 400,000 units. Actual annual production was as follows:

Year	Units
1	120,000
2	90,000
3	110,000
4	80,000

Required:

1. Complete a separate depreciation schedule for each of the alternative methods. Round your answers to the nearest dollar.
   a. Straight-line.
   b. Units-of-production.
   c. Double-declining-balance.

Method:				
Year	**Computation**	**Depreciation Expense**	**Accumulated Depreciation**	**Net Book Value**
At acquisition				
1				
2				
etc.				

2. Assuming that the machine was used directly in the production of one of the products that the company manufactures and sells, what factors might management consider in selecting a preferable depreciation method in conformity with the expense principle?

Explaining Depreciation Policy

E8-12
LO8-3

The 2001 annual report for **General Motors Corporation** contained the following note:

> ### NOTE 3. SIGNIFICANT ACCOUNTING POLICIES
>
> *Property, Net*
>
> Property, plant, and equipment, including internal use software, is recorded at cost. Major improvements that extend the useful life of property are capitalized. Expenditures for repairs and maintenance are charged to expense as incurred. At January 1, 2001, we adopted the straight-line method of depreciation for real estate, facilities, and equipment placed in service after that date. Assets placed in service before January 1, 2001, continue to be depreciated using accelerated methods. The accelerated methods accumulate depreciation of approximately two-thirds of the depreciable cost in the first half of the estimated useful lives of property groups as compared to the straight-line method, which allocates depreciable costs equally over the estimated useful lives of property groups.

Required:
Why do you think the company changed its depreciation method for real estate, facilities, and equipment placed in service after January 1, 2001, and subsequent years?

Interpreting Management's Choice of Different Depreciation Methods for Tax and Financial Reporting

E8-13
LO8-3

A recent annual report for **FedEx** includes the following information:

> For financial reporting purposes, we record depreciation and amortization of property and equipment on a straight-line basis over the asset's service life or related lease term if shorter. For income tax purposes, depreciation is computed using accelerated methods when applicable.

Required:
Explain why FedEx uses different methods of depreciation for financial reporting and tax purposes.

Computing Depreciation and Book Value for Two Years Using Alternative Depreciation Methods and Interpreting the Impact on Cash Flows

E8-14
LO8-3, 8-7

Schrade Company bought a machine for $96,000 cash. The estimated useful life was four years and the estimated residual value was $6,000. Assume that the estimated useful life in productive units is 120,000. Units actually produced were 43,000 in Year 1 and 45,000 in Year 2.

Required:

1. Determine the appropriate amounts to complete the following schedule. Show computations, and round to the nearest dollar.

| | Depreciation Expense for | | Net Book Value at the End of | |
Method of Depreciation	Year 1	Year 2	Year 1	Year 2
Straight-line				
Units-of-production				
Double-declining-balance				

2. Which method would result in the lowest EPS for Year 1? For Year 2?
3. Which method would result in the highest amount of cash outflows in Year 1? Why?
4. Indicate the effects of (*a*) acquiring the machine and (*b*) recording annual depreciation on the operating and investing activities sections of the statement of cash flows (indirect method) for Year 1 (assume the straight-line method).

E8-15
LO8-4, 8-5

Inferring Asset Impairment and Recording Disposal of an Asset

In a recent 10-K report, **United Parcel Service** states it "is the world's largest package delivery company, a leader in the U.S. less-than-truckload industry, and the premier provider of global supply chain management solutions." The following note and data were reported:

NOTE 1—SUMMARY OF ACCOUNTING POLICIES

Impairment of Long-Lived Assets

. . . we review long-lived assets for impairment when circumstances indicate the carrying amount of an asset may not be recoverable based on the undiscounted future cash flows of the asset. . . .

	Dollars in Millions
Cost of property and equipment (beginning of year)	$39,151
Cost of property and equipment (end of year)	40,620
Capital expenditures during the year	2,328
Accumulated depreciation (beginning of year)	21,190
Accumulated depreciation (end of year)	22,339
Depreciation expense during the year	1,923
Cost of property and equipment sold during the year	840
Accumulated depreciation on property sold	774
Cash received on property sold	53

Required:

1. Reconstruct the journal entry for the disposal of property and equipment during the year.
2. Compute the amount of property and equipment that United Parcel wrote off as impaired during the year. (**Hint:** Set up T-accounts.)

E8-16
LO8-5

Recording the Disposal of an Asset at Three Different Sale Prices

FedEx is the world's leading express-distribution company. In addition to the world's largest fleet of all-cargo aircraft, the company has more than 650 aircraft and 55,000 vehicles and trailers that pick up and deliver packages. Assume that FedEx sold a delivery truck that had been used in the business for three years. The records of the company reflected the following:

Delivery truck cost	$35,000
Accumulated depreciation	23,000

Required:
1. Give the journal entry for the disposal of the truck, assuming that the truck sold for
   a. $12,000 cash
   b. $12,400 cash
   c. $11,500 cash
2. Based on the three preceding situations, explain the effects of the disposal of an asset.

Recording the Disposal of an Asset at Three Different Sale Prices

E8-17

LO8-5

Marriott International is a worldwide operator and franchiser of hotels and related lodging facilities totaling nearly $1.5 billion in net property and equipment. Assume that Marriott replaced furniture that had been used in the business for five years. The records of the company reflected the following regarding the sale of the existing furniture:

Furniture (cost)	$8,000,000
Accumulated depreciation	7,700,000

Required:
1. Give the journal entry for the disposal of the furniture, assuming that it was sold for
   a. $300,000 cash
   b. $900,000 cash
   c. $100,000 cash
2. Based on the three preceding situations, explain the effects of the disposal of an asset.

Inferring Asset Age and Recording Accidental Loss on a Long-Lived Asset (Straight-Line Depreciation)

E8-18

LO8-3, 8-5

On January 1 of the current year, the records of Sitake Corporation showed the following regarding a truck:

Equipment (estimated residual value, $9,000)	$25,000
Accumulated depreciation (straight-line, three years)	6,000

On December 31 of the current year, the delivery truck was a total loss as the result of an accident.

Required:
1. Based on the data given, compute the estimated useful life of the truck.
2. Give all journal entries with respect to the truck on December 31 of the current year. Show computations.

Computing the Acquisition and Depletion of a Natural Resource

E8-19

LO8-6

Freeport-McMoRan Copper & Gold Inc., headquartered in Phoenix, Arizona, is "a premier U.S.-based natural resource company with an industry leading global portfolio of mineral assets, significant oil and natural gas resources and a growing production profile." At the end of a recent year, its assets include approximately 104 billion pounds of copper, 29 million ounces of gold, 3 billion pounds of molybdenum, 283 million ounces of silver, 860 million pounds of cobalt, and 390 million barrels of estimated oil and natural gas reserves. Its annual revenues exceed $21.4 billion.

Assume that in February 2016, Freeport-McMoRan paid $800,000 for a mineral deposit in Indonesia. During March, it spent $70,000 in preparing the deposit for exploitation. It was estimated that 1,000,000 total cubic yards could be extracted economically. During 2016, 60,000 cubic yards were extracted. During January 2017, the company spent another $6,000 for additional developmental work that increased the estimated productive capacity of the mineral deposit.

Required:
1. Compute the acquisition cost of the deposit in 2016.
2. Compute depletion for 2016.
3. Compute the net book value of the deposit after payment of the January 2017 developmental costs.

Computing and Reporting the Acquisition and Amortization of Three Different Intangible Assets

E8-20

LO8-6

Trotman Company had three intangible assets at the end of 2016 (end of the accounting year):

a. Computer software and Web development technology purchased on January 1, 2015, for $70,000. The technology is expected to have a four-year useful life to the company.

b. A patent purchased from Ian Zimmer on January 1, 2016, for a cash cost of $6,000. Zimmer had registered the patent with the U.S. Patent and Trademark Office five years ago.

c. A trademark purchased for $13,000 on November 1, 2016. Management decided the trademark has an indefinite life.

Required:

1. Compute the acquisition cost of each intangible asset.
2. Compute the amortization of each intangible at December 31, 2016. The company does not use contra-accounts.
3. Show how these assets and any related expenses should be reported on the balance sheet and income statement for 2016.

E8-21
LO8-6

Computing and Reporting the Acquisition and Amortization of Three Different Intangible Assets

Springer Company had three intangible assets at the end of 2017 (end of the accounting year):

a. A copyright purchased on January 1, 2017, for a cash cost of $14,500. The copyright is expected to have a 10-year useful life to Springer.

b. Goodwill of $65,000 from the purchase of the Hartford Company on July 1, 2016.

c. A patent purchased on January 1, 2016, for $48,000. The inventor had registered the patent with the U.S. Patent and Trademark Office on January 1, 2012.

Required:

1. Compute the acquisition cost of each intangible asset.
2. Compute the amortization of each intangible at December 31, 2017. The company does not use contra-accounts.
3. Show how these assets and any related expenses should be reported on the balance sheet and income statement for 2017. (Assume there has been no impairment of goodwill.)

E8-22
LO8-6

Recording Leasehold Improvements and Related Amortization

Starbucks Corporation is the leading roaster and retailer of specialty coffee, with over 21,000 company-operated and licensed stores worldwide. Assume that Starbucks planned to open a new store on Commonwealth Avenue near Boston University and obtained a 10-year lease starting January 1. The company had to renovate the facility by installing an elevator costing $325,000. Amounts spent to enhance leased property are capitalized as intangible assets called Leasehold Improvements. The elevator will be amortized over the useful life of the lease.

Required:

1. Give the journal entry to record the installation of the new elevator.
2. Give any adjusting entries required at the end of the annual accounting period on December 31 related to the new elevator. Show computations.

E8-23
LO8-3

(Chapter Supplement) Recording a Change in Estimate

Refer to E8-7.

Required:

Give the adjusting entry that should be made by Hulme Company at the end of 2017 for depreciation of the manufacturing equipment, assuming no change in the original estimated life or residual value. Show computations. Round answer to the nearest dollar.

E8-24
LO8-2, 8-3

(Chapter Supplement) Recording and Explaining Depreciation, Improvements, and Changes in Estimated Useful Life and Residual Value (Straight-Line Depreciation)

At the end of the annual accounting period, December 31, Year 1, O'Connor Company's records reflected the following for Machine A:

Cost when acquired	$30,000
Accumulated depreciation	10,200

During January Year 2, the machine was renovated at a cost of $15,500. As a result, the estimated life increased from five years to eight years, and the residual value increased from $4,500 to $6,500. The company uses straight-line depreciation.

Required:
1. Give the journal entry to record the renovation.
2. How old was the machine at the end of Year 1?
3. Give the adjusting entry at the end of Year 2 to record straight-line depreciation for the year.
4. Explain the rationale for your entries in requirements 1 and 3.

(Chapter Supplement) Computing the Effect of a Change in Useful Life and Residual Value on Financial Statements and Cash Flows (Straight-Line Depreciation)

E8-25
LO8-3, 8-7

Burbank Company owns the building occupied by its administrative office. The office building was reflected in the accounts at the end of last year as follows:

Cost when acquired	$330,000
Accumulated depreciation (based on straight-line depreciation, an estimated life of 50 years, and a $30,000 residual value)	78,000

During January of this year, on the basis of a careful study, management decided that the total estimated useful life should be changed to 30 years (instead of 50) and the residual value reduced to $22,500 (from $30,000). The depreciation method will not change.

Required:
1. Compute the annual depreciation expense prior to the change in estimates.
2. Compute the annual depreciation expense after the change in estimates.
3. What will be the net effect of the change in estimates on the balance sheet, net income, and cash flows for this year?

 **connect**   **PROBLEMS**

Explaining the Nature of a Long-Lived Asset and Determining and Recording the Financial Statement Effects of Its Purchase (AP8-1)

P8-1
LO8-1, 8-2

On January 2, Summers Company bought a machine for use in operations. The machine has an estimated useful life of eight years and an estimated residual value of $2,600. The company provided the following expenditures:

a. Invoice price of the machine, $85,000.
b. Freight paid by the vendor per sales agreement, $1,000.
c. Installation costs, $2,400 paid in cash.
d. Payment was made as follows:

On January 2:

- The installation costs were paid in cash.
- Summers Company common stock, par $1; 2,000 shares (market value, $3.50 per share).
- Note payable, $60,000; 11.5 percent (principal plus interest due April 1 of the current year).
- Balance of invoice price to be paid in cash by January 12.

On January 12:

- Summers Company paid the balance due.

Required:

1. What are the classifications of long-lived assets? Explain their differences.
2. Record the purchase on January 2 and the subsequent payment on January 12. Show computations.
3. Indicate the accounts, amounts, and effects (+ for increase and − for decrease) of the purchase and subsequent cash payment on the accounting equation. Use the following structure:

Date	Assets	=	Liabilities	+	Stockholders' Equity

4. Explain the basis you used for any questionable items.

P8-2
LO8-2, 8-3

Analyzing the Effects of Repairs, an Addition, and Depreciation (AP8-2)

A recent annual report for **FedEx** included the following note:

> **NOTE 1: DESCRIPTION OF BUSINESS AND SUMMARY OF SIGNIFICANT ACCOUNTING POLICIES**
>
> *PROPERTY AND EQUIPMENT.* Expenditures for major additions, improvements and flight equipment modifications are capitalized when such costs are determined to extend the useful life of the asset or are part of the cost of acquiring the asset. Expenditures for equipment overhaul costs of engines or airframes prior to their operational use are capitalized as part of the cost of such assets as they are costs required to ready the asset for its intended use. Maintenance and repairs costs are charged to expense as incurred. . . .

Assume that FedEx made extensive repairs on an existing building and added a new wing. The building is a garage and repair facility for delivery trucks that serve the Denver area. The existing building originally cost $950,000, and by the end of last year, it was half depreciated based on use of the straight-line method, a 20-year estimated useful life, and no residual value. During the current year, the following expenditures related to the building were made:

a. Ordinary repairs and maintenance expenditures for the year, $7,000 cash.
b. Extensive and major repairs to the roof of the building, $122,000 cash. These repairs were completed at the end of the current year.
c. The new wing was completed on December 31 of the current year at a cash cost of $230,000.

Required:

1. Applying the policies of FedEx, complete the following, indicating the effects for the preceding expenditures for the current year. If there is no effect on an account, write NE on the line.

	Building	Accumulated Depreciation	Depreciation Expense	Repairs Expense	Cash
Balance January 1	$950,000	$475,000			
Depreciation		_____	_____		_____
Balance prior to expenditures	950,000	_____	_____		
Expenditure (*a*)	_____	_____	_____	_____	_____
Expenditure (*b*)	_____	_____	_____	_____	_____
Expenditure (*c*)	_____	_____	_____	_____	_____
Balance December 31	_____	_____	_____	_____	_____

2. What was the net book value of the building on December 31 of the current year?
3. Explain the effect of depreciation on cash flows.

Computing the Acquisition Cost and Recording Depreciation under Three Alternative Methods (AP8-3)

At the beginning of the year, Plummer's Sports Center bought three used fitness machines from Advantage, Inc. The machines immediately were overhauled, installed, and started operating. The machines were different; therefore, each had to be recorded separately in the accounts.

	Machine A	Machine B	Machine C
Amount paid for asset	$11,000	$30,000	$8,000
Installation costs	500	1,000	500
Renovation costs prior to use	2,500	1,000	1,500

By the end of the first year, each machine had been operating 4,800 hours.

Required:
1. Compute the cost of each machine.
2. Give the entry to record depreciation expense at the end of Year 1, assuming the following:

Machine	ESTIMATES Life	Residual Value	Depreciation Method
A	5 years	$1,000	Straight-line
B	60,000 hours	2,000	Units-of-production
C	4 years	1,500	Double-declining-balance

P8-3
LO8-2, 8-3

Inferring Depreciation Amounts and Determining the Effects of a Depreciation Error on Key Ratios (AP8-4)

Best Buy Co., Inc., headquartered in Richfield, Minnesota, is one of the leading consumer electronics retailers, operating more than 1,200 stores in the United States, Canada, China, and Mexico. The following was reported in a recent annual report:

P8-4
LO8-1, 8-3

CONSOLIDATED BALANCE SHEETS		
($ in millions)	Current Year	Prior Year
ASSETS		
Property and Equipment		
Land and buildings	$ 766	$ 757
Leasehold improvements	2,318	2,154
Fixtures and equipment	4,701	4,447
Property under capital lease	120	95
	7,905	7,453
Less accumulated depreciation	4,082	3,383
Net property and equipment	3,823	4,070

Required:
1. Assuming that Best Buy did not sell any property, plant, and equipment in the current year, what was the amount of depreciation expense recorded during the current year?
2. Assume that Best Buy failed to record depreciation during the current year. Indicate the effect of the error (i.e., overstated or understated) on the following ratios:
   a. Earnings per share.
   b. Fixed asset turnover.
   c. Current ratio.
   d. Return on assets.

P8-5

LO8-1, 8-3

Evaluating the Effect of Alternative Depreciation Methods on Key Ratios from an Analyst's Perspective

You are a financial analyst for **Ford Motor Company** and have been asked to determine the impact of alternative depreciation methods. For your analysis, you have been asked to compare methods based on a machine that cost $106,000. The estimated useful life is 13 years and the estimated residual value is $2,000. The machine has an estimated useful life in productive output of 200,000 units. Actual output was 20,000 in Year 1 and 16,000 in Year 2. (Round results to the nearest dollar.)

Required:

1. For years 1 and 2 only, prepare separate depreciation schedules assuming:
   a. Straight-line method.
   b. Units-of-production method.
   c. Double-declining-balance method.

Method:_____				
Year	Computation	Depreciation Expense	Accumulated Depreciation	Net Book Value
At acquisition				
1				
2				

2. Evaluate each method in terms of its effect on cash flow, fixed asset turnover, and EPS. Assuming that Ford Motor Company is most interested in reducing taxes and maintaining a high EPS for Year 1, what would you recommend to management? Would your recommendation change for Year 2? Why or why not?

P8-6

LO8-3, 8-5

Recording and Interpreting the Disposal of Three Long-Lived Assets (AP8-5)

During the current year, Merkley Company disposed of three different assets. On January 1 of the current year, prior to the disposal of the assets, the accounts reflected the following:

Asset	Original Cost	Residual Value	Estimated Life	Accumulated Depreciation (straight line)
Machine A	$21,000	$3,000	8 years	$15,750 (7 years)
Machine B	50,000	4,000	10 years	36,800 (8 years)
Machine C	85,000	5,000	15 years	64,000 (12 years)

The machines were disposed of during the current year in the following ways:

a. Machine A: Sold on January 1 for $5,000 cash.
b. Machine B: Sold on December 31 for $10,500; received cash, $2,500, and an $8,000 interest-bearing (12 percent) note receivable due at the end of 12 months.
c. Machine C: On January 1, this machine suffered irreparable damage from an accident. On January 10, a salvage company removed the machine at no cost.

Required:

1. Give all journal entries related to the disposal of each machine in the current year.
2. Explain the accounting rationale for the way that you recorded each disposal.

Inferring Activities Affecting Fixed Assets from Notes to the Financial Statements and Analyzing the Impact of Depreciation on Cash Flows

P8-7
LO8-5, 8-7

Singapore Airlines reported the following information in the notes to a recent annual report (in Singapore dollars):

SINGAPORE AIRLINES

Notes to the Accounts

21. Property, Plant, and Equipment (in $ millions)

The Group

Cost	Beginning of Year	Additions	Disposals	End of Year
Aircraft	19,144.3	1,712.4	2,108.3	18,748.4
Other fixed assets (*summary*)	4,378.3	880.6	199.0	5,059.9
	23,522.6	2,593.0	2,307.3	23,808.3

Accumulated depreciation	Beginning of Year	Depreciation	Impairment Loss	Disposals	End of Year
Aircraft	8,598.2	1,448.1	310.7	1,397.0	8,960.0
Other fixed assets (*summary*)	1,826.4	127.4	27.6	159.8	1,821.6
	10,424.6	1,575.5	338.3	1,556.8	10,781.6

Singapore Airlines also reported the following cash flow details:

Cash Flow from Operating Activities (in $ millions)	Current Year	Prior Year
Profit before taxation	367.9	469.6
Adjustments for		
Depreciation	1,575.5	1,589.1
Impairment loss	338.3	9.8
Surplus (gain) on disposal of fixed assets	(51.2)	(56.0)
Other adjustments (summarized)	(167.0)	42.2
Cash generated from operations	2,063.5	2,054.7

Required:

1. Reconstruct the information in Note 21 using T-accounts for Property, Plant, and Equipment and Accumulated Depreciation:

Property, Plant, and Equipment		Accumulated Depreciation	
Beg. balance			Beg. balance
Additions	Disposals	Disposals	Depreciation expense
			Impairment loss
End. balance			End. balance

2. Compute the amount of cash the company received for disposals and transfers for the current year. Show computations.

3. Compute the percentage of depreciation expense to cash flows from operations for the current year. What do you interpret from the result?

P8-8

LO8-2, 8-3, 8-6

Determining Financial Statement Effects of Activities Related to Various Long-Lived Assets (AP8-6)

During the current year ending on December 31, BSP Company completed the following transactions:

a. On January 1, purchased a patent for $28,000 cash (estimated useful life, seven years).

b. On January 1, purchased the assets (not detailed) of another business for $164,000 cash, including $10,000 for goodwill. The company assumed no liabilities. Goodwill has an indefinite life.

c. On December 31, constructed a storage shed on land leased from D. Heald. The cost was $15,600. The company uses straight-line depreciation. The lease will expire in three years. (Amounts spent to enhance leased property are capitalized as intangible assets called Leasehold Improvements.)

d. Total expenditures for ordinary repairs and maintenance were $5,500 during the current year.

e. On December 31 of the current year, sold Machine A for $6,000 cash. Original cost was $25,000; accumulated depreciation to December 31 of the prior year was $16,000 (on a straight-line basis with a $5,000 residual value and five-year useful life).

f. On December 31 of the current year, paid $5,000 for a complete reconditioning of Machine B acquired on January 1 of the prior year. Original cost, $31,000; accumulated depreciation to December 31 of the prior year was $1,600 (on a straight-line basis with a $7,000 residual value and 15-year useful life).

Required:

1. For each of these transactions, indicate the accounts, amounts, and effects (+ for increase and − for decrease) on the accounting equation. Use the following structure:

Date	Assets	=	Liabilities	+	Stockholders' Equity

2. For each of these assets, except the assets not detailed in (b), compute depreciation and amortization to be recorded at the end of the year on December 31 of the current year.

P8-9

LO8-3, 8-6

Computing Goodwill from the Purchase of a Business and Related Depreciation and Amortization

The notes to a recent annual report from Weebok Corporation indicated that the company acquired another company, Sport Shoes, Inc.

Assume that Weebok acquired Sport Shoes on January 5 of the current year. Weebok acquired the name of the company and all of its assets for $750,000 cash. Weebok did not assume the liabilities. The transaction was closed on January 5 of the current year, at which time the balance sheet of Sport Shoes reflected the following book values and an independent appraiser estimated the following market values for the assets:

Sport Shoes, Inc.

January 5 of the Current Year	Book Value	Market Value*
Accounts receivable (net)	$ 50,000	$ 50,000
Inventory	385,000	350,000
Fixed assets (net)	156,000	208,000
Other assets	4,000	10,000
Total assets	$595,000	
Liabilities	$ 75,000	
Stockholders' equity	520,000	
Total liabilities and stockholders' equity	$595,000	

These values for the purchased assets were provided to Weebok by an independent appraiser.

Required:

1. Compute the amount of goodwill resulting from the purchase. (**Hint:** Assets are purchased at market value in conformity with the cost principle.)
2. Compute the adjustments that Weebok would make at the end of the current year (ending December 31) for the following:
   a. Depreciation of the fixed assets (straight line), assuming an estimated remaining useful life of 10 years and no residual value.
   b. Goodwill (an intangible asset with an indefinite life).

Computing Amortization, Book Value, and Asset Impairment Related to Different Intangible Assets (AP8-7)

P8-10
LO8-3, 8-4, 8-6

Starn Tool Company has five different intangible assets to be accounted for and reported on the financial statements. The management is concerned about the amortization of the cost of each of these intangibles. Facts about each intangible follow:

a. **Patent.** The company purchased a patent at a cash cost of $55,900 on January 1, 2017. The patent has an estimated useful life of 13 years.
b. **Copyright.** On January 1, 2017, the company purchased a copyright for $22,500 cash. It is estimated that the copyrighted item will have no value by the end of 10 years.
c. **Franchise.** The company obtained a franchise from McKenna Company to make and distribute a special item. It obtained the franchise on January 1, 2017, at a cash cost of $14,400 for a 10-year period.
d. **License.** On January 1, 2016, the company secured a license from the city to operate a special service for a period of five years. Total cash expended to obtain the license was $14,000.
e. **Goodwill.** The company started business in January 2014 by purchasing another business for a cash lump sum of $400,000. Included in the purchase price was "Goodwill, $40,000." Company executives stated that "the goodwill is an important long-lived asset to us." It has an indefinite life.

Required:

1. Compute the amount of amortization that should be recorded for each intangible asset at the end of the annual accounting period, December 31, 2017.
2. Give the book value of each intangible asset on December 31, 2018.
3. Assume that on January 2, 2019, the copyrighted item was impaired in its ability to continue to produce strong revenues. The other intangible assets were not affected. Starn estimated that the copyright would be able to produce future cash flows of $17,000. The fair value of the copyright was determined to be $16,000. Compute the amount, if any, of the impairment loss to be recorded.

(Chapter Supplement) Analyzing and Recording Entries Related to a Change in Estimated Life and Residual Value

P8-11
LO8-3

Rungano Corporation is a global publisher of magazines, books, and music and video collections and is a leading direct mail marketer. Many direct mail marketers use high-speed Didde press equipment to print their advertisements. These presses can cost more than $1 million. Assume that Rungano owns a Didde press acquired at an original cost of $400,000. It is being depreciated on a straight-line basis over a 20-year estimated useful life and has a $50,000 estimated residual value. At the end of the prior year, the press had been depreciated for a full six years. At the beginning of January of the current year, a decision was made, on the basis of improved maintenance procedures, that a total estimated useful life of 25 years and a residual value of $73,000 would be more realistic. The accounting period ends December 31.

Required:

1. Compute (*a*) the amount of depreciation expense recorded in the prior year and (*b*) the book value of the printing press at the end of the prior year.
2. Compute the amount of depreciation that should be recorded in the current year. Show computations (round amount to the nearest dollar).
3. Give the adjusting entry for depreciation at December 31 of the current year.

ALTERNATE PROBLEMS

AP8-1
LO8-1, 8-2

Explaining the Nature of a Long-Lived Asset and Determining and Recording the Financial Statement Effects of Its Purchase (P8-1)

On June 1, the Wallace Corp. bought a machine for use in operations. The machine has an estimated useful life of six years and an estimated residual value of $2,000. The company provided the following expenditures:

a. Invoice price of the machine, $60,000.
b. Freight paid by the vendor per sales agreement, $650.
c. Installation costs, $1,500.
d. Payment was made as follows:

On June 1:

- The installation costs were paid in cash.
- Wallace Corp. common stock, par $2; 2,000 shares (market value, $6 per share).
- Balance of the invoice price on a 12 percent note payable; principal and interest are due September 1 of the current year.

On September 1:

- Wallace Corp. paid the balance and interest due on the note payable.

Required:

1. What are the classifications of long-lived assets? Explain their differences.
2. Record the purchase on June 1 and the subsequent payment on September 2. Show computations.
3. Indicate the accounts, amounts, and effects (+ for increase and − for decrease) of the purchase and subsequent cash payment on the accounting equation. Use the following structure:

Date	Assets	=	Liabilities	+	Stockholders' Equity

4. Explain the basis you used for any questionable items.

AP8-2
LO8-2, 8-3

Analyzing the Effects of Repairs, an Addition, and Depreciation (P8-2)

A recent annual report for **AMERCO**, the holding company for **U-Haul International, Inc.**, included the following note:

> NOTES TO CONSOLIDATED FINANCIAL STATEMENTS
>
> **Note 3. Accounting Policies**
>
> *Property, Plant and Equipment*
>
> Property, plant and equipment are stated at cost. Interest expense incurred during the initial construction of buildings and rental equipment is considered part of cost. Depreciation is computed for financial reporting purposes using the straight line or an accelerated method based on a declining balance formula over the following estimated useful lives: rental equipment 2–20 years and buildings and non-rental equipment 3–55 years. We follow the deferral method of accounting based on ASC 908—*Airlines* for major overhauls in which engine and transmission overhauls are capitalized and amortized over three years. Routine maintenance costs are charged to operating expense as they are incurred.

AMERCO subsidiaries own property, plant, and equipment that are utilized in the manufacture, repair, and rental of U-Haul equipment and that provide offices for U-Haul. Assume that AMERCO made extensive repairs on an existing building and added a new wing. The building is a garage and repair facility for rental trucks that serve the Seattle area. The existing building originally cost $330,000, and by the end of its fifth year, the building was one-quarter depreciated on the basis of a 20-year estimated useful life and no residual value. Assume straight-line depreciation. During the sixth year, the following expenditures related to the building were made:

a. Ordinary repairs and maintenance expenditures for the year, $6,000 cash.
b. Extensive and major repairs to the roof of the building, $17,000 cash. These repairs were completed on December 31.
c. The new wing was completed on December 31 at a cash cost of $70,000.

Required:
1. Applying the policies of AMERCO, complete the following, indicating the effects for the preceding expenditures for the sixth year. If there is no effect on an account, write NE on the line.

	Building	Accumulated Depreciation	Depreciation Expense	Repairs Expense	Cash
Balance January 1	$330,000	$82,500			
Depreciation		_____	_____		_____
Balance prior to expenditures	330,000	_____	_____		
Expenditure (*a*)	_____	_____	_____	_____	_____
Expenditure (*b*)	_____	_____	_____	_____	_____
Expenditure (*c*)	_____	_____	_____	_____	_____
Balance December 31	_____	_____	_____		_____

2. What was the book value of the building on December 31 of the sixth year?
3. Explain the effect of depreciation on cash flows.

Computing the Acquisition Cost and Recording Depreciation under Three Alternative Methods (P8-3)

AP8-3
LO8-2, 8-3

At the beginning of the year, Ramos Inc. bought three used machines from Santaro Corporation. The machines immediately were overhauled, installed, and started operating. The machines were different; therefore, each had to be recorded separately in the accounts.

	Machine A	Machine B	Machine C
Cost of the asset	$12,200	$32,500	$21,700
Installation costs	1,600	1,100	1,100
Renovation costs prior to use	600	1,400	1,600

By the end of the first year, each machine had been operating 7,000 hours.

Required:
1. Compute the cost of each machine.
2. Give the entry to record depreciation expense at the end of Year 1 (with separate accumulated depreciation accounts for each machine), assuming the following:

Machine	ESTIMATES Life	Residual Value	Depreciation Method
A	8 years	$1,000	Straight-line
B	33,000 hours	2,000	Units-of-production
C	5 years	1,400	Double-declining-balance

Inferring Depreciation Amounts and Determining the Effects of a Depreciation Error on Key Ratios (P8-4)

AP8-4
LO8-1, 8-3

The Gap, Inc., is a global specialty retailer of casual wear and personal products for women, men, children, and babies under the Gap, Banana Republic, Old Navy, Athleta, and Intermix brands.

The Company operates approximately 3,200 stores across the globe, as well as online. The following is a note from a recent annual report:

Note 2. Additional Financial Statement Information

Property and Equipment

Property and equipment are stated at cost less accumulated depreciation and consist of the following:

($ in millions)	Current Year	Prior Year
Leasehold improvements	$3,220	$3,211
Furniture and equipment	2,560	2,493
Software	1,349	1,173
Land, buildings, and building improvements	1,009	1,106
Construction-in-progress	167	176
Property and equipment, at cost	8,305	8,159
Less: Accumulated depreciation	(5,532)	(5,401)
Property and equipment, net of accumulated depreciation	$2,773	$2,758

Required:

1. Assuming The Gap, Inc., had asset impairment write-offs of $10 million (which increased accumulated depreciation) and sold property, plant, and equipment in the most recent year with a cost of $568 million and an accumulated depreciation of $439 million, what was the amount of depreciation expense recorded in the current year?
2. Assume that The Gap, Inc., failed to record depreciation in the current year. Indicate the effect of the error (i.e., overstated or understated) on the following ratios:
   a. Earnings per share
   b. Fixed asset turnover
   c. Current ratio
   d. Return on assets

AP8-5

LO8-3, 8-5

Recording and Interpreting the Disposal of Three Long-Lived Assets (P8-6)

During the current year ended December 31, Rank Company disposed of three different assets. On January 1 of the current year, prior to their disposal, the asset accounts reflected the following:

Asset	Original Cost	Residual Value	Estimated Life	Accumulated Depreciation (straight line)
Machine A	$24,000	$2,000	5 years	$17,600 (4 years)
Machine B	16,500	5,000	20 years	4,025 (7 years)
Machine C	59,200	3,200	14 years	48,000 (12 years)

The machines were disposed of during the current year in the following ways:

a. Machine A: Sold on January 1 for $6,750 cash.
b. Machine B: Sold on December 31 for $8,000; received cash, $2,000, and a $6,000 interest-bearing (10 percent) note receivable due at the end of 12 months.
c. Machine C: On January 1, this machine suffered irreparable damage from an accident and was scrapped.

Required:

1. Give all journal entries related to the disposal of each machine.
2. Explain the accounting rationale for the way in which you recorded each disposal.

Determining Financial Statement Effects of Activities Related to Various Long-Lived Assets (P8-8)

During the current year ending December 31, Nguyen Corporation completed the following transactions:

a. On January 1, purchased a license for $7,200 cash (estimated useful life, four years).
b. On January 1, repaved the parking lot of the building leased from H. Lane. The cost was $17,800; the estimated useful life was five years with no residual value. The lease will expire in 10 years. (Amounts spent to enhance leased property are capitalized as intangible assets called Leasehold Improvements.)
c. On July 1, purchased another business for $120,000 cash. The transaction included $115,000 for the assets and $24,000 for the liabilities assumed by Nguyen. The remainder was goodwill with an indefinite life.
d. On December 31, sold Machine A for $6,000 cash. Original cost, $21,500; accumulated depreciation (straight line) to December 31 of the prior year, $13,500 ($3,500 residual value and four-year life).
e. Total expenditures during the current year for ordinary repairs and maintenance were $6,700.
f. On December 31, paid $8,000 for a complete reconditioning of Machine B. Original cost, $18,000; accumulated depreciation to December 31 of the prior year, $12,000 (based on the straight-line method using a $2,000 residual value and four-year life).

Required:
1. For each of these transactions, indicate the accounts, amounts, and effects (+ for increase and − for decrease) on the accounting equation. Use the following structure:

Date	Assets	=	Liabilities	+	Stockholders' Equity

2. For each of these assets, except the assets not detailed in (c), compute depreciation and amortization to be recorded at the end of the current year on December 31.

Computing Amortization, Book Value, and Asset Impairment Related to Different Intangible Assets (P8-10)

Carey Corporation has five different intangible assets to be accounted for and reported on the financial statements. The management is concerned about the amortization of the cost of each of these intangibles. Facts about each intangible follow:

a. **Goodwill.** The company started business in January 2014 by purchasing another business for a cash lump sum of $650,000. Included in the purchase price was "Goodwill, $75,000." Company executives stated that "the goodwill is an important long-lived asset to us." It has an indefinite life.
b. **Patent.** The company purchased a patent at a cash cost of $18,600 on January 1, 2016. It is amortized over its expected useful life of 10 years.
c. **Copyright.** On January 1, 2016, the company purchased a copyright for $24,750 cash. It is estimated that the copyrighted item will have no value by the end of 30 years.
d. **Franchise.** The company obtained a franchise from Cirba Company to make and distribute a special item. It obtained the franchise on January 1, 2016, at a cash cost of $19,200 for a 12-year period.
e. **License.** On January 1, 2015, the company secured a license from the city to operate a special service for a period of seven years. Total cash expended to obtain the license was $21,700.

Required:
1. Compute the amount of amortization that should be recorded for each intangible asset at the end of the annual accounting period, December 31, 2016.
2. Give the book value of each intangible asset on January 1, 2019.
3. Assume that on January 1, 2019, the franchise was impaired in its ability to continue to produce strong revenues. The other intangible assets were not affected. Carey estimated that the franchise would be able to produce future cash flows of $13,500. The fair value of the franchise was determined to be $12,000. Compute the amount, if any, of the impairment loss to be recorded.

CON8-1   **Asset Acquisition, Depreciation, and Disposal**

Pool Corporation, Inc., is the world's largest wholesale distributor of swimming pool supplies and equipment. Assume Pool Corporation purchased for cash new loading equipment for the warehouse on January 1 of Year 1, at an invoice price of $72,000. It also paid $2,000 for freight on the equipment, $1,300 to prepare the equipment for use in the warehouse, and $800 for insurance to cover the equipment during operation in Year 1. The equipment was estimated to have a residual value of $3,300 and be used over three years or 24,000 hours.

Required:
1. Record the purchase of the equipment, freight, preparation costs, and insurance on January 1 of Year 1.
2. Create a depreciation schedule assuming Pool Corporation uses the straight-line method.
3. Create a depreciation schedule assuming Pool Corporation uses the double-declining-balance method. Round answers to the nearest dollar.
4. Create a depreciation schedule assuming Pool Corporation uses the units-of-production method, with actual production of 8,000 hours in Year 1; 7,400 hours in Year 2; and 8,600 hours in Year 3.
5. On December 31 of Year 2, the equipment was sold for $22,500. Record the sale of the equipment assuming the company used the straight-line method.

COMPREHENSIVE **PROBLEM (CHAPTERS 6–8)**

COMP8-1   **Complete the requirements for each of the following independent cases:**

Case A. **Dr Pepper Snapple Group, Inc.**, is a leading integrated brand owner, bottler, and distributor of nonalcoholic beverages in the United States, Canada, and Mexico. Key brands include Dr Pepper, Snapple, 7-UP, Mott's juices, A&W root beer, Canada Dry ginger ale, Schweppes ginger ale, and Hawaiian Punch, among others.

The following represents selected data from recent financial statements of Dr Pepper Snapple Group (dollars in millions):

DR PEPPER SNAPPLE GROUP, INC.		
Consolidated Balance Sheets (partial)		
(in millions)	December 31, 2014	December 31, 2013
Assets		
Current assets:		
Cash and cash equivalents	$237	$153
Accounts receivable (net of allowances of $2 and $3, respectively)	61	58

Consolidated Statements of Income (partial)			
		For the Year Ended December 31	
(in millions)	2014	2013	2012
Net sales	$6,121	$5,997	$5,995
...			
Net income	$ 703	$ 624	$ 629

The company also reported bad debt expense of $1 million in 2014, $1 million in 2013, and $2 million in 2012.

1. Record the company's write-offs of uncollectible accounts for 2014.
2. Assuming all sales were on credit, what amount of cash did Dr Pepper Snapple Group collect from customers in 2014?
3. Compute the company's net profit margin (rounded to four decimal places) for the three years presented. What does the trend suggest to you about Dr Pepper Snapple Group?

Case B. Samuda Enterprises uses the aging approach to estimate bad debt expense. At the end of the current year, Samuda reported a balance in accounts receivable of $620,000 and estimated that $12,400 of its accounts receivable would likely be uncollectible. The allowance for doubtful accounts has a $1,500 debit balance at year-end (that is, more was written off during the year than the balance in the account).

1. What amount of bad debt expense should be recorded for the current year?
2. What amount will be reported on the current year's balance sheet for accounts receivable?

Case C. At the end of the current year, the unadjusted trial balance of Samuels, Inc., indicated $6,530,000 in Accounts Receivable, a credit balance of $9,200 in Allowance for Doubtful Accounts, and Sales Revenue (all on credit) of $155,380,000. Based on knowledge that the current economy is in distress, Samuels increased its bad debt rate estimate to 0.3 percent on credit sales.

1. What amount of bad debt expense should be recorded for the current year?
2. What amount will be reported on the current year's balance sheet for accounts receivable?

Case D. Stewart Company reports the following inventory record for November:

INVENTORY			
Date	Activity	# of Units	Cost/Unit
November 1	Beginning balance	100	$16
November 4	Purchase	300	19
November 7	Sale (@ $50 per unit)	200	
November 13	Purchase	500	21
November 22	Sale (@ $50 per unit)	500	

Selling, administrative, and depreciation expenses for the month were $16,000. Stewart's tax rate is 30 percent.

1. Calculate the cost of ending inventory and the cost of goods sold under each of the following methods:
   a. First-in, first-out.
   b. Last-in, first-out.
   c. Weighted average (round unit cost to the nearest penny).
2. Based on your answers in requirement (1):
   a. What is the gross profit percentage under the FIFO method?
   b. What is net income under the LIFO method?
   c. Which method would you recommend to Stewart for tax and financial reporting purposes? Explain your recommendation.
3. Stewart applied the lower of cost or market method to value its inventory for reporting purposes at the end of the month. Assuming Stewart used the FIFO method and that inventory had a market replacement value of $19.50 per unit, what would Stewart report on the balance sheet for inventory? Why?

Case E. Matson Company purchased the following on January 1, 2016:

- Office equipment at a cost of $60,000 with an estimated useful life to the company of three years and a residual value of $15,000. The company uses the double-declining-balance method of depreciation for the equipment.

- Factory equipment at an invoice price of $880,000 plus shipping costs of $20,000. The equipment has an estimated useful life of 100,000 hours and no residual value. The company uses the units-of-production method of depreciation for the equipment.
- A patent at a cost of $330,000 with an estimated useful life of 15 years. The company uses the straight-line method of amortization for intangible assets with no residual value.

The company's year ends on December 31.

1. Prepare a partial depreciation schedule for 2016, 2017, and 2018 for the following assets (round your answers to the nearest dollar):
   a. Office equipment.
   b. Factory equipment. The company used the equipment for 8,000 hours in 2016, 9,200 hours in 2017, and 8,900 hours in 2018.
2. On January 1, 2019, Matson altered its corporate strategy dramatically. The company sold the factory equipment for $700,000 in cash. Record the entry related to the sale of the factory equipment.
3. On January 1, 2019, when the company changed its corporate strategy, its patent had estimated future cash flows of $210,000 and a fair value of $190,000. What would the company report on the income statement (account and amount) regarding the patent on January 1, 2019? Explain your answer.

CASES AND PROJECTS

Annual Report Cases

CP8-1

LO8-1, 8-2, 8-4, 8-6

Finding Financial Information

Refer to the financial statements of **American Eagle Outfitters** in Appendix B at the end of this book.

Required:
For each question, answer it and indicate where you located the information to answer the question. (**Hint:** Use the notes to the financial statements for some of these questions.)

1. How much did the company spend on property and equipment (capital expenditures) in fiscal year 2014 (the year ended January 31, 2015)?
2. What is the typical estimated useful life of leasehold improvements for amortization purposes?
3. What was the original cost of fixtures and equipment held by the company at the end of the most recent reporting year?
4. What was the amount of depreciation expense on property and equipment for the current year? Compare this amount to the change in accumulated depreciation from fiscal year ended 2014 to fiscal year ended 2015. Why would these numbers be different?
5. What is the company's fixed asset turnover ratio for fiscal year ended January 31, 2015?

CP8-2

LO8-1, 8-2, 8-6

Finding Financial Information

Refer to the financial statements of **Urban Outfitters** given in Appendix C at the end of this book.

Required:
For each question, answer it and indicate where you located the information to answer the question. (**Hint:** Use the notes to the financial statements for many of these questions.)

1. What method of depreciation does the company use?
2. What is the amount of accumulated depreciation and amortization at the end of the most recent reporting year?
3. For depreciation purposes, what is the estimated useful life of furniture and fixtures?

4. What was the original cost of leasehold improvements owned by the company at the end of the most recent reporting year?
5. What amount of depreciation and amortization was reported as expense for the most recent reporting year?
6. What is the company's fixed asset turnover ratio (rounded to two decimal places) for the most recent year? What does it suggest?

Comparing Companies within an Industry

Refer to the financial statements of **American Eagle Outfitters** (Appendix B) and **Urban Outfitters** (Appendix C) and the Industry Ratio Report (Appendix D) at the end of this book.

CP8-3
LO8-1, 8-3

Required:
1. Compute the percentage of net fixed assets to total assets (rounded to one decimal place) for both companies for the most recent year. Why do the companies differ?
2. Compute the percentage of gross fixed assets (rounded to one decimal place) that has been depreciated for both companies for the most recent year. Why do you think the percentages differ?
3. Compute the fixed asset turnover ratio (rounded to two decimal places) for the most recent year presented for both companies. Which company has higher asset efficiency? Why?
4. Compare the fixed asset turnover ratio for both companies to the industry average. Are these companies doing better or worse than the industry average in asset efficiency?

Financial Reporting and Analysis Cases

Using Financial Reports: Analyzing the Age of Assets

As stated in its recent annual report, "**Sysco Corporation** . . . is the largest North American distributor of food and related products primarily to the foodservice or food-away-from-home industry. We provide products and related services to approximately 425,000 customers, including restaurants, healthcare and educational facilities, lodging establishments and other foodservice customers." A note to a recent annual report for Sysco contained the following information:

CP8-4
LO8-3

(in thousands)	Current Year
Land	$ 431,694
Buildings and improvements	3,816,387
Fleet and equipment	2,726,415
Computer hardware and software	1,109,379
	8,083,875
Accumulated depreciation	(4,098,257)
	$3,985,618

Depreciation expense (in thousands of dollars) charged to operations was $493,800 in the current year. Depreciation generally is computed using the straight-line method for financial reporting purposes.

Required:
1. What is your best estimate of the average expected life for Sysco's depreciable assets?
2. What is your best estimate of the average age of Sysco's depreciable assets?

Using Financial Reports: Analyzing Fixed Asset Turnover Ratio and Cash Flows

Karl Company operates in both the beverage and entertainment industries. In June 2013, Karl purchased Good Time, Inc., which produces and distributes motion picture, television, and home video products and recorded music; publishes books; and operates theme parks and retail stores. The purchase resulted in $2.7 billion in goodwill. Since then, Karl has undertaken a number of business acquisitions and divestitures (sales of businesses) as the company expands into the entertainment industry. Selected data from a recent annual report are as follows (amounts are in U.S. dollars in millions):

CP8-5
LO8-1, 8-6, 8-7

Property, Plant, Equipment, and Intangibles from the Consolidated Balance Sheet	Current Year	Prior Year
Film costs, net of amortization	$ 1,272	$ 991
Artists' contracts, advances, and other entertainment assets	761	645
Property, plant, and equipment, net	2,733	2,559
Excess of cost over fair value of assets acquired	3,076	3,355
From the Consolidated Statement of Income		
Total revenues	$ 9,714	$10,644
From the Consolidated Statement of Cash Flows		
Income from continuing operations	$ 880	$ 445
Adjustments:		
Depreciation	289	265
Amortization	208	190
Other adjustments (summarized)	$(1,618)	(256)
Net cash provided by continuing operations	(241)	644
From the Notes to the Financial Statements		
Accumulated depreciation on property, plant, and equipment	$ 1,178	$ 1,023

Required:
1. Compute the cost of the property, plant, and equipment at the end of the current year. Explain your answer.
2. What was the approximate age of the property, plant, and equipment at the end of the current year?
3. Compute the fixed asset turnover ratio (rounded to one decimal place) for the current year. Explain your results.
4. What is "excess of cost over fair value of assets acquired"?
5. On the consolidated statement of cash flows, why are the depreciation and amortization amounts added to income from continuing operations?

CP8-6
LO8-1, 8-5, 8-7

Using Financial Reports: Inferring the Sale of Assets

A recent annual report for **Eastman Kodak** reported that the cost of property, plant, and equipment at the end of the current year was $755 million. At the end of the previous year, it had been $751 million. During the current year, the company bought $43 million worth of new equipment. The balance of accumulated depreciation at the end of the current year was $231 million; at the end of the previous year it was $67 million. Depreciation expense for the current year was $174 million. The company reported a $23 million gain on the disposition of property, plant, and equipment. There were no impairment losses during the current year.

Required:
What amount of proceeds did Eastman Kodak receive when it sold property, plant, and equipment during the current year? (**Hint:** Set up T-accounts.)

Critical Thinking Cases

CP8-7
LO8-1, 8-2

Evaluating an Ethical Dilemma: A Real-Life Example

Assume you work as a staff member in a large accounting department for a multinational public company. Your job requires you to review documents relating to the company's equipment purchases. Upon verifying that purchases are properly approved, you prepare journal entries to record the equipment purchases in the accounting system. Typically, you handle equipment purchases costing $100,000 or less.

This morning, you were contacted by the executive assistant to the chief financial officer (CFO). She says that the CFO has asked to see you immediately in his office. Although your boss's boss has attended a few meetings where the CFO was present, you have never met the CFO during your three years with the company. Needless to say, you are anxious about the meeting.

Upon entering the CFO's office, you are warmly greeted with a smile and friendly handshake. The CFO compliments you on the great work that you've been doing for the company. You soon feel a little more comfortable, particularly when the CFO mentions that he has a special project for you. He states that he and the CEO have negotiated significant new arrangements with the company's equipment suppliers, which require the company to make advance payments for equipment to be purchased in the future. The CFO says that, for various reasons that he didn't want to discuss, he will be processing the payments through the operating division of the company rather than the equipment accounting group. Given that the payments will be made through the operating division, they will initially be classified as operating expenses of the company. He indicates that clearly these advance payments for property and equipment should be recorded as assets, so he will be contacting you at the end of every quarter to make an adjusting journal entry to capitalize the amounts inappropriately classified as operating expenses. He advises you that a new account, called Prepaid Equipment, has been established for this purpose. He quickly wraps up the meeting by telling you that it is important that you not talk about the special project with anyone. You assume he doesn't want others to become jealous of your new important responsibility.

A few weeks later, at the end of the first quarter, you receive a voicemail from the CFO stating, "The adjustment that we discussed is $771,000,000 for this quarter." Before deleting the message, you replay it to make sure you heard it right. Your company generates over $8 billion in revenues and incurs $6 billion in operating expenses every quarter, but you've never made a journal entry for that much money. So, just to be sure there's not a mistake, you send an e-mail to the CFO confirming the amount. He phones you back immediately to abruptly inform you, "There's no mistake. That's the number." Feeling embarrassed that you may have annoyed the CFO, you quietly make the adjusting journal entry.

For each of the remaining three quarters in that year and for the first quarter in the following year, you continue to make these end-of-quarter adjustments. The "magic number," as the CFO liked to call it, was $560,000,000 for Q2, $742,745,000 for Q3, $941,000,000 for Q4, and $818,204,000 for Q1 of the following year. During this time, you've had several meetings and lunches with the CFO where he provides you the magic number, sometimes supported with nothing more than a Post-it note with the number written on it. He frequently compliments you on your good work and promises that you'll soon be in line for a big promotion.

Despite the CFO's compliments and promises, you are growing increasingly uncomfortable with the journal entries that you've been making. Typically, whenever an ordinary equipment purchase involves an advance payment, the purchase is completed a few weeks later. At that time, the amount of the advance is removed from an Equipment Deposit account and transferred to the appropriate equipment account. This hasn't been the case with the CFO's special project. Instead, the Prepaid Equipment account has continued to grow, now standing at over $3.8 billion. There's been no discussion about how or when this balance will be reduced, and no depreciation has been recorded for it.

Just as you begin to reflect on the effect the adjustments have had on your company's fixed assets, operating expenses, and operating income, you receive a call from the vice president for internal audit. She needs to talk with you this afternoon about "a peculiar trend in the company's fixed asset turnover ratio and some suspicious journal entries that you've been making."

Required:

1. Complete the following table to determine what the company's accounting records would have looked like had you not made the journal entries as part of the CFO's special project. Comment on how the decision to capitalize amounts, which were initially recorded as operating expenses, has affected the level of income from operations in each quarter.

(amounts in millions of U.S. dollars)	Q1 Year 1 (March 31)		Q2 Year 1 (June 30)		Q3 Year 1 (September 30)		Q4 Year 1 (December 31)		Q1 Year 2 (March 31)	
	With the Entries	Without the Entries	With the Entries	Without the Entries	With the Entries	Without the Entries	With the Entries	Without the Entries	With the Entries	Without the Entries
Property and equipment, net	$38,614	$	$35,982	$	$38,151	$	$38,809	$	$39,155	$
Sales revenues	8,825	8,825	8,910	8,910	8,966	8,966	8,478	8,478	8,120	8,120
Operating expenses	7,628		8,526		7,786		7,725		7,277	
Income from operations	1,197		384		1,180		753		843	

2. Using the publicly reported numbers (which include the special journal entries that you recorded), compute the fixed asset turnover ratio (rounded to two decimal places) for the periods ended Q2–Q4 of Year 1 and Q1 of Year 2. What does the trend in this ratio suggest to you? Is this consistent with the changes in operating income reported by the company?

3. Before your meeting with the vice president for internal audit, you think about the above computations and the variety of peculiar circumstances surrounding the "special project" for the CFO. What in particular might have raised your suspicion about the real nature of your work?

4. Your meeting with internal audit was short and unpleasant. The vice president indicated that she had discussed her findings with the CFO before meeting with you. The CFO claimed that he too had noticed the peculiar trend in the fixed asset turnover ratio, but that he hadn't had a chance to investigate it further. He urged internal audit to get to the bottom of things, suggesting that perhaps someone might be making unapproved journal entries. Internal audit had identified you as the source of the journal entries and had been unable to find any documents that approved or substantiated the entries. She ended the meeting by advising you to find a good lawyer. Given your current circumstances, describe how you would have acted earlier had you been able to foresee where it might lead you.

5. In the real case on which this one is based, the internal auditors agonized over the question of whether they had actually uncovered a fraud or whether they were jumping to the wrong conclusion. *The Wall Street Journal* mentioned this on October 30, 2002, by stating, "it was clear . . . that their findings would be devastating for the company. They worried about whether their revelations would result in layoffs. Plus, they feared that they would somehow end up being blamed for the mess." Beyond the personal consequences mentioned in this quote, describe other potential ways in which the findings of the internal auditors would likely be devastating for the publicly traded company and those associated with it.

Epilogue: This case is based on a fraud committed at **WorldCom** (now called **Verizon**). The case draws its numbers, the nature of the unsupported journal entries, and the CFO's role in carrying out the fraud from a report issued by WorldCom's bankruptcy examiner. Year 1 in this case was actually 2001 and Year 2 was 2002. This case excludes other fraudulent activities that contributed to WorldCom's $11 billion fraud. The 63-year-old CEO was sentenced to 25 years in prison for planning and executing the biggest fraud in the history of American business. The CFO, who cooperated in the investigation of the CEO, was sentenced to five years in prison.

CP8-8
LO8-1, 8-2, 8-7

Evaluating the Impact of Capitalized Interest on Cash Flows and Fixed Asset Turnover from an Analyst's Perspective

You are a financial analyst charged with evaluating the asset efficiency of companies in the hotel industry. Recent financial statements for **Marriott International** include the following note:

---

12.   PROPERTY AND EQUIPMENT

We record property and equipment at cost, including interest and real estate taxes we incur during development and construction. Interest we capitalized as a cost of property and equipment totaled $33 million in 2014, $31 million in 2013, and $27 million in 2012.

We capitalize the cost of improvements that extend the useful life of property and equipment when we incur them. These capitalized costs may include structural costs, equipment, fixtures, floor, and wall coverings.

Required:

1. Assume that Marriott followed this policy for a major construction project this year. How does Marriott's policy affect the following (use + for increase, − for decrease, and NE for no effect)?
   a. Cash flows.
   b. Fixed asset turnover ratio.

2. Normally, how would your answer to requirement (1*b*) affect your evaluation of Marriott's effectiveness in utilizing fixed assets?

3. If the fixed asset turnover ratio decreases due to interest capitalization, does this change indicate a real decrease in efficiency? Why or why not?

Financial Reporting and Analysis Team Project

Team Project: Analysis of Long-Lived Assets

CP8-9
LO8-1, 8-2, 8-3,
8-4, 8-6, 8-7

As a team, select an industry to analyze. Yahoo Finance provides lists of industries at **biz.yahoo.com/p/ industries.html**. Click on an industry for a list of companies in that industry. Alternatively, go to Google Finance at **www.google.com/finance**, search for a company you are interested in, and you will be presented with a list including that company and its competitors. Each team member should acquire the annual report or 10-K for one publicly traded company in the industry, with each member selecting a different company (the SEC EDGAR service at **www.sec.gov** and the company's investor relations website itself are good sources).

Required:

1. List the accounts and amounts of the company's long-lived assets (land, buildings, equipment, intangible assets, natural resources, and/or other) for the last three years.
   a. What is the percentage of each to total assets (rounded to two decimal places)?
   b. What do the results of your analysis suggest about the strategy your company has followed with respect to investing in long-lived assets?
2. What cost allocation method(s) and estimates does the company use for each type of long-lived asset?
3. What percentage of the property, plant, and equipment (rounded to two decimal places) has been used as of the end of the most recent year? (Accumulated Depreciation ÷ Cost)
4. What does the company disclose regarding asset impairment? What was its impairment loss, if any, in the most recent year?
5. Ratio analysis:
   a. What does the fixed asset turnover ratio measure in general?
   b. Compute the ratio for the last three years. Round your answers to two decimal places.
   c. What do your results suggest about the company?
   d. If available, find the industry ratio for the most recent year, compare it to your results, and discuss why you believe your company differs or is similar to the industry ratio.
6. What was the effect of depreciation expense on cash flows from operating activities? Compute the percentage of depreciation expense to cash flows from operating activities (rounded to two decimal places) for each of the past three years.
7. From the statement of cash flows, what were capital expenditures over the last three years? Did the company sell any long-lived assets?

Reporting and Interpreting Liabilities

Starbucks's mission statement is "To inspire and nurture the human spirit—one person, one cup and one neighborhood at a time." In 1971 Starbucks opened its first store in Seattle's Pike Place Market. Today, the company has almost 200,000 employees working in over 21,000 stores spread across 65 countries. In fiscal 2014, Starbucks reported global revenues of $16.4 billion, an 11% increase over the previous year.

Starbucks has ambitious growth plans for the future, intending to open approximately 1,500 stores each year for several years. To be successful, management must focus on a number of critical financing activities. These activities will generate funds to finance the current operating activities of the business and the long-term assets that will permit the company to grow in the future.

UNDERSTANDING THE BUSINESS

Businesses finance the acquisition of assets from two external sources: funds supplied by creditors (debt) and funds provided by owners (equity). The mixture of debt and equity a business uses is called its *capital structure.* In addition to selecting a capital structure, management can select from a variety of sources from which to borrow money, as illustrated by the liability section of the balance sheet from **Starbucks** shown in Exhibit 9.1.

Learning Objectives

After studying this chapter, you should be able to:

9-1   Define, measure, and report current liabilities.

9-2   Compute and interpret the accounts payable turnover ratio.

9-3   Report notes payable and explain the time value of money.

9-4   Report contingent liabilities.

9-5   Explain the importance of working capital and its impact on cash flows.

9-6   Report long-term liabilities.

9-7   Compute and explain present values.

9-8   Apply the present value concept to the reporting of long-term liabilities.

chapter 9

©The McGraw-Hill Companies, Inc./Jill Braaten, photographer

FOCUS COMPANY:

Starbucks

RECORDING AND REPORTING LIABILITIES

www.starbucks.com

What factors do managers consider when they borrow money? Two key factors are risk and cost. From the firm's perspective, debt capital is more risky than equity capital because payments associated with debt are a company's legal obligation. If a company cannot meet a required debt payment (either principal or interest) because of a temporary cash shortage, creditors may force the company into bankruptcy and require the sale of assets to satisfy the debt. As with any business transaction, borrowers and lenders attempt to negotiate the most favorable terms possible. Managers devote considerable effort analyzing alternative borrowing arrangements.

Companies that include debt in their capital structure must also make strategic decisions concerning the balance between short-term and long-term debt. To evaluate a company's capital structure, financial analysts calculate a number of accounting ratios. In this chapter, we will discuss both short-term and long-term debt, as well as some important accounting ratios. We will also introduce present values and discuss the role present values play in how long-term liabilities are reported on a company's balance sheet. In the next chapter, we discuss a special category of long-term debt, bond securities.

EXHIBIT 9.1

Liability Section of Starbucks's Balance Sheets

STARBUCKS

REAL WORLD EXCERPT:

Annual Report

STARBUCKS CORPORATION
CONSOLIDATED BALANCE SHEETS
(in millions)

	Sept. 28, 2014	Sept. 29, 2013
Current liabilities:		
Accounts payable	$ 533.7	$ 491.7
Accrued litigation charge	—	2,784.1
Accrued liabilities	1,514.4	1,269.3
Insurance reserves	196.1	178.5
Deferred revenue	794.5	653.7
Total current liabilities	3,038.7	5,377.3
Long-term debt	2,048.3	1,299.4
Other long-term liabilities	392.2	357.7
Total liabilities	$ 5,479.2	$ 7,034.4

ORGANIZATION of the Chapter

Liabilities Defined and Classified	Current Liabilities	Long-Term Liabilities	Computing Present Values
	• Accounts Payable • Accounts Payable Turnover Ratio • Accrued Liabilities • Notes Payable • Current Portion of Long-Term Debt • Deferred Revenues • Contingent Liabilities Reported on the Balance Sheet • Contingent Liabilities Reported in the Footnotes • Working Capital Management	• Long-Term Notes Payable and Bonds • Lease Liabilities	• Present Value of a Single Amount • Present Value of an Annuity • Accounting Applications of Present Values

LIABILITIES DEFINED AND CLASSIFIED

LEARNING OBJECTIVE 9-1
Define, measure, and report current liabilities.

Most people have a reasonable understanding of the definition of the word *liability*. Accountants formally define liabilities as the probable future sacrifice of economic benefits that arise from past transactions. As Exhibit 9.1 shows, as of September 28, 2014 (**Starbucks**'s fiscal year ends on the Sunday closest to September 30), Starbucks had borrowed on a long-term basis $2,048.3 million. The company has an obligation to pay cash to its creditors at some time in the future based on the borrowing agreements. Because of this obligation, Starbucks must record a long-term liability on its balance sheet.

When a liability is first recorded, it is measured in terms of its current cash equivalent, which is the cash amount a creditor would accept to settle the liability immediately. Although Starbucks borrowed $2,048.3 million, it will repay much more than that because the company must also pay interest on the debt. Interest that will be paid in the future is not included in the reported amount of the liability because it accrues and becomes a liability with the passage of time.

Like most businesses, Starbucks has several kinds of liabilities as well as a wide range of creditors. The list of liabilities on the balance sheet differs from one company to the next because different operating activities result in different types of liabilities. The liability section of Starbucks's balance sheet begins with the caption Current Liabilities. **Current liabilities** are expected to be paid with current assets within the current operating cycle of the business or within one year of the balance sheet date, whichever is longer. Noncurrent liabilities include all other liabilities.

CURRENT LIABILITIES

Many current liabilities have a direct relationship to the operating activities of a business. In other words, specific operating activities are financed, in part, by a related current liability. Some examples from **Starbucks**'s balance sheet (Exhibit 9.1) are:

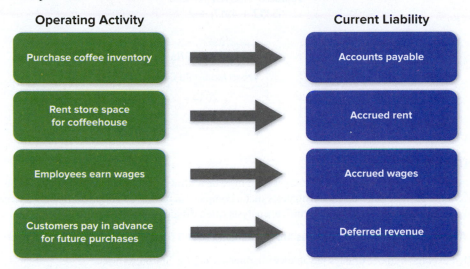

Early in this chapter, we mentioned that Starbucks is opening a lot of new stores each year. As a result, it must buy additional inventory, rent more store space, and hire more employees. By understanding the relationship between operating activities and current liabilities, an analyst can explain changes in the various current liability accounts.

We will now discuss the current liability accounts that are common to most balance sheets.

Accounts Payable

Most companies in the course of running their day-to-day operations purchase goods and services from other businesses. Typically, these purchases are made on credit with cash payments made after the goods and services have been provided. As a result, these transactions create obligations to pay suppliers in the near future. Most companies list such obligations on their balance sheets as **accounts payable** (sometimes called trade accounts payable).

For many companies, buying on credit from suppliers is a relatively inexpensive way to finance the purchase of inventory because interest does not normally accrue on accounts payable. As an incentive to encourage more sales, some suppliers offer generous credit terms that may allow buyers to resell merchandise and collect cash before payment must be made to the supplier.

Some managers may be tempted to delay payment to suppliers as long as possible to conserve cash. This strategy can create problems for suppliers. Most successful companies develop positive working relationships with suppliers to ensure that they receive quality goods and services. A positive relationship can be destroyed by slow payments. In addition, financial analysts become concerned if a business does not meet its obligations to suppliers on a timely basis because such slowness often indicates that a company is experiencing financial difficulties. Both managers and analysts use the accounts payable turnover ratio to evaluate how effectively a company is managing its accounts payable.

KEY RATIO ANALYSIS	Accounts Payable Turnover

LEARNING OBJECTIVE 9-2
Compute and interpret the accounts payable turnover ratio.

? ANALYTICAL QUESTION

How quickly does management pay its suppliers?

% RATIO AND COMPARISONS

The accounts payable turnover ratio is computed as follows:

Accounts Payable Turnover = Cost of Goods Sold ÷ Average Accounts Payable

The 2014 accounts payable turnover ratio for **Starbucks** was:

$$\$6,858.8 \div \$512.7^* = 13.4$$
$$^*(533.7 + 491.7) \div 2$$

COMPARISONS OVER TIME			COMPARISONS WITH COMPETITORS	
Starbucks			**Green Mountain Coffee**	**Dunkin' Brands**
2014	**2013**	**2012**	**2014**	**2014**
13.4	12.4	14.3	8.0	6.2

💡 INTERPRETATIONS

In General   The accounts payable turnover ratio measures how quickly management pays suppliers. A high accounts payable ratio normally suggests that a company is paying its suppliers in a timely manner. To make interpreting the ratio more intuitive, analysts often divide it into the number of days in a year:

Average Number of Days Payables Are Outstanding = 365 Days / Accounts Payable Turnover

The 2014 average number of days payables were outstanding for Starbucks was:

365 Days ÷ 13.4 = 27.2 Days

This means that, on average, Starbucks took 27 days to pay its suppliers in 2014.

Focus Company Analysis   Analyzing the average number of days payables are outstanding indicates that in 2014 Starbucks paid its suppliers more slowly than in 2013 (27.2 days versus 25.5 days), and more quickly than its competitors paid their suppliers. On average, **Green Mountain** took 45.6 days to pay its suppliers and **Dunkin' Brands** took 58.9 days. Suppliers like being paid as soon as possible and may extend benefits (e.g., faster shipments or preferential treatment when supply is limited) to companies that pay quickly.

A Few Cautions   The accounts payable turnover ratio is an average based on all accounts payable. As such, the ratio does not tell us how quickly a company is paying each of its suppliers. It is possible for a company to pay some suppliers quickly and others late and yet still end up with an acceptable ratio. This is not meant to suggest that the ratio is not useful. It simply implies that the more you know about the numbers used to calculate a ratio, the more fully you can understand the ratio's implications.

ACCRUED LIABILITIES
Expenses that have been incurred but have not been paid at the end of the accounting period.

Accrued Liabilities

In many situations, a business incurs an expense in one accounting period and makes the cash payment in a future period. **Accrued liabilities** are expenses that have been incurred before the end of an accounting period but have not been paid. These expenses include items such as rent, utilities, and salaries. The balance sheet for **Starbucks** lists two of these items: accrued litigation charge and accrued liabilities. Accrued liabilities are recorded at the end of the accounting period by recognizing an expense for the period and an associated liability.

Accrued Taxes Payable

Like individuals, corporations must pay taxes on the income they earn. Corporate tax rates are graduated, with large corporations paying a top federal tax rate of 35%. Corporations may also pay state and local income taxes and, in some cases, foreign income taxes. The notes to Starbucks's Annual Report include the following information pertaining to taxes:

INCOME TAXES

Note 13:

Provision for income taxes (*in millions*):

Fiscal Year Ended	Sept. 28, 2014	Sept. 29, 2013	Sept. 30, 2012
Current Taxes:			
U.S. federal	$ 822.7	$616.6	$466.0
U.S. state & local	132.9	93.8	79.9
Foreign	128.8	95.9	76.8
Total current taxes	$1,084.4	$806.3	$622.7

STARBUCKS

REAL WORLD EXCERPT:

Annual Report

For Starbucks and most other corporations, income taxes represent a major cost.

Accrued Compensation and Related Costs

At the end of each accounting period, employees usually have earned salaries that have not yet been paid. Unpaid salaries may be reported as a separate item on the balance sheet (e.g., as accrued compensation) or as a part of a general accrued liabilities account, as is the case with Starbucks. Starbucks reports in the footnotes to its 2014 Annual Report that "accrued compensation and related costs" in the accrued liabilities account amount to $437.9 million. In addition to reporting salaries that have been earned but not paid, companies also must report the cost of unpaid benefits, including retirement programs, vacation time, and health insurance. Starbucks refers to these items as "related costs."

Let's take a closer look at vacation time as an example. Typically, a business grants employees paid vacation time based on the number of months they have worked. The cost of vacation time must be recorded in the year employees earn the vacation time by working rather than the year they actually take vacation. If Starbucks estimates the cost of earned vacation time to be $125,000, accountants make the following adjusting entry at the end of the fiscal year:

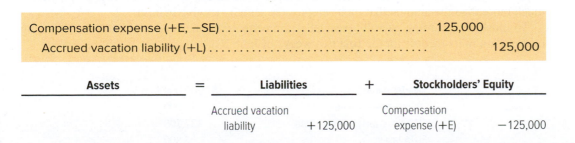

| Compensation expense (+E, −SE) .... | 125,000 | |
| Accrued vacation liability (+L) .... | | 125,000 |

Assets	=	Liabilities	+	Stockholders' Equity
		Accrued vacation liability +125,000		Compensation expense (+E) −125,000

When employees take vacations (for example, next summer), the accountants record the following:

Accrued vacation liability (−L)	125,000
Cash (−A)	125,000

Assets		=	Liabilities	+	Stockholders' Equity
Cash	−125,000		Accrued vacation liability −125,000		

Starbucks does not separately disclose the amount of accrued vacation liability. Instead, the company reports this liability as part of "accrued compensation and related costs." For most companies, the amount of accrued vacation liability is not large enough to warrant its own line item on the balance sheet.

Payroll Taxes

All payrolls are subject to a variety of taxes, including federal, state, and local income taxes; Social Security taxes; and federal and state unemployment taxes. Employees pay some of these taxes and employers pay others. While we will look at only the three largest taxes, reporting is similar for other types of payroll tax.

Kevin P. Casey/AP Photos

Employee Income Taxes Employers are required to withhold income taxes for each employee. The amount of income tax withheld is recorded by the employer as a current liability and remains a liability until the amount is paid to the government (usually quarterly).

Employee and Employer FICA Taxes Social Security taxes are often called **FICA taxes** because they are required by the Federal Insurance Contributions Act. These taxes are imposed in equal amounts on both the employee and the employer. The current Social Security tax rate is 6.2% on the first $117,000 paid to each employee during the year. In addition, a separate 1.45% Medicare tax applies to all employee income. Therefore, the FICA tax rate is 7.65% on income up to $117,000 and 1.45% on income above $117,000. Employees who earn above $200,000 have withheld an "additional Medicare tax" of 0.9%. Unlike all other FICA taxes, this additional Medicare tax is paid only by employees, not by employers. However, employers will withhold this additional tax as part of an employee's payroll deductions.

Employer Unemployment Taxes Employers are charged unemployment taxes through the Federal Unemployment Tax Act (FUTA) and State Unemployment Tax Acts (SUTA). These programs provide financial support to employees who lose their jobs through no fault of their own. Because the rate and specified amount of wages vary by state, we will focus on federal unemployment taxes. The FUTA specifies a federal tax rate of 0.6% on taxable wages up to the first $7,000 for each employee. Employers with a good payment history may receive a credit for taxes paid at the state level, thus reducing their federal tax liability.

Employee compensation expense includes an employee's salary and related costs as well as any funds paid to others on behalf of the employee. As a result, the cost of hiring employees is much more than the amount that those employees actually receive in cash.

To illustrate recording payroll taxes, let's assume that Starbucks accumulated the following information in its records for the first two weeks of June 2014:

Salaries earned	$1,800,000
Income taxes withheld	275,000
FICA taxes (employees' share)	137,700
FUTA taxes	2,300

Companies generally record two journal entries to account for payroll taxes. The first entry records the amount of cash paid to employees and the various deductions withheld from employees' paychecks:

Compensation expense (+E, −SE)...........................	1,800,000	
Liability for income taxes withheld (+L).......................		275,000
FICA payable (+L).......................................		137,700
Cash (−A)...		1,387,300

Assets	=	Liabilities	+	Stockholders' Equity
Cash −1,387,300		FICA payable +137,700		Compensation
		Liability for income		expense (+E) −1,800,000
		taxes withheld +275,000		

The second entry records the taxes that employers must pay from their own funds. Federal and state laws require these tax payments. Assuming all employees earn less than $200,000, the FICA tax amount is equal to the amount that is paid by employees:

Compensation expense (+E, −SE)...........................	140,000	
FICA payable (+L).......................................		137,700
FUTA payable (+L)......................................		2,300

Assets	=	Liabilities	+	Stockholders' Equity
		FICA payable +137,700		Compensation expense (+E) −140,000
		FUTA payable +2,300		

Deferred Revenues

In most business transactions, cash is paid when a product or service is delivered, or soon thereafter. In some cases, however, cash is paid in advance of delivery. You have probably paid for an airline ticket in advance. The airline company receives cash for the ticket you purchased, but it does not provide the service (the flight) until a future date. When a company collects cash before the related revenue has been earned, the cash is called **deferred revenues**, or, occasionally, unearned revenues. A **Starbucks** card, which allows customers to pay for their purchases in advance, is an example of deferred revenues. Advantages for the customer include convenience at the point of sale and the accumulation of loyalty rewards. Advantages for Starbucks include the ability to collect and use customers' cash before they actually purchase anything, while also collecting information on the purchasing habits of individual customers. Starbucks's balance sheet shown in Exhibit 9.1 shows that in 2014 the company collected $794.5 million in cash from customers and has yet to provide those customers with any sort of product or service. Starbucks explains the amount with the following note:

"Revenues from our stored value cards, primarily Starbucks Cards, are recognized when redeemed or when the likelihood of redemption, based on historical experience, is deemed to be remote. Outstanding customer balances are included in deferred revenue on the consolidated balance sheets."

STARBUCKS

REAL WORLD EXCERPT:

Annual Report

Under the revenue recognition principle introduced in Chapter 3, revenue cannot be recorded until it has been earned. Deferred revenues are reported as a liability because cash has been collected from customers but the company has not delivered a product or service, and thus the related revenue has not been earned by the end of the accounting period. The obligation to provide a product or service in the future still exists. These obligations are classified as current or long-term, depending on when a company expects to provide the product or service.

Notes Payable

TIME VALUE OF MONEY
Interest that is associated with the use of money over time.

When a company borrows money, it normally signs a formal written contract with a bank and reports the amount borrowed as a **note payable.** The contract specifies the amount borrowed, the date by which it must be repaid, and the interest rate associated with the borrowing.

Banks and other creditors are willing to lend cash because they will earn interest in return. Earning interest by loaning money to others reflects the **time value of money**. To the borrower, interest reflects the cost of using someone else's money and is therefore an expense. To lenders, interest reflects the benefit of allowing someone else to use their money and is therefore a revenue.

You need three pieces of information to calculate interest: (1) the **principal** (i.e., the cash that was borrowed), (2) the **annual interest rate,** and (3) the **time period for the loan.** The interest formula is:

Principal × Annual Interest Rate × Number of Months / 12 Months = Interest for the Period

To illustrate, assume that on November 1, a company with a December 31 fiscal year-end borrows $100,000 cash for one year. The annual interest rate is 12%. The interest is payable on April 30 and October 31 of the following year. The principal ($100,000) is payable at the maturity date, October 31 of next year. The note is recorded in the accounts as follows:

Cash (+A)	100,000	
Notes payable (+L)		100,000

Assets	=	Liabilities	+	Stockholders' Equity
Cash +100,000		Notes payable +100,000		

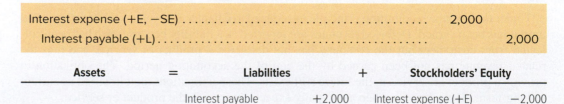

Interest is an expense incurred when companies borrow money. Companies record interest expense for a given accounting period, regardless of when they actually pay the bank cash for interest. In the above example, the company borrowed the money on November 1 so it must record two months of interest expense at December 31, the end of the fiscal year. It does not matter that the company will not actually pay the bank cash for interest until April 30 of next year.

The computation to determine the amount of interest accrued during the two months is:

Principal × Annual Interest Rate × Number of Months / 12 Months = Interest for the Period

$100,000 × 0.12 × 2/12 months = $2,000

The entry to record interest expense and interest payable for the two months is:

Interest expense (+E, −SE)	2,000	
Interest payable (+L)		2,000

Assets	=	Liabilities	+	Stockholders' Equity
		Interest payable +2,000		Interest expense (+E) −2,000

On April 30 of next year, the company would make a $6,000 payment to the bank for interest, which includes the $2,000 accrued and reported at the end of last year plus the $4,000 interest accrued in the first four months of the next year. The following journal entry would be made on April 30:

Interest expense (+E, −SE)	4,000	
Interest payable (−L)	2,000	
Cash (−A)		6,000

Assets		=	Liabilities		+	Stockholders' Equity	
Cash	−6,000		Interest payable	−2,000		Interest expense (+E)	−4,000

Current Portion of Long-Term Debt

The distinction between current and long-term debt is important for both managers and analysts. A company must have sufficient cash on hand to repay current debt. To provide accurate information on how much of its long-term debt is due in the current year, a company must reclassify its long-term debt as a current liability within a year of its maturity date. Assume that a company signed a note to borrow $5 million at the end of December 2015. Half of the loan must be repaid in January 2017 and the other half is due in January 2018. The 2015, 2016, and 2017 year-end balance sheets would report the following:

December 31, 2015	
Long-term liabilities:	
Note payable	$5,000,000
December 31, 2016	
Current liabilities:	
Current portion of long-term note	$2,500,000
Long-term liabilities:	
Note payable	$2,500,000
December 31, 2017	
Current liabilities:	
Current portion of long-term note	$2,500,000

Note in Exhibit 9.1 that **Starbucks** did not report any current portion of long-term debt. This indicates that Starbucks will not pay off any of its long-term debt in 2015. In the footnotes to its 2014 Annual Report, Starbucks explains that its long-term debt consists of bonds, which only pay interest for several years, after which the principal amount is due. Because Starbucks will not pay any of the principal in the coming year, all of the debt is classified as long term. We will cover the accounting for bonds in Chapter 10.

Refinancing Debt: Current or Long-Term Liability?

FINANCIAL ANALYSIS

Instead of repaying a loan from current cash, a company may refinance it either by negotiating a new loan agreement with a new maturity date or by taking out a new loan and using the proceeds to pay off the old loan. If a company intends to refinance a currently maturing loan with a new *long-term* loan and has the ability to do so, the current loan should be classified as a long-term liability. It is not a current liability because current liabilities are short-term obligations that are expected to be paid with current assets within the current operating cycle or one year, whichever is longer.

U.S. GAAP (generally accepted accounting principles) and IFRS (International Financial Reporting Standards) differ slightly in how they treat refinancing of loans. Under IFRS, the actual refinancing must take place by the balance sheet date. Under U.S. GAAP, the intent and ability to refinance must exist before the balance sheet date, but the actual refinancing does not have to have occurred.

SeongJoon Cho/Bloomberg/
Getty Images

LEARNING OBJECTIVE 9-4
Report contingent liabilities.

CONTINGENT LIABILITY
A potential liability that has arisen as the result of a past event; it is not a definitive liability until some future event occurs.

Contingent Liabilities Reported on the Balance Sheet

Some recorded liabilities are based on estimates because the exact amount will not be known until a future date. For example, a **contingent liability** is created when a company offers a warranty with the products it sells. The cost of providing future repair work must be estimated and recorded as a liability (and expense) in the period in which the product is sold.

As an example, assume **Starbucks** estimates that it will have to provide $150,000 of warranty services to customers who purchased coffee brewing and espresso equipment this year. In addition to recording the sale of the brewing and espresso equipment, Starbucks would record the following:

Warranty expense (+E, −SE)		150,000
Warranty payable (+L)		150,000

Assets	=	Liabilities	+	Stockholders' Equity
		Warranty payable +150,000		Warranty expense (+E) −150,000

Contingent Liabilities Reported in the Footnotes

Each of the liabilities that we have discussed is reported on the balance sheet at a specific dollar amount because each involves the probable future sacrifice of economic benefits. Some transactions or events create only a reasonably possible (but not probable) future sacrifice of economic benefits. These situations create contingent liabilities that are reported in the footnotes, but not on a company's balance sheet.

Contingent Liability Examples

Lawsuits   Environmental   Product
                  problems   warranties

Whether a contingent liability is reported on the balance sheet, in the footnotes, or not at all depends on two factors: (1) the probability of a future economic sacrifice and (2) the ability of management to estimate the amount of the liability. The following table illustrates the possibilities:

	Probable	Reasonably Possible	Remote
Amount can be reasonably estimated	Record as liability	Disclose in footnotes	Disclosure not required
Amount cannot be reasonably estimated	Disclose in footnotes	Disclose in footnotes	Disclosure not required

The probabilities of occurrence are defined in the following manner:

- Probable—The future event or events are likely to occur.
- Reasonably possible—The chance of the future event or events occurring is more than remote but less than likely.
- Remote—The chance of the future event or events occurring is slight.

It's a Matter of Degree

INTERNATIONAL PERSPECTIVE

The assessment of future probabilities is inherently subjective, but both U.S. GAAP and IFRS provide some guidance. Under U.S. GAAP, "probable" has been defined as *likely to occur,* which is commonly interpreted to mean having a greater than 70% chance of occurring. Under IFRS, "probable" is defined as *more likely than not to occur,* which implies more than a 50% chance of occurring. This difference means that for some contingent liabilities, IFRS would require the reporting of a liability on the balance sheet whereas GAAP would simply require footnote disclosure.

In summary,

- A liability that both is probable and can be reasonably estimated must be recorded and reported on the balance sheet.
- A liability that is reasonably possible must be disclosed in a footnote whether the amount can be estimated or not.
- Remote contingencies do not require any type of disclosure.

For several years, **Starbucks** reported a contingent liability associated with a legal dispute with **Kraft Foods Group**. In late 2013, Starbucks lost the dispute and was ordered by an arbitrator to pay Kraft over $2 billion. Below are excerpts from Starbucks's 2013 Annual Report:

> "We believe we had valid claims of material breach by Kraft under the Agreement that allowed us to terminate the Agreement and certain other relationships with Kraft without compensation to Kraft.
>
> Kraft denied it had materially breached the Agreement. On November 29, 2010, Starbucks received a notice of arbitration from Kraft putting the commercial dispute between the parties into binding arbitration pursuant to the terms of the Agreement.
>
> . . . prior to receiving the arbitrator's ruling we could not reasonably estimate the possible loss. Accordingly, no loss contingency was recorded for this matter.
>
> On November 12, 2013, the arbitrator ordered Starbucks to pay Kraft $2,227.5 million in damages plus prejudgment interest and attorneys' fees. We have estimated prejudgment interest, which includes an accrual through the estimated payment date, and attorneys' fees to be approximately $556.6 million. As a result, we recorded a litigation charge of $2,784.1 million in our fiscal 2013 operating results."

STARBUCKS

REAL WORLD EXCERPT:

Annual Report

Consistent with the table shown earlier, Starbucks did not initially record a liability because management decided it could not reasonably estimate the amount of the potential loss. Therefore, disclosure in a footnote was sufficient. However, once the arbitrator ruled against Starbucks, the company was required to report a liability on its balance sheet and an associated loss on its income statement.

Working Capital Management

Information about current liabilities is very important to managers and analysts because these obligations must be paid in the near future. Analysts say that a company has **liquidity** if it has the ability to meet its current obligations. A number of financial measures are useful in evaluating liquidity, including the current ratio (introduced in Chapter 2) and the dollar amount of **working capital**. **Working capital** is defined as the dollar difference between current assets and current liabilities. Working capital is important to both managers and financial analysts because it has a significant impact on the health and profitability of a company. **Starbucks** reported current assets of $4,168.7 million and current liabilities of $3,038.7 million at the end of fiscal year 2014, which results in working capital of $1,130.0 million. Working capital reflects the amount Starbucks would have left over if it used all of its current assets to pay off all of its current liabilities.

LIQUIDITY
The ability to pay current obligations.

WORKING CAPITAL
The dollar difference between total current assets and total current liabilities.

The working capital accounts are actively managed to achieve a balance between a company's short-term obligations and the resources to satisfy those obligations. If a business has too little working capital, it runs the risk of not being able to meet its obligations. On the other hand, too much working capital may tie up resources in unproductive assets. Excess inventory, for example, ties up dollars that could be invested more profitably elsewhere in the business and incurs additional costs associated with storage and deterioration.

Changes in working capital accounts are also important to managers and analysts because they have a direct impact on the cash flows from operating activities reported on the statement of cash flows.

FOCUS ON CASH FLOWS

Working Capital and Cash Flows

Many working capital accounts have a direct relationship to income-producing activities. Accounts receivable, for example, are related to sales revenue: Accounts receivable increase when sales are made on credit. Cash is collected when the customer pays the bill. Similarly, accounts payable increase when inventory is purchased on credit. A cash outflow occurs when the account is paid. Changes in working capital accounts that are related to income-producing activities, called operating working capital, must be considered when computing cash flows from operating activities. We discuss how to create the cash flow statement in Chapter 12.

PAUSE FOR **FEEDBACK**

Companies classify liabilities as either current or long term. Our discussion to this point has focused on current liabilities. In the next section, we turn our attention to long-term liabilities. Before you move on, complete the following questions to test your understanding of the concepts we have covered.

SELF-STUDY **QUIZ**

For each of the following events, state whether **Starbucks**'s working capital will increase, decrease, or not change:

1. Starbucks purchases inventory on credit.
2. Starbucks borrows $1,000,000 in long-term debt.
3. Starbucks pays cash to reduce its rent payable account by $750,000.
4. Starbucks pays employee salaries with cash.

After you have completed your answers, check them below.

Solutions to
SELF-STUDY QUIZ

| 1. No change | 2. Increase | 3. No change | 4. Decrease |

LONG-TERM LIABILITIES

Long-term liabilities include all obligations that are not classified as current liabilities, such as long-term notes payable and bonds payable. Typically, a long-term liability will require payment more than one year in the future.

Most companies borrow money on a long-term basis in order to purchase assets, like property or equipment. In some cases, a company may pledge specific assets as security for repayment. If the company defaults on the loan, then the bank has the right to take ownership of the assets. A loan supported by this type of agreement is called **secured debt.** Unsecured debt refers to an agreement in which the bank relies primarily on the borrower's integrity and general earning power to repay the loan.

Long-Term Notes Payable and Bonds

Companies can raise capital directly from a number of financial service organizations including banks, insurance companies, and pension plans. Raising capital from one of these organizations is known as a **private placement.** The resulting liability is often called a **note payable,** which is a written promise to pay a stated sum at one or more specified future dates called the **maturity date(s).**

In many cases, a company's need for capital exceeds the financial ability of any single bank or other creditor. In these situations, the company may issue publicly traded debt called **bonds.** The opportunity to sell a bond security in established markets provides bondholders with an important benefit. Without involving the company, bondholders can sell their bond securities to other investors prior to maturity if they have an immediate need for cash. We will discuss bonds in detail in the next chapter.

Accounting for long-term debt is based on the same concepts used in accounting for short-term notes payable. A liability is recorded when the debt is incurred and interest expense is recorded with the passage of time.

Business operations are global in nature, with many corporations operating manufacturing facilities around the world. In order to support these foreign operations, companies sometimes borrow money from foreign banks. Borrowing money in a foreign currency raises some interesting accounting and management issues.

LEARNING OBJECTIVE 9-6
Report long-term liabilities.

LONG-TERM LIABILITIES
All of the entity's obligations that are not classified as current liabilities.

Borrowing in Foreign Currencies

INTERNATIONAL PERSPECTIVE

Many corporations with foreign operations elect to finance those operations with foreign debt to lessen exchange rate risk. Exchange rate risk exists because the relative value of each nation's currency varies on virtually a daily basis.

A U.S. corporation that conducts business operations in England might decide to borrow British pounds to finance its operations there. The profits from the business, which will be in pounds, can be used to pay off the debt, which is in pounds. If this business earns profits in pounds but pays off debt in dollars, however, it will be exposed to exchange rate risk because the relative value of the dollar and the pound fluctuates.

In attempting to mitigate exchange rate risk, **Amazon.com** states the following in the footnotes to its 2013 Annual Report:

> "We have internationally-focused websites for the United Kingdom, Germany, France, Japan, Canada, China, Italy, Spain, Brazil, India, Mexico, and Australia. Net sales generated from these websites, as well as most of the related expenses directly incurred from those operations, are denominated in local functional currencies."

AMAZON
REAL WORLD EXCERPT:
Annual Report

For reporting purposes, accountants must convert, or translate, foreign debt into U.S. dollars at the end of the accounting period in order to report the debt on a U.S. company's balance sheet. In the same footnote excerpted above, Amazon.com discusses how it does this by stating:

"Assets and liabilities of these subsidiaries are translated into U.S. dollars at period-end exchange rates. . . ."

Lease Liabilities

Companies often lease assets rather than purchase them. For example, leasing extra delivery trucks during a busy period is more economical than owning them if they are not needed during the rest of the year. When a company leases an asset, it enters into a contractual agreement with the owner of the asset. In the language of contracts (and accounting), the party that owns the asset is referred to as the **lessor**. The party that pays for the right to use the asset is referred to as the **lessee**. For accounting purposes, a lessee can lease an asset by signing either an operating lease or a capital lease.

LESSOR
The party that owns a leased asset.

LESSEE
The party that pays for the right to use the leased asset.

OPERATING LEASE
Does not require a lessee to recognize an asset or liability.

CAPITAL LEASE
Does require a lessee to recognize an asset and a liability.

The terms of an **operating lease** are similar to a short-term rental and therefore do not require companies to recognize a lease asset or a lease liability on their balance sheets. In contrast, the terms of a **capital lease** resemble the financing and outright purchasing of an asset and therefore require companies to recognize both a lease asset and a lease liability on their balance sheets. Since managers often prefer to minimize the liabilities they report on their balance sheets, they have an incentive to structure lease contracts so that they are accounted for as operating leases rather than capital leases.

How do accountants determine if a lease should be recorded as an operating lease or a capital lease? GAAP helps guide them through this determination by stating that if a lease meets any of the following four criteria, it is considered a capital lease:

- The lease term is 75% or more of the asset's expected economic life.
- Ownership of the asset is transferred to the lessee at the end of the lease term.
- The lease contract permits the lessee to purchase the asset at a price that is lower than its fair market value.
- When the lease is signed, the present value of the lease payments is 90% or more of the fair market value of the leased asset.

As an example of an operating lease, assume that on December 31, **Starbucks** signs an operating lease contract to rent five delivery trucks for the month of January for $10,000 to be paid at the end of January. No entry is recorded at the time the lease is signed on December 31. Rent expense is recorded in January, when the trucks are actually used.

| Rent expense (+E, −SE) | 10,000 | |
| Cash (−A) | | 10,000 |

Assets	=	Liabilities	+	Stockholders' Equity
Cash −10,000				Rent expense (+E) −10,000

To record a capital lease, it is necessary to determine the current cash equivalent of the required lease payments. Assume that Starbucks signs a four-year lease for new delivery trucks. The accountant has determined that the lease is a capital lease with a current cash equivalent of $250,000. Once the lease is signed, Starbucks records the transaction in a manner similar to the actual purchase of delivery trucks:

Leased equipment (+A) 250,000

   Lease liability (+L) 250,000

Assets	=	Liabilities	+	Stockholders' Equity
Leased equipment +250,000		Lease liability +250,000		

In this example, you were given the current cash equivalent of the lease. In the next section we will learn how accountants compute current cash equivalents, commonly referred to as *present values*.

COMPUTING PRESENT VALUES

Our discussion of capital leases raises an interesting question about liabilities: Is the liability today the amount of cash that will be paid in the future? For example, if I agree to pay you $10,000 five years from now, should I report a liability of $10,000 on my personal balance sheet? If I can earn interest on my money, the answer is "no." To understand why, it is important for you to understand that money invested in an interest-bearing account grows over time. We briefly introduced this concept earlier in the chapter and referred to it as the time value of money. The time value of money plays an important role in how companies report long-term liabilities, such as the capital lease we just discussed as well as bonds, the topic of Chapter 10.

The concept of **present value** (PV) is based on the time value of money. Quite simply, money received today is worth more than money to be received one year from today (or at any other future date) because it can be used to earn interest. If you invest $1,000 today at 10%, you will have $1,100 in one year. In contrast, if you receive $1,000 one year from today, you will lose the opportunity to earn the $100 in interest revenue. The difference between the $1,000 and the $1,100 is the interest that can be earned during the year, which reflects the time value of money.

In one of your math classes, you have probably already solved some problems involving the time value of money. In the typical problem, you are told a certain dollar amount has been deposited in a savings account earning a specified rate of interest. You are asked to compute the dollar amount in the savings account after a certain number of years. This is an example of a **future value** (FV) problem: How much is a given dollar amount today worth in the future if it grows at a specified interest rate? For example, if you deposited $100 today in a savings account that earns 10% interest, how much would you have after one year?

LEARNING OBJECTIVE 9-7
Compute and explain present values.

PRESENT VALUE
The current value of an amount to be received in the future; a future amount discounted for compound interest.

FUTURE VALUE
The sum to which an amount will increase as the result of compound interest.

Present value (PV)   1 year   Future value (FV)

$100 $110

ANSWER: $110

In this chapter we focus on how to solve the opposite problem. In present value problems, you are asked to compute the amount you would need to deposit today at a specified interest rate to have a given dollar amount in the future. For example, if you needed $110 in one year, how much would you need to deposit in a savings account today if the savings account earns 10% interest?

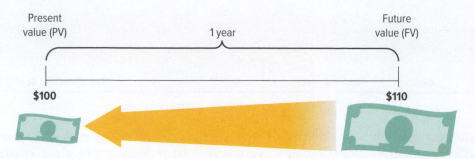

ANSWER: $100

There are two basic types of present value problems: those involving single amounts like the example above and those involving a stream of future amounts. Understanding and being able to compute both types is important when accounting for certain long-term liabilities.

Present Value of a Single Amount

To compute the present value of a single amount, you must discount the amount to be received in the future at i interest rate for n periods. The formula to compute the present value of a single amount is

$$\text{Present value} = \frac{1}{(1+i)^n} \times \text{Amount}$$

While the formula is not difficult to use, most analysts use present value tables, calculators, or Excel. We strongly encourage you to visit Connect for tutorials on how to compute present values using each of these tools.

 GUIDED HELP 9-1

For additional step-by-step video instruction on how to compute present values, go to **www.mhhe. com/libby9e_gh9a**.

For all examples that follow, we provide in the box the inputs required to compute each present value using tables, calculators, and Excel.

Assume that today is January 1, 2016, and you need to make a $1,000 cash payment on December 31, 2018. At an interest rate of 10% per year, how much would you need to deposit today to have exactly $1,000 on December 31, 2018? You could discount the amount year by year to figure out how much you would need to deposit today, but it is easier to use Table E.1, Appendix E, Present Value of $1. For $i = 10\%$, $n = 3$ periods, we find that the present value of $1 is 0.75131. The present value of $1,000 to be paid at the end of three years can be computed as follows:

$$\$1,000 \times 0.75131 = \$751.31$$

| From Table E.1: interest rate (i) = 10%, periods (n) = 3: Factor = 0.75131 |
| Using Excel: rate (i) = .10, nper (n) = 3, pmt = $0, FV = –$1,000 |
| Using Calculator: rate (i) = 10, periods (n) = 3, pmt = $0, FV = –$1,000 |

Once you have computed a present value amount, it is important that you understand what it means. The $751.31 is the amount you would have to deposit today in order to have exactly $1,000 three years from today, assuming an interest rate of 10%. Conceptually, you should be indifferent between paying $751.31 today and paying $1,000 in three years. If you had $751.31 today and did not want to worry about having to come up with $1,000 in three years, you could simply deposit the money in a savings account and at 10% interest it

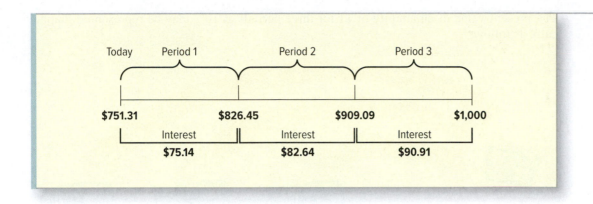

EXHIBIT 9.2

How a Deposit Grows
to $1,000

would grow to $1,000 in three years.[1] How the deposit of $751.31 grows to equal $1,000 is shown in Exhibit 9.2.

PAUSE FOR **FEEDBACK**

SELF-STUDY **QUIZ**

So far we have discussed the first type of present value problems—those involving a single future amount. In the next section, we will discuss annuities, which involve a stream of future amounts. Before you move on, complete the following questions to test your understanding of the present value concepts we have covered so far.

1. If the interest rate in a present value problem increases from 8% to 10%, will the present value increase or decrease?
2. Assuming an annual interest rate of 5%, what amount should you deposit today if you need $10,000 in 10 years?

After you have completed your answers, check them below.

Present Value of an Annuity

Instead of a single amount, many business problems involve multiple cash payments over a number of periods. An **annuity** is a series of consecutive payments characterized by

1. An equal dollar amount each period.

2. Interest periods of equal length (year, half a year, quarterly, or monthly).

3. The same interest rate each period.

Examples of annuities include monthly rent payments on an apartment or quarterly lease payments on a car.

The present value of an annuity is the value now of a series of equal amounts to be received (or paid out) for some specified number of periods in the future. We compute the present value of an annuity by discounting each of the equal periodic amounts back to today.

ANNUITY
A series of periodic cash receipts or payments that are equal in amount each interest period.

---

[1]Though not the focus of this chapter, we provide tables for computing future values in Appendix E. You use future value tables the same way you use present value tables. For example, to compute how much you would have after three years if you deposited $751.31 in a savings account earning 10% interest, you would use Table E.3 ($i = 10\%$, $n = 3$ periods) and multiply $751.31 × 1.33100. The answer: $1,000.

---

1. The present value will decrease.
2. $10,000 × 0.61391 = $6,139.10

The present value of an annuity of $1 for three periods at 10% may be represented graphically as follows:

Present value
of an annuity
$2.49

Assume you purchase a piece of equipment and agree to pay $1,000 cash each December 31 for three years. How much would you need to deposit today at an annual interest rate of 10% to make each $1,000 payment? We could use Table E.1, Appendix E, to calculate the present value as follows:

Year	Amount		Factor from Table E.1, Appendix E, I = 10%		Present Value
1	$1,000	×	0.90909 (n = 1)	=	$ 909.09
2	$1,000	×	0.82645 (n = 2)	=	$ 826.45
3	$1,000	×	0.75131 (n = 3)	=	$ 751.31
			Total present value	=	$2,486.85

We can compute the present value of this annuity more easily, however, by using Table E.2, Appendix E, as follows:

$$\$1,000 \times 2.48685 = \$2,486.85$$

From Table E.2: interest rate (i) = 10%, periods (n) = 3: Factor = 2.48685

Using Excel: rate (i) = .10, nper (n) = 3, pmt = −$1,000, FV = $0

Using Calculator: rate (i) = 10, periods (n) = 3, pmt = −$1,000, FV = $0

Let's now connect the amount we computed above to the three required $1,000 payments. As shown in Exhibit 9.3, if you deposited $2,486.85 today at an interest rate of 10%, that amount would grow to $2,735.54 after one year ($2,486.85 + interest of $248.69). At that point you would make your first $1,000 payment and have $1,735.54 left. The $1,735.54 would grow to $1,909.09 over the next year ($1,735.54 + interest of $173.55). At that point you would make your second $1,000 payment and have $909.09 left. The $909.09 would grow to exactly $1,000 over the next year ($909.09 + interest of $90.91), and you would be able to make your last $1,000 payment. Thus, at an interest rate of 10%, depositing $2,486.85

EXHIBIT 9.3	Beginning of Year	+	Interest Earned During Year	=	End of Year	−	Payment	=	Remaining Balance
	$2,486.85	+	$248.69	=	$2,735.54	−	$1,000.00	=	$1,735.54
Illustration of an Annuity over Time	$1,735.54	+	$173.55	=	$1,909.09	−	$1,000.00	=	$ 909.09
	$ 909.09	+	$ 90.91	=	$1,000.00	−	$1,000.00	=	$ 0

today would allow you to make the three required $1,000 payments at the end of the next three years.[2]

Interest Rates and Interest Periods

The preceding illustrations assumed annual periods for compounding and discounting. Although interest rates are almost always quoted on an annual basis, most compounding periods encountered in business are less than one year. When interest periods are less than a year, the values of n and i must be adjusted to be consistent with the length of the interest period.

To illustrate, 12% interest compounded annually for five years requires the use of $n = 5$ and $i = 12\%$. If compounding is quarterly, however, the interest period is one-quarter of a year (i.e., four periods per year), and the quarterly interest rate is one-quarter of the annual rate (i.e., 3% per quarter). Therefore, 12% interest compounded quarterly for five years requires use of $n = 20$ and $i = 3\%$.

Truth in Advertising	A QUESTION OF ETHICS

Online and television advertisements are easy to misinterpret if the consumer does not understand the time value of money. For example, perhaps you have seen advertisements that promise "No payments for one year!" It is important to realize that "no payments" does not mean "no interest." In almost all cases, during the "no payments" year, interest is accruing (being added to the amount owed) and, depending on the interest rate, can add significantly to the total amount customers must pay back.

Another misleading advertisement relates to lotteries, which often promise to make winners instant millionaires. In some cases, however, the lottery amount is paid out over a long period of time, for example, $25,000 each year for 40 years. The winner will receive $1,000,000 ($25,000 × 40 years), but the present value of this annuity at 8% is only $298,000. While most winners are happy to get the money, they are not really millionaires.

Some consumer advocates argue that consumers should not have to study present value concepts to understand such advertisements. While some of these criticisms may be valid, the quality of information contained in advertisements that include interest rates has improved over time.

Accounting Applications of Present Values

Many business transactions that affect long-term liabilities require accountants to compute present values. We provide three brief examples below before transitioning to accounting for bonds in the next chapter.

Computing the Amount of a Liability with a Single Payment

On January 1, 2016, **Starbucks** bought some new delivery trucks. The company signed a note and agreed to pay $200,000 on December 31, 2017. This type of arrangement is often referred to as a "non-interest-bearing" note since no interest payments are required over the life of the note. Do not confuse "non-interest-bearing" with "no interest." The interest is simply built into the final payment, in this case the $200,000 payment on December 31, 2017. Assume that the market interest rate applicable to the note was determined to be 12%.

To record this transaction, the accountant must first compute the present value of a single amount to be paid in the future. This amount is the present value, or current cash equivalent, which reflects the value of the trucks today. The problem can be shown graphically as follows:

---

[2] To compute the future value of an annuity, you would use Table E.4, Appendix E. For example, at an interest rate of 10 percent, if you deposited $1,000 at the end of each year for three years (with no withdrawals), you would have $3,310 ($1,000 × 3.31000, the future value factor for $n = 3$, $i = 10\%$).

The present value of the $200,000 payment is computed as follows:

$$\$200,000 \times 0.79719 = \$159,438$$

> From Table E.1: interest rate (i) = 12%, periods (n) = 2: Factor = 0.79719
> Using Excel: rate (i) = .12, nper (n) = 2, pmt = $0, FV = −$200,000
> Using Calculator: rate (i) = 12, periods (n) = 2, pmt = $0, FV = −$200,000

Therefore, the journal entry is as follows:

Delivery trucks (+A)...	159,438	
Note payable (+L)		159,438

Assets	=	Liabilities	+	Stockholders' Equity
Delivery trucks +159,438		Note payable +159,438		

After the initial transaction is recorded, Starbucks must record the implied interest expense each year.

December 31, 2016	Interest expense (+E, −SE)	19,133*	
	Note payable (+L)........................		19,133

*$159,438 note payable balance × 0.12 annual interest rate = $19,133.
When added to $159,438, the note payable balance is now $178,571.

Assets	=	Liabilities	+	Stockholders' Equity
		Note payable +19,133		Interest expense (+E) −19,133

December 31, 2017	Interest expense (+E, −SE)	21,429*	
	Note payable (+L)........................		21,429

*$178,571 note payable balance × 0.12 annual interest rate = $21,429.
When added to $178,571, the note payable balance is now $200,000.

Assets	=	Liabilities	+	Stockholders' Equity
		Note payable +21,429		Interest expense (+E) −21,429

At the end of two years, the loan amount must be repaid. The amount owed is the balance of Note Payable, which started at $159,438 and grew as we added interest over the two-year period to now equal exactly $200,000. The journal entry to record full payment of the debt follows:

Note payable (−L)	200,000	
Cash (−A)		200,000

Assets	=	Liabilities	+	Stockholders' Equity
Cash −200,000		Note payable −200,000		

Computing the Amount of a Liability with an Annuity

On January 1, 2016, Starbucks bought several new espresso machines. The company elected to finance the purchase with a note payable to be paid off in three annual payments of $163,685.

Each payment includes principal plus interest on the unpaid balance at 11% per year. The annual payments are due on December 31, 2016, 2017, and 2018. This problem can be shown graphically as follows:

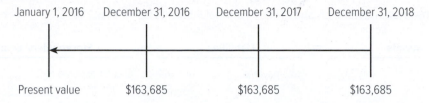

January 1, 2016	December 31, 2016	December 31, 2017	December 31, 2018
Present value	$163,685	$163,685	$163,685

The present value of the note is the amount Starbucks would have to deposit today at 11% interest to cover the three $163,685 payments. This is an annuity because payments are made in three equal installments. The present value of the note is computed as follows:

$$\$163,685 \times 2.44371 = \$399,999$$

> From Table E.2: interest rate $(i) = 11\%$, periods $(n) = 3$: Factor $= 2.44371$
>
> Using Excel: rate $(i) = .11$, nper $(n) = 3$, pmt $= -\$163,685$, FV $= \$0$
>
> Using Calculator: rate $(i) = 11$, periods $(n) = 3$, pmt $= -\$163,685$, FV $= \$0$

The acquisition on January 1, 2016, is recorded as follows:

Espresso machines (+A)	399,999	
Note payable (+L)		399,999

Assets		=	Liabilities		+	Stockholders' Equity
Espresso machines	+399,999		Note payable	+399,999		

At the end of each year over the three-year life of the note, the accountant would enter the following:

December 31, 2016	Note payable (−L).	119,685	
	Interest expense (+E, −SE)	44,000*	
	Cash (−A)		163,685

*$399,999 note payable balance × 0.11 annual interest rate = $44,000.
The remaining payable balance after recording this entry is $280,314.

Assets		=	Liabilities		+	Stockholders' Equity	
Cash	−163,685		Note payable	−119,685		Interest expense (+E)	−44,000

December 31, 2017	Note payable (−L).	132,850	
	Interest expense (+E, −SE)	30,835*	
	Cash (−A)		163,685

*$280,314 note payable balance × 0.11 annual interest rate = $30,835.
The remaining payable balance after recording this entry is $147,464.

Assets		=	Liabilities		+	Stockholders' Equity	
Cash	−163,685		Note payable	−132,850		Interest expense (+E)	−30,835

December 31, 2018	Note payable (−L)............................	147,464	
	Interest expense (+E, −SE)	16,221*	
	Cash (−A).............................		163,685

*$147,464 note payable balance × 0.11 annual interest rate = $16,221.

Assets		=	Liabilities		+	Stockholders' Equity	
Cash	−163,685		Note payable	−147,464		Interest expense (+E)	−16,221

After making the last cash payment of $163,685, the balance in the notes payable account is zero.

Present Values Involving Both an Annuity and a Single Payment

In some business situations, a company may agree to make periodic payments (an annuity) in addition to a single payment at the end of the agreement. Assume Starbucks bought new coffee roasting equipment and agreed to pay the supplier $1,000 per month for 20 months and an additional $40,000 at the end of 20 months. The supplier is charging 12% interest per year, or 1% per month.

In this type of problem, you can determine the present value of the total obligation by **computing the present value of each part**. In other words, you compute the present value of the annuity and the present value of the single payment and add the two amounts together, as follows:

Step 1: Compute the present value of the annuity using Table E.2, Appendix E:

$$\$1{,}000 \times 18.04555 = \$18{,}046$$

> From Table E.2: interest rate (i) = 1%, periods (n) = 20: Factor = 18.04555
> Using Excel / Calculator: see single calculation below

Step 2: Compute the present value of the single payment using Table E.1, Appendix E:

$$\$40{,}000 \times 0.81954 = \$32{,}782$$

> From Table E.1: interest rate (i) = 1%, periods (n) = 20: Factor = 0.81954
> Using Excel / Calculator: see single calculation below

Step 3: Add the two amounts to determine the present value of the total obligation:

	$18,046	(present value of 20 months of annuity payments)
+	32,782	(present value of single sum after 20 months)
	$50,828	(present value of the total obligation)

The $50,828 is the present value of all the cash payments that Starbucks must make under this agreement. Starbucks would record this amount as a liability. This amount can be computed as a single calculation using Excel or a Calculator as follows:

> Using Excel: rate (i) = .01, nper (n) = 20, pmt = −$1,000, FV = −$40,000
> Using Calculator: rate (i) = 1, periods (n) = 20, pmt = −$1,000, FV = −$40,000

GUIDED HELP 9-2

For additional step-by-step video instruction on the present value of an annuity and a single payment, go to **www.mhhe.com/libby9e_gh9b**.

In the next chapter, we will use the present value techniques you have just learned to understand how to account for bonds.

DEMONSTRATION CASE

(Try to answer the questions before proceeding to the suggested solutions that follow.) **Patagonia** completed several transactions during the year. In each case, decide if a liability (or liabilities) should be recorded and, if so, determine the amount. Assume the current date is December 31, and all transactions occurred over the last year.

1. Employees earned salaries of $100,000, which have not been paid at year-end.

2. Patagonia borrowed $100,000 on June 30 at an annual interest rate of 7%. As of December 31, no payments associated with this loan have been made.

3. A customer prepaid $250 for a custom waterproof jacket. The customer will pick up the jacket next month.

4. The company lost a lawsuit for $250,000 but plans to appeal.

5. A new truck was leased for a period equal to 85% of the expected life of the truck.

6. On December 31, a bank loaned money to Patagonia. Patagonia agreed to repay the bank $100,000 on December 31 next year. The annual interest rate is 5%.

7. Patagonia signed a loan agreement that requires it to pay $50,000 per year for 20 years. The annual interest rate is 8%.

SUGGESTED SOLUTION

1. A liability of $100,000 should be recorded.

2. The amount borrowed ($100,000) should be recorded as a liability on June 30. In addition, interest accrued but not paid should be recorded as a liability at year-end. This amount is $100,000 × 7% × 6/12 = $3,500.

3. The amount the customer paid ($250) is a liability until the customer picks up the jacket, at which point the $250 becomes revenue.

4. Unless Patagonia can make a convincing argument that it is not probable it will have to pay the $250,000, the company should record the amount as a liability.

5. The lease covers more than 75% of the estimated life of the truck. It should therefore be accounted for as a capital lease and a liability should be recorded. The amount is the present value of the lease payments (which were not given in the problem).

6. Patagonia should record a liability equal to the present value of the obligation. Using Table E.1, Appendix E ($i = 5\%, n = 1$), the amount is $100,000 × 0.95238 = $95,238.

7. Patagonia should record a liability for the present value of the obligation. Using Table E.2, Appendix E ($i = 8\%, n = 20$), the amount is $50,000 × 9.81815 = $490,908.

Chapter Supplement A

Present Value Computations Using a Calculator or Excel

While the present value tables at the end of this book are useful for educational purposes, most present value problems in business are solved with Excel or a financial calculator. To review how to use Excel or a financial calculator to solve present value problems, go to the videos or use the information below.

Calculating Present Values Using the HP 10BII+

SAMPLE PROBLEM INPUTS:

N = Number of periods:		3
I/YR = Interest rate/period:		10%
PMT = Payments/period:		−$500
FV = Future value:		−$1,000

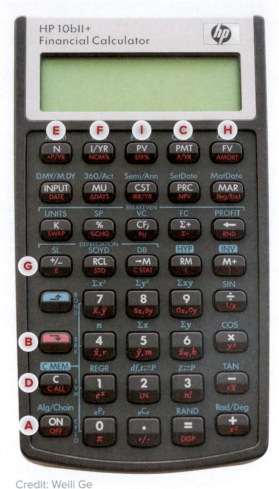

Credit: Weili Ge

Step 1: Turn on, set payments per year to 1, and clear prior inputs:

- Turn your calculator on by pressing the "ON" button (**A**)
- Press "1"
- Press the orange-colored shift key (**B**)
- Press the "P/YR" key (**C**)
- To confirm the change, press the orange-colored shift key (**B**), then press "C ALL" (**D**). You should briefly see "1 P_Yr" on your screen. This step will also clear all prior inputs from your calculator.

Step 2: Enter the number of periods:

- Press "3", then press "N" (**E**)

Step 3: Enter the interest rate per period:

- Press "10", then press "I/YR" (**F**)
- *NOTE: When using an HP 10BII+, you should enter the whole number "10" for 10%, not the decimal 0.10.*

Step 4: Enter the amount of any annuity payments:

- Press "500", then press "+/−" (**G**), then press "PMT" (**C**)
- *NOTE: If you are calculating the present value of a single amount, there are no annuity payments. When there are no annuity payments, skip STEP 4 or press "0" then press "PMT"(**C**).*

Step 5: Enter the future amount:

- Press "1,000", then press "+/−" (**G**), then press "FV" (**H**)

Step 6: Compute the present value:

- Press "PV" (**I**)

ANSWER: $1,994.74

NOTE: If you omit the annuity payment of $500 in STEP 4 and solve for the present value of a single amount ($1,000), the answer is $751.31.

Calculating Present Values Using the HP 12C

SAMPLE PROBLEM INPUTS:

N = Number of periods:	3
I/YR = Interest rate/period:	10%
PMT = Payments/period:	−$500
FV = Future value:	−$1,000

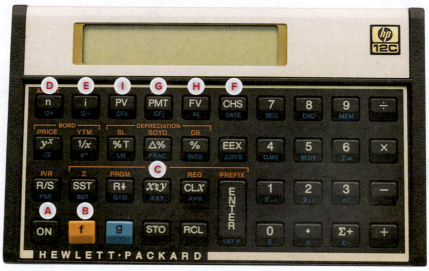

Credit: Weili Ge

Step 1: Turn on and clear prior inputs:

- Turn your calculator on by pressing the "ON" button (**A**)
- Clear inputs by pressing the orange-colored shift key (**B**), then "CLEAR FIN" (**C**)

Step 2: Enter the number of periods:

- Press "3", then press "n" (**D**)

Step 3: Enter the interest rate per period:

- Press "10", then press "i" (**E**)
- *NOTE: When using an HP 12C, you should enter the whole number "10" for 10%, not the decimal 0.10.*

Step 4: Enter the amount of any annuity payments:

- Press "500", then press "CHS" (**F**), then press "PMT" (**G**)
- *NOTE: If you are calculating the present value of a single amount, there are no annuity payments. When there are no annuity payments, skip STEP 4 or press "0", then press "PMT" (**F**).*

Step 5: Enter the future amount:

- Press "1,000", then press "CHS" (**F**), then press "FV" (**H**)

Step 6: Compute the present value:

- Press "PV" (**I**)

ANSWER: $1,994.74

NOTE: If you omit the annuity payment of $500 in STEP 4 and solve for the present value of a single amount ($1,000), the answer is $751.31.

Calculating Present Values Using Excel

SAMPLE PROBLEM INPUTS:

N = Number of periods:		3
I/YR = Interest rate/period:		10%
PMT = Payments/period:		−$500
FV = Future value:		−$1,000

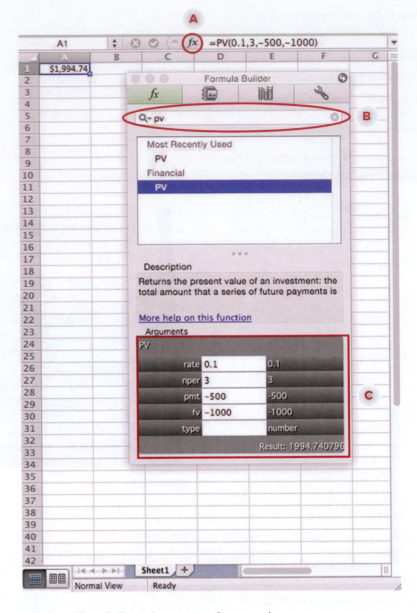

Step 1: Open the Formula Builder:

- Open Excel on your computer
- Click the "fx" function symbol (**A**) in the menu bar to open the Formula Builder

Step 2: Locate the present value (PV) formula:

- In the Formula Builder search bar (**B**), type in "PV"
- Double-click on "PV" shown in the search results

Step 3: Enter the interest rate:

- You will enter inputs directly into boxes in the Formula Builder (**C**)
- In the "rate" box enter .10
- *NOTE: When using Excel, you should enter the decimal .10 and not the whole number "10" for 10%.*

Step 4: Enter the number of periods:

- In the "nper" box enter "3"

Step 5: Enter the amount of any annuity payments:

- In the "pmt" box enter "−500"
- *NOTE: If you are calculating the present value of a single amount, there are no annuity payments. When there are no annuity payments, you would leave the "pmt" box empty or enter "0".*

Step 6: Enter the future amount:

- In the "fv" box enter "−1000"

Step 7: The last box:

- Leave the "type" box empty
- *NOTE: Entering "1" here tells Excel to assume that payments are at the beginning of the period. Entering "0" or leaving this box blank tells Excel to assume that payments are at the end of the period (which is what we want).*

ANSWER: $1,994.74

NOTE: If you omit the annuity payment of $500 in STEP 5 and solve for the present value of a single amount ($1,000), the answer is $751.31.

Chapter Supplement B

Deferred Taxes

In Chapter 8 you learned that companies follow GAAP for financial reporting but the Internal Revenue Code when creating their tax returns. Following different rules can create what are called **temporary tax differences**. Temporary tax differences are the result of a company reporting revenues and expenses on its income statement *in a different time period* than it reports them on its tax return. If the difference between financial reporting and tax reporting will result in a lower tax bill in the future, it results in the creation of an asset. If the difference will result in a higher tax bill in the future, it results in the creation of a liability. We call these assets and liabilities deferred tax assets and deferred tax liabilities. In this chapter supplement, we focus on understanding deferred tax liabilities.

A company creates a **deferred tax liability** when it:

- Reports revenue on this period's income statement that it *does not* report on its tax return until a future period, or
- Reports an expense on this period's tax return that it *does not* report on its income statement until a future period.

Both circumstances result in this period's accounting income reported on the income statement being *higher* than this period's tax income reported on the company's tax return. An example is when a company pays expenses in advance. The company is required to include the advance payment as an expense on its tax return in the period it pays the cash. For financial reporting purposes, the company is required to recognize the advance payment as an asset on its balance sheet until it actually incurs the expense in a future period. When this happens, the company then uses the asset to satisfy the expense.

Another accounting area that often results in a deferred tax liability is depreciation. Many companies use straight-line depreciation for financial reporting purposes and an accelerated depreciation method for tax purposes. Let's consider a simple example. Assume that in the current year, **Starbucks** owns a building that originally cost $10 million. The current book value (cost less accumulated depreciation) on the balance sheet is $8.5 million. For tax purposes, the book value is $6.5 million. The $2 million difference is a result of Starbucks using straight-line depreciation for financial reporting and accelerated depreciation for tax purposes. Starbucks has been able to delay or defer paying federal income taxes by reporting more depreciation on its tax return than it reports on its income statement. The amount of deferred tax liability is computed by multiplying the timing difference by the corporate tax rate (35%):

$$\textbf{Deferred Tax Liability} = \$2 \text{ million} \times .35 = \$700,000$$

If there are no other deferred tax items, Starbucks will report a deferred tax liability on its balance sheet of $700,000.

At the end of the following year, Starbucks would again compare the GAAP book value of the building to the tax book value. Assume that the GAAP book value is $8.2 million and the tax book value is $6 million. The timing difference is $2.2 million, resulting in a deferred tax liability of $770,000 ($2.2 million × .35).

The income tax expense reported under GAAP is the amount needed to complete a journal entry once the company has computed the amount it will pay the IRS for taxes and the change in its deferred taxes. Based on our example, the change in the deferred tax liability for Starbucks is $70,000 ($770,000 − $700,000). Assume the company completes its tax return and determines it owes the IRS $550,000 for taxes. The company would record the following:

Income tax expense (+E, −SE)	620,000	
Deferred taxes (+L)		70,000
Income taxes payable (+L)		550,000

Assets	=	Liabilities	+	Stockholders' Equity
		Deferred taxes +70,000		Income tax expense (+E) −620,000
		Income taxes payable +550,000		

The computation of deferred taxes involves some complexities that are discussed in advanced accounting courses. At this point, you need to understand only that deferred tax assets and liabilities are caused by temporary differences between the income statement and tax return. Each temporary difference has an impact on the income statement in one accounting period and the tax return in another.

CHAPTER **TAKE-AWAYS**

9-1. Define, measure, and report current liabilities.   p. 460

Accountants define liabilities as probable future sacrifices of economic benefits that arise from past transactions. Liabilities are classified on the balance sheet as either current or long term. Current liabilities are short-term obligations that will be paid within the current operating cycle of the business or within one year of the balance sheet date, whichever is longer. Long-term liabilities are all obligations not classified as current.

9-2. Compute and interpret the accounts payable turnover ratio.   p. 462

To compute this ratio, divide cost of goods sold by average accounts payable. This ratio reflects how quickly management is paying its suppliers and is considered to be a measure of liquidity, or a company's ability to meet its short-term obligations.

9-3. Report notes payable and explain the time value of money.   p. 466

Companies sign a note when they borrow money. The note specifies the amount borrowed, when it must be repaid, and the interest rate associated with the loan. Accountants report the amount borrowed, and any unpaid interest, as liabilities. The time value of money refers to the principle that a given amount of money is worth more today than it is in the future due to its earnings potential.

9-4. Report contingent liabilities.   p. 468

A contingent liability is a potential liability that has arisen as the result of a past event. An example is a warranty. The past event is the sale of the item. The potential liability is the possibility that the company will have to honor the warranty. Contingent liabilities are reported on the balance sheet if they can be estimated and are probable. If they are only reasonably possible, then they are reported in the footnotes.

9-5. Explain the importance of working capital and its impact on cash flows.   p. 470

Working capital is defined as current assets minus current liabilities. Working capital is used to fund the operating activities of a business. Changes in working capital accounts affect the statement of cash flows.

9-6. Report long-term liabilities.   p. 471

Any liability that is not a current liability is a long-term liability. Many long-term liabilities are reported on the balance sheet at their present value, which is the amount a company would have to pay today at a given interest rate to satisfy the obligation.

9-7. Compute and explain present values.   p. 473

The present value concept is based on the time value of money. Money received today is worth more than the same amount of money to be received in the future because of interest rates. We can compute the present value of a single amount or the present value of a stream of amounts (called an annuity) using present value tables, Excel, or a financial calculator.

9-8. Apply the present value concept to the reporting of long-term liabilities.   p. 477

A liability involves the payment of some amount at a future date. With long-term liabilities, the reported liability is not the dollar value of the future payment(s), but rather the present value of the future payment(s).

In this chapter, we focused on the reporting of current liabilities and introduced how to compute and interpret present values. In the next chapter, we discuss a firm's capital structure and how long-term liabilities, like bonds, fit into that structure.

Accounts payable turnover is a measure of how quickly a company pays its suppliers. It is computed as follows (see the "Key Ratio Analysis" box in the Current Liabilities section):

$$\text{Accounts Payable Turnover} = \frac{\text{Costs of Goods Sold}}{\text{Average Accounts Payable}}$$

FINDING **FINANCIAL INFORMATION**

Balance Sheet

Under Current Liabilities

Liabilities listed by account title, such as:
   Accounts payable
   Accrued liabilities
   Notes payable
   Current portion of long-term debt

Under Noncurrent Liabilities

Liabilities listed by account title, such as:
   Long-term debt
   Leases
   Deferred taxes
   Bonds

Statement of Cash Flows

Under Operating Activities (indirect method)
   Net income
   + Increases in current liabilities
   − Decreases in current liabilities

Under Financing Activities
   + Increases in long-term liabilities
   − Decreases in long-term liabilities

Income Statement

Liabilities are shown only on the balance sheet, never on the income statement. Transactions affecting liabilities often also affect an income statement account. For example, employee salaries earned but not yet paid affect an income statement account (salary expense) and a balance sheet account (salaries payable).

Notes

Under Summary of Significant Accounting Policies

A brief description of the accounting for certain liabilities.

Under Separate Notes

Additional details about both short-term liabilities (e.g., deferred revenue) and long-term liabilities (notes).

Additional details about contingent liabilities, especially legal issues.

KEY **TERMS**

QUESTIONS

1. Define *liability*. Differentiate between a current liability and a long-term liability.
2. What financial statement is the primary source of information about the liabilities of a company?
3. In their balance sheets, what do companies call obligations to pay suppliers in the near future?
4. What does the *accounts payable turnover ratio* tell you about a company? How is the ratio computed?
5. Define *accrued liability*. What is an example of an accrued liability?
6. Define *note payable*. When must a company reclassify a long-term note payable as a current liability?
7. On April 1 of the current year, a company borrowed $4,000 from a bank. The annual interest rate was 12%. When the company prepares its year-end financial statements on December 31, how much will it report as interest expense associated with this note?
8. Define *deferred revenue*. Why is it a liability?
9. Define *contingent liability*. What conditions must be met in order for a contingent liability to be reported on a company's balance sheet?
10. Define *working capital*. How is working capital computed?
11. When a company signs a capital lease, does it record an asset and/or a liability on its balance sheet?
12. Explain the concept of the time value of money.
13. If you hold a valid contract that will pay you $8,000 cash in 10 years and the going annual rate of interest is 10%, what is the contract's present value? Show your computations.
14. Define *annuity*.
15. Using Table E.1 in Appendix E, fill in the present value factors for the following interest rates and periods:

Present Value Factors

	$i = 5\%$	$i = 10\%$	$i = 14\%$
	$n = 4$	$n = 7$	$n = 10$
PV of $1			
PV of annuity of $1			

16. You purchased a new car and promised to pay the dealership five payments of $8,000 at the end of each of the next five years. The applicable interest rate is 8%. What is the present value of this annuity?

MULTIPLE-CHOICE QUESTIONS

1. What is the present value factor for an annuity of five periods and an interest rate of 10%?
   a. 0.62092   c. 3.79079
   b. 4.32948   d. 7.72173
2. The university golf team needs to buy a car to travel to tournaments. A dealership in Lockhart has agreed to the following terms: $4,000 down plus 20 monthly payments of $750. A dealership in Leander will agree to $1,000 down plus 20 monthly payments of $850. The local bank is currently charging an annual interest rate of 12% for car loans. Which is the better deal, *and why*?
   a. The Leander offer is better because the total payments of $18,000 are less than the total payments of $19,000 to be made to the Lockhart dealership.
   b. The Lockhart offer is better because the cost in terms of present value is less than the present value cost of the Leander offer.
   c. The Lockhart offer is better because the monthly payments are less.
   d. The Leander offer is better because the cash down payment is less.
   e. The Leander offer is better because the cost in terms of present value is less than the present value cost of the Lockhart offer.
3. Which of the following best describes *accrued liabilities*?
   a. Long-term liabilities.
   b. Current amounts owed to suppliers of inventory.

   c. Current liabilities to be recognized as revenue in a future period.
   d. Current amounts owed, but not yet paid, to various parties at the end of an accounting period.
 4. BigFish Company has borrowed $100,000 from the bank to be repaid over the next five years, with payments beginning next month. Which of the following best describes the presentation of this debt in the balance sheet as of today (the date of borrowing)?
   a. $100,000 in the Long-Term Liability section.
   b. $100,000 plus the interest to be paid over the five-year period in the Long-Term Liability section.
   c. A portion of the $100,000 in the Current Liability section and the remainder of the principal in the Long-Term Liability section.
   d. A portion of the $100,000 plus interest in the Current Liability section and the remainder of the principal plus interest in the Long-Term Liability section.
 5. A company is facing a lawsuit from a customer. It is possible, but not probable, that the company will have to pay a settlement that management estimates to be $2,000,000. How would this fact be reported in the financial statements to be issued at the end of the current month?
   a. $2,000,000 in the Current Liability section.
   b. $2,000,000 in the Long-Term Liability section.
   c. In a descriptive narrative in the footnote section.
   d. None because disclosure is not required.
 6. Which of the following transactions would usually cause accounts payable turnover to increase?
   a. Payment of cash to a supplier for merchandise previously purchased on credit.
   b. Collection of cash from a customer.
   c. Purchase of merchandise on credit.
   d. None of the above.
 7. How is working capital calculated?
   a. Current assets multiplied by current liabilities.
   b. Current assets plus current liabilities.
   c. Current assets minus current liabilities.
   d. Current assets divided by current liabilities.
 8. The present value of an annuity of $10,000 per year for 10 years discounted at 8% is what amount?
   a. $5,002   c. $53,349
   b. $67,101   d. $80,000
 9. SmallFish Company borrowed $100,000 at 8% interest for three months. How much interest does the company owe at the end of three months?
   a. $8,000   c. $800
   b. $2,000   d. $200
 10. Fred received a gift from his grandmother of $100,000. She has promised to pay Fred the $100,000 in equal installments at the end of each year for the next 10 years. Fred wants to know how much the $100,000 is worth in today's dollars. Which of the following will Fred need to calculate this amount?
   a. The anticipated interest rate and the present value of $1 table.
   b. The anticipated interest rate and the future value of $1 table.
   c. The anticipated interest rate and the future value table for annuities.
   d. The anticipated interest rate and the present value table for annuities.

MINI-EXERCISES

Understanding Liquidity

M9-1
LO9-1

Which of the following will improve liquidity?
 1. A company purchases a new truck with cash.
 2. A company receives cash from taking out a long-term loan that is due in five years.
 3. A company substantially increases credit sales and expects to collect all of the credit sales in the current account period.
 4. A company purchases inventory on credit but is having trouble selling the inventory as most of it has become obsolete.
 5. A company took out a long-term loan four years ago. The loan is due next month.

M9-2
LO9-2

Computing and Interpreting Accounts Payable Turnover

Nelson Company reported cost of goods sold of $690,000 last year and $720,000 this year. Nelson also reported accounts payable of $250,000 last year and $230,000 this year. Compute this year's accounts payable turnover ratio for Nelson. Interpret the number.

M9-3
LO9-3

Computing Interest Expense

Kieso Company borrowed $600,000 for three months. The annual interest rate on the loan was 11%. Kieso's fiscal year ends on December 31. Kieso borrowed the $600,000 one month prior to the end of its current fiscal year and paid the $600,000 plus interest back two months into its current fiscal year. In regards to this loan, how much interest expense, if any, would Kieso report at the end of its last fiscal year? At the end of its current fiscal year?

M9-4
LO9-3

Recording a Note Payable

Wygant Corporation borrowed $290,000 on October 1 last year. The note carried a 10% interest rate with the principal and interest payable on May 1 this year. Prepare the journal entry to record the note on October 1. Prepare the adjusting entry to record accrued interest on December 31, the end of Wygant's fiscal year.

M9-5
LO9-4

Reporting Contingent Liabilities

Buzz Coffee Shops is famous for its large servings of hot coffee. Last year a customer spilled a cup of hot coffee on himself and decided to file a lawsuit against Buzz for $1,000,000. Buzz's management thinks the chances of the company having to pay anything to the customer are remote. The case went to trial this year, and Buzz was found guilty of serving hot coffee in the wrong type of cup. The judge ordered Buzz to pay the customer $200,000. What is the proper reporting of the lawsuit in each year?

M9-6
LO9-5

Computing Working Capital

The balance sheet for Stevenson Corporation reported the following: noncurrent assets, $240,000; total assets, $360,000; noncurrent liabilities, $176,000; total stockholders' equity, $94,000. Compute Stevenson's working capital.

M9-7
LO9-5

Analyzing the Impact of Transactions on Working Capital

Ospry Company has working capital in the amount of $1,240,000. For each of the following transactions, determine whether working capital will increase, decrease, or remain the same.

a. Paid accounts payable in the amount of $50,000.
b. Recorded accrued salaries in the amount of $100,000.
c. Borrowed $250,000 from a local bank, to be repaid in 90 days.
d. Purchased $20,000 of new inventory on credit.

M9-8
LO9-6

Accounting for Long-Term Liabilities: Leases

StarGaze Company leased a truck for three months. Accounting guidance classifies the lease as an operating lease. StarGaze makes lease payments of $800 at the end of each month. What journal entry will StarGaze enter upon signing the lease? What journal entry will StarGaze enter when it makes its first lease payment of $800 cash to the leasing company?

M9-9
LO9-7

Computing the Present Value of a Single Payment

What is the present value of $500,000 to be paid in 10 years? The annual interest rate is 8%.

M9-10
LO9-7

Computing the Present Value of an Annuity

What is the present value of 10 equal payments of $15,000 to be made at the end of each year for the next 10 years? The annual interest rate is 10%.

Computing the Present Value of a Complex Contract

M9-11
LO9-7

Global Stores is downsizing and must let some employees go. Employees volunteering to leave are being offered a severance package of $118,000 cash, another $129,000 to be paid in one year, and an annuity of $27,500 to be paid each year for six years with the first payment coming at the end of this year. What is the present value of the total severance package, assuming an annual interest rate of 5%?

Computing Present Values and Recording Long-Term Liabilities

M9-12
LO9-8

MoonShine Company signed a note for $50,000 to purchase a new piece of equipment. MoonShine will pay the $50,000 back at the end of two years along with any accrued interest. The annual interest rate on the loan is 6%. Compute the present value of this long-term liability, and provide the journal entry Moon-Shine will record on the day it purchases the piece of equipment and signs the note.

 **EXERCISES**

Identifying Current Liabilities, Computing Working Capital, and Explaining Working Capital

E9-1
LO9-1, 9-4, 9-5

Diane Corporation is preparing its year-end balance sheet. The company records show the following selected amounts at the end of the year:

Total assets	$530,000
Total noncurrent assets	362,000
Liabilities:	
Notes payable (8%, due in 5 years)	15,000
Accounts payable	56,000
Income taxes payable	14,000
Liability for withholding taxes	3,000
Rent revenue collected in advance	7,000
Bonds payable (due in 15 years)	90,000
Wages payable	7,000
Property taxes payable	3,000
Note payable (10%, due in 6 months)	12,000
Interest payable	400
Common stock	100,000

Required:

1. Identify current liabilities and compute working capital. Why is working capital important to management?
2. Would your computation be different if the company reported $250,000 worth of contingent liabilities in the notes to its financial statements? Explain.

Recording Payroll Costs

E9-2
LO9-1

Paul Company completed the salary and wage payroll for the month of March. The payroll provided the following details:

Salaries and wages earned by employees	$200,000
Employee income taxes withheld	40,000
Employee government insurance premiums withheld	1,000
FICA payroll taxes*	15,000

$15,000 each for employer and employees.

Required:

1. Provide the journal entry to record the payroll for March, including employee deductions. Assume employees have been paid, but that Paul has yet to transfer any withholdings to the government.
2. Provide the journal entry to record the employer's payroll taxes, which have not yet been paid to the government.
3. Provide a combined journal entry to show the payment of all amounts owed to governmental agencies.

E9-3

LO9-1

Computing Payroll Costs; Discussion of Labor Costs

Oaks Company has completed the payroll for the month of January, reflecting the following data:

Salaries and wages earned	$86,000
Employee income taxes withheld	10,000
FICA payroll taxes*	6,000

*Assessed on both employer and employee (i.e., $6,000 each).

Required:

1. What was the total labor cost to the company? What was the amount of the employees' take-home pay?
2. List the liabilities and their amounts reported on the company's January 31 balance sheet, assuming the employees have been paid but that no transfers have been made to government agencies.
3. A junior accountant at Oaks stated in a meeting that giving all employees a 5% raise would have cost Oaks $4,300 ($86,000 × .05) in the month of January. Do you agree?

E9-4

LO9-1, 9-3

Recording a Note Payable through Its Time to Maturity with Discussion of Management Strategy

Many businesses borrow money during periods of increased business activity to finance inventory and accounts receivable. **Neiman Marcus** is one of America's most prestigious retailers. Each Christmas season, Neiman Marcus builds up its inventory to meet the needs of Christmas shoppers. A large portion of these Christmas sales are on credit. As a result, Neiman Marcus often collects cash from the sales several months after Christmas. Assume that on November 1 of this year, Neiman Marcus borrowed $4.8 million cash from **Bank of America** to meet short-term obligations. Neiman Marcus signed an interest-bearing note and promised to repay the $4.8 million in six months. The annual interest rate was 8%. All interest will accrue and be paid when the note is due in six months. Neiman Marcus's accounting period ends December 31.

Required:

1. Provide the journal entry to record the note on November 1.
2. Provide any adjusting entry required at the end of the annual accounting period on December 31.
3. Provide the journal entry to record payment of the note and interest on the maturity date, April 30.
4. If Neiman Marcus needs extra cash during every Christmas season, should management borrow money on a long-term basis to avoid the necessity of negotiating a new short-term loan each year?

E9-5

LO9-1, 9-3

Determining Financial Statement Effects of Transactions Involving Notes Payable

Using the data from the previous exercise, complete the following requirements.

Required:

Determine the financial statement effects for each of the following: (*a*) the issuance of the note on November 1, (*b*) the impact of the adjusting entry at the end of the accounting period, and (*c*) payment of the note and interest on April 30. Indicate the effects (e.g., cash + or −) using the format below. You do not need to include amounts, just accounts and the direction in which they are affected.

Date	Assets	Liabilities	Stockholders' Equity

Determining the Impact of Transactions, Including Analysis of Cash Flows

E9-6
LO9-1, 9-3, 9-5

Vernon Company sells a wide range of goods through two retail stores operated in adjoining cities. Vernon purchases most of the goods it sells in its stores on credit, promising to pay suppliers later. Occasionally, a short-term note payable is used to obtain cash for current use. The following transactions were selected from those occurring during the fiscal year, which ends on December 31:

a. Purchased merchandise on credit for $18,000 on January 10.
b. Borrowed $45,000 cash on March 1 from City Bank by signing an interest-bearing note payable. The note is due at the end of six months (August 31) and has an annual interest rate of 10% payable at maturity.

Required:
1. Describe the impact of each transaction on the balance sheet equation. Indicate the effects (e.g., cash + or −) using the format below. You do not need to include amounts, just accounts and the direction in which they are affected.

Date	Assets	Liabilities	Stockholders' Equity

2. What amount of cash is paid on the maturity date of the note?
3. Discuss the impact of each transaction on Vernon's cash flows.

Calculating and Explaining the Accounts Payable Turnover Ratio

E9-7
LO9-2

Skullcandy designs, markets, and distributes audio and gaming headphones, earbuds, and speakers. Last year, Skullcandy reported cost of goods sold of $158 million. This year, cost of goods sold was $117 million. Accounts payable was $23 million at the end of last year and $17 million at the end of this year.

Required:
1. For this year, compute the average number of days that Skullcandy's accounts payable are outstanding.
2. Assume Skullcandy's closest competitor reports that the average number of days that its accounts payable are outstanding is 30. Comment on Skullcandy's number relative to its competitor's number.

Reporting Notes Payable and Calculating Interest Expense

E9-8
LO9-3

North Face is one of the world's most popular outdoor apparel companies. Assume that North Face borrows $2 million from **U.S. Bank** and signs a note promising to pay the $2 million back in nine months, at which time North Face will also pay any accrued interest. The interest rate on the note is 8%.

Required:
1. Prepare the journal entry North Face will record when it signs the note and receives the cash.
2. Prepare the journal entry that North Face will record when it pays off the note and any accrued interest after nine months.

Reporting Contingent Liabilities

E9-9
LO9-4

Jones Soda is a regional soda manufacturer in the Pacific Northwest. Jones is currently facing three lawsuits, summarized below:

a. A customer is suing Jones for $1 million because he claims to have found a piece of glass in his soda. Management deems the probability that Jones will lose the lawsuit and have to pay $1 million as reasonably possible.
b. An employee is suing Jones for $500,000 for an injury she incurred in the parking lot while walking to work. Management deems the probability that Jones will lose the lawsuit as probable, but estimates that a reasonable payout will be $100,000, not $500,000.
c. A customer is suing Jones for $300,000 because her last name is Jones and she claims Jones stole her name. Management deems the probability that Jones will lose the lawsuit and have to pay $300,000 as remote.

Required:

How should Jones report each of the lawsuits in its financial statements and footnotes?

E9-10
LO9-5

Using Working Capital

Super Savers Department Store's balance sheet revealed the following information:

Current assets	$750,000
Noncurrent assets	450,000
Noncurrent liabilities	400,000
Stockholders' equity	380,000

Determine the amount of working capital reported in the balance sheet.

E9-11
LO9-6

Reporting a Long-Term Liability

McDonald's is one of the world's most popular fast-food restaurants, offering good food and convenient locations. Effective management of its properties is a key to its success. As the following note in its annual report indicates, McDonald's both owns and leases property:

> The Company owns and leases real estate primarily in connection with its restaurant business. The Company identifies and develops sites that offer convenience to customers and long-term sales and profit potential to the Company. The Company generally owns the land and building or secures long-term leases for restaurant sites, which ensures long-term occupancy rights and helps control related costs.

Required:

Should McDonald's report lease liabilities on its balance sheet? Explain. If the obligation should be reported as a liability, how should the amount be measured?

E9-12
LO9-6

Evaluating Lease Alternatives

As the new vice president for consumer products at **Whole Foods**, you are attending a meeting to discuss a serious problem associated with delivering merchandise to customers. Bob Smith, director of logistics, summarized the problem: "It's easy to understand; we just don't have enough delivery trucks given our recent growth." Barb Bader from the accounting department responded: "Maybe it's easy to understand, but it's impossible to do anything. Because of Wall Street's concern about the amount of debt on our balance sheet, we're under a freeze and can't borrow money to acquire new assets. There's nothing we can do."

On the way back to your office after the meeting, your assistant offers a suggestion: "Why don't we just lease the trucks we need? That way we can get the assets we want without having to record a liability on the balance sheet."

How would you respond to this suggestion?

E9-13
LO9-7

Computing Four Present Value Problems

On January 1 of this year, Shannon Company completed the following transactions (assume a 10% annual interest rate):

a. Bought a delivery truck and agreed to pay $60,000 at the end of three years.
b. Rented an office building and was given the option of paying $10,000 at the end of each of the next three years or paying $28,000 immediately.
c. Established a savings account by depositing a single amount that will increase to $90,000 at the end of seven years.
d. Decided to deposit a single sum in the bank that will provide 10 equal annual year-end payments of $40,000 to a retired employee (payments starting December 31 of this year).

Required (show computations and round to the nearest dollar):
1. In (a), what is the cost of the truck that should be recorded at the time of purchase?
2. In (b), which option for the office building results in the lowest present value?
3. In (c), what single amount must be deposited in this account on January 1 of this year?
4. In (d), what single sum must be deposited in the bank on January 1 of this year?

Computing a Present Value

An investment will pay $20,000 at the end of the first year, $30,000 at the end of the second year, and $50,000 at the end of the third year. Determine the present value of this investment using a 10% annual interest rate.

E9-14
LO9-7

Computing a Present Value

An investment will pay $15,000 at the end of each year for eight years and a one-time payment of $150,000 at the end of the eighth year. Determine the present value of this investment using a 7% annual interest rate.

E9-15
LO9-7

Computing a Present Value Involving an Annuity and a Single Payment

The Jenkins Corporation has purchased an executive jet. The company has agreed to pay $200,000 per year for the next 10 years and an additional $1,000,000 at the end of the 10th year. The seller of the jet is charging 6% annual interest. Determine the liability that would be recorded by Jenkins.

E9-16
LO9-6, 9-7

Computing a Present Value Involving an Annuity and a Single Payment

You have decided to buy a used car. The dealer has offered you two options:

E9-17
LO9-7

a. Pay $500 per month for 20 months and an additional $10,000 at the end of 20 months. The dealer is charging an annual interest rate of 24%.
b. Make a one-time payment of $14,906, due when you purchase the car.

In present value terms, which offer is a better deal?

Using Present Value Concepts for Decision Making

You have just won the state lottery and have two choices for collecting your winnings. You can collect $100,000 today or receive $20,000 at the end of each year for the next seven years. A financial analyst has told you that you can earn 10% on your investments. Which alternative should you select?

E9-18
LO9-7

Calculating a Retirement Fund

You are a financial adviser working with a client who wants to retire in eight years. The client has a savings account with a local bank that pays 9% annual interest. The client wants to deposit an amount that will provide her with $1,000,000 when she retires. Currently, she has $300,000 in the account. How much additional money should she deposit now to provide her with $1,000,000 when she retires?

E9-19
LO9-7

Determining an Educational Fund

Judge Drago has decided to set up an educational fund for his favorite granddaughter, Emma, who will start college in one year. The judge plans to deposit an amount in a savings account that pays 9% annual interest. He wants to deposit an amount that is sufficient to permit Emma to withdraw $20,000 for tuition starting in one year and continuing each year for a total of four years. How much should he deposit today to provide Emma with a fund to pay for her college tuition?

E9-20
LO9-7

(Chapter Supplement B) Computing Deferred Income Tax

The following information pertains to the Lewis Corporation.

E9-21
LO9-6

	Year 1	Year 2
Income taxes payable	$250,000	$290,000
Increase in deferred tax liability	54,000	58,000

Required:
1. For each year, compute income tax expense (assume that no taxes have been paid).
2. Explain why tax expense is not simply the amount of cash paid during the year.

E9-22
LO9-6

(Chapter Supplement B) Recording Deferred Income Tax

The balance sheet for Nair Corporation provided the following summarized pretax data:

	Year 1	Year 2
Deferred tax liability	$355,000	$463,000

The income statement reported tax expense for Year 2 in the amount of $580,000.

Required:
1. What was the amount of income taxes payable for Year 2?
2. Explain why management incurs the cost of maintaining separate tax and financial accounting records.

E9-23
LO9-7, FUTURE VALUES

Computing Future Values: Deposit Required and Accounting for a Single-Sum Savings Account

On January 1, Alan King decided to deposit $58,800 in a savings account that will provide funds four years later to send his son to college. The savings account will earn 8% annually. Any interest earned will be added to the fund at year-end (rather than withdrawn).

Required (show computations and round to the nearest dollar):
1. How much will be available in four years?
2. Provide the journal entry that Alan should make on January 1.
3. What is the total interest for the four years?
4. Provide the journal entry that Alan should make on (*a*) December 31 of the first year and (*b*) December 31 of the second year.

E9-24
LO9-7, FUTURE VALUES

Computing Future Values: Recording Growth in a Savings Account with Equal Periodic Payments

At the end of each year, you plan to deposit $2,000 in a savings account. The account will earn 9% annual interest, which will be added to the fund balance at year-end. The first deposit will be made at the end of Year 1.

Required (show computations and round to the nearest dollar):
1. Give the required journal entry at the end of Year 1.
2. What will be the balance in the savings account at the end of the 10th year (i.e., after 10 deposits)?
3. What is the interest earned on the 10 deposits?
4. How much interest revenue did the fund earn in the second year? In the third year?
5. Give all required journal entries at the end of the second and third years.

PROBLEMS

P9-1
LO9-1

Recording and Reporting Current Liabilities

Vigeland Company completed the following transactions during Year 1. Vigeland's fiscal year ends on December 31.

Jan.	15	Purchased and paid for merchandise. The invoice amount was $26,500; assume a perpetual inventory system.
Apr.	1	Borrowed $700,000 from Summit Bank for general use; signed a 10-month, 6% annual interest-bearing note for the money.
June	14	Received a $15,000 customer deposit for services to be performed in the future.
July	15	Performed $3,750 of the services paid for on June 14.
Dec.	12	Received electric bill for $27,860. Vigeland plans to pay the bill in early January.
	31	Determined wages of $15,000 were earned but not yet paid on December 31 (disregard payroll taxes).

Required:
1. Prepare journal entries for each of these transactions.
2. Prepare all adjusting entries required on December 31.

Recording and Reporting Current Liabilities with Discussion of Cash Flow Effects (AP9-1)

P9-2
LO9-1, 9-5

Rogers Company completed the following transactions during Year 1. Rogers's fiscal year ends on December 31.

Jan.	8	Purchased merchandise for resale on account. The invoice amount was $14,860; assume a perpetual inventory system.
	17	Paid January 8 invoice.
Apr.	1	Borrowed $35,000 from National Bank for general use; signed a 12-month, 8% annual interest-bearing note for the money.
June	3	Purchased merchandise for resale on account. The invoice amount was $17,420.
July	5	Paid June 3 invoice.
Aug.	1	Rented office space in one of Rogers's buildings to another company and collected six months' rent in advance amounting to $6,000.
Dec.	20	Received a $100 deposit from a customer as a guarantee to return a trailer borrowed for 30 days.
	31	Determined wages of $9,500 were earned but not yet paid on December 31 (disregard payroll taxes).

Required:
1. Prepare journal entries for each of these transactions.
2. Prepare all adjusting entries required on December 31.
3. What is the total amount of liabilities arising from these transactions that will be reported on the fiscal year-end balance sheet?
4. For each transaction, state whether operating cash flows increase, decrease, or are not affected.

Determining Financial Effects of Transactions Affecting Current Liabilities (AP9-2)

P9-3
LO9-1, 9-5

Using data from the previous problem, complete the following:

Required:
For each transaction (including adjusting entries) listed in the previous problem, indicate the effects (e.g., cash + or −) using the format below. You do not need to include amounts, just accounts and the direction in which they are affected.

Date	Assets	Liabilities	Stockholders' Equity

Recording and Reporting Accrued Liabilities and Deferred Revenue with Discussion of Accrual versus Cash Accounting

P9-4
LO9-1

During its first year of operations, Walnut Company completed the following two transactions. The annual accounting period ends December 31.

a. Paid and recorded wages of $130,000 during Year 1; however, at the end of Year 1, three days' wages are unpaid and have not yet been recorded because the weekly payroll will not be paid to employees until January 6 of Year 2. Wages for the three days are $4,000.
b. Collected rent revenue on December 10 of Year 1 of $2,400 for office space that Walnut rented to another company. The rent collected was for 30 days from December 10 of Year 1 to January 10 of Year 2.

Required:
1. With respect to wages, provide the adjusting entry required at the end of Year 1 and the journal entry required on January 6 of Year 2.
2. With respect to rent revenue, provide the journal entry for the collection of rent on December 10 and the adjusting entry required on December 31.

3. What is the total amount of liabilities arising from these transactions that will be reported on the balance sheet on December 31 of Year 1?
4. Explain why the accrual method of accounting provides more useful information to financial analysts than the cash method of accounting.

P9-5
LO9-1

Determining Financial Statement Effects of Transactions Involving Accrued Liabilities and Deferred Revenue

Using the data from the previous problem, complete the following:

Required:
For each transaction (including adjusting entries) listed in the previous problem, indicate the effects (e.g., cash + or −) using the format below. You do not need to include amounts, just accounts and the direction in which they are affected.

Date	Assets	Liabilities	Stockholders' Equity

P9-6
LO9-1, 9-4

Determining Financial Statement Effects of Various Liabilities (AP9-3)

Dell Computers is a leader in the computer industry with over $59 billion in sales each year. A recent annual report for Dell contained the following note:

Warranty

We record warranty liabilities at the time of sale for the estimated costs that may be incurred under our limited warranty. Factors that affect our warranty liability include the number of installed units currently under warranty, historical and anticipated rates of warranty claims on those units, and cost per claim to satisfy our warranty obligation.

1. Assume that estimated warranty costs for the current year are $500 million and that $400 million of warranty work was performed during the year. Provide the journal entries required to recognize warranty expense and the warranty services provided during the year. Assume that all warranty services were paid for with cash.

Walt Disney is a well-recognized brand in the entertainment industry with products ranging from broadcast media to parks and resorts. The following note is from a recent annual report:

Revenue Recognition

For non-expiring, multi-day tickets to our theme parks, we recognize revenue over a three-year period based on estimated usage patterns which are derived from historical usage patterns.

2. Assume that in the current year, Disney collected $90 million in multiday tickets that will be used in the future. Also in the current year, Disney estimates that $5 million worth of multiday tickets that have been sold in the past will not be used (e.g., they have been lost by customers). Provide the journal entries required to recognize (*a*) the receipt of the $90 million in cash and (*b*) the $5 million that Disney estimates will not be used.

P9-7
LO9-2

Calculating and Explaining the Accounts Payable Turnover Ratio (AP9-4)

Columbia Sportswear is an outdoor and active lifestyle apparel and footwear company. Last year, Columbia reported cost of goods sold of $941 million. This year, cost of goods sold was $1,146 million. Accounts payable was $174 million at the end of last year and $214 million at the end of this year.

Required:
1. For this year, compute the average number of days that Columbia's accounts payable are outstanding.
2. Assume the apparel and footwear industry reports an average number of days that accounts payable are outstanding of 72. Comment on Columbia's number relative to the industry average.

P9-8
LO9-3, 9-5

Analyzing the Reclassification of Debt

PepsiCo, Inc., is a dominant player in the beverage, snack food, and restaurant businesses. A recent PepsiCo annual report included the following note:

At year-end, $3.5 billion of short-term borrowings were reclassified as long-term, reflecting PepsiCo's intent and ability to refinance these borrowings on a long-term basis . . . .

As a result of this reclassification, PepsiCo's working capital improved. Do you think the reclassification was appropriate? As a financial analyst, would you use the working capital amount before the reclassification or after the reclassification to evaluate PepsiCo's liquidity?

Making Decisions about Contingent Liabilities

P9-9
LO9-4

For each of the following situations, determine whether the company should (*a*) report a liability on the balance sheet, (*b*) disclose a contingent liability in the footnotes, or (*c*) not report the situation. Justify your conclusions.

1. An automobile company introduces a new car. Past experience demonstrates that lawsuits will be filed as soon as the new model is involved in any accidents. The company can be certain that at least one jury will award damages to people injured in an accident, but it is unable to estimate the amount of any payout.
2. A research scientist determines that the company's best-selling product may infringe on another company's patent. If the other company discovers the infringement and files suit, which is unlikely, your company could lose millions.
3. As part of land development for a new housing project, your company has polluted a natural lake. Under state law, you must clean up the lake once you complete development. The development project will take five to eight years to complete. Current estimates indicate that it will cost $3 million to clean up the lake.
4. Your company has just been notified that it is being sued by a customer. The probability of the customer winning is deemed to be probable, but the amount of any loss cannot be reliably estimated.
5. A key customer is unhappy with the quality of a major construction project. The company believes that the customer is being unreasonable but, to maintain goodwill, has decided to do $250,000 in repairs next year.

Determining Cash Flow Effects (AP9-5)

P9-10
LO9-5

For each of the following transactions, determine whether cash flows from operating activities will increase, decrease, or remain the same:

a. Purchased merchandise on credit.
b. Paid an account payable in cash.
c. Accrued payroll for the month but did not pay it.
d. Borrowed money from the bank. The term of the note is 90 days.
e. Reclassified a long-term note as a current liability.
f. Paid accrued interest expense.
g. Disclosed a contingent liability based on a pending lawsuit.
h. Paid back the bank for money borrowed in (*d*). Ignore interest.
i. Collected cash from a customer for services that will be performed in the next accounting period (i.e., deferred revenues are recorded).

Computing Present Values (AP9-6)

P9-11
LO9-7, 9-8

On January 1, Boston Company completed the following transactions (use a 7% annual interest rate for all transactions):

a. Borrowed $115,000 for seven years. Will pay $6,000 interest at the end of each year and repay the $115,000 at the end of the 7th year.
b. Established a plant remodeling fund of $490,000 to be available at the end of Year 8. A single sum that will grow to $490,000 will be deposited on January 1 of this year.
c. Agreed to pay a severance package to a discharged employee. The company will pay $75,000 at the end of the first year, $112,500 at the end of the second year, and $150,000 at the end of the third year.
d. Purchased a $170,000 machine on January 1 of this year for $34,000 cash. A five-year note is signed for the balance. The note will be paid in five equal year-end payments starting on December 31 of this year.

Required (show computations and round to the nearest dollar):
1. In transaction (*a*), determine the present value of the debt.
2. In transaction (*b*), what single sum amount must the company deposit on January 1 of this year? What is the total amount of interest revenue that will be earned?
3. In transaction (*c*), determine the present value of this obligation.
4. In transaction (*d*), what is the amount of each of the equal annual payments that will be paid on the note? What is the total amount of interest expense that will be incurred?

P9-12
LO9-7

Comparing Options Using Present Value Concepts (AP9-7)

After hearing a knock at your front door, you are surprised to see the Prize Patrol from your state's online lottery agency. Upon opening your door, you learn you have won the lottery of $12.5 million. You discover that you have three options: (1) you can receive $1.25 million per year for the next 10 years, (2) you can have $10 million today, or (3) you can have $4 million today and receive $1 million for each of the next eight years. Your lawyer tells you that it is reasonable to expect to earn an annual return of 10% on investments. All else equal, which option do you prefer? What factors influence your decision?

P9-13
LO9-6

(Chapter Supplement B) Recording and Reporting Deferred Income Tax: Depreciation

Mansfield Corporation purchased a new warehouse at the beginning of Year 1 for $1,000,000. The expected life of the asset is 20 years with no residual value. The company uses straight-line depreciation for financial reporting purposes and accelerated depreciation for tax purposes (the accelerated method results in $100,000 of depreciation each year). The company's federal income tax rate is 34%. The company determined its income tax obligations for Year 1 and Year 2 were $400,000 and $625,000, respectively.

Required:
1. Compute the deferred income tax amount reported on the balance sheet for each year. Explain why the deferred income tax is a liability.
2. Compute income tax expense for each year.

P9-14
LO9-7, FUTURE VALUES

Computing Future Values of a Single Amount and an Annuity (AP9-8)

a. A friend of yours, Grace, wants to purchase a house in five years. To save for the house, Grace decides to deposit $112,000 in a savings account on January 1 of this year. The savings account will earn 6% annually. Any interest earned will be added to the fund at year-end (rather than withdrawn).

b. At the end of each year, a different friend, Claire, plans to deposit $9,000 in a savings account. The account will earn 9% annual interest, which will be added to the fund balance at year-end. Claire will make her first deposit at the end of this year.

Required (show computations and round to the nearest dollar):
1. In (*a*), how much will be available at the end of five years? What is the total interest earned over the four years?
2. In (*b*), what will be the balance in the savings account at the end of the 8th year (i.e., after 8 deposits)? What is the interest earned on the 8 deposits?

ALTERNATE PROBLEMS

AP9-1
LO9-1, 9-5

Recording and Reporting Current Liabilities with Discussion of Cash Flow Effects (P9-2)

Sturgis Company completed the following transactions during Year 1. Sturgis's fiscal year ends on December 31.

Jan.	15	Recorded tax expense for the year in the amount of $125,000. The tax liability owed to the IRS this year was $93,000. Any deferred tax liability is a current liability.
	31	Paid previously accrued interest expense in the amount of $52,000.
Apr.	30	Borrowed $550,000 from Commerce Bank; signed a 12-month, 12% annual interest-bearing note for the money.
June	3	Purchased merchandise for resale on account. The invoice amount was $75,820.
July	5	Paid June 3 invoice in full.
Aug.	31	Signed contract to provide security service to a small apartment complex and collected six months' fees in advance amounting to $12,000.
Dec.	31	Reclassified a long-term liability in the amount of $100,000 as a current liability.
	31	Determined salary and wages of $85,000 earned but not yet paid December 31 (disregard payroll taxes).

Required:

1. Prepare journal entries for each of these transactions.
2. Prepare all adjusting entries required on December 31.
3. What is the total amount of liabilities arising from these transactions that will be reported on the fiscal year-end balance sheet?
4. For each transaction, state whether operating cash flows increase, decrease, or are not affected.

Determining Financial Effects of Transactions Affecting Current Liabilities with Discussion of Cash Flow Effects (P9-3)

AP9-2
LO9-1, 9-5

Using data from problem AP9-1, complete the following:

Required:

For each transaction (including adjusting entries) listed in the previous problem, indicate the effects (e.g., cash + or −) using the format below. You do not need to include amounts, just accounts and the direction in which they are affected.

Date	Assets	Liabilities	Stockholders' Equity

Determining Financial Statement Effects of Various Liabilities (P9-6)

AP9-3
LO9-1, 9-4

Ford Motor Company is one of the world's largest companies, with annual sales of cars and trucks in excess of $144 billion. A recent annual report for Ford contained the following note:

Warranties

Estimated warranty costs are accrued for at the time the vehicle is sold to a dealer. Estimates for warranty cost are made based primarily on historical warranty claim experience.

1. Assume that this year Ford paid cash to service warranty claims in the amount of $4.0 billion. Ford also accrued expenses for warranties in the amount of $3.9 billion. If Ford had a balance in its accrued warranties account of $1.0 billion to start the year, what is the balance at the end of the year?

Bally Total Fitness Holding Corporation operates fitness centers mainly in North America. The following note was contained in a recent annual report for Bally:

Revenue Recognition

As a general principle, revenue is recognized when the following criteria are met: (i) persuasive evidence of an arrangement exists, (ii) delivery has occurred and services have been rendered, (iii) the price to the buyer is fixed or determinable and, (iv) collectability is reasonably assured. Membership revenue is earned on a straight-line basis over the longer of the contractual term or the estimated membership term. The weighted average membership life is 39 months.

2. Assume that Bally collected $23 million in December for "New Year's Resolution" memberships starting January 1 of next year. What is the amount of unearned revenue that should be reported on this year's balance sheet and next year's balance sheet associated with the $23 million?

Calculating and Explaining the Accounts Payable Turnover Ratio (P9-7)

AP9-4
LO9-2

Tootsie Roll Industries, Inc., is engaged in the manufacture and sale of confectionery products. Last year, Tootsie Roll reported cost of goods sold of $352 million. This year, cost of goods sold was $342 million. Accounts payable was $9 million at the end of last year and $12 million at the end of this year.

Required:

1. For this year, compute the average number of days that Tootsie Roll's accounts payable are outstanding.
2. Assume the confectionery products industry reports an average number of days that accounts payable are outstanding of 30. Comment on Tootsie Roll's number relative to the industry average.

Determining Cash Flow Effects (P9-10)

AP9-5
LO9-5

For each of the following transactions, determine whether cash flows from operating activities will increase, decrease, or remain the same:

a. Purchased merchandise for cash.

b. Paid salaries and wages that were earned last period, but not paid last period.

c. Paid taxes to the federal government.

d. Borrowed money from the bank. The term of the note is two years.

e. Withheld FICA taxes from employees' paychecks and immediately paid the government.

f. Recorded accrued interest expense.

g. Paid cash as the result of losing a lawsuit. A contingent liability associated with the liability had been recorded.

h. Paid salaries and wages for the current month in cash.

i. Performed services for a customer who had paid for them in the previous accounting period (i.e., deferred revenue is earned).

AP9-6
LO9-7, 9-8

Computing Present Values (P9-11)

On January 1, Ellsworth Company completed the following transactions (use an 8% annual interest rate for all transactions):

a. Borrowed $2,000,000 to be repaid in five years. Agreed to pay $150,000 interest each year for the five years.

b. Established a plant remodeling fund of $1,000,000 to be available at the end of Year 10. A single sum that will grow to $1,000,000 will be deposited on January 1 of this year.

c. Purchased a $750,000 machine on January 1 of this year and paid cash, $400,000. A four-year note is signed for the balance. The note will be paid in four equal year-end payments starting on December 31 of this year.

Required (show computations and round to the nearest dollar):

1. In transaction (*a*), determine the present value of the debt.

2. In transaction (*b*), what single amount must the company deposit on January 1 of this year? What is the total amount of interest revenue that will be earned?

3. In transaction (*c*), what is the amount of each of the equal annual payments that will be paid on the note? What is the total amount of interest expense that will be incurred?

AP9-7
LO9-7

Comparing Options Using Present Value Concepts (P9-12)

After completing a long and successful career as senior vice president for a large bank, you are preparing for retirement. Visiting the human resources office, you find that you have several retirement options: (1) you can receive an immediate cash payment of $750,000, (2) you can receive $60,000 per year for life (you have a life expectancy of 20 years), or (3) you can receive $50,000 per year for 10 years and then $80,000 per year for life (this option is intended to give you some protection against inflation). You have determined that you can earn 6% annual interest on your investments. All else equal, which option do you prefer and why?

AP9-8
LO9-7, FUTURE VALUES

Computing Future Values (P9-14)

On January 1 of Year 1, Austin Auto Company decided to start a fund to build an addition to its plant. Austin will deposit $320,000 in the fund at each year-end, starting on December 31 of Year 1. The fund will earn 9% annual interest, which will be added to the balance at each year-end. The accounting period ends December 31 of each year.

Required:
Complete the following fund accumulation schedule:

Date	Cash Payment	Interest Earned	Fund Increase	Fund Balance
Dec. 31, Year 1				
Dec. 31, Year 2				
Dec. 31, Year 3				
Total				

 **CONTINUING PROBLEM**

CON9-1 Recording and Reporting Liabilities

Pool Corporation, Inc., is the world's largest wholesale distributor of swimming pool supplies and equipment. It is a publicly traded corporation that trades on the NASDAQ exchange. The majority of Pool's customers are small, family-owned businesses. Pool Corporation completed the following transactions during the current year. Pool's fiscal year ends on December 31.

Sept.	15	Purchased and paid for merchandise for resale. The invoice amount was $125,000. Assume Pool uses a periodic inventory system.
Oct.	1	Borrowed $900,000 from Southwest Bank for general use; signed an 11-month, 5% annual interest-bearing note for the money.
Oct.	5	Received a $40,000 customer deposit from Joe Lipscomb for services to be performed in the future.
Oct.	15	Performed $18,000 of the services paid for by Mr. Lipscomb.
Dec.	12	Received electric bill for $12,000. Pool plans to pay the bill in early January.
	31	Determined wages of $52,000 earned but not yet paid on December 31 (disregard payroll taxes).

Required:

1. Prepare journal entries for each of these transactions.
2. Prepare all adjusting entries required on December 31.

 **CASES AND PROJECTS**

Annual Report Cases

Finding Financial Information

Refer to the financial statements of **American Eagle** given in Appendix B at the end of this book.

CP9-1
LO9-1, 9-2, 9-5, 9-6

Required:

1. What is the amount of accrued compensation and payroll taxes at the end of the most recent reporting year?
2. In Chapter 9 we have used the term "deferred revenue." What term does American Eagle use to reflect cash that it has received for goods or services that it will provide in the future?
3. What is the average number of days that American Eagle accounts payable are outstanding in the most recent reporting year?
4. What is the amount of long-term liabilities at the end of the most recent reporting year?

Finding Financial Information

Refer to the financial statements of **Urban Outfitters** given in Appendix C at the end of this book.

CP9-2
LO9-1, 9-2, 9-5, 9-6

Required:

1. What is the amount of accrued compensation at the end of the most recent reporting year?
2. Does Urban Outfitters report any deferred revenue? (**Hint:** You may need to look in the footnotes.)
3. What is the average number of days that Urban Outfitters accounts payable are outstanding in the most recent reporting year?
4. What is the amount of long-term liabilities at the end of the most recent reporting year?

CP9-3
LO9-2

Comparing Companies within an Industry

Refer to the financial statements of **American Eagle** (Appendix B) and **Urban Outfitters** (Appendix C) and the Industry Ratio Report (Appendix D) at the end of this book.

Required:
1. Compute the average number of days that accounts payable are outstanding for the industry.
2. Compare the average number of days that accounts payable are outstanding for American Eagle and Urban Outfitters to the average number of days that accounts payable are outstanding for the industry. Are Urban Outfitters and American Eagle paying suppliers more quickly or more slowly than the industry average?

Financial Reporting and Analysis Case

CP9-4
LO9-7

Analyzing Hidden Interest in a Real Estate Deal: Present Value

You are researching the housing market in Bloomington, Indiana, and you come upon an advertisement offering to sell a house for $240,000 with a zero interest rate mortgage. All you have to do is agree to make $4,000 payments ($240,000 ÷ 60 months) at the end of each month for five years. If you do so, the advertisement says you will not be charged any interest. When you see the offer, mortgages are typically being granted at a 6% annual interest rate.

Required:
1. If the builder demands a 6% return on investment, what is the actual value of the house? How much "implied" interest will you pay over the five years that you are paying off the house? The present value factor for an annuity with 60 periods and an interest rate of .5% (6%/12 months) is 51.72556.
2. If the builder is actually demanding a 6% return on investment, why would she advertise the mortgage as a "zero interest rate mortgage"?

Critical Thinking Case

CP9-5
LO9-7

Evaluating an Ethical Dilemma: Fair Advertising

A State Lottery Commission ran the following advertisement:

> The Lotto jackpot for this month's drawing is $10 million, which will be paid out to the winning ticket in equal installments at the end of each year over the next 20 years.

Do you agree that the lottery winner has won $10 million? If not, what amount is more accurate? State any assumptions you make.

Financial Reporting and Analysis Team Project

CP9-6
LO9-1, 9-2, 9-3,
9-4, 9-5, 9-6

Team Project: Examining an Annual Report

As a team, select an industry to analyze. Both Yahoo Finance and Google Finance provide information on any given firm's industry. Each team member should acquire the annual report or 10-K for one publicly traded company in the industry, with each member selecting a different company. The annual reports or 10-Ks can be downloaded from the SEC EDGAR website (**www.sec.gov**) or from any individual company's investor relations website.

Required:
Each team member should individually gather the information described below and attempt to answer each question. After completing this individual phase of the project, teams should get together to compare and contrast their answers to each question. At the conclusion of this discussion, each team should write a short report summarizing their analysis and findings.
1. List the accounts and amounts of the company's current liabilities for the last three years.
2. Compute the accounts payable turnover ratio for the last two years.

3. Does your company report any notes payable? If so, is the interest rate on the notes payable reported in the footnotes? What does the interest rate tell you about the risk of loaning funds to the company?

4. Does your company report any contingent liabilities on the balance sheet or in the footnotes? If so, what does the way your company reports its contingent liabilities tell you about management's beliefs about probable payment?

5. What is your company's working capital for the last three years? Any concerns?

6. List the accounts and amounts of the company's long-term liabilities for the last three years.

Reporting and Interpreting Bond Securities

In 1995, **Amazon.com** opened its virtual doors and began selling books online. The company grew rapidly and went public two years later. Today, Amazon does much more than sell books. Its mission is to be "Earth's most customer-centric company where people can find and discover virtually anything they want to buy online." Amazon has over 150,000 full-time and part-time employees worldwide and reported revenues of $89 billion in fiscal 2014. The technology and infrastructure necessary to support Amazon's growth could not have been developed without billions of dollars of investment. One of the strengths of our economic system is the ability of companies to raise large amounts of money from investors. In this chapter, we will discuss how companies raise money from investors by issuing debt securities in the bond markets. The bond markets are where companies go to sell debt securities and where investors go to purchase and trade debt securities. The debt securities purchased and traded in the bond markets are generically referred to as "bonds" by the press and investors. The companies issuing debt securities in the bond markets, however, almost always refer to these securities as "notes" in their financial statements. You will see this distinction in the Real World Excerpts in this chapter. In the next chapter we will discuss money raised from shareholders through the issuance of stock in the equity markets.

For Amazon to maintain its position as an industry leader, it must reinvest large amounts of money in its business. Last year alone, the company spent almost $5 billion building new distribution centers and purchasing new software. Like most large companies, Amazon has

Learning Objectives

After studying this chapter, you should be able to:

10-1 Describe the characteristics of bond securities.

10-2 Report bonds payable and interest expense for bond securities issued at par.

10-3 Compute and analyze the times interest earned ratio.

10-4 Report bonds payable and interest expense for bond securities issued at a discount.

10-5 Report bonds payable and interest expense for bond securities issued at a premium.

10-6 Compute and analyze the debt-to-equity ratio.

10-7 Report the early retirement of bond securities.

10-8 Explain how bond securities are reported on the statement of cash flows.

chapter 10

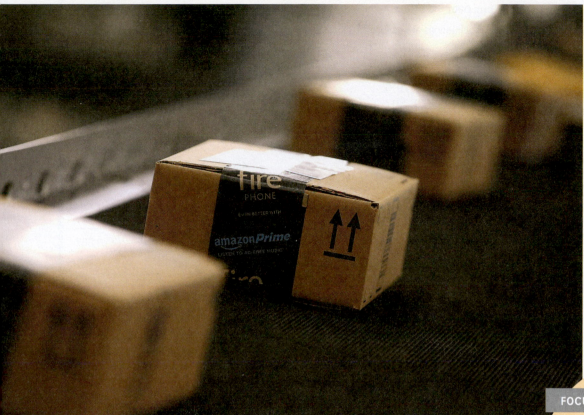

Justin Sullivan/Getty Images

raised capital to support its operations by both selling debt securities in the bond markets and issuing stock in the equity markets. Amazon has disclosed detailed information concerning its long-term debt in the note shown in Exhibit 10.1. Some of the terminology in this note will be new to you. After studying this chapter, you will understand each of the terms used in the note.

UNDERSTANDING THE BUSINESS

A company's capital structure is the mixture of debt and equity it uses to finance its operations. Almost all companies employ some debt in their capital structure, with large companies often borrowing billions of dollars. Borrowing such a large amount from an individual bank is often impractical, so companies issue bond securities (bonds) to the investing public instead. Companies are not the only entities that go to the bond markets to raise capital; governments around the world also issue bonds for the same reason.

After bond securities have been issued, they are traded on established exchanges such as the New York Bond Exchange. The ability to sell a bond on the bond exchange is a significant advantage for investors because it provides them with liquidity, or the ability to convert their investments into cash. If you lend money directly to a corporation for 20 years, you must wait that long before your cash investment is repaid. In contrast, if you lend money by purchasing a bond in the bond markets, you can always sell it to another investor if you need cash before it matures.

The liquidity associated with being able to trade debt securities in the bond markets offers an important advantage to corporations. Most investors are reluctant to lend money for long periods with no opportunity to receive cash prior to

EXHIBIT 10.1

Excerpts from Amazon's
Long-Term Debt Footnote

AMAZON

REAL WORLD EXCERPT:

Annual Report Footnotes

NOTE 6—Long-Term Debt

Total long-term debt obligations are as follows (in millions):

	December 31	
	2014	**2013**
0.65% Notes due on November 27, 2015	$ 750	$ 750
1.20% Notes due on November 29, 2017	1,000	1,000
2.50% Notes due on November 29, 2022	1,250	1,250
2.60% Notes due on December 5, 2019	1,000	
3.30% Notes due on December 5, 2021	1,000	
3.80% Notes due on December 5, 2024	1,250	
4.80% Notes due on December 5, 2034	1,250	
4.95% Notes due on December 5, 2044	1,500	
Other long-term debt	881	967
Total debt	9,881	3,967
Less current portion of long-term debt	(1,520)	(753)
Long-term debt reported on the balance sheet	$8,361	$3,214

maturity. If they do so, they demand a higher interest rate to compensate for the illiquidity. By issuing more liquid debt that investors can easily buy and sell in the bond markets, companies are able to reduce the cost of long-term borrowing.

This chapter begins with a basic overview of the characteristics of bonds before moving on to discuss accounting for bonds from issuance to maturity. The chapter closes with a discussion of the early retirement of bonds.

ORGANIZATION of the Chapter

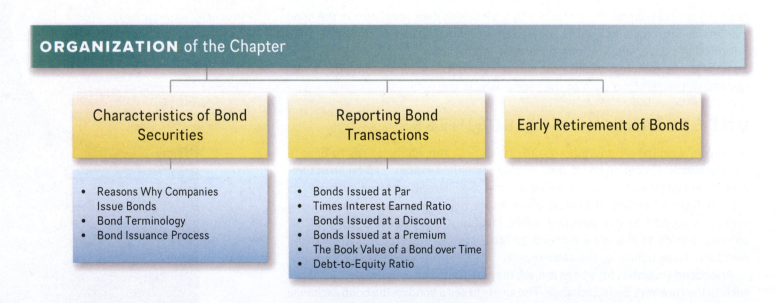

Characteristics of Bond Securities	Reporting Bond Transactions	Early Retirement of Bonds
• Reasons Why Companies Issue Bonds • Bond Terminology • Bond Issuance Process	• Bonds Issued at Par • Times Interest Earned Ratio • Bonds Issued at a Discount • Bonds Issued at a Premium • The Book Value of a Bond over Time • Debt-to-Equity Ratio	

CHARACTERISTICS OF BOND SECURITIES

Why Issue Bonds?

LEARNING OBJECTIVE 10-1

Describe the characteristics of bond securities.

Companies issue both stock and bonds to raise capital. Several reasons why a company might choose to issue bonds instead of stock include:

1. **Stockholders maintain control.** Issuing bonds allows shareholders to maintain their current level of control. Bondholders do not vote or share in any dividend payments made to shareholders.

2. **Interest expense is tax deductible.** Interest associated with bonds is tax deductible. The tax deductibility of interest reduces the net cost of borrowing. In contrast, dividends are not tax deductible.

3. **Issuing bonds can increase the return to shareholders** if a company can borrow at a low interest rate and invest in projects that earn a high rate of return. For example, assume that Drone Delivery, Inc., delivers critical medical supplies to search-and-rescue operations in remote locations. The company has shareholders' equity of $100,000 invested in various types of drone equipment and earns net income of $20,000 per year. Management plans to purchase new drones that will cost $100,000 and are expected to earn an additional $20,000 per year. To fund the purchase of the new drones, should management issue new stock or borrow the money at an interest rate of 8 percent? The following analysis shows that borrowing the money will increase the return to the company's shareholders:

	Option 1: Issue Stock	Option 2: Borrow
Income before interest & taxes	$ 40,000	$ 40,000
Interest (8% × $100,000)		8,000
Income before taxes	40,000	32,000
Income taxes (35%)	14,000	11,200
Net income	$ 26,000	$ 20,800
Stockholders' equity	$200,000	$100,000
Return on equity (income/equity)	13%	20.8%

The above example illustrates why a company might choose to issue bonds instead of stock. So what are the potential disadvantages to issuing bonds? Here are two:

1. **Risk of bankruptcy.** Interest payments to bondholders are fixed charges that must be paid each period whether the corporation earns income or incurs a loss.

2. **Negative impact on cash flows.** Bonds must be repaid at a specified time in the future. Management must be able to generate sufficient cash to repay the debt or have the ability to refinance it.

Bond Terminology

A bond usually requires the payment of interest over its life with repayment of principal on the maturity date. The **bond principal** is (1) the amount a company must pay to bondholders at the maturity date and (2) the amount used to compute the bond's periodic cash interest payments. The bond principal is also called the **face value, par value,** or **maturity value.** All bonds have a face value. For most individual bonds, the face value is $1,000, but it can be any amount.

BOND PRINCIPAL (PAR VALUE, FACE VALUE, MATURITY VALUE)
The amount a company pays bondholders on the maturity date and the amount used to compute the bond's periodic cash interest payments.

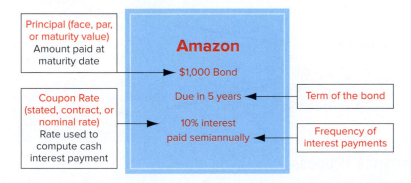

A bond always specifies a **coupon rate** (also called the **stated rate, contract rate,** or **nominal rate**) and the frequency of periodic cash interest payments. These interest payments are sometimes called coupon payments. A bond's coupon rate is always stated in annual terms. This means that, if interest is paid annually, or once per year, the periodic cash interest payment is computed simply as the bond's face value times its coupon rate. If the interest payment is made

COUPON RATE (STATED RATE, CONTRACT RATE, NOMINAL RATE)
The interest rate specified on a bond, and the rate used to compute the bond's periodic cash interest payment.

more frequently, computing the cash interest payment requires that the coupon rate be converted to a rate per interest period before it is multiplied by the bond's face value. For example, the following table reflects how a bond's cash interest payment is calculated when interest is paid annually, semiannually, and quarterly. The face value of the bond is $1,000 and the coupon rate is 8%.

Frequency of Interest Payment	Interest Rate per Interest Period	Cash Payment per Interest Period
Annual (once per year)	8% × 1 = 8%	$1,000 × 8% = $80
Semiannual (twice per year)	8% × 1/2 = 4%	$1,000 × 4% = $40
Quarterly (four times per year)	8% × 1/4 = 2%	$1,000 × 2% = $20

As shown above, if the bond pays interest annually, bondholders will receive one interest payment of $80 during the year. If the bond pays interest semiannually, bondholders will receive a $40 interest payment every six months, for a total of $80 a year. If the bond pays interest quarterly, bondholders will receive a $20 interest payment every three months, for a total of $80 a year. Note that in all cases, $80 in interest is paid per year.

Different types of bonds have different characteristics for good economic reasons. Individual investors have different risk and return preferences. A retired person may be willing to receive a lower interest rate in return for greater security. This type of investor might want a mortgage bond that pledges a specific asset as security in case the company cannot repay the bond. Another type of creditor might be willing to accept a low interest rate and an unsecured status in return for the opportunity to convert the bond into common stock at some point in the future. These types of bonds are called **convertible bonds**. Companies try to design bond features that are attractive to different groups of investors just as automobile manufacturers try to design cars that appeal to different groups of consumers. Some common types of bonds (for example, **debentures** and **callable bonds**) are shown in the illustration below.

CONVERTIBLE BONDS
Bonds that may be converted to other securities of the issuer (usually common stock).

DEBENTURE
An unsecured bond; no assets are specifically pledged to guarantee repayment.

CALLABLE BONDS
Bonds that may be called for early retirement at the option of the issuer.

Bond Type	Characteristics
Unsecured bond (or **debenture**)	No assets are pledged as a guarantee of repayment at maturity
Secured bond	Specific assets are pledged as a guarantee of repayment at maturity
Callable bond	Contains a call feature that allows the bond issuer the option of retiring the bonds early
Convertible bond	Contains a conversion feature that allows the bonds to be converted into shares of the issuer's common stock

INDENTURE
A legal document that describes all the details of a debt security to potential buyers.

PROSPECTUS
A regulatory filing that describes all the details of a debt or equity security to potential buyers.

Bond Issuance Process

When **Amazon** decides to issue securities in the bond markets, it prepares a bond **indenture** and a bond **prospectus**. The indenture is a legal document that specifies all the details of the bond offering. The prospectus is a regulatory document that is filed with the Securities and Exchange Commission. It also specifies all the details of the bond offering. These details include the maturity date, the rate of interest to be paid, the date of each interest payment, and other characteristics of the bonds, such as whether they are callable or convertible. The prospectus also describes any **covenants** designed to protect the creditors. Typical covenants include limitations on new debt that the company might issue in the future, limitations on the payment of dividends to shareholders, or requirements that the company maintain certain minimum accounting ratios, such as the current ratio or the debt-to-equity ratio. Because covenants may limit the company's future actions, management prefers those that are least restrictive. Bondholders, however, prefer more restrictive covenants, which lessen the risk of the investment. As with any business transaction, the final result is achieved through negotiation.

Besides being described in the prospectus, bond covenants are also typically reported in the notes to the financial statements. Amazon recently issued debt securities on the bond markets that do not contain any covenants and informed potential investors of this in its prospectus by stating:

> "The notes do not require us to maintain any financial ratios or specific levels of net worth, revenues, income, cash flow or liquidity and, accordingly, do not protect holders of the notes in the event that we experience significant adverse changes in our financial condition or results of operations."

The prospectus also describes to potential investors how the proceeds from the bond issuance will be used. Amazon used the money for general corporate purposes, one of which included the purchase of land for its new headquarters in Seattle.

When a bond is issued to an investor, the person receives a **bond certificate**. All bond certificates for the same bond issuance, whether an actual paper certificate or an electronic certificate, contain the same information. The certificates show the same maturity date, coupon rate, interest dates, and other characteristics. An independent party, called the **trustee**, is usually appointed to represent the bondholders. A trustee's duties are to ascertain whether the issuing company has fulfilled all provisions of the bond contract.

COVENANTS
Legally binding agreements between a bond issuer and a bondholder.

BOND CERTIFICATE
The document investors receive when they purchase bond securities.

TRUSTEE
An independent party appointed to represent the bondholders.

AMAZON
REAL WORLD EXCERPT:
Annual Report Footnotes

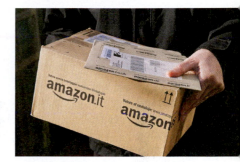

Loop Images Ltd/Alamy

Bond Rating Agencies and Their Assessments of Default Risk

FINANCIAL ANALYSIS

Because of the large amount of money involved and the complexities associated with bonds, several agencies exist to evaluate the risk that a bond issuer will not be able to meet the requirements specified in the prospectus. This risk is called **default risk.** Standard & Poor's, Moody's, and Fitch use letter ratings to specify the quality of a bond. Higher-quality bonds have lower default risk, as shown in the table below. Many banks, mutual funds, and trusts are permitted to invest only in investment-grade bonds.

Standard & Poor's	Moody's	Fitch	Description	Risk
AAA	Aaa	AAA	Highest investment grade	**Low risk**
AA	Aa	AA		
A	A	A		
BBB	Baa	BBB	Lowest investment grade	
BB	Ba	BB	Highest junk bond grade	
B	B	B		
CCC	Caa	CCC		
CC	Ca	CC		
C	C	C		
D	C	DDD	In default or unrated	**High risk**

REPORTING BOND TRANSACTIONS

When **Amazon** issued its bonds, it specified two types of cash payments in the bond contract:

1. **Principal.** As noted in the previous section, this amount is usually a single payment that is made at the end of the bond's life. It is also called the **par value, face value,** or **maturity value.**

2. **Cash interest payments.** These payments, which are sometimes referred to as **coupon payments,** represent an annuity and are computed by multiplying the bond's face value times the coupon rate. The bond contract specifies whether the interest payments are made quarterly, semiannually, or annually. When you are asked to work problems in which interest payments are made more frequently than once a year, be sure and use the interest rate per period in your calculations. For example, consider a bond with the following characteristics:

- Face value: $1,000
- Term: 10 years
- Coupon rate: 6% (annual)
- Interest paid: Semiannually (twice a year)

If you are asked to compute the cash interest payment for this bond, you will need to use an interest rate per period of 3 percent (the semiannual coupon rate). The calculation is:

- Cash interest payment: $30 ($1,000 × 6% × ½ year)

The issuing company does not determine the price at which the bonds sell. Instead, the market determines the price using the present value concepts introduced in the last chapter. To determine the present value of the bond, you compute the present value of the principal (a single payment) and the present value of the interest payments (an annuity) and add the two amounts together.

Investors demand a certain rate of return to compensate them for the risks related to a particular company's bond offering. The demanded rate of return is called the **market interest rate** (also known as the **yield** or **effective interest rate**). Because the market rate is the interest rate investors demand on the day the bonds are issued, it is the rate that should be used in computing the present value of a bond.

On the day a company issues a bond, the market interest rate will either be the same as the coupon rate, greater than the coupon rate, or less than the coupon rate. The relationship between the market interest rate and the bond's coupon rate determines whether the bond is issued at par, at a **premium,** or at a **discount.** When the market interest rate equals the coupon rate, the bond sells at par; when the market interest rate is greater than the coupon rate, the bond sells at a discount; and when the market interest rate is less than the coupon rate, the bond sells at a premium. This relationship can be shown graphically as follows:

In commonsense terms, when a bond's coupon rate is less than the rate investors demand, investors will not buy the bond unless its price is reduced (i.e., a discount must be provided). When a bond's coupon rate is more than investors demand, investors will be willing to pay a premium to buy the bond.

It is important to keep in mind that regardless of whether a bond is issued at par, at a discount, or at a premium, investors will always earn the market rate of return. To illustrate, consider a company that issues three separate bonds on the same day. The bonds are the same except that one has a coupon rate of 8 percent, another a rate of 10 percent, and a third a rate of 12 percent. If the market rate of interest is 10 percent on the date all three bonds are issued, the

---

MARKET INTEREST RATE (YIELD, EFFECTIVE INTEREST RATE)
The rate of return investors demand for a company's bonds on the date the bonds are issued, and the rate used to compute the bond's interest expense each period.

BOND PREMIUM
The difference between the selling price of a bond and the bond's face value when the bond is sold for more than par.

BOND DISCOUNT
The difference between the selling price of a bond and the bond's face value when the bond is sold for less than par.

first bond will be issued at a discount, the second at par, and the third at a premium. As a result, an investor who purchases any one of the bonds will earn the market interest rate of 10 percent.

During the life of the bond, its market price will change as market interest rates change. While this information is reported in the financial press, it does not affect the company's financial statements and the way its interest payments are accounted for from one period to the next. The interest rates that matter for accounting purposes are the bond's **coupon rate** (which does not change over time) and the **market interest rate on the day the bond is issued.**

Bond Information from the Business Press	FINANCIAL ANALYSIS

Bond prices are reported each day in the business press based on transactions that have occurred on the bond exchange. Though formats differ across news outlets, the following is typical of the information you will find:

Issuer	Coupon (%)	Maturity	Current ($)	Yield (%)
Apple	3.45	2024	101.29	3.29
Amazon	2.50	2022	94.92	3.20
Walmart	3.30	2024	101.36	3.13

The above reflects that the Amazon bond pays a coupon rate of 2.5 percent, will mature in the year 2022, and is currently selling for $94.92. The bond's "yield" reflects that investors who purchase the bond at its current price and hold it to maturity will earn a return on their investment of 3.2 percent.

It is important to remember that the current price listed above does not affect Amazon's financial statements—Amazon is not a part of the transaction when one investor decides to sell his or her bond to another investor. For financial reporting purposes, Amazon uses the market interest rate that existed when the bonds were first issued to the public.

In the next section of this chapter, we will see how to account for bonds issued at par, at a discount, and at a premium.

PAUSE FOR FEEDBACK STOP

SELF-STUDY QUIZ

Before we move on, it is important that you understand the new terminology introduced in this chapter. Let's review some of the terms. Define the following:

1. Market interest rate.
2. Synonyms for *market interest rate.*
3. Coupon rate.
4. Synonyms for *coupon rate.*
5. Bond discount.
6. Bond premium.

After you have completed your answers, check them below.

Solutions to

SELF-STUDY QUIZ

1. The market interest rate is the interest rate demanded by investors for a bond at the time the bond is issued. It is the rate investors use in their present value computations to determine how much they will pay for the bond.
2. The market interest rate is also called a bond's *yield* or its *effective interest rate.*
3. Coupon rate is a bond's stated interest rate.
4. Coupon rate is also called the *stated rate, contract rate,* or *nominal rate.*
5. A bond that sells for less than its face value is sold at a discount. This occurs when the coupon rate is less than the market interest rate.
6. A bond that sells for more than its face value is sold at a premium. This occurs when the coupon rate is greater than the market interest rate.

Bonds Issued at Par

Bond Contract	Market Rate	Bond Price
Coupon rate is 10%	Exactly 10%	Par

Bonds sell at their face (par) value when the market interest rate that investors demand is equal to the interest rate stated in the bond contract, or the **coupon rate.** To illustrate, let's assume that on January 1, 2016, **Amazon** issues bonds with a coupon rate of 10 percent and a face value of $100,000. On the date of issuance, investors are willing to pay Amazon $100,000 in cash (which means that the bonds are being sold at par). The bonds start accruing interest on January 1, 2016, and will pay interest each June 30 and December 31. The bonds mature in two years on December 31, 2017.

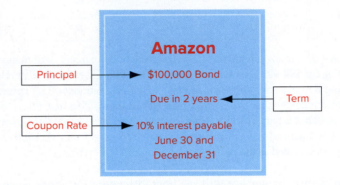

The amount of money a company receives when it sells bonds is the present value of the future cash flows associated with the bonds. In issuing the bonds described above, Amazon agrees to make two types of payments in the future: a single payment of $100,000 when the bond matures in two years and an annuity of $5,000 [$100,000 × (10% × ½ year)] payable twice a year for two years. The 10% in the above equation is the bond's coupon rate. The bond payments can be shown graphically as follows:

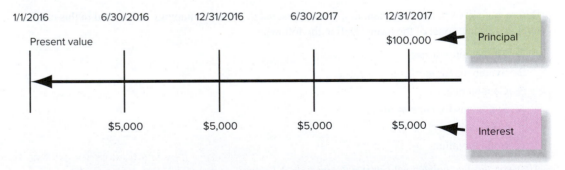

We use the bond's market interest rate per period (in this case 10% ÷ 2 = 5%) to compute the bond's present value. As we discussed in the previous chapter, the present value of the bond payments can be computed using Excel, a financial calculator, or the tables in Appendix E:

	Present Value
Single principal payment at maturity: $100,000 × 0.82270	$ 82,270
+ Annuity cash interest payment: $5,000 × 3.54595	17,730
Issue (sale) price of bonds	$ 100,000

> From Table E.1: interest rate (i) = 5%, periods (n) = 4: Factor = 0.82270
>
> From Table E.2: interest rate (i) = 5%, periods (n) = 4: Factor = 3.54595
>
> Using Excel: rate (i) = .05, nper (n) = 4, pmt = −$5,000, FV = −$100,000
>
> Using Calculator: rate (i) = 5, periods (n) = 4, pmt = −$5,000, FV = −$100,000

When the market rate of interest equals the coupon rate, the present value of the future cash flows associated with a bond always equals the bond's face value amount. Remember a bond's selling price is determined by the present value of its future cash flows, not the face value. On the date Amazon issues the bonds, it records a bond liability equal to the amount investors are willing to pay for the bonds:

Cash (+A)	100,000	
Bonds payable (+L)		100,000

Assets		=	Liabilities		+	Stockholders' Equity
Cash	+100,000		Bonds payable	+100,000		

Bonds may pay interest each month, each quarter, each half-year, or each year. In all cases, to determine the bond's selling price, you would determine the present value of the bond's cash flows using the number of interest periods in the bond's life as well as the market interest rate per period.

PAUSE FOR **FEEDBACK**

SELF-STUDY **QUIZ**

Assume that **Amazon** issues bonds with a face value of $500,000 that will mature in two years. The bonds pay interest at the end of each year. On the date of issuance, the coupon rate and market rate of interest are the same: 8 percent. Compute the selling price of the bonds.

After you have completed your answer, check it below.

Reporting Interest Expense for Bonds Issued at Par

Continuing with our example, the investors who bought the Amazon bonds did so with the expectation that they would earn interest over the life of the bond. Amazon will pay interest at 10 percent per year on the face value of the bonds each June 30 and December 31 until the bond's maturity date. The amount of interest each period will be $5,000 ($100,000 × 0.10 × ½ year). The entry to record each interest payment is as follows:

Interest expense (+E, −SE)	5,000	
Cash (−A)		5,000

Assets		=	Liabilities	+	Stockholders' Equity	
Cash	−5,000				Interest expense (+E)	−5,000

Solution to
SELF-STUDY QUIZ

$500,000 × 0.85734 = $428,670

($500,000 × 0.08) × 1.78326 = <u> 71,330</u>

= $500,000

Interest expense is reported on the income statement. Because interest is related to financing activities rather than operating activities, it is normally not included in operating expenses on the income statement. Instead, interest expense is typically reported just below "income from operations" on the income statement. A portion of the income statement for Amazon shows how interest expense is usually reported.

AMAZON

REAL WORLD EXCERPT:

Partial Income Statement

AMAZON.COM, INC.
CONSOLIDATED STATEMENTS OF INCOME
(in millions, except per share data)

| | Year Ended December 31 | | |
	2014	2013	2012
…			
Income from operations	178	745	676
Interest income	39	38	40
Interest expense	(210)	(141)	(92)
Other income (expense), net	(118)	(136)	(80)
Total non-operating income (expense)	(289)	(239)	(132)
Income before income taxes	(111)	506	544
…			

Bond interest payment dates rarely coincide with the last day of a company's fiscal year. Under the expense recognition principle introduced in Chapter 3, interest expense that has been incurred but not paid must be accrued at the end of the accounting period. If Amazon's fiscal year ended on May 31 instead of December 31, the company would accrue interest for five months and report that amount as interest expense on its income statement and the same amount as interest payable on its balance sheet.

Because interest payments are a legal obligation for the borrower, financial analysts want to be certain that a business is generating sufficient resources to meet its interest obligations. The times interest earned ratio is useful when making this assessment.

KEY RATIO ANALYSIS	Times Interest Earned

LEARNING OBJECTIVE 10-3

Compute and analyze the times interest earned ratio.

? ANALYTICAL QUESTION

Is **Amazon** generating sufficient resources from its profit-making activities to meet its current interest obligations?

% RATIO AND COMPARISONS

The times interest earned ratio is computed as follows:

$$\text{Times Interest Earned} = \frac{\text{Net Income} + \text{Interest Expense} + \text{Income Tax Expense}}{\text{Interest Expense}}$$

The 2014 ratio for Amazon (dollars in millions):

$$[\$(241) + \$210 + \$167] \div \$210 = 0.65$$

COMPARISONS OVER TIME			COMPARISONS WITH COMPETITORS	
Amazon			eBay	Walmart
2014	**2013**	**2012**	**2014**	**2014**
0.7	4.1	5.2	26.8	3.3

🔍 INTERPRETATIONS

In General   Analysts view a high times interest earned ratio more favorably than a low one. The ratio shows the amount of income earned for each dollar of interest expense. A high ratio indicates an extra margin of protection in case profitability deteriorates. Analysts are particularly interested in a company's ability to meet its required interest payments because failure to do so could result in bankruptcy.

Focus Company Analysis   In 2014, profit-making activities for Amazon generated only $0.65 for each dollar of interest. The ratio has declined over time for two reasons: Net income has decreased over time, while interest expense has increased. Given the sharp decline over time, analysts are likely keeping an eye on Amazon's times interest earned ratio. **eBay** and **Walmart** both have higher ratios, indicating a safer margin of error with respect to their ability to pay interest with earnings generated during the period.

A Few Cautions   The times interest earned ratio is often misleading for new or rapidly growing companies, which tend to invest considerable resources to build their capacity for future operations. In such cases, the times interest earned ratio will reflect significant amounts of interest expense associated with borrowing to support expansion plans but not the future income that will likely come from expanding. For this reason, analysts should consider the company's long-term strategy when interpreting this ratio.

Bonds Issued at a Discount

Bonds sell at a discount when the market interest rate is greater than the coupon rate. To illustrate, let's assume that the market interest rate is 12 percent on January 1, 2016, when **Amazon** sells its bonds (which have a face value of $100,000). The bonds mature in two years and have a coupon rate of 10 percent. Interest is payable twice a year on June 30 and December 31. Because the coupon rate (10 percent) is less than the market interest rate (12 percent) on the date of issuance, the bonds sell at a discount.

   To compute what investors will be willing to pay for the bonds given the difference in interest rates, we can use the tables in Appendix E. As in the previous example, the number of periods is four and the interest rate is the market interest rate per period; in this case 6 percent (12% × ½ year). With this information, we can compute the cash issue price of the Amazon bonds as follows:

	Present Value
Single principal payment at maturity:	
$100,000 × 0.79209	$79,209
+ Annuity cash interest payment: $5,000 × 3.46511	17,326
Issue (sale) price of bonds	$96,535

> From Table E.1: interest rate $(i) = 6\%$, periods $(n) = 4$: Factor $= 0.79209$
>
> From Table E.2: interest rate $(i) = 6\%$, periods $(n) = 4$: Factor $= 3.46511$
>
> Using Excel: rate $(i) = .06$, nper $(n) = 4$, pmt $= -\$5,000$, FV $= -\$100,000$
>
> Using Calculator: rate $(i) = 6$, periods $(n) = 4$, pmt $= -\$5,000$, FV $= -\$100,000$

Thus, if the market interest rate is 12 percent on the date of issuance, investors will be willing to pay Amazon $96,535 for the bonds. Some people refer to this price as 96.5, which indicates the selling price was 96.5 percent of the bond's face value (96.5 = $96,535 ÷ $100,000)

There are two acceptable methods for recording a bond that is sold at a discount; both result in the same dollar value being reported on a company's balance sheet. The first method *explicitly* keeps track of the bond discount by incorporating it into the journal entries. The second method *implicitly* keeps track of the bond discount but does not incorporate it into the journal entries. Regardless of the method used, the dollar value reported on the balance sheet (the bond payable book value) is identical, as shown in the example below. Using both methods, the journal entries to record the sale of Amazon's bonds issued at a discount are:

WITH DISCOUNT ACCOUNT			WITHOUT DISCOUNT ACCOUNT		
Cash (+A)	96,535		Cash (+A)	96,535	
Bond discount (+XL, −L)	3,465		Bonds payable (+L)		96,535
Bonds payable (+L)		100,000			

Assets	=	Liabilities	+	Stockholders' Equity		Assets	=	Liabilities	+	Stockholders' Equity
Cash +96,535		Bonds payable +100,000				Cash +96,535		Bonds payable +96,535		
		Bond discount −3,465								

Bonds payable book value: **$96,535**
($100,000 − $3,465)

Bonds payable book value: **$96,535**

Bond discount is a contra-liability account, which is why it is debited in the journal entry above and shown as a negative number under liabilities. This account is not separately disclosed on Amazon's balance sheet. Instead, the balance sheet reports the bonds payable at its book value ($96,535), which is the face value of the bonds less the unamortized discount ($100,000 − $3,465). Note that reporting bonds payable at their book value results in the same amount being reported on the balance sheet ($96,535), regardless of whether a bond discount is explicitly recorded in the journal entry.

While Amazon received only $96,535 when it sold the bonds, it must repay $100,000 when the bonds mature. The $3,465 of additional cash that Amazon must pay at maturity is incrementally reflected in interest expense and added to the book value of the liability each period over the life of the bond. This causes interest expense to reflect the **market interest rate** (also referred to as the **effective interest rate**), while the cash being paid to bondholders each period reflects the **coupon rate.** The accounting method used to record interest expense is referred to as the **effective-interest amortization** method.

Throughout the remainder of Chapter 10 we use the bond discount account in all journal entries. **We duplicate the text and show all journal entries** *without the bond discount account* **in the Chapter Supplement at the end of the chapter.**

EFFECTIVE-INTEREST AMORTIZATION

A method of amortizing a bond discount or bond premium that reflects the effective interest rate a company pays bondholders over the life of a bond.

Reporting Interest Expense on Bonds Issued at a Discount Using Effective-Interest Amortization (with Discount Account)

Under the effective-interest amortization method, a company computes interest expense in a given period by multiplying the bonds payable book value times the market rate of interest on the date of issuance. When bonds are issued at a discount, using a market interest rate that is greater than the coupon rate results in interest expense each period being greater than the cash owed for interest each period. The difference between interest expense and the cash owed for interest is the amount of the bond discount amortized during the period. This process can be summarized as follows:

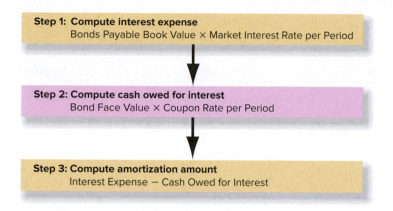

Step 1: Compute interest expense
Bonds Payable Book Value × Market Interest Rate per Period

Step 2: Compute cash owed for interest
Bond Face Value × Coupon Rate per Period

Step 3: Compute amortization amount
Interest Expense − Cash Owed for Interest

Recall that the cash owed for interest is computed by multiplying the bond's face value ($100,000) by the coupon rate per period (10% × ½ year). Thus, Amazon owes bondholders cash of $5,000 each June 30 and again on December 31. The first interest payment on the bonds is made on June 30, 2016. Following the three steps outlined above, interest expense and the amount of the bond discount amortized are:

Step 1: Interest expense: $96,535 × (0.12 × ½ year) = **$5,792**

Step 2: Cash owed for interest: $100,000 × (0.10 × ½ year) = **$5,000**

Step 3: Amortized amount: $5,792 − $5,000 = **$792**

The journal entry Amazon would enter is:

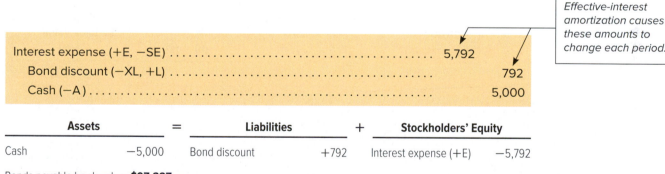

Effective-interest amortization causes these amounts to change each period.

Interest expense (+E, −SE)	5,792	
Bond discount (−XL, +L)		792
Cash (−A)		5,000

Assets		=	Liabilities		+	Stockholders' Equity	
Cash	−5,000		Bond discount	+792		Interest expense (+E)	−5,792

Bonds payable book value: **$97,327**
($100,000 − $3,465 + $792)

Each period, the amortization of the bond discount increases the bond's book value, bringing it closer to the $100,000 that is due at maturity. The amortization of the bond discount can be thought of as the amount of interest earned by the bondholders in a given period that will be paid to them when the bonds mature. During the first interest period, Amazon's bondholders earned interest of $5,792 but received only $5,000 in cash. The additional $792 was added to the book value of the bond and will be paid to bondholders when the bonds mature.

Interest expense for the next interest period must reflect the change in the bonds payable book value. Amazon calculates interest expense for the second half of 2016 by multiplying the bonds payable book value on June 30, 2016 ($97,327) by the market rate of interest per period [$97,327 × (12% × ½ year) = $5,840]. With interest expense equal to $5,840 and cash owed for interest equal to $5,000, the amount of the bond discount amortized on December 31, 2016, is $840:

Interest expense (+E, −SE)	5,840	
Bond discount (−XL, +L)		840
Cash (−A)		5,000

Assets		=	Liabilities		+	Stockholders' Equity	
Cash	−5,000		Bond discount	+840		Int. expense (+E)	−5,840

Bonds payable book value: **$98,167**
($100,000 − $3,465 + $792 + $840)

Notice that interest expense for December 31, 2016, is more than interest expense for June 30, 2016. Amazon effectively borrowed more money during the second half of the year because of the unpaid interest accrued during the first half of the year. Because of the amortization of the bond discount, the book value of the bond and interest expense **increase** each year during the life of the bond. This process can be illustrated with the amortization schedule shown below:

BOND DISCOUNT AMORTIZATION SCHEDULE

Date	(a) Cash Owed for Interest	(b) Interest Expense	(c) Amortization of Bond Discount	(d) Bonds Payable Book Value
	$100,000 × (10% × ½ year)	Beginning of Period Book Value × (12% × ½ year)	(b) − (a)	Beginning Book Value + (c)
01/01/2016				$ 96,535
06/30/2016	$5,000	$5,792	$792	97,327
12/31/2016	5,000	5,840	840	98,167
06/30/2017	5,000	5,890	890	99,057
12/31/2017	5,000	5,943	943	100,000

Coupon rate (10%)

Market interest rate (12%)

Note that:

- Cash owed for interest (column a) is computed by multiplying the bond's face value by the coupon rate per period.

- Interest expense (column b) is computed by multiplying the book value of the bonds at the beginning of the period (column d) by the market interest rate. Note that the book value of a bond at the beginning of a period is the book value of the bond at the end of the previous period.

- Amortization of the bond discount is computed by subtracting cash owed for interest (column a) from interest expense (column b).

- The new book value of the bonds (column d) is computed by adding amortization of the bond discount (column c) to the book value at the beginning of the period.

In summary, under the effective-interest amortization method, interest expense changes each accounting period as the effective amount of the liability changes.

PAUSE FOR FEEDBACK STOP

SELF-STUDY QUIZ

Assume that **Amazon** issued bonds with a face value of $100,000 and a coupon rate of 5 percent. The bonds mature in 10 years and pay interest annually. The bonds were sold when the annual market interest rate was 6 percent at a price of $92,640.

1. What amount of cash was owed for interest at the end of the first year?
2. Using the effective-interest amortization method, what amount of interest expense would Amazon report at the end of the first year?

After you have completed your answers, check them below.

Bonds Issued at a Premium

Bond Contract   **Market Rate**   **Bond Price**

Coupon rate is 10% → Less than 10% → Premium

LEARNING OBJECTIVE 10-5
Report bonds payable and interest expense for bond securities issued at a premium.

Recall that bonds sell at a **discount** when the market interest rate is greater than the bond's coupon rate. When the market interest rate is less than the bond's coupon rate, the bonds sell at a premium. To demonstrate how to account for bonds issued at a **premium**, let's use the same **Amazon** example as before but assume that the market interest rate is now 8 percent while the coupon rate remains the same, at 10 percent. Like before, the bonds are issued on January 1, 2016; pay interest semiannually; and mature in two years.

The present value of the bonds described above can be computed from the tables contained in Appendix E using the factor for four periods and an interest rate of 4 percent per period (8% × ½ year):

	Present Value
Single principal payment at maturity: $100,000 × 0.85480	$ 85,480
+ Annuity cash interest payment: $5,000 × 3.62990	18,150
Issue (sale) price of bonds	$103,630

From Table E.1: interest rate (i) = 4%, periods (n) = 4: Factor = 0.85480

From Table E.2: interest rate (i) = 4%, periods (n) = 4: Factor = 3.62990

Using Excel: rate (i) = .04, nper (n) = 4, pmt = −$5,000, FV = −$100,000

Using Calculator: rate (i) = 4, periods (n) = 4, pmt = −$5,000, FV = −$100,000

---

1. Cash owed for interest: $100,000 × 5% = **$5,000**
2. Interest expense: $92,640 × 6% = **$5,558**

Accounting for bonds issued at a premium is similar to accounting for bonds issued at a discount. Companies can explicitly use a bond premium account in their journal entries or implicitly keep track of the premium amount. We show both side-by-side below, and then, as we did with bond discounts, we present all subsequent journal entries using a bond premium account. **We duplicate the text and show all journal entries *without the bond premium account* in the Chapter Supplement at the end of the chapter.** The January 1, 2016, issuance of Amazon's bonds at a premium would be recorded as follows:

WITH PREMIUM ACCOUNT		WITHOUT PREMIUM ACCOUNT	
Cash (+A) 103,630		Cash (+A) 103,630	
Bond premium (+XL, +L)	3,630	Bonds payable (+L)..................	103,630
Bonds payable (+L)..................	100,000		

Assets	=	Liabilities		+	Stockholders' Equity		Assets	=	Liabilities		+	Stockholders' Equity
Cash +103,630		Bonds payable	+100,000				Cash +103,630		Bonds payable	+103,630		
		Bond premium	+3,630									

Bonds payable book value: **$103,630**
($100,000 + $3,630)

Bonds payable book value: **$103,630**

Like the bond discount account, the bond premium account is not separately disclosed on Amazon's balance sheet. Instead, the balance sheet reports the bonds payable at their book value ($103,630), which is their face value plus the unamortized premium ($100,000 + $3,630). Note that reporting bonds payable at their book value results in the same amount being reported on the balance sheet ($103,630), regardless of whether a bond premium is explicitly recorded in the journal entry.

Reporting Interest Expense on Bonds Issued at a Premium Using Effective-Interest Amortization (with Premium Account)

As with the discount account, the recorded premium of $3,630 must be apportioned to each interest period so that interest expense reflects the market (effective) interest rate that Amazon is actually paying. To compute interest expense and the amount of the premium to be amortized each period, we follow the same three steps that we followed to compute these amounts when the bonds were issued at a discount:

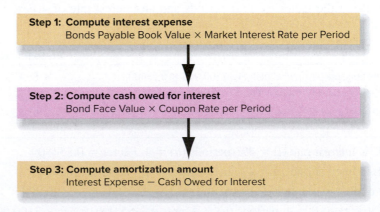

Step 1: Compute interest expense
Bonds Payable Book Value × Market Interest Rate per Period

Step 2: Compute cash owed for interest
Bond Face Value × Coupon Rate per Period

Step 3: Compute amortization amount
Interest Expense − Cash Owed for Interest

Step 1: Interest expense: $103,630 × (0.08 × ½ year) = $4,145

Step 2: Cash owed for interest: $100,000 × (0.10 × ½ year) = $5,000

Step 3: Amortized amount: $4,145 − $5,000 = −$855

The journal entry Amazon would enter is:

Interest expense (+E, −SE) 4,145	
Bond premium (−XL, −L) 855	
Cash (−A)	5,000

Assets		=	Liabilities		+	Stockholders' Equity	
Cash	−5,000		Bond premium	−855		Interest expense (+E)	−4,145

Bonds payable book value: **$102,775**
($100,000 + $3,630 − $855)

The basic difference between effective-interest amortization of a bond discount and a bond premium is that the amortization of a discount **increases** the book value of the liability and the amortization of a premium **decreases** it. Both serve the same purpose: to bring the liability to the bond's face value at the maturity date. The following schedule illustrates the amortization of a premium over the life of a bond.

BOND PREMIUM AMORTIZATION SCHEDULE

Date	(a) Cash Owed for Interest	(b) Interest Expense	(c) Amortization of Bond Premium	(d) Bonds Payable Book Value
	$100,000 × (10% × ½ year)	Beginning of Period Book Value × (8% × ½ year)	(b) − (a)	Beginning Book Value + (c)
01/01/2016				$103,630
06/30/2016	$5,000	$4,145	$(855)	102,775
12/31/2016	5,000	4,111	(889)	101,886
06/30/2017	5,000	4,075	(925)	100,961
12/31/2017	5,000	4,039*	(961)	100,000

*Rounded

Regardless of whether a company issues bonds at par, at a discount, or at a premium, the company will enter the same journal entry when the bonds mature. For our Amazon example, the journal entry would be:

Bonds payable (−L) 100,000	
Cash (−A)	100,000

Assets		=	Liabilities		+	Stockholders' Equity	
Cash	−100,000		Bonds payable	−100,000			

STOP PAUSE FOR **FEEDBACK**

SELF-STUDY **QUIZ**

Assume that **Amazon** issued bonds with a face value of $100,000 and a coupon rate of 9 percent. The bonds mature in 10 years and pay interest annually. The bonds were sold when the annual market interest rate was 8 percent at a price of $106,710.

1. What amount of cash was owed for interest at the end of the first year?
2. Using the effective-interest amortization method, what amount of interest expense would Amazon report at the end of the first year?

After you have completed your answers, check them below.

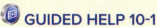 **GUIDED HELP 10-1**

For additional step-by-step instruction on how to account for a bond issued at a premium, go to **www.mhhe.com/libby_gh10a**.

The Book Value of a Bond over Time

Exhibit 10.2 reflects how the book value of a bond changes over its life when the bond is issued at par, at a discount, or at a premium.

EXHIBIT 10.2

The Change in the Book Value of a Bond Over Time

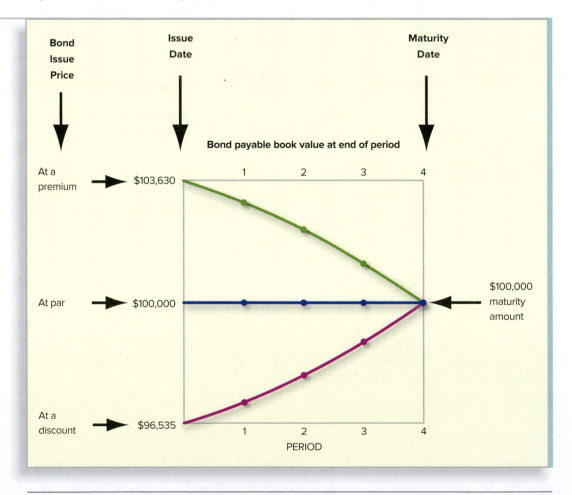

Solutions to
SELF-STUDY QUIZ

1. Cash owed for interest: $100,000 × 9% = **$9,000**
2. Interest expense: $106,710 × 8% = **$8,537**

Zero Coupon Bonds

So far, we have discussed bonds that pay interest over their life and have a principal payment due at the end of their life, which are the most common type of bond issued by companies to raise capital. For a number of reasons, companies may choose to issue bonds that have unique features. The concepts you have learned will help you understand these bonds. For example, a company might issue a bond that does not pay periodic cash interest. These bonds are typically called *zero coupon bonds*. Why would an investor buy a bond that did not pay interest? Our discussion of bond discounts has probably given you a good idea of the answer. The coupon interest rate on a bond can be virtually any amount (including zero) and investors will price the bond so that they earn the market rate of interest. A bond with a zero coupon interest rate is simply a deeply discounted bond that will sell for substantially less than its maturity value.

Let's use the $100,000 **Amazon** bond to illustrate a zero coupon rate. Assume that the market interest rate is 10 percent and the bond does not make any cash interest payments to bondholders over its life. The bond matures in five years. The selling price of the bond is the present value of the maturity amount because no other cash payments will be made over the life of the bond. We can compute the present value with the tables contained in Appendix E, using the factor for five periods and an interest rate of 10 percent:

	Present Value
Single principal payment at maturity: $100,000 × 0.62092	$62,092

From Table E.1: interest rate (i) = 10%, periods (n) = 5: Factor = 0.62092

Using Excel: rate (i) = .10, nper (n) = 5, pmt = $0, FV = −$100,000

Using Calculator: rate (i) = 10, periods (n) = 5, pmt = $0, FV = −$100,000

Accounting for a zero coupon bond is no different than accounting for other bonds issued at a discount. However, the amount of the discount is much larger. For example, the bond discount in the above example is $37,908. Over the five-year life of the bond, this amount will decrease until it is zero at the end of the bond's life.

While zero coupon bonds do not pay cash interest, they have been priced to provide investors with a market rate of interest. Notice that the bonds payable book value in our example ($62,092) is much lower than the maturity value ($100,000). This is because the price investors are willing to pay has been discounted such that when they receive the $100,000 at the end of the five years, they will have earned an interest rate of 10 percent, the market rate of interest on the issue date.

Accounting for Issuance Costs

For the sake of simplicity, the examples in this chapter assume that the company issuing bonds does not incur any issuance costs. This is not typically the case in the business world. When companies issue bonds, they almost always hire another company (or companies) to help them with the offering. These companies are called underwriters, and they charge a fee. Accounting for this fee is quite simple. The amount of the fee is deducted from the proceeds of the bond issuance. As a result, the fee increases the bond discount if the bonds were issued at a discount, and reduces the bond premium if the bonds were issued at a premium.

Reporting Interest Expense Using Straight-Line Amortization

GAAP requires that companies use the effective-interest method to amortize bond discounts and bond premiums. However, GAAP permits companies to use straight-line amortization when results do not materially differ from results computed using the effective-interest method. With **straight-line amortization** a company simply takes the total amount of the discount or

STRAIGHT-LINE AMORTIZATION
An alternative method of amortizing bond discounts and premiums that allocates an equal dollar amount to each interest period. It is only permitted by GAAP under specific circumstances.

the premium at issuance, divides it by the number of periods in the bond's life, and amortizes that amount each period. For example, the total amount of the premium in the Amazon example above was $3,630 and the bonds paid interest over four periods. Using straight-line amortization, Amazon would amortize $907.50 each period over the life of the bonds. The amortization schedule would reflect:

	BOND PREMIUM AMORTIZATION SCHEDULE (STRAIGHT-LINE AMORTIZATION)			
Date	(a)	(b)	(c)	(d)
	Cash Owed for Interest	Interest Expense	Amortization of Bond Premium	Bonds Payable Book Value
	$100,000 × (10% × ½ year)	(a) − (c)	$3,630 ÷ 4 periods	Beginning Book Value + (c)
01/01/2016				$103,630.00
06/30/2016	$5,000.00	$4,092.50	$(907.50)	102,722.50
12/31/2016	5,000.00	4,092.50	(907.50)	101,815.00
06/30/2017	5,000.00	4,092.50	(907.50)	100,907.50
12/31/2017	5,000.00	4,092.50	(907.50)	100,000.00

Other than the amounts, the journal entries using straight-line amortization and effective-interest amortization are the same. Because straight-line amortization is only permitted by GAAP under specific circumstances, we focus on the effective-interest method in this chapter.

KEY RATIO ANALYSIS

 Debt-to-Equity

LEARNING OBJECTIVE 10-6
Compute and analyze the debt-to-equity ratio.

 ANALYTICAL QUESTION

What is the relationship between the amount of capital provided by owners and the amount of capital provided by creditors?

RATIO AND COMPARISONS

The debt-to-equity ratio is computed as follows:

Debt-to-Equity = Total Liabilities ÷ Total Stockholders' Equity

The 2014 ratio for **Amazon** is:

$43,764 ÷ $10,741 = 4.1

COMPARISONS OVER TIME			COMPARISONS WITH COMPETITORS	
Amazon			eBay	Walmart
2014	2013	2012	2014	2014
4.1	3.1	3.0	1.3	1.5

 INTERPRETATIONS

In General   A high ratio indicates that a company relies heavily on debt financing relative to equity financing. Heavy reliance on debt financing increases the risk that a company may not be able to meet its contractual financial obligations (e.g., principal and interest payments) during a business downturn.

Focus Company Analysis   The debt-to-equity ratio for Amazon has increased over the past few years, and in 2014, the ratio reflects that for each dollar of stockholders' equity, Amazon has $4.1 of liabilities. Both **eBay** and **Walmart** have considerably lower amounts of liabilities relative to their stockholders' equity. Given the increase in Amazon's ratio over time, and the fact that its ratio is higher than that of its competitors, analysts would likely keep an eye on this ratio going forward.

A Few Cautions   The debt-to-equity ratio tells only part of the story with respect to the risks associated with a company's debt. It does not help the analyst understand whether the company's operations can support its debt. As a result, most analysts would evaluate the debt-to-equity ratio within the context of the amount of cash the company can generate from operating activities.

EARLY RETIREMENT OF BONDS

Bonds are often issued for long periods, such as 20 or 30 years. As mentioned earlier, bond-holders who need cash prior to the maturity date can simply sell their bond securities on a bond exchange to another investor. This transaction does not affect the books of the company that issued the bonds; it is a transaction between two investors. Some bonds have a **call** feature that allows the issuing company to call (retire) the bonds early. A call feature most often requires the issuing company to pay investors an amount greater than the bond's face value to retire the bonds before their maturity date. The amount is often stated as a percentage of the bond's face value and is described in the bond indenture or bond prospectus.

> **LEARNING OBJECTIVE 10-7**
> Report the early retirement of bond securities.

Assume that several years ago, **Amazon** issued callable bonds with a face value of $100,000. The bonds were issued at a premium, and the call feature allows Amazon to retire the bonds early by paying bondholders 102 percent of face value. If Amazon decides to call the bonds early, it will pay bondholders $102,000 cash and remove the bond liability from its balance sheet. Any difference between the cash paid to retire the bonds and the book value of the bond liability is recorded as a gain or loss on the income statement. For example, if the book value of Amazon's bonds was $101,000 at the time the bonds were retired, Amazon would recognize a loss on early retirement of $1,000 on its income statement; Amazon had to pay bondholders $102,000 cash to remove a $101,000 liability from its balance sheet. The journal entry is:

WITH PREMIUM ACCOUNT			WITHOUT PREMIUM ACCOUNT		
Bond payable (−L)	100,000		Bond payable (−L)	101,000	
Bond premium (−XL, −L)	1,000		Loss on bond call (+Loss, −SE)	1,000	
Loss on bond call (+Loss, −SE)	1,000		Cash (−A)		102,000
Cash (−A)		102,000			

Assets	=	Liabilities	+	Stockholders' Equity		Assets	=	Liabilities	+	Stockholders' Equity
Cash −102,000		Bonds payable −100,000		Loss on		Cash −102,000		Bonds payable −101,000		Loss on
		Bond premium −1,000		bond call −1,000						bond call −1,000

In some cases, a company may elect to retire bonds early by purchasing them on the open market, just as an investor would. This approach is necessary when the bonds do not have a call feature. Even when the bonds have a call feature, retiring them by purchasing them on the open market is attractive when the cost of doing so is less than the cost of paying the call premium. What could cause the price of a bond to fall? The most common cause is a rise in interest rates. As you may have noticed during our discussion of present values, **bond prices move in the opposite direction of interest rates.** If interest rates go up, bond prices fall, and vice versa. If interest rates go up enough, a company may decide that it makes good economic sense to retire its bonds early by purchasing them on the open market.

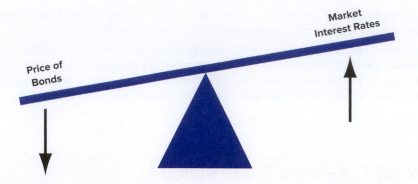

FOCUS ON CASH FLOWS	Bonds Payable

LEARNING OBJECTIVE 10-8

Explain how bond securities are reported on the statement of cash flows.

The cash a company receives when it issues bonds is reported as a cash inflow from financing activities on the statement of cash flows. The repayment of principal is reported as a cash outflow from financing activities. Many students are surprised to learn that the payment of interest is not reported as a financing activity on the statement of cash flows. Interest expense, as well as any gain or loss that results from retiring bonds early, is reported on the income statement and is a component of net income. As a result, GAAP requires that interest payments and any gain or loss from early retirement be reported as operating activities on the statement of cash flows.

EFFECT ON STATEMENT OF CASH FLOWS

In General   Cash paid for interest is a component of net income and is considered a cost of doing business during each accounting period. It is therefore reported in the operating section of the cash flow statement. Cash received from issuing debt and cash paid for principal are financing activities and are therefore reported in the financing section of the cash flow statement, as shown in the following table:

	Effect on Cash Flows
Financing activities:	
Cash received from bondholders when bonds are issued	+
Cash paid to bondholders when bonds mature or are retired	−

Focus Company Analysis   Below is an excerpt from **Amazon**'s cash flow statement showing its financing activities. The excerpt reflects the cash inflows and outflows Amazon experienced during the period associated with issuing and paying back debt. Analysts are particularly interested in the Financing Activities section of the statement of cash flows because it provides important insights about the capital structure of a company.

AMAZON

REAL WORLD EXCERPT:

Cash Flow Statement

AMAZON.COM, INC. CONSOLIDATED STATEMENTS OF CASH FLOWS (in millions)			
	2014	**2013**	**2012**
FINANCING ACTIVITIES			
Repurchase of common stock	—	—	(960)
Proceeds from issuance of long-term debt	6,359	394	3,378
Repayment of long-term debt	(513)	(231)	(82)
Repayment of capital lease obligations	(1,285)	(775)	(486)
Other	(129)	73	409
Net Cash Used in Financing Activities	4,432	(539)	2,259

(*Try to answer the questions below before reading the suggested solution that follows.*)

To raise funds to build a new plant, the managers of Zeus Company decide to issue bonds. The bond prospectus states the following:

> Face value of the bonds: $100,000.
> Date of issue: January 1, 2016; due in 10 years.
> Coupon rate: 12 percent per year, payable semiannually on June 30 and December 31.

The bonds were sold on January 1, 2016, at 106 percent of face value. Assume the annual market rate of interest on the date of issue was 11 percent.

Required:

1. How much cash did Zeus Company receive from the sale of the bonds? Show computations.

2. Were the bonds issued at a discount or a premium? What was the amount of the discount or premium?

3. How much cash does Zeus owe bondholders for interest on June 30, 2016?

4. Assume Zeus uses the effective-interest amortization method. What amount of interest expense will Zeus recognize on June 30, 2016?

SUGGESTED SOLUTION

1. Sale price of the bonds: $100,000 × 1.06 = $106,000.

2. The bonds were issued at a premium. The amount of the premium is $6,000 ($106,000 − $100,000).

3. Cash paid for interest on June 30, 2016: $100,000 × (12% × ½ year) = $6,000.

4. Interest expense recognized on June 30, 2016: $106,000 × (11% × ½ year) = $5,830.

CHAPTER SUPPLEMENT

Accounting for Bonds without a Discount Account or Premium Account

In this chapter supplement we duplicate the text from Chapter 10 but show all journal entries *without* the bond discount or bond premium accounts.

Reporting Interest Expense on Bonds Issued at a Discount Using Effective-Interest Amortization (without Discount Account)

Under the effective-interest amortization method, a company computes interest expense in a given period by multiplying the bonds payable book value times the market rate of interest on the date of issuance. When bonds are issued at a discount, using a market interest rate that is greater than the coupon rate results in interest expense each period being greater than the cash owed for interest each period. The difference between interest expense and the cash owed for interest is the amount of the bond discount amortized during the period. This process can be summarized as follows:

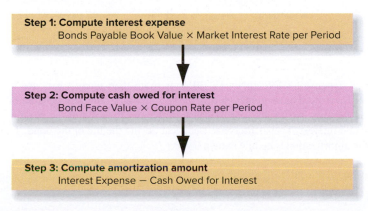

Step 1: Compute interest expense
Bonds Payable Book Value × Market Interest Rate per Period

Step 2: Compute cash owed for interest
Bond Face Value × Coupon Rate per Period

Step 3: Compute amortization amount
Interest Expense − Cash Owed for Interest

Recall that the cash owed for interest is computed by multiplying the bond's face value ($100,000) by the coupon rate per period (10% × ½ year). Thus, **Amazon** owes bondholders cash of $5,000 each June 30 and again on December 31. The first interest payment on the bonds is made on June 30, 2016. Following the three steps outlined above, interest expense and the amount of the bond discount amortized are:

Step 1: Interest expense: $96,535 × (0.12 × ½ year) = **$5,792**

Step 2: Cash owed for interest: $100,000 × (0.10 × ½ year) = **$5,000**

Step 3: Amortized amount: $5,792 − $5,000 = **$792**

The journal entry Amazon would enter is:

Effective-interest amortization causes these amounts to change each period.

Interest expense (+E, −SE)	5,792	
Bonds payable (+L)		792
Cash (−A)		5,000

Assets		=	Liabilities		+	Equity	
Cash	−5,000		Bonds payable	+792		Interest expense (+E)	−5,792

Bonds payable book value: **$97,327**
($96,535 + $792)

Each period, the amortization of the bond discount increases the bond's book value, bringing it closer to the $100,000 that is due at maturity. The amortization of the bond discount can be thought of as the amount of interest earned by the bondholders in a given period that will be paid to them when the bonds mature. During the first interest period, Amazon's bondholders earned interest of $5,792 but received only $5,000 in cash. The additional $792 was added to the book value of the bond and will be paid to bondholders when the bonds mature.

Interest expense for the next interest period must reflect the change in the bonds payable book value. Amazon calculates interest expense for the second half of 2016 by multiplying the bonds payable book value on June 30, 2016 ($97,327) by the market rate of interest per period ($97,327 × (12% × ½ year) = $5,840). With interest expense equal to $5,840 and cash owed for interest equal to $5,000, the amount of the bond discount amortized on December 31, 2016, is $840:

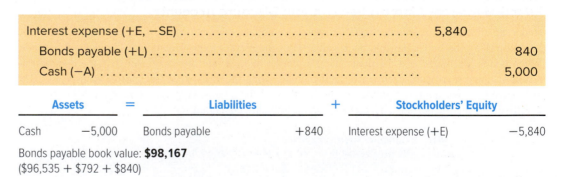

Interest expense (+E, −SE)	5,840	
Bonds payable (+L)		840
Cash (−A)		5,000

Assets		=	Liabilities		+	Stockholders' Equity	
Cash	−5,000		Bonds payable	+840		Interest expense (+E)	−5,840

Bonds payable book value: **$98,167**
($96,535 + $792 + $840)

Notice that interest expense for December 31, 2016, is more than interest expense for June 30, 2016. Amazon effectively borrowed more money during the second half of the year because of the unpaid interest accrued during the first half of the year. Because of the amortization of the bond discount, the book value of the bond and interest expense **increase** each year during the life of the bond. This process can be illustrated with the amortization schedule shown below:

BOND DISCOUNT AMORTIZATION SCHEDULE

Date	(a) Cash Owed for Interest	(b) Interest Expense	(c) Amortization of Bond Discount	(d) Bonds Payable Book Value
	$100,000 × (10% × ½ year)	Beginning of Period Book Value × (12% × ½ year)	(b) − (a)	Beginning Book Value + (c)
01/01/2016				$ 96,535
06/30/2016	$5,000	$5,792	$792	97,327
12/31/2016	5,000	5,840	840	98,167
06/30/2017	5,000	5,890	890	99,057
12/31/2017	5,000	5,943	943	100,000

Coupon rate (10%)

Market interest rate (12%)

Note that:

- Cash owed for interest (column a) is computed by multiplying the bond's face value by the coupon rate per period.
- Interest expense (column b) is computed by multiplying the book value of the bonds at the beginning of the period (column d) by the market interest rate. Note that the book value of a bond at the beginning of a period is the book value of the bond at the end of the previous period.
- Amortization of the bond discount is computed by subtracting cash owed for interest (column a) from interest expense (column b).
- The new book value of the bonds (column d) is computed by adding amortization of the bond discount (column c) to the book value at the beginning of the period.

In summary, under the effective-interest amortization method, interest expense changes each accounting period as the effective amount of the liability changes.

PAUSE FOR **FEEDBACK**

STOP

SELF-STUDY **QUIZ**

Assume that **Amazon** issued bonds with a face value of $100,000 and a coupon rate of 5 percent. The bonds mature in 10 years and pay interest annually. The bonds were sold when the annual market interest rate was 6 percent at a price of $92,640.

1. What amount of cash was owed for interest at the end of the first year?
2. Using the effective-interest amortization method, what amount of interest expense would Amazon report at the end of the first year?

After you have completed your answers, check them below.

1. Cash owed for interest: $100,000 × 5% = **$5,000**
2. Interest expense: $92,640 × 6% = **$5,558**

Solutions to
SELF-STUDY QUIZ

Bonds Issued at a Premium

LEARNING OBJECTIVE 10-5
Report bonds payable and interest expense for bond securities issued at a premium.

Recall that bonds sell at a discount when the market interest rate is greater than the bond's coupon rate. When the market interest rate is less than the bond's coupon rate, the bonds sell at a premium. To demonstrate how to account for bonds issued at a premium, let's use the same **Amazon** example as before but assume that the market interest rate is now 8 percent while the coupon rate remains the same, at 10 percent. Like before, the bonds are issued on January 1, 2016, pay interest semiannually, and mature in two years.

The present value of the bonds described above can be computed from the tables contained in Appendix E using the factor for four periods and an interest rate of 4 percent per period ($8\% \times \frac{1}{2}$ year):

	Present Value
Single principal payment at maturity: $100,000 × 0.85480	$ 85,480
+ Annuity cash interest payment: $5,000 × 3.62990	18,150
Issue (sale) price of bonds	$103,630

> From Table E.1: interest rate (i) = 4%, periods (n) = 4: Factor = 0.85480
>
> From Table E.2: interest rate (i) = 4%, periods (n) = 4: Factor = 3.62990
>
> Using Excel: rate (i) = .04, nper (n) = 4, pmt = −$5,000, FV = −$100,000
>
> Using Calculator: rate (i) = 4, periods (n) = 4, pmt = −$5,000, FV = −$100,000

Accounting for bonds issued at a premium is similar to accounting for bonds issued at a discount. Companies can explicitly use a bond premium account in their journal entries or implicitly keep track of the premium amount. We show both side-by-side below and then, as we did in our discussion of bond discounts, we present all subsequent journal entries without using a bond premium account. The January 1, 2016, issuance of Amazon's bonds at a premium would be recorded as follows:

WITH PREMIUM ACCOUNT			WITHOUT PREMIUM ACCOUNT		
Cash (+A)	103,630		Cash (+A)	103,630	
Bond premium (+XL, +L)		3,630	Bond payable (+L)		103,630
Bonds payable (+L)		100,000			

Assets	=	Liabilities	+	Stockholders' Equity		Assets	=	Liabilities	+	Stockholders' Equity
Cash +103,630		Bonds payable +100,000				Cash +103,630		Bonds payable +103,630		
		Bond premium +3,630								

Bonds payable book value: **$103,630**
($100,000 + $3,630)

Bonds payable book value: **$103,630**

Like the bond discount account, the bond premium account is not separately disclosed on Amazon's balance sheet. Instead, the balance sheet reports the bonds payable at their book value ($103,630), which is their face value plus the unamortized premium ($100,000 + $3,630). Note that reporting bonds payable at its book value results in the same amount being reported on the balance sheet ($103,630), regardless of whether a bond premium is explicitly recorded in the journal entry.

Reporting Interest Expense on Bonds Issued at a Premium Using Effective-Interest Amortization (without Premium Account)

As with a discount, the recorded premium of $3,630 must be apportioned to each interest period so that interest expense reflects the market (effective) interest rate that Amazon is actually paying. To compute interest expense and the amount of the premium we will amortize each period, we follow the same three steps that we followed to compute these amounts when the bonds were issued at a discount:

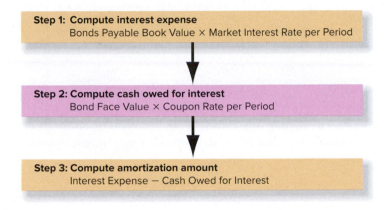

Step 1: Compute interest expense
Bonds Payable Book Value × Market Interest Rate per Period

Step 2: Compute cash owed for interest
Bond Face Value × Coupon Rate per Period

Step 3: Compute amortization amount
Interest Expense − Cash Owed for Interest

Step 1: Interest expense: $103,630 × (0.08 × ½ year) = $4,145

Step 2: Cash owed for interest: $100,000 × (0.10 × ½ year) = $5,000

Step 3: Amortized amount: $4,145 − $5,000 = −$855

The journal entry Amazon would enter is:

Interest expense (+E, −SE)	4,145	
Bonds payable (−L)	855	
Cash (−L)		5,000

Assets	=	Liabilities	+	Stockholders' Equity	
Cash −5,000		Bonds payable −855		Interest expense (+E)	−4,145

Bonds payable book value: **$102,775**
($103,630 − $855)

The basic difference between effective-interest amortization of a bond discount and a bond premium is that the amortization of a discount **increases** the book value of the liability and the amortization of a premium **decreases** it. Both serve the same purpose: to bring the liability to the bond's face value at the maturity date. The following schedule illustrates the amortization of a premium over the life of a bond.

BOND PREMIUM AMORTIZATION SCHEDULE

Date	(a) Cash Owed for Interest	(b) Interest Expense	(c) Amortization of Bond Premium	(d) Bonds Payable Book Value
	$100,000 × (10% × ½ year)	Beginning of Period Book Value × (8% × ½ year)	(b) − (a)	Beginning Book Value + (c)
01/01/2016				$103,630
06/30/2016	$5,000	$4,145	$(855)	102,775
12/31/2016	5,000	4,111	(889)	101,886
06/30/2017	5,000	4,075	(925)	100,961
12/31/2017	5,000	4,039*	(961)	100,000

Coupon rate (10%)

Market interest rate (8%)

*Rounded

Regardless of whether a company issues bonds at par, at a discount, or at a premium, the company will enter the same journal entry when the bonds mature. For our Amazon example, the journal entry would be:

Bonds payable (−L)	−100,000	
Cash (−A)		−100,000

Assets	=	Liabilities	+	Stockholders' Equity
Cash −100,000		Bonds payable −100,000		

STOP   PAUSE FOR **FEEDBACK**

SELF-STUDY **QUIZ**

Assume that **Amazon** issued bonds with a face value of $100,000 and a coupon rate of 9 percent. The bonds mature in 10 years and pay interest annually. The bonds were sold when the annual market interest rate was 8 percent at a price of $106,710.

1. What amount of cash was owed for interest at the end of the first year?
2. Using the effective-interest amortization method, what amount of interest expense would Amazon report at the end of the first year?

After you have completed your answers, check them below.

 **GUIDED HELP 10-2**

For additional step-by-step instruction on how to account for a bond issued at a premium without a premium account, go to **www.mhhe.com/libby9e_gh10b**.

Solutions to
SELF-STUDY QUIZ

1. Cash owed for interest: $100,000 × 9% = **$9,000**
2. Interest expense: $106,710 × 8% = **$8,537**

10-1. Describe the characteristics of bond securities. p. 508

Bond securities are commonly referred to as just "bonds." Bonds have a number of characteristics designed to meet the needs of both the issuing company and the bondholder. We discussed many of those characteristics in this chapter.

Companies issue bonds to raise long-term capital. Bonds offer a number of advantages compared to stock, including the tax deductibility of interest and the fact that control of the company is not diluted when a company issues bonds instead of stock. Bonds do carry additional risk, however, because interest and principal payments are not discretionary.

10-2. Report bonds payable and interest expense for bond securities issued at par. p. 514

Three types of events must be recorded over the life of a typical bond: (1) the receipt of cash when the bond is sold, (2) the periodic payment of interest, and (3) the repayment of the bond's face value at maturity. The amount of cash a company receives when it issues bonds is the present value of the future cash flows associated with the bonds. When the market interest rate and the coupon rate are the same, the bond will sell at par (face value).

10-3. Compute and analyze the times interest earned ratio. p. 516

The times interest earned ratio reflects the amount of income earned for each dollar of interest expense. It is a measure of a company's ability to meet its interest obligations. It is computed by comparing interest expense to net income after adding back interest expense and income tax expense.

10-4. Report bonds payable and interest expense for bond securities issued at a discount. pp. 517 & 529

Bonds are sold at a discount whenever the coupon rate is less than the market interest rate. A discount is the difference between the selling price of a bond and the bond's face value when the bond is sold for less than its face amount. Companies have the option of explicitly keeping track of the bond discount by incorporating it into journal entries or implicitly keeping track of the bond discount and not including it in journal entries. Regardless, the same amount is reported as bonds payable on a company's balance sheet.

10-5. Report bonds payable and interest expense for bond securities issued at a premium. pp. 521 & 532

Bonds are sold at a premium whenever the coupon rate is greater than the market interest rate. A premium is the difference between the selling price of a bond and the bond's face value when the bond is sold for more than its face value. Companies have the option of explicitly keeping track of the bond premium by incorporating it into journal entries or implicitly keeping track of the bond premium and not including it in journal entries. Regardless, the same amount is reported as bonds payable on a company's balance sheet.

10-6. Compute and analyze the debt-to-equity ratio. p. 526

The debt-to-equity ratio compares the amount of debt to the amount of equity on a company's balance sheet. It is an important ratio because of the high risk associated with debt capital; debt capital requires interest and principal payments.

10-7. Report the early retirement of bond securities. p. 527

A company may retire bonds before their maturity date, by either purchasing the bonds in the open market or activating a call feature if the bonds contain such a feature. The difference between the book value of the bonds and the amount paid to retire the bonds is reported as a gain or loss on the company's income statement.

10-8. Explain how bond securities are reported on the statement of cash flows. p. 528

Cash received from issuing bonds and cash paid to retire bonds at maturity are financing cash flows. Cash paid for interest and any gain or loss on the early retirement of bonds are operating cash flows.

KEY **RATIOS**

Times interest earned ratio reflects the amount of income earned for each dollar of interest expense. It is a measure of a company's ability to meet its interest obligations. The ratio is computed as follows (see the "Key Ratio Analysis" box in the Reporting Bond Transactions section):

$$\text{Times Interest Earned} = \frac{\text{Net Income} + \text{Interest Expense} + \text{Income Tax Expense}}{\text{Interest Expense}}$$

Debt-to-equity ratio compares the amount of debt on a company's balance sheet to the amount of equity. The ratio is computed as follows (see the "Key Ratio Analysis" box in the Reporting Bond Transactions section):

$$\text{Debt-to-Equity} = \frac{\text{Total Liabilities}}{\text{Stockholders' Equity}}$$

FINDING **FINANCIAL INFORMATION**

Balance Sheet
Bonds are normally listed as long-term liabilities. An exception occurs when the bonds are within one year of maturity, in which case they are reported as current liabilities with the title "Current Portion of Long-Term Debt."

Income Statement
Issuing bonds and paying off bonds at maturity do not affect the income statement. Recognizing interest expense and any gain or loss from early retirement does affect the income statement. Most companies report interest expense in a separate category on the income statement.

Statement of Cash Flows
Under Financing Activities
  + Cash inflows from issuing bonds
  − Cash outflows from paying off principal when bonds mature or are retired

Under Operating Activities
  − Cash outflows for interest payments activity
  − Cash outflows associated with a loss from early retirement
  + Cash inflows associated with a gain from early retirement

Notes
Under Summary of Significant Accounting Policies
A brief description of how a company accounts for long-term liabilities, including bonds.

Under a Separate Note
Most companies include a separate note where they describe in more detail their accounting for long-term debt, including the type of debt, maturity dates, and interest rates. The note also typically describes any special features associated with the debt, such as whether bonds can be called early. Typically in a company's financial statements and footnotes, bonds are referred to as "notes."

KEY **TERMS**

1. From the perspective of the issuer, what are some advantages of issuing bonds instead of stock?
2. What are the primary characteristics of a bond? For what purposes are bonds usually issued?
3. What is the difference between an unsecured and a secured bond?
4. Differentiate between a bond indenture and a bond prospectus.
5. What is a bond covenant?
6. Differentiate between a bond coupon rate and the market rate of interest.
7. Explain what determines whether a bond is issued at a discount or a premium.
8. When calculating the present value of a bond's future cash flows, do investors use the coupon rate or market interest rate as the discount rate?
9. What is the book value of a bond?
10. What is the formula used for calculating the cash payment bond investors will receive for interest each period? What is the formula used to calculate interest expense each period?
11. How is the debt-to-equity ratio computed? What does the debt-to-equity ratio tell you?
12. When market interest rates increase, do bond prices increase or decrease?

1. Annual interest expense for a single bond issue continues to increase over the life of the bonds. Which of the following explains this?
   a. The market rate of interest has increased since the bonds were sold.
   b. The coupon rate has increased since the bonds were sold.
   c. The bonds were sold at a discount.
   d. The bonds were sold at a premium.
2. Which of the following is **not** an advantage of issuing bonds when compared to issuing additional shares of stock in order to obtain additional capital?
   a. Stockholders maintain proportionate ownership percentages.
   b. Interest expense reduces taxable income.
   c. The payment of interest is flexible and at the discretion of the issuing firm.
   d. All of the above are advantages associated with bonds.
3. A bond with a face value of $100,000 has a coupon rate of 8 percent. The bond matures in 10 years. When the bond is issued, the market rate of interest is 10 percent. What amount will investors pay for this bond?
   a. $100,000   c. $49,157
   b. $87,707   d. $113,421
4. Which account would **not** be included in the debt-to-equity ratio calculation?
   a. Unearned Revenue.   c. Income Taxes Payable.
   b. Retained Earnings.   d. All of the above are included.
5. Which of the following is **false** when a bond is issued at a premium?
   a. The bond will issue for an amount above its par value.
   b. Bonds payable will be credited for an amount greater than the bond's face value.
   c. Interest expense will exceed the cash interest payments.
   d. All of the above are false.
6. A bond with a face value of $100,000 was issued for $93,500 on January 1 of this year. The stated rate of interest was 8 percent and the market rate of interest was 10 percent when the bond was sold. Interest is paid annually. How much interest will be paid on December 31 of this year?
   a. $10,000   c. $7,480
   b. $8,000   d. $9,350
7. To determine whether a bond will be sold at a premium, at a discount, or at face value, one must know which of the following pairs of information?
   a. Face value and the coupon rate on the date the bond is issued.
   b. Face value and the market rate of interest on the date the bond is issued.
   c. The coupon rate and the market rate of interest on the date the bond is issued.
   d. The coupon rate and the stated rate on the date the bond is issued.

8. When using the effective-interest method of amortization, interest expense reported in the income statement is impacted by the
   a. Face value of the bonds.
   b. Coupon rate stated in the bond certificate.
   c. Market rate of interest on the date the bonds were issued.
   d. Both (a) and (b).

9. A bond with a face value of $100,000 is sold on January 1. The bond has a coupon rate of 10 percent and matures in 10 years. When the bond was issued, the market rate of interest was 10 percent. On December 31, the market rate of interest increased to 11 percent. What amount should be reported on December 31 as the bond liability on the balance sheet?
   a. $100,000   c. $94,460
   b. $94,112   d. $87,562

10. When using the effective-interest method of amortization, the book value of a bond changes by what amount on each interest payment date?
    a. Interest expense
    b. Cash interest payment
    c. The difference between interest expense and the cash interest payment
    d. None of the above

| MINI-**EXERCISES** |  connect |

M10-1
LO10-1, 10-2, 10-8

Finding Financial Information

For each of the following items, specify whether the information would be found in the balance sheet, the income statement, the statement of cash flows, or the notes to the statements.
1. The amount of a bond liability.
2. A description of any bond covenants.
3. The coupon rates associated with bond issuances.
4. Interest expense for the period.
5. The maturity dates associated with bond issuances.
6. Cash interest paid for the period.

M10-2
LO10-2

Computing the Price of a Bond Issued at Par

Williams Company plans to issue bonds with a face value of $600,000 and a coupon rate of 8 percent. The bonds will mature in 10 years and pay interest semiannually every June 30 and December 31. All of the bonds are sold on January 1 of this year. Determine the issuance price of the bonds assuming an annual market rate of interest of 8 percent.

M10-3
LO10-3, 10-6

Understanding Financial Ratios

The debt-to-equity and times interest earned ratios were discussed in this chapter. Which is a better indicator of a company's ability to meet its required interest payment? Explain.

M10-4
LO10-3

Computing the Times Interest Earned Ratio

Oak Corporation's financial statements for the current year showed the following:

	Income Statement
Revenues	$800,000
Expenses	(620,000)
Interest expense	(12,600)
Pretax income	167,400
Income tax (30%)	(50,220)
Net income	$117,180

Compute Oak's times interest earned ratio.

Computing the Price of a Bond Issued at a Discount

M10-5
LO10-4

Trew Company plans to issue bonds with a face value of $900,000 and a coupon rate of 6 percent. The bonds will mature in 10 years and pay interest semiannually every June 30 and December 31. All of the bonds are sold on January 1 of this year. Determine the issuance price of the bonds assuming an annual market rate of interest of 8.5 percent.

Recording the Issuance and Interest Payments of a Bond Issued at a Discount (with Discount Account)

M10-6
LO10-4

Coffman Company sold bonds with a face value of $1,000,000 for $940,000. The bonds have a coupon rate of 10 percent, mature in 10 years, and pay interest semiannually every June 30 and December 31. All of the bonds were sold on January 1 of this year. Using a discount account, record the sale of the bonds on January 1 and the payment of interest on June 30 of this year. Coffman uses the effective-interest amortization method. Assume an annual market rate of interest of 11 percent.

(Chapter Supplement) Recording the Issuance and Interest Payments of a Bond Issued at a Discount (without Discount Account)

M10-7
LO10-4

Coffman Company sold bonds with a face value of $1,000,000 for $940,000. The bonds have a coupon rate of 10 percent, mature in 10 years, and pay interest semiannually every June 30 and December 31. All of the bonds were sold on January 1 of this year. Record the sale of the bonds on January 1 and the payment of interest on June 30 of this year, without the use of a discount account. Coffman uses the effective-interest amortization method. Assume an annual market rate of interest of 11 percent.

Computing the Price of a Bond Issued at a Premium

M10-8
LO10-5

Waterhouse Company plans to issue bonds with a face value of $500,000 and a coupon rate of 10 percent. The bonds will mature in 10 years and pay interest semiannually every June 30 and December 31. All of the bonds are sold on January 1 of this year. Determine the issuance price of the bonds assuming an annual market rate of interest of 8 percent.

Recording the Issuance and Interest Payments of a Bond Issued at a Premium (with Premium Account)

M10-9
LO10-5

RKO Company sold bonds with a face value of $850,000 for $910,000. The bonds have a coupon rate of 8 percent, mature in 10 years, and pay interest annually every December 31. All of the bonds were sold on January 1 of this year. Using a premium account, record the sale of the bonds on January 1 and the payment of interest on December 31 of this year. RKO uses the effective-interest amortization method. Assume an annual market rate of interest of 7 percent.

(Chapter Supplement) Recording the Issuance and Interest Payments of a Bond Issued at a Premium (without Premium Account)

M10-10
LO10-5

RKO Company sold bonds with a face value of $850,000 for $910,000. The bonds have a coupon rate of 8 percent, mature in 10 years, and pay interest annually every December 31. All of the bonds were sold on January 1 of this year. Record the sale of the bonds on January 1 and the payment of interest on December 31 of this year, without the use of a premium account. RKO uses the effective-interest amortization method. Assume an annual market rate of interest of 7 percent.

Recording the Issuance and Interest Payments of a Bond Issued at a Discount (Straight-Line Amortization with a Discount Account)

M10-11
LO10-4

Wefald Company sold bonds with a face value of $600,000 for $580,000. The bonds have a coupon rate of 10 percent, mature in 10 years, and pay interest semiannually every June 30 and December 31. All of the bonds were sold on January 1 of this year. Using a discount account, record the sale of the bonds on January 1 and the payment of interest on June 30 of this year. Wefald uses the straight-line amortization method.

(Chapter Supplement) Recording the Issuance and Interest Payments of a Bond Issued at a Discount (Straight-Line Amortization without a Discount Account)

M10-12
LO10-4

Wefald Company sold bonds with a face value of $600,000 for $580,000. The bonds have a coupon rate of 10 percent, mature in 10 years, and pay interest semiannually every June 30 and December 31. All of the bonds were sold on January 1 of this year. Record the sale of the bonds on January 1 and the payment of interest on June 30 of this year, without the use of a discount account. Wefald uses the straight-line amortization method.

M10-13
LO10-7

Interest Rates and the Early Retirement of Debt

If interest rates fell after the issuance of a bond and the company decided to retire the debt early, would you expect the company to report a gain or loss on debt retirement? How would the company's balance sheet and income statement be affected?

M10-14
LO10-8

The Cash Flow Effects of Retiring Bonds and Paying Interest

In what section of the statement of cash flows would you find cash paid for principal when a bond matures? In what section would you find cash paid for interest each period?

EXERCISES

E10-1
LO10-1

Interpreting Information Reported in the Business Press

Apple recently issued a series of bonds with various maturity dates. The information below pertains to one of Apple's bonds:

Issuer	Coupon (%)	Maturity	Current ($)	Yield (%)
Apple	3.45	2024	101.29	3.29

Explain why investors would care about knowing the coupon rate and yield percentages. Assume that over the next several weeks the yield went down to 3.10. How would this decrease affect Apple's financial statements?

E10-2
LO10-1

Evaluating Bond Features

You are a personal financial planner working with a married couple in their early 40s who have decided to invest $100,000 in corporate bonds. You have found two bonds that you think will interest your clients. One is a zero coupon bond issued by **PepsiCo** with an effective interest rate of 9 percent and a maturity date of 2025. It is callable at par. The other is a **Walt Disney** bond that matures in 2093. It has an effective interest rate of 9.5 percent and is callable at 102 percent of par. Which of the two bonds is less likely to be called if interest rates fall over the next few years?

E10-3
LO10-2, 10-4, 10-5

Computing Issue Prices of Bonds Sold at Par, at a Discount, and at a Premium

LaTanya Corporation is planning to issue bonds with a face value of $100,000 and a coupon rate of 8 percent. The bonds mature in seven years. Interest is paid annually on December 31. All of the bonds will be sold on January 1 of this year.

Required:
Compute the issue (sale) price on January 1 of this year for each of the following independent cases (show computations):

a. **Case A:** Market interest rate (annual): 8 percent.
b. **Case B:** Market interest rate (annual): 6 percent.
c. **Case C:** Market interest rate (annual): 9 percent.

E10-4
LO10-2, 10-4, 10-5

Computing Issue Prices of Bonds Sold at Par, at a Discount, and at a Premium

James Corporation is planning to issue bonds with a face value of $500,000 and a coupon rate of 6 percent. The bonds mature in 10 years and pay interest semiannually every June 30 and December 31. All of the bonds will be sold on January 1 of this year.

Required:
Compute the issue (sale) price on January 1 of this year for each of the following independent cases (show computations):

a. **Case A:** Market interest rate (annual): 4 percent.
b. **Case B:** Market interest rate (annual): 6 percent.
c. **Case C:** Market interest rate (annual): 8.5 percent.

Determining the Effects of Issuing Bonds on the Debt-to-Equity Ratio

E10-5
LO10-2, 10-6

On January 1 of this year, Denver Corporation sold bonds with a face value of $300,000 and a coupon rate of 6 percent. The bonds mature in 10 years and pay interest annually every December 31. At the time the bonds were issued, the annual market rate of interest was 6 percent. The company uses the effective-interest amortization method.

Required:
1. When the bonds were issued, did Denver's debt-to-equity ratio increase, decrease, or stay the same?
2. At the end of the first year, when Denver recorded its first interest expense and paid cash to investors for interest, did its debt-to-equity ratio increase, decrease, or stay the same?

Analyzing Financial Ratios

E10-6
LO10-3, 10-6

You have just started your first job as a financial analyst for a large stock brokerage company. Your boss, a senior analyst, has finished a detailed report evaluating bonds issued by two different companies. She stopped by your desk and asked for help: "I have compared two ratios for the companies and found something interesting." She went on to explain that the debt-to-equity ratio for Applied Engineering is much lower than the industry average and that the one for Innovative Engineering is much higher. On the other hand, the times interest earned ratio for Applied Engineering is much higher than the industry average, and the ratio for Innovative Engineering is much lower. Your boss then asked you to think about what the ratios indicate about the two companies so that she could include the explanation in her report. How would you respond to your boss?

Computing the Price of a Bond Issued at a Discount

E10-7
LO10-4

GMAC Corporation is planning to issue bonds with a face value of $250,000 and a coupon rate of 6 percent. The bonds mature in five years and pay interest semiannually every June 30 and December 31. All of the bonds were sold on January 1 of this year. Determine the issuance price of the bonds assuming an annual market rate of interest of 8 percent.

Recording and Reporting a Bond Issued at a Discount (with Discount Account)

E10-8
LO10-4

Park Corporation is planning to issue bonds with a face value of $600,000 and a coupon rate of 7.5 percent. The bonds mature in four years and pay interest semiannually every June 30 and December 31. All of the bonds were sold on January 1 of this year. Park uses the effective-interest amortization method and also uses a discount account. Assume an annual market rate of interest of 8.5 percent.

Required:
1. Provide the journal entry to record the issuance of the bonds.
2. Provide the journal entry to record the interest payment on June 30 of this year.
3. What bonds payable amount will Park report on its June 30 balance sheet?

(Chapter Supplement) Recording and Reporting a Bond Issued at a Discount (without Discount Account)

E10-9
LO10-4

Park Corporation is planning to issue bonds with a face value of $600,000 and a coupon rate of 7.5 percent. The bonds mature in four years and pay interest semiannually every June 30 and December 31. All of the bonds were sold on January 1 of this year. Park uses the effective-interest amortization method and does not use a discount account. Assume an annual market rate of interest of 8.5 percent.

Required:
1. Provide the journal entry to record the issuance of the bonds.
2. Provide the journal entry to record the interest payment on June 30 of this year.
3. What bond payable amount will Park report on its June 30 balance sheet?

E10-10

LO10-4

Preparing a Bond Amortization Schedule for a Bond Issued at a Discount and Determining Reported Amounts

On January 1 of this year, Ikuta Company issued a bond with a face value of $100,000 and a coupon rate of 5 percent. The bond matures in three years and pays interest every December 31. When the bond was issued, the annual market rate of interest was 6 percent. Ikuta uses the effective-interest amortization method.

Required:
1. Complete a bond amortization schedule for all three years of the bond's life.
2. What amounts will be reported on the income statement and balance sheet at the end of Year 1 and Year 2?

E10-11

LO10-4

Interpreting a Bond Amortization Schedule

Santa Corporation issued a bond on January 1 of this year with a face value of $1,000. The bond's coupon rate is 6 percent and interest is paid once a year on December 31. The bond matures in three years. The annual market rate of interest was 8 percent at the time the bond was sold. The following amortization schedule pertains to the bond issued:

	Cash Paid	Interest Expense	Amortization	Balance
January 1, Year 1				$ 948
December 31, Year 1	$60	$76	$16	964
December 31, Year 2	60	77	17	981
December 31, Year 3	60	79	19	1,000

Required:
1. What was the bond's issue price?
2. Did the bond sell at a discount or a premium? How much was the premium or discount?
3. What amount(s) should be shown on the balance sheet for bonds payable at the end of Year 1 and Year 2?
4. Show how the following amounts were computed for Year 2: (*a*) $60, (*b*) $77, (*c*) $17, and (*d*) $981.

E10-12

LO10-4, 10-5

Explaining Why Debt Is Issued at a Price Other Than Par

The annual report of **American Airlines** contained the following note:

> The Company recorded the issuance of $775 million in bonds (net of $25 million discount) as long-term debt on the consolidated balance sheet. The bonds bear interest at fixed rates, with an average effective rate of 8.06 percent, and mature over various periods of time, with a final maturity in 2031.

After reading this note, an investor asked her financial advisor why the company didn't simply sell the notes for an effective yield that equaled the coupon rate, thereby avoiding the need to account for a small discount over the next 20 years. Prepare a written response to this question.

E10-13

LO10-5

Recording and Reporting a Bond Issued at a Premium (with Premium Account)

Park Corporation is planning to issue bonds with a face value of $2,000,000 and a coupon rate of 10 percent. The bonds mature in 10 years and pay interest semiannually every June 30 and December 31. All of the bonds were sold on January 1 of this year. Park uses the effective-interest amortization method and also uses a premium account. Assume an annual market rate of interest of 8.5 percent.

Required:
1. Provide the journal entry to record the issuance of the bonds.
2. Provide the journal entry to record the interest payment on June 30 of this year.
3. What bonds payable amount will Park report on its June 30 balance sheet?

(Chapter Supplement) Recording and Reporting a Bond Issued at a Premium (without Premium Account)

E10-14
LO10-5

Park Corporation is planning to issue bonds with a face value of $2,000,000 and a coupon rate of 10 percent. The bonds mature in 10 years and pay interest semiannually every June 30 and December 31. All of the bonds were sold on January 1 of this year. Park uses the effective-interest amortization method and does not use a premium account. Assume an annual market rate of interest of 8.5 percent.

Required:
1. Provide the journal entry to record the issuance of the bonds.
2. Provide the journal entry to record the interest payment on June 30 of this year.
3. What bonds payable amount will Park report on its June 30 balance sheet?

Preparing a Bond Amortization Schedule for a Bond Issued at a Premium and Determining Reported Amounts

E10-15
LO10-5

On January 1 of this year, Houston Company issued a bond with a face value of $10,000 and a coupon rate of 5 percent. The bond matures in three years and pays interest every December 31. When the bond was issued, the annual market rate of interest was 4 percent. Houston uses the effective-interest amortization method.

Required:
1. Complete a bond amortization schedule for all three years of the bond's life.
2. What amounts will be reported on the income statement and balance sheet at the end of Year 1 and Year 2?

Recording and Analyzing the Cash Flow Effects of a Bond Issued at a Premium (with Premium Account)

E10-16
LO10-5, 10-8

On January 1 of this year, Gateway Company issued bonds with a face value of $1 million and a coupon rate of 9 percent. The bonds mature in 10 years and pay interest semiannually every June 30 and December 31. When the bonds were issued, the annual market rate of interest was 8 percent. Record the issuance of the bonds on January 1 of this year. How will Gateway's statement of cash flows be affected on January 1, June 30, and December 31 of this year?

Recording the Early Retirement of a Bond

E10-17
LO10-7

Several years ago, Walters Company issued bonds with a face value of $1,000,000 at par. As a result of declining interest rates, the company has decided to call the bond at a call premium of 5 percent over par. Record the retirement of the bonds.

Recording the Early Retirement of a Bond Issued at a Discount (with Discount Account)

E10-18
LO10-7

Several years ago, Nicole Company issued bonds with a face value of $1,000,000 for $945,000. As a result of declining interest rates, the company has decided to call the bond at a call premium of 5 percent over par. The bonds have a current book value of $984,000. Record the retirement of the bonds, using a discount account.

(Chapter Supplement) Recording the Early Retirement of a Bond Issued at a Discount (without Discount Account)

E10-19
LO10-7

Several years ago, Nicole Company issued bonds with a face value of $1,000,000 for $945,000. As a result of declining interest rates, the company has decided to call the bond at a call premium of 5 percent over par. The bonds have a current book value of $984,000. Record the retirement of the bonds without using a discount account.

Recording and Reporting a Bond Issued at a Discount (Straight-Line Amortization with Discount Account)

E10-20
LO10-4

On January 1 of this year, Clearwater Corporation sold bonds with a face value of $750,000 and a coupon rate of 8 percent. The bonds mature in 10 years and pay interest annually every December 31. Clearwater uses the straight-line amortization method and also uses a discount account. Assume an annual market rate of interest of 9 percent.

Required:
1. Provide the journal entry to record the issuance of the bonds.
2. Provide the journal entry to record the interest payment on December 31 of this year.
3. What bonds payable amount will Clearwater report on its December 31 balance sheet?

E10-21
LO10-4

(Chapter Supplement) Recording and Reporting a Bond Issued at a Discount (Straight-Line Amortization without Discount Account)

On January 1 of this year, Clearwater Corporation sold bonds with a face value of $750,000 and a coupon rate of 8 percent. The bonds mature in 10 years and pay interest annually every December 31. Clearwater uses the straight-line amortization method and does not use a discount account. Assume an annual market rate of interest of 9 percent.

Required:
1. Provide the journal entry to record the issuance of the bonds.
2. Provide the journal entry to record the interest payment on December 31 of this year.
3. What bonds payable amount will Clearwater report on its December 31 balance sheet?

E10-22
LO10-5

Recording and Reporting a Bond Issued at a Premium (Straight-Line Amortization with Premium Account)

On January 1 of this year, Victor Corporation sold bonds with a face value of $1,400,000 and a coupon rate of 8 percent. The bonds mature in four years and pay interest semiannually every June 30 and December 31. Victor uses the straight-line amortization method and also uses a premium account. Assume an annual market rate of interest of 6 percent.

Required:
1. Provide the journal entry to record the issuance of the bonds.
2. Provide the journal entry to record the interest payment on December 31 of this year.
3. What bonds payable amount will Victor report on its December 31 balance sheet?

E10-23
LO10-5

(Chapter Supplement) Recording and Reporting a Bond Issued at a Premium (Straight-Line Amortization without Premium Account)

On January 1 of this year, Victor Corporation sold bonds with a face value of $1,400,000 and a coupon rate of 8 percent. The bonds mature in four years and pay interest semiannually every June 30 and December 31. Victor uses the straight-line amortization method and does not use a premium account. Assume an annual market rate of interest of 6 percent.

Required:
1. Provide the journal entry to record the issuance of the bonds.
2. Provide the journal entry to record the interest payment on December 31 of this year.
3. What bonds payable amount will Victor report on its December 31 balance sheet?

E10-24
LO10-8

Determining How Bond Transactions Affect the Statement of Cash Flows

A number of events over the life of a bond have effects that are reported on the statement of cash flows. For each of the following events, determine whether the event affects the statement of cash flows and, if so, whether it affects operating, investing, or financing cash flows.

Required:
1. A bond with a face value of $1,000,000 is issued for $960,000.
2. At year-end, $45,000 accrued interest payable is recorded and $1,000 of the bond discount is amortized.
3. Early in the second year, the accrued interest recorded in requirement (2) is paid.
4. The debt matures at the end of the fifth year.

PROBLEMS

Analyzing the Use of Debt

Last year, Arbor Corporation reported the following:

P10-1
LO10-1, 10-6

BALANCE SHEET

Total Assets	$800,000
Total Liabilities	500,000
Total Shareholders' Equity	$300,000

This year, Arbor is considering whether to issue more debt to fund a $100,000 project or to issue additional shares of common stock. Both options will bring in exactly $100,000. Arbor's current debt contracts contain a debt covenant that requires it to maintain a debt-to-equity ratio of 2.0 or less.

Required:
1. Calculate Arbor's current debt-to-equity ratio.
2. Calculate Arbor's debt-to-equity ratio assuming it funds the project using additional debt.
3. Calculate Arbor's debt-to-equity ratio assuming it funds the project by issuing common stock.
4. How do you recommend Arbor fund the project?

Reporting Bonds Issued at Par (AP10-1)

On January 1 of this year, Nowell Company issued bonds with a face value of $100,000 and a coupon rate of 8 percent. The bonds mature in five years and pay interest semiannually every June 30 and December 31. When the bonds were sold, the annual market rate of interest was 8 percent.

P10-2
LO10-2

Required:
1. What was the issue price on January 1 of this year?
2. What amount of interest expense should be recorded on June 30 and December 31 of this year?
3. What amount of cash is owed to investors on June 30 and December 31 of this year?
4. What is the book value of the bonds on December 31 of this year? December 31 of next year?

Comparing Bonds Issued at Par, at a Discount, and at a Premium (AP10-2)

On January 1 of this year, Barnett Corporation sold bonds with a face value of $500,000 and a coupon rate of 7 percent. The bonds mature in 10 years and pay interest annually on December 31. Barnett uses the effective-interest amortization method. Ignore any tax effects. Each case is independent of the other cases.

P10-3
LO10-2, 10-4, 10-5

Required:
Complete the following table. The interest rates provided are the annual market rate of interest on the date the bonds were issued.

	Case A (7%)	Case B (8%)	Case C (6%)
a. Cash received at issuance			
b. Interest expense recorded in Year 1			
c. Cash paid for interest in Year 1			
d. Cash paid at maturity for bond principal			

Computing Issue Prices of Bonds Sold at Par, at a Discount, and at a Premium

Rosh Corporation is planning to issue bonds with a face value of $800,000 and a coupon rate of 8 percent. The bonds mature in four years and pay interest semiannually every June 30 and December 31. All of the bonds will be sold on January 1 of this year.

P10-4
LO10-2, 10-4, 10-5

Required:

Compute the issue (sale) price on January 1 of this year for each of the following independent cases (show computations):

a. **Case A:** Market interest rate (annual): 8 percent.
b. **Case B:** Market interest rate (annual): 6 percent.
c. **Case C:** Market interest rate (annual): 10 percent.

P10-5
LO10-3, 10-4, 10-6

Recording a Bond Issued at a Discount and Determining How the Issuance Affects Ratios

On January 1 of this year, Cunningham Corporation issued bonds with a face value of $200,000 and a coupon rate of 6 percent. The bonds mature in 10 years and pay interest annually every December 31. When the bonds were sold, the annual market rate of interest was 8 percent. The company uses the effective-interest amortization method. By December 31 of this year, the annual market rate of interest had increased to 10 percent.

Required:
1. What is the issuance price of the bonds on January 1?
2. What amount of interest expense is recorded on December 31 of this year?
3. Determine whether the company's debt-to-equity ratio and times interest earned ratio increase, decrease, or stay the same when (*a*) the bonds are issued and (*b*) interest expense is recorded and cash is paid to investors for interest.

P10-6
LO10-4

Recording and Reporting Bonds Issued at a Discount (AP10-3)

PowerTap Utilities is planning to issue bonds with a face value of $1,000,000 and a coupon rate of 10 percent. The bonds mature in 10 years and pay interest semiannually every June 30 and December 31. All of the bonds were sold on January 1 of this year. PowerTap uses the effective-interest amortization method. Assume an annual market rate of interest of 12 percent.

Required:
1. What was the issue price on January 1 of this year?
2. What amount of interest expense should be recorded on June 30 and December 31 of this year?
3. What amount of cash should be paid to investors June 30 and December 31 of this year?
4. What is the book value of the bonds on June 30 and December 31 of this year?

P10-7
LO10-4

Recording and Reporting a Bond Issued at a Discount (with Discount Account) (AP10-4)

Claire Corporation is planning to issue bonds with a face value of $100,000 and a coupon rate of 8 percent. The bonds mature in two years and pay interest quarterly every March 31, June 30, September 30, and December 31. All of the bonds were sold on January 1 of this year. Claire uses the effective-interest amortization method and also uses a discount account. Assume an annual market rate of interest of 12 percent.

Required:
1. Provide the journal entry to record the issuance of the bonds.
2. Provide the journal entry to record the interest payment on March 31, June 30, September 30, and December 31 of this year.
3. What bonds payable amount will Claire report on this year's December 31 balance sheet?

P10-8
LO10-4

(Chapter Supplement) Recording and Reporting a Bond Issued at a Discount (without Discount Account) (AP10-5)

Claire Corporation is planning to issue bonds with a face value of $100,000 and a coupon rate of 8 percent. The bonds mature in two years and pay interest quarterly every March 31, June 30, September 30, and December 31. All of the bonds were sold on January 1 of this year. Claire uses the effective-interest amortization method and does not use a discount account. Assume an annual market rate of interest of 12 percent.

Required:
1. Provide the journal entry to record the issuance of the bonds.
2. Provide the journal entry to record the interest payment on March 31, June 30, September 30, and December 31 of this year.
3. What bonds payable amount will Claire report on this year's December 31 balance sheet?

Recording and Reporting Bonds Issued at a Premium (AP10-6)

P10-9
LO10-5

Cron Corporation is planning to issue bonds with a face value of $700,000 and a coupon rate of 13 percent. The bonds mature in five years and pay interest semiannually every June 30 and December 31. All of the bonds were sold on January 1 of this year. Cron uses the effective-interest amortization method. Assume an annual market rate of interest of 12 percent.

Required:
1. What was the issue price on January 1 of this year?
2. What amount of interest expense should be recorded on June 30 and December 31 of this year?
3. What amount of cash should be paid to investors June 30 and December 31 of this year?
4. What is the book value of the bonds on June 30 and December 31 of this year?

Preparing a Bond Amortization Schedule for a Bond Issued at a Premium

P10-10
LO10-5

On January 1 of this year, Olive Corporation issued bonds. Interest is payable once a year on December 31. The bonds mature at the end of four years. Olive uses the effective-interest amortization method. The partially completed amortization schedule below pertains to the bonds:

Date	Cash	Interest	Amortization	Balance
January 1, Year 1				$48,813
End of Year 1	$3,600	$3,417	$183	48,630
End of Year 2	?	?	?	48,434
End of Year 3	?	?	210	?
End of Year 4	?	3,376	?	48,000

Required:
1. Complete the amortization schedule.
2. When the bonds mature at the end of Year 4, what amount of principle will Olive pay investors?
3. How much cash was received on the day the bonds were issued (sold)?
4. Were the bonds issued at a premium or a discount? If so, what was the amount of the premium or discount?
5. How much cash will be disbursed for interest each period and in total over the life of the bonds?
6. What is the coupon rate?
7. What was the annual market rate of interest on the date the bonds were issued?
8. What amount of interest expense will be reported on the income statement for Year 2 and Year 3?
9. What amount will be reported on the balance sheet at the end of Year 2 and Year 3?

Recording and Reporting a Bond Issued at a Premium (with Premium Account) (AP10-7)

P10-11
LO10-5

Serotta Corporation is planning to issue bonds with a face value of $300,000 and a coupon rate of 12 percent. The bonds mature in two years and pay interest quarterly every March 31, June 30, September 30, and December 31. All of the bonds were sold on January 1 of this year. Serotta uses the effective-interest amortization method and also uses a premium account. Assume an annual market rate of interest of 8 percent.

Required:
1. Provide the journal entry to record the issuance of the bonds.
2. Provide the journal entry to record the interest payment on March 31, June 30, September 30, and December 31 of this year.
3. What bonds payable amount will Serotta report on this year's December 31 balance sheet?

(Chapter Supplement) Recording and Reporting a Bond Issued at a Premium (without Premium Account) (AP10-8)

P10-12
LO10-5

Serotta Corporation is planning to issue bonds with a face value of $300,000 and a coupon rate of 12 percent. The bonds mature in two years and pay interest quarterly every March 31, June 30, September 30, and December 31. All of the bonds were sold on January 1 of this year. Serotta uses the effective-interest amortization method and does not use a premium account. Assume an annual market rate of interest of 8 percent.

Required:
1. Provide the journal entry to record the issuance of the bonds.
2. Provide the journal entry to record the interest payment on March 31, June 30, September 30, and December 31 of this year.
3. What bonds payable amount will Serotta report on this year's December 31 balance sheet?

P10-13

LO10-7

Recording the Early Retirement of a Bond Issued at a Premium (with Premium Account)

Several years ago, Cyclop Company issued bonds with a face value of $1,000,000 for $1,045,000. As a result of declining interest rates, the company has decided to call the bonds at a call premium of 5 percent over par. The bonds have a current book value of $1,010,000. Record the retirement of the bonds, using a premium account.

P10-14

LO10-7

(Chapter Supplement) Recording the Early Retirement of a Bond Issued at a Premium (without Premium Account)

Several years ago, Cyclop Company issued bonds with a face value of $1,000,000 for $1,045,000. As a result of declining interest rates, the company has decided to call the bonds at a call premium of 5 percent over par. The bonds have a current book value of $1,010,000. Record the retirement of the bonds and do not use a premium account.

P10-15

LO10-4

Computing Amounts for a Bond Issued at a Discount and Comparing Effective-Interest Amortization to Straight-Line Amortization

Electrolux Corporation manufactures electrical test equipment. The company's board of directors authorized a bond issue on January 1 of this year with the following terms:

> Face (par) value: $800,000
> Coupon rate: 8 percent payable each December 31
> Maturity date: December 31, end of Year 5
> Annual market interest rate at issuance: 12 percent

Required:

1. Compute the bond issue price.
2. Assume that the company used the straight-line amortization method. Compute the following for Year 1 through Year 5:
   a. Cash payment for bond interest.
   b. Bond interest expense.
3. Assume that the company used the effective-interest amortization method. Compute the following for Year 1 through Year 5:
   a. Cash payment for bond interest.
   b. Bond interest expense.

P10-16

LO10-8

Reporting Bond Transactions on the Statement of Cash Flows

Determine whether each of the following would be reported in the financing activities section of the statement of cash flows and, if so, specify whether it is a cash inflow or outflow.

1. Sale of bonds at a discount.
2. Payment of interest on a bond at maturity.
3. Sale of a bond from one investor to another. Transaction was in cash.

ALTERNATE PROBLEMS

AP10-1

LO10-2

Reporting Bonds Issued at Par (P10-2)

On January 1 of this year, Trucks R Us Corporation issued bonds with a face value of $2,000,000 and a coupon rate of 10 percent. The bonds mature in five years and pay interest semiannually every June 30 and December 31. When the bonds were sold, the annual market rate of interest was 10 percent.

Required:

1. What was the issue price on January 1 of this year?
2. What amount of interest expense should be recorded on June 30 and December 31 of this year?
3. What amount of cash interest should be paid on June 30 and December 31 of this year?
4. What is the book value of the bonds on December 31 of this year? December 31 of next year?

Completing Schedule Comparing Bonds Issued at Par, at a Discount, and at a Premium (P10-3)

On January 1 of this year, Bidden Corporation sold bonds with a face value of $100,000 and a coupon rate of 10 percent. The bonds mature in five years and pay interest semiannually every June 30 and December 31. Bidden uses the effective-interest amortization method. Ignore any tax effects. Each case is independent of the other cases.

Required:
Complete the following table. The interest rates provided next to each case are the annual market rate of interest on the date the bonds were issued.

	At End of Year 1	At End of Year 2	At End of Year 3
Case A: Sold at par (10%)	$	$	$
Interest expense for the year			
Net liability on balance sheet			
Case B: Sold at a discount (12%)			
Interest expense for the year			
Net liability on balance sheet			
Case C: Sold at a premium (8%)			
Interest expense for the year			
Net liability on balance sheet			

AP10-2
LO10-2, 10-4, 10-5

Recording and Reporting Bonds Issued at a Discount (P10-6)

On January 1 of this year, Avaya Corporation issued bonds with a face value of $2,000,000 and a coupon rate of 6 percent. The bonds mature in five years and pay interest annually on December 31. When the bonds were sold, the annual market rate of interest was 7 percent. Avaya uses the effective-interest amortization method.

Required:
1. What was the issue price on January 1 of this year?
2. What amount of interest expense should be recorded on December 31 of this year? December 31 of next year?
3. What amount of cash interest should be paid on December 31 of this year? December 31 of next year?
4. What is the book value of the bonds on December 31 of this year? December 31 of next year?

AP10-3
LO10-4

Recording and Reporting a Bond Issued at a Discount (with Discount Account) (P10-7)

Zues Corporation is planning to issue bonds with a face value of $800,000 and a coupon rate of 4 percent. The bonds mature in two years and pay interest semiannually every June 30 and December 31. All of the bonds were sold on January 1 of this year. Zues uses the effective-interest amortization method and also uses a discount account. Assume an annual market rate of interest of 6 percent.

Required:
1. Provide the journal entry to record the issuance of the bonds.
2. Provide the journal entry to record the interest payment on June 30 and December 31 of this year.
3. What bonds payable amount will Zues report on this year's December 31 balance sheet?

AP10-4
LO10-4

(Chapter Supplement) Recording and Reporting a Bond Issued at a Discount (without Discount Account) (P10-8)

Zues Corporation is planning to issue bonds with a face value of $800,000 and a coupon rate of 4 percent. The bonds mature in two years and pay interest semiannually every June 30 and December 31. All of the bonds were sold on January 1 of this year. Zues uses the effective-interest amortization method and does not use a discount account. Assume an annual market rate of interest of 6 percent.

Required:
1. Provide the journal entry to record the issuance of the bonds.
2. Provide the journal entry to record the interest payment on June 30 and December 31 of this year.
3. What bonds payable amount will Zues report on its December 31 balance sheet?

AP10-5
LO10-4

AP10-6

LO10-5

Recording and Reporting Bonds Issued at a Premium (P10-9)

On January 1 of this year, Thomas Insurance Corporation issued bonds with a face value of $4,000,000 and a coupon rate of 9 percent. The bonds mature in five years and pay interest annually every December 31. When the bonds were sold, the annual market rate of interest was 6 percent. Thomas uses the effective-interest amortization method.

Required:
1. What was the issue price on January 1 of this year?
2. What amount of interest expense should be recorded on December 31 of this year? December 31 of next year?
3. What amount of cash interest should be paid on December 31 of this year? December 31 of next year?
4. What is the book value of the bonds on December 31 of this year? December 31 of next year?

AP10-7

LO10-5

Recording and Reporting a Bond Issued at a Premium (with Premium Account) (P10-11)

Lemond Corporation is planning to issue bonds with a face value of $200,000 and a coupon rate of 10 percent. The bonds mature in three years and pay interest semiannually every June 30 and December 31. All the bonds were sold on January 1 of this year. Lemond uses the effective-interest amortization method and also uses a premium account. Assume an annual market rate of interest of 8.5 percent.

Required:
1. Provide the journal entry to record the issuance of the bonds.
2. Provide the journal entry to record the interest payment on June 30 and December 31 of this year.
3. What bonds payable amount will Lemond report on this year's December 31 balance sheet?

AP10-8

LO10-5

(Chapter Supplement) Recording and Reporting a Bond Issued at a Premium (without Premium Account) (P10-12)

Lemond Corporation is planning to issue bonds with a face value of $200,000 and a coupon rate of 10 percent. The bonds mature in three years and pay interest semiannually every June 30 and December 31. All of the bonds were sold on January 1 of this year. Lemond uses the effective-interest amortization method and does not use a premium account. Assume an annual market rate of interest of 8.5 percent.

Required:
1. Provide the journal entry to record the issuance of the bonds.
2. Provide the journal entry to record the interest payment on June 30 and December 31 of this year.
3. What bonds payable amount will Lemond report on this year's December 31 balance sheet?

CONTINUING PROBLEM

CON10-1

Recording and Reporting Liabilities

Pool Corporation, Inc., is the world's largest wholesale distributor of swimming pool supplies and equipment. It is a publicly traded corporation that trades on the NASDAQ exchange. The majority of Pool's customers are small, family-owned businesses. Assume that Pool borrowed $750,000,000 on January 1 of this year, and that the coupon rate is 5 percent. At the time of the borrowing, the annual market rate of interest was 4 percent. The debt matures in 10 years, and Pool makes interest payments semiannually on June 30 and December 31.

Required:
1. What was the issue price on January 1 of this year?
2. What amount of interest expense should be recorded on June 30 and December 31 of this year?
3. What amount of cash interest should be paid on June 30 and December 31 of this year?
4. What is the book value of the bonds on June 30 and December 31 of this year?

Annual Report Cases

Finding Financial Information

Refer to the financial statements of **American Eagle Outfitters** given in Appendix B at the end of this book.

CP10-1
LO10-1, 10-2

Required:

1. Did American Eagle pay any interest during the year? (**Hint:** You may need to look in the footnotes.)
2. American Eagle has not issued bonds, but it has an agreement to borrow money if needed. What is the total amount the company can borrow under what it calls its "Credit Agreement"?
3. Calculate American Eagle's debt-to-equity ratio.

Finding Financial Information

Refer to the financial statements of **Urban Outfitters** given in Appendix C at the end of this book.

CP10-2
LO10-1, 10-2

Required:

1. Urban Outfitters does not report paying any cash for interest during the year. If it had, where would you find the amount listed?
2. Urban Outfitters has not issued bonds, but it has an agreement to borrow money if needed. What is the total amount the company can borrow under what it calls its "Line of Credit"?
3. Calculate American Eagle's debt-to-equity ratio.

Comparing Companies within an Industry

Refer to the financial statements of **American Eagle** (Appendix B) and **Urban Outfitters** (Appendix C) and the Industry Ratio Report (Appendix D) at the end of this book.

CP10-3
LO10-2, 10-5, 10-7

Required:

1. How do American Eagle's and Urban Outfitters's debt-to-equity ratios compare to the industry average from the Industry Ratio Report?
2. Do you think the debt-to-equity ratio is a meaningful ratio to examine when analyzing American Eagle and Urban Outfitters? Explain.

Analyzing Zero Coupon Bonds from an Actual Company

French energy giant **GDF Suez** recently issued a zero coupon bond. This bond issuance garnered attention because it was the first time in 14 years that a zero coupon bond had been issued in euros. The zero coupon bond has a face value of €500 million and matures in two years. Assume that when the bonds were sold to the public, the annual market rate of interest was 3 percent.

CP10-4
LO10-4

Required:

1. Explain why an investor would buy a bond with a zero coupon (interest) rate.
2. If investors could earn 3 percent on similar investments, how much did GDF Suez receive when it issued the bonds with a face value of €500 million?
3. How much would GDF Suez have received if the annual market rate of interest remained at 3 percent, but the bonds did not mature for 10 years?

Critical Thinking Cases

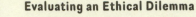

CP10-5

LO10-1

Evaluating an Ethical Dilemma

You work for a small company that is considering investing in a new Internet business. Financial projections suggest that the company will be able to earn in excess of $40 million per year on an investment of $100 million. The company president suggests borrowing the money by issuing bonds that will carry a 7 percent interest rate. He says, "This is better than printing money! We won't have to invest a penny of our own money, and we get to keep $33 million per year after we pay interest to the bondholders." As you think about the proposed transaction, you feel a little uncomfortable about taking advantage of the creditors in this fashion. You feel that it must be wrong to earn such a high return by using money that belongs to other people. Is this an ethical business transaction?

CP10-6

LO10-1

Evaluating an Ethical Dilemma

Assume that you are a portfolio manager for a large insurance company. The majority of the money you manage is from retired school teachers who depend on the income you earn on their investments. You have invested a significant amount of money in the bonds of a large corporation and have just received a call from the company's president explaining that it is unable to meet its current interest obligations because of deteriorating business operations related to increased international competition. The president has a recovery plan that will take at least two years. During that time, the company will not be able to pay interest on the bonds and, she admits, if the plan does not work, bondholders will probably lose more than half of their money. As a creditor, you can force the company into immediate bankruptcy and probably get back at least 90 percent of the bondholders' money. You also know that your decision will cause at least 10,000 people to lose their jobs if the company ceases operations. Given only these two options, what should you do?

Financial Reporting and Analysis Team Project

CP10-7

LO10-1, 10-2, 10-3, 10-4, 10-5, 10-6, 10-8

Team Project: Examining an Annual Report

As a team, select an industry to analyze. Both Yahoo Finance and Google Finance provide information on any given firm's industry. Each team member should acquire the annual report or 10-K for one publicly traded company in the industry, with each member selecting a different company. The annual reports or 10-Ks can be downloaded from the SEC EDGAR website (**www.sec.gov**) or from any individual company's investor relations website.

Required:

Each team member should individually gather the information described below and attempt to answer each question. After completing this individual phase of the project, teams should get together to compare and contrast their answers to each question. At the conclusion of this discussion, each team should write a short report summarizing their analysis and findings.

1. Has your company issued any long-term debt, either bonds or notes? If so, read the footnote and list any unusual features (e.g., callable, convertible, secured by specific collateral, etc.).
2. If your company issued any bond securities (which may be referred to as "notes" in the footnotes), were they issued at par, a premium, or a discount? If they were issued at a premium or discount, does the company use the straight-line or effective-interest amortization method?
3. Ratio analysis:
   a. What does the debt-to-equity ratio measure in general?
   b. Compute the ratio for your company for the last three years.
   c. What do your results suggest about the company?
   d. If available, find the industry ratio for the most recent year, compare it to your results, and discuss why you believe your company differs from or is similar to the industry ratio.
4. Ratio analysis:
   a. What does the times interest earned ratio measure in general?
   b. Compute the ratio for your company for the last three years. If interest expense is not separately disclosed, you will not be able to compute the ratio. If so, state why you think it is not separately disclosed.

    c. What do your results suggest about the company?

    d. If available, find the industry ratio for the most recent year, compare it to your results, and discuss why you believe your company differs from or is similar to the industry ratio.

5. Examine your company's statement of cash flows for the most recent year. Were there any cash inflows or outflows associated with the issuance of debt, payment of interest, or repayment of principal reported on the statement of cash flows? In what section were these inflows and/or outflows reported in the statement of cash flows?

Reporting and Interpreting Stockholders' Equity

Whole Foods Market is a leading retailer of natural and organic foods in the United States. The popular supermarket was incorporated in 1978 and completed its initial public offering in 1992. Whole Foods has over 400 stores in the United States, Canada, and the United Kingdom. In an average week, over 7.7 million customers visit a Whole Foods store. In fiscal 2014, Whole Foods reported revenues of $14.2 billion and net income of $579 million. Whole Foods's growth strategy is to expand primarily through new store openings. In support of this growth plan, the company spent over $700 million in 2014 on capital expenditures.

In this chapter, we study the role that stockholders' equity plays in funding a business and the strategies that managers use to maximize stockholders' wealth.

UNDERSTANDING THE BUSINESS

To some people, the words *corporation* and *business* are almost synonymous. You've probably heard friends refer to a career in business as "the corporate world." Equating business with corporations is understandable because corporations are the dominant form of

Learning Objectives

After studying this chapter, you should be able to:

11-1 Explain the role of stock in the capital structure of a corporation.

11-2 Compute and analyze the earnings per share ratio.

11-3 Describe the characteristics of common stock and report common stock transactions.

11-4 Discuss and report dividends.

11-5 Compute and analyze the dividend yield ratio.

11-6 Discuss and report stock dividends and stock splits.

11-7 Describe the characteristics of preferred stock and report preferred stock transactions.

11-8 Discuss the impact of stock transactions on cash flows.

Jeff Haynes/AFP/Getty Images

Whole Foods Market

ISSUING AND REPORTING
STOCK

www.wholefoodsmarket.com

business organization in terms of volume of operations. If you were to write the names of 10 familiar businesses on a piece of paper, probably all of them would be corporations.

The popularity of the corporate form can be attributed to a critical advantage that corporations have over sole proprietorships and partnerships: They can raise large amounts of capital because both large and small investors can easily participate in their ownership. This ease of participation is related to several factors.

- Shares of stock can be purchased in small amounts. You could buy a single share of Whole Foods stock for about $35 and become one of the owners of this successful company.
- Ownership interests can be easily transferred through the sale of shares on established markets such as the New York Stock Exchange.
- Stock ownership provides investors with limited liability. In the event of bankruptcy, creditors have claims against only the corporation's assets, not the assets of the individual owners.

Many Americans own stock either directly or indirectly through a mutual fund or pension program. Stock ownership offers them the opportunity to earn higher returns than they could depositing money in a bank account or investing in corporate bonds. Unfortunately, stock ownership also involves risks. The proper balance between risk and the expected return on an investment depends on individual preferences.

Exhibit 11.1 presents financial information from **Whole Foods**'s annual report.

EXHIBIT 11.1

Excerpt from Consolidated
Balance Sheets for Whole
Foods Market

WHOLE FOODS

REAL WORLD EXCERPT:

Annual Report

WHOLE FOODS MARKET, INC. Consolidated Balance Sheets (In millions)	September 28, 2014	September 29, 2013
Shareholders' Equity		
Common stock, no par value, 600.0 shares authorized; 377.1 and 375.7 shares issued; 360.4 and 372.4 shares outstanding at 2014 and 2013, respectively	**$2,863**	$2,765
Accumulated other comprehensive income (loss)	**(7)**	1
Retained earnings	**1,668**	1,265
Common stock in treasury, at cost, 16.7 and 3.3 shares at 2014 and 2013, respectively	**(711)**	(153)
Total Shareholders' Equity	**$3,813**	$3,878

Notice that the stockholders' equity section of Whole Foods's balance sheet lists two primary sources of equity:

1. Contributed capital from the sale of stock. This is the amount of money stockholders invested through the purchase of shares. For Whole Foods, contributed capital is the amount in the Common Stock account ($2,863 million for fiscal 2014).

2. Earned capital generated by the company's profit-making activities. Earned capital is kept track of in the Retained Earnings account (sometimes called Accumulated Earnings account). Retained earnings is the cumulative amount of net income the corporation has earned since it organized as a corporation, less the cumulative amount of dividends paid since it organized.

ORGANIZATION of the Chapter

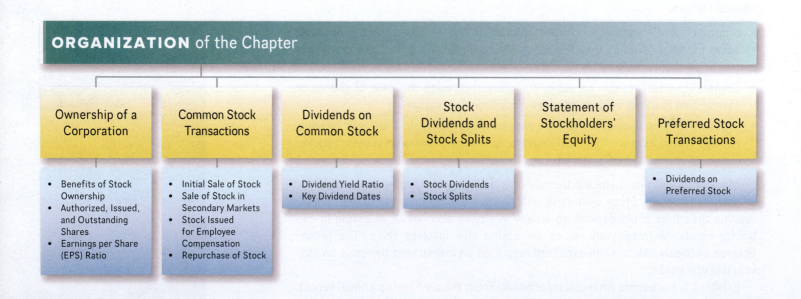

OWNERSHIP OF A CORPORATION

The corporation is the only business form the law recognizes as a separate entity. As a distinct entity, the corporation enjoys a continuous existence separate and apart from its owners. It may own assets, incur liabilities, expand and contract in size, sue others, be sued, and enter into contracts independently of its stockholder owners.

To protect everyone's rights, the creation and governance of corporations are tightly regulated by law. Corporations are created by application to a state government (not the federal government). On approval of the application, the state issues a charter, sometimes called the articles of incorporation. Corporations are governed by a board of directors elected by the stockholders.

Each state has different laws governing the organization of corporations created within its boundaries. **Whole Foods** incorporated in the state of Texas and has its headquarters in Austin, Texas. You will find that an unusually large number of corporations are incorporated in Delaware even though their headquarters are located in a different state. Companies choose Delaware for incorporation because the state has some of the most favorable laws, especially with regard to taxes, for establishing corporations.

Benefits of Stock Ownership

When you invest in a corporation, you are known as a stockholder or shareholder. As a stockholder, you receive shares of stock that you subsequently can sell on established stock exchanges. Owners of common stock receive a number of benefits:

- **A voice in management.** You may vote in the stockholders' meeting on major issues concerning management of the corporation.

- **Dividends.** If a company pays dividends, you receive a proportional share of the distribution of profits.

- **Residual claim.** You will receive a proportional share of the distribution of remaining assets upon the liquidation of the company.

Stockholders, unlike creditors, are able to vote at the annual stockholders' meeting. Each share of stock represents one vote. The following notice of the annual meeting of shareholders was recently sent to all owners of **Whole Foods** stock:

> NOTICE OF ANNUAL MEETING OF SHAREHOLDERS
>
> Notice is hereby given that a meeting of Shareholders of Whole Foods Market, Inc., will be held at the Roosevelt New Orleans, 130 Roosevelt Way, New Orleans, Louisiana 70112, on March 10, 2015, at 8:30 a.m. local time for the following purposes:
>
> 1. To elect the eleven nominees to the board of directors to serve one-year terms;
> 2. To conduct an advisory vote to approve executive compensation;
> 3. To ratify the appointment of Ernst & Young as independent auditor;
> 4. To approve an amendment to the Company's Articles of Incorporation to increase the number of authorized shares;
> 5. To approve an amendment to the Company's Bylaws regarding proxy access; and
> 6. To transact such other business as may properly come before the meeting.
>
> Only shareholders of record at the close of business on January 12, 2015, are entitled to notice of, and to vote at, the meeting.

LEARNING OBJECTIVE 11-1
Explain the role of stock in the capital structure of a corporation.

WHOLE FOODS

REAL WORLD EXCERPT:

Notice of Shareholders' Meeting

This notice also contained several pages of information concerning the people who were nominated to be members of the board of directors as well as a variety of financial information. Because most stockholders do not actually attend the annual meeting, the notice included information about how absentee stockholders can cast their votes using the Internet or a telephone.

Stockholders have ultimate authority in a corporation. The board of directors and, indirectly, all employees are accountable to the stockholders.

Authorized, Issued, and Outstanding Shares

AUTHORIZED NUMBER OF SHARES

The maximum number of shares of stock a corporation can issue as specified in its charter.

ISSUED SHARES

The total number of shares of stock that have been sold.

TREASURY STOCK

A corporation's own stock that has been repurchased. Shares held as treasury stock are considered issued shares but not outstanding shares.

OUTSTANDING SHARES

The total number of shares of stock that are owned by stockholders on any particular date.

The corporate charter specifies the maximum number of shares the corporation is authorized to sell to the public. The financial statements report this number, as well as the number of shares that have been sold to date. Let's look at the share information reported by **Whole Foods** as of September 28, 2014, shown in Exhibit 11.1. For Whole Foods, the maximum number of common shares that can be sold, called the **authorized number of shares**, is 600,000,000. As of September 28, 2014, the company had sold 377,100,000 common shares. Shares that have been sold to the public are called **issued shares**.

For a number of reasons, a company might want to buy back shares that have already been sold to the public. Shares that have been bought back are called **treasury stock**. Shares held as treasury stock are considered issued shares but not **outstanding shares**. Thus, when a company buys back shares, it creates a difference between the number of issued shares and the number of outstanding shares of its stock. As of September 28, 2014, Whole Foods had 360,400,000 shares outstanding and 16,700,000 shares being held as treasury stock. The relationship between Whole Foods's issued, outstanding, and treasury shares is shown below:

Issued shares	377,100,000
Less: Treasury stock	(16,700,000)
Outstanding shares	360,400,000

Knowing the number of shares outstanding is important because this number is used in the calculation of various ratios, including the earnings per share ratio.

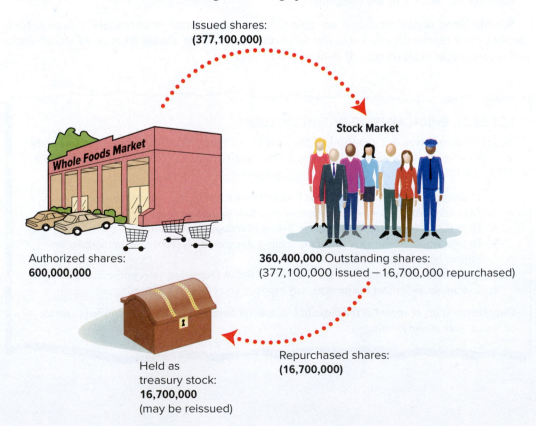

Issued shares:
(377,100,000)

Stock Market

Authorized shares:
600,000,000

360,400,000 Outstanding shares:
(377,100,000 issued − 16,700,000 repurchased)

Held as
treasury stock:
16,700,000
(may be reissued)

Repurchased shares:
(16,700,000)

Earnings per Share (EPS)		KEY RATIO ANALYSIS

 ANALYTICAL QUESTION

How well is a company performing?

 RATIO AND COMPARISONS

Earnings per share is computed as follows:

Earnings per Share = Net Income* ÷ Weighted Average Number of Common Shares Outstanding

*Preferred dividends, if any, should be subtracted from net income.

The 2014 ratio for **Whole Foods**:

\$579 million ÷ 367.8 (million) shares† = \$1.57

†As reported on the income statement.

COMPARISONS OVER TIME			COMPARISONS WITH COMPETITORS	
Whole Foods			**Safeway**	**The Fresh Market**
2014	**2013**	**2012**	**2014**	**2014**
$1.57	$1.48	$1.28	$0.48	$1.30

 INTERPRETATIONS

In General   You have probably seen newspaper headlines announcing a company's earnings. Notice that those news stories normally report earnings on an earnings per share (EPS) basis. EPS is a popular measure because it emphasizes the amount of earnings attributable to a single share of outstanding common stock. Since the number of outstanding shares of common stock changes over time, and is different across firms, using EPS rather than just net income allows analysts and investors to make "apples-to-apples" comparisons across time and across firms. Companies are required to report EPS on their income statements.

Focus Company Analysis   For Whole Foods, the weighted average number of common shares outstanding has stayed relatively constant over the last three years, while net income has increased. This has caused the company's EPS to increase over the three years. Whole Foods also has a higher EPS than **The Fresh Market**, a much smaller competitor with annual sales of \$1.8 billion, and **Safeway**, a much larger competitor with annual sales of \$36 billion. We can compare EPS numbers across firms of different sizes because EPS captures the amount of earnings attributable to a single share of outstanding common stock, regardless of the size of a company or the number of shares of stock outstanding.

A Few Cautions   While EPS is an effective and widely used measure of profitability, it does not necessarily indicate how a company will perform in the future. Stock price is a better indication of expected future performance. For example, if two companies have identical EPS numbers, but the stock price of one company is double that of the other company, investors expect greater future performance from the firm with the higher stock price. EPS is a measure of performance over a prior period, while stock price is an indication of performance over future periods. It is important to keep this in mind when analyzing EPS numbers across time and across firms.

LEARNING OBJECTIVE 11-2
Compute and analyze the earnings per share ratio.

COMMON STOCK TRANSACTIONS

All corporations issue common stock, and some elect to issue a second type of stock called preferred stock. In this section, we discuss common stock. Near the end of the chapter, we will discuss preferred stock.

Common stock is held by investors who are the "owners" of a corporation. Though stockholders are owners and have the right to vote and share in the profitability of the business through dividends, they do not actively participate in managing the business. Instead, they elect a board of directors and it is the board's role to hire and monitor executives who manage a company's activities on a day-to-day basis.

LEARNING OBJECTIVE 11-3
Describe the characteristics of common stock and report common stock transactions.

COMMON STOCK
The basic voting stock issued by a corporation.

Depending on state law, a company's common stock may be required to have a **par value**, a nominal value per share established in the corporate charter. Par value has no relationship to the market value of a stock. For example, **The Fresh Market**'s common stock has a par value of $0.01 per share while its stock price is over $40 per share. **Whole Foods**'s common stock does not have a par value.

Most states require stock to have a par value. The original purpose of this requirement was to protect creditors by specifying a permanent amount of capital that owners could not withdraw before a bankruptcy, which would leave creditors with something in the event that a company did not succeed. This permanent amount of capital is called **legal capital**. Though the requirement to assign a par value and maintain legal capital is embedded in state law, in today's business world it does little to protect creditors. Companies have simply transitioned to assigning an extremely low par value, like $0.01 per share, which means that any legal capital requirements are too low to meaningfully protect creditors. As a result, creditors have adopted other protection mechanisms, like the debt covenants we discussed in Chapter 10, to provide some protection in the event that a company performs poorly.

There are some states that require the issuance of **no-par value stock**. When a corporation issues no-par stock, like Whole Foods, legal capital is as defined by state law.

Initial Sale of Stock

An **initial public offering,** or IPO, involves the very first sale of a company's stock to the public (i.e., when the company first "goes public"). You have probably heard stories of a new company's stock price increasing dramatically the day of its IPO. While investors sometimes earn significant returns on IPOs, they also take significant risks. Once a company's stock has been traded on established markets, additional sales of new stock to the public are called **seasoned offerings.**

Most sales of stock to the public are cash transactions. To illustrate the accounting for an initial sale of stock, assume that **Trader Joe's** sold 100,000 shares of its $1 par value stock for $20 per share. The company would record the following journal entry:

Cash (+A) (100,000 × $20)	2,000,000	
Common stock (+SE) (100,000 × $1)		100,000
Additional paid-in capital (+SE)		1,900,000

Assets		=	Liabilities	+	Stockholders' Equity	
Cash	+2,000,000				Common stock	+100,000
					Additional paid-in capital	+1,900,000

Notice that the Common Stock account is credited for the number of shares sold times the par value per share. The Additional Paid-in Capital account is credited for the remainder, which is the amount "in addition" to par value that the company received when it issued the shares. In rare cases, a corporate charter may specify a "stated value" rather than a "par value." For accounting purposes, the two values are used in the same way. If there is no par or stated value, the entire proceeds from the sale will be entered in the Common Stock account.

Sale of Stock in Secondary Markets

When a company sells stock to the public, the transaction is between the issuing corporation and the investor. Subsequent to the initial sale, investors can sell shares to other investors without directly affecting the corporation. For example, if investor Ed DeHaan sold 1,000 shares of **Whole Foods** stock to investor Amanda Winn, Whole Foods would not record a journal entry. Mr. DeHaan received cash for the shares he sold, and Ms. Winn received stock for the cash she paid. Whole Foods was not a part of the transaction and therefore did not receive or pay anything.

Each business day, *The Wall Street Journal* reports the results of thousands of transactions between investors in secondary markets, such as the New York Stock Exchange (NYSE) and the NASDAQ market. Managers of corporations monitor the price movements of their companies' stock. Stockholders expect to earn money on their investments through both dividends and increases in the stock price. In many instances, senior management has been replaced because of a stock's poor performance in the stock market.

Stock Issued for Employee Compensation

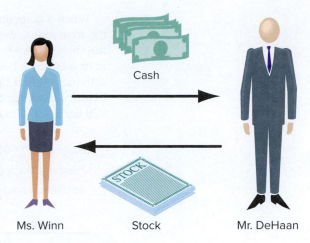

One of the advantages of the corporate form is the ability to separate the management of a business from its ownership. Separation can also be a disadvantage because some managers may not act in the owners' best interests. This potential problem can be addressed in a number of ways. For example, compensation packages can be developed to reward managers for meeting goals that are important to stockholders. Another strategy is to offer managers stock options, which permit them to buy stock at a fixed price.

The holder of a stock option has an interest in a company's performance just as an owner does. Stock option plans are a common form of compensation. **Whole Foods** offers employees stock options as part of their compensation. The options specify that shares may be bought at the then-current market price. Granting a stock option is a form of compensation, even if the grant price and the current stock price are the same. You can think of a stock option as a risk-free investment. If you hold a stock option and the stock price declines, you have lost nothing. If the stock price increases, you can exercise your option at the low grant price and sell the stock at the higher price for a profit.

Companies must estimate and report compensation expense associated with stock options. How managers make these estimates are discussed in more detail in intermediate accounting courses.

Repurchase of Stock

A corporation may want to repurchase its stock from existing stockholders for a number of reasons. One common reason is the existence of an employee bonus plan that provides workers with shares of the company's stock as part of their compensation. Because of Securities and Exchange Commission regulations concerning newly issued shares, most companies find it less costly to give employees repurchased shares than to issue new ones. In addition, if a company were to pay bonuses with newly issued shares each period, it would increase the number of shares in the market, which would decrease the company's stock price. Increasing the number of shares would also dilute existing stockholders' investments, as each share of stock they own would be worth less. By repurchasing shares to fulfill bonus obligations, companies avoid this dilution effect. Stock that has been repurchased and is held by the issuing corporation is called *treasury stock*. Treasury shares have no voting, dividend, or other stockholder rights while they are held as treasury stock.

When companies repurchase shares from the market, they pay cash and receive their own stock. Assume that **Trader Joe's** repurchased 100,000 shares of its stock in the open market when it was selling for $20 per share. To reflect the repurchase, the company would record the following journal entry:

Treasury stock (+XSE, −SE) (100,000 × $20)	2,000,000
Cash (−A)	2,000,000

Assets	=	Liabilities	+	Stockholders' Equity	
Cash −2,000,000				Treasury stock	−2,000,000

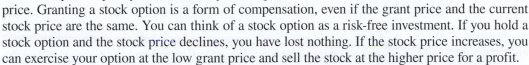

Intuitively, many students expect the Treasury Stock account to be reported as an asset. Such is not the case because a company cannot own itself. The Treasury Stock account is actually a contra-equity account, which is why in Exhibit 11.1 **Whole Foods** shows Common Stock in Treasury as a negative number on its balance sheet. This practice makes sense because treasury stock is considered issued but not outstanding. Thus, when stock is repurchased and held in treasury it is not removed from the Common Stock account but rather is shown as its own separate account within stockholders' equity, and because repurchasing the shares reduced assets (cash), it reduces equity. As the information in Exhibit 11.1 indicates, Whole Foods reported treasury stock in the amount of $711 (million) on its balance sheet as of September 28, 2014.

When a company sells its treasury stock, it does not report an accounting profit or loss on the transaction, even if it sells the stock for more or less than it originally cost to repurchase the shares. GAAP does not permit a corporation to report income or losses from investments in its own stock because transactions with the owners are not considered normal profit-making activities. Based on the previous example, assume that Trader Joe's resells 10,000 shares of treasury stock for $30 per share. Remember that the company had repurchased the stock for $20 per share. Trader Joe's would record the following journal entry when it resells the shares:

Cash (+A) (10,000 × $30)	300,000	
Treasury stock (−XSE, +SE) (10,000 × $20)		200,000
Additional paid-in capital (+SE)		100,000

Assets	=	Liabilities	+	Stockholders' Equity	
Cash +300,000				Treasury stock	+200,000
				Additional paid-in capital	+100,000

If the treasury stock had been resold at $15 per share rather than $30 per share, stockholders' equity would be reduced by the amount of the difference between the repurchase price and the sale price. The journal entry Trader Joe's would record if the sale price were $15 per share is:

Cash (+A) (10,000 × $15)	150,000	
Additional paid-in capital (−SE) (10,000 × $5)	50,000	
Treasury stock (−XSE, +SE) (10,000 × $20)		200,000

Assets	=	Liabilities	+	Stockholders' Equity	
Cash +150,000				Treasury stock	+200,000
				Additional paid-in capital	−50,000

STOP

PAUSE FOR FEEDBACK

We have looked at several transactions involving the sale and repurchase of common stock. In the next section, we will discuss dividends. Before we move on, complete the following questions to test your understanding of the concepts we have covered so far.

SELF-STUDY QUIZ

1. Assume that Apple Produce issued 10,000 shares of its common stock for $150,000 cash. The stock has a par value of $2 per share. Prepare the journal entry to record this transaction.
2. Assume that Apple Produce repurchased 5,000 shares of its stock in the open market when the stock was selling for $12 per share. Record this transaction.
3. If Apple Produce's common stock did not have a par value, how would the journal entries in (1) and (2) change?

After you have completed your answers, check them below.

Solutions to
SELF-STUDY QUIZ

1. Cash (+A)	150,000	
Common stock (+SE) ($2 × 10,000)		20,000
Additional paid-in capital (+SE, remainder)		130,000
2. Treasury stock (+XSE, −SE)	60,000	
Cash (−A)		60,000

3. In journal entry (1), you would credit Common Stock for 150,000. There would be no "Additional Paid-in Capital" account in the transaction. Journal entry (2) would not change.

DIVIDENDS ON COMMON STOCK

Investors buy common stock because they expect a return on their investment. This return can come in two forms: stock price appreciation and dividends. Some investors prefer to buy stocks that pay little or no dividends because companies that reinvest the majority of their earnings tend to increase their future earnings potential, along with their stock price. Wealthy investors in high tax brackets prefer to receive their return in the form of higher stock prices because capital gains may be taxed at a lower rate than dividend income. Other investors, such as retired people who need a steady income, prefer to receive their return in the form of dividends. These people often seek stocks that will pay relatively high dividends, such as utility stocks. Because of the importance of dividends to many investors, analysts often compute the dividend yield ratio to evaluate a corporation's dividend policy.

Dividend Yield

KEY RATIO ANALYSIS

 ANALYTICAL QUESTION

How much does a company pay out in dividends each year relative to its share price?

 RATIO AND COMPARISONS

The dividend yield ratio is computed as follows:

$$\text{Dividend Yield} = \text{Dividends per Share} \div \text{Market Price per Share}$$

The 2014 ratio for **Whole Foods**: $0.48 \div \$37.67 = 1.3\%$

COMPARISONS OVER TIME			COMPARISONS WITH COMPETITORS	
Whole Foods			**Safeway**	**The Fresh Market**
2014	**2013**	**2012**	**2014**	**2014**
1.3%	2.4%	0.6%	2.5%	0.0%
($0.48 ÷ $37.67)	($1.40 ÷ $58.33)	($0.28 ÷ $48.70)		

 INTERPRETATIONS

In General   Investors in common stock can earn a return from both dividends and capital appreciation (increases in the market price of the stock). The dividend yield ratio reflects the return on investment absent any capital appreciation or, said differently, the return attributed solely to the dividends a company pays.

Focus Company Analysis   Whole Foods's stock price at the end of fiscal 2014 was $37.67. If you had invested this amount in Whole Foods and received the dividends that Whole Foods paid out during 2014, your return on investment would have been 1.3 percent. Whole Foods paid a relatively large dividend per share in 2013, which is reflected in its dividend yield ratio being considerably higher in that year. **Safeway**'s stock price per share at the end of fiscal 2014 was similar to that of Whole Foods ($35.13 vs. $37.67). Safeway, however, paid a higher dividend per share ($0.89 vs. $0.48), resulting in a higher dividend yield ratio. **The Fresh Market** has not paid a dividend since 2011, instead choosing to reinvest all earnings in the company to fuel growth. As a result, the company's dividend yield ratio is zero.

A Few Cautions   Remember that the dividend yield ratio tells only part of the return on investment story; it does not reflect capital appreciation as reflected in the increase in a company's stock price over time. Often potential capital appreciation is a much more important consideration. Whole Foods currently reinvests most of its earnings to fuel growth rather than paying out those earnings in the form of dividends. Whole Foods reported earnings in 2014 of $579 million but paid only $170 million to investors as dividends. Analysts should consider a company's dividend yield ratio in conjunction with other return measures when assessing a company's performance.

Key Dividend Dates

The declaration and payment of a dividend involve several key dates. Let's review these dates based on information reported in **Whole Foods**'s 2014 Annual Report.

Date of Declaration	Dividend per Common Share	Date of Record	Date of Payment	Total Amount (in millions)
November 1, 2013	$0.12	January 17, 2014	January 28, 2014	$45
February 24, 2014	$0.12	April 11, 2014	April 22, 2014	$44
June 12, 2014	$0.12	July 3, 2014	July 15, 2014	$44
September 11, 2014	$0.12	September 26, 2014	October 7, 2014	$43

This excerpt contains three important dates:

DECLARATION DATE

The date on which the board of directors officially approves a dividend.

1. **Declaration date.** The **declaration date** is the date on which the board of directors officially approves the dividend. As soon as the board declares a dividend, a liability is created and must be recorded.

RECORD DATE

The date on which the corporation prepares the list of current stockholders who will receive the dividend when paid.

2. **Date of record.** The **record date** follows the declaration; it is the date on which the corporation prepares the list of current stockholders who will receive the dividend payment. The dividend is payable only to those names listed on the record date. No journal entry is made on this date.

PAYMENT DATE

The date on which a cash dividend is paid to the stockholders of record.

3. **Date of payment.** The **payment date** is the date on which cash is disbursed to pay the dividend liability.

These three dates apply for all cash dividends and can be shown graphically as follows:

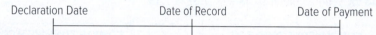

On the declaration date, a company records a liability related to the dividend. To illustrate, on September 11, Whole Foods records the following journal entry. The $43 million is reported in the last column above.

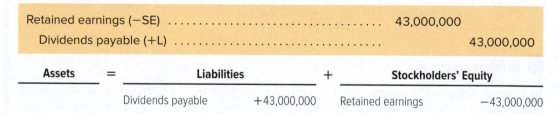

The payment of the liability on October 7 is recorded as follows:

Notice that the declaration and payment of a cash dividend reduce assets (cash) and stockholders' equity (retained earnings) by the same amount. This observation explains the two fundamental requirements for payment of a cash dividend:

1. **Sufficient retained earnings or net income.** The corporation must have accumulated a sufficient amount of retained earnings, or earned a sufficient amount of income during the period, to cover the amount of the dividend.

2. Sufficient cash. The corporation must have sufficient cash to pay the dividend and meet the operating needs of the business. The mere fact that the Retained Earnings account has a large credit balance does not mean that the board of directors can declare and pay a cash dividend. The cash generated in the past by earnings represented in the Retained Earnings account may have been spent to acquire inventory, buy operational assets, and pay liabilities. Consequently, no necessary relationship exists between the balance of retained earnings and the balance of cash on any particular date. Quite simply, retained earnings is not cash.

Investors should be careful to research a company's dividend policy before investing. In the United States, there is no legal obligation for companies to declare dividends, regardless of how profitable the company is. Many very successful companies have never paid dividends while other equally successful companies pay out a large percentage of their earnings each year. The dividend policy for a company is determined by the board of directors. In some other countries, dividend payments are not discretionary and are required by law. In Brazil, for example, companies are legally required to pay out at least 25 percent of their net income in dividends each year.

While U.S. companies are under no legal obligation to declare dividends, once the board of directors declares a dividend (i.e., creates a dividend payable), there is a legal obligation to pay that dividend. In the case of a corporate bankruptcy, dividends payable would be a legally enforceable claim against the company.

| Impact of Dividends on Stock Price | FINANCIAL ANALYSIS |

Another date that is important in understanding dividends has no accounting implications. The date two business days before the date of record is known as the *ex-dividend date*. This date is established by the stock exchanges to account for the fact that it takes time (typically three days) to officially transfer stock from a seller to a buyer. If you buy stock before the ex-dividend date, you will be listed as the owner on the date of record and will receive the dividend. If you buy stock on the ex-dividend date or later, the previous owner will be listed as the owner on the date of record and will therefore receive the dividend.

If you follow stock prices, you will notice that they often fall on the ex-dividend date. The stock is worth less on that date because it no longer includes the right to receive the next dividend.

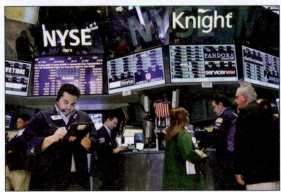

Justin Lane/epa european pressphoto agency b.v./Alamy

PAUSE FOR FEEDBACK

One of the reasons that investors buy common stock is to earn dividends. We have looked at dividends paid in cash. In the next section, we will look at dividends paid in stock. Before we move on, complete the following questions to test your understanding of the concepts we have covered so far.

(continued)

STOCK DIVIDENDS AND STOCK SPLITS

Stock Dividends

LEARNING OBJECTIVE 11-6
Discuss and report stock dividends and stock splits.

STOCK DIVIDEND
A distribution of additional shares of a corporation's own stock on a pro rata basis at no cost to existing stockholders.

Unless stated otherwise, the term *dividend* means a cash dividend. Though cash dividends are by far the most common type of dividend, companies can also distribute additional shares of stock as a dividend. A **stock dividend** is a distribution of additional shares of a company's own stock to its stockholders on a pro rata basis at no cost to the stockholder.

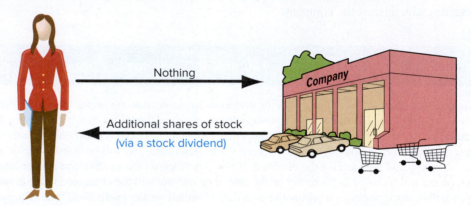

The phrase *pro rata basis* means that each stockholder receives additional shares equal to the percentage of shares held. A stockholder with 10 percent of the outstanding shares would receive 10 percent of any additional shares issued as a stock dividend.

The economic value of a stock dividend is the subject of much debate. In reality, a stock dividend by itself has no economic value. All stockholders receive a pro rata distribution of shares, which means that each stockholder owns exactly the same portion of the company as before. The value of an investment is determined by the percentage of the company that is owned, not the number of shares held. If you get change for a dollar, you do not have more wealth because you hold four quarters instead of one dollar. Similarly, if you own 10 percent of a company, you are not wealthier simply because the company declares a stock dividend and gives you (and all other stockholders) more shares of stock. Both before and after the stock dividend, you own 10 percent of the company.

The stock market reacts immediately when a stock dividend is issued, and the stock price falls. Theoretically, if the stock price was $60 before a stock dividend and the company doubles the number of shares outstanding by issuing a stock dividend, the price of the company's stock should fall to $30. In reality, the fall in price may not be exactly proportional to the number of new shares issued. In some cases, the stock dividend makes the stock more attractive to new investors. Many investors prefer to buy stock in round lots, typically in multiples of 100 shares. An investor with $10,000 might not buy a stock selling for $150, for instance, because she cannot afford to buy 100 shares. However, she might buy the stock if the price were less than $100 as the result of a stock dividend. In such cases, the stock price decrease at the time of a stock dividend will likely not be exactly proportional to the number of new shares issued.

When a company's board of directors declares a stock dividend, the company transfers an amount from the Retained Earnings account (or the Additional Paid-in Capital account) into the Common Stock account to reflect the additional shares issued. The amount transferred depends on whether the stock dividend is classified as a large stock dividend or a small stock dividend.

A large stock dividend involves the distribution of additional shares that amount to more than 20–25 percent of currently outstanding shares. A small stock dividend involves the distribution of shares that amount to less than 20–25 percent of currently outstanding shares. Because a large stock dividend significantly decreases a company's stock price, GAAP requires the amount transferred to the Common Stock account to be based on the par value of the stock. In the case of a small stock dividend, GAAP requires the amount transferred to be based on the market price of the stock, with the par value amount being transferred to the Common Stock account and the excess transferred to the Additional Paid-in Capital account.

To demonstrate how the accounting for stock dividends works, assume **Trader Joe's** declared a large stock dividend that resulted in an additional 50,000,000 shares of $1 par value stock being distributed to stockholders. On the date of declaration, Trader Joe's would record the following journal entry:

Retained earnings (−SE) ($1 par value × 50,000,000)	50,000,000	
Common stock (+SE) ($1 par value × 50,000,000)		50,000,000

Assets	=	Liabilities	+	Stockholders' Equity	
				Retained earnings	−50,000,000
				Common stock	+50,000,000

Now assume Trader Joe's declared a small stock dividend that resulted in an additional 5,000,000 shares being distributed to stockholders. On the date of declaration, Trader Joe's stock was trading at $12 per share. The journal entry Trader Joe's would enter is:

Retained earnings (−SE) ($12 market price × 5,000,000)	60,000,000	
Common stock (+SE) ($1 par value × 5,000,000)		5,000,000
Additional paid-in capital (+SE) (remainder)		55,000,000

Assets	=	Liabilities	+	Stockholders' Equity	
				Retained earnings	−60,000,000
				Common stock	+5,000,000
				Additional paid-in capital	+55,000,000

It is important to note that regardless of whether a stock dividend is classified as large or small, there is no change in the total amount of stockholders' equity. Both large and small stock dividends merely redistribute amounts within the stockholders' equity section of the balance sheet.

Stock Splits

Stock splits are not dividends. While they are similar to a stock dividend in the sense that they distribute additional shares of stock to stockholders, they are quite different in terms of how they impact accounts in the stockholders' equity section of the balance sheet.

Whether a company distributes additional shares of stock by declaring a stock dividend or by initiating a stock split is often determined by state law. In a **stock split**, a company commits to giving stockholders a specified number of additional shares for each share that they currently hold. For example, when a company declares a two-for-one stock split, a stockholder who

STOCK SPLIT
Gives stockholders a specified number of additional shares for each share that they currently hold.

owned one share of stock before the split will own two shares of stock after the split. In essence, the one share has been "split" into two shares. A company's footnotes will state whether the stock split applies to all authorized, issued, and outstanding shares.

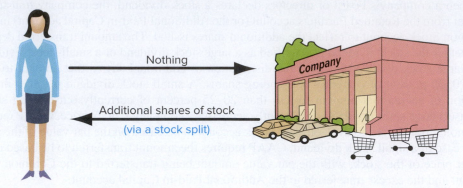

When a company initiates a stock split, it also reduces the par value of its stock so that the total dollar amount in the Common Stock account remains unchanged. For instance, if **Trader Joe's** executes a two-for-one stock split, thereby doubling the number of shares issued, it would reduce the par value of its stock from $1 to $0.50. In contrast to a stock dividend, a stock split does not change any account balances in the stockholders' equity section of the balance sheet.

In both a stock dividend and a stock split, the stockholder receives more shares of stock without having to invest additional resources to acquire the shares. A stock dividend requires a journal entry; a stock split does not but is disclosed in the notes to the financial statements. The comparative effects of a large stock dividend versus a stock split may be summarized as follows:

STOCKHOLDERS' EQUITY			
	Before	**After a 100% Stock Dividend**	**After a 2-for-1 Stock Split**
Number of shares outstanding	300,000	600,000	600,000
Par value per share	$ 1.00	$ 1.00	$ 0.50
Common stock	$300,000	$600,000	$300,000
Retained earnings	650,000	350,000	650,000
Total stockholders' equity	950,000	950,000	950,000

It is quite common for companies to announce a "stock split" but to account for the distribution of additional shares as a large stock dividend. Companies typically do this to avoid changing the par value of their common stock. Such announcements are referred to as initiating a "stock split effected in the form of a stock dividend." Whenever you see this phrase, know that the company has accounted for the transaction as a large stock dividend.

STOP

PAUSE FOR **FEEDBACK**

We have concluded our discussion of common stock by looking at stock dividends and stock splits. In the next section, we will provide a brief introduction to the statement of stockholders' equity and then discuss preferred stock. Before you move on, complete the following questions to test your understanding of the concepts we have covered so far.

SELF-STUDY **QUIZ**

Barton Corporation issued 100,000 shares of common stock (par value $0.10) by declaring a stock dividend. At the time the dividend was declared, Barton's stock was trading at $30 per share.

1. Record this transaction, assuming it is classified as a small stock dividend.
2. Record this transaction, assuming that it is classified as a large stock dividend.
3. If Barton were to distribute the same number of shares by announcing a stock split, what journal entry would be required?

After you have completed your answers, check them below.

STATEMENT OF STOCKHOLDERS' EQUITY

In previous chapters we discussed three of the four financial statements required by GAAP: the income statement, the balance sheet, and the statement of cash flows. The fourth required statement is the statement of stockholders' equity. The purpose of the fourth statement is to show how accounts in the stockholders' equity section of the balance sheet have changed over the accounting period. Common accounts shown are common stock, additional paid-in capital, treasury stock, and retained earnings. The statement of stockholders' (shareholders') equity for **Whole Foods** is shown in Exhibit 11.2. Under GAAP, the statement must show three years of data, but, for illustrative purposes, we show only the latest year.

As you review Exhibit 11.2, you will observe many of the issues discussed in this chapter. Notice for example:

1. Treasury stock was purchased at a cost of $578 (million).

2. Cash dividends totaling $176 (million) were paid, which reduced retained earnings.

3. Net income was $579 (million), which increased retained earnings.

The statement also contains a number of other changes that involve topics typically covered in an intermediate accounting course. Perhaps the most important one is accumulated other comprehensive income (loss), which captures certain items that are reported as a part of comprehensive income, but not net income. Examples of items that are not included in the computation of net income:

1. *Unrealized holding gains or losses from certain types of securities.* Under GAAP, gains and losses from holding certain types of securities are reported on the income statement only when the stock is sold. Unrealized gains and losses that occur before the stock is sold are included in comprehensive income.

2. *Foreign currency translation gains and losses.* Many U.S. companies have foreign subsidiaries that conduct business using foreign currencies. Incorporating the financial statements of these foreign subsidiaries into a U.S. company's financial statements requires the use of a foreign currency exchange rate. Changes in exchange rates from year to year result in foreign currency translation gains and losses. These gains and losses are included in comprehensive income.

We briefly introduce several components of comprehensive income to give you a more complete understanding of the items included on the statement of stockholders' equity. If you choose to take an intermediate accounting course, you will learn a great deal more about these topics.

---

1. Retained earnings (−SE) ($30 × 100,000)	3,000,000	
Common stock (+SE) ($0.10 × 100,000)		10,000
Additional paid-in capital (+SE) (remainder)		2,990,000
2. Retained earnings (−SE) ($0.10 × 100,000)	10,000	
Common stock (+SE) ($0.10 × 100,000)		10,000
3. No journal entry is required in the case of a stock split.		

Solutions to
SELF-STUDY QUIZ

EXHIBIT 11.2   Excerpt from Statement of Shareholders' Equity for Whole Foods

WHOLE FOODS REAL WORLD EXCERPT: Annual Report

WHOLE FOODS MARKET, INC.
Consolidated Statement of Shareholders' Equity
Fiscal year ended September 28, 2014
(in millions)

	Shares Outstanding	Common Stock	Common Stock in Treasury	Accumulated Other Comprehensive Income (Loss)	Retained Earnings	Total Shareholders' Equity
Balances at September 29, 2013	372.4	$2,765	$(153)	$ 1	$1,265	$3,878
Net income	—	—	—	—	579	579
Other comprehensive loss, net of tax	—	—	—	(8)	—	(8)
Dividends ($0.48 per common share)	—	—	—	—	(176)	(176)
Issuance of common stock pursuant to team member stock plans	1.9	21	20	—	—	41
Purchase of treasury stock	(13.9)	—	(578)	—	—	(578)
Tax benefit related to exercise of team member stock options	—	9	—	—	—	9
Share-based payment expense	—	68	—	—	—	68
Balances at September 28, 2014	360.4	$2,863	$(711)	$(7)	$1,668	$3,813

 GUIDED HELP 11-1

For additional step-by-step video instruction on how to create an income statement, statement of stockholders' equity, and balance sheet, go to **www.mhhe.com/libby9e_gh11**.

PREFERRED STOCK TRANSACTIONS

LEARNING OBJECTIVE 11-7

Describe the characteristics of preferred stock and report preferred stock transactions.

PREFERRED STOCK
Stock that has specified rights over common stock.

In addition to common stock, some corporations issue **preferred stock**. The journal entries required to record the issuance and repurchase of preferred stock are the same as the journal entries required to record the issuance and repurchase of common stock. Preferred stock, however, differs from common stock in a number of ways. The most significant differences are:

- **Preferred stock typically does not have voting rights.** Without voting rights, preferred stock does not appeal to investors who want some control over the operations of a corporation. The lack of voting rights is one of the reasons some corporations issue preferred stock to raise capital: Issuing preferred stock permits them to raise money without diluting common stockholders' control. The nearby chart shows the percentage of companies surveyed by *Accounting Trends & Techniques* that include preferred stock in their capital structure.

- **Preferred stock is less risky.** Generally, preferred stock is less risky than common stock because holders receive priority payment of dividends and distribution of assets if the corporation goes out of business. Usually a specified amount per share must be paid to preferred stockholders before any remaining assets can be distributed to the common stockholders.

- **Preferred stock typically has a fixed dividend rate.** For example, "6 percent preferred stock, par value $10 per share" pays an annual dividend of 6 percent of par value, or $0.60 per share. If preferred stock had no par value, the preferred dividend would be specified as $0.60 per share. The fixed dividend is attractive to certain investors who want stable income from their investments.

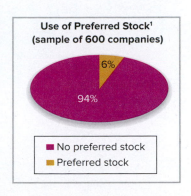

Use of Preferred Stock[1]
(sample of 600 companies)

6%

94%

- No preferred stock
- Preferred stock

What's in a Name?

INTERNATIONAL PERSPECTIVE

It is often confusing when different words are used to describe exactly the same thing. Such is the case with International Financial Accounting Standards (IFRS) and U.S. GAAP. The following table shows how two companies in the same industry use different terms in the stockholders' equity section of their balance sheets to refer to the same accounts. The accounts are the same; only the names differ:

Whole Foods (U.S.) GAAP		Tesco (UK) IFRS
Common stock	=	Share capital
Additional paid-in capital	=	Share premium

Dividends on Preferred Stock

Because investors who purchase preferred stock give up certain advantages that are available to investors who hold common stock, preferred stock offers a dividend preference. The two most common dividend preferences are current and cumulative.

Current Dividend Preference

The **current dividend preference** requires a company to pay current dividends to preferred stockholders before paying dividends to common stockholders. This preference is always a feature of preferred stock. After the current dividend preference has been met and if no other preference is operative, dividends can be paid to the common stockholders. To illustrate, assume Sophia Company has the following stock outstanding:

CURRENT DIVIDEND PREFERENCE
Requires that dividends be paid to preferred stockholders before any dividends are paid to common stockholders.

SOPHIA COMPANY
Preferred stock: 6%, $20 par value, 2,000 shares outstanding = $40,000
Common stock: $10 par value, 5,000 shares outstanding = $50,000

Assuming a current dividend preference only, dividends would be allocated as follows:

Example	Total Dividends	6% Preferred Stock*	Common Stock
No. 1	$ 3,000	$2,400	$ 600
No. 2	18,000	2,400	15,600

Preferred dividend calculation: $20 par value × 0.06 × 2,000 shares = $2,400

CUMULATIVE DIVIDEND PREFERENCE
Requires any unpaid dividends on preferred stock to accumulate. These cumulative preferred dividends must be paid before any common dividends can be paid.

Cumulative Dividend Preference

The **cumulative dividend preference** requires any unpaid dividends on preferred stock to accumulate. This cumulative unpaid amount, known as **dividends in arrears**, must be paid

DIVIDENDS IN ARREARS
Dividends on cumulative preferred stock that have not been paid in prior years.

---

[1]Reprinted with permission from *Accounting Trends & Techniques.* Copyright © 2011 by the American Institute of Certified Public Accountants, Inc.

before any common dividends can be paid. Of course, if the preferred stock is noncumulative, dividends can never be in arrears, and therefore any dividend that is not declared is permanently lost. Preferred stock is usually cumulative.

To illustrate the cumulative dividend preference, assume that Sophia Company's preferred stock in the above example is cumulative and that dividends have been in arrears for two years.

Example	Total Dividends	6% Preferred Stock*	Common Stock
No. 1	$ 8,000	$7,200	$ 800
No. 2	30,000	7,200	22,800

*Preferred dividend calculation:
—Current dividend preference: $20 par value × 0.06 × 2,000 shares = $2,400
—Dividends in arrears: $2,400 × 2 years = $4,800
—Total preferred dividend: $2,400 + $4,800 = $7,200

The existence of dividends in arrears on preferred stock can limit a company's ability to pay dividends to common stockholders and can affect a company's future cash flows. Because dividends are never an actual liability until the board of directors declares them, dividends in arrears are not reported on the balance sheet. Instead, they are disclosed in the notes to the financial statements.

FINANCIAL ANALYSIS

 Preferred Stock and Limited Voting Rights

Though not typical, some preferred stock has special voting rights. For example, the excerpt below is from **Public Storage**'s 2014 Annual Report:

PUBLIC STORAGE

REAL WORLD EXCERPT:

2014 Annual Report

> The holders of our Preferred Shares have general preference rights with respect to quarterly distributions and any accumulated unpaid distributions. Except under certain conditions and as noted below, holders of the Preferred Shares will not be entitled to vote on most matters. In the event of a cumulative arrearage equal to six quarterly dividends, holders of all outstanding preferred shares will have the right to elect two additional members to serve on our board of trustees (the "Board") until the arrearage has been cured. At December 31, 2014, there were no dividends in arrears.

This special voting right allows preferred stockholders to have some say in operational matters if the company has had difficulty paying dividends for an extended period of time.

FOCUS ON CASH FLOWS

 Financing Activities

LEARNING OBJECTIVE 11-8

Discuss the impact of stock transactions on cash flows.

Transactions involving stock have a direct impact on the capital structure of a business. The cash inflows and outflows associated with these transactions are reported in the Financing Activities section of the statement of cash flows.

EFFECT ON STATEMENT OF CASH FLOWS

In General   As reflected in the table below, cash receipts from investors are reported as cash inflows, and cash payments to investors are reported as cash outflows:

	Effect on Cash Flows
Financing activities	
Issuance of stock	+
Purchase of treasury stock	−
Sale of treasury stock	+
Payment of cash dividends	−

Focus Company Analysis   The Financing Activities section of **Whole Foods**'s Statement of Cash Flows is shown in Exhibit 11.3. Notice that for each of the last three years, Whole Foods has paid out a significant amount of cash to purchase treasury shares and to pay dividends.

EXHIBIT 11.3

Excerpt from Statement of Cash Flows for Whole Foods

WHOLE FOODS MARKET
Consolidated Statements of Cash Flows
Fiscal years ended September 28, 2014,
September 29, 2013, and September 30, 2012

(in millions)	2014	2013	2012
Cash Flows from Financing Activities:			
Common stock dividends paid	$(170)	$(508)	$(95)
Issuance of common stock	42	81	370
Purchase of treasury stock	(578)	(125)	(28)
Payments on capital lease obligations	(1)	(2)	—
Other	9	37	50
Net cash provided by (used in) financing activities	$(698)	$(517)	$297

WHOLE FOODS

REAL WORLD EXCERPT:

Annual Report

DEMONSTRATION CASE

(Try to answer the questions before proceeding to the suggested solutions that follow.)

This case focuses on the organization and operations for the first year of Chap 6 Corporation. Chap 6 became a corporation on January 1 of this year. The corporate charter authorized the following stock:

Common stock, no-par value, 20,000 shares
Preferred stock, 5 percent, $100 par value, 5,000 shares

The following summarized transactions, selected from Chap 6's first year of operations, were completed on the dates indicated:

a. January   Sold a total of 8,000 shares of common stock to investors for $50 cash per share.

b. February   Sold 2,000 shares of preferred stock to investors for $102 cash per share.

c. March   Declared, but has yet to pay, a cash dividend of $1 per share of common stock.

d. July   Repurchased 100 shares of preferred stock that was initially sold in February for $104 cash per share.

e. August   Resold 20 shares of the preferred treasury stock for $105 cash per share.

Required:

1. Provide the appropriate journal entries with a brief explanation for each transaction.

2. Prepare the stockholders' equity section of the balance sheet for Chap 6 at the end of Year 1. Assume retained earnings at the end of the current year is $23,000.

SUGGESTED SOLUTION

1. Journal entries:

a. Cash (+A)	400,000	
Common stock (+SE)		400,000
Sale of no-par common stock ($50 × 8,000 shares = $400,000).		
b. Cash (+A)	204,000	
Preferred stock (+SE)		200,000
Additional paid in capital, preferred stock (+SE)		4,000
Sale of $100 par value preferred stock ($102 × 2,000 shares = $204,000).		
c. Retained earnings (−SE).	8,000	
Dividend payable (+L).		8,000
Declared cash dividend ($1 × 8,000 shares = $8,000).		
d. Treasury stock (+XSE, −SE).	10,400	
Cash (−A)		10,400
Repurchased 100 shares of preferred stock ($104 × 100 shares = $10,400).		
e. Cash (+A)	2,100	
Treasury stock (−XSE, +SE).		2,080
Additional paid-in capital, preferred stock (+SE)		20
Resold 20 shares of the preferred treasury stock at $105 ($105 × 20 shares = $2,100).		

2. Stockholders' equity section of the balance sheet:

CHAP 6 CORPORATION
Partial Balance Sheet
At End of Year 1

Stockholders' Equity

Preferred stock, 5% ($100 par value; 5,000 shares authorized,	
2,000 shares issued, 1,920 shares outstanding)	$200,000
Additional paid-in capital, preferred stock	4,020
Common stock (no-par value; 20,000 shares authorized,	
8,000 shares issued and outstanding)	400,000
Retained earnings	23,000
Preferred treasury stock (80 shares)	(8,320)
Total stockholders' equity	$618,700

Chapter Supplement

Accounting for Owner's Equity for Sole Proprietorships and Partnerships

Owner's Equity for a Sole Proprietorship

A *sole proprietorship* is an unincorporated business owned by one person. Only two owner's equity accounts are typically used: (1) a capital account for the proprietor (Hans Solo, Capital) and (2) a drawing (or withdrawal) account for the proprietor (Hans Solo, Drawing).

The capital account of a sole proprietorship serves two purposes: to record investments by the owner and to accumulate the income or loss each accounting period. The drawing account is used to record the owner's withdrawals of cash or other assets from the business. The drawing account is a temporary account that is closed to the owner's capital account at the end of each accounting period. Thus, the capital account reflects the cumulative total of all investments by the owner and all earnings of the entity less all withdrawals from the entity by the owner.

In most respects, the accounting for a sole proprietorship is the same as for a corporation. Exhibit 11.4 presents the recording of selected transactions of Hans Solo Aviation and the statement of owner's equity.

EXHIBIT 11.4

Accounting for Owner's Equity for a Sole Proprietorship

Selected Entries during Year 1

January 1, Year 1

Hans Solo started an aviation business by investing $150,000 of personal savings. The journal entry follows:

Cash (+A)	150,000	
Hans Solo, capital (+OE)		150,000

Assets	=	Liabilities	+	Owner's Equity	
Cash +150,000				Hans Solo, capital	+150,000

During Year 1

Each month during the year, Hans withdrew $1,000 cash from the business for personal living costs. Accordingly, each month the following journal entry was made:

Hans Solo, drawing (−OE)	1,000	
Cash (−A)		1,000

Assets	=	Liabilities	+	Owner's Equity	
Cash −1,000				Hans Solo, drawing	−1,000

Note: At the end of Year 1, after the last withdrawal, the drawing account reflected a debit balance of $12,000.

December 31, Year 1

At the end of Year 1, $418,000 of revenues and $400,000 of expenses were closed to the owner's capital account as follows:

Revenue accounts (−R, closing entry)	418,000	
Expense accounts (−E, closing entry)		400,000
Hans Solo, capital (+OE)		18,000

Assets	=	Liabilities	+	Owner's Equity	
				Close revenue accounts	−418,000
				Close expense accounts	+400,000
				Hans Solo, capital	+18,000

(continued)

EXHIBIT 11.4

Concluded

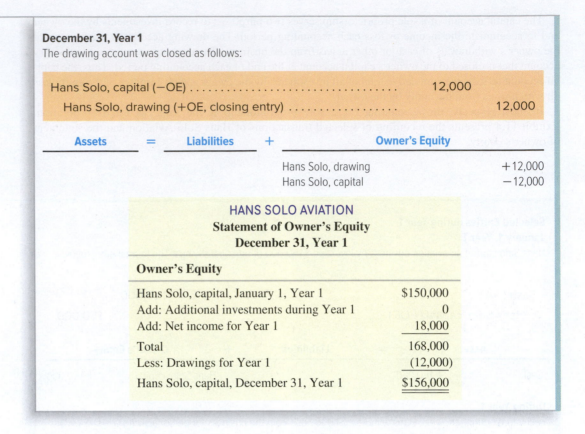

December 31, Year 1

The drawing account was closed as follows:

Hans Solo, capital (−OE)	12,000	
Hans Solo, drawing (+OE, closing entry)		12,000

Assets	=	Liabilities	+	Owner's Equity	
				Hans Solo, drawing	+12,000
				Hans Solo, capital	−12,000

HANS SOLO AVIATION
Statement of Owner's Equity
December 31, Year 1

Owner's Equity	
Hans Solo, capital, January 1, Year 1	$150,000
Add: Additional investments during Year 1	0
Add: Net income for Year 1	18,000
Total	168,000
Less: Drawings for Year 1	(12,000)
Hans Solo, capital, December 31, Year 1	$156,000

Because a sole proprietorship does not pay income taxes, its financial statements do not reflect income tax expense or income taxes payable. Instead, the net income of a sole proprietorship is taxed when it is included on the owner's personal income tax return. Likewise, any withdrawal by the sole proprietor is not recognized as an expense but rather is accounted for as a distribution of profits.

Owners' Equity for a Partnership

The Uniform Partnership Act, which most states have adopted, defines a partnership as "an association of two or more persons to carry on as co-owners of a business for profit." Small businesses and professionals such as accountants, doctors, and lawyers often use the partnership form of business.

A partnership is formed by two or more persons reaching mutual agreement about the terms of the relationship. The law does not require an application for a charter as in the case with a corporation. Instead, the agreement between the partners constitutes a partnership contract. This agreement should specify matters such as division of periodic income, management responsibilities, transfer or sale of partnership interests, disposition of assets upon liquidation, and procedures to be followed in case of the death of a partner. If the partnership agreement does not specify these matters, the laws of the resident state are binding.

The primary advantages of a partnership are (1) ease of formation, (2) complete control by the partners, and (3) lack of income taxes on the business itself. The primary disadvantage is the unlimited liability of each partner for the partnership's debts. If the partnership does not have sufficient assets to satisfy outstanding debt, creditors of the partnership can seize the partners' personal assets.

As with a sole proprietorship, accounting for a partnership follows the same underlying principles as any other form of business organization, except for those entries that directly affect owners' equity. Accounting for partners' equity follows the same pattern as for a sole proprietorship, except that separate capital and drawing accounts are established for each partner. Investments by each partner are credited to that partner's capital account; withdrawals are debited to the respective partner's drawing account. The net income of a partnership is divided among the partners in accordance with the partnership agreement and credited to each account. The respective drawing accounts are closed to the partner capital accounts. After the closing process, each partner's capital account reflects the cumulative total of all of that partner's investments plus that partner's share of the partnership earnings less all that partner's withdrawals.

Exhibit 11.5 presents selected journal entries and a Statement of Owners' Equity for Mirror Image Partners to illustrate the accounting for partnerships.

Selected Entries during Year 1
January 1, Year 1

Hannah and Bob organized Mirror Image Partners on January 1. Hannah and Bob contributed cash to the partnership in the amount of $60,000 and $40,000, respectively, and agreed to divide net income (and any losses) 60 percent and 40 percent, respectively. The journal entry to record the partners' initial contributions was as follows:

Cash (+A)	100,000	
Hannah, capital (+OE)		60,000
Bob, capital (+OE)...................................		40,000

Assets		=	Liabilities	+	Owners' Equity	
Cash	+100,000				Hannah, capital	+60,000
					Bob, capital	+40,000

During Year 1

The partners agreed that Hannah would withdraw $1,000 and Bob $650 per month in cash. Accordingly, each month the following journal entry was made:

Hannah, drawing (−OE)	1,000	
Bob, drawing (−OE)	650	
Cash (−A)		1,650

Assets		=	Liabilities	+	Owners' Equity	
Cash	−1,650				Hannah, drawing	−1,000
					Bob, drawing	−650

December 31, Year 1

At the end of Year 1, $630,000 of revenues and $600,000 of expenses were closed to the owners' capital accounts. The partnership agreement specified Hannah would receive 60 percent of earnings and Bob would receive 40 percent. The closing entry was as follows:

Revenue accounts (−R, closing entry)	630,000	
Expense accounts (−E, closing entry)		600,000
Hannah, capital (+OE) ($30,000 × 0.60)		18,000
Bob, capital (+OE) ($30,000 × 0.40)		12,000

Assets	=	Liabilities	+	Owners' Equity	
				Close revenue accounts	−630,000
				Close expense accounts	+600,000
				Hannah, capital	+18,000
				Bob, capital	+12,000

December 31, Year 1

The journal entry required to close the drawing accounts follows:

Hannah, capital (−OE)	12,000	
Bob, capital (−OE)	7,800	
Hannah, drawing (+OE, closing entry)		12,000
Bob, drawing (+OE, closing entry)		7,800

Assets	=	Liabilities	+	Owners' Equity	
				Close drawing account, Hannah	+12,000
				Close drawing account, Bob	+7,800
				Hannah, capital	−12,000
				Bob, capital	−7,800

EXHIBIT 11.5

Accounting for Owners' Equity for a Partnership

(continued)

EXHIBIT 11.5

Concluded

A separate statement of owners' equity, similar to the following, is customarily prepared to supplement the balance sheet:

MIRROR IMAGE PARTNERS
Statement of Owners' Equity
December 31, Year 1

	Hannah	Bob	Total
Investment, January 1, Year 1	$60,000	$40,000	$100,000
Add: Additional investments during Year 1	0	0	0
Add: Net income for Year 1	18,000	12,000	30,000
Totals	78,000	52,000	130,000
Less: Drawings during Year 1	(12,000)	(7,800)	(19,800)
Owners' equity, December 31, Year 1	$66,000	$44,200	$110,200

Like a sole proprietorship, a partnership does not report an income tax expense on its income statement. Partners must report their share of the partnership profits on their individual tax returns. Also like sole proprietorships, withdrawals by the partners are not recorded as expenses but rather are treated as distributions of profits.

CHAPTER **TAKE-AWAYS**

11-1. Explain the role of stock in the capital structure of a corporation.   p. 557

Issuing stock is one way corporations raise capital. Corporations issue stock by selling it to investors, who then become owners of the corporation. Investors can trade their stock on established stock exchanges.

11-2. Compute and analyze the earnings per share ratio.   p. 559

The earnings per share (EPS) ratio is computed by dividing net income by the weighted average number of common shares outstanding. The EPS ratio facilitates the comparison of a company's earnings over time or with other companies' earnings at a single point in time. By expressing earnings on a per share basis, differences in the size of companies become less important.

11-3. Describe the characteristics of common stock and report common stock transactions. p. 559

Common stock is the basic voting stock issued by a corporation. Usually it has a par value, but no-par stock can also be issued.

A number of key transactions involve common stock: (1) initial sale of stock, (2) treasury stock transactions, (3) cash dividends, and (4) stock dividends and stock splits. Each type of transaction is illustrated in this chapter.

11-4. Discuss and report dividends.   p. 563

Investors earn a return on their stock investment through stock price appreciation or the receipt of cash dividends. Cash dividends are payments to stockholders, typically on a per share basis. A company records a dividend as a liability when its board of directors declares the dividend (i.e., on the date of declaration). The liability is satisfied when the company pays the cash dividend to stockholders (i.e., on the date of payment).

11-5. Compute and analyze the dividend yield ratio.   p. 563

The dividend yield ratio is computed by dividing dividends per share by a stock's market price per share. The dividend yield ratio measures an investor's return on investment attributed to the dividends a company pays. For most companies, the return associated with dividends is very small.

11-6. Discuss and report stock dividends and stock splits.   p. 566

Stock dividends and stock splits are both ways for companies to distribute additional shares of stock to existing owners. When a company initiates a stock dividend, it records a journal entry that transfers the dividend amount from the retained earnings account to the common stock account and, if applicable, the additional paid-in capital account. When a company initiates a stock split, no journal entry is required; rather, the company simply increases the number of shares issued and decreases the par value per share.

11-7. Describe the characteristics of preferred stock and report preferred stock transactions. p. 570

The purpose of preferred stock is the same as that of common stock: to raise capital. Preferred stock differs from common stock in that it is much less common, typically does not have voting rights, and may have a current dividend preference and/or a cumulative dividend preference. A current dividend preference specifies that preferred stockholders will receive dividends before common stockholders. A cumulative preference specifies that preferred stockholders will receive any past unpaid dividends before common stockholders receive current dividends.

11-8. Discuss the impact of stock transactions on cash flows.   p. 572

Any cash inflows or outflows associated with a company's stock are reported in the Financing Activities section of the company's statement of cash flows. Typical inflows are the issuance of stock and the reselling of treasury shares. Typical outflows are the repurchase of treasury shares and the payment of dividends.

This chapter concludes a major section of the book. In the previous several chapters, we have discussed individual sections of the balance sheet. We will now shift our focus to the statement of cash flows. In the next chapter, you will learn how companies report cash transactions on the statement of cash flows, and how companies use information from the balance sheet and income statement to create the statement of cash flows.

KEY **RATIOS**

The **earnings per share ratio** reflects net income on a per share basis. The ratio is computed as follows (see the "Key Ratio Analysis" box in the Ownership of a Corporation section):

$$\text{Earnings per Share} = \frac{\text{Net Income}}{\text{Weighted Average Number of Common Shares Outstanding}}$$

The **dividend yield ratio** measures the return on investment attributable to the dividends a company pays. The ratio is computed as follows (see the "Key Ratio Analysis" box in the Dividends on Common Stock section):

$$\text{Dividend Yield} = \frac{\text{Dividends per Share}}{\text{Market Price per Share}}$$

FINDING **FINANCIAL INFORMATION**

Balance Sheet

Under Current Liabilities
Dividends, once declared by the board of directors, are reported as a liability (usually current).

Under Noncurrent Liabilities
Transactions involving capital stock do not generate noncurrent liabilities.

Under Stockholders' Equity
Typical accounts include:
Common stock
Preferred stock
Additional paid-in capital
Retained earnings
Treasury stock

Income Statement

Capital stock transactions do not affect the income statement. Dividends paid are not an expense. They are a distribution of income and are, therefore, not reported on the income statement. Dividends are taken directly out of stockholders' equity by reducing retained earnings.

Statement of Cash Flows

Under Financing Activities
+ Cash inflows from initial sale of stock
+ Cash inflows from sale of treasury stock
− Cash outflows for dividends
− Cash outflows for purchase of treasury stock

Statement of Stockholders' Equity

This statement reports detailed information concerning stockholders' equity, including
Amounts in each equity account,
Number of shares outstanding,
Impact of transactions such as earning income, payment of dividends, and purchase of treasury stock,
Information concerning any comprehensive gains or losses.

Notes

Under Summary of Significant Accounting Policies
Usually, very little information concerning capital stock is provided in the summary footnote.

Under a Separate Note
Most companies report information about their stock option plans and information about major transactions such as stock dividends or significant treasury stock transactions. A historical summary of dividends paid per share is typically provided. Also, dividends in arrears on preferred stock, if any, would be reported in the footnotes.

KEY **TERMS**

Authorized Number of Shares   p. 558
Common Stock   p. 559
Cumulative Dividend Preference   p. 571
Current Dividend Preference   p. 571
Declaration Date   p. 564
Dividends in Arrears   p. 571

Issued Shares   p. 558
Legal Capital   p. 560
No-Par Value Stock   p. 560
Outstanding Shares   p. 558
Par Value   p. 560
Payment Date   p. 564

Preferred Stock   p. 570
Record Date   p. 564
Stock Dividend   p. 566
Stock Split   p. 567
Treasury Stock   p. 558

QUESTIONS

1. Define the term *corporation* and identify the primary advantages of this form of business organization.
2. What is a corporate charter?
3. Explain each of the following terms: (*a*) authorized shares, (*b*) issued shares, and (*c*) outstanding shares.
4. Differentiate between common stock and preferred stock.

5. Explain the distinction between par value and no-par value stock.
6. Define *additional paid-in capital.*
7. Explain the difference between contributed capital and earned capital. How is each represented in the stockholders' equity section of a company's balance sheet?
8. Define *treasury stock.* Why do corporations acquire treasury stock?
9. How is treasury stock reported on the balance sheet? How is the "gain or loss" on the resale of treasury stock reported on the financial statements?
10. What are the two basic requirements to support the declaration of a cash dividend? What are the effects of a cash dividend on assets and stockholders' equity?
11. Define *stock dividend.* How does a stock dividend differ from a cash dividend?
12. Define *stock split.* How does a stock split differ from a stock dividend?
13. Identify and explain the three important dates with respect to dividends.
14. What are the usual characteristics of preferred stock?
15. Differentiate between cumulative and noncumulative preferred stock.

MULTIPLE-CHOICE QUESTIONS

1. Katz Corporation has issued 400,000 shares of common stock and holds 20,000 shares in treasury. The charter authorized the issuance of 500,000 shares. The company has declared and paid a dividend of $1 per share of common stock. What is the total amount of the dividend paid to common stockholders?
   a. $400,000   c. $380,000
   b. $20,000   d. $500,000
2. Which statement regarding treasury stock is false?
   a. Treasury stock is considered to be issued but not outstanding.
   b. Treasury stock has no voting, dividend, or liquidation rights.
   c. Treasury stock reduces total equity on the balance sheet.
   d. None of the above are false.
3. Which of the following statements about stock dividends is true?
   a. Stock dividends are reported on the statement of cash flows.
   b. Stock dividends are reported on the statement of stockholders' equity.
   c. Stock dividends increase total equity.
   d. Stock dividends decrease total equity.
4. Which order best describes the largest number of shares to the smallest number of shares?
   a. Shares authorized, shares issued, shares outstanding.
   b. Shares issued, shares outstanding, shares authorized.
   c. Shares outstanding, shares issued, shares authorized.
   d. Shares in the treasury, shares outstanding, shares issued.
5. A company issued 100,000 shares of common stock with a par value of $1 per share. The stock sold for $20 per share. By what amount will stockholders' equity increase?
   a. $100,000   c. $2,000,000
   b. $1,900,000   d. No change in stockholders' equity
6. Which of the following dates does not require a journal entry?
   a. Date of declaration.   c. Date of payment.
   b. Date of record.   d. A journal entry is recorded on all of these dates.
7. A company has net income of $225,000 and declares and pays dividends in the amount of $75,000. What is the net impact on retained earnings?
   a. Increase of $225,000   c. Increase of $150,000
   b. Decrease of $75,000   d. Decrease of $150,000
8. Which statement regarding dividends is false?
   a. Dividends represent a distribution of corporate profits to owners.
   b. Both stock and cash dividends reduce retained earnings.
   c. Cash dividends paid to stockholders reduce net income.
   d. None of the above statements are false.

9. When treasury stock is purchased with cash, what is the impact on the balance sheet equation?
   a. No change: The reduction of the asset cash is offset with the addition of the asset treasury stock.
   b. Assets decrease and stockholders' equity increases.
   c. Assets increase and stockholders' equity decreases.
   d. Assets decrease and stockholders' equity decreases.

10. Conceptually, does a 2-for-1 stock dividend immediately increase an investor's personal wealth?
    a. No, because the stock price per share drops by half when the number of shares doubles.
    b. Yes, because the investor has more shares.
    c. Yes, because the investor acquired additional shares without paying a brokerage fee.
    d. Yes, because the investor will receive more in cash dividends by owning more shares.

MINI-EXERCISES

M11-1
LO11-1

Sources of Equity and Retained Earnings

There are two primary sources of equity reported in the stockholders' equity section of a company's balance sheet: contributed capital and earned capital. Earned capital is kept track of in the retained earnings account. What increases retained earnings and what decreases retained earnings?

M11-2
LO11-1

Computing the Number of Unissued Shares

The balance sheet for Ronlad Corporation reported 168,000 shares outstanding, 268,000 shares authorized, and 10,000 shares in treasury stock. How many shares have been issued?

M11-3
LO11-2

Earnings per Share Ratio

How is the earnings per share (EPS) ratio calculated? On what financial statement will an investor find EPS for a given company?

M11-4
LO11-3

Recording the Sale of Common Stock

To expand operations, Aragon Consulting issued 170,000 shares of previously unissued stock with a par value of $1. Investors purchased the stock for $21 per share. Record the sale of this stock. Would your journal entry be different if the par value was $2 per share? If so, record the sale of stock with a par value of $2.

M11-5
LO11-3, 11-7

Comparing Common Stock and Preferred Stock

Your parents have just retired and have asked you for some financial advice. They have decided to invest $100,000 in a company very similar to **Whole Foods**. The company has issued both common and preferred stock. Describe the differences between common stock and preferred stock to your parents.

M11-6
LO11-3

Determining the Effects of Treasury Stock Transactions

Carbide Corporation purchased 20,000 shares of its own stock from investors for $45 per share. The next year, the company resold 5,000 of the repurchased shares for $50 per share, and the following year it resold 10,000 of the repurchased shares for $37 per share. Determine the impact (increase, decrease, or no change) of each of these transactions on the following:

1. Total assets
2. Total liabilities
3. Total stockholders' equity
4. Net income

M11-7
LO11-4

Determining the Amount of a Dividend

Cole Company has 288,000 shares of common stock authorized, 260,000 shares issued, and 60,000 shares of treasury stock. The company's board of directors has declared a dividend of 65 cents per share. What is the total amount of the dividend that will be paid?

Recording Dividends

On April 15 of this year, the board of directors for Jedi Company declared a cash dividend of 65 cents per share payable to stockholders of record on May 20. The dividends will be paid on June 14. The company has 100,000 shares of stock outstanding. Prepare any necessary journal entries for each date.

M11-8
LO11-4

Dividend Yield Ratio

How is the dividend yield ratio calculated? Explain what the dividend yield ratio tells you about a company.

M11-9
LO11-5

Determining the Impact of Stock Dividends and Stock Splits

Reliable Tools, Inc., announced a 100 percent stock dividend. Determine the impact (increase, decrease, no change) of this dividend on the following:

M11-10
LO11-6

1. Total assets
2. Total liabilities
3. Common stock
4. Total stockholders' equity
5. Market value per share of common stock

Assume that instead of announcing a stock dividend, the company announced a 2-for-1 stock split. Determine the impact of the stock split on each of the above.

Reporting Stock Transactions on the Statement of Cash Flows

During the year, University Food Systems issued stock, repurchased stock, declared a cash dividend, and declared a 2-for-1 stock split. How will each of these transactions affect University's statement of cash flows?

M11-11
LO11-8

Mc Graw Hill Education **connect**   **EXERCISES**

Computing Shares Outstanding

In a recent annual report, **Outerwall Inc.** (formerly **Redbox**) disclosed that 60,000,000 shares of common stock have been authorized. At the beginning of the fiscal year, a total of 36,356,357 shares had been issued and the number of shares in treasury stock was 7,171,269. During the year, 558,765 additional shares were issued, and the number of treasury shares increased by 3,034,188. Determine the number of shares outstanding at the end of the year.

E11-1
LO11-1

Computing Number of Shares

The charter of Vista West Corporation specifies that it is authorized to issue 300,000 shares of common stock. Since the company was incorporated, it has sold a total of 160,000 shares (at $16 per share) to the public. It has bought back a total of 25,000. The par value of the stock is $3. When the stock was bought back from the public, the market price was $40.

E11-2
LO11-1, 11-3

Required:
1. Determine the authorized shares.
2. Determine the issued shares.
3. Determine the outstanding shares.

Determining the Effects of the Issuance of Common and Preferred Stock

Tandy Company was issued a charter by the state of Indiana on January 15 of this year. The charter authorized the following:

E11-3
LO11-1, 11-3, 11-7

Common stock, $10 par value, 103,000 shares authorized

Preferred stock, 9 percent, par value $8 per share, 4,000 shares authorized

During the year, the following transactions took place in the order presented:

a. Sold and issued 20,000 shares of common stock at $16 cash per share.
b. Sold and issued 3,000 shares of preferred stock at $20 cash per share.
c. At the end of the year, the accounts showed net income of $60,000. No dividends were declared.

Required:
1. Prepare the stockholders' equity section of the balance sheet at the end of the year.
2. Assume that you are a common stockholder. If Tandy needed additional capital, would you prefer to have it issue additional common stock or additional preferred stock? Explain.

E11-4
LO11-1, 11-2, 11-3

Reporting Stockholders' Equity

The financial statements for Highland Corporation included the following selected information:

Common stock	$1,600,000
Retained earnings	$900,000
Net income	$1,000,000
Shares issued	90,000
Shares outstanding	80,000
Dividends declared and paid	$800,000

The common stock was sold at a price of $30 per share.

Required:
1. What is the amount of additional paid-in capital?
2. What was the amount of retained earnings at the beginning of the year?
3. How many shares are in treasury stock?
4. Compute earnings per share (assume the weighted average shares outstanding is equal to the shares outstanding).

E11-5
LO11-1, 11-3, 11-4

Reporting Stockholders' Equity and Determining Dividend Policy

Tarrant Corporation was organized this year to operate a financial consulting business. The charter authorized the following stock: common stock, par value $10 per share, 11,500 shares authorized. During the year, the following selected transactions were completed:

a. Sold 5,600 shares of common stock for cash at $20 per share.
b. Sold 1,000 shares of common stock for cash at $25 per share.
c. At year-end, the accounts reflected income of $12,000. No dividends were declared.

Required:
1. Provide the journal entries required to record the sale of common stock in (*a*) and (*b*).
2. Prepare the stockholders' equity section of the balance sheet at the end of the year.

E11-6
LO11-1, 11-3

Finding Amounts Missing from the Stockholders' Equity Section

The stockholders' equity section on the balance sheet of **Dillard's**, a popular department store, is shown below. During the year, the company reported net income of $463,909,000 and declared and paid dividends of $10,002,000.

Stockholders' Equity:	Current Year	Last Year
Common stock, Class A—118,529,925 and 117,706,523 shares issued; ? and ? shares outstanding	118,530	117,707
Common stock, Class B (convertible)—4,010,929 shares issued and outstanding	40,000	40,000
Additional paid-in capital	828,796,000	805,422,000
Retained earnings	3,107,344,000	?
Less treasury stock, at cost, Class A—73,099,319 and 61,740,439 shares	(1,846,312,000)	(1,355,526,000)

Required:

Answer the following questions. Show your computations.

1. What amount was reported in the Common Stock (Class A) account at the end of the current year?
2. How many shares of Class A Common Stock were outstanding at the end of last year and the end of the current year?
3. What amount was reported in the Retained Earnings account at the end of last year?
4. At the end of the current year, have the treasury stock transactions increased assets or decreased assets? By how much?
5. During the current year, by what amount did treasury stock transactions increase or decrease stockholders' equity?
6. At the end of the current year, what was the average price paid per share for shares held in treasury stock?

Reporting Stockholders' Equity

Williamson Corporation was organized to operate a tax preparation business. The charter authorized the following stock: common stock, $2 par value, 80,000 shares authorized. During the first year, the following selected transactions were completed:

E11-7
LO11-1, 11-3

a. Sold 50,000 shares of common stock for cash at $50 per share.
b. Repurchased 2,000 shares from a stockholder for cash at $52 per share.

Required:
1. Provide the journal entries required for the transactions in (*a*) and (*b*).
2. Prepare the stockholders' equity section of the balance sheet at the end of the year.

Reporting Stockholders' Equity

Ruth's Chris Steakhouse is the largest upscale steakhouse company in the United States, based on total company- and franchisee-owned restaurants. The company's menu features a broad selection of high-quality USDA prime steaks and other premium offerings. Select information from the company's annual report is shown below:

E11-8
LO11-1, 11-3

a. Common stock, $0.01 par value, 100,000,000 shares authorized, 34,333,858 issued and outstanding at December 31, 2014; 34,990,170 issued and outstanding at December 31, 2013.
b. Additional paid-in capital: $155,455,000 at the end of 2014 and $169,107,000 at the end of 2013.
c. Accumulated deficit: $68,804,000 at the end of 2013.
d. In 2014, net income was $16,455,000 and a cash dividend of $7,138,000 was paid.

Required:
Prepare the stockholders' equity section of the balance sheet at December 31, 2014, using this select information.

Determining the Effects of Transactions on Stockholders' Equity

Quick Fix-It Corporation was organized at the beginning of this year to operate several car repair businesses in a large metropolitan area. The charter issued by the state authorized the following stock:

E11-9
LO11-1, 11-3, 11-7

Common stock, $10 par value, 98,000 shares authorized
Preferred stock, $50 par value, 8 percent, 59,000 shares authorized

During January and February of this year, the following stock transactions were completed:

a. Sold 78,000 shares of common stock at $20 cash per share.
b. Sold 20,000 shares of preferred stock at $80 cash per share.
c. Bought 4,000 shares of common stock from a current stockholder for $20 cash per share.

Required:
Net income for the year was $210,000; cash dividends declared and paid at year-end were $50,000. Prepare the stockholders' equity section of the balance sheet at the end of the year.

E11-10
LO11-2

Computing and Interpreting Earnings per Share

Below is select information from DC United Company's income statement. At the end of Year 1, the weighted average number of common shares outstanding was 132,000.

Income Statement, End of Year 1	
Sales	$942,000
Cost of goods sold	800,000
Operating expenses	80,000
Tax expense	15,000

Required:
Calculate EPS for DC United. Is this a good EPS number?

E11-11
LO11-3, 11-7

Recording Stockholders' Equity Transactions

On-Line Learning Corporation obtained a charter at the beginning of this year that authorized 52,000 shares of no-par common stock and 23,000 shares of preferred stock, par value $10. The corporation was organized by four individuals who purchased a total of 20,000 shares of the common stock. The remaining shares were to be sold to other individuals. During the year, the following selected transactions occurred:

a. Collected $20 cash per share from the four organizers and issued 5,000 shares of common stock to each of them.
b. Sold 6,000 shares of common stock to an outsider at $40 cash per share.
c. Sold 7,000 shares of preferred stock at $30 cash per share.

Required:
 1. Provide the journal entries required to record transactions (*a*) through (*c*).
 2. Is it ethical to sell stock to outsiders at a higher price than the amount paid by the organizers?

E11-12
LO11-1, 11-3, 11-4

Finding Information Missing from an Annual Report

Procter & Gamble has sales in excess of $83 billion and sells products that are part of most of our daily lives, including Crest, Duracell, Olay, Gillette, Tide, and Vicks. A recent annual report for P&G contained the following information:

a. Retained earnings at the end of 2013 totaled $80,197 million.
b. Net income for 2014 was $11,643 million.
c. Par value of the stock is $1 per share.
d. Cash dividends declared in 2014 were $6,850 million.
e. The Common Stock account totaled $4,009 million at the end of 2014 and $4,009 million at the end of 2013.

Required (assume that no other information concerning stockholders' equity is relevant):
 1. Calculate the number of shares issued at the end of 2014.
 2. Calculate the amount of retained earnings at the end of 2014.

E11-13
LO11-3

Recording and Analyzing Treasury Stock Transactions

Rock Bottom Gold Company recently repurchased 7 million shares of its common stock for $47 per share. The intent of the repurchase was to increase earnings per share to be more in line with competitors.

Required:
 1. Determine the impact of the stock repurchase on assets, liabilities, and stockholders' equity.
 2. Prepare the journal entry to record the repurchase.
 3. How will this transaction affect the cash flow statement?

Preparing the Stockholders' Equity Section of the Balance Sheet and Evaluating Dividend Policy

The following account balances were selected from the records of TAC Corporation at the end of the fiscal year after all adjusting entries were completed:

E11-14
LO11-1, 11-3, 11-4, 11-5

Common stock ($20 par value; 100,000 shares authorized, 34,000 shares issued, 32,000 shares outstanding)	$680,000
Additional paid-in capital	163,000
Dividends declared and paid during the year	16,000
Retained earnings at the beginning of the year	75,000
Treasury stock at cost (2,000 shares)	(25,000)

Net income for the year was $30,000. The stock price is currently $22.29 per share.

Required:
1. Prepare the stockholders' equity section of the balance sheet at the end of the fiscal year.
2. Compute and evaluate the dividend yield ratio. Determine the number of shares of stock that received dividends.

Recording and Analyzing Treasury Stock Transactions

During the year the following selected transactions affecting stockholders' equity occurred for Orlando Corporation:

E11-15
LO11-3

a. Apr. 1 Repurchased 200 shares of the company's own common stock at $20 cash per share.
b. Jun. 14 Sold 40 shares of the shares purchased on April 1 for $25 cash per share.
c. Sept. 1 Sold 30 shares of the shares purchased on April 1 for $15 cash per share.

Required:
1. Provide the journal entries to record each of the transactions in (*a*) through (*c*).
2. Describe the impact, if any, that these transactions have on the income statement.

Recording and Analyzing Treasury Stock Transactions

During the year, the following selected transactions affecting stockholders' equity occurred for Navajo Corporation:

E11-16
LO11-3, 11-4, 11-8

a. Feb. 1 Repurchased 160 shares of the company's own common stock at $20 cash per share.
b. Jul. 15 Sold 80 of the shares purchased on February 1 for $21 cash per share.
c. Sept. 1 Sold 50 of the shares purchased on February 1 for $19 cash per share.

Required:
1. Provide the journal entries to record each of the transactions in (*a*) through (*c*).
2. What impact does the purchase of treasury stock have on dividends paid?
3. What impact does the sale of treasury stock for an amount higher than the purchase price have on net income and the statement of cash flows?

Analyzing the Impact of Dividend Policy

Peters and Associates is a small manufacturer of electronic connections for local area networks. Consider the three cases below as independent situations.

E11-17
LO11-2, 11-4, 11-6, 11-8

Case 1: Peters increases its cash dividend by 50 percent, but no other changes occur in the company's operations.

Case 2: The company's income and operating cash flows increase by 50 percent, but this does not change its dividends.

Case 3: Peters issues a 50 percent stock dividend, but no other changes occur.

Required:
1. How will each case affect Peters's statement of cash flows?
2. How will each case affect Peters's earnings per share ratio?

E11-18
LO11-4, 11-7, 11-8

Computing Dividends on Preferred Stock and Analyzing Differences

The records of Hollywood Company reflected the following balances in the stockholders' equity accounts at the end of the current year:

  Common stock, $12 par value, 50,000 shares outstanding
  Preferred stock, 10 percent, $10 par value, 5,000 shares outstanding
  Retained earnings, $216,000

On September 1 of the current year, the board of directors was considering the distribution of an $85,000 cash dividend. No dividends were paid during the previous two years. You have been asked to determine dividend amounts under two independent assumptions (show computations):

a. The preferred stock is noncumulative.
b. The preferred stock is cumulative.

Required:
1. Determine the total and per share amounts that would be paid to the common stockholders and the preferred stockholders under the two independent assumptions.
2. Will the statement of cash flows be affected differently under the two independent assumptions?

E11-19
LO11-4, 11-6, 11-7

Determining the Impact of Dividends

Service Corporation has the following capital stock outstanding at the end of the current year:

  Preferred stock, 6 percent, $15 par value, 8,000 outstanding shares
  Common stock, $8 par value, 30,000 outstanding shares

On October 1 of the current year, the board of directors declared dividends as follows:

  Preferred stock: Cash dividend, payable December 20 of the current year
  Common stock: 50 percent common stock dividend issuable December 20 of the current year

On December 20 of the current year, the market price of Service's preferred stock was $40 per share, and the market price of its common stock was $32 per share.

Required:
Explain how the preferred stock dividend and common stock dividend affect the company's assets, liabilities, and stockholders' equity.

E11-20
LO11-3, 11-4

Recording the Payment of Dividends

A recent annual report for **Nordstrom Inc.** disclosed that the company declared and paid dividends on common stock in the amount of $1.20 per share. During the year, Nordstrom had 1,000,000,000 authorized shares of common stock and 191,200,000 issued shares. There is no treasury stock.

Required:
Assume Nordstrom declared the entire dividend ($1.20 per share) on February 20 and subsequently paid the dividend on March 1. Provide the journal entries to record the declaration and payment of dividends.

E11-21
LO11-3, 11-4

Recording Dividends

Procter & Gamble (P&G) brands touch the lives of people around the world in 180 countries and territories. The P&G community consists of nearly 188,000 employees. In 2014, the company had 10 billion shares of common stock authorized, 4 billion shares issued, and 3 billion shares outstanding. Par value is $1 per share. P&G has been paying a dividend for over 120 years and 2014 marks the 58th consecutive year that the Company has increased its dividend.

Required:
Assume that P&G declared a dividend of $2.45 per share on October 1, 2014, to stockholders of record on October 15. P&G paid the dividend on October 20. Prepare journal entries as appropriate for each date.

Analyzing Stock Dividends

At the beginning of the year, the stockholders' equity section of the balance sheet of Solutions Corporation reflected the following:

Common stock ($12 par value; 65,000 shares authorized, 30,000 shares outstanding)	$360,000
Additional paid-in capital	120,000
Retained earnings	580,000

On February 1, the board of directors declared a 60 percent stock dividend to be issued April 30. The market value of the stock on February 1 was $15 per share. The market value of the stock on April 30 was $18 per share.

Required:
1. For comparative purposes, prepare the stockholders' equity section of the balance sheet (*a*) immediately before the stock dividend and (*b*) immediately after the stock dividend. (*Hint:* Use two columns for this requirement.)
2. Show how the stock dividend affects assets, liabilities, and stockholders' equity.
3. If instead of declaring a stock dividend the company had announced a 3-for-1 stock split for all authorized, issued, and outstanding shares, how would the accounts in the stockholders' equity section of the balance sheet change?

Comparing Stock Dividends and Stock Splits

On July 1, Davidson Corporation had the following capital structure:

Common stock ($1 par value)	$600,000
Additional paid-in capital	900,000
Retained earnings	700,000
Treasury stock	–0–

Required:
Complete the table below for each of the two following independent cases:

Case 1: The board of directors declared and issued a 50 percent stock dividend when the stock was selling at $12 per share.

Case 2: The board of directors announced a 6-for-5 stock split (i.e., a 20 percent increase in the number of shares). The market price prior to the split was $12 per share.

Items	Before Dividend and Split	After Stock Dividend	After Stock Split
Common stock account	$	$	$
Par per share	$1	$	$
Shares outstanding	#	#	#
Additional paid-in capital	$900,000	$	$
Retained earnings	$700,000	$	$
Total stockholders' equity	$	$	$

Comparing Cash Dividends and Stock Dividends

Weili Corporation has 80,000 shares of common stock outstanding with a par value of $8.

Required:
1. Complete the table below for each of the two following independent cases:

   Case 1: The board of directors declared and issued a 40 percent stock dividend when the stock was selling at $25 per share.

   Case 2: The board of directors declared and paid a cash dividend of $2 per share.

Items	Before Dividend and Split	After Stock Dividend	After Cash Dividend
Common stock account	$	$	$
Par per share	$8	$	$
Shares outstanding	#	#	#
Capital in excess of par	$280,000	$	$
Retained earnings	$2,100,000	$	$
Total stockholders' equity	$	$	$

2. Explain how Case 1 and Case 2 will be reported on the statement of cash flows.

E11-25
LO11-1

(Chapter Supplement) Accounting for Equity Transaction for Sole Proprietorships and Partnerships

Case 1: Matsumoto Training Academies is a sole proprietorship. To start the business, the owner, Mr. Tanaka, contributed $500,000 cash. During the year the owner withdrew $30,000 cash. Net income for the year was $45,000.

Case 2: Galaxy Robotics is a partnership with two partners. To start the business, the owners, Mrs. Curtis and Mr. Wilson, each contributed $300,000 cash and agreed to split all earnings 50/50. During the year, Mrs. Curtis withdrew $15,000 cash and Mr. Wilson withdrew $25,000 cash. Net income for the year was $60,000.

Required:
1. Create the statement of owners' equity for Matsumoto Training at the end of the year.
2. Create the statement of owners' equity for Galaxy Robotics at the end of the year.

PROBLEMS

P11-1
LO11-1, 11-2, 11-3, 11-4, 11-6

Finding Missing Amounts (AP11–1)

At the end of the year, the records of NCIS Corporation provided the following selected and incomplete data:

> Common stock ($10 par value); no changes in account during the year.
> Shares authorized: 200,000.
> Shares issued: _____ (all shares were issued at $17 per share. Total cash collected: $2,125,000).
> Treasury stock: 3,000 shares (repurchased at $20 per share).
> The treasury stock was acquired after a stock split was announced.
> Net income: $240,340.
> Dividends declared and paid: $123,220.
> Retained earnings beginning balance: $555,000.

Required:
1. Determine:
   a. The number of authorized shares.
   b. The number of issued shares.
   c. The number of outstanding shares.
2. What is the balance in the Additional Paid-in Capital account?
3. What is earnings per share (EPS)?
4. What was the dividend paid per share?
5. In what section of the balance sheet should treasury stock be reported? What is the amount of treasury stock that should be reported?
6. Assume that the board of directors voted a 2-for-1 stock split. After the stock split, what will be the par value per share? How many shares will be outstanding?

7. Provide the journal entry associated with the stock split above. If no journal entry is required, explain why.
8. Disregard the stock split (assumed above). Assume instead that a 10 percent stock dividend was declared when the market price of the common stock was $21. Provide the journal entry associated with the stock dividend. If no journal entry is required, explain why.

Preparing the Stockholders' Equity Section of the Balance Sheet

P11-2
LO11-1, 11-3, 11-7

Witt Corporation received its charter during January of this year. The charter authorized the following stock:

Preferred stock: 10 percent, $10 par value, 21,000 shares authorized
Common stock: $8 par value, 50,000 shares authorized

During the year, the following transactions occurred in the order given:

a. Issued a total of 40,000 shares of the common stock at $12 cash per share.
b. Sold 5,500 shares of the preferred stock at $16 cash per share.
c. Sold 3,000 shares of the common stock at $15 cash per share and 1,000 shares of the preferred stock at $26 cash per share.
d. Net income for the year was $96,000.

Required:
Prepare the stockholders' equity section of the balance sheet at the end of the year.

Recording Transactions Affecting Stockholders' Equity (AP11-2)

P11-3
LO11-1, 11-3, 11-7

King Corporation began operations in January of the current year. The charter authorized the following stock:

Preferred stock: 10 percent, $10 par value, 40,000 shares authorized
Common stock: $5 par value, 85,000 shares authorized

During the current year, the following transactions occurred in the order given:

a. Issued 66,000 shares of common stock for $9 cash per share.
b. Sold 9,000 shares of the preferred stock at $20 cash per share.
c. Sold 1,000 shares of the preferred stock at $20 cash per share and 2,500 shares of common stock at $10 cash per share.

Required:
Provide the journal entries required to record each of the transactions in (a) through (c).

Recording Transactions and Comparing Par and No-Par Stock

P11-4
LO11-1, 11-3

The following was in the financial press pertaining to **GoDaddy Incorporated**:

April 1, 2015—GoDaddy's (GDDY) stock was sold for $26 per share during its opening day of trading. GoDaddy sold 23 million shares at its IPO.

Required:
1. Record the issuance of stock, assuming the stock was no-par value common stock.
2. Record the issuance of stock, assuming the common stock had a par value of $2 per share.
3. Should a stockholder care whether a company issues par or no-par value stock? Explain.

Preparing the Stockholders' Equity Section after Selected Transactions (AP11-3)

P11-5
LO11-1, 11-3

United Resources Company obtained a charter from the state in January of this year. The charter authorized 200,000 shares of common stock with a par value of $1. During the year, the company earned $590,000. Also during the year, the following selected transactions occurred in the order given:

a. Sold 100,000 shares of the common stock in an initial public offering at $12 cash per share.
b. Repurchased 20,000 shares of the previously issued shares at $15 cash per share.
c. Resold 5,000 of the shares of the treasury stock at $18 cash per share.

Required:

Prepare the stockholders' equity section of the balance sheet at the end of the year.

P11-6

LO11-3, 11-4, 11-6, 11-8

Analyzing Stockholders' Equity Transactions, Including Treasury Stock

1. Explain how a stock dividend differs from a cash dividend.
2. Explain how a large stock dividend differs from a small stock dividend.
3. Explain how reselling treasury stock for more than it was purchased affects the income statement and the statement of cash flows.
4. Explain why a company might purchase treasury stock.

P11-7

LO11-3, 11-8

Analyzing Treasury Stock Transactions

Apple Inc. designs, manufactures, and markets mobile communication and media devices, personal computers, and portable digital music players. In 2014, Apple had the largest market value of any company. Apple has over 92,000 full-time employees. The company's statement of cash flows contained the following information (in millions):

	2014	2013	2012
Cash flows from financing activities:			
Repurchases of common stock	(45,000)	(22,860)	−0−

Required:

1. Prepare the journal entry to record the purchase of treasury stock in 2014.
2. Assume that Apple resold some of the treasury stock. The shares were originally purchased for $9 million and were resold for $10 million. Prepare the journal entry to record the sale of the treasury shares.

P11-8

LO11-4, 11-6, 11-7

Comparing Stock and Cash Dividends (AP11-4)

Chicago Company reported the following information at the end of the current year:

Common stock ($8 par value; 35,000 shares outstanding)	$280,000
Preferred stock, 10% ($15 par value; 8,000 shares outstanding)	120,000
Retained earnings	281,000

The board of directors is considering the distribution of a cash dividend to the two groups of stockholders. No dividends were declared during the previous two years. Assume the three cases below are independent of each other.

Case A: The preferred stock is noncumulative; the total amount of all dividends is $31,000.

Case B: The preferred stock is cumulative; the total amount of all dividends is $36,000.

Case C: The preferred stock is cumulative; the total amount of all dividends is $90,000.

Required:

1. Compute the amount of dividends, in total and per share, that would be payable to each class of stockholders for each case. Show computations.
2. Assume Chicago Company issued a 30 percent common stock dividend on the outstanding shares when the market value per share was $24. Fill in the table below to show how this stock dividend would compare to Case C.

	AMOUNT OF DOLLAR INCREASE (DECREASE)	
Item	**Cash Dividend—Case C**	**Stock Dividend**
Assets	$	$
Liabilities	$	$
Stockholders' equity	$	$

Analyzing Dividend Policy

Heather and Scott, two young financial analysts, were reviewing financial statements for **Google**, one of the world's largest technology companies. Scott noted that the company did not report any dividends in the financing activity section of the statement of cash flows and said, "I have heard that Google is a very profitable company. If it's so profitable, why isn't it paying any dividends?" Heather wasn't convinced that Scott was looking in the right place for dividends but didn't say anything.

Scott continued the discussion by noting, "Sales for Google are up nearly 43 percent over the previous two years, while net income is up over $1 billion compared to last year, and cash flows from operating activities are up over $3 billion to a total of $17 billion."

At that point, Heather noted that the statement of cash flows reported that Google had spent $11 billion in capital expenditures and $15 billion paying back debt. She was confused about whether Google was in a good position to pay dividends or not.

Required:
1. Is Heather's concern that Scott is looking at the wrong section of the statement of cash flows justified?
2. Is there a right time for a company like Google to start paying a dividend?

P11-9
LO11-4, 11-8

Preparing the Stockholders' Equity Section of the Balance Sheet and Evaluating Dividend Policy

The following account balances were selected from the records of Cascade Company at the end of the fiscal year after all adjusting entries were completed:

P11-10
LO11-1, 11-3, 11-4, 11-5

Common stock ($0.01 par value; 200,000 shares authorized, 54,000 shares issued, 52,000 shares outstanding)	$ 540
Additional paid-in capital	456,000
Dividends declared and paid during the year	22,000
Retained earnings at the end of the year	312,000
Treasury stock at cost (2,000 shares)	(15,000)

Net income for the year was $95,000. The stock price is currently $10 per share.

Required:
1. Prepare the stockholders' equity section of the balance sheet at the end of the fiscal year.
2. Compute and evaluate the dividend yield ratio. Determine the number of shares of stock that received dividends.

Recording and Comparing Cash Dividends, Stock Dividends, and Stock Splits

On January 1, Biofuel Corporation had the following capital structure:

P11-11
LO11-4, 11-6, 11-8

Common stock ($0.10 par value)	$ 60,000
Additional paid-in capital	1,900,000
Retained earnings	800,000
Treasury stock	0
Cash flows from financing activities	19,000

Required:
Complete the table below for each of the three following independent cases:

Case 1: The board of directors declared a cash dividend of $0.02 per share.

Case 2: The board of directors declared and issued a 100 percent stock dividend when the stock was selling at $10 per share.

Case 3: The board of directors announced a 2-for-1 stock split. The market price prior to the split was $10 per share.

Items	Before Any Dividends	After Cash Dividend	After Stock Dividend	After Stock Split
Common stock account	$60,000	$	$	$
Par per share	$0.10	$	$	$
Shares outstanding	#	#	#	#
Additional paid-in capital	$1,900,000	$	$	$
Retained earnings	$800,000	$	$	$
Total stockholders' equity	$	$	$	$
Cash flows from financing activities	$19,000	$	$	$

P11-12
LO11-1

(Chapter Supplement) Comparing Stockholders' Equity Sections for Alternative Forms of Organization

Assume for each of the following independent cases that the annual accounting period ends on December 31. Revenues for the year were $144,000. Expenses for the year were $164,000.

Case A: Assume that the company is a *sole proprietorship* owned by Proprietor A. Prior to the closing entries, the capital account reflects a balance of $52,000 and the drawing account shows a balance of $9,000.

Case B: Assume that the company is a *partnership* owned by Partner A and Partner B. Prior to the closing entries, the owners' equity accounts reflect the following balances: A, Capital, $43,000; B, Capital, $43,000; A, Drawings, $5,000; and B, Drawings, $7,000. Profits and losses are divided equally.

Case C: Assume that the company is a *corporation.*

Required:
1. Provide all the closing entries required at December 31 for each of the separate cases.
2. Show how the statement of owners' equity would appear at December 31 for Case A and Case B.

ALTERNATE PROBLEMS

AP11-1
**LO11-1, 11-2, 11-3,
11-4, 11-6**

Finding Missing Amounts (P11-1)

At the end of the year, the records of Duo Corporation provided the following selected and incomplete data:

Common stock: $1,500,000 ($1 par value; no changes in account during the year).
Shares authorized: 5,000,000.
Shares issued: _____ (all shares were issued at $80 per share).
Shares held as treasury stock: 100,000 shares (repurchased at $60 per share).
Net income: $4,800,000.
Dividends declared and paid: $2 per share.
Retained earnings beginning balance: $82,900,000.

Required:
1. Answer the following:
   a. How many issued shares are there?
   b. How many outstanding shares are there?
2. What is the balance in the Additional Paid-in Capital account?
3. What is earnings per share (EPS)?
4. What was the total dividend paid during the year?
5. In what section of the balance sheet should treasury stock be reported? What is the amount of treasury stock that should be reported?

AP11-2
LO11-1, 11-3, 11-7

Recording Transactions Affecting Stockholders' Equity (P11-3)

Granderson Company was granted a charter on January 1 that authorized the following stock:

Common stock: $40 par value, 100,000 shares authorized
Preferred stock: 8 percent; $5 par value; 20,000 shares authorized

During the year, the following transactions occurred in the order given:

a. Sold 30,000 shares of the common stock at $40 cash per share and 5,000 shares of the preferred stock at $26 cash per share.
b. Issued 2,000 shares of preferred stock when the stock was selling at $32.
c. Repurchased 3,000 shares of the common stock sold earlier. Paid $38 cash per share.

Required:
Provide the journal entries required to record each of the transactions in (*a*) through (*c*).

Preparing the Stockholders' Equity Section after Selected Transactions (P11-5)

AP11-3
LO11-1, 11-3

Luther Company obtained a charter from the state in January of this year. The charter authorized 1,000,000 shares of common stock with a par value of $5. During the year, the company earned $429,000. Also during the year, the following selected transactions occurred in the order given:

a. Sold 700,000 shares of the common stock at $54 cash per share.
b. Repurchased 25,000 shares at $50 cash per share.

Required:
Prepare the stockholders' equity section of the balance sheet at the end of the year.

Comparing Stock and Cash Dividends (P11-8)

AP11-4
LO11-4, 11-6, 11-7

Carlton Company reported the following information at the end of the year:

Common stock ($1 par value; 500,000 shares outstanding)	$500,000
Preferred stock, 8% ($10 par value; 21,000 shares outstanding)	210,000
Retained earnings	900,000

The board of directors is considering the distribution of a cash dividend to the two groups of stockholders. No dividends were declared during the previous two years. Assume the three cases below are independent of each other.

Case A: The preferred stock is noncumulative; the total amount of all dividends is $25,000.
Case B: The preferred stock is cumulative; the total amount of all dividends is $25,000.
Case C: The preferred stock is cumulative; the total amount of all dividends is $75,000.

Required:
1. Compute the amount of dividends, in total and per share, that would be payable to each class of stockholders for each case. Show computations.
2. Assume Carlton Company issued a 40 percent common stock dividend on the outstanding shares when the market value per share was $50. Fill in the table below to show how this stock dividend would compare to Case C.

	AMOUNT OF DOLLAR INCREASE (DECREASE)	
Item	**Cash Dividend—Case C**	**Stock Dividend**
Assets	$	$
Liabilities	$	$
Stockholders' equity	$	$

 **connect**

CONTINUING **PROBLEM**

Recording and Reporting Stockholders' Equity Transactions

CON11-1

Pool Corporation, Inc., is the world's largest wholesale distributor of swimming pool supplies and equipment. It is a publicly traded corporation that trades on the NASDAQ exchange under the symbol

POOL. The majority of Pool's customers are small, family-owned businesses. The company issued the following press release:

COVINGTON, La., March 2, 2015 (GLOBE NEWSWIRE)—Pool Corporation (Nasdaq: POOL) announced today that its Board of Directors declared a quarterly cash dividend of $0.22 per share. The dividend will be payable on March 26, 2015, to holders of record on March 12, 2015.

   The Company also announced in its 2014 Annual Report that it had repurchased $132.3 million of its common stock in the open market.

Required:
1. Record the repurchase of shares by Pool assuming all shares were repurchased at one time.
2. Prepare all necessary entries associated with the dividend. Assume that at the time of the dividend, Pool was authorized to issue 100 million shares and had 43 million shares outstanding.

COMPREHENSIVE PROBLEM (CHAPTERS 9–11)

Answer the questions below. Treat each case as being independent from the other cases.

Case A: The charter for Rogers, Incorporated, authorized the following stock:

   Common stock, $10 par value, 103,000 shares authorized
   Preferred stock, 9 percent, $8 par value, 4,000 shares authorized

The company sold 40,000 shares of common stock and 3,000 shares of preferred stock. During the year, the following selected transactions were completed in the order given:

1. Rogers declared and paid dividends in the amount of $10,000. How much was paid to the holders of preferred stock? How much was paid to the common stockholders?
2. Rogers repurchased 5,000 shares of common stock. After this transaction, how many shares of common stock were outstanding?
3. Provide the journal entry if Rogers sold 1,000 shares of treasury stock for $25 per share. The treasury stock was repurchased at $20 per share.
4. Describe how the balance sheet equation (assets = liabilities + stockholders' equity) would be affected if Rogers declared a 2-for-1 stock split.

Case B: Ospry, Inc., has working capital in the amount of $960,000. For each of the following transactions, determine whether working capital will increase, decrease, or remain the same.

1. Paid accounts payable in the amount of $10,000.
2. Recorded rent payable in the amount of $22,000.
3. Collected $5,000 in accounts receivable.
4. Purchased $20,000 of new inventory for cash.

Case C: James Corporation is planning to issue $1,000,000 worth of bonds with a coupon rate of 5 percent. The bonds mature in 10 years and pay interest annually. All of the bonds were sold on January 1 of this year.

Required:
Compute the issue (sale) price on January 1 under each independent assumption below (show computations):

1. Assume an annual market interest rate of 5 percent.
2. Assume an annual market interest rate of 4 percent.
3. Assume an annual market interest rate of 6 percent.

Case D: Miller Bikes is a national chain of upscale bicycle shops. The company has followed a success-ful strategy of locating near major universities. Miller has the opportunity to expand into sev-eral new markets but must raise additional capital. The company has engaged in the following transactions:

- Issued 45,000 additional shares of common stock. The stock has a par value of $1 and sells in the market for $25 per share.
- Issued bonds. These bonds have a face value of $1,000,000 and a coupon rate of 10 percent. The bonds mature in 10 years and pay interest semiannually. The current annual market rate of interest is 8 percent.

Required:
1. Record the sale of the bonds.
2. Record the issuance of the stock.

CASES **AND PROJECTS**

Annual Report Cases

Finding Financial Information

Refer to the financial statements of **American Eagle Outfitters** given in Appendix B at the end of this book. All questions below pertain to the last fiscal year reported in Appendix B.

Required:
1. Does the company report treasury stock? If so, what dollar amount does it report?
2. Did the company repurchase treasury stock during the year?
3. Did the company pay dividends during the year? If so, how much per share?
4. What is the par value of the common stock?

CP11-1
LO11-1, 11-3, 11-4

Finding Financial Information

Refer to the financial statements of **Urban Outfitters** given in Appendix C at the end of this book. All questions below pertain to the last fiscal year reported in Appendix C.

Required:
1. How many shares of common stock are authorized? How many are issued? How many are outstanding?
2. Did the company pay dividends during the year? If so, how much per share?
3. Does the company report treasury stock? If so, what dollar amount does it report?
4. Did the company repurchase any shares of its common stock during the year?
5. What is the par value of the common stock?

CP11-2
LO11-1, 11-3, 11-4, 11-6

Comparing Companies within an Industry

Refer to the financial statements of **American Eagle** (Appendix B) and **Urban Outfitters** (Appendix C).

Required:
1. Calculate the dividend yield ratios for Urban Outfitters (assume the market price of the stock is $40) and American Eagle (assume the market price of the stock is $20) for the most recent reporting year.
2. Why would an investor choose to invest in a stock that does not pay dividends?
3. Using the information from the following table, compare the dividend yield ratios for the industries listed below. Why might an investor care about a firm's dividend yield ratio?

CP11-3
LO11-4, 11-5, 11-6

DIVIDEND YIELD RATIOS FOR VARIOUS INDUSTRIES			
	Beverages	**Tobacco**	**Oil and Gas**
Dividend yield	2.2%	4.8%	9.6%
Example company	**Coca-Cola**	**Philip Morris**	**Exxon Mobil**

Financial Reporting and Analysis Case

CP11-4

LO11-4

Computing Dividends for an Actual Company

A recent annual report for **Apple Inc.** contained the following information (dollars in thousands):

Stockholders' Equity	2014
Common stock, $0.00001 par value, 12.6 billion shares authorized, 5.9 billion shares issued and outstanding	$ 0.059
Additional paid-in capital	23,313
Retained earnings	87,152

In 2014, Apple declared and paid dividends equal to $1.82 per share. Approximately how much cash in total did Apple pay to stockholders for dividends in 2014?

Critical Thinking Cases

CP11-5

LO11-4, 11-6

Evaluating an Ethical Dilemma

You are a member of the board of directors of a large company that has been in business for more than 100 years. The company is proud of the fact that it has paid dividends every year it has been in business. Because of this stability, many retired people have invested large portions of their savings in your common stock. Unfortunately, the company has struggled for the past few years as it tries to introduce new products and is considering not paying a dividend this year. The president wants to skip the dividend in order to have more cash to invest in product development: "If we don't invest this money now, we won't get these products to market in time to save the company. I don't want to risk thousands of jobs." One of the most senior board members speaks next: "If we don't pay the dividend, thousands of retirees will be thrown into financial distress. Even if you don't care about them, you have to recognize our stock price will crash when they all sell." The company treasurer proposes an alternative: "Let's skip the cash dividend and pay a stock dividend. We can still say we've had a dividend every year." The entire board now turns to you for your opinion. What should the company do?

CP11-6

LO11-4

Evaluating an Ethical Dilemma

You are the president of a very successful Internet company that has had a remarkably profitable year. You have determined that the company has more than $10 million in cash generated by operating activities not needed in the business. You are thinking about paying it out to stockholders as a special dividend. You discuss the idea with your vice president, who reacts angrily to your suggestion:

"Our stock price has gone up by 200 percent in the last year alone. What more do we have to do for the owners? The people who really earned that money are the employees who have been working 12 hours a day, six or seven days a week, to make the company successful. Most of them didn't even take vacations last year. I say we have to pay out bonuses and nothing extra for the stockholders."

As president, you know that you are hired by the board of directors, which is elected by the stockholders. What is your responsibility to both groups? To which group would you give the $10 million?

Financial Reporting and Analysis Team Project

Team Project: Examining an Annual Report

CP11-7
LO11-1, 11-3, 11-4,
11-6, 11-7

As a team, select an industry to analyze. Both Yahoo Finance and Google Finance provide information on any given firm's industry. Each team member should acquire the annual report or 10-K for one publicly traded company in the industry, with each member selecting a different company. The annual reports or 10-Ks can be downloaded from the SEC EDGAR website (**www.sec.gov**) or from any individual company's investor relations website.

Required:

Each team member should individually gather the information described below and attempt to answer each question. After completing this individual phase of the project, teams should get together to compare and contrast their answers to each question. At the conclusion of this discussion, each team should write a short report summarizing their analysis and findings.

1. *a.* List the accounts and amounts of the company's stockholders' equity.
   b. From the footnotes, identify any additional information about the accounts you listed that you feel would be important to someone analyzing the company as a potential investment.
2. Examine the statement of cash flows and the statement of stockholders' equity. What amount of stock, if any, was issued in the most recent year? How much cash did the issuance generate for the company?
   a. What was the average market value per share of the issuance?
   b. Recreate the journal entry for the issuance.
3. What amount of treasury stock, if any, did the company repurchase during the year? Did it resell any of its treasury stock?
4. What types of dividends, if any, did the company declare during the year? How much was paid in cash?

Statement of Cash Flows

While once best known for their Shasta and Faygo carbonated soft drinks, **National Beverage** now focuses on its innovative LaCroix sparkling waters, Rip It energy products, and Everfresh juices. These products bring its well-known reputation for flavor variety to the growing number of health-conscious consumers. Its diverse product lines can meet all of the beverage needs of a wide variety of consumers and retailers. However, for its strategy to earn profits for shareholders, National Beverage must also be a cost-effective producer and distributor. It maintains product quality and cost discipline through centralized purchasing and by owning and operating all of its production and bottling facilities. Its 12 plants, strategically located near customer distribution centers in different markets, reduce distribution costs and allow National Beverage to tailor its products and media promotions to regional tastes.

Although it may seem puzzling, growing profitable operations do not always ensure positive cash flow. As we have seen in earlier chapters, this occurs because the timing of revenues and expenses does not always match cash inflows and outflows. As a consequence, National Beverage must carefully manage cash flows as well as profits. For the same reasons, financial analysts must consider the information provided in National Beverage's cash flow statement in addition to its income statement and balance sheet.

UNDERSTANDING THE BUSINESS

Clearly, net income is important, but cash flow is also critical to a company's success. Cash flow permits a company to expand operations, replace worn assets, take advantage of new

Learning Objectives

After studying this chapter, you should be able to:

12-1 Classify cash flow statement items as part of net cash flows from operating, investing, and financing activities.

12-2 Report and interpret cash flows from operating activities using the indirect method.

12-3 Analyze and interpret the quality of income ratio.

12-4 Report and interpret cash flows from investing activities.

12-5 Analyze and interpret the capital acquisitions ratio.

12-6 Report and interpret cash flows from financing activities.

12-7 Understand the format of the cash flow statement and additional cash flow disclosures.

chapter 12

Sara Stathas/Alamy

investment opportunities, and pay dividends to its owners. Some Wall Street analysts go so far as to say "Cash flow is king." Both managers and analysts need to understand the various sources and uses of cash that are associated with business activity.

The cash flow statement focuses attention on a firm's ability to generate cash internally, its management of operating assets and liabilities, and the details of its investments and its external financing. It is designed to help both managers and analysts answer important cash-related questions such as these:

- Will the company have enough cash to pay its short-term debts to suppliers and other creditors without additional borrowing?
- Is the company adequately managing its accounts receivable and inventory?
- Has the company made necessary investments in new productive capacity?
- Did the company generate enough cash flow internally to finance necessary investments, or did it rely on external financing?
- Is the company changing the makeup of its external financing?

We begin our discussion with an overview of the statement of cash flows. Then we examine the information reported in each section of the statement in depth. The chapter ends with a discussion of additional cash flow disclosures.

FOCUS COMPANY:

National Beverage Corporation

PRODUCING HEALTHIER BEVERAGES FOR CUSTOMERS AND CASH FLOWS FOR SHAREHOLDERS

www.nationalbeverage.com

ORGANIZATION of the Chapter

Classifications of the Statement of Cash Flows	Reporting and Interpreting Cash Flows from Operating Activities	Reporting and Interpreting Cash Flows from Investing Activities	Reporting and Interpreting Cash Flows from Financing Activities	Completing the Statement and Additional Disclosures
• Cash Flows from Operating Activities • Cash Flows from Investing Activities • Cash Flows from Financing Activities • Net Increase (Decrease) in Cash • Relationships to the Balance Sheet and Income Statement • Preliminary Steps in Preparing the Cash Flow Statement	• Reporting Cash Flows from Operating Activities— Indirect Method • Interpreting Cash Flows from Operating Activities • Quality of Income Ratio	• Reporting Cash Flows from Investing Activities • Interpreting Cash Flows from Investing Activities • Capital Acquisitions Ratio	• Reporting Cash Flows from Financing Activities • Interpreting Cash Flows from Financing Activities	• Statement Structure • Supplemental Cash Flow Information

LEARNING OBJECTIVE 12-1
Classify cash flow statement items as part of net cash flows from operating, investing, and financing activities.

CASH EQUIVALENTS
Short-term investments with original maturities of three months or less that are readily convertible to cash and whose value is unlikely to change.

CLASSIFICATIONS OF THE STATEMENT OF CASH FLOWS

Basically, the statement of cash flows explains how the amount of cash on the balance sheet at the beginning of the period has become the amount of cash reported at the end of the period. For purposes of this statement, the definition of cash includes cash and cash equivalents. **Cash equivalents** are short-term, highly liquid investments that are both

1. Readily convertible to known amounts of cash and

2. So near to maturity there is little risk that their value will change if interest rates change.

Generally, only investments with original maturities of three months or less qualify as a cash equivalent under this definition.[1] Examples of cash equivalents are Treasury bills (a form of short-term U.S. government debt), money market funds, and commercial paper (short-term notes payable issued by large corporations).

As you can see in Exhibit 12.1, the statement of cash flows reports cash inflows and outflows in three broad categories: (1) operating activities, (2) investing activities, and (3) financing activities. Together, these three cash flow categories explain the change in cash from the beginning balance to the ending balance on the balance sheet.

---

[1] **Original maturity** means original maturity to the entity holding the investment. For example, both a three-month Treasury bill and a three-year Treasury note purchased three months from maturity qualify as cash equivalents. A Treasury note purchased three years ago, however, does not become a cash equivalent when its remaining maturity is three months.

EXHIBIT 12.1

Consolidated Statement
of Cash Flows

NATIONAL BEVERAGE CORP.
Consolidated Statement of Cash Flows*
Year Ended May 3, 2014
(In thousands)

Cash flows from operating activities:

Net income	$ 43,635
Adjustments to reconcile net income to net cash provided by (used in) operating activities:	
Depreciation and amortization	10,063
Changes in assets and liabilities:	
Accounts receivable	5,864
Inventories	(4,680)
Prepaid expenses	(2,699)
Accounts payable	1,345
Accrued expenses	(259)
Net cash provided by operating activities	53,269

Cash flows from investing activities:

Purchases of property, plant, and equipment	(12,124)
Proceeds from disposal of property, plant, and equipment	62
Purchase of short-term investments	(1,463)
Proceeds from sale of short-term investments	2,443
Net cash used by investing activities	(11,082)

Cash flows from financing activities:

Repayment of principal on long-term debt	(22,772)
Proceeds from issuance of long-term debt	—
Repurchase of stock	(7,024)
Proceeds from issuance of stock	—
Payment of cash dividends	(726)
Net cash used by financing activities	(30,522)
Net Increase (Decrease) in Cash and Equivalents	11,665
Cash and Equivalents—Beginning of Year	18,267
Cash and Equivalents—End of Year	$ 29,932

Certain amounts have been adjusted for pedagogical purposes.

NATIONAL BEVERAGE CORP.

REAL WORLD EXCERPT:

Annual Report

Cash Flows from Operating Activities

Cash flows from operating activities (cash flows from operations) are the cash inflows and outflows that relate directly to revenues and expenses reported on the income statement. There are two alternative approaches for presenting the operating activities section of the statement:

1. The **direct method** reports the components of cash flows from operating activities as gross receipts and gross payments.

Inflows	Outflows
Cash received from	**Cash paid for**
Customers	Purchase of services (electricity, etc.)
Dividends and interest on investments	and goods for resale
	Salaries and wages
	Income taxes
	Interest on liabilities

CASH FLOWS FROM OPERATING ACTIVITIES (CASH FLOWS FROM OPERATIONS)
Cash inflows and outflows directly related to earnings from normal operations.

DIRECT METHOD
A method of presenting the operating activities section of the statement of cash flows that reports components of cash flows from operating activities as gross receipts and gross payments.

The difference between the inflows and outflows is called **net cash provided by (used by) operating activities. National Beverage** experienced a net cash inflow of $53,269 (all amounts in thousands) from its operations for the fiscal year ended May 3, 2014 (hereafter 2014). Though the FASB recommends the direct method, it is rarely used in the United States. Many financial executives have reported that they do not use it because it is more expensive to implement than the indirect method. Both the FASB and the IASB are considering a proposal to require this method, but intense opposition from the preparer community continues.

INDIRECT METHOD
A method of presenting the operating activities section of the statement of cash flows that adjusts net income to compute cash flows from operating activities.

2. The **indirect method** starts with net income from the income statement and then eliminates noncash items to arrive at net cash inflow (outflow) from operating activities.

> Net income
> +/− Adjustments for noncash items
> ――――――――――――――――――
> Net cash inflow (outflow) from operating activities

Ninety-nine percent of large U.S. companies, including National Beverage, use the indirect method.[2] Notice in Exhibit 12.1 that in the year 2014, National Beverage reported positive net income of $43,635 but generated positive cash flows from operating activities of $53,269. Why should income and cash flows from operating activities differ? Remember that on the income statement, revenues are recorded when they are earned, without regard to when the related cash inflows occur. Similarly, expenses are matched with revenues and recorded without regard to when the related cash outflows occur.

For now, the most important thing to remember about the two methods is that they are simply alternative ways to arrive at the same number. The total amount of **cash flows from operating activities is always the same** (an inflow of $53,269 in National Beverage's case), **regardless of whether it is computed using the direct or indirect method,** as illustrated below.

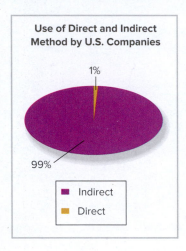

Use of Direct and Indirect Method by U.S. Companies

1%

99%

- Indirect
- Direct

Direct		Indirect	
Cash collected from customers	$646,999	Net income	$43,635
Cash payments for interest	(1,326)	Depreciation	10,063
Cash payments to suppliers	(426,815)	Changes in operating assets and liabilities	(429)
Cash payments for other expenses	(146,115)		
Cash payments for income taxes	(19,474)		
Net cash provided by operating activities	$ 53,269	Net cash provided by operating activities	$53,269

Cash Flows from Investing Activities

CASH FLOWS FROM INVESTING ACTIVITIES
Cash inflows and outflows related to the acquisition or sale of productive facilities and investments in the securities of other companies.

Cash flows from investing activities are cash inflows and outflows related to the purchase and disposal of long-lived productive assets and investments in the securities of other companies. Typical cash flows from investing activities include:

Inflows	Outflows
Cash received from	**Cash paid for**
Sale or disposal of property, plant, and equipment	Purchase of property, plant, and equipment
Sale or maturity of investments in securities	Purchase of investments in securities

The difference between these cash inflows and outflows is called **net cash provided by (used by) investing activities.**

――――――――――――――――――

[2]*Accounting Trends & Techniques* (New York: American Institute of CPAs, 2012).

For **National Beverage**, this amount was an outflow of $11,082 for the year 2014. Most of the activity was related to purchases and sales of short-term investments and the purchase and sale of property, plant, and equipment. Since total purchases exceeded cash collected from sales, there was a net cash outflow.

Cash Flows from Financing Activities

Cash flows from financing activities include exchanges of cash with creditors (debtholders) and owners (stockholders). Usual cash flows from financing activities include the following:

Inflows	Outflows
Cash received from	**Cash paid for**
Borrowing on notes, mortgages, bonds, etc., from creditors	Repayment of principal to creditors (excluding interest, which is an operating activity)
Issuing stock to owners	Repurchasing stock from owners
	Dividends to owners

The difference between these cash inflows and outflows is called **net cash provided by (used by) financing activities.**

National Beverage experienced a net cash outflow from financing activities of $30,522 for the year 2014. The Financing Activities section of its statement shows that National Beverage paid $22,772 in principal on long-term debt, $726 in dividends, and $7,024 for stock repurchases.[3]

Net Increase (Decrease) in Cash

The combination of **the net cash flows from operating activities, investing activities, and financing activities must equal the net increase (decrease) in cash** for the reporting period. For the year 2014, **National Beverage** reported a net increase in cash of $11,665, which explains the change in cash on the balance sheet from the beginning balance of $18,267 to the ending balance of $29,932.

Net cash provided by operating activities	$53,269
Net cash used in investing activities	(11,082)
Net cash used in financing activities	(30,522)
Net increase in cash and cash equivalents	11,665
Cash and cash equivalents at beginning of period	18,267
Cash and cash equivalents at end of period	$29,932

Beginning and ending balances from the balance sheet

PAUSE FOR **FEEDBACK**

We just discussed the three main sections of the cash flow statement: Cash Flows from Operating Activities, which are related to earning income from normal operations; Cash Flows from Investing Activities, which are related to the acquisition and sale of productive assets; and Cash Flows from Financing Activities, which are related to external financing of the enterprise. The net cash inflow or outflow for the year is the same amount as the increase or decrease in cash and cash equivalents for the year on the balance sheet. To make sure you understand the appropriate classifications of the different cash flows, answer the following questions before you move on.

(continued)

---

[3]This description was simplified to eliminate discussion of stock options and cash flow hedges.

To give you a better understanding of the statement of cash flows, we now discuss National Beverage's statement in more detail, including the way in which it relates to the balance sheet and income statement. Then we examine how each section of the statement describes a set of important decisions made by National Beverage's management. Last, we examine how financial analysts use each section to evaluate the company's performance.

Relationships to the Balance Sheet and Income Statement

Preparing and interpreting the cash flow statement requires an analysis of the balance sheet and income statement accounts that relate to the three sections of the cash flow statement. In previous chapters, we emphasized that companies record transactions as journal entries that are posted to T-accounts, which are used to prepare the income statement and the balance sheet. But companies cannot prepare the statement of cash flows using the amounts recorded in the T-accounts because those amounts are based on accrual accounting. Instead, they must analyze the numbers recorded under the accrual method and adjust them to a cash basis. To prepare the statement of cash flows, they need the following data:

1. **Comparative balance sheets** used in calculating the cash flows from all activities (operating, investing, and financing).

2. A **complete income statement** used primarily in calculating cash flows from operating activities.

3. **Additional details** concerning selected accounts where the total change amount in an account balance during the year does not reveal the underlying nature of the cash flows.

Our approach to preparing and understanding the cash flow statement focuses on the changes in the balance sheet accounts. It relies on a simple manipulation of the balance sheet equation:

$$\text{Assets} = \text{Liabilities} + \text{Stockholders' Equity}$$

First, assets can be split into cash and noncash assets:

$$\text{Cash} + \text{Noncash Assets} = \text{Liabilities} + \text{Stockholders' Equity}$$

If we move the noncash assets to the right side of the equation, then:

$$\text{Cash} = \text{Liabilities} + \text{Stockholders' Equity} - \text{Noncash Assets}$$

Category	Transaction	Cash Effect	Other Account Affected
Operating	Collect accounts receivable	+Cash	−Accounts Receivable (A)
	Pay accounts payable	−Cash	−Accounts Payable (L)
	Prepay rent	−Cash	+Prepaid Rent (A)
	Pay interest	−Cash	−Retained Earnings (SE)
	Sale for cash	+Cash	+Retained Earnings (SE)
Investing	Purchase equipment for cash	−Cash	+Equipment (A)
	Sell investment securities for cash	+Cash	−Investments (A)
Financing	Pay back debt to bank	−Cash	−Notes Payable—Bank (L)
	Issue stock for cash	+Cash	+Common Stock and Additional Paid-in-Capital (SE)

EXHIBIT 12.2

Selected Cash Transactions and Their Effects on Other Balance Sheet Accounts

Given this relationship, the changes (Δ) in cash between the beginning and the end of the period must equal the changes (Δ) in the amounts on the right side of the equation between the beginning and the end of the period:

$$\Delta \text{ Cash} = \Delta \text{ Liabilities} + \Delta \text{ Stockholders' Equity} - \Delta \text{ Noncash Assets}$$

Thus, **any transaction that changes cash must be accompanied by a change in liabilities, stockholders' equity, or noncash assets.** Exhibit 12.2 illustrates this concept for selected cash transactions.

Preliminary Steps in Preparing the Cash Flow Statement

Based on this logic, we use the following preliminary steps to prepare the cash flow statement:

1. Determine the change in each balance sheet account. From this year's ending balance, subtract this year's beginning balance (i.e., last year's ending balance).

2. Classify each change as relating to operating (O), investing (I), or financing (F) activities by marking them with the corresponding letter. Use Exhibit 12.3 as a guide.

The balance sheet accounts related to earning income (operating items) should be marked with an O. These accounts are often called **operating assets and liabilities.** The accounts that should be marked with an O include the following:

- Most current assets (other than short-term investments, which relate to investing activities, and cash).[4]

- Most current liabilities (other than amounts owed to investors and financial institutions,[5] all of which relate to financing activities).

- Retained Earnings because it increases by the amount of net income, which is the starting point for the operating section. (Retained Earnings also decreases by dividends declared and paid, which is a financing outflow noted by an F.)

In Exhibit 12.3, all of the operating assets and liabilities have been marked with an O. These items include:

- Accounts Receivable
- Inventories

---

[4]Certain noncurrent assets such as long-term receivables from customers and noncurrent liabilities such as postretirement obligations to employees are considered to be operating items. These items are covered in more advanced accounting classes.

[5]Examples of the accounts excluded are Dividends Payable, Short-Term Debt to Financial Institutions, and Current Maturities of Long-Term Debt. Current maturities of long-term debt are amounts of debt with an original term of more than one year that are due within one year of the statement date. Certain noncurrent liabilities involving payables to suppliers, to employees, or for taxes are also considered to be operating liabilities. These items are covered in more advanced accounting classes.

EXHIBIT 12.3

Comparative Balance Sheet and Current Income Statement

NATIONAL BEVERAGE CORP.

REAL WORLD EXCERPT:

Annual Report

Related Cash Flow Section			
Change in Cash			
I			
O			
O			
O			
I†			
O			
O			
F			
F			
F			
O and F			

NATIONAL BEVERAGE CORP.
Consolidated Balance Sheet
(In thousands)

	May 3, 2014	April 27, 2013	*Change*
Assets			
Current assets:			
Cash and cash equivalents	$ 29,932	$ 18,267	+11,665
Short-term investments	2,685	3,665	−980
Accounts receivable	58,205	64,069	−5,864
Inventories	43,914	39,234	+4,680
Prepaid expenses	8,405	5,706	+2,699
Total current assets	143,141	130,941	
Property, plant, and equipment, net	79,700	77,701	+1,999
Total assets	$222,841	$208,642	
Liabilities and Stockholders' Equity			
Current liabilities:			
Accounts payable	$ 45,606	$ 44,261	+1,345
Accrued expenses	18,917	19,176	−259
Total current liabilities	64,523	63,437	
Long-term debt	52,117	74,889	−22,772
Stockholders' equity:			
Common stock	894	1,054	−160
Additional paid-in capital	24,570	31,434	−6,864
Retained earnings	80,737	37,828	+42,909
Total stockholders' equity	106,201	70,316	
Total liabilities and stockholders' equity	$222,841	$208,642	

†*The Accumulated Depreciation account is also related to operations because it relates to depreciation.*

NATIONAL BEVERAGE CORP.
Consolidated Statements of Income
For the Fiscal Year Ended May 3, 2014
(In thousands)

Net sales	$641,135
Cost of sales	423,480
Gross profit	217,655
Operating expenses:	
Selling, general, and administrative expense	143,157
Depreciation and amortization expense	10,063
Total operating expenses	153,220
Operating income	64,435
Interest expense	(1,326)
Income before provision for income taxes	63,109
Provision for income taxes	19,474
Net income	$ 43,635

Certain balances have been adjusted to simplify the presentation.

- Prepaid Expenses
- Accounts Payable
- Accrued Expenses

As we have noted, retained earnings is also relevant to operations.

The balance sheet accounts related to investing activities should be marked with an I. These include all of the remaining assets on the balance sheet. In Exhibit 12.3 these items include:

- Short-Term Investments
- Property, Plant, and Equipment, Net

The balance sheet accounts related to financing activities should be marked with an F. These include all of the remaining liability and stockholders' equity accounts on the balance sheet. In Exhibit 12.3 these items include:

- Long-Term Debt
- Common Stock
- Additional Paid-in Capital
- Retained Earnings (for decreases resulting from dividends declared and paid)

Next, we use this information to prepare each section of the statement of cash flows.

REPORTING AND INTERPRETING CASH FLOWS FROM OPERATING ACTIVITIES

> **LEARNING OBJECTIVE 12-2**
> Report and interpret cash flows from operating activities using the indirect method.

As noted above, the operating section can be prepared in two formats, and nearly all U.S. companies choose the indirect method. As a result, we discuss the indirect method here and the direct method in Supplement A at the end of the chapter.

Recall that:

1. Cash flow from operating activities is always the **same** regardless of whether it is computed using the direct or indirect method.

2. The investing and financing sections are always presented in the **same** manner regardless of the format of the operating section.

Reporting Cash Flows from Operating Activities—Indirect Method

Exhibit 12.3 shows **National Beverage**'s comparative balance sheet and income statement. Remember that the indirect method starts with net income and converts it to cash flows from operating activities. This involves adjusting net income for the differences in the timing of accrual basis net income and cash flows. The general structure of the operating activities section is:

Operating Activities
Net income
Adjustments to reconcile net income to cash flow from operating activities:
  +Depreciation and amortization expense
  −Gain on sale of investing asset
  +Loss on sale of investing asset
  +Decreases in operating assets
  +Increases in operating liabilities
  −Increases in operating assets
  −Decreases in operating liabilities
Net Cash Flow from Operating Activities

To keep track of all the additions and subtractions made to convert net income to cash flows from operating activities, it is helpful to set up a schedule to record the computations. We will construct a schedule for National Beverage in Exhibit 12.4.

EXHIBIT 12.4

National Beverage Corp.: Schedule for Net Cash Flow from Operating Activities, Indirect Method (dollars in thousands)

CONVERSION OF NET INCOME TO NET CASH FLOW FROM OPERATING ACTIVITIES		
Items	**Amount**	**Explanation**
Net income, accrual basis	$43,635	From income statement.
Add (subtract) to convert to cash basis:		
Depreciation and amortization	+10,063	Add back because depreciation and amortization expense does not affect cash.
Accounts receivable decrease	+5,864	Add because cash collected from customers is more than accrual basis revenues.
Inventory increase	−4,680	Subtract because purchases are more than cost of goods sold expense.
Prepaid expense increase	−2,699	Subtract because cash prepayments for expenses are more than accrual basis expenses.
Accounts payable increase	+1,345	Add because cash payments to suppliers are less than amounts purchased on account (borrowed from suppliers).
Accrued expenses decrease	−259	Subtract because cash payments for expenses are more than accrual basis expenses.
Net cash provided by operating activities	$53,269	Reported on the statement of cash flows.

We begin our schedule presented in Exhibit 12.4 with net income of $43,635 taken from National Beverage's income statement (Exhibit 12.3). Completing the operating section using the indirect method involves two steps:

Step 1: **Adjust net income for depreciation and amortization expense and gains and losses on sale of investing assets such as property, plant, and equipment and investments.** Recording depreciation and amortization expense does not affect the cash account (or any other operating asset or liability). It affects a noncurrent investing asset (Property, plant, and equipment, net). **Since depreciation and amortization expense is subtracted in computing net income but does not affect cash, we always add it back** to convert net income to cash flow from operating activities. In the case of National Beverage, we need to remove the effect of depreciation and amortization expense by adding back $10,063 to net income (see Exhibit 12.4).

If National Beverage had sold property, plant, and equipment at a gain or loss, the amount of cash received would be classified as an investing cash inflow. Since all of the cash received is an investing cash flow, an adjustment must also be made in the operating activities section to avoid double counting the gain or loss. **Gains on sales of property, plant, and equipment are subtracted and losses on such sales are added** to convert net income to cash flow from operating activities. We illustrate the relevant computations and adjustments for gains and losses on the sale of long-term assets in Supplement B at the end of the chapter.[6]

Step 2: **Adjust net income for changes in assets and liabilities marked as operating (O).** Each **change** in operating assets (other than cash and short-term investments) and liabilities (other than amounts owed to owners and financial institutions) causes a difference between net income and cash flow from operating activities.[7] When converting net income to cash flow from operating activities, apply the following general rules:

- Add the change when an operating asset decreases or an operating liability increases.
- Subtract the change when an operating asset increases or an operating liability decreases.

---

[6]Other similar additions and subtractions are discussed in more advanced accounting courses.

[7]As noted earlier, certain noncurrent assets, such as long-term receivables from customers, and noncurrent liabilities, such as postretirement obligations to employees, are considered to be operating items. These items are covered in more advanced accounting classes.

Understanding what makes these assets and liabilities increase and decrease is the key to understanding the logic of these additions and subtractions.

Change in Accounts Receivable

We illustrate this logic with the first operating item (O) listed on National Beverage's balance sheet (Exhibit 12.3), accounts receivable. Remember that the income statement reflects sales revenue, but the cash flow statement must reflect cash collections from customers. As the following accounts receivable T-account illustrates, when sales revenues are recorded, accounts receivable increases, and when cash is collected from customers, accounts receivable decreases.

Accounts Receivable (A)			
Beginning balance	64,069		
Sales revenue (on account)	641,135	Collections from customers	646,999
Ending balance	58,205		

Change $5,864 { (brace spanning Beginning balance through Ending balance)

In the National Beverage example, sales revenue reported on the income statement is less than cash collections from customers by $641,135 − $646,999 = ($5,864). Because more money was collected from customers, this amount must be added to net income to convert to cash flows from operating activities. Note that this amount is also the same as the **change** in the accounts receivable account:

Ending balance	$58,205
− Beginning balance	64,069
Change	($ 5,864)

This same underlying logic is used to determine adjustments for the other operating assets and liabilities.

To summarize, the income statement reflects revenues of the period, but cash flow from operating activities must reflect cash collections from customers. Sales on account increase the balance in accounts receivable, and collections from customers decrease the balance.

Accounts Receivable (A)			
Beginning	64,069		
		Decrease	5,864
Ending	58,205		

If Accounts Receivable:
- **Increases** ($ is Lower) → **Subtract**
- **Decreases** ($ is Higher) → **Add**

The balance sheet for National Beverage Corp. (Exhibit 12.3) indicates a **decrease** in accounts receivable of $5,864 for the period, which means that cash collected from customers is higher than revenue. To convert to cash flows from operating activities, the amount of the decrease (the increased collections) must be **added** in Exhibit 12.4. (An increase is subtracted.)

Change in Inventory

The income statement reflects merchandise sold for the period, whereas cash flow from operating activities must reflect cash purchases. As shown in the Inventories T-account, purchases of goods increase the balance in inventory, and recording merchandise sold decreases the balance in inventory.

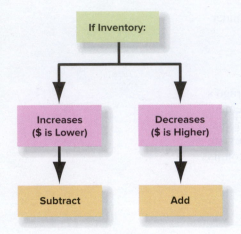

Inventories (A)			Inventories (A)	
Beg. balance			Beg.	39,234
Purchases	Costs of goods sold		Increase	4,680
End. bal.			End.	43,914

National Beverage's balance sheet (Exhibit 12.3) indicates that inventory **increased** by $4,680, which means that the amount of purchases is more than the amount of merchandise sold. The increase (the extra goods purchased) must be **subtracted** from net income to convert to cash flow from operating activities in Exhibit 12.4. (A decrease is added.)

Change in Prepaid Expenses

The income statement reflects expenses of the period, but cash flow from operating activities must reflect the cash payments. Cash prepayments increase the balance in prepaid expenses, and recording of expenses decreases the balance in prepaid expenses.

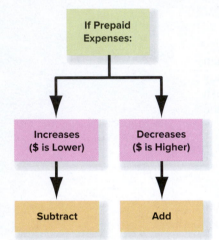

Prepaid Expenses (A)			Prepaid Expenses (A)	
Beg. bal.			Beg.	5,706
Cash prepayments	Services used (expense)		Increase	2,699
End. bal.			End.	8,405

The National Beverage balance sheet (Exhibit 12.3) indicates a $2,699 **increase** in prepaid expenses, which means that new cash prepayments are more than the amount of expenses. The increase (the extra prepayments) must be **subtracted** from net income in Exhibit 12.4.

Change in Accounts Payable

Cash flow from operations must reflect cash purchases, but not all purchases are for cash. Purchases on account increase accounts payable and cash paid to suppliers decreases accounts payable.

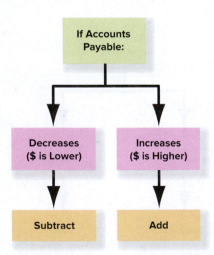

Accounts Payable (L)			Accounts Payable (L)	
Cash payments	Beg. bal.		Beg.	44,261
	Purchases on account		Increase	1,345
	End. bal.		End.	45,606

National Beverage's accounts payable **increased** by $1,345, which means that cash payments were less than purchases on account. This increase (the extra purchases on account) must be **added** in Exhibit 12.4. (A decrease is subtracted.)

Change in Accrued Expenses

The income statement reflects all accrued expenses, but the cash flow statement must reflect actual payments for those expenses. Recording accrued expenses increases the balance in the liability accrued expenses and cash payments for the expenses decrease accrued expenses.

Accrued Expenses (L)			Accrued Expenses (L)	
Pay off accruals	Beg. bal.			Beg.	19,176
	Accrued expenses		Decrease	259	
	End. bal.			End.	18,917

National Beverage's accrued expenses (Exhibit 12.3) **decreased** by $259, which indicates that cash paid for the expenses is more than accrual basis expenses. The decrease (the higher cash paid) must be **subtracted** in Exhibit 12.4. (An increase is added.)

Summary

We can summarize the typical additions and subtractions that are required to reconcile net income with cash flow from operating activities as follows:

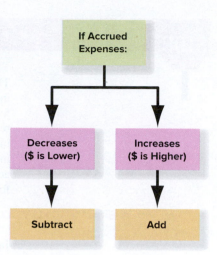

ADDITIONS AND SUBTRACTIONS TO RECONCILE NET INCOME TO CASH FLOW FROM OPERATING ACTIVITIES

Item	When Item Increases	When Item Decreases
Depreciation and amortization	+	NA
Gain on sale of long-term asset	−	NA
Loss on sale of long-term asset	+	NA
Accounts receivable	−	+
Inventory	−	+
Prepaid expenses	−	+
Accounts payable	+	−
Accrued expense liabilities	+	−

Notice again in this table that to reconcile net income to cash flows from operating activities, you must:

- **Add the change when an operating asset decreases or an operating liability increases.**
- **Subtract the change when an operating asset increases or an operating liability decreases.**

The cash flow statement for National Beverage (Exhibit 12.1) shows the same additions and subtractions to reconcile net income to cash flows from operating activities described in Exhibit 12.4.

Classification of Interest on the Cash Flow Statement

INTERNATIONAL PERSPECTIVE

U.S. GAAP and IFRS differ in the cash flow statement treatment of interest received and interest paid as follows:

	Interest Received	Interest Paid
U.S. GAAP	Operating	Operating
IFRS	Operating or Investing	Operating or Financing

   Under U.S. GAAP, interest paid and received are both classified as operating cash flows because the related revenue and expense enter into the computation of net income. This makes it easier to compare net income to cash flow from operations. It also benefits the financial statement user by ensuring comparability across companies. IFRS, on the other hand, allows interest received to be classified as either operating or investing and interest paid to be classified as either operating or financing. This recognizes that interest received results from investing activities, whereas interest paid, like dividends paid, involves payments to providers of financing. However, the alternative classifications may be confusing to financial statement readers.

STOP

PAUSE FOR **FEEDBACK**

The indirect method for reporting cash flows from operating activities reports a conversion of net income to net cash flow from operating activities. The conversion involves additions and subtractions for (1) expenses (such as depreciation expense) and revenues that do not affect current assets or current liabilities and (2) changes in each of the individual current assets (other than cash and short-term investments) and current liabilities (other than short-term debt to financial institutions and current maturities of long-term debt, which relate to financing), which reflect differences in the timing of accrual basis net income and cash flows. To test whether you understand these concepts, answer the following questions before you move on.

SELF-STUDY **QUIZ**

Indicate which of the following items taken from **Dr Pepper Snapple Group**'s cash flow statement would be added (+), subtracted (−), or not included (NA) in the reconciliation of net income to cash flow from operations.

_____ 1. Increase in inventories.   _____ 4. Decrease in accounts receivable.

_____ 2. Proceeds from issuance of notes payable.   _____ 5. Increase in accounts payable.

_____ 3. Amortization expense.   _____ 6. Increase in prepaid expenses.

After you have completed your answers, check them below.

 GUIDED HELP 12-1

For additional step-by-step video instruction on preparing the operating section of the statement of cash flows using the indirect method, go to **http://www.mhhe.com/libby9e_gh12a**.

Interpreting Cash Flows from Operating Activities

The operating activities section of the cash flow statement focuses attention on the firm's ability to generate cash internally through operations and its management of current assets and current liabilities (also called **working capital**). Most analysts believe that this is the most important section of the statement because, in the long run, operations are the only source of cash. That is, investors will not invest in a company if they do not believe that cash generated from operations will be available to pay them dividends or expand the company. Similarly, creditors will not lend money if they do not believe that cash generated from operations will be available to pay back the loan. For example, many dot-com companies crashed when investors lost faith in their ability to turn business ideas into cash flows from operations.

A common rule of thumb followed by financial and credit analysts is to avoid firms with rising net income but falling cash flow from operations. Rapidly rising inventories or receivables often predict a slump in profits and the need for external financing. A true understanding of the meaning of the difference requires a detailed understanding of its causes.

In the year 2014, **National Beverage** reported that cash flow from operations was higher than net income. What caused this relationship? To answer these questions, we must carefully analyze how National Beverage's operating activities are reported in its cash flow statement. To properly interpret this information, we also must learn more about the beverage industry. National Beverage normally reports higher cash flow from operations than net income because of the effect of depreciation and amortization, which reduces income but is not a cash outflow. At the same time, it carefully manages the assets and liabilities that enter into the operating cash flow calculation, keeping those total changes to a minimum. Many analysts compute the quality of income ratio as a general sign of the ability to generate cash through operations.

mauritius images GmbH/Alamy

Solutions to
SELF-STUDY QUIZ

1. −,   2. NA,   3. +,   4. +,   5. +,   6. −.

Quality of Income Ratio

 ANALYTICAL QUESTION

How much cash does each dollar of net income generate?

 RATIO AND COMPARISONS

> **LEARNING OBJECTIVE 12-3**
> Analyze and interpret the quality of income ratio.

$$\text{Quality of Income Ratio} = \frac{\text{Cash Flow from Operating Activities}}{\text{Net Income}}$$

National Beverage Corp.'s ratio for the year 2014 was:

$$\frac{53,269}{43,635} = 1.22\ (122\%)$$

COMPARISONS OVER TIME			COMPARISONS WITH COMPETITORS	
National Beverage			**Coca-Cola**	**PepsiCo**
2012	**2013**	**2014**	**2014**	**2014**
0.86	0.86	1.22	1.49	1.60

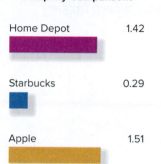

Selected Focus
Company Comparisons

Home Depot	1.42
Starbucks	0.29
Apple	1.51

 INTERPRETATIONS

In General   The quality of income ratio measures the portion of income that was generated in cash. All other things equal, a higher quality of income ratio indicates greater ability to finance operating and other cash needs from operating cash inflows. A higher ratio also indicates that it is less likely that the company is using aggressive revenue recognition policies to increase net income, and therefore is less likely to experience a decline in earnings in the future. When this ratio does not equal 1.0, analysts must establish the sources of the difference to determine the significance of the findings. There are four potential causes of any difference:

1. **The corporate life cycle (growth or decline in sales).** When sales are increasing, receivables and inventory normally increase faster than accounts payable. This often reduces operating cash flows below income, which, in turn, reduces the ratio. When sales are declining, the opposite occurs, and the ratio increases.

2. **Seasonality.** Seasonal (from quarter to quarter) variations in sales and purchases of inventory can cause the ratio to deviate from 1.0 during particular quarters.

3. **Changes in revenue and expense recognition.** Aggressive revenue recognition or failure to accrue appropriate expenses will inflate net income and reduce the ratio.

4. **Changes in management of operating assets and liabilities.** Inefficient management will increase operating assets and decrease liabilities, reducing operating cash flows and the quality of income ratio. More efficient management, such as shortening of payment terms, will have the opposite effect.

Focus Company Analysis   During the past three years, National Beverage's quality of income ratio has increased from 0.86 to 1.22. Its ratio is below those of **Coca-Cola** and **PepsiCo**. National Beverage's lower ratio would generally be judged negatively by analysts and would prompt them to read the management's discussion and analysis section of the annual report to determine its causes.

A Few Cautions   The quality of income ratio can be interpreted based only on an understanding of the company's business operations and strategy. For example, a low ratio for a quarter can be due simply to normal seasonal changes. However, it also can indicate obsolete inventory, slowing sales, or failed expansion plans. To test for these possibilities, analysts often analyze this ratio in tandem with the accounts receivable turnover and inventory turnover ratios.

The cash flow statement often gives outsiders the first hint that financial statements may contain errors and irregularities. The importance of this indicator as a predictor is receiving more attention in the United States and internationally. *Investors Chronicle* reported on an accounting fraud at a commercial credit company, suggesting that

INVESTORS CHRONICLE
REAL WORLD EXCERPT

> . . . a look at **Versailles**'s cash flow statement—an invaluable tool in spotting creative accounting—should have triggered misgivings. In the company's last filed accounts . . . Versailles reported operating profits of . . . $25 million but a cash outflow from operating activities of $24 million . . . such figures should . . . have served as a warning. After all, what use is a company to anyone if it reports only accounting profits which are never translated into cash?

As noted in earlier chapters, unethical managers sometimes attempt to reach earnings targets by manipulating accruals and deferrals of revenues and expenses to inflate income. Since these adjusting entries do not affect the cash account, they have no effect on the cash flow statement. A growing difference between net income and cash flow from operations can be a sign of such manipulations. This early warning sign has signaled some famous bankruptcies, such as that of **W. T. Grant** in 1975. The company had inflated income by failing to make adequate accruals of expenses for uncollectible accounts receivable and obsolete inventory. The more astute analysts noted the growing difference between net income and cash flow from operations and recommended selling the stock long before the bankruptcy.

Source: James Chapman, "Creative Accounting: Exposed!," *Investors Chronicle,* March 2, 2001.

LEARNING OBJECTIVE 12-4
Report and interpret cash flows from investing activities.

REPORTING AND INTERPRETING CASH FLOWS FROM INVESTING ACTIVITIES

Reporting Cash Flows from Investing Activities

Preparing this section of the cash flow statement requires an analysis of the accounts related to property, plant, and equipment; intangible assets; and investments in the securities of other companies. Normally, the relevant balance sheet accounts include Short-Term Investments and long-term asset accounts such as Long-Term Investments and Property, Plant, and Equipment. The following relationships are the ones that you will encounter most frequently:

Related Balance Sheet Account(s)	Investing Activity	Cash Flow Effect
Property, plant, and equipment and intangible assets (patents, etc.)	Purchase of property, plant, and equipment or intangible assets for cash	Outflow
	Sale of property, plant, and equipment or intangible assets for cash	Inflow
Short- or long-term investments (stocks and bonds of other companies)	Purchase of investment securities for cash	Outflow
	Sale (maturity) of investment securities for cash	Inflow

Remember that:

- **Only purchases paid for with cash or cash equivalents are included.**
- **The amount of cash that is received from the sale of assets is included, regardless of whether the assets are sold at a gain or loss.**

Items	Cash Inflows (Outflows)	Explanation
Purchase of property, plant, and equipment	$(12,124)	Payment in cash for equipment
Proceeds from disposal of property, plant, and equipment	62	Receipt of cash from sale of equipment
Purchase of short-term investments	(1,463)	Payment in cash for new investments
Proceeds from sale of short-term investments	2,443	Receipt of cash from sale of investments
Net cash inflow (outflow) from investing activities	$(11,082)	Reported on the statement of cash flows

EXHIBIT 12.5

National Beverage Corp.: Schedule for Net Cash Flow from Investing Activities (dollars in thousands)

In **National Beverage**'s case, the balance sheet (Exhibit 12.3) shows two investing assets (noted with an I) that have changed during the period: Property, Plant, and Equipment, Net, and Short-Term Investments. To determine the causes of these changes, accountants need to search the related company records.

Property, Plant, and Equipment, Net

Analysis of National Beverage Corp.'s records reveals that the company purchased new property, plant, and equipment for $12,124 in cash, which is a cash outflow. The company also sold old equipment for $62 in cash, an amount equal to its net book value. This is a cash inflow. These investing items are listed in the schedule of investing activities in Exhibit 12.5. These items, less the amount of depreciation expense added back in the Operations section ($10,063), explain the increase in property, plant, and equipment, net, of $1,999.

Property, Plant, and Equipment, Net (A)			
Beginning	77,701	Sold	62
Purchased	12,124	Depreciation	10,063
Ending	79,700		

Investments

National Beverage's records indicate that it purchased $1,463 in short-term investments during the year for cash, which is an investing cash outflow. The company also sold short-term investments for $2,443, an amount equal to their net book value. These investing items are listed in the schedule of investing activities in Exhibit 12.5. They explain the $980 decrease in short-term investments reported on the balance sheet. Changes in long-term investments would be treated in the same fashion.

Short-Term Investments (A)			
Beginning	3,665		
Purchased	1,463	Sold	2,443
Ending	2,685		

The net cash flow from investing activities resulting from these four items is an $11,082 outflow (see Exhibit 12.5).

Interpreting Cash Flows from Investing Activities

Two common ways to assess a company's ability to internally finance its expansion needs are the capital acquisitions ratio and free cash flow.

KEY RATIO ANALYSIS

Capital Acquisitions Ratio

LEARNING OBJECTIVE 12-5
Analyze and interpret the capital acquisitions ratio.

? ANALYTICAL QUESTION

To what degree was the company able to finance purchases of property, plant, and equipment with cash provided by operating activities?

% RATIO AND COMPARISONS

$$\text{Capital Acquisitions Ratio} = \frac{\text{Cash Flow from Operating Activities}}{\text{Cash Paid for Property, Plant, and Equipment}}$$

National Beverage's ratio for 2014 was

$$\frac{53,269}{12,124} = 4.39$$

Examine the ratio using two techniques:

COMPARISONS OVER TIME National Beverage			COMPARISONS WITH COMPETITORS	
			Coca-Cola	PepsiCo
2012	**2013**	**2014**	**2014**	**2014**
3.81	4.15	4.39	4.41	3.67

💡 INTERPRETATIONS

In General   The capital acquisitions ratio reflects the portion of purchases of property, plant, and equipment financed from operating activities (without the need for outside debt or equity financing or the sale of other investments or fixed assets). A high ratio indicates less need for outside financing for current and future expansion. It benefits the company because it provides the company opportunities for strategic acquisitions, avoids the cost of additional debt, and reduces the risk of bankruptcy that comes with additional leverage (see Chapter 10).

Focus Company Analysis   National Beverage's capital acquisitions ratio has increased from 3.81 to 4.39 in recent years. It generates more than sufficient cash to meet its investing needs. As a consequence, when credit markets tightened during the recent financial meltdown, National Beverage's investment plans were unaffected. National Beverage has also maintained a ratio that is nearly as high or higher than its larger competitors, **Coca-Cola** and **PepsiCo**.

A Few Cautions   Since the needs for investment in plant and equipment differ dramatically across industries (for example, airlines versus pizza delivery restaurants), a particular firm's ratio should be compared only with its prior years' figures or with other firms in the same industry. Also, a high ratio may indicate a failure to update plant and equipment, which can limit a company's ability to compete in the future.

Selected Focus Company Comparisons

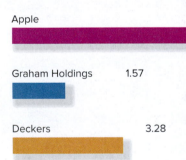

Apple	6.24
Graham Holdings	1.57
Deckers	3.28

FINANCIAL ANALYSIS

Free Cash Flow

FREE CASH FLOW
Cash Flows from Operating Activities less Dividends less Capital Expenditures.

Managers and analysts often calculate **free cash flow**[8] as a measure of a firm's ability to pursue long-term investment opportunities. Free cash flow is normally calculated as follows:

$$\text{Free Cash Flow} = \text{Cash Flow from Operating Activities} \\ - \text{Dividends} - \text{Capital Expenditures}$$

---

[8] An alternative definition that does not subtract dividends and interest is often called the **total cash flow of the firm** in finance.

Any positive free cash flow is available for additional capital expenditures, investments in other companies, and mergers and acquisitions without the need for external financing or reductions in dividends to shareholders. While free cash flow is considered a positive sign of financial flexibility, it also can represent a hidden cost to shareholders. Sometimes managers use free cash flow to pursue unprofitable investments just for the sake of growth or to obtain perquisites (such as fancy offices and corporate jets) that do not benefit the shareholders. In these cases, the shareholders would be better off if free cash flow were paid as additional dividends or used to repurchase the company's stock on the open market.

REPORTING AND INTERPRETING CASH FLOWS FROM FINANCING ACTIVITIES

LEARNING OBJECTIVE 12-6
Report and interpret cash flows from financing activities.

Reporting Cash Flows from Financing Activities

Financing activities are associated with generating capital from creditors and owners. This section of the cash flow statement reflects changes in two current liabilities, Notes Payable to Financial Institutions (often called short-term debt) and Current Maturities of Long-Term Debt, as well as changes in long-term liabilities and stockholders' equity accounts. These balance sheet accounts relate to the issuance and retirement of debt and stock and the payment of dividends. The following relationships are the ones that you will encounter most frequently:

Related Balance Sheet Account(s)	Financing Activity	Cash Flow Effect
Short-term debt (notes payable)	Borrowing cash from banks or other financial institutions	Inflow
	Repayment of loan principal	Outflow
Long-term debt	Issuance of bonds for cash	Inflow
	Repayment of bond principal	Outflow
Common stock and additional paid-in capital	Issuance of stock for cash	Inflow
	Repurchase (retirement) of stock with cash	Outflow
Retained earnings	Payment of cash dividends	Outflow

Remember that:

- **Cash repayments of principal are cash flows from financing activities.**

- **Interest payments are cash flows from operating activities.** Since interest expense is reported on the income statement, the related cash flow is shown in the operating section.

- **Dividend payments are cash flows from financing activities.** Dividend payments are not reported on the income statement because they represent a distribution of income to owners. Therefore, they are shown in the financing section.

- **If debt or stock is issued for other than cash, it is not included in this section.**

To compute cash flows from financing activities, you should review changes in debt and stockholders' equity accounts. In the case of **National Beverage Corp.**, the analysis of changes in the balance sheet (Exhibit 12.3) finds that only long-term debt, common stock, and additional paid-in capital changed during the period (noted with an F).

Short- and Long-Term Debt

When there is additional borrowing or principal repayments on long-term debt owed to financial institutions and investors, those amounts are financing cash flows. The appropriate amounts are determined by analyzing the long-term debt account. For 2014, the company repaid $22,772

EXHIBIT 12.6

National Beverage Corp.:
Schedule for Net Cash Flow
from Financing Activities
(dollars in thousands)

Items	Cash Inflows (Outflows)	Explanation
Cash flows from financing activities:		
Repayment of principal on long-term debt	(22,772)	Cash payments of principal on long-term debt
Proceeds from issuance of long-term debt	—	Cash proceeds from issuing long-term debt
Purchase of treasury stock	(7,024)	Cash payments to repurchase common stock
Proceeds from issuance of stock	—	Cash proceeds from issuing common stock
Payment of cash dividends	(726)	Cash payments of dividends to shareholders
Net cash used in financing activities	(30,522)	Reported on the statement of cash flows

in principal on long-term debt. This amount is listed in the schedule of financing activities in Exhibit 12.6. There were no additional borrowings on long-term debt.

Long-Term Debt (L)			
		Beginning	74,889
Retire (repay)	22,772	Issue (borrow)	0
		Ending	52,117

If the company had borrowed or repaid short-term debt to financial institutions, it would be treated in the same fashion.

Common Stock and Additional Paid-in Capital

National Beverage's change in common stock and additional paid-in capital resulted from two decisions. National Beverage did not issue any outstanding stock during the year. But the company did repurchase common stock for $7,024 in cash, which is a financing cash ouflow.[9] This accounts for the $7,024 decrease in common stock and additional paid-in capital. The amount is listed as an outflow in the schedule of financing activities in Exhibit 12.6.

Common Stock (SE)			
		Beginning	1,054
Repurchase	160	Issue	
		Ending	894

Additional Paid-in Capital (SE)			
		Beginning	31,434
Repurchase	6,864	Issue	
		Ending	24,570

Retained Earnings

Finally, retained earnings should be analyzed. Retained earnings rise when income is earned and fall when dividends are declared and paid. National Beverage earned $43,635 in income and paid $726 in dividends during 2014. National Beverage's dividend payment is listed on the schedule of financing activities in Exhibit 12.6.

Retained Earnings (SE)			
		Beginning	37,828
Dividends	726	Net Income	43,635
		Ending	80,737

Interpreting Cash Flows from Financing Activities

The long-term growth of a company is normally financed from three sources: internally generated funds (cash from operating activities), the issuance of stock, and money borrowed on a

---

[9]This description was simplified to eliminate discussion of stock options and cash flow hedges.

long-term basis. As we discussed in Chapter 10, companies can adopt a number of different capital structures (the balance of debt and equity). The financing sources that management uses to fund growth will have an important impact on the firm's risk and return characteristics. The statement of cash flows shows how management has elected to fund its growth. This information is used by analysts who wish to evaluate the capital structure and growth potential of a business.

PAUSE FOR FEEDBACK

As we just discussed, the investing section of the statement of cash flows includes cash payments to acquire fixed assets and short- and long-term investments and cash proceeds from the sale of fixed assets and short- and long-term investments. Cash inflows from financing activities include cash proceeds from the issuance of short- and long-term debt and common stock. Cash outflows include cash principal payments on short- and long-term debt, cash paid for the repurchase of the company's stock, and cash dividend payments. Check your understanding of these concepts by answering the following questions before you move on.

SELF-STUDY QUIZ

Indicate which of the following items taken from the cash flow statement of **Dr Pepper Snapple Group** would be reported in the Investing section (I) or the Financing section (F) and whether the amount would be an inflow (+) or an outflow (−).

_____ 1. Purchases of short-term investments.

_____ 2. Proceeds from issuance of note payable (to bank).

_____ 3. Cash dividends paid.

_____ 4. Proceeds from issuance of common stock.

_____ 5. Proceeds from sale of property, plant, and equipment.

After you have completed your answers, check them below.

 GUIDED HELP 12-2

For additional step-by-step video instruction on preparing the investing and financing sections of the statement of cash flows using the indirect method, go to **http://www.mhhe.com/libby9e_gh12b**.

COMPLETING THE STATEMENT AND ADDITIONAL DISCLOSURES

Statement Structure

Refer to the formal statement of cash flows for **National Beverage Corp.** shown in Exhibit 12.1. As you can see, it is a simple matter to construct the statement after the detailed analysis of the accounts and transactions has been completed (shown in Exhibits 12.4, 12.5, and 12.6). Exhibit 12.7 summarizes the general structure of the statement for companies that use the indirect method for the operating section. As you can see, when the **net increase or decrease in cash and cash equivalents** is added to the cash and cash equivalents taken from the beginning-of-period amount on the balance sheet, it equals the end-of-period cash and cash equivalents amount reported on the balance sheet. Companies also must provide two other disclosures related to the cash flow statement.

> **LEARNING OBJECTIVE 12-7**
> Understand the format of the cash flow statement and additional cash flow disclosures.

1. I−, 2. F+, 3. F−, 4. F+, 5. I+.

EXHIBIT 12.7

Structure of the Statement of Cash Flows (Indirect Method)

Statement of Cash Flows (Indirect Method)

Operating Activities:
Net Income
+ Depreciation and amortization expense
− Gain on sale of long-term asset
+ Loss on sale of long-term asset
+ Decreases in operating assets
+ Increases in operating liabilities
− Increases in operating assets
− Decreases in operating liabilities
Net Cash Flow from Operating Activities

Investing Activities:
− Purchase of property, plant, and equipment or intangible assets
+ Sale of property, plant, and equipment or intangible assets
− Purchase of investment securities
+ Sale (maturity) of investment securities
Net Cash Flow from Investing Activities

Financing Activities:
+ Borrowing from bank or other financial institution
− Repayment of loan principal
+ Issuance of bonds for cash
− Repayment of bond principal
+ Issuance of stock
− Repurchase (retirement) of stock
− Payment of (cash) dividends
Net Cash Flow from Financing Activities

Net increase or decrease in cash and cash equivalents
Cash and cash equivalents at beginning of period
Cash and cash equivalents at end of period

Supplemental Cash Flow Information

Two additional required cash flow disclosures are normally listed at the bottom of the statement or in the notes. **United Airlines** discloses this information in a note.

UNITED AIRLINES

REAL WORLD EXCERPT:

Annual Report

16. Statement of Consolidated Cash Flow—Supplemental Disclosures

Supplemental disclosures of cash flow information and non-cash investing and financing activities for the years ended December 31 are as follows (in millions):

	YEAR ENDED DECEMBER 31,		
	2014	**2013**	**2012**
Cash paid (refunded) during the period for:			
Interest (net of amounts capitalized)	748	752	766
Income taxes	(16)	(15)	4
Non-cash transactions:			
Net property and equipment acquired through issuance of debt	1,114	229	544

Noncash Investing and Financing Activities

Certain transactions are important investing and financing activities but have no cash flow effects. These are called **noncash investing and financing activities**. For example, the purchase of a $100,000 building with a $100,000 mortgage given by the former owner does not cause either an inflow or an outflow of cash. As a result, these noncash activities are not listed in the three main sections of the cash flow statement. However, supplemental disclosure of these transactions is required, in either narrative or schedule form. **National Beverage**'s statement of cash flows does not list any noncash investing and financing activities.

NONCASH INVESTING AND FINANCING ACTIVITIES
Transactions that do not have direct cash flow effects; reported as a supplement to the statement of cash flows in narrative or schedule form.

Cash Paid for Interest and Income taxes

Companies that use the indirect method of presenting cash flows from operations also must provide two other figures: **cash paid for interest** and **cash paid for income taxes.**

Epilogue

Our more detailed analysis of **National Beverage**'s cash flow indicates the causes of the difference between net income and cash flows from operations. In fact, it was a normal consequence of depreciation and amortization as well as careful management of operating assets and liabilities. Our further analysis of National Beverage's investing and financing activities indicates that the cash needs to maintain its investment strategy should continue to be more than met by operations. Check the company's latest quarterly reports to update this information.

DEMONSTRATION   CASE

During an earlier year (ended April 30), **National Beverage Corp.** reported net income of $24,742 (all numbers in thousands of dollars). The company also reported the following activities:

a. Purchased equipment for $6,658 in cash.

b. Disposed of equipment for $167 in cash, its net book value on the date of sale.

c. Purchased short-term investments for $109,450.

d. Sold short-term investments for $112,450, their net book value on the date of sale.

e. Issued stock for $950 in cash.

f. Repurchased treasury stock for $305 in cash.

g. Depreciation of equipment was $8,891 for the year.

Its comparative balance sheet is presented below.

NATIONAL BEVERAGE CORP.
Balance Sheet
Year ended April 30

(dollars in thousands)	Current Year	Prior Year
Assets		
Current assets:		
Cash and cash equivalents	$ 84,140	$ 51,497
Short-term investments	—	3,000
Accounts receivable	53,735	49,186
Inventories	39,612	38,754
Prepaid expenses	5,552	12,009
Total current assets	183,039	154,446
Equipment, net	79,381	81,781
Total assets	$262,420	$236,227

(continued)

(dollars in thousands)	Current Year	Prior Year
Liabilities and Stockholders' Equity		
Current liabilities:		
Accounts payable	$ 48,005	$ 49,803
Accrued expenses	44,403	41,799
Total current liabilities	92,408	91,602
Stockholders' equity:		
Contributed capital	9,803	9,158
Retained earnings	160,209	135,467
Total stockholders' equity	170,012	144,625
Total liabilities and stockholders' equity	$262,420	$236,227

Required:

Based on this information, prepare the cash flow statement using the indirect method. Evaluate cash flows reported in the statement.

SUGGESTED SOLUTION

NATIONAL BEVERAGE CORP.
Statement of Cash Flows
Year ended April 30
(dollars in thousands)

Cash flows from operating activities:	
Net income	$ 24,742
Adjustments to reconcile net income to cash flow from operating activities:	
Depreciation and amortization	8,891
Changes in assets and liabilities:	
Accounts receivable	(4,549)
Inventory	(858)
Prepaid expenses	6,457
Accounts payable	(1,798)
Accrued expenses	2,604
Net cash provided by operating activities	35,489
Cash flows from investing activities:	
Purchases of property, plant, and equipment	(6,658)
Proceeds from disposal of property, plant, and equipment	167
Purchase of short-term investments	(109,450)
Proceeds from sale of short-term investments	112,450
Net cash used in investing activities	(3,491)
Cash flows from financing activities:	
Purchase of treasury stock	(305)
Proceeds from issuance of stock	950
Net cash provided by financing activities	645
Net increase in cash and cash equivalents	32,643
Cash and cash equivalents at beginning of period	51,497
Cash and cash equivalents at end of period	$ 84,140

National Beverage reported positive profits and even higher cash flows from operations for the year. This difference between the two is caused primarily by decreases in prepaid expenses and depreciation. This also suggests that National Beverage is carefully managing its current assets and current liabilities so that it has more than sufficient cash on hand to cover the costs of purchases of additional equipment without the need to borrow additional funds. This cash can be used for future expansion or to pay future dividends to stockholders.

Chapter Supplement A

Reporting Cash Flows from Operating Activities—Direct Method

The **direct method** presents a summary of all operating transactions that result in either a debit or a credit to cash. It is prepared by adjusting each item on the income statement from an accrual basis to a cash basis. We will complete this process for all of the revenues and expenses reported in **National Beverage**'s income statement in Exhibit 12.3 and accumulate them in a new schedule in Exhibit 12.8.

Converting Revenues to Cash Inflows

When sales are recorded, accounts receivable increase, and when cash is collected, accounts receivable decrease. Thus, the following formula will convert sales revenue amounts from the accrual basis to the cash basis:

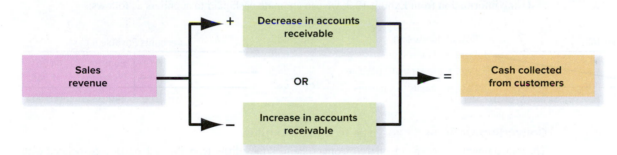

Using information from **National Beverage**'s income statement and balance sheet presented in Exhibit 12.3, we can compute cash collected from customers as follows:

		Accounts Receivable (A)		
Net sales	$641,135	Beg.	64,069	
+Decrease in accounts receivable	5,864			Decrease 5,864
Cash collected from customers	$646,999	End.	58,205	

Converting Cost of Goods Sold to Cash Paid to Suppliers

Cost of goods sold represents the cost of merchandise sold during the accounting period. It may be more or less than the amount of cash paid to suppliers during the period. In **National Beverage**'s case, inventory increased during the year because the company bought more merchandise from suppliers than it sold

Cash flows from operating activities	
Cash collected from customers	$646,999
Cash payments to suppliers	(426,815)
Cash payments for other expenses	(146,115)
Cash payments for interest	(1,326)
Cash payments for income taxes	(19,474)
Net cash provided by operating activities	$ 53,269

EXHIBIT 12.8

National Beverage Corp.: Schedule for Net Cash Flow from Operating Activities, Direct Method (dollars in thousands)

to customers. If the company paid cash to suppliers of inventory, it must have paid more cash to suppliers than the amount of cost of goods sold, so the increase in inventory must be added to compute cash paid to suppliers.

Typically, companies owe their suppliers money (an accounts payable balance will appear on the balance sheet). To convert cost of goods sold to cash paid to suppliers, the borrowing and repayments represented by the accounts payable must also be considered. Borrowing increases cash and accounts payable and repayment decreases cash and accounts payable, so National Beverage's increase in accounts payable must also be subtracted in the computation. Cost of goods sold can therefore be converted to a cash basis in the following manner:

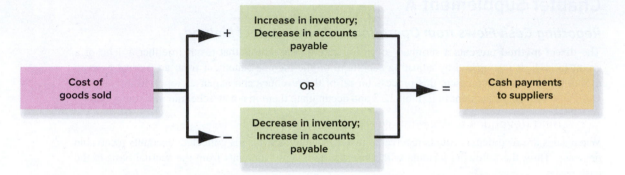

Using information from Exhibit 12.3, we can compute cash paid to suppliers as follows:

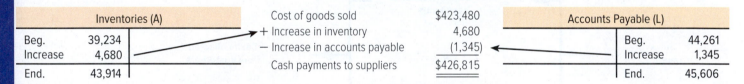

Inventories (A)		
Beg.	39,234	
Increase	4,680	
End.	43,914	

Cost of goods sold	$423,480
+ Increase in inventory	4,680
− Increase in accounts payable	(1,345)
Cash payments to suppliers	$426,815

Accounts Payable (L)		
	Beg.	44,261
	Increase	1,345
	End.	45,606

Converting Operating Expenses to a Cash Outflow

The total amount of an expense on the income statement may differ from the cash outflow associated with that activity. Some expenses are paid before they are recognized as expenses (e.g., prepaid rent). When prepayments are made, the balance in the asset prepaid expenses increases; when expenses are recorded, the balance in prepaid expenses decreases. When **National Beverage**'s prepaid expenses increased by $2,699 during the period, it paid more cash than it recorded as operating expenses. The increase must be added in computing cash paid for expenses.

Some other expenses are paid for after they are recognized (e.g., accrued expenses). In this case, when expenses are recorded, the balance in the liability accrued expenses increases; when payments are made, the balance in accrued expenses decreases. When National Beverage's accrued expenses decreased by $259, it paid more cash than it recorded as operating expenses. The decrease must be added in computing cash paid for expenses.

Generally, other expenses can be converted from the accrual basis to the cash basis in the following manner:

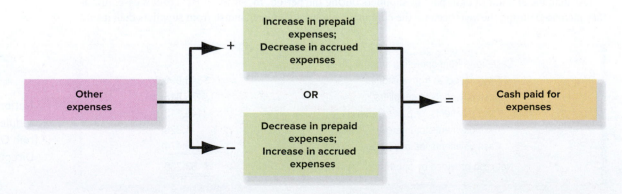

Using information from Exhibit 12.3, we can compute cash paid for expenses for National Beverage as follows:

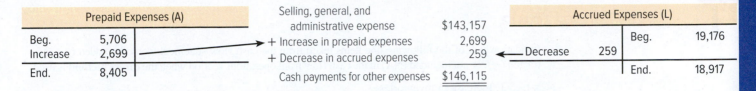

Prepaid Expenses (A)			Selling, general, and administrative expense	$143,157		Accrued Expenses (L)		
Beg.	5,706		+ Increase in prepaid expenses	2,699			Beg.	19,176
Increase	2,699		+ Decrease in accrued expenses	259	← Decrease 259			
End.	8,405		Cash payments for other expenses	$146,115			End.	18,917

National Beverage also reports $1,326 of interest expense.[10] Since there is no interest payable balance, we can see that interest expense must be equal to cash payments for interest expense.

Interest expense	$1,326
No changes in interest payable	0
Cash payments for interest	$1,326

The same logic can be applied to income taxes. National Beverage presents income tax expense of $19,474. Since there is no balance in Income Taxes Payable (or change in Deferred Taxes), income taxes paid must be the same as income tax expense.

Income tax expense	$19,474
No change in taxes payable	0
Cash payments for income taxes	$19,474

These amounts of the operating cash inflows and outflows are accumulated in Exhibit 12.8.

To summarize, the following adjustments must commonly be made to convert income statement items to the related operating cash flow amounts:

Income Statement Account	+/− Change in Balance Sheet Account(s)	= Operating Cash Flow
Sales revenue	+Decrease in Accounts Receivable (A) −Increase in Accounts Receivable (A)	= Collections from customers
Interest/Dividend revenue	+Decrease in Interest/Dividends Receivable (A) −Increase in Interest/Dividends Receivable (A)	= Collections of interest/dividends on investments
Cost of goods sold	+Increase in Inventory (A) −Decrease in Inventory (A) −Increase in Accounts Payable (L) +Decrease in Accounts Payable (L)	= Payments to suppliers of inventory
Other expenses	+Increase in Prepaid Expenses (A) −Decrease in Prepaid Expenses (A) −Increase in Accrued Expenses (L) +Decrease in Accrued Expenses (L)	= Payments to suppliers of services (e.g., rent, utilities, wages, interest)
Income tax expense	+Increase in Prepaid Income Taxes (Deferred Taxes) (A) −Decrease in Prepaid Income Taxes (Deferred Taxes) (A) −Increase in Income Taxes Payable (Deferred Taxes) (L) +Decrease in Income Taxes Payable (Deferred Taxes) (L)	= Payments of income taxes

It is important to note again that the net cash inflow or outflow is the same regardless of whether the direct or indirect method of presentation is used (in National Beverage's case, an inflow of $53,269). The two methods differ only in terms of the details reported on the statement.

---

[10]Certain amounts have been adjusted to simplify the presentation.

STOP

PAUSE FOR **FEEDBACK**

SELF-STUDY **QUIZ**

Indicate which of the following line items taken from the cash flow statement would be added (+), subtracted (−), or not included (NA) in the cash flow from operations section when the **direct method** is used.

_____ 1. Increase in inventories.

_____ 2. Payment of dividends to stockholders.

_____ 3. Cash collections from customers.

_____ 4. Purchase of plant and equipment for cash.

_____ 5. Payments of interest to debtholders.

_____ 6. Payment of taxes to the government.

After you have completed your answers, check them below.

Chapter Supplement B

Adjustment for Gains and Losses on Sale of Long-Term Assets—Indirect Method

As noted earlier, the Operating Activities section of the cash flow statement prepared using the indirect method may include an adjustment for gains and losses on the sale of long-term assets reported on the income statement. As discussed in Chapter 8, when property, plant, and equipment with an original cost of $10,000 and accumulated depreciation of $4,000 is sold for $8,000 cash, the following entry is made.

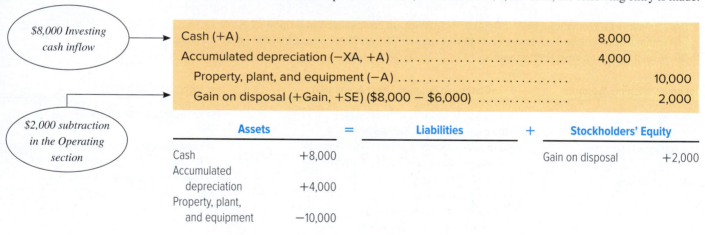

$8,000 Investing cash inflow

Cash (+A)	8,000	
Accumulated depreciation (−XA, +A)	4,000	
Property, plant, and equipment (−A)		10,000
Gain on disposal (+Gain, +SE) ($8,000 − $6,000)		2,000

$2,000 subtraction in the Operating section

Assets		=	Liabilities	+	Stockholders' Equity	
Cash	+8,000				Gain on disposal	+2,000
Accumulated depreciation	+4,000					
Property, plant, and equipment	−10,000					

The $8,000 inflow of cash is an investing cash inflow, but the reported gain of $2,000 is also shown on the income statement. Because the gain is included in the computation of income, it is necessary to remove (subtract) the $2,000 gain from the Operating Activities section of the statement to avoid double counting.

Cash flows from operating activities

Net income	43,635
Adjustments to reconcile net income to cash flow from operating activities:	
. . .	. . .
Gain on disposal of property, plant, and equipment	(2,000)
. . .	. . .
Net cash flow provided by operating activities	. . .

Cash flows from investing activities

Purchases of property, plant, and equipment	. . .
Proceeds from disposal of property, plant, and equipment	8,000
. . .	. . .
Net cash used in investing activities	. . .

If the company had sold the same asset for $5,000 cash, the following entry would be made:

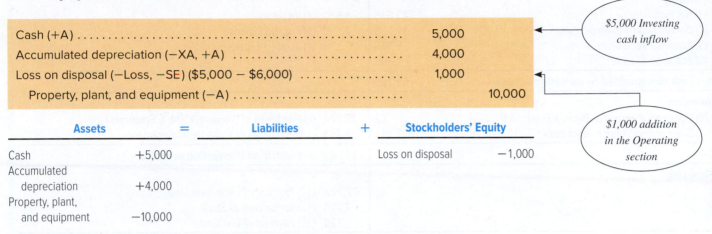

Cash (+A)	5,000	
Accumulated depreciation (−XA, +A)	4,000	
Loss on disposal (−Loss, −SE) ($5,000 − $6,000)	1,000	
Property, plant, and equipment (−A)		10,000

$5,000 Investing cash inflow

$1,000 addition in the Operating section

Assets		=	Liabilities	+	Stockholders' Equity	
Cash	+5,000				Loss on disposal	−1,000
Accumulated depreciation	+4,000					
Property, plant, and equipment	−10,000					

On the cash flow statement, the loss of $1,000 must be removed (added back) in the computation of cash from operating activities, and the total cash collected of $5,000 must be shown in the investing activities section of the statement.

Cash flows from operating activities

Net income	$43,635
Adjustments to reconcile net income to cash flow from operating activities:	
. . .	. . .
Loss on disposal of property, plant, and equipment	1,000
. . .	. . .
Net cash flow provided by operating activities	. . .

Cash flows from investing activities

Purchases of property, plant, and equipment	. . .
Proceeds from disposal of property, plant, and equipment	5,000
. . .	. . .
Net cash used in investing activities	. . .

Chapter Supplement C

T-Account Approach (Indirect Method)

When we began our discussion of preparing the statement of cash flows, we noted that changes in cash must equal the sum of the changes in all other balance sheet accounts. Based on this idea, we used the following three steps to prepare the statement of cash flows:

1. Determine the change in each balance sheet account. From this year's ending balance, subtract this year's beginning balance (i.e., last year's ending balance).
2. Identify the cash flow category or categories to which each account relates.
3. Create schedules that summarize operating, investing, and financing cash flows.

Instead of creating separate schedules for each section of the statement, many accountants prefer to prepare a single large T-account to represent the changes that have taken place in cash subdivided into the three sections of the cash flow statement. Such an account is presented in Panel A of Exhibit 12.9. The cash account in Panel A shows increases in cash as debits and decreases in cash as credits. Note how

EXHIBIT 12.9 T-Account Approach to Preparing the Statement of Cash Flows (Indirect Method)

Panel A: Changes in Cash Account

Cash (A)				
Operating				
(1) Net Income	43,635	4,680	(4) Inventory	
(2) Depreciation and Amortization	10,063	2,699	(5) Prepaid Expense	
(3) Accounts Receivable	5,864	259	(7) Accrued Expenses	
(6) Accounts Payable	1,345			
Net cash flow provided by operating activities	53,269			
Investing				
(9) Disposals of Property, Plant, & Equipment	62	12,124	(8) Purchases of Property, Plant, & Equipment	
(11) Sales of Short-term Investments	2,443	1,463	(10) Purchases of Short-term Investments	
		11,082	**Net cash used in investing activities**	
Financing				
		22,772	(12) Payment of Long-Term Debt	
		7,024	(13) Repurchase of Stock	
		726	(14) Payment of Dividends	
		30,522	**Net cash used in financing activities**	
Net increase in cash and cash equivalents	11,665			

Panel B: Changes in Noncash Accounts

Accounts Receivable (A)			
Beg. bal	64,069		
		(3) Decrease 5,864	
End. bal	58,205		

Inventory (A)			
Beg. bal	39,234		
(4) Increase	4,680		
End. bal	43,914		

Prepaid Expenses (A)			
Beg. bal	5,706		
(5) Increase	2,699		
End. bal	8,405		

Accounts Payable (L)			
	Beg. bal	44,261	
	(6) Increase	1,345	
	End. bal	45,606	

Accrued Expenses (L)			
	Beg. bal	19,176	
(7) Increase 259			
	End. bal	18,917	

Property, Plant, & Equipment, Net (A)			
Beg. bal	77,701	(2) Depreciation	10,063
(8) Purchases	12,124	(9) Disposals	62
End. bal	79,700		

Short-Term Investments (A)			
Beg. bal	3,665		
(10) Purchases	1,463	(11) Disposals 2,443	
End. bal	2,685		

Long-Term Debt (L)			
	Beg. bal	74,889	
(12) Payments 22,772	Borrowings	0	
	End. bal	52,117	

Common Stock (SE)			
		Beg. bal	1,054
(13) Stock repurchased 160	Stock issued		0
		End. bal	894

Additional Paid-In Capital (SE)			
	Beg. bal	31,434	
(13) Stock repurchased 6,864	Stock issued	0	
	End. bal	24,570	

Retained Earnings (SE)			
	Beg. bal	37,828	
(14) Dividends 726	(1) Net income	43,635	
	End. bal	80,737	

each section matches the three schedules that we prepared for **National Beverage**'s cash flows presented in Exhibits 12.4, 12.5, and 12.6. Panel B includes the same T-accounts for the noncash balance sheet accounts we used in our discussion of each cash flow statement section in the body of the chapter. Note how each change in the noncash balance sheet accounts has a number referencing the change in the cash account that it accompanies. The statement of cash flows presented in Exhibit 12.1 can be prepared in proper format based on the information in the cash flow T-account.

12-1. Classify cash flow statement items as part of net cash flows from operating, investing, and financing activities.   p. 602

The cash flow statement has three main sections: Cash Flows from Operating Activities, which are related to earning income from normal operations; Cash Flows from Investing Activities, which are related to the acquisition and sale of productive assets; and Cash Flows from Financing Activities, which are related to external financing of the enterprise. The net cash inflow or outflow for the year is the same amount as the increase or decrease in cash and cash equivalents for the year on the balance sheet. Cash equivalents are highly liquid investments with original maturities of three months or less.

12-2. Report and interpret cash flows from operating activities using the indirect method.   p. 609

The indirect method for reporting cash flows from operating activities reports a conversion of net income to net cash flow from operating activities. The conversion involves additions and subtractions for (1) noncurrent accruals, including expenses (such as depreciation expense) and revenues that do not affect current assets or current liabilities, and (2) changes in each of the individual current assets (other than cash and short-term investments) and current liabilities (other than short-term debt to financial institutions and current maturities of long-term debt, which relate to financing), which reflect differences in the timing of accrual basis net income and cash flows.

12-3. Analyze and interpret the quality of income ratio.   p. 615

The quality of income ratio (Cash Flow from Operating Activities ÷ Net Income) measures the portion of income that was generated in cash. A higher quality of income ratio indicates greater ability to finance operating and other cash needs from operating cash inflows. A higher ratio also indicates that it is less likely that the company is using aggressive revenue recognition policies to increase net income.

12-4. Report and interpret cash flows from investing activities.   p. 616

Investing activities reported on the cash flow statement include cash payments to acquire fixed assets, intangibles, and short- and long-term investments and cash proceeds from the sale of fixed assets, intangibles, and short- and long-term investments.

12-5. Analyze and interpret the capital acquisitions ratio.   p. 618

The capital acquisitions ratio (Cash Flow from Operating Activities ÷ Cash Paid for Property, Plant, and Equipment) reflects the portion of purchases of property, plant, and equipment financed from operating activities without the need for outside debt or equity financing or the sale of other investments or fixed assets. A high ratio benefits the company because it provides the company with opportunities for strategic acquisitions.

12-6. Report and interpret cash flows from financing activities.   p. 619

Cash inflows from financing activities include cash proceeds from the issuance of short- and long-term debt and common stock. Cash outflows include cash principal payments on short- and long-term debt, cash paid for the repurchase of the company's stock, and cash dividend payments. Cash payments associated with interest are a cash flow from operating activities.

12-7. Understand the format of the cash flow statement and additional cash flow disclosures.   p. 621

The statement of cash flows splits transactions that affect cash into three categories: Operating, Investing, and Financing Activities. The operating section is most often prepared using the indirect method that begins with Net Income and adjusts the amount to eliminate noncash transactions. Noncash investing and financing activities are investing and financing activities that do not involve cash. They include, for example, purchases of fixed assets with long-term debt or stock, exchanges of fixed assets, and exchanges of debt for stock. These transactions are disclosed only as supplemental disclosures to the cash flow statement along with cash paid for taxes and interest under the indirect method.

Throughout the preceding chapters, we emphasized the conceptual basis of accounting. An understanding of the rationale underlying accounting is important for both preparers and users of financial statements. In Chapter 13, we bring together our discussion of the major users of financial statements and how they analyze and use these statements. We discuss and illustrate many widely used analytical techniques discussed in earlier chapters, as well as additional techniques. As you study Chapter 13, you will see that an understanding of accounting rules and concepts is essential for effective analysis of financial statements.

KEY **RATIOS**

The **quality of income ratio** indicates what portion of income was generated in cash. It is computed as follows (see the "Key Ratio Analysis" box in the Reporting and Interpreting Cash Flows from Operating Activities section):

$$\text{Quality of Income Ratio} = \frac{\text{Cash Flow from Operating Activities}}{\text{Net Income}}$$

The **capital acquisitions ratio** measures the ability to finance purchases of plant and equipment from operations. It is computed as follows (see the "Key Ratio Analysis" box in the Reporting and Interpreting Cash Flows from Investing Activities section):

$$\text{Capital Acquisitions Ratio} = \frac{\text{Cash Flow from Operating Activities}}{\text{Cash Paid for Property, Plant, and Equipment}}$$

FINDING **FINANCIAL INFORMATION**

Balance Sheet

Changes in Assets, Liabilities, and
   Stockholders' Equity

Income Statement

Net Income and Noncurrent Accruals

Statement of Cash Flows

Cash Flows from Operating Activities

Cash Flows from Investing Activities

Cash Flows from Financing Activities

Separate Schedule (or note):

   Noncash investing and financing activities

   Interest and taxes paid

Notes

Under Summary of Significant
   Accounting Policies:
     Definition of cash equivalents

Under Separate Note (if not listed on cash
   flow statement):
     Noncash investing and financing activities
     Interest and taxes paid

KEY **TERMS**

Cash Equivalents   p. 602
Cash Flows from Financing
   Activities   p. 605
Cash Flows from Investing
   Activities   p. 604

Cash Flows from Operating
   Activities (Cash Flows from
   Operations)   p. 603
Direct Method   p. 603
Free Cash Flow   p. 618

Indirect Method   p. 604
Noncash Investing and Financing
   Activities   p. 623

QUESTIONS

1. Compare the purposes of the income statement, the balance sheet, and the statement of cash flows.
2. What information does the statement of cash flows report that is not reported on the other required financial statements?
3. What are cash equivalents? How are purchases and sales of cash equivalents reported on the statement of cash flows?
4. What are the major categories of business activities reported on the statement of cash flows? Define each of these activities.
5. What are the typical cash inflows from operating activities? What are the typical cash outflows from operating activities?
6. Under the indirect method, depreciation expense is added to net income to report cash flows from operating activities. Does depreciation cause an inflow of cash?
7. Explain why cash payments during the period for purchases and for salaries are not specifically reported as cash outflows on the statement of cash flows, under the indirect method.
8. Explain why a $50,000 increase in inventory during the year must be included in developing cash flows from operating activities under both the direct and indirect methods.
9. Compare the two methods of reporting cash flows from operating activities in the statement of cash flows.
10. What are the typical cash inflows from investing activities? What are the typical cash outflows from investing activities?
11. What are the typical cash inflows from financing activities? What are the typical cash outflows from financing activities?
12. What are noncash investing and financing activities? Give two examples. How are they reported on the statement of cash flows?
13. How is the sale of equipment reported on the statement of cash flows under the indirect method?

MULTIPLE-CHOICE QUESTIONS

1. In what order do the three sections of the statement of cash flows usually appear when reading from top to bottom?
   a. Financing, Investing, Operating
   b. Investing, Operating, Financing
   c. Operating, Financing, Investing
   d. Operating, Investing, Financing
2. Total cash inflow in the operating section of the statement of cash flows should include which of the following?
   a. Cash received from customers at the point of sale.
   b. Cash collections from customer accounts receivable.
   c. Cash received in advance of revenue recognition (unearned revenue).
   d. All of the above.
3. If the balance in prepaid expenses has increased during the year, what action should be taken on the statement of cash flows when following the indirect method, and why?
   a. The change in the account balance should be subtracted from net income because the net increase in prepaid expenses did not impact net income but did reduce the cash balance.
   b. The change in the account balance should be added to net income because the net increase in prepaid expenses did not impact net income but did increase the cash balance.
   c. The net change in prepaid expenses should be subtracted from net income to reverse the income statement effect that had no impact on cash.
   d. The net change in prepaid expenses should be added to net income to reverse the income statement effect that had no impact on cash.
4. Consider the following: Net income = $10,000, depreciation expense = $2,000, accounts receivable increased by $800, inventory decreased by $100, and accounts payable increased by $500. Based on this information alone, what is cash flow from operating activities?
   a. $12,000
   b. $11,600
   c. $11,800
   d. $13,400

5. Which of the following would **not** appear in the investing section of the statement of cash flows?
   a. Purchase of inventory.
   b. Sale of obsolete equipment used in the factory.
   c. Purchase of land for a new office building.
   d. All of the above would appear in the investing section.

6. Which of the following items would **not** appear in the financing section of the statement of cash flows?
   a. The repurchase of the company's own stock.
   b. The receipt of dividends.
   c. The repayment of debt.
   d. The payment of dividends.

7. Which of the following is **not** added to net income when computing cash flows from operations under the indirect method?
   a. The net increase in accounts payable.
   b. The net decrease in accounts receivable.
   c. Depreciation expense reported on the income statement.
   d. All of the above are added to net income.

8. Consider the following: Issued common stock for $18,000, sold office equipment for $1,200, paid cash dividends of $4,000, purchased investments for $2,000, paid accounts payable of $4,000. What was the net cash inflow (outflow) from financing activities?
   a. $20,000   c. ($20,000)
   b. $14,000   d. ($14,000)

9. Consider the following: Issued common stock for $18,000, sold office equipment for $1,200, paid cash dividends of $4,000, purchased investments for $2,000, purchased new equipment for $4,000. What was the net cash inflow (outflow) from investing activities?
   a. $20,200   c. ($10,800)
   b. ($2,800)   d. ($4,800)

10. The **total** change in cash as shown near the bottom of the statement of cash flows for the year should agree with which of the following?
    a. The difference in retained earnings when reviewing the comparative balance sheet.
    b. Net income or net loss as found on the income statement.
    c. The difference in cash when reviewing the comparative balance sheet.
    d. None of the above.

MINI-**EXERCISES**    connect

M12-1
LO12-1

Matching Items Reported to Cash Flow Statement Categories (Indirect Method)

MillerCoors Brewing Company is the world's fifth largest brewer. In the United States, its tie to the magical appeal of the Rocky Mountains is one of its most powerful trademarks. Some of the items included in its recent annual consolidated statement of cash flows presented using the **indirect method** are listed here. Indicate whether each item is disclosed in the Operating Activities (O), Investing Activities (I), or Financing Activities (F) section of the statement or use (NA) if the item does not appear on the statement. (**Note:** This is the exact wording used on the actual statement.)

_____ 1. Purchase of stock. [This involves repurchase of the company's own stock.]
_____ 2. Principal payment on long-term debt.
_____ 3. Proceeds from sale of properties.
_____ 4. Inventories (decrease).
_____ 5. Accounts payable (decrease).
_____ 6. Depreciation, depletion, and amortization.

Determining the Effects of Account Changes on Cash Flow from Operating Activities (Indirect Method)

M12-2
LO12-2

Indicate whether each item would be added (+) or subtracted (−) in the computation of cash flow from operating activities using the indirect method.

_____ 1. Accrued expenses (increase).
_____ 2. Inventories (increase).
_____ 3. Accounts receivable (decrease).
_____ 4. Accounts payable (decrease).
_____ 5. Depreciation, depletion, and amortization.

Matching Items Reported to Cash Flow Statement Categories (Direct Method)

M12-3
LO12-1

Telstra, Australia's largest telecommunications and media company, has net revenue of more than $26 billion (Australian). Some of the items included in its recent annual consolidated statement of cash flows presented using the **direct method** are listed here. Indicate whether each item is disclosed in the Operating Activities (O), Investing Activities (I), or Financing Activities (F) section of the statement or use (NA) if the item does not appear on the statement. (**Note:** This is the exact wording used on the actual statement.)

_____ 1. Receipts from customers.
_____ 2. Dividends paid.
_____ 3. Payment for share buy-back (repurchase of company stock).
_____ 4. Proceeds from sale of property, plant, and equipment.
_____ 5. Repayments of borrowings (bank debt).
_____ 6. Income taxes paid.

Analyzing the Quality of Income Ratio

M12-4
LO12-3

Casey Corporation reported net income of $102,000, depreciation expense of $2,000, and cash flow from operations of $86,500. Compute the quality of income ratio. What does the ratio tell you about the company's ability to finance operating and other cash needs from operating cash inflows?

Computing Cash Flows from Investing Activities

M12-5
LO12-4

Based on the following information, compute cash flows from investing activities.

Cash collections from customers	$550
Sale of used equipment	400
Depreciation expense	200
Purchase of short-term investments	635

Computing Cash Flows from Financing Activities

M12-6
LO12-6

Based on the following information, compute cash flows from financing activities.

Purchase of short-term investments	$ 500
Dividends paid	700
Interest paid	300
Additional short-term borrowing from bank	1,200

Reporting Noncash Investing and Financing Activities

M12-7
LO12-7

Which of the following transactions qualify as noncash investing and financing activities?

_____ Purchase of building with mortgage payable.
_____ Additional short-term borrowing from bank.
_____ Dividends paid in cash.
_____ Purchase of equipment with short-term investments.

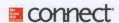

E12-1

LO12-1

Matching Items Reported to Cash Flow Statement Categories (Indirect Method)

Reebok International Ltd. is a global company that designs and markets sports and fitness products, including footwear, apparel, and accessories. Some of the items included in its recent annual consolidated statement of cash flows presented using the **indirect method** are listed here.

Indicate whether each item is disclosed in the Operating Activities (O), Investing Activities (I), or Financing Activities (F) section of the statement or use (NA) if the item does not appear on the statement. (**Note:** This is the exact wording used on the actual statement.)

_____ 1. Dividends paid.

_____ 2. Repayments of long-term debt.

_____ 3. Depreciation and amortization.

_____ 4. Proceeds from issuance of common stock to employees.

_____ 5. [Change in] Accounts payable and accrued expenses.

_____ 6. Cash collections from customers.

_____ 7. Net repayments of notes payable to banks.

_____ 8. Net income.

_____ 9. Payments to acquire property and equipment.

_____ 10. [Change in] Inventory.

E12-2

LO12-1

Matching Items Reported to Cash Flow Statement Categories (Direct Method)

EMC Corporation helps store, manage, protect, analyze, and secure information for companies that use cloud computing. Some of the items included in its recent annual consolidated statement of cash flows presented using the **direct method** are listed here.

Indicate whether each item is disclosed in the Operating Activities (O), Investing Activities (I), or Financing Activities (F) section of the statement or use (NA) if the item does not appear on the statement. (**Note:** This is the exact wording used on the actual statement.)

_____ 1. Sales of short- and long-term available-for-sale securities (investments).

_____ 2. Interest paid.

_____ 3. Additions to property, plant, and equipment.

_____ 4. Income taxes paid.

_____ 5. Issuance of EMC's common stock.

_____ 6. Payment of long-term and short-term obligations.

_____ 7. Dividends and interest received.

_____ 8. Cash received from customers.

_____ 9. Purchases of short- and long-term available-for-sale securities.

_____ 10. Net income.

E12-3

LO12-1

Matching Items Reported to Cash Flow Statement Categories (Direct Method)

Woolworths Limited is one of the largest retailers in Australia and New Zealand. Some of the items included in its recent annual consolidated statement of cash flows presented using the **direct method** are listed here.

Indicate whether each item is disclosed in the Operating Activities (O), Investing Activities (I), or Financing Activities (F) section of the statement or use (NA) if the item does not appear on the statement. (**Note:** This is the exact wording used on the actual statement.)

_____ 1. Proceeds from the sale of property, plant, and equipment.

_____ 2. Interest received.

_____ 3. Payments for intangible assets.

_____ 4. Payments to suppliers and employees.

_____ 5. Proceeds from external borrowings.

_____ 6. Dividends paid.

_____ 7. Income tax paid.

_____ 8. Receipts from customers.

_____ 9. Payments for purchase of investments.

_____ 10. Proceeds from the issue of equity securities.

Determining Cash Flow Statement Effects of Transactions

Stanley Furniture Company is a Virginia-based furniture manufacturer. For each of the following first-year transactions, indicate whether **net cash inflows (outflows)** from operating activities (NCFO), investing activities (NCFI), or financing activities (NCFF) are affected and whether the effect is an inflow (+) or outflow (−), or use (NE) if the transaction has no effect on cash. (**Hint:** Determine the journal entry recorded for the transaction. The transaction affects net cash flows *if and only if* the account Cash is affected.)

E12-4

LO12-1

_____ 1. Recorded an adjusting entry to record accrued salaries expense.

_____ 2. Paid cash to purchase new equipment.

_____ 3. Collected payments on account from customers.

_____ 4. Recorded and paid interest on debt to creditors.

_____ 5. Declared and paid cash dividends to shareholders.

_____ 6. Sold used equipment for cash at book value.

_____ 7. Prepaid rent for the following period.

_____ 8. Repaid principal on revolving credit loan from bank.

_____ 9. Purchased raw materials inventory on account.

_____ 10. Made payment to suppliers on account.

Determining Cash Flow Statement Effects of Transactions

Hewlett-Packard is a leading manufacturer of computer equipment for the business and home markets. For each of the following recent transactions, indicate whether **net cash inflows (outflows)** from operating activities (NCFO), investing activities (NCFI), or financing activities (NCFF) are affected and whether the effect is an inflow (+) or outflow (−), or use (NE) if the transaction has no effect on cash. (**Hint:** Determine the journal entry recorded for the transaction. The transaction affects net cash flows *if and only if* the account Cash is affected.)

E12-5

LO12-1

_____ 1. Purchased raw materials inventory on account.

_____ 2. Prepaid rent for the following period.

_____ 3. Purchased new equipment by signing a three-year note.

_____ 4. Recorded an adjusting entry for expiration of a prepaid expense.

_____ 5. Recorded and paid income taxes to the federal government.

_____ 6. Purchased investment securities for cash.

_____ 7. Issued common stock for cash.

_____ 8. Collected payments on account from customers.

_____ 9. Sold equipment for cash equal to its net book value.

_____ 10. Issued long-term debt for cash.

Comparing the Direct and Indirect Methods

To compare statement of cash flows reporting under the direct and indirect methods, enter check marks to indicate which items are used with each method.

E12-6

LO12-1

Cash Flows (and Related Changes)	STATEMENT OF CASH FLOWS METHOD	
	Direct	Indirect
1. Accounts payable increase or decrease		
2. Payments to employees		
3. Cash collections from customers		
4. Accounts receivable increase or decrease		
5. Payments to suppliers		
6. Inventory increase or decrease		
7. Wages payable, increase or decrease		
8. Depreciation expense		
9. Net income		
10. Cash flows from operating activities		
11. Cash flows from investing activities		
12. Cash flows from financing activities		
13. Net increase or decrease in cash during the period		

E12-7
LO12-2

Reporting Cash Flows from Operating Activities (Indirect Method)

The following information pertains to Peak Heights Company:

Income Statement for Current Year		
Sales		$93,000
Expenses		
Cost of goods sold	$51,875	
Depreciation expense	6,000	
Salaries expense	12,000	69,875
Net income		$23,125
Partial Balance Sheet	**Current Year**	**Prior Year**
Accounts receivable	$10,500	$11,000
Inventory	13,000	8,000
Salaries payable	2,250	800

Required:
Present the operating activities section of the statement of cash flows for Peak Heights Company using the indirect method.

E12-8
LO12-2

Reporting and Interpreting Cash Flows from Operating Activities from an Analyst's Perspective (Indirect Method)

Rodriguez Company completed its income statement and comparative balance sheet for the current year and provided the following information:

Income Statement for Current Year		
Service revenue		$54,000
Expenses		
Salaries	$46,000	
Depreciation	4,500	
Amortization of copyrights	200	
Other expenses	9,700	60,400
Net loss		$ (6,400)

(continued)

Partial Balance Sheet	Current Year	Prior Year
Accounts receivable	$ 8,000	$13,000
Salaries payable	12,000	1,000
Other accrued liabilities	1,000	2,800

In addition, Rodriguez bought a small service machine for $5,000.

Required:
1. Present the operating activities section of the statement of cash flows for Rodriguez Company using the indirect method.
2. What were the major reasons that Rodriguez was able to report a net loss but positive cash flow from operations? Explain why the reasons for the difference between cash flow from operations and net income are important to financial analysts.

Reporting and Interpreting Cash Flows from Operating Activities from an Analyst's Perspective (Indirect Method)

E12-9
LO12-2

Time Warner Inc. is a leading media and entertainment company with businesses in television networks, filmed entertainment, and publishing. The company's recent annual report contained the following information (dollars in millions):

Net loss	$(13,402)
Depreciation, amortization, and impairments	34,790
Decrease in receivables	1,245
Increase in inventories	5,766
Decrease in accounts payable	445
Additions to equipment	4,377

Required:
1. Based on this information, compute cash flow from operating activities using the indirect method.
2. What were the major reasons that Time Warner was able to report a net loss but positive cash flow from operations? Explain why the reasons for the difference between cash flow from operations and net income are important to financial analysts.

Reporting and Interpreting Cash Flows from Operating Activities with Loss on Sale of Equipment (Indirect Method)

E12-10
LO12-2

Parra Company completed its income statement and comparative balance sheet for the current year and provided the following information:

Service revenue		$125,000
Expenses:		
Salaries	$92,000	
Depreciation	8,500	
Utilities	8,000	
Loss on sale of equipment	2,500	111,000
Net income		$ 14,000

Partial Balance Sheet	Current Year	Prior Year
Accounts receivable	$14,000	$24,000
Salaries payable	19,000	8,000
Other accrued liabilities	7,000	9,000
Land	52,000	57,000

Required:
Present the operating activities section of the statement of cash flows for Parra Company using the indirect method.

E12-11

LO12-2

Inferring Balance Sheet Changes from the Cash Flow Statement (Indirect Method)

A recent statement of cash flows for **Colgate-Palmolive** reported the following information (dollars in millions):

Operating Activities	
Net income	$2,554
Depreciation	421
Cash effect of changes in	
Receivables	(130)
Inventories	(130)
Other current assets	54
Payables	199
Other	(72)
Net cash provided by operations	$2,896

Required:

Based on the information reported on the statement of cash flows for Colgate-Palmolive, determine whether the following accounts increased or decreased during the period: Receivables, Inventories, Other Current Assets, and Payables.

E12-12

LO12-2

Inferring Balance Sheet Changes from the Cash Flow Statement (Indirect Method)

A recent statement of cash flows for **Apple** contained the following information (dollars in millions):

Operations	
Net income	$25,922
Depreciation	1,814
Changes in assets and liabilities	
Accounts receivable	143
Inventories	275
Other current assets	(1,391)
Accounts payable	2,515
Deferred revenue	1,654
Other current liabilities	4,495
Other adjustments	2,102
Cash generated by operations	$37,529

Required:

For each of the asset and liability accounts listed on the statement of cash flows, determine whether the account balances increased or decreased during the period.

E12-13

(Chapter Supplement B) Computing and Reporting Cash Flow Effects of Sale of Plant and Equipment

During two recent years Perez Construction, Inc., disposed of the following plant and equipment:

	Year 1	Year 2
Plant and equipment (at cost)	$ 75,000	$13,500
Accumulated depreciation on equipment disposed of	40,385	3,773
Cash received	17,864	12,163
Gain (loss) on sale	(16,751)	2,436

Required:
1. Determine the cash flow from the sale of property for each year that would be reported in the investing activities section of the cash flow statement.
2. Perez uses the indirect method for the operating activities section of the cash flow statement. What amounts related to the sales would be added or subtracted in the computation of Net Cash Flows from Operating Activities for each year?

(Chapter Supplement B) Computing and Reporting Cash Flow Effects of the Sale of Equipment   **E12-14**

During the period, Sanchez Company sold some excess equipment at a loss. The following information was collected from the company's accounting records:

From the Income Statement	
Depreciation expense	$ 1,500
Loss on sale of equipment	2,300
From the Balance Sheet	
Beginning equipment	82,500
Ending equipment	72,000
Beginning accumulated depreciation	43,000
Ending accumulated depreciation	41,000

No new equipment was bought during the period.

Required:
1. For the equipment that was sold, determine its original cost, its accumulated depreciation, and the cash received from the sale. (Use the equipment and accumulated depreciation T-accounts to infer the book value of the equipment sold.)
2. Sanchez Company uses the indirect method for the Operating Activities section of the cash flow statement. What amount related to the sale would be added or subtracted in the computation of Net Cash Flows from Operating Activities?
3. What amount related to the sale would be added or subtracted in the computation of Net Cash Flows from Investing Activities?

Analyzing Cash Flows from Operating Activities; Interpreting the Quality of Income Ratio   **E12-15**
LO12-2, 12-3

A recent annual report for **PepsiCo** contained the following information for the period (dollars in millions):

Net income	$6,462
Depreciation and amortization	2,737
Increase in accounts receivable	666
Increase in inventory	331
Increase in prepaid expense	27
Increase in accounts payable	520
Decrease in taxes payable	340
Increase in other current liabilities	589
Cash dividends paid	3,157
Treasury stock purchased	2,489

Required:
1. Compute cash flows from operating activities for PepsiCo using the indirect method.
2. Compute the quality of income ratio.
3. What were the major reasons that PepsiCo's quality of income ratio did not equal 1.0?

E12-16

LO12-4, 12-6

Reporting Cash Flows from Investing and Financing Activities

Oering's Furniture Corporation is a Virginia-based manufacturer of furniture. In a recent year, it reported the following activities:

Net income	$ 5,135
Purchase of property, plant, and equipment	1,071
Borrowings under line of credit (bank)	1,117
Proceeds from issuance of stock	11
Cash received from customers	37,164
Payments to reduce long-term debt	46
Sale of marketable securities	219
Proceeds from sale of property and equipment	6,894
Dividends paid	277
Interest paid	90
Purchase of treasury stock (stock repurchase)	2,583

Required:

Based on this information, present the cash flows from investing and financing activities sections of the cash flow statement.

E12-17

LO12-2, 12-4, 12-6

Preparing a Statement of Cash Flows (Indirect Method)

Shallow Waters Company was started several years ago by two diving instructors. The company's comparative balance sheets and income statement are presented below, along with additional information.

	Current Year	Prior Year
Balance Sheet at December 31		
Cash	$ 3,900	$4,500
Accounts receivable	1,300	800
Prepaid expenses	100	250
Equipment	700	0
	$ 6,000	$5,550
Wages payable	$ 650	$1,100
Contributed capital	1,600	1,400
Retained earnings	3,750	3,050
	$ 6,000	$5,550
Income Statement for Current Year		
Lessons revenue	$34,550	
Wages expense	30,200	
Other expenses	3,650	
Net income	$ 700	

Additional Data:

a. Prepaid expenses relate to rent paid in advance.
b. Other expenses were paid in cash.
c. Purchased equipment for $700 cash at the end of the prior year to be used starting in current year.
d. An owner contributed capital by paying $200 cash in exchange for the company's stock.

Required:

Prepare the statement of cash flows for the year ended December 31, current year, using the indirect method.

Preparing a Statement of Cash Flows (Indirect Method)

Computer Service and Repair was started five years ago by two college roommates. The company's comparative balance sheets and income statement are presented below, along with additional information.

E12-18
LO12-2, 12-4, 12-6

	Current Year	Prior Year
Balance Sheet at December 31		
Cash	$ 3,250	$4,000
Accounts receivable	700	500
Prepaid expenses	100	50
Equipment	350	0
Accumulated depreciation	(50)	0
	$ 4,350	$4,550
Wages payable	$ 350	$1,100
Short-term note payable	250	0
Common stock	1,000	1,000
Retained earnings	2,750	2,450
	$ 4,350	$4,550
Income Statement for Current Year		
Service revenue	$34,000	
Depreciation expense	50	
Salaries expense	30,000	
Other expenses	3,650	
Net income	$ 300	

Additional Data:

a. Prepaid expenses relate to rent paid in advance.
b. Other expenses were paid in cash.
c. Purchased equipment for $350 cash at the beginning of the current year and recorded $50 of depreciation expense at the end of the current year.
d. At the end of the current year, the company signed a short-term note payable to the bank for $250.

Required:
Prepare the statement of cash flows for the year ended December 31, current year, using the indirect method.

Reporting and Interpreting Cash Flows from Investing and Financing Activities with Discussion of Management Strategy

E12-19
LO12-4, 12-5, 12-6

Gibraltar Industries is a Buffalo, New York–based manufacturer of high-value-added steel products. In a recent year, it reported the following activities:

Acquisitions (investments in other companies)	$(109,248)
Increase in inventories	(10,101)
Depreciation and amortization	26,181
Long-term debt reduction	(76,658)
Net cash provided by operating activities	46,695
Net income	16,523
Net proceeds from issuance of common stock	34
Net proceeds from sale of property and equipment	1,226
Proceeds from long-term debt	73,849
Proceeds from sale of other equity investments	69,368
Purchases of property, plant, and equipment	(11,552)

Required:

1. Based on this information, present the cash flows from investing and financing activities sections of the cash flow statement.
2. Compute the capital acquisitions ratio. What does the ratio tell you about Gibraltar's ability to finance purchases of property, plant, and equipment with cash provided by operating activities?
3. What purpose do you think Gibraltar's management had in mind for the cash generated by selling other equity investments?

E12-20

LO12-5, 12-7

Reporting Noncash Transactions on the Statement of Cash Flows; Interpreting the Effect on the Capital Acquisitions Ratio

An analysis of Courtney Corporation's operational asset accounts provided the following information:

a. Acquired a large machine that cost $36,000. Courtney paid for it by giving a $15,000, 12 percent interest-bearing note due at the end of two years and 500 shares of its common stock, with a par value of $10 per share and a market value of $42 per share.

b. Acquired a small machine that cost $12,700. Full payment was made by transferring a tract of land that had a book value of $12,700.

Required:

1. Show how this information should be reported on the statement of cash flows.
2. What would be the effect of these transactions on the capital acquisitions ratio? How might these transactions distort one's interpretation of the ratio?

E12-21

(Chapter Supplement A) Reporting Cash Flows from Operating Activities from an Analyst's Perspective (Direct Method)

Refer to the information for Peak Heights Company in Exercise 12-7.

Required:

Present the operating activities section of the statement of cash flows for Peak Heights Company using the direct method.

E12-22

(Chapter Supplement A) Reporting and Interpreting Cash Flows from Operating Activities from an Analyst's Perspective (Direct Method)

Refer to the information for Rodriguez Company in Exercise 12-8.

Required:

1. Present the operating activities section of the statement of cash flows for Rodriguez Company using the direct method. Assume that other accrued liabilities relate to other expenses on the income statement.
2. What were the major reasons that Rodriguez was able to report a net loss but positive cash flow from operations? Why are the reasons for the difference between cash flow from operations and net income important to financial analysts?

E12-23

(Chapter Supplement A) Reporting and Interpreting Cash Flows from Operating Activities from an Analyst's Perspective (Direct Method)

Refer to the following summarized income statement and additional selected information for Trumansburg, Inc.:

Income Statement	
Revenues	$150,800
Cost of sales	55,500
Gross margin	95,300
Salary expense	55,400
Depreciation and amortization	33,305
Other expense	9,600
Net loss before tax	(3,005)
Income tax expense	1,500
Net loss	$ (4,505)

Other information:

Decrease in receivables	$ 800
Decrease in inventories	230
Increase in prepaid expenses	1,500
Increase in accounts payable	1,750
Decrease in accrued liabilities	602
Increase in income taxes payable	1,280

Required:

1. Based on this information, compute cash flow from operating activities using the direct method. Assume that prepaid expenses and accrued liabilities relate to other expense.
2. What were the major reasons that Trumansburg was able to report a net loss but positive cash flow from operations? Why are the reasons for the difference between cash flows from operations and net income important to financial analysts?

(Chapter Supplement C) Preparing a Statement of Cash Flows, Indirect Method: T-Account Method   **E12-24**

Golf Universe is a regional and online golf equipment retailer. The company reported the following for the current year:

Purchased a long-term investment for cash, $15,000.

Paid cash dividend, $12,000.

Sold equipment for $6,000 cash (cost, $21,000; accumulated depreciation, $15,000).

Issued shares of no-par stock, 500 shares at $12 per share cash.

Net income was $20,200.

Depreciation expense was $3,000.

Its comparative balance sheet is presented below.

	Balances 12/31/Current Year	Balances 12/31/Prior Year
Cash	$ 19,200	$ 20,500
Accounts receivable	22,000	22,000
Merchandise inventory	75,000	68,000
Investments	15,000	0
Equipment	93,500	114,500
Accumulated depreciation	(20,000)	(32,000)
Total	$204,700	$193,000
Accounts payable	$ 14,000	$ 17,000
Wages payable	1,500	2,500
Income taxes payable	4,500	3,000
Notes payable	54,000	54,000
Contributed capital	106,000	100,000
Retained earnings	24,700	16,500
Total	$204,700	$193,000

Required:

1. Following Chapter Supplement C, complete a T-account worksheet to be used to prepare the statement of cash flows for the current year.
2. Based on the T-account worksheet, prepare the statement of cash flows for the current year in proper format.

PROBLEMS

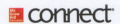 **connect**

P12-1

LO12-1, 12-2, 12-4, 12-6

Preparing a Statement of Cash Flows (Indirect Method) (AP12-1)

Sharp Screen Films, Inc., is developing its annual financial statements at December 31, current year. The statements are complete except for the statement of cash flows. The completed comparative balance sheets and income statement are summarized as follows:

	Current Year	Prior Year
Balance sheet at December 31		
Cash	$ 73,250	$ 63,500
Accounts receivable	15,250	21,350
Merchandise inventory	23,450	18,000
Property and equipment	209,250	160,350
Less: Accumulated depreciation	(57,450)	(45,750)
	$263,750	$217,450
Accounts payable	$ 16,500	$ 19,000
Wages payable	2,000	2,700
Note payable, long-term	56,300	71,000
Contributed capital	103,950	65,900
Retained earnings	85,000	58,850
	$263,750	$217,450
Income statement for current year		
Sales	$205,000	
Cost of goods sold	123,500	
Depreciation expense	11,700	
Other expenses	43,000	
Net income	$ 26,800	

Additional Data:

a. Bought equipment for cash, $48,900.
b. Paid $14,700 on the long-term note payable.
c. Issued new shares of stock for $38,050 cash.
d. Dividends of $650 were declared and paid.
e. Other expenses all relate to wages.
f. Accounts payable includes only inventory purchases made on credit.

Required:

1. Prepare the statement of cash flows using the indirect method for the year ended December 31, current year.
2. Based on the cash flow statement, write a short paragraph explaining the major sources and uses of cash by Sharp Screen Films during the current year.

P12-2

LO12-1, 12-2, 12-4, 12-6

Preparing a Statement of Cash Flows (Indirect Method) (AP12-2)

BG Wholesalers is developing its annual financial statements at December 31, current year. The statements are complete except for the statement of cash flows. The completed comparative balance sheets and income statement are summarized:

	Current Year	Prior Year
Balance sheet at December 31		
Cash	$ 37,000	$ 29,000
Accounts receivable	32,000	28,000
Merchandise inventory	41,000	38,000
Property and equipment	132,000	111,000
Less: Accumulated depreciation	(41,000)	(36,000)
	$201,000	$170,000
Accounts payable	$ 36,000	$ 27,000
Accrued wages expense	1,200	1,400
Note payable, long-term	38,000	44,000
Contributed capital	88,600	72,600
Retained earnings	37,200	25,000
	$201,000	$170,000
Income statement for current year		
Sales	$120,000	
Cost of goods sold	70,000	
Other expenses	37,800	
Net income	$ 12,200	

Additional Data:

a. Bought equipment for cash, $21,000.
b. Paid $6,000 on the long-term note payable.
c. Issued new shares of stock for $16,000 cash.
d. No dividends were declared or paid.
e. Other expenses included depreciation, $5,000; wages, $20,000; taxes, $6,000; other, $6,800.
f. Accounts payable includes only inventory purchases made on credit. Because there are no liability accounts relating to taxes or other expenses, assume that these expenses were fully paid in cash.

Required:

1. Prepare the statement of cash flows for the year ended December 31, current year, using the indirect method.
2. Based on the cash flow statement, write a short paragraph explaining the major sources and uses of cash during the current year.

(Chapter Supplement A) Preparing a Statement of Cash Flows (Direct Method) (AP12-3)   **P12-3**

Use the information concerning Sharp Screen Films, Inc., provided in Problem 12-1 to fulfill the following requirements.

Required:

1. Prepare the statement of cash flows using the direct method for the year ended December 31, current year.
2. Based on the cash flow statement, write a short paragraph explaining the major sources and uses of cash by Sharp Screen Films during the current year.

P12-4   **(Chapter Supplement A) Comparing Cash Flows from Operating Activities (Direct and Indirect Methods)**

Omega Company's accountants have just completed the income statement and balance sheet for the year and have provided the following information (dollars in thousands):

INCOME STATEMENT		
Sales revenue		$22,600
Expenses		
Cost of goods sold	$10,500	
Depreciation expense	2,000	
Salaries expense	4,070	
Rent expense	3,200	
Insurance expense	1,100	
Utilities expense	850	
Interest expense on bonds	450	
Loss on sale of investments	650	22,820
Net loss		$ (220)

SELECTED BALANCE SHEET ACCOUNTS		
	Prior Year	**Current Year**
Merchandise inventory	$ 65	$150
Accounts receivable	620	440
Accounts payable	212	285
Salaries payable	23	38
Rent payable	10	4
Prepaid rent	7	6
Prepaid insurance	4	17

Other Data:
The company issued $30,000, 8 percent bonds payable at par during the year.

Required:
1. Prepare the cash flows from operating activities section of the statement of cash flows using the direct method.
2. Prepare the cash flows from operating activities section of the statement of cash flows using the indirect method.

P12-5
LO12-2, 12-4, 12-6   **(Chapter Supplement B) Preparing a Statement of Cash Flows with Gain on Sale of Equipment (Indirect Method)**

XS Supply Company is developing its annual financial statements at December 31, current year. The statements are complete except for the statement of cash flows. The completed comparative balance sheets and income statement are summarized:

	Current Year	**Prior Year**
Balance sheet at December 31		
Cash	$ 34,000	$ 29,000
Accounts receivable	35,000	28,000
Merchandise inventory	41,000	38,000
Property and equipment	121,000	100,000
Less: Accumulated depreciation	(30,000)	(25,000)
	$201,000	$170,000

	Current Year	Prior Year
Accounts payable	$ 36,000	$ 27,000
Wages payable	1,200	1,400
Note payable, long-term	38,000	44,000
Contributed capital	88,600	72,600
Retained earnings	37,200	25,000
	$201,000	$170,000
Income statement for current year		
Sales	$120,000	
Gain on sale of equipment	1,000	
Cost of goods sold	70,000	
Other expenses	38,800	
Net income	$ 12,200	

Additional Data:

a. Bought equipment for cash, $31,000. Sold equipment with original cost of $10,000, accumulated depreciation of $7,000, for $4,000 cash.
b. Paid $6,000 on the long-term note payable.
c. Issued new shares of stock for $16,000 cash.
d. No dividends were declared or paid.
e. Other expenses included depreciation, $12,000; wages, $13,000; taxes, $6,000; and other, $7,800.
f. Accounts payable includes only inventory purchases made on credit. Because there are no liability accounts relating to taxes or other expenses, assume that these expenses were fully paid in cash.

Required:

1. Prepare the statement of cash flows for the year ended December 31, current year, using the indirect method.
2. Evaluate the statement of cash flows.

(Chapter Supplement C) Preparing a Statement of Cash Flows, Indirect Method, Using the T-Account Approach

P12-6

Hanks Company is developing its annual financial statements at December 31, current year. The statements are complete except for the statement of cash flows. The completed comparative balance sheets and income statement are summarized as follows:

	Current Year	Prior Year
Balance sheet at December 31		
Cash	$ 33,000	$ 18,000
Accounts receivable	26,000	28,000
Merchandise inventory	39,000	36,000
Fixed assets (net)	80,000	72,000
	$178,000	$154,000
Accounts payable	$ 27,000	$ 21,000
Wages payable	1,500	1,000
Note payable, long-term	42,000	48,000
Common stock, no par	78,500	60,000
Retained earnings	29,000	24,000
	$178,000	$154,000
Income statement for current year		
Sales	$ 80,000	
Cost of goods sold	(43,000)	
Expenses	(30,000)	
Net income	$ 7,000	

Additional Data:

 a. Bought fixed assets for cash, $12,000.
 b. Paid $6,000 on the long-term note payable.
 c. Sold unissued common stock for $18,500 cash.
 d. Declared and paid a $2,000 cash dividend.
 e. Incurred the following expenses: depreciation, $4,000; wages, $12,000; taxes, $2,000; and other, $12,000.

Required:

 1. Prepare the statement of cash flows T-accounts using the indirect method to report cash flows from operating activities.
 2. Prepare the statement of cash flows.
 3. Prepare a schedule of noncash investing and financing activities if necessary.

ALTERNATE PROBLEMS

AP12-1
LO12-1, 12-2, 12-4, 12-6

Preparing a Statement of Cash Flows (Indirect Method) (P12-1)

Ingersol Construction Supply Company is developing its annual financial statements at December 31, current year. The statements are complete except for the statement of cash flows. The completed comparative balance sheets and income statement are summarized as follows:

	Current Year	Prior Year
Balance sheet at December 31		
Cash	$ 34,000	$ 29,000
Accounts receivable	45,000	28,000
Merchandise inventory	32,000	38,000
Property and equipment	121,000	100,000
Less: Accumulated depreciation	(30,000)	(25,000)
	$202,000	$170,000
Accounts payable	$ 36,000	$ 27,000
Wages payable	2,200	1,400
Note payable, long-term	40,000	46,000
Contributed capital	86,600	70,600
Retained earnings	37,200	25,000
	$202,000	$170,000
Income statement for current year		
Sales	$135,000	
Cost of goods sold	70,000	
Other expenses	37,800	
Net income	$ 27,200	

Additional Data:

 a. Bought equipment for cash, $21,000.
 b. Paid $6,000 on the long-term note payable.
 c. Issued new shares of stock for $16,000 cash.
 d. Dividends of $15,000 were declared and paid in cash.
 e. Other expenses included depreciation, $5,000; wages, $20,000; taxes, $6,000; and other, $6,800.
 f. Accounts payable includes only inventory purchases made on credit. Because there are no liability accounts relating to taxes or other expenses, assume that these expenses were fully paid in cash.

Required:
1. Prepare the statement of cash flows using the indirect method for the year ended December 31, current year.
2. Evaluate the statement of cash flows.

Preparing a Statement of Cash Flows (Indirect Method) (P12-2)

AP12-2
LO12-1, 12-2, 12-4, 12-6

Audio House, Inc., is developing its annual financial statements at December 31, current year. The statements are complete except for the statement of cash flows. The completed comparative balance sheets and income statement are summarized as follows:

	Current Year	Prior Year
Balance sheet at December 31		
Cash	$ 64,000	$ 65,000
Accounts receivable	15,000	20,000
Inventory	22,000	20,000
Property and equipment	210,000	150,000
Less: Accumulated depreciation	(60,000)	(45,000)
	$251,000	$210,000
Accounts payable	$ 8,000	$ 19,000
Taxes payable	2,000	1,000
Note payable, long-term	86,000	75,000
Contributed capital	75,000	70,000
Retained earnings	80,000	45,000
	$251,000	$210,000
Income statement for Current Year		
Sales	$190,000	
Cost of goods sold	90,000	
Other expenses	60,000	
Net income	$ 40,000	

Additional Data:

a. Bought equipment for cash, $60,000.
b. Borrowed an additional $11,000 and signed an additional long-term note payable.
c. Issued new shares of stock for $5,000 cash.
d. Dividends of $5,000 were declared and paid in cash.
e. Other expenses included depreciation, $15,000; wages, $20,000; and taxes, $25,000.
f. Accounts payable includes only inventory purchases made on credit.

Required:
1. Prepare the statement of cash flows for the year ended December 31, current year, using the indirect method.
2. Based on the cash flow statement, write a short paragraph explaining the major sources and uses of cash during the current year.

(Chapter Supplement A) Preparing a Statement of Cash Flows (Direct Method) (P12-3)

AP12-3

Use the information concerning Ingersol Construction Supply Company provided in Alternate Problem 12-1 to fulfill the following requirements.

Required:
1. Prepare the statement of cash flows using the direct method for the year ended December 31, current year.
2. Evaluate the statement of cash flows.

CON12-1

LO12-1, 12-2, 12-4, 12-6, 12-7

Preparing the Statement of Cash Flows (Indirect Method)

Presented in alphabetical order below are the line items including the subtotals and totals from **Pool Corporation**'s recent statement of cash flows prepared using the indirect method. Using these line items, prepare Pool Corporation's statement of cash flows in good form for the year ended December 31 following the format presented in Exhibit 12.1.

Accounts payable	$ 6,402
Accrued expenses and other current liabilities	20,682
Acquisition of businesses	(5,934)
Amortization	1,559
Cash and cash equivalents at beginning of year	9,721
Cash and cash equivalents at end of year	17,487
Change in cash and cash equivalents	7,766
Depreciation	9,746
Loss on sale of property and equipment	263
Net cash provided by operating activities	75,103
Net cash used in financing activities	(41,759)
Net cash used in investing activities	(25,578)
Net income	71,993
Other financing activities	944
Other operating assets	8,635
Payments of cash dividends	(26,470)
Payments on long-term debt and other long-term liabilities	(149)
Payments on revolving line of bank credit	(700,749)
Prepaid expenses	(2,951)
Proceeds from revolving line of bank credit	749,349
Proceeds from stock issued under share-based compensation plans	13,085
Product inventories	(35,339)
Purchases of property and equipment	(19,844)
Purchases of treasury stock	(77,769)
Receivables	(5,887)
Sale of property and equipment	200

Annual Report Cases

CP12-1

LO12-2, 12-4, 12-6

Finding Financial Information

Refer to the financial statements of **American Eagle Outfitters** given in Appendix B at the end of this book.

Required:

1. On the statement of cash flows, what was the largest item (in absolute value) listed under "Adjustments to reconcile net income to net cash provided by operating activities"? Explain the direction of its effect in the reconciliation.
2. What was the largest "Changes in assets and liabilities" in the operating section of the cash flow statement? Explain the direction of its effect in the reconciliation.
3. Examine American Eagle Outfitters's investing and financing activities. List the company's three largest uses of cash over the past three years. List two major sources of cash for these activities.

Finding Financial Information

CP12-2
LO12-2, 12-4, 12-6

Refer to the financial statements of **Urban Outfitters** given in Appendix C at the end of this book.

Required:
1. Does Urban Outfitters use the direct or indirect method to report cash flows from operating activities?
2. What amount of tax payments did the company make during the most recent reporting year? (**Hint:** The statement of cash flows may be helpful to answer this question.)
3. Explain why the "share-based compensation" and "depreciation and amortization" items were added in the reconciliation of net income to net cash provided by operating activities.
4. Has the company paid cash dividends during the last three years? How do you know?
5. What was free cash flow for the year ended January 31, 2015?

Comparing Companies within an Industry

CP12-3
LO12-3, 12-5

Refer to the financial statements of **American Eagle Outfitters** (Appendix B) and **Urban Outfitters** (Appendix C) and the Industry Ratio Report (Appendix D) at the end of this book.

Required:
1. Compute the quality of income ratio for both companies for the most recent reporting year. Which company has a better quality of income ratio?
2. Compare the quality of income ratio for both companies to the industry average. Are these companies producing more or less cash from operating activities relative to net income than the average company in the industry?
3. Compute the capital acquisitions ratio for both companies for the most recent reporting year. Compare their abilities to finance purchases of property, plant, and equipment with cash provided by operating activities.
4. Compare the capital acquisitions ratio for both companies to the industry average. How does each company's ability to finance the purchase of property, plant, and equipment with cash provided by operating activities compare with that of other companies in the industry?

Financial Reporting and Analysis Cases

Preparing a Complex Statement of Cash Flows (Indirect Method)

CP12-4
LO12-1, 12-2, 12-4, 12-6

Rocky Mountain Chocolate Factory manufactures an extensive line of premium chocolate candies for sale at its franchised and company-owned stores in malls throughout the United States. Its balance sheet for the first quarter of a recent year is presented along with an analysis of selected accounts and transactions:

ROCKY MOUNTAIN CHOCOLATE FACTORY, INC.
Balance Sheets

Assets	May 31 (Unaudited)	February 29
Current assets		
Cash and cash equivalents	$ 921,505	$ 528,787
Accounts and notes receivable—trade, less allowance for doubtful accounts of $43,196 at May 31 and $28,196 at February 29	1,602,582	1,463,901
Inventories	2,748,788	2,504,908
Deferred tax asset	59,219	59,219
Other	581,508	224,001
Total current assets	5,913,602	4,780,816
Property and equipment—at cost	14,010,796	12,929,675
Less accumulated depreciation and amortization	(2,744,388)	(2,468,084)
	11,266,408	10,461,591

(continued)

Assets	May 31 (Unaudited)	February 29
Other assets		
Notes and accounts receivable due after one year	$ 100,206	$ 111,588
Goodwill and other intangibles, net of accumulated amortization		
of $259,641 at May 31 and $253,740 at Feb. 29	330,359	336,260
Other	574,130	624,185
	1,004,695	1,072,033
	$18,184,705	$16,314,440
Liabilities and Equity		
Current liabilities		
Short-term debt	$ 0	$ 1,000,000
Current maturities of long-term debt	429,562	134,538
Accounts payable—trade	1,279,455	998,520
Accrued liabilities	714,473	550,386
Income taxes payable	11,198	54,229
Total current liabilities	2,434,688	2,737,673
Long-term debt, less current maturities	4,193,290	2,183,877
Deferred income taxes	275,508	275,508
Stockholders' Equity		
Common stock—authorized 7,250,000 shares, $0.03 par		
value; issued 3,034,302 shares at May 31 and at Feb. 29	91,029	91,029
Additional paid-in capital	9,703,985	9,703,985
Retained earnings	2,502,104	2,338,267
	12,297,118	12,133,281
Less common stock held in treasury, at cost—129,153		
shares at May 31 and at February 29	1,015,899	1,015,899
	11,281,219	11,117,382
	$18,184,705	$16,314,440

The accompanying notes are an integral part of these statements.

Analysis of Selected Accounts and Transactions:

a. Net income was $163,837. Notes and accounts receivable due after one year relate to operations.

b. Depreciation and amortization totaled $282,205.

c. No "other" noncurrent assets (which relate to investing activities) were purchased this period.

d. No property, plant, and equipment were sold during the period. No goodwill was acquired or sold.

e. Proceeds from issuance of long-term debt were $4,659,466, and principal payments were $2,355,029. (Combine the current maturities with the long-term debt in your analysis.)

f. No dividends were declared or paid.

g. Ignore the "deferred tax asset" and "deferred income taxes" accounts.

Required:
Prepare a statement of cash flows for the year using the indirect method.

CP12-5
LO12-2

Making a Decision as a Financial Analyst: Analyzing Cash Flow for a New Company

Carlyle Golf, Inc., was formed in September of last year. The company designs, contracts for the manufacture of, and markets a line of men's golf apparel. A portion of the statement of cash flows for Carlyle follows:

CURRENT YEAR	
Cash flows from operating activities	
Net income	$(460,089)
Depreciation	3,554
Noncash compensation (stock)	254,464
Deposits with suppliers	(404,934)
Increase in prepaid assets	(42,260)
Increase in accounts payable	81,765
Increase in accrued liabilities	24,495
Net cash flows	$(543,005)

Management expects a solid increase in sales in the near future. To support the increase in sales, it plans to add $2.2 million to inventory. The company did not disclose a sales forecast. At the end of the current year, Carlyle had less than $1,000 in cash. It is not unusual for a new company to experience a loss and negative cash flows during its start-up phase.

Required:
As a financial analyst recently hired by a major investment bank, you have been asked to write a short memo to your supervisor evaluating the problems facing Carlyle. Emphasize typical sources of financing that may or may not be available to support the expansion.

Critical Thinking Case

Ethical Decision Making: A Real-Life Example

CP12-6
LO12-1, 12-2, 12-6

In a February 19, 2004, press release, the Securities and Exchange Commission described a number of fraudulent transactions that **Enron** executives concocted in an effort to meet the company's financial targets. One particularly well-known scheme is called the "Nigerian barge" transaction, which took place in the fourth quarter of 1999. According to court documents, Enron arranged to sell three electricity-generating power barges moored off the coast of Nigeria. The "buyer" was the investment banking firm of **Merrill Lynch**. Although Enron reported this transaction as a sale in its income statement, it turns out this was no ordinary sale. Merrill Lynch didn't really want the barges and had only agreed to buy them because Enron guaranteed, in a secret side deal, that it would arrange for the barges to be bought back from Merrill Lynch within six months of the initial transaction. In addition, Enron promised to pay Merrill Lynch a hefty fee for doing the deal. In an interview on National Public Radio on August 17, 2002, Michigan Senator Carl Levin declared, "(T)he case of the Nigerian barge transaction was, by any definition, a loan."

Required:
1. Discuss whether the Nigerian barge transaction should have been considered a loan rather than a sale. As part of your discussion, consider the following questions. Doesn't the Merrill Lynch payment to Enron at the time of the initial transaction automatically make it a sale, not a loan? What aspects of the transaction are similar to a loan? Which aspects suggest that the four criteria for revenue recognition (summarized near the end of Chapter 3) were not fulfilled?
2. The income statement effect of recording the transaction as a sale rather than a loan is fairly clear: Enron was able to boost its revenues and net income. What is somewhat less obvious, but nearly as important, are the effects on the statement of cash flows. Describe how recording the transaction as a sale rather than as a loan would change the statement of cash flows.
3. How would the two different statements of cash flows (described in your response to requirement 2) affect financial statement users?

Financial Reporting and Analysis Team Project

CP12-7
LO12-1, 12-2, 12-3,
12-4, 12-5, 12-6

Team Project: Analyzing Cash Flows

As a team, select an industry to analyze. Yahoo Finance provides lists of industries at **biz.yahoo.com/p/ industries.html**. Click on an industry for a list of companies in that industry. Alternatively, go to Google Finance at **www.google.com/finance** and search for a company you are interested in. You will be presented with a list including that company and its competitors. Each team member should acquire the annual report or 10-K for one publicly traded company in the industry, with each member selecting a different company (the SEC EDGAR service at **www.sec.gov** and the company's investor relations website itself are good sources).

Required:

On an individual basis, each team member should write a short report answering the following questions about the selected company. Discuss any patterns across the companies that you as a team observe. Then, as a team, write a short report comparing and contrasting your companies.

1. Which of the two basic reporting approaches for cash flows from operating activities did the company adopt?
2. What is the quality of income ratio for the most current year? What were the major causes of differences between net income and cash flow from operations?
3. What is the capital acquisitions ratio for the three-year period presented in total? How is the company financing its capital acquisitions?
4. What portion of the cash from operations in the current year is being paid to stockholders in the form of dividends?

Analyzing Financial Statements

The history of **The Home Depot** is an unusual success story. Founded in 1978 in Atlanta, The Home Depot has grown to be America's largest home improvement retailer, with over 2,200 stores in the United States, Canada, and Mexico. Financial statements for The Home Depot are presented in Exhibit 13.1. As you can see, The Home Depot has grown both sales and net income over the last three years. As you analyze Exhibit 13.1 and read other disclosures in this chapter, it is helpful to keep in mind that "fiscal 2014" for The Home Depot ended on February 1, 2015. Similarly, "fiscal 2013" ended on February 2, 2014, and "fiscal 2012" ended on February 3, 2013.

With the recent improvement in the company's financial results, would you want to invest in The Home Depot? A number of professional analysts think you should, including those who work for **Jefferson Research**, an investment research and advisory firm. In a report in which they recommended buying stock in The Home Depot, they wrote: "Home Depot, Inc., is showing strong Earnings Quality, Cash Flow Quality, Operating Efficiency and Balance Sheet Quality, and Valuation suggests a lower amount of price risk. When combined, Home Depot deserves a BUY rating."

Learning Objectives

After studying this chapter, you should be able to:

13-1 Explain how a company's business strategy affects financial statement analysis.

13-2 Discuss ways to analyze financial statements.

13-3 Compute and interpret component percentages.

13-4 Compute and interpret profitability ratios.

13-5 Compute and interpret asset turnover ratios.

13-6 Compute and interpret liquidity ratios.

13-7 Compute and interpret solvency ratios.

13-8 Compute and interpret market ratios.

chapter 13

RiverNorthPhotography/Getty Images

Professional analysts consider a large number of factors in developing the type of recommendation contained in the Jefferson Research report, including information reported in a company's financial statements. In this chapter, we use accounting information and a variety of analytical tools to study The Home Depot and its major competitor, **Lowe's**.

UNDERSTANDING THE BUSINESS

Companies spend billions of dollars each year preparing, auditing, and publishing their financial statements. These statements are then made available to current and prospective investors. Most companies no longer mail this information to investors, but rather make it available online. **The Home Depot**'s financial information is available from its Investor Relations website at **www.homedepot.com**.

The reason that The Home Depot and other companies spend so much money to provide information to investors is simple: Financial statements help people make better economic decisions. In fact, published financial statements are designed primarily to meet the needs of external decision makers, including present and potential owners, investment analysts, and creditors.

EXHIBIT 13.1

The Home Depot Financial Statements

THE HOME DEPOT, INC., AND SUBSIDIARIES
Consolidated Statements of Earnings
(amounts in millions, except per share data)

	Fiscal Year Ended		
	February 1, 2015	February 2, 2014	February 3, 2013
Net Sales	$83,176	$78,812	$74,754
Cost of Sales	54,222	51,422	48,912
Gross Profit	28,954	27,390	25,842
Operating Expenses:			
Selling, General and Administrative	16,834	16,597	16,508
Depreciation and Amortization	1,651	1,627	1,568
Total Operating Expenses	18,485	18,224	18,076
Operating Income	10,469	9,166	7,766
Interest and Other (Income) Expense:			
Interest and Investment Income	(337)	(12)	(20)
Interest Expense	830	711	632
Other	—	—	(67)
Interest and Other, net	493	699	545
Earnings before Provision for Income Taxes	9,976	8,467	7,221
Provision for Income Taxes	3,631	3,082	2,686
Net Earnings	$ 6,345	$ 5,385	$ 4,535
Weighted Average Common Shares	1,338	1,425	1,499
Basic Earnings per Share	$ 4.74	$ 3.78	$ 3.03
Diluted Weighted Average Common Shares	1,346	1,434	1,511
Diluted Earnings per Share	$ 4.71	$ 3.76	$ 3.00

THE HOME DEPOT, INC., AND SUBSIDIARIES
Consolidated Balance Sheets
(amounts in millions, except share and per share data)

	February 1, 2015	February 2, 2014
ASSETS		
Current Assets:		
Cash and Cash Equivalents	$ 1,723	$ 1,929
Receivables, net	1,484	1,398
Merchandise Inventories	11,079	11,057
Other Current Assets	1,016	895
Total Current Assets	15,302	15,279
Property and Equipment, at cost	38,513	39,064
Less Accumulated Depreciation and Amortization	15,793	15,716
Net Property and Equipment	22,720	23,348
Goodwill	1,353	1,289
Other Assets	571	602
Total Assets	$39,946	$40,518

	February 1, 2015	February 2, 2014
LIABILITIES AND STOCKHOLDERS' EQUITY		
Current Liabilities:		
Short-Term Debt	$ 290	$ —
Accounts Payable	**5,807**	5,797
Accrued Salaries and Related Expenses	**1,391**	1,428
Sales Taxes Payable	**434**	396
Deferred Revenue	**1,468**	1,337
Income Taxes Payable	**35**	12
Current Installments of Long-Term Debt	**38**	33
Other Accrued Expenses	**1,806**	1,746
Total Current Liabilities	**11,269**	10,749
Long-Term Debt, excluding current installments	**16,869**	14,691
Other Long-Term Liabilities	**1,844**	2,042
Deferred Income Taxes	**642**	514
Total Liabilities	**30,624**	27,996
STOCKHOLDERS' EQUITY		
Common Stock, par value $0.05; authorized: 10 billion shares; issued: 1.768 billion shares at February 1, 2015, and 1.761 billion shares at February 2, 2014; outstanding: 1.307 billion shares at February 1, 2015, and 1.380 billion shares at February 2, 2014	**88**	88
Paid-In Capital	**8,885**	8,402
Retained Earnings	**26,995**	23,180
Accumulated Other Comprehensive (Loss) Income	**(452)**	46
Treasury Stock, at cost, 461 million shares at February 1, 2015, and 381 million shares at February 2, 2014	**(26,194)**	(19,194)
Total Stockholders' Equity	**9,322**	12,522
Total Liabilities and Stockholders' Equity	**$39,946**	$40,518

EXHIBIT 13.1

continued

THE HOME DEPOT, INC., AND SUBSIDIARIES
Consolidated Statements of Cash Flows
(amounts in millions)

	Fiscal Year Ended		
	February 1, 2015	February 2, 2014	February 3, 2013
CASH FLOWS FROM OPERATING ACTIVITIES:			
Net Earnings	**$6,345**	$5,385	$4,535
Reconciliation of Net Earnings to Net Cash Provided by Operating Activities:			
Depreciation and Amortization	**1,786**	1,757	1,684
Stock-Based Compensation Expense	**225**	228	218
Gain on Sales of Investments	**(323)**	—	—
Goodwill Impairment	**—**	—	97

continued

	February 1, 2015	February 2, 2014	February 3, 2013
EXHIBIT 13.1			
concluded			
Changes in Assets and Liabilities, net of the effects of acquisitions:			
Receivables, net	$ **(81)**	$ (15)	$ (143)
Merchandise Inventories	**(124)**	(455)	(350)
Other Current Assets	**(199)**	(5)	93
Accounts Payable and Accrued Expenses	**244**	605	698
Deferred Revenue	**146**	75	121
Income Taxes Payable	**168**	119	87
Deferred Income Taxes	**159**	(31)	107
Other Long-Term Liabilities	**(152)**	13	(180)
Other	**48**	(48)	8
Net Cash Provided by Operating Activities	**8,242**	7,628	6,975
CASH FLOWS FROM INVESTING ACTIVITIES:			
Capital Expenditures, net of $217, $46, and $98 of non-cash capital expenditures in fiscal 2014, 2013, and 2012, respectively	**(1,442)**	(1,389)	(1,312)
Proceeds from Sales of Investments	**323**	—	—
Payments for Businesses Acquired, net	**(200)**	(206)	(170)
Proceeds from Sales of Property and Equipment	**48**	88	50
Net Cash Used in Investing Activities	**(1,271)**	(1,507)	(1,432)
CASH FLOWS FROM FINANCING ACTIVITIES:			
Proceeds from Short-Term Borrowings, net	**290**	—	—
Proceeds from Long-Term Borrowings, net of discount	**1,981**	5,222	—
Repayments of Long-Term Debt	**(39)**	(1,289)	(32)
Repurchases of Common Stock	**(7,000)**	(8,546)	(3,984)
Proceeds from Sales of Common Stock	**252**	241	784
Cash Dividends Paid to Stockholders	**(2,530)**	(2,243)	(1,743)
Other Financing Activities	**(25)**	(37)	(59)
Net Cash Used in Financing Activities	**(7,071)**	(6,652)	(5,034)
Change in Cash and Cash Equivalents	**(100)**	(531)	509
Effect of Exchange Rate Changes on Cash and Cash Equivalents	**(106)**	(34)	(2)
Cash and Cash Equivalents at Beginning of Year	**1,929**	2,494	1,987
Cash and Cash Equivalents at End of Year	**$1,723**	$1,929	$2,494
SUPPLEMENTAL DISCLOSURE OF CASH PAYMENTS MADE FOR:			
Interest, net of interest capitalized	$ **782**	$ 639	$ 617
Income Taxes	**$3,435**	$2,839	$2,482

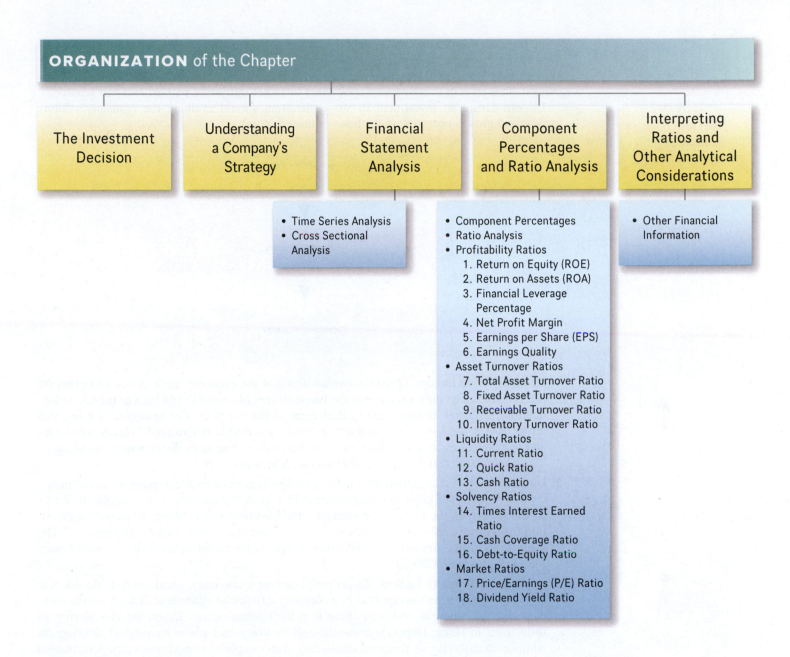

ORGANIZATION of the Chapter

The Investment Decision

Understanding a Company's Strategy

Financial Statement Analysis
- Time Series Analysis
- Cross Sectional Analysis

Component Percentages and Ratio Analysis
- Component Percentages
- Ratio Analysis
- Profitability Ratios
  1. Return on Equity (ROE)
  2. Return on Assets (ROA)
  3. Financial Leverage Percentage
  4. Net Profit Margin
  5. Earnings per Share (EPS)
  6. Earnings Quality
- Asset Turnover Ratios
  7. Total Asset Turnover Ratio
  8. Fixed Asset Turnover Ratio
  9. Receivable Turnover Ratio
  10. Inventory Turnover Ratio
- Liquidity Ratios
  11. Current Ratio
  12. Quick Ratio
  13. Cash Ratio
- Solvency Ratios
  14. Times Interest Earned Ratio
  15. Cash Coverage Ratio
  16. Debt-to-Equity Ratio
- Market Ratios
  17. Price/Earnings (P/E) Ratio
  18. Dividend Yield Ratio

Interpreting Ratios and Other Analytical Considerations
- Other Financial Information

THE INVESTMENT DECISION

Of the people who use financial statements, investors are perhaps the single largest group. They often rely on the advice of professional analysts, who develop recommendations on widely held stocks such as **The Home Depot**. Investors who use analysts' reports pay close attention to their recommendations. As this book was being written, professional analysts issued the following investment recommendations for The Home Depot:

Strong Buy	10
Buy	1
Hold	9
Underperform	0
Sell	0

Source: NASDAQ.com.

Perhaps the most important thing to notice about this summary of investment recommendations is the degree of disagreement. Currently, 10 analysts strongly recommend buying more Home Depot stock, while 9 others recommend holding Home Depot stock only if one already owns it. This level of disagreement shows that financial analysis is part art and part science.

In considering an investment in stock, investors should evaluate the company's future income and growth potential on the basis of three factors:

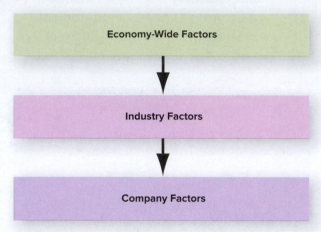

1. **Economy-wide factors.** Often the overall health of the economy has a direct impact on the performance of an individual company. Investors should consider data such as the unemployment rate, general inflation rate, and changes in interest rates. For example, in a research report issued by **Zacks Investment Research**, an analyst determined "Heavy job losses and reduced access to credit have led to a sharp fall in consumer discretionary spending on big-ticket items." *(Zacks Investment Research, September 1, 2014)*

2. **Industry factors.** Certain events can have a major impact on each company within an industry but only a minor impact on other companies outside the industry. For example, the Zacks report states, "In the home improvement retail business, Home Depot faces stiff competition from **Lowe's**, **Sherwin-Williams Company** and other home supply retailers. . . ." The analyst report goes on to state, "This may weigh on the company's results." *(Zacks Equity Research, March 19, 2012)*

3. **Individual company factors.** To properly analyze a company, good analysts do not rely solely on the information reported in a company's financial statements. They visit the company, buy its products, and read about it in the business press. If you are considering an investment in Home Depot, you should visit its stores and assess its product offerings in addition to analyzing its financial statements. An example of company-specific information is contained in the Zacks report, which states that ". . . the company has implemented significant changes in its store operations to make them simpler and more customer-friendly." *(Zacks Equity Research, October 30, 2014)*

Besides considering these factors, investors should understand a company's business strategy when evaluating its financial statements. A company's business strategy directly affects the accounts you will see on its financial statements.

UNDERSTANDING A COMPANY'S STRATEGY

LEARNING OBJECTIVE 13-1
Explain how a company's business strategy affects financial statement analysis.

Financial statement analysis involves more than just "crunching numbers." Before you start looking at numbers, you should know what you are looking for. While financial statements reflect transactions, each of those transactions is the result of a company's operating decisions as it implements its business strategy.

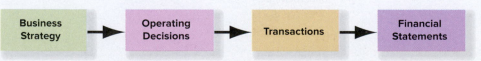

Businesses can earn a high rate of return by following different strategies. There are two fundamental strategies:

1. **Product differentiation.** Under this strategy, companies offer products with unique benefits, such as high quality or unusual style or features. These unique benefits allow a company to charge higher prices. In general, a product differentiation strategy results in higher profit margins but lower inventory turnover.

2. **Cost differentiation.** Under this strategy, companies attempt to operate more efficiently than their competitors, which permits them to offer lower prices to attract customers. In general, a cost differentiation strategy results in lower profit margins but higher inventory turnover.

You can probably think of a number of companies that have followed one of these two basic strategies. Here are some examples:

The best place to start financial analysis is with a solid understanding of a company's business strategy. To evaluate how well a company is doing, you must know what managers are trying to do. You can learn a great deal about a company's business strategy by reading its annual report or 10-K, especially the letter from the president and management's discussion and analysis (MD&A). It also is useful to read articles about the company in the business press. **The Home Depot**'s business strategy is described in its 10-K report as follows:

Operating Strategy

Over the past several years, we have maintained a consistent strategic framework comprised of three key initiatives—Customer Service; Product Authority; and Disciplined Capital Allocation, Productivity and Efficiency—tied together through our Interconnected Retail initiative. In fiscal 2014, we focused on continuing to enhance our capability to deliver a superior interconnected retail experience for our customers. As customers increasingly expect to be able to buy how, when and where they want, we believe that providing a seamless shopping experience across multiple channels, featuring innovative and expanded product choices, will be a key enabler for future success. Becoming a best-in-class interconnected retailer is growing in importance as the line between online and in-store shopping continues to blur. Our interconnected retail initiative supports and connects the three other key initiatives of our long-standing strategic framework, with the overall goal of strengthening the connectivity between our stores and our online channels and our connectivity with our customers.

THE HOME DEPOT

REAL WORLD EXCERPT:

10-K Report

This description of The Home Depot's strategy serves as a guide for our financial analysis. By understanding what management is trying to accomplish, we are better able to evaluate its progress in meeting its goals.

With management's stated goals in mind, we can attach more meaning to the information contained in The Home Depot's financial statements.

FINANCIAL STATEMENT ANALYSIS

Analyzing financial data without a basis for comparison is not informative. For example, would you be impressed with a company that earned $1 million last year? You are probably thinking, "It depends." A $1 million profit might be very good for a company that lost money the year before but not good for a company that made $500 million the preceding year. It might be good for a small company but not for a very large company. And it might be considered good if all the other companies in the industry lost money the same year but not good if they all earned much larger profits.

As you can see from this simple example, financial results cannot be evaluated in isolation. To properly analyze the information reported in financial statements, you must develop appropriate comparisons. The task of finding appropriate comparisons requires judgment and is not always easy. Financial analysis is a sophisticated skill, not a mechanical process.

There are two general methods for making financial comparisons. The first compares a company to itself in prior years. The second compares a company to other companies at a point in time.

1. **Comparing across time.** In this type of analysis, which is often referred to as "time-series analysis," information on a single company is compared over time. For example, a key measure of performance for most companies is the change in sales volume each year. The time-series chart below shows that **The Home Depot**'s sales have been trending upward, though at different rates depending on the year. The notes to the financial statements help us understand the improvement in sales in the current year:

THE HOME DEPOT

REAL WORLD EXCERPT:

10-K Report

> The positive comparable store sales for fiscal 2014 reflect a number of factors, including the execution of our key initiatives, continued strength in our maintenance and repair categories, and an improved U.S. home improvement market. All of our departments posted positive comparable store sales for fiscal 2014. Further, our comparable store customer transactions increased 3.5% for fiscal 2014 and comparable store average ticket increased 1.8% for fiscal 2014, due in part to strong sales in big ticket purchases, such as appliances and water heaters, and sales growth in our services business.

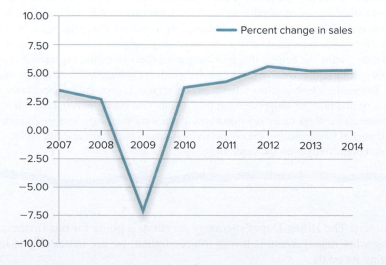

In the current environment, The Home Depot is experiencing more customers in its stores and those customers are spending more money on their average purchases. Notice that our understanding of the reported numbers is directly tied to understanding The Home Depot's business strategy.

2. **Comparing across companies.** In this type of analysis, which is often referred to as "cross-sectional analysis," information for multiple companies is compared at a point in time. We have seen that financial results are often affected by industry and economy-wide factors. By comparing a company with other companies in the same line of business, an analyst can gain better insight into its performance. For example, the graph below compares The Home Depot with one of its closest competitors, **Lowe's**, during fiscal 2014. The gross profit percentage and growth in sales are essentially the same for both companies, but net income as a percentage of sales is higher for The Home Depot, indicating more efficient business operations.

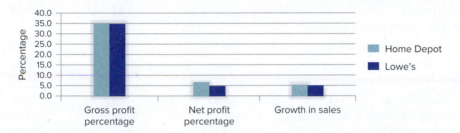

Finding comparable companies is often difficult. Few companies do the exact same thing as their competitors. For example, **American Apparel**, **Gap**, **Nordstrom**, **Target**, and **Walmart** are all apparel retailers, but not all could be considered comparable companies for purposes of financial analysis. These retailers offer different levels of quality and appeal to different types of customers.

The federal government has developed the North American Industry Classification System (NAICS) for use in reporting economic data. The system assigns a specific industry code to each corporation based on its business operations. Analysts often use these six-digit codes to identify companies that have similar business operations. In addition, you can find multiple online resources, such as Google Finance or Yahoo Finance, that provide averages for many common accounting ratios for various industries. Because of the diversity of companies included in any given industry classification, and the potential difference in how ratios are calculated, these data should be used with great care. For this reason, some analysts prefer to compare two companies that are very similar instead of using industry-wide comparisons.

COMPONENT PERCENTAGES AND RATIO ANALYSIS

Component Percentages

All analysts use various tools to analyze a company's financial statements. Two popular tools are **component percentages** and **ratio analysis**. Component percentages express each item on a financial statement as a percentage of a single base amount. The base amount on the income statement is net sales. To compute component percentages on the income statement, each amount reported is divided by net sales. The base amount on the balance sheet is total assets. To compute component percentages on the balance sheet, each amount is divided by total assets.

Exhibit 13.2 shows a component percentage analysis for **The Home Depot**'s income statement. The percentages reported in Exhibit 13.2 were calculated by taking the dollar amounts reported on The Home Depot's income statement shown in Exhibit 13.1 and dividing them by net sales. If you simply reviewed the dollar amounts on the income statement, you might miss important insights. For example, selling, general, and administrative expense increased by $237 million in fiscal 2014. This increase might seem to reflect a decline in operating efficiency until it is compared with sales productivity. A component percentage analysis provides an important insight: This expense category decreased as a percent of sales (from 21.06% in

EXHIBIT 13.2

Component Percentages for
The Home Depot

| | COMPONENT PERCENTAGES* | | |
| | February 1, 2015 | February 2, 2014 | February 3, 2013 |
Income Statement	(fiscal 2014)	(fiscal 2013)	(fiscal 2012)
Net sales	100.00%	100.00%	100.00%
Cost of Sales	65.19	65.25	65.43
Gross profit	34.81	34.75	34.57
Operating Expenses:			
Selling, General, and Administrative	20.24	21.06	22.08
Depreciation and Amortization	1.98	2.06	2.10
Total Operating Expenses	22.22	23.12	24.18
Operating Income	12.59	11.63	10.39
Interest and Other (Income) Expense:			
Interest and Investment Income	(0.41)	(0.01)	(0.03)
Interest Expense	1.00	0.90	0.85
Other	0.00	0.00	(0.09)
Interest and Other, net	0.59	0.89	0.73
Earnings, before Provision for Income Taxes	12.00	10.74	9.66
Provision for Income Taxes	4.37	3.91	3.59
Net Earnings	7.63	6.83	6.07

*Numbers are rounded.

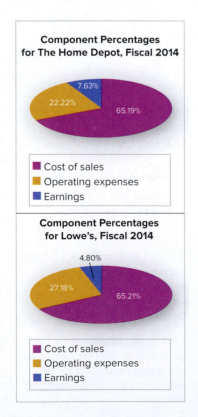

**Component Percentages
for The Home Depot, Fiscal 2014**

7.63%
22.22%
65.19%

■ Cost of sales
■ Operating expenses
■ Earnings

**Component Percentages
for Lowe's, Fiscal 2014**

4.80%
27.18%
65.21%

■ Cost of sales
■ Operating expenses
■ Earnings

fiscal 2013 to 20.24% in fiscal 2014) during that period. In other words, The Home Depot has actually done a good job of keeping selling, general, and administrative expense in line with its sales activity.

The component analysis (in Exhibit 13.2) also reflects that net income has increased as a percentage of sales from fiscal 2012 to fiscal 2014. In general, this reflects that The Home Depot is operating more efficiently across time. You can see this improvement in operating efficiency by examining the decrease in operating expenses as a percentage of sales over the three-year period.

Many analysts use graphics software to help them analyze companies. Graphic representation is especially useful when communicating findings during meetings or in printed form. The nearby pie charts summarize key 2014 data from Exhibit 13.2, along with comparable data from **Lowe's**, a key competitor.

Ratio Analysis

Component percentages are a type of ratio. Ratios simply express the proportionate relationship between two amounts. With component percentages, both the numerator and the denominator of the ratio came from the same financial statement, either the income statement or the balance sheet. This does not have to be the case. As an example, assume you want to know how effective a company is using its assets to generate net income. Answering this question is difficult if you only know that the company earned net income of $500,000. Comparing income to total assets provides additional insights. If total assets are $5 million, for example, then the relationship of earnings to assets is $500,000 ÷ $5,000,000 = 10%. This measure indicates a different level of performance than would be the case if total assets were $250 million. Ratio analysis helps decision makers identify significant relationships and make meaningful comparisons between companies.

Of the many ratios that can be computed using a company's financial statements, analysts use only those that can be helpful in a given situation. Comparing cost of goods sold to property, plant, and equipment is not meaningful because these items have no natural relationship. Instead, an analyst will often compute certain widely used ratios and then decide which additional ratios could be relevant to a particular decision. Research and development costs as a percentage of sales is not a meaningful ratio for some companies, for example, but it is useful when analyzing companies that depend on new products, such as a pharmaceutical company.

When you compute ratios, remember a basic fact about financial statements: Balance sheet amounts are as of a specific point in time while income statement amounts relate to a period of time. In comparing an income statement amount to a balance sheet amount, you should express the balance sheet as an average of the beginning and ending balances. In practice, some analysts simply use the ending balance sheet amount, an approach that is appropriate only if there is not a significant difference between the beginning and ending balances. For consistency, we always use average amounts.

Financial statement analysis involves a lot of judgment; not all ratios are helpful in a given situation. We will discuss several ratios that are appropriate to most situations. They can be grouped into the categories shown in Exhibit 13.3.[1]

Profitability Ratios

Profitability is a primary measure of the overall success of a company. **Profitability ratios** focus on net income and how it compares to other amounts reported on the financial statements. Return on equity is a widely used measure of profitability.

LEARNING OBJECTIVE 13-4
Compute and interpret profitability ratios.

PROFITABILITY RATIOS
Ratios that compare income with one or more primary activities.

1. Return on Equity (ROE)

Return on equity relates income earned to the investment made by a company's owners. This ratio reflects the simple fact that investors expect to earn a return on the money they invest in a company. The return on equity ratio is computed as follows:

$$\text{Return on Equity (ROE)} = \frac{\text{Net Income}}{\text{Average Total Stockholders' Equity}}$$

$$\text{Home Depot 2014} = \frac{\$6{,}345}{\$10{,}922^*} = 58.09\%$$

$$^*\frac{(\$9{,}322 + \$12{,}522)}{2} = \$10{,}922$$

The Home Depot earned 58.09 percent on the owners' investment. Another way to interpret this number is to say that, on average, for every $1.00 equity investors contributed to The Home Depot, the company earned 58 cents in fiscal 2014. Was this return good or bad? To answer this question, we need to compare 58.09 percent to what The Home Depot's ROE was in prior years, or to its competitors' ROE in 2014. ROE for **Lowe's** was 24.73 percent in fiscal 2014. Clearly, The Home Depot produced a better return than its main competitor.

We can gain additional insight by examining The Home Depot's ROE from fiscal 2012 to fiscal 2014:

	2014	2013	2012
ROE	58.09%	35.55%	25.42%

This comparison indicates consistent improvement in The Home Depot's performance as measured by its ROE.

Justin Sullivan/Getty Images

---

[1]The numbers for The Home Depot used throughout the following examples are taken from the financial statements in Exhibit 13.1.

EXHIBIT 13.3

Widely Used Accounting Ratios

RATIO	BASIC COMPUTATION*
Profitability Ratios	
1. Return on equity (ROE)	$\dfrac{\text{Net Income}}{\text{Average Total Stockholders' Equity}}$
2. Return on assets (ROA)	$\dfrac{\text{Net Income}}{\text{Average Total Assets}}$
3. Financial leverage percentage	Return on Equity — Return on Assets
4. Net profit margin	$\dfrac{\text{Net Income}}{\text{Net Sales Revenue}}$
5. Earnings per share (EPS)	$\dfrac{\text{Net Income}}{\text{Weighted Average Number of Common Shares Outstanding}}$
6. Earnings quality	$\dfrac{\text{Cash Flows from Operating Activities}}{\text{Net Income}}$
Asset Turnover Ratios	
7. Total asset turnover	$\dfrac{\text{Net Sales Revenue}}{\text{Average Total Assets}}$
8. Fixed asset turnover	$\dfrac{\text{Net Sales Revenue}}{\text{Average Net Fixed Assets}}$
9. Receivable turnover ratio	$\dfrac{\text{Net Credit Sales}}{\text{Average Net Receivables}}$
10. Inventory turnover ratio	$\dfrac{\text{Cost of Goods Sold}}{\text{Average Inventory}}$
Liquidity Ratios	
11. Current ratio	$\dfrac{\text{Current Assets}}{\text{Current Liabilities}}$
12. Quick ratio	$\dfrac{\text{Cash \& Cash Equivalents} + \text{Net Accounts Receivable} + \text{Marketable Securities}}{\text{Current Liabilities}}$
13. Cash ratio	$\dfrac{\text{Cash \& Cash Equivalents}}{\text{Current Liabilities}}$
Solvency Ratios	
14. Times interest earned ratio	$\dfrac{\text{Net Income} + \text{Interest Expense} + \text{Income Tax Expense}}{\text{Interest Expense}}$
15. Cash coverage ratio	$\dfrac{\text{Cash Flows from Operating Activities}}{\text{Interest Paid}}$
16. Debt-to-equity ratio	$\dfrac{\text{Total Liabilities}}{\text{Total Stockholders' Equity}}$
Market Ratios	
17. Price/Earnings (P/E) ratio	$\dfrac{\text{Market Price per Share}}{\text{Earnings per Share}}$
18. Dividend yield ratio	$\dfrac{\text{Dividends per Share}}{\text{Market Price per Share}}$

We list the basic computation for each ratio. Analysts sometimes adjust these basic computations depending on the analysis they are conducting.

2. Return on Assets (ROA)

Another test of profitability compares income to the total assets used to generate the income. Return on assets is computed as follows:

$$\text{Return on Assets (ROA)} = \frac{\text{Net Income}}{\text{Average Total Assets}}$$

$$\text{Home Depot 2014} = \frac{\$6,345}{\$40,232^*} = 15.77\%$$

$$\frac{^*(\$39,946 + \$40,518)}{2} = \$40,232$$

This implies that, on average, for every $1.00 of assets reported on The Home Depot's balance sheet, the company earned 16 cents in fiscal 2014. The ROA for Lowe's was 8.36 percent, considerably lower than the ROA for The Home Depot. This comparison indicates that The Home Depot is utilizing its assets more effectively than Lowe's.

Some analysts modify the basic ROA computation listed above by adding interest expense (net of tax) to the numerator of the ratio. The logic for making this adjustment is that the denominator of the ratio includes resources (assets) provided by both owners and creditors, so the numerator should include the return that was available to both groups. Interest expense is therefore added back because it was previously deducted in the computation of net income. Note, too, that when making this adjustment, interest expense is measured net of income tax. The net of tax amount is used because interest is deductible for tax purposes, so we need to adjust interest expense for the tax savings associated with using debt.

3. Financial Leverage Percentage

Financial leverage percentage measures the advantage or disadvantage that occurs when a company's return on equity differs from its return on assets. This percentage is computed by subtracting ROA from ROE. The financial leverage percentage is positive when a company earns a return on its debt that exceeds the interest rate it pays on the debt. Most companies have positive leverage, though if they borrow money and make poor investments it is possible to have negative leverage.

Financial leverage percentage is computed as follows:

$$\text{Financial Leverage Percentage} = \text{Return on Equity} - \text{Return on Assets}$$

$$\text{Home Depot 2014} = 58.09\% - 15.77\% = 42.32\%$$

The Home Depot's financial leverage percentage indicates that it earned a considerably higher return on borrowed funds than it paid to borrow those funds. Note that a company's financial leverage percentage can be enhanced either by investing effectively (i.e., earning a high return on investment) or by borrowing effectively (i.e., paying a low rate of interest).

Lowe's financial leverage percentage (16.37 percent) is lower than The Home Depot's. This is not surprising because Lowe's ROE and ROA are lower than The Home Depot's.

4. Net Profit Margin

The net profit margin reflects net income as a percent of sales. It is computed as follows:

$$\text{Net Profit Margin} = \frac{\text{Net Income}}{\text{Net Sales Revenue}}$$

$$\text{Home Depot 2014} = \frac{\$6,345}{\$83,176} = 7.63\%$$

For fiscal 2014, each dollar of The Home Depot's sales generated just under 8 cents of profit. In comparison, Lowe's earned just under 5 cents for each dollar of sales. These numbers reflect that for each dollar of sales, The Home Depot is subtracting approximately 92 cents in expenses while Lowe's is subtracting approximately 95 cents.

While profit margin is a good measure of operating efficiency, you should be careful not to analyze it in isolation because it does not consider the resources needed to earn income. It is very difficult to compare profit margins for companies in different industries. For example, profit margins are low in the food industry while profit margins in the jewelry industry are high. Both types of business can be quite profitable, however, because a high sales volume can compensate for a low profit margin. Grocery stores have low profit margins, but they generate a high sales volume from their relatively inexpensive stores and inventory. Although jewelry stores earn comparatively more profit from each sales dollar, they require a large investment in luxury stores and very expensive inventory.

The trade-off between profit margin and sales volume can be stated in simple terms: Would you prefer to have 5 percent of $1,000,000 or 10 percent of $100,000? As you can see, a larger profit margin is not always better in terms of total dollars earned.

5. Earnings per Share (EPS)

The earnings per share ratio is a measure of return on investment that is based on the number of common shares outstanding. EPS is computed as follows:

$$\text{Earnings per Share (EPS)} = \frac{\text{Net Income}}{\text{Weighted Average Number of Shares Outstanding}}$$

$$\text{Home Depot 2014} = \frac{\$6,345}{1,338} = \$4.74 \text{ per share}$$

You can obtain the weighted average number of shares outstanding from the bottom of a company's income statement (see Exhibit 13.1). Earnings per share is probably the single most widely reported ratio, and it is the only ratio required by GAAP. Analysts develop their own estimates of EPS and the stock price of a company may change significantly if the actual EPS differs from the estimate.

6. Earnings Quality

Most financial analysts are concerned about the quality of a company's earnings because some accounting procedures can be used to report higher income. For example, a company that uses LIFO and short estimated lives for depreciable assets will report lower earnings than an identical company that uses FIFO and longer estimated lives. One method of evaluating the quality of a company's earnings is to compare its reported earnings to its cash flows from operating activities, as follows:

$$\text{Earnings Quality} = \frac{\text{Cash Flows from Operating Activities}}{\text{Net Income}}$$

$$\text{Home Depot 2014} = \frac{\$8,242}{\$6,345} = 1.30$$

A general rule of thumb is that an earnings quality ratio that is higher than 1 is considered to indicate high-quality earnings because each dollar of income is supported by one or more dollars of cash flows. A ratio that is below 1 represents lower-quality earnings.

A research report from **Jefferson Research**, an investment research and advisory firm, discusses the issue of earnings quality for The Home Depot:

> Earnings quality has long been analyzed and used by investors as a measure of the fundamental quality of the company and its future prospects. Companies may be including certain items that increase reported earnings and often the amount of cash flow supporting the earnings may be weak. Jefferson adjusts for these kinds of items and other anomalies to produce an adjusted earnings number that more accurately reflects ongoing business fundamentals at Home Depot. Reported earnings are compared to the Jefferson adjusted earnings as a means to gauge earnings quality. Also measured is the amount of cash flow that underpins earnings.

THE HOME DEPOT

REAL WORLD EXCERPT:

Jefferson Research

PAUSE FOR **FEEDBACK**   STOP

SELF-STUDY **QUIZ**

We have discussed several measures of profitability. Next we will discuss asset turnover ratios. Before you move on, complete the following questions to test your understanding of the concepts we have covered so far.

Show how to compute the following ratios:

1. Return on equity =
2. Return on assets =
3. Net profit margin =

After you have completed your answers, check them below.

Asset Turnover Ratios

LEARNING OBJECTIVE 13-5
Compute and interpret asset turnover ratios.

Asset turnover ratios focus on capturing how efficiently a company uses its assets. For example, acquiring and selling inventory is a key activity for many companies. The inventory turnover ratio helps analysts evaluate a company's ability to sell its inventory. Another example is the receivable turnover ratio, which helps analysts evaluate a company's ability to collect its receivables. These and other asset turnover ratios are discussed below.

ASSET TURNOVER RATIOS
Ratios that capture how efficiently a company uses its assets.

Solutions to
SELF-STUDY QUIZ

1. $$\dfrac{\text{Net income}}{\text{Average Total Stockholders' Equity}}$$

2. $$\dfrac{\text{Net Income}}{\text{Average Total Assets}}$$

3. $$\dfrac{\text{Net Income}}{\text{Net Sales Revenue}}$$

7. Total Asset Turnover Ratio

The total asset turnover ratio captures how well a company uses its assets to generate revenue. The ratio is computed as follows:

$$\text{Total Asset Turnover} = \frac{\text{Net Sales Revenue}}{\text{Average Total Assets}}$$

$$\text{Home Depot 2014} = \frac{\$83,176}{\$40,232^*} = 2.07$$

$$^*\frac{(\$39,946 + \$40,518)}{2} = \$40,232$$

A total asset turnover ratio of 2.07 implies that, on average, each dollar of assets on **The Home Depot**'s balance sheet generates $2.07 of revenue. **Lowe's** total asset turnover ratio is 1.74. Comparing the two indicates that The Home Depot is more efficient than Lowe's at using its assets to generate revenue. As the table below indicates, The Home Depot has also improved its total asset turnover ratio from fiscal 2012 to fiscal 2014.

	2014	2013	2012
Total Asset Turnover	2.07	1.93	1.83

8. Fixed Asset Turnover Ratio

Whereas the total asset turnover ratio captures how well a firm uses *all* of its assets to generate revenues, the fixed asset turnover ratio focuses more narrowly on how well a company uses its *fixed assets* to generate revenues. The term *fixed assets* is synonymous with property, plant, and equipment. The ratio is computed as follows:

$$\text{Fixed Asset Turnover} = \frac{\text{Net Sales Revenue}}{\text{Average Net Fixed Assets}}$$

$$\text{Home Depot 2014} = \frac{\$83,176}{\$23,034^*} = 3.61$$

$$^*\frac{(\$22,720 + \$23,348)}{2} = \$23,034$$

Lowe's fiscal 2014 fixed asset turnover ratio is 2.75. Once again, The Home Depot's ratio is higher, indicating it is more efficient at using its fixed assets to generate revenues. For each dollar The Home Depot invested in property, plant, and equipment, the company was able to generate $3.61 in sales revenue, while Lowe's could generate only $2.75.

9. Receivable Turnover Ratio

Being able to efficiently collect accounts receivable is critical to a company. Analysts know this and therefore keep close watch on a company's receivable turnover ratio. The receivable turnover ratio is computed as follows:

$$\text{Receivable Turnover Ratio} = \frac{\text{Net Credit Sales}^*}{\text{Average Net Receivables}}$$

$$\text{Home Depot 2014} = \frac{\$83,176}{\$1,441^\dagger} = 57.72 \text{ Times}$$

$$^\dagger\frac{(\$1,484 + \$1,398)}{2} = \$1,441$$

If credit sales are not reported separately (which is typically the case), use total net sales as an approximation.

A high receivable turnover ratio suggests that a company collects its accounts receivable many times during a year. The Home Depot, on average, collects its accounts receivable over 57 times a year. Granting credit to customers with poor credit and ineffective collection efforts will produce a low receivable turnover ratio. While a very low ratio is obviously a problem, a very high ratio also can be troublesome because it suggests an overly stringent credit policy that could cause lost sales and profits.

The receivable turnover ratio is often converted to a time basis known as the *average days to collect*. The computation is as follows:

$$\text{Average Days to Collect Receivables} = \frac{\text{Days in a Year}}{\text{Receivable Turnover Ratio}}$$

$$\text{Home Depot 2014} = \frac{365}{57.72} = 6.32 \text{ Days}$$

The Home Depot's average days to collect ratio implies that it takes the company an average of just over 6 days to collect its accounts receivable. Although the receivable turnover ratio normally provides useful insights, the one for The Home Depot is not meaningful. It is highly unlikely that The Home Depot collects cash from its credit customers in just 6 days. Because we did not know the amount of The Home Depot's credit sales, we used total sales as an approximation. In this case, the approximation is not reasonable. Most customers use a bank credit card such as MasterCard or Visa. From The Home Depot's perspective, a sales transaction involving a bank credit card is recorded as a cash sale because the credit card company quickly transfers cash to The Home Depot and then takes on the responsibility of collecting from the customer. As a result, many of The Home Depot's sales are actually cash sales, invalidating the assumption that total sales are a reasonable proxy for credit sales. This situation illustrates that ratio analysis involves more than the mere computation of numbers. Analysts must evaluate the results based on their understanding of the business.

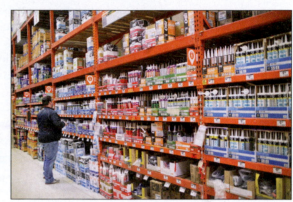
Scott Olson/Getty Images

10. Inventory Turnover Ratio

Like the receivable turnover ratio, the inventory turnover ratio is a measure of operating efficiency. It is computed as follows:

$$\text{Inventory Turnover Ratio} = \frac{\text{Cost of Goods Sold}}{\text{Average Inventory}}$$

$$\text{Home Depot 2014} = \frac{\$54,222}{\$11,068^*} = 4.90 \text{ Times}$$

$$\frac{^*(\$11,079 + \$11,057)}{2} = \$11,068$$

Because a company normally realizes profit each time inventory is sold, an increase in this ratio is usually favorable. If the ratio is too high, however, it may be an indication that sales were lost because desired items were not in stock. A company must balance the cost of holding inventory with the potential cost of losing a sale.

On average, The Home Depot's inventory was acquired and sold to customers 4.9 times during the year. The inventory turnover ratio is critical for The Home Depot because of its business strategy. It wants to be able to offer customers the right product when they need it at a price that beats the competition. Inventory turnover for Lowe's was 4.07. Historically, The Home Depot has enjoyed an advantage over Lowe's in terms of inventory management. The Home Depot's effectiveness in inventory management means that the company is able to tie up less money in carrying inventory compared to Lowe's.

Turnover ratios vary significantly from one industry to the next. Companies in the food industry (grocery stores and restaurants) have high inventory turnover ratios because their inventory is subject to rapid deterioration. Companies that sell expensive merchandise (automobiles and high-fashion clothes) have much lower ratios because although sales of those items are infrequent, customers want to have a selection to choose from when they do buy.

Like the receivable turnover ratio, the inventory turnover ratio is often converted to a time basis. The computation is:

$$\text{Average Days to Sell Inventory} = \frac{\text{Days in a Year}}{\text{Inventory Turnover Ratio}}$$

$$\text{Home Depot 2014} = \frac{365}{4.90} = 74.49 \text{ Days}$$

Using Ratios to Analyze the Operating Cycle In Chapter 3, we introduced the concept of a company's operating cycle, which is the time it takes for a company to pay cash to its suppliers, sell goods to its customers, and collect cash from its customers. Analysts are interested in the operating cycle because it helps them evaluate a company's cash needs and is a good indicator of operating efficiency.

The operating cycle for most companies involves three distinct phases: the acquisition of inventory, the sale of the inventory, and the collection of cash from the customer. We have discussed several ratios that are helpful when evaluating a company's operating cycle:

Ratio*	Operating Activity
Accounts payable turnover ratio	Purchase of inventory
Inventory turnover ratio	Sale of inventory
Receivable turnover ratio	Collection of cash from customers

We discussed the accounts payable turnover ratio in Chapter 9. The inventory turnover ratio and the receivable turnover ratio are discussed in this chapter.

Each of the ratios measures the number of days it takes, on average, to complete an operating activity. We have already computed two of the needed ratios for The Home Depot, so if we compute the accounts payable turnover ratio, we can analyze the company's operating cycle:

$$\text{Accounts Payable Turnover Ratio} = \frac{\text{Cost of Goods Sold}}{\text{Average Accounts Payable}}$$

$$\text{Home Depot 2014} = \frac{\$54,222}{\$5,802^*} = 9.35 \text{ Times}$$

$$\frac{^*(\$5,807 + \$5,797)}{2} = \$5,802$$

$$\text{Average Days to Pay Payables} = \frac{\text{Days in Year}}{\text{Accounts Payable Turnover Ratio}}$$

$$\text{Home Depot 2014} = \frac{365}{9.35} = 39.04 \text{ Days}$$

The number of days it takes The Home Depot to complete each phase of its operating cycle are:

Ratio	Time
Average days to pay payables	39.04 days
Average days to sell inventory	74.49 days
Average days to collect receivables	6.32 days

Examining each phase of the operating cycle helps us understand the cash needs of the company. The Home Depot, on average, pays for its inventory 39 days after it receives it. It takes, on average, 81 days (74.49 + 6.32) for it to sell its inventory and collect cash from its customers. Therefore, The Home Depot must invest cash in its operating activities for just over 42 days (81 days − 39 days) between the time it pays its vendors and the time it collects from its customers. Companies prefer to minimize the time between paying vendors and collecting cash from customers because it frees up cash for other productive purposes. The Home Depot could reduce this time by slowing payments to creditors or by increasing how quickly it turns over its inventory.

The DuPont Model

The **DuPont model** brings together several of the ratios we have discussed so far and reflects how these ratios are related. The model is:

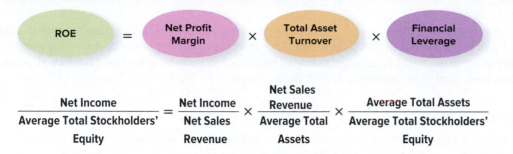

$$\frac{\text{Net Income}}{\text{Average Total Stockholders' Equity}} = \frac{\text{Net Income}}{\text{Net Sales Revenue}} \times \frac{\text{Net Sales Revenue}}{\text{Average Total Assets}} \times \frac{\text{Average Total Assets}}{\text{Average Total Stockholders' Equity}}$$

In mathematical terms, canceling out like items on the right side of the above equation shows that the left and right sides are equivalent. Examining the additional information on the right side of the DuPont model allows an analyst to tell a much richer story about a company's profitability than can be told by examining just ROE. For example, a company can increase its ROE by increasing its net profit margin or by increasing the revenue it generates from its asset base (its total asset turnover). A company can also *leverage up* its return to stockholders by borrowing funds and investing them in such a way that the return exceeds the cost of borrowing. This leverage effect is captured by the financial leverage ratio.

The DuPont model is a useful way to analyze a company's performance. Understanding it will also help you start to make connections between other ratios. For example, multiplying just the net profit margin and the total asset turnover ratio creates a company's ROA ratio.

Liquidity Ratios

Liquidity refers to a company's ability to meet its short-term obligations. Because most short-term obligations will be paid with current assets, **liquidity ratios** focus on the relationship between current assets and current liabilities. The ability to pay current liabilities is an important factor in evaluating a company's short-term financial strength. In this section, we discuss three ratios that are used to measure liquidity: the current ratio, the quick ratio, and the cash ratio.

11. Current Ratio

The current ratio measures to what extent a company's total current assets cover its total current liabilities on a specific date. It is computed as follows:

$$\text{Current Ratio} = \frac{\text{Current Assets}}{\text{Current Liabilities}}$$

$$\text{Home Depot 2014} = \frac{\$15,302}{\$11,269} = 1.36$$

A ratio greater than 1 implies that a company's current assets are sufficient to cover its current liabilities. If a company's current ratio is less than 1, analysts will want to understand how the company intends to meet its short-term obligations. At the end of fiscal 2014, **The Home Depot** had $1.36 in current assets for each $1.00 in current liabilities. Most analysts would judge that ratio to be quite strong.

To properly use the current ratio, analysts must understand the nature of a company's business. Many manufacturing companies have developed sophisticated systems to minimize the amount of inventory they must hold. These systems, called *just-in-time inventory,* are designed to have an inventory item arrive just when it is needed. While these systems work well in manufacturing processes, they do not work as well in retailing. Customers expect to find merchandise in the store when they want it, and it has proven difficult to precisely forecast consumer behavior. As a result, most retailers have comparatively high current ratios because they must

LEARNING OBJECTIVE 13-6
Compute and interpret liquidity ratios.

LIQUIDITY RATIOS
Ratios that measure a company's ability to meet its currently maturing obligations.

carry large inventories. The Home Depot, for example, maintains an inventory of 40,000 different products in a typical store.

The optimal level of the current ratio depends on the business environment in which a company operates. If cash flows are predictable and stable, the current ratio can be low, even less than 1. For example, **Procter & Gamble**, a strong and fiscally conservative company, has a current ratio of 0.94. When cash flows are highly variable, a higher current ratio is desirable.

Analysts become concerned if a company's current ratio is high compared to that of other companies in its industry. A firm is operating inefficiently when it ties up too much money in inventory or accounts receivable. It is also important to keep in mind that current assets other than cash need to be converted to cash before they can be used to satisfy current obligations.

12. Quick Ratio

The quick ratio, sometimes referred to as the **acid test,** is a more stringent test of short-term liquidity than is the current ratio. The quick ratio compares quick assets, defined as *cash and near-cash assets,* to current liabilities. Quick assets include cash, net accounts receivable, and marketable securities. Inventory is omitted from quick assets because of the uncertainty of the timing of cash flows from its sale. Prepaid expenses are also excluded from quick assets. The quick ratio is computed as follows:

Erik S. Lesser/Bloomberg/Getty Images

$$\text{Quick Ratio} = \frac{\text{Cash \& Cash Equivalents} + \text{Net Accounts Receivable} + \text{Marketable Securities}}{\text{Current Liabilities}}$$

$$\text{Home Depot 2014} = \frac{(\$1{,}723 + \$1{,}484 + \$0)}{\$11{,}269} = 0.28$$

The quick ratio is a measure of whether the highly liquid assets of a company, those that can be converted to cash quickly, are sufficient to cover current liabilities. The Home Depot has 28 cents in cash and near-cash assets for every $1.00 in current liabilities. This margin of safety is typical of the retail industry and would be considered a good margin in light of the large amount of cash The Home Depot generates from its operating activities ($8.2 billion). In comparison, the quick ratio for **Lowe's** is significantly lower (0.06).

13. Cash Ratio

Cash is the lifeblood of a business. Without cash, a company cannot pay its employees or meet its obligations to creditors. Even a profitable business will fail without sufficient cash. One measure of the adequacy of available cash, called the *cash ratio,* is computed as follows:

$$\text{Cash Ratio} = \frac{\text{Cash \& Cash Equivalents}}{\text{Current Liabilities}}$$

$$\text{Home Depot 2014} = \frac{\$1{,}723}{\$11{,}269} = 0.15$$

In fiscal 2014, Lowe's cash ratio was 0.05, which was considerably lower than The Home Depot's cash ratio of 0.15. The Home Depot's cash ratio indicates that the company has on hand 15 cents of cash for each $1.00 of current liabilities. Would analysts be concerned about this number? Not likely. It is important to keep in mind that not all of The Home Depot's current liabilities need to be paid immediately. It therefore does not need to keep enough cash on hand at any point in time to cover all of its short-term obligations. Looking at the bigger picture, the Home Depot's statement of cash flows shows that the company generated $8.2 billion in cash from its operating activities. As a result, it is highly likely that The Home Depot will have sufficient cash on hand when the time comes to meet any given current liability. Many analysts believe the cash ratio should not be too high because holding excess cash is usually uneconomical. It is far better to invest the cash in productive assets or reduce debt.

SELF-STUDY QUIZ

We have discussed several measures of liquidity. Next we will discuss solvency ratios. Before you move on, complete the following questions to test your understanding of the concepts we have covered so far.

Show how to compute the following ratios:

1. Current ratio =
2. Quick ratio =
3. Cash ratio =

After you have completed your answers, check them below.

Solvency Ratios

Solvency refers to a company's ability to meet its long-term obligations. **Solvency ratios** measure this ability and include the times interest earned, cash coverage, and debt-to-equity ratios.

> **LEARNING OBJECTIVE 13-7**
> Compute and interpret solvency ratios.

> **SOLVENCY RATIOS**
> Ratios that measure a company's ability to meet its long-term obligations.

14. Times Interest Earned Ratio

Interest payments are a fixed obligation. If a company fails to make required interest payments, creditors may force it into bankruptcy. Because of the importance of meeting interest payments, analysts often compute a ratio called *times interest earned:*

$$\text{Times Interest Earned} = \frac{\text{Net Income} + \text{Interest Expense} + \text{Income Tax Expense}}{\text{Interest Expense}}$$

$$\text{Home Depot 2014} = \frac{(\$6{,}345 + \$830 + \$3{,}631)}{\$830} = 13.02 \text{ Times}$$

The times interest earned ratio compares the income available to pay interest in a period to a company's interest obligation for the same period. Interest expense and income tax expense are added back in the numerator because these amounts are available to pay interest. The times interest earned ratio represents a margin of protection for creditors. In fiscal 2014, **The Home Depot** generated $13.02 in income for each $1.00 of interest expense, a high ratio that indicates a secure position for creditors.

Some analysts believe that the times interest earned ratio is flawed because interest expense is paid in cash, not with net income. These analysts prefer to use the cash coverage ratio.

15. Cash Coverage Ratio

Given the importance of having enough cash on hand to make required interest payments, it is easy to understand why many analysts use the cash coverage ratio. It is computed as follows:

$$\text{Cash Coverage Ratio} = \frac{\text{Cash Flows from Operating Activities}}{\text{Interest Paid}}$$

$$\text{Home Depot 2014} = \frac{\$8{,}242}{\$782} = 10.54 \text{ Times}$$

---

1. Current Assets ÷ Current Liabilities
2. (Cash & Cash Equivalents + Net Accounts Receivable + Marketable Securities) ÷ Current Liabilities
3. Cash & Cash Equivalents ÷ Current Liabilities

Solutions to
SELF-STUDY QUIZ

The Home Depot's cash coverage ratio shows that the company generated $10.54 in cash for every $1.00 of interest paid, which is strong coverage. Some analysts modify the basic cash coverage ratio by adding back to the numerator interest paid and income taxes paid. These amounts are typically disclosed separately at the bottom of a company's statement of cash flows, as they are for The Home Depot in Exhibit 13.1.

16. Debt-to-Equity Ratio

The debt-to-equity ratio expresses a company's debt as a proportion of its stockholders' equity. It is computed as follows:

$$\text{Debt-to-Equity Ratio} = \frac{\text{Total Liabilities}}{\text{Total Stockholders' Equity}}$$

$$\text{Home Depot 2014} = \frac{\$30,624}{\$9,322} = 3.29$$

In fiscal 2014, for each $1.00 of stockholders' equity, The Home Depot had $3.29 of liabilities. By comparison, **Lowe's** debt-to-equity ratio was 2.19.

Debt is risky for a company because specific interest payments must be made even if the company has not earned sufficient income to pay them. In contrast, dividends are always at the company's discretion and are not legally enforceable until they are declared by the board of directors. Thus, equity capital is associated with fewer contractual payments than is debt.

Despite the risk associated with debt, however, most companies obtain significant amounts of resources from creditors because of the advantages of financial leverage discussed earlier. In addition, interest expense is a deductible expense on a company's income tax return. Weighing these benefits against the contractual obligations that accompany debt results in companies using a mix of debt and equity financing. Analysts evaluate this mix by computing the debt-to-equity ratio.

Market Ratios

LEARNING OBJECTIVE 13-8

Compute and interpret market ratios.

Several ratios, often called **market ratios**, relate the current price per share of a company's stock to the return that accrues to stockholders. Analysts find these ratios helpful because they are based on the current value of an owner's investment in a company.

MARKET RATIOS

Ratios that relate the current price per share of a company's stock to the return that accrues to stockholders.

17. Price/Earnings (P/E) Ratio

The price/earnings (P/E) ratio measures the relationship between the current market price of a company's stock and its earnings per share. At the end of fiscal 2014, **The Home Depot**'s stock was trading at $104.43 per share. EPS for fiscal 2014 was $4.74. With this information, we can compute The Home Depot's P/E ratio as follows:

$$\text{Price/Earnings Ratio} = \frac{\text{Market Price per Share}}{\text{Earnings per Share}}$$

$$\text{Home Depot 2014} = \frac{\$104.43}{\$4.74} = 22.03$$

This P/E ratio indicates that The Home Depot's stock was selling at a price that was just over 22 times its earnings per share. The P/E ratio reflects the stock market's assessment of a company's future performance. A high ratio indicates that earnings are expected to grow rapidly. Lowe's P/E ratio is 25.00. The P/E ratios for The Home Depot and Lowe's indicate that the market expects them to perform well in the future.

In economic terms, the value of a stock is determined by calculating the present value of the company's future earnings. Thus, a company that expects to increase its earnings in the future is worth more than one that cannot grow its earnings (assuming other factors are the same). However, while a high P/E ratio and good growth prospects are considered favorable, there are risks. When a company with a high P/E ratio does not meet the level of earnings expected by the market, the negative impact on its stock can be dramatic.

18. Dividend Yield Ratio

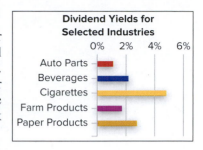

Dividend Yields for Selected Industries

When investors buy stock, they can earn a return on their investment through dividends or price appreciation. The dividend yield ratio reflects the return on investment absent any capital appreciation, or, said differently, the return attributed solely to the dividends a company pays. Not all companies report the cash dividend they paid per share on their income statement or statement of cash flows, so you may need to search their 10-K to find the information. The Home Depot paid dividends of $1.16 per share in fiscal 2014. At the end of fiscal 2014 its stock price was $104.43 per share. Its dividend yield ratio is computed as follows:

$$\text{Dividend Yield Ratio} = \frac{\text{Dividends per Share}}{\text{Market Price per Share}}$$

$$\text{Home Depot 2014} = \frac{\$1.16}{\$104.43} = 1.11\%$$

In recent years, the dividend yield for The Home Depot has been less than 2 percent. The dividend yield for most stocks is not high compared to alternative investments. Investors are willing to accept low dividend yields if they expect that the price of a stock will increase while they own it. Investors who bought The Home Depot stock did so knowing they would receive a dividend, but they also were expecting its stock price to increase. In contrast, stocks with low growth potential tend to offer much higher dividend yields than do stocks with high growth potential. Stocks with high dividend yields often appeal to retired investors who need current income rather than future growth potential.

The dividend yield for **Lowe's** is similar to that for The Home Depot, 1.28 percent in fiscal 2014. The nearby chart shows average dividend yields for several different industries.

PAUSE FOR FEEDBACK

SELF-STUDY QUIZ

We have discussed several solvency and market ratios. Next we will discuss important analytical considerations. Before you move on, complete the following questions to test your understanding of the concepts we have covered so far.

Show how to compute the following ratios:

1. Cash coverage ratio =

2. Debt-to-equity ratio =

3. Price/earnings ratio =

After you have completed your answers, check them below.

 GUIDED HELP 13-1

For additional step-by-step video instruction on calculating ratios, go to **http://www.mhhe.com/ libby9e_gh13**.

---

1. Cash Coverage Ratio = Cash Flows from Operating Activities ÷ Interest Paid
2. Debt-to-Equity Ratio = Total Liabilities ÷ Total Stockholders' Equity
3. Price/Earnings Ratio = Market Price per Share ÷ Earnings per Share

Solutions to
SELF-STUDY QUIZ

INTERPRETING RATIOS AND OTHER ANALYTICAL CONSIDERATIONS

Except for earnings per share, the computation of financial ratios has not been standardized by the accounting profession. Thus, analysts must decide which ratios to use and how to compute them based on their decision objective. When using ratios computed by others, analysts are careful to note how each ratio is computed.

As we have seen, ratios can be interpreted only by comparing them to other ratios or a benchmark value. Some ratios, by their very nature, are unfavorable at either very high or very low values. For example, a very low current ratio may indicate an inability to meet short-term obligations, while a very high current ratio may indicate excessive current assets. Furthermore, an optimal ratio for one company may not be optimal for another. Comparing ratios for two firms is appropriate only if the companies are comparable in terms of their industry, operations, and accounting policies.

Because ratios are based on the aggregation of information, they may obscure underlying factors that are of interest to the analyst. For example, a current ratio that is considered optimal can obscure a short-term liquidity problem in a company with a large amount of inventory but a minimal amount of cash with which to meet short-term obligations. Examining multiple ratios, like the quick ratio and cash ratio in conjunction with the current ratio, can uncover this type of problem.

In other cases, analysis cannot uncover obscured problems. For example, consolidated statements include financial information about a parent company and its subsidiaries. The parent company could have a low current ratio and the subsidiary a high one, but when their statements are consolidated, their current ratios are in effect averaged and can fall within an acceptable range. The fact that the parent company could have a serious liquidity problem is obscured.

A company's accounting policy choices will influence its ratios. This is important because different companies rarely use exactly the same accounting policies. For example, two companies that purchase the exact same asset will report different net income amounts if one uses accelerated deprecation while the other uses straight-line depreciation. These different amounts will influence any ratios that include net income. Analysts who do not understand how a company's accounting choices influence its ratios could draw inappropriate conclusions. It is therefore critical that analysts understand a company's accounting policies before interpreting its ratios. A company's accounting policies are described in the footnotes to its financial statements.

Other Financial Information

Understanding the broader economic environment in which a company operates is important when interpreting its ratios. Some things that analysts commonly consider are:

1. **Rapid growth.** Growth in total sales does not always indicate that a company is successful. Total sales can increase as a result of a company selling more at its existing stores, or it can increase as a result of a company opening new stores. Growth driven by new-store sales might obscure the fact that existing stores are not meeting customer needs and are experiencing declining sales. To help analysts sort out what is driving sales growth, companies often report a figure called "comparable store sales growth." This figure captures the growth in sales for stores that have been in existence for some period of time, typically 13 months or more. **The Home Depot** discusses comparable store sales growth in its 2014 10-K:

> Net Sales increased 5.5% to $83.2 billion for fiscal 2014 from $78.8 billion for fiscal 2013. Our total comparable store sales increased 5.3% in fiscal 2014, driven by a 3.5% increase in our comparable store customer transactions and a 1.8% increase in our comparable store average ticket.

2. Uneconomical expansion. In the pursuit of growth, some companies will open stores in less desirable locations. These poor locations can cause a company's average productivity to decline. One measure of productivity in the retail industry is sales volume per square foot of selling space. The Home Depot reports sales volume per square foot in its 10-K report:

Year	Sales per Square Foot
2014	$352
2013	334
2012	319
2011	299
2010	289

As the table shows, sales per square foot has grown each of the last five years, a good sign that The Home Depot is not opening stores in undesirable locations.

3. Subjective factors. Remember that analyzing a company involves much more than simply analyzing its financial statements and ratios. To get a sense for how a company is implementing its strategy, analysts will often visit individual stores and perhaps talk to customers and suppliers. Information obtained during these visits helps analysts better understand how a company's strategy is actually being implemented in its stores. With this understanding, analysts are better able to interpret a company's current financial information as well as make more informed predictions about future performance.

Insider Information   **A QUESTION OF ETHICS**

A company's accountants often are aware of important financial information before it is made available to the public. This is called *insider information.* Some people might be tempted to buy or sell stock based on insider information, but to do so is a serious criminal offense. The Securities and Exchange Commission has brought a number of cases against individuals who traded on insider information. Their convictions resulted in large fines and time served in jail.

In some cases, determining whether something is insider information is difficult. For example, an individual could overhear a comment made in the company elevator by two executives. Is this insider information? A well-respected Wall Street investment banker offers good advice on dealing with such situations: "If you are not sure if something is right or wrong, apply the newspaper headline test. Ask yourself how you would feel to have your family and friends read about what you had done in the newspaper." Interestingly, many people who have spent time in jail and lost small fortunes in fines because of insider trading say that the most difficult part of the process was telling their families.

To uphold the highest ethical standard, many public accounting firms have adopted rules that prevent their staff from investing in companies that they audit. Such rules are designed to ensure that a company's auditors will not be tempted to engage in insider trading.

CHAPTER TAKE-AWAYS

13-1. Explain how a company's business strategy affects financial statement analysis.   p. 664

Financial statements reflect transactions. Transactions are the result of a company carrying out its operating decisions as it implements its business strategy. Thus, an understanding of a company's business strategy provides the context for conducting financial statement analysis.

13-2. Discuss ways to analyze financial statements.   p. 666

Analysts use financial statements to understand a company's current and past performance, as well as to make predictions about future performance. The data reported in a company's financial statements can be used for either time-series analysis (comparing a single company over time) or cross-sectional analysis (comparing similar companies at a point in time).

13-3. Compute and interpret component percentages.   p. 667

Component percentages express each item on a financial statement as a percentage of a single base amount. The base amount on the income statement is net sales. To compute component percentages on the income statement, each amount reported is divided by net sales. The base amount on the balance sheet is total assets. To compute component percentages on the balance sheet, each amount is divided by total assets. Component percentages are evaluated by comparing them over time for a single company or by comparing them with percentages for similar companies at a point in time.

13-4. Compute and interpret profitability ratios.   p. 669

Profitability ratios focus on net income and how it compares to other amounts reported on the financial statements. Exhibit 13.3 lists these ratios and shows how to compute them. Profitability ratios are evaluated by comparing them over time for a single company or by comparing them with ratios for similar companies at a point in time.

13-5. Compute and interpret asset turnover ratios.   p. 673

Asset turnover ratios focus on capturing how efficiently a company uses its assets. Exhibit 13.3 lists these ratios and shows how to compute them. Asset turnover ratios are evaluated by comparing them over time for a single company or by comparing them with ratios for similar companies at a point in time.

13-6. Compute and interpret liquidity ratios.   p. 677

Liquidity ratios focus on evaluating a company's ability to meet its short-term obligations. Exhibit 13.3 lists these ratios and shows how to compute them. Liquidity ratios are evaluated by comparing them over time for a single company or by comparing them with ratios for similar companies at a point in time.

13-7. Compute and interpret solvency ratios.   p. 679

Solvency ratios focus on evaluating a company's ability to meet its long-term obligations. Exhibit 13.3 lists these ratios and shows how to compute them. Solvency ratios are evaluated by comparing them over time for a single company or by comparing them with ratios for similar companies at a point in time.

13-8. Compute and interpret market ratios.   p. 680

Market ratios relate the current price per share of a company's stock to the return that accrues to stockholders. Exhibit 13.3 lists these ratios and shows how to compute them. Market ratios are evaluated by comparing them over time for a single company or by comparing them with ratios for similar companies at a point in time.

FINDING FINANCIAL INFORMATION

Balance Sheet

Ratios are not reported on the balance sheet. Analysts do, however, use balance sheet information to compute some ratios. Most analysts use an average of the beginning and ending amounts for balance sheet accounts when comparing balance sheet numbers to income statement numbers.

Income Statement

Earnings per share is the only ratio that is required to be reported on the financial statements. It is reported at the bottom of the income statement.

Statement of Cash Flows

Ratios are not reported on the statement of cash flows. Analysts do, however, use cash flow information to compute some ratios.

Statement of Stockholders' Equity

Ratios are not reported on the statement of stockholders' equity. Analysts do, however, use amounts from this statement to compute some ratios.

Notes

Under Summary of Significant Accounting Policies

This note describes a company's accounting policies. Understanding a company's accounting policies is critical to interpreting its ratios, especially when comparing ratios across companies.

Under Separate Notes

There is a vast amount of information reported in a company's footnotes. At times, you will need to retrieve information from a footnote in order to calculate a specific ratio.

KEY TERMS

Asset Turnover Ratios   p. 673
Component Percentage   p. 667
Liquidity Ratios   p. 677

Market Ratios   p. 680
Profitability Ratios   p. 669
Ratio Analysis   p. 667

Solvency Ratios   p. 679

QUESTIONS

1. Who are the primary users of financial statements?
2. When considering an investment in stock, investors should evaluate the company's future income and growth potential on the basis of what three factors?
3. How does product differentiation differ from cost differentiation?
4. What are the two general methods for making financial comparisons?
5. What are component percentages? Why are they useful?
6. What is ratio analysis? Why is it useful?
7. What do profitability ratios focus on? What is an example of a profitability ratio and how is it computed?
8. What do turnover ratios focus on? What is an example of a turnover ratio and how is it computed?
9. What do liquidity ratios focus on? What is an example of a liquidity ratio and how is it computed?
10. What do solvency ratios focus on? What is an example of a solvency ratio and how is it computed?
11. What do market ratios focus on? What is an example of a market ratio and how is it computed?
12. Explain how a company's accounting policy choices can affect its ratios.
13. Explain why rapid growth in total sales might not necessarily be a good thing for a company.

MULTIPLE-CHOICE QUESTIONS

1. A company has total assets of $500,000 and noncurrent assets of $400,000. Current liabilities are $40,000. What is the current ratio?
   a. 12.5
   b. 10.0
   c. 2.5
   d. Cannot be determined without additional information.
2. Which of the following would **not** change the receivables turnover ratio for a retail company?
   a. Increases in the retail prices of inventory.
   b. A change in credit policy.
   c. Increases in the cost incurred to purchase inventory.
   d. None of the above.

3. Which of the following ratios is used to analyze liquidity?
   a. Earnings per share.   c. Current ratio.
   b. Debt-to-equity ratio.   d. Both (a) and (c).
4. Positive financial leverage indicates
   a. Positive cash flow from financing activities.
   b. A debt-to-equity ratio higher than 1.
   c. A rate of return on assets exceeding the interest rate on debt.
   d. A profit margin in one year exceeding the previous year's profit margin.
5. If a potential investor is analyzing three companies in the same industry and wishes to invest in only one, which ratio is least likely to affect the investor's decision?
   a. Earnings per share.
   b. Price/earnings ratio.
   c. Dividend yield ratio.
   d. All of the above will likely affect the investor's decision.
6. A company has quick assets of $300,000 and current liabilities of $150,000. The company purchased $50,000 in inventory on credit. After the purchase, the quick ratio would be
   a. 2.0   c. 1.5
   b. 2.3   d. 1.75
7. The inventory turnover ratio for Natural Foods Stores is 14.6. The company reported cost of goods sold in the amount of $1,500,000 and total sales of $2,500,000. What is the average amount of inventory for Natural Foods?
   a. $102,740   c. $100,000
   b. $171,233   d. $60,000
8. Given the following ratios for four companies, which company is **least** likely to experience problems paying its current liabilities promptly?

	Quick Ratio	Receivable Turnover Ratio
a.	1.2	58
b.	1.2	25
c.	1.0	55
d.	.5	60

9. A decrease in selling and administrative expenses would impact what ratio?
   a. Fixed asset turnover ratio.
   b. Times interest earned ratio.
   c. Debt-to-equity ratio.
   d. Current ratio.
10. A creditor is **least** likely to use what ratio when analyzing a company that has borrowed funds on a long-term basis?
   a. Cash coverage ratio.
   b. Debt-to-equity ratio.
   c. Times interest earned ratio.
   d. Dividend yield ratio.

MINI-**EXERCISES**    connect

M13-1   **Inferring Financial Information Using Component Percentages**

LO13-3   A large retailer reported revenue of $1,665,000. The company's gross profit percentage was 44 percent. What amount of cost of goods sold did the company report?

Inferring Financial Information Using Component Percentages

M13-2
LO13-3

A consumer products company reported a 5.4 percent increase in sales from Year 1 to Year 2. Sales in Year 1 were $29,600. In Year 2, the company reported cost of goods sold in the amount of $9,107. What was the gross profit percentage in Year 2?

Computing the Return on Equity Ratio

M13-3
LO13-4

Compute the return on equity ratio for Year 2 given the following data:

	Year 2	Year 1
Net income	$ 183,000	$ 159,000
Stockholders' equity	1,100,000	1,250,000
Total assets	2,460,000	2,630,000
Interest expense	42,000	32,000

Computing the Financial Leverage Percentage

M13-4
LO13-4

Compute the financial leverage percentage for Year 2 given the following data:

	Year 2	Year 1
Return on equity	21.00%	26.00%
Return on assets	6.00	8.00
Profit margin	12.00	12.00

Analyzing the Inventory Turnover Ratio

M13-5
LO13-5

A manufacturer reported an inventory turnover ratio of 8.6 during last year. This year, management introduced a new inventory control system that was expected to reduce average inventory levels by 25 percent without affecting sales. Given this estimate, would you expect the inventory turnover ratio to increase or decrease this year relative to last year? Explain.

Using the Current Ratio to Infer Financial Information

M13-6
LO13-6

Stacy Company reported total assets of $1,400,000 and noncurrent assets of $480,000. The company also reported a current ratio of 3.5. What amount of current liabilities did the company report?

Analyzing Financial Relationships

M13-7
LO13-4, 13-6

Ramesh Company has prepared preliminary financial results that are now being reviewed by the accountants. You notice that the current ratio is 2.4 and the quick ratio is 3.7. You recognize that this is unusual. Does it imply that a mistake has been made? Explain.

Calculating the Times Interest Earned Ratio

M13-8
LO13-7

In the current year, Pringle Company reported Sales of $1,420,000, Interest Expense of $12,000, Income Tax Expense of $13,000, and Net Income of $52,000. What is Pringle's times interest earned ratio?

Inferring Financial Information Using a Ratio

M13-9
LO13-8

An Internet company earned $6.50 per share and paid dividends of $3.50 per share. The company reported a dividend yield of 5 percent. What was the price of the stock?

Analyzing the Impact of Accounting Alternatives

M13-10
LO13-4, 13-5, 13-6

Youngstown Corporation is considering changing its inventory method from FIFO to LIFO. Assume that inventory prices have been increasing. All else equal, what impact would you expect the change to have on the following ratios: net profit margin, fixed asset turnover ratio, current ratio, and quick ratio?

EXERCISES

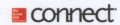

E13-1
LO13-1, 13-2, 13-3,
13-5, 13-6, 13-7

Using Financial Information to Identify Companies

The following selected financial data pertain to four unidentified companies:

	COMPANIES			
	1	2	3	4
Balance Sheet Data (component percentage)				
Cash	3.5%	4.7%	8.2%	11.7%
Accounts receivable	16.9	28.9	16.8	51.9
Inventory	46.8	35.6	57.3	0.0
Property and equipment	18.3	21.7	7.6	18.7
Income Statement Data (component percentage)				
Cost of goods sold	78.0%	77.5%	55.8%	0.0%
Profit before taxes	2.1	0.7	1.2	3.2
Selected Ratios				
Current ratio	1.3	1.5	1.6	1.2
Inventory turnover ratio	3.6	9.8	1.5	N/A*

*N/A = Not applicable

The above financial information pertains to the following companies:

a. High-end clothing store
b. Advertising agency
c. Wholesale candy company
d. Car manufacturer

Required:
Match each company with its financial information.

E13-2
LO13-1, 13-2, 13-3,
13-5, 13-6, 13-7

Using Financial Information to Identify Companies

The following selected financial data pertain to four unidentified companies:

	COMPANIES			
	1	2	3	4
Balance Sheet Data (component percentage)				
Cash	7.3%	21.6%	6.1%	11.3%
Accounts receivable	28.2	39.7	3.2	22.9
Inventory	21.6	0.6	1.8	27.5
Property and equipment	32.1	18.0	74.6	25.1
Income Statement Data (component percentage)				
Cost of goods sold	84.7%	0.0%	0.0%	56.6%
Profit before taxes	1.7	3.2	2.4	6.9
Selected Ratios				
Current ratio	1.5	1.2	0.6	1.9
Inventory turnover ratio	27.4	N/A*	N/A*	3.3

*N/A = Not applicable

The above financial information pertains to the following companies:

a. Travel agency
b. Hotel
c. Meat processing company
d. Drug company

Required:
Match each company with its financial information.

Using Financial Information to Identify Companies

The following selected financial data pertain to four unidentified companies:

E13-3
LO13-1, 13-2, 13-3, 13-5, 13-6, 13-7

	COMPANIES			
	1	**2**	**3**	**4**
Balance Sheet Data (component percentage)				
Cash	5.1%	8.8%	6.3%	10.4%
Accounts receivable	13.1	41.5	13.8	4.9
Inventory	4.6	3.6	65.1	35.8
Property and equipment	53.1	23.0	8.8	35.7
Income Statement Data (component percentage)				
Cost of goods sold	0.0%	0.0%	54.8%	77.5%
Profit before taxes	0.3	16.0	3.9	1.5
Selected Ratios				
Current ratio	0.7	2.2	1.9	1.4
Inventory turnover ratio	N/A*	N/A*	1.4	15.5

*N/A = Not applicable

The above financial information pertains to the following companies:

a. Cable TV company
b. Grocery store
c. Accounting firm
d. High-end jewelry store

Required:
Match each company with its financial information.

Using Financial Information to Identify Companies

The following selected financial data pertain to four unidentified companies:

E13-4
LO13-1, 13-2, 13-3, 13-5, 13-6, 13-7

	COMPANIES			
	1	**2**	**3**	**4**
Balance Sheet Data (component percentage)				
Cash	11.6%	6.6%	5.4%	7.1%
Accounts receivable	4.6	18.9	8.8	35.6
Inventory	7.0	45.8	65.7	26.0
Property and equipment	56.0	20.3	10.1	21.9
Income Statement Data (component percentage)				
Cost of goods sold	43.3%	63.6%	85.9%	84.2%
Profit before taxes	2.7	1.4	1.1	0.9
Selected Ratios				
Current ratio	0.7	2.1	1.2	1.3
Inventory turnover ratio	30.0	3.5	5.6	16.7

The above financial information pertains to the following companies:

a. Full-line department store
b. Wholesale fish company
c. Automobile dealer (low-priced used cars)
d. Restaurant

Required:
Match each company with its financial information.

E13-5
LO13-3

Calculating Component Percentages

Compute the component percentages for **Lowe's** income statement below. Discuss any trends you observe.

LOWE'S COMPANIES, INC.						
Consolidated Statements of Earnings						
(in millions, except per share and percentage data)						
	Fiscal Years Ended on					
	January 30, 2015	**% Sales**	**January 31, 2014**	**% Sales**	**February 1, 2013**	**% Sales**
Net sales	$56,223	100.00%	$53,417	100.00%	$50,521	100.00%
Cost of sales	36,665		34,941		33,194	
Gross margin	19,558		18,476		17,327	
Expenses:						
Selling, general, and administrative	13,281		12,865		12,244	
Depreciation	1,485		1,462		1,523	
Interest—net	516		476		423	
Total expenses	15,282		14,803		14,190	
Pre-tax earnings	4,276		3,673		3,137	
Income tax provision	1,578		1,387		1,178	
Net earnings	$ 2,698		$ 2,286		$ 1,959	

E13-6
LO13-4, 13-5, 13-6, 13-7

Matching Each Ratio with Its Computational Formula

Match each ratio or percentage with its computation.

Ratios or Percentages	**Definitions**
1. Net profit margin	A. Net Income ÷ Net Sales Revenue
2. Inventory turnover ratio	B. Days in Year ÷ Receivable Turnover Ratio
3. Average days to collect receivables	C. Net Income ÷ Average Total Stockholders' Equity
4. Dividend yield ratio	D. Net Income ÷ Weighted Average Number of Common Shares Outstanding
5. Return on equity	E. Return on Equity − Return on Assets
6. Current ratio	F. (Cash & Cash Equivalents + Net Accounts Receivable + Marketable Securities) ÷ Current Liabilities
7. Debt-to-equity ratio	
8. Price/earnings ratio	G. Current Assets ÷ Current Liabilities
9. Financial leverage percentage	H. Cost of Goods Sold ÷ Average Inventory
10. Receivable turnover ratio	I. Net Credit Sales ÷ Average Net Receivables
11. Average days to sell inventory	J. Days in Year ÷ Inventory Turnover Ratio
12. Earnings per share	K. Total Liabilities ÷ Total Stockholders' Equity
13. Return on assets	L. Dividends per Share ÷ Market Price per Share
14. Quick ratio	M. Market Price per Share ÷ Earnings per Share
15. Times interest earned ratio	N. Net Income ÷ Average Total Assets
16. Cash coverage ratio	O. Cash Flows from Operating Activities ÷ Interest Paid
17. Fixed asset turnover	P. Net Sales Revenue ÷ Average Net Fixed Assets
	Q. (Net Income + Interest Expense + Income Tax Expense) ÷ Interest Expense

Computing Turnover Ratios

E13-7
LO13-3, 13-5

Procter & Gamble is a multinational corporation that manufactures and markets many household products. Last year, sales for the company were $83,062 (all amounts in millions). The annual report did not disclose the amount of credit sales, so we will assume that 90 percent of sales were on credit. The average gross profit on sales was 49 percent. Additional account balances were:

	Ending	Beginning
Accounts receivable (net)	$6,386	$6,508
Inventory	6,759	6,909

Required:
Compute Procter & Gamble's receivable turnover ratio and its inventory turnover ratio. On average, how many days does it take for the company to collect its accounts receivable and sell its inventory?

Computing Turnover Ratios

E13-8
LO13-3, 13-5

Sales for the year for Victor Company were $1,000,000, 70 percent of which were on credit. The average gross profit on sales was 40 percent. Additional account balances were:

	Ending	Beginning
Accounts receivable (net)	$60,000	$45,000
Inventory	25,000	70,000

Required:
Compute the turnover for the accounts receivable and inventory, the average days to collect receivables, and the average days to sell inventory.

Analyzing the Impact of Selected Transactions on the Current Ratio

E13-9
LO13-6

Assume current assets totaled $120,000 and the current ratio was 1.5 before the following independent transactions:

(1) Purchased merchandise for $40,000 on short-term credit.
(2) Purchased a delivery truck for $25,000. Paid $3,000 cash and signed a two-year interest-bearing note for the balance.

Required:
Compute the current ratio after each transaction.

Analyzing the Impact of Selected Transactions on the Current Ratio

E13-10
LO13-6

The Bombay Company, Inc., sold a line of home furnishings that included furniture, wall decor, and decorative accessories. Bombay operated through a network of retail locations throughout the United States and Canada, as well as through its direct-to-customer operations and international licensing arrangements. The company was forced to file for bankruptcy. In its last financial statement prior to bankruptcy, Bombay reported current assets of $161,604,000 and current liabilities of $113,909,000.

Required:
Determine the impact of the following independent transactions on the current ratio for Bombay:

1. Sold long-term assets for cash.
2. Accrued severance pay and benefits for employees who were terminated.
3. Wrote down the carrying value of certain inventory items that were deemed to be obsolete.
4. Acquired new inventory; supplier was not willing to provide normal credit terms, so an 18-month interest-bearing note was signed.

Inferring Financial Information from Ratios

E13-11
LO13-3, 13-5

Dollar General Corporation operates general merchandise stores that feature quality merchandise at low prices. All stores are located in the United States, predominantly in small towns in 24 midwestern and southeastern states. In the current year, the company reported average inventories of $1,668 million and an inventory turnover ratio of 8.0. Average total fixed assets were $2,098 million, and the fixed asset turnover ratio was 9.0. What amount did Dollar General report as gross profit in the current year?

E13-12

LO13-5, 13-6, 13-7

Computing Liquidity and Solvency Ratios

Cintas designs and manufactures uniforms for corporations throughout the United States and Canada. The company's stock is traded on the NASDAQ. Selected information from the company's financial statements follows.

CINTAS (in millions)		
	Current Year	**Last Year**
Select Income Statement Information		
Net revenue	$4,552	$4,316
Cost of goods sold	2,637	2,529
Selling, general, and administrative expenses	1,303	1,222
Interest expense	72	70
Income tax expense	233	184
Net income	374	315
Select Statement of Cash Flows Information		
Cash paid for interest	65	69
Cash flows from operating activities	608	553
Select Balance Sheet Information		
Cash and equivalents	513	352
Marketable securities	—	6
Accounts receivable	508	505
Inventories	251	240
Prepaid expense and other current assets	26	25
Accounts payable	150	121
Current accrued expenses	377	342
Current portion of long-term debt	1	8
Other current liabilities	102	85
Long-term debt	1,300	1,301

Required:
Compute the following ratios:

- Receivable turnover ratio (assume that all sales were credit sales)
- Inventory turnover ratio
- Current ratio
- Cash ratio
- Times interest earned ratio
- Cash coverage ratio

E13-13

LO13-8

Inferring Financial Information Using Market Ratios

Wakon Company earned $3.25 per share and paid dividends of $0.75 per share. The company reported a dividend yield of 3 percent. What was the price of Wakon's stock?

Analyzing Ratios (AP13-1)

Company X and Company Y are two giants of the retail industry. Both offer full lines of moderately priced merchandise. In the last fiscal year, annual sales for Company X totaled $53 billion and annual sales for Company Y totaled $20 billion. Compare the two companies as a potential investment based on the following ratios:

Ratios for Current Year	Company X	Company Y
P/E	11.0	12.9
Gross profit margin	28.6	39.3
Profit margin	2.8	5.7
Current ratio	2.0	1.4
Cash coverage ratio	0.7	2.2
Debt-to-equity	1.4	2.0
Return on equity	12.0	27.8
Return on assets	5.2	9.3
Dividend yield	Not applicable	1.4
Earnings per share	$5.17	$5.20

P13-1
LO13-1, 13-2, 13-3, 13-4, 13-6, 13-7, 13-8

Analyzing an Investment by Comparing Selected Ratios (AP13-2)

You have the opportunity to invest $10,000 in one of two companies from a single industry. The only information you have is below. Which company would you select? Justify your choice.

Ratios for Current Year	Company A	Company B	Industry Average
Current	1.30	1.00	1.20
Quick	0.80	0.75	0.80
Debt-to-equity	0.90	3.45	1.10
Inventory turnover	18.20	12.00	12.20
Price/earnings	22.01	19.20	21.25
Dividend yield	1.84	1.02	1.04

P13-2
LO13-2, 13-5, 13-6, 13-7, 13-8

Calculating Profitability, Turnover, Liquidity, and Solvency Ratios (AP13-3)

Using the financial information presented in Exhibit 13.1, calculate the following ratios for **The Home Depot**:

- Return on equity
- Return on assets
- Total asset turnover
- Inventory turnover
- Current ratio
- Quick ratio
- Cash coverage ratio
- Debt-to-equity ratio

P13-3
LO13-4, 13-5, 13-6, 13-7

P13-4
LO13-3, 13-4, 13-5, 13-6, 13-7

Computing Ratios and Comparing Alternative Investment Opportunities (AP13-4)

The current year financial statements for Blue Water Company and Prime Fish Company are presented below.

	Blue Water	Prime Fish
Balance Sheet		
Cash	$ 41,000	$ 21,000
Accounts receivable (net)	38,000	31,000
Inventory	99,000	40,000
Property & equipment (net)	140,000	401,000
Other assets	84,000	305,000
Total assets	$ 402,000	$ 798,000
Current liabilities	$ 99,000	$ 49,000
Long-term debt (interest rate: 10%)	65,000	60,000
Capital stock ($10 par value)	148,000	512,000
Additional paid-in capital	29,000	106,000
Retained earnings	61,000	71,000
Total liabilities and stockholders' equity	$ 402,000	$ 798,000
Income Statement		
Sales revenue (1/3 on credit)	$ 447,000	$ 802,000
Cost of goods sold	(241,000)	(400,000)
Operating expenses	(161,000)	(311,000)
Net income	$ 45,000	$ 91,000
Other data		
Per share stock price at end of current year	$ 22	$ 15
Average income tax rate	30%	30%
Dividends declared and paid in current year	$ 33,000	$ 148,000

Both companies are in the fish catching and manufacturing business. Both have been in business approximately 10 years, and each has had steady growth. The management of each has a different viewpoint in many respects. Blue Water is more conservative, and as its president has said, "We avoid what we consider to be undue risk." Neither company is publicly held.

Required:
1. Compute as many ratios from Exhibit 13.3 as possible. You will not be able to compute all ratios. You will need to use year-end balances (not averages) for all ratios.
2. Based on the ratios you computed, which company is more efficient at collecting its accounts receivables and turning over its inventory?

P13-5   **Computing Differences and Comparing Financial Statements Using Percentages (AP13-5)**
LO13-3, 13-6

The comparative financial statements for Prince Company are below:

	Year 2	Year 1
Income Statement		
Sales revenue	$190,000	$167,000
Cost of goods sold	112,000	100,000
Gross profit	78,000	67,000
Operating expenses and interest expense	56,000	53,000
Pretax income	22,000	14,000
Income tax	8,000	4,000
Net income	$ 14,000	$ 10,000

	Year 2	Year 1
Balance Sheet		
Cash	$ 4,000	$ 7,000
Accounts receivable (net)	14,000	18,000
Inventory	40,000	34,000
Property and equipment (net)	45,000	38,000
Total assets	$103,000	$97,000
Current liabilities (no interest)	$ 16,000	$17,000
Long-term liabilities (Interest rate: 10%)	45,000	45,000
Common stock ($5 par value, 6,000 shares outstanding)	30,000	30,000
Retained earnings	12,000	5,000
Total liabilities and stockholders' equity	$103,000	$97,000

Required:
1. Complete the following columns for each item in the preceding comparative financial statements:

INCREASE (DECREASE) from Year 1 to Year 2

Amount	Percent

2. By what amount did the current ratio change from Year 1 to Year 2?

Computing Comparative Financial Statements and DuPont Ratios (AP13-6)

P13-6
LO13-3, 13-4, 13-5

Use the data given in P13-5 for Prince Company.

Required:
1. Compute component percentages for Year 2.
2. Compute the ratios in the DuPont model for Year 2.

Analyzing Financial Statements Using Ratios

P13-7
LO13-4, 13-6, 13-8

Use the data in P13-5 for Prince Company. Assume that the stock price per share is $28 and that dividends in the amount of $3.50 per share were paid during Year 2. Compute the following ratios:

- Earnings per share
- Current ratio
- Quick ratio
- Cash ratio
- Price/earnings ratio
- Dividend yield ratio

Analyzing the Impact of Alternative Inventory Methods on Selected Ratios

P13-8
LO13-4, 13-5, 13-6, 13-7

Company A uses the FIFO method to account for inventory and Company B uses the LIFO method. The two companies are exactly alike except for the difference in inventory cost flow assumptions. Costs of inventory items for both companies have been rising steadily in recent years, and each company has increased its inventory each year. Ignore tax effects.

Required:
Identify which company will report the higher amount for each of the following ratios. If it is not possible to determine, explain why.

1. Net profit margin
2. Earnings per share

3. Inventory turnover
4. Current ratio
5. Quick ratio
6. Debt-to-equity ratio

P13-9

LO13-4, 13-5, 13-6, 13-7

Computing and Analyzing Ratios

California Pizza Kitchen opened its first restaurant in Beverly Hills in 1985. Almost immediately after the first location opened, it expanded from California to more than 250 locations in more than 30 states and 11 countries. California Pizza Kitchen completed an initial public offering in August 2000. Several years ago, Golden Gate Capital completed the acquisition of California Pizza Kitchen and, as a result of the acquisition, the company's common stock is no longer publicly traded.

Required:

1. Compute the following ratios for Year 3 using information from the company annual report that was issued before California Pizza Kitchen was acquired.
   a. Return on equity
   b. Net profit margin
   c. Inventory turnover
   d. Current ratio
   e. Quick ratio
   f. Debt-to-equity ratio
   g. Price/earnings ratio (assume a market price per share of $1.12)

2. Does California Pizza Kitchen's inventory turnover ratio seem reasonable to you?

CALIFORNIA PIZZA KITCHEN, INC., AND SUBSIDIARIES			
Consolidated Statements of Operations			
(amounts in thousands, except for per share data)			
	Year 3	**Year 2**	**Year 1**
Revenues:			
Restaurant sales	$630,606	$652,185	$665,616
Royalties from licensing agreement	6,122	7,739	6,580
Domestic franchise revenues	3,100	2,684	2,757
International franchise revenues	2,403	2,078	2,121
Total revenues	642,231	664,686	677,074
Costs and expenses:			
Food, beverage, and paper supplies	148,732	154,181	165,526
Labor	237,133	247,350	247,276
Direct operating and occupancy	142,420	141,973	140,367
Cost of sales	528,285	543,504	553,169
General and administrative	50,731	50,791	51,642
Depreciation and amortization	37,006	40,181	40,299
Pre-opening costs	3,269	1,843	4,478
Loss on impairment of property and equipment	18,702	22,941	13,336
Store closure costs	1,708	539	1,033
Litigation, settlement, and other costs	8,759	1,609	736
Total costs and expenses	648,460	661,408	664,693
Operating (loss)/income	(6,229)	3,278	12,381
Interest expense, net	(16)	(788)	(1,324)
(Loss)/income before income tax (benefit)/ provision	(6,245)	2,490	11,057
Income tax (benefit)/provision	(5,839)	(2,091)	2,395
Net (loss)/income	$ (406)	$ 4,581	$ 8,662

	Year 3	Year 2	Year 1
Net (loss)/income per common share:			
Basic	$ (0.02)	$ 0.19	$ 0.34
Diluted	$ (0.02)	$ 0.19	$ 0.34
Weighted average shares used in calculating net (loss)/income per common share:			
Basic	24,488	24,064	25,193
Diluted	24,488	24,143	25,211

CALIFORNIA PIZZA KITCHEN, INC., AND SUBSIDIARIES
Consolidated Balance Sheets
(in thousands, except for share data)

	Year 3	Year 2
Assets		
Current assets:		
Cash and cash equivalents	$ 21,230	$ 21,424
Other receivables	11,594	12,541
Inventories	5,827	5,557
Current deferred tax asset, net	8,225	7,076
Prepaid rent	231	4,957
Other prepaid expenses	2,518	2,031
Total current assets	49,625	53,586
Property and equipment, net	241,446	255,416
Noncurrent deferred tax asset, net	22,101	25,011
Goodwill	4,622	4,622
Other intangibles, net	4,837	4,714
Other assets	8,313	6,909
Total assets	$330,944	$350,258
Liabilities and Stockholders' Equity		
Current liabilities:		
Accounts payable	$ 17,075	$ 11,263
Accrued compensation and benefits	23,273	23,201
Accrued rent	20,424	19,287
Deferred rent credits	4,058	3,745
Other accrued liabilities	13,690	10,915
Gift card liability	14,577	20,640
Store closure reserve	54	326
Total current liabilities	93,151	89,377
Long-term debt	—	22,300
Other liabilities	9,886	7,728
Deferred rent credits, net of current portion	33,177	32,478
Income taxes payable, net of current portion	319	9,125
Commitments and contingencies		
Stockholders' equity:		
Common stock—$0.01 par value, 80,000,000 shares authorized, 24,579,797 and 24,195,800 shares issued and outstanding at the end of Year 3 and Year 2, respectively	246	242
Additional paid-in capital	179,563	174,000
Retained earnings	14,602	15,008
Total stockholders' equity	194,411	189,250
Total liabilities and stockholders' equity	$330,944	$350,258

P13-10

LO13-8

Identifying Companies Based on the Price/Earnings Ratio

The price/earnings ratio provides important information concerning the stock market's assessment of the growth potential of a business. The following are price/earnings ratios for selected companies. Match the company with its ratio and explain how you made your selections. If you are not familiar with a company, you should visit its website.

Company	Price/Earnings Ratio
1. **American Airlines**	A. 77
2. **Facebook**	B. 29
3. **Starbucks**	C. 10
4. **Yahoo**	D. 1
5. **Patriot Coal**	E. 5

ALTERNATE **PROBLEMS**

AP13-1

LO13-1, 13-2, 13-3, 13-4, 13-6, 13-7, 13-8

Analyzing Ratios (P13-1)

Coke and Pepsi are well-known international brands. **Coca-Cola** sells more than $46 billion worth of products each year while annual sales of **PepsiCo** products exceed $67 billion. Compare the two companies as a potential investment based on the following ratios:

Ratio	Coca-Cola	PepsiCo
P/E	65.0	26.5
Gross profit margin	69.3	58.4
Net profit margin	12.2	8.8
Quick	0.4	0.7
Current	0.6	1.1
Debt-to-equity	0.7	0.4
Return on equity	27.4	29.1
Return on assets	28.0	16.6
Dividend yield	1.0	1.6

AP13-2

LO13-2, 13-5, 13-6, 13-7, 13-8

Analyzing an Investment by Comparing Selected Ratios (P13-2)

You have the opportunity to invest $10,000 in one of two companies from a single industry. The only information you have is below. Which company would you select? Justify your choice.

Ratios for Current Year	Company A	Company B	Industry Average
Current	1.00	1.02	1.20
Quick	0.80	0.79	0.95
Debt-to-equity	1.25	1.34	0.70
Inventory turnover	8.20	14.00	18.20
Price/earnings	4.01	9.20	21.25
Dividend yield	1.74	2.24	6.04

Calculating Profitability, Turnover, Liquidity, Solvency, and Market Ratios (P13-3)

AP13-3

LO13-4, 13-5, 13-6, 13-7, 13-8

Using the financial information presented in Exhibit 13.1, calculate the following ratios for **The Home Depot**:

- Net profit margin
- Earnings quality
- Receivable turnover
- Cash ratio
- Times interest earned
- Price/earnings ratio (assume a market price per share of $100)

Computing and Interpreting Ratios (P13-4)

AP13-4

LO13-5, 13-6, 13-7

Tabor Company has just prepared the following comparative annual financial statements for the current year:

TABOR COMPANY Comparative Income Statement For the Years Ended December 31		
	Current Year	**Last Year**
Sales revenue (one-half on credit)	$110,000	$99,000
Cost of goods sold	52,000	48,000
Gross profit	$ 58,000	$51,000
Expenses (including $4,000 interest expense each year)	40,000	37,000
Pretax income	$ 18,000	$14,000
Income tax expense (30%)	5,400	4,200
Net income	$ 12,600	$ 9,800

TABOR COMPANY Comparative Balance Sheet At December 31		
	Current Year	**Last Year**
Assets		
Cash	$ 49,500	$ 18,000
Accounts receivable	37,000	32,000
Inventory	25,000	38,000
Property & equipment (net)	95,000	105,000
Total assets	$206,500	$193,000
Liabilities		
Accounts payable	$ 42,000	$ 35,000
Income taxes payable	1,000	500
Note payable, long-term	40,000	40,000
Stockholders' equity		
Capital stock ($5 par value)	90,000	90,000
Retained earnings	33,500	27,500
Total liabilities and stockholders' equity	$206,500	$193,000

Required:

1. For the current year, compute the turnover, liquidity, and solvency ratios in Exhibit 13.3. Assume cash flows from operating activities were $14,600 and cash paid for interest was $3,800.
2. Comment on the turnover ratios. Any concerns?

AP13-5
LO13-3, 13-6

Computing Differences and Comparing Financial Statements Using Percentages (P13-5)

The comparative financial statements for Summer Corporation are below:

	Year 2	Year 1
Income Statement		
Sales revenue	$453,000	$447,000
Cost of goods sold	250,000	241,000
Gross profit	203,000	206,000
Operating expenses (including interest on bonds)	167,000	168,000
Pretax income	36,000	38,000
Income tax	10,800	11,400
Net income	$ 25,200	$ 26,600
Balance Sheet		
Cash	$ 6,800	$ 3,900
Accounts receivable (net)	42,000	29,000
Merchandise inventory	25,000	18,000
Prepaid expenses	200	100
Property and equipment (net)	130,000	120,000
	$204,000	$171,000
Accounts payable	$ 17,000	$ 18,000
Income taxes payable	1,000	1,000
Bonds payable (Interest rate: 10%)	70,000	50,000
Common stock ($10 par value)	100,000	100,000
Retained earnings	16,000	2,000
	$204,000	$171,000

Required:

1. Complete the following columns for each item in the preceding comparative financial statements:

INCREASE (DECREASE) from Year 1 to Year 2	
Amount	Percent

2. By what amount did the current ratio change from Year 1 to Year 2?

AP13-6
LO13-3, 13-4, 13-5

Computing Comparative Financial Statements and DuPont Ratios (P13-6)

Use the data given in AP13-5 for Summer Corporation.

Required:

1. Compute component percentages for Year 2.
2. Compute the ratios in the DuPont model for Year 2.

Computing Ratios

CON13-1

Pool Corporation, Inc., is the world's largest wholesale distributor of swimming pool supplies and equipment. It is a publicly traded corporation that trades on the NASDAQ exchange under the symbol POOL. The majority of Pool's customers are small, family-owned businesses.

Required:
1. Using the SEC EDGAR service at **www.sec.gov**, download the current annual report for Pool Corporation.
2. Compute the following ratios:
   a. Return on assets
   b. Net profit margin
   c. Inventory turnover ratio
   d. Current ratio
   e. Cash coverage ratio
   f. Debt-to-equity ratio
   g. Price/earnings ratio (**Hint:** You will need to go to another source, such as Google Finance, to get the market price per share.)

Annual Report Cases

Computing Ratios

CP13-1
LO13-4, 13-5, 13-6, 13-7, 13-8

Refer to the financial statements of **American Eagle Outfitters** given in Appendix B at the end of this book. Compute the following ratios for fiscal 2014: return on equity, basic earnings per share, net profit margin, inventory turnover, current ratio, debt-to-equity ratio, price/earnings ratio, and dividend yield. Assume the stock price is $16.

Computing Ratios

CP13-2
LO13-4, 13-5, 13-6, 13-7, 13-8

Refer to the financial statements of **Urban Outfitters** given in Appendix C at the end of this book. Compute the following ratios for fiscal 2014: return on equity, basic earnings per share, net profit margin, inventory turnover, current ratio, debt-to-equity ratio, price/earnings ratio, and dividend yield. Assume the stock price is $40.

Comparing Companies within an Industry

CP13-3
LO13-2, 13-4, 13-5, 13-6, 13-7, 13-8

Refer to the financial statements of **American Eagle** (Appendix B) and **Urban Outfitters** (Appendix C) and the Industry Ratio Report (Appendix D) at the end of this book. Compute the following ratios for fiscal 2014: return on equity, basic earnings per share, net profit margin, inventory turnover, current ratio, debt-to-equity ratio, price/earnings ratio, and dividend yield. Assume the stock price is $40 for Urban Outfitters and $16 for American Eagle. Compare the ratios for each company to the industry average ratios.

Financial Reporting and Analysis Cases

CP13-4
LO13-1, 13-5

Interpreting Financial Results Based on Corporate Strategy

In this chapter, we discussed the importance of analyzing financial results based on an understanding of the company's business strategy. Using the DuPont model, we illustrated how different strategies could earn high returns for investors. Assume that two companies in the same industry adopt fundamentally different strategies. One manufactures high-end consumer electronics. Its products employ state-of-the-art technology, and the company offers a high level of customer service both before and after the sale. The other company emphasizes low cost with good performance. Its products utilize well-established technology but are never innovative. Customers buy these products at large, self-service warehouses and are expected to install the products using information contained in printed brochures. Which of the DuPont model ratios would you expect to differ for these companies as a result of their different business strategies?

CP13-5
LO13-5

Inferring Information from the DuPont Model Ratios

In this chapter, we discussed the DuPont model. Using that framework, find the missing amount in each of the following cases:

Case 1: ROE is 10 percent; net income is $200,000; the total asset turnover ratio is 5; and net sales are $1,000,000. What is the amount of average stockholders' equity?

Case 2: Net income is $1,500,000; net sales are $8,000,000; average stockholders' equity is $12,000,000; ROE is 22 percent; and the total asset turnover ratio is 8. What is the amount of average total assets?

Case 3: ROE is 15 percent; the net profit margin is 10 percent; the total asset turnover ratio is 5; and average total assets are $1,000,000. What is the amount of average stockholders' equity?

Case 4: Net income is $500,000; ROE is 15 percent; the total asset turnover ratio is 5; net sales are $1,000,000; and financial leverage is 2. What is the amount of average total assets?

Critical Thinking Case

CP13-6
LO13-5

Evaluating an Ethical Dilemma

Barton Company requested a large loan from First Federal Bank to acquire a tract of land for future expansion. Barton reported current assets of $1,900,000 ($430,000 in cash) and current liabilities of $1,075,000. First Federal denied the loan request for a number of reasons, including the fact that the current ratio was below 2:1. When Barton was informed of the loan denial, the controller of the company immediately paid $420,000 that was owed to several trade creditors. The controller then asked First Federal to reconsider the loan application. Based on these abbreviated facts, would you recommend that First Federal approve the loan request? Why? Are the controller's actions ethical?

Financial Reporting and Analysis Team Project

CP13-7
**LO13-3, 13-4, 13-5,
13-6, 13-7**

Team Project: Examining an Annual Report

As a team, select an industry to analyze. Both Yahoo Finance and Google Finance provide information on any given firm's industry. Each team member should acquire the annual report or 10-K for one publicly traded company in the industry, with each member selecting a different company. The annual reports or 10-Ks can be downloaded from the SEC EDGAR website (**www.sec.gov**) or from any individual company's investor relations website.

Required:

Each team member should individually gather the information described below and attempt to answer each question. After completing this individual phase of the project, teams should get together to compare and contrast their answers to each question. At the conclusion of this discussion, each team should write a short report summarizing their analysis and findings.

Compute and interpret each of the ratios in Exhibit 13.3. Most of the information you need will be in the financial statements, though some may come from the footnotes or management's discussion and analysis section.

Reporting and Interpreting Investments in Other Corporations

In 2013, **Amazon.com** founder Jeffrey Bezos purchased for $250 million *The Washington Post* and some other assets owned by **The Washington Post Company**, ending 80 years of control of the newspaper by the Graham family. The remaining assets of the Washington Post Company adopted **Graham Holdings Company** as its new name to expand the Graham Holdings Company investments. The best known of these is **Kaplan, Inc**., the king of admissions test preparation and other services that helped or will help you prepare for the SAT, GMAT, LSAT, Certified Public Accountant, or Chartered Financial Analyst exams. In addition to test preparation, Kaplan offers K–12 services for children and post-secondary education and professional training at Kaplan Higher Education. As a diversified company, Graham Holdings also owns media operations in television broadcasting and *Slate, The Root,* and *Foreign Policy* magazines; **SocialCode**, a marketing technology and solutions company for firms such as Facebook, Twitter, Pinterest, and Instagram; and a variety of other smaller operations ranging from home health care services to industrial products manufacturing.

The company has achieved its diversity by investing in the stock of other companies and acquiring other businesses. In 2014, it acquired nine businesses for $210 million and spent over $49.9 million to invest in other companies. As its long-term investment strategy, Graham Holdings analyzes the earnings potential and strength of the management teams of businesses it is interested in acquiring. The result is a diverse group of businesses, but with common goals and values. Each acquired business retains its own identity, workplace culture, and management team responsible for its operations.*

Learning Objectives

After studying this material, you should be able to:

A-1 Analyze and report investments in debt securities held to maturity.

A-2 Analyze and report passive investments in securities using the fair value method.

A-3 Analyze and report investments involving significant influence using the equity method.

A-4 Analyze and report investments in controlling interests.

Based upon information from Graham Holdings Company, "Investor Relations," July 3, 2014.

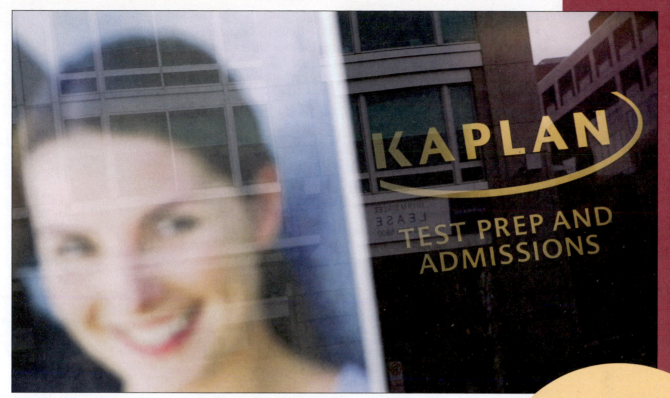

Kristoffer Tripplaar/Alamy

FOCUS COMPANY:

Graham Holdings Company

INVESTMENT STRATEGIES IN A DIVERSIFIED COMPANY

www.ghco.com

UNDERSTANDING THE BUSINESS

Many strategic factors motivate managers to invest in securities. A company that has extra cash and simply wants to earn a return on the idle funds can invest those funds in the stocks and bonds of other companies, either long or short term. We say these investments are *passive* because the managers are not interested in influencing or controlling the other companies. **Graham Holdings**'s 2014 and 2013 comparative balance sheets, shown in Exhibit A.1, include the short-term account "Investments in Available-for-Sale Securities."

Sometimes a company decides to invest in another company with the purpose of influencing that company's policies and activities. Graham Holdings's balance sheet reports these types of investments as "Investments in Affiliates." Finally, managers may determine that controlling another company, by either purchasing it directly or becoming the majority shareholder, is desirable. If the acquired company goes out of existence, its assets and liabilities are added at fair value to the assets and liabilities of the buyer. If the acquired company continues as a separate legal entity, the two companies' financial reports are combined into consolidated financial statements, as Graham Holdings has done (see the title to its **consolidated** balance sheet).

In this appendix, we discuss the accounting for four types of investments. First, we discuss using the amortized cost method to account for passive investments in bonds. Second, we examine the fair value method of accounting for passive investments. Third, we present the equity method used to account for stock investments involving significant influence. The appendix closes with a discussion of accounting for mergers and consolidated statements.

EXHIBIT A.1

Graham Holdings Company
Consolidated Balance Sheet
(Condensed)

GRAHAM HOLDINGS COMPANY
Consolidated Balance Sheets (condensed)

(in millions)	As of December 31, 2014	As of December 31, 2013
Assets		
Current assets		
Cash and other current assets	$1,464	$1,180
Investments in available-for-sale securities	227	522
Total current assets	1,691	1,702
Property, plant, and equipment, net and other noncurrent assets	2,070	2,224
Investments in affiliates	20	16
Goodwill and other intangible assets, net	1,971	1,869
Total assets	$5,752	$5,811
Liabilities and Equity		
Total liabilities and redeemable preferred stock	$2,611	$2,511
Common stockholders' equity:		
Common stock and capital in excess of par value	324	308
Retained earnings	6,009	4,783
Accumulated other comprehensive income, net of taxes		
Net unrealized gains (losses) on available-for-sale securities	52	174
Other	402	526
Treasury stock	(3,646)	(2,491)
Total common stockholders' equity	3,141	3,300
Total liabilities and equity	$5,752	$5,811

ORGANIZATION of the Appendix

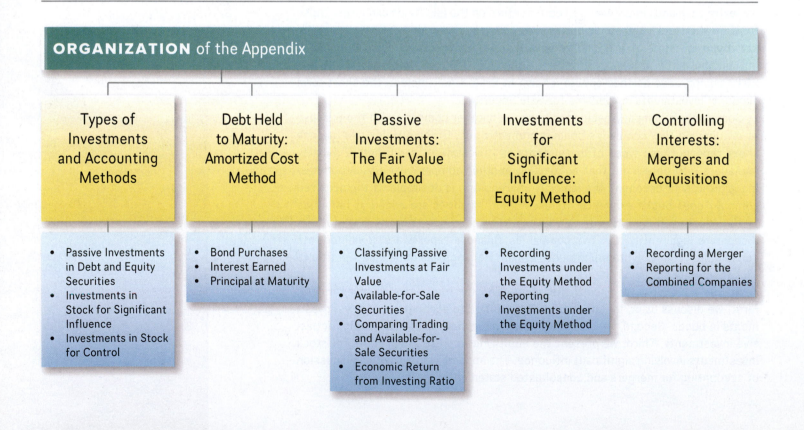

Types of Investments and Accounting Methods	Debt Held to Maturity: Amortized Cost Method	Passive Investments: The Fair Value Method	Investments for Significant Influence: Equity Method	Controlling Interests: Mergers and Acquisitions
• Passive Investments in Debt and Equity Securities • Investments in Stock for Significant Influence • Investments in Stock for Control	• Bond Purchases • Interest Earned • Principal at Maturity	• Classifying Passive Investments at Fair Value • Available-for-Sale Securities • Comparing Trading and Available-for-Sale Securities • Economic Return from Investing Ratio	• Recording Investments under the Equity Method • Reporting Investments under the Equity Method	• Recording a Merger • Reporting for the Combined Companies

TYPES OF INVESTMENTS AND ACCOUNTING METHODS

The accounting methods used to record investments are directly related to how much is owned and how long management intends to hold the investments. The investment categories and the appropriate measuring and reporting methods are summarized as follows.

Passive Investments in Debt and Equity Securities

Passive investments are made to earn a return on funds that may be needed for future short-term or long-term purposes. This category includes both investments in debt (bonds and notes) and equity securities (stock). Debt securities are always considered passive investments. If the company intends to hold the securities until they reach maturity, the investments are measured and reported at amortized cost. If they are to be sold before maturity, they are reported using the fair value method.

For investments in equity securities, the investment is presumed passive if the investing company owns less than 20 percent of the outstanding voting shares of the other company. The fair value method is used to measure and report the investments.

Investments in Stock for Significant Influence

Significant influence is the ability to have an important impact on the operating, investing, and financing policies of another company. Significant influence is presumed if the investing company owns from 20 to 50 percent of the outstanding voting shares of the other company. However, other factors may also indicate that significant influence exists, such as membership on the board of directors of the other company, participation in the policy-making processes, evidence of material transactions between the two companies, an interchange of management personnel, or technological dependency. The equity method is used to measure and report this category of investments.

Investments in Stock for Control

Control is the ability to determine the operating and financing policies of another company through ownership of voting stock. Control is presumed when the investing company owns more than 50 percent of the outstanding voting stock of the other company. Acquisition accounting and consolidation are applied to combine the companies.

Investment Category	Investment in Debt Securities of Another Entity		Investment in the Voting Common Stock of Another Entity		
	Passive		**Passive**	**Significant Influence**	**Control**
Level of Ownership	Held to maturity	Not held to maturity	<20% of outstanding shares	20–50% of outstanding shares	>50% of outstanding shares
Measuring and Reporting Method	Amortized cost method	Fair value method		Equity method	Acquisition accounting and consolidation

LEARNING OBJECTIVE A-1
Analyze and report investments in debt securities held to maturity.

HELD-TO-MATURITY INVESTMENTS
Investments in debt securities that management has the ability and intent to hold until maturity.

AMORTIZED COST METHOD
Reports investments in debt securities held to maturity at cost minus any premium or plus any discount.

DEBT HELD TO MATURITY: AMORTIZED COST METHOD

When management plans to hold a debt security (such as a bond or note) until its maturity date (when the principal is due), it is reported in an account appropriately called **held-to-maturity investments**. Debt securities should be classified as held-to-maturity investments if management has the intent and the ability to hold them until maturity. These investments in debt instruments are listed at cost adjusted for the amortization of any discount or premium (**amortized cost method**), not at their fair value. We now illustrate accounting for investments in bonds issued by another company.

Bond Purchases

On the date of purchase, a bond may be acquired at the maturity amount (at **par**), for less than the maturity amount (at a **discount**), or for more than the maturity amount (at a **premium**).[1] The total cost of the bond, including all incidental acquisition costs such as transfer fees and broker commissions, is debited to the Held-to-Maturity Investments account.

To illustrate accounting for bond investments, assume that on July 1, 2016, **Graham Holdings** paid the par value of $100,000 for 8 percent bonds that mature on June 30, 2021.[2] Interest at 8 percent is paid each June 30 and December 31. Management plans to hold the bonds for five years, until maturity.

The journal entry to record the purchase of the bonds follows:

Held-to-Maturity Investments (+A).............................	100,000	
Cash (−A)		100,000

Assets		=	Liabilities	+	Stockholders' Equity
Held-to-Maturity Investments	+100,000				
Cash	−100,000				

Interest Earned

The bonds in this illustration were purchased at par or face value. Since no premium or discount needs to be amortized, the book value remains constant over the life of the investment. In this situation, revenue earned from the investment each period is measured as the amount of interest collected in cash or accrued at year-end. The following journal entry records the receipt of interest on December 31:

Cash (+A) [$100,000 × 0.08 × 6/12]	4,000	
Interest Revenue (+R, +SE)		4,000

Assets		=	Liabilities	+	Stockholders' Equity	
Cash	+4,000				Interest Revenue (+R)	+4,000

The same entry is made on succeeding interest payment dates.

Principal at Maturity

When the bonds mature on June 30, 2021, the journal entry to record receipt of the principal payment would be:

---

[1] The determination of the price of the bond is based on the present value techniques discussed in Chapter 9. Many analysts refer to a bond price as a **percentage of par.** For example, *The Wall Street Journal* might report that an ExxonMobil bond with a par value of $1,000 is selling at 82.97. This means it would cost $829.70 (82.97 percent of $1,000) to buy the bond.

[2] When bond investors accept a rate of interest on a bond investment that is the same as the stated rate of interest on the bonds, the bonds will sell at par (i.e., at 100 or 100% of face value). For illustration of the journal entries of a bond purchased at other than par value, see Supplement A at the end of this appendix.

| Cash (+A) .... | 100,000 | |
| Held-to-Maturity Investments (−A) .... | | 100,000 |

Assets	=	Liabilities	+	Stockholders' Equity
Cash +100,000				
Held-to-Maturity Investments −100,000				

If the bond investment must be sold before maturity, any difference between market value (the proceeds from the sale) and net book value would be reported as a gain or loss on sale. If management **intends** to sell the bonds before the maturity date, they are treated in the same manner as investments in stock classified as available-for-sale securities, which we discuss in the next section.

PASSIVE INVESTMENTS: THE FAIR VALUE METHOD

When the investing company owns debt securities or less than 20 percent of the outstanding voting stock of another company, the investment is considered passive. Among the assets and liabilities on the balance sheet, only passive investments in marketable securities (other than debt held to maturity) are **required** to be reported using the **fair value method** on the date of the balance sheet. Fair value is a security's current market value (the amount that would be received in an orderly sale). Before we discuss the specific accounting for these investments, we should consider the implications of using fair value:

1. **Why are passive investments reported at fair value on the balance sheet?** Two primary factors determine the answer to this question:

   - **Relevance.** Analysts who study financial statements often attempt to forecast a company's future cash flows. They want to know how a company can generate cash for purposes such as expansion of the business, payment of dividends, or survival during a prolonged economic downturn. One source of cash is the sale of securities from its passive investments portfolio. The best estimate of the cash that could be generated by the sale of these securities is their current fair value.

   - **Measurability.** Accountants record only items that can be measured in dollar terms with a high degree of reliability (an unbiased and verifiable measurement). Determining the fair value of most assets is very difficult because they are not actively traded. For example, **Graham Holdings**'s balance sheet reports its headquarters building in terms of its original cost less accumulated depreciation in part because of the difficulty in determining an objective fair value for it. Contrast the difficulty of determining the value of a building with the ease of determining the value of **Berkshire Hathaway** stock owned by Graham Holdings. A quick look at *The Wall Street Journal* or an Internet financial service is all that is necessary to determine the current price because these securities are traded each day on established stock exchanges.

2. **When the investment account is adjusted to reflect changes in fair value, what other account is affected when the asset account is increased or decreased?** Under the double-entry method of accounting, every journal entry affects at least two accounts. One account is the investment account. The other account affected is for **unrealized holding gains (losses)**

FAIR VALUE METHOD
Reports securities at their current market value (the amount that would be received in an orderly sale).

Studio Works/Alamy

UNREALIZED HOLDING GAINS (LOSSES)
Amounts associated with price changes of securities that are currently held.

that are recorded whenever the fair value of investments changes. These are unrealized because no actual sale has taken place; simply by holding the security, the value has changed. If the value of the investments increases by $100,000 during the year, an adjusting journal entry records the increase in the investment account and an unrealized holding gain for $100,000. If the value of the investments decreases by $75,000 during the year, an adjusting journal entry records the decrease in the investment account and an unrealized holding loss of $75,000. The financial statement treatment of the unrealized holding gains or losses depends on the classification of the passive investments.

Classifying Passive Investments at Fair Value

Depending on management's intent, passive investments at fair value may be classified as trading securities or available-for-sale securities.

Trading Securities

TRADING SECURITIES

All investments in stocks or bonds that are held primarily for the purpose of active trading (buying and selling) in the near future (classified as short term).

Trading securities are actively traded with the objective of generating profits on short-term changes in the price of the securities. This approach is similar to the one taken by many mutual funds. The portfolio manager actively seeks opportunities to buy and sell securities. Trading securities are classified as **current assets** on the balance sheet.

Available-for-Sale Securities

AVAILABLE-FOR-SALE SECURITIES

All passive investments other than trading securities and debt held to maturity (classified as either short term or long term).

Most companies do not actively trade the securities of other companies. Instead, they invest to earn a return on funds they may need for future operating purposes. Other than debt securities to be held to maturity, these debt and equity investments are called **available-for-sale securities**. They are classified as current or noncurrent assets on the balance sheet depending on whether management intends to sell the securities during the next year.

Trading securities (TS for short) are most commonly reported by financial institutions that actively buy and sell short-term investments to maximize returns. Most corporations, however, invest in short- and long-term available-for-sale securities (AFS, for short). We will focus on this category in the next section by analyzing **Graham Holdings**'s investing activities.

Available-for-Sale Securities

Graham Holdings's annual report contains the following information concerning this investment portfolio:

GRAHAM HOLDINGS COMPANY

REAL WORLD EXCERPT:
Annual Report

> **2. Summary of Significant Accounting Policies**
>
> **Investments in Available-for-Sale Securities.** The Company's investments in marketable equity securities are classified as available-for-sale and, therefore, are recorded at fair value in the Consolidated Financial Statements, with the change in fair value during the period excluded from earnings and recorded net of income taxes as a separate component of other comprehensive income. If the fair value of a marketable equity security declines below its cost basis and the decline is considered other than temporary, the Company will record a write-down, which is included in earnings.

For simplification, let's assume that Graham Holdings had no passive investments at the end of 2014. In the following illustration, we will apply the accounting policy used by Graham Holdings for 2015, 2016, and 2017.

Purchase of Securities

At the beginning of 2015, Graham Holdings purchases for cash 15,000 shares of Internet News[3] (INews for short) common stock for $10 per share (a total of $150,000). There were 100,000 outstanding shares, so Graham Holdings owns 15 percent of INews (15,000 shares ÷ 100,000 shares), which is treated as a passive investment. Such investments are recorded initially at cost:

| Investments in AFS Securities (+A).............................. | 150,000 | |
| Cash (−A) .... | | 150,000 |

Assets	=	Liabilities	+	Stockholders' Equity
Investments in AFS Securities	+150,000			
Cash	−150,000			

Dividends Earned

Investments in equity securities earn a return from two sources: (1) dividend income and (2) price increases. Dividends earned are reported as investment income on the income statement and are included in the computation of net income for the period. Graham Holdings received a $1 per share cash dividend from INews totaling $15,000 ($1 × 15,000 shares).

| Cash (+A) .... | 15,000 | |
| Dividend Revenue (+R, +SE)................................. | | 15,000 |

Assets		=	Liabilities	+	Stockholders' Equity	
Cash	+15,000				Dividend Revenue (+R)	+15,000

This entry is the same for both the trading securities and available-for-sale securities. Price increases (or decreases) are analyzed both at year-end and when a security is sold.

Year-End Valuation

At the end of the accounting period, these passive investments are reported on the balance sheet at fair value, the amount that would be received in an orderly sale.

For 2015 Assume that INews had an $8 per share fair value at the end of the year. That is, the investment had lost value ($10 − $8 = $2 per share) for the year. However, because the investment has not been sold, the loss is an unrealized loss, not a realized loss.

Reporting the AFS investment at fair value requires adjusting the asset Investments in AFS Securities **up or down** to fair value at the end of each period.[4] The gain is credited or the loss is debited to the Net Unrealized Gains (Losses) account to complete the entry. For available-for-sale securities, the Net Unrealized Gains (Losses) account is reported in the stockholders' equity section of the balance sheet under **Accumulated Other Comprehensive Income** (denoted as **OCI**). Thus, the balance sheet remains in balance. Only when the security is sold are any realized gains or losses included in net income.

---

[3]Internet News is a fictitious company.

[4]Companies often keep the asset value at cost and record the change in fair value in a related valuation allowance that is added or subtracted from the asset. This does not change the financial statement presentation.

The following chart is used to compute any unrealized gain or loss in the AFS portfolio:

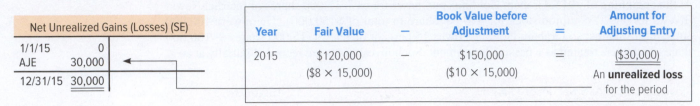

		Net Unrealized Gains (Losses) (SE)
1/1/15	0	
AJE	30,000	
12/31/15	30,000	

Year	Fair Value	—	Book Value before Adjustment	=	Amount for Adjusting Entry
2015	$120,000 ($8 × 15,000)	—	$150,000 ($10 × 15,000)	=	($30,000) An **unrealized loss** for the period

The adjusting entry (AJE) at the end of 2015 is recorded as follows:

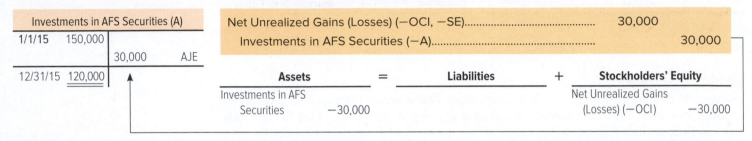

Investments in AFS Securities (A)		
1/1/15	150,000	
		30,000 AJE
12/31/15	120,000	

Net Unrealized Gains (Losses) (−OCI, −SE)... 30,000
Investments in AFS Securities (−A).. 30,000

Assets	=	Liabilities	+	Stockholders' Equity
Investments in AFS Securities −30,000				Net Unrealized Gains (Losses) (−OCI) −30,000

On the 2015 Balance Sheet:

Assets
Investments in AFS
Securities $120,000

Stockholders' Equity
Accumulated Other
Comprehensive Income:
Net unrealized gains
(losses)   (30,000)

On the 2015 balance sheet, Graham Holdings would report an investment in available-for-sale securities of $120,000. It would also report under Accumulated Other Comprehensive Income its net unrealized loss on available-for-sale securities of $30,000. The only item reported on the income statement for 2015 would be investment income of $15,000 from the dividends earned, classified under Other Items.

For 2016 Now let's assume that the INews securities were held through the next year, 2016. At the end of 2016, the stock had an $11 per share fair value. The adjustment for 2016 would be computed as follows:

Net Unrealized Gains (Losses) (SE)		
1/1/15	0	
AJE	30,000	
12/31/15	30,000	
	45,000	AJE
	15,000	12/31/16

Year	Fair Value	—	Book Value before Adjustment	=	Amount for Adjusting Entry
2016	$165,000 ($11 × 15,000)	—	$120,000 ($8 × 15,000)	=	$45,000 An **unrealized gain** for the period

The adjusting entry at the end of 2016 would be:

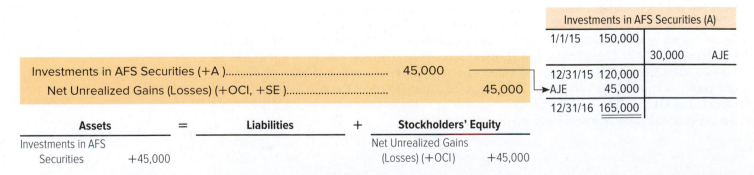

Investments in AFS Securities (+A).. 45,000
Net Unrealized Gains (Losses) (+OCI, +SE)................................. 45,000

Assets	=	Liabilities	+	Stockholders' Equity
Investments in AFS Securities +45,000				Net Unrealized Gains (Losses) (+OCI) +45,000

Investments in AFS Securities (A)		
1/1/15	150,000	
		30,000 AJE
12/31/15	120,000	
AJE	45,000	
12/31/16	165,000	

On the 2016 balance sheet, Graham Holdings would report under Assets an investment in available-for-sale securities of $165,000 and under Accumulated Other Comprehensive Income its net unrealized gain on available-for-sale securities of $15,000 (fair value − cost).

Sale of Securities

When available-for-sale securities are sold, Cash is increased and **two** accounts on the balance sheet are eliminated:

- Investments in AFS Securities (A)
- Net Unrealized Gains (Losses) (OCI, SE)

Let's assume that at the end of 2017 Graham Holdings sold all of its AFS securities investment in INews for $13 per share. The company would receive $195,000 in cash ($13 × 15,000 shares) for stock it paid $150,000 for in 2015 ($10 × 15,000 shares). The gain or loss on sale is computed as follows:

Proceeds from sale − Investment cost = Gain if positive (Loss if negative)

In our example, a gain on sale of $45,000 (proceeds of $195,000 − cost of $150,000) would be recorded and reported on the income statement. The Investment in AFS securities of $165,000 and the credit balance of $15,000 in Net Unrealized Gains (Losses) would be eliminated.

Cash (+A)	195,000	
Net Unrealized Gains (Losses) (−OCI, −SE)	15,000	
Investment in AFS Securities (−A)		165,000
Gain on Sale of Investments (+Gain, +SE)		45,000

Assets		=	Liabilities	+	Stockholders' Equity	
Investments in AFS Securities	−165,000				Net Unrealized Gains (Losses) (−OCI)	−15,000
Cash	+195,000				Gain on Sale of Investment (+Gain)	+45,000

Comparing Trading and Available-for-Sale Securities

The reporting impact of unrealized holding gains or losses depends on whether the investment is classified as an available-for-sale security or a trading security.

Available-for-Sale Portfolio

As we learned in the previous section, for available-for-sale securities, the balance in net unrealized holding gains and losses is reported as a separate **component of stockholders' equity** (under Accumulated Other Comprehensive Income, as illustrated in Exhibit A.1 for Graham Holdings Company).

It is not reported on the income statement and does not affect net income. At the time of sale, the difference between the proceeds from the sale and the **original cost** of the investment is recorded as a gain or loss on sale of available-for-sale securities. At the same time, the Investments in AFS Securities and Net Unrealized Gains (Losses) accounts are eliminated.

Trading Securities Portfolio

For trading securities, the amount of the adjustment to record net unrealized holding gains and losses is **included on each period's income statement.** Net holding gains increase and net holding losses decrease net income. This also means that the amount recorded as net unrealized gains and losses on trading securities is closed to Retained Earnings at the end of the period. Thus, when selling a trading security, Cash and only *one* other balance sheet account are affected: Investments in TS. Also, only the difference between the cash proceeds from the

On the 2016 Balance Sheet:	
Assets	
Investments in AFS	
Securities	$165,000
Stockholders' Equity	
Accumulated Other	
Comprehensive Income:	
Net unrealized gains	
(losses)	15,000

sale and the **book value** (not cost) of the Investments in TS is recorded as a gain or loss on sale of trading securities. In the illustration above, assuming the investment was in trading securities, the realized gain from the sale of the investments in 2017 would be $30,000 ($195,000 proceeds − $165,000 book value). **Note that total income reported for the three years is the same $60,000 for both trading securities and available-for-sale securities. Only the allocation across the three periods differs.**

Exhibit A.2 provides comparative journal entries and financial statement balances for the transactions illustrated for **Graham Holdings** from 2015 to 2017.

EXHIBIT A.2	Comparison of Accounting for Trading Securities and Available-for-Sale Portfolios

PART A: ENTRIES	TRADING SECURITIES		AVAILABLE-FOR-SALE SECURITIES	
2015:				

• Purchase (for $150,000 cash)	Investments in TS (+A) 150,000
	    Cash (−A).....................................
		150,000	Investments in AFS Securities (+A) 150,000
			    Cash (−A) ....
				150,000

• Receipt of dividends ($15,000 cash)	Cash (+A)....................................... 15,000
	    Dividend Revenue (+R, +SE)..................
		15,000	Cash (+A)....................................... 15,000
			    Dividend Revenue (+R, +SE).................
				15,000

• Year-end adjustment to fair value (= $120,000)	Net unrealized loss (+Loss, −SE)................. 30,000
	    Investments in TS (−A)........................
		30,000	Net unrealized gains (losses) (−OCI, −SE)......... 30,000
			    Investments in AFS Securities (−A)............
				30,000

2016:				

• Year-end adjustment to fair value (= $165,000)	Investments in TS (+A) 45,000
	    Net unrealized gain (+Gain, +SE).............
		45,000	Investments in AFS Securities (+A)............... 45,000
			    Net unrealized gains (losses) (+OCI, +SE)......
				45,000

2017:				

• Sale (for $195,000)	*One balance sheet account is eliminated:*
	Cash (+A)....................................... 195,000
	    Investments in TS (−A)........................
	    Gain on sale of investments (+Gain, +SE) ......
		165,000
		30,000
			Two balance sheet accounts are eliminated:
			Cash (+A)....................................... 195,000
			Net unrealized gains (losses) (−OCI, −SE)......... 15,000
			    Investments in AFS Securities (−A)............
			    Gain on sale of investments (+Gain, +SE)......
				165,000
				45,000

PART B: FINANCIAL REPORTING	TRADING SECURITIES				AVAILABLE-FOR-SALE SECURITIES			
• **Balance Sheet:**	**Assets**	**2017**	**2016**	**2015**	**Assets**	**2017**	**2016**	**2015**
	Investments in TS	0	165,000	120,000	Investments in AFS Securities	0	165,000	120,000
					Stockholders' Equity Accumulated other comprehensive income:			
					Net unrealized gains (losses)	0	15,000	(30,000)
• **Income Statement:**		**2017**	**2016**	**2015**		**2017**	**2016**	**2015**
	Dividend revenue	0	0	15,000	Dividend revenue	0	0	15,000
	Gain on sale	30,000	—	—	Gain on sale	45,000	—	—
	Net unrealized gains (losses)		45,000	(30,000)				

Income in	Trading Securities		Available-for-Sale Securities
2015	$15,000	dividend revenue	$15,000 dividend revenue
	(30,000)	unrealized loss	—
2016	45,000	unrealized gain	—
2017	30,000	realized gain	45,000 realized gain
Total	$60,000		$60,000

Reporting the Fair Value of Investments

FINANCIAL ANALYSIS

Accounting standards require that companies disclose the measurements used to determine the fair values of assets on the balance sheet. The fair value of an asset is the amount that would be received in an orderly sale. To measure fair value, the standard recognizes three approaches in order of decreasing reliability:

- Level 1: Quoted prices in active markets for identical assets.

- Level 2: Estimates based on other observable inputs (e.g., prices for similar assets).

- Level 3: Estimates based on unobservable estimates (the company's own estimates of factors that market participants would consider).

Fair value should be determined using the **most** reliable method available (Level 1 if possible). The reporting company must then disclose the amounts determined under each approach in a note to the financial statements. The following is the note provided in the most recent annual report of **Microsoft Corporation**.

Note 6 – Fair Value Measurements

Assets and Liabilities Measured at Fair Value on a Recurring Basis

The following tables present the fair value of our financial instruments that are measured at fair value on a recurring basis:

(in millions)	Level 1	Level 2	Level 3
June 30, 2014			
Assets			
Mutual funds	$ 590	$ 0	$ 0
Commercial paper	0	189	0
Certificates of deposit	0	1,197	0
U.S. government and agency securities	66,288	745	0
Foreign government bonds	139	3,210	0
Mortgage-backed securities	0	1,015	0
Corporate notes and bonds	0	6,863	0
Municipal securities	0	332	0
Common and preferred stock	9,552	1,825	14
Derivatives	5	348	7
Total	$76,574	$15,724	$21

MICROSOFT CORPORATION

REAL WORLD EXCERPT:

Annual Report

Companies also have the option of accounting for other financial assets (such as notes receivable) and financial liabilities (such as bonds payable) at fair value. Thus far, application of this **fair value option** has been limited mostly to banks and other financial institutions.

FINANCIAL ANALYSIS	Proposed Changes to Measuring Certain Investments

As this appendix is being written, the Financial Accounting Standards Board is deliberating on issues raised regarding the measurement of investments in equity securities. The tentative decision is that all investments in **equity** securities, regardless of whether they are classified as current or noncurrent, trading or available-for-sale, should be measured at fair value with subsequent adjustments recognized in net income. The exceptions are for investments meeting the equity method accounting criteria (discussed in the next section) and those without a readily determinable fair value. This is a departure from the current practice of having only adjustments to fair value for trading securities recognized in net income of the current period.

PAUSE FOR **FEEDBACK**

Passive investments other than debt held to maturity are recorded at cost and adjusted to **fair value** at year-end. The resulting unrealized gain or loss is recorded.

- For trading securities, the net unrealized gains and losses are reported in net income.
- For available-for-sale securities, the net unrealized gains and losses are reported as a component of stockholders' equity in other comprehensive income.

Any dividends earned are reported as revenue, and any gains or losses on sales of passive investments are reported on the income statement. To see if you understand passive investments accounting and reporting, answer the following questions.

SELF-STUDY **QUIZ**

In 2016, Rosa Food Corporation acquired 5,000 shares (10%) of the outstanding voting equity shares of another company for $100,000 to be held as long-term available-for-sale securities. At the end of 2016, the fair value of the stock was $22 per share. At the end of 2017, the fair value of the stock was $17 per share. On January 2, 2018, Rosa Food sold the entire investment for $120,000 cash.

1. Record the purchase.	

2. Record the adjusting entry at the end of 2016.
   a. What would be reported on the balance sheet for the investment?
   b. What would be reported on the income statement for the investment?	

3. Record the adjusting entry at the end of 2017.	
4. Record the sale in 2018.	

5. If the investment was held as trading securities,
   a. What would be reported on the balance sheet for the investment at the end of 2016?
   b. What would be reported on the 2016 income statement for the investment?	

After you have completed your answers, check them at the bottom of the next page.

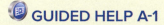 **GUIDED HELP A-1**

For additional step-by-step video instruction on accounting for and reporting available-for-sale securities as investments at fair value, go to **http://www.mhhe.com/libby9e_gha**.

Economic Return from Investing	KEY RATIO ANALYSIS

Both corporate and individual investors need to monitor the performance of their securities portfolios. Normally, this is done using the economic return from investing ratio, which provides a percentage of what was earned plus any realized and/or unrealized gains or losses on the portfolio.

 ANALYTICAL QUESTION

During the period, how much was earned per dollar invested in securities?

 RATIO AND COMPARISONS

$$\text{Economic Return from Investing} = \frac{\text{Dividends and Interest Received} + \text{Change in Fair Value*}}{\text{Fair Value of Investments (beginning of period)}}$$

*Ending balance of Investments − Beginning balance of Investments

The 2015 ratio for our hypothetical investment:

$$\frac{\$15,000 \text{ Dividends} - \$30,000 \text{ Unrealized Loss}}{\$150,000} = -0.10 \ (-10.0\%)$$

The 2016 ratio for our hypothetical investment:

$$\frac{\$0 \text{ Dividends} + \$45,000 \text{ Unrealized Gain}}{\$120,000} = +0.375 \ (+37.5\%)$$

The 2017 ratio for our hypothetical investment:

$$\frac{\$0 \text{ Dividends} - \$15,000 \text{ Unrealized Loss} + \$45,000 \text{ Realized Gain}}{\$165,000} = +0.182 \ (18.2\%)$$

 INTERPRETATIONS

In General   Economic investment returns contain two parts: the effect of dividends received, called the *dividend yield,* and the effect of the change in fair value, called the *capital gain* or *loss.* Note that from an economic standpoint, you have earned the capital gain or loss whether you have sold the securities or not since you had the opportunity to convert the gain or loss into cash by selling. If you look at the numerator of the ratio each year, you will see that it matches the amount of income reported each year under trading securities in Exhibit A.2, Part B. This is why many analysts believe that the accounting for trading securities better reflects the economics of investing.

(*continued*)

Solutions to

SELF-STUDY QUIZ

1.	Investments in AFS securities (+A)	100,000		
	Cash (−A)		100,000	
2.	Investments in AFS securities (+A)	10,000		
	Net unreal. gains (losses) (+OCI, +SE).		10,000	[$110,000 fair value − $100,000 cost = +$10,000]

    a. Under noncurrent assets: Investments in AFS securities $110,000
        Under stockholders' equity
        (other comprehensive income): Net unrealized gain $ 10,000
    b. No dividend revenue or realized gains and losses on sales of investments would be reported on the income statement.

3.	Net unrealized gains (losses) (−OCI, −SE)	25,000		[($17 × 5,000 shares) − $110,000
	Investments in AFS securities (−A)		25,000	book value = −$25,000]
4.	Cash (+A)	120,000		
	Investments in AFS securities (−A)		85,000	
	Net unrealized gains (losses) (+OCI, +SE).		15,000	
	Gain on sale of investments (+Gain, +SE).		20,000	

  5. *a.* Under current assets: Investments in AFS securities $110,000
    b. Under other items: Net unrealized gain $ 10,000
    There were no dividends reported.

Note that the denominator each year is the beginning balance of investments for the year (or the ending balance from the prior year). For 2015, the denominator $150,000 is the balance of the first purchase of 2015, $120,000 is the ending balance of 2015 (and beginning balance for 2016), and $165,000 is the ending balance of 2016 (and beginning balance for 2017).

A Few Cautions   Computations for realistic portfolios are more complex if securities are bought and sold throughout the year. This affects the computation of the denominator of the ratio.

INVESTMENTS FOR SIGNIFICANT INFLUENCE: EQUITY METHOD

LEARNING OBJECTIVE A-3

Analyze and report investments involving significant influence using the equity method.

When **Graham Holdings** invests cash in securities that are reported on its balance sheet as Investments in Available-for-Sale Securities, it is a passive investor. However, when the company reports Investments in Affiliates on its balance sheet, it is taking a more active role as an investor. For a variety of reasons, an investor may want to exert influence (presumed by owning 20 to 50 percent of the outstanding voting stock) without becoming the controlling shareholder (presumed when owning more than 50 percent of the voting stock). Examples follow:

EQUITY METHOD

Used when an investor can exert significant influence over an affiliate; the method permits recording the investor's share of the affiliate's income.

- A retailer may want to influence a manufacturer to be sure that it can obtain certain products designed to its specifications.

- A manufacturer may want to influence a computer consulting firm to ensure that it can incorporate the consulting firm's cutting-edge technology in its manufacturing processes.

- A manufacturer may recognize that a parts supplier lacks experienced management and could prosper with additional managerial support.

INVESTMENTS IN AFFILIATES (OR ASSOCIATED COMPANIES)

Investments in stock held for the purpose of influencing the operating and financing strategies of the entity for the long term.

The **equity method** must be used when an investor can exert significant influence over an affiliate. On the balance sheet these long-term investments are classified as **investments in affiliates (or associated companies)**. Graham Holdings reported investments in affiliates in the notes to its 2014 financial statements.

GRAHAM HOLDINGS COMPANY

REAL WORLD EXCERPT:
Annual Report

2. Summary of Significant Accounting Policies

Investments in Affiliates. The Company uses the equity method of accounting for its investments in and earnings or losses of affiliates that it does not control, but over which it exerts significant influence. . . .

4. Investments

Investments in Affiliates. . . . At December 31, 2014, the Company held a 40% interest in Residential Home Health Illinois, a 42.5% interest in Residential Hospice Illinois and interests in several other affiliates.

Recording Investments under the Equity Method

Under the equity method, the investor's 20 to 50 percent ownership of a company presumes significant influence over the affiliate's process of earning income. As a consequence, the investor reports its portion of the affiliate's net income as its income and increases the investment account by the same amount. Similarly, the receipt of dividends by the investor is treated as a reduction of the investment account, not revenue. A summary follows:

- *Net income of affiliates:* If affiliates report positive results of operations for the year, the investor then records investment income equal to its percentage share of the affiliates' net income and increases its asset account Investments in Affiliates (or Associated Companies). If the affiliates report net losses, the investor records the opposite effect.

- *Dividends paid by affiliates:* If affiliates declare and pay dividends during the year (a financing decision), the investor reduces its investment account and increases cash when it receives its share of the dividends.

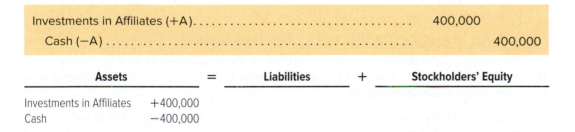

Investments in Affiliates (A)	
Beginning balance	
Purchases	Sales
Company's % share of affiliates' net income (credit Equity in Affiliate Earnings [↑ income])	Company's % share of affiliates' net losses (debit Equity in Affiliate Losses [↓ income]
	Company's % share of affiliates' dividends declared for the period (debit Cash)
Ending balance	

Purchase of Stock

For simplification, let's assume that, at the beginning of 2015, **Graham Holdings** had no long-term investments in companies over which it exerted significant influence. In 2015, Graham Holdings purchased 40,000 shares of the outstanding voting common stock of Internet News (INews) for $400,000 in cash. Since INews had 100,000 shares of common stock outstanding, Graham Holdings acquired 40 percent and was presumed to have significant influence over the affiliate. Therefore, Graham Holdings must use the equity method to account for this investment. The purchase of the asset would be recorded at cost.

Investments in Affiliates (+A).....................................	400,000	
Cash (−A)		400,000

Assets	=	Liabilities	+	Stockholders' Equity
Investments in Affiliates +400,000				
Cash −400,000				

Earnings of Affiliates

Because the investor can influence the process of earning income for the affiliates, the investor company bases its investment income on the affiliates' earnings rather than the dividends affiliates pay. During 2015, INews reported a net income of $500,000 for the year. Graham Holdings's percentage share of INews's income was $200,000 (40% × $500,000) and is recorded as follows:

Investments in Affiliates (+A).....................................	200,000	
Equity in Affiliate Earnings (+R, +SE)		200,000

Assets	=	Liabilities	+	Stockholders' Equity	
Investments in Affiliates +200,000				Equity in Affiliate Earnings (+R) +200,000	

If the affiliates report a net loss for the period, the investor records its percentage share of the loss by decreasing the investment account and recording Equity in Affiliate Loss. The Equity in Affiliate Earnings (or Loss) is reported in the Other Items section of the income statement, with interest revenue, dividend revenue, and interest expense.

Dividends Received

Because Graham Holdings can influence the dividend policies of its equity-method investments, any dividends it receives should **not** be recorded as investment income. Instead, dividends received reduce its investment account. During 2015, INews declared and paid a cash dividend of $1 per share to stockholders. Graham Holdings received $40,000 in cash ($1 × 40,000 shares) from INews.

Cash (+A)	40,000	
Investments in Affiliates (−A).................................		40,000

Assets		=	Liabilities	+	Stockholders' Equity
Investments in Affiliates	−40,000				
Cash	+40,000				

In summary, the effects for 2015 are reflected in the following T-accounts:

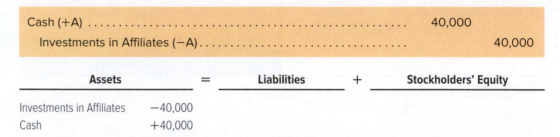

Investments in Affiliates (A)					Equity in Affiliate Earnings (R)		
1/1/15	0					0	1/1/15
Purchase	400,000						
Share of affiliate's net earnings	200,000	40,000	Share of affiliate's dividends			200,000	Share of affiliate's net earnings
12/31/15	560,000					200,000	12/31/15

Reporting Investments under the Equity Method

The Investments in Affiliates account is reported on the balance sheet as a long-term asset. However, as these last two entries show, the investment account does not reflect either cost or fair value. Instead, the following occurs:

- The investment account is increased by the cost of shares that were purchased and the proportional share of the affiliates' net income.

- The account is reduced by the amount of dividends received from the affiliate companies and the proportional share of any affiliates' net losses and the cost of shares that were sold.

At the end of the accounting period, accountants **do not adjust the investment account to reflect changes in the fair value** of the securities that are held.[5] When the securities are sold, the difference between the cash received and the book value of the investment is recorded as a gain or loss on the sale of the investment and is reported on the income statement in the Other Items section.

---

[5]FAS 159 (ASC 825-10) does allow companies to elect fair value treatment for equity method investments, but few companies are expected to take the election.

If between 20 and 50 percent of the outstanding voting shares are owned, significant influence over the affiliate firm's operating and financing policies is presumed, and the equity method is applied. Under the **equity method,** the investor records the investment at cost on the acquisition date. Each period thereafter, the investment amount is increased (or decreased) by the proportionate interest in the income (or loss) reported by the affiliate corporation and decreased by the proportionate share of the dividends declared by the affiliate corporation.

SELF-STUDY QUIZ

To test your understanding of these concepts, answer the following questions.

At the beginning of 2016, Weld Company purchased 30 percent (20,000 shares) of the outstanding voting stock of another company for $600,000 cash. During 2016, the affiliate declared and paid $50,000 in dividends. For 2016, the affiliate reported net income of $150,000. The stock had a fair value of $34 per share on December 31, 2016. Answer the following questions.

1. Record the purchase.	
2. Record the receipt of dividends in 2016.	
3. Record Weld's equity in the affiliate's earnings for 2016.	
4. Record any year-end adjustment to the investments account.	
5. What would be reported on the balance sheet for the investment in the affiliate at the end of 2016? (*Hint:* Construct a T-account.)	
6. What would be reported on the 2016 income statement for the investment in the affiliate?	

After you have completed your answers, check them below.

1.	Investments in Affiliates (+A)............	600,000		
	Cash (−A)........................		600,000	
2.	Cash (+A)...........................	15,000		[$50,000 total
	Investments in Affiliates (−A).........		15,000	dividends × 30%]
3.	Investments in Affiliates (+A)............	45,000		[$150,000 net
	Equity in Affiliate Earnings (+R, +SE) ..		45,000	income × 30%]
4.	There is no other year-end adjustment related to the stock's fair value under the equity method.			
5.	Under Long-Term Assets: Investments in Affiliates $630,000			
6.	Under Other Items on Weld's			
	income statement: Equity in Affiliate Earnings $45,000			

Investments in Affiliates (A)			
1/1/16	0		
Purchase	600,000		
Share of affiliate's			Share of affiliate's
net earnings	45,000	15,000	dividends
12/31/16	630,000		

A QUESTION OF ETHICS

Transaction Structuring: Selecting Accounting Methods for Minority Investments

Managers can choose freely between LIFO and FIFO or accelerated depreciation and straight-line depreciation. In the case of minority (≤50% owned) investments, investments of less than 20 percent of a company's outstanding stock are usually accounted for under the fair value method and investments of 20 to 50 percent are accounted for under the equity method.

However, managers may be able to structure the acquisition of stock in a manner that permits them to use the accounting method that they prefer. For example, a company that wants to use the fair value method could purchase only 19.9 percent of the outstanding stock of another company and achieve the same investment goals as it would with a 20 percent investment. Why might managers want to avoid using the equity method? Most managers prefer to minimize variations in reported earnings. If a company were planning to buy stock in a firm that reported large earnings in some years and large losses in others, it might want to use the fair value method to avoid reporting its share of the affiliate's earnings and losses.

Analysts who compare several companies must understand management's reporting choices and the way in which differences between the fair value and equity methods can affect earnings. Auditors will review management's application of the fair value and equity method to investments near to the 20 percent ownership level to determine if the proper method was used.

FOCUS ON CASH FLOWS

Investments

Many of the effects of applying the fair value method to passive investments and the equity method to investments held for significant influence affect net income but not cash flow. These items require adjustments under the indirect method when converting net income to cash flows from operating activities.

In General   Investments have a number of effects on the statement of cash flows:

1. The cash resulting from the sale or purchase is reflected in the Investing Activities section.
2. In the Operating Activities section, there are a number of adjustments to net income:

    a. Any gain (loss) on the sale is subtracted from (added to) net income.

    b. Any unrealized holding gain (loss) on trading securities is subtracted from (added to) net income.

    c. Equity in affiliate earnings (losses) is subtracted from (added to) net income because no cash was involved in the recording of the revenue under the equity method.

    d. Any dividends received from an affiliate are added to net income because, when cash was received, no revenue was recorded under the equity method.

EFFECT ON THE STATEMENT OF CASH FLOWS	
	Effect on Cash Flows
Operating activities	
Net income	$xxx
Adjusted for	
Gains/losses on sale of investments	−/+
Net unrealized holding gains/losses on trading securities	−/+
Equity in net earnings/losses of affiliated companies	−/+
Dividends received from affiliated companies	+
Investing Activities	
Purchase of investments	−
Sale of investments	+

CONTROLLING INTERESTS: MERGERS AND ACQUISITIONS

Before we discuss financial reporting issues for situations in which a company owns more than 50 percent of the outstanding common stock of another corporation, we should consider management's reasons for acquiring this level of ownership. The following are some of the reasons for acquiring control of another corporation:

1. **Vertical integration.** In this type of acquisition, a company acquires another at a different level in the channels of distribution. For example, oil companies such as **ExxonMobil** are active at vertical integration, from locating oil deposits, drilling and extracting the crude, transporting it, refining it into various petroleum products, and distributing the fuel to company-owned retail stations.

2. **Horizontal growth.** These acquisitions involve companies at the same level in the channels of distribution. For example, in early 2015, **Heinz** announced its plans to merge with **Kraft Foods** in a $45 billion deal that will create the world's fifth largest food and beverage company.

3. **Synergy.** The operations of two companies together may be more profitable than the combined profitability of the companies as separate entities. The Heinz-Kraft merger is expected to provide for $1.5 billion in annual cost savings. In addition, Heinz earns 60 percent of its sales from regions beyond North America, whereas Kraft's sales are mostly in North America. The merger will provide opportunities to sell Kraft brands globally, realizing higher profits.

Scott Olson/Getty Images

Understanding why one company has acquired control over other companies is a key factor in understanding the company's overall business strategy.

Recording a Merger

The simplest way to understand the statements that result from the purchase of another company is to consider the case of a simple **merger**, where one company purchases all of the assets and liabilities of another and the acquired company goes out of existence as a separate corporation. We will consider the case where **Graham Holdings** acquires all of the assets and liabilities of INews for $1,000,000 cash.

The **acquisition method** is the only method allowed by U.S. GAAP and IFRS for recording a merger or acquisition. It requires that the assets and liabilities of INews be recorded by Graham Holdings on its books at their **fair value** on the date of the merger. So the acquiring company, in this case Graham Holdings, must go through a two-step process, often called the **purchase price allocation,** to determine how to record the acquisition:

MERGER
Occurs when one company purchases all of the net assets of another and the acquired company goes out of existence.

ACQUISITION METHOD
Records assets and liabilities acquired in a merger or acquisition at their fair value on the transaction date.

Step 1: **Estimate the fair value of the acquired company's tangible assets, identifiable intangible assets, and liabilities.** This includes all assets and liabilities, regardless of whether and at what amount they were recorded on the books of the acquired company.

Step 2: **Compute goodwill, the excess of the total purchase price over the fair value of the assets minus the liabilities listed in Step 1.**

GOODWILL (COST IN EXCESS OF NET ASSETS ACQUIRED)
For accounting purposes, the excess of the purchase price of a business over the fair value of the acquired business's assets and liabilities.

For our example, assume that INews owned two assets (equipment and a patent) and had one liability (a note payable). Graham Holdings followed the two steps and produced the following:

Step 1:   Estimate the fair value of the acquired company's tangible assets, identifiable intangible assets, and liabilities.

Fair value of INews's—	Equipment	$350,000	} $950,000 total assets
	Patents	600,000	
	Note Payable	100,000	

Step 2: Compute goodwill as follows:

Purchase price for INews	$1,000,000
Less: Fair value of assets ($950,000) minus liabilities ($100,000)	850,000
Goodwill purchased	$ 150,000

Graham Holdings would then account for the merger by recording the assets and liabilities listed above and reducing cash for the amount paid as follows:

Equipment (+A)	350,000	
Patents (+A)	600,000	
Goodwill (+A)	150,000	
Note Payable (+L)		100,000
Cash (−A)		1,000,000

Assets		=	Liabilities		+	Stockholders' Equity
Equipment	+350,000		Note Payable	+100,000		
Patents	+600,000					
Goodwill	+150,000					
Cash	−1,000,000					

In summary, when performing a purchase price allocation, it is important to remember two points:

- The book values on the acquired company's balance sheet are irrelevant unless they represent fair value.
- Goodwill is reported only if it is acquired in a merger or acquisition transaction.

In a recent annual report, Graham Holdings describes GAAP for recording mergers and acquisitions in the following note:

2. Summary of Significant Accounting Policies

Business Combinations. The purchase price of an acquisition is allocated to the assets acquired, including intangible assets, and liabilities assumed, based on their respective fair values at the acquisition date. Acquisition-related costs are expensed as incurred. The excess of the cost of an acquired entity over the net of the amounts assigned to the assets acquired and liabilities assumed is recognized as goodwill. The net assets and results of operations of an acquired entity are included in the Company's Consolidated Financial Statements from the acquisition date.

Reporting for the Combined Companies

After the merger, **Graham Holdings** will treat the acquired assets and liabilities in the same manner as if they were acquired individually. For example, the company will depreciate the $350,000 added to equipment over its remaining useful life and amortize the $600,000 for patents over their remaining useful life. As we noted in Chapter 8, goodwill is considered to have an indefinite life. As a consequence, it is not amortized, but, like all long-lived assets, goodwill is reviewed for possible impairment of value. Recording an impairment loss would increase expenses for the period and reduce the amount of goodwill on the balance sheet.

When a company acquires another, and both companies continue their separate legal existence, **consolidated financial statements** must be presented. The parent company is the company that gains control over the other company. The subsidiary company is the company that the parent acquires. When the parent buys 100 percent of the subsidiary, the resulting consolidated financial statements look the same as they would if the companies were combined into one in a simple merger as discussed above. The procedures involved in preparation of consolidated statements are discussed in advanced accounting courses.

PAUSE FOR **FEEDBACK**

Mergers and ownership of a controlling interest in another corporation (more than 50 percent of the outstanding voting shares) must be accounted for using the acquisition method. The acquired company's assets and liabilities are measured at their fair values. Any amount paid above the fair value of the net assets is reported as goodwill by the buyer. To make sure you understand how to apply these concepts, answer the following questions.

SELF-STUDY **QUIZ**

Lexis Corporation purchased 100 percent of **Nexis Company** for $10 and merged Nexis into Lexis. On the date of the merger, the fair value of Nexis's other assets was $11 and the fair value of Nexis's liabilities was $4. What amounts would be added to Lexis's balance sheet as a result of the merger for:

1. Goodwill?
2. Other Assets (excluding Goodwill)?

After you have completed your answers, check them below.

Solutions to
SELF-STUDY QUIZ

1. Purchase Price ($10) − Fair Value of Net Assets ($11 − $4) = Goodwill $3.
2. Nexis's other assets (at fair value) = $11.

DEMONSTRATION   **CASE A**

PASSIVE INVESTMENTS USING FAIR VALUE METHOD

(Try to resolve the requirements before proceeding to the suggested solution that follows.) Howell Equipment Corporation sells and services a major line of farm equipment. Both sales and service operations have been profitable. The following transactions affected the company during 2016:

a. Jan. 1 Purchased 2,000 shares of common stock of Dear Company at $40 per share to be held as available-for-sale securities. This purchase represented 1 percent of the shares outstanding.

b. Dec. 28 Received $4,000 cash dividend on the Dear Company stock.

c. Dec. 31 Determined that the current market price of the Dear stock was $39.

Required:

1. Prepare the journal entry for each of these transactions.

2. What accounts and amounts will be reported on the balance sheet at the end of 2016? On the income statement for 2016?

3. Assuming management intends to trade these shares actively instead of holding them as available-for-sale securities, what accounts and amounts will be reported on the balance sheet at the end of 2016? On the income statement for 2016?

SUGGESTED SOLUTION FOR CASE A

1.

a.	Jan.	1	Investments in AFS securities (+A)...............		80,000	
			Cash (−A) [2,000 shares × $40 per share].......			80,000
b.	Dec.	28	Cash (+A)		4,000	
			Dividend revenue (+R, +SE)..................			4,000
c.	Dec.	31	Net unrealized gains (losses) (−OCI, −SE)		2,000	
			Investments in AFS securities (−A).............			2,000

Year	Fair Value	−	Book Value before Adjustment	=	Amount for Adjusting Entry
2016	$78,000 ($39 × 2,000 shares)	−	$80,000	=	($2,000) An unrealized loss for the period

2. On the Balance Sheet:

Current or Noncurrent Assets

Investments in AFS securities
($80,000 cost − $2,000 adjustment) $78,000

Stockholders' Equity

Other comprehensive income:
Net unrealized gain (loss)   (2,000)

On the Income Statement:

Other Items

Dividend revenue $4,000

3. Assuming trading securities:

On the Balance Sheet:

Current Assets

Investments in TS
($80,000 cost − $2,000 adjustment) $78,000

On the Income Statement:

Other Items

Dividend revenue $4,000
Net unrealized gain (loss)   (2,000)

DEMONSTRATION   CASE B

INVESTMENTS WITH SIGNIFICANT INFLUENCE USING EQUITY METHOD

On January 1, 2016, Connaught Company purchased 40 percent of the outstanding voting shares of London Company on the open market for $85,000 cash. London declared and paid $10,000 in cash dividends on December 1 and reported net income of $60,000 for the year.

Required:

1. Prepare the journal entries for 2016.

2. What accounts and amounts were reported on Connaught's balance sheet at the end of 2016? On Connaught's income statement for 2016?

SUGGESTED SOLUTION FOR CASE B

1.

Jan. 1 Investments in affiliates (+A).....................	85,000	
Cash (−A)		85,000
Dec. 1 Cash (+A) (40% × $10,000).....................	4,000	
Investments in affiliates (−A).................		4,000
Dec. 31 Investments in affiliates (+A) (40% × $60,000)....	24,000	
Equity in affiliate earnings (+R, +SE)...........		24,000

2. On the Balance Sheet:

Noncurrent Assets

Investments in affiliates

($85,000 − $4,000 + $24,000) $105,000

On the Income Statement:

Other Items

Equity in affiliate earnings $24,000

DEMONSTRATION   **CASE C**

MERGER USING ACQUISITION METHOD

On January 1, 2016, Ohio Company purchased 100 percent of the outstanding voting shares of Allegheny Company in the open market for $85,000 cash and Allegheny was merged into Ohio Company. On the date of acquisition, the fair value of Allegheny Company's plant and equipment was $89,000 and the fair value of a note payable was $10,000. Allegheny had no other assets or liabilities.

Required:

1. Analyze the merger to determine the amount of goodwill purchased.

2. Give the journal entry that Ohio Company should make on the date of the acquisition. If none is required, explain why.

3. Should Allegheny Company's assets be included on Ohio's balance sheet at book value or fair value? Explain.

SUGGESTED SOLUTION FOR CASE C

1.

Purchase price for Allegheny Company	$85,000	
Less: Fair value of net assets purchased	79,000	($89,000 − $10,000)
Goodwill	$ 6,000	

2.

Jan. 1, 2016 Plant and Equipment (+A)	89,000	
Goodwill (+A)..........................	6,000	
Notes Payable (+L)		10,000
Cash (−A)		85,000

3. Allegheny Company's assets should be included on the postmerger balance sheet at their fair values as of the date of acquisition. The cost principle applies as it does with all asset acquisitions.

Appendix Supplement

Held-to-Maturity Bonds Purchased at Other Than Par Value: Amortized Cost Method

Bond Purchases

On the date of purchase, a bond may be acquired at the maturity amount (at par), for less than the maturity amount (at a discount), or for more than the maturity amount (at a premium). The total cost of the bond, including all incidental acquisition costs such as transfer fees and broker commissions, is debited to the Held-to-Maturity Investments account.

To illustrate accounting for bond investments acquired **at other than par,** assume that on July 1, 2016, **Graham Holdings** paid $92,277 cash for an 8 percent, 5-year $100,000 bond that paid interest semiannually (on June 30 and December 31). The bond's yield was 10 percent. The $92,277 represents the present value of the bond on the purchase date, computed as follows:

Present value of the bond investment = Present value of the face + Present value of the interest annuity

$$\$92,277 = (\$100,000 \times 0.6139) + (\$4,000 \times 7.7217)$$

$$[n = 10 \text{ periods; interest rate} = 5\%]$$

Management intends to hold the bonds until maturity. The journal entry to record the purchase of the bonds follows:

Held-to-Maturity Investments (+A)	92,277	
Cash (−A)		92,277

Assets		=	Liabilities	+	Stockholders' Equity
Held-to-Maturity Investments	+92,277				
Cash	−92,277				

Interest Earned

The bonds in this illustration were purchased at a discount that will need to be amortized over the life of the investment. Using the effective interest amortization method (discussed in Chapter 10), the cash received is based on the face amount of the bond ($100,000) multiplied by the stated rate of interest for half of a year (4 percent). Revenue earned is computed by multiplying the present value of the bond times the market rate for half of a year (5 percent). The following journal entry records the receipt of interest on December 31, 2016:

Cash (+A)	4,000	
Held-to-Maturity Investments (+A)	614	
Interest Revenue (+R, +SE)		4,614

Assets		=	Liabilities	+	Stockholders' Equity	
Held-to-Maturity Investments	+614				Interest Revenue (+R)	+ 4,614
Cash	+4,000					

The amount reported on the balance sheet at December 31, 2016, is $92,891 ($92,277 + $614), which will be the present value of the bond used in determining interest revenue on the next payment date of June 30, 2017. If the bond investment must be sold before maturity, any difference between market value on the date of sale and net book value would be reported as a gain or loss on sale.

A-1. Analyze and report investments in debt securities held to maturity.   p. A-3

When management intends to hold an investment in a debt security (such as a bond or note) until it matures, the held-to-maturity security is recorded at cost when acquired and reported at amortized cost on the balance sheet. Any interest earned during the period is reported on the income statement.

A-2. Analyze and report passive investments in securities using the fair value method.   p. A-5

Acquiring debt securities not held to maturity or less than 20 percent of the outstanding voting shares of another company's common stock is presumed to be a passive investment. Passive investments may be classified as:

- Trading securities (which are actively traded to maximize return) **or**
- Available-for-sale securities (which earn a return but are not as actively traded) depending on management's intent.

The investments are recorded at cost and adjusted to **fair value** at year-end. The resulting unrealized gain or loss is recorded as follows:

- For trading securities, the net unrealized gains and losses are reported in net income.
- For available-for-sale securities, the net unrealized gains and losses are reported as a component of stockholders' equity in other comprehensive income.

Any dividends earned are reported as revenue, and any gains or losses on sales of passive investments are reported on the income statement.

A-3. Analyze and report investments involving significant influence using the equity method.   p. A-14

If between 20 and 50 percent of the outstanding voting shares are owned, significant influence over the affiliate firm's operating and financing policies is presumed, and the equity method is applied. Under the **equity method,** the investor records the investment at cost on the acquisition date. Each period thereafter, the investment amount is increased (or decreased) by the proportionate interest in the income (or loss) reported by the affiliate corporation and decreased by the proportionate share of the dividends declared by the affiliate corporation.

A-4. Analyze and report investments in controlling interests.   p. A-19

Mergers occur when one company purchases all of the net assets of another and the target company ceases to exist as a separate legal entity. Mergers and ownership of a controlling interest of another corporation (more than 50 percent of the outstanding voting shares) must be accounted for using the acquisition method. The acquired company's assets and liabilities are measured at their fair values on the date of the transaction. Any amount paid above the fair value of the assets less liabilities is reported as goodwill by the buyer.

Each year, many companies report healthy profits but file for bankruptcy. Some investors consider this situation to be a paradox, but sophisticated analysts understand how this situation can occur. These analysts recognize that the income statement is prepared under the accrual concept (revenue is reported when earned and the related expense is matched with the revenue). The income statement does not report cash collections and cash payments. Troubled companies usually file for bankruptcy because they cannot meet their cash obligations (for example, they cannot pay their suppliers or meet their required interest payments). The income statement does not help analysts assess the cash flows of a company. The statement of cash flows, discussed in Chapter 12, is designed to help statement users evaluate a company's cash inflows and outflows.

KEY **RATIO**

Economic return from investing measures the performance of a company's securities portfolios. Investment returns include both dividends received and any change in the fair value. A high or rising ratio suggests that a firm's securities portfolio is improving. It is computed as follows (see the "Key Ratio Analysis" box in the Passive Investments section):

$$\text{Economic Return from Investing} = \frac{\text{Dividends and Interest Received} + \text{Change in Fair Value*}}{\text{Fair Value of Investments (beginning of period)}}$$

*Ending Balance of Investments − Beginning Balance of Investments

FINDING **FINANCIAL INFORMATION**

Balance Sheet

Current Assets:
Investment in trading securities
Investment in available-for-sale securities

Noncurrent Assets:
Investment in available-for-sale securities
Investment in affiliates (or associated companies)
Investments held to maturity

Stockholders' Equity
Other comprehensive income:
    Net unrealized gains (losses) (on available-for-sale
        securities)

Statement of Cash Flows

Operating Activities:
Net income adjusted for:
    Gains/losses on sale of investments
    Equity in earnings/losses of affiliates
    Dividends received from affiliates
    Net unrealized gains (losses) on trading securities

Investing Activities:
Purchase/sale of investments

Income Statement

Under "Other Items":
Dividend (and interest) revenue
Loss or gain on sale of investments
Net unrealized gains (losses) (on trading
    securities)
Equity in affiliate earnings/losses

Notes

In Various Notes:
Accounting policies for investments
Details on securities held as trading
    and available-for-sale securities and
    investments in affiliates

KEY **TERMS**

Acquistion Method   p. A-19
Amortized Cost Method   p. A-3
Available-for-Sale Securities   p. A-6
Equity Method   p. A-14
Fair Value Method   p. A-5

Goodwill (Cost in Excess of Net Assets
    Acquired)   A-19
Held-to-Maturity Investments   p. A-3
Investments in Affiliates (or Associated
    Companies)   p. A-14

Merger   p. A-19
Trading Securities   p. A-6
Unrealized Holding Gains (Losses)
    p. A-5

QUESTIONS

1. Explain the difference between a short-term investment and a long-term investment.
2. Explain the difference in accounting methods used for passive investments, investments in which the investor can exert significant influence, and investments in which the investor has control over another entity.
3. Explain how bonds held to maturity are reported on the balance sheet.
4. Explain the application of the cost principle to the purchase of capital stock in another company.
5. Under the fair value method, when and how does the investor company measure revenue?
6. Under the equity method, why does the investor company measure revenue on a proportionate basis when income is reported by the affiliate company rather than when dividends are declared?
7. Under the equity method, dividends received from the affiliate company are not recorded as revenue. To record dividends as revenue involves double counting. Explain.
8. When one company acquires control of another, how are the acquired company's assets and liabilities recorded?
9. What is goodwill?

1. Company X owns 40 percent of Company Y and exercises significant influence over the management of Company Y. Therefore, Company X uses what method of accounting for reporting its ownership of stock in Company Y?
   a. The amortized cost method.
   b. The equity method.
   c. The fair value method.
   d. Consolidation of the financial statements of companies X and Y.

2. Company W purchases 10 percent of Company Z and Company W intends to hold the stock for at least five years. At the end of the current year, how would Company W's investment in Company Z be reported on Company W's December 31 (year-end) balance sheet?
   a. At the December 31 fair value in the long-term assets section.
   b. At original cost in the current assets section.
   c. At the December 31 fair value in the current assets section.
   d. At original cost in the long-term assets section.

3. Dividends received from stock that is reported as an available-for-sale security in the long-term assets section of the balance sheet are reported as which of the following?
   a. An increase to cash and a decrease to the investment in stock account.
   b. An increase to cash and an increase to revenue.
   c. An increase to cash and an unrealized gain on the income statement.
   d. An increase to cash and an unrealized gain on the balance sheet.

4. Realized gains and losses are recorded on the income statement for which of the following transactions in trading securities and available-for-sale securities?
   a. When adjusting a trading security to its fair value.
   b. Only when recording the sale of a trading security.
   c. When adjusting an available-for-sale security to its fair value.
   d. When recording the sale of either a trading security or an available-for-sale security.

5. When recording dividends received from a stock investment accounted for using the equity method, which of the following statements is true?
   a. Total assets are increased and net income is increased.
   b. Total assets are increased and total stockholders' equity is increased.
   c. Total assets and total stockholders' equity do not change.
   d. Total assets are decreased and total stockholders' equity is decreased.

6. When using the equity method of accounting, when is revenue recorded on the books of the investor company?
   a. When a dividend is received from the affiliate.
   b. When the fair value of the affiliate stock increases.
   c. When the affiliate company reports net income.
   d. Both (a) and (c).

7. Bott Company acquired 500 shares of stock of Barus Company at $53 per share as a long-term investment. This represents 10 percent of the outstanding voting shares of Barus. During the year, Barus paid stockholders $3 per share in dividends. At year-end, Barus reported net income of $60,000. Barus's stock price at the end of the year was $55 per share. For Bott Company, the amount of investments reported on the balance sheet at year-end and the amount reported on the income statement for the year are:

	Balance Sheet	**Income Statement**
a.	$26,500	$1,500
b.	$27,500	$1,500
c.	$27,500	$6,000
d.	$26,500	$6,000

8. Bott Company acquired 500 shares of stock of Barus Company at $53 per share as a long-term investment. This represents 40 percent of the outstanding voting shares of Barus. During the year, Barus paid stockholders $3 per share in dividends. At year-end, Barus reported net income of

$60,000. Barus's stock price at the end of the year was $55 per share. For Bott Company, the amount of investments reported on the balance sheet at year-end and the amount reported on the income statement for the year are:

	Balance Sheet	Income Statement
a.	$27,500	$ 0
b.	$27,500	$ 0
c.	$27,500	$24,000
d.	$49,000	$24,000

9. Which of the following is true regarding the economic return from investing ratio?
   a. This ratio is used to evaluate how efficiently a company manages its total assets.
   b. This ratio is used to evaluate the efficiency of a company given the capital contributed by owners.
   c. This ratio is used to evaluate the financing strategy of a company.
   d. This ratio is used to evaluate the performance of a company's investment portfolio.

10. Lamichael Company purchased 100 percent of the outstanding voting shares of Darrell Corporation in the open market for $230,000 cash and Darrell was merged into Lamichael Company. On the date of acquisition, the fair value of Darrell Corporation's property and equipment was $300,000 and the fair value of its long-term debt was $130,000. Darrell has no other assets or liabilities. What amount of goodwill would Lamichael record related to the purchase of Darrell Corporation?
    a. No goodwill should be recorded by Lamichael.
    b. $170,000
    c. $60,000
    d. $40,000

MINI-EXERCISES

MA-1
LO A-1, A-2, A-3, A-4

Matching Measurement and Reporting Methods

Match the following. Answers may be used more than once:

Measurement Method

A. Amortized cost
B. Equity method
C. Acquisition method and consolidation
D. Fair value method

____ 1. Less than 20 percent ownership.
____ 2. Current fair value.
____ 3. More than 50 percent ownership.
____ 4. At least 20 percent but not more than 50 percent ownership.
____ 5. Bonds held to maturity.
____ 6. Original cost less any amortization of premium or discount with the purchase.
____ 7. Original cost plus proportionate part of the income of the affiliate less proportionate part of the dividends declared by the affiliate.

MA-2
LO A-1

Recording a Bond Investment

James Company purchased $800,000, 8 percent bonds issued by Heidi Company on January 1 of the current year. The purchase price of the bonds was $900,000. Interest is payable semiannually each June 30 and December 31. Record the purchase of the bonds on January 1 of the current year.

MA-3
LO A-2

Recording Available-for-Sale Securities Transactions

During December of the current year, James Company acquired some of the 50,000 outstanding shares of the common stock, par $12, of Andrew Corporation as available-for-sale investments. The accounting period for both companies ends December 31. Give the journal entries for each of the following transactions that occurred during the current year:

Dec. 2	Purchased 6,250 shares of Andrew common stock at $15 per share.
Dec. 15	Andrew Corporation declared and paid a cash dividend of $2 per share.
Dec. 31	Determined the current market price of Andrew stock to be $12 per share.

Recording Trading Securities Transactions

MA-4
LO A-2

Using the data in MA-3, assume that James Company purchased the voting stock of Andrew Corporation for the trading securities portfolio instead of the available-for-sale securities portfolio. Give the journal entries for each of the transactions listed.

Determining Financial Statement Effects of Available-for-Sale Securities Transactions

MA-5
LO A-2

Using the following categories, indicate the effects of the transactions listed in MA-3 assuming the securities are available for sale. Use + for increase and − for decrease and indicate the amounts.

	Balance Sheet			Income Statement		
Transaction	Assets	Liabilities	Stockholders' Equity	Revenues/ Gains	Expenses/ Losses	Net Income

Determining Financial Statement Effects of Trading Securities Transactions

MA-6
LO A-2

Using the following categories, indicate the effects of the transactions listed in MA-3 assuming the securities are trading securities. Use + for increase and − for decrease and indicate the amounts.

	Balance Sheet			Income Statement		
Transaction	Assets	Liabilities	Stockholders' Equity	Revenues/ Gains	Expenses/ Losses	Net Income

Recording Equity Method Securities Transactions

MA-7
LO A-3

On January 1 of the current year, PurchaseAgent.com acquired 35 percent (800,000 shares) of the common stock of E-Transaction Corporation. The accounting period for both companies ends December 31. Give the journal entries for each of the following transactions that occurred during the current year for PurchaseAgent.com:

| July. 2 | E-Transaction declared and paid a cash dividend of $5 per share. |
| Dec. 31 | E-Transaction reported net income of $400,000. |

Determining Financial Statement Effects of Equity Method Securities

MA-8
LO A-3

Using the following categories, indicate the effects of the transactions listed in MA-7. Use + for increase and − for decrease and indicate the amounts.

	Balance Sheet			Income Statement		
Transaction	Assets	Liabilities	Stockholders' Equity	Revenues/ Gains	Expenses/ Losses	Net Income

Recording a Merger

MA-9
LO A-4

England Textile Company acquired Belgium Fabric Company for $660,000 cash when Belgium's only assets, property and equipment, had a book value of $660,000 and a fair value of $750,000. England also assumed Belgium's bonds payable of $175,000. After the merger, Belgium would cease to exist as a separate legal entity. Record the acquisition.

MA-10
LO A-2

Computing and Interpreting Economic Return from Investing Ratio

N.M.S. Company held available-for-sale securities and reported the following information at the end of each year:

Year	Dividend Revenue	Ending Fair Value of Investments
2016	$1,500	$64,000
2017	3,000	70,000
2018	4,200	82,000
2019	3,500	80,000

Compute the economic return from investing ratio for 2017, 2018, and 2019. What do the results suggest about N.M.S. Company?

MA-11
LO A-4

Interpreting Goodwill Disclosures

The Walt Disney Company owns theme parks, movie studios, television and radio stations, newspapers, and television networks, including ABC and ESPN. Its balance sheet recently reported goodwill in the amount of $24 billion, which is almost 35 percent of the company's total assets. This percentage is very large compared to that of most companies. Explain why you think Disney has such a large amount of goodwill reported on its balance sheet.

EXERCISES

EA-1
LO A-1

Recording Bonds Held to Maturity

Macy's, Inc., operates nearly 850 Macy's and Bloomingdale's department stores globally. The company does more than $28 billion in sales each year.

Assume that as part of its cash management strategy, Macy's purchased $12 million in bonds at par for cash on July 1 of the current year. The bonds pay 8 percent interest annually, with payments on June 30 and December 31, and mature in 10 years. Macy's plans to hold the bonds until maturity.

Required:
1. Record the purchase of the bonds on July 1 of the current year.
2. Record the receipt of interest on December 31 of the current year.

EA-2
LO A-2, A-3

Comparing Fair Value and Equity Methods

Company A purchased a certain number of Company B's outstanding voting shares at $20 per share as a long-term investment. Company B had outstanding 20,000 shares of $10 par value stock. Complete the following table relating to the measurement and reporting by Company A after acquisition of the shares of Company B stock.

Questions	Fair Value Method	Equity Method
a. What level of ownership by Company A of Company B is required to apply the method?	_____%	_____%

For *b, e, f,* and *g,* assume the following:		
Number of shares acquired of Company B stock	2,500	7,000
Net income reported by Company B in first year	$59,000	$59,000
Dividends declared by Company B in first year	$12,000	$12,000
Market price at end of first year, Company B stock	$ 17	$ 17

Questions	Fair Value Method	Equity Method
b. At acquisition, the investment account on the books of Company A should be debited at what amount?	$_____	$_____
c. When should Company A recognize revenue earned on the stock of Company B? Explanation required.	_____	_____
d. After the acquisition date, how should Company A change the balance of the investment account with respect to the stock owned in Company B (other than for disposal of the investment)? Explanation required.	_____	_____
e. What is the balance in the investment account on the balance sheet of Company A at the end of the first year?	$_____	$_____
f. What amount of revenue from the investment in Company B should Company A report at the end of the first year?	$_____	$_____
g. What amount of unrealized loss should Company A report at the end of the first year?	$_____	$_____

Recording Transactions in the Available-for-Sale Securities Portfolio

EA-3
LO A-2

On June 30, 2016, Slick Rocks, Inc., purchased 7,000 shares of Sandstone stock for $15 per share. Management recorded the stock in the available-for-sale securities portfolio. The following information pertains to the price per share of Sandstone stock:

	Price
12/31/2016	$17
12/31/2017	14
12/31/2018	18

Slick Rocks sold all of the Sandstone stock on February 14, 2019, at a price of $20 per share. Prepare any journal entries that are required by the facts presented in this case.

Recording Transactions in the Trading Securities Portfolio

EA-4
LO A-2

Using the data in EA-3, assume that Slick Rocks management purchased the Sandstone stock for the trading securities portfolio instead of the available-for-sale securities portfolio. Prepare any journal entries that are required by the facts presented in the case.

Reporting Gains and Losses in the Available-for-Sale Securities Portfolio

EA-5
LO A-2

On March 10, 2015, Dearden, Inc., purchased 15,000 shares of Jaffa stock for $35 per share. Management recorded it in the available-for-sale securities portfolio. The following information pertains to the price per share of Jaffa stock:

	Price
12/31/2015	$33
12/31/2016	36
12/31/2017	32

Dearden sold all of the Jaffa stock on September 12, 2018, at a price of $30 per share. Prepare any journal entries that are required by the facts presented in this case.

Reporting Gains and Losses in the Trading Securities Portfolio

EA-6
LO A-2

Using the data in EA-5, assume that Dearden management purchased the Jaffa stock for the trading securities portfolio instead of the available-for-sale securities portfolio. Prepare any journal entries that are required by the facts presented in the case.

EA-7

LO A-3

Recording and Reporting an Equity Method Investment

Gioia Company acquired some of the 65,000 shares of outstanding common stock (no par) of Tristezza Corporation during the current year as a long-term investment. The annual accounting period for both companies ends December 31. The following transactions occurred during the current year:

Jan. 10	Purchased 17,875 shares of Tristezza common stock at $11 per share.
Dec. 31	a. Received the current year financial statements of Tristezza Corporation that reported net income of $80,000.
	b. Tristezza Corporation declared and paid a cash dividend of $0.60 per share.
	c. Determined the market price of Tristezza stock to be $10 per share.

Required:
1. What accounting method should the company use? Why?
2. Give the journal entries for each of these transactions. If no entry is required, explain why.
3. Show how the long-term investment and the related revenue should be reported on the current year's financial statements (balance sheet and income statement) of the Gioia Company.

EA-8

LO A-3

Interpreting the Effects of Equity Method Investments on Cash Flow from Operations

Using the data in EA-7, answer the following questions.

Required:
1. On the current year cash flow statement, how would the investing section of the statement be affected by the preceding transactions?
2. On the current year cash flow statement (indirect method), how would the equity in the earnings of the affiliated company and the dividends from the affiliated company affect the operating section? Explain the reasons for the effects.

EA-9

LO A-4

Determining the Appropriate Accounting Treatment for an Acquisition

The notes to recent financial statements of **Colgate-Palmolive** contained the following information (dollar amounts in millions):

> **3. Acquisitions and Divestitures**
>
> On June 20, 2011, the Company . . . finalized the Company's acquisition from Unilever of the Sanex personal care business . . . for an aggregate purchase price of $966 . . . . This strategic acquisition is expected to strengthen Colgate's personal care business in Europe, primarily in the liquid body cleansing and deodorants business. Total purchase price consideration of $966 has been allocated to the net assets acquired based on their respective fair values at June 20, 2011 . . . .

Assume that Colgate-Palmolive acquired 100 percent of the fair value of the net assets of **Sanex** in a recent year for $1,377 million in cash. Sanex's assets at the time of the acquisition had a book value of $625 million and a fair value of $1,036 million. Colgate-Palmolive also assumed Sanex's liabilities of $70 million (book value and fair value of the liabilities are the same). Prepare the entry on the date of acquisition as a merger.

EA-10

LO A-2

Analyzing and Interpreting the Economic Return from Investing Ratio

Kukenberger, Inc., reported the following in its portfolio of available-for-sale securities:

Year	Dividends Received	Ending Fair Value of Investment Portfolio
2015	$24,550	$836,451
2016	23,906	759,999
2017	24,399	806,345
2018	25,538	845,160

Required:
1. Determine the economic return from investing ratio for the years 2016, 2017, and 2018.
2. What do your results suggest about Kukenberger's investment portfolio?

(Appendix Supplement) Recording Bonds Held to Maturity (Purchased at a Premium)

EA-11
LO A-1

Macy's, Inc., operates nearly 850 Macy's and Bloomingdale's department stores nationwide. The company does more than $24 billion in sales each year.

Assume that, as part of its cash management strategy, Macy's purchased as a long-term investment $12 million in 10-year bonds for $13,785,600 cash on July 1 of the current year. The bonds pay 8 percent interest semiannually on June 30 and December 31. The market rate on the bonds on the date of purchase was 6 percent.

Required:
1. Record the purchase of the bonds on July 1 of the current year.
2. Record the receipt of interest on December 31 of the current year (including applying the effective interest amortization method).

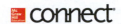

PROBLEMS

Determining Financial Statement Effects for Bonds Held to Maturity (APA-1)

PA-1
LO A-1

Starbucks is a global company that provides high-quality coffee products. Assume that as part of its expansion strategy, Starbucks plans to open numerous new stores in Mexico in three years. The company has $7 million to support the expansion and has decided to invest the funds in corporate bonds until the money is needed. Assume that Starbucks purchased bonds with $7 million face value at par for cash on July 1 of the current year. The bonds pay 7 percent interest each June 30 and December 31 and mature in three years. Starbucks plans to hold the bonds until maturity.

Required:
1. What accounts are affected when the bonds are purchased on July 1 of the current year?
2. What accounts are affected when interest is received on December 31 of the current year?
3. Should Starbucks prepare a journal entry if the fair value of the bonds decreased to $6,000,000 on December 31 of the current year? Explain.

Recording Passive Investments (APA-2)

PA-2
LO A-2

On March 1, 2016, Rain Technology purchased 20,000 shares of Lightyear Services Company for $10 per share. The following information applies to the stock price of Lightyear Services:

	Price
12/31/2016	$ 8
12/31/2017	14
12/31/2018	17

Required:
1. Prepare journal entries to record the facts in the case, assuming that Rain purchased the shares for the trading securities portfolio.
2. Prepare journal entries to record the facts in the case, assuming that Rain purchased the shares for the available-for-sale securities portfolio.

Recording Passive Investments

PA-3
LO A-2

Below are selected T-accounts for the RunnerTech Company.

Balance Sheet Accounts

(In Other Investments) Investments in AFS Securities			
1/1	5,587		
Purchase	19,000		
AJE	?	15,239	Sale
12/31	14,558		

(In Other Comprehensive Income) Net Unrealized Gains (Losses)—AFS			
		1,565	1/1
Sale	?	?	AJE
		5,683	12/31

Income Statement Accounts

Dividend Revenue		
	?	Earned
	7,771	12/31

Gain on Sale of Investments		
	2,384	Sale
	2,384	12/31

Required:

Complete the following journal entries and answer the following questions:

a. Purchased available-for-sale securities for cash. Prepare the journal entry.
b. Received cash dividends on the investments. Prepare the journal entry.
c. Sold AFS investments at a gain. Prepare the journal entry.
d. At year-end, the AFS portfolio had a fair value of $14,558. Prepare the adjusting entry.
e. What would be reported on the balance sheet related to the AFS investments on December 31?
f. What would be reported on the income statement for the year?
g. How would year-end reporting change if the investments were categorized as trading securities instead of available-for-sale securities?

PA-4
LO A-2

Reporting Passive Investments (APA-3)

During January 2016, Optimum Glass Company purchased the following securities as its long-term available-for-sale securities investment portfolio:

D Corporation common stock: 14,000 shares (95,000 outstanding) at $11 per share
F Corporation bonds: $400,000 (20-year, 7 percent) purchased at par (not to be held to maturity)

Subsequent to acquisition, the following data were available:

	2016	2017
Net income reported at December 31:		
D Corporation	$ 31,000	$ 41,000
F Corporation	$360,000	$550,000
Dividends and interest paid during the year:		
D Corporation common stock cash dividends (per share)	$ 0.50	$ 0.70
F Corporation bonds interest	$ 28,000	$ 28,000
Fair value at December 31:		
D Corporation common stock (per share)	$ 10.00	$ 11.50
F Corporation bonds	$375,000	$385,000

Required:

1. What accounting method should be used for the investment in D common stock? F bonds? Why?
2. Give the journal entries for the company for each year in parallel columns (if none, explain why) for each of the following:
   a. Purchase of the investments.
   b. Income reported by D and F Corporations.

  c. Dividends and interest received from D and F Corporations.

  d. Fair value effects at year-end.

 3. For each year, show how the following amounts should be reported on the financial statements:

  a. Long-term investments.

  b. Stockholders' equity—net unrealized losses/gains.

  c. Revenues.

Recording Passive Investments and Investments for Significant Influence

PA-5
LO A-2, A-3

On August 4, 2015, Jeffrey Corporation purchased 2,000 shares of Kevin Company for $180,000. The following information applies to the stock price of Kevin Company:

	Price
12/31/2015	$85
12/31/2016	91
12/31/2017	94

Kevin Company declares and pays cash dividends of $3.50 per share on June 1 of each year.

Required:

 1. Prepare journal entries to record the facts in the case, assuming that Jeffrey purchased the shares for the trading securities portfolio.

 2. Prepare journal entries to record the facts in the case, assuming that Jeffrey purchased the shares for the available-for-sale securities portfolio.

 3. Prepare journal entries to record the facts in the case, assuming that Jeffrey used the equity method to account for the investment. Jeffrey owns 30 percent of Kevin and Kevin reported $30,000 in income each year.

Comparing Methods to Account for Various Levels of Ownership of Voting Stock

PA-6
LO A-2, A-3

Company T had outstanding 25,000 shares of common stock, par value $10 per share. On January 1 of the current year, Company P purchased some of these shares as a long-term investment at $25 per share. At the end of the current year, Company T reported the following: income, $45,000, and cash dividends declared and paid during the year, $16,500. The fair value of Company T stock at the end of the current year was $22 per share.

Required:

 1. For each of the following cases (Case A and Case B, shown in the tabulation), identify the method of accounting that Company P should use. Explain why.

 2. Give the journal entries for Company P at the dates indicated for each of the two independent cases (Case A and Case B), assuming that the investments will be held long term. If no entry is required, explain why. Use the following format:

Tabulation of Items	Case A: 3,000 Shares Purchased	Case B: 8,750 Shares Purchased
1. Accounting method?		
2. Journal entries:		
a. To record the acquisition at January 1.		
b. To recognize the income reported by Company T for current year.		
c. To recognize the dividends declared and paid by Company T.		
d. To recognize fair value effect at end of current year.		

3. Complete the following schedule to show the separate amounts that should be reported on the current year's financial statements of Company P:

	Dollar Amounts	
	Case A	Case B
Balance sheet		
Investments		
Stockholders' equity		
Income statement		
Dividend revenue		
Equity in earnings of affiliate		

4. Explain why assets, stockholders' equity, and revenues for the two cases are different.

PA-7

LO A-2, A-3

Comparing the Fair Value and Equity Methods (APA-4)

Surge Corporation had outstanding 120,000 shares of no-par common stock. On January 10 of the current year, Crash Company purchased a block of these shares in the open market at $25 per share for long-term investment purposes. At the end of the current year, Surge reported net income of $175,000 and cash dividends of $1.00 per share. At December 31 of the current year, Surge stock was selling at $23 per share. This problem involves two separate cases:

Case A: Purchase of 15,000 shares of Surge common stock.
Case B: Purchase of 48,000 shares of Surge common stock.

Required:
1. For each case, identify the accounting method that the company should use. Explain why.
2. For each case, in parallel columns, give the journal entries for each of the following (if no entry is required, explain why):
   a. Acquisition.
   b. Revenue recognition.
   c. Dividends received.
   d. Fair value effects.
3. For each case, show how the following should be reported on the current year's financial statements:
   a. Long-term investments.
   b. Stockholders' equity.
   c. Revenues.
4. Explain why the amounts reported in requirement (3) are different for the two cases.

PA-8

LO A-3

Recording Investments for Significant Influence

Below are selected T-accounts for William Company.

Investments in Affiliates			
1/1	56,432		
Purchase	15,685		
Share of			Share of
affiliate net			affiliate
income	?	8,564	dividends
12/31	67,450		

Equity in Affiliate Earnings			
		0	1/1
			Share of
			affiliate net
		?	income
		3,897	12/31

Required:
Complete the following journal entries and answer the following questions:

a. Purchased additional investments in affiliated companies for cash. Prepare the journal entry.
b. Received cash dividends on the investments. Prepare the journal entry.
c. At year-end, the investments in affiliates account had a fair value of $62,000; the affiliate also reported $8,120 in net income for the year. Prepare the adjusting entry.

d. What would be reported on the balance sheet related to the investments in affiliates on December 31?

e. What would be reported on the income statement for the year?

Determining Cash Flow Statement Effects of Investments for Significant Influence (APA-5)

PA-9

LO A-3

During the current year, Bradford Company purchased some of the 90,000 shares of common stock, par $6, of Hall, Inc., as a long-term investment. The annual accounting period for each company ends December 31. The following transactions occurred during the current year:

Jan. 7	Purchased 40,500 shares of Hall stock at $30 per share.
Dec. 31	*a.* Received the current year financial statements of Hall, which reported net income of $215,000.
	b. Hall declared and paid a cash dividend of $1.50 per share.
	c. Determined that the current market price of Hall stock was $41 per share.

Required:

Indicate how the Operating Activities and Investing Activities sections of the cash flow statement (indirect method) will be affected by each transaction.

Analyzing Goodwill and Reporting a Merger (APA-6)

PA-10

LO A-4

On January 4, David Company acquired all of the net assets (assets and liabilities) of William Company for $145,000 cash. The two companies merged, with David Company surviving. On the date of acquisition, William's balance sheet included the following.

Balance Sheet at January 4	William Company
Cash	$23,000
Property and equipment (net)	70,000
Total assets	$93,000
Liabilities	$16,000
Common stock (par $5)	41,000
Retained earnings	36,000
Total liabilities and stockholders' equity	$93,000

The property and equipment had a fair value of $85,000. William also owned an internally developed patent with a fair value of $3,000. The book values of the cash and liabilities were equal to their fair values.

Required:

1. How much goodwill was involved in this merger? Show computations.

2. Give the journal entry that David would make to record the merger on January 4.

Interpreting the Economic Return from Investing Ratio

PA-11

LO A-2

Apple, Inc., designs and markets innovative hardware, software, peripherals, and services, including the iPhone®, iPad®, Mac®, iPod®, Apple TV®, and Apple Watch®, The following information was reported in a recent annual report for available-for-sale securities:

	(DOLLARS IN MILLIONS)	
	Current Year	Prior Year
AFS investment portfolio	$121,251*	$81,570
Investment income	522	415

*The increase in the portfolio was due to $1,031 fair value change and $38,650 in additional purchases of AFS securities acquired on the last day of the year.

Required:

1. Compute the economic return from investing ratio for the current year.

2. What do the results in requirement (1) suggest about Apple, Inc.?

ALTERNATE PROBLEMS

APA-1

LO A-1

Determining Financial Statement Effects for Bonds Held to Maturity (PA-1)

Sonic Corp. operates and franchises a chain of quick-service drive-in restaurants in most of the United States. Customers order at a drive thru, dine on the patio, or drive up to a canopied parking space. A carhop then delivers the food to the customer. Assume that Sonic has $15 million in cash to support future expansion and has decided to invest the funds in corporate bonds until the money is needed. Sonic purchases bonds with $15 million face value for $15.7 million cash on January 1 of the current year. The bonds pay 9 percent interest annually, with payments on each June 30 and December 31, and mature in four years. Sonic plans to hold the bonds until maturity.

Required:

1. What accounts were affected when the bonds were purchased on January 1 of the current year?
2. What accounts were affected when interest was received on June 30 of the current year?
3. Should Sonic prepare a journal entry if the fair value of the bonds increased to $16,300,000 on December 31 of the current year? Explain.

APA-2

LO A-2

Recording Passive Investments (PA-2)

On September 15, 2016, Hill-Nielson Corporation purchased 7,000 shares of Community Communications Company for $32 per share. The following information applies to the stock price of Community Communications:

	Price
12/31/2016	$34
12/31/2017	25
12/31/2018	21

Required:

1. Prepare journal entries to record the facts in the case, assuming that Hill-Nielson purchased the shares for the trading securities portfolio.
2. Prepare journal entries to record the facts in the case, assuming that Hill-Nielson purchased the shares for the available-for-sale securities portfolio.

APA-3

LO A-2

Reporting Passive Investments (PA-4)

During January 2017, Pentagon Company purchased 12,000 shares of the 200,000 outstanding common shares (no-par value) of Square Corporation at $25 per share. This block of stock was purchased as a long-term investment. Assume that the accounting period for each company ends December 31. Subsequent to acquisition, the following data were available:

	2017	2018
Income reported by Square Corporation at December 31	$40,000	$60,000
Cash dividends declared and paid by Square Corporation during the year	$60,000	$80,000
Market price per share of Square common stock on December 31	$ 28	$ 27

Required:

1. What accounting method should Pentagon Company use? Why?
2. Give the journal entries for the company for each year (use parallel columns) for the following (if none, explain why):
   a. Acquisition of Square Corporation stock.
   b. Net income reported by Square Corporation.
   c. Dividends received from Square Corporation.
   d. Fair value effects at year-end.
3. For each year, show how the following amounts should be reported on the financial statements:
   a. Long-term investments.
   b. Stockholders' equity—net unrealized loss/gain.
   c. Revenues.

Comparing the Fair Value and Equity Methods (PA-7)

APA-4
LO A-2, A-3

Cardinal Company purchased, as a long-term investment, some of the 200,000 shares of the outstanding common stock of Arbor Corporation. The annual accounting period for each company ends December 31.
   The following transactions occurred during the current year:

Jan. 10	Purchased shares of common stock of Arbor at $12 per share as follows:
	Case A—30,000 shares
	Case B—80,000 shares
Dec. 31	a. Received the current year financial statements of Arbor Corporation; the reported net income was $90,000.
	b. Received a cash dividend of $0.60 per share from Arbor Corporation.
	c. Determined that the current market price of Arbor stock was $9 per share.

Required:

1. For each case, identify the accounting method that the company should use. Explain why.
2. Give the journal entries for each case for these transactions. If no entry is required, explain why. (**Hint:** Use parallel columns for Case A and Case B.)
3. Give the amounts for each case that should be reported on the financial statements for the current year. Use the following format:

	Case A	Case B
Balance sheet (partial)		
Investments		
Investments in common stock, Arbor Corporation		
Stockholders' equity		
Net unrealized gain or loss		
Income statement (partial)		
Dividend revenue		
Equity in earnings of affiliate		

Determining Cash Flow Statement Effects of Passive Investments and Investments for Significant Influence

APA-5
LO A-2, A-3

For each of the transactions in APA-4, indicate how the operating activities and investing activities sections of the cash flow statement (indirect method) will be affected.

APA-6
LO A-4

Analyzing Goodwill and Reporting a Merger (PA-10)

On June 1, Gamma Company acquired all of the net assets of Pi Company for $140,000 cash. The two companies merged, with Gamma Company surviving. On the date of acquisition, Pi Company's balance sheet included the following:

Balance Sheet at June 1	Pi Company
Inventory	$ 13,000
Property and equipment (net)	165,000
Total assets	$178,000
Liabilities	$ 82,000
Common stock (par $1)	65,000
Retained earnings	31,000
Total liabilities and stockholders' equity	$178,000

On the date of acquisition, the inventory had a fair value of $12,000 and the property and equipment had a fair value of $180,000. The fair value of the liabilities equaled their book value.

Required:
1. How much goodwill was involved in this merger? Show computations.
2. Give the journal entry that Gamma Company would make to record the merger on June 1.

CONTINUING PROBLEM

CONA-1   Accounting for Passive Investments

Pool Corporation, Inc., is the world's largest wholesale distributor of swimming pool supplies and equipment. Assume Pool Corporation purchased for cash 400,000 shares of **The Walt Disney Company** on November 21, 2016, at $48 per share as an investment. The following information applies to the stock price of Disney:

	Price per Share
12/31/2016	$45
12/31/2017	41
12/31/2018	49

On September 15, 2019, Pool Corporation sold all of the Disney securities at $50 per share.

Required:
1. Prepare journal entries to record the facts in the case, assuming that Pool Corporation purchased the shares for the trading securities portfolio.
2. Prepare journal entries to record the facts in the case, assuming that Pool Corporation purchased the shares for the available-for-sale securities portfolio.

CASES **AND PROJECTS**

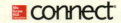

Annual Report Cases

CPA-1
LO A-1, A-2, A-4

Finding Financial Information

Refer to the financial statements of **American Eagle Outfitters** in Appendix B at the end of this book.

Required:
1. What types of securities are included in the short-term investments and the long-term investments reported on the company's balance sheet as of the end of fiscal 2014 (statement dated January 31, 2015)? (**Hint:** The notes to the financial statements may be helpful for this question.)

2. What is the balance of goodwill reported by the company at January 31, 2015? What does the change in goodwill from February 1, 2014, imply about corporate acquisition activities in the 2014 fiscal year? Do the notes to the financial statements indicate any acquisition or disposition activity in either fiscal 2013 or 2014? If so, what were the activities?

Finding Financial Information

Refer to the financial statements of **Urban Outfitters** in Appendix C at the end of this book.

CPA-2
LO A-1, A-2

Required:
1. What is the balance in short-term and long-term marketable securities reported by the company on January 31, 2015? What types of securities are included in these accounts? (**Hint:** The notes to the financial statements may be helpful for this question.)
2. How much cash did the company use to purchase marketable securities during the year ended January 31, 2015?

Financial Reporting and Analysis Cases

Using Financial Reports: Analyzing the Financial Effects of the Fair Value and Equity Methods

On January 1 of the current year, Sheena Company purchased 30 percent of the outstanding common stock of Maryn Corporation at a total cost of $485,000. Management intends to hold the stock for the long term. On the current year's December 31 balance sheet, the investment in Maryn Corporation was $556,000, but no additional Maryn stock was purchased. The company received $90,000 in cash dividends from Maryn. The dividends were declared and paid during the current year. The company used the equity method to account for its investment in Maryn. The market price of Sheena Company's share of Maryn stock increased during the current year to a total value of $550,000.

CPA-3
LO A-2, A-3

Required:
1. Explain why the investment account balance increased from $485,000 to $556,000 during the current year.
2. What amount of revenue from the investment was reported during the current year?
3. If Sheena did not have significant influence over Maryn and used the fair value method, what amount of revenue from the investment should have been reported in the current year?
4. If Sheena did not have significant influence over Maryn and used the fair value method, what amount should be reported as the investment in Maryn Corporation on the current year's December 31 balance sheet?

Using Financial Reports: Interpreting International Goodwill Disclosures

Diageo is a major international company located in London, best known for its Smirnoff, Johnnie Walker, and Guinness brands of spirits. Its financial statements are accounted for under IFRS. A recent annual report contained the following information concerning its accounting policies.

CPA-4
LO A-4

> Acquired brands and other intangible assets are recognised when they are controlled through contractual or other legal rights, or are separable from the rest of the business, and the fair value can be reliably measured.
>
> Intangible assets that are regarded as having limited useful economic lives are amortised on a straight-line basis over those lives and reviewed for impairment whenever events or circumstances indicate that the carrying amount may not be recoverable. Goodwill and intangible assets that are regarded as having indefinite useful economic lives are not amortised. These assets are reviewed for impairment at least annually or when there is an indication that the assets may be impaired. To ensure that assets are not carried at above their recoverable amounts . . . Amortisation and any impairment writedowns are charged to other operating expenses in the income statement.

Required:
Discuss how this accounting treatment compares with procedures used in this country.

Critical Thinking Cases

CPA-5
LO A-4

Evaluating an Ethical Dilemma: Using Inside Information

Assume that you are on the board of directors of a company that has decided to buy 80 percent of the outstanding stock of another company within the next three or four months. The discussions have convinced you that this company is an excellent investment opportunity, so you decide to buy $10,000 worth of the company's stock for your personal portfolio. Is there an ethical problem with your decision? Would your answer be different if you planned to invest $500,000? Are there different ethical considerations if you don't buy the stock but recommend that your brother do so?

CPA-6
LO A-4

Evaluating an Acquisition from the Standpoint of a Financial Analyst

Assume that you are a financial analyst for a large investment banking firm. You are responsible for analyzing companies in the retail sales industry. You have just learned that a large West Coast retailer has acquired a large East Coast retail chain for a price more than the net book value of the acquired company. You have reviewed the separate financial statements for the two companies before the announcement of the acquisition. You have been asked to write a brief report explaining what will happen when the financial results of the companies are consolidated under the acquisition method.

Financial Reporting and Analysis Team Project

CPA-7
LO A-2, A-3, A-4

Team Project: Examining an Annual Report

Working together as a team, select an industry to analyze. Yahoo Finance provides lists of industries at **biz.yahoo.com/p/industries.html**. Click on an industry for a list of companies in that industry. Alternatively, go to Google Finance at **www.google.com/finance** and search for a company you are interested in. You will be presented with a list including that company and its competitors. Each team member should acquire the annual report or 10-K for one publicly traded company in the industry, with each member selecting a different company (the SEC EDGAR service at **www.sec.gov** and the company's investor relations website itself are good sources).

Required:
On an individual basis, each team member should write a short report answering the following questions about the selected company. Discuss any patterns across the companies that you as a team observe. Then, as a team, write a short report comparing and contrasting your companies.

On an individual basis, each team member should write a short report that answers the following questions:
1. Determine whether the company prepared consolidated financial statements. If so, did it use the acquisition method? How do you know?
2. Does the company use the equity method for any of its investments?
3. Does the company hold any investments in securities? If so, what is their fair value? Does the company have any unrealized gains or losses?
4. Identify the company's lines of business. Why does management want to engage in these business activities?

UNITED STATES SECURITIES AND EXCHANGE COMMISSION
Washington, D.C. 20549

Form 10-K

☑ **ANNUAL REPORT PURSUANT TO SECTION 13 OR 15(d)
OF THE SECURITIES EXCHANGE ACT OF 1934**

For the Fiscal Year Ended January 31, 2015

OR

☐ **TRANSITION REPORT PURSUANT TO SECTION 13 OR 15(d)
OF THE SECURITIES EXCHANGE ACT OF 1934**

Commission File Number: 1-33338

American Eagle Outfitters, Inc.

(Exact name of registrant as specified in its charter)

Delaware	**No. 13-2721761**
(State or other jurisdiction of incorporation or organization)	*(I.R.S. Employer Identification No.)*
77 Hot Metal Street, Pittsburgh, PA	**15203-2329**
(Address of principal executive offices)	*(Zip Code)*

Registrant's telephone number, including area code:
(412) 432-3300

Securities registered pursuant to Section 12(b) of the Act:

Common Shares, $0.01 par value	New York Stock Exchange
(Title of class)	*(Name of each exchange on which registered)*

Securities registered pursuant to Section 12(g) of the Act:
None

Indicate by check mark if the registrant is a well-known seasoned issuer, as defined in Rule 405 of the Securities Act. YES ☑   NO ☐

Indicate by check mark if the registrant is not required to file reports pursuant to Section 13 or Sections 15(d) of the Act. YES ☐   NO ☑

Indicate by check mark whether the registrant (1) has filed all reports required to be filed by Section 13 or 15(d) of the Securities Exchange Act of 1934 during the preceding 12 months (or for such shorter period that the registrant was required to file such reports), and (2) has been subject to the filing requirements for at the past 90 days. YES ☑   NO ☐

Indicate by check mark whether the registrant has submitted electronically and posted on its corporate Web site, if any, every Interactive Data File required to be submitted and posted pursuant to Rule 405 of Regulation S-T (§232.405 of this chapter) during the preceding 12 months (or for such shorter period that the registrant was required to submit and post such files). YES ☑   NO ☐

Indicate by check mark if disclosure of delinquent filers pursuant to Item 405 of Regulation S-K (§229.405 of this chapter) is not contained herein, and will not be contained, to the best of registrant's knowledge, in definitive proxy or information statements incorporated by reference in Part III of this Form 10-K or any amendment to this Form 10-K.   ☐

Indicate by check mark whether the registrant is a large accelerated filer, an accelerated filer, a non-accelerated filer, or a smaller reporting company. See the definitions of "large accelerated filer," "accelerated filer" and "smaller reporting company" in Rule 12b-2 of the Exchange Act. (Check one):

Large accelerated filer ☑   Accelerated filer ☐   Non-accelerated filer ☐   Smaller reporting company ☐

(Do not check if a smaller reporting company)

Indicate by check mark whether the registrant is a shell company (as defined in Rule 12b-2 of the Act). YES ☐   NO ☑

The aggregate market value of voting and non-voting common equity held by non-affiliates of the registrant as of August 2, 2014 was $1,874,117,608.

Indicate the number of shares outstanding of each of the registrant's classes of common stock, as of the latest practicable date: 195,022,073 Common Shares were outstanding at March 9, 2015.

DOCUMENTS INCORPORATED BY REFERENCE

Part III — Proxy Statement for 2015 Annual Meeting of Stockholders, in part, as indicated.

ITEM 1.   *BUSINESS.*

General

American Eagle Outfitters, Inc., a Delaware corporation (the "Company"), operates under the American Eagle Outfitters ® and aerie ® by American Eagle Outfitters ® brands. Founded in 1977, American Eagle Outfitters is a leading apparel and accessories retailer that operates more than 1,000 retail stores in the U.S. and internationally, online at ae.com and aerie.com and international store locations managed by third-party operators. Through its brands, the Company offers high quality, on-trend clothing, accessories and personal care products at affordable prices. The Company's online business, AEO Direct, ships to 81 countries worldwide.

We have company operated stores in the United States, Canada, Mexico, Hong Kong, China and the United Kingdom. American Eagle Outfitters ® and aerie ® merchandise is also available at international store locations managed by third party operators. As of January 31, 2015, we operated 955 American Eagle Outfitters stores and 101 aerie stand-alone stores. Our third party operated store base has grown to 99 stores in 16 countries and products purchased through our online business, AEO Direct, ship to 81 countries worldwide.

We operated the 77kids by American Eagle Outfitters ® brand until the exit of the business during Fiscal 2012. Our Consolidated Financial Statements reflect the results of 77kids as discontinued operations for all periods presented.

As used in this report, all references to "we," "our" and the "Company" refer to American Eagle Outfitters, Inc. and its wholly owned subsidiaries. "American Eagle Outfitters," "AEO" and the "AEO Brand" refer to our company operated American Eagle Outfitters stores. "aerie" refers to our aerie ® by American Eagle Outfitters ® stores. "AEO Direct" refers to our e-commerce operations, ae.com and aerie.com.

Our financial year is a 52/53 week year that ends on the Saturday nearest to January 31. As used herein, "Fiscal 2015" refers to the 52 week period ending January 30, 2016. "Fiscal 2014" and "Fiscal 2013" refer to the 52 week period ended January 31, 2015 and February 1, 2014, respectively. "Fiscal 2012" refers to the 53 week period ended February 2, 2013. "Fiscal 2011" and "Fiscal 2010" refer to the 52 week periods ended January 28, 2012 and January 29, 2011, respectively.

Information concerning our segments and certain geographic information is contained in Note 2 of the Consolidated Financial Statements included in this Form 10-K and is incorporated herein by reference. Additionally, a five-year summary of certain financial and operating information can be found in Part II, Item 6, Selected Consolidated Financial Data, of this Form 10-K. See also Part II, Item 8, Financial Statements and Supplementary Data.

Brands

American Eagle Outfitters Brand

The American Eagle Outfitters ® brand targets 15 to 25 year old men and women. Denim is the cornerstone of the American Eagle Outfitters ® product assortment, which is complemented by other key categories including pants, shorts, sweaters, fleece, outerwear, graphic t-shirts, footwear and accessories. American Eagle Outfitters ® is honest, real, individual and fun. American Eagle Outfitters ® is priced to be worn by everyone, everyday, delivering value through quality and style.

Gaining market share through differentiated fashion, product innovation, and having the right product, in the right size for every customer are the main focuses within the AEO Brand. Delivering value, variety and versatility to our customers remains a top priority. We strive to offer quality and value at all levels of the assortment, punctuated with promotions.

aerie

The aerie ® brand is a collection of intimates and personal care products for women that want to feel good about who they are, inside and out. The collection is available in 101 stand-alone aerie stores throughout the United States and Canada, online at aerie.com and at select American Eagle Outfitters ® stores. aerie, with bras and undies at the core, and offerings in sleep, swim and apparel is beautiful, feminine, soft, sensuous, yet comfortable and real.

Business Priorities & Strategy

We are focused on delivering results through four near-term priorities: (1) pursuing revenue and profit improvement in both the American Eagle Outfitters and aerie brands through more compelling product assortments, product focused marketing messages and unique customer experiences digitally and in stores; (2) continued evolution of our omni-channel capabilities (flexible fulfilment, full utilization of our omni-channel distribution center and maximizing our investments in technologies and tools); (3) growing our digital business through further site enhancements, expanded product line, improved customer engagement and continued upgrades to our mobile site; and (4) improvement in profitability of our stores and repositioning the store fleet.

AEO Direct & Omni-Channel Capabilities

We sell merchandise via ae.com and aerie.com, which are the digital manifestation of the lifestyle that our brands represent. In addition to purchasing items directly from our digital channels, customers can experience AEO Direct in-store through our Store-to-Door program. This program enables store associates to sell any item available online to an in-store customer in a single transaction. Customers are taking advantage of Store-to-Door by purchasing extended sizes that are not available in-store, as well as finding a certain size or color that happens to be out-of-stock at the time of their visit. The ordered items are shipped to the customer's home free of charge. Additionally, in Fiscal 2014, we began fulfilling online orders at stores through our Buy Online Ship-from-Store program and we plan to further enhance our websites, increase CRM capabilities through personalization, segmentation and customer lifecycle management.

We are focused on delivering an omni-channel approach to customer engagement, which will eventually lead to a single view of the customer and inventory. We have made investments including a re-launched mobile app and enhanced websites. We will continue to invest in initiatives geared towards integration of our shopping channels as well as expanded product line offerings.

Real Estate

We remain focused on real-estate strategies to grow our business and strengthen our financial performance utilizing our most productive formats in the right markets, including underpenetrated markets, AEO Factory stores and aerie side-by-side locations. Also, we will selectively close stores and maintain flexibility within our real estate portfolio through short-term lease extensions.

At the end of Fiscal 2014, we operated in all 50 states, Puerto Rico, Canada, Mexico, Hong Kong, China and the United Kingdom. During Fiscal 2014, we opened 60 new stores, consisting largely of AEO Factory stores and international store openings. These store openings, offset by 70 store closings, brought our total store base to 1,056 stores at the end of Fiscal 2014.

Our stores average approximately 6,200 gross square feet and approximately 5,000 on a selling square foot basis. Our gross square footage increased by approximately 2% during Fiscal 2014.

During Fiscal 2014, we renovated a total of 44 AEO stores through remodels, refurbishes and refreshes. We evaluate each store and determine the appropriate capital spend based on financial performance and non-financial factors including the location and condition of the store, the center and competitors. Remodels result in a newly constructed store, sometimes larger in size, in the most current store design including new storefront, floors, fixtures, marketing and lighting. Refurbishes consist of selective changes that include new store front, floors and fixtures. Refreshes include certain aspects of our current store format, including paint and new fixtures.

In Fiscal 2015, we plan to open approximately 20 to 25 AEO stores primarily in the Factory store format and continue our international expansion. We also plan to remodel and refurbish approximately 25 existing AEO stores and close approximately 50 AEO stores and 20 aerie stores. Our square footage is expected to decline slightly in Fiscal 2015.

The table below shows certain information relating to our historical store growth from continuing operations.

	Fiscal 2014	Fiscal 2013	Fiscal 2012	Fiscal 2011	Fiscal 2010
Consolidated stores at beginning of period	1,066	1,044	1,069	1,077	1,075
Consolidated stores opened during the period	60	64	16	21	25
Consolidated stores closed during the period	(70)	(42)	(41)	(29)	(23)
Total consolidated stores at end of period	**1,056**	**1,066**	**1,044**	**1,069**	**1,077**

	Fiscal 2014	Fiscal 2013	Fiscal 2012	Fiscal 2011	Fiscal 2010
AEO Brand stores at beginning of period	944	893	911	929	938
AEO Brand stores opened during the period	60	64	16	11	14
AEO Brand stores closed during the period	(49)	(13)	(34)	(29)	(23)
Total AEO Brand stores at end of period	**955**	**944**	**893**	**911**	**929**

	Fiscal 2014	Fiscal 2013	Fiscal 2012	Fiscal 2011	Fiscal 2010
aerie stores at beginning of period	122	151	158	148	137
aerie stores opened during the period	—	—	—	10	11
aerie stores closed during the period	(21)	(29)	(7)	—	—
Total aerie stores at end of period	**101**	**122**	**151**	**158**	**148**

Consolidated Store Locations

As of January 31, 2015, we operated 1,056 wholly-owned stores under the American Eagle Outfitters and aerie brands as shown below:

United States, including the Commonwealth of Puerto Rico—920 stores

Alabama	15	Indiana	22	Nebraska	6	Rhode Island	3
Alaska	5	Iowa	11	Nevada	5	South Carolina	15
Arizona	12	Kansas	9	New Hampshire	10	South Dakota	3
Arkansas	8	Kentucky	14	New Jersey	27	Tennessee	25
California	59	Louisiana	14	New Mexico	3	Texas	68
Colorado	11	Maine	6	New York	64	Utah	9
Connecticut	14	Maryland	19	North Carolina	27	Vermont	2
Delaware	5	Massachusetts	28	North Dakota	4	Virginia	27
Florida	57	Michigan	27	Ohio	37	Washington	20
Georgia	31	Minnesota	18	Oklahoma	11	West Virginia	8
Hawaii	4	Mississippi	9	Oregon	11	Wisconsin	20
Idaho	3	Missouri	16	Pennsylvania	59	Wyoming	1
Illinois	30	Montana	2	Puerto Rico	6		

Canada—101 stores

Alberta	11	New Brunswick	3	Ontario	55
British Columbia	12	Newfoundland	1	Quebec	12
Manitoba	2	Nova Scotia	3	Saskatchewan	2

International—35 stores

China	9	Hong Kong	5	Mexico	18	United Kingdom	3

International Operations

As of January 31, 2015, we had 101 company-operated stores in Canada, 18 in Mexico, nine in China, six in Puerto Rico, five in Hong Kong and three in the United Kingdom. We continue to evaluate further opportunities to expand internationally, which may include additional company-operated stores as well as stores operated by third party operators under license, franchise and/or joint venture agreements.

We have agreements with multiple third party operators to expand our brands internationally. Through these agreements, a series of franchised, licensed or other brand-dedicated American Eagle Outfitters stores have opened and expect to continue to open in areas including Eastern Europe, the Middle East, Central and South America, Northern Africa and parts of Asia. These agreements do not involve a significant capital investment or operational involvement from the Company. We plan to continue to increase the number of countries in which we enter into these types of arrangements as part of our strategy for profitable international expansion. As of January 31, 2015, we had 99 stores operated by our third party operators in 16 countries. International third party operated stores are not included in the consolidated store data or the total gross square feet calculation.

Purchasing

We design our merchandise and source its manufacture from third-party factories. During Fiscal 2014, we purchased substantially all of our merchandise from non-North American suppliers.

All of our merchandise suppliers must agree to the terms and conditions of our Master Purchase Agreement (MPA) and to conduct business with us in accordance with the policies and procedures set forth in our Corporate Vendor Manual (the "Manual"). The Manual includes, but is not limited to, policies and procedures covering the following topics: social responsibility; quality assurance; product safety and testing; product labeling and other regulatory requirements; supply chain security; our intellectual property; and our shipping process.

We maintain a quality control department at our distribution centers to inspect incoming merchandise shipments for uniformity of sizes and colors and for overall quality of manufacturing. Periodic inspections are also made by our employees and agents at manufacturing facilities to identify quality issues prior to shipment of merchandise.

Corporate Responsibility

We are firmly committed to the principle that the people who make our clothes should be treated with dignity and respect. We seek to work with apparel suppliers throughout the world who share our commitment to providing safe and healthy workplaces. At a minimum, we require our suppliers to maintain a workplace environment that complies with local legal requirements and meets universally-accepted human rights standards.

Our Vendor Code of Conduct (the "Code"), which is based on universally-accepted human rights principles, sets forth our expectations for suppliers. The Code must be posted in every factory that manufactures our clothes in the local language of the workers. All suppliers must agree to abide by the terms of our Code before we will place production with them.

We maintain an extensive factory inspection program to monitor compliance with our Code. New garment factories must pass an initial inspection in order to do business with us. Once new factories are approved, we continue to review their social compliance performance both through internal audits by our compliance team, and through the use of third-party monitors. We review the outcome of these inspections with factory management with the goal of helping them to continuously improve their performance. Although our primary goal is to remediate issues and build long term relationships with our vendors, in cases where a factory is unable or unwilling to meet our standards, we will take steps up to and including the severance of our business relationship.

In Fiscal 2013, AEO signed the Accord on Fire and Building Safety, aligning with nearly 100 brands, non-governmental organizations (NGOs) and trade unions, to improve workplace safety in Bangladesh. The International Labor Organization (ILO), an organization that gives equal voice to workers, employers and unions, is Chair of the Steering Committee of the Accord. The Accord is a five-year program that will establish in-factory training; facilitate the creation of factory health and safety committees; review existing building regulations and enforcement; and develop a worker complaint process and mechanism for workers to report health and safety risks. AEO is also engaged with the ILO on Better Work programs in Cambodia, Haiti, Indonesia and Vietnam and is a member of the Better Work Buyers Partners.

Security Compliance

During recent years, there has been an increasing focus within the international trade community on concerns related to global terrorist activity and protecting the supply chain. Various security issues and other terrorist threats have brought increased demands from the Bureau of Customs and Border Protection ("CBP") and other agencies within the Department of Homeland Security that importers take responsible action to secure their supply chains. We have been a certified member of the Customs — Trade Partnership Against Terrorism program ("C-TPAT") since 2004. C-TPAT is a voluntary program offered by CBP in which an importer agrees to work with CBP to strengthen overall supply chain security. As part of this program, we are subject to validations by CBP.

Historically, we took significant steps to expand the scope of our security procedures, including, but not limited to: a significant increase in the number of factory audits performed; a revision of the factory audit format to include a review of all critical security issues as defined by CBP; a requirement that all of our international logistics partners, including forwarders, consolidators, shippers and brokers be certified members of C-TPAT; and inspections of all potential production facilities. Additionally, we also evaluate additional oversight options for high-risk security countries and among other things, implemented full third-party audits on an annual basis. In Fiscal 2013, we took the audits one step further, and conducted security audits of our own to validate the results we receive from the third-party audits, and continue with this practice today. We also implemented security training for our domestic logistics partners, along with conducting periodic audits on their facilities as well.

Trade Compliance

We act as the importer of record for substantially all of the merchandise we purchase overseas from foreign suppliers. Accordingly, we have an affirmative obligation to comply with the rules and regulations established for importers by the CBP regarding issues such as merchandise classification, valuation and country of origin. We have developed and implemented a comprehensive series of trade compliance procedures to assure that we adhere to all CBP requirements. In its most recent review and audit of our import operations and procedures, CBP found no material, unacceptable risks of non-compliance.

In addition to CBP requirements, we also ensure compliance with all other government agencies and their corresponding regulations including but not limited to the Federal Trade Commission (FTC), the Consumer Product Safety Commission (CPSC), the Food and Drug Administration (FDA) and U.S. Fish and Wildlife services. We have policies and procedures in place for labeling, packaging, product testing, obtaining required documentation and making appropriate declarations to reduce the risk of non-compliance.

Product Safety

We are strongly committed to the safety and well being of our customers. We require our products to meet applicable laws and regulations. In certain cases, we also voluntarily adopt industry standards and best practices that may be higher than legally required or where no clear laws exist.

To ensure compliance with our product safety standards, we maintain an extensive set of testing protocols for each category of products. All of the products we sell are tested by an independent testing laboratory in accordance with applicable regulatory requirements. In rare cases where a safety issue has been discovered in a product that has reached our store shelves, we respond with a comprehensive recall process.

Merchandise Inventory, Replenishment and Distribution

Merchandise is generally shipped directly from our vendors and routed through third-party transloaders at key ports of entry to our U.S. distribution centers in Warrendale, Pennsylvania, Ottawa, Kansas and most recently Hazelton, Pennsylvania, or to our Canadian distribution center in Mississauga, Ontario. Additionally, an increasing amount of product is shipped directly to stores from our transloaders, by-passing our distribution centers which reduces transit times and lowers operating costs. In 2014, we opened a third-party distribution center in the Netherlands to support our European international store and e-commerce growth. We also operate third-party distribution centers in Mexico

City, Hong Kong and Shanghai. Additionally, we opened a new 1,000,000 square foot omni-channel distribution center in Hazleton, Pennsylvania in July 2014, and will phase out our distribution center in Warrendale, Pennsylvania in Fiscal 2015.

Upon receipt at one of our distribution centers, merchandise is processed and prepared for shipment to the stores or forwarded to a warehouse holding area to be used for store sales replenishment. The allocation of merchandise among stores varies based upon a number of factors, including geographic location, customer demographics and store size. Merchandise is shipped to our stores two to five times per week depending upon the season and store requirements. Our current e-commerce distribution center, located in Ottawa, Kansas, ships merchandise directly to customers in all 50 states and 81 countries worldwide.

Customer Credit

We offer co-branded credit cards (the "AEO or aerie Visa Credit Card") and private label credit cards (the "AEO or aerie Credit Card") under the AEO and aerie brands. These credit cards are issued by a third-party bank (the "Bank") and we have no liability to the Bank for bad debt expense, provided that purchases are made in accordance with the Bank's procedures. Once a customer is approved to receive a Visa Credit Card or private label Credit Card and the card is activated, the customer is eligible to participate in our credit card rewards program. Customers who make purchases at AEO and aerie earn discounts in the form of savings certificates when certain purchase levels are reached. Also, AEO and aerie Visa Credit Card customers who make purchases at other retailers where the card is accepted earn additional reward points to be used at American Eagle Outfitters and aerie. AEO and aerie Credit Card holders will also receive advance notice of American Eagle Outfitters sales events offered throughout the year. The AEO and aerie Credit Cards are accepted at all of our U.S. stores and at ae.com and aerie.com. The AEO Visa and aerie Visa Cards are accepted in all of our stores and AEO Direct sites as well as merchants worldwide that accept Visa ® .

Competition

The retail apparel industry is highly competitive both in stores and on-line. We compete with various individual and chain specialty stores, as well as the casual apparel and footwear departments of department stores and discount retailers, primarily on the basis of quality, fashion, service, selection and price.

Trademarks and Service Marks

We have registered AMERICAN EAGLE OUTFITTERS ® , AMERICAN EAGLE ® , AE ® , AEO ® , LIVE YOUR LIFE ® , aerie ® and the Flying Eagle Design with the United States Patent and Trademark Office. We also have registered or have applied to register these trademarks with the registries of the foreign countries in which our stores and/or manufacturers are located and/or where our product is shipped.

We have registered AMERICAN EAGLE OUTFITTERS ® , AMERICAN EAGLE ® , AEO ® , LIVE YOUR LIFE ® , aerie ® and the Flying Eagle Design with the Canadian Intellectual Property Office. In addition, we have acquired rights in AE tm for clothing products and registered AE ® in connection with certain non-clothing products.

In the United States and in other countries around the world, we also have registered, or have applied to register, a number of other marks used in our business, including our pocket stitch designs.

These registered trademarks are renewable indefinitely, and their registrations are properly maintained in accordance with the laws of the country in which they are registered. We believe that the recognition associated with these trademarks makes them extremely valuable and, therefore, we intend to use and renew our trademarks in accordance with our business plans.

Employees

As of January 31, 2015, we had approximately 38,000 employees in the United States, Canada, Mexico, Hong Kong, China and the United Kingdom of whom approximately 31,000 were part-time and seasonal hourly employees. We consider our relationship with our employees to be good.

Executive Officers of the Registrant

Mary M. Boland , age 57, has served us as Executive Vice President, Chief Financial and Administrative Officer, and Principal Financial Officer since July 2012. Prior to joining the Company, Ms. Boland served Levi Strauss & Co. as Senior Vice President Finance of Global Levi's from 2011 to 2012 and as Senior Vice President Finance of the Americas from 2006 to 2011. Prior to that time, Ms. Boland held a variety of finance positions with General Motors Corporation from 1979 to 2006 including Vice President and Chief Financial Officer, North America from 2003 to 2006.

Jennifer M. Foyle , age 48, has served as our Global Brand President — aerie since January 2015. Prior thereto, Ms. Foyle served as Executive Vice President, Chief Merchandising Officer — aerie from February 2014 to January 2015 and Senior Vice President, Chief Merchandising Officer — aerie from August 2010 to February 2014. Prior to joining the Company, Ms. Foyle was President of Calypso St. Barth from 2009 to 2010. In addition, she held various positions at J. Crew Group, Inc., including Chief Merchandising Officer, from 2003 to 2009.

Charles F. Kessler, age 42, has served as our Global Brand President – American Eagle Outfitters since January 2015. Prior thereto, he served as our Executive Vice President, Chief Merchandising and Design Officer — American Eagle Outfitters from February 2014 to January 2015. Prior to joining us, Mr. Kessler served as Chief Merchandising Officer at Urban Outfitters, Inc. from October 2011 to November 2013 and as Senior Vice President, Corporate Merchandising at Coach, Inc. from July 2010 to October 2011. Prior to that time, Mr. Kessler held various positions with Abercrombie & Fitch Co. from 1994 to 2010, including Executive Vice President, Female Merchandising from 2008 to 2010.

Roger S. Markfield , age 73, has served as Vice Chairman, Executive Creative Director since February 2009 and as a Director since March 1999. From February 2007 to February 2009, Mr. Markfield served as a non-executive officer employee of the Company. Prior to February 2007, he served us as Vice Chairman since November 2003, as President from February 1995 to February 2006, and as Co-Chief Executive Officer of the Company from December 2002 to November 2003. Mr. Markfield also served the Company and its predecessors as Chief Merchandising Officer from February 1995 to December 2002. Mr. Markfield was formerly on the Board of Directors of DSW Inc. from 2008 to 2012.

Simon R. Nankervis , age 48, has served as our Executive Vice President, Global Commercial Operations since January 2015. Prior thereto, he served as our Executive Vice President, Americas and Global Country Licensing from February 2014 to January 2015, Senior Vice President, Americas and Global Country Licensing from April 2013 to February 2014 and as Vice President, International Franchising and Global Business Development from October 2011 to March 2013. Prior to joining us, Mr. Nankervis was Managing Director at Busbrand Pty Ltd, an Australian based international brand management company, from 2002 to 2011.

Michael R. Rempell , age 41, has served as our Executive Vice President and Chief Operations Officer since June 2012. Prior thereto, he served as our Executive Vice President and Chief Operating Officer, New York Design Center, from April 2009 to June 2012, as Senior Vice President and Chief Supply Chain Officer from May 2006 to April 2009, and in various other positions since joining us in February 2000.

Jay L. Schottenstein , age 60, has served as Interim Chief Executive Officer since January 2014. He has also served as Chairman of the Company and its predecessors since March 1992. He served the Company as Chief Executive Officer from March 1992 until December 2002 and prior to that time, he served as a Vice President and Director of the Company's predecessors since 1980. He has also served as Chairman of the Board and Chief Executive Officer of Schottenstein Stores Corporation ("SSC") since March 1992 and as President since 2001. Prior thereto, Mr. Schottenstein served as Vice Chairman of SSC from 1986 to 1992. He has been a Director of SSC since 1982. Mr. Schottenstein also served as Chief Executive Officer from March 2005 to April 2009 and as Chairman of the Board since March 2005 of DSW Inc., a company traded on the New York Stock Exchange. He has also served as an officer and director of various other entities owned or controlled by members of his family since 1976. Mr. Schottenstein also serves as Executive Chairman and Director on the Board of Directors of DSW Inc.

Available Information

Our Annual Reports on Form 10-K, Quarterly Reports on Form 10-Q, Current Reports on Form 8-K and amendments to those reports are available under the "About AEO, Inc." section of our website at www.ae.com. These reports are available as soon as reasonably practicable after such material is electronically filed with the Securities and Exchange Commission (the "SEC").

Our corporate governance materials, including our corporate governance guidelines, the charters of our audit, compensation, and nominating and corporate governance committees, and our code of ethics may also be found under the "About AEO, Inc." section of our website at www.ae.com. Any amendments or waivers to our code of ethics will also be available on our website. A copy of the corporate governance materials is also available upon written request.

Additionally, our investor presentations are available under the "About AEO, Inc." section of our website at www.ae.com. These presentations are available as soon as reasonably practicable after they are presented at investor conferences.

Certifications

As required by the New York Stock Exchange ("NYSE") Corporate Governance Standards Section 303A.12(a), on June 9, 2014 our Chief Executive Officer submitted to the NYSE a certification that he was not aware of any violation by the Company of NYSE corporate governance listing standards. Additionally, we filed with this Form 10-K, the Principal Executive Officer and Principal Financial Officer certifications required under Sections 302 and 906 of the Sarbanes-Oxley Act of 2002.

ITEM 1A.   *RISK FACTORS*

Our ability to anticipate and respond to changing consumer preferences, fashion trends and a competitive environment in a timely manner

Our future success depends, in part, upon our ability to identify and respond to fashion trends in a timely manner. The specialty retail apparel business fluctuates according to changes in the economy and customer preferences, dictated by fashion and season. These fluctuations especially affect the inventory owned by apparel retailers because merchandise typically must be ordered well in advance of the selling season. While we endeavor to test many merchandise items before ordering large quantities, we are still susceptible to changing fashion trends and fluctuations in customer demands.

In addition, the cyclical nature of the retail business requires that we carry a significant amount of inventory, especially during our peak selling seasons. We enter into agreements for the manufacture and purchase of our private label apparel well in advance of the applicable selling season. As a result, we are vulnerable to changes in consumer demand, pricing shifts and the timing and selection of merchandise purchases. The failure to enter into agreements for the manufacture and purchase of merchandise in a timely manner could, among other things, lead to a shortage of inventory and lower sales. Changes in fashion trends, if unsuccessfully identified, forecasted or responded to by us, could, among other things, lead to lower sales, excess inventories and higher markdowns, which in turn could have a material adverse effect on our results of operations and financial condition.

The effect of economic pressures and other business factors

The success of our operations depends to a significant extent upon a number of factors relating to discretionary consumer spending, including economic conditions affecting disposable consumer income such as payroll taxes, employment, consumer debt, interest rates, increases in energy costs and consumer confidence. There can be no assurance that consumer spending will not be further negatively affected by general, local or international economic conditions, thereby adversely impacting our business and results of operations.

Seasonality

Historically, our operations have been seasonal, with a large portion of total net revenue and operating income occurring in the third and fourth fiscal quarters, reflecting increased demand during the back-to-school and year-end holiday selling seasons, respectively. As a result of this seasonality, any factors negatively affecting us during the third and fourth fiscal quarters of any year, including adverse weather or unfavorable economic conditions, could have a material adverse effect on our financial condition and results of operations for the entire year. Our quarterly results of operations also may fluctuate based upon such factors as the timing of certain holiday seasons, the number and timing of new store openings, the acceptability of seasonal merchandise offerings, the timing and level of markdowns, store closings and remodels, competitive factors, weather and general economic conditions.

Our ability to react to raw material cost, labor and energy cost increases

Increases in our costs, such as raw materials, labor and energy may reduce our overall profitability. Specifically, fluctuations in the cost associated with the manufacture of merchandise we purchase from our suppliers impacts our cost of sales. We have strategies in place to help mitigate these costs and our overall profitability depends on the success of those strategies. Additionally, increases in other costs, including labor and energy, could further reduce our profitability if not mitigated.

Our ability to rebalance our store fleet and drive improved performance through new store openings, selective closings and existing store remodels and expansions

Our ability to drive improved performance will depend in part on our ability to rebalance our store fleet and expand and remodel existing stores on a timely and profitable basis. During Fiscal 2015, we plan to open approximately 20 to 25 new American Eagle Outfitters stores primarily in the Factory store format in North America and continue our international expansion. Additionally, we plan to remodel and refurbish 25 existing American Eagle Outfitters stores and close approximately 70 stores during Fiscal 2015. Accomplishing our store rebalancing and expansion goals will depend upon a number of factors, including the ability to obtain suitable sites for new and expanded stores at acceptable costs, the hiring and training of qualified personnel, particularly at the store management level, the integration of new stores into existing operations and the expansion of our buying and inventory capabilities. There can be no assurance that we will be able to achieve our store expansion and rebalancing goals, manage our growth effectively, successfully integrate the planned new stores into our operations or operate our new and remodeled stores profitably.

Our efforts to expand internationally

We are actively pursuing additional international expansion initiatives, which include wholly-owned stores and stores operated by third parties in select international markets. The effect of these arrangements on our business and results of operations is uncertain and will depend upon various factors, including the demand for our products in new markets internationally. Furthermore, although we provide store operation training, literature and support, to the extent that the franchisee, licensee or other operator does not operate its stores in a manner consistent with our requirements regarding our brand and customer experience standards, our business results and the value of our brand could be negatively impacted.

A failure to properly implement our expansion initiatives, or the adverse impact of political or economic risks in these international markets, could have a material adverse effect on our results of operations and financial condition. We have limited prior experience operating internationally, where we face established competitors. In many of these locations, the real estate, labor and employment, transportation and logistics and other operating requirements differ dramatically from those in the locations where we have more experience. Consumer demand and behavior, as well as tastes and purchasing trends, may differ substantially, and as a result, sales of our products may not be successful, or the margins on those sales may not be in line with those we currently anticipate. Any differences that we encounter as we expand internationally may divert financial, operational and managerial resources from our existing operations, which could adversely impact our financial condition and results of operations. In addition, we are increasingly exposed to foreign currency exchange rate risk with respect to our revenue, profits, assets, and liabilities denominated in currencies other than the U.S. dollar. We may in the future use instruments to hedge certain foreign currency risks; however, these measures may not succeed in offsetting all of the negative impact of foreign currency rate movements on our business and results of operations.

As we pursue our international expansion initiatives, we are subject to certain laws, including the Foreign Corrupt Practices Act, as well as the laws of the foreign countries in which we operate. Violations of these laws could subject us to sanctions or other penalties that could have an adverse effect on our reputation, operating results and financial condition.

Our ability to achieve planned store financial performance

The results achieved by our stores may not be indicative of long-term performance or the potential performance of stores in other locations. The failure of stores to achieve acceptable results could result in additional store asset impairment charges, which could adversely affect our results of operations and financial condition.

Our international merchandise sourcing strategy

Our merchandise is manufactured by suppliers worldwide. Although we purchase a significant portion of our merchandise through a single international buying agent, we do not maintain any exclusive commitments to purchase from any one vendor. Because we have a global supply chain, any event causing the disruption of imports, including the insolvency of a significant supplier or a major labor slow-down, strike or dispute including any such actions involving ports, transloaders, consolidators or shippers, could have an adverse effect on our operations. Given the volatility and risk in the current markets, our reliance on external vendors leaves us subject to certain risks should one or more of these external vendors become insolvent. Although we monitor the financial stability of our key vendors and plan for contingencies, the financial failure of a key vendor could disrupt our operations and have an adverse effect on our cash flows, results of operations and financial condition. Other events that could also cause a disruption of imports include the imposition of additional trade law provisions or import restrictions, such as increased duties, tariffs, anti-dumping provisions, increased United States Customs and Border Protection (CBP) enforcement actions, or political or economic disruptions.

We have a Vendor Code of Conduct (the "Code") that provides guidelines for all of our vendors regarding working conditions, employment practices and compliance with local laws. A copy of the Code is posted on our website, www.ae.com , and is also included in our vendor manual in English and multiple other languages. We have a factory compliance program to audit for compliance with the Code. However, there can be no assurance that all violations can be eliminated in our supply chain. Publicity regarding violation of our Code or other social responsibility standards by any of our vendor factories could adversely affect our reputation, sales and financial performance.

We believe that there is a risk of terrorist activity on a global basis. Such activity might take the form of a physical act that impedes the flow of imported goods or the insertion of a harmful or injurious agent to an imported shipment. We have instituted policies and procedures designed to reduce the chance or impact of such actions. Examples include, but are not limited to, factory audits and self-assessments, including audit protocols on all critical security issues; the review of security procedures of our other international trading partners, including forwarders, consolidators, shippers and brokers; and the cancellation of agreements with entities who fail to meet our security requirements. In addition, CBP has recognized us as a validated participant of the Customs — Trade Partnership Against Terrorism program, a voluntary program in which an importer agrees to work with customs to strengthen overall supply chain security. However, there can be no assurance that terrorist activity can be prevented entirely and we cannot predict the likelihood of any such activities or the extent of their adverse impact on our operations.

Our reliance on our ability to implement and sustain information technology systems

We regularly evaluate our information technology systems and are currently implementing modifications and/or upgrades to the information technology systems that support our business. Modifications include replacing legacy systems with successor systems, making changes to legacy systems or acquiring new systems with new functionality. We are aware of inherent risks associated with operating, replacing and modifying these systems, including inaccurate system information and system disruptions. We believe we are taking appropriate action to mitigate the risks through testing, training, staging implementation and in-sourcing certain processes, as well as securing appropriate commercial contracts with third-party vendors supplying such replacement and redundancy technologies; however, there is a risk that information technology system disruptions and inaccurate system information, if not anticipated and/or promptly and appropriately mitigated, could have a material adverse effect on our results of operations.

Our ability to safeguard against security breaches with respect to our information technology systems

Our business employs systems and websites that allow for the storage and transmission of proprietary or confidential information regarding our business, customers and employees including credit card information. Security breaches could expose us to a risk of loss or misuse of this information and potential liability. We may not be able to anticipate or prevent rapidly evolving types of cyber-attacks. Actual or anticipated attacks may cause us to incur increasing costs including costs to deploy additional personnel and protection technologies, train employees and engage third party experts and consultants. Advances in computer capabilities, new technological discoveries or other developments may result in the technology used by us to protect transaction or other data being breached or compromised. Data and security breaches can also occur as a result of non-technical issues including intentional or inadvertent breach by employees or persons with whom we have commercial relationships that result in the unauthorized release of personal or confidential information. Any compromise or breach could result in a violation of applicable privacy and other laws, significant financial exposure and a loss of confidence in our security measures, which could have an adverse effect on our results of operations and our reputation.

Our reliance on key personnel

Our success depends to a significant extent upon our ability to attract and retain qualified key personnel, including senior management. Collective or individual changes in our senior management and other key personnel could have an adverse effect on our ability to determine and execute our strategies, which could adversely affect our business and results of operations. There is a high level of competition for senior management and other key personnel, and we cannot be assured we will be able to attract, retain and develop a sufficient number of qualified senior managers and other key personnel.

Failure to comply with regulatory requirements

As a public company, we are subject to numerous regulatory requirements, including those imposed by the Sarbanes-Oxley Act of 2002, the SEC and the NYSE. In addition, we are subject to numerous domestic and foreign laws and regulations affecting our business, including those related to labor, employment, worker health and safety, competition, privacy, consumer protection, import/export and anti-corruption, including the Foreign Corrupt Practices Act. Although we have put into place policies and procedures aimed at ensuring legal and regulatory compliance, our employees, subcontractors, vendors and suppliers could take actions that violate these requirements, which could have a material adverse effect on our reputation, financial condition and on the market price of our common stock. In addition, recent regulatory developments regarding the use of "conflict minerals," certain minerals originating from the Democratic Republic of Congo and adjoining countries, could affect the sourcing and availability of raw materials used by suppliers and subject us to costs associated with the regulations, including for the diligence pertaining to the presence of any conflict minerals used in our products, possible changes to products, processes or sources of our inputs, and reporting requirements.

Fluctuations in foreign currency exchange rates could adversely impact our financial condition and results of operations

We have foreign currency exchange rate risk with respect to revenues, expenses, assets and liabilities denominated in currencies other than the U.S. dollar. We currently do not utilize hedging instruments to mitigate foreign currency exchange risks. Specifically, fluctuations in the value of the Canadian Dollar, Mexican Peso, Chinese Yuan, Hong Kong Dollar, British Pound and Euro against the U.S. Dollar could have a material adverse effect on our results of operations, financial condition and cash flows.

Other risk factors

Additionally, other factors could adversely affect our financial performance, including factors such as: our ability to successfully acquire and integrate other businesses; any interruption of our key infrastructure systems, including exceeding capacity in our distribution centers; any disaster or casualty resulting in the interruption of service from our distribution centers or in a large number of our stores; any interruption of our business related to an outbreak of a pandemic disease in a country where we source or market our merchandise; extreme weather conditions or changes in climate conditions or weather patterns; the effects of changes in current exchange rates and interest rates; and international and domestic acts of terror.

The impact of any of the previously discussed factors, some of which are beyond our control, may cause our actual results to differ materially from expected results in these statements and other forward-looking statements we may make from time-to-time.

ITEM 5.   *MARKET FOR THE REGISTRANT'S COMMON EQUITY, RELATED STOCKHOLDER MATTERS AND ISSUER PURCHASES OF EQUITY SECURITIES.*

Our common stock is traded on the NYSE under the symbol "AEO". As of March 9, 2015, there were 520 stockholders of record. However, when including associates who own shares through our employee stock purchase plan, and others holding shares in broker accounts under street name, we estimate the stockholder base at approximately 55,000. The following table sets forth the range of high and low closing prices of the common stock as reported on the NYSE during the periods indicated.

For the Quarters Ended	Market Price		Cash Dividends per Common Share
	High	Low	
January 31, 2015	$ 14.63	$ 11.91	$ 0.125
November 1, 2014	$ 14.81	$ 10.42	$ 0.125
August 2, 2014	$ 11.97	$ 10.28	$ 0.125
May 3, 2014	$ 14.85	$ 10.95	$ 0.125
February 1, 2014	$ 16.52	$ 12.77	$ 0.125
November 2, 2013	$ 19.97	$ 13.24	$ 0.125
August 3, 2013	$ 20.48	$ 17.62	$ 0.125
May 4, 2013	$ 22.55	$ 18.38	$ 0.00

During Fiscal 2014 and Fiscal 2013, we paid quarterly dividends as shown in the table above. No cash dividends per common share were paid for the quarter ended May 4, 2013 as the dividend payment was accelerated into the previous quarter. The payment of future dividends is at the discretion of our Board of Directors (the "Board") and is based on future earnings, cash flow, financial condition, capital requirements, changes in U.S. taxation and other relevant factors. It is anticipated that any future dividends paid will be declared on a quarterly basis.

ITEM 6.   *SELECTED CONSOLIDATED FINANCIAL DATA.*

The following Selected Consolidated Financial Data should be read in conjunction with "Management's Discussion and Analysis of Financial Condition and Results of Operations," included under Item 7 below and the Consolidated Financial Statements and Notes thereto, included in Item 8 below. Most of the selected Consolidated Financial Statements data presented below is derived from our Consolidated Financial Statements, if applicable, which are filed in response to Item 8 below. The selected Consolidated Statement of Operations data for the years ended January 28, 2012 and January 29, 2011 and the selected Consolidated Balance Sheet data as of February 2, 2013, January 28, 2012, and January 29, 2011 are derived from audited Consolidated Financial Statements not included herein.

		For the Years Ended(1)			
(In thousands, except per share amounts, ratios and other financial information)	January 31, 2015	February 1, 2014	February 2, 2013	January 28, 2012	January 29, 2011
Summary of Operations (2)					
Total net revenue	$ 3,282,867	$ 3,305,802	$ 3,475,802	$ 3,120,065	$ 2,945,294
Comparable sales increase (decrease)(3)	(5)%	(6)%	9%	4%	(1)%
Gross profit	$ 1,154,674	$ 1,113,999	$ 1,390,322	$ 1,144,594	$ 1,182,151
Gross profit as a percentage of net sales	35.2%	33.7%	40.0%	36.7%	40.1%
Operating income	$ 155,765	$ 141,055	$ 394,606	$ 269,335	$ 339,552
Operating income as a percentage of net sales	4.7%	4.3%	11.4%	8.6%	11.5%
Income from continuing operations	$ 88,787	$ 82,983	$ 264,098	$ 175,279	$ 195,731
Income from continuing operations as a percentage of net sales	2.6%	2.5%	7.6%	5.6%	6.7%
Per Share Results					
Income from continuing operations per common share-basic	$ 0.46	$ 0.43	$ 1.35	$ 0.90	$ 0.98
Income from continuing operations per common share-diluted	$ 0.46	$ 0.43	$ 1.32	$ 0.89	$ 0.97
Weighted average common shares outstanding — basic	194,437	192,802	196,211	194,445	199,979
Weighted average common shares outstanding — diluted	195,135	194,475	200,665	196,314	201,818
Cash dividends per common share	$ 0.50	$ 0.375	$ 2.05	$ 0.44	$ 0.93
Balance Sheet Information					
Total cash and short-term investments	$ 410,697	$ 428,935	$ 630,992	$ 745,044	$ 734,695
Long-term investments	$ —	$ —	$ —	$ 847	$ 5,915
Total assets	$ 1,696,908	$ 1,694,164	$ 1,756,053	$ 1,950,802	$ 1,879,998
Short-term debt	$ —	$ —	$ —	$ —	$ —
Long-term debt	$ —	$ —	$ —	$ —	$ —
Stockholders' equity	$ 1,139,746	$ 1,166,178	$ 1,221,187	$ 1,416,851	$ 1,351,071
Working capital	$ 431,420	$ 512,513	$ 705,898	$ 882,087	$ 786,573
Current ratio	1.94	2.23	2.62	3.18	3.03
Average return on stockholders' equity	7.7%	7.0%	17.6%	11.0%	9.6%
Other Financial Information (2)					
Total stores at year-end	1,056	1,066	1,044	1,069	1,077
Capital expenditures	$ 245,002	$ 278,499	$ 93,939	$ 89,466	$ 75,904
Net sales per average selling square foot(4)	$ 525	$ 547	$ 602	$ 547	$ 526
Total selling square feet at end of period	5,294,744	5,205,948	4,962,923	5,028,493	5,026,144

Net sales per average gross square foot(4)	$ 420	$ 444	$ 489	$ 438	$ 422
Total gross square feet at end of period	6,613,100	6,503,486	6,023,278	6,290,284	6,288,425
Number of employees at end of period	38,000	40,400	40,100	39,600	39,900

(1)   Except for the fiscal year ended February 2, 2013, which includes 53 weeks, all fiscal years presented include 52 weeks.

(2)   All amounts presented are from continuing operations for all periods presented. Refer to Note 15 to the accompanying Consolidated Financial Statements for additional information regarding the discontinued operations of 77kids.

(3)   The comparable sales increase for the period ended February 2, 2013 is compared to the corresponding 53 week period in Fiscal 2011. Additionally, comparable sales for all periods include AEO Direct sales.

(4)   Total net revenue per average square foot is calculated using retail store sales for the year divided by the straight average of the beginning and ending square footage for the year.

ITEM 8.   *FINANCIAL STATEMENTS AND SUPPLEMENTARY DATA.*

Report of Independent Registered Public Accounting Firm

The Board of Directors and Stockholders of
American Eagle Outfitters, Inc.

We have audited the accompanying consolidated balance sheets of American Eagle Outfitters, Inc. as of January 31, 2015 and February 1, 2014, and the related consolidated statements of operations, comprehensive income, stockholders' equity, and cash flows for each of the three years in the period ended January 31, 2015. These financial statements are the responsibility of the Company's management. Our responsibility is to express an opinion on these financial statements based on our audits.

We conducted our audits in accordance with the standards of the Public Company Accounting Oversight Board (United States). Those standards require that we plan and perform the audit to obtain reasonable assurance about whether the financial statements are free of material misstatement. An audit includes examining, on a test basis, evidence supporting the amounts and disclosures in the financial statements. An audit also includes assessing the accounting principles used and significant estimates made by management, as well as evaluating the overall financial statement presentation. We believe that our audits provide a reasonable basis for our opinion.

In our opinion, the financial statements referred to above present fairly, in all material respects, the consolidated financial position of American Eagle Outfitters, Inc. at January 31, 2015 and February 1, 2014, and the consolidated results of its operations and its cash flows for each of the three years in the period ended January 31, 2015, in conformity with U.S. generally accepted accounting principles.

We also have audited, in accordance with the standards of the Public Company Accounting Oversight Board (United States), American Eagle Outfitters, Inc.'s internal control over financial reporting as of January 31, 2015, based on criteria established in Internal Control — Integrated Framework issued by the Committee of Sponsoring Organizations of the Treadway Commission (2013 framework) and our report dated March 11, 2015 expressed an unqualified opinion thereon.

/s/   Ernst & Young LLP

Pittsburgh, Pennsylvania
March 11, 2015

AMERICAN EAGLE OUTFITTERS, INC.
CONSOLIDATED BALANCE SHEETS

(In thousands, except per share amounts)	January 31, 2015	February 1, 2014
Assets		
Current assets:		
Cash and cash equivalents	$ 410,697	$ 418,933
Short-term investments	—	10,002
Merchandise inventory	278,972	291,541
Accounts receivable	67,894	73,882
Prepaid expenses and other	73,848	88,155
Deferred income taxes	59,102	45,478
Total current assets	890,513	927,991
Property and equipment, at cost, net of accumulated depreciation	694,856	632,986
Intangible assets, at cost, net of accumulated amortization	47,206	49,271
Goodwill	13,096	13,530
Non-current deferred income taxes	14,035	24,835
Other assets	37,202	45,551
Total assets	$ 1,696,908	$ 1,694,164
Liabilities and Stockholders' Equity		
Current liabilities:		
Accounts payable	$ 191,146	$ 203,872
Accrued compensation and payroll taxes	44,884	23,560
Accrued rent	78,567	76,397
Accrued income and other taxes	33,110	5,778
Unredeemed gift cards and gift certificates	47,888	47,194
Current portion of deferred lease credits	12,969	13,293
Other liabilities and accrued expenses	50,529	45,384
Total current liabilities	459,093	415,478
Non-current liabilities:		
Deferred lease credits	54,516	59,510
Non-current accrued income taxes	10,456	16,543
Other non-current liabilities	33,097	36,455
Total non-current liabilities	98,069	112,508
Commitments and contingencies	—	—
Stockholders' equity:		
Preferred stock, $0.01 par value; 5,000 shares authorized; none issued and outstanding	—	—
Common stock, $0.01 par value; 600,000 shares authorized; 249,566 shares issued; 194,516 and 193,149 shares outstanding, respectively	2,496	2,496
Contributed capital	569,675	573,008
Accumulated other comprehensive income	(9,944)	12,157
Retained earnings	1,543,085	1,569,851
Treasury stock, 55,050 and 56,417 shares, respectively, at cost	(965,566)	(991,334)
Total stockholders' equity	1,139,746	1,166,178
Total liabilities and stockholders' equity	$ 1,696,908	$ 1,694,164

Refer to Notes to Consolidated Financial Statements

AMERICAN EAGLE OUTFITTERS, INC.
CONSOLIDATED STATEMENTS OF OPERATIONS

	For the Years Ended		
(In thousands, except per share amounts)	January 31, 2015	February 1, 2014	February 2, 2013
Total net revenue	$ 3,282,867	$ 3,305,802	$ 3,475,802
Cost of sales, including certain buying, occupancy and warehousing expenses	2,128,193	2,191,803	2,085,480
Gross profit	1,154,674	1,113,999	1,390,322
Selling, general and administrative expenses	806,498	796,505	834,601
Restructuring charges	17,752	—	—
Loss on impairment of assets	33,468	44,465	34,869
Depreciation and amortization expense	141,191	131,974	126,246
Operating income	155,765	141,055	394,606
Other income, net	3,737	1,022	7,432
Income before income taxes	159,502	142,077	402,038
Provision for income taxes	70,715	59,094	137,940
Income from continuing operations	88,787	82,983	264,098
Loss from discontinued operations, net of tax	(8,465)	—	(31,990)
Net income	$ 80,322	$ 82,983	$ 232,108
Basic income per common share:			
Income from continuing operations	$ 0.46	$ 0.43	$ 1.35
Loss from discontinued operations	(0.04)	—	(0.16)
Basic net income per common share	$ 0.42	$ 0.43	$ 1.19
Diluted income per common share:			
Income from continuing operations	$ 0.46	$ 0.43	$ 1.32
Loss from discontinued operations	(0.04)	—	(0.16)
Diluted net income per common share	$ 0.42	$ 0.43	$ 1.16
Weighted average common shares outstanding — basic	194,437	192,802	196,211
Weighted average common shares outstanding — diluted	195,135	194,475	200,665

Refer to Notes to Consolidated Financial Statements

AMERICAN EAGLE OUTFITTERS, INC.

CONSOLIDATED STATEMENTS OF COMPREHENSIVE INCOME

	For the Years Ended		
(In thousands)	January 31, 2015	February 1, 2014	February 2, 2013
Net income	$ 80,322	$ 82,983	$ 232,108
Other comprehensive (loss) income:			
Foreign currency translation (loss) gain	(22,101)	(17,140)	638
Other comprehensive (loss) income	(22,101)	(17,140)	638
Comprehensive income	$ 58,221	$ 65,843	$ 232,746

Refer to Notes to Consolidated Financial Statements

AMERICAN EAGLE OUTFITTERS, INC.
CONSOLIDATED STATEMENTS OF STOCKHOLDERS' EQUITY

(In thousands, except per share amounts)	Shares Outstanding (1)	Common Stock	Contributed Capital	Retained Earnings	Treasury Stock(2)	Accumulated Other Comprehensive Income (Loss)	Stockholders' Equity
Balance at January 28, 2012	193,848	$ 2,496	$ 552,797	$ 1,771,464	$ (938,565)	$ 28,659	$ 1,416,851
Stock awards	—	—	76,108	—	—	—	76,108
Repurchase of common stock as part of publicly announced programs	(8,407)	—	—	—	(173,554)	—	(173,554)
Repurchase of common stock from employees	(280)	—	—	—	(4,125)	—	(4,125)
Reissuance of treasury stock	7,443	—	(11,054)	(36,213)	125,515	—	78,248
Net income	—	—	—	232,108	—	—	232,108
Other comprehensive income	—	—	—	—	—	638	638
Cash dividends and dividend equivalents ($2.05 per share)	—	—	9,214	(414,301)	—	—	(405,087)
Balance at February 2, 2013	192,604	$ 2,496	$ 627,065	$ 1,553,058	$ (990,729)	$ 29,297	$ 1,221,187
Stock awards	—	—	1,184	—	—	—	1,184
Repurchase of common stock as part of publicly announced programs	(1,600)	—	—	—	(33,051)	—	(33,051)
Repurchase of common stock from employees	(1,059)	—	—	—	(23,385)	—	(23,385)
Reissuance of treasury stock	3,204	—	(56,706)	6,090	55,831	—	5,215
Net income	—	—	—	82,983	—	—	82,983
Other comprehensive income	—	—	—	—	—	(17,140)	(17,140)
Cash dividends and dividend equivalents ($0.375 per share)	—	—	1,465	(72,280)	—	—	(70,815)
Balance at February 1, 2014	193,149	$ 2,496	$ 573,008	$ 1,569,851	$ (991,334)	$ 12,157	$ 1,166,178
Stock awards	—	—	12,372	—	—	—	12,372
Repurchase of common stock from employees	(517)	—	—	—	(7,464)	—	(7,464)
Reissuance of treasury stock	1,884	—	(17,988)	(7,503)	33,232	—	7,741
Net income	—	—	—	80,322	—	—	80,322
Other comprehensive income	—	—	—	—	—	(22,101)	(22,101)

Cash dividends and dividend equivalents ($0.50 per share)	—	—	2,283	(99,585)	—	—	(97,302)
Balance at January 31, 2015	**194,516**	**$ 2,496**	**$ 569,675**	**$ 1,543,085**	**$ (965,566)**	**$ (9,944)**	**$ 1,139,746**

_____

(1)   600,000 authorized, 249,566 issued and 194,516 outstanding, $0.01 par value common stock at January 31, 2015; 600,000 authorized, 249,566 issued and 193,149 outstanding, $0.01 par value common stock at February 1, 2014; 600,000 authorized, 249,566 issued and 192,604 outstanding, $0.01 par value common stock at February 2, 2013. The Company has 5,000 authorized, with none issued or outstanding, $0.01 par value preferred stock at January 31, 2015, February 1, 2014 and February 2, 2013.

(2)   55,050 shares, 56,417 shares, and 56,962 shares at January 31, 2015, February 1, 2014 and February 2, 2013, respectively. During Fiscal 2014, Fiscal 2013, and Fiscal 2012, 1,884 shares, 3,204 shares, and 7,443 shares, respectively, were reissued from treasury stock for the issuance of share-based payments.

Refer to Notes to Consolidated Financial Statements

AMERICAN EAGLE OUTFITTERS, INC.
CONSOLIDATED STATEMENTS OF CASH FLOWS

		For the Years Ended				
(In thousands)		January 31, 2015		February 1, 2014		February 2, 2013
Operating activities:						
Net income	$	80,322	$	82,983	$	232,108
Loss from discontinued operations, net of tax		8,465		—		31,990
Income from continuing operations	$	88,787	$	82,983	$	264,098
Adjustments to reconcile net income to net cash provided by operating activities						
Depreciation and amortization		142,351		134,047		128,397
Share-based compensation		16,070		(6,541)		66,349
Deferred income taxes		(2,279)		20,100		(30,647)
Foreign currency transaction loss (gain)		(495)		1,378		100
Loss on impairment of assets		33,468		44,465		34,869
Changes in assets and liabilities:						
Merchandise inventory		8,586		40,148		35,202
Accounts receivable		3,084		(29,511)		(6,664)
Prepaid expenses and other		14,282		(10,844)		404
Other assets		6,612		(36,089)		(8,165)
Accounts payable		(5,280)		28,568		(10,468)
Unredeemed gift cards and gift certificates		1,238		1,269		1,473
Deferred lease credits		(4,528)		583		(11,073)
Accrued compensation and payroll taxes		20,716		(42,465)		23,018
Accrued income and other taxes		24,826		(25,840)		(7,408)
Accrued liabilities		(9,012)		27,605		20,186
Total adjustments		249,639		146,873		235,573
Net cash provided by operating activities from continuing operations		**338,426**		**229,856**		**499,671**
Investing activities:						
Capital expenditures for property and equipment		(245,002)		(278,499)		(93,939)
Purchase of long-lived assets in a business combination		—		(20,751)		—
Acquisition of intangible assets		(1,264)		(6,835)		(1,125)
Purchase of available-for-sale securities		—		(52,065)		(111,086)
Sale of available-for-sale securities		10,002		162,785		15,500
Net cash (used for) provided by investing activities from continuing operations		**(236,264)**		**(195,365)**		**(190,650)**
Financing activities:						
Payments on capital leases and other		(7,143)		(2,839)		(3,066)
Repurchase of common stock as part of publicly announced programs		—		(33,051)		(173,554)
Repurchase of common stock from employees		(7,464)		(23,386)		(4,125)
Net proceeds from stock options exercised		7,305		6,197		76,401
Excess tax benefit from share-based payments		742		8,833		13,279
Cash used to net settle equity awards		—		—		—
Cash dividends paid		(97,224)		(72,280)		(403,490)
Net cash used for financing activities from continuing operations		**(103,784)**		**(116,526)**		**(494,555)**
Effect of exchange rates on cash		(7,578)		(8,151)		504
Cash flows of discontinued operations						
Net cash provided by (used for) operating activities		963		—		(24,616)
Net cash used for investing activities		—		—		(780)
Net cash used for financing activities		—		—		—
Effect of exchange rates on cash		—		—		—
Net cash provided by (used for) discontinued operations		**963**		**—**		**(25,396)**
Net decrease in cash and cash equivalents		**(8,237)**		**(90,186)**		**(210,426)**
Cash and cash equivalents — beginning of period	$	418,933	$	509,119		719,545
Cash and cash equivalents — end of period	$	410,697	$	418,933	$	509,119

Refer to Notes to Consolidated Financial Statements

AMERICAN EAGLE OUTFITTERS, INC.

NOTES TO CONSOLIDATED FINANCIAL STATEMENTS

FOR THE YEAR ENDED JANUARY 31, 2015

1.   Business Operations

American Eagle Outfitters, Inc. (the "Company"), a Delaware corporation, operates under the American Eagle Outfitters ® ("AEO") and aerie ® by American Eagle Outfitters ® ("aerie") brands. The Company operated 77kids by American Eagle Outfitters ® ("77kids") until its exit in Fiscal 2012.

Founded in 1977, American Eagle Outfitters is a leading apparel and accessories retailer that operates more than 1,000 retail stores in the U.S. and internationally, online at ae.com and aerie.com and international store locations managed by third-party operators. Through its brands, the Company offers high quality, on-trend clothing, accessories and personal care products at affordable prices. The Company's online business, AEO Direct, ships to 81 countries worldwide.

Merchandise Mix

The following table sets forth the approximate consolidated percentage of total net revenue from continuing operations attributable to each merchandise group for each of the periods indicated:

	For the Years Ended		
	January 31, 2015	February 1, 2014	February 2, 2013
Men's apparel and accessories	39%	40%	39%
Women's apparel and accessories (excluding aerie)	53%	52%	52%
aerie	8%	8%	9%
Total	100%	100%	100%

2.   Summary of Significant Accounting Policies

Principles of Consolidation

The Consolidated Financial Statements include the accounts of the Company and its wholly-owned subsidiaries. All intercompany transactions and balances have been eliminated in consolidation. At January 31, 2015, the Company operated in one reportable segment.

The Company exited its 77kids brand in Fiscal 2012. These Consolidated Financial Statements reflect the results of 77kids as discontinued operations for all periods presented.

Fiscal Year

Our financial year is a 52/53 week year that ends on the Saturday nearest to January 31. As used herein, "Fiscal 2015" refers to the 52 week period ending January 30, 2016. "Fiscal 2014" and "Fiscal 2013" refer to the 52 week period ended January 31, 2015 and February 1, 2014, respectively. "Fiscal 2012" refers to the 53 week period ended February 2, 2013. "Fiscal 2011" and "Fiscal 2010" refer to the 52 week periods ended January 28, 2012 and January 29, 2011, respectively.

Estimates

The preparation of financial statements in conformity with accounting principles generally accepted in the United States of America ("GAAP") requires the Company's management to make estimates and assumptions that affect the reported amounts of assets and liabilities and disclosure of contingent assets and liabilities at the date of the financial statements and the reported amounts of revenues and expenses during the reporting period. Actual results could differ from those estimates. On an ongoing basis, our management reviews its estimates based on currently available information. Changes in facts and circumstances may result in revised estimates.

Recent Accounting Pronouncements

In May 2014, the Financial Accounting Standard Board ("FASB") issued Accounting Standards Update ("ASU") No. 2014-09, *Revenue from Contracts with Customers* ("ASU 2014-09"). ASU 2014-09 is a comprehensive new revenue recognition model that expands disclosure requirements and requires a company to recognize revenue to depict the transfer of goods or services to a customer at an amount that reflects the consideration it expects to receive in exchange for those goods or services. ASU 2014-09 is effective for annual reporting periods beginning after December 15, 2016 and early adoption is not permitted. Accordingly, the Company will adopt ASU 2014-09 on January 29, 2017. The Company does not expect a material impact of the adoption of this guidance on the Company's consolidated financial condition, results of operations and cash flows.

AMERICAN EAGLE OUTFITTERS, INC.

NOTES TO CONSOLIDATED FINANCIAL STATEMENTS — (Continued)

In July 2013, the FASB issued ASU No. 2013-11, *Income Taxes (Topic 740): Presentation of an Unrecognized Tax Benefit When a Net Operating Loss Carryforward, a Similar Tax Loss, or a Tax Credit Carryforward Exists* ("ASU 2013-11"). ASU 2013-11 requires an entity to present an unrecognized tax benefit, or a portion of an unrecognized tax benefit, in the financial statements as a reduction to a deferred tax asset for a net operating loss carryforward, a similar tax loss, or a tax credit carryforward. To the extent a net operating loss carryforward, a similar tax loss, or a tax credit carryforward is not available at the reporting date under the tax law of the applicable jurisdiction to settle any additional income taxes that would result from the disallowance of a tax position or the tax law of the applicable jurisdiction does not require the entity to use, and the entity does not intend to use, the deferred tax asset for such purpose, the unrecognized tax benefit should be presented in the financial statements as a liability and should not be combined with deferred tax assets. ASU No. 2013-11 is effective for financial statements issued for annual reporting periods beginning after December 15, 2013 and interim periods within those years. The Company adopted ASU 2013-11 on February 2, 2014 with no significant impact to its Consolidated Financial Statements.

Foreign Currency Translation

In accordance with Accounting Standards Codification ("ASC") 830, *Foreign Currency Matters* , assets and liabilities denominated in foreign currencies were translated into United States dollars ("USD") (the reporting currency) at the exchange rates prevailing at the balance sheet date. Revenues and expenses denominated in foreign currencies were translated into USD at the monthly average exchange rates for the period. Gains or losses resulting from foreign currency transactions are included in the results of operations, whereas, related translation adjustments are reported as an element of other comprehensive income in accordance with ASC 220, *Comprehensive Income* (refer to Note 11 to the Consolidated Financial Statements).

Cash and Cash Equivalents, Short-term Investments and Long-term Investments

Cash includes cash equivalents. The Company considers all highly liquid investments purchased with a remaining maturity of three months or less to be cash equivalents.

As of February 1, 2014, short-term investments include treasury bills and term-deposits purchased with a maturity of greater than three months, but less than one year.

Long-term investments are included within other assets on the Company's Consolidated Balance Sheets. As of January 31, 2015 and February 1, 2014, the Company held no long-term investments.

Refer to Note 3 to the Consolidated Financial Statements for information regarding cash and cash equivalents and investments.

Other-than-Temporary Impairment

The Company evaluates its investments for impairment in accordance with ASC 320, *Investments — Debt and Equity Securities* ("ASC 320"). ASC 320 provides guidance for determining when an investment is considered impaired, whether impairment is other-than-temporary, and measurement of an impairment loss. An investment is considered impaired if the fair value of the investment is less than its cost. If, after consideration of all available evidence to evaluate the realizable value of its investment, impairment is determined to be other-than-temporary, then an impairment loss is recognized in the Consolidated Statement of Operations equal to the difference between the investment's cost and its fair value. Additionally, ASC 320 requires additional disclosures relating to debt and equity securities both in the interim and annual periods as well as requires the Company to present total OTTI with an offsetting reduction for any non-credit loss impairment amount recognized in other comprehensive income ("OCI").

There was no net impairment loss recognized in earnings for all years presented.

Merchandise Inventory

Merchandise inventory is valued at the lower of average cost or market, utilizing the retail method. Average cost includes merchandise design and sourcing costs and related expenses. The Company records merchandise receipts at the time which both title and risk of loss for the merchandise transfers to the Company.

The Company reviews its inventory levels to identify slow-moving merchandise and generally uses markdowns to clear merchandise. Additionally, the Company estimates a markdown reserve for future planned permanent markdowns related to current inventory. Markdowns may occur when inventory exceeds customer demand for reasons of style, seasonal adaptation, changes in customer preference, lack of consumer acceptance of fashion items, competition, or if it is determined that the inventory in stock will not sell at its currently ticketed price. Such markdowns may have a material adverse impact on earnings, depending on the extent and amount of inventory affected. The Company also estimates a shrinkage reserve for the period between the last physical count and the balance sheet date. The estimate for the shrinkage reserve, based on historical results, can be affected by changes in merchandise mix and changes in actual shrinkage trends.

AMERICAN EAGLE OUTFITTERS, INC.

NOTES TO CONSOLIDATED FINANCIAL STATEMENTS — (Continued)

Property and Equipment

Property and equipment is recorded on the basis of cost with depreciation computed utilizing the straight-line method over the assets' estimated useful lives. The useful lives of our major classes of assets are as follows:

Buildings	25 years
Leasehold improvements	Lesser of 10 years or the term of the lease
Fixtures and equipment	5 years

In accordance with ASC 360, *Property, Plant, and Equipment* , the Company's management evaluates the value of leasehold improvements and store fixtures associated with retail stores, which have been open for a period of time sufficient to reach maturity. The Company evaluates long-lived assets for impairment at the individual store level, which is the lowest level at which individual cash flows can be identified. Impairment losses are recorded on long-lived assets used in operations when events and circumstances indicate that the assets might be impaired and the undiscounted cash flows estimated to be generated by those assets are less than the carrying amounts of the assets. When events such as these occur, the impaired assets are adjusted to their estimated fair value and an impairment loss is recorded separately as a component of operating income under loss on impairment of assets.

During Fiscal 2014, the Company recorded pre-tax asset impairment charges of $33.5 million that includes $25.1 million for the impairment of 79 retail stores recorded as a loss on impairment of assets in the Consolidated Statements of Operations. Based on the Company's evaluation of current and future projected performance, it was determined that these stores would not be able to generate sufficient cash flow over the expected remaining lease term to recover the carrying value of the respective stores' assets. Additionally, the Company recorded $8.4 million of impairment charges related to corporate assets.

During Fiscal 2013, the Company recorded asset impairment charges of $44.5 million consisting of $25.2 million for the impairment of 69 retail stores and $19.3 million for the Company's Warrendale, Pennsylvania Distribution Center, recorded as a loss on impairment of assets in the Consolidated Statements of Operations. The retail store impairments were recorded based on the results of the Company's evaluation of stores that considered performance during the holiday selling season and a significant portfolio review in the fourth quarter of Fiscal 2013 that considered current and future performance projections and strategic real estate initiatives. The Company determined that these stores would not be able to generate sufficient cash flow over the expected remaining lease term to recover the carrying value of the respective stores assets.

During Fiscal 2012, the Company recorded asset impairment charges of $34.9 million consisting of the impairment of 52 retail stores, which is recorded as a loss on impairment of assets in the Consolidated Statements of Operations. This impairment was recorded based on the results of the Company's evaluation of stores that considered performance during the holiday selling season and strategic decisions made in the fourth quarter of Fiscal 2012 regarding the rebalancing of our store fleet. The Company determined that these stores would not be able to generate sufficient cash flow over the expected remaining lease term to recover the carrying value of the respective stores assets. Additionally, the Company recorded $16.6 million of store asset impairment charges related to 77kids stores, which is included in Discontinued Operations.

Refer to Note 15 to the Consolidated Financial Statements for additional information regarding the discontinued operations for 77kids.

When the Company closes, remodels or relocates a store prior to the end of its lease term, the remaining net book value of the assets related to the store is recorded as a write-off of assets within depreciation and amortization expense.

Refer to Note 7 to the Consolidated Financial Statements for additional information regarding property and equipment.

Goodwill

The Company's goodwill is primarily related to the acquisition of its importing operations, Canadian business and recently acquired operations in Hong Kong and China. In accordance with ASC 350, *Intangibles- Goodwill and Other* ("ASC 350"), the Company evaluates goodwill for possible impairment on at least an annual basis and last performed an annual impairment test as of January 31, 2015. As a result of the Company's annual goodwill impairment test, the Company concluded that its goodwill was not impaired.

Intangible Assets

Intangible assets are recorded on the basis of cost with amortization computed utilizing the straight-line method over the assets' estimated useful lives. The Company's intangible assets, which primarily include trademark assets, are amortized over 15 to 25 years.

The Company evaluates intangible assets for impairment in accordance with ASC 350 when events or circumstances indicate that the carrying value of the asset may not be recoverable. Such an evaluation includes the estimation of undiscounted future cash flows to be generated by those assets. If the sum of the estimated future undiscounted cash flows are less than the carrying amounts of the assets, then the assets are impaired and are adjusted to their estimated fair value. No intangible asset impairment charges were recorded during Fiscal 2014, Fiscal 2013 or Fiscal 2012.

Refer to Note 8 to the Consolidated Financial Statements for additional information regarding intangible assets.

AMERICAN EAGLE OUTFITTERS, INC.

NOTES TO CONSOLIDATED FINANCIAL STATEMENTS — (Continued)

Deferred Lease Credits

Deferred lease credits represent the unamortized portion of construction allowances received from landlords related to the Company's retail stores. Construction allowances are generally comprised of cash amounts received by the Company from its landlords as part of the negotiated lease terms. The Company records a receivable and a deferred lease credit liability at the lease commencement date (date of initial possession of the store). The deferred lease credit is amortized on a straight-line basis as a reduction of rent expense over the term of the original lease (including the pre-opening build-out period). The receivable is reduced as amounts are received from the landlord.

Self-Insurance Liability

The Company is self-insured for certain losses related to employee medical benefits and worker's compensation. Costs for self-insurance claims filed and claims incurred but not reported are accrued based on known claims and historical experience. Management believes that it has adequately reserved for its self-insurance liability, which is capped through the use of stop loss contracts with insurance companies. However, any significant variation of future claims from historical trends could cause actual results to differ from the accrued liability.

Co-branded Credit Card and Customer Loyalty Program

The Company offers a co-branded credit card (the "AEO Visa Card") and a private label credit card (the "AEO Credit Card") under the AEO and aerie brands. These credit cards are issued by a third-party bank (the "Bank") in accordance with a credit card agreement ("the Agreement"). The Company has no liability to the Bank for bad debt expense, provided that purchases are made in accordance with the Bank's procedures. We receive cash from the Bank in accordance with the Agreement and based on card activity. We recognize revenue for such cash receipts when the amounts are fixed or determinable and collectability is reasonably assured. The revenue is recorded in other revenue, which is a component of total net revenue in our Consolidated Statements of Operations.

Once a customer is approved to receive the AEO Visa Card or the AEO Credit Card and the card is activated, the customer is eligible to participate in the credit card rewards program. Customers who make purchases at AEO and aerie earn discounts in the form of savings certificates when certain purchase levels are reached. Also, AEO Visa Card customers who make purchases at other retailers where the card is accepted earn additional discounts. Savings certificates are valid for 90 days from issuance.

Points earned under the credit card rewards program on purchases at AEO and aerie are accounted for by analogy to ASC 605-25, Revenue Recognition, *Multiple Element Arrangements* ("ASC 605-25"). The Company believes that points earned under its point and loyalty programs represent deliverables in a multiple element arrangement rather than a rebate or refund of cash. Accordingly, the portion of the sales revenue attributed to the award points is deferred and recognized when the award is redeemed or when the points expire. Additionally, credit card reward points earned on non-AEO or aerie purchases are accounted for in accordance with ASC 605-25. As the points are earned, a current liability is recorded for the estimated cost of the award, and the impact of adjustments is recorded in cost of sales.

The Company offers its customers the AEREWARDS ® loyalty program (the "Program"). Under the Program, customers accumulate points based on purchase activity and earn rewards by reaching certain point thresholds during three-month earning periods. Rewards earned during these periods are valid through the stated expiration date, which is approximately one month from the mailing date of the reward. These rewards can be redeemed for a discount on a purchase of merchandise. Rewards not redeemed during the one-month redemption period are forfeited. The Company determined that rewards earned using the Program should be accounted for in accordance with ASC 605-25. Accordingly, the portion of the sales revenue attributed to the award credits is deferred and recognized when the awards are redeemed or expire.

Income Taxes

The Company calculates income taxes in accordance with ASC 740, *Income Taxes* ("ASC 740"), which requires the use of the asset and liability method. Under this method, deferred tax assets and liabilities are recognized based on the difference between the Consolidated Financial Statement carrying amounts of existing assets and liabilities and their respective tax bases as computed pursuant to ASC 740. Deferred tax assets and liabilities are measured using the tax rates, based on certain judgments regarding enacted tax laws and published guidance, in effect in the years when those temporary differences are expected to reverse. A valuation allowance is established against the deferred tax assets when it is more likely than not that some portion or all of the deferred taxes may not be realized. Changes in the Company's level and composition of earnings, tax laws or the deferred tax valuation allowance, as well as the results of tax audits, may materially impact the Company's effective income tax rate.

The Company evaluates its income tax positions in accordance with ASC 740 which prescribes a comprehensive model for recognizing, measuring, presenting and disclosing in the financial statements tax positions taken or expected to be taken on a tax return, including a decision whether to file or not to file in a particular jurisdiction. Under ASC 740, a tax benefit from an uncertain position may be recognized only if it is "more likely than not" that the position is sustainable based on its technical merits.

The calculation of the deferred tax assets and liabilities, as well as the decision to recognize a tax benefit from an uncertain position and to establish a valuation allowance require management to make estimates and assumptions. The Company believes that its assumptions and

AMERICAN EAGLE OUTFITTERS, INC.

NOTES TO CONSOLIDATED FINANCIAL STATEMENTS — (Continued)

estimates are reasonable, although actual results may have a positive or negative material impact on the balances of deferred tax assets and liabilities, valuation allowances or net income.

Revenue Recognition

Revenue is recorded for store sales upon the purchase of merchandise by customers. The Company's e-commerce operation records revenue upon the estimated customer receipt date of the merchandise. Shipping and handling revenues are included in total net revenue. Sales tax collected from customers is excluded from revenue and is included as part of accrued income and other taxes on the Company's Consolidated Balance Sheets.

Revenue is recorded net of estimated and actual sales returns and deductions for coupon redemptions and other promotions. The Company records the impact of adjustments to its sales return reserve quarterly within total net revenue and cost of sales. The sales return reserve reflects an estimate of sales returns based on projected merchandise returns determined through the use of historical average return percentages.

	For the Years Ended		
(In thousands)	January 31, 2015	February 1, 2014	February 2, 2013
Beginning balance	$ 2,205	$ 4,481	$ 2,929
Returns	(79,813)	(85,871)	(86,895)
Provisions	80,857	83,595	88,447
Ending balance	$ 3,249	$ 2,205	$ 4,481

Revenue is not recorded on the purchase of gift cards. A current liability is recorded upon purchase, and revenue is recognized when the gift card is redeemed for merchandise. Additionally, the Company recognizes revenue on unredeemed gift cards based on an estimate of the amounts that will not be redeemed ("gift card breakage"), determined through historical redemption trends. Gift card breakage revenue is recognized in proportion to actual gift card redemptions as a component of total net revenue. For further information on the Company's gift card program, refer to the Gift Cards caption below.

The Company recognizes royalty revenue generated from its franchise agreements based upon a percentage of merchandise sales by the franchisee. This revenue is recorded as a component of total net revenue when earned.

Cost of Sales, Including Certain Buying, Occupancy and Warehousing Expenses

Cost of sales consists of merchandise costs, including design, sourcing, importing and inbound freight costs, as well as markdowns, shrinkage and certain promotional costs (collectively "merchandise costs") and buying, occupancy and warehousing costs.

Design costs are related to the Company's Design Center operations and include compensation, travel, supplies and samples for our design teams, as well as rent and depreciation for the Company's Design Center. These costs are included in cost of sales as the respective inventory is sold.

Buying, occupancy and warehousing costs consist of compensation, employee benefit expenses and travel for the Company's buyers and certain senior merchandising executives; rent and utilities related to the Company's stores, corporate headquarters, distribution centers and other office space; freight from the Company's distribution centers to the stores; compensation and supplies for the Company's distribution centers, including purchasing, receiving and inspection costs; and shipping and handling costs related to our e-commerce operation. Gross profit is the difference between total net revenue and cost of sales.

Selling, General and Administrative Expenses

Selling, general and administrative expenses consist of compensation and employee benefit expenses, including salaries, incentives and related benefits associated with the Company's stores and corporate headquarters. Selling, general and administrative expenses also include advertising costs, supplies for our stores and home office, communication costs, travel and entertainment, leasing costs and services purchased. Selling, general and administrative expenses do not include compensation, employee benefit expenses and travel for the Company's design, sourcing and importing teams, the Company's buyers and the Company's distribution centers as these amounts are recorded in cost of sales.

Advertising Costs

Certain advertising costs, including direct mail, in-store photographs and other promotional costs are expensed when the marketing campaign commences. As of January 31, 2015 and February 1, 2014, the Company had prepaid advertising expense of $6.6 million and $9.0 million, respectively. All other advertising costs are expensed as incurred. The Company recognized $94.2 million, $87.0 million and $90.0 million in advertising expense during Fiscal 2014, Fiscal 2013 and Fiscal 2012, respectively.

AMERICAN EAGLE OUTFITTERS, INC.

NOTES TO CONSOLIDATED FINANCIAL STATEMENTS — (Continued)

Store Pre-Opening Costs

Store pre-opening costs consist primarily of rent, advertising, supplies and payroll expenses. These costs are expensed as incurred.

Other Income, Net

Other income, net consists primarily of interest income/expense, foreign currency transaction gain/loss and realized investment gains/losses.

Gift Cards

The value of a gift card is recorded as a current liability upon purchase and revenue is recognized when the gift card is redeemed for merchandise. The Company estimates gift card breakage and recognizes revenue in proportion to actual gift card redemptions as a component of total net revenue. The Company determines an estimated gift card breakage rate by continuously evaluating historical redemption data and the time when there is a remote likelihood that a gift card will be redeemed. The Company recorded gift card breakage of $7.0 million, $7.3 million and $8.9 million during Fiscal 2014, Fiscal 2013 and Fiscal 2012, respectively.

Legal Proceedings and Claims

The Company is subject to certain legal proceedings and claims arising out of the conduct of its business. In accordance with ASC 450, *Contingencies* ("ASC 450"), the Company records a reserve for estimated losses when the loss is probable and the amount can be reasonably estimated. If a range of possible loss exists and no anticipated loss within the range is more likely than any other anticipated loss, the Company records the accrual at the low end of the range, in accordance with ASC 450. As the Company believes that it has provided adequate reserves, it anticipates that the ultimate outcome of any matter currently pending against the Company will not materially affect the consolidated financial position, results of operations or consolidated cash flows of the Company.

Supplemental Disclosures of Cash Flow Information

The table below shows supplemental cash flow information for cash amounts paid during the respective periods:

| | For the Years Ended | | |
| | January 31, 2015 | February 1, 2014 | February 2, 2013 |
(In thousands)			
Cash paid during the periods for:			
Income taxes	$ 38,501	$ 65,496	$ 142,009
Interest	$ 638	$ 387	$ 348

Segment Information

In accordance with ASC 280, *Segment Reporting* ("ASC 280"), the Company has identified three operating segments (American Eagle Outfitters ® Brand retail stores, aerie ® by American Eagle Outfitters ® retail stores and AEO Direct) that reflect the Company's operational structure as well as the business's internal view of analyzing results and allocating resources. All of the operating segments have been aggregated and are presented as one reportable segment, as permitted by ASC 280.

The following tables present summarized geographical information:

| | For the Years Ended | | |
| | January 31, 2015 | February 1, 2014 | February 2, 2013 |
(In thousands)			
Total net revenue:			
United States	$ 2,895,310	$ 2,954,635	$ 3,131,233
Foreign(1)	387,557	351,167	344,569
Total net revenue	$ 3,282,867	$ 3,305,802	$ 3,475,802

---

(1)   Amounts represent sales from American Eagle Outfitters and aerie international retail stores, AEO Direct sales that are billed to and/or shipped to foreign countries and international franchise revenue.

AMERICAN EAGLE OUTFITTERS, INC.

NOTES TO CONSOLIDATED FINANCIAL STATEMENTS — (Continued)

(In thousands)	January 31, 2015	February 1, 2014
Long-lived assets, net:		
United States	$ 664,734	$ 614,284
Foreign	90,424	81,503
Total long-lived assets, net	$ 755,158	$ 695,787

Reclassifications

Certain reclassifications have been made to the Consolidated Financial Statements for prior periods in order to conform to the current period presentation.

3. Cash and Cash Equivalents, Short-term Investments and Long-term Investments

The following table summarizes the fair market value of our cash and marketable securities, which are recorded on the Consolidated Balance Sheets:

(In thousands)	January 31, 2015	February 1, 2014
Cash and cash equivalents:		
Cash	370,692	$ 330,013
Money-market	40,005	25,696
Treasury bills	—	63,224
Total cash and cash equivalents	410,697	$ 418,933
Short-term investments:		
Treasury bills	—	$ 10,002
Total short-term investments	—	$ 10,002
Total	410,697	$ 428,935

Proceeds from the sale of available-for-sale securities were $10.0 million, $162.8 million and $15.5 million for Fiscal 2014, Fiscal 2013 and Fiscal 2012, respectively. Purchases of available-for-sale securities for Fiscal 2013 and Fiscal 2012 were $52.1 million and $111.1 million, respectively. At January 31, 2015 and February 1, 2014, the fair value of all available for sale securities approximated par, with no gross unrealized holding gains or losses.

4. Fair Value Measurements

ASC 820, *Fair Value Measurement Disclosures* ("ASC 820"), defines fair value, establishes a framework for measuring fair value in accordance with GAAP, and expands disclosures about fair value measurements. Fair value is defined under ASC 820 as the exit price associated with the sale of an asset or transfer of a liability in an orderly transaction between market participants at the measurement date.

Financial Instruments

Valuation techniques used to measure fair value under ASC 820 must maximize the use of observable inputs and minimize the use of unobservable inputs. In addition, ASC 820 establishes this three-tier fair value hierarchy, which prioritizes the inputs used in measuring fair value. These tiers include:

- *Level 1* — Quoted prices in active markets for identical assets or liabilities.

- *Level 2* — Inputs other than Level 1 that are observable, either directly or indirectly, such as quoted prices for similar assets or liabilities; quoted prices in markets that are not active; or other inputs that are observable or can be corroborated by observable market data for substantially the full term of the assets or liabilities.

- *Level 3* — Unobservable inputs (i.e., projections, estimates, interpretations, etc.) that are supported by little or no market activity and that are significant to the fair value of the assets or liabilities.

As of January 31, 2015 and February 1, 2014, the Company held certain assets that are required to be measured at fair value on a recurring basis. These include cash equivalents and investments.

AMERICAN EAGLE OUTFITTERS, INC.

NOTES TO CONSOLIDATED FINANCIAL STATEMENTS — (Continued)

In accordance with ASC 820, the following tables represent the fair value hierarchy for the Company's financial assets (cash equivalents and investments) measured at fair value on a recurring basis as of January 31, 2015 and February 1, 2014:

| | | Fair Value Measurements at January 31, 2015 | | |
| | | Quoted Market Prices in Active Markets for Identical Assets | Significant Other Observable | Significant Unobservable Inputs |
(In thousands)	Carrying Amount	(Level 1)	Inputs (Level 2)	(Level 3)
Cash and cash equivalents				
Cash	$ 370,692	$ 370,692	$ —	$ —
Money-market	40,005	40,005	—	—
Total cash and cash equivalents	$ 410,697	$ 410,697	$ —	$ —
Total short-term investments	—	—	—	—
Total	$ 410,697	$ 410,697	$ —	$ —

| | | Fair Value Measurements at February 1, 2014 | | |
| | | Quoted Market Prices in Active Markets for Identical Assets | Significant Other Observable | Significant Unobservable Inputs |
(In thousands)	Carrying Amount	(Level 1)	Inputs (Level 2)	(Level 3)
Cash and cash equivalents				
Cash	$ 330,013	$ 330,013	$ —	$ —
Treasury bills	63,224	63,224	—	—
Money-market	25,696	25,696	—	—
Total cash and cash equivalents	$ 418,933	$ 418,933	$ —	$ —
Short-term investments				
Treasury bills	$ 10,002	$ 10,002	$ —	$ —
Total short-term investments	$ 10,002	$ 10,002	$ —	$ —
Total	$ 428,935	$ 428,935	$ —	$ —

In the event the Company holds Level 3 investments, a discounted cash flow model is used to value those investments. There were no Level 3 investments at January 31, 2015 or February 1, 2014.

Non-Financial Assets

The Company's non-financial assets, which include goodwill, intangible assets and property and equipment, are not required to be measured at fair value on a recurring basis. However, if certain triggering events occur, or if an annual impairment test is required and the Company is required to evaluate the non-financial instrument for impairment, a resulting asset impairment would require that the non-financial asset be recorded at the estimated fair value. As a result of the Company's annual goodwill impairment test performed as of January 31, 2015, the Company concluded that its goodwill was not impaired.

Certain long-lived assets were measured at fair value on a nonrecurring basis using Level 3 inputs as defined in ASC 820. During Fiscal 2014 and Fiscal 2013, certain long-lived assets related to the Company's retail stores and corporate assets were determined to be unable to recover their respective carrying values and were written.

AMERICAN EAGLE OUTFITTERS, INC.

NOTES TO CONSOLIDATED FINANCIAL STATEMENTS — (Continued)

5.   Earnings per Share

The following is a reconciliation between basic and diluted weighted average shares outstanding:

| | For the Years Ended | | |
| | January 31, 2015 | February 1, 2014 | February 2, 2013 |
(In thousands, except per share amounts)			
Weighted average common shares outstanding:			
Basic number of common shares outstanding	194,437	192,802	196,211
Dilutive effect of stock options and non-vested restricted stock	698	1,673	4,454
Dilutive number of common shares outstanding	195,135	194,475	200,665

Equity awards to purchase approximately 2.3 million, 1.7 million and 1.5 million shares of common stock during the Fiscal 2014, Fiscal 2013 and Fiscal 2012, respectively, were outstanding, but were not included in the computation of weighted average diluted common share amounts as the effect of doing so would have been anti-dilutive.

Additionally, for Fiscal 2014, approximately 1.9 million of performance-based restricted stock awards were not included in the computation of weighted average diluted common share amounts because the number of shares ultimately issued is contingent on the Company's performance compared to pre-established performance goals. For Fiscal 2013, approximately 1.8 million of performance-based restricted stock awards were not included in the computation of weighted average diluted common share amounts because the number of shares ultimately issued is contingent on the Company's performance compared to pre-established performance goals.

Refer to Note 12 to the Consolidated Financial Statements for additional information regarding share-based compensation.

6.   Accounts Receivable

Accounts receivable are comprised of the following:

(In thousands)	January 31, 2015	February 1, 2014
Franchise and license receivable	$ 24,945	$ 22,943
Merchandise sell-offs and vendor receivables	12,953	16,106
Credit card program receivable	9,637	15,000
Marketing cost reimbursements	4,640	6,063
Gift card receivable	4,453	986
Landlord construction allowances	3,354	11,626
Other Items	7,912	1,158
Total	$ 67,894	$ 73,882

7.   Property and Equipment

Property and equipment consists of the following:

(In thousands)	January 31, 2015	February 1, 2014
Land	$ 17,495	$ 17,986
Buildings	201,024	140,600
Leasehold improvements	571,312	600,572
Fixtures and equipment	852,408	732,228
Construction in progress	42,470	102,974
Property and equipment, at cost	$ 1,684,709	$ 1,594,360
Less: Accumulated depreciation	(989,853)	(961,374)
Property and equipment, net	$ 694,856	$ 632,986

AMERICAN EAGLE OUTFITTERS, INC.

NOTES TO CONSOLIDATED FINANCIAL STATEMENTS — (Continued)

Depreciation expense is summarized as follows:

	For the Years Ended		
(In thousands)	January 31, 2015	February 1, 2014	February 2, 2013
Depreciation expense	$ 132,529	$ 116,761	$ 122,756

Additionally, during Fiscal 2014, Fiscal 2013 and Fiscal 2012, the Company recorded $6.4 million, $14.6 million and $3.7 million, respectively, related to asset write-offs within depreciation and amortization expense.

8.   Intangible Assets

Intangible assets include costs to acquire and register the Company's trademark assets. The following table represents intangible assets as of January 31, 2015 and February 1, 2014:

(In thousands)	January 31, 2015	February 1, 2014
Trademarks, at cost	$ 59,385	$ 58,121
Less: Accumulated amortization	(12,179)	(8,850)
Intangible assets, net	$ 47,206	$ 49,271

Amortization expense is summarized as follows:

	For the Years Ended		
(In thousands)	January 31, 2015	February 1, 2014	February 2, 2013
Amortization expense	$ 3,465	$ 2,714	$ 1,952

The table below summarizes the estimated future amortization expense for intangible assets existing as of January 31, 2015 for the next five Fiscal Years:

(In thousands)	Future Amortization
2015	3,404
2016	3,473
2017	3,472
2018	3,452
2019	3,433

9.   Other Credit Arrangements

In December 2014, the Company entered into a new Credit Agreement ("Credit Agreement") for five-year, syndicated, asset-based revolving credit facilities (the "Credit Facilities"). The Credit Agreement provides senior secured revolving credit for loans and letters of credit up to $400 million, subject to customary borrowing base limitations. The Credit Facilities provide increased financial flexibility and take advantage of a favorable credit environment.

All obligations under the Credit Facilities are unconditionally guaranteed by certain subsidiaries. The obligations under the Credit Agreement are secured by a first-priority security interest in certain working capital assets of the borrowers and guarantors, consisting primarily of cash, receivables, inventory and certain other assets, and will be further secured by first-priority mortgages on certain real property.

As of January 31, 2015, the Company was in compliance with the terms of the Credit Agreement and had $8.1 million outstanding in stand-by letters of credit. No loans were outstanding under the Credit Agreement on January 31, 2015.

The Credit Facilities replace the Company's syndicated, unsecured, revolving credit facility in the amount of $150.0 million.

Additionally, the Company has borrowing agreements with two separate financial institutions under which it may borrow an aggregate of $155.0 million USD for the purposes of trade letter of credit issuances. The availability of any future borrowings under the trade letter of credit facilities is subject to acceptance by the respective financial institutions.

As of January 31, 2015, the Company had outstanding trade letters of credit of $13.7 million.

AMERICAN EAGLE OUTFITTERS, INC.

NOTES TO CONSOLIDATED FINANCIAL STATEMENTS — (Continued)

10. Leases

The Company leases all store premises, some of its office space and certain information technology and office equipment. The store leases generally have initial terms of 10 years and are classified as operating leases. Most of these store leases provide for base rentals and the payment of a percentage of sales as additional contingent rent when sales exceed specified levels. Additionally, most leases contain construction allowances and/or rent holidays. In recognizing landlord incentives and minimum rent expense, the Company amortizes the items on a straight-line basis over the lease term (including the pre-opening build-out period).

A summary of fixed minimum and contingent rent expense for all operating leases follows:

| | For the Years Ended | | |
| | January 31, 2015 | February 1, 2014 | February 2, 2013 |
(In thousands)			
Store rent:			
Fixed minimum	$ 279,640	$ 260,668	$ 250,844
Contingent	6,733	6,576	9,758
Total store rent, excluding common area maintenance charges, real estate taxes and certain other expenses	$ 286,373	$ 267,244	$ 260,602
Offices, distribution facilities, equipment and other	15,449	17,153	14,960
Total rent expense	$ 301,822	$ 284,397	$ 275,562

In addition, the Company is typically responsible under its store, office and distribution center leases for tenant occupancy costs, including maintenance costs, common area charges, real estate taxes and certain other expenses.

The table below summarizes future minimum lease obligations, consisting of fixed minimum rent, under operating leases in effect at January 31, 2015:

(In thousands)	Future Minimum Lease Obligations
Fiscal years:	
2015	287,091
2016	259,106
2017	229,489
2018	199,208
2019	173,388
Thereafter	549,046
Total	1,697,328

11. Other Comprehensive Income

The accumulated balances of other comprehensive income included as part of the Consolidated Statements of Stockholders' Equity follow:

(In thousands)	Before Tax Amount	Tax Benefit (Expense)	Accumulated Other Comprehensive Income
Balance at January 28, 2012	$ 28,659	—	$ 28,659
Foreign currency translation gain	638	—	638
Balance at February 2, 2013	$ 29,297	—	$ 29,297
Foreign currency translation loss	(17,140)	—	(17,140)
Balance at February 1, 2014	$ 12,157	—	$ 12,157
Foreign currency translation loss	(22,101)	—	(22,101)
Balance at January 31, 2015	$ (9,944)	—	$ (9,944)

AMERICAN EAGLE OUTFITTERS, INC.

NOTES TO CONSOLIDATED FINANCIAL STATEMENTS — (Continued)

12.   Share-Based Payments

The Company accounts for share-based compensation under the provisions of ASC 718, *Compensation — Stock Compensation* ("ASC 718"), which requires the Company to measure and recognize compensation expense for all share-based payments at fair value. Total share-based compensation expense included in the Consolidated Statements of Operations for Fiscal 2014 and Fiscal 2012 was $16.1 million ($9.9 million, net of tax) and $66.3 million ($40.9 million, net of tax), respectively. Total share-based compensation expense included in the Consolidated Statements of Operations for Fiscal 2013 was a net benefit of $6.5 million ($4.1 million, net of tax).

ASC 718 requires recognition of compensation cost under a non-substantive vesting period approach for awards containing provisions that accelerate or continue vesting upon retirement. Accordingly, for awards with such provisions, the Company recognizes compensation expense over the period from the grant date to the date retirement eligibility is achieved, if that is expected to occur during the nominal vesting period. Additionally, for awards granted to retirement eligible employees, the full compensation cost of an award must be recognized immediately upon grant.

At January 31, 2015, the Company had awards outstanding under three share-based compensation plans, which are described below.

Share-based compensation plans

2014 Stock Award and Incentive Plan

The 2014 Plan was approved by the stockholders on May 29, 2014. The 2014 Plan authorized 11.5 million shares for issuance, in the form of options, stock appreciation rights ("SARS"), restricted stock, restricted stock units, bonus stock and awards, performance awards, dividend equivalents and other stock based awards. The 2014 Plan provides that the maximum number of shares awarded to any individual may not exceed 4.0 million shares per year for options and SARS and no more than 1.5 million shares may be granted with respect to each of restricted shares of stock and restricted stock units plus any unused carryover limit from the previous year. The 2014 Plan allows the Compensation Committee of the Board to determine which employees receive awards and the terms and conditions of the awards that are mandatory under the 2014 Plan. The 2014 Plan provides for grants to directors who are not officers or employees of the Company, which are not to exceed in value $300,000 in any single calendar year ($500,000 in the first year a person becomes a non-employee director). Through January 31, 2015, approximately 46,700 shares of restricted stock and approximately 23,400 shares of common stock had been granted under the 2014 Plan to employees and directors. Approximately 62% of the restricted stock awards are performance-based and are earned if the Company meets established performance goals. The remaining 38% of the restricted stock awards are time-based and vest over three years.

2005 Stock Award and Incentive Plan

The 2005 Plan was approved by the stockholders on June 15, 2005. The 2005 Plan authorized 18.4 million shares for issuance, of which 6.4 million shares are available for full value awards in the form of restricted stock awards, restricted stock units or other full value stock awards and 12.0 million shares are available for stock options, SAR, dividend equivalents, performance awards or other non-full value stock awards. The 2005 Plan was subsequently amended in Fiscal 2009 to increase the shares available for grant to 31.9 million without taking into consideration 9.1 million non-qualified stock options, 2.9 million shares of restricted stock and 0.2 million shares of common stock that had been previously granted under the 2005 plan to employees and directors (without considering cancellations as of January 31, 2009 of awards for 2.9 million shares). The 2005 Plan provides that the maximum number of shares awarded to any individual may not exceed 6.0 million shares per year for options and SAR and no more than 4.0 million shares may be granted with respect to each of restricted shares of stock and restricted stock units plus any unused carryover limit from the previous year. The 2005 Plan allows the Compensation Committee of the Board to determine which employees receive awards and the terms and conditions of the awards that are mandatory under the 2005 Plan. The 2005 Plan provides for grants to directors who are not officers or employees of the Company, which are not to exceed 20,000 shares per year (not to be adjusted for stock splits). Through January 31, 2015, 17.1 million non-qualified stock options, 10.4 million shares of restricted stock and 0.4 million shares of common stock had been granted under the 2005 Plan to employees and directors (without considering cancellations to date of awards for 13.1 million shares). Approximately 95% of the options granted under the 2005 Plan vest over three years, 4% vest over one year and 1% vest over five years. Options were granted for ten and seven year terms. Approximately 62% of the restricted stock awards are performance-based and are earned if the Company meets established performance goals. The remaining 38% of the restricted stock awards are time-based and vest over three years. The 2005 Plan terminated on May 29, 2014 with all rights of the awardees and all unexpired awards continuing in force and operation after the termination.

1999 Stock Incentive Plan

The 1999 Stock Option Plan (the "1999 Plan") was approved by the stockholders on June 8, 1999. The 1999 Plan authorized 18.0 million shares for issuance in the form of stock options, stock appreciation rights ("SAR"), restricted stock awards, performance units or performance shares. The 1999 Plan was subsequently amended to increase the shares available for grant to 33.0 million. Additionally, the 1999 Plan provided that the maximum number of shares awarded to any individual may not exceed 9.0 million shares. The 1999 Plan allowed the Compensation Committee to determine which employees and consultants received awards and the terms and conditions of these awards. The 1999 Plan provided for a grant of 1,875 stock options quarterly (not to be adjusted for stock splits) to each director who is not an officer or employee of the Company starting in August 2003. The Company ceased making these quarterly stock option grants in June 2005. Under this

AMERICAN EAGLE OUTFITTERS, INC.

NOTES TO CONSOLIDATED FINANCIAL STATEMENTS — (Continued)

plan, 33.2 million non-qualified stock options and 6.7 million shares of restricted stock were granted to employees and certain non-employees (without considering cancellations to date of awards for 9.7 million shares). Approximately 33% of the options granted were to vest over eight years after the date of grant but were accelerated as the Company met annual performance goals. Approximately 34% of the options granted under the 1999 Plan vest over three years, 23% vest over five years and the remaining grants vest over one year. All options expire after 10 years. Performance-based restricted stock was earned if the Company met established performance goals. The 1999 Plan terminated on June 15, 2005 with all rights of the awardees and all unexpired awards continuing in force and operation after the termination.

Stock Option Grants

The Company grants both time-based and performance-based stock options under the 2005 Plan. Time-based stock option awards vest over the requisite service period of the award or to an employee's eligible retirement date, if earlier. Performance-based stock option awards vest over three years and are earned if the Company meets pre-established performance goals during each year.

A summary of the Company's stock option activity under all plans for Fiscal 2014 follows:

| | For the Year Ended January 31, 2015 | | | |
| | Options | Weighted-Average Exercise Price | Weighted-Average Remaining Contractual Term | Aggregate Intrinsic Value |
	(In thousands)		*(In years)*	*(In thousands)*
Outstanding — February 1, 2014	3,925	$ 17.65		
Granted	126	$ 14.50		
Exercised(1)	(613)	$ 12.07		
Cancelled	(1,048)	$ 23.66		
Outstanding — January 31, 2015	2,390	$ 16.28	1.8	$ 514
Vested and expected to vest — January 31, 2015	2,380	$ 16.29	1.8	$ 514
Exercisable — January 31, 2015(2)	509	$ 13.03	3.5	$ 513

(1) Options exercised during Fiscal 2014 ranged in price from $8.09 to $14.05.

(2) Options exercisable represent "in-the-money" vested options based upon the weighted average exercise price of vested options compared to the Company's stock price at January 31, 2015.

The weighted-average grant date fair value of stock options granted during Fiscal 2014, Fiscal 2013 and Fiscal 2012 was $3.99, $4.17 and $3.72, respectively. The aggregate intrinsic value of options exercised during Fiscal 2014, Fiscal 2013 and Fiscal 2012 was $1.3 million, $3.9 million and $57.4 million, respectively. Cash received from the exercise of stock options and the actual tax benefit realized from share-based payments was $7.3 million and ($0.5) million, respectively, for Fiscal 2014. Cash received from the exercise of stock options and the actual tax benefit realized from share-based payments was $6.2 million and $8.7 million, respectively, for Fiscal 2013. Cash received from the exercise of stock options and the actual tax benefit realized from share-based payments was $76.4 million and $14.1 million, respectively, for Fiscal 2012.

The fair value of stock options was estimated at the date of grant using a Black-Scholes option pricing model with the following weighted-average assumptions:

| | For the Years Ended | | |
Black-Scholes Option Valuation Assumptions	January 31, 2015	February 1, 2014	February 2, 2013
Risk-free interest rates(1)	1.5%	0.3%	0.6%
Dividend yield	3.1%	2.0%	2.8%
Volatility factors of the expected market price of the Company's common stock(2)	41.2%	34.4%	41.2%
Weighted-average expected term(3)	4.5 years	2.5 years	4.0 years
Expected forfeiture rate(4)	8.0%	8.0%	8.0%

(1) Based on the U.S. Treasury yield curve in effect at the time of grant with a term consistent with the expected life of our stock options.

(2) Based on a combination of historical volatility of the Company's common stock and implied volatility.

(3) Represents the period of time options are expected to be outstanding. The weighted average expected option terms were determined based on historical experience.

AMERICAN EAGLE OUTFITTERS, INC.

NOTES TO CONSOLIDATED FINANCIAL STATEMENTS — (Continued)

(4)   Based on historical experience.

As of January 31, 2015, there was $0.4 million of unrecognized compensation expense related to nonvested stock option awards that is expected to be recognized over a weighted average period of 2.1 years.

Restricted Stock Grants

Time-based restricted stock awards are comprised of time-based restricted stock units. These awards vest over three years. Time-based restricted stock units receive dividend equivalents in the form of additional time-based restricted stock units, which are subject to the same restrictions and forfeiture provisions as the original award.

Performance-based restricted stock awards include performance-based restricted stock units. These awards cliff vest at the end of a three year period based upon the Company's achievement of pre-established goals throughout the term of the award. Performance-based restricted stock units receive dividend equivalents in the form of additional performance-based restricted stock units, which are subject to the same restrictions and forfeiture provisions as the original award.

The grant date fair value of all restricted stock awards is based on the closing market price of the Company's common stock on the date of grant.

A summary of the activity of the Company's restricted stock is presented in the following tables:

| | Time-Based Restricted Stock Units | | Performance-Based Restricted Stock Units | |
| | For the year ended January 31, 2015 | | For the year ended January 31, 2015 | |
(Shares in thousands)	Shares	Weighted-Average Grant Date Fair Value	Shares	Weighted-Average Grant Date Fair Value
Nonvested — February 1, 2014	1,155	$ 20.13	2,395	$ 16.85
Granted	1,506	14.11	1,314	14.21
Vested	(648)	18.08	(604)	15.34
Cancelled/Forfeited	(417)	17.56	(670)	16.05
Nonvested — January 31, 2015	1,596	15.95	2,435	16.02

As of January 31, 2015, there was $16.2 million of unrecognized compensation expense related to nonvested time-based restricted stock unit awards that is expected to be recognized over a weighted average period of 1.9 years. Additionally, there was $2.8 million of unrecognized compensation expense related to performance-based restricted stock unit awards which will be recognized as achievement performance goals are probable over a one to three year period.

As of January 31, 2015, the Company had 8.9 million shares available for all equity grants.

13.   Retirement Plan and Employee Stock Purchase Plan

The Company maintains a profit sharing and 401(k) plan (the "Retirement Plan"). Under the provisions of the Retirement Plan, full-time employees and part-time employees are automatically enrolled to contribute 3% of their salary if they have attained 20 1/2 years of age. In addition, full-time employees need to have completed 60 days of service and part-time employees must complete 1,000 hours worked to be eligible. Individuals can decline enrollment or can contribute up to 50% of their salary to the 401(k) plan on a pretax basis, subject to IRS limitations. After one year of service, the Company will match 100% of the first 3% of pay plus an additional 50% of the next 3% of pay that is contributed to the plan. Contributions to the profit sharing plan, as determined by the Board, are discretionary. The Company recognized $10.5 million, $9.6 million and $15.8 million in expense during Fiscal 2014, Fiscal 2013 and Fiscal 2012, respectively, in connection with the Retirement Plan. In Fiscal 2014, the Company announced a change to the Retirement Plan effective January 1, 2015. The Company will match 100% of the first 3% of pay plus an additional 25% of the next 3% of pay that is contributed to the plan.

The Employee Stock Purchase Plan is a non-qualified plan that covers all full-time employees and part-time employees who are at least 18 years old and have completed 60 days of service. Contributions are determined by the employee, with the Company matching 15% of the investment up to a maximum investment of $100 per pay period. These contributions are used to purchase shares of Company stock in the open market.

AMERICAN EAGLE OUTFITTERS, INC.

NOTES TO CONSOLIDATED FINANCIAL STATEMENTS — (Continued)

14. **Income Taxes**

The components of income before income taxes from continuing operations were:

| | For the Years Ended | | |
	January 31, 2015	February 1, 2014	February 2, 2013
(In thousands)			
U.S.	$ 193,167	$ 157,669	$ 381,131
Foreign	(33,665)	(15,592)	20,907
Total	$ 159,502	$ 142,077	$ 402,038

The significant components of the Company's deferred tax assets and liabilities were as follows:

	January 31, 2015	February 1, 2014
(In thousands)		
Deferred tax assets:		
Rent	$ 28,323	$ 27,458
Deferred compensation	16,109	22,654
Foreign tax credits	15,546	13,436
Accruals not currently deductible	9,899	9,059
Employee compensation and benefits	9,609	2,799
Net Operating Loss	9,179	4,226
State tax credits	7,595	6,215
Inventories	6,939	11,234
Deferred Revenue	5,150	124
Foreign and state income taxes	3,774	3,255
Loyalty Reserve	2,908	3,196
Capital loss carryforward	—	16,207
Other	3,871	844
Gross deferred tax assets	118,902	120,707
Valuation allowance	(10,563)	(20,601)
Total deferred tax assets	$ 108,339	$ 100,106
Deferred tax liabilities:		
Property and equipment	$ (30,054)	$ (23,595)
Prepaid expenses	(3,227)	(4,544)
Other	(1,921)	(1,654)
Total deferred tax liabilities	$ (35,202)	$ (29,793)
Total deferred tax assets, net	$ 73,137	$ 70,313
Classification in the Consolidated Balance Sheet:		
Current deferred tax assets	$ 59,102	$ 45,478
Noncurrent deferred tax assets	14,035	24,835
Total deferred tax assets	$ 73,137	$ 70,313

The net decrease in deferred tax assets and liabilities was primarily due to an increase in the deferred tax liability for property and equipment basis differences.

AMERICAN EAGLE OUTFITTERS, INC.

NOTES TO CONSOLIDATED FINANCIAL STATEMENTS — (Continued)

Significant components of the provision for income taxes from continuing operations were as follows:

	For the Years Ended		
(In thousands)	January 31, 2015	February 1, 2014	February 2, 2013
Current:			
Federal	$ 66,229	$ 29,794	$ 143,612
Foreign taxes	(792)	(50)	6,939
State	9,447	9,162	18,845
Total current	74,884	38,906	169,396
Deferred:			
Federal	$ (1,178)	$ 20,611	$ (26,063)
Foreign taxes	(85)	695	(1,486)
State	(2,906)	(1,118)	(3,907)
Total deferred	(4,169)	20,188	(31,456)
Provision for income taxes	$ 70,715	$ 59,094	$ 137,940

At February 1, 2014, the Company had a valuation allowance of $16.2 million related to capital loss carryforwards. During the fiscal year ended January 31, 2015, the Company utilized all of its capital loss carryforwards and released the $16.2 million valuation allowance associated with the capital loss carryforward.

As a result of additional tax deductions related to share-based payments, tax benefits have been recognized as contributed capital for Fiscal 2014, Fiscal 2013 and Fiscal 2012 in the amounts of ($0.5 million), $8.7 million and $14.1 million, respectively.

The Company repatriated the earnings of its Canadian subsidiaries as of January 31, 2015. Upon distribution of the earnings, the Company was subject to income and withholding taxes offset by U.S. foreign tax credits resulting in no material impact on tax expense. It is Management's position to indefinitely reinvest accumulated earnings of our Canadian subsidiaries outside of the United States to the extent not repatriated in Fiscal 2014.

As of January 31, 2015, the Company had state and foreign net operating loss carryovers that could be utilized to reduce future years' tax liabilities, totaling $10.3 million. A portion of these net operating loss carryovers begin expiring in the year 2018 and some have an indefinite carryforward period. Management believes it is more likely than not that the foreign net operating loss carryovers will not reduce future years' tax liabilities in certain foreign jurisdictions. As such a valuation allowance of $7.2 million has been recorded on the deferred tax assets related to the cumulative foreign net operating loss carryovers.

As of January 31, 2015, the gross amount of unrecognized tax benefits was $12.6 million, of which $9.1 million would affect the effective income tax rate if recognized. The gross amount of unrecognized tax benefits as of February 1, 2014 was $14.6 million, of which $9.7 million would affect the effective income tax rate if recognized.

The following table summarizes the activity related to our unrecognized tax benefits:

	For the Years Ended		
(In thousands)	January 31, 2015	February 1, 2014	February 2, 2013
Unrecognized tax benefits, beginning of the year balance	$ 14,601	$ 17,250	$ 31,578
Increases in current period tax positions	2,166	2,294	2,458
Increases in tax positions of prior periods	—	440	—
Settlements	(73)	—	(4,809)
Lapse of statute of limitations	(471)	(453)	(1,592)
Decreases in tax positions of prior periods	(3,614)	(4,930)	(10,385)
Unrecognized tax benefits, end of the year balance	$ 12,609	$ 14,601	$ 17,250

Unrecognized tax benefits decreased by $2.0 million during Fiscal 2014, decreased $2.6 million during Fiscal 2013 and decreased by $14.3 million during Fiscal 2012. The unrecognized tax benefit changes were primarily related to federal and state income tax settlements and other changes in income tax reserves. Over the next twelve months the Company believes it is reasonably possible the unrecognized tax

AMERICAN EAGLE OUTFITTERS, INC.

NOTES TO CONSOLIDATED FINANCIAL STATEMENTS — (Continued)

benefits could decrease by as much as $5.6 million as the result of federal and state tax settlements, statute of limitations lapses, and other changes to the reserves.

The Company records accrued interest and penalties related to unrecognized tax benefits in income tax expense. Accrued interest and penalties related to unrecognized tax benefits included in the Consolidated Balance Sheet were $1.6 million and $1.9 million as of January 31, 2015 and February 1, 2014, respectively. During Fiscal 2012, the Company recognized a net benefit of $4.8 million in the provision for income taxes related to the reversal of accrued interest and penalties primarily due to federal and state income tax settlements. An immaterial amount of interest and penalties were recognized in the provision for income taxes during Fiscal 2014 and Fiscal 2013.

The Company and its subsidiaries file income tax returns in the U.S. federal jurisdiction and various state and foreign jurisdictions. The Internal Revenue Service ("IRS") examination of the Company's U.S. federal income tax return for the tax year ended January 2012 was completed in February 2014. Accordingly, all years prior to the tax year ended January 2013 are no longer subject to U.S. federal income tax examinations by tax authorities. Additionally, the Company is participating in the IRS's Compliance Assurance Process (CAP) for the years ended February 1, 2014 and January 31, 2015. The Company does not anticipate that any adjustments will result in a material change to its financial position, results of operations or cash flow. With respect to state and local jurisdictions and countries outside of the United States, with limited exceptions, generally, the Company and its subsidiaries are no longer subject to income tax audits for tax years before 2008. Although the outcome of tax audits is always uncertain, the Company believes that adequate amounts of tax, interest and penalties have been provided for any adjustments that are expected to result from these years.

The Company has foreign tax credit carryovers in the amount of $19.3 million and $13.4 million as of January 31, 2015 and February 1, 2014, respectively. The foreign tax credit carryovers begin to expire in Fiscal 2019 to the extent not utilized. No valuation allowance has been recorded on the foreign tax credit carryovers as the Company believes it is more likely than not that the foreign tax credits will be utilized prior to expiration.

The Company has state income tax credit carryforwards of $11.7 million and $10.7 million as of January 31, 2015 and February 1, 2014, respectively. These income tax credits can be utilized to offset future state income taxes and have a carryforward period of 10 to16 years. They will begin to expire in Fiscal 2018.

A reconciliation between the statutory federal income tax rate and the effective income tax rate from continuing operations follows:

	For the Years Ended		
	January 31, 2015	February 1, 2014	February 2, 2013
Federal income tax rate	35%	35%	35%
State income taxes, net of federal income tax effect	4	4	3
Valuation allowance changes, net	6	4	(1)
Tax settlements	(1)	(2)	(3)
Other	—	1	—
	44%	42%	34%

15. Discontinued Operations

In Fiscal 2012, the Company exited the 77kids business. These Consolidated Financial Statements reflect the results of 77kids as a discontinued operation for all periods presented.

In connection with the exit of the 77kids business, the Company became secondarily liable for obligations under lease agreements for 21 store leases assumed by the third party purchaser. In Fiscal 2014, the third party purchaser did not fulfill its obligations under the leases, resulting in the Company becoming primarily liable. The Company was required to make rental and lease termination payments and received reimbursement from the $11.5 million stand-by letter of credit provided by the third party purchaser. The Company has incurred $13.7 million in expense above the letter of credit proceeds to terminate store leases. The cash outflow for termination costs are expected to be paid in the first quarter of Fiscal 2015.

In accordance with ASC 460, *Guarantees* ("ASC 460"), as the Company became primarily liable under the leases upon the third party purchaser's default, the remaining amounts to exit the lease agreements have been accrued in our Consolidated Financial Statements related to these guarantees.

Costs associated with exit or disposal activities are recorded when incurred. A summary of the pre-tax exit and disposal costs recognized within Loss from Discontinued Operations on the Consolidated Income Statement for 77kids are as follows. There were no exit or disposal costs recognized in Fiscal 2013 related to 77kids.

AMERICAN EAGLE OUTFITTERS, INC.

NOTES TO CONSOLIDATED FINANCIAL STATEMENTS — (Continued)

	For the Years Ended		
(In thousands)	January 31, 2015	February 1, 2014	February 2, 2013
Non-cash charges			
Asset impairments	$ —	$ —	$ 16,623
Cash charges			
Lease-related charges	$ 13,673	$ —	$ 7,768
Inventory charges	—	—	10,237
Severence charges	—	—	3,439
Total charges	$ 13,673	$ —	$ 38,067

A rollforward of the liabilities for the exit of the 77kids brand recognized in the Consolidated Balance Sheets is as follows:

(In thousands)	January 31, 2015
Accrued liability as of February 1, 2014	$ —
Add: Costs incurred	25,173
Less: Cash payments	(10,537)
Accrued liability as of January 31, 2015	$ 14,636

The tables below present the significant components of 77kids' results included in Loss from Discontinued Operations on the Consolidated Statements of Operations for the years ended January 31, 2015, February 1, 2014 and February 2, 2013.

	For the Years Ended		
	January 31, 2015	February 1, 2014	February 2, 2013
Total net revenue	$ —	$ —	$ 20,117
Loss from discontinued operations, before income taxes(1)	$ (13,673)	$ —	$ (51,839)
Income tax benefit	5,208	—	19,849
Loss from discontinued operations, net of tax	$ (8,465)	$ —	$ (31,990)
Loss per common share from discontinued operations:			
Basic	$ (0.04)	$ —	$ (0.16)
Diluted	$ (0.04)	$ —	$ (0.16)

(1)   Loss from discontinued operations is presented net of the reversal of non-cash lease credits for Fiscal 2012

16.   Restructuring Charges

During the 13 weeks ended November 1, 2014, the Company undertook restructuring aimed at strengthening the store portfolio and reducing corporate overhead, including severance and office space consolidation. These changes are aimed at driving efficiencies and aligning investments in areas that help fuel the business.

Costs associated with restructuring activities are recorded when incurred. A summary of costs recognized within Restructuring Charges on the Consolidated Income Statement for Fiscal 2014 are included in the table as follows.

(In thousands)	For the year ended January 31, 2015
Cash restructuring charges	
Office space consolidation charges	$ 8,571
Severance and related employee costs	7,816
Other corporate items	1,365
Total restructuring charges	$ 17,752

AMERICAN EAGLE OUTFITTERS, INC.

NOTES TO CONSOLIDATED FINANCIAL STATEMENTS — (Continued)

The Company also incurred non-cash corporate office and other asset impairment charges of $8.4 million. This charge is included within Loss on Impairment of Assets on the Consolidated Income Statement. Also included in Loss on Impairment of Assets is $25.1 million of store asset impairments resulting from evaluation of current and future projected performance.

A rollforward of the liabilities recognized in the Consolidated Balance Sheet is as follows:

(In thousands)	January 31, 2015
Accrued liability as of February 1, 2014	$ —
Add: Costs incurred, excluding non-cash charges	17,752
Less: Cash payments	(5,296)
Accrued liability as of January 31, 2015	$ 12,456

17. Quarterly Financial Information — Unaudited

The sum of the quarterly EPS amounts may not equal the full year amount as the computations of the weighted average shares outstanding for each quarter and the full year are calculated independently.

(In thousands, except per share amounts)	Fiscal 2014 Quarters Ended			
	May 3, 2014	August 2, 2014	November 1, 2014	January 31, 2015
Total net revenue	$ 646,129	$ 710,595	$ 854,290	$ 1,071,853
Gross profit	$ 225,845	$ 237,547	$ 315,472	$ 375,810
Income from continuing operations	3,866	5,813	9,035	70,073
Loss from discontinued operations, net of tax	—	—	—	(8,465)
Net income	$ 3,866	$ 5,813	$ 9,035	$ 61,608
Basic per common share amounts:				
Income from continuing operations	$ 0.02	$ 0.03	$ 0.05	$ 0.36
Loss from discontinued operations, net of tax	—	—	—	(0.04)
Basic net income per common share	$ 0.02	$ 0.03	$ 0.05	$ 0.32
Diluted per common share amounts:				
Income from continuing operations	$ 0.02	$ 0.03	$ 0.05	$ 0.36
Loss from discontinued operations, net of tax	—	—	—	(0.04)
Diluted net income per common share	$ 0.02	$ 0.03	$ 0.05	$ 0.32

(In thousands, except per share amounts)	Fiscal 2013 Quarters Ended			
	May 4, 2013	August 3, 2013	November 2, 2013	February 1, 2014
Total net revenue	$ 679,477	$ 727,313	$ 857,305	$ 1,041,707
Gross profit	$ 263,609	$ 245,495	$ 298,875	$ 306,020
Income from continuing operations	27,976	19,594	24,903	10,510
Loss from discontinued operations, net of tax	—	—	—	—
Net income	$ 27,976	$ 19,594	$ 24,903	$ 10,510
Basic per common share amounts:				
Income from continuing operations	$ 0.14	$ 0.10	$ 0.13	$ 0.05
Loss from discontinued operations, net of tax	—	—	—	—
Basic net income per common share	$ 0.14	$ 0.10	$ 0.13	$ 0.05
Diluted per common share amounts:				
Income from continuing operations	$ 0.14	$ 0.10	$ 0.13	$ 0.05
Loss from discontinued operations, net of tax	—	—	—	—
Diluted net income per common share	$ 0.14	$ 0.10	$ 0.13	$ 0.05

UNITED STATES
SECURITIES AND EXCHANGE COMMISSION
Washington, DC 20549

FORM 10-K

☒ ANNUAL REPORT PURSUANT TO SECTION 13 OR 15(d) OF THE SECURITIES EXCHANGE ACT OF 1934

For the fiscal year ended January 31, 2015

☐ TRANSITION REPORT PURSUANT TO SECTION 13 OR 15(d) OF THE SECURITIES EXCHANGE ACT OF 1934

For the transition period from _____ to _____

Commission File No. 000-22754

URBAN OUTFITTERS, INC.
(Exact Name of Registrant as Specified in Its Charter)

Pennsylvania	23-2003332
(State or Other Jurisdiction of Incorporation or Organization)	(I.R.S. Employer Identification No.)
5000 South Broad Street, Philadelphia, PA	19112-1495
(Address of Principal Executive Offices)	(Zip Code)

Registrant's telephone number, including area code: (215) 454-5500

Securities registered pursuant to Section 12(b) of the Act:

Title of Each Class	Name of Exchange on Which Registered
Common Shares, $.0001 par value	The NASDAQ Global Select Market LLC

Securities registered pursuant to Section 12(g) of the Act: None

---

Indicate by checkmark if the registrant is a well-known seasoned issuer, as defined in Rule 405 of the Securities Act.   Yes ☒   No ☐

Indicate by checkmark if the registrant is not required to file reports pursuant to Section 13 or Section 15(d) of the Act.   Yes ☐   No ☒

Indicate by checkmark whether the registrant (1) has filed all reports required to be filed by Section 13 or 15(d) of the Securities Exchange Act of 1934 during the preceding 12 months (or for such shorter period that the registrant was required to file such reports), and (2) has been subject to such filing requirements for the past 90 days.   Yes ☒   No ☐

Indicate by check mark whether the registrant has submitted electronically and posted on its corporate website, if any, every Interactive Data File required to be submitted and posted pursuant to Rule 405 of Regulation S-T during the preceding 12 months (or for such shorter period that the registrant was required to submit and post such files).   Yes ☒   No ☐

Indicate by checkmark if disclosure of delinquent filers pursuant to Item 405 of Regulation S-K is not contained herein, and will not be contained, to the best of Registrant's knowledge, in definitive proxy or information statements incorporated by reference in Part III of this Form 10-K or any amendment to this Form 10-K.   ☒

Indicate by checkmark whether the registrant is a large accelerated filer, an accelerated filer, a non-accelerated filer, or a smaller reporting company. See the definitions of "large accelerated filer," "accelerated filer" and "smaller reporting company" in Rule 12b-2 of the Exchange Act.

Large accelerated filer ☒   Accelerated filer ☐

Non-accelerated filer ☐ (Do not check if a smaller reporting company)   Smaller reporting company ☐

Indicate by a checkmark whether the registrant is a shell company (as defined in Rule 12b-2 of the Act).   Yes ☐   No ☒

The aggregate market value of the voting and non-voting common equity held by non-affiliates computed by reference to the price at which the common equity was last sold, or the average bid and asked price of such common equity, as of the last business day of the registrant's most recently completed second fiscal quarter, was $3,614,766,155.

The number of shares outstanding of the registrant's common stock on March 25, 2015 was 131,723,233.

DOCUMENTS INCORPORATED BY REFERENCE

Certain information required by Items 10, 11, 12, 13 and 14 is incorporated by reference into Part III hereof from portions of the Proxy Statement for the registrant's 2015 Annual Meeting of Shareholders.

Item 5. Market for Registrant's Common Equity, Related Shareholder Matters and Issuer Purchases of Equity Securities

Our common shares are traded on the NASDAQ Global Select Market under the symbol "URBN." The following table sets forth, for the periods indicated below, the reported high and low sale prices for our common shares as reported on the NASDAQ Global Select Market.

Market Information

	High	Low
Fiscal 2015		
Quarter ended April 30, 2014	$ 38.84	$ 33.95
Quarter ended July 31, 2014	$ 37.40	$ 32.23
Quarter ended October 31, 2014	$ 40.67	$ 29.11
Quarter ended January 31, 2015	$ 36.99	$ 27.89
Fiscal 2014		
Quarter ended April 30, 2013	$ 44.15	$ 38.18
Quarter ended July 31, 2013	$ 44.96	$ 38.11
Quarter ended October 31, 2013	$ 44.15	$ 35.00
Quarter ended January 31, 2014	$ 40.45	$ 35.26

Holders of Record

On March 25, 2015 there were 120 holders of record of our common shares.

Dividend Policy

Our current credit facility includes certain limitations on the payment of cash dividends on our common shares. We have not paid any cash dividends since our initial public offering and do not anticipate paying any cash dividends on our common shares in the foreseeable future.

Securities Authorized for Issuance Under Equity Compensation Plans

All equity compensation plans have been approved by security holders of the Company. See Note 9, "Share-Based Compensation," for details of the Company's equity compensation plans and outstanding awards.

Item 6. Selected Financial Data

The following table sets forth selected consolidated income statement and balance sheet data for the periods indicated. The selected consolidated income statement and balance sheet data for each of the five fiscal years presented below is derived from our consolidated financial statements. The data presented below should be read in conjunction with Item 7: Management's Discussion and Analysis of Financial Condition and Results of Operations and the Consolidated Financial Statements of the Company and the related notes thereto, which appear elsewhere in this Annual Report on Form 10-K. The results of operations for past accounting periods are not necessarily indicative of the results to be expected for any future accounting period.

	Fiscal Year Ended January 31,				
	2015	2014	2013	2012	2011
	(in thousands, except share amounts and per share data)				
Income Statement Data:					
Net sales	$ 3,323,077	$ 3,086,608	$ 2,794,925	$ 2,473,801	$ 2,274,102
Gross profit	1,174,930	1,161,342	1,031,531	860,536	936,620
Income from operations	365,385	426,831	374,285	284,725	414,203
Net income	232,428	282,360	237,314	185,251	272,958
Net income per common share—basic	$ 1.70	$ 1.92	$ 1.63	$ 1.20	$ 1.64
Weighted average common shares outstanding—basic	136,651,899	147,014,869	145,253,691	154,025,589	166,896,322
Net income per common share—diluted	$ 1.68	$ 1.89	$ 1.62	$ 1.19	$ 1.60
Weighted average common shares outstanding—diluted	138,192,734	149,225,906	146,663,731	156,191,289	170,333,550
Balance Sheet Data:					
Working capital	$ 455,377	$ 663,150	$ 622,089	$ 363,526	$ 592,953
Total assets	1,888,741	2,221,214	1,797,211	1,483,708	1,794,321
Total liabilities	560,772	527,044	442,623	417,440	382,773
Total shareholders' equity	$ 1,327,969	$ 1,694,170	$ 1,354,588	$ 1,066,268	$ 1,411,548

REPORT OF INDEPENDENT REGISTERED PUBLIC ACCOUNTING FIRM

To the Board of Directors and Shareholders of
Urban Outfitters, Inc.
Philadelphia, Pennsylvania

We have audited the accompanying consolidated balance sheets of Urban Outfitters, Inc. and subsidiaries (the "Company") as of January 31, 2015 and 2014, and the related consolidated statements of income, comprehensive income, shareholders' equity, and cash flows for each of the three years in the period ended January 31, 2015. These financial statements are the responsibility of the Company's management. Our responsibility is to express an opinion on these financial statements based on our audits.

We conducted our audits in accordance with the standards of the Public Company Accounting Oversight Board (United States). Those standards require that we plan and perform the audit to obtain reasonable assurance about whether the financial statements are free of material misstatement. An audit includes examining, on a test basis, evidence supporting the amounts and disclosures in the financial statements. An audit also includes assessing the accounting principles used and significant estimates made by management, as well as evaluating the overall financial statement presentation. We believe that our audits provide a reasonable basis for our opinion.

In our opinion, such consolidated financial statements present fairly, in all material respects, the financial position of Urban Outfitters, Inc. and subsidiaries as of January 31, 2015 and 2014, and the results of their operations and their cash flows for each of the three years in the period ended January 31, 2015, in conformity with accounting principles generally accepted in the United States of America.

We have also audited, in accordance with the standards of the Public Company Accounting Oversight Board (United States), the Company's internal control over financial reporting as of January 31, 2015, based on the criteria established in *Internal Control—Integrated Framework (2013)* issued by the Committee of Sponsoring Organizations of the Treadway Commission and our report dated April 1, 2015, expressed an unqualified opinion on the Company's internal control over financial reporting.

/s/ DELOITTE & TOUCHE LLP

Philadelphia, Pennsylvania
April 1, 2015

URBAN OUTFITTERS, INC.

Consolidated Balance Sheets
(in thousands, except share and per share data)

		January 31, 2015		January 31, 2014
ASSETS				
Current assets:				
Cash and cash equivalents	$	154,558	$	242,058
Marketable securities		104,246		281,813
Accounts receivable, net of allowance for doubtful accounts of $850 and $1,711, respectively		70,458		55,161
Inventories		358,237		311,207
Prepaid expenses and other current assets		102,863		75,968
Deferred income taxes		18,755		28,773
Total current assets		809,117		994,980
Property and equipment, net		889,232		806,909
Marketable securities		104,448		366,422
Deferred income taxes and other assets		85,944		52,903
Total Assets	$	1,888,741	$	2,221,214
LIABILITIES AND SHAREHOLDERS' EQUITY				
Current liabilities:				
Accounts payable	$	156,090	$	137,036
Accrued compensation		45,007		41,085
Accrued expenses and other current liabilities		152,643		153,709
Total current liabilities		353,740		331,830
Deferred rent and other liabilities		207,032		195,214
Total Liabilities		560,772		527,044
Commitments and contingencies (see Note 13)				
Shareholders' equity:				
Preferred shares; $.0001 par value, 10,000,000 shares authorized, none issued		—		—
Common shares; $.0001 par value, 200,000,000 shares authorized, 130,502,864 and 147,309,575 shares issued and outstanding, respectively		13		15
Additional paid-in-capital		—		97,684
Retained earnings		1,343,383		1,597,439
Accumulated other comprehensive loss		(15,427)		(968)
Total Shareholders' Equity		1,327,969		1,694,170
Total Liabilities and Shareholders' Equity	$	1,888,741	$	2,221,214

The accompanying notes are an integral part of these consolidated financial statements.

URBAN OUTFITTERS, INC.

Consolidated Statements of Income
(in thousands, except share and per share data)

		Fiscal Year Ended January 31,			
		2015	**2014**		**2013**
Net sales	$	3,323,077	$ 3,086,608	$	2,794,925
Cost of sales		2,148,147	1,925,266		1,763,394
Gross profit		1,174,930	1,161,342		1,031,531
Selling, general and administrative expenses		809,545	734,511		657,246
Income from operations		365,385	426,831		374,285
Interest income		2,319	2,713		2,126
Other income		580	1,088		862
Other expenses		(4,834)	(3,114)		(1,701)
Income before income taxes		363,450	427,518		375,572
Income tax expense		131,022	145,158		138,258
Net income	$	232,428	$ 282,360	$	237,314
Net income per common share:					
Basic	$	1.70	$ 1.92	$	1.63
Diluted	$	1.68	$ 1.89	$	1.62
Weighted-average common shares outstanding:					
Basic		136,651,899	147,014,869		145,253,691
Diluted		138,192,734	149,225,906		146,663,731

The accompanying notes are an integral part of these consolidated financial statements.

URBAN OUTFITTERS, INC.

Consolidated Statements of Comprehensive Income
(in thousands)

	Fiscal Year Ended January 31,		
	2015	2014	2013
Net income	$ 232,428	$ 282,360	$ 237,314
Other comprehensive (loss) income:			
Foreign currency translation	(14,128)	7,194	1,455
Change in unrealized (losses) gains on marketable securities, net of tax	(331)	620	1,275
Total other comprehensive (loss) income	(14,459)	7,814	2,730
Comprehensive income	$ 217,969	$ 290,174	$ 240,044

The accompanying notes are an integral part of these consolidated financial statements.

URBAN OUTFITTERS, INC.

Consolidated Statements of Shareholders' Equity
(in thousands, except share data)

	Common Shares			Additional Paid-in Capital	Retained Earnings	Accumulated Other Comprehensive Loss	Total
	Number of Shares	Par Value					
Balances as of January 31, 2012	144,633,007	$ 15	$	—	$ 1,077,765	$ (11,512)	$ 1,066,268
Comprehensive income	—	—		—	237,314	2,730	240,044
Share-based compensation	—	—		10,892	—	—	10,892
Stock options and awards	1,382,760	—		30,671	—	—	30,671
Excess tax benefit from share-based awards	—	—		6,713	—	—	6,713
Balances as of January 31, 2013	146,015,767	$ 15	$	48,276	$ 1,315,079	$ (8,782)	$ 1,354,588
Comprehensive income	—	—		—	282,360	7,814	290,174
Share-based compensation	—	—		15,742	—	—	15,742
Stock options and awards	1,603,628	—		35,218	—	—	35,218
Excess tax benefit from share-based awards	—	—		9,540	—	—	9,540
Share repurchases	(309,820)	—		(11,092)	—	—	(11,092)
Balances as of January 31, 2014	147,309,575	$ 15	$	97,684	$ 1,597,439	$ (968)	$ 1,694,170
Comprehensive income	—	—		—	232,428	(14,459)	217,969
Share-based compensation	—	—		16,736	—	—	16,736
Stock options and awards	723,083	—		10,693	—	—	10,693
Excess tax benefit from share-based awards	—	—		3,822	—	—	3,822
Share repurchases	(17,529,794)	(2)		(128,935)	(486,484)	—	(615,421)
Balances as of January 31, 2015	130,502,864	$ 13	$	—	$ 1,343,383	$ (15,427)	$ 1,327,969

The accompanying notes are an integral part of these consolidated financial statements.

URBAN OUTFITTERS, INC.

Consolidated Statements of Cash Flows

(in thousands)

	Fiscal Year Ended January 31,		
	2015	2014	2013
Cash flows from operating activities:			
Net income	$ 232,428	$ 282,360	$ 237,314
Adjustments to reconcile net income to net cash provided by operating activities:			
Depreciation and amortization	138,110	132,664	118,664
(Benefit) provision for deferred income taxes	(2,221)	(28,505)	22,248
Excess tax benefits from stock option exercises	(3,822)	(9,540)	(6,713)
Share-based compensation expense	16,736	15,742	10,892
Loss on disposition of property and equipment, net	3,189	2,368	616
Changes in assets and liabilities:			
Receivables	(18,393)	(15,368)	(2,917)
Inventories	(68,992)	(27,713)	(32,237)
Prepaid expenses and other assets	(23,257)	2,985	16,057
Payables, accrued expenses and other liabilities	48,543	68,162	31,756
Net cash provided by operating activities	322,321	423,155	395,680
Cash flows from investing activities:			
Cash paid for property and equipment	(229,804)	(186,101)	(168,875)
Cash paid for marketable securities	(405,659)	(727,987)	(372,689)
Sales and maturities of marketable securities	830,297	451,866	207,576
Net cash provided by (used in) investing activities	194,834	(462,222)	(333,988)
Cash flows from financing activities:			
Proceeds from the exercise of stock options	10,693	35,218	30,671
Excess tax benefits from stock option exercises	3,822	9,540	6,713
Share repurchases related to share repurchase program	(611,475)	(10,695)	—
Share repurchases related to taxes for share-based awards	(3,947)	(397)	—
Net cash (used in) provided by financing activities	(600,907)	33,666	37,384
Effect of exchange rate changes on cash and cash equivalents	(3,748)	2,132	978
(Decrease) increase in cash and cash equivalents	(87,500)	(3,269)	100,054
Cash and cash equivalents at beginning of period	242,058	245,327	145,273
Cash and cash equivalents at end of period	$ 154,558	$ 242,058	$ 245,327
Supplemental cash flow information:			
Cash paid during the year for:			
Income taxes	$ 144,892	$ 159,628	$ 103,006
Non-cash investing activities—Accrued capital expenditures	$ 18,771	$ 20,889	$ 15,055

The accompanying notes are an integral part of these consolidated financial statements.

URBAN OUTFITTERS, INC.

NOTES TO CONSOLIDATED FINANCIAL STATEMENTS

(in thousands, except share and per share data)

1. Nature of Business

Urban Outfitters, Inc. (the "Company" or "Urban Outfitters"), which was founded in 1970, was incorporated in the Commonwealth of Pennsylvania in 1976. The principal business activity of the Company is the operation of a general consumer product retail and wholesale business selling to customers through various channels including retail stores, websites, catalogs and mobile applications. As of January 31, 2015 and 2014, the Company operated 546 and 511 stores, respectively. Stores located in the United States totaled 464 as of January 31, 2015 and 442 as of January 31, 2014. Operations in Europe and Canada included 50 stores and 32 stores as of January 31, 2015, respectively, and 44 stores and 25 stores as of January 31, 2014, respectively. In addition, the Company's Wholesale segment sold and distributed apparel to approximately 1,600 better department and specialty retailers worldwide.

2. Summary of Significant Accounting Policies

Fiscal Year-End

The Company operates on a fiscal year ending January 31 of each year. All references to fiscal years of the Company refer to the fiscal years ended on January 31 in those years. For example, the Company's fiscal 2015 ended on January 31, 2015.

Principles of Consolidation

The Consolidated Financial Statements include the accounts of the Company and all of its subsidiaries. All inter-company transactions and accounts have been eliminated in consolidation.

Use of Estimates

The preparation of financial statements, in conformity with accounting principles generally accepted in the United States, requires management to make estimates and assumptions that affect the reported amounts of assets and liabilities and disclosure of contingent assets and liabilities at the date of the financial statements and the reported amounts of net sales and expenses during the reporting period. Actual results could differ from those estimates.

Cash and Cash Equivalents

Cash and cash equivalents are defined as cash and short-term highly liquid investments with maturities of less than three months at the time of purchase. These short-term highly liquid investments are both readily convertible to known amounts of cash and so near their maturity that they present insignificant risk of changes in value because of changes in interest rates. As of January 31, 2015 and 2014, cash and cash equivalents included cash on hand, cash in banks, money market accounts and marketable securities with maturities of less than three months at the time of purchase.

Marketable Securities

All of the Company's marketable securities as of January 31, 2015 and January 31, 2014 are classified as available-for-sale and are carried at fair value, which approximates amortized cost. Interest on these securities, as well as the amortization of discounts and premiums, is included in interest income in the Consolidated Statements of Income. Unrealized gains and losses on these securities (other than mutual funds held in the rabbi trust) are considered temporary and therefore are excluded from earnings and are reported as a component of "Other comprehensive (loss) income" in the Consolidated Statements of Comprehensive Income and in accumulated other comprehensive loss in shareholders' equity until realized. Mutual funds held in the rabbi trust have been accounted for under the fair value option, which results in all unrealized gains and losses being recorded in "Interest income" in the Consolidated Statements of Income. Other than temporary impairment losses related to credit losses are considered to be realized losses. When available-for-sale securities are sold, the cost of the securities is specifically identified and is used to determine the realized gain or loss. Securities classified as current assets have maturity dates of less than one year from the balance sheet date. Securities classified as non-current assets have maturity dates greater than one year from the balance sheet date.

During the first quarter of fiscal 2014, the Company sold all of its remaining auction rate securities ("ARS") for approximately $4,580 in cash. The Company's ARS had a par value and a recorded fair value of $4,925 and $4,330, respectively, prior to the sale.

Accounts Receivable

Accounts receivable primarily consists of amounts due from our wholesale customers as well as credit card receivables outstanding with third-party credit card vendors. The activity of the allowance for doubtful accounts for the years ended January 31, 2015, 2014 and 2013 was as follows:

	Balance at beginning of year	Additions	Deductions	Balance at end of year
Year ended January 31, 2015	$ 1,711	4,666	(5,527)	$ 850
Year ended January 31, 2014	$ 1,681	4,400	(4,370)	$ 1,711
Year ended January 31, 2013	$ 1,614	5,019	(4,952)	$ 1,681

Inventories

Inventories, which consist primarily of general consumer merchandise held for sale, are valued at the lower of cost or market. Cost is determined on the first-in, first-out method and includes the cost of merchandise and import related costs, including freight, import taxes and agent commissions. A periodic review of inventory is performed in order to determine if inventory is properly stated at the lower of cost or market. Factors related to current inventories such as future expected consumer demand and fashion trends, current aging, current and anticipated retail markdowns or wholesale discounts, and class or type of inventory are analyzed to determine estimated net realizable value.

URBAN OUTFITTERS, INC.

NOTES TO CONSOLIDATED FINANCIAL STATEMENTS—(Continued)
(in thousands, except share and per share data)

Criteria utilized by the Company to quantify aging trends include factors such as average selling cycle and seasonality of merchandise, the historical rate at which merchandise has sold below cost during the average selling cycle, and the value and nature of merchandise currently priced below original cost. A provision is recorded to reduce the cost of inventories to the estimated net realizable values, if appropriate. The Company's estimates generally have been accurate and its reserve methods have been applied on a consistent basis. The Company expects the amount of its reserves and related inventories to increase over time as it increases its sales. The majority of inventory at January 31, 2015 and 2014 consisted of finished goods. Unfinished goods and work-in-process were not material to the overall net inventory value.

Property and Equipment

Property and equipment are stated at cost and primarily consist of store related leasehold improvements, buildings and furniture and fixtures. Depreciation is typically computed using the straight-line method over five years for furniture and fixtures, the lesser of the lease term or useful life for leasehold improvements, three to ten years for other operating equipment and 39 years for buildings. Major renovations or improvements that extend the service lives of our assets are capitalized over the extension period or life of the improvement, whichever is less.

The Company reviews long-lived assets for possible impairment whenever events or changes in circumstances indicate the carrying amount may not be recoverable. This determination includes evaluation of factors such as future asset utilization and future net undiscounted cash flows expected to result from the use of the assets.

Deferred Rent

Rent expense from leases is recorded on a straight-line basis over the lease period. The net excess of rent expense over the actual cash paid is recorded as deferred rent. In addition, certain store leases provide for contingent rentals when sales exceed specified break-point levels that are weighted based upon historical cyclicality. For leases where achievement of these levels is considered probable based on cumulative lease year revenue versus the established breakpoint at any given point in time, the Company accrues a contingent rent liability and a corresponding rent expense.

Operating Leases

The Company leases its retail stores under operating leases. Many of the lease agreements contain rent holidays, rent escalation clauses and contingent rent provisions or some combination of these items.

The Company recognizes rent expense on a straight-line basis over the lease period commencing on the date that the premises are available from the landlord. The lease period includes the construction period required to make the leased space suitable for operating during which time the Company is not permitted to occupy the space. For purposes of calculating straight-line rent expense, the commencement date of the lease term reflects the date the Company takes possession of the building for initial construction and setup.

The Company classifies tenant improvement allowances in its consolidated financial statements under deferred rent and amortizes them on a straight-line basis over the related lease period. Tenant improvement allowance activity is presented as part of cash flows from operating activities in the accompanying Consolidated Statements of Cash Flows.

Revenue Recognition

Revenue is recognized by the Retail segment at the point-of-sale for merchandise the customer takes possession of at the retail store or when merchandise is shipped to the customer, net of estimated customer returns. Revenue is recognized by the Wholesale segment when merchandise is shipped to the customer, net of estimated customer returns. Revenue is presented on a net basis and does not include any tax assessed by a governmental or municipal authority. Payment for merchandise in the Company's Retail segment is tendered by cash, check, credit card, debit card or gift card. Therefore, the Company's need to collect outstanding accounts receivable for its Retail segment is negligible and mainly results from returned checks or unauthorized credit card transactions. The Company maintains an allowance for doubtful accounts for its Wholesale segment accounts receivable, which management reviews on a regular basis and believes is sufficient to cover potential credit losses and billing adjustments.

The Company accounts for a gift card transaction by recording a liability at the time the gift card is issued to the customer in exchange for consideration from the customer. A liability is established and remains on the Company's books until the card is redeemed by the customer, at which time the Company records the redemption of the card for merchandise as a sale, or when it is determined the likelihood of redemption is remote. The Company determines the probability of the gift cards being redeemed to be remote based on historical redemption patterns. Revenues attributable to the reduction of gift card liabilities for which the likelihood of redemption becomes remote are included in sales and are not material. The Company's gift cards do not expire.

Sales Return Reserve

The Company records a reserve for estimated product returns where the sale has occurred during the period reported, but the return is likely to occur subsequent to the period reported. The reserve for estimated product returns is based on the Company's most recent historical return trends. If the actual return rate or experience is materially higher than the Company's estimate, additional sales returns would be recorded in the future. The activity of the sales returns reserve for the years ended January 31, 2015, 2014 and 2013 was as follows:

	Balance at beginning of year	Additions	Deductions	Balance at end of year
Year ended January 31, 2015	$ 17,089	80,390	(77,675)	$ 19,804
Year ended January 31, 2014	$ 14,448	64,313	(61,672)	$ 17,089
Year ended January 31, 2013	$ 10,967	49,412	(45,931)	$ 14,448

Cost of Sales

Cost of sales includes the following: the cost of merchandise; obsolescence and shrink provisions; store occupancy costs including rent and depreciation; delivery expense; inbound and outbound freight; customs related taxes and duties; inventory acquisition and purchasing costs; design costs; warehousing and handling costs and other inventory acquisition related costs.

URBAN OUTFITTERS, INC.

NOTES TO CONSOLIDATED FINANCIAL STATEMENTS—(Continued)
(in thousands, except share and per share data)

Selling, General and Administrative Expenses

Selling, general and administrative expenses includes expenses such as: direct selling and selling supervisory expenses; marketing expenses; various corporate expenses such as information systems, finance, loss prevention, talent acquisition, home office and executive management expenses; share-based compensation expense; and other associated general expenses.

Shipping and Handling Revenues and Costs

The Company includes shipping and handling revenues in net sales and shipping and handling costs in cost of sales. The Company's shipping and handling revenues consist of amounts billed to customers for shipping and handling merchandise. Shipping and handling costs include shipping supplies, related labor costs and third-party shipping costs.

Advertising

The Company expenses the costs of advertising when the advertising occurs, except for direct-to-consumer advertising, which is capitalized and amortized over its expected period of future benefit. Advertising costs primarily relate to our Retail segment marketing expenses which are comprised of web marketing, catalog printing, paper, postage and other costs related to production of photographic images used in our catalogs and on our websites and mobile applications. The catalog printing, paper, postage and other costs are amortized over the period in which the customer responds to the marketing material determined based on historical customer response trends to a similar season's advertisement. Amortization rates are reviewed on a regular basis during the fiscal year and may be adjusted if the predicted customer response appears materially different than the historical response rate. The Company has the ability to measure the response rate to direct marketing early in the course of the advertisement based on its customers' reference to a specific catalog or by product placed and sold. The average amortization period for a catalog and related items are typically one to two months. If there is no expected future benefit, the cost of advertising is expensed when incurred. Advertising costs reported as prepaid expenses were $2,146 and $2,067 as of January 31, 2015 and 2014, respectively. Advertising expenses were $103,882, $91,615 and $81,944 for fiscal 2015, 2014 and 2013, respectively.

Start-up Costs

The Company expenses all start-up and organization costs as incurred, including travel, training, recruiting, salaries and other operating costs, and are included in selling, general and administrative expenses in the Consolidated Statements of Income.

Website Development Costs

The Company capitalizes applicable costs incurred during the application and infrastructure development stage and expenses costs incurred during the planning and operating stage. During fiscal 2015, 2014 and 2013, the Company did not capitalize any internally generated internal-use software development costs because substantially all costs were incurred during the planning and operating stages, and costs incurred during the application and infrastructure development stage were not material.

Income Taxes

The Company utilizes a balance sheet approach to provide for income taxes. Under this method, deferred tax assets and liabilities are recognized for the expected future tax consequences of net operating loss carryforwards and temporary differences between the carrying amounts and the tax bases of assets and liabilities. Investment tax credits or grants are accounted for in the period earned. The Company files a consolidated United States federal income tax return (see Note 8, "Income Taxes," for a further discussion of income taxes). The effect of a change in tax rates on deferred tax assets and liabilities is recognized in income in the period that includes the enactment date.

Net Income Per Common Share

Basic net income per common share is computed by dividing net income by the weighted-average number of common shares outstanding. Diluted net income per common share is computed by dividing net income by the weighted-average number of common shares and common share equivalents outstanding. Common share equivalents include the effect of stock options, stock appreciation rights ("SAR's"), restricted stock units ("RSU's") and performance stock units ("PSU's").

Comprehensive Income and Accumulated Other Comprehensive Loss

Comprehensive income is comprised of two subsets—net income and other comprehensive income/loss. Amounts included in accumulated other comprehensive loss relate to foreign currency translation adjustments and unrealized gains or losses on marketable securities. The foreign currency translation adjustments are not adjusted for income taxes because these adjustments relate to non-U.S. subsidiaries for which foreign earnings have been designated as permanently reinvested. Accumulated other comprehensive loss consisted of foreign currency translation losses of ($15,516) and ($1,388) as of January 31, 2015 and January 31, 2014, respectively, and unrealized gains, net of tax, on marketable securities of $89 and $420 as of January 31, 2015 and January 31, 2014, respectively. The tax effect of the unrealized (losses) on marketable securities recorded in comprehensive income was ($201), ($378) and ($672) during fiscal 2015, 2014 and 2013, respectively. Gross realized gains and losses are included in other income in the Consolidated Statements of Income and were not material to the Company's Consolidated Financial Statements for all three years presented.

Foreign Currency

The financial statements of the Company's foreign operations are translated into U.S. dollars. Assets and liabilities are translated at current exchange rates as of the balance sheet date, equity accounts at historical exchange rates, while income statement accounts are translated at the average rates in effect during the year. Translation adjustments are not included in determining net income, but are included in "Accumulated other comprehensive loss" within shareholders' equity. Remeasurement gains and losses included in operating results for fiscal years 2015, 2014 and 2013 were not material.

Concentration of Credit Risk

Financial instruments that potentially subject the Company to concentrations of credit risk consist principally of cash, cash equivalents, marketable securities and accounts receivable. The Company manages the credit risk associated with cash, cash equivalents and marketable securities by investing in high-quality securities held with reputable trustees and, by policy, limiting the amount of credit exposure to any one issuer or issue, as well as providing limitations on investment maturities. The Company's investment policy requires that its cash, cash equivalents and marketable securities are invested in corporate and municipal bonds rated "BBB" or better, commercial paper and federally insured or guaranteed investment vehicles such as certificates of deposit, United States treasury bills and federal government agencies. Receivables from third-party credit cards are processed by financial institutions, which are monitored for financial stability. The Company regularly evaluates the financial condition of its Wholesale segment customers. The Company's allowance for doubtful accounts reflects current market conditions and management's

URBAN OUTFITTERS, INC.

NOTES TO CONSOLIDATED FINANCIAL STATEMENTS—(Continued)
(in thousands, except share and per share data)

assessment regarding the collectability of its accounts receivable. The Company maintains cash accounts that, at times, may exceed federally insured limits. The Company has not experienced any losses from maintaining cash accounts in excess of such limits. Management believes that it is not exposed to any significant risks related to its cash accounts.

Recently Issued Accounting Pronouncements

In May 2014, the Financial Accounting Standards Board issued an accounting standards update that clarifies the principles for recognizing revenue from contracts with customers. The update outlines a single comprehensive model for entities to use in accounting for revenue arising from contracts with customers and supersedes most current revenue recognition guidance, including industry-specific guidance. The update states that an entity should recognize revenue to depict the transfer of promised goods or services to customers in the amount that reflects the consideration to which the entity expects to be entitled in exchange for those goods and services. Entities are required to apply the following steps when recognizing revenue under the update: (1) identify the contract(s) with a customer; (2) identify the performance obligation in the contract; (3) determine the transaction price; (4) allocate the transaction price to the performance obligations in the contract; and (5) recognize revenue when (or as) the entity satisfies a performance obligation. The update is effective for the Company beginning February 1, 2017. The update allows for a "full retrospective" adoption, meaning the update is applied to all periods presented, or a "modified retrospective" adoption, meaning the update is applied only to the most current period presented in the financial statements. Early adoption is not permitted. The Company is currently evaluating the adoption method to apply and the impact that the update will have on its financial position, results of operations, cash flows and financial statement disclosures.

3. Marketable Securities

During all periods shown, marketable securities are classified as available-for-sale. The amortized cost, gross unrealized gains (losses) and fair values of available-for-sale securities by major security type and class of security as of January 31, 2015 and 2014 are as follows:

	Amortized Cost		Unrealized Gains		Unrealized (Losses)		Fair Value
As of January 31, 2015							
Short-term Investments:							
Corporate bonds	$	56,594	$	20	$	(24)	$ 56,590
Municipal and pre-refunded municipal bonds		30,509		41		(2)	30,548
Certificates of deposit		11,127		5		—	11,132
Treasury bills		2,033		3		—	2,036
Commercial paper		3,938		2		—	3,940
		104,201		71		(26)	104,246
Long-term Investments:							
Corporate bonds		46,754		22		(40)	46,736
Municipal and pre-refunded municipal bonds		42,840		113		(6)	42,947
Certificates of deposit		3,066		—		—	3,066
Treasury bills		7,111		9		—	7,120
Mutual funds, held in rabbi trust		3,816		16		(54)	3,778
Federal government agencies		799		2		—	801
		104,386		162		(100)	104,448
	$	208,587	$	233	$	(126)	$ 208,694
As of January 31, 2014							
Short-term Investments:							
Corporate bonds	$	100,856	$	56	$	(41)	$ 100,871
Municipal and pre-refunded municipal bonds		85,000		98		(2)	85,096
Certificates of deposit		35,844		13		(1)	35,856
Treasury bills		24,873		10		—	24,883
Commercial paper		35,101		7		(1)	35,107
		281,674		184		(45)	281,813
Long-term Investments:							
Corporate bonds		208,446		268		(162)	208,552
Municipal and pre-refunded municipal bonds		125,934		415		(8)	126,341
Certificates of deposit		4,000		—		(2)	3,998
Treasury bills		21,551		21		—	21,572
Mutual funds, held in rabbi trust		1,591		108		(33)	1,666
Federal government agencies		4,287		6		—	4,293
		365,809		818		(205)	366,422
	$	647,483	$	1,002	$	(250)	$ 648,235

URBAN OUTFITTERS, INC.

NOTES TO CONSOLIDATED FINANCIAL STATEMENTS—(Continued)
(in thousands, except share and per share data)

Proceeds from the sale and maturities of available-for-sale securities were $830,297, $451,866 and $207,576 in fiscal 2015, 2014 and 2013, respectively. The Company included in "Interest income," in the Consolidated Statements of Income, a net realized gain of $237 during fiscal 2015, a net realized loss of $101 during fiscal 2014 and a net realized gain of $248 during fiscal 2013. Amortization of discounts and premiums, net, resulted in a reduction of "Interest income" of $6,696, $10,932 and $5,276 for fiscal years 2015, 2014 and 2013, respectively. Mutual funds represent assets held in an irrevocable rabbi trust for the Company's Non-qualified Deferred Compensation Plan ("NQDC"). These assets are a source of funds to match the funding obligations to participants in the NQDC but are subject to the Company's general creditors. The Company elected the fair value option for financial assets for the mutual funds held in the rabbi trust resulting in all unrealized gains and losses being recorded in "Interest income" in the Consolidated Statements of Income and not as a component of accumulated Other comprehensive (loss) income.

The following tables show the gross unrealized losses and fair value of the Company's marketable securities with unrealized losses that are not deemed to be other-than-temporarily impaired aggregated by the length of time that individual securities have been in a continuous unrealized loss position, at January 31, 2015 and January 31, 2014, respectively.

	January 31, 2015					
	Less Than 12 Months		12 Months or Greater		Total	
Description of Securities	Fair Value	Unrealized Losses	Fair Value	Unrealized Losses	Fair Value	Unrealized Losses
Corporate bonds	$ 55,384	$ (63)	$ 383	$ (1)	$ 55,767	$ (64)
Municipal and pre-refunded municipal bonds	4,672	(8)	—	—	4,672	(8)
Certificates of deposit	1,600	—	—	—	1,600	—
Treasury bills	—	—	—	—	—	—
Commercial paper	747	—	—	—	747	—
Mutual funds, held in rabbi trust	3,778	(54)	—	—	3,778	(54)
Federal government agencies	—	—	—	—	—	—
Total	$ 66,181	$ (125)	$ 383	$ (1)	$ 66,564	$ (126)

	January 31, 2014					
	Less Than 12 Months		12 Months or Greater		Total	
Description of Securities	Fair Value	Unrealized Losses	Fair Value	Unrealized Losses	Fair Value	Unrealized Losses
Corporate bonds	$ 147,731	$ (203)	$ —	$ —	$ 147,731	$ (203)
Municipal and pre-refunded municipal bonds	6,291	(10)	—	—	6,291	(10)
Certificates of deposit	12,746	(3)	—	—	12,746	(3)
Treasury bills	6,606	—	—	—	6,606	—
Commercial paper	6,640	(1)	—	—	6,640	(1)
Mutual funds, held in rabbi trust	1,666	(33)	—	—	1,666	(33)
Federal government agencies	1,753	—	—	—	1,753	—
Total	$ 183,433	$ (250)	$ —	$ —	$ 183,433	$ (250)

As of January 31, 2015 and 2014, there were a total of 172 and 219 securities with unrealized loss positions within the Company's portfolio, respectively.

4. Fair Value

The Company utilizes a hierarchy that prioritizes fair value measurements based on the types of inputs used for the various valuation techniques (market approach, income approach and cost approach that relate to its financial assets and financial liabilities). The levels of the hierarchy are described as follows:

•   Level 1: Observable inputs such as quoted prices in active markets for identical assets or liabilities.

•   Level 2: Inputs other than quoted prices that are observable for the asset or liability, either directly or indirectly; these include quoted prices for similar assets or liabilities in active markets and quoted prices for identical or similar assets or liabilities in markets that are not active.

•   Level 3: Unobservable inputs that reflect the Company's own assumptions.

Management's assessment of the significance of a particular input to the fair value measurement requires judgment and may affect the valuation of financial assets and liabilities and their placement within the fair value hierarchy. The Company's financial assets that are accounted for at fair value on a recurring basis are presented in the table below:

	Marketable Securities Fair Value as of January 31, 2015			
	Level 1	Level 2	Level 3	Total
Assets:				
Corporate bonds	$ 103,326	$ —	$ —	$ 103,326
Municipal and pre-refunded municipal bonds	—	73,495	—	73,495
Certificates deposit	—	14,198	—	14,198
Treasury bills	9,156	—	—	9,156
Commercial paper	—	3,940	—	3,940
Mutual funds, held in rabbi trust	3,778	—	—	3,778
Federal government agencies	801	—	—	801
	$ 117,061	$ 91,633	$ —	$ 208,694

URBAN OUTFITTERS, INC.

NOTES TO CONSOLIDATED FINANCIAL STATEMENTS—(Continued)
(in thousands, except share and per share data)

| | Marketable Securities Fair Value as of January 31, 2014 | | | |
	Level 1	Level 2	Level 3	Total
Assets:				
Corporate bonds	$ 309,423	$ —	$ —	$ 309,423
Municipal and pre-refunded municipal bonds	—	211,437	—	211,437
Certificates deposit	—	39,854	—	39,854
Treasury bills	46,455	—	—	46,455
Commercial paper	—	35,107	—	35,107
Mutual funds, held in rabbi trust	1,666	—	—	1,666
Federal government agencies	4,293	—	—	4,293
	$ 361,837	$ 286,398	$ —	$ 648,235

Level 1 assets consist of financial instruments whose value has been based on inputs that use, as their basis, readily observable market data that are actively quoted and are validated through external sources, including third-party pricing services and brokers.

Level 2 assets consist of financial instruments whose value has been based on quoted prices for similar assets and liabilities in active markets as well as quoted prices for identical or similar assets or liabilities in markets that are not active.

Level 3 assets consist of financial instruments where there is no active market. The Company has no Level 3 assets as of January 31, 2015. During the first quarter of fiscal 2014, the Company sold all of its remaining ARS for $4,580 in cash. The Company's ARS had a par value and a recorded fair value of $4,925 and $4,330, respectively, prior to the sale in April 2013. Accordingly, the level 3 rollforward for fiscal 2015 and 2014 is not presented.

The fair value of cash and cash equivalents (Level 1) approximate carrying value since cash and cash equivalents consist of short-term highly liquid investments with maturities of three months or less. As of January 31, 2015 and 2014, cash and cash equivalents included cash on hand, cash in banks, money market accounts and marketable securities with maturities of less than three months at the time of purchase.

5. Property and Equipment

Property and equipment is summarized as follows:

| | January 31, | |
	2015	2014
Land	$ 15,197	$ 15,042
Buildings	239,115	185,605
Furniture and fixtures	410,265	375,429
Leasehold improvements	794,995	809,789
Other operating equipment	180,397	161,933
Construction-in-progress	182,595	93,240
	1,822,564	1,641,038
Accumulated depreciation	(933,332)	(834,129)
Total	$ 889,232	$ 806,909

Depreciation expense for property and equipment for fiscal years ended 2015, 2014 and 2013 was $131,414, $121,732 and $113,388, respectively.

6. Accrued Expenses and Other Current Liabilities

Accrued expenses and other current liabilities consist of the following:

| | January 31, | |
	2015	2014
Gift certificates and merchandise credits	$ 47,943	$ 44,311
Sales return reserves	19,804	17,089
Accrued construction	18,717	20,939
Accrued sales taxes	12,171	12,379
Accrued rents and estimated property taxes	11,121	10,850
Other current liabilities	42,887	48,141
Total	$ 152,643	$ 153,709

7. Line of Credit Facility

On March 27, 2014, the Company amended and restated its existing line of credit facility with Wells Fargo Bank, National Association (the "Line"). The Line is a five-year $175.0 million revolving credit facility with an accordion feature allowing for an increase of up to $50.0 million at our discretion. The Line contains a sub-limit for borrowings by the Company's subsidiaries that are guaranteed by the Company. Under the terms of the Line, at the Company's option, the aggregate principal balance of the amounts advanced or portions thereof will bear interest at (a) the base rate, or (b) the applicable LIBOR Rate plus a margin that can range from 0.50% to 1.50%. The Line subjects

URBAN OUTFITTERS, INC.

NOTES TO CONSOLIDATED FINANCIAL STATEMENTS—(Continued)
(in thousands, except share and per share data)

the Company to various restrictive covenants, including maintenance of certain financial covenants. As of January 31, 2015, there were no borrowings under the Line and the Company was in compliance with all covenants. Outstanding letters of credit under the Line totaled approximately $83,533 as of January 31, 2015.

8. Income Taxes

The components of income before income taxes are as follows:

	Fiscal Year Ended January 31,		
	2015	2014	2013
Domestic	$ 328,479	$ 375,793	$ 340,536
Foreign	34,971	51,725	35,036
	$ 363,450	$ 427,518	$ 375,572

The components of the provision for income tax expense/ (benefit) are as follows:

	Fiscal Year Ended January 31,		
	2015	2014	2013
Current:			
Federal	$ 109,978	$ 139,848	$ 93,625
State	19,665	20,530	15,746
Foreign	3,600	13,285	6,639
	$ 133,243	$ 173,663	$ 116,010
Deferred:			
Federal	$ (3,295)	$ (15,171)	$ 23,285
State	1,372	(6,225)	(722)
Foreign	(298)	(7,109)	(315)
	(2,221)	(28,505)	22,248
	$ 131,022	$ 145,158	$ 138,258

The Company's effective tax rate was different than the statutory U.S. federal income tax rate for the following reasons:

	Fiscal Year Ended January 31,		
	2015	2014	2013
Expected provision at statutory U.S. federal tax rate	35.0%	35.0%	35.0%
State and local income taxes, net of federal tax benefit	3.7	2.2	3.1
Foreign taxes	(2.4)	(2.7)	(1.7)
Other	(0.3)	(0.5)	0.4
Effective tax rate	36.0%	34.0%	36.8%

The significant components of deferred tax assets and liabilities as of January 31, 2015 and 2014 are as follows:

	January 31,	
	2015	2014
Deferred tax liabilities:		
Prepaid expense	$ (3,732)	$ (2,813)
Depreciation	(51,774)	(48,362)
Other temporary differences	(1,728)	(634)
Gross deferred tax liabilities	(57,234)	(51,809)
Deferred tax assets:		
Deferred rent	70,023	66,579
Inventories	8,137	5,624
Accounts receivable	2,844	3,063
Net operating loss carryforwards	4,003	2,601
Tax uncertainties	3,363	3,372
Accrued salaries and benefits	31,747	28,045
Other temporary differences	5,839	9,413
Gross deferred tax assets, before valuation allowances	125,956	118,697
Valuation allowances	(45)	(54)
Net deferred tax assets	$ 68,677	$ 66,834

URBAN OUTFITTERS, INC.

NOTES TO CONSOLIDATED FINANCIAL STATEMENTS—(Continued)
(in thousands, except share and per share data)

Net deferred tax assets are attributed to the jurisdictions in which the Company operates. As of January 31, 2015 and 2014, respectively, $43,330 and $39,513 were attributable to U.S. federal, $16,097 and $17,092 were attributed to state jurisdictions and $9,250 and $10,229 were attributed to foreign jurisdictions.

As of January 31, 2015, certain non-U.S. subsidiaries of the Company had net operating loss carryforwards for tax purposes of approximately $853 that expire from 2016 through 2033 and approximately $12,866 that do not expire. Certain U.S. subsidiaries of the Company had state net operating loss carryforwards for tax purposes of approximately $1,307 that expire from 2018 through 2031. As of January 31, 2015, the Company had a full valuation allowance for certain foreign net operating loss carryforwards where it was uncertain the carryforwards would be utilized. The Company had no valuation allowance for certain other foreign and state net operating loss carryforwards where management believes it is more likely than not the tax benefit of these carryforwards will be realized. As of January 31, 2015 and 2014, the non-current portion of net deferred tax assets aggregated $49,922 and $38,061, respectively.

The cumulative amount of the Company's share of undistributed earnings of non-U.S. subsidiaries for which no deferred taxes have been provided was $240,704 as of January 31, 2015. These earnings are deemed to be permanently re-invested to finance growth programs. It is not practical to estimate the income tax liability that might be incurred if such earnings were remitted to the United States.

A reconciliation of the beginning and ending balances of the total amounts of gross unrecognized tax benefits is as follows:

Tax Benefit Reconciliation	January 31,		
	2015	2014	2013
Balance at the beginning of the period	$ 4,835	$ 7,895	$ 8,664
Increases in tax positions for prior years	2,518	1,026	419
Decreases in tax positions for prior years	(12)	(305)	(929)
Increases in tax positions for current year	352	521	635
Settlements	(620)	(3,190)	(13)
Lapse in statute of limitations	(184)	(1,112)	(881)
Balance at the end of the period	$ 6,889	$ 4,835	$ 7,895

The total amount of net unrecognized tax benefits that, if recognized, would impact the Company's effective tax rate were $4,952 and $2,416 as of January 31, 2015 and 2014, respectively. The Company accrues interest and penalties related to unrecognized tax benefits in income tax expense in the Consolidated Statements of Income, which is consistent with the recognition of these items in prior reporting periods. During the years ended January 31, 2015, 2014 and 2013, the Company recognized expense/(benefit) of $408, ($1,992) and $541, respectively, related to interest and penalties. The Company accrued $1,486 and $1,078 for the payment of interest and penalties as of January 31, 2015 and 2014, respectively.

The Company files income tax returns in the U.S. federal jurisdiction and various state and foreign jurisdictions. Certain federal, foreign and state jurisdictions are subject to audit from fiscal 2005 to 2014. It is possible that a state or foreign examination may be resolved within twelve months. Due to the potential for resolution of federal and foreign audit and state examinations, and the expiration of various statutes of limitation, it is possible that the Company's gross unrecognized tax benefits balance may change within the next twelve months by a range of zero to $2,450.

9. Share-Based Compensation

The Company's 2008 Stock Incentive Plan can authorize up to 10,000,000 common shares, which can be granted as RSU's, unrestricted shares, incentive stock options, nonqualified stock options, PSU's or SAR's. Awards under this plan generally expire seven or ten years from the date of grant, thirty days after termination of employment or six months after the date of death or termination due to disability of the grantee. As of January 31, 2015, there were 5,102,199 common shares available to grant under the 2008 Stock Incentive Plan.

A lattice binomial pricing model ("the Model") was used to estimate the fair value of stock options and SAR's. The Model allows for assumptions such as the risk-free rate of interest, volatility and exercise rate to vary over time reflecting a more realistic pattern of economic and behavioral occurrences. The Company uses historical data on exercise timing to determine the expected life assumption. The risk-free rate of interest for periods within the contractual life of the award is based on U.S. Government Securities Treasury Constant Maturities over the expected term of the equity instrument. The expected volatility is based on a weighted-average of the implied volatility and the Company's most recent historical volatility.

Based on the Company's historical experience, it has assumed an annualized forfeiture rate of 5% for its unvested share-based awards granted during the fiscal years ended January 31, 2015, 2014 and 2013. For share-based awards granted in previous years that remain unvested, an annualized forfeiture rate of 5% has been assumed. The Company will record additional expense if the actual forfeiture rate is lower than it estimated, and will record a recovery of prior expense if the actual forfeiture is higher than estimated.

Share-based compensation expense, included in "Selling, general and administrative expenses" in the Consolidated Statements of Income, for the fiscal years ended January 31, 2015, 2014 and 2013 was as follows:

	Fiscal Year Ended January 31,		
	2015	2014	2013
Stock Options	$ 1,377	$ 2,621	$ 2,214
Stock Appreciation Rights	2,244	2,918	2,578
Performance Stock Units (1)(2)	12,991	9,956	6,124
Restricted Stock Units	124	247	(24)
Total	$ 16,736	$ 15,742	$ 10,892

(1)   Includes the reversal of $1,396 of previously recognized compensation expense in fiscal 2015, related to 163,336 PSU's that will not vest as the achievement of the related performance target is not probable.

(2)   Includes the reversal of $3,418 of previously recognized compensation expense in fiscal 2013, related to 320,200 PSU's that will not vest as the achievement of the related performance target is not probable.

URBAN OUTFITTERS, INC.

NOTES TO CONSOLIDATED FINANCIAL STATEMENTS—(Continued)
(in thousands, except share and per share data)

The total tax benefit associated with share-based compensation expense for the fiscal years ended January 31, 2015, 2014 and 2013 was $6,367, $5,976 and $3,921, respectively.

Stock Options

The Company may grant stock options which generally vest over a period of three to five years. Stock options become exercisable over the vesting period in installments determined by the administrator, which can vary depending upon each individual grant. Stock options granted to non-employee directors generally vest over a period of one year. The following weighted-average assumptions were used in the Model to estimate the fair value of stock options at the date of grant:

	Fiscal Year Ended January 31,		
	2015	2014	2013
Expected life, in years	3.4	3.5	3.6
Risk-free interest rate	1.1%	0.6%	0.5%
Volatility	33.0%	36.0%	45.0%
Dividend rate	—	—	—

The following table summarizes the Company's stock option activity for the fiscal year ended January 31, 2015:

	Shares	Weighted-Average Exercise Price	Weighted-Average Contractual Terms (years)	Aggregate Intrinsic Value
Awards outstanding at beginning of year	2,813,194	$ 31.55	2.3	14,502
Granted	100,000	35.85		
Exercised	(422,187)	25.33		
Forfeited or Expired	(26,617)	40.56		
Awards outstanding at end of year	2,464,390	32.69	1.6	$ 8,547
Awards outstanding expected to vest	2,458,921	32.69	1.6	$ 8,120
Awards exercisable at end of year	2,355,015	$ 32.54	1.6	$ 8,538

The following table summarizes other information related to stock options during the years ended January 31, 2015, 2014 and 2013:

	Fiscal Year Ended January 31,		
	2015	2014	2013
Weighted-average grant date fair value—per share	$ 7.02	$ 9.67	$ 7.71
Intrinsic value of awards exercised	$ 4,852	$ 30,450	$ 19,544
Net cash proceeds from the exercise of stock options	$ 10,693	$ 35,218	$ 30,671

The Company recognized tax benefits related to stock options of $1,898, $10,312 and $6,532 for the fiscal years ended January 31, 2015, 2014 and 2013, respectively. Total unrecognized compensation cost of stock options granted but not yet vested, as of January 31, 2015, was $254, which is expected to be recognized over the weighted-average period of 0.3 year.

Stock Appreciation Rights

The Company may grant SAR's which generally vest over a five year period. Each vested SAR entitles the holder the right to the differential between the value of the Company's common share price at the date of exercise and the value of the Company's common share price at the date of grant. There were no SAR's granted during the fiscal year ended January 31, 2015. The following weighted-average assumptions were used in the Model to estimate the fair value of SAR's at the date of grant:

	Fiscal Year Ended January 31,		
	2015	2014	2013
Expected life, in years	—	5.6	5.0
Risk-free interest rate	—	1.0%	0.9%
Volatility	—	46.0%	48.2%
Dividend rate	—	—	—

The following table summarizes the Company's SAR activity for the fiscal year ended January 31, 2015:

URBAN OUTFITTERS, INC.

NOTES TO CONSOLIDATED FINANCIAL STATEMENTS—(Continued)
(in thousands, except share and per share data)

	Awards	Weighted-Average Exercise Price	Weighted-Average Remaining Contractual Term (years)	Aggregate Intrinsic Value
Awards outstanding at beginning of year	1,102,475	$ 31.33	5.7	
Granted	—	—		
Exercised	(75,650)	28.87		
Forfeited or Expired	(133,417)	35.70		
Awards outstanding at end of year	893,408	30.89	4.6	$ 3,990
Awards outstanding expected to vest	873,671	30.89	4.6	$ 3,791
Awards exercisable at end of year	498,675	$ 30.57	4.6	$ 2,164

The following table summarizes other information related to SAR's during the years ended January 31, 2015, 2014 and 2013:

	Fiscal Year Ended January 31,		
	2015	2014	2013
Weighted-average grant date fair value—per share	$ —	$ 14.11	$ 11.85
Intrinsic value of awards exercised	$ 654	$ 848	$ —

The Company recognized tax benefit related to SAR's of $66 and $305 for the fiscal years ended January 31, 2015 and 2014, respectively. There were no tax benefits related to SAR's for the fiscal year ended January 31, 2013. Total unrecognized compensation cost of SAR's granted, but not yet vested, as of January 31, 2015, was $1,998, which is expected to be recognized over the weighted-average period of 1.7 years.

Performance Stock Units

The Company may grant PSU's which vest based on the achievement of various company performance targets and external market conditions. The fair value of the PSU's are determined using a Monte Carlo simulation. Once the Company determines that it is probable that the performance targets will be met, compensation expense is recorded for these awards. If any of these performance targets are not met, the awards are forfeited. Each PSU is equal to one common share with varying maximum award value limitations. PSU's typically vest over a five year period.

The following table summarizes the Company's PSU activity for the fiscal year ended January 31, 2015:

	Shares	Weighted-Average Fair Value
Non-vested awards outstanding at beginning of year	3,709,225	$ 20.48
Granted	867,500	23.40
Vested	(278,324)	17.12
Forfeited	(306,192)	20.69
Non-vested awards outstanding at end of year	3,992,209	$ 21.32

The weighted-average grant date fair value of PSU's awarded during the fiscal years ended January 31, 2015, 2014 and 2013 was $23.40, $25.13 and $18.22, per share, respectively. No PSU's vested during the fiscal years ended January 31, 2014 and 2013. Unrecognized compensation cost related to unvested PSU's as of January 31, 2015 was $40,917, which is expected to be recognized over a weighted-average period of 3.1 years.

Restricted Stock Units

The Company may grant RSU's which vest based on the achievement of specified service and external market conditions. RSU's typically vest over a three to five year period.

The following table summarizes the Company's RSU activity for the fiscal year ended January 31, 2015:

	Shares	Weighted-Average Fair Value
Non-vested awards outstanding at beginning of year	10,000	$ 39.06
Granted	—	—
Vested	(5,000)	39.06
Forfeited	—	—
Non-vested awards outstanding at end of year	5,000	$ 39.06

URBAN OUTFITTERS, INC.

NOTES TO CONSOLIDATED FINANCIAL STATEMENTS—(Continued)
(in thousands, except share and per share data)

The Company recognized tax benefits related to RUS's of $7 for the fiscal year ended January 31, 2015. There were no tax benefits related to RSU's for the fiscal years ended January 31, 2014 and 2013, respectively. There were no RSU's granted during the fiscal years ended January 31, 2015 and January 31, 2013. The weighted-average grant date fair value of RSU's awarded during the fiscal year ended January 31, 2014 was $39.06 per share. No RSU's vested during the fiscal year ended January 31, 2014. Unrecognized compensation cost related to unvested RSU's as of January 31, 2015 was $13, which is expected to be recognized over a weighted-average period of 0.1 year.

10. Shareholders' Equity

On May 27, 2014, the Company's Board of Directors authorized the repurchase of 10,000,000 common shares under a new share repurchase program. Under this authorization, the Company repurchased and subsequently retired 7,718,531 common shares at a total cost of $258,160 during fiscal 2015. The average cost per share of these repurchases for fiscal 2015 was $33.45, including commissions.

On August 27, 2013, the Company's Board of Directors authorized the repurchase of 10,000,000 common shares under a share repurchase program. The Company repurchased and subsequently retired all of the remaining 9,699,700 outstanding shares available under this authorization during the first quarter of fiscal 2015 at a total cost of $353,315 for an average cost per share of $36.43, including commissions.

In addition to the shares repurchased under the share repurchase programs, during the fiscal years ended January 31, 2015 and January 31, 2014 the Company acquired and subsequently retired 111,563 and 9,520 common shares at a total cost of $3,947 and $397, respectively, from employees to meet minimum statutory tax withholding requirements.

As a result of the share repurchase activity during fiscal 2015, the Company reduced the balance of additional paid-in-capital by $128,935, which resulted in a reduction of retained earnings of $486,484.

On February 23, 2015, the Company's Board of Directors authorized the repurchase of 20,000,000 common shares under a new share repurchase program.

11. Other Comprehensive Income (Loss) and Accumulated Other Comprehensive Income (Loss)

The following tables present the change in accumulated other comprehensive income (loss), by component, net of tax, for the fiscal years ended January 31, 2015 and 2014, respectively:

	Fiscal Year Ended January 31, 2015		
	Foreign Currency Translation	Unrealized Gains and (Losses) on Available-for-Sale Securities	Total
Beginning Balance	$ (1,388)	$ 420	$ (968)
Other comprehensive income (loss) before reclassifications	(14,128)	(568)	(14,696)
Amounts reclassified from accumulated other comprehensive income (loss)	—	237	237
Net current-period other comprehensive income/(loss)	(14,128)	(331)	(14,459)
Ending Balance	$ (15,516)	$ 89	$ (15,427)

	Fiscal Year Ended January 31, 2014		
	Foreign Currency Translation	Unrealized Gains and (Losses) on Available-for-Sale Securities	Total
Beginning Balance	$ (8,582)	$ (200)	$ (8,782)
Other comprehensive income (loss) before reclassifications	7,194	519	7,713
Amounts reclassified from accumulated other comprehensive income (loss)	—	101	101
Net current-period other comprehensive income/(loss)	7,194	620	7,814
Ending Balance	$ (1,388)	$ 420	$ (968)

All unrealized gains and losses on available-for-sale securities reclassified from accumulated other comprehensive loss were recorded in "Interest income" in the Consolidated Statements of Income.

12. Net Income Per Common Share

The following is a reconciliation of the weighted-average common shares outstanding used for the computation of basic and diluted net income per common share:

	Fiscal Year Ended January 31,		
	2015	2014	2013
Basic weighted-average common shares outstanding	136,651,899	147,014,869	145,253,691
Effect of dilutive options, stock appreciation rights, restricted stock units and performance stock units	1,540,835	2,211,037	1,410,040
Diluted weighted-average shares outstanding	138,192,734	149,225,906	146,663,731

URBAN OUTFITTERS, INC.

NOTES TO CONSOLIDATED FINANCIAL STATEMENTS—(Continued)
(in thousands, except share and per share data)

For the fiscal years ended January 31, 2015, 2014 and 2013, awards to purchase 1,015,895 common shares ranging in price from $35.12 to $46.02, 151,625 common shares ranging in price from $37.65 to $46.02 and 2,440,525 common shares ranging in price from $28.49 to $39.58, respectively, were excluded from the calculation of diluted net income per common share because the impact would be anti-dilutive.

As of January 31, 2015 and 2014, 2,216,899 and 1,752,200 contingently issuable awards, respectively, were excluded from the calculation of diluted net income per common share as they did not meet certain performance criteria.

13. Commitments and Contingencies

Leases

The Company leases its stores, certain fulfillment and distribution facilities, and offices under non-cancelable operating leases. The following is a schedule by year of the future minimum lease payments for operating leases with original terms in excess of one year:

Fiscal Year	
2016	$ 254,733
2017	241,639
2018	226,884
2019	207,603
2020	184,806
Thereafter	720,574
Total minimum lease payments	$ 1,836,239

Amounts noted above include commitments for 22 executed leases for stores not opened as of January 31, 2015. The majority of our leases allow for renewal options between five and ten years upon expiration of the initial lease term. The store leases generally provide for payment of direct operating costs including real estate taxes. Certain store leases provide for contingent rentals when sales exceed specified levels. Additionally, the Company has entered into store leases that require a percentage of total sales to be paid to landlords in lieu of minimum rent.

Rent expense consisted of the following:

	Fiscal Year Ended January 31,		
	2015	2014	2013
Minimum and percentage rentals	$ 234,982	$ 205,759	$ 186,804
Contingent rentals	3,901	5,542	5,714
Total	$ 238,883	$ 211,301	$ 192,518

The Company also has commitments for un-fulfilled purchase orders for merchandise ordered from our vendors in the normal course of business, which are liquidated within 12 months, of $466,008. The majority of the Company's merchandise commitments are cancellable with no or limited recourse available to the vendor until the merchandise shipping date. The Company also has commitments related to contracts with construction contractors, fully liquidated upon the completion of construction, which is typically within 12 months, of $12,056.

Benefit Plans

Full and part-time U.S. based employees who are at least 18 years of age are eligible after three months of employment to participate in the Urban Outfitters 401(k) Savings Plan (the "Plan"). Under the Plan, employees can defer 1% to 25% of compensation as defined. The Company makes matching contributions in cash of $0.25 per employee contribution dollar on the first 6% of the employee contribution. The employees' contribution is 100% vested while the Company's matching contribution vests at 20% per year of employee service. The Company's contributions were $1,708, $1,770 and $1,483 for fiscal years 2015, 2014 and 2013, respectively.

On November 27, 2012, the Company's Board of Directors approved the terms of the NQDC, which became effective as of February 1, 2013. The NQDC provides certain employees who are limited in their participation under the Plan the opportunity to defer compensation as defined within the NQDC. The Company's matching contributions are calculated to provide $0.25 per employee contribution dollar on the first 6% of total compensation deferred under the combination of both the Plan and the NQDC. Employee contributions are 100% vested on the contribution date and the Company's matching contribution is 100% vested upon crediting to participants' accounts on an annual basis. The Company made a matching contribution of $100 during fiscal 2015. The NQDC obligation was $3,778 as of January 31, 2015. The Company has purchased investments to fund the NQDC obligation. The investments had an aggregate market value of $3,778 as of January 31, 2015, and are included in "Marketable securities" in the Consolidated Balance Sheets (see Note 3, "Marketable Securities").

Contingencies

The Company is party to various legal proceedings arising from normal business activities. Management believes that the ultimate resolution of these matters will not have a material adverse effect on the Company's financial position, results of operations or cash flows.

URBAN OUTFITTERS, INC.

NOTES TO CONSOLIDATED FINANCIAL STATEMENTS—(Continued)
(in thousands, except share and per share data)

14. Related Party Transactions

Drinker Biddle & Reath LLP ("DBR"), a law firm, provided general legal services to the Company. Fees paid to DBR during fiscal 2015, 2014 and 2013 were $2,752, $2,637 and $1,902, respectively. Harry S. Cherken, Jr., a director of the Company, is a partner at DBR. Amounts due to DBR as of January 31, 2015 and 2014 were approximately $203 and $380, respectively.

The McDevitt Company, a real estate company, acted as a broker in substantially all of the Company's new real estate transactions during fiscal 2015 in the United States. The Company has not paid any compensation to The McDevitt Company, but the Company has been advised that The McDevitt Company has received commissions from other parties to such transactions. Wade L. McDevitt is the brother-in-law of Scott Belair, one of the Company's directors, and is president and the sole shareholder of The McDevitt Company. Mr. McDevitt's wife, Wendy McDevitt, is an employee of the Company. In addition, Mr. McDevitt owns McDevitt Corporation Limited, a United Kingdom entity, and McDevitt Netherlands BV, a Dutch entity. During fiscal 2015 and 2014, the Company paid real estate commissions of $295 and $518 to West St. Consulting a United Kingdom entity owned by an employee of McDevitt Corporation Limited. The Company also paid commissions of $300 and $562 during fiscal 2015 and 2014 to HED Real Estate BV, a Dutch entity owned by three employees of McDevitt Netherlands BV. There were no amounts paid to West St. Consulting or HED Real Estate BV during fiscal 2013. The Company has been advised that West St. Consulting and HED Real Estate BV have entered into arrangements to share a portion of these commissions with McDevitt Corporation Limited and McDevitt Netherlands BV.

The Addis Group ("Addis"), an insurance brokerage and risk management consulting company, acted as the Company's commercial insurance broker and risk management consultant for the years ended January 31, 2015, 2014 and 2013. The Company has not paid any compensation to Addis for such services, but has been advised that Addis has received commissions from other parties to such transactions. Scott Addis, the brother-in-law of Richard A. Hayne, Chairman of the Board of the Company, Chief Executive Officer and President, is the President of The Addis Group. There were no amounts due to or from Addis as of January 31, 2015 and January 31, 2014.

15. Segment Reporting

The Company is a global retailer of lifestyle-oriented general merchandise with two reportable segments—"Retail" and "Wholesale." The Company's Retail segment consists of the aggregation of its five brands operating through 546 stores under the retail names "Urban Outfitters," "Anthropologie," "Free People," "Terrain" and "Bhldn" and includes their direct-to-consumer channels. Each of the Company's brands, which include the retail stores and direct-to-consumer channels, are considered an operating segment. Net sales from the Retail segment accounted for more than 93% of total consolidated net sales for the fiscal years ended, January 31, 2015, 2014 and 2013, respectively. The remaining net sales are derived from the Company's Wholesale segment that distributes apparel to its Retail segment and to approximately 1,600 better department and specialty retailers worldwide.

The Company has aggregated its brands into the Retail segment based upon their shared management, customer base and economic characteristics. Reporting in this format provides management with the financial information necessary to evaluate the success of the segments and the overall business. The Company evaluates the performance of the segments based on the net sales and pre-tax income from operations (excluding intercompany charges) of the segment. Corporate expenses include expenses incurred and directed by the corporate office that are not allocated to segments. The principal identifiable assets for each reporting segment are inventories and property and equipment.

Other assets are comprised primarily of general corporate assets, which principally consist of cash and cash equivalents, marketable securities, deferred taxes and prepaid expenses, which are typically not allocated to the Company's segments. The Company accounts for intersegment sales and transfers as if the sales and transfers were made to third parties making similar volume purchases.

The Company's omni-channel strategy enhances its customers' brand experience by providing a seamless approach to the customer shopping experience. The Company has substantially integrated all available shopping channels, including stores, websites (online and through mobile devices) and catalogs. The Company's investments in areas such as marketing campaigns and technology advancements are designed to generate demand for the omni-channel and not the separate store or direct-to-consumer channels. Store sales are primarily fulfilled from that store's inventory, but may also be shipped from any of the Company's fulfillment centers or from a different store location if an item is not available at the original store. Direct-to-consumer orders are primarily shipped to the Company's customers through its fulfillment centers, but may also be shipped from any store, or a combination of fulfillment centers and stores depending on the availability of a particular item. Direct-to-consumer orders may also be picked up at a store location. As the Company's customers continue to shop across multiple channels, the Company has adapted its approach towards meeting this demand. Due to the availability of like product in a variety of shopping channels, the Company now sources these products utilizing single stock keeping units based on the omni-channel demand rather than the demand of the separate channels. These and other technological capabilities allow the Company to better serve its customers and help it to complete a sale that otherwise may not have occurred due to out-of-stock positions. As a result of changing customer behavior and the substantial integration of the operations of the Company's store and direct-to-consumer channels, the Company manages and analyzes its performance based on a single omni-channel rather than separate channels and believes that the omni-channel results present the most meaningful and appropriate measure of the Company's performance.

The accounting policies of the reportable segments are the same as the policies described in Note 2, "Summary of Significant Accounting Policies." Both the Retail and Wholesale segments are highly diversified. No one customer constitutes more than 10% of the Company's total consolidated net sales. A summary of the information about the Company's operations by segment is as follows:

URBAN OUTFITTERS, INC.

NOTES TO CONSOLIDATED FINANCIAL STATEMENTS—(Continued)
(in thousands, except share and per share data)

	Fiscal Year		
	2015	2014	2013
Net sales			
Retail operations	$ 3,097,274	$ 2,908,981	$ 2,646,284
Wholesale operations	237,491	185,792	154,957
Intersegment elimination	(11,688)	(8,165)	(6,316)
Total net sales	$ 3,323,077	$ 3,086,608	$ 2,794,925
Income from operations			
Retail operations	$ 354,326	$ 414,734	$ 366,139
Wholesale operations	55,403	42,191	35,783
Intersegment elimination	(1,079)	(837)	(610)
Total segment operating income	408,650	456,088	401,312
General corporate expenses	(43,265)	(29,257)	(27,027)
Total income from operations	$ 365,385	$ 426,831	$ 374,285
Depreciation expense for property and equipment			
Retail operations	$ 130,383	$ 120,960	$ 112,645
Wholesale operations	1,031	772	743
Total depreciation expense for property and equipment	$ 131,414	$ 121,732	$ 113,388
Inventories			
Retail operations	$ 314,940	$ 282,590	
Wholesale operations	43,297	28,617	
Total inventories	$ 358,237	$ 311,207	
Property and equipment, net			
Retail operations	$ 885,200	$ 802,965	
Wholesale operations	4,032	3,944	
Total property and equipment, net	$ 889,232	$ 806,909	
Cash paid for property and equipment			
Retail operations	$ 228,682	$ 184,255	$ 168,530
Wholesale operations	1,122	1,846	345
Total cash paid for property and equipment	$ 229,804	$ 186,101	$ 168,875

The Company has foreign operations in Europe and Canada. Revenues and long-lived assets, based upon the Company's domestic and foreign operations, are as follows:

	Fiscal Year		
	2015	2014	2013
Net Sales			
Domestic operations	$ 2,870,140	$ 2,685,042	$ 2,423,155
Foreign operations	452,937	401,566	371,770
Total net sales	$ 3,323,077	$ 3,086,608	$ 2,794,925
Property and equipment, net			
Domestic operations	$ 745,504	$ 655,866	
Foreign operations	143,728	151,043	
Total property and equipment, net	$ 889,232	$ 806,909	

INDUSTRY RATIO REPORT
Retail Family Clothing Stores

Liquidity

Current Ratio	2.03
Quick Ratio	0.98

Activity

Inventory Turnover	5.03
Days to Sell Inventory	87.02 days
Receivables Turnover	78.20
Average Collection Period	10.02 days
Fixed Asset Turnover	6.60
Total Asset Turnover	2.02
Accounts Payable Turnover	11.19

Profitability

Gross Profit Margin	35.15%
Operating Profit Margin	7.62%
Net Profit Margin	3.75%
Return on Equity	11.34%
Return on Assets	6.86%
Quality of Income	2.01

Leverage

Times Interest Earned	71.24981
Total Debt/Total Equity	0.43
Total Assets/Total Equity	2.45

Dividends

Dividend Payout	34.95%
Dividend Yield	1.41%

Other

Advertising-to-Sales	3.97%
Sales Growth	1.6%
Capital Acquisitions Ratio	2.46
Price/Earnings	22.06

COMPANIES USED IN INDUSTRY ANALYSIS

Company Name	Ticker Symbol
Abercrombie & Fitch Co.	ANF
Aeropostale, Inc.	ARO
American Eagle Outfitters, Inc.	AEO
Buckle, Inc.	BKE
Children's Place, Inc.	PLCE
Destination XL Group, Inc.	DXLG
Gap, Inc.	GPS
Lands' End, Inc.	LE
Nordstrom, Inc.	JWN
Ross Stores, Inc.	ROST
Stage Stores, Inc.	SSI
Stein Mart, Inc.	SMRT
TJX Companies, Inc.	TJX
Urban Outfitters, Inc.	URBN

TABLE E.1

Present Value of $1

Periods	1.0%	2.0%	3.0%	3.75%	4.0%	4.25%	5.0%	6.0%	7.0%
1	0.99010	0.98039	0.97087	0.96386	0.96154	0.95923	0.95238	0.94340	0.93458
2	0.98030	0.96117	0.94260	0.92902	0.92456	0.92013	0.90703	0.89000	0.87344
3	0.97059	0.94232	0.91514	0.89544	0.88900	0.88262	0.86384	0.83962	0.81630
4	0.96098	0.92385	0.88849	0.86307	0.85480	0.84663	0.82270	0.79209	0.76290
5	0.95147	0.90573	0.86261	0.83188	0.82193	0.81212	0.78353	0.74726	0.71299
6	0.94205	0.88797	0.83748	0.80181	0.79031	0.77901	0.74622	0.70496	0.66634
7	0.93272	0.87056	0.81309	0.77283	0.75992	0.74725	0.71068	0.66506	0.62275
8	0.92348	0.85349	0.78941	0.74490	0.73069	0.71679	0.67684	0.62741	0.58201
9	0.91434	0.83676	0.76642	0.71797	0.70259	0.68757	0.64461	0.59190	0.54393
10	0.90529	0.82035	0.74409	0.69202	0.67556	0.65954	0.61391	0.55839	0.50835

Present Value of $1

Periods	1.0%	2.0%	3.0%	3.75%	4.0%	4.25%	5.0%	6.0%	7.0%
11	0.89632	0.80426	0.72242	0.66701	0.64958	0.63265	0.58468	0.52679	0.47509
12	0.88745	0.78849	0.70138	0.64290	0.62460	0.60686	0.55684	0.49697	0.44401
13	0.87866	0.77303	0.68095	0.61966	0.60057	0.58212	0.53032	0.46884	0.41496
14	0.86996	0.75788	0.66112	0.59726	0.57748	0.55839	0.50507	0.44230	0.38782
15	0.86135	0.74301	0.64186	0.57568	0.55526	0.53562	0.48102	0.41727	0.36245
16	0.85282	0.72845	0.62317	0.55487	0.53391	0.51379	0.45811	0.39365	0.33873
17	0.84438	0.71416	0.60502	0.53481	0.51337	0.49284	0.43630	0.37136	0.31657
18	0.83602	0.70016	0.58739	0.51548	0.49363	0.47275	0.41552	0.35034	0.29586
19	0.82774	0.68643	0.57029	0.49685	0.47464	0.45348	0.39573	0.33051	0.27651
20	0.81954	0.67297	0.55368	0.47889	0.45639	0.43499	0.37689	0.31180	0.25842
25	0.77977	0.60953	0.47761	0.39838	0.37512	0.35326	0.29530	0.23300	0.18425
30	0.74192	0.55207	0.41199	0.33140	0.30832	0.28689	0.23138	0.17411	0.13137

Present Value of $1

Periods	8.0%	9.0%	10.0%	11.0%	12.0%	13.0%	14.0%	15.0%	20.0%	25.0%
1	0.92593	0.91743	0.90909	0.90090	0.89286	0.88496	0.87719	0.86957	0.83333	0.80000
2	0.85734	0.84168	0.82645	0.81162	0.79719	0.78315	0.76947	0.75614	0.69444	0.64000
3	0.79383	0.77218	0.75131	0.73119	0.71178	0.69305	0.67497	0.65752	0.57870	0.51200
4	0.73503	0.70843	0.68301	0.65873	0.63552	0.61332	0.59208	0.57175	0.48225	0.40960
5	0.68058	0.64993	0.62092	0.59345	0.56743	0.54276	0.51937	0.49718	0.40188	0.32768
6	0.63017	0.59627	0.56447	0.53464	0.50663	0.48032	0.45559	0.43233	0.33490	0.26214
7	0.58349	0.54703	0.51316	0.48166	0.45235	0.42506	0.39964	0.37594	0.27908	0.20972
8	0.54027	0.50187	0.46651	0.43393	0.40388	0.37616	0.35056	0.32690	0.23257	0.16777
9	0.50025	0.46043	0.42410	0.39092	0.36061	0.33288	0.30751	0.28426	0.19381	0.13422
10	0.46319	0.42241	0.38554	0.35218	0.32197	0.29459	0.26974	0.24718	0.16151	0.10737

Present Value of $1

Periods	8.0%	9.0%	10.0%	11.0%	12.0%	13.0%	14.0%	15.0%	20.0%	25.0%
11	0.42888	0.38753	0.35049	0.31728	0.28748	0.26070	0.23662	0.21494	0.13459	0.08590
12	0.39711	0.35553	0.31863	0.28584	0.25668	0.23071	0.20756	0.18691	0.11216	0.06872
13	0.36770	0.32618	0.28966	0.25751	0.22917	0.20416	0.18207	0.16253	0.09346	0.05498
14	0.34046	0.29925	0.26333	0.23199	0.20462	0.18068	0.15971	0.14133	0.07789	0.04398
15	0.31524	0.27454	0.23939	0.20900	0.18270	0.15989	0.14010	0.12289	0.06491	0.03518
16	0.29189	0.25187	0.21763	0.18829	0.16312	0.14150	0.12289	0.10686	0.05409	0.02815
17	0.27027	0.23107	0.19784	0.16963	0.14564	0.12522	0.10780	0.09293	0.04507	0.02252
18	0.25025	0.21199	0.17986	0.15282	0.13004	0.11081	0.09456	0.08081	0.03756	0.01801
19	0.23171	0.19449	0.16351	0.13768	0.11611	0.09806	0.08295	0.07027	0.03130	0.01441
20	0.21455	0.17843	0.14864	0.12403	0.10367	0.08678	0.07276	0.06110	0.02608	0.01153
25	0.14602	0.11597	0.09230	0.07361	0.05882	0.04710	0.03779	0.03038	0.01048	0.00378
30	0.09938	0.07537	0.05731	0.04368	0.03338	0.02557	0.01963	0.01510	0.00421	0.00124

TABLE E.2

Present Value of Annuity of $1

Periods	1.0%	2.0%	3.0%	3.75%	4.0%	4.25%	5.0%	6.0%	7.0%
1	0.99010	0.98039	0.97087	0.96386	0.96154	0.95923	0.95238	0.94340	0.93458
2	1.97040	1.94156	1.91347	1.89287	1.88609	1.87936	1.85941	1.83339	1.80802
3	2.94099	2.88388	2.82861	2.78831	2.77509	2.76198	2.72325	2.67301	2.62432
4	3.90197	3.80773	3.71710	3.65138	3.62990	3.60861	3.54595	3.46511	3.38721
5	4.85343	4.71346	4.57971	4.48326	4.45182	4.42073	4.32948	4.21236	4.10020
6	5.79548	5.60143	5.41719	5.28507	5.24214	5.19974	5.07569	4.91732	4.76654
7	6.72819	6.47199	6.23028	6.05790	6.00205	5.94699	5.78637	5.58238	5.38929
8	7.65168	7.32548	7.01969	6.80280	6.73274	6.66378	6.46321	6.20979	5.97130
9	8.56602	8.16224	7.78611	7.52077	7.43533	7.35135	7.10782	6.80169	6.51523
10	9.47130	8.98259	8.53020	8.21279	8.11090	8.01089	7.72173	7.36009	7.02358

Present Value of Annuity of $1

Periods	1.0%	2.0%	3.0%	3.75%	4.0%	4.25%	5.0%	6.0%	7.0%
11	10.36763	9.78685	9.25262	8.87979	8.76048	8.64354	8.30641	7.88687	7.49867
12	11.25508	10.57534	9.95400	9.52269	9.38507	9.25039	8.86325	8.38384	7.94269
13	12.13374	11.34837	10.63496	10.14236	9.98565	9.83251	9.39357	8.85268	8.35765
14	13.00370	12.10625	11.29607	10.73962	10.56312	10.39090	9.89864	9.29498	8.74547
15	13.86505	12.84926	11.93794	11.31530	11.11839	10.92652	10.37966	9.71225	9.10791
16	14.71787	13.57771	12.56110	11.87017	11.65230	11.44031	10.83777	10.10590	9.44665
17	15.56225	14.29187	13.16612	12.40498	12.16567	11.93315	11.27407	10.47726	9.76322
18	16.39827	14.99203	13.75351	12.92046	12.65930	12.40590	11.68959	10.82760	10.05909
19	17.22601	15.67846	14.32380	13.41731	13.13394	12.85938	12.08532	11.15812	10.33560
20	18.04555	16.35143	14.87747	13.89620	13.59033	13.29437	12.46221	11.46992	10.59401
25	22.02316	19.52346	17.41315	16.04320	15.62208	15.21734	14.09394	12.78336	11.65358
30	25.80771	22.39646	19.60044	17.82925	17.29203	16.77902	15.37245	13.76483	12.40904

Present Value of Annuity of $1

Periods	8.0%	9.0%	10.0%	11.0%	12.0%	13.0%	14.0%	15.0%	20.0%	25.0%
1	0.92593	0.91743	0.90909	0.90090	0.89286	0.88496	0.87719	0.86957	0.83333	0.80000
2	1.78326	1.75911	1.73554	1.71252	1.69005	1.66810	1.64666	1.62571	1.52778	1.44000
3	2.57710	2.53129	2.48685	2.44371	2.40183	2.36115	2.32163	2.28323	2.10648	1.95200
4	3.31213	3.23972	3.16987	3.10245	3.03735	2.97447	2.91371	2.85498	2.58873	2.36160
5	3.99271	3.88965	3.79079	3.69590	3.60478	3.51723	3.43308	3.35216	2.99061	2.68928
6	4.62288	4.48592	4.35526	4.23054	4.11141	3.99755	3.88867	3.78448	3.32551	2.95142
7	5.20637	5.03295	4.86842	4.71220	4.56376	4.42261	4.28830	4.16042	3.60459	3.16114
8	5.74664	5.53482	5.33493	5.14612	4.96764	4.79877	4.63886	4.48732	3.83716	3.32891
9	6.24689	5.99525	5.75902	5.53705	5.32825	5.13166	4.94637	4.77158	4.03097	3.46313
10	6.71008	6.41766	6.14457	5.88923	5.65022	5.42624	5.21612	5.01877	4.19247	3.57050

Present Value of Annuity of $1

Periods	8.0%	9.0%	10.0%	11.0%	12.0%	13.0%	14.0%	15.0%	20.0%	25.0%
11	7.13896	6.80519	6.49506	6.20652	5.93770	5.68694	5.45273	5.23371	4.32706	3.65640
12	7.53608	7.16073	6.81369	6.49236	6.19437	5.91765	5.66029	5.42062	4.43922	3.72512
13	7.90378	7.48690	7.10336	6.74987	6.42355	6.12181	5.84236	5.58315	4.53268	3.78010
14	8.24424	7.78615	7.36669	6.98187	6.62817	6.30249	6.00207	5.72448	4.61057	3.82408
15	8.55948	8.06069	7.60608	7.19087	6.81086	6.46238	6.14217	5.84737	4.67547	3.85926
16	8.85137	8.31256	7.82371	7.37916	6.97399	6.60388	6.26506	5.95423	4.72956	3.88741
17	9.12164	8.54363	8.02155	7.54879	7.11963	6.72909	6.37286	6.04716	4.77463	3.90993
18	9.37189	8.75563	8.20141	7.70162	7.24967	6.83991	6.46742	6.12797	4.81219	3.92794
19	9.60360	8.95011	8.36492	7.83929	7.36578	6.93797	6.55037	6.19823	4.84350	3.94235
20	9.81815	9.12855	8.51356	7.96333	7.46944	7.02475	6.62313	6.25933	4.86958	3.95388
25	10.67478	9.82258	9.07704	8.42174	7.84314	7.32998	6.87293	6.46415	4.94759	3.98489
30	11.25778	10.27365	9.42691	8.69379	8.05518	7.49565	7.00266	6.56598	4.97894	3.99505

TABLE E.3
Future Value of $1

Periods	1.0%	2.0%	3.0%	3.75%	4.0%	4.25%	5.0%	6.0%	7.0%
1	1.01000	1.02000	1.03000	1.03750	1.04000	1.04250	1.05000	1.06000	1.07000
2	1.02010	1.04040	1.06090	1.07641	1.08160	1.08681	1.10250	1.12360	1.14490
3	1.03030	1.06121	1.09273	1.11677	1.12486	1.13300	1.15763	1.19102	1.22504
4	1.04060	1.08243	1.12551	1.15865	1.16986	1.18115	1.21551	1.26248	1.31080
5	1.05101	1.10408	1.15927	1.20210	1.21665	1.23135	1.27628	1.33823	1.40255
6	1.06152	1.12616	1.19405	1.24718	1.26532	1.28368	1.34010	1.41852	1.50073
7	1.07214	1.14869	1.22987	1.29395	1.31593	1.33824	1.40710	1.50363	1.60578
8	1.08286	1.17166	1.26677	1.34247	1.36857	1.39511	1.47746	1.59385	1.71819
9	1.09369	1.19509	1.30477	1.39281	1.42331	1.45440	1.55133	1.68948	1.83846
10	1.10462	1.21899	1.34392	1.44504	1.48024	1.51621	1.62889	1.79085	1.96715

Future Value of $1

Periods	1.0%	2.0%	3.0%	3.75%	4.0%	4.25%	5.0%	6.0%	7.0%
11	1.11567	1.24337	1.38423	1.49923	1.53945	1.58065	1.71034	1.89830	2.10485
12	1.12683	1.26824	1.42576	1.55545	1.60103	1.64783	1.79586	2.01220	2.25219
13	1.13809	1.29361	1.46853	1.61378	1.66507	1.71786	1.88565	2.13293	2.40985
14	1.14947	1.31948	1.51259	1.67430	1.73168	1.79087	1.97993	2.26090	2.57853
15	1.16097	1.34587	1.55797	1.73709	1.80094	1.86699	2.07893	2.39656	2.75903
16	1.17258	1.37279	1.60471	1.80223	1.87298	1.94633	2.18287	2.54035	2.95216
17	1.18430	1.40024	1.65285	1.86981	1.94790	2.02905	2.29202	2.69277	3.15882
18	1.19615	1.42825	1.70243	1.93993	2.02582	2.11529	2.40662	2.85434	3.37993
19	1.20811	1.45681	1.75351	2.01268	2.10685	2.20519	2.52695	3.02560	3.61653
20	1.22019	1.48595	1.80611	2.08815	2.19112	2.29891	2.65330	3.20714	3.86968
25	1.28243	1.64061	2.09378	2.51017	2.66584	2.83075	3.38635	4.29187	5.42743
30	1.34785	1.81136	2.42726	3.01747	3.24340	3.48564	4.32194	5.74349	7.61226

Future Value of $1

Periods	8.0%	9.0%	10.0%	11.0%	12.0%	13.0%	14.0%	15.0%	20.0%	25.0%
1	1.08000	1.09000	1.10000	1.11000	1.12000	1.13000	1.14000	1.15000	1.20000	1.25000
2	1.16640	1.18810	1.21000	1.23210	1.25440	1.27690	1.29960	1.32250	1.44000	1.56250
3	1.25971	1.29503	1.33100	1.36763	1.40493	1.44290	1.48154	1.52088	1.72800	1.95313
4	1.36049	1.41158	1.46410	1.51807	1.57352	1.63047	1.68896	1.74901	2.07360	2.44141
5	1.46933	1.53862	1.61051	1.68506	1.76234	1.84244	1.92541	2.01136	2.48832	3.05176
6	1.58687	1.67710	1.77156	1.87041	1.97382	2.08195	2.19497	2.31306	2.98598	3.81470
7	1.71382	1.82804	1.94872	2.07616	2.21068	2.35261	2.50227	2.66002	3.58318	4.76837
8	1.85093	1.99256	2.14359	2.30454	2.47596	2.65844	2.85259	3.05902	4.29982	5.96046
9	1.99900	2.17189	2.35795	2.55804	2.77308	3.00404	3.25195	3.51788	5.15978	7.45058
10	2.15892	2.36736	2.59374	2.83942	3.10585	3.39457	3.70722	4.04556	6.19174	9.31323

Future Value of $1

Periods	8.0%	9.0%	10.0%	11.0%	12.0%	13.0%	14.0%	15.0%	20.0%	25.0%
11	2.33164	2.58043	2.85312	3.15176	3.47855	3.83586	4.22623	4.65239	7.43008	11.64153
12	2.51817	2.81266	3.13843	3.49845	3.89598	4.33452	4.81790	5.35025	8.91610	14.55192
13	2.71962	3.06580	3.45227	3.88328	4.36349	4.89801	5.49241	6.15279	10.69932	18.18989
14	2.93719	3.34173	3.79750	4.31044	4.88711	5.53475	6.26135	7.07571	12.83918	22.73737
15	3.17217	3.64248	4.17725	4.78459	5.47357	6.25427	7.13794	8.13706	15.40702	28.42171
16	3.42594	3.97031	4.59497	5.31089	6.13039	7.06733	8.13725	9.35762	18.48843	35.52714
17	3.70002	4.32763	5.05447	5.89509	6.86604	7.98608	9.27646	10.76126	22.18611	44.40892
18	3.99602	4.71712	5.55992	6.54355	7.68997	9.02427	10.57517	12.37545	26.62333	55.51115
19	4.31570	5.14166	6.11591	7.26334	8.61276	10.19742	12.05569	14.23177	31.94800	69.38894
20	4.66096	5.60441	6.72750	8.06231	9.64629	11.52309	13.74349	16.36654	38.33760	86.73617
25	6.84848	8.62308	10.83471	13.58546	17.00006	21.23054	26.46192	32.91895	95.39622	264.69780
30	10.06266	13.26768	17.44940	22.89230	29.95992	39.11590	50.95016	66.21177	237.37631	807.79357

TABLE E.4

Future Value of Annuity of $1

Periods	1.0%	2.0%	3.0%	3.75%	4.0%	4.25%	5.0%	6.0%	7.0%
1	1.00000	1.00000	1.00000	1.00000	1.00000	1.00000	1.00000	1.00000	1.00000
2	2.01000	2.02000	2.03000	2.03750	2.04000	2.04250	2.05000	2.06000	2.07000
3	3.03010	3.06040	3.09090	3.11391	3.12160	3.12931	3.15250	3.18360	3.21490
4	4.06040	4.12161	4.18363	4.23068	4.24646	4.26230	4.31013	4.37462	4.43994
5	5.10101	5.20404	5.30914	5.38933	5.41632	5.44345	5.52563	5.63709	5.75074
6	6.15202	6.30812	6.46841	6.59143	6.63298	6.67480	6.80191	6.97532	7.15329
7	7.21354	7.43428	7.66246	7.83861	7.89829	7.95848	8.14201	8.39384	8.65402
8	8.28567	8.58297	8.89234	9.13255	9.21423	9.29671	9.54911	9.89747	10.25980
9	9.36853	9.75463	10.15911	10.47503	10.58280	10.69182	11.02656	11.49132	11.97799
10	10.46221	10.94972	11.46388	11.86784	12.00611	12.14622	12.57789	13.18079	13.81645

Future Value of Annuity of $1

Periods	1.0%	2.0%	3.0%	3.75%	4.0%	4.25%	5.0%	6.0%	7.0%
11	11.56683	12.16872	12.80780	13.31288	13.48635	13.66244	14.20679	14.97164	15.78360
12	12.68250	13.41209	14.19203	14.81212	15.02581	15.24309	15.91713	16.86994	17.88845
13	13.80933	14.68033	15.61779	16.36757	16.62684	16.89092	17.71298	18.88214	20.14064
14	14.94742	15.97394	17.08632	17.98135	18.29191	18.60879	19.59863	21.01507	22.55049
15	16.09690	17.29342	18.59891	19.65565	20.02359	20.39966	21.57856	23.27597	25.12902
16	17.25786	18.63929	20.15688	21.39274	21.82453	22.26665	23.65749	25.67253	27.88805
17	18.43044	20.01207	21.76159	23.19497	23.69751	24.21298	25.84037	28.21288	30.84022
18	19.61475	21.41231	23.41444	25.06478	25.64541	26.24203	28.13238	30.90565	33.99903
19	20.81090	22.84056	25.11687	27.00471	27.67123	28.35732	30.53900	33.75999	37.37896
20	22.01900	24.29737	26.87037	29.01739	29.77808	30.56250	33.06595	36.78559	40.99549
25	28.24320	32.03030	36.45926	40.27112	41.64591	43.07648	47.72710	54.86451	63.24904
30	34.78489	40.56808	47.57542	53.79924	56.08494	58.48553	66.43885	79.05819	94.46079

Future Value of Annuity of $1

Periods	8.0%	9.0%	10.0%	11.0%	12.0%	13.0%	14.0%	15.0%	20.0%	25.0%
1	1.00000	1.00000	1.00000	1.00000	1.00000	1.00000	1.00000	1.00000	1.00000	1.00000
2	2.08000	2.09000	2.10000	2.11000	2.12000	2.13000	2.14000	2.15000	2.20000	2.25000
3	3.24640	3.27810	3.31000	3.34210	3.37440	3.40690	3.43960	3.47250	3.64000	3.81250
4	4.50611	4.57313	4.64100	4.70973	4.77933	4.84980	4.92114	4.99337	5.36800	5.76563
5	5.86660	5.98471	6.10510	6.22780	6.35285	6.48027	6.61010	6.74238	7.44160	8.20703
6	7.33593	7.52333	7.71561	7.91286	8.11519	8.32271	8.53552	8.75374	9.92992	11.25879
7	8.92280	9.20043	9.48717	9.78327	10.08901	10.40466	10.73049	11.06680	12.91590	15.07349
8	10.63663	11.02847	11.43589	11.85943	12.29969	12.75726	13.23276	13.72682	16.49908	19.84186
9	12.48756	13.02104	13.57948	14.16397	14.77566	15.41571	16.08535	16.78584	20.79890	25.80232
10	14.48656	15.19293	15.93742	16.72201	17.54874	18.41975	19.33730	20.30372	25.95868	33.25290

Future Value of Annuity of $1

Periods	8.0%	9.0%	10.0%	11.0%	12.0%	13.0%	14.0%	15.0%	20.0%	25.0%
11	16.64549	17.56029	18.53117	19.56143	20.65458	21.81432	23.04452	24.34928	32.15042	42.56613
12	18.97713	20.14072	21.38428	22.71319	24.13313	25.65018	27.27075	29.00167	39.58050	54.20766
13	21.49530	22.95338	24.52271	26.21164	28.02911	29.98470	32.08865	34.35192	48.49660	68.75958
14	24.21492	26.01919	27.97498	30.09492	32.39260	34.88271	37.58107	40.50471	59.19592	86.94947
15	27.15211	29.36092	31.77248	34.40536	37.27971	40.41746	43.84241	47.58041	72.03511	109.68684
16	30.32428	33.00340	35.94973	39.18995	42.75328	46.67173	50.98035	55.71747	87.44213	138.10855
17	33.75023	36.97370	40.54470	44.50084	48.88367	53.73906	59.11760	65.07509	105.93056	173.63568
18	37.45024	41.30134	45.59917	50.39594	55.74971	61.72514	68.39407	75.83636	128.11667	218.04460
19	41.44626	46.01846	51.15909	56.93949	63.43968	70.74941	78.96923	88.21181	154.74000	273.55576
20	45.76196	51.16012	57.27500	64.20283	72.05244	80.94683	91.02493	102.44358	186.68800	342.94470
25	73.10594	84.70090	98.34706	114.41331	133.33387	155.61956	181.87083	212.79302	471.98108	1054.79118
30	113.28321	136.30754	164.49402	199.02088	241.33268	293.19922	356.78685	434.74515	1181.88157	3227.17427

A

Account A standardized format that organizations use to accumulate the dollar effect of transactions on each financial statement item.

Accounting A system that collects and processes (analyzes, measures, and records) financial information about an organization and reports that information to decision makers.

Accounting Cycle The process used by entities to analyze and record transactions, adjust the records at the end of the period, prepare financial statements, and prepare the records for the next cycle.

Accounting Entity The organization for which financial data are to be collected.

Accounting Period The time period covered by the financial statements.

Accounts Receivable (Trade Receivables, Receivables) Open accounts owed to the business by trade customers.

Accrual Basis Accounting Records revenues when earned and expenses when incurred, regardless of the timing of cash receipts or payments.

Accrued Expenses Previously unrecorded expenses that need to be adjusted at the end of the accounting period to reflect the amount incurred and its related payable account.

Accrued Liabilities Expenses that have been incurred but have not been paid at the end of the accounting period.

Accrued Revenues Previously unrecorded revenues that need to be adjusted at the end of the accounting period to reflect the amount earned and its related receivable account.

Acquisition Cost The net cash equivalent amount paid or to be paid for an asset.

Acquisition Method Records assets and liabilities acquired in a merger or acquisition at their fair value on the transaction date.

Actuaries Statisticians who specialize in assessing risks and probabilities.

Additional Paid-In Capital (Paid-In Capital, Contributed Capital in Excess of Par) The amount of contributed capital less the par value of the stock.

Adjusting Entries Entries necessary at the end of the accounting period to measure all revenues and expenses of that period.

Aging of Accounts Receivable Method Estimates uncollectible accounts based on the age of each account receivable.

Allowance for Doubtful Accounts (Allowance for Bad Debts, Allowance for Uncollectible Accounts) Contra-asset account containing the estimated uncollectible accounts receivable.

Allowance Method Bases bad debt expense on an estimate of uncollectible accounts.

Amortization Systematic and rational allocation of the acquisition cost of an intangible asset over its useful life.

Amortized Cost Method Reports investments in debt securities held to maturity at cost minus any premium or plus any discount.

Annuity A series of periodic cash receipts or payments that are equal in amount each interest period.

Asset Turnover Ratios Ratios that capture how efficiently a company uses its assets.

Assets Probable future economic benefits owned by the entity as a result of past transactions.

Audit An examination of the financial reports to ensure that they represent what they claim and conform with generally accepted accounting principles.

Authorized Number of Shares The maximum number of shares of a corporation's stock that can be issued as specified in the charter.

Available-for-Sale Securities All passive investments other than trading securities and debt held to maturity (classified as either short term or long term).

Average Cost Method Uses the weighted average unit cost of the goods available for sale for both cost of goods sold and ending inventory.

B

Bad Debt Expense (Doubtful Accounts Expense, Uncollectible Accounts Expense, Provision for Uncollectible Accounts) Expense associated with estimated uncollectible accounts receivable.

Balance Sheet (Statement of Financial Position) Reports the amount of assets, liabilities, and stockholders' equity of an accounting entity at a point in time.

Bank Reconciliation Process of verifying the accuracy of both the bank statement and the cash accounts of a business.

Bank Statement A monthly report from a bank that shows deposits recorded, checks cleared, other debits and credits, and a running bank balance.

Basic Accounting Equation (Balance Sheet Equation) Assets = Liabilities + Stockholders' Equity.

Board of Directors Elected by the shareholders to represent their interests; its audit committee is responsible for maintaining the integrity of the company's financial reports.

Bond Certificate The document investors receive when they purchase bond securities.

Bond Discount The difference between the selling price of a bond and the bond's face value when a bond is sold for less than par.

Bond Premium The difference between the selling price of a bond and the bond's face value when a bond is sold for more than par.

Bond Principal (Par Value, Face Value, Maturity Value) The amount a company pays bondholders on the maturity date and the amount used to compute the bond's periodic cash interest payments.

C

Callable Bonds Bonds that may be called for early retirement at the option of the issuer.

Capital Lease *Does* require a lessee to recognize an asset and a liability.

Capitalized Interest Interest expenditures included in the cost of a self-constructed asset.

Cash Money or any instrument that banks will accept for deposit and immediate credit to a company's account, such as a check, money order, or bank draft.

Cash Basis Accounting Records revenues when cash is received and expenses when cash is paid.

Cash Equivalents Short-term investments with original maturities of three months or less that are readily convertible to cash and whose value is unlikely to change.

Cash Flows from Financing Activities Cash inflows and outflows related to external sources of financing (owners and creditors) for the enterprise.

Cash Flows from Investing Activities Cash inflows and outflows related to the acquisition or sale of productive facilities and investments in the securities of other companies.

Cash Flows from Operating Activities (Cash Flows from Operations) Cash inflows and outflows directly related to earnings from normal operations.

Closing Entries Made at the end of the accounting period to transfer balances in temporary accounts to Retained Earnings and to establish a zero balance in each of the temporary accounts.

Common Stock The basic voting stock issued by a corporation.

Component Percentage Expresses each item on a particular financial statement as a percentage of a single base amount.

Contingent Liability A potential liability that has arisen as the result of a past event; it is not a definitive liability until some future event occurs.

Contra-Account An account that is an offset to, or reduction of, the primary account.

Contributed Capital Cash (and sometimes other assets) provided from the owners to the business.

Convertible Bonds Bonds that may be converted to other securities of the issuer (usually common stock).

Copyright Exclusive right to publish, use, and sell a literary, musical, or artistic work.

Corporate Governance The procedures designed to ensure that the company is managed in the interests of the shareholders.

Cost (Historical Cost) The cash-equivalent value of an asset on the date of the transaction.

Cost-Effectiveness Requires that the benefits of accounting for and reporting information should outweigh the costs.

Cost of Goods Sold Equation $BI + P - EI = CGS$.

Coupon Rate (Stated Rate, Contract Rate, Nominal Rate) The interest rate specified on a bond, and the rate used to compute the bond's periodic cash interest payment.

Covenant A legally binding agreement between a bond issuer and a bondholder.

Credit The right side of an account.

Credit Card Discount Fee charged by the credit card company for its services.

Cumulative Dividend Preference Requires any unpaid dividends on preferred stock to accumulate. These cumulative preferred dividends must be paid before any common dividends can be paid.

Current Assets Assets that will be used or turned into cash within one year. Inventory is always considered a current asset regardless of the time needed to produce and sell it.

Current Dividend Preference Requires that dividends be paid to preferred stockholders before any dividends are paid to common stockholders.

Current Liabilities Short-term obligations that will be paid in cash (or other current assets) within the current operating cycle or one year, whichever is longer.

D

Debenture An unsecured bond; no assets are specifically pledged to guarantee repayment.

Debit The left side of an account.

Declaration Date The date on which the board of directors officially approves a dividend.

Declining-Balance Depreciation Method that allocates the net book value (cost minus accumulated depreciation) of an asset over its useful life based on a multiple of the straight-line rate, thus assigning more depreciation to early years and less depreciation to later years of an asset's life.

Deferred Expenses Previously acquired assets that need to be adjusted at the end of the accounting period to reflect the amount of expense incurred in using the asset to generate revenue.

Deferred (Unearned) Revenues Previously recorded liabilities (from collecting cash from customers in the past) that need to be adjusted at the end of the period to reflect the amount of revenue earned by providing goods or services over time to customers.

Deferred Tax Asset Asset created when differences in financial reporting and tax reporting

cause accounting income to be lower than tax income in a given period.

Deferred Tax Items Timing differences caused by reporting revenues and expenses according to GAAP on a company's income statement and according to the Internal Revenue Code on the tax return.

Deferred Tax Liability Is created when differences in financial reporting and tax reporting cause accounting income to be higher than tax income in a given period.

Defined Benefit Pension Plans Require companies to provide a defined amount to an employee during retirement.

Defined Contribution Pension Plans Require companies to contribute a defined amount to a retirement fund.

Depletion Systematic and rational allocation of the cost of a natural resource over the period of its exploitation.

Depreciation The process of allocating the cost of buildings and equipment (but not land) over their productive lives using a systematic and rational method.

Direct Labor The earnings of employees who work directly on the products being manufactured.

Direct Method A method of presenting the operating activities section of the statement of cash flows that reports components of cash flows from operating activities as gross receipts and gross payments.

Dividends in Arrears Dividends on cumulative preferred stock that have not been paid in prior years.

E

Earnings Forecasts Predictions of earnings for future accounting periods, prepared by financial analysts.

Effective-Interest Amortization A method of amortizing a bond discount or bond premium that reflects the effective interest rate a company pays bondholders over the life of a bond.

Effective Interest Rate (Yield) The rate of return investors demand for a company's bonds on the date the bonds are issued; also called the market interest rate.

Effective Tax Rate The tax rate reflected on a company's income statement.

Equity Method Used when an investor can exert significant influence over an affiliate; the method permits recording the investor's share of the affiliate's income.

Estimated Useful Life The expected service life of an asset to the present owner.

Expense Recognition Principle (or Matching Principle) Requires that expenses be recorded when incurred in earning revenue.

Expenses Decreases in assets or increases in liabilities from ongoing operations incurred to generate revenues during the period.

F

Factory Overhead Manufacturing costs that are not raw material or direct labor costs.

Fair Value Method Reports securities at their current market value (the amount that would be received in an orderly sale).

Faithful Representation Requires that the information be complete, neutral, and free from error.

Financial Accounting Standards Board (FASB) The private sector body given the primary responsibility to work out the detailed rules that become generally accepted accounting principles.

Finished Goods Inventory Manufactured goods that are complete and ready for sale.

First-In, First-Out (FIFO) Method An inventory costing method that assumes that the first goods purchased (the first in) are the first goods sold.

Form 8-K The report used by publicly traded companies to disclose any material event not previously reported that is important to investors.

Form 10-K The annual report that publicly traded companies must file with the SEC.

Form 10-Q The quarterly report that publicly traded companies must file with the SEC.

Franchise A contractual right to sell certain products or services, use certain trademarks, or perform activities in a geographical region.

Free Cash Flow Cash Flows from Operating Activities less Dividends less Capital Expenditures.

Future Value The sum to which an amount will increase as the result of compound interest.

G

Gains Result from disposing of assets for more than the reported book value.

Generally Accepted Accounting Principles (GAAP) The measurement and disclosure rules used to develop the information in financial statements.

Going Concern Assumption States that businesses are assumed to continue to operate into the foreseeable future (also called the continuity assumption).

Goods Available for Sale The sum of beginning inventory and purchases (or transfers to finished goods) for the period.

Goodwill (Cost in Excess of Net Assets Acquired) For accounting purposes, the excess of the purchase price of a business over the fair value of the acquired business's assets and liabilities.

Gross Profit (Gross Margin) Net sales less cost of goods sold.

H

Held-to-Maturity Investments Investments in debt securities that management has the ability and intent to hold until maturity.

I

Improvements Expenditures that increase the productive life, operating efficiency, or capacity of an asset and are recorded as increases in asset accounts, not as expenses.

Income before Income Taxes (Pretax Earnings) Revenues minus all expenses except income tax expense.

Income Statement (Statement of Income, Statement of Earnings, Statement of Operations, Statement of Comprehensive Income) Reports the revenues less the expenses of the accounting period.

Indenture A legal document that describes all the details of a debt security to potential buyers.

Indirect Method A method of presenting the operating activities section of the statement of cash flows that adjusts net income to compute cash flows from operating activities.

Institutional Investors Managers of pension, mutual, endowment, and other funds that invest on the behalf of others.

Intangible Assets Assets that have special rights but not physical substance.

Internal Controls Processes by which a company provides reasonable assurance regarding the reliability of the company's financial reporting, the effectiveness and efficiency of its operations, and its compliance with applicable laws and regulations.

Inventory Tangible property held for sale in the normal course of business or used in producing goods or services for sale.

Investments in Affiliates (or Associated Companies) Investments in stock held for the purpose of influencing the operating and financing strategies of the entity for the long term.

Issued Shares The total number of shares of stock that have been sold.

J

Journal Entry An accounting method for expressing the effects of a transaction on accounts in a debits-equal-credits format.

L

Last-In, First-Out (LIFO) Method An inventory costing method that assumes that the most recently purchased units (the last in) are sold first.

Leasehold Improvements Modifications that a lessee makes to a leased property.

Legal Capital The permanent amount of capital defined by state law that must remain invested in the business; serves as a cushion for creditors.

Lenders (Creditors) Suppliers and financial institutions that lend money to companies.

Lessee The party that pays for the right to use the leased asset.

Lessor The party that owns a leased asset.

Liabilities Probable future sacrifices of economic benefits arising from a present obligation to transfer cash, goods, or services as a result of a past transaction.

Licenses and Operating Rights Obtained through agreements with governmental units or agencies; permit owners to use public property in performing their services.

LIFO Liquidation A sale of a lower-cost inventory item from beginning LIFO inventory.

LIFO Reserve A contra-asset for the excess of FIFO over LIFO inventory.

Liquidity The ability to pay current obligations.

Liquidity Ratios Ratios that measure a company's ability to meet its currently maturing obligations.

Long-Lived Assets Tangible and intangible resources owned by a business and used in its operations over several years.

Long-Term Liabilities All of the entity's obligations that are not classified as current liabilities.

Losses Result from disposing of assets for less than the reported book value cost.

Lower of Cost or Market (LCM) Valuation method departing from the cost principle; it serves to recognize a loss when net realizable value drops below cost.

M

Market Interest Rate (Yield, Effective Interest Rate) The rate of return investors demand for a company's bonds on the date the bonds are issued, and the rate used to compute the bond's interest expense each period.

Market Ratios Ratios that relate the current price per share of a company's stock to the return that accrues to stockholders.

Material Amounts Amounts that are large enough to influence a user's decision.

Merchandise Inventory Goods held for resale in the ordinary course of business.

Merger Occurs when one company purchases all of the net assets of another and the acquired company goes out of existence.

Mixed-Attribute Measurement Model Applied to measuring different assets and liabilities of the balance sheet.

Monetary Unit Assumption States that accounting information should be measured and reported in the national monetary unit without any adjustment for changes in purchasing power.

N

Natural Resources Assets occurring in nature, such as mineral deposits, timber tracts, oil, and gas.

Net Book Value (Carrying or Book Value) The acquisition cost of an asset less accumulated depreciation, depletion, or amortization.

Net Realizable Value The expected sales price less selling costs (e.g., repair and disposal costs).

Net Sales The top line reported on the income statement. Net Sales = Sales Revenue − (Credit card discounts + Sales discounts + Sales returns and allowances).

Noncash Investing and Financing Activities Transactions that do not have direct cash flow effects; reported as a supplement to the statement of cash flows in narrative or schedule form.

No-Par Value Stock Capital stock that has no par value specified in the corporate charter.

Notes (Footnotes) Provide supplemental information about the financial condition of a company, without which the financial statements cannot be fully understood.

Notes Receivable Written promises that require another party to pay the business under specified conditions (amount, time, interest).

O

Off-Balance-Sheet Financing Structuring contracts to avoid reporting liabilities.

Operating (Cash-to-Cash) Cycle The time it takes for a company to pay cash to suppliers, sell goods and services to customers, and collect cash from customers.

Operating Income (Income from Operations) Net sales less cost of goods sold and other operating expenses.

Operating Lease *Does not* require a lessee to recognize an asset or liability.

Ordinary Repairs and Maintenance Expenditures that maintain the productive capacity of an asset during the current accounting period only and are recorded as expenses.

Outstanding Shares The total number of shares of stock that are owned by stockholders on any particular date.

Overfunded When the plan's assets are greater than its liability.

P

Paid-In Capital (Additional Paid-in Capital, Contributed Capital in Excess of Par) The amount of contributed capital less the par value of the stock.

Par Value (1) The nominal value per share of capital stock as specified in the corporate charter. (2) Also, another name for bond principal, or the maturity amount of a bond.

Patent Granted by the federal government for an invention; gives the owner the exclusive right to use, manufacture, and sell the subject of the patent.

Payment Date The date on which a cash dividend is paid to the stockholders of record.

Pension An amount of money paid to a retired employee.

Percentage of Credit Sales Method Bases bad debt expense on the historical percentage of credit sales that result in bad debts.

Periodic Inventory System An inventory system in which ending inventory and cost of goods sold are determined at the end of the accounting period based on a physical inventory count.

Permanent (Real) Accounts The balance sheet accounts that carry their ending balances into the next accounting period.

Perpetual Inventory System An inventory system in which a detailed inventory record is maintained, recording each purchase and sale during the accounting period.

Post-Closing Trial Balance Prepared as an additional step in the accounting cycle to check that debits equal credits and all temporary accounts have been closed.

Preferred Stock Stock that has specified rights over common stock.

Present Value The current value of an amount to be received in the future; a future amount discounted for compound interest.

Press Release A written public news announcement normally distributed to major news services.

Primary Objective of Financial Reporting to External Users To provide useful economic information about a business to help external parties make sound financial decisions.

Private Investors Individuals who purchase shares in companies.

Profitability Ratios Ratios that compare income with one or more primary activities.

Prospectus A regulatory filing that describes all the details of a debt or equity security to potential buyers.

Public Company Accounting Oversight Board (PCAOB) The private sector body given the primary responsibility to work out detailed auditing standards.

Purchase Discount Cash discount received for prompt payment of an account.

Purchase Returns and Allowances A reduction in the cost of purchases associated with unsatisfactory goods.

R

Ratio Analysis An analytical tool that measures the proportional relationship between two financial statement amounts.

Raw Materials Inventory Items acquired for the purpose of processing into finished goods.

Record Date The date on which the corporation prepares the list of current stockholders who will receive the dividend when paid.

Relevant Information Information that can influence a decision; it is timely and has predictive and/or feedback value.

Residual (or Salvage) Value The estimated amount to be recovered by the company, less disposal costs, at the end of an asset's estimated useful life.

Retained Earnings Cumulative earnings of a company that are not distributed to the owners and are reinvested in the business.

Revenue Recognition Principle Revenues are recognized (1) when the company transfers promised goods or services to customers (2) in the amount it expects to receive.

Revenues Increases in assets or settlements of liabilities from the major or central ongoing operations of the business.

S

Sales (or Cash) Discount Cash discount offered to encourage prompt payment of an account receivable.

Sales Returns and Allowances A reduction of sales revenues for return of or allowances for unsatisfactory goods.

Sarbanes-Oxley Act A law that strengthens U.S. financial reporting and corporate governance regulations.

Securities and Exchange Commission (SEC) The U.S. government agency that determines the financial statements that public companies must provide to stockholders and the measurement rules that they must use in producing those statements.

Separate Entity Assumption States that business transactions are separate from the transactions of the owners.

Solvency Ratios Ratios that measure a company's ability to meet its long-term obligations.

Specific Identification Method An inventory costing method that identifies the cost of the specific item that was sold.

Statement of Cash Flows (Cash Flow Statement) Reports inflows and outflows of cash during the accounting period in the categories of operating, investing, and financing.

Statement of Stockholders' Equity Reports the way that net income and the distribution of dividends affected the financial position of the company during the accounting period.

Statutory Tax Rate The rate tax law says a company should pay given its level of income.

Stock Dividend A distribution of additional shares of a corporation's own stock on a pro rata basis at no cost to existing stockholders.

Stock Split Gives stockholders a specified number of additional shares for each share that they currently hold.

Stockholders' Equity (Shareholders' or Owners' Equity) The financing provided by the owners and the operations of the business.

Straight-Line Amortization An alternative method of amortizing bond discounts and premiums that allocates an equal dollar amount to each interest period. It is only permitted by GAAP under specific circumstances.

Straight-Line Depreciation Method that allocates the depreciable cost of an asset in equal periodic amounts over its useful life.

T

T-account A tool for summarizing transaction effects for each account, determining balances, and drawing inferences about a company's activities.

Tangible Assets Assets that have physical substance.

Technology Includes costs for computer software and Web development.

Temporary (Nominal) Accounts Income statement (and sometimes dividends declared) accounts that are closed to Retained Earnings at the end of the accounting period.

Temporary Tax Differences Result from companies reporting revenues and expenses on their income statements in a different time period than they report them on their tax returns.

Time Period Assumption The long life of a company can be reported in shorter time periods.

Time Value of Money Interest that is associated with the use of money over time.

Trademark An exclusive legal right to use a special name, image, or slogan.

Trading Securities All investments in stocks or bonds that are held primarily for the purpose of active trading (buying and selling) in the near future (classified as short term).

Transaction (1) An exchange between a business and one or more external parties to a business or (2) a measurable internal event such as the use of assets in operations.

Transaction Analysis The process of studying a transaction to determine its economic effect on the business in terms of the accounting equation.

Treasury Stock A corporation's own stock that has been repurchased. Shares held as treasury stock are considered issued shares but not outstanding shares.

Trial Balance A list of all accounts with their balances to provide a check on the equality of the debits and credits.

Trustee An independent party appointed to represent the bondholders.

U

Underfunded When a defined benefit pension plan's liability is greater than its assets.

Units-of-Production Depreciation Method that allocates the depreciable cost of an asset over its useful life based on the relationship of its periodic output to its total estimated output.

Unqualified (Clean) Audit Opinion Auditor's statement that the financial statements are fair presentations in all material respects in conformity with GAAP.

Unrealized Holding Gains (Losses) Amounts associated with price changes of securities that are currently held.

W

Work in Process Inventory Goods in the process of being manufactured.

Working Capital The dollar difference between total current assets and total current liabilities.